THE ROUGH GUIDE TO

Argentina

D0032152

written and researched by

Stephen Keeling, Shafik Meghji, Sorrel Moseley-Williams and
Madelaine Triebe

**ROUGH
GUIDES**

roughguides.com

Contents

OPPOSITE LAGO PERITO MORENO, PATAGONIA **PREVIOUS PAGE** IGLESIA SAN FRANCISCO, SALTA

Introduction to
Argentina

Studded with outstanding natural wonders and endowed with one of the world's most stylish cities, Argentina is a vast and varied land. Tapering from the Tropic of Capricorn towards the tip of Antarctica, it encompasses a staggering diversity of terrains, from the lush wetlands of the Litoral and the bone-dry Andean plateaux of the northwest to the end-of-the-world archipelago of Tierra del Fuego. Its most emblematic landscapes are the verdant flatlands of the Pampas and the dramatic steppe of Patagonia, whose very name evokes windswept plains inhabited by hardy pioneers.

At first glance, Argentina may seem less "exotic" than the rest of South America, and its inhabitants will readily, and rightly, tell you how powerful an influence Europe has been on their nation. It has been quipped that Argentina is the most American of all European countries and the most European of all American countries, but it actually has a very special character all of its own, distilled into the national ideal of **Argentinidad**, characterized by proud, defiant passion. While there is a lot of truth in the clichés – Argentine society really is dominated by **football**, politics and living life in the fast lane (literally, when it comes to driving) – not everyone dances the **tango**, or is obsessed with **Evita** or gallops around on a horse. Wherever you go, though, you're bound to be wowed by Argentines' zeal for so many aspects of their own culture and curiosity about the outside world.

One of Argentina's top attractions is the leviathan metropolis of **Buenos Aires**, the most fascinating of all South American capitals. It's a riveting place just to wander about, people-watching, shopping or simply soaking up the unique atmosphere. Its many barrios (neighbourhoods) are startlingly different – some are decadently old-fashioned, others daringly modern – but all of them ooze character. The other main cities worth visiting are colonial **Salta** in the northwest, beguiling **Rosario** – the birthplace of Che Guevara – and **Ushuaia**, which, in addition to being the world's most southerly city, enjoys a fabulous waterfront setting on the Beagle Channel.

ABOVE FIELD OF SUGAR CANE, GRAN CHACO

Metres	
5000	
4000	
3000	
2000	
1500	
1000	
400	
200	
0	

BOLIVIA

PARAGUAY

BRAZIL

La Quiaca

RN-40

Jujuy

RN-34

Salta

RN-81

Puerto Iguazú

Cafayate

Formosa

RN-16

RN-12

Tucumán

Resistencia

Posadas

Santiago del Estero

Corrientes

RN-40

RN-9

RN-11

Catamarca

RN-34

Río Paraná

RN-14

La Rioja

BRAZIL

Laguna Mar Chiquita

URUGUAY

San Juan

Córdoba

Concordia

Río Uruguay

Santa Fe

Mendoza

RN-9

San Luis

Rosario

RN-7

Gualeguaychú

RN-7

San Antonio de Areco

Colonia del Sacramento

San Rafael

BUENOS AIRES

RN-188

La Plata

CHILE

RN-55

Santa Rosa

RN-3

RN-2

RN-40

Mar del Plata

PACIFIC OCEAN

RN-22

Bahía Blanca

San Martín de los Andes

Neuquén

Río Negro

RN-3

Carmen de Patagones

Bariloche

ATLANTIC OCEAN

El Bolsón

Península Valdés

Río Chubut

Puerto Madryn

Esquel

Trelew

RN-25

RN-3

RP-43

Comodoro Rivadavia

RN-40

Perito Moreno

Puerto Deseado

Argentine Antarctic Territory

Puerto San Julián

El Calafate

Puerto Santa Cruz

Puerto Natales

Río Gallegos

Falkland Islands (Islas Malvinas)

N

Punta Arenas

RN-3

0   200
kilometres

Straits of Magellan

Ushuaia

Cape Horn

CORDILLERA DE LOS ANDES

ARGENTINA

But the country's real trump cards outside the capital are the sheer size of the **land** and the diverse **wildlife** inhabiting it. In theory, by hopping on a plane or two you could spot howler monkeys and toucans in northern jungles in the morning, then watch the antics of penguins tobogganing into the icy South Atlantic in the afternoon. Argentina hosts hundreds of bird species – including the Andean condor and three varieties of flamingo – plus pumas, armadillos, llamas, foxes and tapirs roaming the country's forests and mountainsides and the dizzying heights of the altiplano, or *puna*. Lush tea plantations and parched salt flats, palm groves and icebergs, plus the world's mightiest waterfalls, are just some of the scenes that will catch you unawares if you were expecting Argentina to be one big cattle ranch. Dozens of these biosystems are protected by an extensive network of national and provincial **parks and reserves**.

For **getting around** and seeing these marvels, you can generally rely on a well-developed infrastructure inherited from decades of domestic tourism. Thanks in part to an increasing number of boutique hotels, the range and quality of **accommodation** has improved no end in the last decade. Among the best lodgings are the beautiful ranches known as **estancias** – or *fincas* in the north – that function as luxury resorts. In most places, you'll be able to rely on the services of top-notch tour operators, who will not only show you the sights but also fix you up with a staggering range of **outdoor adventures**: horseriding, trekking, white-water rafting, kayaking, skiing and hang-gliding, along with more relaxing pursuits such as wine tasting, birdwatching or photography safaris. Argentina offers such a hallucinating variety it's all but impossible to take in on one trip – don't be surprised if you find yourself longing to return to explore the bits you didn't get to see the first time around.

RIGHT PARQUE PROVINCIAL ISCHIGUALASTO

Where to go

Argentina has many attractions that could claim the title of natural wonders of the world: the prodigious waterfalls of **Iguazú**; the spectacular **Glaciar Perito Moreno**; unforgettable whale-watching off **Península Valdés**; or the handsome lakes and mountains around **Bariloche** – indeed, **Patagonia** in general. Yet many of the country's most rewarding destinations are also its least known, such as the **Esteros del Iberá**, a huge reserve of lily-carpeted lagoons offering close-up encounters with cormorants and caymans; or **Antofagasta de la Sierra**, a remote village set amid frozen lakes mottled pink with flamingoes; or **Laguna Diamante**, a high-altitude mirror of sapphire water reflecting a wondrous volcano. In any case, climate and distance will rule out any attempt to see every corner; it's more sensible and rewarding to concentrate on one or two sections of the country.

Unless you're visiting Argentina as part of a South American tour, **Buenos Aires** is likely to be your point of entry, as it has the country's only *bona fide* international airport, Ezeiza. It is one of the world's top urban experiences, with an intriguing blend of European architecture and a vernacular flair that includes houses painted in the colours of legendary football team Boca Juniors. The city's museums are eclectic enough to suit all interests – Latin American art, colonial silverware, dinosaurs and ethnography are just four subjects on offer – and you can round off a day's sightseeing with a tango show, a bar tour or a meal at one of the dozens of fabulous restaurants.

CRIOLLO CULTURE

Most closely translated as "creole", **criollo** refers to a way of life born in the Americas, but with Old World roots. In Argentina, it is a byword for that which is absolutely Argentine – the culture of the countryside and the gaucho. Key aspects of this include the food – *asado* barbecues, of course, but also maize-based stews like *locro*; clothing – such as baggy riding trousers called *bombachas* and the espadrille-like *alpargatas*; horses – be they for rounding up cattle or playing polo; and a decidedly anti-authoritarian streak in the national character. Even the wealthiest city-dweller is usually keen to prove that he or she is fundamentally a *criollo*, never happier than when sipping a *mate* by the fire.

Due north lies the **Litoral**, an expanse of subtropical watery landscapes that shares borders with Uruguay, Brazil and Paraguay. Here are the photogenic **Iguazú waterfalls** and Jesuit missions whose once-noble ruins are crumbling into the jungle – with the exception of well-groomed **San Ignacio Miní**. Immediately west of the Litoral extends the **Chaco**, one of Argentina's most infrequently visited regions, reserved for those with an ardent interest in **wildlife**, so be prepared for fierce summer heat and poor infrastructure. A highlight in the country's landlocked **northwest** is the **Quebrada de Humahuaca**, a fabulous gorge lined with rainbow-hued rocks; it winds up to the oxygen-starved altiplano, where llamas and their wild relatives munch wiry grass. Nearby, in the **Valles Calchaquíes**, a chain of stunningly scenic valleys, high-altitude vineyards produce the delightfully flowery torrontés wine.

Sprawling across Argentina's broad midriff to the west and immediately south of Buenos Aires are **the Pampas**, arguably the country's most archetypal landscape. Formed by horizon-to-horizon plains interspersed with the odd low sierra, this subtly beautiful scenery is punctuated by small towns, the occasional ranch and countless clumps of pampas grass (*cortaderas*). Part arid, part wetland, the Pampas are grazed by millions of cattle and planted with soya and wheat fields of incomprehensible size. The Pampas are also where you'll glimpse traditional **gaucho culture**, most famously in the charming pueblo of **San Antonio de Areco**. Here, too, are some of the classiest estancias, offering a combination of hedonistic luxury and horseback adventures. On the Atlantic Coast a string of fun beach resorts includes long-standing favourite **Mar del Plata**.

As you head further west, the Central Sierras loom: the mild climate, clear brooks and sylvan idylls of these ancient highlands have attracted holiday-makers since the late nineteenth century, and within reach of **Córdoba**, the country's colonial-era second city, are some of the oldest resorts on the continent. Keep going west and you'll get to the **Cuyo**, with the highest Andean peaks as a snowcapped backdrop; here you can discover one of Argentina's most enjoyable cities, the regional capital of **Mendoza**, also the country's **wine capital**. From here, the scenic **Alta Montaña** route climbs steeply to the Chilean border, passing **Cerro Aconcagua**, now well established as a fantasy challenge for mountaineers worldwide. Just south, **Las Leñas** is a ski-and-snowboard resort where celebrities show off their winter wear, while the nearby black-and-red lava wastes of

Author picks

Rough Guides authors covered every corner of Argentina for this new edition, from the gale-swept shores of the Beagle Channel to the spray-drenched viewing platforms at the Iguazú Falls. These are their personal picks.

Road trips The world's eighth-largest country is laced by roads that pass through an astonishing variety of landscapes. Most famously, Ruta 40 (p.490) skirts the Andes to zip through Patagonia and beyond. We also like the two-day Cafayate–Cachi circuit (p.315) and the polychrome Quebrada de Humahuaca (p.299).

Meet the ancestors Enjoy cakes in the Welsh teahouses of Gaiman (p.459) and Trevelin (p.417), wander through colourful Genoese Boca (p.82), sup locally brewed beer in Germanic Villa General Belgrano (p.203) and Bariloche (p.397) and get a taste of indigenous Calchaquí and Kolla cultures in the northwest (p.294 & p.319).

Breathtaking views Picking Argentina's finest view is an impossible task, but our favourites include Glaciar Perito Moreno (p.476) and Monte Fitz Roy (p.483) in Patagonia, Cerro Catedral (p.406) in the Lake District, and, of course, the Iguazú Falls (p.259) in the Northeast.

Wildlife encounters Argentina is a wildlife haven, with whales off Península Valdés (p.450), Magellanic penguins at Punta Tombo (p.461) and vicuñas in the northwest (p.327) – just make sure the coatis don't steal your lunch at the Iguazú Falls (p.265).

Favourite wines Argentina is one of the world's leading producers of vino, and the quality improves every harvest. Visit the Mendoza region (p.335) – home to numerous world-class vineyards specializing in Argentina's signature grape, malbec – or tour the torrontés and tannat producers of Cafayate (p.316).

Most romantic estancia The marvellous estancia of *La Bamba* (p.145) may have been the setting for a film about a tragic love story but that shouldn't put off honeymooners. The wild isolation of Patagonia (p.440) or the colonial charms of the northwest (p.278) also lend themselves to memorable holiday trysts.

> Our author recommendations don't end here. We've flagged up our favourite places – a perfectly sited hotel, an atmospheric café, a special restaurant – throughout the guide, highlighted with the ★ symbol.

FROM TOP MAGELLAN PENGUINS AT PUNTA TOMBO (P.461); WOMAN CYCLING ON RUTA 40 (P.490); *CIERVO ROJO*, VILLA GENERAL BELGRANO (P.203)

TANGO, ARGENTINA'S BLUES

Tango is not only a dance, or even an art form, it is a powerful symbol, closely associated with Argentina around the world. Essentially and intrinsically linked to Buenos Aires and its multicultural history, it nonetheless has ardent fans all around the country. Rosario and, to a lesser extent, Córdoba, the country's two biggest cities after the capital, have a strong tango culture, complete with **milongas** (tango dance halls) and shops to buy the right garb and footwear. And don't be surprised to find villagers in some remote hamlet, hundreds of kilometres from Buenos Aires, listening to a scratchy recording of **Carlos Gardel** – the 1930s heart-throb still regarded as the best tango singer. Some experts argue that tango's success can be put down to its perfect representation of the Argentine psyche: a unique blend of nostalgia, resignation and heartbroken passion.

La Payunia, one of the country's hidden jewels, are all but overlooked. Likewise, **San Juan** and **La Rioja** provinces are relatively uncharted territories, but their marvellous hill-and-dale landscapes reward exploration, along with their underrated wineries. The star attractions are a brace of parks: **Parque Nacional Talampaya**, with its giant red cliffs, and the nearby **Parque Provincial Ischigualasto**, usually known as the **Valle de la Luna** on account of its intriguing moonscapes.

Argentina cherishes the lion's share of the wild, sparsely populated expanses of **Patagonia** (the rest belongs to Chile) and possesses by far the more worthwhile half of the remote archipelago of **Tierra del Fuego**. These are lands of seemingly endless arid steppe hemmed in for the most part by the southern leg of the Andes, a row of majestic volcanoes and craggy peaks interspersed by deep glacial lakes. An almost unbroken series of national parks running along these Patagonian and Fuegian cordilleras makes for some of the best trekking anywhere on the planet. You should certainly include the savage granite peaks of the Fitz Roy massif in **Parque Nacional Los Glaciares** in your itinerary, but consider also the less frequently visited araucaria (monkey puzzle) forests of **Parque Nacional Lanín** or the peerless trail network of **Parque Nacional Nahuel Huapi**. On the

Atlantic side of Patagonia, **Península Valdés** is a must-see for its world-class marine fauna, including sea elephants and orcas. If you have a historical bent, you may like to trace the region's associations with Darwin and his captain Fitz Roy in the choppy **Beagle Channel** off Ushuaia, or track down the legacy of Butch Cassidy, who lived near Cholila, or of the Welsh settlers whose influence can still be felt in communities like **Gaiman**, **Trelew** and – further inland – Trevelin.

When to go

Given the size of Argentina, you're unlikely to flit from region to region, and, if you can, you should try and visit each area at the optimal time of year. Roughly falling from September to November, the Argentine **spring** is perfect just about everywhere, although in the far south icy gales may blow. **Summer** (Dec–Feb) is the only time to climb the highest Andean peaks, such as Aconcagua, and also the most reliable time of year to head for Tierra del Fuego, though it can snow there any time of year. Buenos Aires is liable to be very hot and sticky in December and January, and you should certainly avoid the lowland parts of the north at this time of year, as temperatures can be scorching and roads flooded by heavy storms. **Autumn** (March and April) is a great time to visit Mendoza and San Juan provinces for the wine harvests, and Patagonia and Tierra del Fuego to witness the eye-catching red and orange hues of the beech groves. The **winter** months of June, July and August are obviously the time to head for the Andean ski resorts, but blizzards can cut off towns in Patagonia, and many places close from Easter through to October, so it's not a good time to tour the southerly region. Temperatures in the north of the country should be pleasant at this time of year, though Buenos Aires can come across as somewhat bleak in July and August, despite a plethora of indoor attractions.

A final point to bear in mind: the **national holiday seasons** are roughly January, Easter and July, when transport and accommodation can get booked up and rates are hiked, sometimes almost doubling.

AVERAGE TEMPERATURES AND RAINFALL

	Jan	Feb	Mar	Apr	May	Jun	Jul	Aug	Sep	Oct	Nov	Dec
BARILOCHE												
Max/Min (°C)	22/6	22/6	19/4	15/2	10/1	7/-1	6/-1	8/-1	11/-1	14/1	17/4	20/5
Rainfall (mm)	20	20	40	60	140	150	140	110	60	40	20	30
BUENOS AIRES												
Max/Min (°C)	29/17	28/17	26/16	22/12	18/8	14/5	14/6	16/6	18/8	21/10	24/13	28/16
Rainfall (mm)	79	71	109	89	76	61	56	51	79	86	84	99
SALTA												
Max/Min (°C)	27/17	27/16	25/15	23/12	20/7	19/4	20/3	23/5	23/7	27/12	28/14	28/14
Rainfall (mm)	170	140	100	30	8	3	3	5	8	25	61	127
USHUAIA												
Max/Min (°C)	15/6	14/5	12/4	10/2	6/0	5/-1	5/-1	6/-1	9/-1	11/2	13/4	13/5
Rainfall (mm)	31	33	48	50	55	55	46	61	40	35	35	41

25

things not to miss

It's not possible to see everything Argentina has to offer in one trip – and we don't suggest you try. What follows, in no particular order, is a selective taste of the country's highlights: vibrant cities, dramatic landscapes, spectacular wildlife and more. Each one has a page reference to take you straight into the Guide, where you can find out more. Coloured numbers refer to chapters in the Guide.

1 RUTA DE LOS SIETE LAGOS
Page 410
Seven Patagonian lakes – their sparkling waters emerald, ultramarine, cobalt, turquoise, cerulean, sapphire and indigo – linked by a rugged mountain road: a magical route best explored in a 4WD.

2 CARNIVAL IN THE LITORAL
Page 242
Like their neighbours across the river in Uruguay and Brazil, the people of the northeast do know how to party, not least in Gualeguaychú in the lead-up to Lent.

3 TALAMPAYA
Page 386
The undisputed highlight of La Rioja Province is a World Heritage Site dominated by giant cliffs of deep pink sandstone – once home to dinosaurs, now the protected habitat of condors, guanacos and foxes.

4 GLACIAR PERITO MORENO
Page 476
A visit to one of the world's last advancing glaciers is a treat for the eyes and the ears; count impossible shades of blue as you listen to a chorus of cracks, thuds and whines.

5 BIRDLIFE AT THE ESTEROS DEL IBERÁ
Page 237

The shimmering lagoons of these vital wetlands attract myriad birds, from tiny hummingbirds to majestic herons.

6 CUEVA DE LAS MANOS PINTADAS
Page 496

A prehistoric mural, an early finger-printing exercise or ancient graffiti? Whatever it is, this delicate tableau of many hands is one of the continent's most enchanting archeological sites.

7 WINTER SPORTS
Pages 365, 408 & 509

Las Leñas for the jet-set après-ski, Cerro Catedral for traditional pistes and Tierra del Fuego for the world's most southerly resorts – winter sports in Argentina combine great snow with a lot of showing off.

8 LA RECOLETA CEMETERY
Page 90

The prestigious resting place of Argentina's great and good – even Evita sneaked in – this cemetery is one of the world's most exclusive patches of real estate.

9 SAN TELMO, BUENOS AIRES
Page 78

Take a stroll down the cobbled streets of this bohemian neighbourhood full of tango bars and antique shops, talented street performers and decaying grandeur.

10 CLIMBING ACONCAGUA
Page 356

Despite frigid temperatures and extreme altitude – 6959m – the highest peak outside the Himalayas can be climbed with the right preparation and a knowledgeable guide, making for a world-class mountaineering experience.

11 THE PAMPAS
Page 137

Rugged gauchos, nodding pampas grass and herds of contented cattle are the famous inhabitants of Argentina's most archetypal landscape.

12 VOLCÁN LANÍN
Page 430

Despite the unappealing meaning of its native name – "he who choked himself to death" – this perfect symmetrical cone of a volcano is both a beauty to behold and a treat to climb.

13 TIGRE AND THE PARANÁ DELTA
Page 133

Take a boat or paddle a kayak around the swampy islets and muddy creeks of Tigre – a subtropical Venice right on the capital's doorstep.

14 DINOSAUR FOSSILS IN NEUQUÉN
Page 438

The world's biggest dinosaurs once roamed Neuquén Province – nothing will convey their immensity more than standing underneath their skeletons or seeing their giant footprints in the rock.

15 ANDEAN CAMELIDS
Page 555

Shaggy llamas and silky-fleeced alpacas, imposing guanacos and delicate vicuñas – all four distant relatives of the camel can be spotted along Argentina's cordillera.

16 QUEBRADA DE HUMAHUACA
Page 299

Whitewashed settlements nestled against polychrome mountains, dazzling salt flats, lush valleys and cactus forests, windswept steppe and deep gorges – some of the planet's most incredible scenery.

22

23

22 TREKKING IN THE ANDES
Page 482
South America's great mountain range offers world-class trekking, not least in the Fitz Roy sector of the Parque Nacional Los Glaciares.

23 IGUAZÚ FALLS
Page 259
Known simply as the Cataratas, the world's most awe-inspiring set of waterfalls is set among dense jungle, home to brightly coloured birds and butterflies.

24 ELEPHANT SEALS AT VALDÉS
Page 450
Península Valdés is a natural wonder and home to a staggering array of wildlife – but for many the giant blubbery elephant seals steal the show.

25 TRADITIONAL HANDICRAFTS
Page 125
Argentina's looms, kilns and workshops produce fine ponchos, pots and silverware, as well as world-class leatherware, jewellery and, great for souvenirs, *mate* paraphernalia.

Itineraries

The following itineraries will take you to every corner of the country, via both well-known sights and less visited ones, from the crashing Patagonia glaciers to off-the-beaten-track villages. Given the size of the country and cost of internal flights, don't worry if you can't complete the list – just visiting some will give you a good flavour of what Argentina has to offer.

WONDERS OF NATURE

Much of Argentina's "wow" nature highlights are in Patagonia, but there are unmissable sights further north, too, if you can spare a month or so.

❶ **Península Valdés** Watch whales, seals and sea lions basking in the rich, cool waters off this peninsula in Chubut, northern Patagonia. See p.450

❷ **Punta Tombo** The biggest colony of penguins in South America is a delightful sight, and the trip there will likely take you past guanacos, armadillos and more. See p.461

❸ **Ushuaia** At the very end of the road, Ushuaia sits on the Beagle Channel, teeming with birds, sea lions and giant crabs, and provides a base for exploring nearby Tierra del Fuego national park. See p.507

❹ **Glaciar Perito Moreno** Justifiably one of Argentina's most visited sights. Watch enormous chunks of blue ice carve off the city-sized glacier and even don crampons to walk on top of it. See p.476

❺ **Fitz Roy** The northern part of Los Glaciares national park provides some of the country's best trekking, among jagged peaks and turquoise lakes. See p.482

❻ **Quebrada de Humahuaca** Up in the dry northwest, the multicoloured hues of the pinnacles and strata of Humahuaca make it the pick of the region's sights. See p.299

❼ **Iguazú** The enormous Iguazú waterfalls by the Brazilian border, set in subtropical rainforest, make a steamy, stunning contrast to the icy southern sights. See p.259

❽ **Esteros del Iberá** An enchanting, little-visited ecosystem in Corrientes Province whose marshes are filled with an array of wildlife. See p.237

❾ **The Paraná Delta** A surprisingly verdant riverine community, right on Buenos Aires' doorstep, makes for a gentle but impressive end to a tour of Argentina's natural highlights. See p.133

RUTA 40

Like Route 66 in the US, Argentina's Ruta 40 – the country's longest highway, running from Patagonia to Bolivia – has a legendary status, inspiring songs, books and of course road trips. Count on six weeks if you want to take in all 5224km.

❶ **Cabo Vírgenes** La Cuarenta's beginning by the Strait of Magellan, marked by a lighthouse, heralds the start of a zigzagging route through the windswept Patagonian steppe. See p.491

ABOVE VOLCANO, LA PAYUNA

❷ Cueva de los Manos Pintadas Just off the Ruta 40, in the Patagonia wilderness, this World Heritage Site is one of South America's finest examples of ancient rock art. **See p.496**

❸ Bariloche Gateway to the Nahuel Huapi park, Argentina's Lake District has pristine alpine-like scenery, dramatic mountain lakes and ancient trees. **See p.397**

❹ La Payunia A remote land of rosy lava, ebony gorges, deep karstic caves and flamingo-flecked lagoons in Mendoza Province. **See p.368**

❺ Laguna Diamante Often inaccessible, this lagoon rewards the adventurous. Enjoy a picnic on the banks of a crystalline brook as you admire the silhouette of Volcán Maipo. **See p.359**

❻ Cuesta de Miranda The road in La Rioja Province winds through polychrome mountains that contrast with the verdant vegetation along the riverbanks below. **See p.385**

❼ Belén Stop off at this Catamarca highland village for a top-notch poncho – methods of weaving have been maintained since pre-Hispanic times. **See p.325**

❽ Salinas Grandes Ringed by mountains, this area of snow-white salt flats is a good place to spot llamas and vicuñas. **See p.302**

WINE AND DINE

Wherever you travel in Argentina, you can find excellent-quality food and drink. Beef plays a part, of course, but there's more to the country's culinary offering. Allow two to three weeks.

❶ Buenos Aires The country's capital has, unsurprisingly, the most cosmopolitan selection of restaurants – including its famous *puertas cerradas* – with inventive cooking at reasonable prices easy to track down. **See p.112**

❷ The Pampas Stay on an estancia to enjoy the best barbecued beef you're likely to taste anywhere, right in the fertile heartland where it comes from. **See p.145**

❸ Mendoza Spend your days – and nights if you wish – at a bodega, tasting fine malbec wines with the snowcapped Andes as a backdrop. **See p.335**

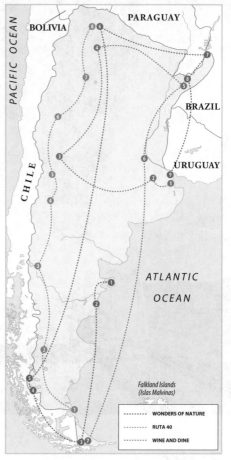

❹ Salta A good place to try the distinctive northwestern cuisine, including the classic empanada, a pasty filled with meat or vegetables, or *locro* stew. **See p.281**

❺ Estancia Santa Inés Set among plantations of *mate*, the tea-like beverage drunk avidly throughout Argentina, this estancia in verdant Misiones also serves delicious food. **See p.253**

❻ Rosario Vibrant and stylish Rosario overlooks the Río Paraná and is an excellent place to dine on the local river fish, such as *dorado*, *boga* and *surubí*. **See p.216**

❼ Ushuaia The capital of Argentine Tierra del Fuego is the best place to sample *centolla* (king crab), plucked fresh from the Beagle Channel. **See p.507**

DRIVING TOWARDS FITZ ROY, EL CHALTÉN, PATAGONIA

Basics

Getting there

Though some visitors reach Argentina overland from a neighbouring country and a tiny handful arrive by boat, the overwhelming majority of travellers first set foot on Argentine soil at Buenos Aires' international airport, Ezeiza.

In general, airfares to Argentina tend to be quite high, but they do vary widely depending on the routing and the **season**. The highest fares are between December and February, around Easter and in July and August, Argentines' winter holiday season. You'll get the best prices during the low season: March to June and September to November. Note also that flying at weekends often hikes return fares; price ranges quoted in this section assume midweek travel.

Flights from the UK and Ireland

Several airlines offer regular scheduled flights **from the UK** to Buenos Aires, via another European city, São Paulo or the US (trips via the US can be marginally less expensive, but are usually longer). British Airways (**W** ba.com) is currently the only airline to fly direct from London. Iberia (**W** iberia.com) via Madrid skimps on the creature comforts but is often the cheapest. Adult **fares** from London to Buenos Aires usually start at around £650 in the low season, rising to well over £1000 in the high season.

There are no direct flights **from Ireland** to Argentina. If you're trying to keep costs down, consider flying to London with an economy airline and making a connection there. For less hassle, though, and only a fraction more money, you're better off flying direct to New York or Miami and catching an onward flight from there.

In addition to fares, it's worth paying attention to the **routes** used by different airlines. The shortest and most convenient routes from London, often via São Paulo or Madrid, entail a total travelling time of around sixteen hours. Apart from minimizing the length of the flight, another reason to check the routes is that many airlines allow you to take **stopovers** on the way –

sometimes for free, sometimes for a surcharge of around ten percent. Potential stopovers include Bogotá, Rio and São Paulo in South America; Boston, Chicago, Dallas, Houston, Miami, Newark and Washington DC in the US; and Frankfurt, Madrid, Milan, Paris and Rome in Europe.

Flights from the US and Canada

Several airlines, including American Airlines (**W** aa .com), United (**W** united.com) and Aerolíneas Argentinas (**W** aerolineas.com.ar), offer daily non-stop **flights from the US** to Buenos Aires. Typical **fares** start at around US$1200 from New York, Chicago or Washington in low season, rising to US$1700 in the high season. Flying times to Buenos Aires are around eleven hours from New York and Chicago, and nine from Miami.

There's less choice if you're flying **from Canada**, with Air Canada (**W** aircanada.com) offering the only flight into the country – from Toronto via Santiago de Chile (with connections from other major Canadian cities). You'll be able to put together a considerably more flexible itinerary if you look for connecting flights with a US carrier. Direct flights from Toronto take around thirteen hours and **prices** start at Can$1200 in low season; from Vancouver the journey time is at least eighteen hours, at a similar fare.

Note that a reciprocity fee of US$92 charged to Canadians is payable before entering Argentina (**W** reciprocidad.provincianet.com.ar). There is no way around this and airline staff are hot on payments, so do buy online before you check in (see p.47).

Flights from Australia, New Zealand and South Africa

The best flight deals to Argentina from Australia and New Zealand are offered by Aerolíneas Argentinas (**W** aerolineas.com.ar) and LAN (**W** lan.com) in conjunction with Qantas (**W** qantas.com), Air New Zealand (**W** airnz.co.nz) and Emirates (**W** emirates .co.nz), with a stopover in Santiago. In **Australia**, flights to Argentina leave from Sydney, plus a

---

ROUND-THE-WORLD TICKETS

If Argentina is only one stop on a longer journey, you might want to consider buying a **round-the-world (RTW)** ticket. Some travel agents can sell you an "off-the-shelf" RTW ticket that will have you touching down in about half a dozen cities (Buenos Aires is on many itineraries). Alternatively, you can have a travel agent assemble an RTW ticket for you; in this case the ticket can be tailored to your needs but is usually more expensive.

couple a week that depart from Melbourne. There are no direct flights **from New Zealand**, so you will need to go either via Sydney or with LAN via Santiago. Flights **from South Africa** to Argentina leave from Cape Town and Johannesburg and usually go via São Paulo, taking sixteen or seventeen hours; South African Airways (**W**flysaa .com) leaves from Johannesburg, for example.

Airfares depend on both the season and duration of stay. Fares from Australia normally start around Aus$2000 in low season. The lowest return fares from Cape Town or Johannesburg cost around ZAR8500.

Australians must also pay the reciprocity fee of US$100 before entering Argentina.

DISCOUNT AGENTS

Adventure World Australia **T** 1300 295 049, **W** adventureworld .com.au; New Zealand **T** 0800 238368, **W** adventureworld.co.nz. Agents for a vast array of international adventure travel companies that operate trips to South America.

Bridge the World UK **T** 0800 988 6884, **W** bridgetheworld.com. Specializing in RTW tickets, with good deals aimed at backpackers.

North South Travel UK **T** 01245 608291, **W** northsouthtravel .co.uk. Friendly, competitive travel agency, offering discounted fares worldwide. Profits are used to support projects in the developing world, especially the promotion of sustainable tourism.

STA Travel UK **T** 0333 321 0099; US **T** 1 800 781 4040, Australia **T** 134 782; New Zealand **T** 0800 474400; South Africa **T** 0861 781781; **W** statravel.com. Worldwide specialists in independent travel; also student IDs, travel insurance, car rental, rail passes and more. Good discounts for students and under-26s.

Trailfinders UK **T** 020 7368 1200, Ireland **T** 01 677 7888; **W** trailfinders.com. One of the best-informed and most efficient agents for independent travellers.

Travel Cuts Canada **T** 1 800 667 2887; **W** travelcuts.com. Canadian youth and student travel firm.

USIT Ireland **T** 01 602 1906, Australia **T** 1 800 092 499; **W** usit.ie. Ireland's main student and youth travel specialist tour operator.

A BETTER KIND OF TRAVEL

At Rough Guides we are passionately committed to travel. We believe it helps us understand the world we live in and the people we share it with – and of course tourism is vital to many developing economies. But the scale of modern tourism has also damaged some places irreparably, and climate change is accelerated by most forms of transport, especially flying. All Rough Guides' flights are carbon-offset, and every year we donate money to a variety of environmental charities.

ADVENTURE TOUR SPECIALISTS

Adventures Abroad Canada **T** 1 800 665 3998, **W** adventures -abroad.com. Adventure specialist offering mainly cultural tours to Argentina, combined with Chile or Brazil.

Contours Australia **T** 1300 135 391, **W** contourstravel.com.au. Specialists in tailored city stopover packages and tours, including self-drive tours through the Lake District and Mendoza wine tours.

Dragoman UK **T** 01728 861133, **W** dragoman.com. Extended overland journeys; shorter camping and hotel-based safaris, too.

Exodus Travels UK **T** 0845 869 8275, **W** exodus.co.uk; US **T** 1 844 227 9087, **W** exodustravels.com. Adventure-tour operator taking small groups for specialist programmes, including walking, biking, overland, adventure and cultural trips. Among its tours is a two-week Fitz Roy and Torres del Paine (Chile) trip.

TOURS

Explore! UK **T** 01252 883591, **W** explore.co.uk. Small-group tours, treks, expeditions and safaris. Offers two-week tours of Patagonia.

Journey Latin America UK **T** 02034 681042, **W** journey latinamerica.co.uk. Specialist in flights, packages and tailor-made trips to Latin America, including a sixteen-day self-drive trip to Salta.

MacDermott's Argentina Argentina **T** 011 4773 2522, **W** mac dermottsargentina.com. Bespoke horseback adventures around the country, specializing in Andes crossings and treks in Salta and Mendoza.

Tucan Travel UK **T** 0800 804 8435, **W** tucantravel.com. Group holidays in Argentina, plus a range of overland expeditions in the rest of South America.

Wilderness Travel US **T** 1 800 368 2794, **W** wildernesstravel .com. Specialist in hiking, cultural and wildlife adventures in Patagonia.

Wildlife Worldwide UK **T** 01962 302086, **W** wildlifeworldwide .com. Tailor-made trips for wildlife and wilderness enthusiasts. Twelve-day trip in the northeast, including Iguazú and Esteros del Iberá.

World Expeditions UK **T** 0800 0744 135, **W** worldexpeditions .co.uk; Australia **T** 612 8270 8400, **W** worldexpeditions.com.au. Australian-owned adventure company whose trips include an Aconcagua ascent for hardcore adventurers and special tours for travellers over 55.

Getting around

Distances are immense in Argentina, and you are likely to spend a considerable portion of your budget on travel. Ground transport (mostly bus) is best for giving a true impression of the scale of the country and for appreciating the landscape. However, you may want to cover some big distances, particularly to and around Patagonia, in which case travelling by domestic flights can often save a day or more. The inter-city bus network is extensive but services in remote areas can be poor and infrequent; in these places, it is worth considering

car rental. Train services are run-down and limited and not generally a viable method of getting around.

By bus

By far the most common and straightforward method of transport in Argentina is the **bus** (colectivo or *bus* for local journeys, *micro* for long-distance journeys). There are hundreds of private companies, most of which concentrate on one particular region, although some, such as Vía TAC and El Rápido, run nationwide.

Many buses are modern, plush Brazilian-built models designed for long-distance travel. Breakdowns do happen, but in general your biggest worry will be what movie the driver has chosen to "entertain" you with (usually subtitled Hollywood action flicks, played with the sound either turned off or at thunderous volume). On longer journeys, snacks and hot meals are served (included in the ticket price), although these vary considerably in quality and tend towards sweet-toothed tastes. *Cama, ejecutivo* and *suite* are the luxury services, with wide, fully reclinable seats; *semi-cama* services offer a little less comfort, with narrower seats that only extend part of the way back. These former services usually cost between twenty and forty percent more than the *semi-cama* (regular) services, and are well worth the extra, particularly over long distances. On minor routes, you'll have less choice of buses, though most are decent with plenty of legroom. Many services turn the air conditioning up beyond most people's levels of endurance; take a jumper on board.

Buying tickets (*boletos* or *pasajes*) is normally a simple on-the-spot matter, but you must plan in advance if travelling in the high season (mid-Dec to Feb) or around long weekends, especially if you're taking a long-distance bus from Buenos Aires or any other major city to a particularly popular holiday destination. In these cases you should buy your ticket a week beforehand; note that prices rise during peak times. Some destinations have both direct (*directo* or *rápido*) and slower services that stop at all intermediary points, and though most services call into the bus terminal (*terminal de ómnibus*), this is not always the case: some drop you on the road outside the centre. Similarly, when heading to Buenos Aires, check that the bus' final destination is **Retiro**, the central bus terminal (see p.105), otherwise you might end up in a suburban terminal such as Liniers.

There's usually some kind of **left-luggage office** (*guardamaleta* or *guardaequipaje*) at terminals, or, if you have a few hours to kill between connections, the company with whom you have your onward ticket will usually store your pack free of charge, enabling you to look around town unencumbered.

If you are planning to travel a lot by bus, it may be worth investing in a **South Pass**, which allows unlimited travel in the Southern Cone and Andean countries over a set number of days, though you will have to be clocking up quite a few kilometres to make it worthwhile, with prices starting at $2940 per trip and a minimum of three trips (☎0800 555 28737, ⌨ argentinabybus.com).

By air

Argentina's most important domestic **airport** is Buenos Aires' Aeroparque Jorge Newbery, which has **flights** to all the country's provincial capitals and major tourist centres. People who want to get an overview of Argentina's tremendous variety in a limited time may rely heavily on domestic flights to combat the vast distances involved – what takes twenty or more hours by bus might take only one or two by plane. As a rule, you'll find **prices** are the same whether you buy your ticket direct from the airline office or from the plentiful travel agencies in most towns and cities. Availability can be a problem on tourist routes such as those around Patagonia or during the holidays, and if these feature in your itinerary you are advised to book as far in advance as possible. Some deals booked in advance are good value, although non-residents usually pay a considerably higher tariff than Argentines. Domestic **departure taxes** are always included in the price of the ticket.

Aerolíneas Argentinas (☎0810 2228 6527, ⌨ aerolineas.com.ar) is the national flag carrier, with the biggest destination network. The company has faced many problems over the past decade or so and its once excellent reputation has been tarnished, but in many places it will be your only option. Its main rival in Argentina these days is Chilean flag carrier **LAN** (☎0810 999 9526, ⌨ lan.com), which has an Argentine subsidiary (LAN Argentina) operating flights to the country's major tourist destinations.

The military also provides civilian services – the Air Force's **LADE** (☎0810 810 5233, ⌨ lade.com.ar) is one of the cheapest methods of travel in the country and flies to isolated, often unexpected places, mostly destinations in Patagonia. However, routings can be convoluted, and you might find a flight stops four or five times between its original departure point and final destination. Timetables change frequently (up to once a month) and services can be cancelled at the last moment if the

Air Force needs the plane. That said, it's worth asking at LADE offices as you travel round just in case they've something useful.

There are other small airlines in operation, such as Salta-based Andes (📞0810 7772 6337, 🌐andes online.com), which connects the city with a few destinations, including Buenos Aires, Iguazú and Puerto Madryn. Another is Alas (📞011 4313 6954, 🌐alas.uy), a Uruguay-based low-cost airline that launched in 2016, serving Montevideo and Punta del Este in Uruguay and Asunción in Paraguay from Buenos Aires.

One factor to bear in mind is the possible disruption caused by **volcanic eruptions** in the Andes. Huge clouds of ash billowed out of a Chilean volcano throughout much of 2011, showering grit and dust onto the Lake District and causing havoc farther afield. Bariloche airport was closed for several months while other airports around the country, including both of the capital's, were repeatedly shut down as a precaution, sometimes for a couple of days at a time. Airports were also affected in 2013 and 2015 by Copahue and Villarrica volcanoes respectively.

By car

You are unlikely to want or need a **car** for your whole stay in Argentina, but you'll find one pretty indispensable if you want to explore some of the more isolated areas of Patagonia, Tierra del Fuego, the Northwest, Mendoza or San Juan. If possible, it makes sense to get a group together, not just to keep costs down but also to share the driving,

which can be arduous and potentially dangerous, especially on unsurfaced roads. Approximately thirty percent of roads are paved in Argentina, but some of the less important of these routes are littered with potholes. Unsurfaced roads can be extremely muddy after rain, and may be impassable, even to 4WDs, after prolonged wet spells. A 4WD is not usually necessary, but can be useful on minor roads in mountainous areas, when you're likely to encounter snow, or on Ruta 40 in Patagonia. Outside major cities, most accidents (often the most serious ones) occur on unsurfaced gravel roads (*ripio*).

Altitude can also be a problem in the high Andes – you may need to adjust the fuel intake. One thing worth noting: flashing your lights when driving is a warning to other vehicles *not* to do something, as opposed to the British system, where it is used to signal concession of right of way. You can be fined for not wearing **seatbelts** (both in the front and back), although many Argentines display a cavalier disregard of this law.

Car rental

To **rent a car**, you need to be over 21 (25 with some agencies) and hold a driver's licence – an international one is not usually necessary. Bring a credit card and your passport for the **deposit**. Before you drive off, check that you've been given insurance, tax and ownership papers, check carefully for dents and paintwork damage and get hold of a 24hr emergency telephone number. Also, pay close attention to the small print, most notably what you're liable for in the event of an accident: the list of people with grievances after renting a car and spending considerably

---

DRIVING ON DIRT ROADS

Driving on gravel is much like driving on snow – fine in a straight line but difficult on bends or when braking. To keep safe, stick to the Highway Code and follow this **advice**:

- On unpaved sections, follow the most recently used tracks and never exceed 70km/hr (you'll often creep along at 40km/hr).
- Slow down and move as far right as possible when approaching an oncoming vehicle to avoid windscreen or headlight damage.
- Overtake with caution – dust and stones thrown up will obscure visibility.
- Go downhill in a low gear – the rear will skid if you go too fast.
- Slow down in strong winds, especially crosswinds – in a high-clearance 4WD the wind may get underneath – and be careful opening doors, as they can be wrenched from their hinges.
- Give help if you see someone has broken down: offering to give them a lift or taking a message to the next town could be vital.
- Refuel whenever you see a pump – the next may be hundreds of kilometres away.
- Take plenty of provisions with you (especially drinking water), plus warm clothing in case you are stranded overnight.
- Always allow more time than you need to get from A to B, as the distances are huge.

ADDRESSES

Addresses are nearly always written with the street name followed by the street number – thus, San Martín 2443; with avenues (avenidas), the abbreviation "**Av**" or "**Avda**" appears before the name – thus, Av San Martín 2443. The relatively rare abbreviation "**c/**" for calle (street) is used only to avoid confusion in a city that has streets named after other cities – thus c/Tucumán 564, Salta or c/Salta 1097, Tucumán – or where streets are numbered rather than named – c/24, for example. If the name is followed by "**s/n**" (sin número), it means the building is numberless, frequently the case in small villages and for larger buildings such as hotels or town halls. Sometimes streets whose names have been officially changed continue to be referred to by their former names, even in written addresses. In most cities, **blocks** (*cuadras* or *manzanas*) go up in 100s, making it relatively easy to work out on a map where a hotel at no. 977 or a restaurant at no. 2233 is located.

more than they intended is a long one. Your insurance will not normally cover you for flipping the car, or smashed windscreens or headlights.

Car-rental **costs** are high in Argentina, though rates between different agencies can vary considerably. Small, local firms often give very good deals – up to half the price of the global rental names – and it doesn't necessarily hold that the local branch of an international agency will be up to the standards you expect. The main cities offer the most economical prices, while costs are highest in Patagonia; **unlimited mileage** deals are usually your best option, as per-kilometre charges can otherwise exceed your daily rental cost many times over. Unfortunately, there are relatively few places in Argentina where you can rent a vehicle and drop it in another specified town without being clobbered with a high relocation fee. Book as early as possible if you're travelling in high season to popular holiday destinations, as demand usually outstrips supply. It's fairly straightforward to take a vehicle into **Chile** but it is essential to have the correct paperwork from the rental firm. Many provide this free of charge, particularly those in towns near the border.

If you plan to do a lot of driving, consider a membership with the **Automóvil Club Argentino (ACA)**, which has a useful **emergency breakdown** towing and repair service and offers discounts at a series of lodges across the country (many of which are in need of an overhaul). You can join in Buenos Aires at Av del Libertador 1850 (daily 9am–7pm; ☎011 4808 4000, ⓦ www.aca.org.ar), or at any of the ACA service stations.

Taxis

There are two main types of taxi in Argentina: regular **urban taxis** that you can flag down in the street; and **remises**, or minicab radio taxis, that you must book by phone or at their central booking booth. Urban taxis are fitted with meters – make sure they use them – and each municipality has its own rates.

Remises operate with rates fixed according to the destination and are less expensive than taxis for out-of-town and long-distance trips. Often, it makes more sense to hire a *remís* for a day than to rent your own car: it can be more economical, you save yourself the hassle of driving and you'll normally get the sights pointed out for you along the way.

In some places, such as in the northwest, **shared taxis** (*taxis colectivos*) also run on fixed routes between towns: they wait at a given collection point, each passenger pays a set fee and the colectivos leave when full (some carry destination signs on their windscreen, others don't, so always ask around). They often drop you at a place of your choice at the other end, making them a faster and more convenient alternative to buses, often for only marginally more money. *Taxis colectivos* also drive up and down fixed routes within certain cities: flag one down and pay your share (usually posted on the windscreen).

By boat

Boat services in Argentina fall into two broad categories: those that serve as a functional form of transport, and (with some overlap) those that you take to enjoy tourist sights. The two **ferry services** you are most likely to use are the comfortable ones from Buenos Aires to Colonia del Sacramento in Uruguay (also served by the speedier hydrofoil) and the much more spartan Chilean ones that transport foot passengers and vehicles across the Strait of Magellan into Tierra del Fuego at Punta Delgada and Porvenir. There are also several practical river crossings throughout the Litoral region, for example connecting Concordia with Salto in Uruguay, or linking Goya in Corrientes with Reconquista in Santa Fe, as well as numerous crossings from Misiones to neighbouring Paraguay and Brazil. Tigre, just northwest of the capital, tends towards the pleasure-trips end of the market, and offers boat trips around the Delta and to Isla Martín

García; there is, however, one small ferry that crosses the river to Carmelo in Uruguay.

In Patagonia, most **boat trips** are designed purely for their scenic value, including ones that give access to the polar scenery of the Parque Nacional Los Glaciares and the alpine Parque Nacional Nahuel Huapi.

By rail

Argentina's **train network**, developed through British investment in the late nineteenth century and nationalized by the Perón administration in 1948, collapsed in 1993 when government subsidies were withdrawn. The railways are now in a pitiful state, with very little in the way of long-distance services – there's a handful in Buenos Aires Province (see p.130), cheaper than the bus but considerably less savoury. The government has announced a plethora of measures and licences intended to reinvigorate the system and to introduce new, modern services, most notably a controversial US$4 billion bullet train connecting Buenos Aires, Rosario and Córdoba, the licence for which has been awarded but which is still on hold indefinitely at the time of writing. Currently, Buenos Aires to Rosario takes a hardly speedy six and a half hours.

You're far less likely to want to use Argentine trains as a method of getting from place to place, however, than you are to try one of the country's **tourist trains**, where the aim is simply to travel for the fun of it. There are two principal lines: La Trochita (see p.418), the Old Patagonian Express from Esquel; and the Tren a las Nubes (see p.293), one of the highest railways in the world, climbing through the mountains from Salta towards the Chilean border.

Cycling

Most towns with a tourist infrastructure have at least one place that rents out **bicycles** for half- or full-day visits to sights at very reasonable prices. These excursions can be great fun, but remember to bring spare inner tubes and a pump, especially if you're cycling off surfaced roads, and check that the brakes and seat height are properly adjusted. Dedicated bike paths have appeared; Buenos Aires now has a substantial 155km, and also a free bike hire scheme (see p.108). Don't expect much consideration from other vehicles on the road, though. There are almost no places that rent out **motorbikes**.

Argentina is also a popular destination for more serious cyclists, and expeditions along routes such as the arduous, partly unsurfaced RN-40 attract mountain-biking devotees who often value physical endurance above the need to see sights (most points of interest off RN-40 lie a good way west along branch roads, which deters most people from visiting more than one or two). Trips such as these need to be planned thoroughly, and should only be attempted by experienced expedition cyclists with top-quality equipment and plenty of spares.

Hitchhiking

Hitchhiking always involves an element of risk, but it can also be one of the most rewarding ways to travel, especially if you can speak at least elementary conversational Spanish. It is getting trickier to hitchhike in Argentina: some truck drivers are prohibited by company rules from picking you up, others are reluctant as it often invalidates car insurance or you become the liability of the driver. In general, it is not advisable for women travelling on their own to hitchhike in Argentina, and it isn't normal to head out of large urban areas by hitch-hiking: you're far better off catching a local bus out to an outlying service station or road checkpoint and trying from there. In the south of the country, hitching is still generally very safe. In places such as Patagonia, where roads are few and traffic sparse, you'll often find yourself part of a queue, especially in summer. If you do try to hitchhike, always travel with sufficient reserves of water, food, clothes and shelter; you can get stranded for days in some of the more isolated spots.

Accommodation

Accommodation in Argentina runs the gamut from campsites and youth hostels to fabulously luxurious estancias (ranches) and opulent hotels offering every conceivable amenity. Between these two extremes you'll find a whole variety of establishments, including charming old colonial houses with balconies and dark and seedy hotels that lack so much as a window. Informal room rental is also common in towns with seasonal influxes of tourists but too few hotels to cope, while Airbnb has taken off in recent years, especially in Buenos Aires.

Prices vary considerably depending on where you are in the country. The standard given throughout this Guide reflects double room rates in high season, but not over bank holidays or the festival season. Areas receiving large numbers of foreign visitors, particularly Buenos Aires and Patagonia, have seen prices rise sharply in recent years; less-visited areas offer less variety but also much better bargains. Even in the capital, however, you can expect to pay slightly less for comparable accommodation than you would in most European countries or North America. Single travellers on a budget and seeking more privacy than is available at a youth hostel will find things harder, although the number of places offering per-person prices appears to be on the rise, especially at resorts and estancias where meals or activities are included. Discounts can sometimes be negotiated, particularly if you are staying for a longer period. Bear in mind that the 21% IVA tax is often not included in quoted prices, while places aimed at foreigners may quote in US$ rather than pesos. If paying with cash dollars, you may be able to strike a deal on the exchange rate (see "Costs", p.45) in more remote areas, though it's best to check when reserving.

Hotels

Most towns in Argentina will have at least one **hotel**, though in many places these are unimaginative, rather drab places. If you are on a budget, and the option is available, you might do better to head for a hostel, most of which provide good-value private rooms as well as dorms. Posadas and bed and breakfasts can be more attractive in the middle of the range, while small boutique or designer hotels – which have popped up in significant numbers in Argentina in the past few years – often have a lot more individuality than the standard plush but monotonous five-star places aimed at business travellers.

Posadas, hosterías and B&Bs

The use of the term **posada** usually denotes a fairly idiosyncratic place, often with a slightly rustic feel, but generally comfortable or even luxurious. In a similar vein, the term **hostería** is frequently used for smallish, upmarket hotels – oriented towards tourists rather than businessmen.

A similar type of accommodation, particularly common around Buenos Aires, is **B&Bs** (the English term is used), which tend to be chic, converted townhouses with an exclusive but cosy atmosphere – price-wise they tend to be mid- to top-range options, and generally offer far more attractive surroundings than standard hotels at the same price.

Hostels

Youth hostels are known as *albergues juveniles* or *albergues de la juventud* in Argentina, though the term "(youth) hostel" is frequently used instead – *albergue* is normally taken to mean *albergue transitorio* (short-stay hotels where rooms are rented by the hour, also known as *telos*). There is an extensive chain of mostly reliable hostels in Argentina affiliated with Hostelling International (HI), as well as a good number of independent hostels, which vary more in quality, but when they are good – particularly in Buenos Aires, Mendoza and Salta – they are among the country's best. Accommodation is generally in **dormitories**, though most places also have several double **rooms**, often en suite. Facilities vary, too, from next to nothing to swimming pools, internet access, washing machines, cable TV and patios with barbecue equipment.

Note you sometimes see the term "**hostal**" used as a seemingly general term for hotels – both youth hostels and high-rise modern hotels call themselves *hostales*. The pricing standard throughout this Guide reflects the cheapest dorm bed in high season.

Youth hostel associations

The local office of Hostelling International is in Buenos Aires, at Florida 835 (☎011 4511 8723, ⓦhostelsofargentina.com). Associated hostels give a ten percent discount – usually a few pesos a night – to holders of HI cards, but they rarely require that you possess a card in order to stay there. Membership for non-Argentines is US$20 a year, and also gives you discounts with some bus companies and other businesses.

Residenciales and hospedajes

Basic **hospedajes** and **residenciales** are sometimes forgotten as an accommodation option, given that they often aren't very fancy or trendy in Argentina and are not usually recommended by tourist offices. However, they can be far more welcoming, clean and secure than one-star hotels; a few of them stand out as some of Argentina's best budget accommodation. Furnishings tend to be basic, with little more than a bed, perhaps a desk and chair and a fan in each room – though some are far less austere than others and there is even the odd one with cable TV. Most places offer private bathrooms. There's little difference between *residenciales* and *hospedajes* – indeed, the same establishment may be described in different accommodation lists as both, or even as a hotel or hostel. The only real difference is that *hospedajes* tend to be part of a family house.

Estancias

A very different experience to staying in a hotel is provided by Argentina's many **estancias** (ranches, or **fincas** as they are known in the north of the country) that are open to visitors. Guests usually stay in the *casco*, or farmhouse, which can be anything from a simple family home to an extravagant castle-like residence. Estancias are nearly always family-run, the income from tourism tending to serve as a supplement to the declining profits earned from the land itself. Accommodation is generally luxurious, with bags of character, and a stay is a mini-vacation in itself; for about US$300–700 a day you are given four meals, invariably including a traditional *asado*, with activities such as horseriding and swimming also usually part of the price. Many places offer experiences that reflect the local area, from cattle herding and branding in the Pampas to wine tasting in Mendoza to observing caymans in the Litoral.

You can **book** your estancia accommodation either by approaching them directly or through certain travel agencies; a comprehensive one in Buenos Aires is Estancias Argentinas, at Roque Sáenz Peña 616, 9th floor (☎011 4343 2366, ⓦestanciasargentinas.com).

Cabañas

Popular in resort towns, self-catering *cabañas* are small, chalet-style buildings that can vary from miniature suburban villas with cable TV and microwaves to pleasingly simple and rustic wooden constructions. If you have been staying in a lot of hotels or doing some hardcore camping, *cabañas* can be fun and relaxing places to take a break for a few days. They are often very good value for money for small groups, although a few of the simpler ones can also be surprisingly affordable options for couples or even single travellers. They are usually grouped together in outfits of between two and ten cabins; many campsites also offer basic ones as an alternative to tents.

Camping

There are plenty of places to camp throughout Argentina, with most towns and villages having their own municipal **campsites** (*campings*), but standards vary wildly. At the major resorts, there are usually plenty of privately owned, well-organized sites, with facilities ranging from provisions stores to volleyball courts and TV rooms. Some are attractive, but mostly they seem to take the fun out of camping and you're more likely to wake up to a view of next door's 4WD than the surrounding countryside. They are, however, good places to meet other travellers and generally offer a high degree of security. There are also simpler campsites, though at nearly all of them showers, electric light and barbecue facilities are standard. A campsite with no, or very limited, facilities is referred to as a *camping libre*. Municipal sites can be rather desolate and sometimes not particularly safe: it's usually a good idea to check with locals as to the security of the place before pitching a tent. The price, and pricing system vary greatly from place to place, but expect to pay around $50–100 per person; camping prices given in this Guide are per person pitching your own tent, unless otherwise specified.

Food and drink

Argentine food can be summed up with one word: beef. And not just any beef, but the best in the world – succulent, cherry-red meat raised on some of the greenest, most extensive pastures known to cattle. The *asado*, or barbecue, is an institution, as much a part of the Argentine way of life as football, fast driving and tango.

Where to eat

Apart from generic *restaurantes* (or *restoranes*), you will come across *parrillas* (for steak and beef), *marisquerías* (for seafood), *confiterías* (cafés for coffee, cakes, snacks or simple meals), *comedores* (simple local canteens), *pizzerías*, *bodegones* (unpretentious restaurants that theoretically serve a house wine) and *cantinas* (neighbourhood places often dishing up Italian food, such as home-made pasta). By South American standards the quality of restaurants is high, and though by international standards they are not always cheap, they often represent good value. If you're on a tight budget, make lunch your main meal, and take advantage of the **menú del día** or **menú ejecutivo** – usually set meals for about $100 – and in the evening try **tenedor libre** restaurants where you can eat as much as you like for a set price at self-service buffets. Up your budget to $200 or so a head and you can dine a la carte at most mid-range restaurants, wine included. Argentina also has a fair sprinkling of gourmet locales (*restaurantes cocina de autor*),

ASADO BASICS

The term **asado** (from *asar*, to roast) originally referred to slowly grilled or roasted brisket, but now is applied to any **barbecued meat**. Since barbecues are an integral part of life, it's good to know your way around the beef-eating vocabulary, especially as *carne* in Argentina isn't cut in the same way as in the rest of the world – cuts are sliced through bone and muscle rather than across them.

Argentines like their meat **well done** (*cocida*), and indeed, some are better cooked through. If you prefer it medium, ask for *a punto*, and for rare – which really requires some insistence – *jugosa* or *muy jugosa*. Before you get to the steaks, you'll be offered **achuras**, or offal, and different types of sausage. **Chorizos** are excellent pork sausages, while **morcilla**, blood sausage, is an acquired taste. **Provoleta**, sliced provolone cheese, grilled on the barbecue till crispy on the edges, is on most menus and a classic starter. Otherwise, it's beef all the way.

After these "appetizers" you move on to the **beef** cuts, such as **tira de asado** or **asado de tira** (ribs; also called *costillar* or *asado a secas*). These can be fatty, but explode with a meaty taste. Next is the muscly but delicious **vacío** (flank), often preferred by home barbecue masters. But save some room for the prime cuts: **bife ancho** is entrecôte; **bife angosto** or **lomito** is sirloin; **cuadril** is a lump of rumpsteak; **lomo**, one of the luxury cuts and often kept in reserve, is fillet steak; **bife de chorizo** (not to be confused with *chorizo* sausage) is what the French call a *pavé*. Aficionados call **entraña**, a sinewy cut, the main delicacy. Rarely barbecued, **peceto** (eye round steak) is a tender lump of flesh, roasted with potatoes (*peceto al horno con papas*) or sliced cold for *vitel tonné* – a classic Italian starter, adopted by Argentines, that's topped with a tuna and anchovy mayonnaise.

Lightly salted meat is usually best served with nothing on it but the traditional condiments of **chimichurri** – olive oil mixed with salt, garlic, chilli pepper, vinegar and bay leaf – and **salsa criolla**, similar but also with onion and tomato; everyone jealously guards their secret formulas for both these "magic" dressings.

concentrated in, but by no means limited to, Buenos Aires. In these, your per-head bill will cost more like $400, though this still compares well with cities in other industrialized countries and you get fabulous food, wine, ambience and service. You should try and splash out at least once during your visit. *Restaurantes a puertas cerradas* or closed door restaurants (see box, p.114), whose address is given out on reservation, are often run out of the cook's own home. They can offer an intimate and often experimental dining experience that steers away from beef.

When to eat

Argentines tend to have four meals a day, given that dinner time begins far later than in Europe or the US. **Breakfast** is usually served up until around 10am, and **lunch** from around noon until 3pm. Hardly any restaurants open for **dinner** before 8pm, so if you think you're going to be starving by this time, do as the locals do and either have a hearty lunch or take **merienda**: tea and snacks squeezed in before dinner at a café or *confitería* in the late afternoon. In Buenos Aires – and in the hotter months in the rest of the country – few people turn up for dinner before 10 or even 11pm. Don't be surprised to see people pouring into restaurants well after midnight: Argentines, and Porteños in particular, are night owls.

What to eat

While beef is the most prominent feature on many menus, it's by no means the whole story. In general, you seldom have a bad meal in Argentina. That said, imagination, innovation and a sense of subtle flavour are sometimes lacking, with Argentines preferring to eat the wholesome but often bland dishes their immigrant forebears cooked. At the other end of the spectrum, there is some very (some might say overly) inventive *cordon bleu* cooking being concocted by daring young chefs across the country, especially in Buenos Aires and Mendoza. Fast food is extremely popular, but you can also snack on delicious local specialities such as empanadas or home-made pizza if you want to avoid the ubiquitous multinational chains.

Snacks

If you're feeling peckish during the day there are plenty of **minutas** (quick meals) to choose from. The **lomito** (as opposed to *lomo* – the name of the steak cut itself) is a nourishing sandwich filled with a juicy slice of steak, often made with delicious **pan árabe** (pitta bread); the **chivito** (originally Uruguayan) refers to a similar kind of sandwich made with a less tender cut; though it translates as "kid", or baby goat, it's made with beef. Other street foods include the **choripán**, a local version of the hot dog made with pork sausages (*chorizos*), and the **tostado** (or *tostado mixto*), a toasted cheese and ham sandwich, often daintily thin and sometimes (in the provinces) called a *carlitos*. **Milanesas** refer to breaded veal escalopes served in a sandwich, hamburger-style. **Empanadas** are small pastries with savoury fillings, usually stuffed with beef, cheese and/or vegetables, although the fillings are as varied as the cook's imagination.

Parrillas, pizza and pasta

The three Ps – *parrillas*, pizza and pasta – are the mainstays of Argentine cuisine, both at home and in restaurants. **Parrillas** are simply barbecues (or the restaurants that employ them) where you can try the traditional *asado* (see box, p.33). Usually there's a set menu (the **parrillada**), though the establishments themselves vary enormously. At many, especially in big cities, the decor is stylish, the staff laidback, the crockery delicate and the meat served tidily. Elsewhere, especially in smaller towns, *parrillas* are more basic, and you're likely to be served by burly, sweaty grill-men who spend all their time carving hunks of flesh and hurling them onto wooden platters. Portions in *parrillas* are generally very large, intended for sharing, and accompaniments like fries or salad are ordered separately, again served family style on large platters to share.

Mass immigration from Italy since the middle of the nineteenth century has had a profound influence on Argentine food and drink – the abundance of **fresh pasta** (*pasta casera*) is just one example. Ravioli and cannelloni fillings tend to be a little unexciting (lots of cheese, including ricotta, but seldom meat), the sauces are not exactly memorable (mostly tomato and onion) and the pasta, whether stuffed or plain, itself cooked beyond *al dente*, yet it's a reliable staple and rarely downright bad. **Pizzas** are very good on the whole, though the toppings tend to lack originality, especially away from the capital. One popular ingredient regularly used as a garnish may be unfamiliar to visitors: the **palmito**, a sweet, crunchy heart of palm. Argentine pizzas are nearly always of the thick-crust variety, wood-oven baked and very big, meant to be divided between a number of diners.

Regional cuisine

Although you will find *parrillas* throughout Argentina, different regions have their own specialities, too. Probably the most noteworthy regional cuisine is found in the Argentine **Northwest**, where, as well as the juiciest empanadas, you can find *humitas* – steamed creamed sweetcorn, served in parcels made from corncob husks, and *locro*, a hearty stew based on maize, with onions, beans, squash and meat thrown in. **Andean** *quinoa* is a frequent ingredient in everything from soups to empanadas. **Patagonia**, meanwhile, is famed for its barbecued lamb, staked around the fire, and jams made from local fruit such as the *calafate* berry.

Other cuisines

In addition to the Italian cooking available all over the country, **Spanish** restaurants serve tapas and familiar dishes such as *paella*, while specifically Basque restaurants are also fairly commonplace; these are often the places to head for fish or seafood. **Chinese** and, increasingly, **Korean** restaurants are found in many Argentine cities, but they rarely serve anything remotely like authentic Asian food and specialize in *tenedor libre* buffet dinners. You can find excellent **sushi** and **Peruvian food** in Buenos Aires, where nearly every national cuisine from Armenian to Vietnamese via Mexican, Polish and Thai is also occasionally available, but such variety is rare in the provinces.

Arab and **Middle Eastern** food, including favourites such as kebabs and *kepe* (seasoned ground raw meat), is more widespread, as is **German** cuisine such as sauerkraut (*chucrút*) and frankfurters, along with Central and Eastern European food, often served in *choperías*, or beer gardens. **Welsh tearooms** are a speciality in Chubut, Patagonia.

Vegetarian food

As a **vegetarian** in Argentina you shouldn't have too many problems in the capital, the larger cities or Patagonian resorts, all of which are relatively cosmopolitan. A number of **restaurants** completely dedicated to non-meat-eaters do exist and many places have a few good non-meat dishes. The exceptions are *parrillas*, though the sight and smell of entire animals roasting on the grill is unlikely to appeal to vegetarians anyway.

In the smaller provincial towns, however, vegetarian food tends to be a lot simpler and you will likely have to adjust to a diet of pizza, pasta, empanadas and salads, with very little variety in the toppings and fillings. The good news is that these fillings are often tasty options such as spinach, **acelga** (Swiss chard – similar to spinach, but slightly more bitter) and ricotta. Other foods to keep an eye out for are **fainá** – a fairly bland but agreeable Genovese speciality made with chickpea dough, often served on top of pizza – and **milanesas de soja** (breaded soya "cutlets"), while *milanesas* of vegetables like **berenjena** (aubergine) and **calabaza** (squash) are also quite popular.

When all the cheese gets a bit much, look out for the popular *tenedor libres*, which usually feature a good smattering of veggies, as do Middle Eastern restaurants. Another possibility would be to self-cater – supermarkets are usually fairly well stocked with vegetables, seasonings and soy products.

You should always check the ingredients of a dish before ordering, as the addition of small amounts of meat is not always referred to on menus. Don't be surprised if your *"no como carne"* (I don't eat meat) is dismissed with a glib *"no tiene mucha"* (It doesn't contain much) and be particularly on your guard for the seemingly ever-present **jamón** (ham).

Vegans will have a hard time outside of Buenos Aires, as pretty much everything that doesn't contain meat contains cheese or pastry. On the upside though, salad ingredients are sourced locally, so they tend to be fresh and tasty. Waiters will rarely be familiar with veganism, but will usually try to accommodate your requests.

Desserts

Argentines have a fairly sweet tooth and love anything with sugar, especially *dulce de leche* (see box below). Even breakfast tends to be dominated by sweet things such as sticky croissants (*medialunas*) or **chocolate con churros**, Andalucían-style hot chocolate with fritters, sometimes filled with *dulce de leche*. All kinds of cakes and biscuits, including *alfajores* (maize-flour cookie sandwiches, filled with jam or *dulce de leche*, sometimes coated with chocolate), pastries called **facturas** and other sweet treats are popular with Argentines of all ages.

However, for dessert you'll seldom be offered anything other than the tired trio of **flan** (a kind of crème caramel, religiously served with a thick custard or *dulce de leche*), **budín de pan** (a syrupy

version of bread pudding) and fresh fruit salad (*ensalada de frutas*). In Andean regions, or in *criollo* eateries, you'll most likely be served **dulce vigilante**, a slab of neutral, pallid cheese called *quesillo* eaten with sweet potato (*batata*), quince (*membrillo*), spaghetti squash (*cayote/alcayote*), squash (*zapallo*) or lime (*lima*). *Panqueques*, or crêpes, are also popular.

With such a large Italian community it is not surprising that superb *helado* (**ice cream**) is easy to come by in Argentina. Even the tiniest village has at least one *heladería artesanal*. If you're feeling really self-indulgent, you might like your cone dipped in chocolate (*bañado*). Some of the leading ice-cream makers offer an overwhelming range of flavours (*sabores*). Chocolate chip (*granizado*) is a favourite, and raspberry mousse (*mousse de frambuesa*) is also delicious.

Drinks

Fizzy drinks (*gaseosas*) are extremely popular with people of all ages and often accompany meals. All the big-brand names are available, along with local brands such as Paso de los Toros, which makes tonic water and fizzy grapefruit (*pomelo*) drinks. You will often be asked if you want **mineral water** – either still (*agua sin gas*) or carbonated – (*agua con gas* or *soda*) – with your meal, but you can ask for **tap water** (*agua de la llave* or *agua del grifo*), which is safe to drink in most places, though this may raise eyebrows. Although none is grown in the country, good **coffee** is easy to come by. You will find very decent espressos, or delicious *café con leche*, in most cafés. **Tea** is usually made from teabags; Argentine tea is strong rather than subtle, and is served with either milk or lemon; you need to ask for milk if you want it, and it usually comes hot. **Herbal teas** (*infusiones*) are all the rage, camomile (*manzanilla*) being the most common. **Mate** is a whole world

---

DULCE DE LECHE

Dulce de leche, a sticky, sweet goo made by laboriously boiling large quantities of vanilla-flavoured milk and sugar until they almost disappear, is claimed by Argentines as a national invention, although similar concoctions are made in Brazil, France and Italy. Something called *manjar* is produced in Chile, but Argentines regard it as far inferior. The thick caramel is eaten with a spoon, spread on bread or biscuits, used to fill cakes, biscuits and fritters or dolloped onto other desserts. Some of the best flavours of ice cream are variations on the *dulce de leche* theme. Although some people still make their own, most people buy it ready-made, in jars. While all Argentines agree that *dulce de leche* is fabulous, there is no consensus on a particular brand: the divisions between those who favour Havanna and those who would only buy Chimbote run almost as deep as those between supporters of Boca Juniors and River Plate. Foreigners are advised to maintain a diplomatically neutral stance on the issue.

unto itself, with its own etiquette and rituals (see box, p.252). **Fruit juices** (*jugos*) and **shakes** (*licuados*) can be excellent, though freshly squeezed orange juice is often sold at ridiculously high prices.

Beer

Argentina's **beer** is more thirst-quenching than alcoholic and mostly comes as fairly bland lager, with Quilmes dominating the market and Heineken producing a big-selling beer in the country; imported brands are fairly common in the cities, though more expensive. Regional brews are sometimes worth trying: in Mendoza, the Andes brand crops up all over, while Salta's own brand is also good, and a kind of stout (*cerveza negra*) can sometimes be obtained in the Northwest. **Craft beer** (*cerveza artesanal*) is increasingly available, particularly around Bariloche and El Bolsón, often coming in a surprising array of flavours and served at dedicated bars (*cervecerías*), though a number of craft beer pubs have sprouted up in Buenos Aires recently, too. Usually when you ask for a beer it comes in large litre bottles, meant for sharing; a small bottle is known as a *porrón*. If you want draught beer, ask for a *chopp* (or a *liso* in Santa Fe province).

Wine

The produce of Argentina's **vineyards**, ranging from gutsy plonk to some of the world's prize-winning **wines**, is widely available both in the country and abroad. Many vintages are excellent and not too expensive. Unfortunately, many restaurants still have limited, unimaginative wine lists, which don't reflect Argentina's drift away from mass-produced table wines to far superior single or multi-varietals (for more on wine, see box, p.349). It can be difficult to order wine by the glass, and half-bottles too are rare but on the increase. Cheaper wine is commonly made into **sangría** or its fruitier, white wine equivalent, **clericó**.

Spirits

Don't be surprised to see home-grown variants (*nacionales*) of whisky, gin, brandy, port, sherry and rum, none of which is that good; familiar imported brands (*importados*) can be very dear, however. It's far better to stick to the locally distilled **aguardientes**, or firewaters, some of which (from Catamarca, for example) are deliciously grapey. **Fernet Branca**, a bitter spirit, is the most popular, a demonic-looking brew the colour of molasses with a medicinal taste, usually combined with Coke and consumed in huge quantities – it's generally regarded as the gaucho's favourite tipple.

The media

In terms of newspaper circulation, Argentina is Latin America's most literate nation, and it has a diverse and generally high-quality press. Its television programming is a rather chaotic amalgam of light-entertainment shows and sports, and its radio services tend to fall into one of two categories: urban mainstream commercial channels or amateur ones designed to serve the needs of local rural communities.

Newspapers and magazines

In the past, the fortunes of the print **press** in Argentina have varied greatly, depending on the prevailing political situation. Overbearing state control and censorship characterized much of the twentieth century, but the current situation is far more dynamic, and a resilient streak of investigative journalism provides a constant stream of stories revolving around official corruption. Self-censorship, though, is fairly widespread, and deep criticism of the country's institutions is pretty muted in favour of a generally patriotic stance.

The *Buenos Aires Herald* (Ⓦ buenosairesherald .com) is South America's most prestigious **English-language daily** and dates back to 1876. Although the quality of the writing and editing can be inconsistent, the *Herald* is useful for getting the low-down on current events in Argentina and for catching up on international news and sports, as it features stories from the wires as well as syndicated articles from the likes of *The New York Times* and Reuters newswire. It is still associated in many minds with the old-style Anglo-Argentine elite, but it won international plaudits for its stand on human rights issues in the years of the military dictatorship. The *Herald* is easily available in the capital, but don't expect to find it often outside major cities and tourist centres. Look out also for English-language website *The Bubble* (Ⓦ bubblear.com), which takes a more light-hearted approach to the news that's written by and aimed at young immigrants and visitors. If you have some Spanish, the most accessible of the **national dailies** is *Clarín* (Ⓦ clarin .com.ar), the paper with the highest circulation. Despite its mass-market appeal, it is surprisingly highbrow, with politics on page three, followed by a fair-sized economics section, with celebrities usually kept in their place – that is, the "*Espectáculos*" supplement, which also has good listings of what's on. The country's major **broadsheet** is *La Nación* (W lanacion.com.ar), the favoured reading of the upper and educated classes. Conservative in some ways, it is also the most international, outward-looking and arguably best written of the Spanish-language newspapers. At the other extreme, *Página 12* (W pagina12.com.ar) is a left-leaning paper, originally anti-establishment, that was former president Cristina Fernández de Kirchner's government's biggest fan. Popular with students and intellectuals, it requires a good knowledge of the Spanish language and Argentine politics.

Argentina's **regional press** is also strong, though the quality varies enormously across the country. A handful of local dailies, such as Mendoza's *Los Andes* (W losandes.com.ar), Córdoba's *La Voz del Interior* (W lavoz.com.ar) and Rosario's *La Capital* (W lacapital .com.ar), are every bit as informative and well written as the leading national newspapers, and they contain vital information about tourist attractions, cultural events and travel news. Outside Buenos Aires, you pay a supplement for the nationals, and dailies often don't arrive till late in the day.

International publications such as *Time*, *Newsweek*, *The Economist* and the *Miami Herald* are sold at the kiosks on Calle Florida, outside the *Alvear Palace Hotel* in Recoleta in Buenos Aires, and at the capital's airports, as are some imported European and US magazines. However, check the cover as they can often be long past their publication date; they are also usually so expensive that unless you're really desperate, it's probably better to buy the *BA Herald*.

Radio

Argentina's most popular **radio** station, La 100 (99.9FM), plays a fairly standard formula of Latin pop, whereas Rock & Pop (95.9FM) veers more, as its name would imply, towards rock. Classical can be heard on Radio Clásica (96.7FM). Towns are blessed with a remarkable number of small-time radio stations, which are listened to avidly by locals, though they're rarely likely to appeal to foreign visitors.

Television

There are five national free-to-air **television stations**, mostly showing a mix of football, soap operas (*telenovelas*) and chat shows. Even if you can't understand much, these shows can provide a fascinating glimpse into certain aspects of society. Cable TV, offering many more channels, is common in mid-range and even budget hotels; the channels you get depend on the cable provider, but often

include CNN or BBC World in English, with a myriad of channels playing movies, sports and (mostly American) TV shows, frequently subtitled. Argentine cable news channels include Clarín's TN (*Telenoticias*) and the unique Crónica, a budget Buenos Aires-based news channel that provides live, unedited coverage of anything that happens in the city; indeed, it is said that the Crónica vans often arrive before the police do.

Festivals

The bulk of Argentina's festivals are found in the Northwest, owing to its attachment to tradition and its high proportion of ethnic communities. Pre-Columbian revivals, Catholic and secular celebrations are observed that are a blend of indigenous and imported customs, so subtly melded that the elements are indistinguishable. On the whole, holidays such as Christmas and Easter are more religious, family-focused occasions than they are in Europe and the US. Although some traditions – such as the European custom of eating chocolate eggs at Easter – are starting to take off, the festivals are generally a lot less commercial, and the run-up to them doesn't start two months beforehand.

What follows is a selective list of some of the major festivals, though wherever you travel you'll come across events celebrating minor saints or local produce; public holidays are observed nationwide (see box, p.53).

A festival calendar

JANUARY

6: Procession in honour of the Virgin Mary, Belén, Catamarca. A pilgrimage procession up to a hilltop statue of the Virgin.

Last week: Festival de Cosquín, Córdoba. Large folklore music festival. A rock music version takes place a couple of weeks later.

FEBRUARY

2: Virgen de la Candelaria, Humahuaca, Jujuy. This major religious festival includes a procession, special masses and a folk music festival to serenade the Virgin.

Early Feb: Fiesta Nacional del Queso, Tafí del Valle, Tucumán. A lively celebration of the country's cheeses.

6: Pachamama festival, Purmamarca and Amaicha, Jujuy. Pachamama, the Mother Earth deity dear to the indigenous peoples of the Northwest, is celebrated in these festivities.

First weekend: Fiesta de la Manzana y la Semilla, Rodeo, San Juan. A major regional folk festival.

Mid-Feb: Feria Artesanal y Ganadera de la Puna, Antofagasta de la Sierra, Catamarca. Vibrant Northwest craft festival.

Five days preceding Ash Wednesday: Carnaval, nationwide. Celebrated throughout Argentina – especially in Gualeguaychú, Entre Ríos, which hosts the country's premier parades – with a double bank holiday.

Weekend following Shrove Tuesday: Serenata Cafayateña, Cafayate, Salta. Popular folk jamboree.

MARCH

First weekend: Fiesta de la Vendimia, Mendoza. Grape harvest festival in the country's main wine region.

17: St Patrick's Day, Buenos Aires. The Irish saint's day, celebrated with much gusto in the capital; Argentina has the highest Irish immigrant population in a non-English-speaking country.

18 & 19: Pilgrimage of Puerta de San José, near Belén, Catamarca. A major pilgrimage, with night vigils and processions, converges on this tiny village.

18 & 19: Quema de Cardones and Fiesta Patronal de San José, Cachi, Salta. Villagers gather to pay tribute to the saint after whom their church is named, burning *cardón* cacti as an offering on the first day; activities on the second day are tamer, such as raising the national flag in the main square in José's name.

APRIL

2: Día de las Malvinas (officially known as Día del Veterano de Guerra y de los Caídos en la Guerra de las Malvinas), nationwide. Ceremonies to remember the Falklands conflict are held throughout Argentina.

Variable (sometimes in March): Semana Santa (Holy Week). Celebrated throughout Argentina; highlights include the pilgrimage to El Señor de la Peña, Aimogasta (in La Rioja), the procession of the Virgen de Punta Corral, from Punta Corral to Tumbaya (in Jujuy), and Maundy Thursday in Yavi (also in Jujuy).

MAY

4: San Francisco de Paula celebrations, Uquía, Jujuy. This tiny village eats, drinks and makes merry in honour of its patron saint.

JUNE

21: St John's Day, Salta and Jujuy. A major feast day throughout the region with pagan roots, this is the winter solstice celebrated with northwest Argentine style by lighting bonfires.

JULY

25: San Santiago, Quebrada de Humahuaca, Jujuy. Ceremonies take place in villages around the valley in tribute to the patron saint of livestock.

AUGUST

Early Aug: Fiesta Nacional de la Nieve, Bariloche. A five-day festival of snow, with parades, races and evening skiing.

15: Assumption, Casabindo. Festivities culminate in Argentina's only bullfight, a bloodless *corrida*.

Mid-Aug: World Tango Festival, Buenos Aires. Lasting around two weeks, the world's largest tango festival attracts aficionados from all over.

30: Santa Rosa de Lima, Purmamarca. Parishioners show their continued faith in Santa Rosa with a parade and dancers in traditional dress stepping to Sikuri music.

SEPTEMBER

6–15: Fiesta Señor y Virgen del Milagro, Salta. Major religious event, climaxing in a huge procession.

OCTOBER

Early Oct: Oktoberfest, Villa General Belgrano. For ten days, this alpine resort is awash with beer in this answer to the famous German festival.

First Sun: Our Lady of the Rosary, Iruya. Highly photogenic masked event that's one of the most fascinating in the Northwest region.

20 (approx): Fiesta de la Ollas, or "Manca Fiesta", La Quiaca. Literally, a "cooking-pot" festival with crafts and music.

NOVEMBER

1 & 2 All Souls' Day and the Day of the Dead, Quebrada de Humahuaca and Antofagasta de la Sierra, Jujuy. Death is remembered in this colourful, joyful pagan and Catholic festival. Villagers from around the region dress up, prepare food for their departed and make merry for two days.

10 (or nearest weekend): Fiesta de la Tradición, San Antonio de Areco. Lively gaucho festival.

DECEMBER

24: Christmas Eve, Buenos Aires. A great time to be in the capital, when the sky explodes with fireworks.

Sports

Argentines suffer an incurable addiction to sport; many go rigid at the thought of even one week without football (soccer), and you'll hear informed and spirited debate in bars on subjects as diverse as tennis, rugby, basketball and the uniquely Argentine equestrian sport of pato.

Football

Ever since two teams of British merchants lined up against each other at the Buenos Aires Cricket Club for a kick-about in 1867, *fútbol* has been an integral part of Argentine identity. The incredible atmosphere generated by the passion of the fans makes attending a match one of the highlights of many people's visits to Argentina, and it is certainly worth setting aside time to do so, even if you're not normally a fan. There are twenty teams in the Primera División, the country's top flight, including the "Big Five": River Plate, Boca Juniors, Independiente, San

Lorenzo and Racing Club (all based in Buenos Aires but supported around the country). If you can catch the *superclásico*, the derby between Boca and River, then you're in for a real treat.

The domestic league's year is split into two **seasons** – allowing for two champions and two sets of celebrations. The first season runs from August to December and is known as the *apertura* (opening); the second, from February to June, is the *clausura* (closing); fixtures are mostly played on Sunday afternoons and evenings. In addition, there are two South American club championships – the Copa Libertadores and Copa Sudamericana, roughly equivalent to Europe's UEFA Champions League and Europa League, respectively. These are generally dominated by teams from Argentina, Brazil and Colombia, with a leg played in each country, usually a midweek fixture. If you're lucky, you may even get the chance to see the national side (*la selección*) strutting their stuff in a friendly or World Cup qualifier.

You can usually buy **tickets** at the grounds on match day, although some games sell out in advance, notably the matches between the big five and top-of-the-table clashes. For these, you can get tickets two days before the game at the stadium (be prepared for a scrum) or further in advance for some games from Ticketek (☎011 5237 7200, ❽ticketek.com.ar). Many Buenos Aires-based tour agencies, hotels and hostels provide a ticket and transfer service, for a premium.

Tickets for spectators are either in the *popular* or the more expensive *platea*, with the price depending on your vantage point and the game's importance, although it always compares favourably with the cost of European match tickets. The *popular* are the standing-only **terraces**, where young men, the hardcore home fans, sing and swear their way through the match. This is the most colourful part of the stadium, but it's also the area where you're most likely to be pick-pocketed, charged by police or faced with the wrath of the equally hardcore away-team fans (in the *visitantes* section, where you can often buy the cheapest tickets, though it's standing room only). Unless you're pretty confident, or with someone who is, you may be better off heading to the relative safety of the *platea* **seats**, from where you can photograph the *popular* and enjoy the match sitting down. Don't be surprised if someone's in the seat allocated to you on the ticket – locals pay scant regard to official seating arrangements so sit elsewhere. After major wins, the Obelisco in central Buenos Aires is the epicentre of raucous **celebrations**.

It's advisable to turn up an hour or so before the match in order to avoid the rush, and not to hang around the stadium afterwards, when trouble sometimes brews. Dress down, avoid flaunting the colours of either side and take the minimum of valuables.

Polo and pato

Although it's mainly a game for *estancieros* and wealthy families from Recoleta, **polo** is nonetheless far less snobbish or exclusive in Argentina than in Britain or the US; there are some 150 teams and 5000 club members nationwide. You don't need an invitation from a member or a double-barrelled surname to see the world's top polo players; simply turn up and buy a ticket during the open championship in November and December, played at the **Campo de Polo** in Palermo, Buenos Aires. Even if the rules go over your head, the game is exciting and aesthetically pleasing, with hooves galloping over impeccably trimmed grass.

The sport is at least as hard as it looks, but if you're confident on horseback and determined to have a go, many estancias (listed throughout the text) offer lessons as part of their accommodation and activity packages. Alternatively, contact the Asociación Argentina de Polo at Arévalo 3065, Buenos Aires (☎011 4777 8005, ❽aapolo.com), which can also provide match information.

Less glamorous, the curious sport of **pato** has been played by gauchos since the early 1600s and is in fact the national sport. Named after the trussed duck that once served as the "ball" – a leather version with six handles is now used – pato is a sort of lacrosse on horse-back, which also has its national tournament in November and December each year, played at the **Campo Argentino de Pato** in San Miguel, just outside the city limits. For more information on pato and a fixture list, see the national federation's website, ❽pato.org.ar.

Rugby

Argentina's national **rugby** squad, the Pumas, is currently ranked fifth in the world and in 2012 took part in the southern hemisphere Rugby Championship (formerly the Tri Nations) for the first time; this success has seen the sport's popularity rise significantly. You may be able to catch the burly Pumas playing test series at home (all over the country) or in World Cup qualifiers. See the website of the Unión Argentina de Rugby (❽uar.com.ar) for upcoming fixtures.

Outdoor activities

Argentina is a highly exciting destination for outdoors enthusiasts: world-class fly-fishing, horseriding, trekking and rock-climbing opportunities abound, as do options for white-water rafting, skiing, ice climbing and even – for those with sufficient stamina and preparation – expeditions onto the Southern Patagonian Ice Cap.

Nature tourism

Argentina's network of national and provincial parks offers wonderful opportunities for nature tourism across this country's range of ecosystems (see pp.553–557). Highlights for **wildlife viewing** include the Península Valdés, a superb destination for the marine wildlife and fauna of the Patagonian steppe (see p.450), the humid swamplands of Esteros del Iberá (see p.237), and the subtropical jungles of Iguazú (see p.259).

For an overview of the national park system, visit the **National Park Headquarters** in Buenos Aires at Santa Fe 690 (Mon–Fri 8am–8pm; ☎011 4311 0303, Ⓦ parquesnacionales.gov.ar). There is an underfunded and not terribly helpful information office on the ground floor that may be able to provide some introductory leaflets, and they can give you tips if you're intending to visit some of the more isolated places like Baritú, Perito Moreno, San Guillermo and Santiago del Estero's Copo, which have limited infrastructure and require some planning. A wider range of free material is available at each individual park, but these are of variable quality – many only have a basic map and a brief park description. Each national park has its own **intendencia**, or park administration, although

---

ARGENTINA'S TOP TREKKING ROUTES

El Bolsón region p.413.
La Cueva de las Manos Pintadas p.496.
Fitz Roy sector, Parque Nacional Los Glaciares p.482.
Parque Nacional Los Alerces p.418.
Parque Nacional Calilegua p.310.
Parque Nacional Lanín p.430.
Parque Nacional Nahuel Huapi p.402.
Parque Nacional Perito Moreno p.493.
Parque Nacional El Rey p.311.
Parque Nacional Tierra del Fuego p.515.
Parque Provincial Talampaya p.386.

---

these are often in the principal access town, not within the park itself. An information office or visitors' centre is often attached. Argentina's **guardaparques**, or national park rangers, are some of the most professional on the continent: generally friendly, they are well trained and dedicated to jobs that are demanding and often extremely isolated. All have a good grounding in the wildlife of the region and are happy to share their knowledge, although don't expect them all to be professional naturalists – some are, but ranger duties often involve more contact with the general public than with the wildlife.

A good port of call in the capital for nature enthusiasts is the **Fundación Vida Silvestre**, located at Defensa 251, 6th floor office K, Buenos Aires (Mon–Fri 10am–1pm & 2–6pm; ☎011 4343 4086, Ⓦ vidasilvestre.org.ar), a committed and highly professional environmental organization, and an associate of the WWF. Visit its shop for back issues of its beautiful magazine (in Spanish) and for books and leaflets on wildlife and ecological issues, as well as for information on its nature reserves.

Argentina has an incredible diversity of birdlife – you can see some ten percent of all the world's bird species here. **Birdwatchers** should visit the headquarters of the country's well-respected birding organization, **Aves Argentinas**, at Matheu 1246, Buenos Aires (nearest subway station is Pichincha on Linea E; Mon–Fri 10.30am–1.30pm & 2.30–8.30pm; ☎011 4943 7216, Ⓦ avesargentinas .org.ar). It has an excellent library and a shop, and organizes regular outings and **birding safaris**.

Trekking

Argentina offers some truly marvellous **trekking**, and it is still possible to find areas where you can trek for days without seeing a soul. Trail quality varies considerably, and many are difficult to follow, so always get hold of the best **map** available and ask for information as you go; the Club Andino in Bariloche (see p.399) can offer excellent advice and sell you maps. Most of the best treks are in the national parks – especially the ones in Patagonia – but you can often find lesser-known but equally superb options in the lands bordering them. Most people head for the savage granite spires of the **Fitz Roy** region around El Chaltén, an area whose fame has spread so rapidly over the last ten years that it now holds a similar status to Chile's renowned Torres del Paine. Tourist pressures are starting to tell, however, at least in the high season (late Dec to Feb), when campsites are packed. The other principal trekking destination is the mountainous

PROTECTING ARGENTINA'S NATURAL WONDERS

When visiting natural parks and wild areas, always be **environmentally responsible**. Stick to marked trails, camp only at authorized sites, take – don't burn – all litter with you, bury toilet waste at least 30m away from all water sources and use detergents and toothpastes as sparingly as possible. Above all, pay attention to the fire risk. Every year, fires destroy huge swathes of forest, and virtually all these are started by hand: some deliberately, but most because of unpardonable negligence. One prime culprit is the cigarette butt, often casually tossed out of a car window, but just as bad are campfires that are poorly tended or poorly extinguished. Woodland becomes tinder-dry in summer droughts, and, especially in places such as Patagonia, it is vulnerable to sparks carried by the strong winds. Fires can easily turn into infernos that blaze for weeks on end as there are limited water resources to put them out, and much fire-damaged land never regenerates its growth. Many parks have a ban on campfires and trekkers are asked to take stoves on which to do their cooking; please respect this. Others ban fires during high-risk periods. The most environmentally responsible approach is to avoid lighting campfires at all: even dead wood has a role to play in often-fragile ecosystems. Choose a spot on stony or sandy soil, use only fallen wood and always extinguish the fire with water, not earth.

area of **Parque Nacional Nahuel Huapi**, south of Bariloche. This area has the best infrastructure, with a network of generally well-marked trails and mountain refuges. In the north of the country, some of the best trekking is in **Jujuy Province**, especially in Calilegua, where the habitat ranges from subtropical to bald mountain landscape.

Camping is possible in many national parks, and sites are graded according to three categories: *camping libre* sites, which are free but have no or very few services (perhaps a latrine and sometimes a shower block); *camping organizado* sites, which have more services, including electricity and often some sort of restaurant; and *camping agreste* sites, which are run as concessions and usually provide hot water, showers, toilets, places for lighting a campfire and barbecue, and a small shop. While free camping is more common in Patagonia, it's best to check at nearby towns or villages where you can pitch up and for how long.

You should always be well prepared for your trips, even for half-day hikes. Good-quality, **water- and windproof clothing** is vital: temperatures plummet at night and often with little warning during the day. Keep spare dry layers of clothing and socks in a plastic bag in your pack. **Boots** should provide firm ankle support and have the toughest soles possible (Vibram soles are recommended). Gore-Tex boots are only waterproof to a degree: they will not stay dry when you have to cross swampland. A **balaclava** is sometimes more useful than a woollen hat. Make sure that your **tent** is properly waterproofed and that it can cope with high winds (especially for Patagonia). You'll need a minimum of a three-season sleeping bag, to be used in conjunction with a solid or semi-inflatable foam mattress (essential, as the

ground will otherwise suck out all your body heat). Also bring high-factor **sunblock** and lip salve, plus good **sunglasses** and a hat or cap.

Park authorities often require you to carry a **stove** for cooking. The Camping Gaz models that run on butane cylinders (refills are fairly widely available in *ferretería* hardware shops) are not so useful in exposed areas, where you're better off with a high-pressure petrol stove such as an MSR, although these are liable to clog with impurities in the fuel, so filter it first. Telescopic hiking poles save your knees from a lot of strain and are useful for balance. Miner-style **head torches** are preferable to regular hand-held ones, and gaffer tape makes an excellent all-purpose emergency repair tool. Carry a **first-aid kit** and a **compass**, and know how to use both. And always carry plenty of **water** – aim to have at least two litres on you at all times. Pump-action **water filters** can be very handy, as you can thus avoid the hassle of having to boil suspect water.

Note also that, in the national parks, especially on the less-travelled and overnight routes, you should inform the **park ranger** (*guardaparque*) of your plans, not forgetting to report your safe arrival at your destination – the ranger will send a search party out for you if you do not arrive. You'd be advised to buy all your camping equipment before you leave home: quality gear is relatively expensive in Argentina, and there are few places that rent decent equipment, even in some of the key trekking areas.

Climbing

For **climbers**, the Andes offer incredible variety. You do not always have to be a technical expert, but you should always take preparations seriously. You can often arrange a climb close to the date – though it's best to bring as much high-quality gear with you as you can. The climbing season is fairly short – November to March in some places, though December to February is the best time. The best-known challenge is South America's highest peak, **Cerro Aconcagua** (6962m), accessed from the city of Mendoza (see p.356). Not considered the most technical challenge, this peak nevertheless merits top-level expedition status, as the altitude and storms claim several victims a year. Only slightly less lofty are nearby Cerro Tupungato (6750m), just to the south; Cerro Mercedario (6770m), just to the north; cerros Bonete (6872m) and Pissis (6793m) on the provincial border between La Rioja and Catamarca; and Ojos del Salado, the highest active volcano in the world (6885m), a little further north into Catamarca. The last three can be climbed from Fiambalá, but Ojos is most normally climbed from the Chilean side of the border. The most famous volcano to climb is the elegant cone of **Cerro Lanín** (3776m), which can be ascended in two days via the relatively straightforward northeastern route (see p.430). Parque Nacional Nahuel Huapi, near Bariloche, offers the **Cerro Catedral** massif and **Cerro Tronador** (3554m). Southern Patagonia is also a highly prized climbing destination. One testing summit is **San Lorenzo** (3706m), which, from the Argentine side, can best be approached along the valley of Río Oro, although the summit itself is usually climbed from across the border in Chile. Further south are the inspirational granite spires of the **Fitz Roy** massif (3405m) and **Cerro Torre** (3102m), which have few equals on the planet in terms of technical difficulty and scenic grandeur.

On all of these climbs, but especially those over 4000m, make sure to acclimatize thoroughly, and be fully aware of the dangers of *puna*, or altitude sickness (see p.48).

CLIMBING CONTACTS IN ARGENTINA

Centro Andino Buenos Aires Rivadavia 1255, Buenos Aires ☎ 011 4381 1566, ⓦ caba.org.ar. Offers climbing courses, talks and slideshows. Its website has a useful page of links to other Argentine climbing clubs.
Club Andino Bariloche (CAB) 20 de Febrero 30, Bariloche, Río Negro ☎ 02944 422266, ⓦ clubandino.org. The country's oldest and most famous mountaineering club, with excellent specialist knowledge of guides and Patagonian challenges.

Fishing

As a destination for **fly-fishing** (*pesca con mosca*), Argentina is unparalleled, with Patagonia drawing in professionals from around the globe. Trout,

introduced in the early twentieth century, is the sport's mainstay, but there is also fishing for landlocked and even Pacific salmon. The most famous places to go are those where the world's largest sea-running brown trout (*trucha marrón*) are found: principally the **Río Grande** and other rivers of eastern and central Tierra del Fuego, and the Río Gallegos on the mainland. The reaches of the Río Santa Cruz near Comandante Luís Piedra Buena have some impressive specimens of steelhead trout (sea-running rainbows, or *trucha arcoíris*), and the area around Río Pico is famous for its brook trout. The Patagonian **Lake District** – around Junín de los Andes, San Martín de los Andes, Bariloche and Esquel – is the country's most popular trout-fishing destination, offering superb angling in delightful scenery.

The **trout-fishing season** runs from mid-November to Easter. Regulations change slightly from year to year, but **permits** are valid country-wide. They can be purchased at national park offices, some *guardaparque* posts, tourist offices and at fishing equipment shops, which are fairly plentiful – especially in places like the north Patagonian Lake District. With your permit, you are issued a **booklet** detailing the regulations of the type of fishing allowed in each river and lake in the region, the restrictions on catch-and-release and the number of specimens you are allowed to take for eating. Argentine law states that permit holders are allowed to fish any waters they can reach without crossing private land. You are, in theory at least, allowed to walk along the bank as far as you like from any public road, although in practice you may find that owners of some more prestigious beats try to obstruct you from doing this.

For more **information** on fly-fishing in Argentina, contact the Asociación Argentina de Pesca con Mosca, Lerma 452, Buenos Aires (☎ 011 4773 0821, ⓦ aapm.org.ar).

Horseriding

Given the archetypal image of the gaucho on horseback, it's no surprise that Argentina is a great place to learn **horseriding**. Whether you want a laidback walk around a Pampas farm, an overnight escape in the sierras of Córdoba or an Andes crossing on horseback, all levels are catered for. Do note that Argentine *criollo* horses respond to neck reining, a style used in Western riding where the reins are held in one hand. MacDermott's Argentina specializes in bespoke **horseriding holidays** around the country, and regularly undertakes Andes crossings (☎ 011 4773 2522, ⓦ macdermottsargentina.com).

Skiing

Argentina's **ski resorts** are not on the same scale as those of Europe or North America and attract mainly domestic and Latin American tourists (from Chile and Brazil), as well as a smattering of foreigners who are looking to ski during the northern summer. However, infrastructure is constantly being upgraded and it's easy to rent gear. The main **skiing season** is July and August, although in some resorts it is possible to ski from mid-June to early October. Snow conditions vary from year to year, but you can often find excellent powder.

The most prestigious resort for downhill skiing is modern **Las Leñas** (see p.365), which also offers the most challenging skiing and once hosted World Cup races. Following this are **Chapelco**, near San Martín de los Andes (see p.422), where you also have extensive cross-country options, and the Bariloche resorts of **Cerro Catedral** and **Cerro Otto** (see p.408), which are the longest-running in the country, with wonderful panoramas of the Nahuel Huapi region – albeit with rather too many people. Ushuaia's **Cerro Castor** (see p.509) is an up-and-coming if pricey resort, with some fantastic cross-country possibilities and expanding downhill facilities; the resort is 25km from Ushuaia so it's a good choice if you want to combine skiing with sightseeing. Bariloche and Las Leñas are the best destinations for those interested in après-ski.

Rafting

Though it does not have the same range of extreme options as neighbouring Chile, Argentina nevertheless has some beautiful **white-water rafting** possibilities, ranging from grades II to V. Many of these are offered as day-trips, and include journeys through enchanting monkey puzzle tree scenery on the generally sedate **Río Aluminé** (see p.434); along the turbulent and often silty **Río Mendoza** (see p.344); through deep canyons carved by the **Río Juramento** in Salta (see p.288); on the **Río Manso** in the Alpine-like country south of Parque Nacional Nahuel Huapi; and along the similar but less-visited **Río Corcovado**, south of Esquel (see p.416). Esquel can also be used as a base for rafting on Chile's fabulous, world-famous **Río Futaleufú** (see p.418), a turquoise river that flows through temperate rainforest and tests rafters with rapids of grade V. You do not need previous rafting experience to enjoy these, but you should obviously be able to swim. Pay heed to operators' safety instructions, and ensure your safety gear (especially helmets and life-jackets) fits well.

Culture and etiquette

Argentina's mores reflect its overwhelmingly European ancestry, and, apart from getting used to the late dining hours, most travellers from the West will have little trouble fitting in.

Society generally displays a pleasing balance between formal politeness and casual tolerance. When it comes to dress, Argentines are quite conservative and take great pride in appearance, but in bigger cities in particular, you will see examples of many different styles and sub-cultures. Particularly outlandish clothing might raise eyebrows out in the provinces, but probably no more than it would in, say, deepest Wisconsin or Wiltshire. One area of etiquette that will probably be new to you is the very Argentine custom of drinking *mate*, which comes with its own set of rules (see box, p.252), but foreigners will be given lots of leeway here, as in other areas of social custom – a *faux pas* is more likely to cause amusement than offence.

Rules, regulations and bureaucracy

Argentines' rather cavalier attitude towards **rules** and considerations of health and safety is probably the biggest culture shock many foreigners have to deal with; the most obvious example of this is the anarchy you'll see on roads, but you will also likely come across things such as loose wiring in hotels or wobbly cliff-top fencing. A complaint will probably get you no more than a shrug of the shoulders, though there are signs of a change in attitudes. Many visitors actually find the lack of regulations liberating.

Another difference is the Kafka-esque **bureaucracy** that you will encounter if you're in the country for any length of time – when obtaining a visa, say, or picking up a parcel from the post office. Do not lose your temper if faced with red tape – this will hinder rather than help.

Sexual harassment and discrimination

Women planning on travelling alone to the country can do so with confidence. Some **machista** attitudes do persist but the younger generation is shedding gender differences with alacrity and few people will find it strange that you are travelling unaccompanied. You will probably find you are the target of comments in the street and chat-up lines (called *piropos*) more frequently than you are accustomed to, but those responsible will not persist if you make it clear you're not interested. Such attentions are almost never hostile or physical – Italian-style bottom pinching is very rare here.

Greetings

When **greeting** people or taking your leave, it is normal to kiss everyone present on the cheek (just once, always the right cheek); some men may also emphasize their masculinity by slapping each other on the back, or clasp hands then bump fists. Shaking hands tends to be the preserve of conservative businessmen or very formal situations, though some Argentines may offer a hand rather than a cheek if they know you're foreign; if in doubt, watch the locals.

Drinking and smoking

Argentine attitudes to **drinking** tend to be similar to those in southern Europe: alcohol is fine in moderation, and usually taken with food. Public drunkenness occurs more frequently among the young than it used to, though equally a group of friends might make a litre of beer last all night. **Smoking** is fairly common among all sexes and classes, although it is illegal to smoke in enclosed public areas throughout the country.

Shopping

You will find no real tradition of **haggling** in Argentina, although you can always try it when buying pricey artwork or antiques. Expensive services such as excursions and car rental are also obvious candidates for bargaining, while hotel rates can be beaten down off-season, late at night or if you're paying in cash (*en efectivo*). But try and be reasonable, especially in the case of already low-priced crafts or high-quality goods and services that are obviously worth every centavo.

Tipping

Tipping is not widespread in Argentina, with a couple of exceptions. It's normal to give hairdressers and beauticians a five to ten percent tip and you should add a gratuity of ten percent to restaurant bills if service is not included. Note that a service charge is not the same as the ambiguous *cubiertos* charge you might see on your bill; this literally means "cutlery",

and is there to cover a bread basket and tap water. It isn't charged everywhere and can vary between $10 and $50 depending on the establishment. It is another, slightly sneaky, way for restaurants to earn a bit extra. Unofficial assistants who hang around taxi ranks to open and close doors also expect a small amount, as do hotel porters and the people who load and unload long-distance bus luggage.

Travel essentials

Children

Argentines love children and you will generally find them helpful and understanding if you're travelling as a family. Most hotels have triple rooms or suites with connecting rooms to accommodate families and will be able to provide a cot if you have a small child (ask when you reserve).

When it comes to **eating out**, only the very snootiest restaurants will turn children away or look pained when you walk in; the vast majority will do their best to make sure you and your offspring are comfortable and entertained. Highchairs are sometimes, but not always, provided. It is quite normal to see children out with their parents until late – you may well see families strolling home at 1 or 2am, especially in summer. Bring any **children's medicines** that you are likely to need with you, and if your child gets sick, go to a private hospital, preferably in one of the larger cities, where you will be attended by a pediatrician rapidly and professionally. **Breastfeeding** in public is fine. Supplies such as

---

STUDENT CARDS

These are not as useful as they can be in some countries, as museums and the like often refuse to give **student discounts**. Some bus companies, however, do give a ten- to fifteen-percent discount for holders of **ISIC cards**, as do certain hotels, laundries and outdoor gear shops, and even one or two ice-cream parlours. Al Mundo, Argentina's student travel agency (☎0810 777 2728, ⊛almundo.com.ar), issues a booklet that lists partners throughout the country. The international student card often suffices for a discount at youth hostels in the country, though membership of the Youth Hostelling Association may entitle you to even lower rates (see p.31).

nappies/diapers are widely available, but changing facilities are relatively nonexistent, so you will have to get used to changing on the move.

Argentina's **natural attractions** may be your best bet for entertaining your kids – the country has little in the way of amusement parks or specific family destinations, and the ones that do exist are generally rather poor. Consider the waterfalls and jungle critters at Iguazú, the boat rides and glaciers of Parque Nacional Los Glaciares or the whales and penguins near Península Valdés. Areas that provide sports such as skiing and rafting may also be worth considering. Buenos Aires' somewhat sophisticated attractions will mostly appeal more to adults, but there is enough to keep younger ones amused for a couple of days, including a planetarium (see p.99) and a natural history museum (see p.103). Rosario (see p.216) is unusual among Argentine cities for the amount of child-centred attractions it has – and it's fun for their parents too. Wherever you go, remember the distances in Argentina are vast and travel times can be lengthy – do not be too ambitious in planning your itinerary. Avoid the summer heat unless you will be spending most of your time in Patagonia.

Costs

Given Argentina's turbulent economy over the past fifteen years, costs can fluctuate (see box below), but it certainly can't be described as a cheap destination – and with inflation unofficially estimated at around thirty percent it's getting more expensive all the time. But the quality of what is on offer is mostly pretty good, and outside Buenos Aires and the main tourist destinations you can find real bargains in shops and hotels.

Adhering to a reasonable **daily budget** is not impossible, but there are considerable regional variations. As a rule of thumb, the further south you travel the more you will need to stretch your budget. Roughly speaking, on average you'll need to plan on spending at least $4000/US$220/£170 a week on a tight budget (sharing a dorm, eating snacks, limiting other spending), or double that if staying in budget accommodation but not stinting. To live in the lap of luxury, though, you could easily burn through $50,000/US$2800/£2200 in a week.

Camping and self-catering are good ways of **saving money**, though the now-extensive network of youth hostels enables you to pay little without sleeping rough. Out of season, at weekends and during slow periods it is a good idea to bargain hotel prices down. You can save money on **food** by having your main meal at lunchtime – especially by opting for the set menu (usually called *menú ejecutivo*). Picnicking is another option; local produce is often world-class and an alfresco meal of bread, cheese, ham or salami with fresh fruit and a bottle of table wine in a great location is a match for any restaurant feast.

Long-distance **transport** will eat up a considerable chunk of your expenses, particularly if you use internal flights; buses are usually (but not always) cheaper but take far longer. They vary in condition and price from one category to another, though you may find the cheaper fares are a false economy – better companies usually give you free food and drink (of varying quality) on lengthy journeys, while spacious *coche cama* comfort overnight enables you to save the price of a room and is worthwhile for covering the longest distances over less interesting terrain. City transport – including taxis and *remises* (radio taxis) – is inexpensive, but then most cities are compact enough to walk around anyway.

Hotels, restaurants and big stores may ask for a hefty handling fee for credit-card payments (as high as twenty percent), while many businesses – and hotels in particular – will give you a fair-sized

---

ARGENTINA'S ECONOMY AND EXCHANGE RATES

The economic situation in Argentina has been volatile in recent years, and it is advisable to check the latest before you travel. Until the end of 2015, the economy acted within two exchange rates – an **official rate** (around nine pesos to the US dollar), and a **black market** ("blue") rate (nudging 14 pesos to the dollar). However, President Mauricio Macri **devalued the peso** almost immediately upon taking office in December 2015. That took the peso to around 14 to the dollar, though at the time of writing, it's too early to say how effective his measure has been at stabilizing the economy and wiping out the "blue" currency market.

Given the unpredictable exchange rate, prices in this Guide were updated as late as possible. While they are therefore helpful for comparing price ranges, fluctuations are still very likely, so readers should always **check before booking**.

Note that hotels and other types of commerce, especially at the luxury end of the market, often quote in US dollars rather than Argentine pesos.

discount for cash payments (*en efectivo* or *contado*) on the quoted price, though they may need prompting. Be aware that some costs, such as air travel and entrance fees, might operate on a **dual pricing structure** – one price for Argentine residents (including foreigners) and another, often as much as three times more, for non-residents.

All prices in this book are quoted in Argentine pesos ($) unless otherwise noted.

Crime and personal safety

With the effects of economic crises in 2001 and 2009 still lingering, Argentina has lost the reputation it enjoyed for many years as a totally safe destination. However, any concern you have should be kept in perspective – the likelihood of being a victim of crime remains small, because most of the more violent crime (concentrated in the big cities) tends to be directed at wealthy locals rather than foreign visitors.

In Buenos Aires, highly publicized incidents of violence and armed robbery have increased over the years but the vast majority of visitors have no problems. Some potential pitfalls are outlined here – not to induce paranoia, but on the principle that to be forewarned is to be forearmed.

The usual precautions should be taken, particularly in the capital, provincial cities such as Rosario and Córdoba, and some of the northern border towns (near the frontiers with Paraguay and Brazil). A basic rule is to carry only what you need for that day, and conceal valuable items such as cameras and jewellery. Always be cautious when withdrawing cash from ATMs. These are often located inside a bank rather than on the street; it's normal to queue outside a single-booth, enclosed ATM if it is already in use to offer the user privacy. If you're not sure about the wisdom of walking somewhere, play it safe and take a cab – but call radio taxis or hail them in the street, rather than taking a waiting one. Remember that pickpockets most commonly hang around subte (subway) stations and bus terminals (particularly Retiro in the capital), and on crowded trains and buses.

EMERGENCY NUMBERS

Ambulance ☎ 107
Fire ☎ 100
Police ☎ 911
Tourist police (policía turística) in Buenos Aires ☎ 0800 999 5000 or ☎ 011 4346 5748

Theft from **hotels** is rare, but do not leave valuables lying around. Use the hotel safe if there is one. Compared with other Latin American countries, you're unlikely to have things stolen on long-distance **buses** (luggage is checked in and you get a ticket for each item), but it makes sense to take your daypack with you when you disembark for meal stops, and, particularly at night, to keep your bag by your feet rather than on the overhead rack. Pilfering from checked-in luggage on **flights** is quite common – don't leave anything of value in outside pockets, and lock your bag where possible. **Car theft** is a common occurrence; if you are renting a car, check the insurance will cover you, and always park in a car park or where someone will keep an eye on it. When driving in the city, keep windows closed and doors locked.

Drugs are frowned upon, although perhaps not as much as in other parts of South America. Drug use, particularly of marijuana and cocaine, is fairly common among the younger generation, and quite openly celebrated in some popular song lyrics. Despite court rulings in 2009, interpreted as a step towards decriminalization, both Argentine society at large and the police don't draw much of a line between soft drugs and hard drugs, and the penalties for either are stiff. As everywhere else, there are many slang words for drugs: common ones for marijuana include *porro*, *maconia* and *yerba;* for cocaine, *merca* and *falopa*.

Drugs of all kinds are available everywhere, but we strongly advise against buying or using them – quite apart from the risks inherent in the substances themselves, doing so may bring you into contact with some very dangerous people.

If you are unlucky enough to be the victim of a **robbery** (*asalto*) or lose anything of value, you will need to make a report at the nearest police station for insurance purposes. This is usually a time-consuming but fairly straightforward process. Check that the report includes a comprehensive account of everything lost and its value, and that the police add the date and an official stamp (*sello*). These reports do not cost anything.

Scams

As elsewhere in Latin America, you should be aware of the possibility of **scams**. A popular one, especially in the tourist areas of Buenos Aires, is having mustard, ice cream or some similar substance "spilt" over you. Some person then offers to help clean it off – cleaning you out at the same time. If this happens to you, push them off, get away from them fast and make as much noise as possible, shouting "thief!" ("*ladrón!*"), "police!" ("*policía!*") or for help ("*socorro!*" or "*auxilio!*"). Another well-worked scam involves a regular cab picking you up from the taxi rank outside the airport, driving off the airport grounds (so they're no longer on CCTV), then the driver taking a call on his mobile phone and suddenly saying that he has to drop you off and can't take you to your destination. He leaves you stranded at the side of the road to be picked up by a "random" cab he's in league with, who'll fleece you. Easily avoided: always make sure you take an official, booked *remís* rather than waiting for a regular cab.

Note, too, that though the police are entitled to check your documents, they have no right to inspect your money or travellers' cheques: anyone who does is a con artist, and you should ask for their identification or offer to be taken to the police station (*comisaría*). If you ever do get "arrested", never get into a vehicle other than an official police car.

Electricity

220V/50Hz is standard throughout the country. Two different types of sockets are found: increasingly rare two-pronged with round pins, which are different to the two-pin European plugs; and three-pronged, with flat pins, two of which are slanted (Australian adaptors usually work alright with these). Electrical shops along calles Talcahuano and Florida, in Buenos Aires, sell adaptors, useful if you haven't brought one with you.

Entry requirements

Citizens of the US, Canada, Australia, the UK, Ireland, New Zealand and most European countries do not currently need a **visa** for tourist trips to Argentina of up to ninety days. All visitors need a valid **passport** and, at international airports, have their thumbprint and photo digitally recorded on arrival; passports are stamped on arrival wherever you enter. In theory, this could be for thirty or sixty days, but in practice it's almost always ninety. If you are travelling alone with a child you must obtain a notarized document before travel certifying both parents' permission for the child to travel (check with the embassy).

Citizens of Australia and Canada must pay a reciprocity fee (because Argentines are charged a fee or must obtain a visa to visit their countries) of US$100 for the former and US$92 for the latter. The payment is valid for multiple entry for twelve months for Australians; Canadian citizens can use it for multiple entries over a ten-year period. Anyone needing to pay must do so online in advance at

virtual.provincianet.com.ar. The rules do change frequently, so it's best to check the government website for the latest (argentina.gob.ar) – at the time of writing, for example, US citizens' US$160 reciprocity fee had been waived for a 90-day trial period, expected to be extended indefinitely. Be sure to keep a hard copy of your proof of purchase on you to avoid any problems.

On entering the country you will be given a **customs declaration form** to fill in, and all luggage is scanned on arrival at international airports. Duty is not charged on used personal effects, books and other articles for noncommercial purposes, up to the value of US$300. You might be required to declare any valuable electronic items such as laptops and mobile phones, but Customs are really looking for large quantities of goods or illicit items.

You can **extend your stay** for a further ninety days by presenting your passport at the main immigration department, Dirección de Migraciones in Buenos Aires, at Av Antártida Argentina 1350, Retiro (011 4317 0200). This costs $600 and must be done on weekdays between 8am and 1pm; be prepared for a possibly lengthy wait. You can do this extension, called a *prórroga*, only once. Alternatively, you could try leaving the country (the short hop to Colonia del Sacramento in Uruguay is a good option) and returning to get a fresh stamp. This usually works, but may be frowned upon if done repeatedly, and the provision of an extra stamp is totally at the discretion of the border guards. If you do overshoot your stay, you pay a $600 fine at Migraciones, who will give you a form that allows you to leave the country within ten days. Do bear in mind that if you do this your stay in the country will be illegal and could potentially cause you problems. If you are crossing into **Chile**, make sure your papers are in order, as Chilean officials are considerably more scrupulous.

When leaving the country, you must obtain an **exit stamp**. At certain border controls, particularly in the north of the country, it is often up to you to ensure that the bus driver stops and waits while you get this – otherwise drivers may not stop, assuming that all passengers are Argentine nationals and don't need stamps. In some places (for example, Clorinda) your Argentine exit stamp is actually given on the far side of the border, but check this with the driver beforehand.

Visas for work or study must be obtained in advance from your consulate. Extensive paperwork, much of which must be legalized by the Home Office then translated into Spanish by a certified translator, is required – allow plenty of time before departure to start the process. The websites listed below have details of what documentation is needed; you could also contact the consulate directly.

Although checks are extremely rare, visitors are legally obliged to carry their passport as ID. You might get away with carrying a photocopy, but don't forget to copy your entrance stamp and landing card as well.

ARGENTINE EMBASSIES AND CONSULATES ABROAD

Australia Embassy: John McEwan House, Floor 2, 7 National Circuit, Barton ACT 2600 ☎ 02 6273 9111, ⓦ eaust.mrecic.gov.ar; Consulate: 44 Market St, Floor 20, Sydney, NSW ☎ 02 9262 2933, ⓦ csidn.cancilleria.gov.ar.

Canada Embassy: 90 Sparks St, Suite 910, Ottawa, ON K1P 5B4 ☎ 613 236 2351, ⓦ ecana.mrecic.gov.ar; Consulates: 2000 Peel St, 7th floor, Suite 600, Montréal, PQ H3A 2W5 ☎ 514 842 6582, ⓦ cmrea.mrecic.gov.ar; 5001 Yonge St, Suite 201, Toronto, ON M2N 6P6 ☎ 416 955 9075, ⓦ ctoro.mrecic.gov.ar.

New Zealand Embassy: Sovereign Assurance Building, Level 14, 142 Lambton Quay, PO Box 5430, Wellington ☎ 04 472 8330, ⓦ enzel.mrecic.gob.ar.

UK Embassy: 65 Brook St, London W1K 4AH ☎ 020 7318 1300, ⓦ argentine-embassy-uk.org; Consulate: 27 Three Kings Yard, London W1K 4DF ☎ 020 7318 1340, ⓦ clond.mrecic.gov.ar.

US Embassy: 1600 New Hampshire Ave NW, Washington DC 20009 ☎ 202 238 6400, ⓦ embassyofargentina.us; Consulates: 245 Peachtree Center Ave, Suite 2101, Atlanta, GA 30303 ☎ 404 880 0805, ⓦ catla.cancilleria.gov.ar; 205 N Michigan Ave, Suite 4209, Chicago, IL 60601 ☎ 312 819 2610, ⓦ cchic.cancilleria.gov.ar; 2200 West Loop South, Suite 1025, Houston, TX 77027 ☎ 713 871 8935, ⓦ chous.cancilleria.gov.ar; 5055 Wilshire Blvd Suite 210, Los Angeles, CA 90036 ☎ 323 954 9155, ⓦ clang.cancilleria.gov.ar; 1101 Brickell Ave, Suite 900 North Tower, Miami, FL 33132 ☎ 305 373 1598, ⓦ consuladoargentinoenmiami.org; 12 W 56th St, New York, NY 10019 ☎ 212 603 0400, ⓦ cnyor.cancilleria.gov.ar.

EMBASSIES IN ARGENTINA

Australia Buenos Aires Villanueva 1400, C1426BMJ ☎ 011 4779 3500.
Canada Buenos Aires Tagle 2828, C1425EEH ☎ 011 4808 1000.
New Zealand Buenos Aires Carlos Pellegrini 1427, 5th floor, CP1011 ☎ 011 4328 0747.
UK Buenos Aires Dr Luis Agote 2412, C1425EOF ☎ 011 4808 2200.
US Buenos Aires Av Colombia 4300, C1425GMN ☎ 011 5777 4533.

Health

Travel to Argentina doesn't raise any major **health** worries and with a small dose of precaution and a handful of standard vaccinations or updates (tetanus, polio, typhoid and hepatitis A) you are unlikely to encounter any serious problems. There have been highly publicized outbreaks of **dengue fever** in the far north; other mosquito-related illnesses to be aware of are yellow fever, malaria and (in the far north) zika. There was also a large number of (again, much publicized) cases of swine flu in mid-2009. Yet a bout of **travellers' diarrhoea**, as your body adjusts to local microorganisms in the food and water, is the most you're likely to have to worry about. The **tap water** in Argentina is generally safe to drink, if sometimes heavily chlorinated, but you may prefer to err on the side of caution in rural areas in the north of the country. Mineral water is good and widely available.

Argentine **pharmacies** are plentiful, well stocked and a useful port of call for help with minor medical problems; the staff may offer simple diagnostic advice and will often help dress wounds, but if in doubt consult a doctor. Medicines and cosmetic products are fairly expensive, however, as they are mostly imported, so if you have room, take plenty of supplies.

The easiest way to get treatment for more serious ailments is to visit the outpatient department of a **hospital**, where treatment will usually be free. In Buenos Aires, the Hospital de Clínicas José de San Martín, Av Córdoba 2351 (☎011 5950 8000), is a particularly efficient place to receive medical advice and prescriptions; you can simply walk in and, for a small fee, make an on-the-spot appointment with the relevant specialist department – English-speaking doctors can usually be found. For a list of English-speaking doctors throughout the country, contact your embassy in Buenos Aires. For **medical emergencies or ambulances** in Argentina, dial ☎107.

Among the nasty complaints that exist on Argentine territory are Chagas' disease, cholera, malaria, dengue, hantavirus, yellow fever and rabies, though all are rare, mostly confined to remote locations off the tourist trail. That said, each is sufficiently serious that you should be aware of their existence and of measures you should take to avoid infection. For up-to-date information on current health risks in Argentina, check ⓦ cdc.gov and ⓦ who.int.

The incidence of **HIV/AIDS** is similar to that in most developed countries. As some of the condoms sold in Argentina are of pretty poor quality, it's wise to bring a reliable brand with you.

Puna (altitude sickness)

Altitude sickness is a potentially – if very rarely – fatal condition encountered at anything over 2000m, but likeliest and most serious at altitudes of 4000m and above. It can cause severe difficulties, but a little preparation should help you avoid the worst of its effects. In many South American countries, it is known by the Quechua word *soroche* but in Argentina it is most commonly, and confusingly, called *puna* (the local word for altiplano, or high Andean steppes). You'll also hear the verb *apunar* and the word *apunamiento*, referring to the state of suffering from *puna*, whether affecting humans or vehicles (which also need to be adjusted for these heights).

First, to avoid the effects of the *puna*, don't rush anywhere – walk slowly and breathe steadily – and make things easier on yourself by not smoking. Whenever possible, **acclimatize**: it's better to spend a day or two at around 2000m and then 3000–3500m before climbing to 4000m or more, rather than force the body to cope with a sudden reduction in oxygen levels. Make sure you're fully **rested**; an all-night party isn't the best preparation for a trip up into the Andes. Alcohol is also best avoided both prior to and during high-altitude travel; the best thing to **drink** is plenty of still water – never fizzy because it froths over and can even explode at high altitudes – or coca tea, made from coca leaves and readily available in supermarkets in the northwest. **Eating**, too, needs some consideration: digestion uses up considerable quantities of oxygen, so snacking is preferable to copious meals. Carry supplies of high-energy cereal bars, chocolate, dried fruit (local raisins, prunes and dried apricots are delicious), walnuts or cashews, crackers and biscuits, and avoid anything that ferments in the stomach, such as milk, fresh fruit and vegetables, juices, or acidic foods – they're guaranteed to make you throw up if you're affected. The best form of sugar to ingest is honey, because it's the least acidic. Grilled meat is fine, so *asados* are alright, but don't overindulge.

Minor symptoms of the *puna*, such as headaches or a strange feeling of pressure inside the skull, nausea, loss of appetite, insomnia or dizziness, are nothing to worry about, but more severe problems, such as persistent migraines, repeated vomiting, severe breathing difficulties, excessive fatigue and a marked reduction in the need to urinate are cause for more concern. If you suffer from any of these, return to a lower altitude and seek medical advice at once. Severe respiratory problems should be treated immediately with oxygen, carried by tour operators on excursions to 3000m or more as a legal requirement, but you're unlikely ever to need it.

Sunstroke and sunburn

You should take the sun very seriously in Argentina. The north of the country, especially the Chaco region and La Rioja Province, is one of the hottest regions of Latin America in summer – temperatures regularly rocket above 40°C; extended siestas taken by locals are wise precautions against the debilitating effects of the midday heat. Where possible, avoid excessive activity between about 11am and 4pm, and when you do have to be out in the sun, wear sunscreen and a hat. You should also drink plenty of liquids – but not alcohol – and always make sure you have a sufficient supply of water when embarking on a hike. Throughout the country, the sun can be extremely fierce and even people with darker skin should use a much higher factor sunscreen than they might normally: you should always use factor 15 or above as a sensible precaution. Remember that the cooler temperatures in the south are deceptive – ozone depletion and long summer days here can be more hazardous than the fierce heat of the north.

MEDICAL RESOURCES FOR TRAVELLERS

Canadian Society for International Health ☎ 613 241 5785, Ⓦ csih.org. Extensive list of travel health centres.

CDC ☎ 1 800 232 4636, Ⓦ cdc.gov/travel. Official US government travel health site.

International Society for Travel Medicine ☎ 1 404 373 8282, Ⓦ istm.org. Has a full list of travel health clinics.

Hospital for Tropical Diseases Travel Clinic UK ☎ 0845 155 5000, ☎ 020 3477 5999 (Travel Clinic), Ⓦ www.thehtd.org. A GP referral is required for those seeking advice and vaccines before travelling to tropical countries.

MASTA (Medical Advisory Service for Travellers Abroad) UK ☎ 0300 100 4200, Ⓦ masta-travel-health.com. Lists clinics in the UK.

Tropical Medical Bureau Ireland ☎ 01 2715 200, Ⓦ tmb.ie. Health clinic offering vaccinations for travellers.

Travellers' Medical and Vaccination Centre ☎ 1300 658 844, Ⓦ traveldoctor.com.au. Lists travel clinics in Australia, New Zealand and South Africa.

World Health Organization Ⓦ who.int. The United Nations' public health bureau, WHO monitors disease outbreaks around the world.

Insurance

It is a good idea to take out an **insurance policy** before travelling, though always check first to see whether you are already covered by your home insurance, provincial health plan or student/employment insurance. In Argentina, insurance is more important to cover theft or loss of belongings and repatriation than medical treatment – the country has a state medical system that is free for emergencies. It is perfectly adequate, though the technology is not the latest and waits can be long. Most well-off Argentines use private healthcare, which is very good and cheaper than the equivalent in the US or Europe. Make sure your travel insurance policy includes coverage for any adventure sports you may

ROUGH GUIDES TRAVEL INSURANCE

Rough Guides has teamed up with WorldNomads.com to offer great **travel insurance** deals. Policies are available to residents of over 150 countries, with cover for a wide range of **adventure sports**, 24-hour emergency assistance, high levels of medical and evacuation cover and a stream of **travel safety information**. Roughguides.com users can take advantage of their policies online 24/7, from anywhere in the world – even if you're already travelling. And since plans often change when you're on the road, you can extend your policy and even claim online. Roughguides.com users who buy travel insurance with WorldNomads.com can also leave a positive footprint and donate to a community development project. For more information, go to ⓦ **roughguides.com/travel-insurance**.

be planning, such as scuba diving, white-water rafting or skiing – you will probably have to pay a premium to have this included. You should keep all receipts in case you need to make a claim, and in the event you have anything stolen, you must obtain an official statement from the police (see p.46).

Internet

All upmarket hotels offer wi-fi, as do most hostels and mid-market hotels. Cafés with wi-fi are common in Buenos Aires, less so in the interior, and it's simply a case of asking for a password rather than signing into a cloud. Otherwise, you can access the internet via internet cafés, or in *locutorios* (see p.54), found in most towns. Rates vary considerably, from $3 to $15 an hour, with the highest rates in Patagonia.

The Spanish keyboard is prevalent; if you have problems locating the "@" symbol (called *arroba* in Spanish), hold the "Alt" key down and type 64.

Laundry

Most towns and cities have a plentiful supply of **laundries** (*lavanderías* or *lavaderos*), especially since not everyone has a washing machine. Some also do dry-cleaning, though you may have to go to a *tintorería*. Self-service places are almost unheard of; you normally give your name and leave your washing to pick it up later (the service is fast by European standards); some places will deliver to wherever you're staying. Laundry is either charged by weight or itemized, but **rates** are not excessive, especially compared with the high prices charged by most hotels. Furthermore, the quality is good and the service is usually reliable. One important word of vocabulary to know is **planchado** (ironed).

LGBT travellers

Thanks to progress in recent years, including the **equal marriage law** (which includes full adoption

rights) passed in 2010, the attitude in Argentina towards LGBT people is quite open, despite this being an overwhelmingly Roman Catholic nation. Violent manifestations of **homophobia** are rare, especially now that the Church and the military exert less influence; homosexual acts between consenting adults have long been legal. A piece of legislation passed by parliament in 2003 afforded all citizens protection from discrimination, making a specific reference to sexual orientation (and making it illegal for hoteliers to turn away same-sex couples, for example).

LGBT associations are springing up in the major cities, notably in Buenos Aires, where nightlife and meeting places are very open (see p.120). Rural areas still do their best to act as if homosexuality doesn't exist, though, and it's best to act a little more discreetly there.

RESOURCES FOR LGBT TRAVELLERS IN ARGENTINA

G-Maps 360 ⓦ gmaps360.com. A helpful site with up-to-date listings on LGBT-friendly hotels, bars, clubs and restaurants in Buenos Aires.

Gay Guide ⓦ gayguide.net. A helpful site for trip planning, bookings and general information about international travel.

The Gay Guide ⓦ thegayguide.com.ar. Online guide offering insight into lodging, Gay Pride, bars and tours for gay male travellers in Buenos Aires.

Nexo ⓦ nexo.org. Serious site reporting on the latest LGBT news and cultural events in Argentina.

Hadrianus Buenos Aires ☎ 011 15 6421 2028, ⓦ hadrianus.com .ar, ✉ info@hadrianus.com.ar. Small, friendly company focusing on city tours and longer holidays around the country, as well as tickets and accommodation.

Living and working in Argentina

Many foreigners choose to stay in Argentina long-term, and if you want to take the plunge you will be in good company, particularly if you settle in Buenos Aires or one of the key travel destinations such as Ushuaia or Mendoza. **Organizations** that cater to immigrants to Argentina include the lively internet forum ⓦbaexpats.org, the Facebook group Buenos Aires Expats Hub (ⓦfacebook.com/groups/BuenosAiresExpatHub) and the Mendoza Expats Club (ⓦmendozaexpats.org).

Tourist **visas** are valid for ninety days. You are usually allowed to renew your visa once, although this does mean an encounter with the bureaucratic immigration services. Many medium-term residents simply leave the country every three months (usually hopping across to Colonia, in Uruguay), to get a new stamp, but this approach might not be tolerated over many years (see p.47). Obtaining a **residence permit** is time-consuming and it's usually granted only if you have an Argentine spouse or child, or are hired and sponsored by an Argentine company.

As far as **working** is concerned, remember Argentines themselves compete for the few jobs on offer and your entry into the employment market may not be looked on kindly; also, unless you are on a contract with an international firm or organization, you will be paid in pesos, which will inevitably add up to a pretty low salary by global standards. If you're determined anyway, many English-speaking foreigners do the obvious thing and **teach English**. Training in this is an advantage but by no means necessary; the demand for native English-speaking teachers is so high that many soon build up a roster of students via the odd newspaper ad and word of mouth. **Working in tourism** is another possibility – a fair proportion of agencies and hotels are run by foreigners. Also worth considering is translation, if you have the language ability.

There are plenty of agencies aimed at foreigners which can help if you need a **place to live** – one is ⓦalojargentina.com – offering accommodation in apartments, university residences and B&B-type establishments; more are listed on the expat forums and websites mentioned above, or you could try ⓦbuenosaires.craigslist.org. Apartments aimed at locals are advertised in newspapers or rented through *inmobiliarías* (estate agents) and are cheaper, but you will need somebody who owns property to be your guarantor and be prepared to sign a two-year contract.

Mail

Argentina's rather unreliable **postal service**, Correo Argentino (☎011 4891 9191, ⓦcorreoargentino .com.ar), is the *bête noire* of many a hapless expat. Not only is it costly to send post to North America or Europe (starting at $8 for a postcard), but many items also never arrive. If you want to **send mail abroad**, always use the *certificado* (registered post) system, which costs about $99 for a letter, but increases chances of arrival. Safer still is Correo Argentino's *encomienda* system (around $300 for a package under 1kg to North America or Europe), a **courier-style** service; if you are sending something important or irreplaceable, it is highly recommended that you use this service or a similar international one such as UPS (☎0800 222 2877) or DHL (☎0810 122 2345). Packets over 2kg need to be examined by the customs (*Aduana*) at the Centro Postal Internacional at Antártida Argentina 1900 y Comodoro Py in Retiro, Buenos Aires (Mon–Fri 10am–5pm). For regular airmail, expect delivery times of one to two weeks – the quickest deliveries, unsurprisingly, are those out of Buenos Aires. You are not permitted to seal envelopes with sticky tape: they must be gummed down (glue is usually available at the counter). The good news is that as well as post offices, many *locutorios*, lottery kiosks and small stores deal with mail, which means you don't usually have to go very far to find somewhere open.

Receiving mail is generally even more fraught with difficulties than sending it. Again, a courier-style service is your best bet; if not, make sure the sender at least registers the letter or parcel. All **parcels** go to the international post office at Antártida Argentina 1900 in Retiro, and you will receive a card informing you that it is there; you will have to pay customs duties and should expect a long wait. If you are elsewhere in the country, you must find out where your nearest customs office is. All post offices keep **poste restante** for at least a month. Items should be addressed clearly, with the recipient's surname in capital letters and underlined, followed by their first name in regular script, then "Poste Restante" or "Lista de Correos", Correo Central, followed by the rest of the address. Buenos Aires city is normally referred to as Capital Federal to distinguish it from its neighbouring province. Bring your passport to collect items ($40/item plus $8/day of storage) – and a book, as you'll need to queue for a few hours.

To send **packages within Argentina**, your best bet is to use the *encomienda* services offered by bus companies (seal boxes in brown paper to prevent casual theft). This isn't a door-to-door service like the post: the recipient must collect the package from its end destination (bring suitable ID). By addressing the package to yourself, this system makes an excellent and remarkably good-value way of reducing the weight in your pack while travelling, but be aware that companies usually keep an *encomienda* for only one month before returning it to its original sender. If sending an *encomienda* to Buenos Aires, check whether it gets held at the Retiro bus station (the most convenient) or at a bus depot elsewhere in the capital.

Maps

There are a number of **country maps** available outside Argentina; Reise Know-How and Freytag & Berndt produce particularly helpful ones. For Buenos Aires city maps, look into Streetwise's pocket-size version or National Geographic's, which is clear, reliable and easy to fold. It is also worth investing in a Guía T map book, the capital's A–Z that includes helpful bus routes and sights.

Within Argentina, **road maps** can be obtained at bookshops and kiosks in all big towns and cities or at service stations. Many maps aren't up to date: it's often a good idea to buy a couple of maps and compare them as you go along, always checking with the locals to see whether a given road does exist and is passable, especially with the vehicle you intend to use. The most reliable maps are those produced by **ACA** (Automóvil Club), which does individual maps for each province, to varying degrees of accuracy. These are widely available at ACA offices, kiosks on Calle Florida in the capital and service stations. Glossy and fairly clear – but at times erratic – regional road maps (Cuyo, Northwest, Lake District, etc) are produced by **AutoMapa** and are often available at petrol stations and bookshops. Slightly more detailed but a tad less accurate is the mini-atlas *Atlas Vial* published by **YPF**, the national petrol company, and sold at its service stations.

For 1:100,000 Ordnance Survey-style maps, the Instituto Geográfico Nacional at Av Cabildo 381 in Buenos Aires is the place to go (Mon–Fri 8.30am–4pm; ☎011 4576 5576 ext 152, ⓦign.gob.ar). These topographical and colour satellite maps are great to look at and very detailed, but they are only really practical for trekkers who are used to maps of this type.

Country maps can be found at the University of Texas's Perry–Castañeda Library: ⓦlib.utexas .edu/maps/argentina.html. A good interactive map of Buenos Aires capital can be found at ⓦmapa .buenosaires.gov.ar.

Money

Notes come in 2, 5, 10, 20, 50, 100, 200 and 500 denominations, while 1 and 2 peso coins and 50,

CURRENCY NOTATION

When you see the $ sign in Argentina – and throughout this book – you can safely assume that the currency being referred to is the Argentine peso. Where a price is quoted in US dollars, the normal notation in Argentina – and the notation we use – is US$.

25, 10 and 5 (rare) centavo coins are in circulation. Sometimes people are loath to give change, as coins used to be in short supply and the old habit is hard to break, so it's a good idea to have plenty of loose change on your person. Ask for small denomination notes when exchanging if possible, break bigger ones up at places where they obviously have plenty of change (busy shops, supermarkets and post offices), and withdraw odd amounts from ATMs ($190, $340, etc) to avoid getting your cash dispensed in $100 bills only – trying to buy a drink, an empanada or a postcard with a crisp $100 note will be a frustrating ordeal and won't make you many friends.

Taxes

IVA (*Impuesto de Valor Agregado*) is the Argentine equivalent of VAT or **sales tax**, and at 21 percent is usually included in the price for goods and services except food or medicines. The major exceptions are some hotels, which quote their rates before tax, plus airfares and car rental fees. It is worth knowing that foreigners can often get IVA reimbursed on many purchases, though this is practical only for bigger transactions (over US$70). Check Global Blue (ⓦglobalblue.com) for information on refund offices, usually found in international airports and terminals. Shops in the more touristy areas will volunteer information and provide the necessary forms, but finding the final paperwork completed, signed and stamped to get your money back, at your point of exit (international airports), is a laborious task; ask for instructions when you check in, as you must display your purchases before check-in and then go through the often frustratingly slow formalities once you've been given your boarding pass.

ATMs and credit and debit cards

ATMs (*cajeros automáticos*) are plentiful in Argentina. It's rare that you'll find a town or even a village without one, though you can sometimes be caught out in very remote places, especially in the Northwest, so never rely completely on them. Most machines take all credit cards or display those that can be used: you can nearly always get money out with Visa or MasterCard, or with any cards linked to the Plus or Cirrus systems. Most ATMs are either Banelco or LINK – test the networks to see which works best with your card. Machines are mostly multilingual though some of them use Spanish only, so you might need to have a phrasebook handy if you don't speak the language.

Credit cards (*tarjetas de crédito*) are a very handy source of funds, and can be used either in the abundant ATMs (this can be expensive) or for purchases. Visa, MasterCard and American Express are all widely used and recognized. Be warned that you must show your ID when making a purchase with plastic, and, especially in small establishments in remote areas, the authorization process can take ages and may not succeed at all. Using your **debit card**, which is not liable to interest payments like credit cards, is usually the best method to get cash and the flat transaction fee is generally quite small – your bank will able to advise on this. Make sure you have a card and PIN that are designed to work overseas and advise your bank before you depart. Bear in mind that all use of credit cards and ATMs will be at the official exchange rate (see p.45).

Opening hours

Most **shops and services** are open Monday to Friday 9am to 7pm, and Saturday 10am to 8pm. Outside the capital, they may close at some point during the afternoon for between one and five hours. As a rule, the further north you go, the longer the siesta – often offset by later closing times in the evening. Supermarkets seldom close during the day and are generally open much later, often until 8 or even 10pm, and on Saturday afternoons. Large shopping malls don't close before 10pm and their food and drink sections (*patios de comida*) may stay open as late as midnight. Many of them open on Sundays too. *Casas de cambio* more or less follow shop hours. However, **banks** only open on weekdays: opening times depend on the region. In hotter areas, banks open as early as 7am or 8am, but close by noon or 1pm; whereas in many other areas, including Buenos Aires, they're open from 10am to 3pm.

The opening hours of **attractions** are indicated in the Guide; however, bear in mind that these often change from one season to another. If you are going out of your way to visit something, it is best to check if its opening times have changed. **Museums** are a law unto themselves, each one having its own timetable, but all commonly close one day a week, usually Monday. Several Buenos Aires museums close for at least a month over January and February. **Tourist offices** are forever adjusting their opening times, but the trend is towards longer hours and opening daily. **Post offices**' hours vary; most should be open between 9am and 6pm on weekdays, with siestas in the hottest places. Outside these hours, many *locutorios* will deal with mail.

PUBLIC HOLIDAYS

Argentina has no shortage of public holidays dotted throughout the calendar. Most services run even on these *feriados*, with the possible exceptions of Christmas Day and May Day. Bear in mind that some of these holidays move to the following Monday (or sometimes to another convenient date) if they fall on a weekend and that "bridges" are conceded when certain holidays fall on a Tuesday or Thursday, to form long weekends. There are also several local public holidays, specific to a city or province, throughout the year (those specific to certain communities and non-Christian faiths are also respected by state-run services). Many offices close for the whole of Semana Santa (Holy Week), the week leading up to Easter, while the Thursday is optional, as is New Year's Eve. Easter Monday is not normally a holiday.

January 1 New Year's Day
Final Monday and Tuesday before Lent (usually Feb) Carnival
Friday before Easter Good Friday
March 24 Truth and Justice Day, in commemoration of the 1976 coup
April 2 Malvinas Veterans' Day
May 1 Labour Day
May 25 Day of the Revolution

June 20 Day of the Flag (anniversary of General Belgrano's death)
July 9 Independence Day
August 17 Anniversary of San Martín's death
October 12 Day of Respect for Cultural Diversity
November 20 Day of National Sovereignty
December 8 Immaculate Conception
December 25 Christmas Day

CALLING HOME FROM ABROAD

Note that the initial zero is omitted from the area code when dialling the UK, Ireland, Australia and New Zealand from abroad.

Australia international access code + 61
New Zealand international access code + 64
UK international access code + 44
US and Canada international access code + 1
Ireland international access code + 353
South Africa international access code + 27

Phones

Argentina operates a GSM 850/1900 **mobile phone** network, in common with much of Latin America. Most modern mobile phones are tri- or quad-band so should work fine, but if yours is older you should check with your phone provider to confirm it will work. Local mobile numbers are prefixed by the area code, like fixed lines, and then 15. If you are dialling an Argentine mobile number from abroad, omit the 15 and dial 9 before the area code. If you're likely to use your phone a lot, it may be worth getting an **Argentine SIM card** to keep costs down. These can be obtained before you travel from various providers, or, cheaper still – though you'll need some Spanish here – you could get a pre-paid SIM (*chip*) from a local operator such as Movistar (Ⓦmovistar.com.ar) or Personal (Ⓦpersonal.com.ar). Movistar is preferable as it will activate your service straight away, whereas you may have to wait a day or two with other providers. It has a large customer service centre in Buenos Aires at Santa Fe 1844 (Mon–Fri 9am–9pm).

In many ways it's just as cheap and straight-forward to make calls from the public call centres known as **locutorios**. Although they are not as ubiquitous as they once were, they are still widely found throughout the country. You'll be assigned a cabin with a meter, with which you can monitor your expenditure. Make as many calls as you want and then pay at the counter. You can get significant discounts on international calls with pre-paid phonecards, available at the *locutorios*. If you are travelling with a laptop, tablet or smartphone, it is even cheaper to use an internet phone service such as Skype, utilizing the free wi-fi provided by most hotels.

Photography

Digital memory cards are widely available, although generally more expensive than in places like the US and Europe, especially in the more remote locations and for the larger-memory cards. Most mid-sized towns have places where you can burn photos onto DVDs or CDs. Standard photographic **film** is also still available, but you're advised to bring specialist films (eg slide film, black-and-white, low-light ISO/ASA ratings) from home. The same goes for all camera spares and supplies. **Developing** and printing are usually of decent quality but are also quite expensive, and outside Buenos Aires the situation is erratic. A constant, however, is that you should watch out where you take photos: sensitive border areas and all military installations, including many civilian airports, are camera **no-go areas**, so watch out for signs and take no risks.

Time

Argentina hasn't – it seems – settled on a stable pattern of **time zones**. Officially, there's supposed to be a unified national time zone (3hr behind GMT), but some provinces have been known to operate separate systems. For the latest information you're best off checking the official government site (Ⓦwww.hidro.gov.ar), or Wikipedia (Ⓦen.wikipedia.org/wiki/Time_in_Argentina).

Tourist information

The main **national tourist board** (Ⓦargentina.travel) is in Buenos Aires and is a useful stop for maps and general information. Piles of leaflets, glossy brochures and maps are dished out at provincial and municipal **tourist offices** (*oficinas de turismo*) across the country, which vary enormously in quality of service and quantity of information. Don't rely on staff speaking any language other than Spanish, or on the printed info being translated into foreign languages. In addition, every province maintains a **casa de provincia** (provincial tourist office) in Buenos Aires.

CASAS DE PROVINCIAS IN BUENOS AIRES

Buenos Aires Av Callao 237 (Mon–Fri 9am–5pm; ☎ 0800 555 2722).
Catamarca Av Córdoba 2080 (Mon–Fri 9am–5pm; ☎ 011 4374 6894).
Chaco Av Callao 328 (Mon–Fri 10am–4.30pm; ☎ 011 4372 5209).
Chubut Sarmiento 1172 (Mon–Fri 10am–6pm; ☎ 011 4382 2009).

Córdoba Av Callao 332 (Mon–Fri 9am–6pm; ☎ 011 4372 8859).
Corrientes Maipú 271 (Mon–Fri 8.30am–8.30pm;
☎ 011 4394 7418).
Entre Ríos Suipacha 844 (Mon–Fri 9am–3pm; ☎ 011 4328 5985).
Formosa H. Yrigoyen 1429 (Mon–Fri 9am–3pm; ☎ 011 4383 0376).
Jujuy Av Santa Fe 967 (Mon–Fri 10am–7pm; ☎ 011 4393 1295).
La Pampa Suipacha 346 (Jan & Feb Mon–Fri 9am–3.30pm;
March–Dec Mon–Fri 8am–6pm; ☎ 011 4326 0511 ext. 2527).
La Rioja Callao 745 (Mon–Fri 9am–6pm; ☎ 011 4813 3417).
Mendoza Av Callao 445 (Mon–Fri 9am–5pm; ☎ 011 4371 7301).
Misiones Av Córdoba 323, 5th floor (Mon–Fri 8am–noon;
☎ 011 4317 3722).
Neuquén Maipú 48 (Mon–Fri 9am–4pm; ☎ 011 4343 2324).
Río Negro Tucumán 1916 (Mon–Fri 10am–4pm; ☎ 011 4371 7273).
Salta Av Pte Roque S. Peña 933 (Mon–Fri 10am–3pm;
☎ 011 4326 2456).
San Juan Sarmiento 1251 (Mon–Fri 9am–5pm;
☎ 011 4382 9241).
San Luís Azcuénaga 1087 (Mon–Fri 9am–6pm;
☎ 011 5778 1621).
Santa Cruz 25 de Mayo 279 (Mon–Fri 9.30am–3.30pm;
☎ 011 4331 2931).
Santa Fe 25 de Mayo 178 (Mon–Fri 9.30am–6pm;
☎ 011 4342 0408).
Santiago del Estero Florida 274 (Mon–Fri 10am–6pm;
☎ 011 4326 9418).
Tierra del Fuego Sarmiento 745 783 (Mon–Fri 10am–4pm;
☎ 011 4322 7343).
Tucumán Suipacha 140 (Mon–Fri 9am–4pm; ☎ 011 432 0010
ext. 124).

USEFUL WEBSITES

Argentina – LANIC Ⓦ lanic.utexas.edu/la/argentina. A great
resource covering every imaginable aspect of life in Argentina, invaluable
both to travellers and researchers.
Argentina Parques Nacionales Ⓦ parquesnacionales.gob.ar.
Spanish-only site for the country's national park system, with information
and news on all the parks.
The Bubble Ⓦ bubblear.com. Light-hearted online news resource
that helps to unravel the country's complex politics in English.
Ciudad de Buenos Aires Ⓦ turismo.buenosaires.gob.ar.
Comprehensive official city site, with listings for bars, clubs, restaurants,
shops, theatres, all searchable by genre and area. A good section on tours,
including suggested circuits designed around famous literary, cultural and
historical figures linked to the capital.
Directorio de Museos Argentinos Ⓦ cultura.gob.ar/museos.
Useful searchable official database of most of the country's museums,
including practicalities.
Pick Up The Fork Ⓦ pickupthefork.com. Irreverent food blog in
English devoted mainly to eating in Buenos Aires.
Planeta Argentina Ⓦ planeta.com/argentina.html. Articles and
advice relating to ecotourism in Argentina.
El Portal del Tango Ⓦ elportaldeltango.com. Lots of background
on the national dance.

South American Explorers Ⓦ saexplorers.org/explore
/Argentina. Useful if dated site set up by the experienced
non-profit-making organization South American Explorers, aimed at
scientists, explorers and travellers to South America.
Travel Blog Ⓦ travelblog.org/South-America/Argentina and
Travel Pod Ⓦ travelpod.com/travel-blog-country/Argentina
/tpod.html. Two decent travel sites with forums, photos, hotel
options etc.

Travellers with disabilities

Argentina does not have a particularly sophisticated
infrastructure for travellers with disabilities, but
most Argentines are extremely willing to help
anyone experiencing problems and this helpful
attitude goes some way to making up for deficien-
cies in facilities.

Things are beginning to improve, and it is in
Buenos Aires that you will find the most notable
changes: there are now pavement-to-road ramps in
many parts of the city, though unfortunately the
pavements themselves don't tend to be in great
condition. Public transport is less problematic, with
many buses that now circulate in the city offering
low-floor access, though you won't find lifts in all
subte stations. Laws demand that all new hotels
provide at least one wheelchair-accessible room,
and that all accommodation provides full wheelchair access, including lifts, wide doorways and
roll-in showers.

Outside Buenos Aires, finding facilities for
disabled travellers is pretty much a hit-and-miss
affair, although there have been some notable
improvements at major **tourist attractions** such as
the Iguazú Falls, where new ramps and walkways
have been constructed, making the vast majority of
the Falls area accessible by wheelchair. The local
Hostelling International office (see p.31) can offer
information on access at its hostels.

CONTACTS FOR TRAVELLERS WITH DISABILITIES

Access-Able Ⓦ access-able.com. Online resources for travellers with
disabilities.
Accessible Journeys US ☎ 800 846 4537, Ⓦ disabilitytravel.com.
Travel tips and programmes for groups or individuals.
Irish Wheelchair Association Ireland ☎ 01 818 6400, Ⓦ iwa.ie.
Information and listings for wheelchair users travelling abroad.
**Society for the Advancement of Travellers with Handicaps
(SATH)** US ☎ 212 447 7284, Ⓦ sath.org. Advice on travelling with
certain conditions.
Tourism for All Vitalise UK ☎ 0845 124 9971, Ⓦ tourismforall.org
.uk. Lists of accessible accommodation abroad worldwide and
information on financial help for holidays.

Buenos Aires

PAINTED BUILDINGS, CAMINITO, BOCA

1

Buenos Aires

Of all South America's capitals, Buenos Aires – aka Capital Federal, CABA, Baires, BsAs or simply BA – has the most going for it. Seductive and cultured, sophisticated yet earthy, eclectic but with a strong identity, it never bores, seldom sleeps and invariably mesmerizes its visitors. Influenced by the great European cities, Buenos Aires nonetheless has its own distinct personality enhanced by proud traditions, including football, tango and *mate*. On one flank lap the caramel-hued waters of the Río de la Plata, the world's widest estuary: signs of BA's regained prosperity include wharves stacked high with containers and the ever-busier cruise-ship terminus. To the west and south, the verdant Pampas – historically the source of the city's food and wealth – meld seamlessly into its vast suburbs.

Modern Buenos Aires enjoys an incomparable **lifestyle**. Elegant restaurants, glamorous bars, historic cafés and heaving nightclubs, plus a world-class opera house, countless theatres, avant-garde galleries and French-style palaces all underscore its attachment to the arts and its eternal sense of style. Its proud inhabitants, known as Porteños, are extravagant and well groomed but they are also hospitable. Another boon is the abundance of **parks and gardens**, plus the many **trees** lining the streets and providing shade in the lively **plazas** that dot the huge metropolis; they add welcome splashes of colour, particularly when ablaze with yellow, pink and mauve blooms in spring and autumn. The squadrons of vociferous songbirds that populate the greenery help visitors forget that this is the fifth-largest metropolitan area in the Americas: there are nearly fourteen million inhabitants in the **Gran Buenos Aires** area, which spills well beyond the city's defining boundary of multi-lane ring roads into Buenos Aires Province (see Chapter 2).

On the map and from the air the metropolitan area looks dauntingly huge, yet the compact centre and relative proximity of the main sights mean you don't have to travel far to gain an overview. Of the city's 48 **barrios** you will most probably visit only the half-dozen most central. During the week, the **city centre** (San Nicolás and Monserrat) and the stretch along pedestrianized Calle Florida are hectic, but the *fin-de-siècle* elegance of **Avenida de Mayo** and the bohemian café culture of **Avenida Corrientes** offer a contrasting atmosphere. Beyond the converted docklands of **Puerto Madero**, east of downtown, lies the unexpectedly wild **Reserva Ecológica**, one of the city's green lungs.

Highlights

❶ San Telmo Historic barrio, appreciated for its mellow charm and seductive ambience. Every Sunday impromptu tango provides the soundtrack for visits to treasure-packed antique stalls. **See p.78**

❷ Football Tricky footwork and colourful passion is on display at Boca Juniors' Bombonera or River Plate's Monumental – and in the surrounding streets. **See p.82 & p.101**

❸ Cementerio de la Recoleta Join the feral cats and prowl around one of the world's most exclusive cemeteries, where Evita's final (for now) resting place lurks discreetly among eminent tombs, extravagant mausoleums and elaborate sculptures. **See p.91**

❹ MALBA Ogle the best of contemporary Latin American painting and sculpture showcased in a stunning example of cutting-edge architecture. **See p.95**

❺ Palermo Viejo Argentina's most famous writer, Borges, loved its authentic lowlife, but today's glitterati flock here for trendy shops, gourmet restaurants and boutique guesthouses. See p.95

❻ Tango Listen to alfresco *bandoneón* players, admire a showcase extravaganza at a glitzy venue or attend a humble neighbourhood *milonga* and learn the basic eight steps. **See p.121**

HIGHLIGHTS ARE MARKED ON THE MAP ON P.60

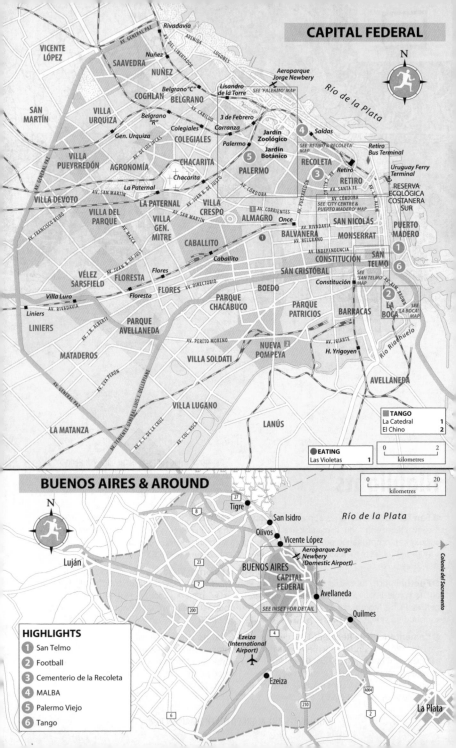

CAPITAL FEDERAL

VICENTE
LÓPEZ

SAAVEDRA
NUÑEZ
Nuñez

SAN
MARTÍN

COGHLAN
VILLA
URQUIZA
BELGRANO
Belgrano "C"
*Lisandro
de la Torre*

*Belgrano
"R"*
COLEGIALES
3 de Febrero
Carranza

*Aeroparque
Jorge Newbery*
SEE 'PALERMO' MAP

Río de la Plata

N

VILLA
PUEYRREDÓN
Gen. Urquiza
COLEGIALES
Palermo
5
PALERMO
**Jardín
Zoológico
Jardín
Botánico**

4 *Saldas*
SEE 'RETIRO & RECOLETA'
MAP
3
RECOLETA

Retiro
*Retiro
Bus Terminal*

AGRONOMÍA
CHACARITA
La Paternal
Chacarita

RETIRO
AV. SANTA FE
*Uruguay Ferry
Terminal*

VILLA DEVOTO
LA PATERNAL
VILLA
GEN.
MITRE
VILLA
CRESPO
ALMAGRO
AV. CORRIENTES
Once

AV. CÓRDOBA
SEE 'CITY CENTRE &
PUERTO MADERO' MAP

RESERVA
ECOLÓGICA
COSTANERA
SUR

PUERTO
MADERO

VILLA
DEL
PARQUE
CABALLITO
Caballito
BALVANERA
AV. RIVADAVIA
AV. BELGRANO
SAN NICOLÁS
MONSERRAT

1

VÉLEZ
SARSFIELD
FLORESTA
Flores
FLORES
Caballito
SAN CRISTÓBAL
Constitución
AV. INDEPENDENCIA
CONSTITUCIÓN
BOEDO

SAN
TELMO
SEE
'SAN TELMO'
MAP

6

Villa Luro
Liniers
AV. RIVADAVIA
Floresta
PARQUE
CHACABUCO
PARQUE
PATRICIOS
BARRACAS
2
LA
BOCA
SEE
'LA BOCA'
MAP

LINIERS
PARQUE
AVELLANEDA
AV. PERITO MORENO
NUEVA
POMPEYA
AV. IRIARTE
H. Yrigoyen
Río Riachuelo

MATADEROS
VILLA SOLDATI

AVELLANEDA

VILLA LUGANO
LANÚS

LA MATANZA

BUENOS AIRES & AROUND

N

0   20
kilometres

Río de la Plata

27
Tigre
8
San Isidro
Olivos
Vicente López
*Aeroparque Jorge
Newbery
(Domestic Airport)*

Luján
23
BUENOS AIRES
CAPITAL
FEDERAL
SEE INSET FOR DETAIL

Avellaneda
Quilmes

7
200
*Ezeiza
(International
Airport)*
4

Colonia del Sacramento

Ezeiza
210
A004

6
2
La Plata

The older **south** of the city begins just beyond the central Plaza de Mayo. The narrow streets are lined with some of the capital's finest architecture, typified by late nineteenth-century townhouses with ornate Italianate facades. Increasingly gentrified, **San Telmo** is primarily known for its cutting-edge artists, lively antiques and artisan fair, and touristy tango haunts, while resolutely working-class **La Boca**, further south, is so inextricably linked with its football team, Boca Juniors, that many buildings are painted blue and yellow. The **north** of the city is leafier and wealthier; you can ogle the French-style palaces of **Retiro**, stay in one of the top-end hotels of **Recoleta** or head to **Palermo** to shop or dine. City **museums** are dotted between La Boca and Palermo, with themes as varied as contemporary Latin American art, *mate* cups and Eva Perón.

Brief history

While European conquistadors are attributed with discovering the Buenos Aires area in 1516, the land was, of course, already inhabited when they arrived. The **Querandí** – a tribe of hunter-gatherers who roamed the Pampas – and other indigenous peoples in the vicinity didn't take entirely kindly to Spanish attempts to found a city on their land, and the first successful permanent settlement didn't exist until 1580.

Buenos Aires was named in honour of **Nuestra Señora de Santa María de los Buenos Ayres**, who blessed the good winds that helped those Spanish sailors first land on the banks of the Río de la Plata estuary. Though the Spanish found the horses and cattle they brought over from Europe thrived, the fertility of the land made little impression on them. They were more interested in precious metals, and named the settlement's river the **Plata** (silver) in the belief that it flowed from the lands of silver and gold in the Andes.

Expansion was slow, however, and Buenos Aires remained a distant outpost of the Spanish-American empire for the next two centuries, with **smuggling** being the mainstay of the local economy. In 1776, in an attempt to shore up its empire, Spain gave the Argentine territories **Viceroyalty status**, with Buenos Aires as the capital. It was too little, too late: boosted by the defeat of two attempted British invasions, the people of the Viceroyalty declared **independence** in 1810, freeing the area from the last vestiges of colonial hindrance.

Immigration and growth

The industrial revolution gave Buenos Aires the opportunity to exploit and export the great riches of the Pampas, thanks to technological advances such as railways and refrigeration – which enabled Europeans to dine on Argentine beef for the first time. Few cities in the world have experienced a period of such astonishing **growth** as that which spurred Buenos Aires between 1870 and 1914. Massive foreign investment – most notably from the British – poured into the city and Buenos Aires' stature leapt accordingly. European **immigrants**, over half of whom were Italians, flocked to the capital, and the city's population doubled between 1880 and 1890. Most of the old town was razed and an eclectic range of new buildings went up in a huge grid pattern. The standard of living of Buenos Aires' middle class equalled or surpassed that of many European countries, while the incredible wealth of the city's elite was almost without parallel anywhere. At the same time, however, much of the large working-class community endured appalling conditions in the city's overcrowded *conventillos*, or tenement buildings.

Modern troubles

By the mid-twentieth century the period of breakneck development had come to a close as the country slid into political turmoil and economic **crisis**. In September 1945, Buenos Aires saw the first of what was to become a regular fixture – a massive **demonstration** that filled the city centre. Rallies of almost religious fervour in support of Perón and his wife Eva or **Evita**, who delivered their speeches on the balcony of the Casa Rosada, followed at regular intervals until Evita's death and Perón's deposition. Eight years of military dictatorship that followed saw the city in lockdown, with the mothers

1

and grandmothers of the disappeared (see box, p.66) one of the few visible signs of the turmoil underneath the surface. Since the return to democracy in 1982, Buenos Aires has been the most visible face of the country's economic rollercoaster. The temporary stabilization of the currency in the 1990s brought a new upsurge in spending by those who could afford it – smart new shopping malls, restaurants and cinema complexes sprung up around the city. But Buenos Aires entered the twenty-first century in retreat, as a grinding **recession** led to weeks of protests and looting that came to a horrendous head in December 2001, when widespread rioting led to dozens of deaths. Demonstrations and roadblocks by unemployed *piqueteros* became part of the fabric of everyday life during the messy recovery that followed, with the sad sight of *cartoneros* (cardboard collectors) rooting through rubbish the most obvious example of the economic problems, and growing crime an inevitable offshoot of this rise in poverty.

As the focus of national **bicentenary** celebrations in 2010 – and despite being hit by the global financial crisis – Buenos Aires is in relatively good shape. Long overdue repairs have been carried out, welfare plans have reduced (though not eradicated) the worst poverty, exclusive bus lanes on major avenues have freed up some traffic problems and **international tourism** continues to be an engine of growth. Problems remain, however – crime, shantytowns, flooding in big storms, power outages and politically motivated roadblocks are some key issues that top voters' agendas. Protests – such as the ones led by the Qom indigenous community to fight for ancestral land rights in the north of the country (see p.269) – are also common occurrences.

Regardless, Buenos Aires seems confident of its future. Led for eight years by former Boca football club chairman Mauricio Macri, elected the nation's president in November 2015, the capital remains in the hands of his Cambiemos ("Let's Change") party.

The city centre

An eclectic, chaotic mix of old-fashioned cafés, grand nineteenth-century public edifices, high-rise office blocks and tearing traffic, Buenos Aires' **city centre** exudes energy and elegance – though it can be shabby in parts. Its heart is the spacious, palm-dotted **Plaza de Mayo**, the ideal place to begin a tour of the area and explore its historical and political connections; its mismatched medley of buildings includes the famous **Casa Rosada**, or government house. Ambling westwards from the plaza will take you along **Avenida de Mayo**, the city's major boulevard, offering an impressive display of Art Nouveau and Art Deco architecture. At its western end, Avenida de Mayo opens onto the **Plaza del Congreso**, presided over by the **Congreso Nacional** building, the seat of the federal parliament.

From Plaza del Congreso, Avenida Callao will take you northwards to **Avenida Corrientes**. Now a busy commercial artery, Corrientes was famous in the twentieth century as the hub of the city's left-leaning café society. Though less plotting goes on here today, it's still the place for a dose of culture, lined with no end of bookshops, music shops, cinemas and theatres. A short detour north from Corrientes will take you to **Plaza Lavalle**, a grassy square most notable for the magnificent opera house that looms over its eastern edge, the regal **Teatro Colón**.

East from Plaza Lavalle, you'll hit the enormous **Avenida 9 de Julio** – the city's multi-lane central nerve. Presiding at its heart is the stark white **Obelisco**, a 67m stake through the intersection of avenidas 9 de Julio and Corrientes. Crossing east over 9 de Julio, you head into a densely packed and busy zone known as the **microcentro** (the Argentine term for downtown), whose two main streets are pedestrianized **Lavalle** and **Florida**, where you'll be swept along by a stream of human traffic past elegant *galerías* (arcades) and stores of every kind. Buenos Aires' small financial district – called, in homage to London, "**La City**" – makes up the southeast corner of the microcentro, while to the northeast sits "**El Bajo**", home to more bars and restaurants.

Plaza de Mayo

1

Packed with some of Buenos Aires' best-known historical landmarks, not least the presidential palace, **Plaza de Mayo** is a microcosm of the city's past: it's been bombed by the military and crowded with Evita's *descamisados* (literally "the shirtless ones", or manual workers), and for many years it has been the scene of the Madres de Plaza de Mayo's weekly demonstration (see box, p.66). Although it still attracts small, noisy protests, including an eternal group of Malvinas/Falklands veterans demanding greater compensation, it's usually sedately filled with gossiping old men batting away flocks of street sellers flogging candied peanuts and Argentine flags, and crisscrossed by harried Porteños late for a meeting. At its centre stands the **Pirámide de Mayo**, a snow-white obelisk erected in 1811 to mark the first anniversary of the May 25 Revolution, when a junta overthrew the Spanish viceroy, declared Buenos Aires' independence from Spain and set about establishing the city's jurisdiction over the rest of the territory. The headscarves painted on the ground around the pyramid echo those worn by the Madres.

Casa Rosada

Balcarce 50 · Guided visits Sat, Sun & bank hols 10am–6pm; 40min · Free · ☎ 011 4344 3804, ⓦ visitas.casarosada.gob.ar

Perón, Evita, Maradona and Galtieri have all addressed the crowds from the balcony of the unmissable **Casa de Gobierno**, otherwise known as the **Casa Rosada**, or "Pink House", the rose-hued government palace that occupies the east end of the square. The practice of painting buildings pink was common in the nineteenth century, particularly in the countryside, where you'll still see many estancias this colour, and was originally achieved with the use of ox blood, for both decorative and practical reasons – the blood acted as a fixative for the whitewash to which it was added. After being a muted rose for many years, followed by a brief phase in a shocking pink – a legacy of the flamboyant Menem era – the building was restored in 2007 to a deep puce colour, patented as "Casa de Gobierno pink". It has been strikingly lit at night since the bicentenary celebrations in 2010 (see box below).

The present structure, a typically Argentine blend of French and Italian Renaissance styles, developed in an organic fashion. It stands on the site of the city's Spanish fort, begun in 1594 and converted in 1776 to the viceroy's palace. In 1862, President Bartolomé Mitre moved government ministries to the building, remodelling it once again. The final touch – the central arch – was added in 1885, unifying the facade. You can explore the building on a **guided visit** (prebooking required; bring ID). Highlights of the tour include the Salón de los Bustos, the Patio de las Palmeras and the famous balcony.

Behind the Casa Rosada, Plaza Colón features a gigantic Argentine flag and used to house a Carrara marble statue of **Cristóbal Colón** (Christopher Columbus). Former president Cristina Fernández de Kirchner, however, took umbrage with Cristóbal, replacing him with Juana Azurduy, a Bolivian freedom fighter, in the form of a 15m-tall bronze created by Andrés Zerneri and gifted by Bolivia's Evo Morales.

CENTENARY AND BICENTENARY

On May 25, 1810, locals gathered in **Plaza de Mayo** to demand the withdrawal of the viceroy and to form the **Primera Junta** – the first move in throwing off the yoke of Spanish rule and creating an independent nation.

The centenary in 1910 was cause for great celebration: Argentina had gone from being a small colonial backwater to one of the world's richest countries, still in the throes of an unprecedented immigration and building boom, and bursting with confidence. Several foreign nations gifted **monuments**, many of which are still standing in Buenos Aires, including the Torre Monumental from Britain (see p.87) and the Monumento de los Españoles from Spain (see p.100).

Argentina has failed to live up to its original heady economic promise, but in 2010 its citizens nonetheless passionately celebrated their two-hundredth birthday, with lasting legacies of the party in Buenos Aires including the **Museo del Bicentenario** (see p.66).

1

CITY CENTRE AND PUERTO MADERO

Recoleta

Laundry

Teatro Nacional Cervantes

AVENIDA CORDOBA

Callao

DEL CARMEN

Museo Judío

Sinagoga Central

Palacio de las Aguas Corrientes

DELLEPIANE

PLAZA LAVALLE

Teatro Colón

AVENIDA CALLAO

Palacio de Justicia

Tribunales

CERRITO

9 DE JULIO

CARLOS PELLEGRINI

Centro Cultural Ricardo Rojas

Callao

Teatro General San Martín

TALCAHUANO

Uruguay

Arteplex Centro

AVENIDA CORRIENTES

Obelisco

Carlos Pellegrini

Pharmacy

AYACUCHO

Centro Cultural San Martín

RODRIGUEZ PEÑA

MONTEVIDEO

PARANA

URUGUAY

RIVADAVIA

LIBERTAD

AVENIDA

RIOBAMBA

MITRE

SUIPACHA

Congreso

Gaumont

RIVADAVIA

Congreso Nacional

PLAZA DEL CONGRESO

Saenz Peña

EleBaires

AVENIDA DE MAYO

Palacio Barolo

Teatro Avenida

Av. De Mayo

ALSINA

CEBALLOS

PEÑA

ALSINA

LIMA

MORENO

MORENO

AVENIDA BELGRANO

Moreno

VENEZUELA

SARANDI

COMBATE DE LOS POZOS

AVENIDA ENTRE RIOS

SOLIS

VIRREY

PTE. SAENZ

SAN JOSE

SANTIAGO DEL ESTERO

SALTA

BERNARDO DE IRIGOYEN

TACUARI

CONSTITUCIÓN

Independencia (Line E)

Independencia (Line C)

ACCOMMODATION				EATING			
725 Buenos Aires	5	NH Jousten	4	180 Burger Bar	1	Confitería La Ideal	12
Castelar	9	O'Rei	3	La Americana	17	Las Cuartetas	11
Chile	8	Sportsman	7	Arturito	10	La Giralda	8
Esplendor	1	V&S Hostel Club	2	Bice	4	El Globo	19
Faena Hotel & Universe	13			Cabaña Las Lilas	15	Green Eat	3
Hostel Punto Cero	6			Cadore	6	Güerrín	9
Ibis Buenos Aires	11			Café Tortoni	18	i Fresh Market	21
Milhouse	10			Chila	20	Laurak Bat	22
Moreno	12			Chiquilín	13	New Brighton	14

			NIGHTLIFE		TANGO		SHOPPING	
Parrilla Peña	2	Asia de Cuba	9	Club Gricel	11	Abasto	2
Patio San Ramón	16	Bahrein	2	Confitería La Ideal	3	Galerías Pacífico	1
La Paz	7	Bebop Club	7	Piazzola Centro de Artes	5	El Gauchito	4
Siga La Vaca	23	Estadio Luna Park	1			Librería Ávila	6
Tomo 1	5	Maluco Beleza	4			Musimundo	5
		Palacio Alsina	6			Zivals	3
		Pan y Teatro	10				
		La Trastienda	8				

1

Museo del Bicentenario

Paseo Colón 100 • Wed–Sun 10am–6pm • Free • ☎ 011 4344 3802, 🌐 museobicentenario.gob.ar

Uniformed grenadiers guard the Casa Rosada's own museum, the **Museo del Bicentenario**, which opened in May 2011, a year after the national bicentenary it was intended to celebrate (see box, p000). An impressive subterranean structure behind the presidential palace, enhanced by handsome brick arches, it covers the role of the Casa Rosada in the city's history, highlighting the various constructions occupying the site and the presidency past and present – with carefully chosen film footage relating Argentine political history from a Peronist and, above all, Kirchnerist slant. Posters of the Peróns, plus clothing, furniture, writing instruments and even porcelain and carriages used by various holders of the office since 1810, help illustrate this slick propaganda.

Along with temporary exhibitions, the museum hosts *Ejercicio Plástico* ("Plastic Exercise"), a sensual mural painted in 1933 by the Mexican artist David Alfaro Siqueiros, assisted by Argentine painters Spilimbergo, Berni and Castagnino (all three of whom contributed to the fantastic frescoes that decorate Galerías Pacífico mall in the microcentro; see p.72) and the Uruguayan Enrique Lázaro. To enter the capsule containing it you must don protective footwear covers. At the far end of the museum there is a decent café and a gift shop where you can treat yourself to Casa Rosada-related souvenirs.

MADRES AND ABUELAS DE PLAZA DE MAYO

Many of those arrested – and, in many cases, tortured and executed – during the **1976–83 dictatorship** that is also known as the **"Dirty War"** (see p.541) were young people in their teens and 20s who were kidnapped from their homes and streets with no acknowledgement from the authorities as to their whereabouts. In 1976 some of their mothers, frustrated by the intimidating silence they faced when they tried to find out what had happened to their children, started what would become the **Madres de Plaza de Mayo (Mothers of Plaza de Mayo) movement**. When it became apparent that pregnant prisoners were kept alive to give birth to babies that were then adopted by "Dirty War" supporters – estimated to be around 500 children – the **Abuelas de Plaza de Mayo (Grandmothers of Plaza de Mayo)** NGO was also founded.

Just a handful of women in the beginning, the Madres and Abuelas met weekly in **Plaza de Mayo**, the historic centre of the city, as much to support each other as to embarrass the regime into providing answers; wearing white headscarves emerged as a means of identification. As their numbers grew, so did their defiance – standing their ground and challenging the military to carry out its threat to fire on them in front of foreign journalists, for instance. Some were themselves "disappeared" after the "Blond Angel of Death" – notorious torturer Alfredo Astiz – infiltrated the group, posing as the brother of a *desaparecido* (disappeared). He was sentenced to life imprisonment in October 2011.

In 1982, during the Malvinas/Falklands crisis, the Madres were accused of being anti-patriotic for their stance **against the war**, a conflict they maintained was an attempt by the regime to divert attention away from its murderous acts. With the return to democracy in 1983, the Madres were disappointed by the Alfonsín government's reluctance to delve too deeply into what had happened during the "Dirty War", as well as by the later granting of immunity to many of those accused of kidnapping, torture and murder. The group rejected monetary "compensation" and both the Madres and the respect in which they are held were key in finally getting amnesty laws overturned in 2005. The Madres and Abuelas continue to protest, walking around the Pirámide de Mayo every Thursday at 3.30pm, and some have branched into other areas of social protest and human rights: the emblem of the white headscarf was at the forefront of the movement to demand the **non-payment of the country's foreign debt**, for example.

Today both human rights organizations are renowned for their work, a relentless task which has included setting up a DNA database that can be accessed by those grandchildren who doubt their origins. To date, the Abuelas have reunited 119 adults with their birth families, which recently included the grandson of lead activist Estela Barnes de Carloto.

Cabildo

Bolívar 65 • Tues, Wed & Fri 10.30am–5pm, Thurs 10.30am–8pm, Sat & Sun 10.30am–6pm • $15 • Tours (English) Wed–Sun 11.30am • ☎ 011 4342 6729, ⓦ cabildonacional.cultura.gob.ar

At the opposite end of the square from the Casa Rosada is the **Cabildo**, the only colonial-era civil construction to survive the rebuilding craze of the 1880s. Its simple, unadorned lines, green and white shuttered facade and colonnaded front, dating from the mid-eighteenth century, stand in stark contrast to the more ornate nineteenth-century buildings around it. The Spanish administrative headquarters, it now houses a small **museum** whose modest collection includes standards captured during the 1806 British invasion, watercolours by Enrique Pellegrini and original plans of the city and the fort. Although the museum was painstakingly restored at great cost in time for the 2010 bicentenary (aptly so, since it is dedicated to the May Revolution), it is the building's interior that makes a visit worthwhile, in particular the upper galleries' exhibits of various relics from the colonial period onwards, such as huge keys and sturdy wooden doors. Behind the Cabildo, a patio area with an ornamental well hosts a café and small artisans' fair (Thurs & Fri 11am–4pm).

Catedral Metropolitana

San Martín 27 • Mon–Fri 7.30am–6.45pm, Sat & Sun 9am–7pm • Tours (Spanish) Mon–Fri 11.30am & 4pm, Sat & Sun 4pm; 1hr • Free • ⓦ catedralbuenosaires.org.ar

The **Catedral Metropolitana**, with its severe Neoclassical facade, is not a particularly beautiful church, but it's in the spotlight for being the most recent place of employment for Jorge Bergoglio – also known as **Pope Francis I** – before he moved to the Vatican. This, its central location, its status as Buenos Aires' main cathedral and its housing the **mausoleum** to Independence hero General José de San Martín (see p.532) inside – solemnly guarded, and frequently mobbed by schoolchildren on history trips – ensures a steady stream of visitors.

The cathedral assumed its final form over many years. Built and rebuilt since the sixteenth century, the present building was completed in the mid-nineteenth century, complete with Venetian mosaic floors, gilded columns and a silver-plated altar. The twelve columns at the entrance represent the twelve Apostles; above them sits a carved tympanum whose bas-relief depicts the arrival of Jacob and his family in Egypt.

Naturally, it became the focus of jubilant celebrations and international attention when Bergoglio, ex-Archbishop of Buenos Aires, was anointed pope in 2013. He is the first Latin American pontiff and the first to hail from outside Europe in 1300 years.

Avenida de Mayo

Walking west from Plaza de Mayo leads you to one of the capital's grandest thoroughfares, **Avenida de Mayo**, a wide, tree-lined boulevard flanked with ornamental street lamps and offering a stunning ten-block vista between Plaza de Mayo and Plaza del Congreso. Part of an 1880s project to remodel the city along the lines of Haussmann's Paris, Avenida de Mayo is notable for its architectural melange; many buildings are topped with decorative domes and ornamented with elaborate balustrades and sinuous caryatids. Unimpressed with the city's European pretensions, Borges called it one of the saddest places in Buenos Aires, yet even he couldn't resist the charm of its **confiterías** and traditional restaurants, a handful of which remain open.

Casa de la Cultura

Av de Mayo 575 • Tues–Sun 2–8pm • Tours Sat 4pm & 5pm, Sun hourly 11am–4pm; 1hr • Free • ☎ 011 4323 9699, ⓦ buenosaires.gob.ar /cultura/casadelacultura

Just half a block west of Plaza de Mayo, there's the magnificent, French-influenced **La Prensa** building, an extravaganza of grand wrought-iron doors, curvaceous lamps and a steep mansard roof. The building – now the headquarters of the city's culture secretariat

1

and renamed the **Casa de la Cultura** – was originally built as the head office of the once-influential national newspaper *La Prensa*. You can peek at the opulent interior – all ornamental glass and elaborate woodwork – or take advantage of a free guided tour organized by the city government at the weekend. Occasional concerts and other events are held in the opulent Salón Dorado ("Gilded Hall").

Café Tortoni

Av de Mayo 825 • ☎ 011 4342 4328, ⓦ cafetortoni.com.ar

The fact that the **Café Tortoni** (see p.117) is on every tourist's must-visit list – some days you even have to queue to get in – has spoilt the atmosphere and hiked the prices, but *Tortoni*, which has existed in some form or other for over 150 years, is still worth stopping by for a *cortado*. Famous for its literary and artistic connections – notable habitués included poets Alfonsina Storni and Rubén Darío, writer Jorge Luis Borges and tango singer Carlos Gardel – its heavy brown columns and Art Nouveau-mirrored walls undeniably exude an elegance no longer found in many of its rivals.

Museo Mundial del Tango

Av de Mayo 833 (entrance Rivadavia 830, 1st floor) • Mon–Fri 2.30–7.30pm • $20 • ⓦ anacdeltango.org.ar/museo_interior.asp

The fine **Palacio Carlos Gardel** is home to the Academia Nacional del Tango, and the ambitiously named **Museo Mundial del Tango**. The musty museum traces the history of tango (in Spanish, though an English-speaking guide may be available) through interesting displays such as Tita Merello's glittering dress and a photo of men dancing tango together in 1910 – women were rarely allowed to dance in those days, except in brothels.

Palacio Barolo

Av de Mayo 1370 • $195 • ⓦ pbarolo.com.ar • Tours (Spanish and English) Mon–Sat hourly 11am–6pm; 1hr • ⓦ palaciobarolotours.com.ar

Continuing up Avenida de Mayo will take you over the wide Avenida 9 de Julio and past a clutch of old-fashioned hotels, cafés and government institutions dressed in belle époque Art Deco splendour. On the south side of the street stands the avenue's most fantastical building, the **Palacio Barolo** – named after the extremely wealthy farmer of Italian origin who had it built. Designed by Italian architect Mario Palanti and constructed between 1919 and 1923, its unusual top-heavy form is an example of the eclectic style popular at the time. Created as a monument to Dante's *Divine Comedy* (of which Barolo was a great admirer), it is full of references to the epic poem – its different sections represent Hell, Purgatory and Heaven, its height in metres equals the number of songs (100) and it has 22 floors, the same as the number of stanzas in each canto. Moreover, in early June, the roof's tip aligns with the Southern Cross constellation – said to represent the "entrance to heaven". Book onto a fascinating guided tour of the building, which is mostly taken up by offices, for detailed explanations of its history and symbolism.

Plaza del Congreso

At its western extremity, Avenida de Mayo opens up to encircle the **Plaza del Congreso**, a three-block-long wedge of grass dotted with statues, a fountain, swooping pigeons and a number of benches. It is dominated by the grandiose building of the Congreso Nacional, the federal parliament. There is also an allegorical monument to Argentina's history as a republic and its parliamentary institutions.

Congreso Nacional

Hipólito Yrigoyen 1849 • Guided visits (English) Mon, Tues, Thurs & Fri 11am & 4pm; 1hr • Free • Take ID • ⓦ senado.gov.ar/web/museo /visitaguiada.php

Plaza del Congreso's western end is presided over by the Greco-Roman **Congreso Nacional** building, inaugurated in 1906 and designed by Vittorio Meano, who was also one of the architects of the Teatro Colón (see p.124). The northern wing is where the

Lower Chamber (the Diputados or Members of Parliament) sits, while the southern wing is used by the Upper Chamber of senators. Tours include a visit to the marble Salón Azul, in the centre of the building under the copper cupola; look up to see the giant 2000kg chandelier featuring figures representing the Republic and all its provinces.

Monumento a los dos Congresos

Plaza del Congreso's most striking monument is the exuberant **Monumento a los dos Congresos**, a series of sculptural allegories atop heavy granite steps and crowned by the triumphant figure of the Republic, erected to commemorate the 1813 Assembly and the 1816 Declaration of Independence. The plaza is traditionally the final rallying point for many political demonstrations – it was the site of a mass illegal encampment of farmers protesting the government's increase in export taxes in 2008 – and the sculpture has now been surrounded by a high fence to prevent the constant reappearance of fresh graffiti. You'll also see a greening bronze statue in the square, a rain-streaked version of Rodin's *The Thinker*. Next to it, a white block marks *kilómetro cero* – the point from which all roads that lead from Buenos Aires are measured.

Avenida Corrientes

Running parallel to Avenida de Mayo, four blocks north of Plaza del Congreso, **Avenida Corrientes** is another of the city's principal arteries, sweeping down to the lower grounds of El Bajo. It's not so much the architecture that is of note as the atmosphere generated by its bustling mix of cafés, bookshops, cinemas, theatres and pizzerias. For years, **cafés** such as *La Paz*, on the corner of Corrientes and Montevideo, and the austere *La Giralda*, two blocks west, have been the favoured meeting places of left-wing intellectuals and bohemians – and good places to observe Porteño talent whiling away hours over a single tiny coffee.

Corrientes' **bookshops**, many of which stay open till the small hours, have always been as much places to hang out in as to buy from – in marked contrast to almost every other type of shop in the city, where you'll be accosted by sales assistants as soon as you cross the threshold. The most basic places are simply one long room open to the street with piles of books slung on tables and huge handwritten price labels, whereas Liberarte (at no. 1555) and its ilk take literature more seriously. Almost as comprehensive as the bookshops are the street's pavement kiosks, proffering a mind-boggling range of newspapers, magazines and books on subjects from psychology and sex to tango and politics.

Teatro General San Martín

Av Corrientes 1530/Sarmiento 2715 • Box office daily 10am–10pm • ⓦ complejoteatral.gob.ar

The glass front of the **Teatro General San Martín** on Avenida Corrientes signals one of the city's most important cultural spaces. As well as the namesake theatre (see p.123), this municipal complex includes an arthouse cinema and a small free gallery that often has worthwhile exhibitions showcasing Argentine photographers, among other subjects. At the back of the theatre is a large 1960s building, inaugurated by Perón, that is home to the eclectic **Centro Cultural General San Martín**, a space for cutting-edge art, theatre and dance, and a major venue for conventions and academic debates.

Obelisco

The much-photographed centrepiece of Buenos Aires' cityscape, the iconic 68m-tall **Obelisco** dominates the busy intersection between Corrientes and Avenida 9 de Julio known as Plaza de la República. Erected in 1936 in just 31 days, it commemorates four key events in the city's history: the first and second foundings; the first raising of the flag in 1812; and the naming of Buenos Aires as Capital Federal in 1880. Its giant scale and strategic location also make it a magnet for carloads of celebrating fans after a major football victory. At the Plaza, you will also see representations in bronze of the

1

country's provinces and the flags of Buenos Aires and Argentina, raised in 2008 to commemorate 25 years since the return to democracy.

Plaza Lavalle

A short walk northwest from the Obelisco along Diagonal Roque Sáenz Peña takes you past a row of fountains and patio cafés – popular places to take a coffee break – to **Plaza Lavalle**. Stretching for three blocks, the plaza is a pleasant green space, notable for its fine collection of native and exotic trees, many over a hundred years old. Among the pines, magnolias and jacarandas stands an ancient *ceibo*, a tall tree with a twisted trunk whose bright red spring blossom resembling coral is Argentina's national flower.

The plaza began life as a public park, inaugurated in 1827 by British immigrants, and thirty years later was the departure point for the first Argentine train journey, made by the locomotive *La Porteña* to Floresta in the capital's west; the original engine can still be seen in the Complejo Museográfico in Luján (see p.139). Nowadays the plaza is practically synonymous with the law courts that surround it; this part of the city is often referred to as **Tribunales**.

Palacio de Justicia

The western end of Plaza Lavalle is dominated by the **Palacio de Justicia**, seat of the Supreme Court. In a loose and heavy-handed interpretation of Neoclassicism, heavily adorned with pillars, the building stands as something of a monument to architectural uncertainty, which some see as a metaphor for Argentina's state of justice. Busy lawyers rush to and from the court, with those wishing to further their law knowledge catered to by numerous stallholders whose tables are covered with pamphlets and secondhand books explaining every conceivable aspect of Argentine law.

Teatro Colón

Cerrito 628 • **Box office** Mon–Sat 10am–8pm, Sun 10am–6pm • **Tours** Daily 9am–5pm; 50min • $180 • ⑩ teatrocolon.org.ar

The handsome **Teatro Colón**, resplendent with its grand but restrained French Renaissance exterior, stands on the eastern side of Plaza Lavalle, between Viamonte and Tucumán, with its main entrance on the plaza. Famed as an opera house – though it also hosts ballet and classical recitals (see p.171) – the Teatro Colón (named after Christopher Columbus) is Argentina's most prestigious cultural institution and is considered to have some of the best acoustics of any opera house in the world; Luciano Pavarotti was a big fan. Most of the twentieth century's major opera and ballet stars appeared here, from Caruso and Callas to Nijinsky and Nureyev, while classical music recitals were given by the likes of Toscanini and Rubinstein. More recent performers have included Plácido Domingo, Lang Lang, Joshua Bell and Daniel Barenboim. The interior features an Italian Renaissance-style central hall, the beautiful gilded and mirrored Salón Dorado (allegedly inspired by Versailles) and the stunning auditorium itself, whose five tiers of balconies culminate in a huge dome decorated with frescoes by Raúl Soldi during the 1966 restoration of the theatre.

The theatre, first inaugurated on May 25, 1908, was again closed for a costly refurbishment in time for the 2010 bicentenary, complete with air conditioning and impeccably restored gold leaf. The celebratory concert held on May 24 featured *Swan Lake* and the second act of Puccini's *La Bohème*. Check the website or enquire at the box office (*boletería*) for both guided visits and tickets for performances; it is located in the narrow passageway, Pasaje de Carruajes (formerly used for carriages), that cuts sideways through the building at Tucumán 1171.

Sinagoga Central and Museo Judío

Libertad 761–769 • Tues–Thurs 11am–6pm, Fri 11am–5pm • Tours every 40min; 1hr • $35 • Take ID • ⑩ museojudio.org.ar

At the northeastern end of the plaza near Avenida Córdoba is the **Sinagoga Central**, a

JEWISH BUENOS AIRES

Argentina is home to one of the largest **Jewish communities** in the world, estimated at around 185,000; this is still only around one third of its peak figure in the 1950s, though, since when many have migrated to Israel, Europe and the United States. The majority live in Buenos Aires; the more well-to-do in Belgrano, and the lower-middle classes in Once. The latter is where you'll find most of the city's kosher restaurants, especially on the streets around Pueyrredón between Córdoba and Corrientes. Approximately fifty-four synagogues dot the city, including the large Central Synagogue (see opposite), along with more than seventy Jewish educational institutions.

The first Jewish **immigrants** arrived in Argentina in the early seventeenth century but were officially excluded from colonial society by the Spanish authorities. Following independence, Jews were openly allowed to settle and began moving in from France and other Western European countries in the early nineteenth century. Jewish refugees later fled here in large numbers from pogroms and persecution in Russia and Eastern Europe, and were commonly known as "rusos", a term still often used erroneously to refer to all Jews (two-thirds of whom are Ashkenazi).

In 1938 the foreign minister under President Ortiz signed an infamous circular that effectively instructed Argentine consulates not to issue visas to Jews seeking asylum from Nazi Germany. Perón's government was one of the first to recognize the State of Israel, but he openly admired Mussolini, covertly hampered Jewish immigration and notoriously allowed Nazi war criminals to settle in Argentina, including Adolf Eichmann, an SS officer who masterminded the systematic massacre of Jews in Central Europe. In 1960 Eichmann was abducted from a Buenos Aires suburb, where he worked for Mercedes Benz, by Mossad and Shin Bet agents and whisked off for trial and execution in Jerusalem.

The Jewish community was the target of two of the country's most murderous **terrorist attacks**: a bomb explosion at the Israeli Embassy in 1992, in which 29 people died, and another at the headquarters of AMIA, the Argentine Jewish association, in 1994, which killed 85. In 2006, Argentine prosecutors officially accused the Iranian government and Hezbollah of ordering the bombings, a charge Teheran adamantly denies, but the crimes have never been properly resolved. A monument in Plaza Lavalle remembers those who lost their lives in both attacks – another, in the Plaza Embajada de Israel, at the corner of Arroyo and Suipacha in Retiro, focuses on the loss of life in the 1992 atrocity, with one lime tree representing each victim.

Investigations were set back in January 2015 when federal prosecutor **Alberto Nisman** was found dead in his apartment, a case that rocked Argentina and led to global speculation about the cause of his death.

neo-Byzantine edifice housing the main synagogue of Argentina's Jewish community, and the country's first, founded in 1862. Well-informed guides (English-speakers available) will take you around the handsome interior of the synagogue (men are provided with a kippa) and the **Museo Judío**, a small museum of religious artefacts mostly imported from Europe, providing an explanation of the history of Argentina's large Jewish community (see box above). There are also audioguides in English, Spanish, Hebrew, Portuguese and French. Some of the finest objects are two sixteenth-century Torahs from Morocco and a set of paintings depicting Polish Jews on their arrival in the Pampas. The museum holds occasional exhibitions of Judaism-related contemporary art, too. You might like to sample Jewish specialities at the on-site kosher bar-restaurant, *Mench* (Mon–Thurs 11am–8pm, Fri 11am–2pm).

The microcentro

The **microcentro** – bounded by avenidas Corrientes, Alem, de Mayo and 9 de Julio – is the core of downtown, the nerve centre of the modern city, a fast-moving, noisy district packed with offices, banks, bars, hotels and shops. Few people other than business visitors opt to stay here, but you're bound to come here once or twice to eat or drink, make travel arrangements, shop and take in the sights. The microcentro's key thoroughfares are pedestrianized **Calle Florida**, which runs from Plaza de Mayo to Plaza

1

San Martín in Retiro (see p.85), and partly pedestrianized, cheap and cheerful **Calle Lavalle**, which bisects Florida halfway along its length.

Calle Florida

At the start of the twentieth century, **Florida** was one of the city's most elegant streets – the obligatory route for a stroll following tea at its very own branch of Harrods. Nowadays over a million people a day tramp its length, and cutting your way through its stream of foot traffic requires determination. But this traffic is Florida's most appealing quality; there's always a lively buzz about the place, as a handful of street performers do their best to charm a few pesos from the passers-by. Unofficial vendors have been banned from peddling their wares by city decree, but some still try and sell bootleg DVDs or cheap leather wallets. This is also where *arbolitos* or illegal exchange houses (see box, p.45) encourage tourists to part with their dollars or euros at the "blue" (which confusingly means black market) rate by shouting out "cambio" to passers-by.

Florida commences at Plaza de Mayo and, save for the elegant facade of the ICBC Bank (formerly the **Banco de Boston**) at no. 99, which is particularly impressive when lit up at night, its initial blocks are mostly taken up with bookshops, clothes shops, exchange offices and fast-food outlets, packed with office workers at lunchtime. Vestiges of Florida's more sophisticated past remain in its **galerías**, or shopping arcades, such as the Art Nouveau **Galería Güemes** at no. 165, which features a series of beautiful glass cupolas, or in its cafés – though the historic **Richmond confitería** at Florida 468 reopened as a sportswear store to widespread consternation in 2011.

Towards the northern (Retiro) end of Florida, the crowds become thinner and the stores more upmarket – at no. 877 you'll see the impressive shell that once housed the local Harrods. Until the 1960s, this was a fully operational branch of the famous British department store, with visitors flocking to marvel at its full-size double-decker bus, and once even a live Indian elephant shipped in for an exhibition. Despite occasional rumblings that it will reopen, and its intermittent use as an exposition hall and pop-up arts and events venue, it has been shuttered for years.

Galerías Pacífico

Florida 753 • ⓦ galeriaspacifico.com.ar

The most notable of Florida's arcades, the **Galerías Pacífico** offers a glitzy retailing opportunity within a vaulted and attractively frescoed building built as a branch of the Paris department store Le Bon Marché at the end of the nineteenth century. The first floor is home to the **Centro Cultural Borges** (see p.124), a large space offering a worthwhile selection of photography and painting exhibitions from both Argentine and foreign artists. Florida's last two blocks before it spills into Plaza San Martín are filled with leather and handicraft stores; look out also for the fine decorative facade and door of the Centro Naval on the corner of Avenida Córdoba.

La City

Buenos Aires' financial district, **La City**, takes up the southeastern quarter of the microcentro's grid of streets. Its atmosphere serves as a barometer of the country's economic ups and downs – from frantic money changing during hyperinflation in the 1980s, via the noisy pot-banging demonstrations that followed the savings withdrawal freeze in 2001–02, to the renewed currency speculation of 2012; you can still see the scars of the crisis protests on the battered bank shutters. The tight confines and endless foot traffic make it difficult to look up, but if you do you'll be rewarded with an impressive spread of grand facades crowned with domes and towers. La City was once known as the *barrio inglés*, in reference to the large number of British immigrants who set up business here. Indeed, the first financial institutions were built in a rather Victorian style; it seems that the Porteño elite thought their houses should be French and their banks British.

Basílica de Nuestra Señora de la Merced and Convento de San Ramón Nonato

1

Reconquista 269 • Mon–Fri noon–4pm • Free • Ⓦ conventosanramon.org.ar

The City district hosts one of the most beautiful churches in Buenos Aires, the **Basílica de Nuestra Señora de la Merced** at Reconquista and Perón, which has been favoured by important political and military figures through the ages. The main structure dates from 1783, while the sandy coloured facade – the tympanum shows General Belgrano after he defeated the Spanish in battle in 1812 – was added in 1905. Every centimetre of the sombre interior is ornamented with gilt or tiles. Attached to the basilica is one of the city's best-kept secrets, the **Convento de San Ramón Nonato**. At its heart is a charming courtyard where you can eat in the restaurant under the arches.

Puerto Madero

More water than dry land, **Puerto Madero**, Buenos Aires' newest and glossiest barrio, centres on a defunct port directly to the east of the historical centre. Here four enormous oblong *diques*, or docks, run parallel to the Río de la Plata, connecting on either side to the Dársena Sur (Southern Harbour), near La Boca, and the Dársena Norte (Northern Harbour), near Retiro: ferries depart for Uruguay from both harbours. Lining these docks – which are officially numbered one to four, Dock One being the most southerly – is a series of restored brick and iron warehouses, originally used to hold grain from the Pampas before it was shipped. By 1898, before the port was even fully finished, it was already insufficient in scale to cope with the volume of maritime traffic, and a new port was constructed to the north. For most of the twentieth century, Puerto Madero sat as a forlorn industrial relic, but in the 1990s private money was injected and it began to be converted into a voguish mix of restaurants, luxury apartments and offices. While this dockside development is upmarket and somewhat lacking in colour, it's nonetheless a relaxing place to stroll, and there are far worse ways to spend a lazy summer afternoon than sitting on a terrace here, sipping a *clericó*, watching rowers cut through the water and enjoying the gentle river breeze. Docks Three and Four host the pick of the barrio's restaurants and bars.

GETTING AROUND   **PUERTO MADERO**

On foot Puerto Madero is within easy walking distance of downtown – head east along Av Belgrano, c/Juan Domingo Perón or c/Viamonte – though the train tracks sandwiched between avenidas Alicia Moreau de Justo and Eduardo Madero can be awkward to cross on foot.

By bus If legs feel weary at the thought of walking the 24-block length of Puerto Madero, hop on one of several buses, including the #111, which run parallel to Av Alicia Moreau de Justo.

The docks

It's logical to begin your tour of Puerto Madero on the western (or city) side of the docks, which is flanked by a walkway along its entire length. The focal point – and best way to cross to the eastern side of the docks – is Spanish architect Santiago Calatrava's striking white bridge, dubbed the **Puente de la Mujer** (the "women's bridge"). Unveiled in 2001, its graceful curve – said to echo the outstretched leg of a tango dancer – is a mesmerizing sight, especially when lit at night. The area's main attraction is the splendid collection of national and international art at the Colección Fortabat, at the northernmost end of the docks.

Museum ships

Av Alicia Moreau de Justo 500 and 980 • Daily 10am–7pm (except rainy days) • $5 each • Ⓦ ara.mil.ar

Two of the handsomest sights in docks Four and Three respectively are two well-maintained **museum ships** – the Buque Museo Corbeta *ARA Uruguay*, built at the

1

Cammell Laird shipyard in Birkenhead in 1874, and the Argentine navy's first training ship; and the Buque Museo Fragata *ARA Presidente Sarmiento*, built at the same British shipyard and the Argentine navy's flagship from 1899 to 1938. Both sailing ships (a corvette and a frigate) have been declared historic monuments.

Colección de Arte Amalia Lacroze de Fortabat

Olga Cossettini 141 • Tues–Sun noon–9pm • $25 • ☎ 011 4310 6600, ⓦ coleccionfortabat.org.ar

Since opening in 2008, the **Colección de Arte Amalia Lacroze de Fortabat** has become one of the barrio's star attractions. Located at the far northern end of Dock Four, it is housed in a purpose-built pavilion that looks rather like a giant sliding-top bread bin. A state-of-the-art blend of glass and aluminium (the sliding top is a retractable roof with protective panels that open as sunlight diminishes), the pavilion is the tip of the iceberg: below water level is a breathtakingly huge space showcasing the best private art collection on display in Latin America.

The museum was founded by Amalia Lacroze de Fortabat, who married well, twice – first an Argentine lawyer and later a cement magnate, Alfredo Fortabat, whose immense fortune she inherited in the 1970s.

The foreign works

Perhaps the surest sign of Amalia Lacroze de Fortabat's importance both as a personality and art collector is her 1968 portrait by Andy Warhol that kicks off the display, alongside two earlier portraits by Catalan painter Vidal-Quadras. The place of honour must go to *Juliet and her Nurse*, a magnificent oil by Turner depicting Venice's St Mark's Square, which manages to dominate the main exhibition room, a splendid unadorned space the length of a city block. There's also a handful of Dalí works.

The Argentine and Uruguayan works

Many of Argentina's major nineteenth- and twentieth-century artists are represented, several of them strongly influenced by European artistic movements such as Impressionism (for example, Fernando Fader's *Entre duraznos floridos* – "Among peach trees in blossom", 1915) and Symbolism (several works by Xul Solar). Like the Turner, many of the works depict famous sights in Europe such as Venice (see Rómulo Macció's *Puente de los Suspiros* – "Bridge of Sighs", 1998) or London (Nicolás García Uriburu's *Coloration of Trafalgar Square Fountains*, 1974). Several Argentine artists developed their own idiosyncratic styles, though – especially as the twentieth century advanced: many of the works by leading artist Antonio Berni (1905–81) are typically *criollo* (native), depicting among other things a rustic lunch or a country girl fondling a pumpkin. Uruguayans Blanes and Figari also get a look-in: the former's *La cautiva* ("The captive girl", 1880) is a scene from Argentina's own Wild West, while the latter's *En el patio* ("In the patio", undated) is a colonial vignette.

Costanera Sur

Running along Puerto Madero's eastern edge (known as "Puerto Madero Este"), the **Costanera Sur** is a sweeping avenue flanked by elegant balustrades, originally built as a riverside promenade at the beginning of the twentieth century. The avenue essentially lost its *raison d'être* in the 1970s when the government devised a project to reclaim land from the river. Dykes were constructed and the water drawn off but the project was never completed, leaving the suddenly inaptly named Costanera cut off from the river. However, the drained land unexpectedly became a haven for wildlife – now the Reserva Ecológica (see p.76). Just outside the reserve, it's worth pausing to see the flamboyant **Fuente de las Nereidas**, a large and elaborate marble fountain created by Tucumán sculptor Lola Mora in 1902. The fountain depicts a naked Venus perched coquettishly on the edge of a shell supported by two straining sea nymphs. The fountain was

CLOCKWISE FROM TOP LEFT CASA ROSADA (P.63); GLASS SODA SIPHONS, SAN TELMO ANTIQUES MARKET (P.79); PIRÁMIDE DE MAYO, PLAZA DE MAYO (P.63); *PLAZA DORREGO BAR*, SAN TELMO (P.118) >

1

originally destined for Plaza de Mayo, but its seductive display was thought too risqué to be in such proximity to the cathedral.

Faena Arts Center

Aime Paine 1169 • Daily 2–8pm • Free • ☎ 011 4010 9233, ☒ faenaartscenter.org

One of hotelier Alan Faena's lavish projects, this contemporary space – located in a converted grain storage unit with stunning three-storey ceilings – hosts exhibits and installations, films and technology as well as collaborations between Faena and art studios.

Reserva Ecológica Costanera Sur

Av Tristán Achaval Rodríguez 1550 • Tues–Sun 8am–5pm • Guided walks (Spanish; 2hr) April–Oct 10.30am & 3.30pm; Nov–March Sat & Sun 9.30am & 4pm • Guided bird-spotting tour (Spanish; 3hr) monthly, every second Fri • Free • ☎ 011 4315 4129, ☒ buenosaires.gob.ar

The **Reserva Ecológica** is a strange but wonderful place, a fragment of wild and watery grassland stretching for 2km alongside the Costanera. Having self-seeded with grassland after the landfill project was abandoned in 1984, the 3.5-square-kilometre reserve offers a juxtaposition of urban and natural scenes, whether factory chimneys glimpsed through fronds of pampas or the city skyline over a lake populated by ducks and herons. Inside the reserve, the visitors' centre explains the park's development and serves as the starting point for ranger-guided walks along the park's many trails. Full-moon nocturnal tours (weather permitting; dates of tours and sign-up deadlines are listed on the website) allow you to spot all manner of creatures, mainly birds, which keep a low daytime profile. There is a surprising diversity of flora and fauna, with over two hundred species of bird visiting during the year. Aquatic species include ducks, herons, elegant black-necked swans, skittish coots, the common gallinule and the snail hawk, a bird of prey that uses its hooked beak to pluck freshwater snails out of their shells. The park is also home to small mammals, such as the easily spotted coypu, an aquatic rodent, and reptiles such as monitor lizards. The reserve's vegetation includes the *ceibo*, with its bright red flowers, but the most dominant plant is the *cortadera*, or pampas grass.

The south

Described by Borges as "an older, more solid world", **the south** is where Buenos Aires best preserves its traditions. Immediately south of the Plaza de Mayo lies the barrio of **Monserrat**, packed with historic buildings, churches and a few noteworthy museums. Heading south through Monserrat, you'll emerge into the cobbled streets and alleyways of **San Telmo**, where grand nineteenth-century mansions testify to the days when the barrio was home to wealthy landowners. San Telmo is best visited on a Sunday, when its central square, Plaza Dorrego, is the scene of a fascinating **antiques fair**, although plenty of antiques stores are open during the week. At the southern end of the barrio, there's tranquil **Parque Lezama** – a good spot for observing local life, and home to an important history museum. Beyond Parque Lezama, and stretching all the way to the city's southern boundary, the Río Riachuelo, the quirky barrio of **La Boca** is a great place to spend an hour or two, wandering its colourful streets and soaking up its idiosyncratic atmosphere.

Monserrat

Monserrat, sometimes known as Barrio Sur, is the city's oldest district and, together with neighbouring San Telmo, is one of the most rewarding areas to explore on foot. A good starting point for delving into its grid of narrow streets and historic buildings is along **Calle Defensa**, named in honour of the barrio's residents, who, during the British invasions of 1806 and 1807, defended the city from troops by pouring boiling water and oil on them as they marched down the street.

Basílica de San Francisco de Asís

Alsina 380 • Mon–Fri 8am–7pm • Free • ☎ 011 4331 0625

On the corner of Alsina and Defensa stands the neo-Baroque **Basílica de San Francisco de Asís**. Dating from 1754, it was one of a number of churches burnt by angry Peronists in March 1955 in reaction to the navy's murderous bombing of an anti-Church, pro-Perón trade union rally in the Plaza de Mayo. The basilica was eventually restored, reopening in 1967. An oak column from the original altarpiece, destroyed by the fire, is preserved in the adjoining Franciscan monastery, where monks sell bee-derived products, including honey and soap.

Museo de la Ciudad

Defensa 223 • Mon–Fri 11am–7pm, Sat & Sun 10am–8pm • $5; free Mon & Wed • ⓦ museodelaciudad.buenosaires.gov.ar

Half a block west of the Basilica de San Francisco de Asís, on the first floor of a handsome private residence, is the imaginative **Museo de la Ciudad**. Half the museum is given over to a permanent display of children's toys through the ages, so it's worthwhile if you have youngsters to entertain. Look out for the toy farm reinvented as an Argentine estancia – dancing gauchos, bucking broncos and all. The rest of the museum is devoted to regularly changing exhibitions designed to illustrate everyday aspects of Porteño life, such as holidays or football. The objects are accompanied by witty descriptions in Spanish. Downstairs, a salón open to the street holds larger items, such as rescued doors and a traditional barrow from which *vendedores ambulantes* (hawkers) would have sold their wares, decorated in the *filete* style (see box, p.80).

Farmacia de la Estrella

Defensa 201 • Mon–Fri 8am–7pm • Free

At the corner with Alsina, **Farmacia de la Estrella**, a beautifully preserved old pharmacy, describes itself as a living museum and is considered part of the Museo de la Ciudad, yet it is a working chemist's, specializing in homeopathy. Founded in 1834, it boasts an opulent interior of heavy walnut fittings and quirky old-fashioned medical murals and mirrors, finished off with a stunning frescoed ceiling.

Basílica de Santo Domingo

Defensa 422 • Mon–Fri 8am–7pm • Free • ☎ 011 4331 1668

Along Defensa, on the corner of Avenida Belgrano, you'll find the **Basílica de Santo Domingo**, an austere twin-towered structure whose glory is somewhat overshadowed by the elevated mausoleum to General Belgrano that dominates the tiled patio at its front. The square on which the basilica stands was taken by the British on June 27, 1806, on which date Catholicism was outlawed (briefly, as it turned out). In the corner to the left of the altar as you enter, you can see the flags from British regiments captured by General Liniers when the city was retaken two months later.

Manzana de las Luces

Perú 272 • Daily 10am–9pm • $35 • Guided visits (to tunnels and Sala de Representantes) Mon–Fri 3pm, Sat & Sun 3pm, 4.30pm & 6pm; 40min • ☎ 011 4342 3964

Taking up the whole block bounded by Alsina, Peru, Moreno and Bolívar – the latter one block west of Defensa – is the complex of buildings known as the **Manzana de las Luces**, or "block of enlightenment". Dating from 1662, the complex originally housed a Jesuit community, and has been home to numerous official institutions throughout its history. The tour (in Spanish, with summary explanations given in English) generally visits the inner patio, tunnels constructed to connect the churches (and later used for smuggling), some of the surrounding chambers – including one that hosted a nineteenth-century political assassination – and the reconstructed **Sala de Representantes**, a semicircular chamber where the first provincial legislature sat. Opposite the statue of General Roca at Av Julio Roca 600, the **Mercado de las Luces**

1

(Mon–Fri 10.30am–7.30pm, Sun 2–7.30pm) has stalls set up in one of the Jesuit corridors, selling antiques, crystals, candles and other artisan products.

The block also encompasses the elite Colegio Nacional, where the nation's future politicians are schooled, and Buenos Aires' oldest church, the **Parroquia de San Ignacio Loyola**, on the corner of Bolívar and Alsina, which dates from 1675. Apart from the rather Baroque Altar Mayor, the church's interior is fairly simple, an arrangement that makes one of its most notable icons, the beautiful seventeenth-century Nuestra Señora de las Nieves, all the more arresting.

Museo Etnográfico Juan Bautista Ambrosetti

Moreno 350 • Tues–Fri 1–7pm, Sat & Sun 3–7pm; closed Jan • $20 voluntary donation • ⓦ museoetnografico.filo.uba.ar

Part of the Universidad de Buenos Aires, the fascinating **Museo Etnográfico Juan Bautista Ambrosetti** has some international anthropological exhibits, though its real interest lies in its well-displayed collection from pre-Columbian South America. Ambrosetti himself gained fame by discovering the pre-Incan ruins of Tilcara (see p.302) in 1908.

Ground floor

The ground-floor rooms display the impressive jewellery, pots and tools of the few native groups, such as the Mapuche, whose territory reached from modern Chile to the Pampas. Their textiles and jewellery are particularly noteworthy, with distinctive headbands and chest pieces featuring heavy silver frills. There are also exhibits on the Yámana (or Yaghan) and other peoples of Tierra del Fuego (see p.524). Panels (and pamphlets in English) provide some context to exhibits.

Upper floor

The upper floor deals with different themes relating to the culture, religion and trade of various other pre-Columbian South American peoples, including the Inca. Of particular note are a fine Huari tunic covered in the symbols used instead of a written language, and religious costumes from present-day Bolivia made of jaguar skin, an animal that represented power and wisdom. There are many fascinating examples of the gradual Hispanicization of the indigenous people, where Christian motifs and European materials were melded with native American beliefs – look out for the wooden statue of Jesus wearing a jaguar pelt.

San Telmo

You have to be very hard-hearted not to be seduced by the romantically crumbling facades and cobbled streets of **San Telmo**, a neighbourhood proud of its reputation as the guardian of the city's traditions. A small, roughly square-shaped barrio, San Telmo is bounded to the north by Avenida Chile (six blocks south of Plaza de Mayo), to the west by Calle Piedras, to the east by Paseo Colón and to the south by Parque Lezama. Like neighbouring Monserrat, its main artery is **Calle Defensa**, once the main thoroughfare between the Plaza de Mayo and the city's port.

The barrio's appearance of decaying luxury is the result of reverse gentrification. When the city's grand mansions were abandoned by their patrician owners after a yellow fever epidemic in 1871, they were soon converted into *conventillos* (tenements) by landlords keen to make a quick buck from newly arrived immigrants. This sudden loss of cachet preserved many of the barrio's original features: whereas much of the north, centre and west of the city was variously torn down, smartened up or otherwise modernized, San Telmo's inhabitants adapted the neighbourhood's buildings to their needs. It's still largely a working-class area, and well-heeled Palermo-dwellers may warn you off coming here, but the area's superb architecture also attracts bohemians, students, backpackers and artists. Together with rising rents, the recent appearance of designer clothing and home-wares stores among the traditional antiques shops is an indication that San Telmo may be going up in the world again – though this latterday gentrification is not a development that everyone welcomes.

San Telmo is one of Buenos Aires' major tourist attractions, particularly for its Sunday antiques market, the **Feria de San Telmo**. While the neighbourhood's central square, Plaza Dorrego, is at the heart of the fair, artisans also pitch up stands across several blocks on adjoining Calle Defensa. This is the barrio most closely associated with **tango**, and the place where many of the best-known tango shows and bars have their home. At the southern end of the barrio, the palm-lined Parque Lezama, containing the city's well-organized **Museo Histórico Nacional**, makes a restful spot to end a tour of the neighbourhood.

Calle Defensa
Leading south from Plaza de Mayo, Defensa runs through Monserrat (see p.76) and then straight on through San Telmo to Parque Lezama. On weekends, vehicles are banned and replaced with solely human traffic as visitors wend their way past performance artists and buskers to visit the cobbled lane's antiques stores and bars.

1

FILETEADO OR FILETE ART

As you wander around the city, look out for examples of **fileteado** or **filete art**, particularly on shop signs. Characterized by ornate lettering, heavy shading and the use of scrolls and flowers entwined with the azure and white of the national flag, this distinctive art form first made its appearance on the city transport system in the early twentieth century. Often associated with tango, its origins are murky, but it seems to have been introduced by Italian immigrants. Banned from public transport in 1975 – the authorities felt bus destinations and numbers should be unadorned – it moved onto signs above stores and cafés as well as more traditional canvases. Today it is synonymous with Porteño identity, particularly in the south of the city, and is recognized internationally; in 2015 it was added to the UNESCO Intangible Cultural Heritage list. As well as tango stars, a popular subject is the pithy saying, including the classic *si tomás para olvidar, pagá primero* ("if you drink to forget, pay first") and the more obscure *si querés la leche fresca, atá la vaca a la sombra* ("if you want fresh milk, tie the cow up in the shade").

A stroll here is more about soaking up the atmosphere than visiting specific sites; musicians, eccentric buskers and inventive puppeteers add to the ambience.

Mercado Municipal
Mon–Sat 7am–2pm & 4.30–9pm, Sun 7am–7pm

Don't miss the fabulous iron-roofed **Mercado Municipal**, more usually known as Mercado de San Telmo, between Carlos Calvo and Estados Unidos, a thriving city-centre food market and one of the few of its kind left in the city. In addition to piles of colourful fruit and veg, old-fashioned butcher stalls and other food vendors, the market also features all manner of curios, minor antiques and junk, plus vintage clothing and accessories, and collectables like old gramophone records, coins and posters.

El Zanjón de granados
Defensa 755 • **Guided visits** Mon–Fri noon, 2pm & 3pm; 1hr • $180 • **Short guided visits** Sun every 20min 11am–6pm; 40min • $150 • ⊕ 011 4361 3002, ⓦ elzanjon.com.ar

El Zanjón de granados is a typical example of a pre-yellow-fever-era mansion that was turned into a *conventillo* (see p.575). The well-run visits take you underground through layers of history to see the reconstructed and tastefully lit tunnels where the city's water once flowed, and the cisterns the inhabitants used, though the tour price might seem a bit steep to see old water tanks.

Plaza Dorrego
At the core of San Telmo on the corner of Defensa and Humberto 1°, **Plaza Dorrego** is a tiny square surrounded by elegant mansions, most of them now converted into bars and antiques shops. During the week, cafés set up tables in the square, and on Sunday it becomes the setting for the city's long-running antiques market, **Feria de San Pedro Telmo** (10am–5pm; ⓦ feriadesantelmo.com). Overflowing with antique *yerba mate* gourds, jewel-coloured soda syphons, vintage watches and ancient ticket machines from the city's buses, the two dozen tightly packed stalls make for fascinating browsing, albeit through occasionally heavy crowds. There are no real bargains to be had – the stallholders and habitués are far too canny to let a gem slip through their fingers – but among the jumble you may find your own souvenir of Buenos Aires. The market's pickpockets are also canny – one famously swiped the bag of former US President George W. Bush's daughter despite the presence of six security guards – so be careful with your belongings.

As the stallholders start packing away their wares on Sunday afternoons, Plaza Dorrego becomes – weather permitting – the setting of a free outdoor **milonga** (tango dance; see box, p.10). There's a refreshing informality to this regular event, frequented by tourists, locals and tango fanatics alike, which might encourage even those with only a rudimentary knowledge of tango to take the plunge.

Museo de Arte Moderno de Buenos Aires (MAMBA)

Av San Juan 350 • Tues–Fri 11am–7pm, Sat, Sun & public hols (including Mon) 11am–8pm • $15, free on Tues • ☎ 011 4361 6919, ⓦ museos.buenosaires.gob.ar/museoartemoderno

1

On the corner of Calle Defensa and Avenida San Juan, a main east–west artery, the **Museo de Arte Moderno de Buenos Aires** showcases a permanent collection of mostly Argentine art from the 1920s to the present day. Housed in the late nineteenth-century Nobleza Piccardo tobacco factory, with a distinctive brick facade adorned with elegant arches, the collection features big national names, such as Enio Iommi, Emilio Pettoruti, Guillermo Kuitca and Xul Solar. Closed for renovation for many years, it reopened in late 2010, and has since shown off national and international treasures by the likes of Paul Klee, Julio Le Parc, Henri Matisse and Juan del Prete; it also includes a sculpture patio, bookshop and auditorium. One outstanding architectural detail is a futuristic staircase that resembles the charred skeleton of a mythical beast.

Parque Lezama

The southern stretch of Defensa takes you through a slightly more run-down – and perhaps more authentic – part of San Telmo, with its own neighbourhood cafés and stores, though there are some outstanding antiques shops, too. Four blocks on from Plaza Dorrego, you will reach the classic café *Bar Británico* (see p.118), overlooking the **Parque Lezama**, a lively green expanse. On a bluff towering over Paseo Colón, the park is generally regarded as the site of Buenos Aires' founding by **Pedro de Mendoza** in 1536. The conquistador's statue looms over you as you enter the park from the corner of Defensa and Brasil; a bronze of Mendoza thrusts his sword into the ground, while behind him a bas-relief shows an indigenous man, throwing up his hands in surrender. The park looks at its best in early evening, when the sun filters through its trees, children run along its paths and groups of old men play cards or chess at stone tables.

Iglesia Ortodoxa Rusa

Brasil 313 • Sat 5–8pm, Sun 10am–12.30pm • Free • **Guided tours** (call ahead for English-speaking guide) every second Sun of month, 4pm; 1hr • $15 • Women must wear ankle-length skirts and a head scarf to be allowed entry; men must wear trousers • ☎ 011 4361 4274, ⓦ iglesiarusa.org.ar

Overlooking the north end of the park is the exotic-looking **Iglesia Ortodoxa Rusa**, conspicuous for its crown of five bright-blue curvaceous onion domes, typical of Russian Orthodox churches. Dedicated to the Holy Trinity, it was built in 1899 and contains a large set of valuable icons donated by Tsar Nicolas II just as his empire was falling into terminal decline.

Museo Histórico Nacional

Defensa 1600 • Wed–Sun 11am–6pm • $20; free Wed • Guided tours (English) Wed–Fri 2pm • ☎ 011 4307 1182 • ⓦ cultura.gob.ar/museos/museo-historico-nacional

Within the park, though entered via Defensa 1600, the **Museo Histórico Nacional**, founded in 1887, is housed in a magnificent colonial building painted a startling deep red and covered with elaborate white mouldings that resemble piped cake-icing. The museum takes a tour through Argentina's history, concentrating mainly on the tumultuous nineteenth century, featuring portraits of big names from Argentina's formative years as well as maps and important paintings of historical, rather than artistic, interest. But, when it is on display, the high point of the collection is the stunning **La Tarja de Potosí**, an elaborate silver and gold shield given to General Belgrano in 1813 by the women from Potosí (a silver-mining town in Upper Peru, now Bolivia) in recognition of his role in their country's struggle for independence from Spain. Almost as tall as a man, it's a delicately worked and intricate piece complete with tiny figures symbolizing the discovery of America.

1

La Boca

The barrio is easily reached on foot from Parque Lezama or by bus #86 from Plaza de Mayo, buses #64 and #152 from Plaza Italia or #53 from Constitución; it's also on the route of the city government's tour bus (see p.106)

More than any other barrio in Buenos Aires, **La Boca** and its inhabitants seem to flaunt their idiosyncrasies. Located in the capital's southeastern corner, this working-class riverside neighbourhood has been nicknamed the "República de la Boca" since 1882, when a group of local youths declared the barrio's secession from the country. Even today, its residents – many new immigrants from other South American countries – have a reputation for playing by their own rules and are most famous for their brightly coloured wooden and corrugated-iron houses. The district was originally the favoured destination for Italian immigrants, and house colours derive from the Genoese custom of painting homes with the paint left over from boats. La Boca's other most characteristic emblem is its football team, **Boca Juniors**, the country's most popular club and probably the most famous one abroad.

Named after the *boca*, or mouth, of the Río Riachuelo, which snakes along its southern border, La Boca is an irregularly shaped barrio, longer than it is wide. Its main thoroughfare is Avenida Almirante Brown, which cuts through the neighbourhood from Parque Lezama to the towering iron **Puente Transbordador** that straddles the Riachuelo. Apart from some excellent pizzerias, there's little to detain you along the avenue: the majority of La Boca's attractions are packed into the grids of streets on either side. Even then, there's not a great deal to see as such, and unless you plan to visit all the museums an hour or two will suffice; morning is the ideal time to go, when the light best captures the district's bright hues and before the tour buses arrive.

Be warned that La Boca remains a poor neighbourhood and has an unfortunate reputation for crime, with muggings a fairly common occurrence. There's no need to be paranoid, but it is advisable to stick strictly to the main tourist district and follow the advice of the police who patrol the area; don't wear expensive watches or jewellery, and keep cameras out of sight.

La Bombonera

Brandsen 805 • ☎ 011 5777 1200, ⊛ bocajuniors.com.ar/el-club/la-bombonera

The true heart of La Boca is Boca Juniors' stadium, **La Bombonera**. Built in 1940, it was remodelled in the 1990s and the name – literally "the chocolate box" – refers to its compact structure; although Boca has more fans than any other Argentine team, the stadium's capacity is smaller than most of its rivals'. This is the place where many of the country's best young players cut their teeth before heading to Europe on lucrative deals – the Bombonera's most famous veteran is Diego Maradona (see box opposite), who retains a VIP seat at the stadium. Seeing a game here is an incredible experience, even for non-fans.

Just inside the stadium entrance, there's a large painting by famous local artist Benito Quinquela Martín (see p.84) entitled *Orígen de la bandera de Boca* ("the origin of Boca's flag"), which illustrates one of the club's most famous anecdotes. Though the exact date and circumstances of the event are disputed, all agree that Boca Juniors chose the colours of its strip from the flag of the next ship to pass through its then busy port. As the boat was Swedish, the distinctive blue and yellow strip was selected.

Around the stadium, a huddle of shops sell Boca souvenirs and decent quality knock-off shirts while, on the pavement outside, stars with the names of Boca players past and present, some featuring their footprints, were laid as part of the club's centenary celebrations in 2005. Some of the neighbouring houses have taken up the blue and yellow theme, too, with facades painted like giant football shirts.

Museo de la Pasión Boquense

Daily 10am–6pm • $115 • **Tours** Every 30min; 1hr 30min • $150 (includes entry) • **Short tours** Every 30min; 45min • $130 (includes entry) • ⓦ museoboquense.com

If you don't get the opportunity to watch a match, check out the **Museo de la Pasión Boquense** and its **stadium tour**. The museum, built into the stadium structure, offers a modern audiovisual experience, including a 360-degree film that puts you in the boots of a Boca player and a charming model of how La Boca would have looked and sounded in the 1930s. The full tour (usually in Spanish, English and Portuguese) includes the stands, pitch and press conference room and even takes in the players' jacuzzi and dressing room, complete with statues of the Virgin Mary.

Caminito and around

From La Bombonera it's a short walk southwards to La Boca's other nerve centre: **Caminito**. A former train siding now transformed into a pedestrian street and open-air art museum, Caminito, which runs diagonally between the riverfront and Calle Lamadrid, is the barrio's (and possibly the city's) most famous street. Lined with the

---

EL DIEGO

Few people have captured the imagination of the Argentine public as much as **Diego Armando Maradona**. A bull of a player with exceptional close control, balance and on-field vision, the diminutive no. 10 was the finest footballer of his generation and arguably of all time – though the latter title is now seriously contested by his compatriot, Lionel Messi. Born in a poor neighbourhood on the outskirts of Buenos Aires, Maradona's playing career (1976–97) was peerless. He made his first-team, first-division debut for club **Argentinos Juniors** in 1976, when he was just 15. Maradona wore the colours of seven clubs in total, including **Boca Juniors**, **Barcelona** and, most famously, **Napoli**, where he is still venerated as the player who brought southern Italy's poorer brother glory and silverware. He also led Argentina to win the World Cup in 1986, a campaign that included one of the most celebrated of all World Cup games, the quarter-final played against England, just four years after the South Atlantic conflict. Maradona scored two goals, including the infamous "Hand of God" goal, in which he tapped the ball in with his hand, and a second, legitimate goal considered to be one of the finest ever scored.

Like many geniuses, though, Maradona was flawed – in his case, by the excesses of alcohol and, particularly, drugs. He was suspended in 1991 for testing positive for cocaine, and then again for the banned substance ephedrine during the 1994 World Cup. After a low point in 2004 when he was hospitalized following a cocaine-induced heart attack, he bounced back to host his own talk show in 2005, where guests included Pele and Maradona's friend Fidel Castro. In 2008 he surprised many when he took over as coach of Argentina's national side, and during qualifications for the 2010 World Cup was criticized for his tactics (or lack of them) – which led him to more notoriety, this time when he launched an obscenity-laden tirade against the press following Argentina's qualification. He lost his job after a humiliating 4-0 defeat by Germany in the South Africa finals, but was then appointed manager of Al-Wasl FC, based in Dubai, earning £2.7 million a year. Though he was sacked for poor results, these days he's the UAE sports ambassador, still based in Dubai.

1

best-kept examples of Boca's coloured houses, it's very photogenic but not very lived-in – a life-size museum or a tourist trap, depending on your point of view. The street was "founded" by the barrio's most famous artist, **Benito Quinquela Martín**, who painted epic and expressive scenes of the neighbourhood's daily life. Quinquela Martín rescued the old siding from oblivion after the rail company removed the tracks in 1954. He encouraged the immigrants' tradition of painting their houses in bright colours and took the name for the street from a famous 1920s tango.

Caminito may have lost its original charm, but the bold blocks of rainbow-coloured walls, set off with contrasting window frames and balconies, are still an arresting sight. Down the middle of the street, there's an **arts and crafts fair**, dominated by garish paintings of the area. Tango musicians frequently perform along the street, too, accompanied by the sound of cameras clicking and a collecting hat. At the western end of Caminito, Calle Garibaldi runs past and on south, a charmingly ramshackle street with a slew of coloured corrugated-iron buildings, less done up than those of Caminito.

Vuelta de Rocha and Puente Transbordador

The eastern end of Caminito leads to Avenida Pedro de Mendoza and the Riachuelo, which bulges dramatically at this point, creating a curvaceous but often malodorous inlet known as the **Vuelta de Rocha**. The view from Avenida Pedro de Mendoza is of a jumbled but majestic mass of boats, factories and bridges: directly south, across the river, there's the working-class suburb of Avellaneda, while to your left there's one of Buenos Aires' major landmarks, the massive iron **Puente Transbordador** ("transport bridge"), built in the early years of the twentieth century and now out of use. Next to the transport bridge is Puente Nicolás Avellaneda – a very similar construction built in 1939. This functioning bridge is one of the major causeways in and out of the city. Far below it, small rowing boats still ferry passengers to and from Avellaneda. Avenida Pedro de Mendoza itself is lined with cafés catering to the hordes of visiting tourists, and there are also two excellent **art museums** (see below).

Fundación Proa

Av Pedro de Mendoza 1929 • Tues–Sun 11am–7pm • $40 • Guided tours (Spanish) Tues–Sun noon; 1hr • ☏ 011 4104 1000, ⓦ proa.org

The first of the art museums on Avenida Pedro de Mendoza is **Fundación Proa**. Set inside a converted mansion – all Italianate elegance outside and modern, angular galleries within – Proa has no permanent collection but hosts some fascinating and diverse exhibitions, usually with a Latin American theme, ranging from 1980s Argentine art to pre-Columbian Aztec sculpture. Shows have also been dedicated to non-Latin American artists, such as Louise Bourgeois and Marcel Duchamp. Refuel at the top-floor café, which offers a lovely view of the harbour.

Museo de Bellas Artes de La Boca Quinquela Martín

Av Pedro de Mendoza 1835 • Tues–Fri 10am–6pm, Sat & Sun 11.15am–6pm • $20 voluntary contribution • ☏ 011 4301 1080

A short stroll east along Avenida Pedro de Mendoza from the Fundación Proa brings you to another art museum, the long-established **Museo de Bellas Artes de La Boca**. Founded in 1938 by local lad Benito Quinquela Martín on the site of his studio (now also a school), it houses many of his major works, as well as those of contemporary Argentine artists. It's the perfect setting for a display of Quinquela Martín's work, since you can actually see much of his subject matter simply by peering out of the windows of the gallery or climbing up to the viewpoint on the roof. More than anyone, Quinquela Martín conveyed the industrial grandeur of La Boca, dedicating himself to painting scenes of everyday life. Indeed, he was so associated with the city's least salubrious neighbourhood that, like the tango, he did not garner respect with the Argentine establishment until he had become famous abroad.

The north

1

A combination of extravagant elegance and an authentic lived-in feel pervades **the north** of Buenos Aires, where the four residential barrios of most interest to visitors – Retiro, Recoleta, Palermo and Belgrano – each retain a distinctive character. Nearest to the centre, **Retiro** and **Recoleta** have chic streets lined with boutiques, art galleries and smart cafés, although the dockside fringes and the dodgy bits near the city's biggest train station, also called Retiro, are just as down at heel as parts of the southern barrios, if not more so. Recoleta is associated primarily with its magnificent **cemetery** where, among other national celebrities, Evita is buried. Both barrios also share an extraordinary concentration of French-style **palaces**, tangible proof of the obsession of the city's elite at the beginning of the twentieth century with established European cities. Many of these palaces can be visited and some of them house the area's opulent museum collections, but they are also sights in themselves.

Palermo and **Belgrano**, further north, are large districts composed of a mixture of tall apartment buildings, tree-lined boulevards, little cobbled streets and grandiose Neocolonial houses. Many of Buenos Aires' best **restaurants** and **shops** are here, so you should plan a visit in this direction at least once. It's worth making a day of it to check out the beautiful **parks** and **gardens**, attend a game of polo (see p.39), or to see another beguiling side of the city in, for example, Palermo Soho, a district of lively cafés, boutiques and art galleries. Beyond these northern barrios lies the **Zona Norte**, a riverine world of suburbs where the Capital Federal blends into the subtropical Paraná Delta.

Retiro

Retiro is easily reached on foot from the city centre, and is connected to the subte via San Martín and Retiro stations, both on Line C

Squeezed between the city centre to the south, Recoleta to the west and mostly inhospitable docklands to the north and east, **Retiro** gets its name from a hermit's *retiro* (retreat) that was hidden among dense woodland here in the sixteenth century, when Buenos Aires was little more than a village. Today it's surprisingly varied for such a small barrio: commercial **art galleries** and airline offices outnumber other businesses along the busy streets around the end of Calle Florida near the barrio's focal point, Plaza San Martín, while west of busy Avenida 9 de Julio lies a smart, quiet residential area.

Lying at Retiro's aristocratic heart, **Plaza San Martín** is one of the city's most enticing green spaces, flanked by opulent patrician buildings. More outstanding examples of the barrio's palaces, which reflect how wealthy Porteños of the late nineteenth century yearned for their city to be a New World version of Paris, are clustered around **Plaza Carlos Pellegrini**, one of the city's most elegant squares. For most Porteños, the barrio's name has become synonymous with the train terminal, **Estación Retiro**, which still retains some original Edwardian features. Next to it is the city's major bus terminal, a modern and fairly efficient complex, and beyond that urban wasteland and a shantytown called Villa 31.

Estación Retiro

Av del Libertador 50

A massive complex of rail terminals, **Estación Retiro** is in fact three train stations in one: General San Martín, General Belgrano and General Mitre. The third of these is also by far the most impressive, a massive stone and metal structure completed in 1915 by Charles John Dudley, a British constructor based in Liverpool. Decorated with Royal Doulton porcelain tiles, it is a majestic, airy edifice with an iron roof that, at the time, was the largest of its kind in the world. The entire station, and the immediate vicinity in front of it, underwent renovation in 2013, and it's worth a visit for the splendid café alone, *Café Retiro*. This is also the place to come if you plan to take the train to Tigre and the Paraná Delta (see p.133).

1

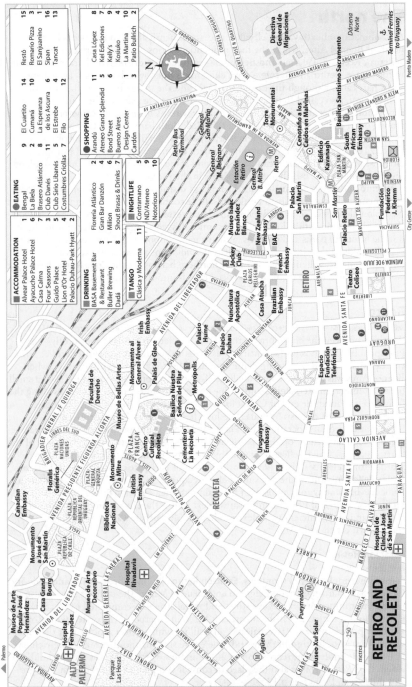

RETIRO AND RECOLETA

■ **ACCOMMODATION**

Alvear Palace Hotel	1
Ayacucho Palace Hotel	6
Casa Calma	7
Four Seasons	5
Guido Palace	4
Lion d'Or Hotel	3
Palacio Duhau-Park Hyatt	2

● **EATING**

Bengal	1
La Biela	6
Brasero Atlántico	7
Club Danés	5
Club Sirio Libanés	4
Costumbres Criollas	7
El Cuartito	9
Cumaná	2
La Esperanza de los Ascurra	8
El Estrebe	5
Filo	7
Restó	15
Romario Pizza	3
El Sanjuanino	1
Sipan	16
Tancat	13

● **SHOPPING**

Arandú	14
Ateneo Grand Splendid	10
Bond Street	8
Buenos Aires Design Center	11
Cardon	12
Casa López	11
Kel Ediciones	5
Kelly's	6
Kosiuko	4
La Martina	10
Patio Bullrich	2

■ **DRINKING**

BASA Basement Bar & Restaurant	2
Buller Brewing	4
Dadá	3

Florería Atlántico	8
Gran Bar Danzón	7
Milion	

■ **TANGO**

Clásica y Moderna	11

■ **NIGHTLIFE**

Contramano	5
ND/Ateneo	9
Notorious	10

Shout Brasas & Drinks	8

0 ——— 250
metres

CHARLES THAYS: BUENOS AIRES' LANDSCAPE ARTIST

1

In the 1880s, French botanist and **landscape architect Charles Thays** (1849–1934) travelled to South America to study its rich flora, particularly the continent's hundreds of endemic tree species. He initially settled in Argentina, where his services were in great demand as municipal authorities across the country sought to smarten their cities up. They, like their European and North American counterparts, were spurred by the realization that the country's fast-growing urban sprawls needed parks and gardens to provide vital breathing spaces and recreational areas.

In 1890, Thays was appointed director of parks and gardens in Buenos Aires, in no small part due to his adeptness at transforming open plazas formerly used for military parades, or *plazas secas*, into shady *plazas verdes*, or green squares, such as Plaza San Martín. He also designed the capital's botanical garden and the zoo – which he planted with dozens of *tipas* (also known as *palo rosa*, or rosewood) – as well as Palermo's Parque 3 de Febrero, Belgrano's Barrancas, Córdoba's Parque Sarmiento and Parque San Martín, Tucumán's Parque 9 de Julio and, most impressive of them all, Mendoza's Parque General San Martín. Thays received countless private commissions, too, including the garden of Palacio Hume, on Avenida Alvear in Recoleta, and the layout of the exclusive residential estate known as Barrio Parque, in Palermo Chico.

Despite his French origins, he preferred the informal English style of landscaping, and also experimented with combinations of native plants such as jacarandas, *tipas* and *palo borracho* (a spiky-trunked relative of the *ceibo* with handsome pink flowers) with Canary Island palms, planes and lime trees. Oddly enough, given the high regard in which he was held and his contributions to the greening of Buenos Aires, the lone plaza named in his honour, Plaza Carlos Thays, in Palermo, is disappointingly barren, and definitely not the best example of landscaping the city has to offer.

Plaza San Martín

Immediately southeast of the train stations, leafy **Plaza San Martín** plays many roles: romantic meeting place, picnic area for office workers, children's playground and many people's arrival point in downtown Buenos Aires, owing to the main train and bus terminals nearby. Plaza San Martín was designed by Argentina's most important landscape architect, Frenchman **Charles Thays** (see box above), and created especially for a monument to **General San Martín** that was moved to its southwestern corner in 1910 for the country's centenary. Aligned with Avenida Santa Fe, the imposing bronze equestrian statue stands proudly on a high marble pedestal decorated with scenes representing national liberation. The Libertador points west, showing the way across the Andes. The plaza's lush lawns are a favourite sunbathing spot in the warmer months, but when it gets baking hot you can always cool down on a bench beneath the luxuriant palms, *ceibos*, monkey puzzles, lime trees and acacias.

Cenotafio a los Caídos en Malvinas

The more open, northern half of Plaza San Martín slopes down to Avenida del Libertador, which runs through northern Buenos Aires all the way to Tigre. The **Cenotafio a los Caídos en Malvinas** stands on the brow of the slope, a sombre cenotaph comprising 25 black marble plaques inscribed with the 649 names of the country's fallen during the 1982 Falklands conflict, its eternal flame partly symbolizing Argentina's persistent claim over the South Atlantic islands. It is permanently guarded by a rotation of the army, navy and air force, and is the scene of both remembrance ceremonies and demonstrations on April 2 each year, the day on which Argentina began its brief occupation of the islands. The monument was deliberately placed opposite the former Plaza Británica – called the Plaza Fuerza Aérea Argentina since 1982.

Torre Monumental (Torre de los Ingleses)

At the centre of the Plaza Fuerza Aérea Argentina, opposite Plaza San Martín, there are echoes of London's Big Ben in the 76m-high **Torre de los Ingleses**, the Anglo-Argentine community's contribution to the city's 1910 centenary celebrations – though it wasn't inaugurated until 1916. During and after the 1982 conflict there was talk of

1

demolishing the tower; instead, it was officially renamed Torre Monumental, though no one really calls it that. The lift that used to carry visitors to the top has been out of operation for many years, so the only way to enjoy it is from outside.

Basílica del Santísimo Sacramento

San Martín 1035 • Mon–Fri 10am–1pm & 2–7pm • Free

The **Basílica del Santísimo Sacramento** lurks east of the Plaza San Martín, at the end of a narrow *pasaje* and rather dwarfed by the skyscrapers surrounding it. It was built with some of the vast fortune of Mercedes Castellanos de Anchorena, a matriarchal figure who married into one of Argentina's wealthiest and most influential landowning clans (hence the Argentine expression "as rich as an Anchorena"). Consecrated in 1916, the basilica is still regarded as the smartest place to get married in Buenos Aires. It was designed by French architects, with a white marble dome and five slender turrets; it's no coincidence that it looks so much like Paris's Sacré Coeur. Inside, no expense was spared: red onyx from Morocco, marble from Verona and Carrara, red sandstone from the Vosges, glazed mosaic tiles from Venice and bronze from France were imported to decorate Anchorena's monument to devotion. Down in the crypt and behind a protective grille is her **mausoleum**, an ostentatious yet doleful concoction of marble angels guarded by a demure Virgin Mary.

Edificio Kavanagh

San Martín and Florida 1065

The **Edificio Kavanagh** sums up the social – and architectural – evolution in twentieth-century Buenos Aires. It is rumoured that Corina Kavanagh sold most of her property in the country to erect what, when it went up in 1935, was to be the tallest building (120m) in South America. It is also rumoured that she deliberately built it in front of the Basílica del Santísimo Sacramento to conceal her bitter rival's masterpiece. The two facades of its distinctive flat-iron shape – it's built in a wedge formed by the two streets – were hailed at the time by the American Institute of Architects as the world's best example of Rationalist architecture. Over the years the apartment building has been inhabited by many of the city's rich and famous; it is not open to the public.

Círculo Militar ex Palacio Paz

Av Santa Fe 750 • Guided visits only: Tues 3pm, Wed–Fri 11am & 3pm (Spanish); Thurs 3.30pm (English); 1hr • $100 • ⓦ palaciopaz.com.ar

Press baron José Paz, founder of daily newspaper *La Prensa* and related by marriage to the Anchorenas, wanted his Buenos Aires home to look like the Louvre in Paris, so he commissioned **Palacio Paz** – now known as the Círculo Militar – to be built by a French architect between 1902 and 1914. Sadly, however, Paz died in 1912, without ever seeing the finished building. The palace runs along the southwest side of Plaza San Martín, and access (on guided tours only) is via magnificent wrought-iron gates at Av Santa Fe 750. It remains the largest single house ever built in Argentina, and its main facade is an uncanny replica of the Sully wing of the Louvre, with steeply stacked slate roofs, a double row of tiny windows and a colonnaded ground floor.

Inside, the eighteen rooms open to the public – less than one-sixth of the whole building – are decorated in an eclectic range of French styles, from Gothic to Empire, including a scaled-down copy of the Hall of Mirrors in Versailles, but the *pièce de résistance* is the great Hall of Honour, a cavernous, circular room lined with several types of European marble and crowned with a stained-glass dome from which the Sun King beams down. Pianist Arthur Rubinstein entertained guests in the little music room and the Prince of Wales dined here during his visit to the city in 1925, but the Paz family fell on hard times in the late 1930s, most of the original furniture was sold off and the palace was divided between the Círculo Militar, an officers' club, and the **Museo de Armas de la Nación** (Mon–Fri 1–7pm; $40; ⓦ museodearmas.com.ar). The latter now houses an exhibition of armour, weapons and military uniforms, some dating back to the Wars of Independence.

Palacio San Martín

Arenales 761 • Guided visits (English & Spanish) Thurs 3pm; 1hr • Free • ☎ 011 4819 8092

Just north of the Círculo Militar and northwest of Plaza San Martín, at Arenales and Esmeralda, **Palacio San Martín** is a particularly extravagant example of the city's ostentatious palaces. Built in 1905 for the **Anchorena** family, it was originally known as the Palacio Anchorena. Mercedes Castellanos de Anchorena lived here with her family for twenty years, until the Great Depression left them penniless. The enormous building is actually divided up into three subtly different palaces, all sharing a huge Neoclassical entrance and ceremonial courtyard. Its overall structure is based on a nineteenth-century Parisian banker's mansion, with slate mansard roofs, colonnades and domed attics, while the neo-Baroque interior is inspired by the eighteenth-century Hotel de Condé, also in Paris. Fashionable Art Nouveau details, such as ornate stained-glass windows and wrought-iron staircases, were also incorporated.

After the palace and its accumulated treasures were hurriedly sold off in 1927, the government turned it into the Ministry of Foreign Affairs, International Trade and Worship, and renamed it Palacio San Martín. Since the 1980s, when the ministry moved into the larger plate-glass building across Calle Esmeralda, the palace has been reserved for state ceremonies, and is open to the public for tours only. Some of the original furniture and paintings have been recovered, but the guided visits are above all a rare opportunity to witness the opulent interior of a Porteño palace. The gilt mirrors, marble fireplaces and chandeliers are all on a grandiose scale, yet they still look lost in the cavernous rooms, with their polished parquet floors, inlaid wooden panelling and ceilings richly decorated with oil paintings.

Museo de Arte Hispanoamericano Isaac Fernández Blanco

Suipacha 1422 • Tues–Fri 1–7pm, Sat & Sun 11am–7pm • $20, free Wed • ⓦ buenosaires.gob.ar/museofernandezblanco

Two blocks north and one west of Palacio San Martín, the **Museo de Arte Hispanoamericano Isaac Fernández Blanco** is one of the city's undisputed cultural highlights. The museum occupies the **Palacio Noel**, a stunning Neocolonial house built in the 1920s by architect Martín Noel, who later donated it to the city. Its style imitates eighteenth-century Lima Baroque, a backlash against the slavish imitation of Parisian palaces fashionable at the time. With plain white walls, lace-like window-grilles, dark wooden bow windows and wrought-iron balconies, it's the perfect residence for the superb collection of **Spanish-American art** inside. Most of the artefacts on display, all favourably presented, were produced in the seventeenth and early eighteenth centuries, in Peru or Alto Perú (present-day Bolivia).

The collection, spread over three floors, highlights the culture of many of the peoples who made up early South America, from Jesuits in the jungle to prosperous colonial *criollos* (Spanish-Americans). One of the most striking pieces, on the ground floor, is a fantastic eighteenth-century silver sacrarium, embellished with a portrait of Christ on a copper plaque. Other high points of this huge and varied collection include a Luso-Brazilian silver votive lamp, polychrome furniture – the work of Bolivian craftsmen – and fine Jesuit/Guaraní statues, all carved from wood. There's also an extensive display of anonymous paintings from the **Cusqueña School** – one of the most prodigious in colonial South America. Its masters, based in the Peruvian city of Cusco and especially active in the eighteenth century, produced subtle oil paintings, mostly of religious, devotional subjects, which combined sombre understatement with a startling vitality and mixed traditional Catholic imagery with indigenous motifs.

Plaza Carlos Pellegrini and around

The elegant triangle of **Plaza Carlos Pellegrini** is a centre of Retiro's well-heeled residential streets west of Avenida 9 de Julio, and near it you'll find a variety of spectacular buildings that share a common theme: their meticulous French style. Between 1910 and 1925, the obsession with turning Buenos Aires into the "Paris of the

1

South" reached a fever pitch in this part of the city, making this neighbourhood one of the more exclusive, something it remains to this day. The many feats of **Carlos Pellegrini**, president in the 1890s and the plaza's namesake, include founding both the Banco Nación and Argentina's influential **Jockey Club**; the latter's national headquarters occupy the massive honey-coloured **Palacio Unzué de Casares**, on the north side of the plaza at Avenida Alvear 1345. Opposite, on the south side of the plaza, stands the **Palacio Celedonio Pereda**, named after a member of the oligarchy who wanted a carbon copy of the Palais Jacquemart-André in Paris. The Porteño palace, now used by the Brazilian Embassy, is a uniformly successful replica, classical columns and all.

Half a block north, at Cerrito 1455, the **Mansion Álzaga Unzué** now forms a luxurious annexe of the *Four Seasons* hotel (see p.111). It's a faultless duplicate of a Loire chateau, built in attractive red brick and cream limestone and topped with a shiny slate mansard roof. Back on the other side of Arroyo, on Plaza Carlos Pellegrini's south corner, the Louis XIV-style **Palacio Ortiz Basualdo** has been the location of the French Embassy since 1925. This magnificent palace – which has some slightly incongruous detailing, including Art Nouveau balconies, monumental Ionic pilasters and bulging Second Empire corner turrets – mercifully escaped demolition in the 1950s when Avenida 9 de Julio was widened, though it did have to be altered considerably to accommodate the highway. From Plaza Carlos Pellegrini, Avenida Alvear leads due northwest to Recoleta.

Recoleta

The subte skirts the southern edge of Recoleta, but the barrio is within walking distance (or a short cab ride) of the city centre

The well-heeled barrio of **Recoleta** is, for most Porteños, intrinsically tied to the magnificent **La Recoleta Cemetery** (see opposite) at its heart. In around 1720, drawn to the area's tranquillity, which was deemed perfect for meditation or "recollection" (hence the name), Franciscan monks set up a monastery here. It wasn't until the cholera and yellow fever epidemics of 1867 and 1871 (see p.78) that the city's wealthy moved to Recoleta, from hitherto fashionable San Telmo. Although many of its residents have left for the northern suburbs in recent years, a Recoleta address still has cachet; **Avenida Alvear** is Buenos Aires' swankiest street. Scattered throughout the barrio are a host of **restaurants** and bars, ranging from some of the city's most traditional to trendy joints that come and go.

Recoleta's other notable attractions include one of the capital's few remaining colonial buildings, the gleaming white **Basílica Nuestra Señora del Pilar**, plus the **Centro Cultural de Recoleta** and the country's biggest and richest collection of nineteenth- and twentieth-century art, at the **Museo Nacional de Bellas Artes** (see p.92).

Avenida Alvear

Only five blocks in length, stretching from Plaza Carlos Pellegrini to Plaza San Martín de Tours, **Avenida Alvear** is one of the city's shortest but most exclusive avenues, lined with expensive **art galleries**. It is home to international designer boutiques like Hermés, although government import restrictions imposed in 2012 left many of these stock-less and shuttered. At the time of writing, it was too early to tell if the change of government would open the economy up to imports again. At the corner of Ayacucho lies the city's most famous and traditional luxury hotel, the French Art Deco **Alvear Palace** (see p.111), built in 1932.

Two blocks south, opposite elegant apartment buildings between Montevideo and Rodriguez Peña, are three palaces that were home to some of Argentina's wealthiest families at the beginning of the twentieth century. Although none is open to the public, the exteriors are worth a peek for their splendid architecture. The northernmost, behind a Charles Thays-designed garden, is the **Residencia Maguire**, formerly known as **Palacio Hume**. This perfectly symmetrical Art Nouveau creation, embellished with intricate wrought-iron work, now looks a little the worse for wear. It was originally built for British rail-engineer Alexander Hume, but was sold to the Duhau family in the 1920s, who staged the city's first-ever art exhibition inside. The Duhau family also built the middle palace, the **Palacio Duhau**, now the *Park Hyatt* (see p.111), an austere imitation of an eighteenth-century French Neoclassical *palais*. The third palace, the severely Neoclassical **Nunciatura Apostólica** on the corner of Montevideo, was designed by a French architect for a member of the Anchorena family. Nowadays it's the seat of the Vatican's Argentina representative, and was used by Pope John Paul II during his visits to the country.

Cementerio de la Recoleta

Junín 1760 • Daily 7am–5.30pm • $100 • Guided tours (English) Tues & Thurs 11am; 1hr

One of the world's most remarkable burial grounds, **Cementerio de la Recoleta** presents an exhilarating panorama of Argentine history. The giant vaults – ninety have been declared national historical monuments – stacked along avenues inside the high walls resemble the rooftops of a fanciful Utopian town from above. The necropolis is a city within a city, a lesson in architectural styles and fashions, and a great place to wander, exploring its narrow streets and wide avenues of yews and cypress trees.

The **tombs** themselves range from simple headstones to bombastic masterpieces built in a variety of styles including Art Nouveau, Art Deco, Secessionist, Neoclassical, neo-Byzantine and even neo-Babylonian. The oldest monumental grave, dating from 1836, is that of **Juan Facundo Quiroga**, the much-feared La Rioja *caudillo* (local leader) immortalized in the Latin American classic *Facundo* by Argentine statesman and writer Domingo Sarmiento, also buried here. Facundo's tomb stands straight ahead of the gateway. Next to it, inscribed with a Borges poem, stands the solemn granite mausoleum occupied by several generations of the eminent Alvear family. The vast majority of tombs in Recoleta belong to similar patrician families of significant means – but not all. Perhaps the most incongruous statue in the cemetery is that of a boxer, in the northwest sector – the final resting place of **Luis Ángel Firpo**, who fought Jack Dempsey for the world heavyweight title in 1923. Military heroes, many of them Irish or British seafarers who played a key part in Argentina's struggle for independence, are also buried here, such as **Admiral William Brown**. An Argentine hero of Irish origins, at the beginning of the nineteenth century Brown decimated the Spanish fleet in the River Plate estuary. An unusual monument decorated with a beautiful miniature of his frigate, the *Hercules*, is a highlight of the cemetery's central plaza.

Basílica Nuestra Señora del Pilar

Junín 1892 • Mon–Sat 10.30am–6.15pm, Sun 2.30–6.15pm • Free • ⓦ basilicadelpilar.org.ar

Just north of the cemetery gates is the stark white silhouette of the **Basílica Nuestra Señora del Pilar**. Built in the early eighteenth century by Jesuits, it's the

EVITA'S FINAL RESTING PLACE

Recoleta cemetery's most famous resident is undoubtedly **Eva Perón**, second wife of President Juan Perón and one of Argentina's most enduring figures (see box, p.540), who died in 1952. Given the snobbishness surrounding the cemetery – the authorities who preside over it treat it more like a gentlemen's club than a burial ground – it's hardly surprising that Porteño high society tried to prevent Evita's family from laying her to rest here. Nevertheless, her family's plain, polished black granite vault, pithily marked **Familia Duarte** and containing poignant quotes on bronze plaques from her speeches, has been her resting place since the 1970s – with the coffin supposedly inside concrete to prevent it from disappearing. Unlike many other graves, it's not signposted (the cemetery authorities are still uneasy about her presence), but you can locate it by following the signs to Sarmiento's, over to the left when you come in, then counting five alleyways farther away from the entrance, and looking out for the pile of bouquets by the vault.

1

second-oldest church in Buenos Aires and effectively the parish church for the Recoleta elite. The sky-blue Pas-de-Calais ceramic tiles atop its single slender turret were restored in the 1930s, along with the plain facade. The interior was also remodelled, and the monks' cells turned into side chapels, each decorated with a gilded reredos and polychrome wooden saints. These include statues of San Pedro de Alcántara and the Virgen de la Merced, all attributed to a native artist known simply as "José". The magnificent Baroque silver altarpiece, embellished with an Inca sun and other pre-Hispanic details, was made by craftsmen from Alto Perú. Equally admirable is the fine altar crucifix allegedly donated to the city by King Carlos III of Spain. It is possible to visit the cloisters above the church (same hours as church; free) via the staircase three altars to the left. The rooms, once home to the Franciscan monks, now hold a collection of religious paintings and artefacts, including some impressive colonial and *criollo* silverware.

Centro Cultural Recoleta

Junín 1930 • Tues–Fri 1.30–8.30pm, Sat & Sun 11.30am–9pm • Free • ⓦ centroculturalrecoleta.org

Immediately north of Basílica Nuestra Señora del Pilar, the **Centro Cultural Recoleta** is one of the city's leading **arts centres**, a good deal bigger and more impressive inside than its modest front suggests. The building, which dates from the 1730s, is one of Buenos Aires' oldest, and originally housed the area's Franciscan monks. The building was extensively, but tastefully, remodelled in the 1980s and retains its former cloisters. These cool, white, arched hallways and simple rooms make an excellent setting for the changing art, photography and audiovisual exhibitions the centre hosts. There are also a number of auditoriums for theatre, dance and music, including the **Sala Villa Villa**, the home of the internationally renowned Argentine theatre troupe Fuerza Bruta when in town.

Plaza San Martín de Tours and Feria Plaza Francia

Opposite the Centro Cultural Recoleta, grassy **Plaza San Martín de Tours** is shaded by three of the biggest rubber trees in the city, an impressive sight with their huge buttress roots, contorted like arthritic limbs. A 100-year-old rubber tree, the famous Gran Gomero, shelters the terrace of nearby *La Biela* (see p.117), on the corner of Avenida Quintana. One of the city's most traditional *confiterías*, La Biela gets its name, which means "connecting-rod", from being the favourite haunt of racing drivers in the 1940s and 50s, and was a frequent guerrilla target in the 1970s, owing to its wealthy patrons. On the other side of the cultural centre, in **Plaza Francia**, buskers, jugglers and groups practising the fluid Brazilian martial art of *capoeira* entertain crowds during the **Feria Plaza Francia**, also known as the Feria Hippy, at weekends (9am–7pm; free; ⓦ feriaplazafrancia.com), while artisans sell hand-crafted wares including *mate* gourds, jewellery and leather at stalls arranged along the wide paths.

Museo Nacional de Bellas Artes

Av del Libertador 1473 • Tues–Fri 12.30–8.30pm, Sat & Sun 9.30am–8.30pm • Tours (English) Tues, Wed, Fri & Sat 1pm • Free • ⓦ mnba.gob.ar

Argentina's principal art museum, the **Museo Nacional de Bellas Artes** occupies an unassuming, slightly gloomy, brick-red Neoclassical building half a kilometre due north of Recoleta Cemetery. Like the barrio's architecture, the museum's contents, comprising mostly nineteenth- and twentieth-century paintings and some sculpture, are resoundingly European; the Old World influences on even the Argentine art on display are clearly evident.

Only about a tenth of the museum's collection of 11,000 exhibits is on display at any time. The whole of the ground floor is given over to **international art**, dominated by French, Dutch and Italian masters such as Degas and Rubens. Later masters as varied as Pollock, Picasso and Italo-Argentine Lucio Fontana also feature. In a room by itself, the wide-ranging **Hirsch bequest** – left to the nation by the wealthy Belgrano landowners and art collectors – includes some fabulous European paintings, sculptures, furniture and other art objects spanning several centuries, including a Spanish retable (an ornamental screen behind the altar) and a portrait by Rembrandt of his sister.

The upper-floor galleries are an excellent introduction to **Argentine art**, containing a selection of the country's major artists. The works span from pre-Columbian terracotta and textiles, through nineteenth-century European imitators such as Prilidiano Pueyrredón and Eduardo Sívori to the Argentine artists in the twentieth century who tried to break away from this imitative tendency and create a movement of their own. Accessed via a short staircase, vast Room 107 covers Argentine art from the 1920s, featuring contemporary masters such as Guillermo Kuitca and Xul Solar (who has a museum dedicated to his works in Recoleta; see below).

Museo Nacional de Arte Decorativo

Av del Libertador 1902 • Tues–Sun 2–7pm • $20; free Tues • Tours (English) Tues–Fri 2.30pm; 45min • $30 • ⓦ mnad.org

There's no finer example of the decadent decor money could buy in early twentieth-century Buenos Aires than that on display in the **Museo Nacional de Arte Decorativo**, with its remarkable collection of art and furniture. The museum is housed in **Palacio Errázuriz**, one of the city's most original private mansions, albeit of typically French design. The two-storey palace was built in 1911 for a Chilean diplomat and his patrician Argentine wife, and was turned into a museum in 1937. Designed by René Sergent, a French architect and proponent of the Academic style, it has three contrasting facades. The western one, on Sánchez de Bustamante, is inspired by the Petit Trianon at Versailles; the long northern side of the building with its Corinthian pillars, on Avenida del Libertador, is based on the palaces on Paris's Place de la Concorde; and the eastern end, near the entrance, is dominated by an enormous semicircular stone porch, supported by four Tuscan columns. The coach house, now a restaurant and tearoom, *Croque Madame*, sits just beyond the monumental wrought-iron and bronze gates, in the style of Louis XVI.

The interior is as French as the exterior, especially the Regency ballroom, lined with gilded Rococo panels and huge mirrors, all stripped from a Parisian house. The couple's extravagant taste in **art** – Flemish furniture and French clocks, Sèvres porcelain, bronzes by Bourdelle, and paintings, old and modern, ranging from El Greco (*Christ Bearing the Cross*) to Manet (*The Sacrifice of the Rose*) – is reflected and preserved. In the basement resides a Gothic chapel, transferred from the Château de Champagnette in France. Temporary exhibitions of ancient and contemporary art are also held down here, or in the garden in the summer, as are classical concerts.

Floralis Genérica

Av Figueroa Alcorta 2263

Behind the Museo Nacional de Bellas Artes lurk the massive Doric columns of the Facultad de Derecho (Law Faculty), next to which it's hard to miss the 25m-high aluminium-and steel bloom named **Floralis Genérica**, one of the city's newer sculptures. Argentine architect **Eduardo Catalano** donated this work to the city as a tribute to all flowers and a symbol of "hope for the country's new spring". A system of light sensors and hydraulics closes the petals at sunset and opens them again at 8am, but they stay open on May 25, September 21 (the beginning of spring), Christmas Eve and New Year's Eve.

Museo Xul Solar

Laprida 1212 • Tues–Fri noon–8pm, Sat noon–7pm; closed Jan • $30 • ⓦ xulsolar.org.ar

The **Museo Xul Solar**, deep in residential Recoleta several blocks northwest of the Cementario de la Recoleta, is housed in the "Fundación Pan Klub", an early twentieth-century townhouse where, for the last twenty years of his life, eccentric Porteño artist Xul Solar (1888–1963) lived. The house was remodelled in the 1990s, and its award-winning design is as exciting as the display of Solar's paintings and other works. The space contains work spanning nearly five decades and is on several different levels,

1

built of timber and glass, each dedicated to a specific period in the artist's career. As well as paintings, there's a set of "Pan Altars", multicoloured mini-retables designed for his "universal religions" – Solar once told Borges that he had "founded twelve new religions since lunch". Other curiosities include a piano whose keyboard he replaced with three rows of painted keys with textured surfaces, created both for blind pianists and to implement his notion of the correspondence of colour and music.

Palermo

Part of subte Line D runs underneath Avenida Santa Fe, one of Palermo's main arteries between Agüero and Carranza. Otherwise, take one of the many buses that also traverse Santa Fe or avenidas Las Heras and Del Libertador, such as #10, #38 or #93

Much of **Palermo**, Buenos Aires' largest barrio, is vibrantly green and appealingly well kempt: ornate balconies overflow with jasmine and roses, grand apartment blocks line wide avenues, and plane trees, palms and jacarandas shade older, cobbled streets; its beautifully landscaped parks, some of the biggest in the world, come alive with locals practising in-line skating, playing football or walking their dogs.

Palermo takes its name from an Italian farmer, Giovanni Palermo, who in 1590 turned these former flood plains into vineyards and orchards. The barrio began to take on its present-day appearance when large parks and gardens were laid out at the end of the nineteenth century; the process of gentrification continued and Palermo is now regarded as a distinctly classy place to live.

Given its sizeable proportions – it stretches all the way from Avenida Coronel Díaz on the border with Recoleta, an area unofficially known as **Barrio Norte**, west to Chacarita, and to Colegiales and Belgrano to the north – it's not surprising that the barrio isn't completely homogeneous. The bit of Palermo around Plaza República de Chile that juts into Recoleta is known as **Palermo Chico** and contains some significant museums such as the **Museo de Arte Latinoamericano de Buenos Aires (MALBA)**, a must for fans of modern art.

About ten blocks west, **Palermo Viejo** is a traditional neighbourhood with lovely old houses along cobbled streets, but it's become such a varied and trendy place, full of funky cafés and avant-garde art galleries, that the area has been unofficially subdivided. The section around Plaza Cortázar is now known as **Palermo Soho**, while across the railway tracks, people in the media work, eat and drink in a cluster of TV studios, restaurants and bars that has been christened **Palermo Hollywood**. Much of north Palermo is taken up by parks, such as the grand **Parque Tres de Febrero**, giving the area its soubriquet the "**Bosques de Palermo**" (Palermo woods). At the barrio's northern edge is **Las Cañitas**, a zone of upmarket bars and restaurants, focused on the corner of Báez and Arévalo.

Museo de Arte Popular José Hernández

Av del Libertador 2373 • Tues–Fri 1–6.30pm, Sat & Sun 10am–7.30pm • $10; free Wed • ⓦ museohernandez.buenosaires.gob.ar

A very different kind of art from that on display at the Museo de Arte Decorativo can be found further along Avenida del Libertador, in a rambling Neocolonial house, home

---

DOG WALKERS

Along the wide avenues and in the many parks of Barrio Norte and Palermo, you'll often be treated to one of Buenos Aires' more characteristic sights: the *paseador de perros*, or professional **dog walkers**. Joggers holding seven or eight prized pedigrees on leashes are surprising enough, but these dilettantes are rightly held in contempt by the beefy specialists who confidently swagger along towed by twenty to thirty dogs. These invariably athletic young men and women are not paid just to take all manner of aristocratic breeds for a stroll, with the inevitable pit stops along the way, but must brush and groom them and look out for signs of ill health; many dog walkers have veterinary training. They perform these vital duties every weekday – the dogs' owners usually manage such chores themselves at the weekend.

1

to the **Museo de Arte Popular José Hernández.** José Hernández wrote the great gaucho classic *Martín Fierro* (1872), a revolutionary epic poem that made *campo* (peasant) culture respectable, and in this vein the museum's purpose is to highlight the value of **popular crafts**, housed in two buildings separated by a shady patio. In the basement of the first building is an impressive but unimaginatively presented display of mostly nineteenth-century rural silverware; spurs, stirrups, saddles, knives and gaucho weaponry stand side by side with a large collection of fine silver *mate* ware. Upstairs, and across the courtyard, changing exhibits of lovingly made crafts such as tablecloths, jewellery and ceramic figures are displayed, many with a strong Catholic influence.

Museo de Arte Latinoamericano de Buenos Aires (MALBA)

Av Figueroa Alcorta 3415 • Mon & Thurs–Sun noon–8pm, Wed noon–9pm • $75; Wed $36 • ⓦ malba.org.ar

One of the city's best museums, the **Museo de Arte Latinoamericano de Buenos Aires (MALBA)**, two blocks north of the Museo de Arte Popular, is housed in a modern, glass-fronted, purpose-built building that is an attraction in its own right; its airy, spacious galleries contrasting with the dark nooks and crannies of the city's more traditional art museums.

The permanent **Costantini collection**, on the first floor up, concentrates on the best Latin American art of the twentieth century. It is arranged chronologically, beginning around 1910, when the Modernist movement in Latin America heralded the start of a real sense of regional identity. This is exemplified in paintings such as a series by Argentine master Xul Solar, a Frida Kahlo self-portrait and Brazilian Tarsila do Amaral's Mexican-influenced *Abaporu*. Dark political undercurrents run through the 1930s to 1950s and the work of Antonio Berni and the Chilean Roberto Matta, while Catholic traditions are given a Surrealist twist in Remedios Varo's votive box *Icono*. Things get more conceptual from the 1960s on, with the moving installations of Julio Le Parc and the LSD-splashed "end of art" collages by the "Nueva Figuración" movement.

Upstairs, temporary exhibitions generally feature the collected works of a prominent modern or contemporary artist. Andy Warhol, Mario Testino and Yayoi Kusama have featured in recent years. MALBA also has its own small arthouse cinema (see website for programme), a great café (daily 9am–9pm), a bookshop and a fun gift shop.

Palermo Viejo

The nearest subte stations to Palermo Viejo are Scalabrini Ortíz and Plaza Italia, on Line D

Palermo Viejo is Buenos Aires' most fashionable place to live, shop or have an evening out. The part of the city most closely linked to Borges, where he lived and began writing poetry in the 1920s, its architecture has changed little since then. Bounded by avenidas Santa Fe, Córdoba, Juan B. Justo and Raúl Scalabrini Ortíz, it's a compact oblong of narrow streets, most of them still cobbled and lined with brightly painted one- or two-storey Neocolonial villas and townhouses, many of them recently restored, some of them hidden behind luxuriant gardens full of bougainvillea and jasmine. Part run-down, part gentrified, it's a leafy district with a laidback bohemian ambience, and many of its stylish houses have been converted into bars, cafés and boutiques. Large communities from Poland, Ukraine, Lebanon and Armenia live here, alongside an Italian contingent and some old Spanish families, and they all have their shops, churches and clubs, adding to the district's colour. The area also boasts a dazzling blend of outstanding **cafés**, serving waffles, burgers and brunch, and has succeeded in luring the city's residents and visitors alike away from more superficial districts such as Puerto Madero and Las Cañitas.

Palermo Viejo's epicentre is **Plaza Inmigrantes de Armenia**, which used to be called Plaza Palermo Viejo, a park-like square dominated by a children's playground, huge lime trees and a crafts fair around its edges at weekends (Sat & Sun 10am–8pm). It vies with nearby **Plaza Serrano** for title of the barrio's most popular cultural and social focal point, whose official name (used on maps but unknown by most taxi drivers) is Plaza Cortázar, after Argentine novelist Julio Cortázar, who frequented this part of the city in the 1960s and

1

PALERMO

0 250
metres

Museo Nacional de Aeronáutica

Aeroparque

AUTOPISTA ARTURO U ILLIA

AVENIDA INTENDENTE CANTILO

Club Alemán de Equitación

AVENIDA DORREGO

Velódromo Municipal

AVENIDA JOSÉ BELISARIO ROLDÁN

AVENIDA PRESIDENTE FIGUEROA ALCORTA

AVENIDA CASARES

Parque Jorge Newbery

Planetario Galileo Galilei

AVENIDA CASARES

AVENIDA ADOLFO BERRO

AVENIDA SARMIENTO

Museo de Arte Popular José Hernández

Plaza Alemania

J.F.SEGUÍ

AVENIDA DEL LIBERTADOR

Monumento a Sarmiento

Jardín Japonés

Tennis Club Argentina

AVENIDA ALSINA

Museo Sívori

Lago de Palermo

Patio Andaluz

Paseo del Rosedal

Parque 3 de Febrero

Monumento de los Españoles

REPÚBLICA DE LA INDIA

Plaza Intendente Seeber

Jardín Zoológico

LAFINUR

CERVIÑO

AVENIDA COLOMBIA

AVENIDA SARMIENTO

Club Gimnasia y Esgrima

AVENIDA INFANTA ISABEL

AVENIDA PRESIDENTE PEDRO MONTT

DARREGUEYRA

J.F.SEGUÍ

DESMARÍA

CERVIÑO

US Embassy

Sociedad Rural Argentina

AVENIDA PRES FIGUEROA ALCORTA

AVENIDA DORREGO

GODOY CRUZ

SINCLAIR

JUNCAL

BERUTI

AVENIDA INTENDENTE BULLRICH

Centro Cultural Islámico Rey Fahd

Campo Hípico Militar

CERVIÑO

Palermo

AUGUSTÍN MÉNDEZ

TORNQUIST

Hipódromo

Argentino

AVENIDA ERNESTO

AVENIDA DEL LIBERTADOR

Campo Argentino de Polo

LAS CAÑITAS

ARÉVALO

HUERGO

Estación Palermo

AVENIDA SANTA FE

CHARCAS

BONPLAND

Buenos Aires Lawn Tennis Club

MIGUELETES

MAURE

OLLEROS

5 DE PALERMO

SOLDADO DE LA INDEPENDENCIA

ORTEGA Y GASSET

ARCE

BÁEZ

SANTOS DUMONT

AVENIDA CHENAUT

AVENIDA DORREGO

L. M. CAMPOS

Carranza

CONCEPCIÓN ARENAL

AJ CARRANZA

DR EMILIO RAVIGNANI

AV VALENTÍN ALSINA

MIGUELETES

MAURE

11 TEMATIĒNZ

AV. LUIS MARÍA CAMPOS

GOROSTIAGA

1º DE SEPTIEMBRE

3 DE FEBRERO

AVENIDA CABILDO

JORGE NEWBERY

TTE. BENJAMÍN MATIENZO

BELGRANO

MIGUELETES

VIRREY LORETO

ZABALA

AVENIDA VIRREY VÉRTIZ

TEODORO GARCÍA

AV. FEDERICO LACROZE

Amauta

Australian Embassy

CIUDAD DE LA PAZ

ZAPATA

AMENÁBAR

OLLEROS

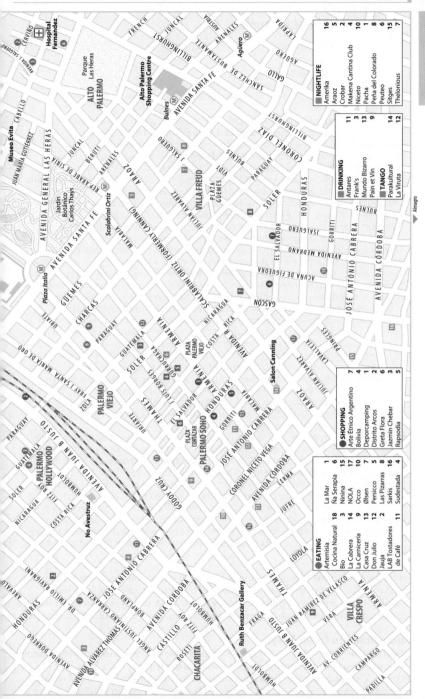

1

NIGHTLIFE	
Amerika	16
Araoz	5
Crobar	2
Makena Cantina Club	4
Niceto	10
Pacha	1
Peña del Colorado	8
Peuteo	6
Sitges	15
Thelonious	7

DRINKING	
Antares	11
Frank's	3
Mundo Bizarro	13
Pain et Vin	9

TANGO	
Parakultural	14
La Viruta	12

SHOPPING	
Arte Étnico Argentino	7
Bolivia	4
Deporcamping	1
Distrito Arcos	2
Greta Flora	6
Jazmín Chebar	3
Rapsodia	5

EATING	
Artemisia	1
Cocina Natural	18
Bio	3
La Cabrera	14
La Carnicería	6
Casa Cruz	13
Don Julio	12
Jauja	2
LAB Tostadores de Café	16
La Mar	15
Na Serapia	17
Ninina	10
NOLA	7
Occo	8
Ølsen	9
Persicco	3
Las Pizarras	11
Sarkis	4
Sudestada	

▶ Almagro

1

BORGES AND BUENOS AIRES

This city that I believed was my past,
is my future, my present;
the years I have spent in Europe are an illusion,
I always was (and will be) in Buenos Aires.

Jorge Luis Borges, "Arrabal", from Fervor de Buenos Aires (1921)

There's no shortage of literary works inspired by Argentina's capital city, but no writer has written so passionately about it as **Jorge Luis Borges**. Though he was born in the heart of Buenos Aires, in 1898, it was the city's humbler barrios that most captivated Borges' imagination. His early childhood was spent in **Palermo**, now a more upmarket neighbourhood that was somewhat marginal at the start of the twentieth century. Borges' middle-class family inhabited one of the few two-storey houses on their street, **Calle Serrano** (now officially renamed Calle J. L. Borges in Palermo Viejo), and, though his excursions were strictly controlled, from behind the garden wall Borges observed the colourful street life that was kept tantalizingly out of his reach. In particular, his attention was caught by men who gathered to drink and play cards in the local *almacén* (a store-cum-bar) on his street corner. With their tales of knife fights and air of lawlessness, these men appeared time and again in Borges' early short stories, and, later, in *Doctor Brodie's Report*, a collection published in 1970.

Borges' writing talent surfaced at a precocious age: at 6 he wrote his first short story, and when he was 11, *El País* newspaper published his translation of Oscar Wilde's *The Happy Prince*. However, it was not until he returned from Europe in 1921, where he had been stranded with his family during World War I, that Borges published his first book, *Fervor de Buenos Aires*, a collection of **poems** that attempted to capture the essence of the city. Enthused by his re-encounter with Buenos Aires at an age at which he was free to go where he wanted, Borges set out to explore the marginal corners of the city. His wanderings took him to the outlying barrios and poorer areas of the city centre with their tenement buildings and bars frequented by prostitutes. With the notable exception of La Boca, which he appears to have regarded as too idiosyncratic – and, perhaps, too obviously picturesque – Borges felt greatest affection for the **south** of Buenos Aires. His exploration of the area that he regarded as representing the heart of the city took in not only the traditional houses of San Telmo and Monserrat, with their patios and decorative facades, but also the humbler streets of Barracas, a largely industrial working-class neighbourhood, and Constitución, where, in a gloomy basement in Avenida Juan de Garay, he set one of his most famous short stories, *El Aleph*.

For a writer as sensitive to visual subtlety as Borges – many of his early poems focus on the city's atmospheric evening light – it seems particularly tragic that he should have gone virtually blind in his 50s. Nonetheless, from 1955 to 1973, Borges was **Director of the National Library**, then located in Monserrat, where his pleasure at being surrounded by books – even if he could no longer read them – was heightened by the fact that his daily journey to work took him through one of his favourite parts of the city, from his apartment in Maipú along pedestrianized Florida. As Borges' fame grew, he spent considerable periods of time away from Argentina, though he claimed always to return to Buenos Aires in his dreams. Borges died in 1986 in Geneva, and is buried in Plainpalais cemetery. Borges pilgrims in Buenos Aires will find a commemorative plaque at no. 2108 on Calle Serrano, inscribed with a stanza from his *Mythical Foundation of Buenos Aires*.

set his Surrealist novel *Hopscotch* (see p.566) here. Its centre also hosts a weekend crafts fair (Sat & Sun 10am–8pm), and is surrounded by trattorias, cafés and bars, some doubling as arts centres and galleries. Among them, a rash of independent designer shops sell upmarket bohemian clothes, jewellery and furnishings – hence the **Soho** nickname.

Jardín Botánico Carlos Thays

Av Santa Fe 3951 • Tues–Fri 8am–6.45pm, Sat & Sun 9.30am–6.45pm; closes 5.45pm in winter • Free • ⓦ buenosaires.gob.ar/jardinbotanico

The entrance to Buenos Aires' charming **botanical garden** is at Plaza Italia, east of Palermo Viejo and near the Plaza Italia subte station. Established at the end of the nineteenth century, the layout was completed by Charles Thays in 1902 and is now

1

named after the ubiquitous landscape artist (see p.87). He divided the garden into distinct areas representing the regions of Argentina and further afield. Most trees are labelled with their Latin and common names, as well as where they are found.

Zoo Buenos Aires

Sarmiento and Las Heras • Daily 10am–6pm • $190, free for under-12s and pensioners • ⓦ zoobuenosaires.com.ar

Just over the road from the botanical garden, Buenos Aires' **zoo** offers the chance to see a variety of South American fauna close up, including the four native camelids (guanacos, llamas, vicuñas and alpacas), as well as condors, *maras* ("Patagonian hares", actually a type of rodent) and capybaras. It was also landscaped by Thays, and its monumental pavilions and cages, built around 1905, include a fabulous replica of the temple to the goddess Lakshmi in Mumbai, a Chinese temple, a Byzantine portico and a Japanese pagoda. Borges fondly wrote that the zoo "smelled of toffee and tiger", a description that still holds true. The zoo fell into disrepute in 2012 when its polar bear died from overheating; it is still looking into improving welfare standards.

Outside the zoo, traditional **mateos** (horse and carriages), decorated with the ribbons and swirls of *filete* art (see box, p.80), cart off the romantically minded on trips around Palermo's parks.

Museo Evita

Lafinur 2988 • Tues–Sun 11am–7pm • $50 • ⓦ museoevita.org

For many Argentines, the **Museo Evita**, opened in 2003, was a long time coming. Located a block east from the zoo, in an attractive early twentieth-century building that was once a hotel, it was bought in 1948 by Evita's Social Aid Foundation to be set up as emergency temporary accommodation for homeless families. The well-laid-out museum traces Evita's life and passions, as well as the daily life of the families who were given shelter here, with helpful info sheets in English in each room. Despite its uncritical stance and glossing over of the less salubrious facts in Evita's life, such as her Nazi sympathies, the museum has some interesting pieces, including magazines featuring her when she was Eva Duarte the radio star, and videos of the extraordinary scenes in the city after she died. A small space on the ground floor is given over to minor temporary exhibitions, while – with a separate entrance next door – an excellent **restaurant** serves top-notch meals best taken on the patio.

Parque Tres de Febrero and around

Avenidas Libertador and Sarmiento

Parque Tres de Febrero is one of the biggest and most popular parks in the city, a wonderful place to stroll on a sunny afternoon. Another Palermo fixture designed by Thays, it was originally envisioned by President Sarmiento, who believed that parks were a civilizing influence and wanted something for Buenos Aires that would be on the scale of New York's Central Park or London's Hyde Park. With its beautifully tended trees, lawns and patios dotted with sculptures, it's at its most serene during the week. Although the wide pathways running along the banks of the boating lake become rather crowded with joggers, cyclists and in-line skaters at weekends and on public holidays, that's also the time to see Porteños at play. You'll see typical scenes of families drinking *mate* under the shade of palms or rubber trees, but perhaps also less expected sights, such as tai chi classes.

The park's features include an **Andalucian patio**, decorated with vibrant ceramic tiles and donated by the city of Seville, and a **Rosedal** (rose garden) that showcases new and colourful varieties of the flower.

Planetario Galileo Galilei

Av Sarmiento close to c/Iraola • Tues–Fri 9am–5pm, Sat & Sun 11.30am–7pm • $50 • ⓦ planetario.gob.ar

The far northeastern tip of Parque Tres de Febrero, at Avenida Sarmiento, serves as the setting for the UFO-shaped **Planetario Galileo Galilei**. In the entrance hall you can see

1

WALKING TOURS OF BUENOS AIRES

The tourism secretariat organizes **free walking tours** (English and Spanish), usually focusing on a particular barrio or theme, such as Evita, Gardel, modern art, or the pope – check online for the monthly schedule (Ⓦturismo.buenosaires.gob.ar). **ANDA tours** (Ⓦandatravel.com.ar) organizes responsible-tourism visits with a difference, which include stop-offs at community organizations, while **Buenos Tours** (Ⓦbuenostours.com) offers private guided walkabouts. **Buenos Aires Cultural Concierge** (Ⓦbaculturalconcierge.com) deals in specialist tours such as Jewish Heritage or Cool Architecture. If you're in Buenos Aires for a flying visit, opt in to one of these specialist walking tours to capture the city's essence in a heartbeat:

Circuito Papal Ⓦturismo.buenosaires.gob.ar. Taking in Monserrat or Flores barrios, the city government's pope tour follows the trail of Francis, visiting his barber shop, churches and childhood hangouts. Tues 3pm; in Spanish. Free.

Foto Ruta ☎011 15 6030 8881, Ⓦfoto-ruta.com. Instagram fans will love this interactive tour that teaches you tricks of the photography trade then puts them into practice by snapping BA's architectural gems. Four tours daily; in English. US$95.

Graffiti Mundo ☎011 15 3683 3219, Ⓦgraffitimundo.com. The city's original street art tour explains the artists and political messages behind the work

before stopping off at its very own graffiti gallery, Galería Union (Costa Rica 5829, Ⓦgaleriaunion.com). Daily; in English. US$25.

Parrilla Tour ☎011 15 5808 9687, Ⓦparrillatour.com. This "meat and greet" introduces three traditional steakhouses in Palermo or San Telmo. Daily, lunch or dinner; in English. US$69.

Shop Hop Ⓦshop-buenosaires.com. Personal shopper Sophie Lloyd creates bespoke shopping tours at off-the-radar boutiques and stores depending on your need for leather, accessories, craft wares, or something else. Daily; in English. From US$155.

an alarmingly huge metal meteorite, discovered in the Chaco in the 1960s (see p.272), and in the evenings from around 7pm (weather permitting) local astronomy enthusiasts cluster around telescopes to peer at the night sky. Shows such as "Cosmic Collisions," a visually appealing video, take place daily ($50).

Jardín Japonés

Casares 2966 • Daily 10am–6pm • $50 • Ⓦjardinjapones.org.ar

To the east of the park, and with its own entrance on Plaza de la República Islámica de Irán, the **Jardín Japonés** was donated to the city by Buenos Aires' small Japanese community in 1979 and contains beautifully landscaped gardens, including a bonsai section, a lake of huge koi carp, and a temple-like café. It is at its best in the springtime, when the almond trees are in blossom and the azaleas are out.

Monumento de los Españoles

Av Del Libertador and Sarmiento

The busy rotunda to the park's southeast is taken up by the most glorious monument in the city, the **Monumento de los Españoles**, whose fine bronze sculptures symbolize the Andes, the Chaco, the Pampas and the Río de la Plata. Its allegorical figures, including the dainty angel at the top, are sculpted from Carrara marble.

Belgrano

Belgrano can be reached via the subte Line D (Juramento stop), or by train from Retiro (stops Belgrano C or Belgrano R)

North of Palermo, leafy **Belgrano** is largely residential, apart from the lively shopping streets on either side of its main artery, Avenida Cabildo. Named after General Manuel Belgrano (see p.531), hero of Argentina's struggle for independence, it was founded as a separate town in 1855. Over the next decade or two lots of wealthy Porteños built their summer or weekend homes here, and it was incorporated into Buenos Aires during the city's whirlwind expansion in the 1880s. Many Anglo-Argentines settled in the barrio in those years, and it became popular with the city's sizeable Jewish community in the 1950s. More recently, Taiwanese and Korean immigrants have settled in **Barrio Chino**, Buenos Aires' small Chinatown, which stretches along Arribeños between Juramento and Olazába. The central part of the barrio is known as **Belgrano C**, whose nucleus lies at the junction of avenidas Cabildo and Justamento. As well as stores, cafés and galleries, there's a clutch of minor museums here.

Museo de Arte Español Enrique Larreta

Juramento 2291 • Mon–Fri 1–7pm, Sat & Sun 10am–8pm • $10, free Thurs • ⓦ buenosaires.gob.ar/museolarreta • Juramento subte

The **Museo de Arte Español Enrique Larreta**, located in a well-restored, whitewashed colonial building, is home to a priceless collection of **Spanish art** amassed by an aristocratic Uruguayan exile, **Enrique Larreta**. From around 1900 to 1916, Larreta spent many of his days in Spain; during that time he visited churches and monasteries, buying up artworks for his Belgrano home, most of them from the Renaissance – statues and paintings of saints, but also furniture, porcelain, silverware and tapestries, all of which are displayed in this house, which he bequeathed to the city.

El Monumental

Av Pte Figueroa Alcorta 7597 • **Museum** Daily 10am–7pm; closes early on match days • $115 • **Tours** Daily, hourly 10am–5pm; 1hr • $150 (includes entry) • ⓦ cariverplate.com.ar/museo-river

The huge concrete stands of **El Monumental**, the country's largest sporting stadium, rise up on the eastern edge of Belgrano, on the border with residential barrio Nuñez. Home to Boca Juniors' bitter rivals, **River Plate** football club, it was remodelled for the 1978 World Cup and can seat 70,000. Matches at the Monumental (see p.38) are a glorious riot of red and white shirts, banners and streamers.

River has its own **museum**, an audiovisual experience that makes every effort to be bigger and better than the Boca museum in the Bombonera (see p.82), although it's less tourist-friendly – both the tour and museum are in Spanish only. Highlights are a "time machine" that takes you through a tunnel relating the history of the club through the twentieth century, with plenty of fascinating historical and cultural context, and era-appropriate TVs showing River's greatest goals. On site there is also a comprehensive souvenir shop, and a surprisingly upmarket café.

Zona Norte

Immediately surrounding the city limits as you cross the Avenida General Paz ring road, the Capital Federal spreads into greater Buenos Aires. Largely residential, the most appealing suburbs are those to the city's north – the **Zona Norte**, an affluent suburban world of riverine villas where the subtropical heart that lies beneath Buenos Aires' European veneer starts to show through. Most worth visiting is San Isidro, which preserves a village-like charm and historic quarter that can be accessed via the Tren de la Costa (see box, p.136) or taxi (about $250).

The west

West of central Buenos Aires a vast, mostly residential area spreads out for over a dozen kilometres towards Avenida General Paz. Sights here are scattered; perhaps the neighbourhoods' greatest appeal lies in their relative lack of tourists, offering a prize glimpse into the lives of ordinary working- and middle-class Porteños. Architecture fans shouldn't miss the stunning **Palacio de las Aguas Corrientes** in the barrio of **Balvanera**, the neighbourhood just south of Recoleta. Northwest of Palermo, the barrio of **Chacarita** is best known for its namesake **cemetery**, where tango singer Carlos Gardel is buried. **Caballito**, right in the heart of the city, has an entertaining natural

1

history museum and old-fashioned indoor food market selling fresh produce. Finally, right at Buenos Aires' fringes, the hugely enjoyable gaucho fair – the **Feria de Mataderos** – is quite simply one of the best days out in the city.

Balvanera

Balvanera is well connected to the subte network; get off at Plaza de Miserere on lines A or H, or Corrientes on lines B or H

Just west of the city centre, **Balvanera** is a commercial, somewhat downmarket barrio, home to many of the city's recent South American immigrants. It has two focal points: **Once**, a noisy shopping area around the Once (de Septiembre) train station, traditionally patronized by the city's less-well-heeled Jewish community and a good place to pick up bargains, including football shirts, reggaeton CDs and carnival gear; and **Abasto**, focused on the enormous Abasto food market turned shopping mall (see p.123).

Palacio de las Aguas Corrientes

Avenidas Córdoba and Riobamba • **Museum** Mon–Fri 9am–1pm • Free

Other than shopping, the main point of interest in Balvanera is the spectacular **Palacio de las Aguas Corrientes**, right on the Recoleta border. Every bit as palatial as the name suggests, it has been described quite accurately as a cross between London's Victoria and Albert Museum and the Uffizi in Florence. Somewhat incongruously, it is home to twelve giant tanks that supplied Buenos Aires with water from 1894 until 1978. An impressive feat of engineering, it was planned and built in Europe, down to the glazed coloured ceramics that dot the facade, all manufactured by Royal Doulton of London, but painted in Buenos Aires. Inside, a small museum explains the building's history.

Chacarita

Dominated by railway lines, **Chacarita** takes its name from the days when the barrio was home to a small farm (*chacra*) run by Jesuits. Nowadays, the neighbourhood is synonymous with the enormous **Cementerio de Chacarita**.

Cementerio de Chacarita

Av Guzmán 780 • Daily 7am–6pm • $100 • Federico Lacroze subte, line B

Less aristocratic than Recoleta's cemetery, but impressive nonetheless, the **Cementerio de Chacarita** contains the city's other most-visited tomb, that of **Carlos Gardel** (see box, p.560). Lying at the northern end of Avenida Corrientes, with the monumental main entrance on Avenida Guzmán, the cemetery covers a good third of the barrio; at one square kilometre, it's Argentina's largest. Immediately facing the entrance, a section of grand mausoleums comes quite close to the Baroque splendour of Recoleta.

Gardel's tomb

By far the best sight in the cemetery is **Gardel's tomb**, on the corner of calles 6 and 33, a brisk five-minute walk to the left of the entrance and a little towards the middle. It is topped by a life-sized statue of the great tango singer in typical rakish pose: hand in pocket, hair slicked back and with characteristic wide grin. Every inch of the surrounding stonework is plastered with plaques of gratitude and flowers placed there by the singer's devotees. There is a pilgrimage to his graveside every year on the anniversary of his death (June 24). Many visitors light a cigarette and place it in the hand of the statue; you will often see a dog-end still dangling between his index and middle fingers.

Caballito

An unassuming, mostly middle-class barrio, **Caballito** lies at the very centre of the metropolis. Narrow Plaza Primera Junta, on Line A of the subte, is the barrio's core, while Avenida Rivadavia, flanked by high-rise apartment blocks and shopping malls, runs east–west through it.

Museo Argentino de Ciencias Naturales

Angel Gallardo 490 • Daily 2–7pm • $15 • Ⓦ www.macn.secyt.gov.ar

Caballito's main attraction is the natural science museum, the **Museo Argentino de Ciencias Naturales**, in the circular Parque del Centenario. The museum is of note for its impressive **paleontological** collection, with many specimens from Argentina – you can see a spiky-necked amargasaurus from Neuquén and a 15m patagosaurus sauropod from Chubút. There is also a host of the later **megafauna** – giant herbivorous mammals that evolved in South America when the region broke away from other continents – such as giant sloths and creepy glyptodonts, a forerunner of today's armadillo. These megafauna were wiped out around three million years ago, after South America reconnected with North America and more successful fauna such as the sabre-toothed tiger and, later, humans arrived.

Mataderos

Lying just inside the boundary of Capital Federal, around 6km southwest of Caballito, **Mataderos** is a barrio with a gory past. For many years, people came to Mataderos to drink the fresh blood of animals killed in the numerous slaughterhouses from which the area takes its name, in the belief that this would cure illnesses such as tuberculosis. The slaughterhouses have long gone, but Mataderos is still home to the **Mercado de Liniers**, better known as the livestock cattle auction (Ⓦ mercadodeliniers.com.ar), whose faded pink walls and arcades provide the backdrop for one of Buenos Aires' most fabulous weekend events, the **Feria de Mataderos** (see box below).

ARRIVAL AND DEPARTURE   BUENOS AIRES

Buenos Aires is well served by numerous international and domestic **flights**. It is also a transport hub for the rest of the country, with frequent daily **bus** services to and from most towns and cities. Limited **train** services join the capital to the provinces, while fast and slow **ferries** cross the Río de la Plata to neighbouring Uruguay (see box, p.104).

BY PLANE

For airport enquiries, call ☎ 011 5480 6111.

EZEIZA AIRPORT

All international flights, with the exception of a few from neighbouring countries, arrive 22km southwest of the city centre at Ministro Pistarini Airport or – as everyone calls it – Ezeiza, in reference to the outlying neighbourhood in which it is situated. In comparison with some Latin American airports, arriving at Ezeiza is relatively stress-free: touting for taxis is banned inside the airport, and the tourist information stand (daily 8am–8pm) has good information on accommodation in the city. Change a little money here, either at privately run exchange booths strategically placed before you exit Arrivals or in the small branch of Banco Nación in the

FERIA DE MATADEROS

The Sunday **Feria de Mataderos** (Lisandro de la Torre & Av de los Corrales, 11am–sunset; Ⓦ feriademataderos.com.ar; buses #55, #92 & #141) is a celebration of Argentina's rural traditions. This busy fair attracts thousands of locals and tourists for its blend of folk music, traditional crafts and regional food such as *locro*, empanadas and *tortas fritas*, mouthwatering fried cakes. You can also try your hand at regional dances such as the *chamamé* and *chacarera*. The undoubted highpoint, however, is the display of **gaucho skills** in which riders participate in events such as the *sortija*, in which, galloping at breakneck speed and standing rigid in their stirrups, they attempt to spear a small ring strung on a ribbon. Take cash – artisan wares here are good quality and often cheaper than in the central stores, but stallholders do not accept credit cards. In February, the fair takes place from 6pm on Saturday evenings instead of on Sunday.

1

TRIPS TO URUGUAY FROM BUENOS AIRES

From Buenos Aires, it's easy to reach the Portuguese colonial historic town of **Colonia del Sacramento** in Uruguay (4–5 daily; 55min–2hr 45min) or visit pleasant **Montevideo**, the capital of Argentina's *rioplatense* neighbour (5 daily; 2hr 35min). Both destinations are served by Buquebus, whose ferries and catamarans leave from Dársena Norte in Puerto Madero (☎011 4317 4100, ⊚buquebus.com), while Colonia Express (☎011 4316 6500, ⊚coloniaexpress.com) also reaches **Punta del Este** and **Piriápolis** (both 3 daily; 2hr with bus) in summer, departing from the less swanky Dársena Sur terminal, near La Boca.

Note that, while Dársena Norte is within walking distance of downtown, the route involves negotiating a rather bewildering skein of busy roads and overgrown rail-tracks, so taking a taxi is advisable. The #140 bus, which goes through west Palermo, stops a block away. Dársena Sur is located near an underpass, so taking a taxi is strongly recommended.

To the east of Buenos Aires, boats cross the Río de la Plata to the small **Isla Martín García**, an Argentine territory in Uruguayan waters. Once used as a penal colony, it is now mostly given over to a nature reserve (visits via Cacciola Viajes in Tigre; ☎011 4749 0931, ⊚cacciolaviajes.com).

arrivals hall; they all use the official rate. Change most of your money in the city, if you can. ATMs are also available (again, you will get the official rate).

Taxis and remises If you want to take a taxi or *remís* (radio cab) into the city (around $450), ask at one of the official taxi/*remís* stands immediately outside the arrivals exit. It may be worth comparing prices. Unofficial taxi drivers congregate outside the terminal (they are not allowed inside) and, while these offer cheaper rates – as low as half the *remís* rate – they tend to be less secure and scams of various descriptions have been reported, so they are best avoided, especially by first-time visitors with no Spanish.

Express buses Buses are operated by Manuel Tienda León (☎011 4314 3636, ⊚tiendaleon.com). Running non-stop between Ezeiza and the centre every 30min during the day and hourly at night, these shuttles cost $175 and take approximately 50min (longer during rush hour), making them fair value for solo travellers. They drop you at the company's main terminal at San Martín and Av Madero in Retiro barrio; you can get a transfer from there to anywhere downtown or within the inner barrios with one of their taxis. If you are transferring to a domestic flight (some destinations also leave from Ezeiza; check first), you could get a Manuel Tienda León bus ($75; 9am–midnight) to the Aeroparque Metropolitano Jorge Newbery. If you are staying in a part of the city near the domestic airport, such as Palermo or Belgrano, you might consider using this service and taking a taxi for the final stretch. Finally, there's the local bus #8 ($7 with a SUBE card, $14 without), which runs between Ezeiza and Boca, entering the city via Rivadavia and continuing past Congreso, Plaza de Mayo and San Telmo; it takes at least 2hr, and leaves frequently beyond the entrance to the airport. Ensure you have change for ticket machines, as notes are not accepted, and be warned that the buses can become very full (not advisable if you have lots of luggage) and obvious tourists may be perceived as easy targets by pickpockets.

AEROPARQUE

Buenos Aires' other airport is Aeroparque Metropolitano Jorge Newbery, usually known as Aeroparque, on the Costanera Norte, around 6km north of the city centre. Most domestic flights and some flights from Brazil and Uruguay arrive here. Manuel Tienda Léon also runs a bus shuttle service from here to the centre ($75; 9am–midnight); a taxi will set you back about $100 (again, it's better to go with an official, booked car rather than take one from the rank outside), or you could catch the local bus ($6.50; the #33 will take you to Paseo Colón, the #45 down 9 de Julio and the #160 near Palermo Soho). The Ar Bus shuttle (⊚arbus.com.ar) runs between the airport to Retiro bus station, Microcentro ($45; Carlos Pellegrini & Lavalle), Alto Palermo shopping mall and Belgrano ($45; Av Maipú & Zufriategui). Aeroparque also has a tourist information booth (daily 8am–8pm).

Destinations Bariloche (up to 10 daily; 2hr 20min); Catamarca (1 daily; 2hr 30min); Córdoba (10 daily; 1hr 15min); Corrientes (1 daily; 1hr 20min); El Calafate (5 daily; 3hr 20min); Formosa (2 daily; 1hr 45min); Jujuy (2 daily; 2hr 15min); La Rioja (1 daily; 1hr 55min); Mar del Plata (3 daily; 1hr); Mendoza (up to 14 daily; 1hr 50min); Neuquén (6 daily; 1hr 55min); Posadas (2 daily; 1hr 30min); Puerto Iguazú (10 daily; 1hr 50min); Puerto Madryn (5 weekly; 1hr 50min); Resistencia (3 daily; 1hr 30min); Río Gallegos (3 daily; 3hr 15min); Salta (7 daily; 2hr); San Juan (3 daily; 1hr 55min); San Luis (2 daily; 1hr 30min); San Martín de los Andes (5 weekly; 2hr 20min); San Rafael (1 daily; 1hr 50min); Santiago del Estero (2 daily; 1hr 40min); Trelew (3 daily; 2hr); Tucumán (4 daily; 1hr 55min); Ushuaia (4 daily; 3hr 40min).

AIRLINES

Aerolíneas Argentinas, Perú 2 ☎011 4340 2000 or ☎0810 222 86527; Air Canada, Av Córdoba 656 ☎011 4327 3640; Air France, San Martín 334, 23rd floor ☎011 4317 4711; Alitalia,

Suipacha 1111, 28th floor ☎0810 777 2548; American Airlines, Santa Fe 881 ☎011 4318 1111; Andes, Av Córdoba 673, 4th floor ☎011 5237 2803; Avianca, Carlos Pellegrini 1163, 4th floor ☎011 4394 5990; British Airways, Viamonte 570, 1st floor ☎0800 222 0075; Delta, Reconquista 737, 2nd floor ☎0800 666 0133; Gol ☎0810 266 3131; Iberia, Carlos Pellegrini 1163, 1st floor ☎011 4131 1000; KLM, San Martín 344 ☎0880 122 3014; LADE, Perú 710 ☎011 5129 9001; LAN, Cerrito 866 ☎0810 999 9526; Lufthansa, Marcelo T. de Alvear 590, 6th floor ☎011 4319 0600; Qantas, Av Madero 900, 27th floor ☎011 4114 5800; Sol ☎0810 444 4765; South African Airways, Pellegrini 1141, 5th floor ☎011 5556 6666; TAM, Cerrito 1030 ☎0800 333 3333; United Airlines, Pellegrini 527 ☎0810 777 8648.

BY BUS

Retiro terminal If you are travelling to Buenos Aires by bus from other points in Argentina, or on international services from neighbouring countries, you will arrive at Buenos Aires' huge long-distance bus terminal (☎011 4310 0700, ⓦtebasa.com.ar), Terminal de Retiro, located in the barrio of that name at the corner of Av Antártida and Ramos Mejía. There are decent if pricey facilities at the terminal, including toilets, shops, cafés and left luggage, though the general ambience is a little seedy. Retiro is centrally placed and it's not a strenuous walk from hotels in the Florida/Retiro area of the city, although at night this is not recommended – a shantytown is next door and robberies are common.

Taxis Black and yellow taxis are plentiful and Retiro subte station is two blocks away, outside the adjoining train station (see below).

Local buses Dozens of local buses or colectivos leave from stands along Ramos Mejía, though actually finding the one you want might be a rather daunting first taste of local bus transport. Buses #5 or #50 will take you to Congreso and that section of Avenida de Mayo, a fairly promising hunting ground for accommodation, so ideal if you haven't booked ahead.

Information If you are departing from Retiro, check the comprehensive website (ⓦretiro.com.ar) for companies, destinations and timetables. You can then call individual companies to make a reservation. Alternatively, visit the terminal itself, where the 150 or so companies all have conveniently numbered ticket booths and there is a useful information desk. These long-distance buses, called *micros*, offer *servicio semi-cama* or slightly reclining seats; *ejecutivo* is a more comfortable if slightly more expensive option. Depending on the distance, a snack or hot meal and sparkling wine is part of the package.

Destinations All major and minor cities across Argentina are served, with buses leaving hourly to popular destinations such as Córdoba, Mar del Plata, Mendoza and Rosario. International destinations such as Asunción (Paraguay), Lima (Peru), Rio de Janeiro (Brazil) and Santiago de Chile (Chile) also depart on a daily basis.

BY TRAIN

Few tourists arrive in Buenos Aires by train these days; although plans are afoot to reinstate long-distance services (possibly with high-speed connections), currently most trains are suburban only. The main exceptions are trains from the Atlantic coast and some towns in Buenos Aires Province, such as Tandil or Azul – which arrive at Constitución in the south of the city, at General Hornos 11 (Ferrobaires ☎0810 666 8736, ⓦferrobaires.gba.gov.ar) – and trains from Rosario – which arrive at Retiro, on Av Ramos Mejía (SOFSE ☎0800 222 8736, ⓦsofse.gob.ar). Both terminals have subte stations and are served by numerous local bus routes.

Destinations La Plata (every 30min; 1hr); Mar del Plata (3 weekly; 6hr 10min); Rosario (1 daily; 6hr 20min).

INFORMATION AND TOURS

INFORMATION

Tourist kiosks The city has numerous tourist kiosks; staff have some specialist knowledge and can provide maps and a few leaflets. The most central one is just off the Plaza de Mayo at Av Diagonal Roque Sáenz Peña and Florida (Mon–Fri 10am–6pm, Sat & Sun 9am–6pm). There are other kiosks at Plaza San Martín at Florida and Marcelo T. de Alvear (Mon–Fri 10am–5pm, Sat & Sun 9am–6pm); Retiro bus terminal, at c/10 local 83 (daily 7.30am–2.30pm); in Recoleta, at Quintana 596, near the cemetery (Mon–Fri 10am–5pm, Sat & Sun 9am–6pm); and in Puerto Madero, by Dock 4 (Mon–Fri 10am–5pm, Sat & Sun 9am–6pm). Also check out the office run by the tourism ministry at Santa Fe 883, or call its information line (☎011 4313 0187; daily 7.30am–7pm; English spoken). For emergency assistance, call the tourism police free on ☎0800 999 5000 or visit Av Corrientes 436.

Websites Visit the city's comprehensive website for ideas of where to go and what to do (ⓦturismo.buenosaires .gob.ar); the national tourism ministry's website is also insightful (ⓦargentina.travel).

English-language information A great source of English-language information is the daily *Buenos Aires Herald* newspaper (ⓦbuenosairesherald.com). Also check out The Bubble (ⓦbubblear.com), an online platform providing a lighter-hearted take on current affairs.

Maps If you are planning to stay a while and travel by public transport, a combined street map and bus atlas such as *Guía "T"* is a useful accessory. It's widely available from central kiosks and occasionally, at knockdown prices, from hawkers on the buses or trains. You can find an excellent city map online at ⓦmapa.buenosaires.gob.ar.

1

GETTING AROUND

Buenos Aires may seem like a daunting city to get around, but it's actually served by an extensive, inexpensive and generally efficient **public transport** service – albeit not the world's cleanest, quietest or most modern. The easiest part of this system to come to grips with is undoubtedly the underground rail system, or **subte**, which serves the city centre, the north and the west of the city. You may also want to familiarize yourself with a few bus routes, as **buses** are the only form of public transport that serves the outlying barrios. However, as **taxis** are plentiful and relatively cheap, you'll likely find them the most convenient means to get around.

THE SUBTE

Buenos Aires' underground rail system, or subte (see box below), is reasonably efficient and the quickest way to get from the centre to outlying points such as Caballito, Plaza Italia (Palermo) or Chacarita, though the trains vary from grubby old hand-me-downs to brand-new with the a/c blasting. The main flaw in the subte's design is that it's shaped like a fork, meaning journeys across town involve going down one "prong" and changing at least once before heading back up to your final destination. However, the new east–west line H was recently completed, as were line B extensions that make travelling more efficient (see map, p.109).

Lines Using the subte is straightforward. There are six lines, plus a "premetro" system which serves the far southwestern corner of the city, linking up with the subte at the end of line E. Lines A, B, D and E run from the city centre outwards, while line C, which runs north–south between Retiro and Constitución, connects them all. Line H is a new east–west line that starts at Las Heras and ends west at Hospitales. Check the name of the last station on the line you are travelling on to ensure you're heading in the right direction; directions to station platforms are given by this final destination.

Tickets Tickets are purchased from *boleterías* (ticket booths) at each station. A single trip (*viaje*) ticket ($7.50) will take you anywhere on the system. If you'll be in the city a while, it's worth investing in a "SUBE" magnetic card, which costs $30 from kiosks (w sube.gob.ar). Charge it with cash in advance then use it on the subte and buses, saving you the hassle of finding the correct change.

BUSES

Peak hours aside, when traffic is increasingly gridlocked, Buenos Aires' **buses** (colectivos) are the best way of reaching outlying barrios for those on a limited budget. Unfortunately, they are also noisy, prone to belching out clouds of exhaust smoke and driven with scant regard for traffic laws – standing, or even sitting, can be an ordeal, and is certainly an experience. Don't expect the driver to be helpful if you're not sure where you're going, wait for you to sit down before accelerating, or wait to stop before opening doors. From a visitor's point of view, possibly the most daunting thing about bus travel in BA is the sheer number of routes – almost two hundred wend their way around the vast capital. Invest in a combined street and bus-route map (see p.105), however, and you shouldn't have too much trouble.

Metrobus Metrobus lanes, constructed in 2013, have helped to ease public transport in central BA significantly. While the buses themselves are the same, allocating them separate lanes has made a big difference to transport times along key avenues such as 9 de Julio, Cabildo and Juan B. Justo; for instance, you can now get from the Obelisco to San Telmo (along 9 de Julio) in seven minutes. Check online (w buenosaires.gob.ar/movilidad/metrobus) to find out where new routes are planned, as construction continues. Buses run day and night.

Tickets Trips within the city cost between $6 and $6.50; once beyond the centre and into Gran Buenos Aires, fares increase slightly. Porteños spent years scrabbling around for coins to pay, but using a SUBE card is now commonplace. If you insist on using cash, note that machines only accept coins.

Bus tours The city government runs daily bus routes (w buenosairesbus.com) with audio in English and other languages, beginning in Roque Sáenz Peña and Suipacha (8.40am–7pm, every 20min; 3hr) and stopping at various points of interest, such as Monserrat, Boca, the Reserva Ecológica and the Rosedal in Palermo. It costs $260 per day or $350 for two days and you can get on and off as many times as

---

SUBTE HERITAGE

Inaugurated in 1913, Buenos Aires' **subte** (short for *subterráneo*) is the oldest in the Spanish-speaking world. And it shows: many of the stations along renovated Line A, which runs between Plaza de Mayo and the residential neighbourhood of Flores, are beautifully decorated with tile murals, depicting anything from famous battles to Gaudí masterpieces. Perú station, on Avenida de Mayo, is straight out of the early twentieth century, complete with Victorian lamps and adverts for long-gone products. Ancient carriages with elegantly lit wood-framed interiors trundled along Line A for decades but in 2013 were replaced by modern Chinese models fitted with air conditioning and automatic doors.

1

you like or stay on board for the three-hour duration. If you're planning to cover lots of ground it represents good value compared to taxis. Also check out L'Open (⌨ lopentour.com .ar), which, as well as running day tours, operates at night.

TAXIS AND REMISES

Taxis The sheer volume of black-and-yellow taxis touting business on Buenos Aires' streets is a characteristic sight and – other than during sudden downpours or in the outer barrios – it's rare that it takes more than a few minutes to flag down a cab. The meter starts at $20.20 and clocks up $2.02 every couple of blocks, still making it a relatively affordable way of getting around the central neighbourhoods. Note also that, thanks to Argentina's rampant inflation (see box, p.45), fares go up every six months. Taxi rides are sometimes white-knuckle affairs – drivers range from amiable characters who drive carefully and engage in lively conversation to maniacs who seem to want to involve you and others on the streets in some road-borne suicide pact. Regardless of road skills, drivers are generally trustworthy, despite occasional reports of accomplices being used to rob passengers or a sleight of hand

passing out a fake $50 bill. Radio taxis are regarded as more secure and better quality than the unaffiliated type – they are distinguished by the company name on the side and can be hailed in the street or ordered by telephone, the latter with a $10 add-on fee. Premium (☎ 011 4374 6666, ⌨ taxipremium .com) has good-quality cars, all with air conditioning, at the same price as other taxis.

Remises *Remises* are plain cars that can be booked through an office. They're cheaper and usually more comfortable than taxis for getting to the airport (and they tend to have larger boots). Call Reminor (☎ 011 4639 1101) or VLZ (☎ 011 4139 7788).

BICYCLES

EcoBici (⌨ buenosaires.gob.ar/ecobici). After constructing 140km of bike lanes or *bicisendas*, the city government also set up a free public bike-sharing scheme known as EcoBici. Visitors can take advantage of the roughly 3000 bright yellow bikes (helmets not included) – which are available all day, every day – by simply presenting a photocopy of their passport details and arrivals stamp at any EcoBici kiosk.

ACCOMMODATION

Buenos Aires' popularity with international visitors means much of the city's best **accommodation** – at all levels – is frequently full. With around half of all the country's hotels in the capital, you will always be able to find somewhere to stay, but if you're fussy about where you lay your head, you're advised to reserve in advance. At the budget end, there are dozens of **hostels**, mostly cheerful, well-run places in converted nineteenth-century mansions or modern purpose-built constructions. If you baulk at dormitory living, consider a private room at a hostel or a costlier but homely **B&B**, which tend to be a better deal than the city-centre budget and mid-market **hotels**, many of which can be dull at best, grim at worst. Airbnb also offers heaps of great, well-priced options, given that Argentines are often keen to receive dollars in an offshore account; the plus side for visitors is that you might end up with a private plunge pool for the same price as a bog-standard hotel room. The city has also seen a surge in upmarket **boutique hotels**, altogether more pleasant (though naturally more expensive) places to stay, catering principally to international visitors and scattered throughout the central neighbourhoods. The label "boutique" can be misleading, as anywhere else; often it just means small and vaguely trendy, but is no guarantee of comfort or quality of service. Wherever you spend the night, a fan or air conditioning is really a

---

DRIVING IN BUENOS AIRES

A number of both international and national **car rental** companies (see p.28) operate in Buenos Aires, but given the comprehensive public transport system and the abundance of taxis, there's little point in renting a car simply to tour the city. If, however, you're taking a road trip that starts in Buenos Aires, it might be worthwhile.

You'll need nerves of steel when driving in BA due to the lack of lane control and Porteños' lax attitude towards traffic lights. The good news is that the city is simple to navigate as the streets are one way, with the direction of traffic (which mostly alternates street by street) marked on road signs with an arrow. There are a few exceptions, though – notably avenidas 9 de Julio and Del Libertador. Some streets within the centre, mostly around the financial district, are closed to private traffic during the day.

The local technique for crossing the city's numerous traffic-light-less intersections at night is to slow down and flash your lights to warn drivers of your approach. In theory the vehicle coming from the right has right of way, but be prepared to give way if the other driver looks more determined and never take it for granted that a speeding bus will respect your trajectory. As for parking in the street, it's allowed wherever the curb is not painted yellow, but it's safer to park in an *estacionamiento* (car park) – look out for the large "E" signs.

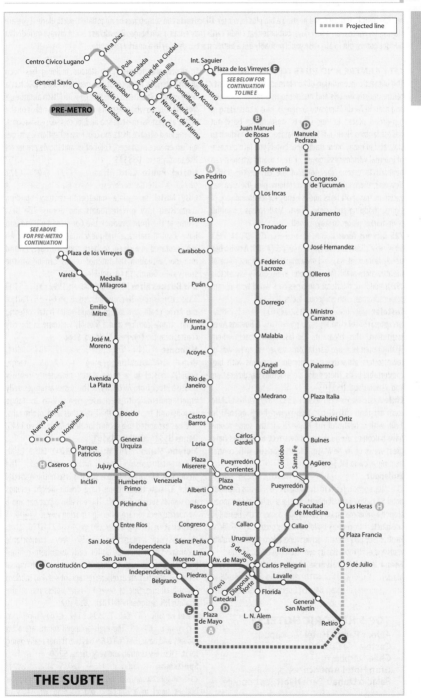

Projected line

Centro Cívico Lugano
Ana Díaz
Pola
Escalada
Larrazábal
Nicolás Descalzi
Gabino Ezeiza
General Savio
Parque de la Ciudad
Presidente Illia
Int. Saguier
Plaza de los Virreyes **E**
Balbastro
Mariano Acosta
Somellera
Ana María Janer
Ntra. Sra. de Fátima
F. de la Cruz

SEE BELOW FOR CONTINUATION TO LINE E

PRE-METRO

B
Juan Manuel de Rosas

D
Manuela Pedraza

A
San Pedrito
Echeverría
Congreso de Tucumán
Los Incas
Flores
Juramento
Tronador
José Hernández
Carabobo
Federico Lacroze
Olleros

SEE ABOVE FOR PRE-METRO CONTINUATION

Plaza de los Virreyes **E**
Varela
Medalla Milagrosa
Puán
Dorrego
Ministro Carranza
Emilio Mitre
Primera Junta
Malabia
José M. Moreno
Acoyte
Angel Gallardo
Palermo
Avenida La Plata
Río de Janeiro
Medrano
Plaza Italia
Boedo
Castro Barros
Scalabrini Ortiz
Nueva Pompeya
Sáenz
Hospitales
General Urquiza
Loria
Carlos Gardel
Bulnes
Córdoba
Santa Fe
Agüero
Parque Patricios
H Caseros
Jujuy
Plaza Miserere
Pueyrredón Corrientes
Inclán
Humberto Primo
Venezuela
Plaza Once
Pueyrredón
Pichincha
Alberti
Pasteur
Facultad de Medicina
Las Heras **H**
Entre Ríos
Pasco
Callao
Callao
San José
Congreso
Uruguay
Plaza Francia
Independencia
Sáenz Peña
Tribunales
San Juan
Lima
9 de Julio
C Constitución
Moreno
Av. de Mayo
Carlos Pellegrini
9 de Julio
Independencia
Piedras
Lavalle
Belgrano
Perú
Florida
Bolívar
Catedral
D
Diagonal Norte
General San Martín
E
Plaza de Mayo
A
L. N. Alem
B
Retiro
C

THE SUBTE

1

requirement in summer, and heating a big plus in winter. **Discounts** can sometimes be negotiated, particularly if you are staying for more than a few days, but note that credit cards may entail a surcharge. **Breakfast** is not always included at budget hotels, but in any case you'll probably get a better start to the day in a nearby *confitería*.

CITY CENTRE AND PUERTO MADERO

The biggest concentration of accommodation is in the city centre, mostly hostels and budget to mid-range hotels on and around Av de Mayo and Congreso, plus a sprinkling of top-range places in the streets surrounding busy but pedestrianized Florida. It is not a laidback area in which to stay, and in many more traditional hotels you face a choice of internal windowless rooms, or front rooms where it can be hard to escape the noise of the city-centre traffic. However, there are plenty of exceptions, plus the area has excellent transport links and is handy for its abundance of sights, shopping and banks. Puerto Madero has a handful of upmarket places to stay, as well.

725 Buenos Aires Roque Sáenz Peña 725 ☎ 011 4131 8016, ⓦ 725continental.com; map pp.64–65. A swish bar, trendy restaurant, spa and swimming pool are just some of the attractions at this fabulous hotel, in an equally remarkable 1920s building; the decor combines dark wood with vibrant colour schemes, with gorgeous results. US$150

Castelar Av de Mayo 1152 ☎ 011 4383 5000, ⓦ castelarhotel.com.ar; map pp.64–65. A Buenos Aires institution, this pleasant, old-fashioned hotel, where Spanish poet Federico García Lorca stayed when he was in town, offers attractive and soundproof rooms with big, comfortable beds. There's also a glamorous bar downstairs and a sauna/spa. US$105

Chile Av de Mayo 1297 ☎ 011 4383 7877, ⓦ hotelchile.com.ar; map pp.64–65. Well-known hotel opened in 1906 with a beautiful Art Nouveau facade; some rooms have balconies overlooking a side street and others have great views of Av de Mayo. All are spacious, with central heating, a/c and TV. $640

Esplendor San Martín 780 ☎ 011 5256 8800, ⓦ esplendorhoteles.com; map pp.64–65. In this boutique hotel 52 rooms, including very spacious suites, are arranged around a luminous atrium, taking up a corner of the beautiful, late nineteenth-century building mostly occupied by Galerías Pacífico (see p.72). Avant-garde works adorn the immaculate walls and each room has its own luxurious decor. $1700

Faena Hotel & Universe Marta Salotti 445, Puerto Madero Este ☎ 011 4010 9000, ⓦ faenahoteland universe.com; map pp.64–65. Buenos Aires' hotel for the

in-crowd, this former grain-storage building has been given a serious Philippe Starck makeover and now has a belle époque jazz bar, a café stuffed with kitsch antiques, a floor-to-ceiling white restaurant with unicorn heads on the walls, an east Asian-style spa and, of course, swish rooms. It's the kind of place that's too cool for a reception – you get an "experience manager". Celebrities and movie producers like to stay here. US$515

Hostel Punto Cero Rivadavia 1777 ☎ 011 4371 0072, ⓦ hoteldoscongresos.com; map pp.64–65. A busy hostel in a late nineteenth-century building comprising fifty private rooms and dorms. The best rooms at the front overlook the Congreso building and have a spiral staircase and mezzanine within them. All are decorated in a clean, modern style with a/c, TV and mini-bar, although the interior rooms can be on the stuffy side. Dorms $140; doubles $400

Ibis Buenos Aires Hipólito Yrigoyen 1592 ☎ 011 5300 5555, ⓦ ibis.com/buenosaires; map pp.64–65. Part of the Accor chain, the *Ibis* is a good-value hotel, offering clean, simple comfort and a friendly welcome in the city centre, near the Congreso building. $660

Milhouse Hipólito Yrigoyen 959 ☎ 011 4345 9604, ⓦ milhousehostel.com; map pp.64–65. Large, popular hostel in a three-storey nineteenth-century house a block from Av de Mayo. The hostel arranges daily entertainment, both in-house events such as tango lessons and trips to football matches and nightclubs, and has expanded to a second locale at Av de Mayo 1245. Dorms US$16; doubles US$61

Moreno Moreno 376, Monserrat ☎ 011 6091 2000, ⓦ morenobuenosaires.com; map pp.64–65. The stunning Art Deco facade tells you this is something special – the 37 sumptuous rooms have double-height ceilings and names such as Big Loft. There is also a jazz bar and a wonderful deck terrace, offering amazing views. $1400

NH Jousten Av Corrientes 280 ☎ 011 4321 6750, ⓦ nh-hoteles.com; map pp.64–65. Very comfortable accommodation in a beautiful early twentieth-century building, popular with business travellers but with appeal for all; it also has an excellent restaurant serving modern Spanish cuisine. One of several central hotels run by the Spanish NH designer hotel chain. US$102

O'Rei Lavalle 733 ☎ 011 4394 7112, ⓦ hotelorei.com.ar; map pp.64–65. The high-ceilinged rooms are a bit gloomy and basic, but the *O'Rei* has two things really going for it – it's very central, and very cheap. $260

Sportsman Rivadavia 1425 ☎ 011 4381 8021, ⓦ hotelsportsman.com.ar; map pp.64–65. Popular budget hotel in a rambling old building with lots of

---

TOP 5 HISTORIC HOTELS

Alvear Palace Hotel See opposite
Castelar See above
Chile See above
Gran Hotel América See opposite
Palacio Duhau-Park Hyatt See opposite

character, though the interior is beginning to show its age. There's a range of rooms, all with fans and some with shared bathrooms; the nicest are the en-suite doubles at the front, which have balconies. Dorms $310; doubles $400

V&S Hostel Club Viamonte 887 ☎011 4322 0994, ⓦhostelclub.com; map pp.64–65. This luxurious hostel is centrally located in a 1910 French-style mansion. A bar and giant TV top the list of amenities, as well as all kinds of interesting organized excursions to keep you occupied. In addition to dormitory accommodation there are three great-value double rooms with private bathrooms and balconies. Dorms US$16; doubles US$50

SAN TELMO

Most accommodation in the south is in the barrio of San Telmo, a magnet for travellers as much for its cobbled streets and prettily crumbling buildings as for its budget hotels and youth hostels. The area around Constitución station has some interesting accommodation options, too, as well as plenty of less salubrious budget joints.

★**Circus Hostel** Chacabuco 1020, San Telmo ☎011 4300 4983, ⓦhostelcircus.com; map p.79. *Circus* successfully bridges the gap between hostel and hotel, offering the ambience and friendliness of the former with the comforts of the latter – the beds have decent mattresses, each room has its own bathroom, and there is even a smart decked pool. The street has other hostels, so is a good place to try your luck if you haven't booked anything. Dorms US$13; doubles US$52

Gran Hotel América Bernardo de Irigoyen 1608, San Telmo ☎011 4307 8785, ⓦgranhotelamerica.com.ar; map p.79. A stone's throw from Constitución station, this reasonably priced hotel was where famous tango composer Angel Villoldo entertained his lady friends. Some of the rooms are a bit gloomy and noisy but the large, airy triples are a good deal. $230

★**Patios de San Telmo** Humberto Primo 773, San Telmo ☎011 4307 0965, ⓦpatiosdesantelmo.com.ar; map p.79. A former *conventillo* given a new lease of life, this thirty-room hotel offers queen-size beds, high ceilings and wooden floorboards as well as numerous patios around the property. Scandinavian-style rooms include luxurious touches such as bathrobes; some even have a jacuzzi. Kick back by the heated rooftop swimming pool all year round. US$105

RETIRO AND RECOLETA

These two barrios are where the city's top-flight luxury hotels tend to be located, although some cheaper options exist too. Recoleta is the perfect location, with plenty to offer – restaurants, bars and shops – and still within walking distance (about 20min) of the microcentro, but with less hustle and bustle.

Alvear Palace Hotel Av Alvear 1891, Recoleta ☎011 4808 2100, ⓦalvearpalace.com; map p.86. Once the choice of wealthy landowners and now the favourite of politicians and royalty, the *Alvear* is still BA's luxury hotel *par excellence*, despite the trendy new upstarts. It offers fabulously decorated rooms in Louis XV style and all the extras you would expect, including a personal butler. Excellent restaurants, too. Also check out sister hotel *Alvear Art*, a more relaxed affair, in Retiro. US$575

Ayacucho Palace Hotel Ayacucho 1408, Recoleta ☎011 4806 1815, ⓦayacuchohotel.com.ar; map p.86. Housed in a smart French-style building, the rooms in this hotel are clean, comfortable and come with a/c in a good location near the centre of Recoleta. $890

Casa Calma Suipacha 1015, Retiro ☎011 4312 5000, ⓦcasacalmahotel.com; map p.86. One of the few boutique hotels in the area, *Casa Calma* lives up to its "quiet house" name, and takes a decidedly ecological approach, with hanging gardens and environmentally friendly toiletries. Many bathrooms have jacuzzis, and you can ask for massages in your room. There's also an honesty bar. US$250

Four Seasons Posadas 1086, Recoleta ☎011 4321 1200, ⓦfourseasons.com/buenosaires; map p.86. Part of the international chain, this fantastically luxurious hotel is divided between a modern block and a belle époque mansion, which looks like a French chateau inside and out. Sunday brunch, open to the public (noon–3pm, $600), is served in *Nuestro Secreto* restaurant next door to the latter. US$545

Guido Palace Guido 1780, Recoleta ☎011 4812 0341; map p.86. Not exactly a palace, more a functional hotel, slightly worn at the edges, but cheap for the area. Its central Recoleta location is its big selling point. $580

Lion d'Or Hotel Pacheco de Melo 2019, Recoleta ☎011 4803 8992, ⓦhotel-liondor.com.ar; map p.86. Homely and friendly place, with a variety of appealing, tastefully decorated rooms, which vary considerably in size, style and price. They range from an internal single with shared bath to a lovely, spacious triple with a fireplace and balcony. $860

Palacio Duhau-Park Hyatt Av Alvear 1661, Recoleta ☎011 5171 1234, ⓦbuenosaires.park.hyatt.com; map p.86. The Duhau family home on the city's most desirable street (see p.90) is now a hyper-luxury hotel, with huge rooms decorated with soothing woods and marble baths. The giant, superbly lit indoor swimming pool, restaurant, *vinoteca* and *Oak Bar* mean you never need to leave the building if you don't want to. US$560

PALERMO

Away from the blasting horns and spluttering buses of the centre, Palermo is a greener, more relaxed neighbourhood in which to stay. Known for its happening nightlife scene, there are some fabulous, if expensive, small hotels, agreeable B&Bs and fun hostels, all with the added benefit of being close to the city's most exciting bars, restaurants and boutiques. A taxi to the centre costs about $100.

1

The Clubhouse Costa Rica 4651 ☎011 4832 5276, ⓦ clubhouseba.com; map pp.96–97. Good taste and luxury reign at this chic five-suite guesthouse in the heart of Soho. Kick back in the two elegant living rooms and bar; the outdoor swimming pool and lush garden are magnets for US and British immigrants in summer, given their private members' club status. US$150

Eco Pampa Hostel Guatemala 4778 ☎011 4831 2435, ⓦ hostelpampa.com.ar; map pp.96–97. Dubbing itself the city's first green hostel – the vibrant lime-hued facade sets the tone – *Eco Pampa* is comfortable as well as ecofriendly, with its leafy terrace and low-energy computers. Dorms US$19; doubles US$80

Fierro Soler 5862 ☎011 3200 6800, ⓦ fierrohotel .com; map pp.96–97. This trendy boutique hotel a few blocks from Hollywood's buzz has comfort at its heart, offering spacious rooms and extremely comfy queen-size beds. Enjoy breakfast or brunch at *Uco*, a top restaurant, and make use of the lush back garden and rooftop swimming pool. US$270

Home Honduras 5860 ☎011 4779 1006, ⓦ homebuenosaires.com; map pp.96–97. Owned and run by a British record producer and his Irish-Argentine wife, this masterpiece of modern architecture and hotel design is simply incredible: from the wallpaper in each room to the swimming pool and deck, the attention to detail is breathtaking. US$170

Legado Mítico Gurruchaga 1848 ☎011 4833 1300, ⓦ legadomitico.com; map pp.96–97. In a prime Palermo Viejo location, this delightful boutique hotel has nine spacious, immaculately designed en suites, each one themed around a different Argentine icon, including Che, Borges and Evita. The breakfast room and library feel like gentlemen's clubs, and service is consistently good. It has an equally good sister hotel in Salta (see p.289). US$302.50

Magnolia Julián Álvarez 1746 ☎011 4867 4900, ⓦ magnoliahotelboutique.com; map pp.96–97. At this gorgeous Art Nouveau townhouse with period furnishings, nothing is too much trouble – from the welcome glass of wine on arrival to help with all you need during your stay. Breakfast is excellent and copious. US$210

Nuss El Salvador 4916 ☎011 4833 6222, ⓦ nusshotel .com; map pp.96–97. This utterly classy boutique hotel in a converted convent at the corner of Borges houses 22 beautiful rooms, ranging from the smallest size, superior category, to sizeable suites. The convent's inner courtyard has been preserved, adding to the sense of space and airiness, while the top-floor deck with its plunge pool and a small gym and spa is refreshed by the majestic plane trees in the neighbouring street. US$230

Posada Palermo Salguero 1655 ☎011 4826 8792, ⓦ posadapalermo.com; map pp.96–97. Wonderful B&B in a more residential corner of Palermo, away, but not far, from the nerve centre of Soho; this typical *casa chorizo* (kind of elongated townhouse found in most Argentine cities) offers smart rooms, a homely atmosphere and a great breakfast, including home-made preserves. US$140

★Querido B&B Ramírez de Velasco 934 ☎011 4854 6297, ⓦ queridobuenosaires.com; map pp.96–97. A welcoming B&B in leafy Villa Crespo barrio (a few blocks west of Palermo Soho), *Querido's* eclectic interior gives it a homely feel. Owned by an in-the-know Anglo-Brazilian couple, each of the seven rooms is individually designed. A gem of a spot. US$115

EATING

Buenos Aires is Latin America's second **gastronomic capital** (after Lima) and, with many places offering excellent quality for the price, eating out here counts as a highlight of any visit to Argentina. In addition to the ubiquitous **pizza** and **pasta** restaurants common to the country as a whole, the capital offers a number of cuisines, ranging from Armenian and Basque to Southeast Asian and Mexican. Foodie fashions are enthusiastically adopted; Peruvian haute cuisine and mini gourmet restaurants in the intimate space of someone's house (*puertas cerradas*) are all the rage (see box, p.114). The city's crowning glory, however – though you have to be a meat eater – is its **parrillas**, whose top-end representatives offer the country's choicest beef cooked on an *asador criollo* – staked around an open fire – or on a grill, also called a *parrilla*. There are plenty of humbler places, too, where you can enjoy a succulent *parrillada* in a lively atmosphere.

OPENING HOURS

Though most restaurants open in the evening at around 8pm, it's worth bearing in mind that Porteños don't normally dine until 10pm; many restaurants suddenly go from empty to full between 9.30pm and 10pm. Kitchens generally close around midnight during the week, though at weekends many keep serving till the small hours. Plenty of *confiterías* and pizzerias also open throughout the night, so you shouldn't have trouble satisfying your hunger at any time.

RESTAURANTS

Excellent meals can be had throughout Buenos Aires but, with some exceptions, the centre and the south are best for the city's most traditional restaurants, while the north is the place for more innovative or exotic cooking. Puerto Madero, the recently renovated port area, is knee-deep in big, glitzy themed restaurants, though – a couple of decent places notwithstanding – these are hardly the capital's most exciting eating options and are usually the most expensive. You'll find a far more original crop of restaurants across the board in Palermo Soho and Hollywood as well as in Las Cañitas. Villa Crespo is starting to pull rank with smaller restaurants and trendy sandwich shops.

CITY CENTRE

180 Burger Bar Suipacha 749 ☎ 011 4328 7189; map pp.64–65. Bang on trend with BA's burger obsession, *180* turns out bespoke burgers by the dozen every weekday lunchtime for city workers. Choose your beef or veggie patty, select a salsa and bun, then slap on a variety of toppings for a fast yet fresh meal. A contemporary if petite interior makes this bar a break from the burger norm. Mon–Fri noon–4pm.

Arturito Corrientes 1124 ☎ 011 4382 0227; map pp.64–65. An old-fashioned haven reigned over by courteous white-jacketed waiters, *Arturito* is a Corrientes landmark, and its *bife de chorizo con papas* (rump steak and chips) is an unquestionably good deal. Daily noon–4pm & 8pm–1am.

Chiquilín Sarmiento 1599 ☎ 011 4373 5163; map pp.64–65. A classic Porteño restaurant, popular with tourists, serving traditional dishes in a friendly and stylish atmosphere. The *pollo al verdeo* (chicken with spring onions) is good, but it's the revered *bife* ($110) that brings most people in. Daily noon–3am.

Las Cuartetas Corrientes 838 ☎ 011 4326 0171; map pp.64–65. A pared-down pizza and empanada joint where you can grab a slice of delicious and cheap pizza at the counter and kill time after the cinema over a cold Quilmes. Mon–Thurs & Sun 11am–1am, Fri & Sat 11am–2am.

El Globo Hipólito Yrigoyen 1199 ☎ 011 4381 3926; map pp.64–65. One of several Spanish restaurants in the area, *El Globo* has a gorgeously old-fashioned interior and serves generous portions of classic dishes such as *gambas al ajillo* (spicy prawns) and *puchero* (stew). About $200 for two courses. Daily noon–3pm & 8pm–midnight.

★**Güerrín** Corrientes 1368 ☎ 011 4371 8141; map pp.64–65. A quintessential Porteño pizza experience, the traditional order is a portion of *muzzarella* and *fainá* to eat at the counter, accompanied by a glass of sweet Moscato. A vast pizza emporium that soars above Corrientes, some locals hold that the pies served in the restaurant area are a notch above the counter versions; however, all are inexpensive. Daily noon–2am.

Laurak Bat Belgrano 1144, Monserrat ☎ 011 4381 0682; map pp.64–65. A moderately priced Basque restaurant within *Club Vasco* boasting specialities such as *abadejo al pil-pil* (haddock in garlic sauce). On the go? Stop by the in-house tapas bar. Mon–Thurs noon–3.30pm & 8pm–midnight, Fri & Sat noon–3.30pm & 8pm–1am.

Parrilla Peña Rodríguez Peña 682 ☎ 011 4371 5643; map pp.64–65. Knowledgeable liveried waiters serve up some of the juiciest meat in town, as well as great salads at this great-value, no-nonsense *parrilla*. Mon–Sat noon–4pm & 8pm–midnight.

FIVE GREAT PARRILLAS

Cabaña Las Lilas See below
La Cabrera See p.115
Don Julio See p.115
La Carnicería See p.115
Parrilla Peña See below

Patio San Ramón Reconquista 269 ☎ 011 4343 0290; map pp.64–65. Generously portioned, well-cooked and well-priced food with daily specials such as *pollo al horno con puré de batata* (roast chicken with sweet potato purée). The real attraction, however, is the stunning location – the patio of an old convent where, among palm trees and birdsong, it's easy to forget you're in the heart of the financial district. Mon–Fri noon–4pm.

★**Tomo 1** Carlos Pellegrini 525, 1st floor Hotel Panamericano ☎ 011 4326 6695; map pp.64–65. Considered one of Buenos Aires' best haute cuisine restaurants, this is an elegant but refreshingly unpretentious place where the emphasis is squarely placed on the exquisitely cooked food, such as chilled melon soup and quail with pistachios. Splash out on the dinner menu with wine pairings (around $1200). Mon–Fri noon–3pm & 7pm–12.30am, Sat 7.30pm–12.30am.

PUERTO MADERO

Bice Av Alicia M. de Justo 192 ☎ 011 4315 6216; map pp.64–65. Style often triumphs over content in Puerto Madero, but the excellent pasta and gnocchi ($200) at this highly regarded, if expensive, Italian restaurant will not disappoint. Daily noon–4pm & 7pm–1am.

Cabaña Las Lilas Av Alicia M. de Justo 516 ☎ 011 4313 1336; map pp.64–65. The place to splurge on some of the finest steak around; the *ojo de bife*, best savoured from a shaded veranda on the waterfront, will set you back what it would cost to eat for a week in a standard *parrilla*. Popular with tourists; reservations advisable. Daily noon–3pm & 8pm–midnight.

Chila Av Alicia M. de Justo 1160 ☎ 011 4343 6067, ⊛ chilaweb.com.ar; map pp.64–65. Led by Argentina's top female chef, this highly accoladed establishment offers two delectable tasting menus that deal with *nueva cocina argentina* and local produce. Pricey, at $1400 for seven courses, but worth it. Tues–Sun 8pm–midnight.

i Fresh Market Macacha Guemes 300 ☎ 011 5775 0330; map pp.64–65. By Dique 3, this is a relaxed place for lunch or *merienda*, with a selection of inventive sandwiches and salads plus a range of yummy *licuados* (fruit shakes) and herbal teas to accompany; meals such as pasta and steak are also available. A bit expensive, but not outrageous. Daily 8am–midnight.

Siga La Vaca Av Alicia M. de Justo 1714 ☎ 011 4315 6801; map pp.64–65. At this upmarket *tenedor libre* you

1

can eat till you drop for a reasonable sum; the fixed rate (about $280, less at lunchtime) includes a carafe of wine, salads and, of course, a mountain of meat. As with all *tenedores libres*, go for quantity, variety and speed, rather than quality. Daily noon–1am.

SAN TELMO AND LA BOCA

★**Aramburu Bis** Humberto Primo 1207, San Telmo ☎011 4304 5697; map p.79. For the epitome of a contemporary Argentine bistro with a market-to-table approach, shabby chic surroundings and a great wine list, *Aramburu Bis* – spearheaded by top chef Gonzalo Aramburu – is the place. Mon–Sat 12.30–11.30pm.

★**El Baqueano** Chile 499, San Telmo ☎011 4342 0802; map p.79. This respected and award-winning restaurant sources local ingredients, including indigenous meats, to create gourmet dishes such as *falso bife de chorizo*, made from *pacú* fish, and ñandú (Argentine ostrich) stuffed with liquor-soaked fruit. Excellent wine list, too. Six-course tasting menu $650. Tues–Sat 7–11pm.

Café San Juan Av San Juan 450, San Telmo ☎011 4300 1112; map p.79. A small, good-value, family-run joint whose huge portions and fresh-from-the-market meals mean it's always full, especially since a reality TV show was made about owner-chef Leandro Cristobal. Try the "hunter's-style" rabbit. Tues–Sun 12.30–4pm & 7pm–midnight.

Desnivel Defensa 855, San Telmo ☎011 4307 2489; map p.79. Backpackers pile in to this no-frills *parrilla*, which offers meat-laden dishes at rock-bottom prices. Quality can be hit and miss, but bellies will be filled regardless. Mon 8pm–1am, Tues–Fri noon–5pm & 7pm–1am, Sat noon–1am, Sun noon–midnight.

El Obrero Caffarena 64, La Boca ☎011 4362 9912; map p.82. With sports souvenirs decorating the walls and tango musicians sauntering between tables at weekends, the atmosphere at this hugely popular and moderately priced *bodegón* that opened in 1954 is as appealing as the simple home-cooked food, such as great *milanesas* (veal escalope). Mon–Sat noon–10pm.

RETIRO AND RECOLETA

Bengal Arenales 837, Retiro ☎011 4314 2926; map p.86. Although this smart restaurant offers Indian specialities, including a decent rogan josh, it really excels in its Mediterranean Italian dishes, with a focus on fish. The ambience is posh but the attentive service is not snobbish, and the wine and food, albeit not budget-priced, are impeccable. Mon–Fri noon–4pm & 8pm–late, Sat 8pm–late.

Brasero Atlántico Arroyo 882, Retiro ☎011 4393 7450; map p.86. At this latest venue from the award-winning team behind *Florería Atlántico* bar, Argentine staples receive an update. Beetroot or oxtail conserves are starters for sharing, while grilled veggies are the perfect partner to a T-bone steak for your main. Mon–Fri noon–4pm & 7pm–1am, Sat 1–5pm & 7pm–1am.

★**Club Danés** Alem 1074 12th floor, Retiro

RESTAURANTES A PUERTAS CERRADAS

A dining phenomenon that works perfectly in Buenos Aires, closed-door restaurants, or *restaurantes a puertas cerradas*, are extremely popular. Chefs – many aspiring to be the next Francis Mallmann, Argentina's most renowned culinary export besides beef – set up in their home, rather than forking out exorbitant amounts on rent and taxes for a traditional restaurant. This means they have total culinary freedom, trying experimental fixed menus in a more casual environment. It also means they aren't subject to health-and-safety inspections and are technically illegal, but given that they've been operating openly for well over a decade (and giving your guests food poisoning will not help you in the crowded online *puertas cerradas* marketplace), the risk is almost non-existent.

Note that the addresses are only given out on reservation, so they're not included on this Guide's maps.

30 Sillas Colegiales ☷treintasillas.com.ar. In the game for a decade, Ezequiel Gallardo changes his menu weekly, keeping the focus on modern Argentine dishes.

Casa Félix Chacarita ☷colectivofelix.com. Inspired by his travels, Diego Félix serves up vegetarian and pescetarian menus, sourcing herbs and greens from his organic back garden.

Jueves a la Mesa San Telmo ☷juevesalamesa .wordpress.com. US yoga teacher Meghan Lewis set up this weekly veggie dinner, which dabbles in African flavours and is eaten around a communal table.

Paladar Villa Crespo ☷paladarbuenosaires.com.ar. Dine out on a five-course tasting menu expertly paired with wines selected by sommelier Ivana Piñar, in the comfort of her living room.

Toro 777 Villa Crespo ☷toro777.com.ar. One of the city's more economical *puertas cerradas*, Guillermo Coria draws on experience working in Spain to concoct a five-course menu that changes weekly.

1

⊙011 4312 9266; map p.86. One of several migrant community clubs in BA, this is one of the best, food wise. This lunch-only Danish restaurant serves a mean *smörrebrod* – lots of herrings and blue cheese – and other specialities in an airy dining room with unbeatable river views. Mon–Fri noon–3pm.

Club Sirio Libanés Ayacucho 1496, Recoleta ⊙011 4806 5764; map p.86. The Syrian and Lebanese community also has its own club, and this palatial place, open since the 1930s, offers an excellent and varied menu. About $300 for dinner. Mon–Sat 8.30pm–1am.

El Cuartito Talcahuano 937, Retiro ⊙011 4816 1758; map p.86. Classic BA pizzeria, famed for its delicious dough and *fugazzeta* – a local type of pizza slathered with lots of onions and cheese, but no tomatoes. Seats are uncomfortable, the atmosphere noisy and service variable, but that's part of the experience. Daily noon–1am.

La Esperanza de los Ascurra Vicente López 1661 local 15, Recoleta ⊙011 3533 7122; map p.86. Head up to the first floor for this well-priced Spanish-style, family-run tapas bar that also produces its own craft beer and wine. Expect *cañas* on tap and abundant burrata salads. Tues–Sat 6pm–12.30am.

El Estrebe Peña 2475, Recoleta ⊙011 4803 0282; map p.86. What eating out in Buenos Aires is all about – white tablecloths, pictures by gaucho artist Florencio Molina Campos on the walls, enormous *copas* of velvety red-purple Malbec, and thick, tender steaks at reasonable prices. Daily noon–4pm & 7.30pm–midnight.

Filo San Martín 975, Retiro ⊙011 4311 0312; map p.86. Offers up a vast Italian menu on equally vast premises. Imaginative pizzas and pastas, as well as other Italian-inspired dishes such as baby squid form *Filo's* repertoire. Mon–Sat noon–late.

★**Restó** Montevideo 938, Recoleta ⊙011 4813 2375; map p.86. Set back from the street in the building housing the Central Society of Architects, this appropriately stylish little French restaurant serves quail and duck, while dessert includes the signature muscovado sugar ice cream. The three-course set menus cost around $450. Mon–Fri noon–3pm, Thurs & Fri 8–11pm.

Romario Pizza Vicente López 2102, Recoleta ⊙011 4511 4444; map p.86. You can savour *Romario's* great, reasonably priced pizzas in an outdoor seating area from where Recoleta in full swing can be observed. Part of a decent chain famed for its roller-skating delivery boys and girls. Daily noon–4pm & 8pm–late.

El Sanjuanino Posadas 1515, Recoleta ⊙011 4804 2909; map p.86. This inexpensive restaurant is the place to try traditional dishes like empanadas, *locro* and *humita*, as well as more exotic ones like pickled *vizcacha* (chinchilla). Daily noon–4pm & 7pm–1am.

Sipan Paraguay 624, Retiro ⊙011 4315 0763; map p.86. Stylish if compact, pricey yet delicious Nikkei (Japanese–Peruvian) dishes include ultra-fresh ceviche and sushi, as well as a number of delicious takes on the classic Peruvian sautéed beef dish *lomo saltado*. Mon–Wed noon–4pm & 8pm–midnight, Thurs–Sat noon–4pm & 8pm–1am.

Tancat Paraguay 645, Retiro ⊙011 4312 5442; map p.86. A beautifully decorated and lit Spanish–Catalan *tasca*, where *cañas* (small glasses of draught beer), varied tapas and other mainstays, like grilled baby squid, are genuine; service is brisk, it gets busy and can be noisy, but that adds to the authenticity. Moderately priced, unless you opt for seafood. Mon–Sat noon–late.

PALERMO

Artemisia Cocina Natural Costa Rica 5893 ⊙011 4773 2641; map pp.96–97. One of BA's best non-meat restaurants, the vegetarian and fish dishes here make no sacrifices flavour-wise. Even die-hard carnivores will enjoy *Artemisia's* twist on polenta lasagne or lime- and coriander-spiked *abadejo* (haddock). Food is freshly cooked, so don't go if you're in a hurry – but it's worth the wait. Service can be grouchy. About $250 for dinner. Also pop by for tea and a slice of orange cake. Tues–Sat 10am–late, Sun 10am–5pm.

Bio Humboldt 2192 ⊙011 4774 3880; map pp.96–97. Vegetarian and organic restaurant with lots of wholesome ingredients – wholemeal empanadas, quinoa risotto, tofu salad and so on – with a good-value ($120) lunch with drink. Daily 10am–midnight.

La Cabrera Cabrera 5099 & 5127 ⊙011 4831 7002; map pp.96–97. This fantastic *parrilla* serves hard-to-beat *bife de chorizo* (the half portion feeds two) with an array of delicious tapas-style garnishes; it's so popular the owners opened two more restaurants on the same block. Take advantage of forty percent off during happy hour (daily 7–8pm). Its only downfall is that it's become very touristy. Mon, Sat & Sun 12.30–4.30pm & 8.30pm–1am, Tues–Thurs 8.30pm–1am, Fri 8.30pm–2am.

★**La Carnicería** Thames 2317, Palermo Soho ⊙011 2071 7199; map pp.96–97. This hip *parrilla* led by a Colombian chef rethinks beef. The short and sweet menu specializes in smoked and daily cuts sourced from grass-fed cattle, and dishes are served on wooden boards. *Provoleta* with peaches is a must for a starter. $290 for two courses. Tues–Fri 8pm–late, Sat & Sun 1–3.30pm & 8pm–late.

Casa Cruz Uriarte 1658 ⊙011 4833 1112; map pp.96–97. After a management takeover, this stylish brasserie is more relaxed these days. The menu changes monthly, dealing in modern Argentine cuisine, and includes an assortment of grilled *provoletas*. Also home to a great wine cellar. Around $450 for two courses. Mon–Fri noon–4pm, 7pm–midnight, Sat noon–1am.

★**Don Julio** Guatemala 4699 ⊙011 4832 6058; map pp.96–97. This authentic family-run steakhouse is busy

1

every night thanks to its delicious grass-fed beef, fantastic service and superb wine list. With the grill taking centre stage in this former butcher, order the *vacío* (flank steak). Daily noon–4pm & 7pm–1am.

★**La Mar** Cebichería Arevalo 2024 ☎011 4776 5543; map pp.96–97. From Peru's culinary godfather Gastón Acurio comes the BA version of *La Mar*. A vast patio and pisco bar await, and of course some of the best seafood and Peruvian dishes in town. Ceviche to share $150. Tues–Sat noon–4pm & 8pm–2am, Sun noon–5pm.

Ña Serapia Las Heras 3357 ☎011 4801 5307; map pp.96–97. An unexpectedly traditional and rustic hole in the wall in Barrio Norte, *Ña Serapia* styles itself as a *pulpería* and serves delicious regional dishes including *locro* and tamales at bargain prices. The empanadas are excellent. Daily 11am–midnight.

NOLA Gorriti 4389 ☎011 6350 1704; map pp.96–97. For classy southern fried chicken with Creole flair backed up with craft beers, head to this popular gastro-pub. Mon–Fri 5pm–midnight, Sat & Sun 1pm–midnight.

Ølsen Gorriti 5870 ☎011 4776 7677; map pp.96–97. This airy, stylish restaurant serves exciting cuisine with a Scandinavian touch, such as salmon pizza or goat's-cheese ravioli. There are around forty different kinds of vodka and all manner of cocktails to kick things off. Still a hot brunch spot, so book ahead. About $400 for two courses. Tues–Sat 12.30pm–midnight, Sun 10am–midnight.

Las Pizarras Thames 2296 ☎011 4775 0625; map pp.96–97. Casual yet classy restaurant that's all about the fabulous food. Run by a chef who worked in London and Barcelona, the market-to-table menu is written up on blackboards (*pizarras*); it's a bit of a lottery, but that's part of the fun. Tues–Sun 8pm–midnight.

Sarkis Thames 1101 ☎011 4772 4911; map pp.96–97. Spartan decor, but excellent tabbouleh, *keppe crudo* (raw meat with onion – tastier than it sounds) and falafel at this popular budget restaurant serving a fusion of Armenian and Turkish cuisines. Daily noon–3pm & 8pm–1am.

Sudestada Guatemala 5602 ☎011 4776 3777; map pp.96–97. Smart Southeast Asian establishment where the menu includes tasty curries and other regional specialities at reasonable prices, all in modern, minimalist surroundings. Go for the two-course lunch deal ($130). Mon–Sat noon–4pm & 8pm–late.

CAFÉS, CONFITERÍAS AND SNACKS

You can learn a lot about Porteños from a little discreet people-watching in cafés. People stream through all day, from office workers grabbing a *medialuna* in the morning, to ladies of leisure taking afternoon tea, to students gossiping over a beer in the evenings. They're not the hotbed of revolutionary activity they were in the 1970s, but they're still in many ways where you'll find authentic Buenos Aires – over a *cortado*, an espresso with a dash of milk, usually served with a welcomingly hydrating glass of water and a tiny biscuit. *Confiterías* are traditional tearooms that also specialize in biscuits, cakes and pastries to accompany the tea and coffee, although the dividing line between these, regular cafés and even restaurants (many serve full-blown meals, at reasonable prices) can be quite blurred. Can't live without your flat white? BA is going through a caffeine revolution, with contemporary New

HELADERÍAS

One institution in Buenos Aires, and indeed the rest of the country, serves as a constant reminder of Argentina's strong Italian inheritance: the **heladería**, or ice-cream parlour. Ubiquitous, varied, extremely popular and the subject of fierce debate as to which is the best, these minefields of gelato-style temptation serve millions of cones and cups daily, dispatching delivery boys on motorbikes to satisfy the needs of those who require a kilo of helado but can't be bothered to buy in person (or are averse to queuing).

Cadore Corrientes 1695, city centre; map pp.64–65. Some experts have declared this the best place for ice cream in the city – despite much competition – and the *dulce de leche* flavour above all. It's certainly one of the most traditional and this is the only branch. Daily noon–late.

★**Jauja** Cerviño 3901, Palermo Botánico; map pp.96–97. The capital is now blessed with a branch of Patagonia's pride and joy ice-cream parlour from El Bolsón (see p.414). Wild berry sorbets, including unusual ones such as rosehip, elderberry and *calafate*, are especially good; also give refreshing *yerba mate* or raspberry lemonade a whirl. Daily noon–late.

Occo Dorrego 1581, Palermo Hollywood; map pp.96–97. A tiny spot, where clients spill out onto the street to devour original flavours such as orange, carrot and ginger or Kinder egg pieces and chocolate. Daily noon–11pm.

Persicco Salguero 2591, Palermo Botánico ☎011 4807 7005, plus other branches; map pp.96–97. This small, family-run chain of stylish parlours – part modern, part retro – dishes out fabulous ice creams and sorbets, with emphasis on chocolate flavours. They also serve excellent cakes, croissants and coffees. Mon–Thurs & Sun 9am–midnight, Fri & Sat 9am–2am.

York- and London-style cafés serving up serious beans teamed with cookies or muffins.

CITY CENTRE

★**La Americana** Callao 83; map pp.64–65. A Callao landmark, serving up juicy baked empanadas – some say they're the city's best – to be consumed standing up at metal counters. Daily 6.30am–2.30am.

Café Tortoni Av de Mayo 825 ☎011 4342 4328; map pp.64–65. Buenos Aires' most famous café (see p.68) exudes pure elegance, but is now a tourist trap. Some evenings it hosts live jazz or tango in *La Bodega* downstairs, but there are many far more authentic venues around. Daily 8am–1am.

★**Confitería La Ideal** Suipacha 384; map pp.64–65. Another emblematic café, though not as famous as *Tortoni*; it is just as beautiful, if a little worn at the edges. The main reason to visit is tango: take a class in the salon upstairs or check out the *milonga* (see p.121). Don't be put off by the low-profile entrance. Daily 8.30am–8pm.

La Giralda Av Corrientes 1453; map pp.64–65. Brightly lit and austerely decorated Corrientes café famous for its *chocolate con churros*. A perennial hangout for students and intellectuals and a good place to experience Porteños' passion for conversation. Daily 8am–midnight.

Green Eat Reconquista 690; map pp.64–65. A contemporary option for a quick and healthy lunch, to eat in or take away, from salads to sushi, soup and sandwiches. You can get fresh juices, too. Mon–Fri 10am–6pm.

New Brighton Sarmiento 645; map pp.64–65. The classic Anglo-Porteño *Brighton*, which first opened its doors in 1908 as a tailor, was recently renovated and reopened, retaining many of its original features. Wood panelling and stained glass help re-create a belle époque atmosphere, with a café at the front and expensive restaurant at the back. Mon–Sat 8am–midnight.

La Paz Av Corrientes 1599; map pp.64–65. The classic Corrientes (and Porteño) café; less sumptuous but also with fewer tourists than *Tortoni*. *La Paz* was once the favourite hangout of left-wing intellectuals and writers and it's still a good place to meet friends or read a book over a coffee. Daily 8am–1am.

SAN TELMO

Abuela Pan Bolívar 707; map p.79. Homely vegetarian café and wholefood store offering a daily menu with options such as tofu burgers, stuffed aubergines and vegetarian sushi. Mon–Fri 8am–7pm.

★**Coffee Town** Mercado de San Telmo; map p.79. The hut that's slap-bang in the middle of this food and vintage market is one of the city's finest spots for coffee. Sit in and soak up the ambience or take away. Daily 8am–9pm.

La Poesía Chile 502; map p.79. Self-consciously traditional café-bar with wooden tables and a mind-boggling choice of sandwiches and *picadas*. Tango is the usual soundtrack. Daily 8am–late.

Pride Balcarce 869; map p.79. A "heterosexual-friendly" spot, this gay café is a favourite not only for its perfect flat white but also its generally attractive clientele. Mon–Fri 9am–8pm, Sat & Sun 11am–8pm.

RETIRO AND RECOLETA

La Biela Quintana 596, Recoleta; map p.86. Institutional *confitería* that's more appealing for its history than for its overpriced *lomitos* and coffee, served in the elegant bistro interior or in the shade of a gigantic gum tree on the terrace. Daily 8am–late.

Costumbres Criollas Libertador 308, Retiro; map p.86. A small restaurant specializing in excellent *empanadas tucumanas* and regional dishes such as *locro* and tamales. Worth seeking out for a snack if you have an hour or two to kill in the vicinity of Retiro. Daily 9am–midnight.

Cumaná Rodríguez Peña 1149, Recoleta; map p.86. Popular with students and office workers, this is a good place to try *mate*, served from 4pm to 7.30pm with a basket of crackers. There's also a selection of regional food, such as empanadas and *cazuelas* (casseroles), on the menu. Daily noon–late.

PALERMO

★**LAB Tostadores de Café** Humboldt 1542; map pp.96–97. Starting out as roasters supplying beans to cafés, *LAB* then decided to showcase how they make coffee. Mon–Sat 9am–7pm.

Ninina Gorriti 4738; map pp.96–97. For a contemporary ambience teamed up with healthy kale juice or devilishly good brownies, this airy space attracts trendy twenty-somethings, families and US expats. Mon–Fri 8am–midnight, Sat & Sun 9am–midnight.

OTHER BARRIOS

Las Violetas Av Rivadavia 3899, Almagro; subte Castro Barros, line A; map p.60. Rescued from closure by popular demand, this *confitería*-restaurant is a monument to the Porteño heyday of the 1920s, with its fine wood panelling, gorgeous stained glass, Carrara marble tabletops and impressive columns; it was a favourite hangout of writers such as Roberto Arlt. The glory days of this *confitería's* high tea are long gone, but drop by for a quick *cortado* and soak up the design and architecture. Daily 6am–1am.

DRINKING

If you've come to Buenos Aires eager to experience the city after dark, you will not leave disappointed. Porteños are consummate night owls, and though nightlife peaks from Thursday to Saturday, you'll find plenty of nocturnal activities

1

during the rest of the week too. Worthwhile venues are spread all over the city, but certain areas offer an especially large selection of night-time diversions. The city's young and affluent head to Palermo's **Soho** and **Hollywood** to strut their stuff year-round; the downtown streets around Reconquista and 25 de Mayo offer a walkable circuit of bars and restaurants as well as the odd Irish pub, while **San Telmo** harbours some charismatic bars in among the tango spectacles. Though some bars open all day, most don't really get going until around midnight. Increasingly, the smoother bars run so-called "after offices" on weekdays to fill the early evening slot, but these are almost invariably rather sleazy.

BARS AND PUBS

Buenos Aires has no shortage of great **bars**, ranging from noisy Irish **pubs** to eminently cool places where the chic sip wine, cocktails and craft beer. Most of the former and their ilk are clustered in downtown in Retiro or San Telmo; the latter variety – and a trendier drinking scene – are located over Palermo Viejo, Soho or Hollywood. Note that smoking is banned in public spaces, including bars and restaurants.

SAN TELMO

★**Bar Británico** Av Brasil 399 ☎011 4361 2107; map p.79. Long-established bohemian bar overlooking Parque Lezama, reopened in 2007 after a sustained neighbourhood campaign to save it from closure. It retains the table where Ernesto Sábato wrote *On Heroes and Tombs*. Daily 9am–8pm.

Gibraltar Perú 895 ☎011 4362 5310; map p.79. Popular both with expats and locals who like hanging out with Brit expats, *Gibraltar* is a relaxed British-style pub, with a friendly atmosphere, adequate bar service, pool table and great bar food, including fish and chips and Thai curries. Daily noon–4am.

Plaza Dorrego Bar Defensa 1098 ☎011 4111 5724; map p.79. Most traditional of the bars around San Telmo's central square, a sober wood-panelled place where the names of countless customers have been etched on its wooden tables and walls, and piles of empty peanut shells adorn the tables; mostly frequented by tourists these days. Daily 8am–1am.

RETIRO AND RECOLETA

BASA Basement Bar & Restaurant Basavilbaso 1328, Retiro ☎011 4893 9444; map p.86. A smart place, *BASA* attracts a white-collar working crowd, which morphs into serious drinks aficionados jostling for space at the gleaming bar from 10pm. Mon–Fri noon–3.30pm & 7pm–2am, Sat 8pm–3am.

Buller Brewing Pres. Ortíz 1827, Recoleta ☎011 4808 9061; map p.86. The shiny stainless-steel vats and whiff of malt tell you that this pub brews its own excellent beer, which runs the gamut from pale ale to creamy stout. Daily noon–late.

Dadá San Martín 941, Retiro ☎011 4314 4787; map p.86. Small, hip and attractive bar, playing jazz soundtracks, serving reasonable food and offering a cooler alternative to the nearby Irish joints. Mon–Sat 8am–late.

Florería Atlántico Arroyo 872, Retiro ☎011 4313 6093; map p.86. With a speakeasy front sporting a florist and wine store, open the fridge door to step into this award-winning basement bar. Whipping up excellent cocktails and superb bar food, it attracts BA's hippest drinkers. Daily 7pm–late.

Gran Bar Danzón Libertad 1161, 1st floor, Retiro ☎011 4811 1108; map p.86. Fashionable after-office bar and restaurant with sharply dressed staff and a very comprehensive wine list. Elegant and popular, even midweek. Mon–Fri 7pm–late, Sat & Sun 8pm–late.

★**Milion** Paraná 1048, Recoleta ☎011 4815 9925; map p.86. Drop by this beautifully converted mansion for fabulous cocktails such as basil mojito in one of the host of candlelit rooms – or pick a spot on the marble staircase. Mon–Thurs & Sun 10am–2am, Fri & Sat 10am–4am.

★**Shout Brasas & Drinks** Maipú 981 ☎011 4313 2850; map p.86. A hip wine and cocktail bar in a French-style mansion, there's plenty to shout about here. Knowledgeable staff, a superb food menu and attention to detail ensure its place as a top spot for a drink. Daily 6pm–2am, Sat 8pm–3am.

PALERMO

Antares Armenia 1447 ☎011 4833 9611; map pp.96–97. Home-brewed Kölsch, porter, stout and barley beer, to name just a few, accompany tapas and simple dishes in a roomy, converted storehouse in Soho. Jazz, blues and rock music add to the ambience. Also sister pubs in Las Cañitas and San Telmo. Daily 7pm–4am.

Frank's Arévalo 1445 🖳franks-bar.com; map pp.96–97. To access this off-centre Hollywood speakeasy, follow the clues for the password via social media (in Spanish). Once you're in – via a phone booth – kick back in a 1930s-style bar which cocktails aficionados adore. Wed–Sat 9pm–4am.

Mundo Bizarro Gorriti 5132 ☎011 4832 5654; map pp.96–97. The name means "strange world" and this bar is grungy for super-trendy Palermo: expect low lighting, decent cocktails and a quirky crowd. Daily 8pm–late.

★**Pain et Vin** Gorriti 5132 ☎011 4832 5654, 🖳bit.ly /PainEtVin; map pp.96–97. This airy Soho wine bar stocks bottles from small producers and holds weekly tastings in English and Spanish (dates online). Snap up a bottle of something delicious and sip it on site, teamed up with the best sourdough sandwiches in town. Tues–Sun noon–10pm.

NIGHTLIFE

Porteños live for going out at night with their friends, whether it's to go clubbing or to catch a live gig. In terms of nightclubs, Buenos Aires stands head and shoulders above any other city in Argentina and all tastes are catered for. Venues offering **live music**, including folk, jazz, tango (see p.121) and rock, are scattered all over the city and differ enormously in style and ambience, though the quality is invariably high. For gigs by local bands, check the *Sí* supplement in *Clarín* on Fridays (W clarin.com) and the *Buenos Aires Herald*'s arts section. As well as larger venues like Luna Park or the outdoor GEBA, international stars often play at football stadiums, particularly River Plate's Monumental – these gigs are widely advertised and best booked through a **ticket agency** (see p.121). Smaller venues generally sell tickets on the door. If folk music is your thing, check out W folkloreclub.com.ar. Classical music and opera are accounted for on p.124. Websites with worthwhile dance clubs and live music **listings** include W vuenozairez.com, W wipe.com.ar and W buenosaliens.com.

LIVE MUSIC

Bebop Club Moreno 364, Monserrat ☎ 011 4331 3409; map pp.64–65. The name says it all: local jazz and blues acts perform nightly Tues–Sun in this cool basement space which opened in 2014. Tues–Sun 8pm–late.

Estadio Luna Park Madero 420, San Nicolás ☎ 011 5279 5279, W lunapark.com.ar; map pp.64–65. Wonderful Art Deco edifice whose huge capacity lends itself to big sell-out events like boxing fights, the Chinese state circus and acts ranging from well-known international names like the Pet Shop Boys to big Argentine folk stars like Horacio Guarany. See website for schedule. Mon–Sat 10am–late.

Makena Cantina Club Fitz Roy 1519, Palermo Hollywood ☎ 011 4772 8281, W makenacantinaclub .com.ar; map pp.96–97. Soul, funk and even gospel make the cut at this small yet popular club that will have you dancing your socks off until dawn. Tues–Sun 9pm–late.

Mitos Argentinos Humberto 1° 489, San Telmo ☎ 011 4362 7810, W mitosargentinos.com.ar; map p.79. The main attraction of this old mansion is the offbeat nature of the bands playing here, with Argentine tribute bands often the star act. Fri & Sat 8pm–late.

★**ND/Ateneo** Paraguay 918, Retiro ☎ 011 4328 2888, W ndteatro.com.ar; map p.86. Folk, rock, tango, jazz, modern classical – all the big national and South American names play here at some point. The medium-sized theatre also hosts film screenings and recitals. Check website for schedule and times.

Notorious Av Callao 966, Recoleta ☎ 011 4815 8473; map p.86. This spot hosts interesting, small-scale concerts – blues, jazz, tango, Latin – throughout the year. Mon–Sat noon–4pm & 9pm–1am, Sun 9pm–midnight.

Pan y Teatro Las Casas 4095, Boedo ☎ 011 4922 0055, W panyteatro.com.ar; map pp.64–65. This beautifully restored grocer's shop serves an original blend of Italian and *criollo* food and puts on shows, including tango, classical music and jazz. Tues–Sun 8am–late.

★**Peña del Colorado** Güemes 3657, Palermo ☎ 011 4822 1038, W lapeniadelcolorado.com.ar; map pp.96–97. Famed for its past-midnight *guitarreadas* (bring your guitar, play and sing) that "finish when the candles burn out", the *Colorado* is the city's most traditional folk venue – there is also a *mate* bar, a restaurant and even tango shows. Daily 8pm–4am.

Thelonious Salguero 1884, Palermo ☎ 011 4829 1562, W thelonious.com.ar; map pp.96–97. The odd soul or blues concert is given here, but, as the name implies, this is a jazz club, and regarded as the city's best; the music is always mesmerizing, the acoustics are faultless and the food is decent. Thurs–Sat noon–late.

La Trastienda Balcarce 460, Monserrat ☎ 011 4342 7650, W latrastienda.com; map pp.64–65. Trendy live music in a late nineteenth-century mansion, with a wide-ranging roster of acts including rock, jazz, salsa and tango. Tues–Sun 8pm–late.

NIGHTCLUBS

Music in dance clubs varies from the cheesiest commercial house and revered Eighties pop to cutting-edge tunes mixed by DJs of international standing. Although Buenos Aires has some great home-grown DJs, trends in dance music tend to follow those of Europe (particularly London) and the US, and clubbers are almost always young and affluent. If you're in town in November, don't miss the big annual Creamfields shindig (W creamfieldsba.com). At the other end of the spectrum, *bailantas* are events where the predominant music is *cumbia villera* – a version of Colombia's famous, repetitive *cumbia* rhythm that's the Argentine equivalent of gangsta rap, glorifying drugs and crime. Cheap, alcoholic and rowdy, *bailantas* can be fun but are not recommendable unless you go in the company of a regular. Drunkenness and drug-taking are frowned upon by wider society but pretty common in clubs.

Costs Prices range wildly from free (particularly for women) to $100 or more, with prices sometimes including a drink. Making friends with PRs on the door, or subscribing to mailing lists on clubs' websites, is key to future invites and gaining cheaper or faster access.

Opening hours Traditionally clubs don't get going until around 3am but – to the relief of those who like to get at least some sleep, perhaps – there has been a tendency in BA to go out a bit earlier in recent times. Check Facebook pages for the most up-to-date events.

1

LGBT BUENOS AIRES

Buenos Aires is increasingly considered the major urban LGBT tourist destination in Latin America and its annual pride march in November (ⓦmarchadelorgullo.org.ar) is one of the continent's biggest. Although the scene can be a disappointment for those looking for specifically gay and lesbian locales, for others that's part of the attraction. There is an increasing open-mindedness on the part of Argentina's inhabitants and authorities – in 2010 it became the first country in Latin America to sanction same-sex marriage as well as equal rights in terms of inheritance and adoptions – and PDAs are consequently the norm in BA.

Palermo is the nearest the city comes to a gay neighbourhood, but that's due to its cosmopolitan ambience. As in many Latin American cities, exclusively LGBT places are not always the best places to go out in any case, especially when it comes to restaurants; anywhere trendy, with a mixed crowd, will most likely prove a better option. Though the city doesn't have a specific gay district, the long-established heart of LGBT Buenos Aires is the corner of avenidas Pueyrredón and Santa Fe, where nondescript *Confitería El Olmo* is the place to hang out on Friday and Saturday evenings for free entrance flyers or discount vouchers for clubs. Meanwhile, those looking for a cultural hub should head to *Casa Brandon* (L.M. Drago 236, Palermo; Wed–Sun 8pm–3am) for its art gallery, workshops and cinema. For gay *milongas*, try *La Marshall* (ⓣ011 4912 9043, ⓦlamarshallmilonga.com.ar), which takes place at Riobamba 416 in the centre at 11.30pm on Fridays – though, as with all *milongas* (see box, p.122), you should check it hasn't moved on before setting out.

CITY CENTRE AND PUERTO MADERO

Asia de Cuba Pierina de Alessi Cossettini 750, Puerto Madero ⓦasiadecuba.com.ar; map pp.64–65. Famous for its fashion and VIP crowd, this place starts the night off as a sushi bar then turns into an exclusive disco. Not as cool as it used to be. Mon, Tues & Sun 12.30pm–1am, Wed–Sat 12.30pm–late.

Bahrein Lavalle 345, city centre ⓦbahreinba.com; map pp.64–65. Uber-cool club in a beautifully renovated townhouse dripping with antique furnishings. Drum'n'bass on Fridays, house and techno the rest of the week. Occasionally attracts big international names. Fri–Sun midnight–late.

Maluco Beleza Sarmiento 1728, city centre ⓣ011 4373 0959; map pp.64–65. Long-running Brazilian club, playing a mix of lambada, afro, samba and reggae to a lively crowd of Brazilians and Braziliophiles. Wednesday is Brazilian music only, with a *feijoada* (traditional stew) served; book ahead. Wed–Sun 10pm–late.

PALERMO

Araoz Araoz 2424 ⓣ011 5977 9222, ⓦclubaraoz.com .ar; map pp.96–97. Slotted into a residential area, somehow this busy venue never receives complaints about its electronica, house and hip-hop nights. Fri & Sat 11pm–6am.

Crobar Paseo de la Infanta Isabel ⓣ011 4778 1500, ⓦcrobar.com.ar; map pp.96–97. Large and flashy complex of bars and dancefloors playing mainstream dance music that attracts a smartly dressed clientele. Fri & Sat 10pm–late.

★**Niceto** Niceto Vega 5510 ⓣ011 4779 9396, ⓦnicetoclub.com; map pp.96–97. Most famous for its

Thursday-night "Club 69" party, complete with friendly, diverse crowd, outlandish podium dancers and house music played by the city's most acclaimed resident DJs. Thurs–Sat 8.30pm–7am.

COSTANERA NORTE

Pacha Av Rafael Obligado 6151 ⓣ011 4788 4288; map pp.96–97. Big and glitzy like its Ibiza namesake, *Pacha* attracts a lively crowd, including a sprinkling of Argentine celebrities, and its Saturday "Clubland" nights just keep on going. International dance music DJs often play here. Fri–Sat midnight–late.

LGBT NIGHTLIFE

With gay clubs running the gamut between fun drag shows and electronic music nights, there are plenty of places to go out and meet new people. The streets, plazas and parks of Buenos Aires can be cruisey, making them likelier places to meet people than bars or discos, where people tend to go out in groups of friends. Most venues stock a free LGBT city map, *Gmaps 360* (ⓦgmaps360.com), with all the latest locales. Women are less well catered for than men, but good information about events and venues for lesbians can be found at ⓦlafulana.org.ar.

Amerika Gascón 1040, Palermo ⓦameri-k.com.ar; map pp.96–97. One of the city's biggest and best-known gay discos, with three dancefloors playing house and Latin music. Thurs–Sun midnight–late.

Contramano Rodríguez Peña 1082 ⓦcontramano .com; map p.86. One of the longest-running discos aimed at an older crowd, with shows on Saturdays and bears night on Sundays. Fri–Sun midnight–late.

★**Palacio Alsina** Alsina 940 ⓦpalacioalsina.net; map

pp.64–65. This palatial converted industrial building stages LGBT nights on Fridays and Sundays, usually starting around midnight and attracting some of the most beautiful people in the city. Also the base for "Fiesta Dorothy!", a monthly party, that's one of the city's most fun. Fri & Sun midnight–late.
Peuteo Gurruchaga 1867; map pp.96–97. This

guys-facing bar features house DJs and is frequented by pretty twenty-somethings. Wed–Sun 9pm–3am.
Sitges Av Córdoba 4119; map pp.96–97. Large, bright trendy bar, frequented by a mixed but invariably young crowd. Always bursting at the seams, with late-night weekend shows. Thurs–Sun 6pm–late.

ARTS AND ENTERTAINMENT

There's a superb range of **cultural events** on offer in Argentina's capital, ranging from avant-garde theatre to blockbuster movies and grand opera with a wealth of options in between. One of the best features of Porteño cultural life is the strong tradition of **free** or very cheap events, including film showings at the city's museums and cultural centres, tango and a series of enthusiastically attended outdoor events put on by the city government every summer; street performers are also of very high quality.

LISTINGS

A plethora of listings is given in the entertainment sections of *Buenos Aires Herald*, *Clarín* and *La Nación*. Numerous independent listings sheets are also available in bars, bookshops and kiosks throughout the city; also try tourist kiosks for pamphlets and magazines. *Time Out Buenos Aires* also provides helpful information in English, though it isn't necessarily up to date given its biannual publication. *Arte al Día* (⊚ artealdia.com) shares art exhibition details. The website ⊚ mundoteatral.com.ar is an excellent source for info on shows, with a focus on offbeat performances.

TICKETS

You can buy tickets at discounted prices for theatre, cinema and music events at the various centralized *carteleras* (ticket agencies) in the centre, such as Cartelera Baires, Av Corrientes 1382, local 24 (Mon 10am–6pm, Tues & Wed 1–8pm, Thurs & Fri 1–9pm, Sat 2–11pm, Sun 2–9pm; ☎ 011 4372 5058, ⊚ carterabaires.com). Alternatively, Ticketek (☎ 011 5237 7200, ⊚ ticketek.com.ar) sells tickets to many upcoming concerts, plays and sporting events, bookable over the phone or online with a credit card. Their most central outlet is at Tucumán 633 (Mon–Sat 9am–8.30pm).

TANGO

Tango is so strongly associated with Buenos Aires that a visit to the city isn't complete unless you immerse yourself in it at least once. The most accessible way to experience it is via *espectáculos de tango*. These rather expensive *cena* shows (dinner followed by a show) are performed by professionals who put on a highly skilled and choreographed display. Many hotels and hostels offer excursions to them, and they're mostly attended by foreign visitors. Porteños who are tango fans tend to prefer to go either to music recitals – with no dancing – or to *milongas* (see box, p.122) to dance themselves. A *milonga* refers to a moveable event rather than a specific venue, so the days, times and locations of these change frequently; many are

situated in the city's outer barrios. *Tangauta* (⊚ tangauta .net) is a free magazine with listings, which can generally be picked up at tourist kiosks, hotels and cultural centres. There are also regular tango festivals, with a host of free shows and hundreds of classes and *milongas* – the biggest is the Tango World Championship and Festival, held in August (⊚ festivales.buenosaires.gob.ar).

CITY CENTRE

Club Gricel La Rioja 1180, San Cristóbal (Urquiza subte) ☎ 011 4957 7157, ⊚ clubgrcieltango.com.ar; map pp.64–65. Small, friendly, authentic club holding daily classes and *milongas*. Mon & Wed–Sat from 8pm, Sun from 6pm.
★ **Confitería La Ideal** Suipacha 384, 1st floor ☎ 011 4328 7750; map pp.64–65. An oasis of elegance a few blocks from busy Corrientes, *La Ideal* (see p.429) has a stunning salon, which is undoubtedly one of the most traditional and consistently popular places to dance. There is an exhaustive programme of classes and *milongas* every day. See the website for details and times.
Piazzola Centro de Artes Galería Güemes, Florida 165 ☎ 011 4344 8200, ⊚ piazzollatango.com; map pp.64–65. In a renovated theatre in the lovely Galería Güemes, this is one of the most central *cena* show locations, with a dinner and exciting programme for around $1330 ($835 show only). Daily from 8.30pm.

SAN TELMO

Bar Sur Estados Unidos 299 ☎ 011 4362 6086, ⊚ bar -sur.com.ar; map p.79. One of San Telmo's more reasonably priced tango shows ($1000 with dinner, $700 without). The quality of the shows can vary, but it's an intimate space where audience participation is encouraged towards the end of the evening. Daily 8pm–2am.
Centro Cultural Torquato Tasso Defensa 1575 ☎ 011 4307 6506, ⊚ torquatotasso.com.ar; map p.79. This friendly San Telmo neighbourhood cultural centre has top-quality tango recitals, some of them free. See the website for details and times.

1

MILONGAS

Tango has gained a whole new audience in recent years, with an increasing number of young people filling the floors of social clubs, *confiterías* and traditional dancehalls for regular events known as **milongas**. Many hold classes beforehand, and even if you don't dance yourself, it's still worth going to one: the spectacle of couples slipping almost trance-like around the dancefloor is a captivating sight. Apart from the skill and composure of the dancers, one of the most appealing aspects of the *milonga* is the absence of class and, especially, age divisions; indeed, most younger dancers consider it an honour to be partnered by older and more experienced dancers.

STRUCTURE AND ETIQUETTE

While the setting for a *milonga* can range from a sports hall to an elegant salon, the **structure** – and **etiquette** – of the dances varies little. Once the event gets under way, it is divided into musical sets, known as *tandas*, which will cover the three subgenres of tango: tango "proper"; *milonga* – a more uptempo sound; and waltz. Each is danced differently and occasionally there will also be an isolated interval of salsa, rock or jazz. The invitation to dance comes from the man, who will nod towards the woman whom he wishes to partner. She signals her acceptance with an equally subtle gesture and only then will her new partner approach her table. Once on the dancefloor, the couple waits eight *compases*, or bars, and then begins to dance, circulating in an anticlockwise direction around the dancefloor. The woman follows the man's lead by responding to *marcas*, or signs, to indicate the move he wishes her to make. The more competent she is, the greater number of variations and personal touches she will add. Though the basic steps of the tango may not look very difficult, it entails a rigorous attention to posture and a subtle shifting of weight from leg to leg, essential to avoid losing balance. The couple will normally dance together until the end of a set, which lasts for four or five melodies. Once the set is finished, it is good tango etiquette for the woman to thank her partner, who, if the experience has been successful and enjoyable, is likely to ask her to dance again later in the evening.

CLASSES AND CLOTHING

Watching real tango danced is the kind of experience that makes people long to do it themselves. Unfortunately, a *milonga* is not the best place to take your first plunge; unlike, say, salsa, even the best partner in the world will find it hard to carry a complete novice through a tango. In short, if you can't bear the thought of attending a *milonga* without dancing, the answer is to take some **classes** – reckon on taking about six to be able to hold your own on the dancefloor. There are innumerable places in Buenos Aires offering classes, including cultural centres, bars and *confiterías* and, for the impatient or shy, there are private teachers. If you're going to take classes, it's important to have an appropriate pair of **shoes** with a sole that allows you to swivel (no rubber soles). For women, it's not necessary to wear heels but it is important that the shoes support the instep. At a *milonga*, however, a pair of well-polished heels is the norm, and will act as a signal that you are there to dance. Any woman at a *milonga* who doesn't intend to dance should make that clear in her choice of dress and footwear; go dressed to kill and you'll spend the night turning down invitations from bemused-looking men.

Señor Tango Vieytes 1655, Barracas ☎ 011 4303 0231, ⓦ senortango.com.ar; map pp.64–65. Large and very professional *tanguería* in the quiet southern barrio of Barracas. Daily dinner and a spectacle of a show that traces the history of tango and incorporates trapezes, 1980s tango fusion and even horses; $600 for dinner, drinks and show. Daily from 8.30pm.

Taconeando Balcarce 725 ☎ 011 4307 6696, ⓦ taconeando.com; map p.79. Smaller, more informal *cena* show; a good option if you want to see a show rather than a *milonga* but also want to avoid the larger, more commercial options; US$60 with dinner, US$40 without. See the website for details and times.

El Viejo Almacén Av Independencia 299 ☎ 011 4307 7388, ⓦ viejoalmacen.com.ar; map p.79. Probably the most famous of San Telmo's *tanguerías*, housed in an attractive nineteenth-century building. Occasionally hosts nationally famous tango singers, otherwise slickly executed dinner and dance shows. US$140 with dinner, US$90 without. Daily from 8pm.

RECOLETA AND PALERMO

Clásica y Moderna Callao 892, Recoleta ⓦ clasicaymoderna.com; map p.86. The dark, brick interior has been converted from a bookshop into a café-restaurant with great food and live tango and other acts, including top names. Daily, from 9.30pm.

★ **Parakultural** Salón Canning, Scalabrini Ortiz 1331,

Palermo ⓦparakultural.com.ar; map pp.96–97. Young, bohemian organization that puts on the coolest *milongas* and shows in town at a rotating and eclectic set of venues, including this huge place. Classes are also offered. See the website for details and times.

★ **La Viruta** Armenia 1366, Palermo ☎011 4832 4105, ⓦ lavirutatango.com; map pp.96–97. Huge, long-running institution with *milongas* (Sat & Sun) and shows (Thurs & Fri) that mix tango with folklore, salsa and even rock'n'roll. The action begins at midnight, with classes during the afternoon and evening. Tues–Sun from 6pm.

OUTER BARRIOS

La Catedral Sarmiento 4006, Almagro (Carlos Gardel subte) ☎011 15 5325 1630, ⓦ lacatedralclub.com; map p.60. Popular *milonga* in a former warehouse that attracts both locals and foreign "tango tourists" in the heart of tango barrio Almagro. Daily from 6pm.

El Chino Beazley 3566, Nueva Pompeya ☎011 4911 0215; map p.60. This bar and *parrilla* in a traditional barrio in the southwest of the city (take buses #15 or #188 from the centre) is probably the most authentic place to hear tango sung by the talented staff and a crowd of locals and regulars. It's even been the subject of a movie, *Bar El Chino*. Fri & Sat from 9pm.

CINEMA

Porteños are keen and knowledgeable cinema-goers and there are dozens of cinemas in the city showing everything from the latest Hollywood releases to Argentine films and arthouse cinema. Foreign films are usually subtitled. Traditionally, cinemas showing purely mainstream stuff were concentrated on Calle Lavalle, while arthouse flicks were more common on Avenida Corrientes. However, both are increasingly losing out to the multiplex cinemas in the city's various shopping malls, which offer excellent visuals and acoustics, though in a blander atmosphere. Ticket prices vary but generally cost $80. You can also find free or very cheap showings at museums and cultural centres.

Abasto Shopping Av Corrientes 3200, Almagro ⓦ abasto-shopping.com.ar. Enormous modern cinema at the Abasto shopping centre, featuring a good mix of international and local movies; usually one of the main hosts of April's enthusiastically attended international and independent film festival, BAFICI.

Arteplex Centro Av Corrientes 1145, city centre ⓦ cinesarteplex.com. The most central of a small local chain of arthouse cinemas, and one of the last remaining cinemas on Corrientes; there's a bar and DVD store inside too.

Gaumont Rivadavia 1635, Balvanera ☎011 4371 3050. One of several "Espacio INCAA" showcase cinemas run by the Instituto Nacional de Cine y Artes Audiovisuales, the Argentine national cinema institute. If your Spanish is

up to it, this is the place to catch the best examples of the country's strong national film industry.

THEATRE

Theatre is very strongly represented, with Avenida Corrientes standing up well in comparison to New York's Broadway and London's West End – although obviously almost all plays are in Spanish. Away from the major theatrical venues you'll find a good spread of international and Argentine theatre, both classic and contemporary, ranging from serious drama to reviews and musicals. Elsewhere, the city is dotted with innumerable independent venues, with stages in bars and tiny auditoriums at the back of shopping centres; the terms "Off Corrientes" and "Off Off Corrientes" found in press listings are based on those used in New York and London. Tickets tend to cost around $150, and some theatres will do a half-price show midweek. Some of the more noteworthy theatres are listed below; for what's on, consult the listings sections of *Buenos Aires Herald*, *Clarín* or *La Nación*.

★ **No Avestruz** Humboldt 1857, Palermo Hollywood ☎011 4777 6956, ⓦ noavestruz.com.ar. Outstanding venue hosting independent theatre; also serves delicious food.

Teatro General San Martín Corrientes 1500, city centre ☎011 4371 0111, ⓦ teatrosanmartin.com.ar. Excellent modern venue with several auditoriums and a varied programme that usually includes one or two Argentine plays as well as international standards such as Pinter or Brecht. Also hosts contemporary dance events, ballet, children's theatre and arthouse cinema in the Sala Leopoldo Lugones, while a cultural centre with free exhibitions is tucked behind.

Teatro Nacional Cervantes Libertad 815, city centre ⓦ teatrocervantes.gov.ar. This grand old-fashioned theatre, superb inside and out, presents a broad programme of old and new Argentine and foreign works, with a particular emphasis on plays from Spain.

Teatro Ópera Allianz Corrientes 860, city centre ⓦ operaallianz.com. This fabulous Art Deco theatre, which in its heyday billed Edith Piaf and Josephine Baker, has undergone a recent revival focusing on a music and dance programme, usually of very high quality.

CULTURAL CENTRES AND ART GALLERIES

Buenos Aires' numerous cultural centres are one of the city's greatest assets. Every neighbourhood has its own modest centre – good places to find out about free tango classes and generally offering a mixture of art exhibitions, film and cafés – while the major institutions such as the Centro Cultural Borges and the Centro Cultural Recoleta put on some of the city's best exhibitions. Buenos Aires also has some prestigious commercial art galleries, the majority of

1

which are based in Retiro and Recoleta, particularly around Plaza San Martín and nearby Suipacha and Arenales. During May or June, the contemporary art fair Arte BA (ⓦarteba.org), held in La Rural exhibition centre in Palermo, showcases work from Buenos Aires' most important galleries.

British Arts Centre (BAC) Suipacha 1333, Retiro ☎011 4393 6941, ⓦbritishartscentre.org.ar. The place to head if you're nostalgic for a bit of Hitchcock or *Monty Python* – regular English-language film and video showings, as well as plays by the likes of Harold Pinter. Mon–Fri 3–9pm.

Centro Cultural Borges Viamonte & San Martín, Retiro ☎011 5555 5359, ⓦccborges.org.ar. Large space above the Galerías Pacífico shopping centre. Excellent photography exhibitions in spacious galleries, as well as painting, theatre, dance, and arthouse cinema. Mon–Sat 10am–9pm, Sun noon–9pm.

Centro Cultural Kirchner Sarmiento 151, San Nicolás ☎0800 333 9300, ⓦculturalkirchner.gob.ar. The seat of the national symphony orchestra, the city's newest cultural centre opened in 2015, hosts exhibitions and concerts. Free. Thurs–Sun 2–8pm.

Centro Cultural Recoleta Junín 1930, Recoleta ☎011 4803 1040, ⓦcentroculturalrecoleta.org. One of the city's best cultural centres (see p.92). Free entry. Tues–Fri 2–9pm, Sat & Sun noon–9pm.

Centro Cultural Ricardo Rojas Corrientes 2038, Almagro ☎011 4954 5521, ⓦrojas.uba.ar. Affiliated with the University of Buenos Aires, this friendly cultural centre and gallery space offers free events including live music and bargain film showings, usually alternative or arthouse. Free entry. Mon–Sat 10am–8pm.

Espacio Fundación Telefónica Arenales 1540, Recoleta ☎011 4333 1300, ⓦespacio.fundacion telefonica.com.ar. A high-tech art centre that lays emphasis on communications media, as you would expect for a foundation run by a telecoms company. This sleek, modern space stages small, mostly avant-garde exhibitions of work by contemporary Argentine artists, and houses an excellent media library. Free entry. Mon–Sat 2–8.30pm.

Fundación Federico J. Klemm Marcelo T. de Alvear 626, Retiro ☎011 4312 4443, ⓦfundacionfjklemm .org. The late Argentine art maverick Federico Klemm was a kind of self-fashioned Andy Warhol, producing bizarre portraits of modern-day Argentine celebrities in mythic and homoerotic poses. Klemm was also a collector of modern art, and on display is a serious collection of works by Picasso, Dalí, Mapplethorpe and Warhol himself – to name just a few – as well as major Argentine artists such as Berni and Kuitca. Free entry. Mon–Fri 11am–8pm.

Goethe Institut Corrientes 319, city centre ☎011 4318 5600, ⓦgoethe.de/buenosaires. Smart German cultural institute whose library is stocked with German and English books, as well as German movies and plays on offer. Free entry. Mon–Fri 9am–6pm; closed during summer.

Ruth Benzacar Gallery Juan Ramírez de Velasco, Villa Crespo ☎011 4857 3322, ⓦruthbenzacar.com. This prestigious gallery has temporary exhibitions featuring international artists as well as Argentines. Free entry. Mon–Fri 2–7pm.

CLASSICAL MUSIC, OPERA AND BALLET

Argentina has a number of excellent classical performers, including opera singers such as tenors Marcelo Álvarez and soprano María Cristina Kiehr, ballet dancers like Iñaki Urlezaga, and musicians such as pianist and conductor Daniel Barenboim. Keeping a lower media profile, but equally acclaimed, is concert pianist and multiple Grammy Award-winner Martha Argerich; she presides over her own international piano competition in Buenos Aires. Classical performances have seen something of a revival in recent years, boosted by frequent free and outdoor performances, especially in summer. Some of the best concerts are small-scale affairs held at museums, churches and the like, such as those held at the Museo de Arte Hispanoamericano Isaac Fernández Blanco (see p.89), though larger venues are also exciting, and none is more spectacular than the Teatro Colón. For updates on classical music concerts, visit ⓦwww.musicaclasicaargentina.com.

Casa de la Cultura Av de Mayo 575, city centre. Free classical concerts, mostly chamber music, are held in the marvellous Salón Dorado in the *La Prensa* building; look out for flyers and posters.

★**La Scala de San Telmo** Pasaje Giuffra 371 & Defensa, San Telmo ☎011 4362 1187, ⓦlascala.org.ar. Not Milan, but this sumptuous bijou theatre hosts tango, jazz and other music genres, plus some excellent operas and classical concerts.

Teatro Avenida Av de Mayo 1222, city centre ☎011 4362 1187, ⓦbalirica.org.ar. This stylish theatre, opened only a few months after the Colón in 1908, is the home to Buenos Aires Lírica, which puts on a number of operas here every season.

Teatro Coliseo Marcelo T. de Alvear 1125, San Nicolás ☎011 4816 3789. The most important venue for ballet, musicals and classical music after the Colón, which it replaced during the latter's renovation; also offers occasional free recitals.

★**Teatro Colón** Cerrito 628, city centre ☎011 4378 7100, ⓦteatrocolon.org.ar. Buenos Aires' most glamorous venue is one of the world's great opera houses, acoustically in the top five, showcasing world-class opera, ballet and classical music (see p.70). Since it reopened for the bicentenary it has been attracting top international performers, including Joshua Bell, Riccardo Muti and Renée Fleming.

SHOPPING

Shopping in Buenos Aires is a pleasure unmatched elsewhere in South America. While goods tend to be more Western and familiar than those you will come across in, say, Bolivia or Peru, you can nonetheless count on finding some highly original items to take home. The best **handicrafts** are found in their home provinces rather than in Buenos Aires, but if you miss out on your trip around the country, you can always visit the many good craft markets in the capital. Typical Argentine goods include *mate* paraphernalia, polo wear, wine and world-class leatherware. A box of widely available Havanna *alfajores* (see p.35) makes a good gift, or take a jar or two of *dulce de leche* away with you to satisfy cravings. **Opening hours** are usually around 10am–7pm between Monday and Friday, with smaller stores closing Saturday afternoon and Sunday. Malls open daily until 9pm.

SHOPPING MALLS

Over the past decade or two, shopping malls have partly superseded small shops and street markets, but those in Buenos Aires are among the most tastefully appointed in the world. Several malls, such as Abasto, are housed in revamped buildings of historical and architectural interest in their own right. On a practical level, malls are air-conditioned, and they're among the few places where you'll find that rarity in Buenos Aires – public toilets.

Abasto Av Corrientes 3200, Almagro (subte Carlos Garde) ⓦwww.abasto-shopping.com.ar; map pp.64–65. This grand building, dating from the 1880s, was once the city food market; now it's the daddy of all the central malls. As well as a twelve-screen cinema, it has hundreds of designer and cheaper stores, an enormous food hall, an amusement arcade and a hands-on museum for children, the Museo de los Niños (Tues–Sun 1–8pm; $40 for adults, $100 for children; ⓦwww.museoabasto.org.ar). Daily 10am–10pm.

Bond Street Av Santa Fe 1670, Recoleta ⓦgaleriabondstreet.com; map p.86. The alternative mall, full of local teenagers skulking around skate stores and tattoo parlours; there're also a few surf shops in the surrounding streets. A good place to pick up flyers for live music and clubs. Daily 9am–9pm.

Buenos Aires Design Center Av Pueyrredón 2501, Recoleta ⓦdesignrecoleta.com.ar; map p.86. Right next to the Centro Cultural de Recoleta, this mall is dedicated to shops selling the latest designs, mostly for the home, from Argentina and elsewhere. Mon–Sat 10am–9pm, Sun noon–9pm.

Distrito Arcos Paraguay 4979, Palermo ⓦdistritoarcos.com.ar; map pp.96–97. Design is the focus of the city's newest shopping complex, which fits snugly into the bottom of a railway viaduct. Stores here are high-street outlets. Daily 9am–9pm.

Galerías Pacífico Florida 750, city centre ⓦgaleriaspacifico.com.ar; map pp.64–65. BA's most central mall, with fashion boutiques and bookshops in a beautiful building decorated with murals by leading Argentine artists. Also home to Centro Cultural Borges, a food court and a children's play area. Mon–Sat 10am–9pm, Sun noon–9pm.

Patio Bullrich Libertador 750, Retiro ⓦshoppingbullrich.com.ar; map p.86. Once a thoroughbred horse market, this is one of the most upmarket malls, and a good place to find designer clothes and leather. Daily 10am–9pm.

WHERE TO SHOP

Avenida Santa Fe, which runs from Plaza San Martín through Recoleta and Palermo, is one of the city's main high streets, with a good mix of stores to suit all budgets. **Palermo Soho** is the place to head for independent **designer clothing** stores and one-off boutiques, while **malls** scattered throughout the city house both Argentine and international chains. Villa Crespo houses numerous outlets, though prices don't tend to vary wildly from the high street. Most stores are within a four-block radius. For **leather goods**, head to **Centro del Cuero**, Murillo 500–700, Villa Crespo (Malabia subte), a three-block stretch of around thirty warehouse stores and some boutiques selling leather clothing both wholesale and direct to the public; this is the place to pick up a bargain, but prices are mostly unmarked so be prepared to haggle.

Shops selling **books** and **music** are strung along **Avenida Corrientes** between 9 de Julio and Callao. Others stretch out on Florida north of **Avenida Córdoba**, together with a bevy of craft, T-shirt and leather stores aimed at tourists, many of them in covered arcades or *galerías*. Contemporary **art** is on sale at the scores of smart galleries that line **Retiro**, with several along **Avenida Alvear**, while those looking for colonial paintings and **antiques** should head for **San Telmo**. For outdoor gear, there is a whole row of **camping** and **fishing** shops along the 100 to 200 block of **Calle Paraná**, just off Corrientes. If you're heading south, bear in mind that Ushuaia and many Patagonian towns are just as well stocked as Buenos Aires, although prices may be higher down there.

1

CLOTHING AND ACCESSORIES

Buenos Aires has plenty of inventive designers, selling both unique tailored designs and classic attire. However, prices are often eye-watering these days, and the quality of domestic goods, except at the highest end, is not always the best – don't expect your nifty outfits to hold together for long. On the upside, you can get some bargains by shopping at outlets clustering around Villa Crespo, near Palermo Soho – visit ⓦguiaqueens.com for a comprehensive list – while leather continues to be good value at all price levels. You can find high-quality leather boots, jackets and wallets – and bags to take it all home in.

Arandú Ayacucho 1924, Recoleta ☎011 4800 1575, ⓦarandu.com; map p.86. Traditional *tabalartería* (leatherware shop) selling boots, ponchos, silverware and accessories, everything you may need for a trip to the *campo* (countryside). Look out for shoes and bags made from soft, attractively mottled skin of the *carpincho* (capybara). Mon–Sat 10am–7pm.

Bolivia Gurruchaga 1581, Palermo ☎011 4832 6284, ⓦboliviaonline.com.ar; map pp.96–97. Hip men's clothes, perfect for all-night dancing. Floral shirts, grungy tops, zipped jackets and other casual attire for guys who prefer not to take things too seriously. Mon–Fri 10am–7pm.

Cardón Sante Fe 1399, Recoleta ☎011 4813 8983, ⓦcardon.com.ar; map p.86. With the slogan "*cosas nuestras*" ("our things"), Cardón, beloved of the Argentine landowning classes, sells smart khaki and white clothing and *carpincho* (capybara) leather shoes, jackets and belts. Perfect for polo matches or estancia stays. Other branches are listed on the website. Mon–Fri 10am–7pm.

Casa López Marcelo T. de Alvear 640, Retiro ⓦwww .casalopez.com.ar; map p.86. Regarded as the city's best exporter of classic leather goods – bags, wallets, briefcases and clothing – the quality is excellent but it has prices to match. Mon–Fri 9am–8pm, Sat & Sun 10am–6.30pm.

Deporcamping Santa Fe 4830, Palermo ☎011 4773 3382, ⓦdeporcamping.com; map pp.96–97. Limited but decent-quality range of trekking clothes and boots, as well as other camping gear such as tents, mats, sleeping bags and stoves. Mon–Sat 9am–8pm.

Greta Flora Acuña de Figueroa 1612, Palermo ☎011 6079 4810, ⓦgretaflora.com; map pp.96–97. Everything a tango aficionado needs to dance the night away, from sling-backs to court shoes and vertiginous numbers in an array of pastels, floral prints and sexier colours. Signature footwear is topped with a leather flower. Mon–Sat 10am–7.30pm.

Jazmín Chebar El Salvador 4702, Palermo ☎011 4833 4242, ⓦjazminchebar.com.ar; map pp.96–97. One of the country's best-known designers, creating clothes for women that are voguish yet still soft and feminine. Expensive but top quality. Mon–Sat 10am–8.30pm, Sun 1–7pm.

Kosiuko Santa Fe 1756, Recoleta ☎011 4815 8740, ⓦkosiuko.com.ar; map p.86. Very cool shop (there are branches at most malls too) where affluent young Porteños go to get gear for the weekend's hanging out. Lots of individual items made with a real flair – you're bound to find something irresistible. Women's, men's and children's ranges. Mon–Sat 10am–9pm.

La Martina Paraguay 661, Retiro ⓦlamartina.com; map p.86. Well-established Argentine polo brand named after ten-goal demi-god Adolfo Cambiaso's mother. As well as polo equipment, stores carry the kind of clothes that people wear to matches (think pastel blouses and lozenge-patterned sweaters). The floor spaces are laid out beautifully, with the polo boots and piles of cashmere set off by dark wood fittings and leather sofas. Mon–Sat 10am–8pm.

Rapsodia Honduras 4872, Palermo ⓦrapsodia.com .ar; map pp.96–97. Although it markets a variety of clothes, many with a bohemian twist, Rapsodia is most famous for its range of jeans, which are cut in ways that seem to flatter all shapes and sizes. Branches in most of the malls. Daily 10am–9pm.

BOOKS AND MUSIC

Corrientes is the traditional place to head for books and music, though there are also a number of antique bookshops housed on the ground floors of Av de Mayo's Art Nouveau concoctions. Upmarket bookshops, with good foreign-language and glossy coffee-table sections, can be found around Florida, Córdoba and Santa Fe.

Ateneo Grand Splendid Santa Fe 1860, Recoleta ⓦwww.yenny-elateneo.com/local/grand-splendid; map p.86. Easily the largest bookshop in Latin America and a strong contender for the most beautiful bookshop in the world, this store is housed in a former theatre, built in 1919 and inspired by the Opéra Garnier in Paris. There is a café located on the former stage, from where you can admire the sumptuousness of it all. Daily 10am–midnight.

Kel Ediciones Marcelo T. de Alvear 1369, Recoleta ☎011 4814 3788, ⓦkelediciones.com; map p.86. This long-running all-English bookshop has mostly fairly mainstream stock but it's big enough for anyone to find that perfect accompaniment to a long-distance bus journey. Daily 10am–7pm.

Librería de Ávila Alsina 500, Monserrat ☎011 4331 8989; map pp.64–65. Allegedly the site of the city's first bookshop, this wonderful sprawling antique bookshop is worth a visit as much for the ambience as the books – which include a great selection on Argentina. Daily 10am–7pm.

Musimundo Florida 301, city centre ☎0810 888 5555,

1

Ⓦmusimundo.com; map pp.64–65. Argentina's major record chain, stocking everything from techno to tango. Branches throughout the city, and online delivery also possible. Daily 9am–9pm.

Walrus Books Estados Unidos 617, San Telmo Ⓣ011 4300 7135 Ⓦwalrus-books.com.ar; map p.79. Excellent English-language new and secondhand booksop, with the emphasis on quality literature and nonfiction from around the world. Tues–Sun noon–8pm.

Zivals Av Callao 395, city centre Ⓣ011 4371 6978, Ⓦzivals.com.ar; map pp.64–65. Small but well-stocked music store, particularly good for tango. There's a strong selection of CDs and DVDs as well as books and sheet music, and the staff are very knowledgeable about the best tango recordings. Daily 9am–9.30pm.

ARTS AND CRAFTS

The city's markets – such as the Sunday fairs in Recoleta, San Telmo and Mataderos, along with some of the *casas de provincias* (see p.54), are where you'll find handicrafts, including unique ceramics, wooden masks or alpaca-wool items, usually at far better value than the mass-produced alternatives. Local arts and crafts are also available at a number of central stores.

Arte Étnico Argentino El Salvador 4656, Palermo Ⓣ011 4832 0516, Ⓦarteetnicoargentino.com; map pp.96–97. Mostly pricey rugs and tapestries from the north, plus rustic furniture made from native wood. A fantastic shop – just go and look at the chairs hanging from the main ceiling like wooden bats – in every sense. Mon–Fri 11am–7pm, Sat 11am–2pm.

El Gauchito Carabelas 306, San Nicolás Ⓣ011 4326 8503; map pp.64–65. A stone's throw from the Obelisco, this reassuringly long-running store is an authentic vendor of gaucho clothing, artwork, antique and modern crafts for the home and many other goods emanating from Argentina's pampas heartlands. Mon–Sat 10am–7pm.

Kelly's Paraguay 431, Retiro Ⓣ011 4311 9189; map p.86. Colourful store that sells a variety of ponchos from different provinces, ceramics and, of course, *mate* gourds. Mon–Sat 10.30am–7.30pm.

DIRECTORY

Banks and exchange There is an entire row of bureaux de change in the financial district, near the corner of San Martín and Sarmiento – you will only receive the official rate at both banks and exchanges, and opening hours are generally Mon–Fri 10am–3pm. This is also where you'll find the central bank branches, with similar hours. At other times, look out for the branches of exchange company Metropolis at Corrientes 2557, Florida 506 and Quintana 576, which are also open at weekends. ATMs are widespread.

Embassies and consulates Australia, Villanueva 1400 Ⓣ011 4779 3500; Brazil, Cerrito 1350 Ⓣ011 4515 2400; Canada, Tagle 2828 Ⓣ011 4808 1000; Chile, Roque Saenz Peña 547, 2nd floor Ⓣ011 4331 6228; France, Cerrito 1399 Ⓣ011 4819 2400; Irish Republic, Av del Libertador 1068 Ⓣ011 5787 0755; New Zealand, Carlos Pellegrini 1427, 5th floor Ⓣ011 5070 0700; Peru, San Martín 128 Ⓣ011 4341 0006; South Africa, Marcelo T. de Alvear 590, 8th floor Ⓣ011 4317 2900; UK, Dr Luis Agote 2412 Ⓣ011 4808 2200; Uruguay, Las Heras 1907, 4th floor Ⓣ011 4807 3040; US, Av Colombia 4300 Ⓣ011 5777 4533.

Hospitals Hospital de Clínicas José de San Martín (public), Av Córdoba 2351, Balvanera Ⓣ011 5950 8000; Hospital de Infecciosas F.J. Muñiz (public), Uspallata 2272, Parque Patricios Ⓣ011 4304 8794; Hospital Británico (private),

Perdriel 74, Constitución Ⓣ011 4309 6400; Hospital Italiano (private), Perón 1490, Almagro Ⓣ011 4959 0200. The Argentine medical emergency number is Ⓣ107.

Language learning There are a number of organizations which provide Spanish immersion programmes, often with cultural and social activities as part of the language learning. These include EleBaires, Av de Mayo 1370, 3rd floor office 10 (Ⓣ011 4383 7706, Ⓦelebaires.com), and Amauta, Federico Lacroze 2129 (Ⓣ011 4777 2130, Ⓦamautaspanish.com).

Laundry Laverap, Suipacha 722 Ⓣ011 4322 3458, though you can find laundries on every other corner. Many *lavaderos* will also pick up and deliver free of charge.

Pharmacies There are plenty of pharmacies in the city, including the 24hr Farmacity, Corrientes 1820; for more branches see Ⓦfarmacity.com.ar.

Police Tourist police Corrientes 436 Ⓣ011 4346 5748, emergencies Ⓣ911. There's a special number that visitors can call if they have been robbed or need other emergency assistance – Ⓣ0800 999 2838.

Post offices Perón 321 (Mon–Fri 10am–6pm). There are numerous smaller branches throughout the city, open from 10am to 6pm. Outside these hours, there are many post-office counters within stationery shops (*papelerías*), at *locutorios* and at kiosks.

Buenos Aires Province

FIELD OF SUNFLOWERS ON THE OUTSKIRTS OF
THE SIERRA DE LA VENTANA

Buenos Aires Province

Marvellous though Buenos Aires is, you may wish to follow the example of the Porteños and escape the urban mêlée for a few days. Immediately north of the city, and understandably a favourite getaway destination, is the watery labyrinth of the Paraná Delta. Unfolding westwards and southwards, the famed Pampas of Buenos Aires Province form the country's agricultural heartland; unfairly neglected by many tourists, these fertile grassy plains offer a fascinating window into Argentina's traditional gaucho culture and rural life. The country's beaches are not world famous, but two dozen popular resorts fringe the province's Atlantic coast; some are worth checking out for their restful serenity, others for their frenetic nightlife.

The **Paraná Delta**'s main town, **Tigre**, is akin to a subtropical Little Venice; wooden launches chug along opaque canals lined with timber bungalows and subtropical thickets instead of Renaissance palaces and piazzas.

The province's inland landscape, the **pampa húmeda**, is dominated by farmland – whose beef and soy provide the bulk of the country's exports – peppered with picturesque gaucho settlements: **San Antonio de Areco**, a charming example with cobbled streets and well-preserved nineteenth-century architecture, within striking distance of several traditional and luxurious **estancias** (see box, p.145). Closer to Buenos Aires, the mini-city of **Luján** exposes the country's spiritual heart, with a mass display of religious devotion in honour of Argentina's patron saint, the Virgin of Luján. A little further west from the capital is the appealingly quiet town of **Mercedes**, famed for its authentic *pulpería* (a traditional bar-cum-store), while south is **Tandil**, whose museums and rugged setting make it a highly worthwhile stop-off en route to Patagonia overland. In a predominantly flat province, to reach anything approaching a mountain you should head for the western reaches, where you'll find the Pampas' most dramatic relief, the **Sierra de la Ventana** range, 580km southwest of Buenos Aires.

The coastal route starts south of **La Plata**, the pleasant provincial capital. Another 260km southeast, the point where the silty Río de la Plata flows out into the cool waters of the South Atlantic Ocean marks the beginning of the country's seaside **resorts**, popular with local families in the summer. In January and February much of the national capital pulls down its shutters and heads for the coast; if crowds and 24-hour parties aren't your thing, visit in December or March when hotel prices drop by half or more. Two major resorts along the Interbalnearia, **Pinamar** and **Villa Gesell**, tend to attract younger holiday-makers, while **Mar del Plata** is the liveliest, with vast crowds packing its beaches by day and flocking to its numerous restaurants and clubs at night. If you hanker after peace and quiet, head to a more isolated spot such as exclusive **Cariló**, bucolic **Mar de las Pampas** or sleepy **Mar del Sur**. Of course, if you're after pristine white sands, tropical drinks and warm seas, you're better off heading to Brazil.

A *LANCHA COLECTIVA* ON THE PARANÁ DELTA

Highlights

❶ Tigre and the Paraná Delta Like having the Everglades on the doorstep of Manhattan – Tigre and the nearby islets offer a vivid green reminder that Buenos Aires is a subtropical city. **See p.133**

❷ San Antonio de Areco This postcard-perfect pampas town is a goldmine of rural culture and traditional crafts – and home to one of the country's main gaucho festivals. **See p.141**

❸ Estancias The fertile Pampas provide the ideal setting for many of the country's best-appointed and most famous ranches, giving visitors a taste of country life within easy access of Buenos Aires. **See p.145**

❹ Tandil This green and hilly town denotes where the Pampas landscape starts to change, offering a plethora of outdoor activities and gentle hikes, as well as restaurants serving delicious local charcuterie. **See p.147**

❺ Sierra de la Ventana The craggy Sierra de la Ventana range in the west of the province has a well-earned reputation for enjoyable riding, cosy but rustic chalets and delicious *picadas*. **See p.152**

❻ Small beach resorts The intimate yet fashionable resorts of Cariló, Mar de las Pampas and Mar del Sur offer quiet sands, aromatic pine forests and long walks along the oceanfront. **See p.160, p.163 & p.172**

HIGHLIGHTS ARE MARKED ON THE MAP ON P.132

GETTING AROUND   BUENOS AIRES PROVINCE

Buenos Aires is one of Argentina's easiest provinces to get around: it is crisscrossed with a dense network of roads and railways, making it straightforward to negotiate using public transport.

By train While Capital Federal has recently got some new – and much needed – commuter train carriages, the province has yet to see any new additions to stock. Journey times aren't improving much either; the BA–to Mar del Plata route, once popular with summer travellers, now takes longer than it did twenty-odd years ago, and has been reduced to just five weekly services. Train travel might be economical, but it certainly isn't the safest or fastest way to get around the province. Check ⓦ ferrobaires.gba.gov.ar for destinations, timetables and fares.

By bus Travel by long-distance coach is the norm, and it tends to be more comfortable and safer than the other public transport options. Bear in mind that bus services to smaller coastal towns are reduced out of season. Check bus timetables and fares on ⓦ plataforma10.com.

By boat Given the network of rivers and streams in the Paraná Delta, travelling by water bus or *lancha colectiva* is the norm within the area. While the most helpful information can be acquired from the Estación Fluvial water taxi terminal in Tigre itself (see p.135), you

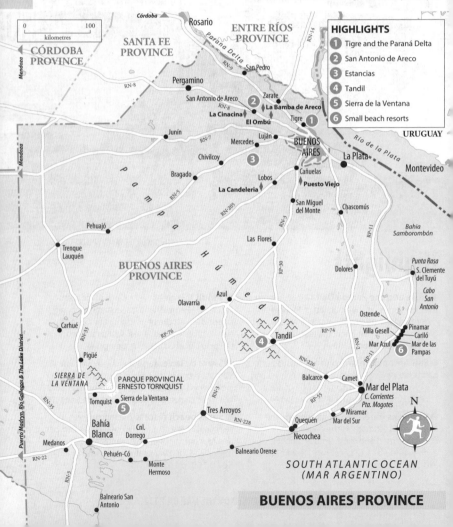

HIGHLIGHTS

1 Tigre and the Paraná Delta
2 San Antonio de Areco
3 Estancias
4 Tandil
5 Sierra de la Ventana
6 Small beach resorts

BUENOS AIRES PROVINCE

can research companies and their points of call at Ⓦvivitigre.gob.ar.

By car When driving around the province's motorways, expect to pay tolls. This can vary between a few pesos and $50 depending on the route and season; always carry cash, as credit cards aren't accepted at booths. The helpful journey calculator on Ⓦ ruta0.com highlights petrol stations, tollbooths and bathroom stops, and can even calculate the cost of your trip depending on the petrol used.

The Paraná Delta

2

One of the world's most beautiful and unusual suburban landscapes, the **Paraná Delta** lies just 21km north of Avenida General Paz, the ring road that divides the city of Buenos Aires from its namesake province. Constantly shifting as sediment from tropical Brazil is deposited by the mighty Río Paraná, the Delta region is a wonderfully seductive maze of lush green islands separated by rivers and streams. Lining the banks, traditional houses on stilts peep out from behind screens of subtropical vegetation. The Delta begins at the port of Diamante in Entre Ríos Province, some 450km to the northwest of the city, and its one thousand square kilometres are divided into three administrative sections. The most visited area is the first section, most of which lies within a one-hour-thirty-minute boat trip from the picturesque town of **Tigre**, itself just 34km northwest of downtown Capital Federal. Travel beyond here into the wide Río Paraná de las Palmas, and you may be forgiven for thinking you've stumbled onto an Amazon tributary. At this point the Delta widens, inhabitants and amenities are more dispersed and *isleños* (as island dwellers are known) rely on electric generators, kerosene lamps and floating supermarkets. The abundance of water and warm climate mean mosquitoes are a real problem in and around the Delta, so come prepared – once you're ensconced on an island, you have to depend on floating supermarkets to stock up on repellent, or indeed any other goods.

Tigre

Sitting on an island bounded by the ríos Luján, Reconquista and Tigre, **TIGRE** owes its poetic name to the jaguars – popularly known as *tigres* in Latin America – that inhabited the Delta region until the beginning of the twentieth century. Primarily seen as a departure point for excursions to the Delta, the town itself is sometimes overlooked by tourists. At first glance it's a bit of a hotchpotch, but don't be put off by initial impressions – Tigre offers a vivacious mix of faded glamour and day-trip brashness. Bars and restaurants around the refurbished riverside area provide perfect vantage points for an unhurried contemplation of the comings and goings of Delta life.

El Tigre (as it is also known) lies along the western bank of the Río Luján, one of the Delta's main arteries, and the town is divided in half by the smaller Río Tigre, which runs north–south through its centre. Riverside avenues flank both sides of the Río Tigre. A good place to begin a tour of the area by foot is around the **Estación Fluvial** boat terminal, immediately north of the bridge over the Río Tigre. The point of contact between island and mainland life, the Estación bustles with activity, particularly at weekends.

However, the most enjoyable part of Tigre to explore is on the western side of the river. Over the bridge, follow riverside Avenida Lavalle north to the confluence of the river with the Río Luján, where Lavalle merges with **Paseo Victorica**, a delightful riverside avenue lined with bars and restaurants.

Brief history

Tigre was first documented in 1635 under the name of El Pueblo de las Conchas ("Seashell Village"), a small settlement that functioned as a defensive outpost against Portuguese invasions. The town became a favoured summer retreat of the Porteño

DELTA BOAT TRIPS

There are many ways to go messing about on the Delta, particularly in summer (Dec–Feb) when you should plan ahead and make reservations. In the capital, various tour companies organize day-trips, including Tangol (☎011 4363 6000, ⓦtangol.com), while companies in Tigre itself offer **paseos**, or round-trip tours. They generally last around an hour and inevitably don't go far into the Delta, but if you're pressed for time they do at least give a taste of river life. Touristy catamarans as well as the better, smaller *lanchas* (launches) run regular *paseos* (11am–5pm; from $80), some from the Estación Fluvial and some from around the international terminal opposite at Lavalle 520.

A second option is the frequent **passenger services**, *lanchas colectivas*, run by three companies – Interisleña, Delta and Jilgüero; these are used by Delta residents to go about their daily business – picking up supplies, taking children to school – and go to all points. If you have a specific destination in mind, phone the tourist office at the Estación Fluvial (see opposite) (not the companies themselves) for the timetable. Most routes are one way, but all three companies also do round trips to the Paraná de las Palmas in the second section, lasting about four hours (Delta 10.30am; Jilgüero 12.30pm; Interisleña 2.30pm). All cost $90–140; again, confirm the timetable with the tourist office in Tigre and, if possible, avoid weekends, when boats are packed and trips take much longer. If you want to do some **walking**, you will need to take one of the regular services to Rama Negra and/or Tres Bocas ($90 & $80 return), where you can disembark and wander for a considerable distance thanks to a public riverside path and wooden footbridges that cross from island to island.

A third, if more expensive, option is to hire a private taxi boat to your destination. Some operators, such as Marsili (stand 9, ☎011 15 4413 4150) and El Fer II (stand 2, ☎011 15 6286 6514), also work out of the Estación Fluvial and should be booked in advance.

elite in the late nineteenth century, from when its sumptuous mansions and palatial rowing clubs mostly date. Back then social life revolved around events at the *Tigre Club*, home to Argentina's first casino, and the grand *Tigre Hotel*, whose clientele included opera singer Enrico Caruso and the Prince of Wales. The town's decline as a glamorous destination was partly due to the closure of the casino in 1933 (a law prohibited casinos in the vicinity of the capital) and in part a result of the growing popularity of Mar del Plata (see p.164), made more accessible thanks to the arrival of the railway and improved roads. The *Tigre Hotel* was demolished in 1940, although the elegant *Tigre Club* still stands at the apex of the island and has been reinvented as the excellent Museo de Arte Tigre.

Delta Terra

Arroyo Rama Negra Chico • Fri–Sun 10am–5pm • Tours (Spanish) 11.30am & 3pm; 1hr 15min • $80 • ☎011 4731 0588, ⓦ deltaterra.com.ar

A conservation-focused private nature reserve, **Delta Terra** is home to flora and fauna typically found in the Delta. You can wander freely through the bamboo and weeping willows that cover the island or join the guided tour, which will point out key species and native plants such as *pindó* and *curupí*. Bird spotting, short treks and kayaking are some of the options available on a day-trip; the reserve also houses an animal sanctuary.

Parque de la Costa

Vivanco 1509 • Jan & Feb Tues–Sun 11am–9pm; March–Dec Sat & Sun 11am–7pm • $60–350 (varies according to age, season and ticket type) • ☎011 4002 6000, ⓦ parquedelacosta.com.ar

On the same side of the river as the Estación Fluvial you'll find the **Parque de la Costa**, one of Latin America's largest amusement parks, with roller-coasters, carousels and arcades. Dodgems and a pirate ship also feature, and there's also a water park, Aquafan, for aquatic relief.

Puerto de Frutos

Río Luján 1648 • Mon–Fri 10am–6pm, Sat & Sun 10am–7pm • ⓦ puertodefrutos-arg.com.ar

Located alongside the Río Luján is the fascinating **Puerto de Frutos**. A Tigre institution, the "Fruit Port" has declined somewhat in importance since the days when fruit cultivation was the region's main source of income. Even so, it's still a working port, where you can watch boats being unloaded with wood, wicker – which grows in abundance in the Delta – and other goods in the small docks. The port also operates as a craft market, with rustic furniture and wickerwork the chief products, and fills up at weekends with Porteños keen for homeware bargains or a spot of lunch.

2

Museo Naval de la Nación

Paseo Victorica 602 • Jan & Feb Mon 8.30am–5.30pm, Tues–Fri 8.30am–5.30pm, Sat & Sun 10.30am–6.30pm; March–Dec Mon 8.30am–5.30pm, Tues–Fri 8.30am–5.30pm, Sat & Sun 10.30am–6.30pm • $20 • ☎ 011 4749 0608

The **Museo Naval de la Nación** is housed in the old naval workshops on Paseo Victorica and holds exhibits relating to the country's maritime history, as well as to Argentine naval history from the British invasions of 1806 to the Falklands/Malvinas conflict of 1982.

Museo de Arte Tigre (MAT)

Paseo Victorica 972 • Wed–Fri 9am–7pm, Sat & Sun noon–7pm • $30 • Tours Wed–Fri 11am & 5pm, Sat & Sun 1pm, 3pm & 5pm; 45min • ☎ 011 4512 4528, ⓦ mat.gov.ar

At the far end of Paseo Victorica is the **Museo de Arte Tigre** or **MAT**, housed in a vast turreted and balustraded structure dating from between 1910 and 1927. The building (formerly the Tigre Club casino) was influenced by grand European hotels of the same period. Inside, the opulent mansion – with its marble staircase, gigantic chandeliers and delicate ceiling frescoes – is a setting to rival any of the capital's art museums. The art itself – mostly by Argentines or on Argentine themes, with many gauchos in evidence – is arranged into topics such as Tigre, the human figure and architecture. Interesting temporary exhibitions have included loans from the prestigious MALBA in Palermo (see p.95).

ARRIVAL AND DEPARTURE   TIGRE

By train Trains depart regularly for Tigre from Retiro station (Línea Mitre; 50min; $3 with a SUBE card), terminating at Tigre's station on the riverbank, just a block south of the Estación Fluvial. For substantially more pesos (there's a separate "tourist" fare), you can transfer to the Tren de la Costa (see box, p.136) at Olivos, which drops you at the entrance to the Parque de la Costa.

By boat The small Cacciola Viajes ferry (Lavalle 520, ☎ 011 4749 0931, ⓦ cacciolaviajes.com) travels daily between Tigre and Carmelo in Uruguay.

By car From Buenos Aires city, it's a 45min drive to Tigre along RN-9.

INFORMATION AND ACTIVITIES

Tourist information There are so many ways of seeing the Delta that it can seem slightly bewildering, and not surprisingly the excellent Estación Fluvial tourist office (daily 8am–6pm; ☎ 0800 888 84473, ⓦ vivitigre.gob.ar) is often busy, especially at weekends. They have good maps and can help you find your way through the labyrinth of trips available. There are also kiosks representing assorted hotels and restaurants at Estación Fluvial, and various boat companies' ticket offices.

Kayaking and rowing Sudeste, based on Río Espera in the Delta itself (☎ 011 15 3860 4018, ⓦ sudeste-kayak.com.ar),

offers half-day, day and overnight guided tours in kayaks, some even crossing over to neighbouring Uruguay. Puro Remo (Lavalle 235; ☎ 011 15 3218 6540, ⓦ puroremo.com .ar) gives you a choice between kayaks and rowing boats with wooden oars. Note that you must take a guide or instructor with you for safety reasons and should reserve ahead.

Wakeboarding To train with a South American wakeboarding champion, check out Gabriela Díaz's school which caters for all ages and levels (Río San Antonio, Gustavito pier; ☎ 011 4728 0031, ⓦ wakeschool.com.ar; from $890).

ACCOMMODATION

Tigre and the Delta can easily be visited on a day-trip, but an overnight stay offers a full break from the hectic pace of Buenos Aires. The most attractive options are in the Delta itself. The first section, closer to Tigre, is easy to get to; one

2

THE TREN DE LA COSTA

The **Tren de la Costa** (daily every 30min 7.20am–9pm; $20 for a *boleto turístico* one way, allowing you to get off and on as many times as you like – tickets should be bought before you get on board; ☎ 011 4794 9159, ⊚ eltrendelacosta.com.ar) runs north from the leafy suburb of Olivos to Tigre in the Paraná Delta, a 25-minute trip if you undertake it in one go. It's a more attractive option for getting to Tigre – it runs parallel to the waterfront, mostly through green parkland and past grandiose suburban mansions and villas – and also presents a number of enticing stop-offs, with eleven restored or purpose-built stations along the route.

The trip starts in the Olivos terminus, known as **Estación Maipú**; to get here, first take a commuter train from Retiro or Belgrano in Capital Federal (see p.105) to Olivos' Estación Mitre (30min; $3 with SUBE card). From here, take the walkway across Avenida Maipú to the red-brick station (many of the stations are modelled on those from the British Victorian era and still sport quaint old-school arm signals, even if they aren't in use).

As well as hopping-off points for the wealthy suburbs of Olivos and San Isidro, many of the Tren de la Costa's stations hold their own appeal. **Estación Borges**, the nearest to Olivos' marina, is referred to as the "station of the arts" – it's home to an art café with open-air sculptures. **Anchorena** station has been christened "Estación Tango" and sits alongside a cultural centre that puts on tango shows and classes; it's also the station closest to the river, and borders a riverside park. **Estación Barrancas** hosts an antiques fair (Sat & Sun 10am–6pm) and provides access to a cycle path, which runs north to San Isidro. **Estación San Isidro**, with its upmarket shopping mall, is conveniently located near the suburb's historic quarter. North of here, you pass through four more riverside stations – Punta Chica, Marina Nueva, San Fernando and Canal – before arriving at the northern terminus, **Estación Delta**, close to Tigre's fruit market (see p.135) and opposite the entrance to the Parque de la Costa.

of the most accessible places to stay is the area known as **Tres Bocas**, a 30min boat trip from the Estación Fluvial. For greater peace and quiet you should journey out into the second section, or more isolated areas such as Arroyo Las Cañas, to appreciate the charm of the Delta's wilds. Getting to most Delta destinations requires a bit of forward planning, so you should ring ahead for a reservation and transport arrangements. In addition to the hotels detailed below, there are plenty of houses and *cabañas* available to rent for weekends or longer stays – see ⊚ vivitigre.gob.ar for a list.

TIGRE

★**Casona La Ruchi** Lavalle 557 ☎ 011 4749 2499, ⊚ casonalaruchi.com.ar. This fabulous old family home is now a B&B with enormous wood-floored bedrooms, huge balconies, a swimming pool in the garden and exceptionally friendly owners, though only shared bathrooms are available. $900

Hotel Agustín García Av Liniers 1547 ☎ 011 4749 0140, ⊚ hotelagustingarcia.com.ar. Simple, old-fashioned town hotel, with rooms sleeping one to five people. Also has its own restaurant. $740

THE DELTA

La Becasina Arroyo Las Canas ☎ 011 4728 1253, ⊚ labecasina.com. In the second, quieter section of the Delta, close to Nordelta, these thoroughly luxurious bungalows are the area's closest approximation of a jungle lodge. $2905 per person

Bonanza Deltaventura Río Carapachay, Km13 ☎ 011 5245 9929, ⊚ deltaventura.com. At an isolated spot on the Carapachay River, *Deltaventura* is the place to go for serious peace and quiet, with only four rooms and around 3km worth of trails, where you can trek, birdwatch and canoe. It can also be visited as a day-trip ($300, including lunch). $1800

Los Pecanes Felicaria and Canal Dos ☎ 011 4728 1932, ⊚ hosterialospecanes.com. An appealing, family-run *hostería* an hour and thirty minutes away out on the Arroyo Felicaria in the quieter second section of the Delta. $1140

★**Villa Julia** Paseo Victorica 800 ☎ 011 4749 0242, ⊚ villajuliaresort.com.ar. A 1910 house carefully converted into a luxury hotel, using many of the original floors, fittings and furniture alongside modern comforts such as soft pillows and a/c. The suites' wide balconies look out over the river, and the hotel has its own elegant restaurant. $890

La Viña Casas Isleñas Arroyo Caraguatá 775 ☎ 011 15 6176 3306, ⊚ islavinia.com. A former vineyard, this century-old property has been converted to include three apartments for a self-catering experience. $1750

EATING AND DRINKING

There are plenty of **restaurants** in Tigre, the pick of them along Paseo Victorica. You'll also find lots of cheap and cheerful *parrillas* near the entrance to the Parque de la Costa, while the above-average café at the Estación Fluvial prepares imaginative sandwiches. On the Delta itself, there are a number of eating options including some quite upmarket ones. However, there's not much in the way of **nightlife** in the Delta – which is kind of the point.

TIGRE

Boulevard Sáenz Peña Boulevard Saénz Peña 1700 ☎011 5197 4776, ⓦboulevardsaenzpena.com.ar. This cute spot is located on the prettiest street in Tigre, and serves delightful home cooking. Try the abundant prawn salad, or the brie and fig sandwiches on ciabatta that's baked in-house. Wed & Thurs 10am–7pm, Fri & Sat 10am–7pm & 8.30pm–midnight, Sun 10.30am–5pm.

Heladería Vía Toscana Paseo Victorica 470 ☎011 4749 2972. This ice-cream parlour has a lovely Victorian-style garden where you can enjoy cones and tubs of home-made ice cream and idly watch river life. Daily noon–midnight.

Il Novo María del Luján Paseo Victorica 611 ☎011 4731 9613 ⓦilnovomariadelujan.com. Tigre's most upmarket restaurant is situated in an elegant dining room on the riverbank. Soothing peach-hued decor offers a pleasant setting and the service is good (except at the very busiest times, when it can be slow). The extensive menu features river fish and an array of well-prepared meat dishes. Daily 8.30am–1am.

La Terraza Paseo Victorica 134 ☎011 4371 2916, ⓦlaterrazatigre.com.ar. This classy *parrilla* has outside seating areas both on the pavement and on the first floor, where you get great views of the river. The meat has a good reputation and there is an excellent wine list to match. Tues–Sun 10am–1am.

THE DELTA

Alpenhaus Rama Negra ☎011 3378 9061, ⓦalpenhaus.com.ar. As the name suggests, this place serves up classic Germanic dishes, such as hams and sauerkraut, with plenty of tarts and strudels on offer for the sweet-toothed. Mon–Fri 11am–5pm, Sat & Sun 11am–6.30pm.

Gato Blanco Río Capitán ☎011 4728 0390, ⓦgato-blanco.com. One of the most upmarket restaurants in the whole Delta, its *ojo de bife* (a tender steak) is famous, as is the sole. Make sure you check the times of launches to get back or you might find yourself stranded after your leisurely lunch. Daily noon–4pm.

The pampa húmeda

Stretching for a couple of hundred kilometres west and northwest of Buenos Aires city, the **pampa húmeda** ("wet pampa") is the country's most fertile and valuable land. It is dotted with several sites of interest, including **Luján**, at the very beginning of RN-5, less than 70km west of the Capital Federal. This is Argentina's leading religious site, thanks to its vast basilica, purpose-built to house an image of the country's patron saint, the Virgin of Luján. Further along RN-5, **Mercedes** stands out for its authentic *pulpería*, largely unchanged since the nineteenth century. *Pulperías*, essentially provisions stores with a bar attached, performed an important social role in rural Argentina and enjoy an almost mythical status in gaucho folklore.

The most notable destination in the province, though, is **San Antonio de Areco**, a charming market town to the capital's northwest, along RN-8. Known colloquially as Areco, it has retained a remarkably authentic feel despite its popularity with tourists; if you visit only one pampas town during your stay in Argentina, this is the one. As the recognized centre of pampas tradition, Areco puts on a popular gaucho festival in November, and has some highly respected artisans and an extremely attractive and unusually well-preserved historic centre. Like other destinations in the *pampa húmeda*, it is close to Buenos Aires and a potential day-trip from the capital, but spending a night – especially at an estancia – will give you a better feel for the interior's much slower pace of life. Areco and its neighbours are also useful stopping-off points on the way to the Litoral, Córdoba or the Northwest.

The small town of **Lobos**, to the capital's southwest, is another popular weekend destination for Porteños, primarily for its lakeside setting. Further afield and better suited for a longer stay (or a stopover on the way to Patagonia), **Tandil** is an appealing

2

THE GAUCHO

The Pampas, the vast expanse of flat grassland that radiates out from Buenos Aires, forms one of the country's most famous features. Similarly, the **gaucho**, who once roamed them on horseback, *facón* (knife) clenched between his teeth, leaving a trail of broken hearts and gnawed steak bones behind him, is as important a part of the collective romantic imagination of Argentina as the Wild West cowboy is in the US. The popular depiction of this splendid, freedom-loving figure – whose real life must have been lonely and brutal – was crystallized in José Hernández's epic poem *Martín Fierro*, which every Argentine learns by heart at school. It's a way of life whose time has passed, but the gaucho's legacy remains. You're unlikely to witness knife fights over a woman, but you can still visit well-preserved *pulperías* (traditional bars), stay at estancias and watch weather-beaten old *paisanos* (folk from the countryside) playing cards and chuckling behind their huge handlebar moustaches. The term "gaucho" is still a compliment, while gaucho garb – beret or *boina*, knotted scarf, checked shirt, ornate belt (*tirador*), baggy trousers (*bombachas*), boots or espadrilles (*alpargatas*) and a poncho – is considered almost chic. A *gauchada* means a good deed or an act of macho heroism, altruistic courage or, at least, heartfelt generosity. Shrines of red flags dedicated to the semi-mythical Gauchito Gil (see box, p.238), one of the most famous gauchos of all, are often seen by the roadside throughout the country.

town of cobbled streets with its own tradition of pampas culture. The main attraction is the nearby mountain scenery, perfect for riding and long rambles.

Luján

Founded in 1756 on the site of a shrine containing a tiny ceramic figure of the Virgin Mary, **LUJÁN**, about 70km west of Buenos Aires, is now one of the major religious centres in Latin America. The **Virgin of Luján** (see box opposite) is the patron saint of Argentina, and the epic basilica erected in her honour in 1887 in Luján attracts around eight million visitors a year. This neo-Gothic edifice is one of the most memorable – though not the most beautiful – churches in Argentina. The town's other major attraction, the vast **Complejo Museográfico Enrique Udaondo**, is a multiplex museum with an important historical section, and is also Argentina's largest transport museum. Away from the museums and the basilica grouped around the central square, Luján is like any other provincial town, with some elegant, early twentieth-century townhouses and less-elegant modern buildings.

For a real flavour of Luján in full religious swing, you should visit at the weekend, when up to nine Masses are held a day – but, unless you desperately want to take part, avoid visiting during the annual **pilgrimages**, when the town is seriously overcrowded. These take place on May 8, the day of the Coronation of the Virgin; the last Sunday of September for the Gaucho pilgrimage, when up to a million gauchos come to honour the Virgin of Luján; the first Sunday of October, meanwhile, is dedicated to the Peregrinación Juvenil a Pie a Luján, when young pilgrims in their thousands walk here from Buenos Aires; and December 8, when smaller pilgrimages mark the Immaculate Conception, a national holiday.

Basílica de Nuestra Señora de Luján

Plaza Belgrano • Daily 8am–8pm • Free • **Mass** (30min) Mon–Sat 8am, 10am, 11am, 3pm, 5pm & 7pm, Sun also at 9am, 12.30pm & 3.30pm • **Crypt** Mon–Fri 10am–5pm, Sat & Sun 10am–6.30pm • $10 • ⓦ basilicadelujan.org.ar

The town's main drag, Avenida Nuestra Señora de Luján, rolls up like a tarmac carpet to the door of the **Basílica de Nuestra Señora de Luján**, at the far end of Luján's main square, Plaza Belgrano. At busy times, all you need to do to visit the Virgin is go with the flow. Begun in 1890 but not completed until 1937, the basilica is a mammoth edifice, built using a pinkish stone quarried in Entre Ríos. In true neo-Gothic style,

THE MIRACLE OF THE VIRGIN OF LUJÁN

In 1630, a Portuguese ship that docked in Buenos Aires on its way from Brazil contained a simple terracotta image of the **Virgin** made by an anonymous Brazilian craftsman. The icon had been ordered by a merchant from Santiago del Estero and, after unloading, it was transported by cart towards his estancia. After the cart paused near **Luján**, so the story goes, it could not be moved. Packages were taken off the cart in an attempt to lighten the load, but only when the tiny package containing the Virgin was removed would the cart budge. This was taken as a sign that the Virgin had decided on her own destination. A small chapel was built and the first pilgrims began to arrive.

The Virgin has been moved over the centuries, although according to legend it took three attempts and several days of prayer the first time. In 1872, Luján's Lazarist order – a religious body founded in Paris in 1625 with an emphasis on preaching to the rural poor – was entrusted with the care of the Virgin by the archbishop of Buenos Aires. In 1875, a member of the order, **Padre Jorge María Salvaire**, was almost killed in one of the last indigenous raids on Azul. Praying to the Virgin, he promised that if he survived he would promote her cult, write her history and build a temple in her name. He survived and the foundation stone to the basilica was laid in 1890.

The original terracotta Virgin is now barely recognizable: a protective bell-shaped silver casing was placed around it in the late nineteenth century. Sky-blue and white robes, the colours of the Argentine flag, were added, as well as a Gothic golden surround. The face of the original statue can now just about be seen, peering through a tiny gap in the casing. Even if you don't visit Luján itself, you cannot avoid seeing images of the Virgin: she is the patron saint of roads and paths, and almost every bus all over the country sports Luján figures and stickers.

everything about the basilica points heavenwards, from its remarkably elongated twin spires, which stand 106m tall, to the acute angles of the architraves surrounding the three main doors. At the centre of the facade, a large circular stained-glass window depicts the Virgin. The basilica's nineteen bells were cast in Milan from the bronze of World War I cannons. One of the two heavy crosses on the spires fell from a height of 100m at midnight on June 13, 2000; no one was harmed, but both crosses were replaced for safety reasons.

On busy days, entering through one of the heavy bronze doors is a bit like stepping onto a religious conveyor belt, as you get caught up in a seemingly endless stream of pilgrims, some on their knees, making their way to the **Camarín de la Virgen**. For a closer look at the Virgin, head up the stairs to the chamber behind the main altar, where you can observe her from behind. Positioned on a marble pedestal and swathed in robes and adornments, the statue at the centre of all the fuss is hard to see; most people gather around the replica in front of the altar below. The outside wall of the chamber is covered with dozens of plaques of all shapes and sizes – including heart-shaped ex votos – thanking the "Virgencita" for prayers answered. The **crypt** below the basilica holds another replica, explains the history and harbours reproductions of Virgins from all over the world, in particular from Latin America and Eastern Europe.

Complejo Museográfico Provincial Enrique Udaondo

Lezica y Torrezuri 917 and Plaza Belgrano • Wed–Fri 11.30am–5pm, Sat & Sun 10.30am–6pm • ☎ 02323 420245 • $3

West of the plaza in a cluster of mustard-and-white colonial buildings the **Complejo Museográfico Provincial Enrique Udaondo** claims to be the most important museum complex in South America. This is debatable, but it's certainly one of the continent's biggest. Its principal collections are housed within the Museo Histórico Colonial, inside the Casa del Virrey and the Cabildo on the western side of Plaza Belgrano, and the Museo de Transportes, at the northern end of the plaza, between Avenida Nuestra Señora de Luján and Lezica y Torrezuri.

2

Museo Colonial e Histórico

The **Museo Colonial e Histórico** is misleadingly named, since its exhibits cover a wider period. Access to the main collection is via the admittedly totally colonial **Cabildo** next door, a two-storey galleried building dating from 1772. The leaders of the short-lived British invasion, General William Beresford and Colonel Dennis Pack, were held at the Cabildo after their surrender in August 1806. Trophies captured during the quashing of the invasion, notably the staff of the 71st Highland Regiment, are displayed. An internal door leads onto a pretty courtyard with a marble well in the centre and an elegant wooden balustrade around the first floor of its green-and-white walls. Other rooms here feature displays on the gaucho (including some fine silver *mate* vessels), nineteenth-century fashion, and the disastrous and bloody War of the Triple Alliance against Paraguay.

Museo de Transportes

Argentina's largest transport museum and the first such in Latin America, the **Museo de Transportes** offers less a chronology of the evolution of transport than a display of some of the country's most historically significant planes, trains and carriages. The museum's two most outstanding exhibits are *La Porteña*, Argentina's first steam locomotive, whose maiden journey between Plaza Lavalle and Floresta in Buenos Aires took place in 1857, and the *Plus Ultra*, the hydroplane with which Ramón Franco, General Franco's brother, made the first crossing of the South Atlantic in 1926.

ARRIVAL AND INFORMATION   LUJÁN

By train There are frequent trains from the capital (Once station), changing at Moreno and terminating at Luján's train station, a couple of kilometres' walk southeast of the centre at Av España and Belgrano.

By bus The fastest way to reach Luján is on the #57 bus (Atlántida company) from Buenos Aires' Plaza Italia (every 20min; 1hr 15min). It arrives at the bus terminal on Av Nuestra Señora de Luján 600 (☎02323 420044), a

couple of blocks north of Plaza Belgrano.

Tourist information The town's tourist office is housed in a building known as La Cúpula, which stands in a park area on the riverbank between Lavalle and San Martín, a block west of Plaza Belgrano (Mon–Fri 9am–5pm, Sat & Sun 10am–6pm; ☎02323 427082, ⌨lujantur.com). In addition to maps and hotel lists, it has detailed info on the phenomenon of the Virgin and the basilica's history and importance.

EATING

La Chakana Defensa y Cortínez ☎02323 15 4042 1235. A Colombian chef offers a refreshing mix of traditional Argentine dishes and international classics at this delightful restaurant set among woods. Fri & Sun 8.30pm–midnight, Sat noon–3.30pm & 8.30pm–midnight.

L'Eau Vive Constitución 2112 ☎02323 421774, ⌨leauvivedeargentina.com.ar. Luján's most famous restaurant is a long way out of the centre, fifteen blocks east along Av San Martín from Plaza Colón and most easily

reached by taxi. The restaurant's main claim to fame is that it is run exclusively by nuns. The cooking, based on a traditional French menu with an emphasis on rich meat dishes, is generally excellent. Tues–Sat noon–2.30pm & 8.30pm–10pm, Sun noon–2.30pm.

La Recova San Martín 1 ☎02323 422280. Conveniently located next to the tourist office, this pleasant restaurant offers outdoor seating and a simple, reasonably priced menu that focuses on pasta. Daily 12.30–3pm & 8pm–midnight.

Mercedes

Peaceful and cultured, the well-preserved provincial town of **MERCEDES**, 100km northwest of Capital Federal along RN-5, was founded in 1752 as a fortress to protect the city from attacks by the Puelche. It's easy to find your way around – the main drag, Avenida 29, crosses central **Plaza San Martín**, which hosts the grand Italianate **Palacio Municipal** and large Gothic **Basílica Catedral Nuestra Señora de Mercedes** and is a hub of activity – especially in the evening, when locals fill the tables that spill out of its inviting *confiterías*. Mercedes' main draw, though, is its unmissable *pulpería*.

Pulpería "Lo de Cacho"
At the end of Av 29, two dozen blocks north of Plaza San Martín • Sat & Sun 11am–3pm & 8–11.30pm

The sign outside Mercedes' big attraction claims this to be the last *pulpería*. Known locally as "*Lo de Cacho*" (Cacho's place), it was run, until his death in 2009 at the age of 70, by the self-styled last *pulpero*, Cacho Di Catarina. The gloomy interior, which has hardly changed since it opened its doors in 1850, harbours a collection of dusty bottles, handwritten notices – included an original wanted poster for the biggest gaucho outlaw of them all, Juan Moreira, who was killed by a police posse in nearby Lobos – and gaucho paraphernalia: it doesn't require much imagination to conjure up visions of the knife fights the late Cacho claimed to have witnessed in his youth. His family still runs the bar in his name and musicians frequently drop in for a glass of Vasco Viejo wine and impromptu jamming, much of it dedicated to the sorely missed Cacho. To get to the *pulpería*, best visited in the evening for a beer and a *picada* featuring renowned local salami, take a *remís* or the local bus that runs towards the park from Avenida 29. A few blocks beyond the last stop, the road becomes unsealed and on the left-hand corner you'll see the simple white building, a sign saying "*pulpería*" painted on its side.

ARRIVAL AND INFORMATION
MERCEDES

By bus Mercedes' bus terminal, served by regular buses from the capital (the fastest way to get here), is south of the town centre, from where it's a 20min walk to Plaza San Martín. There's a local bus from the terminal to the centre, but it is infrequent, so if you don't fancy the walk you may be better off taking one of the bus station taxis (☎ 02324 420651).

By train Regular trains leave from the capital's Once station, though you need to change at Moreno and the journey takes close to three hours. The train station is along Av España, eight blocks north of the centre.

Tourist information The tourist office (Av 29 and c/26; Mon 7am–1pm, Tues–Fri 7am–6pm, Sat & Sun 10am–5pm; ☎ 02324 421080, ⓦ mercedes.gob.ar) doesn't have much printed information, but the staff are enthusiastic and knowledgeable, and can provide you with a town map.

ACCOMMODATION

There's a free municipal **campsite** in Parque Municipal Independencia (República del Chile and Calle 62; ☎ 0810 333 0997) on the edge of town; take any local bus from Avenida 29. Mercedes hosts a motorbike rally at the end of March, the only time you might have trouble finding space to pitch your tent.

Gran Hotel Mercedes Av 29 and c/16 ☎ 02324 425987, ⓦ granhotelmercedes.com.ar. It looks stern and unpromising from the outside, but the rooms are quite comfortable and have a/c and TV, while facilities include a restaurant and bar area. **$850**

Hostal del Sol Av 2 and Av 3 ☎ 02324 433400, ⓦ hotelhostaldelsol.com. This good-value place on the western edge of town offers large, comfortable rooms in a tranquil setting. **$990**

EATING AND DRINKING

Mercedes is the national capital of **salami** and even hosts a salami festival in September. You should certainly try some while you are here – the *salamín picado grueso* is favoured by locals, although its high fat content might be off-putting; the *pulpería Lo de Cacho* (see above) is one of the best places to sample some. Though the town isn't overflowing with any gastronomic wonders, you can keep hunger at bay or quench your thirst.

La Recova Plaza San Martín s/n. Of the *confiterías* around the plaza – all good for coffee, sandwiches and snacks – this is one of the nicest, housed in the only building in the square to retain an old-fashioned *revoca*

(arcade). Daily noon–5.30pm & 8.30pm–midnight.
La Vieja Esquina C/25 and c/28 ☎ 02324 423351. A charming traditional corner bar that also sells deli produce, and is famed for its excellent *picadas*. Daily noon–11.30pm.

San Antonio de Areco
Delightful **SAN ANTONIO DE ARECO**, the national capital of gaucho traditions, hosts the annual **Fiesta de la Tradición** (see box, p.143), the country's most important festival celebrating pampas culture. Despite its modest promotion as a tourist destination,

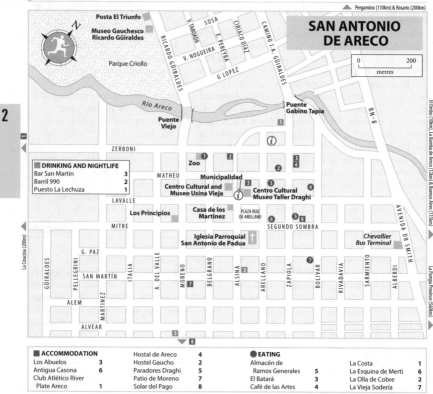

Pergamino (110km) & Rosario (200km)

SAN ANTONIO DE AREO

Posta El Triunfo

Museo Gauchesco Ricardo Güiraldes

Parque Criollo

Río Areco

Puente Viejo

Puente Gabino Tapia

ZERBONI

Zoo

MATHEU

Municipalidad

Centro Cultural and Museo Usina Vieja

Centro Cultural Museo Taller Draghi

LAVALLE

Casa de los Martinez

Los Principios

PLAZA RUIZ DE ARELLANO

MITRE

SEGUNDO SOMBRA

Iglesia Parroquial San Antonio de Padua

Chevallier Bus Terminal

G. PAZ

SAN MARTÍN

ALEM

ALVEAR

■ DRINKING AND NIGHTLIFE	
Bar San Martin	3
Barril 990	2
Puesto La Lechuza	1

■ ACCOMMODATION				● EATING			
Los Abuelos	3	Hostal de Areco	4	Almacén de		La Costa	1
Antigua Casona	6	Hostel Gaucho	2	Ramos Generales	5	La Esquina de Merti	6
Club Atlético River		Paradores Draghi	5	El Batará	3	La Olla de Cobre	2
Plate Areco	1	Patio de Moreno	7	Café de las Artes	4	La Vieja Sodería	7
		Solar del Pago	8				

playing on its appealing setting by the banks of the peaceful Río Areco, the town has retained a genuine feel. You may not find Areco full of galloping gauchos outside festival week, but you still have a good chance of spotting estancia workers on horseback, sporting traditional berets, or coming across *paisanos* propping up the bar of a traditional *boliche* establishment (see p.146). Areco has a prestigious literary connection: the town was the setting for Ricardo Güiraldes' Argentine classic *Don Segundo Sombra* (1926), a novel influential in changing the gaucho's image from that of an undesirable outlaw to a symbol of national values.

The town's only real sights are a few museums, the most important being the **Museo Gauchesco Ricardo Güiraldes**. But what makes Areco memorable is the harmonious architectural character of the town's centre: all cobbled streets and faded Italianate and colonial facades punctuated by elaborate wrought-iron grilles and delicately arching lamps. Some excellent **artisans** also work in *talleres* (workshops), and while weaving and leatherwork are well represented, silversmiths are the highlight.

Areco's traditional gaucho atmosphere extends to the surrounding area, where you will find some of Argentina's most famous **estancias**, offering a luxurious accommodation alternative to staying in Areco itself. The town and its surroundings were hit by terrible floods in late 2009, and many sights have recovered over the past few years, after extensive and costly restoration work.

Plaza Ruiz de Arellano

Areco's main square, the leafy **Plaza Ruiz de Arellano**, six blocks west of the bus terminal, is named after José Ruiz de Arellano, whose estancia stood on the site now occupied by the town and who built Areco's founding chapel (see below) on the south side of the square. Among the elegant *fin-de-siècle* residences that flank the plaza, there is the Italianate **municipalidad**, to the north, painted a particularly delicate version of the pink that characterizes so many of Areco's buildings. On the northwest corner of the square stands a typically colonial two-storey construction built in 1720 and known as the **Casa de los Martínez**, after the local family who once inhabited it. The building's handsome but rather plain green-and-white exterior is dominated by the original railings of a balcony, running around the first floor.

Parroquia San Antonio de Padua

Mitre 366 • Daily 9am–6pm • ☎ 02326 452268

José Ruiz de Arellano's original **chapel**, a simple adobe construction, was declared a parish church in 1730; it was rebuilt in 1792, then again in 1870, in keeping with the town's growing importance. Of no great architectural note, the current version is nonetheless a pleasingly simple white construction, with clear Italian influences. The exterior is dominated by a statue of St Anthony himself, who stands within a niche clad with blue-and-white tiles that echo those of the church's small bell-shaped dome. The inside is admittedly impressive, with a high vaulted ceiling.

Centro Cultural y Museo Taller Draghi

Lavalle 387 • Mon–Sat 10am–12.30pm & 3.30–6.30pm, Sun 10am–12.30pm; free guided visits 11am, 5pm & 6pm • $20 • ☎ 02326 454219, Ⓦ draghiplaterosorfebres.com

Bang opposite Parroquia San Antonio de Padua church, one of Areco's most renowned silversmith families runs the **Centro Cultural y Museo Taller Draghi**. The centre displays some fine pieces made in the *platería criolla* style, which first emerged around 1750 when local craftsmen, who had previously worked according to Spanish and Portuguese tradition, began developing their own style. Fantastically ornate yet sturdy, in keeping with the practical use to which the items are put – at least in theory – the style is still commonly used to produce gaucho knives (*facones*), belts (*rastras*), *yerba mate* gourds and stirrups. The museum/workshop mixes the creations of the late Juan José Draghi – who produced pieces for international figures such as the king and queen of Spain – with a collection of nineteenth-century silver spurs, bridles and swords that have been his inspiration. As there's little in the way of labels, it's hard to tell which is antique and which modern, but the helpful guide on hand will put you straight. Draghi died in 2008, but his sons Mariano and Patricio inherited his skills and now run the workshop. Among Draghi's finest work are the *mates*, which come in their original chalice shape (based on those used in churches) with finely wrought silver stems of cherubs and flowers. Such *mates* are now for decoration only, being expensive – not to mention likely to scald your fingers if filled with hot water.

FIESTA DE LA TRADICIÓN

One of Argentina's most original and enjoyable festivals, San Antonio de Areco's **Fiesta de la Tradición** began in 1939 on an initiative of then-mayor José Antonio Güiraldes. The actual Día de la Tradición is November 10 – the birthday of José Hernández, author of Argentina's gaucho text *par excellence*, *Martín Fierro* – but celebrations last for a week and are organized to run from weekend to weekend, either the first or second week in November, depending on the weather. Activities, including exhibitions, dances, music recitals and shows of gaucho skills, last throughout the week, although the high point is the final Sunday, which begins with dancing and a procession of gauchos dressed in their traditional loose trousers tapered at the ankle (*bombachas*), ornamented belts and wide-brimmed hats or berets. An *asado con cuero*, a barbecue on which meat – ususally beef – is cooked around a fire with its skin on, takes place at noon in the Parque Criollo (at a reduced price for gauchos) and is followed by an extensive display of gaucho skills, including *jineteadas*, Argentine bronco riding.

Centro Cultural & Museo Usina Vieja

Alsina 66 • Tues–Sun 11.15am–4.45pm • $5 • ☎ 02326 454722

A block north of Plaza Ruiz de Arellano is the **Centro Cultural y Museo Usina Vieja**. The restored building originally housed Areco's first electrical generator and has been declared a national industrial monument. Now housing a cultural centre, the building also contains the **Museo Usina Vieja**, an eclectic collection – mainly supplied through local donations – of everyday items, from clothing to record players and even the town's old telephone switchboard. There's also a good display of the nationally famous **gaucho cartoons** of Florencia Molino Campos, first published in almanacs and now adorning hotel walls the length of the country.

Parque Criollo and Museo Gauchesco Ricardo Güiraldes

Ricardo Güiraldes s/n • Museum daily 10am–5pm • Guided visits 11.30am & 3pm • Free • ☎ 02326 455839

After crossing the brick **Puente Viejo** you reach the rather scrubby **Parque Criollo**, less a park than a kind of exhibition ground, used during the Fiesta de la Tradición as the setting for the main displays of gaucho skills, and within the grounds is the **Museo Gauchesco Ricardo Güiraldes**. The entrance to the park and the museum is via the *Pulpería La Blanqueada*, once a staging post on the old Camino Real, which linked Buenos Aires with Alto Perú. It was the setting for the first encounter between Fabio, the young hero of Güiraldes' much-loved novel, and his mentor, Don Segundo Sombra. The *pulpería* closed in the 1930s but original features have been retained, including the traditional grille that separated the owner from his customers' knives and light fingers.

The museum – one of the constructions that suffered in the 2009 flooding and reopened in 2015 – is housed in a 1930s reproduction of an old estancia. Its collection mixes gaucho paraphernalia – *mate* gourds, silverware and *boleadoras* (lasso balls) – with objects deemed to be fascinating because of their famous owners – General Rosas' bed, W.H. Hudson's books, and so on. Of interest are black-and-white photos of the original gauchos who inspired Güiraldes, and the branding irons they used – each landowner had his own, somewhat cabalistic symbol, worn in various forms as a badge of pride by his men as well as his cattle.

ARRIVAL AND INFORMATION · SAN ANTONIO DE ARECO

By bus Most buses from Buenos Aires and Rosario stop at the pink Nueva Chevallier terminal (☎ 02326 453904) at General Paz and Av Dr Smith, six blocks east of Areco's town centre. It's an easy and enjoyable stroll into town along Segundo Sombra, which brings you to Areco's main square, Plaza Ruiz de Arellano. If you're carrying a lot of luggage – or heading for an estancia – take a *remís* (☎ 02326 456225).

Tourist information The tourist office at Arellano and Zerboni (daily 8am–7pm; ☎ 02326 453165) has useful information, including maps, lists of hotels and artisan workshops. There's also a small office in the municipalidad building (Sat & Sun 9am–8pm) on Plaza Ruiz de Arellano, to cope with the extra influx of Porteños escaping Capital Federal at the weekend.

ACCOMMODATION

Areco is easily visited as a day-trip from Buenos Aires, but many museums and workshops close during the afternoon, which can prove frustrating. Staying overnight gives you the chance to explore the town at a leisurely pace and enjoy it at its best, in the morning and evening. Several cafés also double up as simple *hospedajes* (see p.31). If you plan on visiting during the Fiesta de la Tradición celebrations, book a few weeks in advance; the tourist office can provide information on homestays. The countryside around Areco is home to a couple of the province's most traditional **estancias** (see box opposite).

Los Abuelos Zapiola and Zeboni ☎ 02326 456390. A decent option if you're after a more modern type of hotel, and reasonably priced. Rooms have TV and fans (extra for a/c), with balconies looking out over the Río Areco. **$800**

Antigua Casona Segunda Sombra 495 ☎ 02325 15 416030, ⊛ antiguacasona.com. An 1897-built B&B with a rustic edge and a lovely patio where a good breakfast is served. An outdoor swimming pool is the perfect antidote to summer heat. **$1200**

Club Atlético River Plate Areco Costanera s/n ☎ 02326 453590, ⊛ riverplateareco.com. The best campsite within easy reach of Areco is approached by following Zerboni west

2

THE ESTANCIAS OF BUENOS AIRES PROVINCE

Estancias are Argentina's haciendas or ranches, mostly wealthy farms set up to raise livestock on extensive swathes of green pasture, dotted with the odd ombú tree. The owners, or *estancieros*, effectively make up the country's aristocracy, and still employ large numbers of *peones* (ranch hands), some of them regarded as latter-day gauchos, to look after their cattle and, occasionally, sheep. The main buildings, known as *cascos*, range from simple colonial-style farmsteads to ornate mansions, with architecture inspired by French chateaux, English country homes or Italianate palaces. Scattered all over the country, but with the greatest concentration in Buenos Aires Province, above all around San Antonio de Areco in the north and Cañuelas and Lobos in the south, many of them take in paying guests. This can be either for a *día de campo*, during which visitors take part in outdoor activities, such as horseriding or even a polo class, and enjoy three or four hearty meals, or overnight stays in often luxurious rooms for a complete estancia experience.

La Bamba de Areco 12km from Areco (120km from Capital Federal) ☎ 011 4519 4996, ⊕ labambadeareco.com. *La Bamba* was used in María Luisa Bemberg's film *Camila* – the story of the ill-fated romance between wealthy socialite Camila O'Gorman and a priest – and is one of Argentina's most distinctive estancias. The Río Areco runs through the grounds, so guests can fish as well as ride, although "shows" in the *pulpería* and immaculate living rooms make the place seem Disneyfied. Well worth the visit to see horse whisperer Martín Tatta work his charms. Day-trips from US$200. US$790

La Candelaria RN-205 Km14.5, Lobos ☎ 02227 494132 ⊕ estanciacandelaria.com. For the ultimate in royal stays, book into this unexpected and extremely luxurious castle located close to Lobos. Each of the 22 rooms has been carefully designed to show off the best of rural style – and it works. Book in for a polo clinic, a talk about the sport of kings or even for a private four-chukka exhibition match in the stunning grounds. Full board. US$200

La Cinacina Zerboni s/n, San Antonio de Areco; follow Bartolomé Mitre five blocks west of the main plaza to the end of the street ☎ 02326 452773, ⊕ lacinacina.com.ar While large tour groups roll in for relatively affordable "days in the country", you can stay

the night, in pretty, light, country-style rooms for the full experience at a good price. US$2100

El Ombú Ruta 31, Areco ☎ 02326 492080, ⊕ estanciaelombu.com. Arguably the most luxurious estancia near Areco, with sumptuously decorated rooms and a lovely tiled and ivy-covered veranda. As well as offering horseriding, *El Ombú* has a small but well-maintained swimming pool and a games room. Other activities include helping out with – or at least observing – farm tasks and, of course, eating delicious *asados*, sometimes served under the shade of the large ombú tree that gives the estancia its name. Directions are on the website; the estancia will arrange a transfer from Buenos Aires. US$100 as a day-visit. US$205 per person

Puesto Viejo Ruta 6 Km83, Cañuelas, 120km south of Buenos Aires ☎ 011 6091 9266, ⊕ puestoviejoestancia.com.ar. Run by an Anglo–Argentine couple, *Puesto Viejo* is primarily a place for those wanting to improve their polo game; lessons cater to all levels, including beginners. However, you don't have to be a polo player or even a fan to stay here – it's a beautiful, laidback place and the room price includes abundant amounts of food and drink, plus one horse-ride a day. Given its function as a polo club, you're bound to catch a match here. There are additional costs for polo lessons and playing matches, which are worth it given the top-notch tutors. US$200 per person

out of town. There's a large swimming pool within the grounds. US$250 per four-person tent

Hostal de Areco Zapiola 25 ☎ 02326 456118, ⊕ hostaldeareco.com.ar. One of the most attractive accommodation options in town: a traditional rose-coloured building with farmhouse-style decor. The hotel has a bar and comfortable communal area with a fireplace, and serves up a delicious breakfast. US$800

Hostel Gaucho Zerboni 308 ☎ 02326 453625. Hostel with decent communal area and a garden equipped with *parrilla*. Dorms US$100; doubles US$350

Paradores Draghi Matheu 380 ☎ 02326 455583 ⊕ paradoresdraghi.com.ar. The family behind the

museum and cultural centre (see opposite) also provides very charming rooms available on a B&B basis behind the workshop – enquire at the museum. US$1100

★**Patio de Moreno** Moreno 251 and San Martín ☎ 02326 455197, ⊕ patiodemoreno.com. Stylish, centrally located boutique hotel with ten modern rooms, many with views onto a pretty garden. There's also a heated swimming pool and a wine bar serving Argentine wares. US$1800

Solar del Pago Hipólito G. Fiore 232 ☎ 02326 15 410252, ⊕ solardelpago.com. Located out of town on RP-41 in the direction of San Andrés de Giles, this hotel affords stunning views of the nearby Pampas. The hotel has a restaurant and spa, as well as disabled access. US$1100

2

EATING

Most of Areco's locals tend to go in for traditional food such as steak and, true to their gaucho roots, regard a pizza as the most exotic dish they are willing to try. That said, you can find some smarter **restaurants** in this prosperous town to vary your meals a little.

Almacén de Ramos Generales Zapiola 143 ☎ 02326 456376, ⓦ ramosgeneralesareco.com.ar. A converted old *almacén* (general store), this bustling place serves *parrilla*, *picadas* and popular specials such as trout in Roquefort sauce with boiled potatoes. Daily noon–3.30pm & 8.30pm–midnight.

El Batará Arellano 59. This down-to-earth little store does *picadas*, featuring a variety of cured cuts and cheese, plus sandwiches on home-made bread. Grab a space on the bench just outside. Daily noon–4pm & 8pm–midnight.

Café de las Artes Bolívar 70. This arty café – as the name suggests – does tasty handmade pasta that even Italians would find authentic, along with meat dishes such as the unusual but delicious pork in blackberry sauce. Summer daily noon–4pm & 8pm–midnight; winter Wed–Sun noon–4pm & 8pm–midnight.

La Costa Zerboni and Belgrano ☎ 02326 452481. This no-nonsense *parrilla* is popular with the locals for its keenly priced, generous servings of grilled meat, salads and hearty desserts like *budín de pan* (bread pudding). Daily noon–4pm & 8pm–midnight.

La Esquina de Merti Arellano 174 and Segundo Sombra ☎ 02326 456705, ⓦ esquinademerti.com.ar. A much-loved place on the main plaza whose walls are adorned with old signs, ads and bottles, making it a tasteful re-creation of a *pulpería*. It serves straightforward Argentine classics and offers a decent set lunch ($150) with drinks included. Daily noon–3pm & 8pm–1am.

La Olla de Cobre Matheu 433 ☎ 02326 453105, ⓦ laolladecobre.com.ar. A small but renowned chocolate factory and sweet shop where you can try handmade chocolates and delicious *alfajores* before buying. Daily 10am–1pm & 3.30–8.30pm.

★ **La Vieja Sodería** Bolívar and General Paz. The pick of Areco's old-style establishments: coloured soda bottles line the walls of this *pulpería*, which serves a wide range of teas and beers, plus snacks including sandwiches and *picadas*. Daily noon–midnight.

DRINKING AND NIGHTLIFE

The best **bars** in Areco are *boliches* – traditional places where estancia workers drink Fernet and play cards. Most *boliches* in the modern sense of the word – **nightclubs** – are out on Avenida Dr Smith, near the bus terminal (usually Fri & Sat only). Also look out for *pulperías* and *almacenes,* traditional bars that are great for a beer and a plate of peanuts; they do serve as tourist attractions, yet maintain an authentic aura.

Bar San Martín Moreno and Alvear. This is a classic *boliche* – and hence a good bet for spotting local characters meeting up for a chat over a Fernet or two. Daily noon–late.

Barril 990 San Martín 381. More a modern pub than a classic *boliche* but occasionally you can hear live music here. Daily noon–late.

Puesto La Lechuza Victorino Althaparro 423 ☎ 02326 15 470136. Down by the riverside, the "Owl" is one of the typical *boliches* serving up *asado* and a likely place to catch folk music and dancing on a Sat evening. Daily 7pm–1am.

Lobos

LOBOS, an old-fashioned country town with picturesque, slightly crumbling houses, is best known for its famous son – Juan Domingo Perón – who was born here in 1895 at the house-turned-museum which now bears the address Perón 482; an archive of his letters and photos is stored there (Wed–Sun 10am–noon & 3–6pm; free; ☎ 02227 422843). About 100km southwest of the capital on RN-205, Lobos is also reachable from Mercedes via RP-41.

Laguna de Lobos

Around 15km southwest of Lobos is a series of lakes known as *lagunas* (lagoons), the area's main attraction. The biggest and best is **Laguna de Lobos**, thought to be named after the resident otters, *lobos de agua* ("river wolves") in Spanish. Excellent sand-smelt fishing, boating, windsurfing and kitesurfing are all possible; equipment can be rented from several places around the lake, where there are also picnic spots shaded by pines and eucalyptus. To get to the *lagunas*, take the local bus from Lobos that runs every few hours from the corner of Alem and 9 de Julio, opposite the train station.

ARRIVAL AND DEPARTURE   **LOBOS**

By train The train terminal is on the corner of 9 de Julio and Alem, around six blocks east of the town's central square, Plaza 1810. There are hourly services to and from Once in Buenos Aires via Merlo (2hr 15min).

By bus Lobos' main bus station for companies such as El Rápido is on the corner of Héroes de Malvinas and Perón. Minibus services, or *combis*, such as Lobos Bus (Buenos Aires 579; ☎ 02227 431346, ⓦ lobosbus.com.ar), have their own smaller terminals around town. Departures from both to Buenos Aires every hour (2hr).

INFORMATION AND ACTIVITIES

Tourist information Lobos' useful tourist office (Mon–Fri 8am–2pm) is in the Edificio Bicentenario, by the train station on Av Alem 149. Smaller, weekend-only information centres can be found by the entrance of the Lagunas, and in the train station (Sat & Sun 9.30am–6.30pm; ☎ 02227 422275, ⓦ lobos.gov.ar).

Polo Lobos is a centre for polo, which is taught at a number of nearby estancias such as *Puesto Viejo* (see box, p.145).

Skydiving There is a large and well-equipped skydiving school, CEPA (☎ 02227 15 614891, ⓦ paracaidismolobos .com), on RP-205 at Km105, just outside Lobos. All levels are catered for, and tandem jumps with instructors are available.

ACCOMMODATION

Aguará Hotel & Spa Los Eucaliptus 296 ☎ 02227 430090, ⓦ aguarahotel.com. A modern hotel just outside of town; spacious rooms, a large, well-tended garden and fine dining can be found here. **$1500**

Camping Club de Pesca ☎ 02227 494089, ⓦ clubdepescalobos.com.ar. Best of the lakeside campsites – rent boats or go fishing from the jetty. **$80**

Tandil

The attractive town of **TANDIL**, many of whose streets are cobbled with stones quarried from nearby, is set among the central section of the **Sistema de Tandilia**, a long range of granite hills. This is also the birthplace of two of Argentina's top tennis players, Juan Martín del Potro and Juan Mónaco. Beginning around 150km northwest of the town and running across the province to Mar del Plata, they seldom rise above 200m; close to Tandil, however, there are craggy peaks of up to 504m. Although this is not wild trekking country, the sierras are ideal for **horseriding** and **mountain biking**. The town itself is well geared for the holiday-makers who come all year on weekend breaks, with some excellent accommodation plus enticing delicatessens and restaurants and a lively feel in the evening. Tandil is popular during Holy Week, when the Vía Crucis (Stations of the Cross) processions take place; they end at Monte Calvario, a small hillock topped by a giant cross, to the east of the town centre.

Plaza Independencia

The central square, **Plaza Independencia**, on the site of the old fort, is overlooked by the grand municipal building and the overblown **Iglesia del Santísimo Sacramento**. Neo-Romanesque in style, this church was inspired by Paris's Sacré Coeur – hence the unusual elongated domes that top the three towers. A block back at 25 de Mayo and Rodríguez, the more attractive **Iglesia Luterana Danesa**, built in the 1870s, stands among cypress trees, with a simple white facade that wouldn't look out of place in Jutland – and a reminder of the multiethnic nature of immigration into Buenos Aires in the late nineteenth century. The streets surrounding the plaza, especially 9 de Julio, have a bustling feel, particularly in the evenings, when they are filled with people out for a stroll, or sitting outside the cafés and ice-cream parlours.

Museo Municipal de Bellas Artes Tandil (MUMBAT)

Chacabuco 357 • Tues–Fri 9am–noon & 5–8pm, Sat & Sun 5–8pm • Free • ☎ 0249 443 2067, ⓦ mumbat.com

In a splendid Art Nouveau palace around the corner from the municipalidad, the surprisingly good **Museo Municipal de Bellas Artes Tandil (MUMBAT)** houses a worthwhile collection of works by some major names in Argentine art, including

2

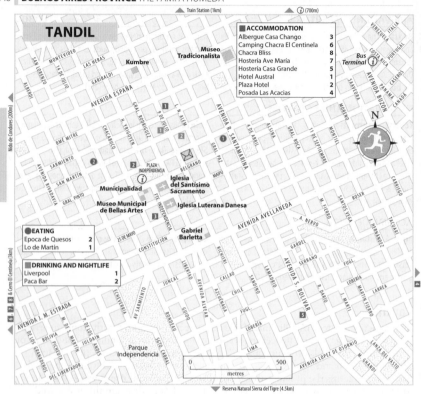

Noé, Gorriarena, Quirós and Ferrari, all belonging to the prestigious Santamarina collection, part of which was bequeathed to the museum's national counterpart in Buenos Aires.

Parque Independencia
Av Avellaneda and Rondeau, 10 blocks south of the centre

The entrance to **Parque Independencia** on Avenida Avellaneda (not to be confused with the plaza of the same name) is marked by the twin towers of a mock-Venetian palazzo, while its central wooded hill is topped by a kitsch Moorish castle. A road snakes around to the summit of the hill, which affords a clear view over the city, and an equally kitsch Moorish bar and restaurant, the *Luz de Luna*, complete with belly dancers.

Museo Histórico Fuerte Independencia
4 de Abril 845 • Tues–Sun: summer 4–8pm; winter 2–6pm • $5 • ☎ 0249 443 5573

North of the town centre, the **Museo Histórico Fuerte Independencia** occupies a handsome old building and consists of a staggeringly large collection of artefacts donated by locals. Although slightly disorganized, the museum is pleasant to wander around and features some curiosities, including photos of the enormous **Piedra La Movediza** (literally "the moving stone"), which rested at an inconceivably steep angle on one of the town's many rocky outcrops, before finally smashing to the valley floor in 1912. Thought to have given Tandil its Mapuche name ("Moving Rock"), the stone is so famous nationally that many Argentines are disappointed to arrive and find that it's no longer there; a cement replica stands in the place where the original once teetered.

The museum's warehouses contain many valuable examples of the huge carts, or *chatas*, once used to transport cereals around Argentina; the enormous wheels in the courtyard, the largest in the country, come from a *chata* that needed fifteen horses to pull it. Look out also for *materas* – huge country hearths – where the gaucho and his clan would take their *mate*, roast their *asado*, stay warm, wash clothes and do everything else.

ARRIVAL AND DEPARTURE   TANDIL

By train The train station (☎0810 666 8736) is at Av Machado and Colón, around twenty blocks northeast of the main square – trains leave Buenos Aires on Tues and Fri at 5pm, returning on Wed and Sun at 11pm (7hr). The return to BA is not recommended as it gets you into dodgy Constitución station late at night.
By bus Tandil's bus terminal (☎0249 443 2092) is around

fifteen blocks east of the main square, at Buzón 650; there are usually plenty of taxis (☎0249 442 2466) waiting to take you into town, or you could take local bus #501.
Destinations Buenos Aires (hourly; 5hr); Mar del Plata (hourly; 3hr); Necochea (4 daily; 3hr); San Miguel del Monte (3 daily; 3hr).

INFORMATION AND ACTIVITIES

Tourist information The main tourist office is east of the city centre, at Av Espora 1120 (summer Mon–Fri 8am–7pm, Sat 10am–7pm, Sun 9am–1pm; winter Mon–Fri 8am–6pm, Sat 10am–6pm, Sun 9am–1pm; ☎0249 443 2073, ⓦturismo.tandil.gov.ar), but there are also smaller, helpful offices at the bus terminal and on Plaza Independencia.
Adventure tour operators Perhaps the best way to explore the region is with the growing number of companies

offering adventure tourism opportunities: Nido de Condores (Necochea 166; ☎0249 442 6519, ⓔncondores@yahoo .com.ar) runs a range of activities including trekking, abseiling, canoeing and mountain biking; Gabriel Barletta (Avellaneda 673; ☎0249 442 7725, ⓔcabalgatasbarletta @yahoo.com.ar) offers adventurous half-day horse rides around the sierras, and regular group swimming sessions. Mountain bikes can be rented at Kumbre (9 de Julio 994; ☎0249 443 4313, ⓦkumbre.com).

ACCOMMODATION

Popular for short breaks throughout the year, Tandil is inundated in January and even more so at Easter, when most **hotels** increase their prices and are often fully booked up to a month beforehand. At other times, there is a good choice of mid-range accommodation. There are also numerous **cabañas** on the outskirts of the town (the tourist office has plenty of leaflets), although you'll need your own transport to reach most of them. **Campsites** are also numerous.

★**Albergue Casa Chango** 25 de Mayo 451 ☎0249 442 2260, ⓦcasa-chango.com.ar. Youth hostel in a large, attractive house, colourfully decorated with an artistic touch. There are several pretty patios perfect for playing chess or chatting with one of the many Argentine students who make up the bulk of the guests. Decent dorms or double rooms. Dorms $180; doubles $580
Camping Chacra El Centinela Av Estrada ☎0249 443 3475, ⓦchacraelcentinela.com.ar. A quiet and attractive wooded campsite 4km west of town along the road out towards Cerro El Centinela, with hot water round the clock and fire pits. Log cabins ($1350) and dorms ($700) are also available. $140
Chacra Bliss Av Estrada, Circuito Turístico Paraje La Porteña ☎0249 15 439 0900, ⓦchacrabliss.com.ar. Shabby chic is the order of the day at this comfy lodge. Splash out on one of two more private *casa de campo* Mexican-style houses ($2500). The delicious breakfast (included) with home-made jams is a highlight. $2200
★**Hostería Ave María** Circuito Turístico Paraje La Porteña ☎0249 442 2843, ⓦavemariatandil.com.ar.

This gorgeous country lodge 7km southwest of the centre is set among stunning grounds, with an avenue of monkey puzzle trees leading to a walnut grove. Peace is guaranteed: the swimming pool is overlooked by eucalyptus; the dozen charming rooms afford sweeping views of the sierras; and you can explore the picturesque surroundings on horseback or in a carriage. Prices include delicious and generous breakfasts and dinners; *asado* is also on the menu. Half-board $3100
Hostería Casa Grande Bolívar 557 ☎0249 443 1719, ⓦhosteriacasagrande.com.ar. Very comfortable *hostería* in a one-storey stone building with its own decent-sized pool and a small spa. There's a recreation area with a bar, a pool table and, unusually for Argentina, a dartboard. $1600
Hotel Austral 9 de Julio 725 ☎0249 442 5606, ⓦhotelaustraltandil.com.ar. A friendly hotel in a modern building in the centre of town. The en-suite rooms are equipped with TV and telephone; the hotel does not offer breakfast but there is an adjoining *confitería*. $750
Plaza Hotel General Pinto 438 ☎02293 427160, ⓦplazahoteldetandil.com.ar. A three-star hotel with an

on-site restaurant and slightly sterile but comfortable rooms that come equipped with a/c. Rooms at the front overlook the plaza. $1200

Posada Las Acacias Brasil 642 ☎0249 442 3373, ⓦposadalasacacias.com.ar. Located at the foot of the sierras and surrounded by acacia trees, this nineteenth-century former country home is quaint yet chic. Enjoy the well-kept garden, hammocks and swimming pool. $1650

EATING

There are plenty of good **restaurants** in Tandil, most of them within a few blocks of Plaza Independencia. The town is also extremely proud of its charcuterie and cheeses, so make a beeline for the twenty or so establishments that form part of the *Circuito del salame y el queso* circuit; visit the comprehensive ⓦturismo.tandil.gov.ar website for more info.

Epoca de Quesos San Martín and 14 de Julio ☎0249 444 8750, ⓦepocadequesos.com. Northwest of the plaza, this delicatessen-cum-pub is one of Tandil's oldest buildings, dating back to 1860, a simple, white construction that originally functioned as a staging post and is now one of the region's foodie hotspots. You can order local specialities, including every conceivable kind of salami, delicious garlic and herb cheeses, strong whisky cheddar, berry conserves and artisan dark stout. There is a charming terrace shaded by vines but the chairs are extremely uncomfortable. Daily 9am–11pm.

Lo de Martín Pinto 965 ☎0249 444 6050. This upmarket *tenedor libre* serves an impressive range of meats, salads and international dishes – try the suckling pig (*lechón*) or the lamb. Daily noon–4pm & 8pm–late.

DRINKING AND NIGHTLIFE

On warm evenings, you'll find people sitting at outdoor tables as **bars** extend out onto the pavements in the centre of town.

Liverpool 9 de Julio and San Martín ☎0249 444 2279. One of the classic bars on the main plaza; its Anglo-inspired interior comes complete with a red phone box and photos of England. Daily 7pm–late.

Paca Bar San Martín 775. For late-night drinking and dancing, try the centrally located *Paca Bar*, which sometimes hosts karaoke nights. Thurs–Sat from midnight.

The Sistema de Tandilia sierras

The green and rocky hills that form **the Sistema de Tandilia sierras**, about 350km from Buenos Aires, are perfect for trekking. The highest peak is the **Sierra Las Animas** (504m), southeast of Tandil town centre, not far from the end of Avenida Brasil. It's a two- to three-hour scramble over rocks to the top, but the peak lies on private land and you must go with a guide; there are several areas of privately owned land in the sierras which you may accidentally wander onto, so check with the tourist office (see p.149), which also has a list of guides, before setting out. More accessible is **Cerro El Centinela**, a smaller peak topped by an upright 7m rock balanced on an unfeasibly tiny base. To get there, head southwest along Avenida J.M. Estrada, the continuation of Avenida Avellaneda; the signposted track to the Cerro lies to the left, about 6km out of town. As the Cerro has been turned into a complex (ⓦcerroelcentinela.com.ar) with all kinds of attractions, it is rather too developed for some tastes. The road stops just a few metres short of the summit, and – should you be feeling hungry – there's a *parrilla*. Nearby is the base of the *aerosilla*, or chairlift (noon–dusk; $95 return), a fifteen-minute ride over the pines of the valley to another, higher peak from where you can enjoy views over the hills as well as burgers and milkshakes at the *Salón de la Cumbre confitería*. You can go on short walks on marked trails near the chairlift.

Reserva Natural Sierra del Tigre

Don Bosco and Suiza • Thurs–Tues 9am–6pm • $20

Several blocks south of Tandil, the **Reserva Natural Sierra del Tigre** is a privately run patch of sierra where you can see indigenous species such as guanaco (cousins to the llama) as well as introduced deer, antelope and wild boar. The *yaguaraté*, a wild cat that

gave the sierra its name, no longer prowls around, but the hills are home to the tiny striped *marí marí* frog, barely the size of a thumb and found only here and in a few other locations in Argentina and Paraguay.

The reserve's highest point is **Cerro Venado** (389m), an easy walk along the unsealed road that winds to the top, from where there are fine views over the surrounding sierra. Near the entrance to the reserve there is a small zoo housing pumas, grey foxes and *ñandúes* (rheas or South American ostriches).

Sierra de la Ventana

In the Western Pampas, towards the border with La Pampa Province, the unremittingly flat landscape is given welcome relief by the modest **Sierra de la Ventana** mountain range, 550km southwest of Buenos Aires. At the same time, the drier, more desert-like features of the *pampa seca* ("dry pampa") herald the start of the long route south into Patagonia. Running from northeast to southwest for 100km or so, the sierra's craggy spine forms a surprising backdrop to the serene Pampas and provides the best opportunities in the province for walking and climbing. The range is named after one of its highest points, the **Cerro de la Ventana**, a 1134m peak pierced by a small "window" (*ventana* in Spanish); it's located within the **Parque Provincial Ernesto Tornquist**, bisected by RP-76, the main highway through the sierra. There are plenty of accommodation options: there's a base camp within the park, but the nearby village of **Sierra de la Ventana**, with its many well-equipped *cabañas*, offers the best setup for visitors; it is situated around 30km southeast of the main park entrance.

Formed principally of sedimentary rock created during the Paleozoic period, the range is notable for its intensely folded appearance and its subtle grey-blue and pink hues. Though the harsh peaks may appear barren, they support an amazing range of **wildlife**, including pumas, foxes, guanacos, armadillos, *vizcachas* (rabbit-like rodents appreciated for their meat) and copper iguanas.

The province's highest peak, **Cerro Tres Picos** (1239m), juts from private land 6km south of Villa Ventana. It's less photogenic than Cerro de la Ventana, but its height, combined with its distance from the nearest base, makes it a more substantial hike. It is usually a two-day trek, overnighting in a cave on the way up. The route passes through land belonging to the Germanic *Estancia Funke* (☏0291 494 0058, ⊛fundacionfunke .org.ar), and you must go with a guide provided by the owners.

GETTING AROUND

SIERRA DE LA VENTANA

The easiest way to travel around the sierras is with your own transport. Otherwise, try the local Condor Estrella service, which runs along RP-76 and stops anywhere along the route, including at both entrances to Parque Provincial

Ernesto Tornquist and the turn-off to Sierra de la Ventana village. Regular buses go from Vila Ventana (departing Mon–Sat 7.15am & 6.50pm, Sun 6.15pm; returning 7.15am & 10pm; 60min; $40).

Parque Provincial Ernesto Tornquist

Daily: summer 8am–6pm; winter 9am–5pm • Free

Walking and climbing activities take place within the 65 square kilometres of **Parque Provincial Ernesto Tornquist**. There are two **entrances** to the park, both just off RP-76. The Bahia Blanca entrance is around 22km from Sierra de la Ventana village, signposted "Acceso a Reserva Provincial". From the Centro de Visitantes (visitor centre) you can also visit the **Reserva Natural Integral**, a strictly controlled sector of the park, where you can see herds of feral horses or explore caves, including one with ancient paintings.

The rest of the park's treks are within the **Monumento Natural**, which includes the much-photographed national monument of Cerro Ventana; the entrance is 5km or so west of the main way in. A well-marked trail to the summit of 1134m **Cerro Ventana** leads northeast from the post. Though the climb to the summit (access 8am/9am–11am; 5hr return trip; $40 access) is not overly demanding, you do need to be quite fit. Follow the park keepers' guidelines and remember that weather conditions can change quickly.

ARRIVAL AND INFORMATION
PARQUE PROVINCIAL ERNESTO TORNQUIST

2

Entry You can visit the reserve in your own vehicle, accompanied by a guide ($60), twice a day, every day, in high season (Dec–Feb) but at weekends only for the rest of the year – it's best to call ahead to check what is accessible.
Visitors' centre Enquire at the Centro de Visitantes, which has a good display of photos of the region's flora and fauna and a useful 3D topographical map. There is a helpful *guardaparques'* post (☎0291 491 0039) at the visitors' centre, which can usually provide you with a sketchy map of the main attractions, as well as indications of the distance, direction and estimated duration of the walks. Organized tours with a guide finish at 2pm.

ACCOMMODATION AND EATING

Campamento Base A few minutes' walk west of the guardaparques' post ☎02914 940286, ✉rhperrando @yahoo.com.ar. This is the best place to stay if you want to start out early for the park. As well as a shady campsite, recognizable from the road by its iron gate, there are dorms with wood-burning stoves for up to six people (plus two vast dorms for up to forty people each). You'll need to bring sleeping bags for all accommodation options. Cooking facilities and hot showers are provided and there is a small shop with a few basics. Camping $100; dorms $130
Hotel El Mirador Just outside the park, on RP-76 at Km226 ☎02914 941338, ⓦcomplejoelmirador.com.ar. This hotel offers pleasant single and double rooms overlooking the sierras as well as attractive and well-equipped wooden cabins (from $2540) that hold from four to eight people. It also has a good restaurant – one of very few eating options in the area, serving up fish, home-made pasta and wild boar (from $130) – and a swimming pool. $1150
Ich-Hutu This restaurant, whose specialities include pickled *escabeche* rabbit with peppers and onion, is just a few kilometres west of the *Hotel El Mirador* along RP-76. Daily noon–midnight.

Sierra de la Ventana village

Some 550km southwest from Capital Federal, **SIERRA DE LA VENTANA** is a delightfully quiet little village with sandy lanes crisscrossed by streams. Divided into several barrios and dissected by both a railway line and the Río Sauce Grande, the village has a rather disjointed layout. Its centre is **Villa Tivoli**, west of the railway tracks; here you'll find most shops and restaurants. By following the rather drab main street, Avenida San Martín, east over the rail tracks, you'll come first to **Barrio Parque Golf**, a mostly residential area of curving streets and chalet-style buildings. Most appealing of all is the aptly named **Villa Arcadia** to the north, separated from Barrio Parque Golf by a bridge over the Río Sauce Grande. Note that, technically, Villa Arcadia is a different district, so you'd need to seek information from its own tourist office (Av San Martín and Roca; ☎0291 491 5303). There are various swimming spots throughout the village, mostly to the north of Avenida San Martín, along the banks of the Río Sauce Grande.

ARRIVAL AND INFORMATION
SIERRA DE LA VENTANA VILLAGE

By bus Coaches from Buenos Aires drop you at the small bus terminal on Av San Martín. For return journeys to the capital, it's best to buy tickets in advance.
Destinations Buenos Aires (Mon–Fri & Sun 1 daily; 8hr); La Plata (1 daily; 7hr).
By train The train station, with services to (1 daily Wed & Fri; 9hr 45min) and from (1 daily Tues & Thurs; 9hr 45min) Buenos Aires' Constitución train station, is at the intersection of avenidas Roca and San Martín.
Tourist information The busy tourist office is right by the train station on Av del Golf, s/n (daily 8am–8pm, although hours may vary slightly according to the season; ☎02914 915303, ⓦsierradelaventana.org.ar).

ACCOMMODATION AND EATING

There is only one hotel to speak of in the vicinity, but there are many **campsites** around the village. The most popular places to stay, on both sides of the river, are **cabañas**, which can represent good value for money and are usually quite cosy and come fully equipped; check with the tourist office for openings. There are few **restaurants** in the village, although there's one very good *parrilla*. A good alternative, especially if you're staying in a *cabaña*, is to visit the popular La Rueda deli (San Martín 256) and put together your own *picada*, selecting from its range of delicious salamis and cheeses.

Balcón del Golf ☎ 02914 915222, ⊛ balcondelgolf .com. *Cabañas* with all mod cons as well as a sauna and pool. To get there, head over the bridge into Villa Arcadia and follow the road straight for about 300m. **$1250**

Pillahuincó Parque Hotel Av Raíces 161, Villa Arcadia ☎ 0291 491 5423, ⊛ hotelpillahuinco.com.ar. This enormous but attractive hotel is set in beautiful grounds with a swimming pool. It organizes trekking and biking excursions in the area and offers half-board, a good idea in view of the lack of restaurants nearby. **$640**

Rali-Hue San Martín 307. This great little *parrilla* does an excellent and good-value *parrillada* for two people. Daily noon–3pm & 7.30pm–midnight.

La Plata

The pleasant and spacious city of **LA PLATA**, the purpose-built provincial capital, was essentially conceived as an administrative centre and in many ways it shows. For many locals it is simply somewhere to go to carry out the dreaded *trámites*, or bureaucratic procedures. In terms of identity, the city undoubtedly suffers from being a mere 58km southeast of Buenos Aires, whose seemingly endless sprawl now laps at its outskirts, practically turning the city that was created as a counterbalance to the capital into its suburb. Nevertheless, La Plata boasts a rich cultural life, partly because it is an important **university town**, with three major institutes drawing students from all over the country. One of the city's chief attractions is its bushy park, the **Paseo del Bosque**, ten blocks northeast of the centre; here you will find the **Museo de La Plata**, famed for some remarkable dinosaur skeletons. You won't need to stay overnight, but it makes for an enjoyable excursion from Buenos Aires.

Brief history

When Buenos Aires became the federal capital in 1880, Buenos Aires Province – by far the wealthiest and most powerful in the republic – was deprived of a centre of government. A year later, the province's newly nominated governor, Dardo Rocha, proposed that a provincial capital be created 50km southeast of the federal capital. The new city's layout was based on a regular numbered street plan within a 5km square and was designed by the French architect Pedro Benoit. An international competition was held to choose blueprints for the most important public buildings, and the winning architects included Germans and Italians as well as Argentines, a mix of nationalities reflected in the city's impressive civic architecture. Argentina's first entirely planned city, **La Plata** was officially founded on November 19, 1882. Electric streetlights were installed in 1884 – the first in Latin America. Unfortunately, however, much of La Plata's carefully conceived architectural identity was lost during the twentieth century, as anonymous modern constructions replaced many original buildings. On a brighter note, some successful attempts have preserved what's left – above all, the old train station, now the wonderful setting for the **Pasaje Dardo Rocha** arts centre, notable not only for its contemporary art museum but also for its stunning interior. The 1990s saw the final completion of the city's grandiose neo-Gothic cathedral, over a century after its foundation stone was laid; this impressive structure, which evokes Notre Dame in Paris, dominates Plaza Moreno at the very heart of the city. Another project that took decades to complete, the **Estadio Único** was finally inaugurated in 2011, in time for the Copa América soccer tournament; the city's sporting pride and joy, in addition to football and other sports events, the stadium hosts major music concerts featuring international artists.

Plaza Moreno and around

La Plata's official centre is **Plaza Moreno**, a vast open square covering four blocks. The city's foundation stone was laid in its centre in 1882, together with a time capsule containing documents and medals relating to the founding of the city. Over the years, a handful of theories circulated, claiming that the buried documents offered proof that La Plata was founded according to a secret Masonic scheme. When the capsule was unearthed on the city's centenary, however, the papers were too damaged to bear out the theory. The contents of the exhumed time capsule can be viewed in the **Museo y Archivo Dardo Rocha** (daily 10am–1pm, 3–6pm; free; ☎0221 427 5591), located in the residence once occupied by La Plata's founder on the western side of the square at Calle 50 no. 933. On the northeastern end of the square is the Germanic **municipalidad**, a broad white edifice dominated by a lofty central clock tower and elegant, arched stained-glass windows.

Catedral de la Inmaculada Concepción

Avenida 51 between calles 14 and 15 • Tues–Sun 11am–7pm • **Museum** Tues–Sun 11am–7pm • Tues–Fri $48, Sat & Sun $55 • ⓦ catedraldelaplataorg.ar

At the southwestern end of Plaza Moreno you can't miss the gigantic, forbidding **Catedral de la Inmaculada Concepción**, which holds the title of South America's largest neo-Gothic church. Designed by Pedro Benoit, and loosely based on the cathedrals of Amiens and Cologne, it features a pinkish brick facade and steep slate roofs. The foundation stone was laid in 1884 but the cathedral wasn't completed until 1932, with its two principal towers not finished until 1999. The cathedral may not be beautiful, but it is certainly imposing, with its soaring, vertigo-inducing interior punctuated by austere ribbed columns, and high windows which make it surprisingly light and airy. The **museum** in the atmospheric crypt is accessed via the *confitería*-cum-*santería* (shop selling religious objects) accessed on either side of the main steps. Along with temporary religious art exhibitions, it features some excellent photographs documenting the cathedral's construction and also gives access to a mirador (viewpoint), in the **Torre de Jesús**, the south tower; 63m high and accessed by two lifts, it offers great views of La Plata's distinctive urban plan.

Teatro Argentino de La Plata

Avenida 51 between calles 9 and 10 • Box office Tues–Sun 10am–8pm • Guided tours hourly Mon–Fri 9am–3pm; 1hr • ☎ 0221 429 1732, ⓦ teatroargentino.gba.gov.ar

Two blocks northeast of Plaza Moreno is the site where the grand Italianate **Teatro Argentino de La Plata**, second in national importance after Buenos Aires' Teatro Colón, once stood. Sadly, it was razed to the ground by a suspicious fire in the 1970s and rebuilt as an octagonal concrete monolith. Undeniably hideous, the structure is impressively vast – you can take a guided tour – and the theatre puts on a decent selection of concerts, operas and plays. Contact the box office or consult the website for programme details.

Plaza San Martín

Avenidas 51 and 53 lead from Plaza Moreno to **Plaza San Martín**, the real hub of city life. This square is more intimate than Plaza Moreno, though it too is flanked by government buildings. At the northeastern end there's the **Casa de Gobierno**, a sturdy, mock Flemish-Renaissance building with a central slate-roofed dome; to the southwest you'll find the German Renaissance-style **Palacio Legislativo**, its grand Neoclassical entrance sitting slightly awkwardly on a more restrained facade.

Pasaje Dardo Rocha

Plaza San Martín s/n • Daily 9am–10pm • Free

More interesting than the square's civic edifices is the **Pasaje Dardo Rocha**, on its northwestern side. This elegant pitched-roof building, whose three-storey facade mixes French and Italian influences, was built in 1883 as the city's first train station. After the station moved to its current site, the Pasaje was remodelled and it now functions as an important **cultural centre** comprising a small cinema and various art museums, including the worthwhile **Museo de Arte Contemporáneo Latinoamericano**, or **MACLA** (Tues–Fri 10am–8pm, Sat & Sun 2–8pm; free; ⓦ macla.com.ar). The galleries are located around a stunning Doric-columned central hall, where natural light (enhanced by a discreet modern lighting system) filters down through a high glass roof onto a vast sweep of black-and-white-tiled floor.

Paseo del Bosque and around

From Plaza San Martín, Avenida 53 heads northeast past the Casa de Gobierno. After four blocks you come to the monumental Plaza Rivadavia, next to the **Paseo del Bosque**, La Plata's major green space. Before crossing busy Avenida 1 and entering the park, take a small detour along Boulevard 53, a short diagonal road to the right of the plaza, to visit the architecturally exciting Casa Curutchet. The beautifully laid-out park features an artificial lake, a sad zoo and a botanical garden, but the main attraction is the city's most important museum, the Museo de La Plata.

Casa Curutchet

Blvd 53 no. 320 • Mon & Tues 9am–1pm, Wed–Fri 9am–5pm, Sat 1–5pm; closed Jan & hols • $40 • ☎ 0221 482 2631, ⊕ capbacs.com

Halfway along Boulevard 53 stands the angular **Casa Curutchet**, the only Le Corbusier-designed residence built in Latin America (another, Chile's Maison Errazuriz, was commissioned but never completed). Commissioned by local surgeon Pedro Curutchet in 1948, the house is a typical Le Corbusier construction, combining functionality with a playful use of colour and perspective, and was the setting for the 2010 Argentine film *El hombre de al lado* ("The Man Next Door"). The building now houses the Colegio de Arquitectos de la Provincia de Buenos Aires (Buenos Aires Province School of Architects) and is open to visitors.

Museo de La Plata (Museo de Ciencias Naturales)

Paseo del Bosque s/n • Tues–Sun 10am–6pm; open Mon 10am–6pm on public hols • Tours Tues–Fri 11am, Sat & Sun 11am, 1pm, 2pm, 3pm & 4pm • $20 • ⊕ museo.fcnym.unlp.edu.ar

Within the Paseo del Bosque is the first purpose-built museum in Latin America (and something of a relic in itself), the **Museo de La Plata**. Housed in the Universidad Nacional de La Plata's natural science faculty, it is sometimes known as the **Museo de Ciencias Naturales** and is a real treat for anyone with a fondness for old-fashioned museums. Run by the university, the city's only worthwhile museum struggles to live up to its self-proclaimed reputation as one of the world's major natural history collections, but is certainly worth a visit for its picturesque presentation and fascinating contents, including some fabulous dinosaur remains. The exterior is very grand: Neoclassical architecture is set off by a colonnaded entrance and a staircase lined with sculptures of sabre-toothed cats. Inside, the museum is gradually being remodelled and modern audiovisuals make a brief and rather shaky appearance in the first rooms. However, later rooms, such as the six dedicated to zoology, have been deliberately preserved to look just as they did when the museum was first opened in 1888, with the embalmed birds and animals exhibited in glass cases, albeit with new easy-to-read labels.

The museum has 21 rooms, including an impressive **paleontological section** that contains a reproduction of a gigantic diplodocus skeleton, and the original skeleton of a neuquensaurus, an herbivorous dinosaur common in northern Patagonia towards the end of the Cretaceous Period around 71 million years ago. Room VI is dedicated to the beginnings of the **Cenozoic Period**, also known as the Age of Mammals, which extends from around 65 million years ago to the present day. It houses the museum's most important collection: the megafauna, a group of giant herbivorous mammals that evolved in South America at the time when the region was separated from other continents. The room's striking collection of skeletons includes the enormous megatherium, largest of the megafauna, which, when standing upright on its powerful two hind legs, would have reached almost double its already impressive six metres.

Upstairs, a **Latin American ethnology and anthropology** section showcases items used by the continent's main indigenous groups, from the colourful, feathered headdresses of Bolivian carnival participants to the simple wood and leather articles of Tierra del Fuego's Selk'nam (see p.524) indigenous community. A sizeable collection of marvellous pre-Columbian ceramics is let down by the lacklustre display.

ARRIVAL AND INFORMATION   LA PLATA

For a place designed along ultra-rational lines, La Plata can be a challenge to navigate. The prevalence of streets cutting across the blocks is disorientating, and you won't need to walk around for very long to see why it's known as the "**city of diagonals**". While the convergence of similar-looking streets can be confusing, the city is small enough that you're unlikely to go too far off track. It helps to know that all of La Plata's major points of interest lie along or just off avenidas 51 and 53. A brisk walk will get you to all the sights, without any need for public transport.

By train Theoretically, the most appealing place to arrive in La Plata is at the beautiful *fin-de-siècle* train station, on the corner of avenidas 1 and 44, a dozen blocks northwest of the town centre. The train itself, however, which shuttles between here and Constitución in Buenos Aires (every 30min; 1hr 15min), is far from beautiful – in fact it is dirty and, at times, downright dangerous.

By bus At the bus terminal, on Calle 41 between calles 3 and 4, you can catch frequent, safe buses to and from the capital ($30 with SUBE card) and major cities throughout the country. Destinations Bahía Blanca (3 daily; 10hr);

Bariloche (2 daily; 20hr); Buenos Aires (every 15min; 1hr); Córdoba (3 daily; 17hr); Mendoza (2 daily; 12hr).

Tourist information La Plata's tourist office (Mon–Fri 9am–5pm; ☎0221 422 9764, ✆laplata.gov.ar) is in the Palacio Campodónico on Diagonal 79 between calles 5 and 56; there's also an information centre in the Pasaje Dardo Rocha (daily 10am–8pm; ☎0221 427 1535).

2 EATING

As provincial capital, La Plata is large and sophisticated enough to have some culinary breadth. There are some decent **restaurants**, mostly aimed at businessmen, although you'll find local hangouts more convivial – the bulk of these are located around the intersection of calles 10 and 47 along Diagonal 74.

Carne Calle 50 no. 452 between calles 4 and 5 ☎0221 421 9817, ✆carnehamburguesas.com. Located within a restored corner mansion, this trendy burger joint serves up organic *hamburguesas* (combo meal $150) created by one of Argentina's top chefs, Mauro Colagreco. Mon–Sat 11.30am–midnight.

Cervecería Modelo Calles 5 and 54 ☎0221 421 1321, ✆cerveceriamodelo.com.ar. With a seemingly endless menu including everything from hamburgers and liverwurst sandwiches to seafood and *bife de chorizo*, food and service are run-of-the-mill but prices are moderate. No matter, this is where locals come for a beer and *picada* after football matches. Daily 8am–1am.

El Chal Chal Calle 8 no. 1279 between 58 and 59

☎0221 421 4331. This place, named after a native tree, is an upmarket *parrilla*, serving fine cuts of meat and decent wines – though the service can be slow. The generous *parrillada* for two is good value. Mon–Sat noon–4pm & 8pm–midnight.

La Trattoria Intersection of calles 10 and 47 and Diagonal 74 ☎0221 422 6135. This restaurant-cum-café offers great views of the to and fro of La Plata life from its wooden tables. The mainstays are pizza and pasta but you can also have breakfast here, or tea and cakes. Daily 8am–1am.

Vitaminas Diagonal 74 no. 1640 ☎0221 482 1106. A colourful restaurant and bar, serving healthy vegetarian dishes and excellent-value lunchtime specials. Mon–Sat noon–3pm & 8pm–midnight.

The Interbalnearia

The endless string of resorts along the easternmost coast of Buenos Aires Province is connected by RP-11, known as the **Interbalnearia** (literally, the inter-resort road). They include the trendy pair of **Pinamar** and **Villa Gesell** and their smaller, but rapidly growing, satellites **Cariló** and **Mar de las Pampas**, around which sand dunes and pine forests dominate the landscape. The routes from Capital Federal and La Plata run southeast along RN-2 and RP-36 (which joins up with RP-11 after around 90km) respectively, threading through flat pampas, dotted with cows and divided at intervals by tree-lined drives leading to estancias. Tall metal wind-pumps, which extract irrigation water from beneath the surface of the land, inject a little drama into the scene, while giant cardoon thistles – a desiccated brown in summer – sprout in clusters like outsized bouquets.

Pinamar

PINAMAR gets its name from the surrounding pinewoods planted among dunes by the town's founder, Jorge Bunge, in 1943; this attractive setting is now rather spoiled by a mix of high-rise buildings and ostentatious chalet-style constructions. Pinamar stretches southwards along the coast, swallowing up the neighbouring resorts of **Mar de Ostende** and **Valeria del Mar**, laidback places that offer up alternative beaches and dining options as well as a change of scene from their trendy neighbour. They are often cheaper to dine or stay in, too. Long the favourite resort of the Porteño elite, in the 1990s Pinamar symbolized the high-living lifestyle of the Menem era, and the exploits of the politicians and celebrities who holidayed here were staples of the gossip mags. Pinamar fell out of popularity for a while following the high-profile murder of an investigative journalist here in 1997 and the post-2001 economic recession, but has bounced back with a vengeance. It remains a hugely popular summer holiday spot for the upper-middle class and, although it has lost its exclusive crown to nearby places like Cariló, it is considerably more expensive than many other Argentine seaside resorts.

Avenida Bunge and the beach

Pinamar's broad main street, **Avenida Bunge**, is flanked by restaurants and branches of the same boutiques that fill most of the capital's malls. Bunge runs east to west through the town centre, ending at beachfront Avenida del Mar. The attractive **beach** is the town's big draw, its pale sands dotted with delicate lilac shells and, to the north and south of the town centre, bordered by high dunes. Various companies offer excursions by jeep or **quad bike** to the most dramatic section of dunes, where, during the summer, you can try **sandboarding**; ask at the tourist office for details.

ARRIVAL AND INFORMATION
PINAMAR

By plane The closest airport to Pinamar is at Villa Gesell, with flights leaving and departing for Buenos Aires during summer (see p.162).

By train The train station – served by Ferrobaires (☎011 4305 0157), which runs trains to (Sun 4.30pm; 6hr) and from (Fri 4.40pm; 6hr) Buenos Aires' Constitución station – is a couple of kilometres west of town, a short taxi ride away.

By bus All long-distance buses arrive at the terminal at Jason 2250, several blocks west of the town centre, just off Av Bunge. This is also the main arrival and departure point for Mar de Ostende and Valeria del Mar. Visitors should take a taxi from the rank outside, or the local bus (direction Cariló; every 20min; $5), also from outside the terminal.

Destinations Buenos Aires (20 daily; 5hr); Mar del Plata (hourly; 2hr).

Tourist information With glossy brochures advertising golf courses, spas and estate agencies, the tourist office, at Av Bunge and Libertador (Jan & Feb daily 8am–9pm; March–Dec Mon–Sat 8am–8pm, Sun 10am–6pm; ☎02254 517020, ⓦpinamar.tur.ar), is heavily geared towards Pinamar's well-off visitors, but also provides decent maps and guides.

ACCOMMODATION

Hotels in Pinamar and its satellite resorts are plentiful, if generally expensive, with little in the way of decent budget accommodation – though there are a few decent campsites. As in all resorts, reservations are advisable in high season.

PINAMAR

Algeciras Hotel Av del Libertador 75 ☎02254 485550, ⓦalgecirashotel.com.ar. A large and off-putting ugly building houses this luxurious, top-of-the-range place, which has a swimming pool, sauna and child-minding service. $1600

Camping Quimey Lemú 250m north of the entrance to town along RP-11 ☎02254 484949, ⓦquimeylemu .com.ar. One of the best campsites in the area is set in attractive wooded grounds with plenty of facilities. It also has some basic cabins for rent – and tents for rent, too. Camping $100; cabins $570

Las Calas Hotel Boutique Av Bunge 560 ☎02254 405999, ⓦlascalashotel.com.ar. Predominantly designed from wood, this highly regarded designer hotel has an intimate interior courtyard (smoke-free) and spacious rooms. $1700

Hotel Casablanca Av de los Tritones 258 ☎02254 482474, ⓦcasablancapinamar.com.ar. A block from the beach, the *Casablanca* offers light, airy rooms, some with balconies. Closed April–Nov, except Semana Santa. $900

Playas Hotel Av Bunge 250 ☎02254 482236, ⓦplayashotel.com.ar. *Playas* is Pinamar's longest-established hotel, housed in a stately white building. It generally attracts a more mature clientele, with its elegant rooms and bar and quiet grounds. There's a swimming pool and a nine-hole golf course. $1500

Posada Pecos Odiseo 448 and Silenios ☎02254 484386, ⓦposadapecos.com.ar. This charmingly relaxed place has attractive tiled floors and whitewashed walls that lend it a slightly rustic feel. Rooms are comfortable, and very good value. $750

MAR DE OSTENDE

Camping Saint Tropez Quintana 138 ☎02254 482498, ⓦsainttropezpinamar.com.ar. On the border with Ostende, this small but conveniently located campsite that's been running for fifty years also rents out apartments. Camping $300; apartments $700

Hotel Viejo Ostende Biarritz 799, Ostende ☎02254

486081, ⓦviejohotelostende.com.ar. A beautifully preserved reminder of the days when this pioneer hotel hosted literary figures such as Argentine author Adolfo Bioy Casares and French writer Antoine de St-Exupéry. Rooms are quite simple and you pay over the odds for the ambience, but the price includes breakfast and dinner, access to the swimming pool, a beach tent at the *balneario* and a child-minding service, so it is a good deal. **$2000**

EATING

While plenty of **restaurants** are dotted around the town, some of the most appealing are close to or overlooking the beach or along Avenida Bunge. Pedestrians and drivers alike cruise this main drag in the summer months, searching out the hottest spot of the moment.

Paxapoga Av Bunge 48 ☎02254 484985. This traditional upmarket restaurant offers good-value Argentine food plus pricier but well-prepared fish and seafood, including excellent squid. Daily noon–4pm & 8pm–1am.

Tante Av de las Artes 35 ☎02254 494949. The best of Pinamar's cooking is undoubtedly found at this teahouse and restaurant. The wide-ranging menu offers elaborate, mostly Germanic, dishes, including some good vegetarian options, and at teatime there's a number of exotic tea blends with which to wash down some exceptionally good cakes. Daily noon–11.30pm.

Tulumei Av Bunge 64 ☎02254 488696. A small and friendly place with a laidback atmosphere, good music and imaginative seafood dishes. Daily noon–3.30pm & 8pm–late.

Viejo Lobo Avenidas del Mar and Bunge ☎02254 483218. This Pinamar classic – the name means "old salt" – pleases everyone and offers a wide-ranging menu focusing on fish and seafood. Daily noon–4pm & 8.30pm–late.

DRINKING AND NIGHTLIFE

Pinamar's **nightlife** is mostly centred on a handful of bars along Avenida Bunge and the seafront, and the party really kicks off in summer when Porteño teens and twenty-somethings head here to let their hair down. The biggest nightclubs are *Ku* and *El Alma*, on Quintana and Nuestras Malvinas respectively, which play everything from dance to rock and salsa.

Paco Bar Av de las Artes 156 ☎02254 585934. A good, traditional-style bar, its walls and counters stuffed with memorabilia. Daily 7pm–1am.

UFO Point Av del Mar and Tobías. This beachfront bar is one of the most consistently cool places in town, with an Ibiza vibe come sunset, and is where you'll find the best DJs. Daily 10am–7am.

Cariló

Pinamar merges seamlessly with **Mar de Ostende**, **Valeria del Mar** and finally **CARILÓ**, the area's most exclusive resort. Cariló – a former private neighbourhood – has a separate personality, a fact made clear as Calle Bathurst, the paved main street of Valeria del Mar, abruptly turns to a sand track with a sign announcing the entrance to Cariló's exclusive "parque" on Calle Divisadero. Here, houses are larger than their neighbouring counterparts, yet manage to be rather more discreet. An idyllic pine forest dotted with luxury hotels, spas and designer shops, this is where Argentina's rich and powerful come to get pampered, hidden away from the rest of society; as such, it is more expensive than other resorts nearby. The streets are quaintly named; the ones running east–west are named after trees, their "roots" drawing water from the sea, while ones named for birds such as *chingolo* (sparrow) and *carpintero* (woodpecker) run north–south.

While *apart-hotels* and rental homes maintain a tasteful distance from each other, and development is controlled by tight laws, the amount of new construction spiralled in the new millennium – too fast for some locals – and you'll still hear the distant hubbub of building work among the tweeting of birds. Cariló nevertheless remains a peaceful place, where stressed-out professional Porteños come to *desenchufarse* ("unplug themselves"). If you can afford it – and don't mind the snooty attitude of some of its regulars – its varied and thick vegetation, quiet, sandy streets and gourmet restaurants make it an agreeable destination, especially outside the summer season.

ARRIVAL AND INFORMATION

CARILÓ

By bus Cariló is connected by the local Montemar bus to Valeria del Mar, Ostende and Pinamar, where the nearest long-distance bus terminal is located. Alternatively, you can simply stroll along the beach, which runs for 10km or so without interruptions past all of them.

Tourist information Cariló's tourist board, a small wooden hut on the corner of Boyero and Castaño (☎02254 570773), has minimal information, probably since the main office in Pinamar covers all the satellite resorts.

ACTIVITIES

Horseriding and polo The Estancia Dos Montes (☎02254 480045), just west of the village, offers polo and horseriding lessons. For a more leisurely experience, saddle up a pony and trot along the beach with Palenque Maito, based at Paraiso and Tero (☎02267 15 666363).
Sand boarding and dune bashing Whizz around circuits Fomula One-style with Arctic Cat, based just out of the village at the Cariló roundabout on RP-11 (☎02254 470262), or whizz around the plentiful dunes on a 4WD buggy with Motorrad, located at Cerezo between Boyero and Divisadero (☎02254 470109). Try sand boarding in the numerous dunes too; Juan Pasos delivers boards to your door (☎02254 406368).

ACCOMMODATION

Accommodation is all high-end luxury, with nothing near a budget option in sight. Most places – whether hotel, self-catering apartment or *cabaña* – include a wide range of excellent services.

La Hostería Cariló Jacarandá 7167 ☎02254 570704, ⓦhosteriacarilo.com.ar. Decorated with the owner's photography, this outstanding boutique hotel hosts film screenings in its small underground cinema and there are thousands of DVDs behind reception. There's also a swimming pool and the enticing *Tiramisú* restaurant. $1800
Marcin Hotel Laurel and Albatros ☎02254 570888, ⓦhotelmarcin.com.ar. A modern hotel in a multistorey block, offering charming mellow-hued rooms commanding ocean views. $1900

EATING

Cattalina Boyero and Castaño ☎02254 571922. Located in the upmarket Feria del Bosque shopping centre, this is the place to come for excellent Italian pasta dishes served with delicious sauces. Daily noon–4pm & 8pm–late.
Hemingway Lambertiana s/n and the coast ☎02254 571585. A beach club naturally sporting great ocean views and even a spa, this trendy haunt serves up sushi and other fish dishes during summer months; the reduced winter menu focuses on pasta and steak. Oozing luxury, the place even has a downstairs spa. April–Oct Sat & Sun noon–late; Nov–March daily noon–late.

Villa Gesell

A larger coastal hub than Pinamar or Cariló, **VILLA GESELL** is located 370km south of Capital Federal, about 25km further along RP-11 than Pinamar. Separated from Cariló by a (strictly off-limits) nature reserve, the town is named after its founder, Carlos Gesell, a mildly eccentric Porteño of German descent. In 1931, Gesell bought a large swathe of coastal land, largely dominated by still-moving sand dunes. Inspired by methods used in Australia, Gesell managed to stabilize the dunes by planting a mixture of vegetation including tamarisk, acacia and esparto grass. He sold lots, many of which were bought by Germans and Central Europeans escaping World War II. Favoured by hippies in the 1960s and 70s, Gesell has a more laidback feel than its smarter neighbours Pinamar and Cariló and teeters on the edge of being run-down in parts. The resort remains popular with Argentina's middle and working classes, plus teenage groups enjoying holidays away from their parents. If you fancy something livelier, head for one of Villa Gesell's popular **balnearios** spread out along the beach, such as *Amy*, *AfriKa* or *Playa 13 al Sur*, which vie with each other every year to become the season's show-off spot.

The winding streets – many sandy and unsurfaced – can seem complex to manoeuvre, given that they are numbered rather than named, much like La Plata. Avenidas run parallel to the sea, while paseos, calles and alamedas follow the natural course of the land, as per Gesell's designs.

2

Bus Terminal (3km), Mar de las Pampas (12km) & Campsites

Parque Cultural Pinar del Norte and Museo de los Pioneros

Park Av Buenos Aires and alamedas 202, 203 & 204 · Daily 24hr · Free · **Museum** Alameda 201 and c/303 · Summer daily 10am–8pm; winter Tues–Sat 10am–4pm, Sun 2–5pm · $10 · ☎ 02255 470723.

At the northern end of town lies the **Parque Cultural Pinar del Norte**. Designed by Gesell, the park's wooded walkways offer welcome shade on hot days, and the dunes that separate it from the beach to the east are particularly good for sunbathing or picnicking. The house built and used by Gesell has been turned into the small **Museo de los Pioneros**; it is dedicated to Carlos and his father Silvio, a leading economist, and features photos and memorabilia from the city's pioneers.

ARRIVAL AND DEPARTURE
VILLA GESELL

By plane Villa Gesell's airport (☎ 02255 458345) is 3km south from the turn-off to town on RP-11, with regular flights during summer to and from Buenos Aires with Sol (2 daily, summer only; 1hr; ☎ 0810 4444 765, ⊚ sol.com.ar). A shuttle runs from the airport to the town, dropping off at central hotels.

By bus The town's main bus terminal is around 3km south of the centre, at Av 3 and Paseo 140; you'll probably want to get a local bus (#504, which will drop you off close to Av 3) or taxi to the centre.

Destinations Buenos Aires (hourly; 6hr); Mendoza (1 daily; 14hr); Mar del Plata (5 daily; 2hr).

INFORMATION AND ACTIVITIES

Tourist information The popularity of Villa Gesell is reflected by its five tourist offices. The most central one is in the town hall, at Avenida 3 no. 820 between paseos 108 and 109 (daily: summer 8am–11pm; winter 8am–8pm; ☎ 02255 478042, ⊚ turismo.gesell.gob.ar). Other useful ones are at the bus terminal (daily: summer 5am–1am;

winter 8am–8pm), and close to the centre at Paseo 106 and Av 3 (daily 8–10am & 6–11pm).

Bike rental There are various places to rent bikes in town; try Casa Macca, on Av Buenos Aires between Paseo 101 and Av 5 (☎ 02255 468013), or Rodados Luis, on Paseo 107 between avenidas 4 and 5 (☎ 02255 463897).

ACCOMMODATION

As with the other coastal resorts, the cost of accommodation varies considerably according to the season. Many places cut prices by at least fifty percent out of season; others close altogether. It is easier to find budget accommodation here than in

Pinamar, and the tourist office holds a complete list of these as well as Villa Gesell's numerous **campsites**, all of which are some distance from the centre, with some of the nicest among the dunes at the southern end of town.

Camping Mar Dorado Av 3 and Paseo 170 ⓣ02255 470963, ⓦmardorado.com.ar. Set among woods and with its own beach a 15min drive south of town, this is the best campsite in the resort, and plenty of activities are laid on. There are also small yet complete houses for four to six people. Camping **$160**; houses **$900**

Hostel Gesell La Deseada Av 6 no. 1183 ⓣ02255 473276, ⓦladeseadahostel.com.ar. Modern hostel with six shared dorms with bunkbeds, two of which become private double rooms from March onwards. Great views of woodland, and a spacious communal living room. Dorms **$300**; doubles **$550**

Playa Hotel Alameda 205 between calles 303 and 304 ⓣ02255 454570, ⓦhotelplayagesell.com.ar Villa Gesell's oldest hotel is set in wooded grounds near the nature reserve, far from the bustle of the centre. The pretty whitewashed building has pleasant, simply decorated rooms. **$690**

Posada del Sol Av 4 no. 642 ⓣ02255 462086, ⓦgesell.com.ar/posadadelsol. Definitely the most unusual place in town, this very friendly posada has a mini-zoo in its garden in which parrots, flamingos and rabbits wander freely. Rooms are small but comfortable and well equipped. Closed April–Nov. **$700**

Residencial Viya Av 5 no. 582 between paseos 105 and 106 ⓣ02255 462757, ⓦgesell.com.ar/viya. The best of the town's budget places, this charming *residencial* has a pleasant garden and seating area, along with plain but very well-kept rooms. **$320**

Tejas Rojas Costanera no. 848 ⓣ02255 462565, ⓦhoteltejasrojas.com.ar. This beachfront hotel is in a cool, tiled and spacious building and has a swimming pool. Rooms with sea views cost slightly more. Closed Easter–Oct. **$1370**

EATING

Carlitos Av 3 no. 184 ⓣ02255 464611. The self-styled "King of Pancakes" makes crêpes with an exhaustive range of savoury and sweet fillings. A super-sweet *dulce de leche* pancake following on from a fully loaded hamburger should satisfy even the hungriest punters. Daily 11am–11pm.

Curcuma Paseo 104 and Av 4 ⓣ02255 473989. A homely restaurant packing everything from beef brochettes to chop suey into its menu, as well as an exhaustive range of desserts. Daily noon–4pm & 8pm–midnight.

El Estribo Av 3 and Paseo 109 ⓣ02255 466357. The best traditional *parrilla* in town serves delicious *bifes de chorizo* as well as all manner of fish, including sole with boiled potatoes. Daily noon–3pm & 8pm–close.

★**Sutton 212** Paseo 105 no. 212 and Avenida 2 ⓣ02255 460674 ⓦsutton212.com.ar. Sporting funky decor, this *resto-bar* serves up great mid-priced meals including sushi and seafood. Once dinner has been served, Sutton 212 slips on its cocktail bar hat. Summer daily 10am–5am; winter Fri & Sat 5pm–5am.

El Viejo Hobbit Av 8 between paseos 111 and 112 ⓣ02255 465851. Countless pints of home-brew and delicious platters of farmhouse cheeses and fondues in enjoyable, faux-Middle Earth surroundings. Daily 6pm–1.30am.

DRINKING AND NIGHTLIFE

The centre of Villa Gesell's lively nightlife is Avenida 3; families gather at the numerous restaurants, while a younger crowd happily tucks into late-night pizzas and cold beers over the summer months.

Pueblo Limite Av Buenos Aires 2600 ⓣ02255 452825, ⓦpueblolimite.com. The best nightclub in town – though it's the cream of a relatively average crop, given that most big-name DJs are lured to Mar del Plata or Pinamar in summer. Thurs–Sat midnight–6am.

Mar de las Pampas and Mar Azul

MAR DE LAS PAMPAS, 380km south of Capital Federal and just 12km from Villa Gesell, is a haven of relaxing pine forests and pampas grass. The beach isn't as deserted as you might expect, since it is easily accessible from Gesell, but inland you can lose yourself along sandy tracks that meander around dunes and woods. The pine forest setting isn't dissimilar to Cariló's, though Mar de las Pampas is more down-to-earth – for now. There is no real division between it and **MAR AZUL**, a short way south and distinguished from its neighbour only by lesser development. The pair is enjoying a reputation for maintaining the bohemian spirit of Villa Gesell, their much smaller sizes preventing

2

such big crowds in summer, and a handful of *balnearios* such as *Blue Beach* (by the beach on c/34; ☎02255 479599, ⓦbluebeach.comar) cultivating a chilled-out atmosphere.

ARRIVAL AND INFORMATION

By plane The closest airport to Pinamar is at Villa Gesell with flights leaving and departing for Buenos Aires during summer (see p.162).

By train Pinamar (see p.159) has the closest train station, served by Ferrobaires (☎011 4305 0157), which runs trains to (Sun 4.30pm; 6hr) and from (Fri 4.40pm; 6hr) Buenos Aires' Constitución station.

By bus There isn't a bus terminal at Mar de las Pampas or Mar Azul. Visitors from Buenos Aires should buy tickets to Villa Gesell, bearing in mind they sometimes go via Pinamar. From Villa Gesell, there are

MAR DE LAS PAMPAS AND MAR AZUL

regular buses which pass through both villages (every 30min; 30min), leaving from behind the bus terminal at Av 3 and Paseo 140.

On foot You can walk from Villa Gesell, either along the beach or via Avenida 3, but it's an 8km walk. Taking a bus or a taxi is recommended.

Tourist information Gesell's tourist offices (see p.162) have maps and accommodation information for both villages, though you can also pick up information from the Mar de las Pampas booth at Mercedes Sosa and El Lucero (daily: summer 8am–11pm; winter 8am–8pm).

ACCOMMODATION

Aquimequedo Cuyo and Roca, Mar de las Pampas ☎02255 479884, ⓦaquimequedonet.com.ar. The best of the typical Mar de las Pampas *cabañas* complexes, with a heated pool, solarium and gym surrounded by pine forest and eucalyptus trees. $1250

Camping de Ingenieros Av Mar del Plata and c/47, two blocks from Mar Azul's beach ☎02255 479502, ⓦcampingdeingenieros.com.ar. The twin resorts' best campsite nestles among fragrant pine woods just two blocks from Mar Azul's beach. You can sleep in dorms, too. Camping $195; dorms $650

Hostal de las Piedras Intersection of Cuyo, Virazón and Mercedes Sosa, Mar de las Pampas ☎02255 454220, ⓦhostaldelaspiedras.com. This upmarket

hostal has large rooms, each with a private outdoor space. The decor is deliberately rustic, with bare stone walls and cool floor tiles. $1200

Hostería Alamos Av Mar del Plata and c/35, Mar Azul ☎02255 479631, ⓦalamoshosteria .com.ar. Mar Azul's only hotel, just one block from the oceanfront, has pleasantly simple doubles and suites in a Swiss-style building. There is a swimming pool and private parking. $1100

Poetas del Bosque Copacabana and c/45, Mar Azul ☎011 4554 6047, ⓦpoetasdelbosque.com.ar. This decidedly poetic *cabañas* complex, with rooms for two to six people, is idyllically located in the woods for which it's named. $1000

Mar del Plata and around

Big, busy and brash, **MAR DEL PLATA** (or Mardel to initiates) dwarfs every other resort on Argentina's Atlantic coast. At 410km south of Capital Federal, around six million – mostly Argentine – tourists holiday here every year, drawn by its bustling beaches and lively entertainment, earning it the nickname "La Feliz", or the "Happy City". The seventh-biggest city in Argentina, Mardel's primarily a place where the Argentine working classes go to forget their daily grind and chill out for a fortnight every summer. If the thought of seeking an unoccupied towel-sized scrap of sand every morning or queuing for a restaurant every evening makes you shudder, you're better off avoiding the resort in January and February. On the other hand, if you like mixing your beach trips with a spot of culture, nightlife or shopping, you may appreciate the city's cheeky charm. Physically Mar del Plata is favoured by the gentle drama of a sweeping coastline and hilly terrain, and while its rather urban beaches may lack the unspoilt peace of other resorts, they are fun places to hang out and great for people-watching.

Furthermore, Mar del Plata is the only resort worth visiting out of season – while the city folk may breathe a sigh of relief when the last of the tourists leave in late February, it certainly doesn't close down. The city enjoys a rich cultural life that includes several modest but interesting **museums** and **galleries**, and one of Argentina's most important **ports**, appealing for its colourful traditional fishing boats and seafood restaurants.

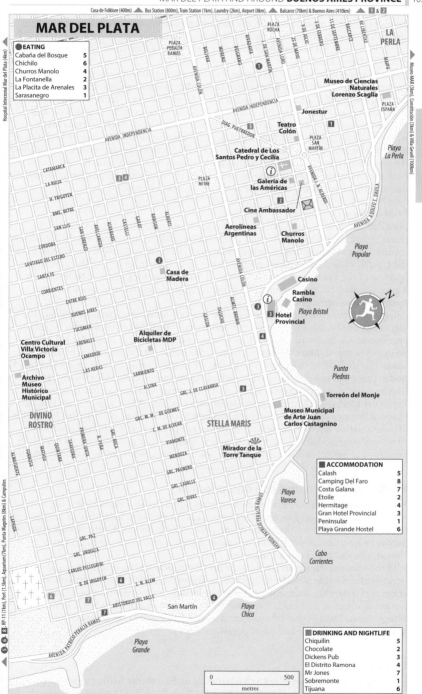

MAR DEL PLATA

EATING

Cabaña del Bosque	5
Chichilo	6
Churros Manolo	4
La Fontanella	2
La Placita de Arenales	3
Sarasanegro	1

PLAZA ROCHA

PLAZA PERALTA RAMOS

LA PERLA

Museo de Ciencias Naturales Lorenzo Scaglia

PLAZA ESPAÑA

Playa La Perla

Jonestur

Teatro Colón

PLAZA SAN MARTÍN

Catedral de Los Santos Pedro y Cecilia

PLAZA MITRE

Galería de las Américas

Cine Ambassador

Aerolíneas Argentinas

Churros Manolo

Playa Popular

Casa de Madera

Casino

Rambla Casino

Playa Bristol

Hotel Provincial

Alquiler de Bicicletas MDP

Centro Cultural Villa Victoria Ocampo

Punta Piedras

Archivo Museo Histórico Municipal

DIVINO ROSTRO

Torreón del Monje

STELLA MARIS

Museo Municipal de Arte Juan Carlos Castagnino

Mirador de la Torre Tanque

Playa Varese

ACCOMMODATION

Calash	5
Camping Del Faro	8
Costa Galana	7
Etoile	2
Hermitage	4
Gran Hotel Provincial	3
Peninsular	1
Playa Grande Hostel	6

Cabo Corrientes

San Martín

Playa Chica

Playa Grande

DRINKING AND NIGHTLIFE

Chiquilin	5
Chocolate	2
Dickens Pub	3
El Distrito Ramona	4
Mr Jones	7
Sobremonte	1
Tijuana	6

0 — 500
metres

2

Hospital Interzonal Mar del Plata (4km) ◀

Museo MAR (5km), Constitución (3km) & Villa Gesell (100km) ▶

◀ 5, 6, 8, RP-11 (1km), Port (1.5km), Aquarium (7km), Punta Mogotes (8km) & Campsites

The oceanfront is dominated by haphazard modern developments, but scattered here and there are some wonderfully quirky buildings, built in a decorative – even fantastical – style known as *pintoresquista*, an eclectic brew of mostly neo-Norman and mock-Tudor architecture.

The official centre is **Plaza San Martín**, but on summer days the city's true heart lies further south, around **Playa Bristol** and the **Rambla Casino**, a pedestrian promenade flanking the grand casino and landmark *Gran Hotel Provincial* (see opposite). Aside from beaches and away from the quiet neighbourhood of **La Perla**, there's little in the way of sightseeing in the city centre. Head south to the hilly streets of **Stella Maris**, where you'll find the Museo Municipal de Arte Juan Carlos Castagnino, or to the quiet residential area of **Divino Rostro**, home to the Villa Victoria cultural centre. South along the coast, a visit to the colourful fishing **port** makes a fine way to end the day – for both the lively bustle of returning fishermen and the majestic (but noisy and smelly) sea lions that have made their home at the port's southern end.

Brief history

Founded in 1874, Mar del Plata was soon developed into a European-style bathing resort, following the vision of Pedro Luro, a successful Basque merchant. As the railway expanded into Buenos Aires Province, Mar del Plata became accessible to visitors from the capital, with the first passenger train arriving in September 1886. The subsequent opening of the town's first hotel in 1888 – the luxurious, long-gone **Hotel Bristol** – was a great occasion for the Buenos Aires elite, many of whom travelled down for the opening on an overnight train.

Regardless, the richest of Argentina's very rich continued to make their regular pilgrimages to Europe, and it took the outbreak of World War I to dampen Argentine enthusiasm for the journey across the Atlantic and to firmly establish Mar del Plata as an exclusive resort. **Mass tourism** began to arrive in the 1930s, helped by improved roads, but took off in the 1940s and 1950s, when the development of union-run hotels under Perón put the city within the reach of Argentina's middle and working classes. The horrified rich then abandoned it for the more genteel Pinamar and Uruguay's Punta del Este, while Menem's peso–dollar parity in the 1990s meant the middle class found it cheaper to sunbathe in Florida and the Caribbean (see p.545). The 2001 crisis and devaluation led to a resurgence in Mardel's popularity; in 2009 the *Gran Hotel Provincial* reopened after lengthy restoration. These days, it attracts a mixed crowd of families, pensioners and twenty-somethings who can't or won't pay to stay in Pinamar.

Plaza San Martín and the microcentro

Plaza San Martín, Mar del Plata's spacious main square, covers four blocks. The inevitable statue of San Martín, by sculptor Luis Perlotti, unusually depicts the general in his old age. At the southern end of the square stands the neo-Gothic **Catedral de los Santos Pedro y Cecilia**, with its French stained-glass windows, designed by Pedro Benoit, chief architect of La Plata (see p.154).

To the south of the square extends the hectic **microcentro**; its main thoroughfare, pedestrianized Calle San Martín, gets so packed with holiday-makers, artisans and street performers on summer evenings it can be difficult to weave your way through. Easier to negotiate is Avenida Luro: eight blocks northwest of Plaza San Martín, it brings you to **Plaza Rocha**, where there is a small **flea market** (Sat & Sun 10am–6pm) selling books, bijouterie and other paraphernalia.

La Perla

Heading northeast from Plaza San Martín along Bartolomé Mitre takes you through the pleasant, hilly barrio of **La Perla**. Despite the relatively quiet neighbourhood, the beach here is almost as busy as the main beaches, though it is regarded as slightly more upmarket.

Inland is La Perla's main square, the Plaza España, where you can visit the **Museo de Ciencias Naturales Lorenzo Scaglia** (Wed–Mon 10am–5.30pm; $25). It houses a decent collection of fossils from all over the world, including Patagonian dinosaurs, as well as a salt- and fresh-water aquarium.

Constitución

From La Perla, continue 3km north up the coast to **Constitución** to unearth **Museo MAR**, the province's landmark contemporary art museum (Camet and López de Gomara; summer Mon, Tues & Thurs–Sun noon–8pm; winter Mon, Tues & Thurs–Sun 10am–8pm; free; ⊕museomar.gob.ar). It includes *Lobo de Alfajores* ("Biscuit Sea Lion"), a spectacular, 10m-high sea lion sculpture designed by favourite local artist Marta Minujín. A three-part installation, it was originally covered with 50,000 *alfajor* wrappers but these days is safely encased in aluminium.

Playa Bristol and Rambla Casino

Playa Bristol, Mar del Plata's iconic beach, lies half a dozen blocks southeast of Plaza San Martín. Together with neighbouring Playa Popular, just to the north, these are by far the city's busiest beaches and in high season their blanket coverage of multi-coloured beach tents resembles a strange nomadic settlement. Dominating the scene are the city's much-loved duo of buildings by leading Argentine architect, Alejandro Bustillo (he notably worked on Bariloche's Centro Cívico; see p.398). The *Gran Hotel Provincial* and Casino Central were the country's biggest hotel and the world's biggest casino building when they were inaugurated in 1950. Inspired by the imperial *Hôtel du Palais* in Biarritz, they form a majestic architectural complex, set off by a harmonious esplanade, the **Rambla Casino**, and a monumental staircase guarded on either side by much-photographed stone sea lions.

Punta Piedras and Torreón del Monje

Follow the bay round to the southeast from Avenida Luro and the coast for about 2km to **Punta Piedras**, crowned by another of the city's landmark buildings, the **Torreón del Monje**. This "monk's tower" is a perfect example of Mar del Plata's peculiar brand of fantasy architecture, which at times makes the city look like a toy village. Built as a folly in 1904 by Ernesto Tornquist, the mock medieval tower is a little overwhelmed by its skyscraper neighbours these days, but it still gives you great views of Playa Bristol and the Rambla Casino from its *confitería*. It is partly accessible by a pedestrian bridge.

Stella Maris

One block inland from Playa Bristol at Avenida Luro, wide Avenida Colón begins to clamber to the hill known as **Loma Stella Maris**, just inland from the Torreón del Monje. This residential area affords fine vistas over the city, particularly from the crest of the hill back down the straight Avenida Colón, while Güemes, which branches off Colón and heads west towards Divino Rostro, has some of the city's most upmarket **shopping**. The barrio is a pleasant place to wander if you're interested in Mar del Plata's *pintoresquista* architecture – dominated by mock-Tudor villas that wouldn't look out of place in Bournemouth. Beyond Stella Maris, the serpentine Avenida Patricio Peralta Ramos winds south along cliffs towards the fishing port (see box, p.168), past three beaches known as Playa Varese, Playa Chica and Playa Grande.

2

Museo Municipal de Arte Juan Carlos Castagnino

Colón 1189 • Mon & Wed–Fri 2–8pm, Sat & Sun 3–8pm • $10 • ☎ 0223 486 1636

The imposing Villa Ortiz Basualdo, an exuberantly turreted and half-timbered Anglo-Norman mansion, houses the **Museo Municipal de Arte Juan Carlos Castagnino**. Local artist Castagnino, born in 1908, painted colourful Expressionist scenes of Mar del Plata. His work forms the basis of the permanent collection, which has also been boosted in recent years by a growing number of contemporary Argentine works.

2

Mirador de la Torre Tanque

Falucho 995 • Mon–Fri 8am–4.45pm • Free • ☎ 0223 451 4681

At the highest point of Stella Maris, you can climb 194 steps to the top of the bizarre, castle-like **Mirador de la Torre Tanque**, a mock-Tudor water tower built in 1943, for great views over the city.

Divino Rostro

Some 3km southwest of Plaza San Martín is the leafy and well-heeled neighbourhood of **Divino Rostro**. The area, also known as Los Troncos, is almost exclusively residential, with little in the way of cafés or bars, but is worth the detour to see the **Centro Cultural Villa Victoria Ocampo**, the former holiday residence of one of Argentina's greatest *femmes de lettres* of the twentieth century. The **Archivo Museo Histórico Municipal Roberto T. Barili**, offering some excellent insight into the coastal city's history, is also nearby.

Centro Cultural Villa Victoria Ocampo

Matheu 1851, between Lamadrid and Arenales • Summer daily 10am–1pm & 5–9pm; winter Tues–Sun noon–6pm • $30 • ☎ 0223 494 2870 (call to check opening times) • Take bus #511 from Av Luro or the Blvd Marítimo and get off on the corner of Alsina and Formosa

Steeped in literary history – its eclectic owner hosted the likes of Borges – the **Centro Cultural Villa Victoria Ocampo** is an architectural curiosity in its own right. Built from Norwegian wood, it is a fine example of the prefabricated housing the British took with them to their colonial outposts. It was shipped to the country in 1912 by the great-aunt of one of Argentina's most famous authors, Victoria Ocampo (1890–1979). Cultural evenings are often dedicated to Indian music, dance and philosophy, which were of particular interest to Ocampo. Born into an aristocratic family and a vehement anti-Peronist, Ocampo became a leading feminist and literary critic, counting Camus and Greene among her close friends. This is also a lovely spot to grab a cup of tea in the café while soaking up the historical ambience and enjoying the well-kept grounds.

IMAGES OF MARDEL: FISHING BOATS AND SEA LIONS

Second only to the Rambla Casino, with its stone sea lions, Mar del Plata's favourite postcard image is that of the striking orange **fishing boats** that depart every morning from its **port**, about 3km south of the city centre. In the early evening you can watch them returning to the Banquina de Pescadores (Fishermen's Wharf) full of crates bursting with sea bass, sole and squid, which are hauled onto the quayside. At the far end of the wharf is the Lobería, a colony of around 800 real-life **sea lions** – they are all males, as you can tell by their distinctive giant manes and loud bark. These *lobos* can be observed from a close (and smelly) distance – a metre or so – all year round, though the colony shrinks in January and February, when large numbers head for the Uruguayan coast to mate. There are also a number of good **seafood restaurants** (see p.170) around the port, mostly grouped close to the Centro Comercial. Buses from the centre of Mar del Plata head to the fishing port; the #511, #551 and #553 can be caught anywhere along Avenida Luro.

Archivo Museo Histórico Municipal Roberto T. Barili

Lamadrid 3870 • Mon–Fri 9am–1pm & 6–9pm, Sat & Sun 6–9pm • $20 • ⓣ 0223 495 1200 • Take bus #511 from Av Luro or the Blvd Marítimo and get off on the corner of Alsina and Formosa

The excellent **Archivo Museo Histórico Municipal Roberto T. Barili**, in a fine Neocolonial villa one block southwest of Centro Cultural Villa Victoria Ocampo, is a goldmine of interesting information on Mar del Plata's history. Its archives include some wonderful photos of the resort's early days when the cognoscenti from Buenos Aires flocked to *Hotel Bristol*, as well as copies of the strict rules enforced on bathers: single men could be fined for being within 30m of women bathers or for using opera glasses on the beach.

2

Punta Magotes

From Avenida Luro and the coast, following the road past the fishing port for 13km south will take you along the **Costanera Sur** (officially Av Martínez de Hoz) and through an area known as **Punta Magotes** – easy to distinguish, with the city's iconic red-and-white-striped lighthouse, the Faro de Punta Magotes, at its extremity. Here you'll find quieter beaches and *balnearios* – including several popular with the surf crowd and a naturist beach – as well as most of the city's campsites.

Aquarium Mar del Plata

Av Martínez de Hoz 5600 • Jan & Feb daily 10am–8.30pm; March daily 10am–7pm; April–Nov Fri–Sun 10am–6pm; Dec daily 10am–6pm • $299 (cheaper online) • ⓣ 0223 467 0700, ⓦ aquarium.com.ar

Besides its beach, Punta Magotes is also home to **Aquarium Mar del Plata**. There are the inevitable sea lion and dolphin shows, but the aquarium's foundation carries out serious conservation and educational work to ensure it's not simply a theme park. If you aren't heading to Patagonia or Antarctica, you may want to take this opportunity to see Magellanic and emperor penguins in the flesh.

ARRIVAL AND DEPARTURE — MAR DEL PLATA

Mar del Plata is well connected by public transport to most points in Argentina, particularly during the summer, when services increase dramatically. From the combined bus and train terminal, bus #511 gets you into the centre of town.

By plane The airport, named for the city's most famous son, tango musician Astor Piazzolla, is 8km northwest of the city centre along Autovía 2; local bus #542 will take you into town. There are flights to Buenos Aires (5 daily; 55min), with more laid on in the height of summer. Aerolíneas Argentinas has its offices at Moreno 2442 (ⓣ 0223 496 0101).

By train Trains from Buenos Aires (Constitución) arrive at Estación Norte, to the northwest of the city centre at Luro and Italia; services are operated by Ferrobaires (ⓣ 011 4306 7919). The main destination is Buenos Aires (1 daily, Mon–Fri; 7hr), though note that this service arrives after dark at dodgy Constitución station.

By bus The bus terminal is located beside the train station at San Juan 152.

Destinations Bahía Blanca (hourly; 5hr 30min); Bariloche (2 daily; 19hr); Buenos Aires (every 20min; 3hr); Córdoba (3 daily; 17hr).

By car If you are travelling by car from Buenos Aires, you have a choice of three routes. Mind-numbingly straight Autovía 2 is the most direct of these, but is also by far the busiest during the summer. RP-29 via Balcarce and the coastal RP-11 are quieter, have lower tolls and meander through more attractive landscape, but add 80km (and a couple of hours) or more to your journey.

GETTING AROUND

By bus Local buses are efficient and routes are well marked at bus stops. Useful routes include #551, #552 and #553, all of which run between Avenida Constitución (the centre of the city's nightlife), downtown and the port. Buses only accept magnetic cards with prepaid credit on them ($50; available at most kiosks), and a one-way ticket costs from $5.90. SUBE cards, the same as in Buenos Aires, can be used on the #531, #532, #533, #562 and #563.

By taxi Taxis are easy to come by and cheap; try Taxi Puerto (ⓣ 0223 489 3222) or Tele Taxi (ⓣ 0223 475 8888).

By bike Rental bikes are available from Alquiler de Bicicletas MDP, at Castelli 1733 (ⓣ 0223 535 5079).

2

INFORMATION AND ACTIVITIES

Tourist information The main office for Emtur, Mar del Plata's tourist information service, is centrally located on Belgrano 2740 (daily: summer 8am–10pm; winter 8am–8pm; ☎0223 494 4140, ⊛turismomardelplata.gob .ar). There's also a useful office by the coast, on the northwest corner of the *Hotel Provincial* on the Blvd Marítimo Peralta Ramos, on the inland side by Av Colón (daily: summer 8am–10pm; winter 8am–8pm; ☎0223 495 1777).

Travel agents and tour operators You'll find several travel agents offering trips around Argentina in Galería de las Américas at San Martín 2648.

Surfing One of Argentina's former surf champs Rulo Penski runs Mar del Plata Surf School at Balneario 8 on Playa Grande (☎0223 15 455 4829). You can also rent boards by the hour ($100) or day ($260).

Paragliding Lessons are available from Luis Ducó from Arcángel (☎0223 463 1167, ⊛parapentes.com; suitable for beginners). Reservce in advance.

ACCOMMODATION

Book ahead if you plan to stay in Mar del Plata during high season. Most of the **budget accommodation** is around the bus terminal, although you can also find some good deals in La Perla. There are numerous **campsites**, many of them just out of town along the Costanera Sur/RP-11 that heads south to Miramar. You can reach the Costanera Sur via bus #511, which passes by the bus and train terminals. Check with the tourist office for addresses and prices.

Calash Falucho 1355 ☎0223 451 6115, ⊛calashmdp .com.ar. On a quiet street near the centre, this friendly, mock-Tudor hotel has rambling hallways, a wooden staircase and simple but light and attractive rooms. There's also a café for guests and a shady seating area outside. $670

Camping Del Faro Av Independencia 2075, Barrio Alfar ☎0223 467 1168, ⊛autocampingdelfaro.com.ar. Located near the lighthouse and some of the best beaches, the site is well equipped with pool, store, laundry, restaurant and shower blocks, and there are also simple *cabañas* and bungalows which sleep up to eight people. Camping $130; *cabañas* and bungalows $700

Costa Galana Av Patricio Peralta Ramos 5725 ☎0223 410 5000, ⊛hotelcostagalana.com. Modern luxury hotel overlooking Playa Grande, with a private tunnel running to the beach. Large, attractively decorated rooms with a/c, all with sea views. $3000

Etoile Santiago del Estero 1869 ☎0223 493 4968, ⊛hoteletoilemdq.com. Three-star hotel with five-star pretensions. The comfortable, spacious, if slightly dog-eared rooms are very reasonably priced. In a central spot; facilities include a gym. $1100

★**Gran Hotel Provincial** Av Peralta Ramos 2502 ☎0223 499 5900, ⊛granhotelprovincial.net. The city's fanciest hotel is housed in the original 1946 building beside the casino, overlooking the seafront. Services include massages, cable TV, 24hr room service, cocktail bar and swimming pool. $2000

Hermitage Av Colón 1643 ☎0223 451 9081, ⊛hermitagehotel.com.ar. A classically elegant hotel, almost lost amid the surrounding modern buildings. Popular with visiting celebrities, the *Hermitage* has suitably luxurious rooms, a pool and spa, and an excellent location. $1700

Peninsular 9 de Julio 2987 ☎0223 495 4151, ⊛hotelpeninsular.com.ar. Colourful hotel located in La Perla neighbourhood. Rooms are functional but comfortable. Discounts offered when paying in cash. $750

Playa Grande Hostel Quintana 168 ☎0223 451 7307, ⊛hostelplayagrande.com.ar. In a large, bright house a couple of blocks from the sea, this is one of Mar del Plata's most reliable hostels. Shared dorms are decent, and there's an on-site surf school. Private doubles available as well. Closed April–Nov, although sister establishment *Playa Grande Suites* (at Alem 3495) is open all year. Dorms $220; doubles $300

EATING

There's a huge number of reasonable **restaurants** in the microcentro, though in high season if you want to avoid queuing up you may prefer to head for the otherwise quiet streets around Castelli and Yrigoyen, southwest of the microcentro, where there are some attractive small bars and restaurants.

★**Cabaña del Bosque** El Cardenal s/n, Bosque Peralta Ramos ☎0223 467 3007. Mar del Plata's most famous café is in a wooden building set in the lush grounds of the Peralta Ramos woods around 10km south of the city centre (accessible by bus #521 or #522). The wildly exotic and rambling interior – decorated with fossils, carved wooden sculptures and stuffed animals – is worth a visit on its own, though the café's fantastic cakes are a pretty enticing attraction too. Daily 9am–8.30pm.

Chichilo Centro Comercial Puerto, Local 17 ☎0223 489 6317, ⊛chichilo.com. One of a clutch of cheap and excellent seafood restaurants that serve up the fresh catch of the day in the port's Centro Comercial; try local *rabas* (squid rings), *lenguado* (sole) or *langostinos* (prawns). Daily noon–4pm & 8pm–midnight.

★**Churros Manolo** Castelli 15 ☎0223 451 3899. Offering fantastic sea views, the coastal branch of *Churros Manolo* is a Mar del Plata institution that does upmarket fast food such as rectangular pizzas and a delicious *brochette mixto* (kebab), but it is best known for its fabulous range of filled *churros* (fried dough). The sister branch at Rivadavia 2371 downtown is busy, too, and a popular spot for *chocolate con churros* after a hard night's clubbing. Daily 8am–1am.

La Fontanella Rawson 2302 ☎0223 494 0533. Named for its pretty fountain, *La Fontanella* is a smart space specializing in *pizza a la piedra* as well as fish and pasta. Daily 11am–midnight.

La Placita de Arenales Arenales 2184 ☎0223 493 2794. Cosy pizza restaurant with photos of the owner with local celebrities hanging from the walls. Serves twelve different types of empanada and specializes in delicious *calzones*. Daily 8pm–1am.

Sarasanegro San Martín 3458 ☎0223 473 0808. One of the city's finer dining places, which mainly deals in fish and seafood. Octopus carpaccio is one highlight; suckling pig with chestnut also makes the menu. Tues–Sat 8.30pm–3am.

DRINKING AND NIGHTLIFE

For many visitors, Mar del Plata's summer **nightlife** is at least as important as its beaches – and if you want to keep up with the locals, you'll need both stamina and transport. The densest concentration of **bars** is along lively Calle Alem, which also has a good selection of late-night restaurants and is swamped by a young crowd, intent on showing off their tans during the summer. Their next port of call is likely to be Constitución, an enormous avenue 4km north of the town centre, housing numerous **nightclubs**, none of which really gets going until well after 2am.

Chiquilin H. Yrigoyen 2899 and Castelli ☎0223 496 0130. Attractive, oak-panelled pub with an eclectic and wide-ranging menu that gives an inventive twist to standard dishes, from pizza to *parrilla*. There's live music some evenings, too. Daily 8pm–4am.

Chocolate Constitución 4445. Large, glossy club, consistently one of Mar del Plata's most highly rated dance destinations. Fri & Sat midnight–6am.

Dickens Pub Diagonal Pueyrredón 3017. A pub that holds regular jazz evenings and is popular with foreign visitors. Mon–Sat 11.30am–4am, Sun 6pm–4am.

El Distrito Ramona H. Yrigoyen 2865. A slightly posey but attractive *resto-bar*, popular with the young and well-to-do keen to get in on the craft beer trend and tuck into pizza or *parrilla*. Daily 7pm–4am.

Mr Jones Alem 3738, between Matheu and Quintana. One of Alem's most popular bars, heaving with bronzed bodies on summer evenings. Next to it is the softer lit, sit-down *Mr Lounge*. Daily 7pm–7am.

Sobremonte Av Constitución 6690. Constitución's most popular club complex, featuring bars and dancefloors ranging from a mock-Mexican *cantina* to the laidback Velvet chill-out room. The music is generally mainstream dance, although international DJs of the stature of Sasha and Deep Dish have played here. Thurs–Sun midnight–late.

Tijuana B. de Irigoyen 3966. An alternative hangout to *Mr Jones* (see above) around the corner – and in a very similar vein. Daily 6pm–late.

ENTERTAINMENT

Mar del Plata is well catered for as far as **theatres** and **cinemas** are concerned; most of them are in the downtown area. **Live music** concerts are a part of the fabric of summer too, with some popular national acts playing outdoors at the *balnearios*, as well as indoors in the theatres. In January and February many of the most successful plays on Buenos Aires' Corrientes strip move to Mardel and entertain hordes of holiday-makers.

Casa de Folklore San Juan 2543 ☎0223 472 3955, 🌐folkloreclub.com.ar. This Mardel institution has a lively agenda, especially in the busy summer months, with gigs by national and international folk musicians nearly every night in Jan and Feb.

Cine Ambassador Córdoba 1673 ☎0223 499 9200. A modern multiplex, this is the resort's main cinema, mostly screening blockbusters, but also the odd indie film.

Teatro Colón H. Yrigoyen 1665 ☎0223 499 6555. Not as majestic or prestigious as its Buenos Aires namesake, Mar del Plata's main theatre, opened in 1893 and renovated three decades later, hosts all manner of shows, ranging from tango extravaganzas to jazz bands, plus folk, flamenco and classical music.

DIRECTORY

Banks and exchange There are many banks on avenidas Independencia, Luro and San Martín. Jonestur, at Luro 3185 (Mon–Fri 10am–7pm, Sat 10am–1pm), exchanges currency and travellers' cheques.

Hospitals Hospital Interzonal Mar del Plata, Juan B. Justo 6701 ☎0223 477 0262.

Laundry Laverap, Av Libertad 5519 ☎0223 474 6884.

Post office The main office is at Luro 2426, on the corner of Santiago del Estero, offering all the usual facilities (☎0223 499 1850); there are numerous other offices throughout the city.

2

Miramar and Mar del Sur

Forty-five kilometres further down RP-11 from Mar del Plata (470km from Buenos Aires), the next resort you come to is popular **MIRAMAR**, a largely modern town dominated by some rather grim high-rise buildings. A more appealing alternative to busy resorts like Mar del Plata is tiny **MAR DEL SUR**, a further 16km southeast. One of Argentina's least-developed beach resorts, Mar del Sur is in many ways one of its most appealing. Although it's increasingly courted by in-the-know Porteños looking for something a little different, the atmosphere remains relaxed, with a safe community feel and the occasional party to inject some life. Its beaches are less frequented than those to the north, and if you venture a short way away from the small clutch of beachgoers grouped around the bottom of Avenida 100 you won't have much trouble finding a stretch of soft sand to yourself. The town's unassuming buildings are dominated by the crumbling faded-pink walls and steeply pitched roof of the ex-**Boulevard Atlantic Hotel**, an elegant, French-influenced construction built in 1886. It's now a wonderfully creepy old building, its once-glamorous rooms taken over by pigeons.

ARRIVAL AND INFORMATION   MIRAMAR AND MAR DEL SUR

By bus Buses arrive at the terminal in Miramar town centre (C/40 between calles 15 & 16). El Rápido del Sur, which serves Mar del Plata, and Expreso Mar del Sur, for Mar del Sur, leave from Av 23 and c/34, three blocks northwest of the plaza. Destinations Buenos Aires (7 daily; 8hr); Mar del Plata (every 30min; 1hr); Necochea (2 daily; 2hr).

Tourist information There's a helpful tourist office in Miramar (daily: summer 7am–11pm; winter 8am–8pm; ☎02291 420190, ⓦ miramar.tur.com.ar) on c/12 1090 between calles 19 and 21.

ACCOMMODATION

Camping La Ponderosa Av La Playa, Mar del Sur ☎0223 474 8759, ⓦ campinglaponderosa.com.ar. A campsite that also rents out dorms, five blocks from the beach and to the west of Mar del Sur town centre. Well equipped with showers, a restaurant and shops. Camping **$100**; four-person dorm **$500**

Hostería Villa del Mar Av 100 and Schweitzer, Mar del Sur ☎02291 491141 ⓦ hosteriamardelsur .com.ar. Open Dec 15–March 15 only, this is the sole hotel on the seafront itself. It has small rooms with sea views and a lovely breakfast area with a hearth – useful for the odd cool day. Double with bunk beds **$500**; double **$900**

Hotel Marina Av 9 no. 744, Miramar ☎02291 420462, ⓦ hotelmarinamiramar.com.ar. One block back from the beach, this decent hotel offers some attractive rooms with balconies and sea views; these cost a few pesos more than the internal rooms but are well worth it. **$800**

La Posada Calles 15 and 98, Mar del Sur ☎02291 491274. A mere two blocks from the beach, this posada has comfortable, simple rooms with shared bathrooms, and it's one of the few places open all year round. **$700**

Posada Las Camelias RP-77 at Km10.5, Miramar ☎011 15 5023 6642, ⓦ posadalascamelias .com.ar. This stunning posada set in large grounds is out of town. It has a gym and swimming pool and staff can organize horseriding along the oceanfront or in the hinterland. **$1100**

EATING

Fortunato C/21 no. 1458, Miramar ☎02291 433223. With friendly service and well-priced, abundant pasta dishes considered the best in town, expect to take leftovers home in a doggy bag. Daily 8am–late.

Makarska Av 100 and Calle 13, Mar del Sur ☎02291 491072. The best place in town is run by Argentines of Croatian origin with a sister restaurant in San Telmo; it does a delicious goulash as well as a tasty vegetable and ricotta strudel. Summer only. Daily noon–4pm & 8pm–late.

Balcarce and the Museo Fangio

The modest agricultural town of **BALCARCE** near the tabletop foothills of the Tandilia range – 417km south of Capital Federal and 60km northwest of Mar del Plata on RN-226 – does not, at first glance, appear to have much to distinguish it from other provincial towns. However, it was the birthplace of legendary Formula One driver **Juan Manuel Fangio** and now houses a spectacular museum that is certainly worth the detour if cars and motor racing are your thing. You can easily visit Balcarce from Mar del Plata (buses every 2hr; 1hr 30min) or the other Atlantic resorts.

Museo Fangio

Dardo Rocha and Mitre • Jan & Feb daily 10am–7pm; March–Dec Mon–Fri 10am–5pm, Sat & Sun 10am–6pm • $95 • ☎ 02266 425540, Ⓦ museofangio.com • Take a taxi from Balcarce bus terminal (Teletaxi ☎ 02266 425076)

The **Museo Fangio** was built in honour of the local boy who won the Formula One World Championship five times in the 1950s, a record not equalled until the twenty-first century (by Michael Schumacher, who notched up seven victories in all). The five floors of the museum are connected by a spiral ramp and tell the fascinating story of Juan Manuel Fangio Déramo – also known as "El Chueco", or "the bandy-legged guy" – in words, pictures and trophies. There are also displays on other prominent drivers, but the cars are the stars here – around fifty of them, in fact, including a red 1954 Maserati 250 and the Brabham BT36 driven by Argentine ex-Formula One driver Carlos Reutemann, who became a Peronist politician. The most impressive, though – and saved for the top floor – is the Mercedes-Benz Silver Arrow that Fangio drove to victory in 1954.

2

Córdoba and the Central Sierras

HORSE AT ESTANCIA LOS POTREROS

Córdoba and the Central Sierras

The Central Sierras are the highest mountain ranges in Argentina away from the Andean cordillera. Their pinkish-grey ridges and jagged outcrops alternate with fertile valleys, wooded with native carob trees, and barren moorlands, fringed with pampas grass – a patchwork that is one of Argentina's most varied landscapes. Formed more than 400 million years before the Andes and sculpted by the wind and rain, the sierras stretch across some 100,000 square kilometres, peaking at Cerro Champaquí. Colonized at the end of the sixteenth century by settlers heading south and east from Tucumán and Mendoza, Córdoba was the region's first city. The Society of Jesus and its missionaries played a pivotal part in its foundation, establishing it at a strategic point along the Camino Real ("Royal Way"), the Spanish route from Alto Perú to the Crown's emerging Atlantic trading posts on the Río de la Plata.

3

From that point on, the Jesuits dominated every aspect of life in the city and its hinterland, until King Carlos III kicked them out of the colonies in 1767. You can still see their handsome temple in the city centre, among other examples of **colonial architecture**. Further vestiges of the Jesuits' heyday, **Santa Catalina** and **Jesús María**, are two of Argentina's best-preserved **Jesuit estancias**, located between Córdoba city and the province's northern border. Slightly north of Santa Catalina is one of the country's most beguiling archeological sites, **Cerro Colorado**, which has hundreds of pre-Columbian petroglyphs.

Northwest from Córdoba city is the picturesque **Punilla Valley**, along which are threaded some of the country's most traditional holiday resorts, such as **La Falda** and **Capilla del Monte**. At the valley's southern end, close to Córdoba city, are two nationally famous resorts: noisy, crowded **Villa Carlos Paz** and slightly quieter **Cosquín**. By contrast, the far north of the province, particularly a stunningly unspoilt area roughly between Capilla del Monte and Santa Catalina, remains little visited: the dramatic rock formations at **Ongamira** and the lovingly restored hamlet of **Ischilín** are just two of the highlights. South of Córdoba, the **Calamuchita Valley** is famed for its popular holiday spots, sedately Germanic **Villa General Belgrano** and rowdy **Santa Rosa de Calamuchita**. **Alta Gracia**, at the entrance to this increasingly urbanized valley, is home to an outstanding historical museum housed in an immaculately restored estancia; Che Guevara spent much of his adolescence in the town.

Southwest of Córdoba a high mountain pass cuts through the sierras, leading to the generally more placid resorts of the **Traslasierra**, a handsome valley in western Córdoba Province, and some stunning scenery in the lee of Cerro Champaquí, accessed from the pretty village of **San Javier**. Along this route lies the province's only national park, the **Quebrada del Condorito**, whose dramatic ravines provide a breeding site for condors.

THE CATHEDRAL, CÓRDOBA

Highlights

❶ Córdoba city Argentina's second city is home to some important colonial architecture, one of South America's oldest universities and a lively nightlife scene. **See p.179**

❷ Jesuit history The province owed its early importance to the Jesuits, whose legacy lives on in the form of estancias, churches and museums, which offer a fascinating insight into early colonial Argentina. **See p.192**

❸ Cerro Colorado Intriguing pre-Columbian pictures are etched onto the side of a cliff in the Reserva Cultural Natural Cerro Colorado. See p.194

❹ Estancias Ride on handsome horses, swim or just relax and enjoy breathtaking views in the unspoilt countryside on an estancia. The best is the Anglo-Argentine *Los Potreros*. **See p.196**

❺ Skydiving and hang-gliding The province's rugged sierras make it a great place for adventure sports, especially skydiving and hang-gliding. **See p.198**

❻ Parque Nacional Quebrada del Condorito This national park offers spectacular mountain views and is a major condor breeding ground. **See p.207**

HIGHLIGHTS ARE MARKED ON THE MAP ON P.178

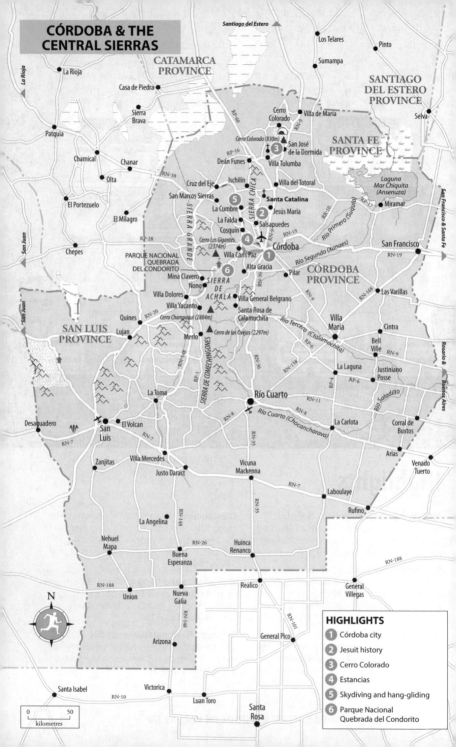

CÓRDOBA & THE CENTRAL SIERRAS

CATAMARCA PROVINCE

SANTIAGO DEL ESTERO PROVINCE

SANTA FE PROVINCE

CÓRDOBA PROVINCE

SAN LUIS PROVINCE

Santiago del Estero

Los Telares

Pinto

Sumampa

La Rioja

Casa de Piedra

Sierra Brava

Cerro Colorado

Villa de María

Selva

Patquia

Chamical

Chanar

Cerro Colorado (830m) ▲

San José de la Dormida

Villa Tulumba

Laguna Mar Chiquita (Ansenuza)

Olta

Deán Funes

Ischilín

Villa del Totoral

Miramar

El Portezuelo

Cruz del Eje

Santa Catalina

El Milagro

San Marcos Sierras

La Cumbre

Jesús María

Salsapuedes

San Francisco

Chepes

La Falda

Cosquín

Cerro Los Gigantes (2374m) ▲

Córdoba

PARQUE NACIONAL QUEBRADA DEL CONDORITO

Villa Carls Paz

Alta Gracia

Pilar

Las Varillas

Mina Clavero

Nono

SIERRA DE ACHALA

Villa General Belgrano

Villa María

Cintra

Villa Dolores

Santa Rosa de Calamuchita

Bell Ville

Villa Yacanto

Cerro Champaquí (2884m) ▲

Quines

Luján

Merlo

Cerro de las Ovejas (2297m) ▲

La Laguna

Justiniano Posse

La Toma

SIERRA DE COMECHINGONES

Río Cuarto

La Carlota

Corral de Bustos

Desaguadero

El Volcán

San Luis

Río Cuarto (Chocancharava)

Arias

Venado Tuerto

Zanjitas

Villa Mercedes

Justo Daract

Vicuña Mackenna

La Angelina

Laboulaye

Rufino

Nehuel Mapa

Buena Esperanza

Huinca Renancó

Unión

Nueva Galia

Realico

General Villegas

Arizona

General Pico

Santa Isabel

Victorica

Luan Toro

Santa Rosa

SIERRA CHICA

SIERRA GRANDE

0	50

kilometres

N

HIGHLIGHTS

1 Córdoba city

2 Jesuit history

3 Cerro Colorado

4 Estancias

5 Skydiving and hang-gliding

6 Parque Nacional Quebrada del Condorito

The province is well served by **public transport** and nearly everywhere is within striking distance of the city of Córdoba, but don't miss out staying at some of the region's excellent estancias. Renting a **car** gives you more freedom, particularly if you want to visit some of the more off-the-beaten-track destinations like Ongamira or Ischilín. The province gets overcrowded in the summer, so try and go in the cooler, drier and quieter months; although night temperatures are low in winter (June–Aug), the days can be mild and sunny.

Córdoba

Around 700km northwest of Buenos Aires, the bustling, modern metropolis of **CÓRDOBA** sits on a curve in the Río Suquía, at its confluence with the tamed La Cañada brook. The jagged silhouettes visible at the western end of its broad avenues announce that the cool heights of the sierras are not far away, and it's here that many of the 1.3 million *cordobeses* take refuge from the sweltering heat during summer. Many people spend only an hour or two here before sprinting off to the nearby resorts. But while Córdoba's excellent location makes it an ideal base for exploring the region, it also has a wide range of services and a fascinating history, and the colonial architecture at its heart remains an attraction in its own right. Moreover, the city is famous for its hospitable, elegant population and its caustically ironic sense of humour, something you'll come to appreciate the longer you stay.

3

Brief history
On July 6, 1573, **Jerónimo Luis de Cabrera**, Governor of Tucumán, declared a new city founded at the fork in the main routes from Chile and Alto Perú to Buenos Aires, calling it Córdoba la Llana de la Nueva Andalucía, after the city of his Spanish ancestors. The Monolito de la Fundación, on the north bank of the Río Suquía nearly 1km northeast of the Plaza San Martín, supposedly marks the precise spot where the city was founded and commands panoramic views.

The Society of Jesus
Almost from the outset the **Society of Jesus** played a crucial role in Córdoba's development (see box, p.192), and King Carlos III of Spain's order to expel the Jesuits from the Spanish empire in 1767 inevitably dealt Córdoba a serious body blow. That, plus the decision in 1776 to make Buenos Aires the headquarters of the newly created Viceroyalty of the Río de la Plata, might well have condemned the city to terminal decline had it not then been made the administrative centre of a huge Intendencia, or viceregal province, stretching all the way to Mendoza and La Rioja. Like so many Argentine cities, Córdoba benefited from the arrival of the railways in 1870 and a period of prosperity followed, still visible in some of the city's lavishly decorated banks and theatres. By the close of the nineteenth century, Córdoba had begun to spread south, with European-influenced urban planning on a huge scale, including the **Parque Sarmiento**. This all coincided with a huge influx of immigrants from Europe and the Middle East.

The twentieth century
In the first half of the twentieth century Córdoba emerged as one of the country's main manufacturing centres. Sadly, the post-2001 crisis boom that occurred in other parts of the country never reached Córdoba, and the industries that once ruled here are now shadows of their former selves. However, in recent years the city has emerged from the doldrums. The local government is investing heavily in arts and culture, and several new museums and cultural spaces have opened up, the latest being the **Centro Cultural Córdoba** (see p.187).

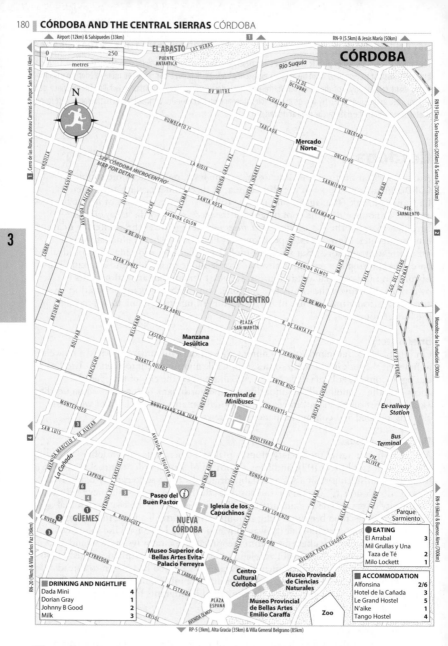

CÓRDOBA

EL ABASTO   LAS HERAS

PUENTE
ANTÁRTICA

Río Suquía

0   250
metres

N

BV MITRE
12 DE
OCTUBRE

HUMBERTO 1°   TABLADA
IGUALDAD

RINCÓN

LIBERTAD

Mercado
Norte   ONCATIVO

SEE 'CÓRDOBA MICROCENTRO'
MAP FOR DETAIL   LA RIOJA

SANTA ROSA

AVENIDA COLÓN

SARMIENTO

CATAMARCA

PTE.
SARMIENTO

9 DE JULIO

DEÁN FUNES

AVENIDA OLMOS

27 DE ABRIL

MICROCENTRO

PLAZA
SAN MARTÍN

25 DE MAYO

R. DE SANTA FE

Manzana
Jesuítica

SAN JERÓNIMO

DUARTE QUIRÓS

ENTRE RÍOS

MONTEVIDEO

BOULEVARD SAN JUAN

Terminal de
Minibuses   CORRIENTES

Ex-railway
Station

SAN LUIS

BOULEVARD A. ILLIA

Bus
Terminal

La Cañada

LAPRIDA

RONDEAU

PJE.
OLIVER

Paseo del (i)
Buen Pastor

Iglesia de los
Capuchinos   SAN LORENZO

Parque
Sarmiento

GÜEMES

A. RODRÍGUEZ

NUEVA
CÓRDOBA

OBISPO ORO

AVENIDA POETA LUGONES

●EATING
El Arrabal   3
Mil Grullas y Una
   Taza de Té   2
Milo Lockett   1

Museo Superior de
Bellas Artes Evita-
Palacio Ferreyra

Centro
Cultural
Córdoba

Museo Provincial
de Ciencias
Naturales

■ACCOMMODATION
Alfonsina   2/6
Hotel de la Cañada   3
Le Grand Hostel   5
N'aike   1
Tango Hostel   4

■ DRINKING AND NIGHTLIFE
Dada Mini   4
Dorian Gray   1
Johnny B Good   2
Milk   3

PLAZA
ESPAÑA

Museo Provincial
de Bellas Artes
Emilio Caraffa

Zoo

RP-5 (3km), Alta Gracia (35km) & Villa General Belgrano (85km)

The microcentro

The city's compact **historic core**, or **microcentro**, wrapped around leafy **Plaza San Martín**, contains all the major **colonial buildings** that sealed the city's importance in the seventeenth and eighteenth centuries. Its elegant **Cabildo** (colonial headquarters) now houses the city museum, which sits conveniently adjacent to the **cathedral**, one of the oldest in the country. Nearby, beyond a handsome Baroque convent, the

Monasterio de Santa Teresa is a group of several well-preserved Jesuit buildings, including the temple and university buildings, which form the **Manzana Jesuítica** ("Jesuits' Block"). East of the Plaza San Martín, the eighteenth-century home of Governor Sobremonte (the city's oldest standing residential building) is now the **Museo Histórico Provincial**, and contains some outstanding colonial paintings, while some interesting examples of nineteenth- and twentieth-century Argentine art are on display in a splendid French-style house, the **Museo Municipal de Bellas Artes**, a couple of blocks northwest of the plaza.

The city's regular Hispano-American grid, centred on Plaza San Martín, is upset only by the winding **La Cañada** brook a few blocks west of the centre, on either side of which snakes one of the city's main thoroughfares, acacia-lined Avenida Marcelo T. de Alvear, which becomes Avenida Figueroa Alcorta after crossing Deán Funes. Street names change and numbering begins level with the Cabildo.

Plaza San Martín

The **Plaza San Martín** has always been the city's focal point. The square is at its liveliest during the *paseo* hour in the early evening, although it is less appealing after dark, when it has a bit of an edge. Originally used for military parades, the shady square was granted its recreational role in the 1870s when the Italianate marble fountains were installed and semitropical shrubberies planted: lush palm-fronds, the prickly, bulging trunks of the *palo borracho* and, in the spring, blazing pink *lapacho* and purple jacaranda blossoms. Watching over all the activity is a monumental bronze **sculpture** of the Liberator himself, which was unveiled in 1916 to mark the centenary of the declaration of independence.

The square's southern edge is dominated by the dowdy Banco Nación and the Teatro Real; more banks sit along the eastern edge. Wedged between shops and the modern municipal offices on the pedestrianized northern side is the diminutive **Oratorio del Obispo Mercadillo**, all that remains of a huge colonial residence built for Bishop Manuel Mercadillo. He had the seat of Tucumán diocese moved from Santiago del Estero to Córdoba at the beginning of the eighteenth century, before becoming the city's first bishop.

The Cabildo

Plaza San Martín • Mon 4–9pm, Tues–Sun 9am–1pm & 4–9pm • Free • ☎ 0351 428 5856

On the pedestrianized western side of Plaza San Martín is the **Cabildo**, or colonial headquarters, a sleekly elegant two-storey building whose immaculate white facade dates to the late eighteenth century. Fifteen harmoniously plain arches, enhanced at night by lighting, alleviate the otherwise sober exterior. Old-fashioned lamps hang in the **Recova**, a fan-vaulted colonnade held up by slender pillars, in front of a row of wooden doors alternating with windows protected by iron grilles. On the pavement in front of the Cabildo, as elsewhere in the historic centre, a clever *trompe-l'oeil* device of mock shadows has been incorporated into the flagstones.

The original Cabildo was built on the same spot at the end of the sixteenth century, but the present facade was added when the Marqués de Sobremonte became governor-mayor in 1784. Put to many different uses throughout its long history – law court, prison, provincial parliament, government offices and police headquarters – nowadays the building and its inner courtyards are mainly used for exhibitions and official receptions. The Recova, meanwhile, houses the tourism office (see p.189) and a souvenir shop.

The cathedral

Plaza San Martín • Daily 8am–noon & 4–7pm • Free • ☎ 0351 422 3446, ⓦ catedraldecordoba.org.ar

Immediately south of the Cabildo, and completing the western flank of Plaza San Martín, is Córdoba's eighteenth-century **cathedral**. One of Argentina's oldest if not its

most beautiful cathedrals, it is part Baroque, part Neoclassical – its most imposing external feature, the immense **cupola**, is surrounded by stern Romanesque turrets that contrast pleasingly with its Baroque curves. However, the building's highly porous, cream-coloured stone suffers badly from ambient pollution and its facade requires regular cleaning.

The cathedral's **bell towers** are decorated at each corner with angelic trumpeters dressed in skirts of exotic plumes. You enter the cathedral first through majestic filigreed wrought-iron gates, past eighteenth-century clergyman and politician Deán Funes' solemn black mausoleum to the left, and then through finely carved **wooden doors** transferred here from the Jesuit temple at the end of the eighteenth century. The first thing you notice is the almost tangible gloom of the interior: scant daylight filters through small stained-glass windows onto an ornate but subdued **floor** of Belgian tiles. The Baroque **pulpit**, in the left-hand aisle, momentarily lifts the atmosphere, as does the decoration of the **ceiling** and **chancel**. This was inspired by the Italian Baroque, but executed in the early twentieth century by local artists of Italian origin, supervised by Emilio Caraffa, whose pictures are displayed at the Museo de Bellas Artes Dr Genaro Pérez (see p.185).

Sitio de Memoria

Pasaje Santa Catalina 64 • Tues–Fri 10am–6pm • Free • ☎ 0351 434 2449, ⓦ apm.gov.ar

On a narrow passageway just off the plaza, between the *cabildo* and the cathedral, the **Sitio de Memoria** is housed in a former secret detention centre – known as D2 – used during the brutal military dictatorship (see p.541). Between 1971 and 1982 around 20,000 people were detained, tortured and (in most cases) killed here by the police. Today it is a moving, upsetting and – when you learn about the ongoing fight for justice by relatives of victims – inspiring museum. Some of the cells and offices have been left as they were found; others feature photos and possessions of victims – a medal from a school sports day, a guitar – and testimony from survivors and relatives. There is a library of books banned under the dictatorship and a film about those forced into exile. One of the most powerful exhibits is a first-hand account from a survivor: hooded during his detention, he only realized where he was when he heard cathedral bells chiming, barely 20m away from his cell.

Monasterio de Santa Teresa

Iglesia Santa Teresa Independencia 146 • Mon–Fri 7am–12.30pm & 4.30–8pm • Free

Immediately southwest of Plaza San Martín, the lavish pink- and cream-coloured **Monasterio de Santa Teresa** is part of a set of buildings dedicated to St Teresa. As it is a working nunnery, only the soberly decorated **Iglesia Santa Teresa**, built in the mid-eighteenth century, is open to the public. Founded by local dignitary Juan de Tejeda, great-nephew of St Teresa of Ávila, the monastery was built out of gratitude for the miraculous recovery of one of his daughters from a fatal disease; after Tejeda's death, his widow and two daughters became nuns and never left. It was designed by Portuguese architects brought over from Brazil, whose influence can be seen in the ornate cross and gabled shape of the church's two-dimensional bell tower.

Museo de Arte Religioso Juan de Tejeda

Independencia 122 • Mon–Fri 9am–1pm, Sat 10am–1.30pm • $10 Mon–Tues, Thurs & Fri, free Wed, $15 Sat • ☎ 0351 428 1540, ⓦ museotejeda.com • Tours (included in entry fee; guides often speak English) Mon–Fri 10am & noon; 1hr

In the northern side of the complex, in a part no longer used by the holy order, the impressive **Museo de Arte Religioso Juan de Tejeda** is entered through an intricate, cream-coloured Baroque doorway, which contrasts with the pink outer walls. Informative guides can show you around the partly restored **courtyards**, the garden of hydrangeas, orange trees, jasmine and pomegranates, and the rooms and cells of the former nuns' quarters. On display alongside all manner of religious artefacts and sacred relics are a very fine polychrome wooden statue of St Peter and some striking paintings from Cusco. Also from Alto Perú is a seat with carved armrests in the shape of jaguars, a symbol of power in pre-Columbian Peru; the original Spanish shield on the seat back was later removed and replaced with the Argentine one. The nuns' devout asceticism and utter isolation is evident in their bare **cells**, lit only by ground-level vents and blocked off by forbidding grilles. Apart from these vents, the austere confessionals positioned against so-called communicating walls were the sisters' only means of contact with the outside world. Life for members of the Carmelite Order, still in residence next door, has barely changed.

Manzana Jesuítica

Obispo Trejo 242 • **Museo Histórico de la Universidad Nacional de Córdoba** Mon–Sat: March 22–Dec 20 9am–6.30pm; Dec 21– March 21 9am–1pm & 4–8pm • $10 • Tours (Spanish; 1hr) March 22–Dec 20 10am & 5pm; Dec 21–March 21 10am & 6pm; call ahead to organize English-language tours • **Museo Montserrat** Tues, Thurs & Fri 9am–2pm & 3–4.30pm, Wed 9am–2pm & 3.15–4.30pm, Sat 10am–1pm • $10, free Wed • Tours (Spanish; 1hr) Tues & Thurs 11am & 3pm, Sat 11am & noon • ☎ 0351 433 2075

Two blocks west and south of Plaza San Martín is the **Manzana Jesuítica**, a whole block, or *manzana*, apportioned to the Society of Jesus a decade after Córdoba was founded. The complex is home to the main offices of the **Universidad Nacional de Córdoba**, the oldest in the country, dating from 1610. Most of the students are now based elsewhere in the city, and much of the campus has been turned into the **Museo Histórico de la Universidad Nacional de Córdoba**. Beyond the harmonious cream- and biscuit-coloured facade are shady patios, ablaze with bougainvillea for much of the year. The **libraries** contain a priceless collection of maps, religious works and late fifteenth-century artefacts, while a ceiling fresco in the **Salon de Grados** shows naked students reaching out to the Muses. Fittingly, this was where applicants for doctorates were quizzed for eight hours a day for three days by their seniors – one wrong answer and they were out.

The Templo de la Compañía de Jesús

The complex is also home to Argentina's oldest surviving Jesuit temple, the **Templo de la Compañía de Jesús**, built by Felipe Lemaire between 1640 and 1675. The almost rustic simplicity of its restored facade, punctuated only by niches used by nesting pigeons, is a foretaste of the severe, single-naved interior, with its roof of Paraguayan cedar in the shape of a barrel. Fifty painted canvas panels huddled around the ceiling and darkened by time depict the figures and legends of the Society of Jesus – at 10m above ground level they're hard to make out without the aid of binoculars. Even more striking is the handsome **Cusqueño altarpiece** and the floridly decorated pulpit. The chapel to the side is dedicated to Our Lady of Lourdes and was known as the Capilla de los Naturales: it was a roofless structure where indigenous churchgoers were graciously allowed to come and pray until the nineteenth century, when it was covered and lined with ornate marble.

The Capilla Doméstica

Another part of the complex is the **Capilla Doméstica**, the residents' private chapel and "gateway to heaven" – at least according to the inscription over the doorway. Its intimate dimensions, finely painted altarpiece and remarkable ceiling are in total contrast with the grandiose austerity of the main temple. The ceiling is a primitive wooden canopy, decorated with rawhide panels that have been painted with natural vegetable pigments. While the main temple is easily accessible, you have to ask the concierge to let you into the chapel.

The Colegio Nacional de Nuestra Señora de Montserrat

The last of the complex's three main Jesuit buildings, a few doors up from the Museo Histórico de la Universidad Nacional de Córdoba, is the prestigious **Colegio Nacional de Nuestra Señora de Montserrat**, founded at a nearby location in the city in 1687 but transferred to its present site in 1782, shortly after the Jesuits' expulsion; the building had been their living quarters, arranged around quadrangles. This all-male bastion of privilege only went co-ed in 1998, amid fierce opposition. The building's studiously Neocolonial appearance – beige-pink facades, a highly ornate doorway, grilled windows and a pseudo-Baroque clock tower looming at the corner with Calle Duarte Quirós – dates from remodelling in the 1920s. Through the embellished doors and the entrance hall with its vivid Spanish majolica floor tiles are the original, seventeenth-century Jesuit cloisters, which now form part of the **Museo Montserrat.**

Teatro del Libertador General San Martín

Av Vélez Sarsfield 365 • ☎ 0351 433 2323

A block southwest of the Colegio Nacional de Nuestra Señora de Montserrat, the austere Neoclassical **Teatro del Libertador General San Martín**, built in 1887, is of world-class calibre, with outstanding acoustics and an elegant, understated interior. The creaking wooden floor, normally steeply tilted for performances, can be lowered to a horizontal position and the seats removed for dances and other social events (see p.191).

Museo Histórico Provincial Marqués de Sobremonte

Rosario de Santa Fe 218 • Mon–Fri 9.30am–2.30pm • $15 (Wed free) • ☎ 0351 433 1661

East of Plaza San Martín, the **Museo Histórico Provincial Marqués de Sobremonte** is a well-preserved and carefully restored showpiece residence and the city's last private colonial house. Built in the middle of the eighteenth century, it was the home of Rafael, Marqués de Sobremonte, between 1784 and 1796. As governor of Córdoba he was responsible for modernizing the city, securing its water supplies and extending it westwards beyond La Cañada.

The building's unassuming exterior, sturdily functional with thickset walls, is embellished by a wrought-iron balcony resting on finely carved wooden brackets, while delicate whitewashed fan vaulting decorates the simple archway of the entrance. Guarding the door are two monstrous creatures, apparently meant to be lions. The leafy **patio** is shaded by a pomegranate tree, supposedly planted when Sobremonte lived here.

The collections

Downstairs, the first rooms to the right house collections of silver and arms, while the rest have been arranged to reflect a nineteenth-century interior; each has an information sheet in English narrating how a typical day there might have passed. Best of all is the museum's outstanding set of paintings of the **Cusco School**, scattered throughout the house. Some of them, such as the *Feast of King David* and *Santa Rita de Cascia*, both downstairs, have been recently and very successfully restored, but others are still in dire need of attention. The portrait of Bishop Salguero de Cabrera displayed in the chapel – dated 1767 and painted at Arequipa, Peru – is a minor masterpiece, while upstairs there is a *Descent from the Cross* featuring a wonderfully lifelike, contrite Mary Magdalene. Also upstairs, the relentless religious imagery is given a more secular counterpoint by a huge map of South America from 1770 that gives an idea of perceptions of regional geography in the era, and a scarlet four-poster bed in the "female" bedroom.

3

Museo de Bellas Artes Dr Genaro Pérez

Av General Paz 33 • Tues–Sun 10am–8pm • Free • ☎ 0351 434 1646, ⓦ museogenaroperez.wordpress.com

To take in Argentine art from the nineteenth and twentieth centuries, head for the **Museo de Bellas Artes Dr Genaro Pérez**, a block west of the Legislatura Provincial. This municipal gallery is housed in a handsome, early twentieth-century building, designed in a French style for the wealthy Dr Tomás Garzón, who bequeathed it to the city in his will. Impeccably restored, and with fine iron and glass details including an intricate lift, the museum is worth a visit for its interior alone, an insight into how the city's prosperous bourgeoisie lived a century ago. Most of the paintings on display belong to the **Escuela Cordobesa**, whose leading master was the museum's namesake **Genaro Pérez** and which produced brooding portraits and local landscapes, some imitating the French Impressionists. Other names to watch out for are those of the so-called **1880s Generation** such as Fidel Pelliza, Andrés Piñero and Emilio Caraffa, the last famous for his supervision of the paintings inside Córdoba cathedral. The **1920s Generation**, markedly influenced by their European contemporaries including Matisse, Picasso and de Chirico, is represented by Francisco Vidal, Antonio Pedone and José Aguilera.

Museo Cripta Jesuítica

Rivera Indarte and Av Colón • Mon–Fri 10am–4pm • $10 • ☎ 0351 434 1228

At the point where pedestrianized Calle Rivera Indarte intercepts noisy Avenida Colón, steps lead down into one of the city's previously hidden treasures. Beneath the hectic street lies the peaceful and mysterious **Cripta Jesuítica**, all that remains of an early eighteenth-century Jesuit novitiate razed to the ground in 1928 during the enlargement of Avenida Colón, and rediscovered by accident in 1989 when telephone cables were being laid under the avenue. The rough-hewn **rock walls** of its three naves, partly lined with bare brick, are a refreshing counterpoint to the cloying decoration of some of the city's other churches, and the space is used for exhibitions, plays and concerts.

Nueva Córdoba and around

South of the historic centre and sliced diagonally by Avenida Hipólito Yrigoyen, **Nueva Córdoba** was laid out in the late nineteenth century. It was designed as an exclusive residential district, but many of Nueva Córdoba's villas and mansions were taken over by bars, cafés, restaurants and offices after the prosperous middle classes moved away from the area to the northwestern suburb of Cerro de las Rosas in the 1940s and 1950s. Architectural styles here are eclectic, to say the least: neo-Gothic churches, mock-Tudor houses, Georgian facades and Second Empire mini-palaces. Today, Nueva Córdoba's bars are frequented by the city's large student population, though far cooler venues are found in neighbouring Güemes.

Paseo del Buen Pastor

Av Hipólito Yrigoyen 325 • **Art Gallery** Daily 10am–9pm • Free • **Dancing Waters** Daily 7pm, 8pm, 9pm & 10pm; Fri & Sat also 11pm • Free • **Chapel** Daily 9am–8pm • Free • ☎ 0351 434 2727

The centrepiece of Nueva Córdoba is the **Paseo del Buen Pastor**, a two-storey cultural centre made of stone and glass on the site of a former women's prison. A source of much civic pride, the building houses a small art gallery, temporary exhibitions on the walls of the covered passage that winds around the building's upper level, and several cafés and restaurants, as well as a tourist information office. There are also much-hyped "**dancing water**" displays when the fountains around the centre's northern end are lit up in garish colours, set to a musical accompaniment. The area around the fountains is the hangout of choice for love-struck teenage couples. The **chapel** is perhaps of most interest, hosting regular music concerts and film screenings. Completed in 1906, its lavishly decorated interior, with murals depicting religious scenes, is a fine example of Italian-influenced *neomanierismo*.

Iglesia de los Capuchinos

Corner Buenos Aires and Obispo Oro • Daily 9am–noon & 4–7.30pm • Free

Opposite the Paseo del Buen Pastor is the **Iglesia de los Capuchinos**, an impressive church mixing neo-Gothic and Romanesque styles, built between 1927 and 1933, which dominates the Nueva Córdoba skyline. Designed by Italian architect Augusto Ferrari, the church's most interesting features adorn its exterior, in particular images of spiders, scorpions and other animals carved out of stone at the base of the columns beside the main entrance. Most notable are statues of hunched men, representing earthly sin, struggling to support the weight of the godly apostles above them. Above the church's central rose window a statue of St Francis keeps watch over the city.

Parque Sarmiento

East of Nueva Córdoba is **Parque Sarmiento**, the city's breathing space. The centre of the park occupies high ground, affording it panoramic views of otherwise flat Nueva Córdoba and the surrounding city. Designed by French landscape architect **Charles Thays** (see box, p.87), who included a boating lake and planted several thousand native and European trees, the park was opened in 1900. This huge open area, crisscrossed by avenues of plane trees, is where the city's main **sports facilities** are located, including tennis courts, jogging routes and an Olympic-sized swimming pool.

Museo Provincial de Bellas Artes Emilio Caraffa

Av Poeta Lugones 411 • Tues–Sun 10am–8pm • $15, Wed free • ☎ 0351 434 3348, ⓦ museocaraffa.org.ar

On the eastern side of the busy Plaza España roundabout, on the fringes of Parque Sarmiento, is the **Museo Provincial de Bellas Artes Emilio Caraffa**, a ponderous Neoclassical pile inaugurated in 1916, and recently enlarged with the addition of a modernist new block. It was designed by Johan Kronfuss, architect of the Legislatura Provincial (see p.338), and is named for the influential 1880s Generation artist who oversaw the decoration of the cathedral interior. Its airy galleries and shady gardens are used for temporary exhibitions.

Centro Cultural Córdoba

Av Poeta Lugones 401 • ☏ 0351 524 3000, ⓦ cba.gov.ar

Housed in an eye-catching, modern glass-and-concrete construction, with an arcing roof that appears to have been designed to tempt skateboarders (an activity that is explicitly banned), the recently opened **Centro Cultural Córdoba** is home to the regional archives and also hosts a range of temporary exhibitions, theatrical performances and film screenings. Immediately behind it is the *Faro* ("*Lighthouse*"), a concrete twist that rises almost 90m into the air.

Museo Provincial de Ciencias Naturales

Av Poeta Lugones 395 • Tues–Sun 10am–5.30pm • $15, Wed free • ☏ 0351 434 4070

On the edge of Parque Sarmiento, the **Museo Provincial de Ciencias Naturales**, the city's natural sciences museum, is geared up for children and families. There are numerous dinosaur skeletons, as well as exhibits on South American megafauna and the province's varied topography.

Museo Superior de Bellas Artes Evita

Av Hipólito Yrigoyen 511 • Tues–Sun 10am–8pm • $15 • ☏ 0351 434 3636

Housed in the Palacio Ferreyra, one of Nueva Córdoba's finest buildings, the **Museo Superior de Bellas Artes Evita** is surrounded by large French-influenced gardens designed by Charles Thays. Once the private residence of the wealthy Ferreyra family, the Palacio was built between 1912 and 1916 in an opulent neo-Bourbon style. It passed into public ownership in 2004, and the museum, which controversially gutted most of the impressive interior of the house, opened in 2007, mixing original features like the grand central staircase with new flooring, lighting and a third floor that feels more chic bar than major art gallery. The result is a bold mix of old and new with spacious rooms featuring five hundred works of art.

The collection

The ground floor focuses on local artists and nineteenth-century Spanish painters while the upper two floors house portrait collections, local landscapes painted between 1920 and 1950 and the eclectic modernist period that followed. Heading up the staircase to the second floor, you pass a silver sculpture of **Evita's head**, a replica made by local artist Juan Carlos Pallarols of the death mask ordered by General Perón following his wife's death in 1952. Other museum highlights include two graphic sketches by Picasso on the top level, and a powerful exhibition about the abuses of the 1970s military dictatorship by Carlos Alonso.

Güemes

Bordering the lively commercial area of Nueva Córdoba, the gentrified barrio of **Güemes** has an altogether different feel. A far older part of town, it's here that Córdoba's mainly Italian population first settled in the 1860s, originally naming the neighbourhood Pueblo Nuevo. Today many of the old low-rise buildings still stand, although some are in desperate need of restoration work. Lined with antique shops, boutiques, trendy restaurants, and craft beer bars, plus ever-increasing numbers of art galleries, Güemes is Córdoba's hip, bohemian neighbourhood. It is something of a cross between San Telmo (see p.78) and Palermo (see p.94) in Buenos Aires, but populated predominantly with locals rather than tourists, and on a much smaller scale.

Every weekend it hosts the **Paseo de las Artes** (Sat, Sun & hols from around 5pm), when the streets around calles Belgrano and Archaval Rodríguez are overtaken by an excellent evening market, with handicraft stalls selling everything from *mate* holders to jewellery, books to leather goods. It's the best time to visit the neighbourhood and when its bars and restaurants are at their liveliest.

Cerro de las Rosas and Chateau Carreras

The prosperous northwestern suburbs of **Cerro de las Rosas** and **Chateau Carreras** are home to many of Córdoba's trendiest nightclubs (see p.190). Avenida Figueroa Alcorta leads out of the El Abasto area, on the northern bank of the Río Suquía. It later becomes Avenida Castro Barros before eventually turning into **Avenida Rafael Núñez**, Cerro de las Rosas' main street, which is lined with shops, cafés and restaurants. Otherwise, it's a mainly residential area of shaded streets and large villas, built on the relatively cool heights of a wooded hill.

Parque San Martín and the Centro de Arte Contemporáneo

Av Cárcano 1750 • **Centro de Arte Contemporáneo** Tues–Sun 2–8pm • $15, Wed free • ☎ 0351 485 8876

On a peninsula formed by the river, the leafy district of **Chateau Carreras** is named after a neo-Palladian mansion built in 1890 for the influential Carreras family. This picturesque building, painted the colour of Parma violets, save for a row of slender white Ionic columns along the front portico, houses the **Centro de Arte Contemporáneo**, which stages temporary exhibitions of contemporary paintings and photographs. The mansion is tucked away in the landscaped woods of **Parque San Martín**, another of the city's green spaces, which, like Parque Sarmiento, was designed by Charles Thays. Incidentally, the area immediately around the museum is regarded as unsafe and it's best not to linger here alone or after dusk. To the east of the park is Córdoba's massive football stadium, built for the 1978 World Cup. Along the avenue, just south of here, are some of the city's most popular nightclubs (see p.190).

ARRIVAL AND DEPARTURE

CÓRDOBA

By plane Córdoba's Aeropuerto Internacional Taravella (☎ 0351 475 0874) is 11km north of the city centre. In addition to domestic flights, there are also several international services to Brazil, Chile and Peru. Minibuses (☎ 0351 475 3083) and taxis (around $160) run into the city. The Aerolíneas Argentinas office is at Av Colón 520 (☎ 0810 2228 6527, ⓦ aerolineas.com.ar).

Destinations Bariloche (1 daily; 2hr 15min); Buenos Aires (2–10 daily; 1hr 15min); Mendoza (1–2 daily; 1hr 5min); Salta (2 weekly; 1hr 25min).

By bus The long-distance bus terminal (☎ 0351 428 4141) is at Blvd Perón 380, several blocks east of the city centre, so you might need to take a bus or a taxi to/from it; stops for city buses and taxi ranks are close to the exit. The long terminal – made up of two linked older and newer sections – has a tourist office branch, banks and ATMs, a pharmacy, restaurants, showers and shops. Tickets for destinations throughout the region and the rest of the country are sold in the basement – advance

booking is advisable. Local buses serving some provincial destinations such as Santa Rosa de Calamuchita, Jesús María and Cerro Colorado leave from the cramped Terminal de Minibuses behind the Mercado Sur on Blvd Arturo Illia, between calles Buenos Aires and Ituzaingó; ticket offices are inside.

Destinations (from long-distance terminal) Alta Gracia (every 15min; 1hr); Buenos Aires (every 30min–1hr; 8hr 45min–11hr); Capilla del Monte (hourly; 1hr 30min); Cosquín (every 30min; 40–50min); Jesús María (every 30min; 1hr 30min); La Cumbre (every 30min–1hr; 2hr 30min); La Falda (every 30min–1hr; 1hr); La Rioja (7 daily; 5–7hr); Mendoza (hourly; 8hr 45min–11hr 30min); Mina Clavero (around 5 daily; 3hr); Nono (around 5 daily; 3hr); Rosario (hourly; 4hr 45min–6hr 45min); Salta (8 daily; 11hr 20min–14hr); San Juan (5 daily; 8hr 25min–9hr 10min); Santa Rosa de Calamuchita (every 30min–1hr; 2hr 20min); Villa Carlos Paz (every 30min; 40min); Villa General Belgrano (every 45min–1hr; 2hr).

GETTING AROUND

By bus The local bus network is pretty poor, but if you do decide to use it, note that you must first buy a token (*cospel*), available at kiosks and newsstands.

By taxi Most of the city sights are within easy reach of each other, in the microcentro; to venture further afield

you're advised to take a taxi rather than brave the city's crammed buses. Recommended companies for *remises* (radio taxis) include Tala Car (☎ 0351 461 7878) and Taxi Com (☎ 0351 464 0000).

By car Avis, Av Jujuy 248 (☎ 0351 424 6185, ⓦ avis.com.ar).

INFORMATION AND TOURS

Tourist office The main tourist office is in the Cabildo (daily 8am–8pm; ☎ 0351 434 1200,

ⓦ cordobaturismo.gov.ar) and has piles of maps and flyers. The municipal tourist authority runs regular free walking tours of downtown sights with English-speaking guides; details of these and other weekly events are pinned on a board here.

Information offices There are several small information offices dotted around town, including at the long-distance bus terminal (daily 7am–9pm; ☎ 0351 433 1982), the airport (daily 8am–8pm; ☎ 0351 434 8390) and the Paseo

del Buen Pastor (daily 8am–8pm; ☎ 0351 434 2727).

City Tour (☎ 0351 15 537 8687) offers sightseeing tours ($100) on a red double-decker bus starting from the Plaza San Martín near the cathedral.

Nativo Viajes (Independencia 174; ☎ 0351 426 4016, ⓦ cordobanativoviajes.com.ar) run day-trips and tours of the province, as well as city tours.

ACCOMMODATION

Córdoba has several good hostels and a couple of boutique hotels, but the majority of accommodation options in the city are functional at best, with the more expensive places catering mainly to business travellers. Rates for all the hotels and guesthouses listed below include breakfast; the hostels tend to charge extra for it.

HOSTELS AND GUESTHOUSES

★**Aldea** Santa Rosa 447 ☎ 0351 426 1312, ⓦ aldeahostelcordoba.com; map p.182. This bright, ambitious hostel has space for 100 or so people and is bursting with extras, including a lively bar, two games rooms, a TV lounge, a leafy patio and a roof terrace. Rates include breakfast, and discounts are available for long stays. Dorms $130; doubles $430

Le Grand Hostel Buenos Aires 547 ☎ 0351 422 7115, ⓦ legrandhostel.com; map p.180. One of the city's biggest hostels – and certainly the brashest – is in a French-style building. There are economical four-, six- and eight-bed dorms, simple but quirkily decorated private rooms (ones with TVs cost $30 extra), guest kitchen, TV lounge and pool table. The attached *Le Grand Suites* annexe has smarter, private en suites. Dorms $72; doubles $330

N'aike Fresnal 5048 ☎ 0351 589 0501, ⓦ naike.com.ar; map p.180. This friendly, well-run guesthouse is located in the quiet Villa Belgrano neighbourhood, a few kilometres northwest of the city centre. There are just six rooms, all with colourful but tasteful decor; four of them have private bathrooms. Guests have access to a kitchen, living room, plunge pool and jacuzzi. $450

Tango Hostel Simon Bolívar 607 ☎ 0351 425 6023, ⓦ tangohostelcordoba.com; map p.180. In a good location, near the Paseo de las Artes, this popular hostel has a collection of no-frills dorms (each with four to eleven beds), as well as a few private rooms (with shared or private bathrooms). Staff can organize excursions and the atmosphere is friendly and sociable. Dorms $100; doubles $360

HOTELS

★**Azur Real Hotel Boutique** San Jerónimo 243 ☎ 0351 424 7133, ⓦ azurrealhotel.com; map p.182. This swish boutique hotel is easily the best place to stay in Córdoba, with classy en suites; the vast, split-level "deluxe" options (around US$229) are well worth splashing out on.

Located in the microcentro, it has stylish *norteño* decor in a beautifully converted building, with a small outdoor splash pool, a sun lounge, a gym and spa, a café and an excellent restaurant. US$160

Gran Hotel Dorá Entre Ríos 70 ☎ 0351 421 2031, ⓦ hoteldora.com.ar; map p.182. Although anything but "gran" and with brown-and-beige decor and furnishings that are firmly stuck in the 1970s, this is a solid mid-range hotel with competitively priced en-suite rooms, plus a pool, gym and restaurant. $700

Hotel de la Cañada Av Marcelo T. de Alvear 580 ☎ 0351 420 8000, ⓦ hoteldelacaniada.com.ar; map p.180. Frequented mainly by business travellers, this hotel is housed in a looming tower block. The en suites are smart, if unremarkable; there's also a sauna, gym, restaurant-bar and small rooftop pool. $900

NH Panorama Av Marcelo T. de Alvear 251 ☎ 0351 410 3900, ⓦ nh-hotels.com; map p.182. Part of the Spanish NH chain, this upper mid-range option has pleasant though slightly anonymous en suites (many have fine views), a small garden, and a rooftop swimming pool. Sister establishment *Urbano*, on the same street at no. 363, has slightly lower rates. US$82

Sacha Mistol Art Hotel Rivera Indarte 237 ☎ 0351 424 2646, ⓦ sachamistol.com; map p.182. A centrally located, stylish boutique hotel, *Sacha Mistol* is based in an elegant building dating back to the 1920s. It has thoughtfully designed and modern en suites, a swimming pool, and an on-site art gallery. A good alternative to *Azur Real*. $1400

Windsor Buenos Aires 214 ☎ 0351 422 4012, ⓦ windsortower.com; map p.182. One of the few hotels with charm in the more expensive price bracket, *Windsor* has a rather fusty British style. All the rooms are comfortable; those in the classy newer wing are slightly fancier (though they also cost a bit more). There's a sauna, pool and gym, plus a slightly pretentious restaurant. US$111

EATING

For many years interesting **restaurants** and **cafés** were disappointingly thin on the ground; thanks to the burgeoning development of Barrio Güemes; however, this is changing. The city also cranks up a gear during university term time. With

3

a couple of notable exceptions, the city centre has little to offer in the evenings, even becoming rather seedy. Nueva Córdoba and Cerro de las Rosas feel safer and have a number of restaurants, but can also be rather colourless. All in all, lively Güemes is the best bet for atmosphere and inventive cuisine.

La Alameda Obispo Trejo 170; map p.182. A long-standing favourite of local students, the grungy *Alameda* serves unexciting but inexpensive food including empanadas ($9) and *humitas* alongside cold beers. Patrons leave scribbled notes and (generally very) minor works of art pinned to the wall. Mon–Sat noon–4/5am.

★**Alfonsina** Duarte Quirós 66 ☎0351 427 2847, ⊛alfonsinaweb.com.ar; map p.182. Busy student-focused restaurant-bar with economical snacks, meals and drinks. It's a particularly popular spot for an early evening *mate*, generally served with home-baked bread (a combo that will set you back $40–50), and there are often live folk-music performances. There are two other branches: at Belgrano 763 and at calles Viamonte and Lima. Mon–Sat 8am–2pm & 6pm–2am, Sun 6pm–2am.

El Arrabal Belgrano 899 and Fructuoso Rivera ☎0351 460 2990, ⊛elarrabalconcert.com.ar; map p.180. Good-value meals – including excellent steaks – are on offer, but the main reason to come here is for the brilliant tango classes and *milongas* ($40–50), and equally good tango shows; a three-course meal and a tango show costs $220. Mon–Sat 10.30am–1.30am, Sun 10.30am–5pm & 6.30pm–1.30am.

La Mamma Santa Rosa and La Cañada ☎0351 421 9191, ⊛lamammarestaurante.com.ar; map p.182. This traditional Italian restaurant is a fine spot for a classy meal: expect formal service, white tablecloths, low lighting, muzak, and authentic pasta ($120–205), risottos and fish dishes. There's also plenty here for vegetarians. Mon–Thurs & Sun noon–3.30pm & 8pm–12.30am, Fri & Sat noon–3.30pm & 8pm–1.30am.

Mil Grullas y Una Taza de Té Galería Caribú, Belgrano 884 ☎0351 469 3604, ⊛milgrullas.tiendanube.com; map p.180. Cute teahouse (and attached shop) in an arty little arcade in the heart of Güemes. Hot, cold and alcoholic drinks – made from over 65 different types of tea, from Nepal to South Africa – are available, plus home-made cakes and pastries. Mon–Fri 10am–10pm, Sat 10am–2pm & 4–10pm, Sun 4–10pm.

Milo Lockett Achaval Rodríguez 225 ☎0351 460 0316; map p.180. Launched by the eponymous Argentine artist and decorated with his quirky designs, this café-bar attracts a slightly older, more family-oriented crowd than some of its neighbours, at least earlier in the evening. The kitchen is helmed by a former Hilton chef, and the food – bagels, wild boar burgers, Thai-style spring rolls ($50–160) – is more inventive than most. Great drinks, too. Wed–Fri 6pm–2am, Sat 5pm–3am, Sun 5pm–midnight.

Novecento Deán Funes 33 ☎0351 423 0660, ⊛novecento.com; map p.182. This atmospheric restaurant, part of the Cabildo complex and with seating in one of the internal patios, is a great place for a weekday breakfast, lunch (mains $85–165) or an (early) *merienda*. Mon–Fri 9am–4pm.

★**Papagayo** Arturo B Mas 69 ☎0351 425 8689, ⊛elpapagayo.com.ar; map p.182. One of the hottest tickets in town, wedged into a narrow but smartly designed space, *Papagayo* specializes in cutting-edge, impeccably presented cuisine. The menu (two courses $200, three courses $230) changes constantly, but expect dishes like tomato carpaccio with burrata and anchovy cream, or olive-oil cake with cardamom sorbet and grapefruit wedges. Mon–Wed 9am–7pm, Thurs & Fri 9am–7pm & 9pm–1am, Sat 9pm–1am.

DRINKING AND NIGHTLIFE

Most of the **nightlife** is concentrated in two outlying areas: El Abasto, a revitalized former warehouse district close to the centre on the northern banks of the Río Suquía that buzzes with **club** and **music venues**, many along Blvd Las Heras, and the even trendier Chateau Carreras area, just south of Cerro de las Rosas, which has a number of flash clubs. The city is also a hub for *cuarteto* (see p.563) music. Unless you're after a dance, though, the best place for a **drink** is the trendy – and rapidly developing – Güemes neighbourhood, which is awash with cool bars, many of them perched on rooftops or tucked away in arcades. As well as those mentioned below, many cafés and restaurants double up as bars in the evening, including *Milo Lockett* (see above). Locals are famous throughout Argentina for their passionate love of Fernet and Coke.

★**Dada Mini** Achával Rodriguez 250 ☎0351 389 7983, ⊛dadamini.com; map p.180. At the end of an arty Güemes arcade, this bar isn't quite as avant-garde as the name would suggest, but it's a great place to spend an evening; friendly, inclusive, chilled-out, and with an extensive range of *tragos* (beer $50–75; cocktails $55–75) and *picadas*. Tues–Fri 7pm–4am, Sat 6.30pm–5am, Sun 6.30pm–2.30am.

Dorian Gray Blvd Las Heras and Av Roque Sáenz Peña, El Abasto ☎0351 15 403 1626, ⊛facebook.com/DorianGrayClub; map p.180. One of Córdoba's most popular clubs, playing techno and house on Fridays, while Saturdays have a more commercial edge. Prominent international DJs, including former *Space* resident Steve Lawler, have played in the past. Fri & Sat 11pm–6am.

Johnny B Good Av Hipólito Yrigoyen 320, Nueva

Córdoba ☎0351 424 3960, ⊛jbgood.com; map p.180. This busy, rather cheesy restaurant-bar serves up North American-style food, a wide range of *tragos* (from $50) and a rock-dominated soundtrack (with live music most weekends). Mon–Thurs 7.30pm–2am, Fri 7.30pm–4am, Sat 11pm–4am, Sun 6pm–3am.

Milk Laprida 139 ☎0351 664 3009; map p.180. Hip cocktail bar in a beautifully restored Güemes townhouse: shabby-chic vintage decor, bearded bartenders, well-mixed drinks (from $50), inventive food, great music, and a packed terrace out back. Wed–Fri 9.30pm–5am, Sat & Sun 6.30pm–5am.

ENTERTAINMENT

Córdoba has a fine performing arts scene, though you will need a good grasp of Spanish to get the most out of its productions.

Teatro del Libertador General San Martín Av Vélez Sarsfield 365 ☎0351 433 2323. One of Argentina's best theatres, the Teatro del Libertador General San Martín dates back to the 1890s and puts on excellent dance shows, operas, musicals and concerts, as well as (Spanish-language) theatrical performances. Box office Tues–Sat 9am–2pm & 3–8pm, Sun 5–8pm.

SHOPPING

Güemes has an array of shops and boutiques selling clothes (often by local designers), antiques, artworks and much more, with more opening up all the time. The neighbourhood's weekend market (see p.187) is a particularly good hunting ground for souvenirs. There are plenty of bookshops in the centre, many of them selling a selection of English-language titles.

Librería Blackpool Deán Funes 395 ☎0351 481 5403, ⊛blackpoolcerro.com.ar. Probably the best bookshop in the city centre, *Librería Blackpool* has a range of English-language novels and non-fiction, as well as a smaller number of books in Italian, French and German, as well as Spanish. Mon–Fri 9am–6.30pm, Sat 9am–1pm.

DIRECTORY

Banks and exchange The best banks for exchanging money are Citibank, at Rivadavia 104, and BBVA, at 9 de Julio 450. ATMs are everywhere, especially around Plaza San Martín.

Laundry There are several branches of Laverap, including a conveniently located one at Chacabuco 313 (☎0351 423 6678).

Post office Av General Paz 201.

The Camino de la Historia

The first 150km stretch of **RN-9** that runs north from Córdoba city towards Santiago del Estero is promoted as the **Camino de la Historia** ("Historical Route"), as it coincides with part of the colonial Camino Real ("Royal Way"), the Spanish road from Lima and Potosí to present-day Argentina. This was the route taken, albeit in the opposite direction, by the region's first European settlers – the founders of Córdoba city – and the **Jesuit missionaries** who quickly dominated the local economy and culture.

Eastwards from the road stretch some of Argentina's most fertile cattle ranches; to the west the unbroken ridge of the Sierra Chica runs parallel to the highway. One of the country's finest Jesuit estancias, now home to the well-presented **Museo Jesuítico Nacional**, can be visited at **Jesús María**, while beautiful **Santa Catalina**, lying off the main road to the north in a bucolic hillside setting, is still inhabited by descendants of the family who moved here at the end of the eighteenth century. Further north, in **Villa Tulumba**, a timeless little place well off the beaten track, the nondescript parish church houses a masterpiece of Jesuit art, the altarpiece that once adorned the Jesuits' temple and, later, Córdoba cathedral. As they developed their intensive agriculture, the Jesuits all but wiped out the region's pre-Hispanic civilizations, but some precious vestiges of their culture, namely intriguing rock paintings, can be seen in the far north of the province, just off RN-9 at **Cerro Colorado**, one of Argentina's finest pre-Columbian sites.

THE JESUITS IN CÓRDOBA PROVINCE

Even today the city of **Córdoba** owes its importance largely to the **Jesuits** who founded a college here in 1613. It would later become South America's second university, the Universidad San Carlos, in 1621, making Córdoba the de facto capital of the Americas south of Lima. In 1640, the Jesuits built a temple (see p.184) at the heart of the city, and for the next 120 years the Society of Jesus dominated life there. Their emphasis on education earned the city the nickname *La Docta* ("the Learned"), and even today Córdoba is still regarded as an erudite kind of place – albeit politically radical.

But while the Jesuits and other missionaries turned Córdoba into the cultural capital of this part of the empire, their presence elsewhere resulted in the decline in numbers of the native population. The indigenous Sanavirones, Comechingones and Abipones resolutely defended themselves from the invaders. Finally conquered, they thwarted attempts by the Spanish to "civilize" them under the system of *encomiendas*, a forced labour system in which indigenous populations were taught Catholicism and Spanish in "exchange" for their toil. Nonetheless, devastated by influenza and other imported ailments, the indigenous population dwindled from several thousand in the late sixteenth century to only a few hundred a century later. Apart from a few archeological finds, such as rock paintings, the only signs of their former presence are the names of villages, rivers and the mountain range to the south of the city, and discernible indigenous features in the *serranos*, or rural inhabitants of the sierras.

Despite their profound effect on the area's original inhabitants, the Jesuits were relatively enlightened by colonial standards, educating their workforce and treating them comparatively humanely. In addition to various monuments in the city itself, you can still visit their estancias, whose produce sustained communities and boosted trade in the whole empire. The Jesuit buildings in Córdoba and four of the remaining estancias around the province – including **Santa Catalina** (see p.194), **Alta Gracia** (see p.201), **Jesús María** (see below) and **Caroya**, near Jesús María – are all UNESCO World Heritage Sites.

Jesús María

Lying just off the busy RN-9, 50km north of Córdoba, **JESÚS MARÍA** is a sleepy little town that comes to life for the annual Festival Nacional de la Doma y el Folklore, a gaucho fiesta with lively entertainment held every evening during the first fortnight of January.

Museo Jesuítico Nacional

Just north of town, near the amphitheatre • Summer Tues–Fri 8am–7pm, Sat & Sun 10am–noon & 3–7pm; winter Tues–Fri 8am–7pm, Sat & Sun 2–6pm • $5 • Tours (English and Spanish) 9am, 10am, 11am, 2.30pm, 3.30pm & 5.30pm; 45min–1hr • ☎ 03525 420126 • Jesús María is reached by regular bus from Córdoba (every 30min; 1hr 30min)

On the town's northern outskirts is the **Museo Jesuítico Nacional**, housed in the former residence and the bodega, or wineries, of a well-restored **Jesuit estancia**. Next to the missionaries' living quarters and the adjoining eighteenth-century church are a colonial *tajamar*, or reservoir, and apple and peach orchards – all that remain of the estancia's once extensive territory, which in the seventeenth and eighteenth centuries covered more than a hundred square kilometres.

In contrast to the bare, rough-hewn granite of the outside walls of the complex, a whitewashed courtyard lies beyond a gateway to the right of the church. Its two storeys of simple arches on three sides set off the bright red roofs, which are capped with the original ceramic tiles, or *musleros*. These slightly convex tiles, taking their name from *muslo*, or thigh, because the tile-makers shaped the clay on their legs, are common to all the Jesuit estancias. The U-shaped *residencia* contains the former missionaries' cells, storehouses and communal rooms, now used for temporary exhibits and various permanent displays of archeological finds, colonial furniture, sacred relics and religious artwork from the seventeenth and eighteenth centuries, along with farming and

CLOCKWISE FROM TOP LEFT TEMPLO DE LA COMPAÑÍA DE JESÚS, CÓRDOBA (P.184); STATUE OF CHE GUEVARA AS A BOY AT THE MUSEUM IN ALTA GRACIA (P.202); HANG-GLIDING FROM CERRO MIRADOR, CUCHI CORRAL (P.198); MIL GRULLAS Y UNA TAZA DE TÉ (P.190) >

wine-making equipment. The local wine, Lagrimilla, is claimed to be the first colonial wine served in the Spanish court – Argentina's earliest vineyards were planted here at the end of the sixteenth century.

Santa Catalina

Around 20km northwest of Jesús María • Tues–Sun: April–Sept 10am–1pm & 2–6pm; Oct–March 10am–2.30pm & 3–7pm • $15, Tues free • ☎ 0351 15 550 3752, ⓦ santacatalina.info • A taxi from Jesús María costs around $200

Some 20km northwest of Jesús María, via RP-66, is **SANTA CATALINA**, the biggest and finest Jesuit **estancia** in the region. Almost completely hidden among the hills, the sprawling yet harmonious set of early eighteenth-century buildings is dominated by its church, whose elegant silhouette and symmetrical towers suddenly and unexpectedly appear as you emerge from the woods. Whitewashed to protect the porous stone from the elements, the brightness of the building almost dazzles you when you approach.

The **church** is dedicated to St Catherine of Alexandria, whose feast day is celebrated with pomp every November 25; the sternly imposing facade is reminiscent of the Baroque churches of southern Germany and Austria. Inside, the austere single nave, whitewashed like the exterior, is decorated with a gilded wooden **retable** that houses an image of St Catherine, and a fine carob-wood pulpit. On the right-hand flank of the church is an overgrown little cemetery, whose outer wall bears a plaque commemorating the Italian composer and organist Domenico Zípoli, who died here in 1726.

ACCOMMODATION AND EATING   SANTA CATALINA

Posada Camino Real 10km north of Santa Catalina ☎ 0351 15 552 5215, ⓦ posadacaminorealweb.com.ar. The rooms at this modern guesthouse are extremely comfortable; horseriding and other activities are laid on and a swimming pool and massages provide welcome relaxation. It's also worth visiting for the gourmet restaurant, which is open to the public (daily noon–3pm & 8–11pm; mains around $120). Rates include half board. **$1600**

Villa Tulumba

95km north of Santa Catalina • A taxi from Córdoba costs around $500–600

VILLA TULUMBA is a tiny hamlet that's home to a Baroque masterpiece: a subtly crafted seventeenth-century **tabernacle**, complete with polychrome wooden cherubs and saints, and decorated with just a hint of gold, inside the otherwise nondescript parish church.

The tabernacle had a circuitous journey to Villa Tulumba. Just after Argentina's independence, Bishop Moscoso, a modernizing anti-Jesuit bishop of Córdoba, decided that his city's cathedral needed a brand-new altarpiece. He asked the parishes in his diocese to collect funds for it, and the citizens of Villa Tulumba were the most generous. As a reward, they were given this tabernacle, which had previously been transferred to Córdoba's cathedral from the city's Jesuit temple after the Society of Jesus was expelled from the Spanish empire by King Carlos III in 1767.

Cerro Colorado

Around 120km north of Jesús María, at the far northern end of the Camino de la Historia

The village of **CERRO COLORADO**, a few houses dotted along a riverbank, nestles in a deep, picturesque valley, surrounded by three looming peaks, Cerro Colorado (830m), Cerro Veladero (810m) and Cerro Inti Huasi (772m), all of which are easily explored on foot and afford fine views of the countryside. The main attraction, though, is the **Reserva Cultural Natural Cerro Colorado**, home to one of Argentina's finest collections of **petroglyphs**.

La Reserva Cultural y Natural Cerro Colorado

Guard post at the entrance to the village • Tues–Sun 9am–1pm & 4–8pm • Free • ☎ 0351 433 3425

La Reserva Cultural y Natural Cerro Colorado is home to some fascinating vestiges of pre-Columbian culture, notably its extensive collection of petroglyphs, several thousand drawings that were scraped and painted by the indigenous inhabitants onto the pink rock face at the base of the mountains and in caves higher up, between 1000 and 1600 AD.

Some of the petroglyphs depict horses, cattle and European figures as well as native llamas, guanacos, condors, pumas and snakes, but few of the abstract figures have been satisfactorily or conclusively interpreted – though your guide will offer convincing theories. The deep depressions, or *morteros*, in the horizontal rock nearby were caused over the centuries by the grinding and mixing of paints. Of the different **pigments** used – chalk, ochre, charcoal, oils and vegetable extracts – the white and black stand out more than the rest, but climatic changes, especially increased humidity, are taking their toll, and many of the rock paintings are badly faded. The petroglyphs are best viewed very early in the morning or before dusk, when the rock takes on blazing red hues and the pigments' contrasts are at their strongest.

There's also a small, free archeological museum (same hours as the reserve), next to the guard post, with photos of the petroglyphs and native flora.

ARRIVAL AND DEPARTURE   CERRO COLORADO

By bus A few direct buses (5 weekly; 3hr 30min) run from Córdoba to Cerro Colorado, but several daily ones (3hr 15min) run from Córdoba to Santa Elena, 11km from Cerro Colorado village; from there take a taxi (around $100) to the village.

By car The reserve is next to the village, 10km down a meandering track off RN-9, west of Santa Elena. Drivers beware: there's a deep ford lurking round a bend, 1km before you enter the village, followed by another in the village itself.

ACCOMMODATION

Hotel Cerro Colorado RP-21 ☎ 03522 15 648990, Ⓦ hotelcerrocolorado.com. This simple, whitewashed hotel is a good-value choice, though not the most inspiring place in the world. It offers clean, if rather bare, en-suite rooms, TV lounge and restaurant-bar. Rates include breakfast. **$400**

The Punilla Valley

Squeezed between the continuous ridge of the Sierra Chica to the east, and the higher peaks of the Sierra Grande to the west, the peaceful **Punilla Valley** is Argentina's longest-established inland tourist area, with idyllic mountain scenery and fresh air, family-friendly resorts and numerous top-class outdoor pursuits.

RN-38 to La Rioja bisects the valley, which stretches northwards for about 100km from horrendously noisy **Villa Carlos Paz**, some 35km along RP-34 west of Córdoba. Tens of thousands of Argentines migrate to this brash inland beach resort every summer in an insatiable quest for sun, sand and socializing – the town is renowned for its mega-clubs and bars. Just north and overlooked by a sugar-loaf hill, El Pan de Azúcar, is **Cosquín**, a slightly calmer place with an annual folk festival. The further north you go, the more tranquil the resorts become: **La Falda**, **La Cumbre** and **Capilla del Monte** have all retained their slightly old-fashioned charm while offering a mixture of high-quality services and a propensity for New Age pursuits. Less crowded, they make for better bases from which to explore the mountains on foot, on horseback or in a vehicle, or to try out some of the adventurous sports on offer. Anyone looking for remote locales to explore should head for the dirt roads between Capilla del Monte and Santa Catalina (see p.200), where from **Ongamira** and **Ischilín** you can discover some of the region's most remarkable landscapes.

3

ESTANCIAS AROUND THE SIERRA CHICA

Although the Jesuit **estancias** in the Sierra Chica are not generally open to guests, a number of estancias around Santa Catalina and the Punilla Valley have opened their doors to visitors. These places are excellent spots to laze away a few days in the countryside, horseriding and swimming; they can also be used as a base for visiting the area's other attractions.

Estancia Dos Lunas Near Ongamira ☎011 2637 5123, ⊛doslunas.com.ar. Lying discreetly off RP-17 in extensive grounds, *Estancia Dos Lunas* is one of the best places to stay in the region. Simple but comfortable rooms are housed in English-style long houses, and there's a large pool with views of the dramatic surroundings, including the peak of Cerro Uritorco. Gourmet cooking, excellent horserides (including full-moon outings), massages and a personal touch are the estancia's major assets. Rates include full board and activities. US$330 per person

★**Estancia Los Potreros** Outside Río Ceballos, 1hr drive northwest of Córdoba ☎011 6091 2692, ⊛estancialospotreros.com. An authentic working estancia that has been in the Anglo-Argentine Begg family for four generations, *Los Potreros* is the place to come if you want to ride horses – the friendly owners will take you on wonderful trips, organize polo lessons, and let you observe or help with farm activities. The horses are so well trained that even reluctant riders *usually* end up happily on horseback. Accommodation is in the attractive adobe *casco* and surrounding cottages, each one with atmospheric period features. Trail rides, staying at local homesteads, and "learn to play polo" weeks also take place throughout the year, but must be arranged in advance. Rates include transfers, horseriding and full board; three-night minimum stay. US$460 per person

Villa Carlos Paz

Brash **VILLA CARLOS PAZ** lies at the southern end of the Punilla Valley, on the southwestern banks of a large, dirty reservoir. It sits at a major junction, that of RP-34, which heads south to Mina Clavero, and RN-38 toll road, which goes north through the valley towards Cruz del Eje and La Rioja. Spoilt by chaotic construction, pollution and overcrowding, the resort is frequently compared to Mar del Plata (see p.164), only without the ocean. The local population of around 85,000 doubles at the height of summer: people whizz around the lake in catamarans and motorboats, or on water skis. In the town centre, amusement arcades and theme parks blare music. The town sprawls in a disorderly way around the lake – the western districts are generally greener and more attractive.

ARRIVAL AND INFORMATION VILLA CARLOS PAZ

By bus Villa Carlos Paz's busy and cramped bus terminal is on Av San Martín, between Belgrano and Maipú.
Destinations Buenos Aires (17 daily; 9hr 30min–12hr); Córdoba (every 30min; 40min).

Tourist information The tourist office is in front of the bus terminal, at Av San Martín 400 (daily: Jan & Feb 7am–10.30pm; March–Dec 7am–9pm; ☎03541 421624, ⊛villacarlospaz.gov.ar/turismo).

ACCOMMODATION AND EATING

During peak periods finding a place to stay can be difficult, even though there are many hotels, but residents often stand by the road advertising rooms for rent. There are dozens of places to eat in the centre.

Cosquín

Some 25km north of Villa Carlos Paz, and barely more appealing, the small, bustling town of **COSQUÍN** nestles in a sweep of the river of the same name and in the lee of the 1260m **Pan de Azúcar**. One of the region's oldest settlements – dating from colonial times – it has been a holiday resort since the end of the nineteenth century. The summit of the sugar-loaf mountain, which affords panoramic views of the valley and mountains beyond, can be reached by a chairlift (*aerosilla*) from the Complejo Aerosilla, which sits about 8km north of town and also houses a bronze monument to **Carlos Gardel**. Alternatively, you can use your legs – from the Complejo Aerosilla it's about half an hour up a steep path.

Cosquín has always been associated nationwide with the **Festival Nacional de Folklore** (🖥aquicosquin.org), held annually in the second half of January and attended by folk artists, ballet troupes and classical musicians from across Argentina.

ARRIVAL AND INFORMATION   COSQUÍN

By bus The bus station, with regular services to and from Córdoba (every 30min; 40–50min) and other Punilla resorts, lies one block west of Plaza San Martín on Presidente Perón.

Tourist information The tourist office is at Plaza San Martín 560 (summer daily 7am–10pm; winter Mon–Fri 7am–2pm & 2.30–7pm, Sat & Sun 10am–1pm & 3pm–7pm; ☎03541 454644, 🖥cosquinturismo.gob.ar).

La Falda and around

Twenty kilometres north of Cosquín and a little more peaceful still, **LA FALDA** serves as a base from which to explore the nearby mountains – a taste of the far finer scenery to come some way up the valley. Today the town is best known for its annual tango festival (🖥lafaldaciudadtango.gob.ar) in July.

Hotel Edén

Av Edén 1400 • Tours (Spanish) daily 9.30am–7pm; 1hr 15min • Night tours (Spanish) Jan–Feb & Easter daily 10pm; rest of year Sat 10pm; 1hr • \$50 • ☎03548 426643, 🖥edenhotellafalda.com

In the early twentieth century La Falda was an exclusive resort, served by the newly built railway and luring the great and the good from as far afield as Europe. A major advertising campaign was conducted here by a German-run luxury hotel, **Hotel Edén**, a magnificent holiday palace built in the 1890s, now a dilapidated and unusual tourist attraction. Much of Argentine high society stayed here in the 1920s and 1930s, as well as such famous international guests as the Prince of Wales and Albert Einstein, and some claim even Adolf Hitler. The state confiscated it from its German owners in the 1940s, after which it fell into decline, but its grandiose design and opulent decor are still discernible, especially in the renovated lobby, wine cellar and *confitería*. The guided tours take you around the faded rooms; night tours are good, creepy fun, though you'll need decent Spanish to understand the ghost stories.

Cerro Banderita

From La Falda, follow Av Edén to its end and then take Austria

For exhilarating views of the valley, head for **Cerro Banderita**, where El Chorrito, a small waterfall among lush vegetation, is the starting point of the steep one-hour climb to the peak; many people do this on horseback, before riding along the mountaintop. Of the longer routes, one of the most impressive takes you east over the Sierra Chica towards **Río Ceballos**; the views into the Punilla Valley from the peak at **Cerro Cuadrado**, 2km from La Falda, are stunning.

ARRIVAL AND DEPARTURE   LA FALDA

By bus The bus station is on Av Buenos Aires, just north of the intersection of avenidas Presidente Kennedy and Edén;

there are frequent buses to and from Córdoba (every 30min–1hr; 1hr) and Carlos Paz (every 30min–1hr; 45min–1hr).

INFORMATION AND TOURS

Tourist information The tourist office is several blocks south of the bus station at Av España 50 (summer daily 10am–10pm; winter Mon–Sat 8am–9pm, Sun 10am–5pm; ☎03548 423007, 🖥turismolafalda.gob.ar).

Tours Several agencies offer tours in the surrounding area, including Polo Tour at Av Edén 412 (☎03548 426101, 🖥polotours.com.ar).

ACCOMMODATION AND EATING

Cabañas Las Ardillas Las Lomas and El Rodeo ☎03548 426254, 🖥lasardillas.net. This complex has a

series of spacious *cabañas* sleeping up to six people, as well as several "suites" – essentially more traditional hotel rooms – with hydrotherapy baths and balconies. There's an outdoor pool, and ample grounds to relax in. *Cabañas* $920; suites $1170

Camping Club del Lago 500m from the Siete Cascadas waterfalls, west of the bus terminal ☎ 03548 15 578511, 🌐 campingclubdel-lago.com. In a pleasant lakeside location, *Camping Club del Lago* provides both spots to pitch your tent and wooden cabins sleeping up to six people, plus a restaurant, a pool, and communal laundry and cooking facilities. Camping $99; cabins $550

La Cumbre and around

Just east of RN-38, 14km north of La Falda, **LA CUMBRE** is a small, leafy town, a great spot for fishing, exploring the mountains, participating in adventure pursuits or just relaxing. Over 1140m above sea level, it enjoys mild summers and cool winters, though is occasionally blanketed in snow. Several trout-rich streams pass through town, among them the Río San Gerónimo, which runs past the central Plaza 25 de Mayo. A British community was established here when the railways were built in the nineteenth century, and La Cumbre's prestigious golf club, its predominantly mock-Tudor villas and its manicured lawns testify to a long-standing Anglo-Saxon presence. But despite the resort's genteel appearance it has become synonymous with **hang-gliding** and **skydiving**; every March international competitions are held here. Cerro Mirador, the cliff-top launching-point for hang-gliding and parasailing, is near the ruined colonial estancia and chapel of **Cuchi Corral**, 8km due west of La Cumbre and worth visiting for the views alone.

El Paraíso

Cruz Chica, 3km north of La Cumbre • Guided visits daily: Jan & Feb 10.30am–1pm & 4–8pm; March & Oct–Dec 3–7pm; April–Sept 2–6pm • $20 • ☎ 03548 15 630043, 🌐 fundacionmujicalainez.org

El Paraíso, a handsome Spanish-style house built in 1915 and with an exquisite garden designed by Charles Thays (see box, p.87), was home to hedonistic writer Manuel "Manucho" Mujica Laínez, whose novel *Bomarzo* is an Argentine classic. Written in 1962, it was turned into an opera whose premiere at the Teatro Colón in Buenos Aires in 1967 was banned by the military dictatorship. The house, where it is said he held frequent orgies, contains a delightful collection of his personal effects, including 15,000 books, paintings and photographs.

Camino de los Artesanos

Running roughly parallel to RN-38 as it heads south to Villa Giardino is the winding **Camino de los Artesanos**, along which you'll find over two dozen establishments selling all manner of crafts – silver- and pewterware, macramé, ceramics, woollens – along with breweries, shops serving *dulce de leche* and home-made cakes, and even places offering yoga and massages.

Candonga

45km south of La Cumbre • Wed–Fri 11.30am–7.30pm, Sat & Sun 11.30am–8.30pm • Free • ☎ 0351 15 529 4778, 🌐 candonga.com.ar • Drive or take a taxi from La Cumbre (around $500)

The old **Estancia Santa Gertrudis** features the splendid eighteenth-century Jesuit chapel of **Candonga** – a historic national monument – with its pristine walls, ochre-tiled roof and rough-hewn stone steps. The majestic curve of its porch, the delicate bell tower and lantern-like cupola fit snugly into the bucolic valley setting, set off by a fast-flowing brook that sweeps through the pampas fields nearby. The estancia serves food, and there are generally rural activities on offer.

ARRIVAL AND DEPARTURE   **LA CUMBRE**

By bus The terminal is at Caraffa and General Paz; there are regular services to and from Córdoba (every 30min–1hr; 2hr 30min) and Capilla del Monte (every 30min–1hr; 30–45min).

INFORMATION AND ACTIVITIES

Tourist information In the former train station at Caraffa 300, 300m southwest of the main square (daily 8am–9/10pm; ☎ 03548 452966, ⓦ lacumbre.gov.ar).
AeroAtelier (Aeroclub La Cumbre, Ruta 38, Km67; ☎ 03548 452544, ⓦ aeroatelier.com) offer skydiving, paragliding and glider flights.

Escuela de Montaña y Escalada George Mallory (25 de Mayo 65; ☎ 03548 451393, ⓔ jorgemallory@yahoo .com) run rock-climbing trips.
El Rosendo (Juan XXIII s/n; ☎ 03548 15 565150) are a good bet for horseriding.

ACCOMMODATION

Hostel La Cumbre San Martín 186 ☎ 03548 451368, ⓦ hostellacumbre.com. This HI-affiliated hostel, in a 1930s British-style townhouse, has tidy four- and six-bed dorms, private rooms, small pool, communal kitchen, and staff who can help organize activities in the surrounding area. Rates include breakfast. Dorms $175; doubles $500

Posada de la Montaña 9 de Julio 753 ☎ 03548 451028. Near the golf course, *Posada de la Montaña* is one of the better mid-range options in La Cumbre, with homely, en-suite rooms and a small pool in the back garden. Rates include breakfast. $900

3

Capilla del Monte

Lively **CAPILLA DEL MONTE**, 17km north of La Cumbre, sits at the confluence of the rivers Calabalumba and Dolores against the bare-sloped Cerro Uritorco, at 1979m the highest peak of the Sierra Chica. It was a resort for Argentina's bourgeoisie at the end of the nineteenth century, as testified by the many luxurious villas, some of them now very dilapidated. These days it attracts more alternative, back-to-nature travellers. The town has few sights, but is an appealing base for mountain treks, hang-gliding and other pursuits. The central Plaza San Martín is a couple of blocks east of RN-38, which runs through the west of the town, parallel to the Río de Dolores. From the plaza, Diagonal Buenos Aires, the commercial pedestrian mall, runs southeast to the quaint former train station on Calle Pueyrredón; it's claimed to be South America's only roofed street, an assertion nowhere else has rushed to contend. Several **balnearios** are found along the Río Calabalumba, including

NATURE'S MEDICINE IN THE CENTRAL SIERRAS

A bewildering variety of vegetation grows on the mountainsides of the Central Sierras, with species from all three of the country's principal phytogeographic zones – the Andes, the Pampas and the Chaco. Many of these plant species are reputed to possess remarkable **medicinal properties**. Perhaps best known is the *peperina*, of which there are two varieties: *Mintostachys verticillata* and *Satureja parvifolia* (or *peperina de la sierra*). Both are highly aromatic and extremely digestive but, in men, diminish sexual potency. The *yerba del pollo* (*Alternanthera pungens*), on the other hand, is a natural cure for flatulence, while ephedrine, a tonic for heart ailments, is extracted industrially from *tramontana* (*Ephedra triandra*), a broom-like bush found at altitudes of 800–1300m.

Anyone suffering from gall bladder problems might do well to drink an infusion of *poleo* (*Lippia turbinata*), a large, aromatic shrub with silvery foliage. Appropriately enough, since Santa Lucia is the patron saint of the blind, the *flor de santa Lucia* (*Commelina erecta*), whose intense blue or lilac blooms carpet the ground to astonishing effect, exudes a sticky substance that can be used as eye drops. The *cola de caballo* (*Equisetum giganteum*) – or "horsetail" – is used to control arterial pressure, thanks to its diuretic powers; its ribbed, rush-like stems grow alongside streams and are crowned with hairy filaments. Whatever you do, however, steer clear of *revienta caballos* (*Solanum eleagnifolium* or *S. sisymbrifolium*), a distant relative of the deadly nightshade. The pretty violet flowers give way to deceptively attractive yellow berries, but the whole plant is highly toxic.

Obviously, you should **seek expert advice** before putting these herbal cures to the test, and they should not be used instead of conventional medicine for the severest of complaints. Pharmaceutical herbs, known as *yuyos*, are sold (usually in dried form) in pharmacies and in stores selling dietetic products throughout the region.

Balneario Calabalumba, at the northern end of General Paz, and *Balneario La Toma*, at the eastern end of Sabattini.

In addition to the fresh air, unspoilt countryside and splendid opportunities for sports pursuits, such as trekking and fishing, many visitors are also drawn by claims of **UFO sightings**, "energy centres" and numerous local **legends**. One such myth asserts that when Calabalumba, the young daughter of a witch doctor, eloped with Uritorco, the latter was turned into a mountain while she was condemned to eternal sorrow, her tears forming the river that flows from the mountainside.

Cerro Uritorco

The path starts 3km from the *Balneario Calabalumba*, northeast of Plaza San Martín • Open daily; you must register at the base of the mountain and set off between 7am and 12.30pm and start your return by 3.30pm • $180 • ☎ 03548 15 575287, ⊕ cerrouritorco.com.ar

The **Cerro Uritorco**, the focus for Capillo del Monte's supposed paranormal activity, is well worth the climb (about 4hr to the top) up a steep, well-trodden path for the grandiose views across the valley to the Sierra de Cuniputo to the west. Only part of the climb is shaded, so take water with you.

Los Terrones

15km outside Capilla del Monte; drive 8km north of town, along RN-38, then head east at Charbonier along a small track towards Sarmiento • Daily 9am–dusk • $78 • ☎ 03548 15 573727, ⊕ losterrones.com

Los Terrones is an amazing formation of multicoloured rocks on either side of a 5km dirt track. You can drive through the privately owned park quickly enough, but it's far better to walk along the signposted path that winds in between the rocks (a 1hr 30min circuit), to more clearly admire the strange shapes, all gnarled and twisted, some of them resembling animals or human forms.

ARRIVAL AND INFORMATION   CAPILLA DEL MONTE

By bus The bus station is at the corner of Corrientes and Rivadavia, 200m south of Plaza San Martín; there are regular services to Córdoba (hourly; 1hr 30min).

Tourist information The dynamic tourist office in the old railway station at Pueyrredón s/n (daily 8am–8pm; ☎ 03548 481903) has details of guides and operators offering treks, horseriding and hang-gliding.

ACCOMMODATION AND EATING

Hostel Los Tres Gómez 25 de Mayo 452 ☎ 03548 482647, ⊕ hostelencapilladelmonte.com. HI-affiliated hostel with a lurid colour scheme – orange walls, lime-green cupboards and a pink pool table are just some of the features. The dorms and private rooms, by contrast, are plain and a little bare. There's a communal kitchen, garden and small restaurant-bar. Breakfast included. Dorms **$190**; doubles **$450**

Hotel Montecassino La Pampa 107 ☎ 03548 482572, ⊕ hotelmontecassino.com.ar. A stately hotel, in a building dating back to 1901, with comfortable en suites

(some with excellent mountain views and costing around $100 extra), a swimming pool and a fine restaurant (open to non-guests). Yoga sessions are on offer, and rates include breakfast. **$1080**

Dos Aguas Santa Cruz 1714 ☎ 03548 633192, ⊕ dosaguas.ar.com. Bringing glamping to Capilla del Monte, *Dos Aguas* has a collection of cool and comfy geodesic tents, as well as larger cabins. There's a pool, plus a guest kitchen, barbecues, and plenty of activities offered – from horseriding to meditation. Camping **$500**; cabins **$950**

Ongamira

ONGAMIRA, 25km northeast of Capilla del Monte and 1400m above sea level, is a remote hamlet famed for its **Grutas**, strange caves amid rock formations sculpted by wind and rain in the reddish sandstone, and painted with black, yellow and white pigments by indigenous groups some six hundred years ago. The drawings depict animals, human figures and abstract geometric patterns, and must be surveyed from a special viewpoint as the extremely fragile stone is gradually crumbling away and many of the paintings have already been lost.

Ischilín

Around 20km north of Ongamira, a dirt road snakes through mesmerizing rocky landscapes and past a polo ground to the once-abandoned village of **ISCHILÍN**. Its spectacular **Plaza de Armas**, not unlike an English village green, is dominated by a venerable algarrobo tree, its gigantic gnarled trunk host to epiphytic cacti and skeins of moss, and by the early eighteenth-century Jesuit church, **Nuestra Señora del Rosario**, with a mustard-yellow facade and a delightfully primitive interior, with a rickety choir balcony made of algarrobo wood.

Casa Museo Fernando Fader

8km south of the village · Wed–Sun noon–5pm · $10

The **Casa Museo Fernando Fader** is in a house built by the painter Fernando Fader, an adoptive Argentine born of German parents who settled here in the vain hope of curing his chronic tuberculosis. His paintings, strongly influenced by Van Gogh and at times Monet, are best seen at the provincial fine-arts museum near Mendoza (see p.350). Only one is on show here, alongside personal effects and furniture, but the mock-Italianate garden is well worth a visit.

3

ACCOMMODATION AND EATING   **ISCHILÍN**

La Rosada ☎ 0351 15 558 7085, ⓦ ischilinposada.com .ar. This charming guesthouse is run by descendants of Fernando Fader; you can stay the night or just enjoy the fine food in the restaurant. There's also a swimming pool. Don't miss the chance of being shown around the village by the owners. Rates include full board. **$1590**

The Calamuchita Valley

One of Córdoba Province's major holiday destinations, where many city folk have weekend or summer homes, the green **Calamuchita Valley** begins 30km south of Córdoba city at the Jesuit estancia town of **Alta Gracia** and stretches due south for over 100km, between the undulating Sierra Chica to the east and the steep Sierra de Comechingones to the west. The varied vegetation that covers the valley's sides provides a perfect habitat for hundreds of species of birds and other fauna. Two large reservoirs, Embalse Los Molinos in the north and Embalse Río Tercero in the south, both dammed in the first half of the twentieth century for water supplies, electricity and recreational angling, give the valley its alternative name, sometimes used by the local tourist authority: **Valle Azul de los Grandes Lagos** ("Blue Valley of the Great Lakes"). It's believed that the area's **climate** has been altered by their creation, with noticeably wetter summers than in the past.

The valley's two main towns could not be more different: **Villa General Belgrano** is a kitsch resort with a strong Germanic identity, whereas **Santa Rosa de Calamuchita**, the valley's rather brash capital, is more youthful and dynamic. Both, however, are good bases for exploring the beautiful Comechingones mountains, whose Camiare name means "mountains and many villages". One of these villages, the quiet hamlet of **La Cumbrecita**, would not look out of place in the Swiss Alps, and is the starting point for some fine hikes. All the villages offer a wide range of accommodation, making them ideal for anyone wanting to avoid big cities like Córdoba.

Alta Gracia

Historic **ALTA GRACIA**, less than 40km south of Córdoba and 3km west of the busy RP-5, lies at the northern entrance of the Calamuchita Valley. It is now rather nondescript, but in the 1920s and 1930s its location made it popular with the wealthy bourgeoisie of Buenos Aires and Córdoba, who built holiday homes. Che Guevara, spent some of his youth here, and revolutionary composer Manuel de Falla fled here from the Spanish Civil War. The original colonial settlement dates from the late sixteenth century, but in 1643 it was chosen as the site for a Jesuit estancia around which the town grew up. After the Jesuits' expulsion in 1767 the estancia fell into ruin, though it was inhabited for a short time in 1810 by Viceroy Liniers, forced to leave Córdoba following the Argentine declaration of independence.

Museo Casa del Virrey Liniers

Plaza Manuel Solares • Jan 3–March 9 Tues–Fri 9am–8pm, Sat & Sun 9.30am–8pm; March 10–Jan 2 Tues–Fri 9am–1pm & 3–7pm, Sat & Sun 9.30am–12.30pm & 3.30–6.30pm • $20, free Wed • Tours (Spanish; ask about English-language tours) 4–8 times Tues–Sun; 30–45min • Free • ☎ 03547 421303, ⓦ museoliniers.org.ar

The **Museo Casa del Virrey Liniers** is housed in the Residencia, the Jesuits' original living quarters and workshops. Entered through an ornate Baroque doorway on Plaza Manuel Solares, the town's main square, the beautifully restored Residencia, with its colonnaded upper storey, forms two sides of a cloistered courtyard. Exhibits consist mainly of furniture and art dating from the early nineteenth century, but there are also some magnificent examples of colonial religious paintings and sculptures. Perhaps the most interesting sections of the museum are the painstakingly re-created kitchen and the *herrería*, or forge, the oldest part of the estancia. The church adjoining the Residencia is still used regularly for Mass; it lies immediately to the south.

Tajamar

Just north of Plaza Manuel Solares

The **Tajamar**, or estancia reservoir, is one of Argentina's earliest hydraulic projects, dating from 1659; it both supplied water for the community and served as a millpond. In its mirror-like surface is reflected the town's emblematic clock tower, erected in 1938 to mark 350 years of colonization in the area (and now home to the tourist office).

Villa Carlos Pellegrini

Avenida Sarmiento leads up a slope from the western bank of the Tajamar into **Villa Carlos Pellegrini**, an interesting district of quaint timber and wrought-iron dwellings, dating from when rich Porteños built summerhouses here in the fashionable so-called *estilo inglés*, a local interpretation of mock-Tudor. Many of them are now sadly dilapidated, but two have been turned into interesting museums.

Museo Casa de Ernesto "Che" Guevara

Avellaneda 501, a 20min walk from Plaza Manuel Solares • Mon 2–6.45pm, Tues–Sun 9am–6.45pm • $75; an $85 joint ticket also covers the Museo Manuel de Falla and the (eminently missable) Museo de Arte Gabriel Dubois • ☎ 03547 428579

One of Villa Carlos Pellegrini's houses, Villa Beatriz, was for several years in the 1930s home to the family of **Che Guevara**. His doctor recommended the dry continental climate of the sierras, and his family rented various houses in Alta Gracia during his adolescence in the vain hope of curing his debilitating asthma. Homage is paid to the young revolutionary-to-be here in the **Museo Casa de Ernesto "Che" Guevara** where evocative photographs, correspondence and all manner of memorabilia – from golf clubs and a typewriter he used as a young man to the ashes of Alberto Granado, with whom he embarked on his famous motorcycle journey around South America – are lovingly displayed.

Museo Manuel de Falla

Av Carlos Pellegrini 1011, a 10min walk from Villa Beatriz • Mon 2–6.45pm, Tues–Sun 9am–6.45pm • $20; a $85 joint ticket also covers the Museo Casa de Ernesto "Che" Guevara and the (eminently missable) Museo de Arte Gabriel Dubois • ☎ 03547 429292

Another house in Villa Carlos Pellegrini, Los Espinillos, was Spanish composer **Manuel de Falla**'s home for four years until his death in 1946; like Che Guevara, he came to the sierras for health reasons, in his case because he suffered from chronic tuberculosis. Now the **Museo Manuel de Falla**, exhibiting his piano and other

CHE GUEVARA

Despite being one of Argentina's most famous sons, **Ernesto "Che" Guevara** is little celebrated in his homeland, with nothing like the number of monuments and museums you might expect for such an international icon. This is no doubt at least in part due to Che fighting his battles elsewhere – primarily, of course, in Cuba, where he is idolized, but also in places like the Congo and Bolivia. It is hard to know whether Argentine authorities ignore his legacy because he was, well, anti-authoritarian, or whether they feel offended that he had the cheek to go and instigate revolution outside of *la gran Argentina*. Whatever his claims to supra-nationality may be, though, Che was certainly Argentine – a fact reflected even in his nickname ("che" being a common interjection, more or less meaning "hey", and very characteristic of the River Plate region).

Che was born to a middle-class family in **Rosario** (see p.216) in 1928, and moved to **Alta Gracia** with his family at the age of 5, going to Deán Funes college in Córdoba before moving on to the Universidad de Buenos Aires to study medicine. Three years later, he set off on his famous **motorbike trip** around South America, during which he was exposed to the continent's poverty and inequalities, as well as the cultural similarities that led him to believe in the need to foster a sense of regional rather than national identity. He did return to Buenos Aires to finish his studies, but a month after graduating he was back on the road, this time heading to Guatemala and a meeting with local radicals which eventually led him to Fidel Castro, Cuba and his status as one of the great revolutionary figures of the twentieth century.

Che, however, saw the Cuban revolution as just the first step in a continent-wide **revolt against US control**, and in 1965 he formally resigned his Cuban citizenship, ministerial position and rank of comandante, and left the country. After an unsuccessful spell leading a Cuban guerrilla contingent supporting rebels in the Congo, Che set off with a small band of supporters for **Bolivia** in 1966 with the aim of fomenting a revolution that would spread throughout the neighbouring states, including Argentina. Bolivia, however, proved to be an exceptionally poor choice; it was the only South American country to have carried out radical land reform, and as such the revolutionary potential of its peasants was fairly low.

Che's group attracted little local support, and soon found itself on the run. On October 8, following a series of gun battles, he was captured by US-trained Bolivian soldiers, and the following day **executed** in the remote hamlet of La Higuera. According to legend, Che's last words were: "Shoot, coward, you are only going to kill a man."

personal effects, the well-preserved house affords fine views of the nearby mountains. Piano and other music recitals are given, normally on Saturday evenings, in the small concert hall in the garden.

ARRIVAL AND INFORMATION ALTA GRACIA

By bus Buses from Córdoba (every 15min; 1hr) pick up and drop off passengers at stops throughout town, as well as at the bus terminal on Calle P. Butori and Av Presidente Perón, around eight blocks west of the Tajamar.

Tourist information You can get a good map of the town at the main tourist office in the clock tower, just off Plaza Manuel Solares (Mon–Fri 7am–8pm, Sat & Sun 8am–8pm; ☎03547 428128, ⓦaltagracia.gov.ar). There's another, smaller office at the bus terminal (Mon–Fri 8am–2pm).

Villa General Belgrano

Around 50km south of Alta Gracia, along attractive corniches skirting the blue waters of the **Embalse Los Molinos**, is the demure resort of **VILLA GENERAL BELGRANO**. The unspoiled countryside surrounding it, the folksy architecture and decor, and the Teutonic traditions of the local population all give the place a distinctly alpine feel. Many residents are of German, Swiss or Austrian origin, some of them descended from escapees from the *Graf Spee*, the pocket battleship scuttled by its captain off the Uruguayan coast on December 13, 1939, after it was surrounded by Allied cruisers during World War II's landmark Battle of the River Plate. The last *Graf Spee* survivor

VILLA GENERAL BELGRANO'S FESTIVALS

Essentially a sedate place favoured by families and older visitors attracted by its creature comforts and hearty food – especially welcome during winter snow – Villa General Belgrano shifts up a gear during its many **festivals**. While the Feria Navideña, or Christmas festival, the Fiesta de Chocolate Alpino, in July, and the Fiesta de la Masa Vienesa, a Holy Week binge of apple strudel and pastries, are all eagerly awaited, the annual climax – during ten days at the beginning of October – is the nationally famous **Oktoberfest**, Villa General Belgrano's answer to Munich's world-renowned beer festival. Stein after stein of foaming Pilsner is knocked back, after which merry revellers stagger down Villa Belgrano's normally genteel streets.

died a few years ago, and you're unlikely to hear German spoken now, but many residents still look distinctly Teutonic, while souvenir shops sell ersatz cuckoo clocks, oompah music CDs, and steins.

Whether or not its kitsch cosiness appeals, Villa General Belgrano is a decent regional base if you'd rather avoid Córdoba, with plentiful accommodation options and easy access to the Sierra de Comechingones. However, if adventure sports or nightclubs are what you're after, you're better off heading for Santa Rosa de Calamuchita (see opposite).

ARRIVAL AND INFORMATION   VILLA GENERAL BELGRANO

By bus Regular services from Buenos Aires (2 daily; 11hr–11hr 40min), Córdoba (every 45min–1hr; 2hr) and Santa Rosa de Calamuchita (every 15–30min; 30min) arrive at the small bus terminal on Av Vélez Sarsfield, 5min northwest of the central square, Plaza José Hernández. Pájaro Blanco (☎03546 461709) runs minibuses to and from La Cumbrecita (7 daily; 45min–1hr); its bus stop is on Av San Martín, 100m north of Plaza José Hernández.

Tourist information Villa General Belgrano's busy tourist office is in the German town hall on the main street, Av Roca 168 (daily 9am–9pm; ☎03546 461215). Above the office is a tower with a viewpoint at the top.

ACCOMMODATION

You're spoilt for choice when it comes to accommodation, although if you're planning to attend the Oktoberfest you should book well ahead and be prepared for steeper prices.

Alburgue el Rincón Alexander Fleming 347 ☎03546 461323, ⓦhostelelrincon.com.ar. This laidback, HI-affiliated hostel offers dorms, en-suite private rooms, and a place to pitch your tent, as well as kitchen access and a small pool. Breakfast costs extra. Camping $100; dorms $140; doubles $520

Posada Nehuen Av San Martín 17 ☎03546 461412, ⓦposadanehuen.com.ar. On the edge of the central square, this guesthouse has a selection of comfortable en suites with TVs, mini-fridges and phones, though the decor throughout is a bit twee. Rates include breakfast but a/c costs extra. $760

Rincón de Mirlos 9km west of the centre, off RP-5 ☎03456 15 516 4254, ⓦrincondemirlos.com.ar. The best of several campsites, signposted 7km west of the centre on the road towards La Cumbrecita. From there it is another 2km through handsome farmland and woods to the bucolic riverside setting, where there are clean dorms, isolated camping pitches among the trees, a restaurant-bar, and long stretches of sandy beach. Breakfast costs extra. Camping $100; dorms $400

Tantra Posada Palotti 36, just off Av Roca ☎03546 462142, ⓦposadatantra.com.ar. In a pleasant whitewashed home with a well-kept garden and a small, curvy swimming pool, this mid-range guesthouse provides a warm welcome and clean, homely en suites. Rates include a good breakfast. $950

EATING

Café Rissen Av Julio A. Roca 36 ☎03546 464100. This café is the place for German-style cakes and pastries ($28–52) – try a slice of black forest gâteau (*selva negra*) or apple strudel. There's also a range of coffees and hot chocolates ($20–72), including several variations featuring alcohol, plus sandwiches, burgers, a few main meals, and – of course – beer. Daily 8am–midnight.

Ciervo Rojo Av Julio A. Roca 210 ☎03546 461345 ⓦconfiteriaelciervorojo.com. Dating back over fifty years, this super-kitsch restaurant feels like a hunting lodge, with deer heads and wood panelling (plus an incongruous row of garden gnomes). The menu features an array of Germanic dishes (mains $105–150) including goulash and *spätzle*, sausages and sauerkraut, and smoked pork steaks. Live oompah music on Saturday nights. Daily 9am–11pm/midnight.

Santa Rosa de Calamuchita and around

In 1700, a community of Dominicans built an estancia and a chapel dedicated to the patron saint of the Americas, Santa Rosa of Lima, after which nothing much else happened in **SANTA ROSA DE CALAMUCHITA**, 11km south of Villa General Belgrano, until the end of the nineteenth century. Then, thanks to its mountainside, riverbank location and its mild climate, the place suddenly took off as a holiday resort, an alternative to its more traditional neighbour to the north. Now it's a highly popular destination and makes an excellent base for exploring the relatively unspoilt mountains nearby. Many of Santa Rosa de Calamuchita's visitors use it as a springboard for adventure sports, from diving and kayaking to jet-skiing and flying, all located at Villa del Dique, 17km away. Less sedate than Villa General Belgrano but more bearable than Villa Carlos Paz, from Christmas until Easter Santa Rosa throbs with dance music blaring from convertibles packed with holiday-makers.

The town's compact centre is built in a curve of the Río Santa Rosa, just south of where the Arroyo del Sauce flows into it. There's no main plaza, but a number of busy streets run off the main Calle Libertad.

3

Museo de Arte Religioso

Libertad • Jan & Feb daily 10am–1pm; March–Aug Wed–Sun 10am–1pm; Sept–Dec Thurs–Sun 10am–1pm • Free

The ruined estancia was demolished at the beginning of the twentieth century, but the beautifully restored **Capilla Vieja** (Old Chapel) now houses the **Museo de Arte Religioso**, where you can see a superb, late seventeenth-century wooden Christ, crafted by local Jesuit artisans, and other works of colonial religious art.

ARRIVAL AND DEPARTURE   SANTA ROSA DE CALAMUCHITA

By bus Regular buses from Córdoba (every 30min–1hr; 2hr 20min) and Villa General Belgrano (every 15–30min; 30min) drop off and pick up passengers at stops along Av Gómez.

INFORMATION AND TOURS

Tourist information The tourist office is at Córdoba and Entre Ríos (daily 8am–10pm; ☎ 03546 429654).
Tours Naturaleza y Aventura (☎ 03546 464144, ⓦ naturalezacba.com.ar) organizes single- and multi-day treks into the Comechingones range, as well as a range of horseriding, 4WD and mountain-biking trips.

ACCOMMODATION AND EATING

Camping Vacacional Miami Outside town on the road to Yacanto ☎ 03546 499613, ⓦ campingmiami.com.ar. This campsite is a good option for budget travellers, offering a mix of camping spots, dorms, wooden huts with shared bathrooms, plus larger en-suite apartments ($685) sleeping up to four, and eye-catching dome-shaped *cabañas* ($1450) sleeping up to six. Guests have access to cooking facilities, and there's a restaurant-bar. Camping $125; dorms $185; huts $475
Hotel Yporá 1km outside town on RP-5 ☎ 03546 421233, ⓦ hotelypora.com. This stylish 1930s hotel has 17 acres of tree-filled grounds, two pools, a tennis court, and a restaurant and bar. The en-suite rooms are smart, if sparsely furnished; all have a/c and plasma TVs. Breakfast included. $1200
La Pulpería de los Ferreyra Libertad 578 ☎ 03546 421769, ⓦ lapulperiaferreyra.com.ar. Aping the look of a *pulpería* (traditional bar), this reliable restaurant focuses on sizeable *asados*, though there are some good fish dishes too (including trout in a black butter sauce). Mains $100–180. Daily noon–3pm & 8pm–midnight.

La Cumbrecita

Around 35km northwest of Villa General Belgrano along a winding scenic track, **LA CUMBRECITA** is a small, peaceful alpine-style village in the foothills of the Comechingones range. Benefiting from a mild microclimate and enjoying views of wild countryside, it has developed as a relatively select holiday resort ever since it was built in 1934 by Swiss, Austrian and German immigrants.

Two paths wind their way through La Cumbrecita, parallel to the Río del Medio that cuts a deep ravine below. The lower one passes a mock-medieval *castillo* on the way to the Río Almbach, which flows into the Río del Medio north of the village; the upper trail climbs the hill to the west of the village, cutting through a well-tended cemetery from where you can enjoy wonderful views of the Lago Esmeralda and the fir-wooded mountains behind.

For some more great vistas, take Avenida San Martín, which leads north from Plaza José Hernández, and keep going until you reach the edge of town; from here the dirt road swings in a westerly direction and climbs through hills that open to views of the Río Segundo Valley.

Mountain walks and balnearios

La Cumbrecita is a perfect base for some of the region's most rewarding **mountain walks**, including some well-trodden but uncrowded trails reaching 2000m or more. Signposted treks lasting between one and four hours each way head off to the eyrie-like *miradores* at casas Viejas, Meierei and Cerro Cristal, while one of the most popular trails climbs from the *castillo*, past *Balneario La Olla*, with its very deep pools of crystal-clear water created by the gushing waterfalls, to the 1715m summit of the unfortunately named Cerro Wank.

Other **balnearios** include *Lago de las Truchas* and *Confluencia* – the former named for the plentiful trout in the stream and the latter renowned for its caves – both with bucolic settings and views up the craggy mountaintops: perfect for cooling off on a hot day.

ARRIVAL AND INFORMATION   LA CUMBRECITA

By bus Pájaro Blanco (☎03546 461709) runs minibuses between Villa General Belgrano (7 daily; 45min–1hr) and Santa Rosa de la Calamuchita (6 daily; 1hr 30min–2hr).

By car Private motor vehicles are banned from the village during the day (summer 9am–7pm; winter 10am–6pm), and many people rent electric buggies to get around.

Distances are walkable, however, and visitors are allowed to drive to their hotel's car park.

Tourist information La Cumbrecita's tourist office is across the bridge over the Río del Medio (daily: summer 9am–7pm; winter 9am–6pm; ☎03546 481088, ⓦlacumbrecita.gov.ar).

ACCOMMODATION AND EATING

Bar Suizo 5min beyond the tourist office, on the main street ☎03546 481067. As you might expect, given the kitsch Germanic design of the place, *Bar Suizo*'s focus is on hearty Central European food (mains $95–150): expect lots of pork-based dishes, sausages, goulash, and trout in butter sauce, plus raclette ($300) and a fine selection of cakes and pastries. Mon–Wed & Fri–Sun 9/10am–10/11pm.

Hotel Solares Pública s/n ☎03546 481019, ⓦhotelsolares.com.ar. Both standard hotel-style double rooms and self-catering apartments ($1390), the latter sleeping up to four with kitchenettes, are on offer at this attractive hotel. Guests can make use of the complex's outdoor barbecue, big swimming pool, and children's play area. Massages are also on offer. $992

The Traslasierra

The most rewarding route from Córdoba to San Luís, capital of the neighbouring province of the same name, is by RP-34 and then RN-20 beyond Villa Carlos Paz. The winding **Nueva Ruta de las Altas Cumbres** climbs past the **Parque Nacional Quebrada del Condorito**, a deep ravine where condors nest in cliffside niches, climbing over a high mountain pass before winding back down a series of hairpin bends. The serene, sunny valleys to the west of the high Sierra Grande and Sierra de Achala, crisscrossed by streams and dotted with oases of bushy palm trees, are known collectively as the **Traslasierra**, literally "across the mountains".

The self-appointed capital of the sub-region, **Mina Clavero**, is a popular little riverside resort. Near **Nono**, a tiny village at the foot of the northern

Comechingones to the south of Mina Clavero, is the oddball **Museo Rocsen**. In a long valley parallel to the Sierra de Comechingones lies the picturesque village of **San Javier**, from where you can climb the highest summit in the Central Sierras, **Cerro Champaquí**.

Parque Nacional Quebrada del Condorito

Around 65km from Villa Carlos Paz, just south of RP-34 • Daily: Sept–May 8am–8pm; June–Aug 9am–4pm • Free • ☎ 03541 486287, ⓦ parquesnacionales.gob.ar

PARQUE NACIONAL QUEBRADA DEL CONDORITO takes its name from the Quebrada de los Condoritos, a misty canyon eroded into the mountains that, in turn, was named for the baby condors reared in its deep ravines.

To get to the park, take RP-34, which sweeps across the eerily desolate landscape of the **Pampa de Achala**, ideal for solitary treks or horse rides. For the first 15km or so, this road, which starts southwest of Villa Carlos Paz, is quite narrow, but several viewpoints have been built at the roadside. From them, you have unobscured vistas of the Icho Cruz and Malambo valleys to the northwest, the distant peak of **Cerro Los Gigantes** (at 2374m the highest mountain in the Sierra Grande and popular with climbers) to the north, and the **Sierra de Achala** to the south. Some 20km further on are the bleak granite moorlands of the Pampa de Achala, reaching just over 2000m above sea level. Here condors, some with wingspans exceeding 3m, can be seen circling majestically overhead.

Hikes within the park

Hikes in the park take between two hours and several days, and there are designated areas where camping (free) is permitted. Register at the Interpretation Centre (1.5km from the park entrance) before setting out; the centre is also a good place to get information about the park and the latest weather conditions. There's little shade and no food or drink on sale within the park boundaries, so bring a hat, sun cream and sustenance.

The hike route is clearly marked with numbered posts, getting steadily more difficult after you pass number ten, which takes you down steep and sometimes slippery paths towards the bottom of the canyon. Many kinds of trees, shrubs and ferns can be spotted, including some endemic species such as rare white gentians, while among the plentiful fauna are various wild cats, frogs, foxes and lizards. Birdlife is prolific, but the stars are the condors themselves, especially their young; if you're lucky you might see condors and their chicks bathing in the water at the bottom of the gorge.

Fundación Cóndor

RP-34, around 9km east of the Interpretation Centre • Daily 9am–5/6pm • Free • ☎ 0351 464 6537, ⓦ fundacion-condor.com.ar

The **Fundación Cóndor** is an independently run centre that provides information on condors and has a striking photo exhibition of the park's flora and fauna. It also has a café, organizes condor-feeding spectacles in the evenings, and can arrange transport to and from the park itself.

ARRIVAL AND ACTIVITIES   PARQUE NACIONAL QUEBRADA DEL CONDORITO

By bus If you're not taking a tour, haven't rented a car or a taxi, and haven't arranged transport via the Fundación Cóndor, it's easiest to reach the park by bus. Services (around 5 daily; 1hr 30min) between Córdoba and La Pampilla pass by the park; ask the driver to drop you off at the entrance.

Guides Guides can be hired in advance from the park's main office, the Intendencia del Parque Nacional Quebrada del Condorito (Resistencia 30 ☎ 03541 486287) in Villa Carlos Paz.

Activities Horseriding trips are offered by Estancia La Granadilla (☎ 03547 48880, ⓦ lagranadilla.com.ar), located close to the park in San Clemente. Trekking, mountain biking and rock climbing can be arranged through agencies in Córdoba (see p.189) and other tourist centres in the province.

Mina Clavero and around

Some 15km west of the Quebrada de los Condoritos, RP-34 begins to snake along narrow corniche roads, which offer stunning views of the Traslasierra Valley and a cluster of extinct volcanic cones in the distance. Just 1.5km up RP-15 north of the junction with RP-34 is **MINA CLAVERO**, wedged between the Sierra Grande and the much lower Sierra de Pocho, to the west. A transport hub at the northern end of the Punilla Valley, it's also a boisterous riverside resort. The place is noteworthy for little else, though, other than its attractive black **ceramics**. The nearby mountains lend themselves to mountain biking, horseriding, trekking and climbing, while trout-fishing is possible in the many brooks.

The balnearios

Mina Clavero is packed during January and February, when people come to relax at the many **balnearios** along the three rivers – Los Sauces, Mina Clavero and Panaholma – that snake through the town. The cleanest bathing area is the Nido de Aguila, set among beautiful rocks on the Río Mina Clavero 1km east of the centre, along Calle Urquiza.

By bus The terminal is on Av Mitre, next to the town hall. There are regular services between here and Córdoba (around 5 daily; 3hr).

Tourist information The tourist office is seven blocks south of the bus terminal, on Av San Martín (daily: summer 8am–10pm; winter 9am–8pm; ☎ 03544 470171, ⊛ minaclavero.gov.ar). There's also a small information office in the bus station (summer only, daily 9am–9pm).

ACCOMMODATION AND EATING

Mina Clavero has a wide choice of **hotels**; out of season, prices can halve. **Restaurants** selling the usual trio of pasta, pizza and *parrilla* line avenidas San Martín and Mitre.

Colina del Valle Camino a Cañada Larga 350 ☎ 03544 471177, ⊛ colinadelvalle.com. Set in expansive gardens, this mid-range hotel has pleasant, high-ceilinged en suites with hot-tub-style baths, a huge outdoor pool and a tennis court. Bike rental, hiking, horseriding and yoga sessions can all be arranged. US$70

Oh La La Hostel J.B. Villanueva 1192 ☎ 03544 472634, ⊛ ohlalahostel.com.ar. This hostel is a decent choice for backpackers, with colourful decor, a large, bare garden, small pool and communal kitchen. Reasonable accommodation is provided in simple dorms and private rooms. Dorms $150; doubles $450

Los Serranitos Cura Gaucho 350, 2km north of town ☎ 03544 470817, ⊛ losserranitos.com.ar. Family-oriented complex with a range of camping spots, basic huts and more comfortable bungalows, plus a large pool, football pitches, volleyball courts, cooking areas, a shop selling provisions, and an internet café. Camping $260; huts $570; bungalows $700

Nono

From the junction with RP-15, RN-20 heads due south through rolling countryside, in the lee of rippling mountains, whose eroded crags change colour from a mellow grey to deepest red, depending on the time of day. Their imposing peak, Cerro Champaquí, lurks to the southeast at the northern end of the Comechingones range. Some 10km south of Mina Clavero you reach the sleepy but picturesque village of **NONO**. Its name is a corruption of the Quichoa *ñuñu*, meaning breasts, an allusion to the bosom-shaped hills poking above the horizon.

Museo Rocsen

Alto de la Quinta, 5km outside the village; take a taxi from Nono or walk (45min–1hr) • Daily 9am–sunset • $45 • ☎ 03544 498218, ⊛ museorocsen.org

One of Argentina's weirdest museums is the hallucinatory **Museo Rocsen**. Its imposing pink-sandstone facade is embellished with a row of 49 statues – from Christ to Mother

Teresa, the Buddha to Che Guevara – representing key figures who, according to the museum's owner and curator, Juan Santiago Bouchon, have changed the course of history. After many years as cultural attaché at the French embassy in Buenos Aires, Bouchon opened his museum in 1969, with the intention of offering "something for everybody". The result is an eclectic collection of more than 30,000 exhibits, from fossils and mummies to a two-headed calf, clocks and cars.

ARRIVAL AND DEPARTURE   NONO

By bus There are regular services between Nono and Córdoba (5 daily; 3hr) via Mina Clavero (10min).

ACCOMMODATION AND EATING

★**Arabela Casas de Campo** Just outside Villa de Las Rosas, a 20min drive south of Nono ☎ 03544 459018, ⓦ complejoarabela.com. This excellent complex has four stylish, fully fitted and secluded *casas de campo* (country houses), each one sleeping up to six people. There's a pool, viewing tower offering lovely vistas, and lots of green space. Birdwatching (55 species have been spotted in the grounds), horseriding and mountain biking are among the activities on offer. **$2400**

Estancia La Lejanía 8km outside Nono ☎ 03544 15 585476, ⓦ lalejania.com. This outstanding French-run hotel has comfortable rooms in a secluded setting with a private riverside beach. The restaurant, which is open to non-guests (daily noon–3pm & 8–11pm; mains $120–200), serves delicious Gallic cuisine accompanied by select Argentine wines from the cellar, and the hotel also offers trekking and horseriding in the nearby mountains. Rates include full board. **$2250**

San Javier

Some 35km south of Mina Clavero, RP-148 branches off RN-20 and heads due south towards **SAN JAVIER**, another 12km away. The tree-lined road takes you through some of the province's most attractive scenery and settlements. If you're driving, though, watch out for the often treacherous *badenes*, very deep fords that suddenly flood after storms; even when dry, their abrupt drop and rough surface can damage a car's undercarriage or tyres.

San Javier is a pretty little place set amid peach orchards, and serves as a base for climbing to the 2884m summit of **Cerro Champaquí**, directly to the east. It has developed as a tourist centre in recent years, offering services such as massages, reiki and even "solar shamanism".

ARRIVAL AND DEPARTURE   SAN JAVIER

By bus There are irregular services between San Javier and Mina Clavero (around 30min); ask locally for the timetable.

ACCOMMODATION

La Constancia 7km east of San Javier on the road to Cerro Champaquí ☎ 03544 15 404317, ⓦ estancialaconstancia.com. This superb hotel – an 1895 building augmented with some modern designer touches – is set in stunning environs. Horseriding, trekking, mountain biking and fishing are among the activities on offer, you can swim in the nearby river, and the food is excellent. Rates include full board. **$3150**

The Litoral and the Gran Chaco

GARGANTA DEL DIABLO WATERFALL, IGUAZÚ

The Litoral and the Gran Chaco

The defining feature of northeastern Argentina is water. Dominated by two of the continent's longest rivers, it's a land of powerful cascades and blue-mirrored lagoons, vast marshes and fertile wetlands teeming with wildlife. The riverine landscapes of the Litoral (meaning "Shore" or "Coastline") – a term generally used to refer to the four provinces of Entre Ríos, Corrientes, Misiones and Santa Fe – range from the caramel-coloured maze of the Paraná Delta, north of Buenos Aires, to the wide translucent curves of the upper Río Paraná, via the gentle sandy banks of the Río Uruguay and the jungle-edged Río Iguazú. All of them exude a seductive subtropical beauty enhanced by the unhurried lifestyle of the locals and a warm, humid climate. *Litoraleños*, as the inhabitants are called, are also fanatical consumers of Argentina's national drink, *mate*, while infectiously lively *chamamé* music can be heard throughout the historic province of Corrientes.

The region's biggest city, and Argentina's third largest, is **Rosario**, home to a dynamic cultural life, fabulous restaurants and some exquisite late nineteenth- and early twentieth-century architecture. However, the **Iguazú Falls**, shared with Brazil, in the far north of Misiones Province, are the region's major attraction by a long chalk: Iguazú's claim to the title of the world's most spectacular waterfalls has few serious contenders. Running a remote second, in terms of the number of visitors, **San Ignacio Miní** is one of the best-preserved ruins of the Jesuit Missions – though some may find picking their way through nearby gothically overgrown **Loreto** and **Santa Ana** a more magical experience. Less well known than Iguazú and San Ignacio are two of Argentina's most unusual attractions: the strange and wonderful **Saltos del Moconá**, the world's most extensive longitudinal waterfalls; and the **Esteros del Iberá**, a vast, bird-filled wetland reserve at the heart of Corrientes Province.

Bordering the Litoral to the northwest, the **Gran Chaco** is a vast, little-visited area of flatlands lying predominantly in western Paraguay and the far north of Argentina. With landscapes varying from brutally desiccated scrub to saturated marshes and boggy lagoons, the main attraction of the Chaco is its **wildlife**, including hundreds of rare bird species.

SAN IGNACIO MINÍ

Highlights

❶ Rosario This flourishing port city on the Río Paraná is home to artsy cafés, galleries, grand belle époque mansions, beaches and superb freshwater fish restaurants. **See p.216**

❷ Esteros del Iberá Glide in a boat across a mirror-like lagoon where capybaras splash, deer trampoline on spongy islets and thousands of birds fly overhead. **See p.237**

❸ Estancia Santa Inés A splendid colonial-style mansion, near its own *yerba mate* plantation, offering hospitality, relaxation, delicious food – and a monkey colony. **See p.253**

❹ San Ignacio Miní The best preserved of all the Jesuit missions features ornate, richly carved ruins in the middle of the jungle. **See p.256**

❺ Garganta del Diablo Of the 250 waterfalls at Iguazú, the "Devil's Throat" is the most powerful, the most dramatic, and of course the wettest. **See p.264**

❻ Saltos del Moconá These extraordinary waterfalls are well worth the effort to reach, assuming the conditions are just right. **See p.267**

HIGHLIGHTS ARE MARKED ON THE MAP ON PP.214–215

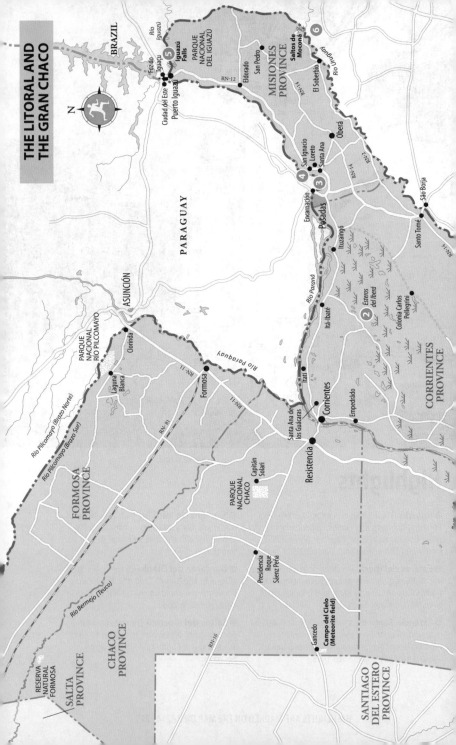

N

BRAZIL

Río Iguazú

Foz do Iguaçu
Ciudad del Este
Puerto Iguazú

5 Iguazú Falls

PARQUE NACIONAL DEL IGUAZÚ

Parque Nacional del Iguazú

RN-12

Eldorado

San Pedro

6
Saltos de Moconá

El Soberbio

Río Uruguay

MISIONES PROVINCE

Oberá

San Ignacio
Loreto
Santa Ana

4

3

Encarnación
Posadas

Ituzaingó

São Borja

Santo Tomé

PARAGUAY

ASUNCIÓN

Río Paraná

Río Paraguay

RN-14

RN-12

Esteros del Iberá

2

Colonia Carlos Pellegrini

Itá-Ibaté

Clorinda

PARQUE NACIONAL RÍO PILCOMAYO

Río Pilcomayo (Brazo Norte)

Río Pilcomayo (Brazo Sur)

Laguna Blanca

Formosa

RN-11

RN-11

Itatí

Santa Ana de los Guácaras

Corrientes

Empedrado

CORRIENTES PROVINCE

RN-81

FORMOSA PROVINCE

Resistencia

Capitán Solari

PARQUE NACIONAL CHACO

Río Bermejo (Teuco)

Presidencia Roque Sáenz Peña

RN-16

Gancedo

Campo del Cielo (Meteorite field)

CHACO PROVINCE

RESERVA NATURAL FORMOSA

SALTA PROVINCE

SANTIAGO DEL ESTERO PROVINCE

BRAZIL

URUGUAY

Tacuarembó

Yapeyú
Uruguaiana
Paso de los Libres
RN-123

Salto
Lago Salto Grande
Concordia
Paysandú
RN-14
Colón
PARQUE NACIONAL EL PALMAR
Palacio San José
Concepción del Uruguay
Fray Bentos
Río Uruguay
RN-14
Villa Paranacito
Gualeguaychú
Paraná Delta

ENTRE RÍOS PROVINCE

Esquina
Río Corrientes
RN-12
La Paz
Río Paraná
Victoria
RN-9
Buenos Aires

Cajastá
Río Paraná
Paraná
Santa Fe

SANTA FE PROVINCE
Río Salado

San Lorenzo
Rosario
①

CÓRDOBA PROVINCE

0   100
kilometres

HIGHLIGHTS

① Rosario
② Esteros del Iberá
③ Estancia Santa Inés
④ San Ignacio Mini
⑤ Garganta del Diablo
⑥ Saltos del Moconá

Rosario

Confident and stylish, with a vibrant cultural scene and a lively nightlife, **ROSARIO** dominates the whole region. With a little over 1.2 million inhabitants, it is Argentina's third-biggest city – Córdoba just beats it to second place. However, Rosario likes to see itself as the most worthy rival to Buenos Aires, 300km southeast – in some ways it is a far smaller version of the capital, but without the hordes of foreign visitors or the political clout. It's also the birthplace of two global superstars, football sensation **Lionel Messi** and revolutionary hero **Che Guevara**.

Geographically the comparison with BA certainly holds: Rosario is a flattish riverside city and major **port**, lying at the heart of a vital agricultural region, its streets lined with shabby but handsome buildings and lilac-blossomed jacaranda trees. Unlike Buenos Aires, however, Rosario has always enjoyed a close relationship with its waterfront; the **Río Paraná**, which swells to an eye-popping 2km wide at this point, features an attractive riverfront that runs for 8km along the city's eastern edge, flanked by high-rise condos, parks, bars and restaurants and, to the north, popular beaches. One of its main attractions is the splendidly unspoilt series of so-called "**delta islands**" with wide sandy beaches, just minutes away from the city by boat. You can also admire some of Argentina's finest turn-of-the-century **architecture** here, with an eclectic spread of styles ranging from English chalets to Catalan Modernism. In addition to the **Museo de Arte Contemporáneo**, housed in a conspicuously converted grain silo on the riverside, the city's most celebrated attraction, nationally at least, is the monolithic **Monumento a la Bandera**, a marble paean to Argentine independence.

Brief history

Rosario lacks an official founding date, with the settlement slowly developing in the eighteenth century around a series of Catholic missions to the local Calchaquí tribes, military outposts and estancias in an area known as Pago de los Arroyos. In 1730 the parish was established with remnants of an old mission chapel dedicated to the **Virgen del Rosario** – the new church was completed in 1762 and gradually lent its name to the settlement, given formal status by the colonial authorities in 1823. Despite its strategic location as a port for goods from Córdoba and Santa Fe provinces, early growth was slow: it wasn't until 1852, when river traffic was freed up, that Rosario was granted city status and finally set on course for expansion. The city's population was boosted further when the **Central Argentine Railway**, owned and largely financed by the British, was completed in 1870, providing a link to Córdoba.

By 1895, Rosario was Argentina's second city, with 91,000 inhabitants – many of them immigrants attracted by the promise of the by now flourishing port, giving the

---

CHE GUEVARA IN ROSARIO

Acknowledgement of Rosario's most famous son, the revolutionary **Ernesto "Che" Guevara**, was a long time in coming; compared with Cuba, where Che made his name and is a hero of gigantic proportions, the Argentine authorities have been reluctant to deify the controversial figure, and it was only in 2008 that a monument to him was erected in his hometown. The bronze statue was unveiled to commemorate what would have been his 80th birthday, but even then, it was funded by almost 15,000 small donations from around the world rather than the government, though they did contribute the space – an out of the way, rather forlorn plaza on 27 de Febrero and Laprida, twelve blocks east of Parque de la Independencia. The statue itself depicts a larger-than-life though not, in truth, very lifelike Che striding purposefully, mounted on a concrete plinth covered in suitably socialist graffiti. Guevara was born in 1928, with his first home the relatively modest (but very middle-class) apartment complex at Entre Ríos 480 in the centre of the city – it's still a private complex with nothing to denote its significance, so you'll have to pay homage from the street outside.

ROSARIO

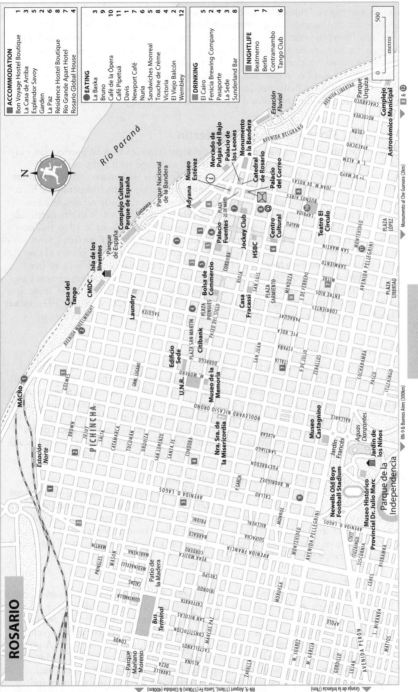

ACCOMMODATION	
Bon Voyage Hostel Boutique	1
La Casa de Arriba	3
Esplendor Savoy	5
Garden	2
La Paz	6
Résidence Hostel Boutique	8
Rio Grande Apart Hotel	7
Rosario Global House	4

● EATING	
La Baska	3
Bruno	9
Café de la Opera	10
Café Pipetuá	11
Davis	1
Newport Café	7
Nuria	6
Sandwiches Monreal	5
Touche de Creme	8
Victoria	4
El Viejo Balcón	2
Wembley	12

■ DRINKING	
El Cairo	5
Fenicia Brewing Company	1
Pasaporte	2
La Sede	4
Sunderland Bar	3

■ NIGHTLIFE	
Beatmemo	7
Berlin	5
Contramambo	6
Tango Club	6

0 — 500 metres

city its soubriquet, "**Hija de los Barcos**" (Daughter of the Ships). In the twentieth century the city became a major **Peronist** stronghold, and the Partido Socialista (Socialist Party) has won every election for mayor since 1989. In 2011 **Mónica Fein** became the first female Socialist candidate to be elected mayor in Argentine history, and was narrowly re-elected in 2015. Other *rosarino* celebrities include leading artists Antonio Berni and Lucio Fontana, three of Argentina's most popular singers – Fito Páez, Juan Carlos Baglietto and Litto Nebbia – and the late cartoonist **Roberto Fontanarrosa**, whose most beloved creation was the hapless gaucho Inodoro Pereyra.

Paseo del Siglo and Plaza San Martín

Rosario's premier shopping street is **Paseo del Siglo** (aka Av Córdoba), pedestrian-only from Paraguay to Plaza 25 de Mayo (see below), and lined with some of the best examples of Rosario's belle époque architecture. Towards its western end lies **Plaza San Martín**, a spacious park dominated by an equestrian statue of the independence hero. On the plaza's west side lies the former Palacio Provincial de Justicia, completed in 1892 and now part of the **Universidad Nacional de Rosario** (UNR). On the north side of Plaza San Martín sits the former police headquarters, completed in 1916 and now the seat of the provincial government of Santa Fe – it's known as **Casa Gris** ("Grey House") after its stark German Neoclassical design. In the southwest corner of the plaza lies the **Museo de la Memoria** (Tues–Fri 10am–6pm, Sat & Sun 5–8pm; free), commemorating the political violence of the 1970s and 1980s. Heading east on Paseo del Siglo, the **Bolsa de Commercio** (at Córdoba 2000), the Rosario Board of Trade, is a gorgeous beaux-arts landmark designed by Raúl Rivero in 1926, while the 1915 **Jockey Club** building at Córdoba and Maipú is one of Argentina's finest Art Deco gems.

4

Plaza 25 de Mayo

Constructed on the site of the first modest chapel built to venerate the Virgen del Rosario, **Plaza 25 de Mayo** is the historic heart of the city. Today the plaza is an elegantly shady space laid out very formally around its central marble column, the **Monumento a la Independencia**. On the southeast of the square, at Córdoba and Buenos Aires, lies the imposing **Palacio del Correo** (central post office), completed in 1938. On the northeast corner is the terracotta-coloured Palacio Municipal, also known as the **Palacio de los Leones** in reference to the majestic sculptured lions that flank the main entrance. It was completed around 1896 and still serves as the city government building.

Basílica Catedral de Nuestra Señora del Rosario

Buenos Aires 789 (Plaza 25 de Mayo) • Mon–Sat 9am–12.30pm & 4.30–8.30pm, Sun 8am–1pm & 5–9.30pm • Free • ☎ 0341 421 0988

Dominating the east side of Plaza 25 de Mayo, the **Basílica Catedral de Nuestra Señora del Rosario** is a late nineteenth-century construction in which domes, towers, columns and pediments are mixed to particularly eclectic effect. Inside, there's a fine Italianate altar carved from Carrara marble and, in the crypt, a wood-carved image of the Virgin of Rosario, shipped over from Cádiz, Spain, in 1773.

Museo Estévez

Santa Fe 748 (Plaza 25 de Mayo) • Wed–Sun 9am–5pm (Dec–Feb Wed–Sun 9am–2pm) • $10 • ☎ 0341 480 2547, Ⓦ museoestevez.gob.ar

Despite its relatively modest facade, the **Museo Estévez** is a real gem, a decorative arts museum housed in a fantastically ornate mansion. It's crammed with artwork donated to the city in the 1960s by its former occupant, Firma Estévez, in memory of her Spanish husband Odilo (who emigrated to Rosario in the 1880s and made a fortune in Argentina by selling the "Yerba 43" *mate* brand). It's a stunning display – every inch of the interior is furnished and ornamented with everything from Egyptian glassware and tiny Greek sculptures to Flemish tapestry and Limoges porcelain, via pre-Hispanic ceramics and

Spanish ivory figures. There's a small but impressive **painting collection**, too, including *Portrait of a Gentleman* by French Neoclassicist Jacques Louis David, and a Goya portrait, *Doña María Teresa Ruiz Apodaca de Sesma*, with strikingly piercing black eyes.

Monumento a la Bandera

Santa Fe 581 • **Crypt & tower** April–Sept Mon 2–6pm, Tues–Sun 9am–6pm; Oct–March Mon 2–7pm, Tues–Sun 9am–7pm • Monument and crypt free; tower view deck (via lift) $12 • ☎ 0341 480 2238, ⓦ monumentoalabandera.gob.ar

Completed in 1957, Rosario's premier historic sight is the **Monumento a la Bandera**, a vast monumental complex honouring the Argentine flag (*bandera*) and the heroes who have fought for it since independence. **General Manuel Belgrano** designed the flag in the city in 1812, lending Rosario the official title of "Cuna de la Bandera" (Birthplace of the Flag). The first section of the monument comprises a 70m tower guarding what was supposed to be Belgrano's tomb (the general remains in Buenos Aires, as per his wishes), overlooking the river and adorned with sculptures; the whole thing is shaped like a ship's prow, representing Argentina sailing towards a glorious future. The observation deck on top of the tower affords stellar views of the river and city. Behind the tower, up the slope, is an amphitheatre-like space (Patio Cívico) leading to the "Propileo", a Modernist Greek temple gateway containing an Eternal Flame ("Llama Votiva") dedicated to those who lost their lives in the wars for independence. Beyond, the **Pasaje Juramento**, lined with dramatic marble figures and fountains by the great sculptor Lola Mora (see box below), links the monument to Plaza 25 de Mayo. The country's major Flag Day celebrations are held at the monument on June 20 each year, but there's a small flag-hoisting ceremony every day at 8.15am. Across the road from the main tower is the **Cenotafio a los Caídos en Malvinas**, completed in 2005 to honour veterans of the Falklands War (see p.544).

4

The Costanera

Stretching over 8km from north to south, Rosario's **Costanera**, or riverfront, is one of the city's most appealing features, offering numerous green spaces and views over the Río Paraná. Its most central park, the **Parque Nacional de la Bandera**, lies just to the east of the Monumento a la Bandera. At the southern end of the park is the **Estación Fluvial** from where regular boat services run to the river islands (see p.222) and cafés line the river. Every weekend (Sat 2–9pm & Sun noon–8pm) there is a flea market selling crafts, antiques and books – the **Mercado de Pulgas del Bajo** – around Avenida Belgrano 500, which runs past the western edge of the park.

LOLA MORA

Dolores Mora Vega de Hernández – better known as **Lola Mora** – was born on November 17, 1866, at El Tala, a tiny village in Salta Province very close to the Tucumán border. She completed her studies in Italy and took to working in **marble**, a medium used for much of her prolific oeuvre of statues and monuments. In addition to works in various towns and cities around the country, she is best known for her invaluable contribution to the Monumento a la Bandera in Rosario (see above); the magnificent Nereidas fountain adorning the Costanera Sur in Buenos Aires (see p.74); and the voluptuous set of allegorical figures – Peace, Progress, Justice, Freedom and Labour – intended for the National Congress building (see p.68) but never placed there, as they were considered too shocking. Instead, the five naked forms can be admired at the Casa de Gobierno in Jujuy (see p.296). Hailed as the country's foremost **sculptor**, Lola had a tragic life, losing her parents at an early age, enduring a turbulent marriage and facing social rejection owing to her bohemian lifestyle and her predilection for portraying shapely female forms. Towards the end of her life, she suffered from ill health and psychological problems. She died in poverty in 1936, shortly after reconciliation with her husband after seventeen years of estrangement and only a few months after the national government agreed to grant her a pension.

Museo de Arte Contemporáneo de Rosario (MACRo)

Estanislao López 2250, at Blvd Oroño · Mon, Tues & Thurs–Sat: summer 3–9pm; rest of year 2–8pm; Sun 10am–1pm & 2–8pm · $10 (includes free entry to Museo Castagnino on Thurs) · ☎ 0341 480 4981, ⓦ castagninomacro.org · Bus #129

At the northern end of the Costanera, a former grain silo complex belonging to the Davis family (taxi drivers still refer to it as "Los Silos Davis") has been turned into a contemporary art gallery, the **Museo de Arte Contemporáneo de Rosario**, or **MACRo**.

The most striking aspects of the museum are its exterior, especially the huge silo cylinders painted in vibrant pink, purple and azure shades, and its riverside location – both the top-floor viewpoint and the Perspex lift shaft leading to it offer fine views of the majestic Paraná. The revolving exhibitions are mostly dedicated to up-and-coming local and national artists, but even if the art leaves you cold the museum is worth a visit for the building, location and café-restaurant, *Davis* (see p.223), where you can enjoy watching boats, barges and bits of vegetation float past.

Balneario La Florida

Eduardo Carrasco 3618 · Daily 9am–8pm · Free · ☎ 0341 453 3491 · Bus #153

Around 8km north of the centre (in the shadow of the giant Rosario–Victoria suspension bridge), Rosario's most popular beach, **Balneario La Florida**, is packed on summer weekends, and has bars, restaurants and shower facilities. At the southern end of the beach area you'll find the **Rambla Cataluña**, lined with glitzy bars, smart restaurants and see-and-be-seen nightclubs that are the summertime focus of Rosario's famed *movida* (nightlife scene). There's also a more exclusive section of the beach, which is cleaner and has more services (Dec–April daily 9am–8pm; entry $35, umbrellas $45, chairs $25).

The Alto Delta islands

Known as the **Alto Delta**, the low-lying riverine **islands** off Rosario's "coast" in fact fall under the jurisdiction of the neighbouring province, Entre Ríos. Like the islands of the Tigre Delta in Buenos Aires (see p.133), they host subtropical vegetation fed by sediment from the Upper Paraná River. The Alto Delta is far less developed than Tigre, however. With the exception of the remote island of **Charigüé**, where there is a small settlement with its own school, police station and a handful of restaurants, the islands are largely uninhabited, though plenty of pleasure boats ply the waters in the summer (see p.222).

Parque de la Independencia

3.5km from Plaza 25 de Mayo · Bus #120 from Entre Ríos; bus #125 from Mitre

Dissected by various avenues and containing several museums, a football stadium and a racetrack, the **Parque de la Independencia** feels like a neighbourhood in itself. **Newell's Old Boys** football club, Lionel Messi's first pro team (see opposite), was founded here in 1903 and named for Isaac Newell, an Englishman who emigrated to Rosario in his teens and went on to pioneer football in Argentina. The park itself was inaugurated in 1902 and is an attractively landscaped space with shady walkways and beautifully laid-out gardens such as the formal **Jardín Francés**, just west of the main entrance on Boulevard Oroño. The park can be reached on foot from the city centre via a particularly attractive walk along the Paseo del Siglo and Oroño, though it can be a hot slog in the summer – you could also take a taxi or a bus.

Museo Castagnino

Av Pellegrini 2202 · Mon & Wed–Sat 2–8pm, Sun 10am–1pm & 2–8pm · $10 (includes free entry to MACRo on Thurs) · ☎ 0341 480 2542, ⓦ castagninomacro.org · Buses #120 & #125

The absorbing **Museo Castagnino** features two permanent art collections, primarily donated by local collectors Juan Bautista Castagnino and Enrique Astengo. The **European painting** collection covers the fifteenth to twentieth centuries and features works by Goya, Pissarro, Sisley and members of the Barbizon school like

LA PULGA ATÓMICA – LIONEL MESSI

The son of a steel factory manager in Rosario, **Lionel Messi** has become one of the greatest football players of all time – the Barcelona striker has won the FIFA Ballon d'Or (world's best player) a record four times. Born in south Rosario's Barrio Las Heras in 1987, at just 4 years old Messi joined local club Grandoli, transferring to Newell's Old Boys at the age of 6. Messi's stellar rise was threatened by a diagnosis of growth hormone deficiency at the age of 10; it seemed Lionel was far too fragile, and simply too small, to go further (thus his later nickname "atomic flea"). Thankfully, Spain's FC Barcelona stepped in, signing Messi in 2000 and allowing him to complete his growth hormone treatment by the age of 14. Messi still regularly visits his family home in Rosario and is afforded god-like status in his hometown (though blasted by the Argentine media for not winning the 2014 World Cup). With so many kids named "Messi", in 2014 the Rosario city government actually banned parents from naming children after the soccer superstar.

Charles-François Daubigny. The **Argentine painting** collection includes examples from major artists such as Lino Enea Spilimbergo and Quinquela Martín, plus Antonio Berni and Lucio Fontana, both born in Rosario (the museum's collection of contemporary art was carved off to create MACRo in 2004). The museum, arranged on two floors with large, well-lit galleries, also puts on some excellent temporary exhibitions.

Museo Histórico Provincial Dr Julio Marc

Av del Museo s/n • Tues–Fri 9am–6pm, Sat & Sun 3–8pm (April–Nov Tues–Fri 9am–6pm, Sat & Sun 2–7pm); closed during Newell's Old Boys football matches • Free • ☎ 0341 472 1457, ⓦ museomarc.gob.ar

Just west of Parque de la Independencia's lake, the **Museo Histórico Provincial Dr Julio Marc** houses a vast and intriguing number of historical exhibits spanning the whole of Latin America. Among its most notable collections are those dedicated to **religious art**, with a stunning eighteenth-century silver altar from Alto Perú, which was used for the Mass given by Pope John Paul II when he visited the city in 1987, and some fine examples of polychrome works in wood, wax and bone, representing the famed Quiteña School (named after the capital of Ecuador). There's also an important collection of **indigenous ceramics**, including some valuable musical pieces known as whistling glasses (*vasos silbadores*) from the Chimú culture of northern Peru and some well-preserved and delicate textiles. Colonial-era furniture is also well represented – look for the beautifully worked travel desk featuring carvings of *conquistadores* and native Americans.

ARRIVAL AND DEPARTURE   ROSARIO

BY PLANE

Rosario's small airport (Aeropuerto Internacional de Rosario-Islas Malvinas; ☎0341 451 3220, ⓦaeropuerto rosario.com) lies around 15km west of the city centre, along RN-9, with 1–6 daily flights to and from Buenos Aires and a handful of other destinations. From the airport, bus #115 runs every 30min into the centre along San Luis, two blocks south of Plaza 25 de Mayo ($7; coins only or MOVI card). Taxi rates are fixed according to destination: it's $185 to anywhere in the centre ($160 to the Terminal de Ómnibus and $1700 to Santa Fe); they'll probably use the meter on the way back. You'll find the major car rental desks in the terminal, plus a Banco Santa Cruz ATM, though don't count on it working (make sure you have pesos as there is nowhere to change money).

Destinations Buenos Aires (1–6 daily; 1hr); Córdoba (1 daily; 55min); El Calafate (4 weekly; 3hr 20min); Mendoza

(2 weekly; 1hr 40min); São Paulo (1–2 daily; 2hr 40min).

BY BUS

Long-distance buses arrive at Rosario's clean and user-friendly Terminal de Ómnibus Mariano Moreno (☎ 0341 437 3030, ⓦ terminalrosario.gob.ar), 4km west of Plaza 25 de Mayo, at Santa Fe and Cafferata. An information kiosk (daily 9am–7pm) can provide you with a list of hotels and a map, and there are also plenty of cafés, internet terminals ($7 for 15min, $18 for 1hr), Banco Municipal ATMs and left luggage facilities ($25–40; daily 24hr). To head into the centre, walk to the corner of Cafferata and Córdoba and catch bus #115, #116, #133 or #142. Otherwise, plenty of taxis pull up outside the front entrance ($40–50 to the centre).

Destinations Buenos Aires (2–3 hourly; 3hr 30min); Córdoba (hourly; 6hr 30min); Corrientes (13 daily; 11–12hr); Paraná (2–3 hourly; 3hr); Posadas (8 daily;

12–15hr); Puerto Iguazú (7 daily; 17–19hr); Resistencia (hourly; 10hr); Salta (8 daily; 15–17hr); Santa Fe (2–3 hourly; 2hr 20min); Victoria (1–2 hourly; 1hr 15min).

BY TRAIN

Trains currently shuttle between ultra-modern Rosario Sur station (San Martín and Battle y Ordóñez) and Retiro in Buenos Aires once a day, departing Buenos Aires at 4.07pm (arriving 10.35pm) and departing Rosario 12.26am (arriving in BA at 6.54am). Retiro to Tucumán trains and Retiro to Córdoba trains also stop at Rosario Norte station

(Aristóbulo del Valle and Callao) once daily in each direction. See ⓦ sofse.gob.ar.

BY BOAT

Passenger boats run to the various islands in the Paraná River throughout the week, with regular services Nov–March from 10am to dusk (1 or 2 departures daily; return $85 adults, $45 children); out of season, services are less frequent. All boats depart from the Estación Fluvial (☎ 0341 447 3838, ⓦ estacionfluvial.com), at De los Inmigrantes 410 on the Costanera.

GETTING AROUND

By bus Rosario's bus system is cheap and easy to use, with bus numbers clearly marked and route maps at most bus stops (ⓦ etr.gov.ar). Fares are $7, but you can only pay with $1 or $2 coins (no change). If you intend to use buses a lot, get a stored-value card (MOVI or *tarjeta magnética*; minimum value $25) – there's a booth selling them at the bus terminal (Mon–Fri 7am–8pm, Sat & Sun 8am–8pm).

You can also buy them at the Centro Municipal at Wheelwright 1486 (the riverfront; Mon–Fri 8am–2pm) and in the centre at Santa Fe 1055 (Mon–Fri 8am–1pm).
By taxi Taxis are easy to hail on the street; the meter starts at $17, adding $0.85 every 100m (Mon–Sat 10pm–6am, and all day Sun/hols, the rate jumps to $19.50 plus $1 every 100m). Most trips across the centre should be no more than $50–60.

INFORMATION AND TOURS

Tourist information There's a helpful tourist information office down by the riverfront, at Belgrano and Buenos Aires (Mon–Sat 9am–7pm, Sun 9am–6pm; ☎ 0341 480 2230, ⓦ rosarioturismo.com). It produces an informative map covering most of the city. See also ⓦ rosariotipica.com.ar.
Bike Rosario Runs bicycle tours and offers bike and kayak rental (Zeballos 327; ☎ 0341 155 713812, ⓦ bikerosario .com.ar). English and French spoken.

River tours One long-established river trip is a 2hr river cruise on the sightseeing boat, *Ciudad de Rosario* (Sat & Sun: winter 2.30pm & 5pm; summer 5pm & 7.30pm; $115; ☎ 0341 449 8688, ⓦ barcocr1.com), while the more intimate Island Explorer dinghies do 2hr trips (Sat & Sun 3pm; $320; ☎ 0341 628 9287, ⓦ islandexplorer.com.ar) from the Estación Fluvial. Sister outfit Rosario Sail (same contacts as Island Explorer) offers 3hr private sailboat trips ($1000/person, minimum 2 people).

ACCOMMODATION

★**Bon Voyage Hostel Boutique** Güemes 2915 ☎ 0341 437 1361, ⓦ bonvoyagehostelboutique.com. Attractive, brightly decorated hostel in the Pichincha neighbourhood, with English-speaking staff, two small dorms, private doubles and free wi-fi. Communal barbecue and filling breakfast included. Dorms $175; doubles $415
La Casa de Arriba Av Córdoba 2889 ☎ 0341 430 0012, ⓦ lacasadearriba.com.ar. Spacious and clean hostel with small dorms, free wi-fi (and use of PlayStation 3), tasty breakfast and well-equipped communal kitchen. Around 15min walk to city centre. $200
★**Esplendor Savoy** San Lorenzo 1022 ☎ 0341 429 6007, ⓦ esplendorhoteles.com. Rosario's belle époque *Savoy* hotel, opened in 1910, was given a respectful makeover by the Fën group in 2009. They created a beautiful boutique hotel that incorporates many of its original features, including the marble staircases, the chandeliers and the crowning cupola, where you can sit and contemplate the street scene below. $1075
Garden Callao 45 ☎ 0341 437 0025, ⓦ hotelgardensa .com. An attractive modern hotel in a quiet area of town.

Rooms have large, comfortable beds, a/c and cable TV, and rates include buffet breakfast and use of a swimming pool. There's also a spacious bar area, and parking is available ($120/day). $635
La Paz Cortada Barón de Mauá 36 ☎ 0341 421 0905, ⓦ hotellapazrosario.com.ar. Plain but adequate rooms with TV, a/c and private bathroom, some with balconies. Prices include buffet breakfast. Parking $100/day. $420
Résidence Hostel Boutique Buenos Aires 1145 ☎ 0341 421 8148, ⓦ residenceboutique.com.ar. Beautifully restored 1911 mansion, blending original pitch pine floors and stucco and cedar-wood fixtures with modern amenities. Free wi-fi. Small, simple dorms and private en-suite rooms available. Dorms $170; doubles $510
★**Río Grande Apart Hotel** Dorrego 1261 ☎ 0341 4241144, ⓦ riograndeapart.com.ar. The best of the city's *apart-hotels*, with bright, roomy suites in a swish, renovated building in a fairly quiet part of the city. Outstanding buffet breakfasts (included), reliable wi-fi and a secure garage. $915
Rosario Global House M. Rodríguez 863 (between

Córdoba and Rioja) **☎**0341 424 4922, **ⓦ**rosarioglobalhouse.com.ar. Another popular hostel, close to the bus station, with pleasant outdoor patio, shared kitchen and a choice of doubles (with bathrooms) and separate male and female dorms. Basic breakfast (coffee, pastries) included. Dorms **$175**; doubles **$480**

EATING

Rosario has plenty of **restaurants** to suit all budgets, both in the city centre and along the Costanera. There are some excellent freshwater fish restaurants specializing in *boga, dorado* (not related to the saltwater fish) and catfish-like *surubí*, but look out also for the "Carlitos". This toasted sandwich – invented here and mostly served in bars – is basically a combination of ham, cheese, olives and (crucially) ketchup, and it has a cult status among *rosarinos*.

La Baska Tucumán 1159 **☎**0341 426 7573. Cheap, piping-hot empanadas stuffed with a range of tasty fillings from prawns and tuna to mushrooms and Roquefort cheese. Daily 11am–2pm & 6–11pm.

Bruno Ovidio Lagos 1599 **☎**0341 421 2396. Long-established, family-run Italian restaurant serving excellent home-made pasta. Tues–Fri 8pm–late, Sat & Sun noon–3pm & 8pm–late.

★**Café de la Ópera** Laprida and Mendoza 787 **☎**0341 421 9402. Beautiful old-fashioned café adjoining the Teatro El Círculo, serving specials like tarragon chicken, along with pasta, omelettes and salads; or you can just have a coffee and a slice of date tart (coffee and pastry sets $23–28). Also hosts lively musical or cabaret events on Fri and Sat from 10pm. Mon–Wed 8am–8pm, Thurs & Fri 8am–midnight, Sat 8am–4pm & 7.30pm–midnight.

Café Pipetuá San Martín 1601 **☎**0341 15 600 7171. Modern, bright café serving excellent coffee and home-made desserts and pastries, notably its banana split, chocolate mousse and famed orange croissants. Mon–Fri 8am–8pm, Sat 9am–1pm.

★**Davis** Estanislao López 2250 **☎**0341 435 7142, **ⓦ**complejodavis.com. Named for the silo that was converted into the fabulous MACRo museum, this waterside bar-restaurant enjoys an incredible location and lively ambience, serving staples such as river fish and salads, as well as a good-value $125 three-course set menu. Mon 12.30pm–1am, Tues–Thurs 9am–1am, Fri & Sat 9am–2am.

Newport Café Córdoba and Maipu **☎**0341 426 1309. This centrally located café has been in business since 1920, and remains the ideal spot to sip a coffee on pedestrianized Córdoba, with a covered terrace opposite the Jockey Club – skip the food, though, which tends to be overpriced. Daily 7am–11.45pm.

Nuria Santa Fe 1026 **☎**0341 480 1911, **ⓦ**nuria.com.ar.

Venerable bakery founded in 1936 with branches all over the city; this branch is a treasure-trove of tempting cakes and pastries, from fruit tarts to lemon pie and chocolate mousse. Mon–Sat 7am–9pm, Sun 7am–2pm.

Sandwiches Monreal San Lorenzo 1295 and Entre Ríos **☎**0341 421 9595, **ⓦ**sandwichesmonreal.com.ar. Local institution specializing in beautifully crafted sandwiches (all white bread, no crusts) stuffed with ham, cheese, tuna and various other combos ($70–185). Sit at the bar or at small tables inside. Mon–Fri 9am–10pm, Sat 9am–1pm & 6–10pm, Sun 6–10pm.

★**Touche de Crème** Laprida 972 **☎**0341 425 4285. Serving the city's best ice cream since 1919, with flavours ranging from coconut and pistachio to Chantilly and "superflan" (a bit like custard cream). Scoops $33–40. Mon–Thurs 4–11pm, Fri 4–11.30pm, Sat 7pm–midnight, Sun 10am–1.30pm & 7–11pm.

Victoria Pte Roca 601 and San Lorenzo **☎**0341 425 7665. Old-school corner café-bar and restaurant with a sober wooden interior and tables on the pavement. Good-value *menú ejecutivo* ($75–100) with a main dish such as pork chops or trout, a dessert and drink. Daily 7am–midnight.

El Viejo Balcón Wheelwright 1815 and Italia **☎**0341 425 5611. One of the city's best *parrillas*, serving up all the usual cuts (such as a *bife de chorizo* for $165) at an attractive riverside location. Daily noon–4pm & 8.30pm–midnight.

Wembley Av Belgrano 2012 **☎**0341 481 1090, **ⓦ**wembleyrestaurant.com.ar. Busy, upmarket restaurant opposite the port, established in 1903 (a reminder of the region's once strong British links). Daily specials include the likes of salmon with capers ($155), though the most successful dishes are the more simply executed grilled river fish ($150) or *parrillada* ($195 for two people). Mon–Sat 10.30am–3pm & 8.30pm–1am, Sun 10.30am–3pm.

DRINKING

★**El Cairo** Sarmiento and Santa Fe **☎**0341 449 0714, **ⓦ**barelcairo.com. A Rosarian institution since 1943, the high-ceilinged *Cairo* fleshes out its claim to be a literary café with artsy events, a library at the back and theatrical-looking velvet curtains; it's also well known in town for being where the great cartoonist Roberto Fontanarrosa came to work. As well as meals (lunch sets are popular; $100–120), there is a huge cocktail menu and a *mate* bar. Mon–Thurs 8am–1am, Fri & Sat 8am–2am, Sun 4pm–1am.

Fenicia Brewing Company Francia 168 (Pichincha) ☎0341 423 2376. Tasty craft beers brewed on the premises by the Californian owners (especially good IPAs; $60), paired with excellent burgers ($75–100) and tempting bar snacks. Tues & Wed 12.30pm–1am, Thurs & Fri 12.30pm–2.30am, Sat 7pm–3am, Sun 7pm–1am.

Pasaporte Maipú 509 and Urquiza ☎0341 448 4097. Stylish bar with outside tables on a pleasant corner down near the riverfront. Coffee, alcoholic drinks and a large selection of filled crêpes. Board games available. Mon–Fri 7am–3am, Sat & Sun 8am–5am.

La Sede Entre Ríos 599 and San Lorenzo ☎0341 425 4071, ⓦ barlasede.com.ar. Elegant and rather literary bar in a fabulous Art Nouveau building – a favourite meeting place for Rosario's artistic celebrities (it was another Roberto Fontanarrosa hangout in the 1990s). Regular theatrical/cabaret evenings. Daily 7pm–1am.

Sunderland Bar Av Belgrano 2010 ☎0341 482 3663. Next to *Wembley* (see p.223), this is another historic place (which is also a restaurant), decorated with antiques, an old piano and Fontanarrosa drawings (you can also try to spot Che Guevara's alleged birth certificate). Established in the 1930s, it survived fires and an extended period of closure to reopen in 2012. The food is good, but it's just as enjoyable for drinks. Mon–Thurs & Sun 11am–midnight, Fri & Sat 11am–2am.

NIGHTLIFE

Rosario is noted for its nightlife, **la movida**, but its **clubs** can be a little disappointing. In summer, when all the action moves to the Rambla Cataluña (see p.220), you're limited to one or two very popular but faceless mega-discos, whose names but not character change with the seasons. The city's popular *milongas* offer a more authentic experience: Rosario has a hard core of **tango** enthusiasts – who dance a slightly showier version of the dance than Porteños – and most nights of the week there is something going on. The tourist office should have a list of current *milongas*.

Beatmemo Oroño 107 ☎0341 223 0757, ⓦ beatmemo .com. Rosario's Anglophile tendencies are on show at this Beatles-themed bar and live venue, an enthusiastic tribute to the 1960s icons, even featuring a small museum (daily 10am–7pm; free) on the fab four. The live acts, however, feature everything from jazz (Mon 9.30pm; $70) to local rock (Tues–Thurs; free–$75). Sun–Wed 8am–1am, Thurs–Sat 8am–3am.

Berlín Pje Simeoni 1128, between Mitre and Sarmiento ☎0341 501 9068. Popular bar and club, with regular cabaret and live bands. Thurs–Sat 10pm–5am.

Contramambo Tango Club Corrientes 1201 and Mendoza ☎0341 421 6536, ⓦ olimporosario.com.ar. Tango classes (free; 8.30pm) followed by a *milonga* every Wed, at the *Olimpo* bar. Beginners (and observers) are welcome, but you'll need to speak Spanish to get the most out of the class. Wed 10pm–late.

ENTERTAINMENT

Teatro El Círculo Laprida 1223 ☎0341 448 3784, ⓦ teatro-elcirculo.com.ar. Rosario's grandest theatre, built in 1904, has an extensive programme of plays, music, opera and dance; check the website for full listings. Tours (generally in Spanish only) of the theatre's ornate interior run Dec–March Mon, Wed, Fri & Sat at 10.30am (1hr 15min; $70).

DIRECTORY

Banks HSBC has a central branch at San Martín 902; Citibank is at Córdoba 1728 (both Mon–Fri 10am–3pm).

Internet access Sicomoro internet café at Laprida 966 is open daily 24hr.

Laundry Lavandería VIP (☎0341 426 3573) at Salta 1525 (Mon–Fri 7.30am–7pm, Sat 7.30am–1pm).

Post office Córdoba 721, on Plaza 25 de Mayo (Mon–Fri 8am–8pm).

Along the Río Paraná

Flowing for some 4880km from southern Brazil to the Río de la Plata, the mighty **Río Paraná** is an attraction in itself, with its lush islands, delicious fish and vast aquatic landscapes – at some points the flood plain is more than 60km across. North of Rosario, **Santa Fe**, the much-overshadowed provincial capital, is at first sight less enticing than its rival, but its faded grandeur and revived dock area merit a stopover. Nearby, the dynamic city of **Paraná** shares not only its name with the river, but also its slow pace and a certain subtropical beauty. Far to the north is **Corrientes**, one of the region's oldest and most dynamic cities, and also the gateway to the Gran Chaco (see p.233).

THE BATTLE OF SAN LORENZO

On February 3, 1813, a newly promoted **Colonel José de San Martín** led his troops to a decisive victory over a larger Spanish colonial force, some 30km north of Rosario in what is now the small riverside town of **San Lorenzo**. San Martín was almost killed in the engagement, the only one he fought on modern Argentine territory. As a result it's been much glorified ever since, despite the fact that very few troops were involved (fewer than 300 on each side) and it made little strategic impact on Argentina's war of independence. Nevertheless, history buffs will enjoy the pilgrimage to the battlefield, now a park in the centre of town dubbed the **Campo de la Gloria**, marked with a concrete memorial comprising two symbolic wings of victory, an eternal flame and nine blocks commemorating the sixteen independence fighters who died. The nearby convent, where San Martín and his troops took shelter, houses the **Museo Conventual San Carlos** (Tues–Fri 8am–6pm, Sat & Sun 10am–6pm; $25), with displays on the battle and San Martín's humble quarters. Buses to San Lorenzo depart Rosario's Terminal de Ómnibus twice every hour and take around forty minutes.

Victoria

Since an impressive 60km road **bridge and causeway** across the Río Paraná flood plain was inaugurated in 2003, the somnolent little market town of **VICTORIA**, northeast of Rosario in Entre Ríos, has been cajoled into life. Founded by immigrants from northern Italy and the Basque country, it seems to relish its status as an up-and-coming holiday resort, with a lavish casino and a thermal baths complex. RN-11 Paraná–Gualeguaychú road bypasses the town to the north, while Avenida Costanera Dr Pedro Radio skirts round the southern edge, following the contours of the **Riacho Victoria** (a tributary of the Paraná), where summer tourists flock to bathe at its sandy beaches. The large main square, leafy **Plaza San Martín**, features an imposing church, the **Nuestra Señora de Áranzazu**, completed in 1872 with a beautifully painted ceiling.

4

Abadía del Niño Dios

RN-11 (Av de los Benedictos) • Guided visits (30min; free; Spanish only) daily 10.15am, 11am, 2.30pm, 3.30pm & 4.30pm • **Shop** Mon–Fri 9am–12.30pm & 2–6.30pm, Sat & Sun 9.30am–6.30pm • Free • ☎ 03436 423171, ⓦ abadiadelninodios.org.ar

Victoria's premier historic and religious site is the **Abadía del Niño Dios**, home to Latin America's oldest Benedictine foundation, dating from 1899. The modern monastery and cheerfully designed church are certainly worth seeing, but the highlight for most visitors is the excellent shop (at the back). This sells delicious and mostly healthy products, true to the Benedictine tradition, ranging from unusual jams and bee products to cheeses and the popular Licores Monacal (liqueurs made with herbs and fruits such as lemon and orange). The abbey sits alongside the main RN-11, 3km north of central Victoria, just beyond the turning to the Rosario bridge/causeway.

ARRIVAL AND INFORMATION
VICTORIA

By bus Victoria's small bus terminal is halfway between the main tourist office and the central plaza, at Junín and L.N. Alem (a short walk from both). Frequent buses shuttle between Rosario and Victoria (1–2 hourly; 1hr 15min).

Tourist information The helpful tourist office (daily 8am–8pm; ☎ 03436 421885, ⓦ victoria.tur.ar) is located on the northwestern edge of town on RN-11, at the corner of 25 de Mayo and Blvd Eva Perón (1.6km from the main plaza).

ACCOMMODATION

El Banco Maipú 13 (at Plaza San Martín) ☎ 03436 427770, ⓦ elbancohotel.com.ar. Enticing boutique hotel in the centre of town, housed in the nineteenth-century premises of the Banco de Italia. The spacious rooms blend original floors, ceilings and windows with modern amenities (a/c, free wi-fi), and breakfast is included. Free parking. $905

Casablanca Felix Cudini s/n ☎ 03436 424131. A hospitable, medium-sized establishment in the southern neighbourhood of Barrio Quinto Cuartel, with large, slightly kitsch rooms, a beautiful garden and swimming pool, plus ample parking space and free wi-fi. $530
Sol Victoria Mastrángelo s/n ☎ 03436 424040, ⓦ hotelsolvictoria.com.ar. The grandest accommodation

option in town, this hotel also houses the casino, overlooking the river. The well-appointed rooms are extremely comfortable, and there is a fine dining room and swimming pool. Various promotional packages including drinks, spa treatments and the like are often available; check the website. $1250

EATING

El Banco Pub Maipú 13 (at Plaza San Martín) ☎03436 427770, ⓦ elbancohotel.com.ar. Attached to the hotel (see p.225), this bar and restaurant occupies what was once an elegant banking hall, serving a decent range of beers and wines, plus burgers and bar snacks. Daily 11am–midnight.

El Jockey L.N. Alem 91 ☎03436 426600, ⓦ eljockeyvictoria.com.ar. One block north of the central square in the 1914 Jockey Club building, this large restaurant is Victoria's classic spot for simple but tasty fish dishes. Daily noon–3.30pm & 6.30pm–midnight.

Santa Fe

The capital of its namesake province, **SANTA FE** was officially founded by Spanish *conquistador* Juan de Garay at Cayastá in 1573, but was moved to the current site in 1653 due to flooding. Its most celebrated moment came in 1853, when the first version of the **Constitution of Argentina** was agreed here (it's been the traditional seat of constitutional conventions ever since). Located 475km north of Buenos Aires, between the banks of the Río Santa Fe and Río Salado (which empties into the Paraná), the city of around half a million inhabitants is an important commercial centre for the surrounding agricultural region. A 2.5km-long road tunnel (cars $15) connects it with

SANTA FE

ACCOMMODATION
Ámbit Boulevard
  Hotel Boutique — 1
Hotel Hernandarias — 2
Los Silos — 3

EATING
Ágora — 1
Las Delicias — 2
España — 3
Triferto Peatonal — 4

DRINKING
Patio de la Cervecería
  Santa Fe — 1

Paraná, around 30km away via RN-168, which in some ways is a more tempting stopover (see p.229). However, beyond its shabby exterior Santa Fe contains a smattering of historic attractions, a revitalized port area and some addictive sweet treats.

Plaza 25 de Mayo

Santa Fe's historic core is anchored by its main square, **Plaza 25 de Mayo**, surrounded by grand buildings in styles ranging from colonial through French Second Empire to nondescript modern. The mammoth **Casa de Gobierno**, completed in French Neoclassical style in 1912, dominates the south end, while on the north side stands the modest eighteenth-century **Catedral Metropolitana Todos los Santos**. Next to the cathedral, Calle San Martín leads north from the plaza, lined by some of the city's most elegant mansions; it becomes a major pedestrianized shopping thoroughfare north of Garay and the **Teatro Municipal 1 de Mayo**, another majestic French-style edifice, completed in 1905.

Iglesia de Nuestra Señora de los Milagros

San Martín 1588 (Plaza 25 de Mayo) • Mon–Fri 6.30am–noon & 6.30–8.30pm, Sat 6–8.30pm, Sun 10am–noon & 6–8.30pm • Free • ☎ 0342 459 5411, ⓦ nsdelosmilagros.com.ar

On the east side of Plaza 25 de Mayo, the **Iglesia de Nuestra Señora de los Milagros** has a pleasingly simple and typically whitewashed colonial facade, rather overwhelmed by the dour Jesuit Colegio de la Inmaculada Concepción (1917) next door. Built around 1670, it is the oldest church in the province; peek inside to see the fine carvings produced by Guaraní artists in the Jesuit missions – most notably the impressive Altar Mayor, produced in Loreto.

Museo Histórico Provincial Brigadier General Estanislao López

San Martín 1490 and 3 de Febrero (Plaza de las Culturas) • March Tues–Fri 8.30am–7.30pm, Sat & Sun 4–7pm; April–Sept Tues–Fri 8.30am–7pm, Sat & Sun 3.30–6.30pm; Oct & Nov Tues–Fri 8.30am–7.30pm, Sat & Sun 4.30–7.30pm; Dec–Feb Tues–Fri 8.30am–12.30pm & 2.30–8.30pm, Sat & Sun 5.30–8.30pm • Free • ☎ 0342 457 3529, ⓦ museobrigadierlopez.gob.ar

Just beyond the southeast corner of Plaza 25 de Mayo, in the adjoining Plaza de las Culturas, you'll find the enlightening **Museo Histórico Provincial Brigadier General Estanislao López**. The history museum is housed in the Casa Diez de Andino, built in the seventeenth century (making it exceptionally old by Argentine standards) and it displays furniture, paintings, silverwork, religious icons and everyday items from that period. Its most notable exhibits are carvings from the Jesuit missions and paintings from the Cusco School, a sixteenth- to eighteenth-century art movement named after the Peruvian city, where indigenous craft workers produced mainly religious art for the Spanish.

Museo Etnográfico y Colonial Juan de Garay

25 de Mayo 1470 (Plaza de las Culturas) • March, April, Oct & Nov Tues–Fri 8.30am–noon & 2–7pm, Sat & Sun 4–7pm; May–Sept Tues–Fri 8.30am–noon & 2–7pm; Dec–Feb Tues–Fri 8.30am–noon & 3.30–8.30pm, Sat & Sun 5.30–8.30pm • Free • ☎ 0342 457 3550, ⓦ museojuandegaray.gob.ar

The bulk of the **Museo Etnográfico y Colonial Juan de Garay**'s well-organized collection comprises historic artefacts recovered from the original site of **Santa Fe La Vieja** at Cayastá. The most commonly recovered pieces were *tinajas*, large ceramic urns – many of them in a surprisingly complete state considering they spent around three hundred years underground – and delicate amulets in the form of shells or the *higa*, a clenched fist symbol, used to ward off the evil eye. There's also a fine ensemble of **indigenous ceramics** with typical zoomorphic forms ranging from birds – especially parrots – and bats, to capybaras, cats and snakes.

Iglesia y Convento de San Francisco

Amenábar 2557 (Plaza de las Culturas) • Tues–Fri 8am–12.30pm & 4–7.30pm, Sat 8am–noon & 4.30–7.30pm • $15 • ☎ 0342 459 3303

Completed around 1688, the **Iglesia y Convento de San Francisco** is notable for its incredibly solid, rustic construction: the whitewashed walls are nearly 2m thick and made

4

of adobe, while the stunning and cleverly assembled interior **ceiling** was constructed using solid wooden beams of Paraguayan cedar, *lapacho*, *algarrobo* and *quebracho colorado* held together not with nails but with wooden pegs. The intricate dome at the centre of the church is a particularly impressive example of the application of this technique and also has a rather light-hearted touch: at the centre a beautifully carved pine cone is suspended. The former convent serves as a museum, containing a life-sized diorama of delegates at the 1853 Constitutional Assembly and an image of **Jesús Nazareno**, a beautifully detailed carving produced in 1650 by one of Spain's most famous *imagineros* (religious image-makers), Alonso Cano. It was presented to the church by Mariana of Austria, Queen of Spain when the city was relocated here from Cayastá.

Puerto Santa Fe

Lying just to the southeast of the city centre where the Río Santa Fe forks towards Laguna Setúbal, the old dock area of **Puerto Sante Fe** is being enthusiastically redeveloped. Its two **diques** (docks) are now home to a casino (wcasinosantafe.com.ar) and luxurious hotel, housed in a giant former grain silo (see below), while the nearby warehouses have been converted into a modern, air-conditioned shopping centre – Shopping La Ribera (wshoppinglaribera.com.ar) – with a food court and cinema complex.

ARRIVAL AND DEPARTURE   SANTA FE

By plane Santa Fe's Aeropuerto Sauce Viejo lies 14km southwest of the city along RN-11 (☎0342 475 0386). There's a small café, a couple of car rental desks and a Banco de Santa Fe (don't count on the ATM working). Austral and Sol fly regularly to Buenos Aires (1–4 daily; 1hr). Frequent local buses (Línea C Verde) run along RN-11 outside the airport into the city centre ($14.50; 45min). Taxis use the meter and tend to take the faster (but more expensive) route via the highway (around $250); reserve a ride in advance with Remises Aeropuerto (☎0342 15 612 8069).

By bus The Terminal de Ómnibus – with cafés, lockers and ATMs – is at Av Belgrano 2910 (☎0342 457 4124, wterminalsantafe.com), just northeast of the town centre and within walking distance of most accommodation.

Destinations Buenos Aires (hourly; 6hr); Córdoba (hourly; 5hr); Posadas (8 daily; 14hr); Puerto Iguazú (2 daily; 20hr); Resistencia (hourly; 7hr); Rosario (2–3 hourly; 2hr 20min).

INFORMATION AND TOURS

Tourist information The main tourist information desk (Mon–Fri 7am–8pm, Sat & Sun 8am–8pm; ☎0342 457 4124, wsantafeturismo.gov.ar) is in the bus terminal, but there are two other kiosks at San Martín 2020 (Mon–Fri 8am–1pm & 4–8pm, Sat 9am–12.30pm & 4–8pm) and Bulevar Gálvez 1150 (daily 8am–8pm; ☎0342 457 4121).

Boat tours At weekends, catamaran trips with Costa Litoral (☎0342 456 4381, wcostalitoral.info) leave from Dique 1 in Puerto Santa Fe to sail around the islands in Laguna Setúbal and the Río Santa Fe (Sat 3/5pm, Sun 11am; $180 return; 2hr) or visit Paraná (Sun 2.30/3pm; $280 return). Times (and prices) tend to change monthly, so check online in advance. Buy tickets in the Costa Litoral café across from the pier.

ACCOMMODATION

Ámbit Boulevard Hotel Boutique Gálvez 1408 and Lavalle ☎0342 455 5702, wambithotel.com.ar. Contemporary boutique hotel converted from a belle époque mansion, with ten brightly decorated rooms, wi-fi, flat-screen TVs, use of bikes and breakfast buffet included. $900
Hotel Hernandarias Rivadavia 2680 ☎0342 452 9752, whotelhernandarias.com. Simple but modern and clean accommodation in a convenient, central location,

with rooms featuring a/c and cable TV. Rates include buffet breakfast, wi-fi and parking. $560
★ **Los Silos** Dique 1, Puerto Santa Fe ☎0342 450 2800, whotellossilos.com.ar. Easily the best hotel in town and part of the Casino Santa Fe complex, this luxury hotel is housed in an enormous former grain silo, complete with bar, swish rooms with fantastic views and a very high rooftop pool. $1245

EATING

Enticing snacks can be found at the **Mercado Norte** (Mon–Sat 8.30am–12.30pm & 5–9pm, Sun 9am–1.30am; wmercadonortesf.com.ar), the renovated indoor market at Santiago del Estero 3100; try the craft beer at *Agosto* or home-made cakes at *Recoletas la Familia*. The US-style food court inside Shopping La Ribera at Puerto Santa Fe knocks out relatively cheap pizza, burgers and sandwiches.

THE SWEET TREATS OF SANTA FE

As well as its beer, Santa Fe is famous in Argentina for *alfajores merengo*, a particularly tempting version of Argentina's favourite *alfajor* cake, coated in crispy, white icing. **Alfajoreria Merengo** (W alfajoresmerengo.com) has been in business since 1851, its founder Don Hermenegildo Zuviría (aka "Merengo" himself) credited with inventing the treat. There are convenient branches in Shopping La Ribera mall (see p.228) and at Gral. López 2632 on Plaza 25 de Mayo (single cakes $15), plus the original café, now *Triferto Peatonal* (see below). Competitor **Alfajores Gayalí** (W gayali.com.ar), founded in 1913, has *Las Delicias* (see below), a dedicated café on Plaza 25 de Mayo, and the *Café Gayalí "Teatro"* at San Martín 2010.

Ágora Santiago del Estero 3102 ☎ 0342 455 1295. This local café in the Mercado Norte knocks out great seafood, lamb burgers, roast chicken and other Argentine staples, with some outdoor seating and an excellent wine list. Tues–Sun 8.30am–4pm & 6pm–1am.

Las Delicias San Martín 2898 and Hipólito Yrigoyen ☎ 0342 453 2126. A traditional *confitería* and the headquarters of Gayalí (see box above), serving good sandwiches and cakes here since 1924, with tiled floors and old coffee machines – also a good place to sip a *liso* and grab some *alfajores* from the connected Gayalí store. Mon–Fri 7am–1.30pm & 3.30–9pm, Sat & Sun 8am–2pm & 4–10pm.

España San Martín 2644 ☎ 0342 400 0472. Justly popular restaurant on the main pedestrian drag, with dishes of the day for $85; expect an eclectic international menu, with a focus on seafood (paella, shellfish casseroles) and local freshwater fish (such as *manubé*, *pacú* and *surubí*). Sit inside the Art Nouveau dining room or on the street terrace. Mains $145–179. Daily 8am–2pm & 7–11pm.

Triferto Peatonal San Martín 2360 ☎ 0342 400 4005, W triferto.com. The original Merengo (see box above) corner café, refurbished in 2002 by its new owners. There are coffee and pastry sets from $45, pizzas for $100–180 and sandwiches for $42–57, but the *alfajores* (still made to the same recipe; from $15) are the real stars. Mon–Sat 7am–1am.

DRINKING

Santa Fe is home to one of South America's largest **breweries**, and the city's beer is renowned throughout the country – locals ask for a *liso*, a draught lager served in a straight glass.

★**Patio de la Cervecería Santa Fe** Calchines 1398 ☎ 0342 15 510 7968, W paseodelacerveceria.com.ar. Founded in 1912, the city's lauded brewery now operates a beer garden right next to the factory, with a pleasant courtyard, beer channelled directly from the vats via the 300m "Cervezoducto", and tasty sandwiches. Ask here about free guided visits to the plant (usually Tues–Sat 5pm, Spanish only; 45min). Mon–Fri 6pm–3am, Sat & Sun noon–3am.

Paraná

Favoured by gentle hilly terrain and bluffs that overlook a handsome, pedestrian-friendly riverfront, **PARANÁ** is a pleasant place to chill out for a day or two. Like Rosario, Paraná lacks a true foundation date: the area was simply settled by Santa Fe residents in the seventeenth century, who regarded the higher ground of the eastern banks of the Paraná River as providing better protection from attack by the area's indigenous inhabitants. Development accelerated when it was the **capital of the Argentine Confederation** (1853–1861), and today it's the capital and largest city of Entre Ríos Province, with a population of around 250,000. In addition to a couple of decent sandy **beaches**, it has a particularly attractive park, the **Parque Urquiza**, whose shady walkways and thick vegetation provide welcome respite from the summer heat.

Plaza 1 de Mayo

Catedral Metropolitana Monte Caseros 51 • Daily 6.30am–8.30pm • Free • ☎ 0343 431 1440

Paraná's main square is **Plaza 1 de Mayo**, ten blocks inland, a tranquil space that comes to life in the evenings. It's ringed by several important buildings – notably the **Palacio Municipal** (1890) and **Antiguo Senado de la Confederación** (1859) – but its outstanding sight is the **Catedral Metropolitana**, completed in 1883 and dedicated to the Virgen del

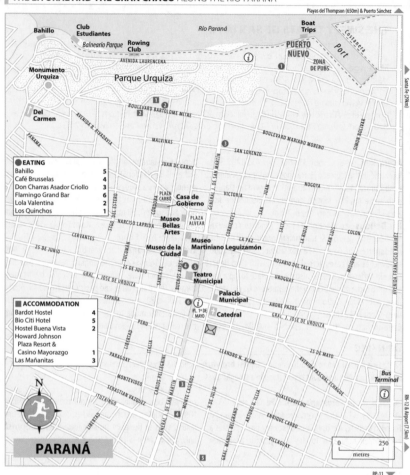

Rosario, a superficially handsome if somehow rather awkward Neoclassical edifice distinguished by an intense blue brick-tiled central dome and rather exotic, almost Byzantine bell towers.

Museo Histórico de Entre Ríos Martiniano Leguizamón

Buenos Aires 285 • Tues–Fri 8am–12.30pm & 3–8pm, Sat 9am–noon & 4–7pm, Sun 9am–noon • Free ($5 donation suggested) • ☎ 0343 420 7869

Pedestrianized Calle San Martín connects Plaza 1 de Mayo to Plaza Alvear, three blocks north, where you'll find the **Museo Histórico de Entre Ríos Martiniano Leguizamón**. Inside there's an eclectic collection of bits and pieces, but you'll need to read Spanish to appreciate the informative labels. Beginning with a tiny section on pre-Hispanic remains, the galleries focus on the history of Entre Ríos Province – and especially its (male) luminaries – from the eighteenth to twentieth centuries, with various tattered flags of the short-lived Republic of Entre Ríos (1820–21), General Artigas' lance and General Urquiza's actual poncho among the more intriguing items. There's also a scale model of the city in the 1850s, a section on Urquiza's great victory at the Battle of Caseros in 1852 (see p.534), and a collection of antique silver *mate* cups.

Museo Provincial de Bellas Artes Dr. Pedro E. Martinez

Buenos Aires 355 (Plaza Alvear) • April–Sept Tues–Fri 8am–1pm & 3–8pm, Sat 10am–noon & 4–7pm, Sun 10am–noon; Oct–March Tues–Fri 8am–1pm & 4–9pm, Sat 10am–noon & 5–8pm, Sun 10am–noon • Free • ☎ 0343 420 7868

Set inside a pink Italianate mansion built in 1900, the **Museo Provincial de Bellas Artes Dr. Pedro E. Martinez** contains a small but intriguing permanent collection of 22 works by lauded Entre Ríos painter **Cesáreo Bernaldo de Quirós** (1879–1968). These include his naturalist *El Viejo Criollo* series and *Grises*, as well as a view of the Puerto Viejo in 1944. Most of the galleries are taken up by temporary art exhibitions with Argentine themes.

Parque Urquiza

Flanking Paraná's riverside, **Parque Urquiza** blankets a fairly narrow but hilly stretch of ground that slopes up from Avenida Laurencena, Paraná's Costanera, to the higher ground of the city. Designed – like so many of Argentina's parks – by landscape gardener Charles Thays, it's particularly attractive and verdant, traversed by serpentine walkways and with fine views over the river, although the area is best avoided at night. At its western end, the **Monumento Urquiza** comprises a marble pillar and statue raised in 1920 to honour General Justo José de Urquiza himself, president of the Argentine Confederation from 1854 to 1860.

Costanera

Playa Club Atlético Estudiantes Daily 8am–7pm • Day fee $300 • ☎ 0343 431 8440, ⓦ caeparana.com.ar

The real hub of Paraná life on summer evenings is the **Costanera**, a boardwalk running for several kilometres along the river, its trees alive with the shrieks of green monk parakeets. The **Balneario Parque**, towards the western end, is a small but sandy public beach, with some shade and a roped-off swimming area (though the muddy waters rarely seem inviting). At either end of the beach are private clubs, **Playa Club Atlético Estudiantes** and **Playa Paraná Rowing Club**; at the former you can become a member for the day, giving you access to cleaner beaches and facilities such as swimming pools and showers (you need a member to sign you in at the swanky Rowing Club). Further west, across the Arroyo Antóníco, is **Puerto Viejo**, the nineteenth-century port area that closed in 1901 due to silting up – until the ruined port buildings are renovated there's not much to see. Walking a couple of kilometres east from Balneario Parque takes you to a series of piers offering boat trips (see below), and to **Puerto Nuevo**, the new port completed in 1907, though this is now rarely used by ships. Instead, you'll find clubs, pubs and seafood restaurants in the streets behind the boardwalk. Keep walking along the coast, through the traditional fishing neighbourhood known as **Puerto Sánchez** (famed in Argentina as the inspiration for the famous *chamamé* folk song by Jorge Méndez), and you'll reach the best beach, **Playas del Thompson**, which is always packed on summer weekends.

4

ARRIVAL, INFORMATION AND TOURS PARANÁ

Paraná does have a small airport, 7.5km southeast of the centre, with a handful of flights to Buenos Aires, and even a train station, but there are few useful routes – you are much more likely to arrive by road.

By bus Paraná's Terminal de Ómnibus (☎ 0343 431 5053) is at Ramírez 2350, around nine blocks east of Plaza 1 de Mayo. Destinations Buenos Aires (hourly; 6hr 45min–8hr); Corrientes (2–3 daily; 8hr 15min); Posadas (9 daily; 9hr 45min–12hr); Puerto Iguazú (3 daily; 15hr 35min); Rosario (2–3 hourly; 3hr); Santa Fe (every 20min; 50min).

Tourist information The most central tourist information kiosk is on Plaza 1 de Mayo (daily 8am–8pm;

☎ 0343 423 0183; ⓦ parana.gob.ar), but there are useful kiosks at the bus terminal (daily 8am–2pm & 4–8pm; ☎ 0343 420 1862) and on the Costanera (Laurencena at San Martín; daily 8am–2pm & 4–8pm; ☎ 0343 420 1837).

Tours For river trips, kayak rental, half-day tours to Santa Fe and Victoria and other local tours, contact Costanera 241 at Buenos Aires 212 (☎ 0343 423 4385, ⓦ costanera241.com.ar).

GETTING AROUND

By bus Numerous buses run into the centre from the Terminal de Ómnibus (#1, #4, #5 & #9). Buses use stored-value cards ("La Tarje Bus"; buy at the terminal) and coins – fares are $6 in cash (coins only) or $4.95 on the card.

By taxi Taxis meters start at $13 and go up $1 every 100m, though rates tend to increase every couple of years.

ACCOMMODATION

Bardot Hostel Monte Caseros 578 ☎0343 422 2832, ✉bardothostel@hotmail.com, ⓦfacebook.com/Bardot.Hostel. Top-notch hostel with slick, modern dorms and amenities which include a bar, pool room, kitchen and lounge with large flat-screen satellite TV. Loads of information on local tours and transport (English spoken). **$220**

Bio Citi Hotel Racedo 233 ☎0343 422 8880, ⓦbiociti.com. Modern budget hotel set in a refurbished building dating from 1890, with simple but bright rooms, all with a/c and bathrooms; wi-fi and light breakfast included, and superior rooms have flat-screen TVs. **$445**

★**Hostel Buena Vista** Mitre 449 ☎0343 455 0847, ⓦhostelbuenavista.com.ar. A truly wonderful hostel close to the waterfront, with two dorms plus private rooms with beds for two to four people and fully equipped kitchen. Free wi-fi and continental breakfast. Dorms **$185**; doubles **$385**

Howard Johnson Plaza Resort & Casino Mayorazgo Etchevehere 33 and Miranda ☎0343 423 0333, ⓦhjmayorazgo.com.ar. Paraná's most luxurious hotel is the *Mayorazgo*, towering over the Costanera. Run by the Howard Johnson chain, it has comfy rooms, two swimming pools and terrific views over the river. Free wi-fi and parking. **$1500**

Las Mañanitas Enrique Carbó 62 ☎0343 407 4753, ⓦlasmanianitas.com.ar. Beautifully converted nineteenth-century property, with twelve simple en-suite rooms with a/c, wi-fi and cable TV. Parking $80/day. **$550**

EATING

Bahillo San Martín 722 ☎0343 422 1324, ⓦbahillo.com. Small, modern ice-cream shop, part of a local chain (founded in Gualeguaychú in 1966), selling tempting scoops of chocolate, lemon, kiwi and numerous other flavours for $25–40. Daily 10am–midnight.

Café Brusselas Buenos Aires 60 ☎0343 423 0339. Paraná lacks the historic cafés of Santa Fe, but this contemporary spot is the best place to linger over coffee in the centre (with blends sourced from Colombia) and sumptuous cakes made from family recipes ($20–45). Mon–Thurs 8am–1.30pm & 4–10pm, Fri 8am–1.30pm & 4–11pm, Sat 8.30am–1pm & 4.30–11pm.

Don Charras Asador Criollo San Martín and San Lorenzo ☎0343 422 5972. Central branch of the long-running traditional *parrilla Don Charras*, grilling sumptuous steaks, but also throwing river fish on the barbecue. Enjoy the a/c inside or the sun outside on the deck. Hearty daily lunch menu for $150. Mon–Thurs 11.30am–3pm & 8.30pm–midnight, Fri–Sun 11.30am–3pm & 8.30pm–1am.

Flamingo Grand Bar San Martín 908 ☎0343 431 1711. Elegant and historic café (given a modern makeover

---

ESTANCIAS OF CORRIENTES PROVINCE

En route between Paraná and Corrientes are a couple of outstanding **estancias** that take in guests – often providing horse rides or hands-on experiences of genuine ranch life. You cannot just turn up on spec but must book ahead; sometimes they will arrange for you to be picked up at the nearest town, airport or bus terminal, even if you have your own car – often the lengthy approach roads are impassable other than by 4WD. Rates for the two options below are full board, and include guided horse rides.

Estancia Buena Vista 5km off RP-30 ☎011 4815 9305, ⓦestanciabuenavista.com.ar. Around 45km northeast of Esquina (which is connected to Buenos Aires by bus), this is a traditional working estate, with large numbers of cattle and sheep. It specializes in game, though, which can be sampled at dinner. Run by a Swiss Argentine, Sara Röhner, and her German-born husband Klaus Liebig, the estancia combines a high level of comfort with old-fashioned *correntino* hospitality. The German-style teas are memorable. **$2500 (US$170)** per person

★**Estancia La Rosita** 11km off RN-12 ☎011 4312 6448, ⓦestancialarosita.com.ar. Some 15km southeast of Esquina, this estate lies among huge pastures dotted with ever-changing lakes and marshes, and is very much a working ranch, with lots of cattle and horses. The house is an agreeable low-rise farmstead, with simple and homely guest rooms. Alicia Cometta de Landgraf runs the place with her sons, who are avid polo players – take a look at the impressive pitch, even if you never get to see or participate in a game. A tank swimming pool and barbecue facilities are added attractions; the food is authentic *criollo*. **$2580 (US$175)** per person in 2005), restaurant and bar on the main square; a great spot for draught beers ($23–46), coffee ($16) or light meals of pastas or steaks (weekday menus $120–140). Daily 8am–midnight.

Lola Valentina Mitre 302 ☏0343 423 5234. Popular local restaurant with old-school waiters in a tranquil, posh part of the city, serving up enormous and tasty river-fish dishes – try the *dorado* in a rich cream and spring onion sauce (sets $95; mains $75–150). Reservations advised at weekends. Cash only. Daily noon–4pm & 8pm–midnight.

Los Quinchos Laurencena 350 ☏0343 423 2045. In a rustic thatched construction by the Costanera, this highly rated if pricey *parrilla* fills up quickly – reservations are advised on summer weekends. Tues–Sun 10am–3pm & 8pm–1am.

Corrientes

Sultry, subtropical and sitting on a 2km-wide bulge in the Río Paraná, **CORRIENTES** is one of the region's oldest and most appealing cities. The Spanish founded the city in 1588, in what was traditional Guaraní territory, as an intermediary port along the river route between Buenos Aires and Asunción. Author **Graham Greene**, who passed through in 1969, was so enamoured he decided to set his novel *The Honorary Consul* here. Today it's the capital of Corrientes Province with a population of around 330,000, and though little has survived from the colonial period – the city is studded with the usual modern blocks and slapdash high rises – a handful of traditional *correntino* buildings remains in the historic centre, Neocolonial edifices with overhanging roofs supported on wooden posts. If you visit from November to February, be aware that both temperatures and humidity can be mercilessly fierce. As a result, locals take the siesta very seriously, not emerging from indoors until dusk on the hottest days. If you must hit the streets on a summer afternoon, though, head

4

for Corrientes' attractive **Costanera**, curving for 2.5km along the river. The historic centre, with **Plaza 25 de Mayo** at its heart, lies close to the Costanera and is where you'll find most of Corrientes' oldest buildings and museums, while the main pedestrianized shopping street is **Calle Junín**, three blocks south.

Corrientes is linked to Resistencia (see p.270), the capital of Chaco Province, 20km to the west, via the impressive Puente General M. Belgrano, a 2.8km cable-stayed bridge across the Río Paraná.

Plaza 25 de Mayo

A leafy square set around the usual equestrian statue of General José de San Martín, **Plaza 25 de Mayo** encapsulates the city's sleepy subtropical ambience. The plaza lies one block south of the Costanera, to which it is linked by the narrow streets of Buenos Aires and Salta, the former in particular lined with fine examples of late nineteenth-century architecture. One of the most striking buildings on the square itself, the pink **Casa de Gobierno**, on the eastern side, was completed in 1886 in an ornate Italianate style (it remains the office of the provincial governor).

At the southern end of the plaza is the **Iglesia de Nuestra Señora de la Merced** (daily 7am–noon & 4–8pm; free), completed in 1905. The church is home to a handsome, hand-carved wooden *retablo*, or altarpiece, with twisted wooden pillars and rich golden inlay work.

Museo de Artesanías Tradicionales Folclóricas de la Provincia

Fray José de la Quintana 905 • Mon–Fri 8am–noon & 3–7pm, Sat 9am–noon & 4–7pm • Free

The **Museo de Artesanías Tradicionales Folclóricas de la Provincia** and its craft workshops, or *talleres*, are housed within a typical colonial Corrientes building just off Plaza 25 de Mayo, built in 1806 for one Don Antonio Mecca. The low, whitewashed residence was constructed around a central patio flanked by a gallery, providing shade from the fierce summer sun. Inside you'll find a selection of local crafts, including fine examples of leatherwork, ceramics and basketwork. Perhaps the most intriguing pieces, sold by craftsmen based in the workshops within, are the carvings of San La Muerte (literally "Saint Death"). These solemn little skeletons carved in wood, gold or bone are carried around – or, in the case of the smallest figures, inserted under the skin – to ensure the bearer a painless death; they're a typical example of the popular cults, many of them inherited from the Guaraní, which coexist in Corrientes with profound Catholic beliefs.

Museo Histórico de Corrientes

9 de Julio 1044 • Tues–Fri 8am–noon & 4–8pm, Sat 8am–noon • Free

Housed in a nineteenth-century Neoclassical mansion two blocks southeast of Plaza 25 de Mayo, the **Museo Histórico de Corrientes** contains a hodgepodge of historic bits and pieces, with treasures such as the Corrientes flag from the Battle of Caáguazú (1841), a door carved by indigenous craftsmen at a Jesuit school in 1826 for the first Casa de Gobierno, religious art and various weapons and personal items belonging to luminaries of the province's history.

Iglesia Santísima Cruz de los Milagros

Plaza de la Cruz • Daily 9am–noon • Free

The **Iglesia Santísima Cruz de los Milagros** is at the southern end of leafy Plaza de la Cruz, several blocks south of Plaza 25 de Mayo. Both the square and the church – a simple pink Italianate construction dating from 1897 – are named after Corrientes' first cross, brought by the Spaniards on the city's founding in 1588. Legend states that the cross gained its epithet, the "Cross of Miracles", when it proved impervious to the attempts of the area's indigenous inhabitants to burn it. A piece of the original cross is preserved as part of the altar within the church.

The Costanera

Corrientes' attractively maintained riverside avenue, the **Avenida Costanera General San Martín** (generally just referred to as "the Costanera") runs from the port, at the northern end of the city, all the way to the Puente General Belgrano. Lined with fine examples of native *lapacho* trees, with exquisite pink blossom in spring, it's a lovely spot on summer evenings, when the heat dissipates a little and locals leave the cool refuge of their homes to pack its promenades for a jog or a stroll, or simply sit sipping *mate* or *tereré* on stone benches. Arts and crafts stalls set up around Punta Tacuara and the information kiosk, and closer to the bridge you'll come to the area known as **Playa Islas Malvinas** (where there's no actual beach, despite the name), with riverside bars and restaurants and a poignant memorial to local soldiers killed in the Falklands War.

ARRIVAL AND INFORMATION
CORRIENTES

By plane Corrientes' Aeropuerto Fernando Piragine Niveyro (☎03783 458340) lies 10km northeast of the city, along RN-12. There are two daily flights to and from Buenos Aires (1hr 30min). Local bus #109 ($5.25) and taxis ($50) shuttle into the city.

By bus The bus terminal (☎03783 442149) is around 4km southeast of Plaza 25 de Mayo, along one of the city's main access roads, Av Maipú. Various local buses, including the #103, run between the terminal and the local bus station on the Costanera, from where you can catch a bus to Resistencia ("Corrientes-Chaco" buses, usually green and white; $7–8). Local buses use a stored-value card (*tarjeta*; buy them at the bus terminal) and coin system (no change given); rides are $5.25 in coins and $4.95 on the card.

Destinations Buenos Aires (12–16 daily, mostly 5–11.30pm; 11hr 10min–14hr 40min); Córdoba (3 daily; 11hr–13hr 45min); Posadas (every 2hr; 4hr–4hr 20min); Puerto Iguazú (7 daily; 8–9hr); Resistencia (hourly; 30min); Rosario (13 daily; 11–12hr).

Tourist information There's a tiny tourist information kiosk (daily 8am–8pm; ☎0379 447 4702, ⓦ ciudaddecorrientes.gov.ar) on the Costanera, where it meets Pellegrini; it has maps, basic information on festivals and tours, and the occasional English-speaker. There are also kiosks on Plaza Cabral (☎0379 4474733), at the airport (☎0379 445 8684) and at the bus terminal (☎0379 447 7600), open similar times.

ACCOMMODATION

There is a good range of accommodation in Corrientes, but note that the city's particularly hot and humid summers make air conditioning almost a necessity. The recommendations below all include free wi-fi and breakfast.

★**La Alondra** 3 de Abril 827 ☎0379 443 0555, ⓦ laalondra.com.ar. Truly original small hotel in a converted family house, with a library, reception and restaurant/bar stacked with antique travel trunks, chandeliers, globes, leather chairs and mahogany bookshelves. The rooms vary a great deal so ask to look at several if possible – they are all decorated in a similar belle époque style, though in a nod to modernity they also have a/c and flatscreen TVs. There's a small gym plus a plunge pool on the main patio. $1445

Bienvenida Golondrina La Rioja 455 ☎0379 443 5316, ⓦ hostelbienvenidagolondrina.com. Still the town's premier hostel, with conventional if comfy dorm rooms and doubles; the pricier ones have a/c. The building is very pleasant – a restored nineteenth-century house with original tiled floors and ceiling frescoes, and walls painted soothing lilac – plus the friendly staff can help arrange river excursions. Dorms $200; doubles $540

Corrientes Plaza Hotel Junín 1549 ☎0379 446 6500, ⓦ hotel-corrientes.com.ar. Overlooking the animated Plaza Cabral, this is a shiny, modern hotel blessed with a

refreshing pool and bright rooms, but noisy a/c. $665

Gran Hotel Guaraní Mendoza 970 ☎0379 443 3800, ⓦ granhotelguarani.com. The doyen of Corrientes' hotels, this is a business-oriented establishment in a modern glass-fronted building, with an inviting pool and bar area (popular with the city's wealthier inhabitants). There are several categories of rooms ranging from standard (actually fairly basic) to VIP and two categories of suites; all have a/c and cable TV. $1265

Hostel Los Lapachos España 531 ☎0379 442 3354, ⓦ loslapachoshostel.com. Modern, friendly hostel in a quiet neighbourhood with a large garden, simple bunk-bed dorms and bright doubles. Shared kitchen and free bikes, but no parking (street only). Dorms $200; doubles $600

La Rozada Suites Placido Martínez 1223 ☎0379 443 3001, ⓦ larozada.com.ar. Beautifully furnished hotel, with local artworks and harmoniously blended features of the original 1890s building (a disused warehouse) giving the place character. The larger suites are duplexes with proper kitchens; the classic rooms are quite a bit smaller,

but still elegant, with great views over the Paraná. Very small (but free) parking area. $\overline{\$920}$
Turismo Hotel Casino Entre Ríos 650 ☎0379 442 9112, Ⓦghturismo.com.ar. This grand hotel (Graham Greene stayed here in the 1960s) is in a good location down by the Costanera. The rooms have been given a luxurious contemporary makeover and there's a huge outdoor swimming pool. $\overline{\$1130}$

EATING

Havanna Mendoza 969 and Irigoyen ☎0379 423 0486, Ⓦhavanna.com.ar. Dependable chain of cafés and chocolate shops housed in a magnificent castle-like mansion built for the Manuel Ferré family (and later used by the Jockey Club) in 1908; enjoy cappuccinos ($45) or their famed *alfajores* ($47) in the cavernous a/c interior or in the shady garden. Mon–Fri 7am–1.30pm & 5–9.30pm, Sat & Sun 8am–1.30pm & 5–9.30pm.
Martha de Bianchetti 9 de Julio 1198 and Mendoza ☎0379 442 3008. Snacks, light meals, fruit juices, ice cream, cakes and coffees are on offer at this wonderfully kitsch and extremely popular *confitería*. The walls drip with over-the-top decoration, gilded mouldings and all manner of baubles. Mon–Sat 6.30am–1pm & 4–10pm.

El Nuevo Típico San Juan 455 (Plaza Italia) ☎0379 454 8666. Housed in an old convent, this is an excellent choice for no-frills, local fish dishes, though the menu offers a wide range of Argentine and international dishes. There's usually a choice of one fish and one meat special for lunch ($75–100); the waiter will let you know. Daily 11am–3pm & 8pm–12.45am.
La Posta Del Río Costanera and Pago Largo ☎0379 444 3846. One of the city's best *parrillas*, with great views of the river – like many such establishments here it specializes in grilled river fish such as *pacú* and *surubí*, and doesn't get going till late in the evenings. Mains from $150. Daily noon–4pm & 8pm–late.

DRINKING AND NIGHTLIFE

A popular nightlife option in Corrientes is a **chamamé show**, held at various restaurants; *chamamé* (see p.562) is perhaps Argentina's most infectious folk music, a lively danceable rhythm punctuated by a rather bloodcurdling cry, known as the *sapucay*.

Parrilla El Quincho Av Juan Pujol 2221 and Pellegrini ☎0379 446 8320. This large *parrilla* is popular with locals for its food and live *chamamé* shows (Fri & Sat nights). Also renowned for its *parrillada*, with plenty of juicy *chorizo* sausage and a wide variety of offal. Tues–Sat 11am–3pm & 9pm–2am, Sun & Mon 11am–3pm.

Yacarú Pora Centenario 4350 ☎0379 445 8800, Ⓦyacarupora.com.ar. Another excellent *parrilla* (it's around $200 for a full *parrillada*), set in an atmospheric hall lined with Guaraní-themed murals and featuring live *chamamé* shows on Wed, Fri and Sat evenings, plus Sun lunchtimes. Daily noon–4pm & 8pm–2am.

The Esteros del Iberá

Covering nearly 13,000 square kilometres, the delicate ecosystem of the **ESTEROS DEL IBERÁ** is a magical landscape of wetlands that offers some of the best opportunities in the country for up-close observation of wildlife. An elongated sliver of land running through the centre of Corrientes Province, in addition to the *esteros* (swamps) that give the area its name, you will see a good many lakes, ponds, streams and wonderful floating islands, formed by a build-up of soil on top of intertwined waterlilies.

For many years this was one of Argentina's wildest and least-known regions, harbouring an isolated community who made their living from hunting and fishing the area's wildlife. Since the **Reserva Natural del Iberá** was created in 1983, covering most of the Esteros region, hunting has been prohibited in the area and many locals have been employed as highly specialized guides, or *baqueanos*, and park rangers, thus helping to preserve the unique environment. The ban on hunting has led to an upsurge in the region's abundant bird and animal population, with an amazingly diverse range of species thriving here (see box, p.241).

Primary access to the region is via **Mercedes**, a picturesque traditional town 246km southeast of Corrientes city. In the heart of the reserve, beside the ecosystem's second-largest lake, the Laguna del Iberá, is the isolated village of **Colonia Carlos Pellegrini** ("Pellegrini"), the centre for guided trips into the wetlands.

Mercedes

The gateway to the Esteros del Iberá, **MERCEDES** is a sprawling agricultural town, its drab, modern outskirts mitigated by an appealing centre of old-fashioned adobe and galleried-roof buildings plus some elegant late nineteenth-century architecture. The town is a hub of traditional country life, too: horses and carts are a common sight on its streets and on Saturdays gauchos come to town, traditionally dressed Corrientes-style, with shallow, wide-brimmed hats, ornate belts and wide *bombachas* (trousers), and accompanied by their wives, who wear frilly, old-fashioned dresses. Some 9km northwest of the town centre (on RN-123) lies the **Santuario Gauchito Gil**, the most important shrine to the legendary Argentine hero (see box, p.238).

The town, built on a regular grid pattern, is centred on **Plaza 25 de Mayo**, a densely planted square with little fountains. At its southern end stands the rather unusual **Iglesia Nuestra Señora de las Mercedes**, a lofty, late nineteenth-century red-brick church whose towers are topped with Moorish domes.

GAUCHITO GIL

Along roadsides throughout Argentina you'll see mysterious **shrines** of varying sizes, smothered in red flags, red candles, empty bottles and other miscellaneous bits and pieces. These are erected in homage to the semi-mythical **Gauchito Gil**, a kind of nineteenth-century gaucho Robin Hood – one of those folkloric figures whose story has some basis in reality yet has undoubtedly been embellished over the years.

Born – perhaps – in 1847 in Corrientes, Antonio Gil refused to fight in that province's civil war and fled to the mountains, robbing from the rich, helping the poor and healing with his hands. Captured by the police, he claimed that he had deserted from the army as he had been told in a dream by a Guaraní god that brothers shouldn't fight each other. An unimpressed sergeant took him out to a spot near Mercedes to execute him. Gil told the sergeant that when he returned to town he would find that his son was seriously ill, but as Gil's blood was innocent it could perform miracles, so the sergeant must pray for his intervention. Unmoved, the sergeant cut Gil's throat. When he returned to town, he found that the situation was indeed as the gaucho had described, but – after fervent prayer – his son made a miraculous recovery.

The sergeant put up the first shrine to thank him, and Gauchito Gil has since been credited with numerous **miracles** and honoured with many **shrines**, all bedecked in the distinctive **red flags** – which may represent his neck scarf soaked in blood – making the shrine look like the aftermath of a left-wing political demonstration. The shrine erected near **Mercedes**, at the place where he was killed, presumably began life as a simple affair, but such is the popularity of **Gauchito Gil** that the site has mushroomed over time into a village of humble restaurants, makeshift sleeping areas and souvenir stalls; there is even a kind of museum exhibiting the offerings made to the Gauchito, such as football shirts, wedding dresses and children's bicycles, along with more conventional rosaries. Simpler offerings, often made by passing motorists to ensure a safe journey, include ribbons and candles. January 8 sees Gauchito Gil pilgrims flock to the main shrine from the whole country.

Fundación Manos Correntinas
San Martín 487 • Mon–Fri 9am–noon & 5–8pm, Sat 9am–noon • ☎ 03773 422671

Three blocks east of Plaza 25 de Mayo, the **Fundación Manos Correntinas** is housed in a beautifully preserved example of the local building style: a low whitewashed adobe-walled construction with a gently sloping red-tiled roof which overhangs the pavement, supported on simple wooden posts. The foundation is a non-profit-making enterprise that functions as an outlet for locally produced crafts. The small but superior collection of goods on sale includes basketwork, simple gourd *mates*, heavy woollens and hand-turned bone and horn buttons.

ARRIVAL AND INFORMATION

By bus Mercedes' bus terminal is six blocks west of Plaza San Martín, on the corner of Av San Martín and El Ceibo, with a left luggage and general information office (daily 24hr). Buses for Pellegrini (☎ 03773 15 462836) normally depart around 1.30pm Mon–Sat (unless it's raining), arriving at 4.30pm; there are return buses at around 5am. These services can be unreliable, though (see p.240).

Destinations Buenos Aires (8 daily; 8hr 50min–10hr 40min); Colón (4 daily; 5hr 30min–8hr); Corrientes (10 daily; 3hr 30min); Paraná (2 daily; 8hr); Resistencia (8 daily; 4–5hr); Rosario (2 daily; 11hr).

MERCEDES

Tourist information There is a tourist office (daily 8am–noon & 4–8pm; ☎ 03773 15 414384), inconveniently located in an isolated building at the western entrance to town (Av San Martín, off RN-119), which can provide useful information and a map of the reserve. There's also a small office at the old train station, the Ex-Estación del Ferrocarril (Mon–Fri 7am–1pm & 2–8pm; ☎ 03773 15 414384), Av Madariaga, 1.5km southwest of Plaza San Martín.

Banks There's an ATM at the Banco de Corrientes, at San Martín 1099 on the corner of Pedro Ferré, three blocks west of Plaza San Martín; stock up here if you are heading to Pellegrini, as it has no banking facilities.

ACCOMMODATION AND EATING

★**La Casa de China** Fray Luís Beltrán 599 and Mitre ☎ 03773 15 627269, ⓦ corrientes.com.ar/lacasa dechina. This fabulous B&B in a tastefully furnished, quiet, nineteenth-century villa has four double rooms with free wi-fi and a/c, plus a beautifully tended garden. Owner María "China" Sánchez herself will prepare delicious meals if given notice. $1000

Che Rhoga San Martín 2296 ☎ 03773 15 407272. Excellent home-cooked food from the chef/owner in a spotless dining room on the edge of town (it's on a major roundabout); everything is good, but the empanadas are extra special. Mains $60–110. Daily noon–4pm & 8pm–1am.

Manantiales Hotel Casino Sarmiento and Juan Pujol ☎ 03773 421700, ⓦ manantialeshoteles.com. Most comfortable, modern hotel in town, with outdoor pool and inviting terrace. Rooms feature slick contemporary design, a/c, flat-screen TVs, free wi-fi and hot tubs (superior rooms only). $945

Torre del Guayaibí RN-123, Km128 ☎ 03773 510210, ⓦ torredelguayaibi.com.ar. Definitely the most atmospheric place to stay in the region, this faux-Gothic castle tower – on a working estancia with gauchos, where you may spot cute capybaras – offers luxurious rooms with canopy beds, wood floors, stone walls, old libraries and ironwork staircases. The downside: you'll need a car to stay here, as it's 15km northwest of Mercedes (it's popular with travellers on private tours). Excellent meals are $200 (lunch) and $300 (dinner); breakfast is included. $1200

Colonia Carlos Pellegrini and around

About 120km northeast of Mercedes, **COLONIA CARLOS PELLEGRINI** lies at the heart of the **Reserva Natural del Iberá**, and is most easily accessed via the largely unpaved but well-maintained RP-40. The journey there takes you through flat, unremarkable land, reminiscent of the African savannah, but with little to prepare you for the wonderfully wild, watery environment of the *esteros* themselves. The village sits on a peninsula on the edges of the **Laguna del Iberá**, a 53-square-kilometre expanse of water. The banks of the sparkling lake (*iberá* means "shining" in Guaraní) are spread with acres of waterlilies, most notably the striking lilac-bloomed *camalotes* and yellow *aguapés*, and dotted with bouncy floating islands formed of matted reeds and grass, known as *embalsados*.

Access to the village is over a temporary-looking – and sounding – narrow bridge and causeway constructed of earth and rock. Just before you cross there's the **Centro de**

Visitantes "Agua Brillante" (visitors' centre) with short trails on either side of the road leading through a small forested area to the south; the densely packed mix of palms, jacarandas, *lapachos* and willows here is a good place to see and hear black howler monkeys. They typically slouch in a ball shape among the branches or swing from tree to tree on lianas. Easiest to see are the yellowish young, often ferried from tree to tree on the backs of their mothers. Birds and butterflies abound, while capybaras often graze on the grass.

The village itself is composed of a small grid of sandy streets, centred on grassy **Plaza San Martín**. There are few services (no petrol station), and no banking facilities, so make sure you bring enough cash with you for your stay.

Excursions into the Esteros del Iberá

Wildlife-spotting excursions in the Esteros del Iberá are generally organized through your accommodation, which take visitors out in their small motorboats, with the boatmen acting as guides. After speeding across the centre of the lake, the boats dip under the causeway bridge, calling in at the visitors' centre to register, before cutting their engines to drift through the narrow streams that thread between the islands on the other side of the lake. This silent approach allows you an incredibly privileged view of the park's wildlife (see box opposite). Sometimes guides will take you onto the floating islands themselves; it's a particularly bizarre experience to feel the ground vibrating beneath your feet as you move. Another trip takes you along the **Río Miriñay**, home to slightly different varieties of flora and fauna to the lake. Enquire also about **horse rides** in the nearby marshes, another excellent way to see birds and the like, especially in the morning.

ARRIVAL AND DEPARTURE   COLONIA CARLOS PELLEGRINI

Self-driving, though possible, is not advised. The roads linking Pellegrini (RP-40 and RP-41) to the main Posadas highway (RN-12) in a northeasterly direction are still mud and gravel tracks and not always viable, especially after rain (in any case, best in a 4WD); whatever you do, enquire about their current state before attempting the journey.

By bus The road between Mercedes and Pellegrini is partially paved (the first 35km so far) and OK to drive (unless very wet), but bus services are often unreliable. Buses (☎ 03773 15 462836) from Mercedes run 1.30pm Mon–Sat, unless it's raining (1.30pm; return 5am; 3hr). Nordestur buses (☎ 03722 445 588) also run from Posadas bus terminal (Tues, Thurs & Sat 8am; return Wed, Fri & Sun 4.30pm; 4hr 30min). Confirm this service is still running before making plans.

By 4WD More dependable and faster transport between

Mercedes and Pellegrini is provided by private 4WD drivers, who tend to charge US$80–100 per trip – an expense alleviated if you have 4 or 5 people to share the ride (hotels in either place can arrange these). From Posadas (3–4hr) it's a lot more expensive – likely over US$250. Recommended operators include Bioiberá (☎ 03773 15 407314, ☹ bioibera.com.ar) and Iberá Wild (☎ 03773 15 413710, ☹ iberawild.com.ar), but it's relatively easy to arrange rides at Mercedes bus station.

INFORMATION AND ACTIVITIES

Tourist information The small Centro de Visitantes (open daily during daylight hours) is immediately to the left just before you cross the bridge, where you can see a small display on the *esteros* and their wildlife.

Boat trips Numerous local guides run boat trips into the

park, and your accommodation may include a free trip. If arranging it yourself, you shouldn't pay more than around $300/person for two hours, though gasoline prices will affect the overall cost.

Kayak rental Nautic Adventures (☹ nauticadventures .net) rents out kayaks for around $100/hour.

ACCOMMODATION

The best **accommodation** is provided by local posadas, most of which offer full board with at least one **boat trip** and other activities included; rates are usually quoted per person, so the prices below are for two people sharing a double room. Note also that only *Irupé Lodge* and *Rincón del Socorro* accept credit cards.

WILDLIFE IN THE ESTEROS DEL IBERÁ

Home to well over three hundred species of **bird** and a mindblowing variety of **reptiles** and **mammals**, the Esteros del Iberá are a paradise for any visitor with an interest in wildlife. Armed with binoculars and a guidebook to South American species, you stand an excellent chance of observing dozens of different varieties in just an hour or two; a good guide will help, too (easily arranged through your accommodation).

BIRDS

A common sight and sound around the Laguna del Iberá are *chajás* (**southern screamers**), large grey birds with a patch of red around the eyes and a look of bashful nervousness. They frequently perch on the trees on the lakeside, nonchalantly chanting "aha-aha" but occasionally emitting a piercing yelp (hence the English name) similar to the sound a dog makes when trodden on. Other large birds include sleek, black **olivaceous cormorants; maguari storks**, with striking black and white plumage, and a tendency to soar on the thermals above the lake; and **striated herons** characterized by a black crown and a lazy disposition. A particularly impressive sight during the spring nesting period is that of the *garzales*, where hundreds of normally solitary herons unite in a spectacular mass gathering. Another magical, if rarer, sight is the elegant *jabirú*, a long-legged relative of the stork with a white body, bright crimson collar and a black head and beak. Different species of **kingfisher** also put on a show of aviation prowess, swooping across the water or diving into it. **Wattled jacanas**, on the other hand, prefer to scuttle over waterlilies and floating weeds, seldom showing off their lemon-tipped wings. Another strange-moving bird is the **giant wood-rail**, or *ipacaá*, whose Guaraní name is onomatopoeic; it croaks plaintively as it tiptoes around near houses, grabbing any food left out for it and scampering off to peck away at it.

REPTILES AND INSECTS

Birds are not the only wonders around the *esteros*. Among the reed beds at the edges of the lake you may catch sight of large **snakes**, such as the handsome **yellow anaconda**, its golden skin dotted with black patches; they can reach up to 3m in length. As you approach the edges of the floating islands, in particular, charcoal-grey **caymans**, or *yacarés*, freeze, often with their ferocious-looking jaws stuck open, or else they suddenly slither into the water, where they observe you with only their eyes peeking above the surface. Another startling spectacle is provided by creepily large **spiders**, which lurk in huge webs among bushes and reeds, waiting for their helpless insect prey. Some guides delight in making it look as though the boat is heading straight for them, so arachnophobes be warned. Rather more appealing are the hundreds of **butterflies**, in every colour imaginable, an enchanting sight you will see all over the region.

MAMMALS

Mammals are well represented, too. **Howler monkeys** – which really growl rather than howl – are much easier to hear than to see, but you might, if you are patient, observe their antics near the visitors' centre or in other tall trees in the area. Listen, too, for the sudden splash of a **capybara**, or *carpincho*, diving into the water. On land, this guinea-pig-like mammal – the world's largest rodent – looks almost ungainly, but they are incredibly graceful as they glide through the water. The floating islands are where the capybaras go to sleep and graze. There, and on the marshy lands and pastures around the more isolated extremes of the lake, you may also spot the rare **marsh deer**, South America's largest, equally at home in the water and on dry land. If you approach them gently, these astonishingly beautiful animals seem to accept your presence and continue grazing lazily on aquatic plants. Rarest of all of the *esteros*' wildlife, and certainly the hardest to spot, is the endangered *aguara-guazú*, or **maned wolf**, a reddish long-legged creature that awkwardly lopes through the vegetation.

4

Camping Municipal del Iberá Immediately to the left as you enter the village from the bridge ☎ 03773 15 432388. The only real budget option in the area, at a pleasant riverside site (albeit one almost entirely bereft of shade) with hot showers till around 8pm. Note that there's a one-time $15 entry fee. **$50**

Irupé Lodge Yacaré and Ysipó ☎ 03773 15 402193, ⓦ ibera-argentina.com. Handsome wooden *hostería* run by Mauricio Lacona and his Swiss-born wife Regi, with eight brightly decorated rooms (plus a family suite) overlooking the lagoon, with its own jetty and launch. Excursions, wi-fi and breakfast included. §3000

Posada Aguapé Yacaré and Ñangapirí ☎ 03773 499412, ⓦ iberaesteros.com.ar. A traditional building set in spacious grounds with twelve appealing en-suite rooms overlooking the lake. There's also a swimming pool and a cosy bar area. Full board and free wi-fi included. §3640

★**Posada de la Laguna** Guazuvirá, between Pinto and Caranday ☎ 03773 499413, ⓦ esterosibera.com. Particularly well situated in a quiet lakeside spot at the eastern edge of the village, this pioneering posada helmed by artist Elsa Güiraldes offers pared-down luxury with a rustic feel. The elegant and spacious but simple en-suite rooms are in a galleried building whose veranda provides a good vantage point for observing the birds that gather around the lake; food (full board) and service are top-notch and the swimming pool is a bonus. Free wi-fi and two activities per day included. §3535

★**Posada Rancho Iberá** Aguara Guazú and Caraguata ☎ 03773 15 412661, ⓦ posadaranchoibera.com.ar. Taty and Marcello host one of the better deals in the village, with simple but comfy a/c rooms and breakfast and boat trips included in the rate. Common room with TV and free wi-fi throughout. §1175

Posada Tupasÿ Yacaré and Ysipó ☎ 03773 427134, ⓦ posadatupasy.com.ar. Basic but cheap accommodation with clean a/c rooms set around an outdoor pool, free (but unreliable) wi-fi and simple breakfast included (full board is $2650). §1325

Rancho de los Esteros Aguara Guazú, at Aguapé ☎ 03773 15 493041, ⓦ ranchodelosesteros.com.ar. Just four handsomely decorated suites in a wonderful ranch operated by the friendly Maita and Julio Dreher, with a traditional gallery, home-made jams and cakes and a selection of excursions included in the rate. §3200

Rancho Inambú Yeruti, between Peguajó and Aguapé ☎ 03773 15 401362, ⓦ ranchoinambu.com.ar. This posada helmed by Jorge Sisi is a typical adobe house, with attractive rooms of various sizes, an airy breakfast room and a bar with a pool table. Rates include breakfast (no full board option), one boat tour and a guided walk. §3000

Rincón del Socorro RP-40 Km83 ☎ 03773 475114, ⓦ rincondelsocorro.com. Five kilometres from the main road (south of the village), this converted cattle ranch, built in 1896, is efficiently run by the hospitable Valeria Verdaguer and Leslie Cook. The traditional main building and luxurious rooms are all decorated with handsome furnishings and splendid photos of Iberá flora and fauna. Food (full board) includes home-grown, organic fruit, vegetables and herbs. §6170

Along the Río Uruguay

Like the Paraná, the **Río Uruguay** rises in southern Brazil, flowing for some 1838km into the Río de la Plata. The well-maintained RN-14 toll road (a fast, four-lane motorway) follows the river at a distance beginning at Ceibas, 160km northwest of Buenos Aires, and runs north towards Iguazú, ending up at the Brazilian border. Side roads lead via bridges to the neighbouring country of **Uruguay** as well as a number of river "resorts"; like many large, continental nations, Argentina has developed a series of holiday towns along its interior rivers, replete with sandy beaches and spas.

The first stop, heading north, is **Gualeguaychú** – home of Argentina's most renowned carnival festivities. Further up is languid and picturesque **Colón**, by far the most attractive of the riverside resorts and boasting the most developed tourist infrastructure, including good hotels and numerous campsites right by its beaches. It is also a convenient base for making a trip to nearby **Parque Nacional El Palmar** and the **Palacio de San José**, once General Urquiza's luxurious residence.

Gualeguaychú

Apart from having a name that sounds like a tongue-twister followed by a sneeze, **SAN JOSÉ DE GUALEGUAYCHÚ**, or just plain Gualeguaychú (its name is possibly derived from the Guaraní words for "tranquil waters"), is most notable for its **Carnaval**, generally regarded as Argentina's most important; during January and February, the town is mobbed with people, particularly at weekends. Gualeguaychú's passion for processions is given further vent in October, when local high-school students take part in the **desfile de carrozas**, in which elaborate floats, constructed by the students

GUALEGUAYCHÚ

themselves, are paraded around the streets. During the rest of the year – with the
exception of long weekends, when it still attracts revellers from Buenos Aires –
Gualeguaychú is a tranquil town with some handsome old buildings in the streets
surrounding its main square, **Plaza San Martín**, and a pleasant *costanera* (its riverfront
on the **Río Gualeguaychú**, a tributary of the Uruguay).

Casa de Haedo

Rivadavia and San José • Wed–Fri 9am–noon & 3.30–6.30pm, Sat 9am–noon & 4–7pm • $10 • 📞 03446 432643

The main site of interest on central Plaza San Martín is the **Casa de Haedo**; officially
Gualeguaychú's oldest building, it dates from around 1808. Built in a primitive
colonial style, the simple whitewashed building opens onto a garden of grapevines
and orchids. Inside, the handful of tiny wood-floored rooms are filled with original
furniture and objects belonging to the Haedos, one of Gualeguaychú's early
patrician families. Among other exhibits, there's a beautiful Spanish representation
of the Virgen del Carmen, made of silver and real hair, and a number of fine pieces
of French porcelain. The house is also notable for having been the temporary home
of Italian hero Giuseppe Garibaldi in 1845, when he ransacked Gualeguaychú for
funds and provisions to assist General Oribe, who was under siege in Montevideo.
Spanish labels only.

Costanera J.J. de Urquiza

Museo Ferroviario Maestra Piccini and Maipú • Mon–Fri 8am–noon & 1–4pm, Sat 8am–noon & 2–6pm, Sun 2–6pm • Free •
📞 03446 437034

The **Costanera J.J. de Urquiza**, quiet during the day and out of season, heaves with life
on summer evenings, when locals and tourists indulge in the obligatory evening stroll
or simply while away the hours on a bench, sipping a *mate*. The southern end of the
Costanera leads to the **old port**, and if you head down this way just before the October
desfile de carrozas (float parade) you will come across scenes of frenetic activity as
students – many of whom barely sleep for the last few days – put the finishing touches
to their floats, which are assembled in huge riverside warehouses. The port was the
termination point for the old railway tracks, which reached Gualeguaychú in 1873. If
you follow the river round to Avenida Parque and walk another 1km, you will come to

4

THE NATION'S CARNIVAL

Gualeguaychú's carnival – officially **Carnaval del País Gualeguaychú** – usually runs from early January to the first weekend in March, with the main events taking place every Saturday at the **Corsódromo** on Ayacucho; it's South America's second-biggest purpose-built carnival stadium (after Rio de Janeiro's), where almost 40,000 spectators pile in to watch Gualeguaychú's *comparsas*, or processions. Though not as spectacular as Rio's carnival, the processions here are well worth experiencing – a huge effort is put into the colourful, skimpy costumes, loud music and thematic floats, and the crowd is always extremely enthusiastic. Compared with Brazilian carnivals the safety levels are far higher, too. Tickets for the main grandstand can be bought at the Corsódromo ticket office (Maestra Piccini 1000 and Ayacucho; daily 9am–9pm; ☎03446 423936, ⓦcarnavaldelpais.com.ar), at special outlets on the Costanera and at the bus terminal, or online (ⓦventas.carnavaldelpais.com.ar). Normal tickets vary in price from $30 to $260 depending on the day and seat location (more expensive VIP seats cost $800–2000).

the Corsódromo and the 1910 train station, now the open-air **Museo Ferroviario**, or railway museum, where an old steam locomotive is displayed along with other relics.

El Patio del Mate

Méndez 284 • Open daily until late • ☎03446 424371

Gualeguaychú's most original retail experience is provided by **El Patio del Mate** down by the Costanera: a shrine to *litoraleños'* most pervasive habit, it sells *mates* carved out of every material imaginable – from simple and functional calabazas or gourds (generally regarded as the best material for *mates*) to elaborate combinations of hoof and hide, best described as gaucho kitsch.

ARRIVAL AND INFORMATION

GUALEGUAYCHÚ

By bus Gualeguaychú's bus terminal (☎03446 427987) is at the corner of Blvd Pedro Jurado and Av General Artigas, 2km from the centre – taxis into town cost $50–70.

Destinations Buenos Aires (hourly; 3hr 30min); Colón (10 daily; 1hr 45min–2hr 20min); Corrientes (3 daily; 10hr 25min–14hr 30min); Montevideo, Uruguay (1 daily; 6hr 20min); Paraná (7 daily; 4hr 20min–6hr); Posadas (2 daily; 10hr 45min); Rosario (2 daily; 4hr 10min–5hr 15min); Victoria (6 daily; 2hr 30min–4hr).

Tourist information Tourist information is available at

the bus terminal (daily 8am–8pm; Dec–March Sun–Thurs 8am–10pm, Fri & Sat 8am–midnight; ☎03446 440706), but the main tourist office (same hours; ☎03446 423668, ⓦgualeguaychuturismo.com) is on the Paseo del Puerto, down by the river. The staff offer information on excursions on the Río Gualeguaychú – such as regular catamaran trips and kayak rental – and on the *jineteadas*, or rodeo events, held in the vicinity throughout the year. There's also a smaller office at 25 de Mayo 718 (Mon–Sat 8am–2pm; ☎03446 437062).

ACCOMMODATION

You'll need to book in advance if you plan to stay during Carnaval, and probably on long weekends, too, when most places also raise their prices. At these times, a number of impromptu notices spring up around town offering rooms to rent. There are numerous **campsites** in Gualeguaychú and the surrounding area; most are along the banks of the Río Gualeguaychú, or out towards the Río Uruguay. All the recommendations below include free wi-fi and breakfast, excluding campsites.

Aguaý Costanera Morrogh Bernard 130 ☎03446 422099, ⓦhotelaguay.com.ar. Swish, modern hotel with top-floor swimming pool and *confitería* overlooking the river, and a reliable ground-floor restaurant that specializes in fish dishes. Spacious, bright rooms all have river-view balconies. **$950**

Balneario Camping Ñandubaysal 15km east of town by RP-42 ☎011 6841 0477, ⓦnandubaysal.com.

Located on the banks of the Río Uruguay, this is an extensive campsite forested with *ñandubay*, a thorny plant typical of the region whose fruit is a favourite of the ñandú (rhea or South American ostrich) – hence the name. **$150**

Buddha Hostel Urquiza 180 ☎03446 431352, ⓦbuddhahostel.com.ar. One of the best of several hostels in town close to the river, with six-bed, ten-bed and

fourteen-bed mixed dorms (clean, with wood-frame bunks). **$185**
Hostel Yinyang Courtet 35 ☎03446 548655. Budget option worth considering, though it is 5km from the river (off Urquiza, on the western edge of town). Cosy dorms, shared kitchen and tranquil garden. **$195**

Puerto Sol San Lorenzo 477 ☎03446 434017, ⓦhotelpuertosol.com.ar. This friendly hotel has comfortable rooms, some looking onto the hotel's interior patio. You can also be taken across the river by boat to the hotel's private section of the Isla Libertad, opposite, for quiet relaxation and a drink. **$820**

EATING

In terms of eating, at least, Gualeguaychú is a town with a split personality – in the summer (Dec–March) all life is centred on the Costanera, which is lined with bars and *parrillas* specializing in freshwater fish, while the rest of the year the action gravitates to the town centre, around 25 de Mayo.

Dacal Andrade, at the Costanera ☎03446 427602. Wonderfully retro and pleasingly reliable since 1962, this classic Costanera *parrilla* has a wide-ranging menu featuring river fish (*surubí* dishes $90–158), pastas ($78–110) and all the usual grilled meats ($86–140). Daily noon–4pm & 8pm–late.
La Paisanita 25 de Mayo 1176 ☎03446 434112. This down-to-earth place is extremely popular with locals for

its *parrilla* and pasta dishes. Daily noon–4pm & 8pm–12.30am.
Terraza Café Costanera and Méndez ☎03446 429373. Contemporary café right on the riverside, with tables overlooking the water or inside (with a/c) – decent coffee, pastries and light snacks. Sun–Thurs 8am–midnight, Fri & Sat 8am–3am.

Colón

Thanks to its tranquil riverside setting, with cobbled or gravel streets and excellent hotels and restaurants, **COLÓN** is easily the most appealing of Entre Ríos' river and thermal spa resorts – it's at the centre of a 14km strip of beaches that attracts hordes of Porteños, up for the weekend, and Uruguayans, who travel across the Puente Internacional General Artigas from Paysandú. It also makes a good base for visiting the wonderfully exotic-looking **Parque Nacional El Palmar**, 60km north, or the grand, European-style **Palacio San José**, about 60km southwest. Every February Colón also hosts an important craft fair, the **Fiesta Nacional de la Artesanía**, with over five hundred exhibitors from Argentina and further afield. The rest of the year, there's no shortage of stores selling **artisan goods** ranging from *mates* and *asado* tableware to local cheese and salami.

Colón spreads along the Río Uruguay, with a narrow strip of beach running for several kilometres alongside its alluring riverside avenue, the **Costanera Gobernador Quirós**. The town's central square, **Plaza Washington**, is twinned with **Plaza Artigas** and together they cover four leafy blocks, ten blocks inland from the riverside; far more elegant and closer to the Río Uruguay, however, is **Plaza San Martín**, east of Plaza Washington along Colón's main commercial street, Avenida 12 de Abril – named after the town's foundation date in 1863.

Termas Colón and Termas Villa Elisa

Termas Colón, Cepeda and Belgrano • Daily 9am–8pm • $130 • ☎03447 424717, ⓦtermascolon.gov.ar • Termas Villa Elisa, RN-130 Km20 • Daily 8am–10pm • $230; parking $30 • ☎03447 480687, ⓦtermasvillaelisa.com

Although there's the simple **Termas Colón** thermal spa complex in town, if you have wheels a better place for a relaxing, therapeutic soak is at **Termas Villa Elisa**, 30km to the northwest. This huge, spacious, state-of-the-art thermal complex has seven pools with mineral waters especially good for sufferers of rheumatism, with massages and refreshments available.

Museo Provincial Molino Forclaz

RP-26 Km3 • Jan & Feb daily 10am–1pm & 5–8pm; March–June & Aug–Dec Mon, Tues, Thurs & Fri 10am–1pm, Sat & Sun 10am–5pm; July daily 10am–5pm • $15 • ☎03447 15 453551, ⓦmolinoforclaz.com.ar

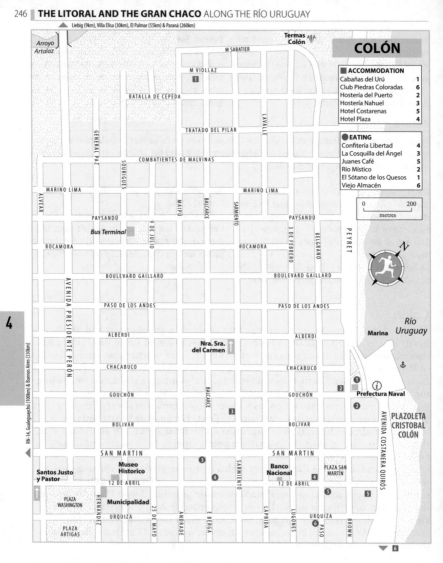

▲ Liebig (9km), Villa Elisa (30km), El Palmar (55km) & Paraná (260km)

COLÓN

ACCOMMODATION

Cabañas del Urú	1
Club Piedras Coloradas	6
Hostería del Puerto	2
Hostería Nahuel	3
Hotel Costarenas	5
Hotel Plaza	4

● EATING

Confitería Libertad	4
La Cosquilla del Ángel	3
Juanes Café	5
Río Místico	2
El Sótano de los Quesos	1
Viejo Almacén	6

Just outside town, the **Museo Provincial Molino Forclaz** preserves the fascinating remains of an old mill, built between 1888 and 1890 by Swiss immigrant Juan Forclaz. The Dutch-style windmill (now bladeless) was designed to grind wheat and corn, and the museum preserves its elaborate machinery and provides background to the community of Swiss settlers in the region.

ARRIVAL AND DEPARTURE

COLÓN AND AROUND

By bus Colón's bus terminal lies fifteen blocks or so northwest of Plaza San Martín, on the corner of Paysandú and Sourigues. There's a café and small tourist information booth, but no ATM. Taxis anywhere in town cost $40–60.

Destinations Buenos Aires (hourly; 4hr 35min–5hr 30min); Corrientes (2 daily; 9hr 35min–11hr); Gualeguaychú (10 daily; 1hr 45min–2hr 20min); Montevideo, Uruguay (2 daily; 6hr); Paraná (6 daily; 3hr 45min–4hr); Rosario (4 daily; 5hr–5hr 25min).

COLÓN'S UNIQUE WINERY

In defiance of Colón's subtropical climate, usually regarded as totally hostile to wine grapes, in 1857 a Swiss immigrant named **Joseph Favre** planted a few **vines** from his homeland just outside the city. Seventeen years later, with his vines not only succeeding, but thriving, he added a handsome **bodega** (winery) in the Piedmontese style – an Italianate villa with ochre walls that would not look out of place in the countryside around Turin. In 1936, the national government banned the commercial production of wine anywhere outside the Cuyo and the Andean Northwest, but Favre's descendants continued making wine for their own consumption. When the law was finally repealed in 1997, Jesús Vulliez, a local descendant of other Swiss immigrants, bought the nineteenth-century bodega and began producing wine for commercial distribution under the label **Bodega Vulliez-Sermet**, planting twelve acres with chardonnay, malbec, merlot, cabernet sauvignon, tannat, syrah and sangiovese vines. If you call ahead, you can tour the beautiful bodega (guided tours daily 11am; 45min; Spanish only), with its impeccably restored interior and cool cellars, and taste the fine red and white wines. The attractive grounds nearby house a large swimming pool and three luxurious **cabañas** sleeping up to six (☏03447 15 645925, ⊛bodegavulliezsermet.com.ar; $1100). To reach the complex from RN-14, take RP-135 Colón–Paysandú road and stay on it for another 200m after the turn-off to Colón.

INFORMATION AND TOURS

Tourist information The tourist office (Av Costanera and Gouchón; daily: high season 7am–9pm, low season 8am–8pm; ☏03447 421233, ⊛colonturismo.net) is in the attractive 1927 Estación Fluvial on the waterfront, two blocks north of Plaza San Martín. It provides useful accommodation information, plus details of the sights around Colón and ways of exploring the river. There's also a small booth in the bus terminal (nominally open daily 8am–7pm; ☏03447 421716).

Tours Excursions to the lush islands in the middle of the Río Uruguay offer opportunities for observing local flora and fauna, especially birdlife, and for sunbathing on a private beach. Trips via motorized dinghies (1–3hr; take sunscreen, swimwear, insect repellent and a jumper on cool evenings; US$20–35) are operated by Ita-i-Corá (☏03447 423360), a wonderfully dynamic outfit whose larger-than-life co-owner, Charlie Adamson, speaks excellent English. Its office is at San Martín 97, on the corner of Plaza San Martín (daily 9am–12.30pm & 3–7.30pm).

ACCOMMODATION

Colón has a fine range of accommodation at all budget levels, though it does become severely overstretched on summer weekends, when bookings should be made weeks ahead. There are also plenty of **campsites**, spread out along the length of Colón's waterfront – if you're looking for something quieter and more rustic, go as far away from the town centre as possible. The recommendations below all include free wi-fi and breakfast.

Cabañas del Urú Mauricio Viollaz 330 ☏03447 424029, ⊛cabaniasdeluru.com.ar. Thatched *cabañas* for 2–6 people, 1.2km north of the centre (500m from the river). Well-appointed "rustic chic" (with cable TV and a/c) and in a quiet, away-from-it-all location, but a shame they are crammed into a tiny garden with an equally small pool. Wi-fi in special zones only. Cash only. **$1050**

Club Piedras Coloradas Juan José Paso and Ansaldi (Costanera) ☏03447 423548, ⊛clubpiedrascoloradas .com. Campsite at the southern edge of the centre, overlooking the river; it has volleyball and basketball courts plus the usual facilities. The site is very well organized but it might be too noisy for many campers – it gets mobbed in summer. Note that camping has a $60 surcharge/person. You can also rent small camper vans for $300/day, plus $30/adult. Per tent **$50**

Hostería del Puerto Alejo Peyret 158 ☏03447 422698, ⊛hosteriadecolon.com.ar. This hotel, housed in a pink colonial building just one block from the port, has a refreshing swimming pool and mostly large, attractively decorated rooms arranged around a central courtyard with an unusual well; some rooms have a river view, but try to avoid the noisy street-side ones. **$870**

Hostería Nahuel Sarmiento 136 ☏03447 422110, ⊛nahuelhosteria.com.ar. This relatively new hotel has clean, stylish rooms (with cable TV and a/c), free parking and very helpful staff. **$600**

Hotel Costarenas Av Quirós and 12 de Abril ☏03447 425050, ⊛hotelcostarenas.com.ar. Undoubtedly Colón's most luxurious hotel, enjoying a prime location overlooking the river (note that the cheapest rooms are small, and have no view). The spa is enticing, the indoor pool a mini-oasis,

4

the gym functional and the restaurant bright and efficient. All rooms are tastefully decorated, though the place lacks character. **$1110**

Hotel Plaza Belgrano and 12 de Abril ☎ 03447 421043, ⓦ hotel-plaza.com.ar. A hotel with an older side, in existence since 1913, offering small, fairly run-of-the-mill but perfectly acceptable rooms, and a newer part with much larger, smartly furnished rooms with LCD TVs and private jacuzzis – for rather higher rates (from $1180). All guests can use the outdoor pool and jacuzzi. **$980**

EATING

Confitería Libertad 12 de Abril 293 ☎ 03447 421004. Get your fix of nostalgia at this old-school bar and café from 1927, with original counter, antique coffee machines and local old boys chatting with the owner. Daily 7am–midnight.

La Cosquilla del Ángel San Martín 304 ☎ 03447 42371. Bright, trendy spot serving contemporary Argentine food, with the home-made breads, gourmet pizzas, tapas, pastas and freshwater fish all excellent. Mon noon–4pm, Wed–Sun noon–midnight.

Juanes Café 12 de Abril and J.J. Paso ☎ 03447 421942. Perfect location on Plaza San Martín, with tasty (if slightly pricey) snacks, sandwiches ($8) and coffee ($20–30). Daily 7am–1am.

Río Místico Gouchón 28 ☎ 03447 425179. Not your typical riverside restaurant; though *Místico* does serve grilled local river fish and decent steaks, what makes it stand apart is the vast selection of craft beers and microbrews on offer (around 32), many of them Argentine and from the Litoral. Daily 8am–1am.

El Sótano de los Quesos Pasaje 29 de Octubre and Peyret, ☎ 03447 427163, ⓦ elsotanodelosquesos.com .ar. Long-standing spot on the waterfront in a building from 1876, with rustic wooden tables outside, and a massive selection of cheese, sausages, cold cuts, beers and wines. Daily 5pm–midnight.

★ **Viejo Almacén** Urquiza 108 at J.J. Paso ☎ 03447 422216. An excellent choice, one block southeast of Plaza San Martín, this stylishly old-fashioned place specializes in excellent river fish – try the grilled *surubí* or *pacú*. Mains $97–205. Daily noon–4pm & 8pm–late.

Palacio San José

RP-39 Km128 (60km southwest of Colón) • Mon–Fri 8am–7.30pm, Sat & Sun 9am–6.30pm; Jan & Feb also Fri 9pm–12.30am • Guided visits (Spanish) 10am, 11am, 3pm & 4pm, plus noon & 2pm at weekends; 1hr • $20 • ☎ 03442 432620, ⓦ palaciosanjose.com

When it was built in the middle of the nineteenth century for local hero General Justo José de Urquiza, the **Palacio San José** was Argentina's most luxurious private residence. *Caudillo* of Entre Ríos Province in the early nineteenth century and its governor from 1841, Urquiza was also the province's largest and wealthiest landowner, possessing a huge *saladero* (meat-salting plant). Restrictions imposed by Buenos Aires on the provinces' freedom to trade led Urquiza to revolt against dictator General Rosas, finally defeating him at the Battle of Caseros, outside Buenos Aires, in 1853. The lavishness of the palace seems clearly intended as a challenge to the Buenos Aires elite's idea of provincial backwardness – it had running water before any building in the capital. The architect was Pedro Fosatti – who also designed the Italian hospitals in Buenos Aires and Montevideo – and, despite the colonial watchtowers that dominate its facade, it shows a strong Italian influence in its elegant Tuscan arches.

The entrance to the palace is at the back of the building, now painted the deep pink of national monuments; to your right as you enter stands a tiny **chapel** lined with spectacular frescoes by nineteenth-century Uruguayan academic painter Juan Manuel Blanes and an imposing 3m-high baptismal font, entirely carved from Carrara marble, a gift from Pope Pius IX (who kept a copy in the Vatican). The palace's 38 rooms are laid out around two vast courtyards. The first of these, the **Patio del Parral**, is named for its grapevines, many of which were brought for Urquiza from France. The rooms in the second courtyard, the **Patio de Honor**, were occupied by Urquiza's most immediate family and important guests. Its most significant room is the dramatically named **Sala de la Tragedia** (Room of Tragedy), Urquiza's bedroom, where, on April 11, 1870, he was assassinated by followers of rival *caudillo* López Jordán. It was turned into a shrine by Urquiza's widow, and traces of blood can still be seen on the door, along with bullets embedded in the wall. Beyond the Patio de Honor extends a small French-style **garden**, from where the Palacio's harmonious facade appears to best advantage.

YAPEYÚ: LAND OF THE LIBERATOR

Celebrated as national hero not just in Argentina but across South America, **José de San Martín** (see p.225) was born in 1778 in the small town of **Yapeyú**, just off RN-14 on the Río Uruguay, some 400km north of Colón. Today the relatively humble ruins of the house in which he was born are preserved within a much grander edifice known as the **Templete**, raised in 1938 (daily 8am–noon & 2–4pm; free; ☎03772 493013) and protected by ceremonial guards; an urn containing the ashes of San Martín's father is also displayed here. The nearby Museo Sanmartiniano (daily 8am–8pm; free) contains assorted **San Martín** memorabilia. Buses connect Yapeyú with **Posadas** (1 daily; 4hr 30min) and **Colón** (1 daily; 5hr).

ARRIVAL AND TOURS

By bus and taxi There is no public transport; take a bus from Colón to Concepción del Uruguay (every 30min; 45min–1hr) then a *remís* (around $250, including wait time) from there. Try Acción (☎03442 427777) or Servi Mas (☎03442 428888). Alternatively, take any Rosario or

PALACIO SAN JOSÉ

Paraná bus from Concepción and ask to get out at Caseros, some 8km from the *palacio*, and take a taxi from there ($70–100). Buses also connect Concepción with Gualeguaychú (11 daily; 1hr 10min).

Parque Nacional El Palmar

RN-14 Km199 (45km north of Colón). There is a *guardaparques*' post at the entrance where you pay and pick up a map • Daily 8am–6pm • $120 • ☎03447 493053 • It's a 10km walk from the entrance to the interpretation centre and campsite, though it should be possible to get a lift with someone entering the park. There are also organized trips – usually half-day tours – from Colón

As you head north from Colón along RN-14, the first sign that you are approaching **PARQUE NACIONAL EL PALMAR** is a sprinkling of tremendously tall palm trees towering above the flat lands that border the highway. The 85-square-kilometre park was set up in 1966 to conserve groves of the **yatay palm**, which once covered large areas of Entre Ríos Province, Uruguay and southern Brazil. Intensive cultivation of the region almost wiped out the palm, and the national park is now the largest remaining reserve of the *yatay*; it is also one of the southernmost palm groves in the world. Though the terrain itself is nondescript rolling grassland, the sheer proliferation of the majestic *yatay* – with many examples over three hundred years old and up to 18m in height – makes for a wonderfully exotic-looking landscape. The park is best appreciated with an overnight stay – the extensive acres of palm forest are absolutely stunning in the late afternoon light, when their exotic forms stand out against the deepening blue sky and reddish gold of the earth.

There are a number of well-signposted trails in the park, taking you along the streams and through palm forests; the longer of these are designed for vehicles, though if you don't mind trekking along several kilometres of gravel road, there's nothing to stop you from doing them on foot. There are great views from **La Glorieta**, a gentle bluff from where you can take in the surrounding sea of palms. Wildlife in the park includes ñandús, armadillos, foxes and capybaras and, particularly around the campsite, *vizcachas* and monitor lizards.

ACCOMMODATION

PARQUE NACIONAL EL PALMAR

Aurora del Palmar RN-14 Km202 ☎03447 15 431689, ⌨auroradelpalmar.com.ar. Just outside the park, well back from the highway, this is an ecology-focused complex set in a mini-grove of *yatay* palms, with a collection of disused train carriages that have been converted into accommodation for up to four people ($1800); there are also more spacious rooms in a colonial-style building nearby, overlooking citrus orchards and a large swimming pool. Guests and non-guests can eat simple meals here and

go on excursions such as horse rides, canoe trips, birdwatching and treks into the park. **$1450**

Camping El Palmar ☎03447 423378, ⌨campingelpalmar.com.ar. The only place to stay inside the park is a spacious and shady campsite with showers and a provisions store; the best pitches have a great view over the Río Uruguay. There is also a decent restaurant in the park (open to all visitors), next door to the interpretation centre. **$80**

4

Misiones Province

The proboscis-shaped territory of **Misiones**, in the extreme northeast of the country, is one of Argentina's smallest, poorest but most beautiful provinces, and has a lot more to offer than the juggernaut that is **Iguazú Falls**, the only place most visitors ever see. What looks odd on the map makes perfect sense on the ground: Misiones' borders are almost completely defined by the wide Paraná and Uruguay rivers. The province's distinctive iron-rich **red earth** ends abruptly just over the border with Corrientes, while the torrent of water that hurtles over the waterfalls at Iguazú must surely mark one of the world's most dramatic and decisive frontiers. Along the Brazilian border, formed by the upper reaches of the Río Uruguay, you can see one of the world's most unusual – if not most powerful – sets of cascades, the **Saltos del Moconá**, weather conditions permitting.

The territory was named for the Jesuit settlements that flourished in the region in the seventeenth and eighteenth centuries; the most impressive mission on Argentine soil is the much-photographed ruin of **San Ignacio Miní**. Misiones became a centre of considerable immigration in the early twentieth century: mostly Ukrainians, Swedes, Japanese and Germans. The province's wildlife-filled **jungle** and its emerald fields and orchards – pale tobacco, vivid lime trees, darker manioc and neatly clipped tea plantations, painting the landscape endless shades of green – are further attractions that make wandering off the beaten tracks of RN-12 and RN-14 infinitely rewarding.

Posadas

4

The steamy, blisteringly hot capital of Misiones, **POSADAS** is a large, sprawling city on the Río Paraná, connected to the city of Encarnacíon in Paraguay via the 2.55km-long Puente Roque González de Santa Cruz. Though it's primarily just a gateway to the more rustic delights of Misiones, the city is a pleasant and prosperous place with a lively feel, some attractive buildings tucked away among the centre's mostly modern constructions, and a revamped **Costanera**, a wonderful place for a stroll or cold drink on a summer's evening. The town also hosts a lively provincial festival, known as the **Estudiantina**, which runs over three weekends in September. During the festival local schools prepare and perform dance routines – all with a strong Brazilian influence.

The historic centre of Posadas is relatively compact, though walking between the central **Plaza 9 de Julio** and the Costanera can be sweaty work in summer. The city's **commercial centre** is concentrated on the streets west of the plaza, with pedestrianized **Calle Bolívar** in particular forming the hub of the clothes shops that make up much of the town's retail activity.

Brief history

The first recorded European presence in the vicinity of modern-day Posadas was a **Jesuit mission** to the local Guaraní, founded in 1615, but the settlement

---

GUARANÍ: VESTIGES OF INDIGENOUS CULTURE IN THE LITORAL

As in parts of neighbouring Corrientes Province, a strong **Guaraní** influence remains in Misiones (known as Tapé or Guayrá in the native tongue), thanks to around 100 small pre-European communities scattered throughout the territory (with around 9000 "pure" **Guaraní**, primarily descendants of those who never moved into the Jesuit missions). Though these communities keep largely to themselves, their influence is echoed above all in the speech of inhabitants in rural areas, where you'll frequently hear a mix of Guaraní and Spanish. Throughout the Litoral, even in urban districts, Guaraní words are a common feature of speech: for example, you may hear a child referred to as a "*gurí*" or a woman as a "*guaina*". Toponyms like San Ignacio Miní, Iguazú, Moconá and Teyú Cuaré are all Guaraní.

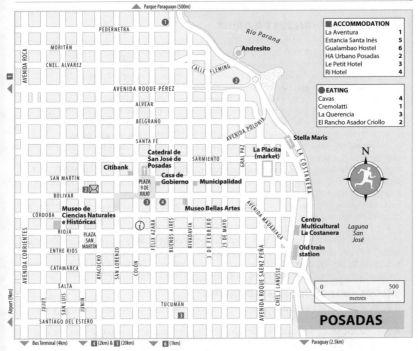

remained insignificant until the end of the Paraguayan War (see p.535). In 1879, the fledgling city was named after **José Gervasio de Posadas**, who, in 1814, had become the first Supreme Director of the Provincias Unidas del Río de la Plata – a title that rather outdid his reign, which lasted only until January of the following year. In 1884 Posadas, by far the most important settlement in the region, became Misiones' provincial capital. Since then it has largely been a quiet backwater, whose fortunes in recent years have been tied to the construction of a road link to Paraguay via the cable-stayed bridge (completed in 1990), its proximity to the massive **Yacyretá Dam** (built in 1994), and the opening of a commuter train to Encarnacíon across the bridge (2014), which has dramatically swelled the city's population.

Plaza 9 de Julio

Beautifully manicured **Plaza 9 de Julio** is flanked to the north by the **Catedral de San José de Posadas**, a two-towered edifice completed in 1937 by super-prolific Alejandro Bustillo, who designed Buenos Aires' Banco Nación, among many other buildings. The plaza's best-looking building, however, is the **Casa de Gobierno**, a pink Neoclassical palace (it's known as "La Rosadita"), completed in 1883.

Museo Municipal de Bellas Artes (Palacio de Mate)

Rivadavia 1846, two blocks east of Plaza 9 de Julio · Mon–Fri 8am–noon & 4–8pm, Sat 5–8pm · $15 · ☎ 0376 444 9074

The city's **Museo Municipal de Bellas Artes** occupies the rather grandly titled Palacio de Mate, with temporary exhibitions by local artists such as Lucas Braulio Areco and Marcos Otaño, alongside a permanent collection of small wooden carvings of laidback Chaco life by Juan de Dios Mena – look out for *Empleado Publico*, the "Public Employee", asleep, with his feet up on his desk. There's also a room of restored murals by René Brusau.

MATE: MORE THAN JUST A DRINK

The herby leaves used in making **mate**, Argentina's national beverage, come from an evergreen tree, *Ilex paraguayensis*, a member of the holly family that grows in northeastern Argentina, southern Brazil and Paraguay. Its leaves and buds are harvested with machetes in the dry southern winter (June–Aug) and used to make *yerba* or *mate*. The **preparation** process for good *yerba* is complex and subtle: first comes the *zapecado*, literally "opening of the eyes", when the *mate* leaves are dry-roasted over a fire, to prevent fermentation and keep the leaves green. They are then coarsely ground, bagged and left to mature in dry sheds for nine months to a year, though this is sometimes artificially accelerated to two months or even less. A milling process then results in either coarse *caá-guazú* "big herb", or the more refined *caá-mini*.

The **vessel** you drink it out of is also called a *mate*, or *matecito*, a hollowed-out gourd that is still used today and comes in two basic **shapes**: the pear-shaped *poro*, traditionally used for *mate* sweetened with sugar, and the squat, satsuma-shaped *galleta*, meant for *cimarrón*, literally "untamed", unsweetened *mate*. Many *mates* are **works of art**, intricately carved or painted, and often made of wood, clay or metal – though connoisseurs claim gourds impart extra flavour to the brew. The *bombilla* – originally a reed or stick of bamboo – is the other vital piece of equipment. Most are now straw-shaped tubes of silver, aluminium or tin, flattened at the end on which you suck, and with a spoon-shaped protuberance at the other; this is perforated to strain the *mate* as you drink it. Optional extras include the *pava hornillo*, a special kettle that keeps the water at the right temperature. A thermos flask is the modern-day substitute for this kettle, and can be replenished at shops and cafés; "hot water available" signs are a common sight all over Argentina, but especially in the Litoral.

THE DOS AND DON'TS OF MATE DRINKING

If you find yourself in a **group** drinking *mate*, it's just as well to know how to avoid gaffes. The *cebador* – from *cebar* "to feed" – is the person who makes the *mate*. After half-filling the *matecito* with *yerba*, the *cebador* thrusts the *bombilla* into the *yerba* and trickles very hot – but not boiling – water down the side of the *bombilla*, to wet the *yerba* from below. The *cebador* always tries the *mate* first – the "fool's *mate*" – before refilling and handing it round to each person present, in turn – always with the right hand and clockwise. Each drinker drains the *mate* through the *bombilla*, without jiggling it around, sipping gently but not lingering, or sucking too hard, before handing it back to the *cebador*. Sucking out of the corner of the mouth is also frowned upon. A little more *yerba* may be added from time to time, but there comes a moment when the *yerba* loses most of its flavour and no longer produces a healthy froth. The *matecito* is then emptied and the process started afresh. Saying *"gracias"* means you've had enough, and the *mate* will be passed to someone else when your turn comes round.

The Costanera

Posadas' **Costanera** is lined with monuments, bars, restaurants and lush mango trees, and is a lovely spot to watch the sunset or wonder about life in Encarnacíon, Paraguay, clearly visible on the opposite bank. It has been much improved in recent years, now running from the beach at **El Brete** all the way to the bridge, and is popular with joggers, dog-walkers and locals who like to set up deckchairs along the grassy banks in the evenings.

The halfway point is marked by a giant, 15m-high steel sculpture of a local Guaraní hero known as **Andresito**, aka Andrés Guazurarí (1778–1821), created in 2013 by local sculptor Gerónimo Rodríguez. Andresito was a general during the wars of independence in Misiones, and later became the adopted son of General Artigas. The southern section of the Costanera features the old train station of 1913 and the new **Centro Multicultural "La Costanera"** (Tues–Fri 8.30am–1pm & 4.30–8.30pm, Sat & Sun 4.30–8.30pm; ☎0376 440 9858), which hosts exhibitions of primarily local art.

Museo Regional Aníbal Cambas

Alberdi 600 (Parque República del Paraguay) • Mon–Fri 8am–noon & 3–7pm, Sat 9am–noon • Free • ☎0376 442 2860

Bordering Parque Paraguayo in the north of the city, the **Museo Regional Aníbal**

Cambas should reopen by the end of 2016 after a mammoth four-year renovation. The original handsome 1940 brick building will be enhanced with spacious galleries covering various aspects of local **history** and **ethnography**, such as objects culled from the ruins of Jesuit missions and artefacts produced by the region's indigenous populations: the Guayaquí, the Chiripá, the Mbyá and the Guaraní.

ARRIVAL AND INFORMATION

POSADAS

By plane The quiet airport (Aeropuerto de Posadas Libertador General San Martín) is around 7km southwest of the centre; bus #28 runs into town from here, or you could take a taxi. There are two daily flights to and from Buenos Aires (1hr 30min).

By train The Posadas–Encarnación International Train (⊕ sofse.gob.ar) is a commuter service that opened in 2014 to connect the Argentine and Paraguayan sides of the river (the line is 8km). Trains depart daily every 30min (7am–6.30pm) and take just 8min; you pass through immigration for both countries on the Argentine side only. Fares are $18 or 7000 Paraguayan guaranies one-way.

By bus Posadas' bus terminal (☎ 03752 454887) is about 4km south of the centre at the intersection of Av Santa

Catalina and RN-12. It's a modern building with good facilities, though no ATM. From the terminal there are numerous local buses (including #24, #25 and #21) heading into the centre (fares are $8; use bills or coins); the taxi ride will cost about $40 (all taxis should use meters).

Destinations Buenos Aires (hourly 5pm–midnight; 12–15hrs); Corrientes (9 daily; 4–5hrs); El Soberbio (7 daily; 5hr 15min); Puerto Iguazú (hourly; 5hr 30min); Resistencia (hourly; 4hr 30min–5hr 30min); Rosario (8 daily; 12–15hrs); San Ignacio (9 daily; 1hr).

Tourist information Posadas' well-stocked tourist office, at Colón 1985 (Mon–Fri 7am–8pm, Sat & Sun 8am–noon & 4.30–8pm; ☎ 03752 447539, ⊕ posadas.gov.ar), has fairly decent maps of both the town and the province.

ACCOMMODATION

Posadas can be extremely hot and sticky during the summer, so you'll need air conditioning. Alternatively, if you have your own transport, consider staying at one of the excellent **estancias** in the surrounding countryside, where you can get to know the locals and enjoy the province's flora and fauna; booking ahead is vital. The recommendations below include breakfast.

★**La Aventura** Zapiola 965 and Urquiza ☎ 0376 446 5555, ⊕ complejolaaventura.com; buses #3 and #13 go from the corner of San Lorenzo and Sarmiento. Swish holiday complex on the outskirts of town, complete with good recreational facilities – including tennis courts and a swimming pool. Choice of plush cabins (2–7 people) and cheaper hotel rooms with cable TV and a/c. Doubles $780; cabins $1480

★**Estancia Santa Inés** RN-105 Km8.5 (20km southeast of Posadas) ☎ 0376 15 466 0456, ⊕ estancia-santaines.com.ar. With marvellous, old-fashioned rooms displaying a fantastic collection of silver *mate* paraphernalia, the estancia's trump card is its exotic setting within a mini-jungle of luxuriant vegetation. You can ride through the *mate* plantations to the huge outdoor pool 5km away, fed by a natural spring, or visit the family's

---

A TASTE OF PARAGUAY: STREET SNACKS, SOUPS AND MATE

The food you find around Argentina is remarkably homogeneous for such a huge country. However, there are **regional variations** that reflect the culinary influence of neighbouring nations more than most Argentines realize or care to admit. The most notable of these cross-border gastronomic influences can be found in the northern reaches bordering **Paraguay**. In the Chaco, northern Corrientes and much of Misiones you will find dishes that are part of the staple diet in Asunción and the rest of Paraguay. **Chipás** – savoury cheese-flavoured lumps of manioc-flour dough – are extremely popular snacks sold on the street, served in restaurants instead of bread and cooked in people's homes. **Sopa paraguaya** is actually not a soup at all, but a hearty maize and cheese dish, said to have been invented during the War of the Triple Alliance, when the beleaguered Paraguayan soldiers needed more sustenance than was provided by their traditional chicken broth, so army cooks thickened it with corn flour. **Borí borí**, on the other hand, *is* a soup, made from chicken, with little balls of maize and cheese floating in it. Last but not least, **tereré**, or cold *mate*, made with iced water or orange juice, is hugely popular in Paraguay, but can also be tasted in the borderlands of northeast Argentina, and is wonderfully refreshing on a hot summer's day.

private chapel, containing handsome Jesuit carvings. No internet access. Cash only. **$4640**

Gualambao Hostel Juan Ambrosetti 1655 ☎ 0376 495 7101, ⊚ gualambaohostel.com.ar. This is just about the cheapest recommendable place in the centre of town: a friendly hostel with clean, small bunk-bed dorms and en-suite doubles, all with a/c, plus shared kitchen. Dorms **$155**; doubles **$360**

HA Urbano Posadas Bolívar 2176 ☎ 0376 444 3800, ⊚ alvarezarguelles.com. Modern, fairly standard business hotel in the centre that offers dependably comfortable rooms with flat-screen TVs and a/c, plus pool and gym. Parking is $15/day and a block away. **$910**

Le Petit Hotel Santiago del Estero 1630 ☎ 0376 443 6031, ⊚ hotellepetit.com.ar. On a quiet, tree-lined street away from the centre, this small, prettily decorated place has simple but adequate rooms with TV and a/c. The friendly owner is also a good source of tourist information. Reservations advisable. **$500**

Ri Hotel Suiza 2051 and Yerbal ☎ 03764 455355, ⊚ rihotelposadas.com. Small hotel offering great value, with simple but cosy apartments featuring bedroom, bathroom and kitchenette, plus a/c and satellite TV. **$530**

EATING

Cavas Bolívar 729 ☎ 0376 443 5514. Formal, contemporary restaurant in the centre, with a selection of local fish (*surubí*) but also decent salmon, substantial salads and chicken dishes in addition to the usual steaks. Daily noon–3pm & 7.30pm–midnight.

★**Cremolatti** Alfonso de Arrechea 892 ☎ 0376 442 1262, ⊚ cremolatti.com.ar. Set just behind the Costanera, this little chain doles out exceptional ice cream in cones or cups (1 scoop $30; 3 scoops $45), with seating on the wooden deck or inside with the a/c. Highlights include the coconut, chocolate and almond flavours. Daily noon–midnight.

La Querencia Bolívar 1849 (Plaza 9 de Julio) ☎ 0376 443 3550, ⊚ laquerenciarestaurante.com. A bustling place with old-school waiters right on the main plaza (in the elegant 1927 Societa Italiana building) that's a surprisingly good deal, particularly as you can easily share some of the dishes. Try the juicy *bife de chorizo* – shipped in from Buenos Aires Province, as local beef is of poorer quality – accompanied by fried manioc for a local touch, or go for the excellent *galetos*, a kind of chicken and vegetable kebab. Mains $140–160. Mon–Sat noon–2.30pm & 8pm–12.30am, Sun noon–2.30pm.

★**El Rancho Asador Criollo** Roque Perez and Bajada Vieja ☎ 0376 442 1666. Modern and stylish *parrilla* right on the Costanera, with great views. It's best for a decent steak and wine, or just a cold beer and live music on a Friday night. Tues–Sun 11.45am–2pm & 7.45pm–1am.

The Jesuit missions

One of the most remarkable episodes in South American history, the creation of **Jesuit missions** in the heart of Guaraní territory in the seventeenth century represents a two-hundred-year experiment in social engineering. They sparked a flowering of wonderful artistic talent and thriving commerce, but ultimately collapsed in tragedy, a series of events memorably fictionalized in the 1986 film *The Mission*. The movie created a surge of interest in the mission ruins north of Posadas (but also in Brazil and Paraguay), a region that was effectively independent until Spain and Portugal brought it under control in the late eighteenth century.

The largest, **San Ignacio Miní**, is also the best preserved in the whole region. Far less well maintained – and much less visited – are the ruins of **Santa Ana** and **Loreto**, south of San Ignacio; these crumbling monuments, set amid thick jungle vegetation, are less dramatic but appealing if only because they attract fewer visitors. All three missions can be visited on a day-trip from Posadas, though it's well worth spending a night in San

---

VISITING THE MISSIONS

If you have your own transport, visiting all the missions should be no problem – the main three are well signed off RN-12, and the link roads are surfaced and in good condition. Travelling by bus, the easiest target is **San Ignacio**; while **Santa Ana** is also possible, **Loreto** is too far off the main road to make it a realistic stop. You'll need your own transport to see **Santa María la Mayor**, which lies just off RP-2 near the village of Santa María (23km east of Concepción de la Sierra), a 2hr drive from Posadas.

Ignacio, visiting the ruins in the morning – the best time for photographs, when the low light enhances the buildings' deep reddish hues – and again at night. The fourth set of Argentine ruins at **Santa María la Mayor** (entry included with tickets to the other missions) is 120km southwest of Posadas, and is for diehards only.

Santa Ana

Daily: April–Oct 7am–6pm; Nov–March 7am–7pm • Admission $150 (includes entry to all 4 Argentine missions, valid for 15 days) • Approximately 40km from Posadas via RN-12; a signposted, surfaced road just south of Santa Ana village (on the right) leads to the entrance; bus stop is further along RN-12 in the village, a 2km walk from the site (flag down buses)

Originally founded in the Tapé region in 1633, the **Santa Ana** mission was transferred, with a population of two thousand Guaraní, to its present site after the *bandeirante* attacks of 1660 (see box opposite). Like all the *reducciones*, Santa Ana is centred on a large square, to the south of which stand the crumbling walls of what was once one of the finest of all Jesuit churches (80m long), built by the Italian architect Brazanelli, whose body was buried underneath the high altar. A lot of work has been carried out on the site, yet the roots and branches of trees are still entangled in the reddish sandstone of the buildings around the plaza, offering a glimpse of the way the ruins must have appeared when they were rediscovered in the late nineteenth century. North of the church, on the site of the original orchard, you can still make out the channels from the *reducción*'s sophisticated irrigation system. The single-room **museum** (same hours) at the entrance contains a few items found on site (tiles, ceramics, iron nails), and a scale model of how it might have looked. Ask here for an English-speaking **guide** (free).

Nuestra Señora de Loreto

April–Oct daily 7am–6pm; Nov–March daily 7am–7pm • Admission $150 (includes entry to all four Argentine missions, valid for 15 days) • Around 6km north of Santa Ana via RN-12; look for turning to Loreto village on the right, and drive a further 3km on surfaced road (no public transport)

The ruins of the **Nuestra Señora de Loreto** mission are even wilder than those of Santa Ana. This site, founded in 1632, was one of the most important of all the Jesuit missions, housing six thousand Guaraní by 1733 and noted not only for its production of cloth and *yerba mate* but also for having the missions' first printing press. Like Santa Ana, Loreto has a single-room **museum** at its entrance, with a scale model of the mission and a few items found on site (candlesticks, glass and the like). When you head out from the visitors' centre to the *reducción* itself, it's actually difficult at first to work out where the buildings are. After a while, though, you begin to see the walls and foundations of the settlement, heavily camouflaged by vegetation and lichen, and on which tall palms have managed, fantastically, to root themselves. Look out for the excavated latrines – site guides (you can ask for one at the entrance; free) proudly point out it's the only mission where these have been found.

San Ignacio

Considering it's home to such a major attraction, the grand Jesuit ruins of **San Ignacio Miní**, the small town of **SAN IGNACIO** is a remarkably low-key place – away from the restaurants and souvenir stands around the ruins themselves, it has little in the way of tourist facilities.

San Ignacio Miní

Around 16km north of Loreto via RN-12 (Alberdi) • $150 (includes entry to all four Argentine missions, valid for 15 days) • April–Oct daily 7am–6pm; Nov–March daily 7am–7pm • **Sound and light show** Daily; summer 8pm; rest of year 6pm • From the San Ignacio bus station walk along RN-12 for six blocks and turn left onto Alberdi, where you'll find the entrance to the site

The most famous of all the Jesuit missions, the ruins of **San Ignacio Miní** occupy six blocks at the northeastern end of San Ignacio. At the entrance, there's an illuminating **museum** with a series of themed rooms depicting various aspects of Guaraní and

THE JESUITS AND THEIR MISSIONS

The first Jesuit **missions** in Argentina were established in 1609, three decades after the order founded by San Ignacio de Loyola first arrived in the region. Though the Jesuits tried to evangelize to other parts of the country over the next 150 years, it was in the subtropical Upper Paraná where they had their greatest success. Known in Spanish as **reducciones**, these missions were largely self-sufficient settlements of indigenous Guaraní who lived and worked under the tutelage of a small number of Jesuit priests. Missions were initially established in three separate zones: the **Guayrá**, corresponding mainly to the modern Brazilian state of Paraná; the **Tapé**, corresponding to the southern Brazilian state of Río Grande do Sul, present-day Misiones Province and part of Corrientes Province; and the **Itatín**, lying between the Upper Paraná and the sierras to the north of the modern Paraguayan city of Concepción. In total, some thirty missions were established.

ENLIGHTENED SLAVE DRIVERS

If the Jesuits were essentially engaged in "civilizing" the area's indigenous inhabitants, they did at least have a particularly enlightened approach to their task – a marked contrast to the harsh methods of procuring native labour practised elsewhere in Latin America. Work was organized on a cooperative basis, with those who could not work provided for by the rest of the community. **Education** and culture also played an important part in mission life, with Guaraní taught to read and write not only in Spanish but also in Latin and Guaraní, and music and artisanship actively encouraged; however, coercion and violence were not unknown, and epidemics periodically ravaged these communities.

The early growth of the missions was impressive, but in 1660 *bandeirantes*, slave traders from São Paulo, attacked, destroying many of the missions, and carrying off their inhabitants, leading the Jesuits to seek more sheltered areas to the west, away from the Guayrá region in particular. The mission population soon recouped – and then surpassed – its former numbers, and also developed a strong standing **army**, making it one of the most powerful military forces in the region. Their most important crop proved to be *yerba mate*, which had previously been gathered from the wild but was now grown on plantations for export; other products sold by the missions included cattle and their hides, sugar, cotton, tobacco, textiles, ceramics and timber. They also exported musical instruments, notably harps and organs from the Reducción de Trinidad in Paraguay.

DECLINE AND FALL

By the end of the seventeenth century, the *reducciones* were among the most populous and successful areas of Argentina. By the 1730s, the larger missions such as Loreto (see opposite) had over six thousand inhabitants – second only to Buenos Aires. Nonetheless, the mission enterprise was beginning to show cracks: a rising number of smallpox epidemics depleted the population, and the Jesuits were becoming the subject of **political resentment**. Settlers in Paraguay and Corrientes were increasingly bitter at the Jesuit hold over the "supply" of Guaraní labour and domination of the market for *yerba mate* and tobacco. Simultaneously, the previous climate of Crown tolerance towards the missions' almost complete autonomy also began to change, with the Jesuits' power and loyalty questioned. Local enemies of the missions took advantage of this, claiming that the Jesuits were hiding valuable silver mines and that foreign Jesuit priests were agents of Spain's enemies. In 1750, Spain and Portugal signed the Treaty of Madrid, according to which Spain gave up its most easterly mission, precipitating the Guaraní War of 1756 (loosely portrayed in *The Mission*); thanks to considerable military resistance by the Jesuits and Guaraní, the treaty was later annulled. The victory proved a double-edged sword, however; the resistance against the Crown only reinforced their image as dangerous rebels and, following earlier expulsions in France, Portugal and Brazil, the Jesuits were **expelled from Argentina** in 1767. Though many of the missions continued to function, their Jesuit priests replaced with Franciscans, thousands of Guaraní returned to the jungle – by 1814 only eight thousand remained. Between 1816 and the 1820s, the now mostly empty Argentine missions were looted and burned by Portuguese/Brazilian and Paraguayan armies. Their magnificent buildings fell into disuse – lumps of stone were used for other constructions and the jungle did the rest – resulting in the ruins that can be visited today.

4

mission life, plus a detailed scale model of the entire *reducción*. Free, detailed guided tours in rapid-fire Spanish depart regularly from the museum – ask if there's an English-speaker (you may have to wait, but with little information around the site, it's worth it). There are also popular **sound and light shows** each evening.

The mission was originally founded in 1610 in the Guayrá region (see box, p.257), in what is now Brazil. After the *bandeirantes* attacked the mission in 1631, the Jesuits moved thousands of kilometres southwards through the jungle, stopping several times en route at various temporary settlements before finally re-establishing the *reducción* at its present site in 1696. It was only rediscovered in 1897.

On entering the settlement itself, you'll come first to rows of simple *viviendas*, or living quarters, a series of six to ten adjoining one-roomed structures, each of which housed a Guaraní family. Like all the mission settlements, these are constructed in a mixture of basaltic rock and sandstone. Passing between the *viviendas*, you arrive at the spacious Plaza de Armas, whose emerald grass provides a stunning contrast with the rich red hues of the sandstone. At the southern end of the plaza, and dominating the entire site, stands the magnificent facade of San Ignacio's **church**, designed, like Santa Ana's, by the Italian architect Brazanelli. The roof and much of the interior have long since crumbled away, but two large chunks of wall on either side of the entrance remain, rising out of the ruins like two great Baroque wings. Though somewhat eroded, many fine details can still be made out: two columns flank either side of the doorway, and much of the walls' surface is covered with decorative bas-relief sculpture executed by Guaraní craftsmen. Most striking are the pair of angels that face each other high up on either side of the entrance, while a more austere touch is added by the prominent insignia of the Jesuit order on the right-hand side of the entrance.

To the left of the main facade, you can wander around the **cloisters** and **priests' quarters**, where a number of other fine doorways and carvings remain. Particularly striking is the doorway connecting the cloisters with the church baptistry, flanked by ribbed columns with heavily moulded bases and still retaining a triangular pediment over the arched doorway.

Casa Museo Miguel Nadasdy

Sarmiento 557 • Sat 7am–7pm, Sun 9am–noon & 3–6pm • Free

The local history and archeology museum, right in the heart of the village, the **Casa Museo Miguel Nadasdy** was renovated in 2015. Inside you'll find a small collection of bits and pieces related to the Jesuit missions (candlesticks, documents, ceramics and the like), plus Guaraní artefacts. Everything is informatively labelled in English. There's also an exhibit on the museum's namesake, a Romanian immigrant who moved here in the 1940s – this was his house, and his private collection now forms the basis of the museum.

Casa de Horacio Quiroga

Horacio Quiroga s/n, via Sargento Cabral, 1km from the centre along a dirt road • Daily 8am–5pm • $40 • ☎ 03752 470130

San Ignacio was once the home of Uruguayan writer **Horacio Quiroga**, known for his rather Gothic short stories and Kipling-inspired jungle tales for children (see p.566), and his house is now a museum, the **Casa de Horacio Quiroga**. Quiroga first visited the region in 1903, taking some of the earliest pictures of the then little-known Jesuit ruins, before moving here permanently in 1910. The museum is composed of two houses – a replica of the first wooden house built by the writer, containing many of his possessions, and a later stone construction actually built by him. The rooms have been enhanced with audio and video clips (all in Spanish and English). At the back of the wooden house there's a small swimming pool built by the writer for his second wife (the first committed suicide, as would Quiroga himself in 1937, and his children after his death). She later left him, at which point Quiroga filled the pool with snakes.

Parque Provincial Teyú Cuaré

7km south of San Ignacio via a single-track gravel road, beyond Club de Río (no public transport) • Daily 24hr • Free

The **Parque Provincial Teyú Cuaré** is a small but enticing park of less than a square kilometre, notable for its golden-hued rocky formations, which jut out over the Paraná, and dense jungle vegetation. A short 200m trail from the guardhouse leads to a fork with a choice of three 600m trails: the first two run down to sensational viewpoints over the river, with the second, steeper, trail emerging on a high rocky cliff, the **Peñón Reina Victoria**, named for its supposed similarity to the profile of the British monarch (rock stairs join this path with the first trail, making a loop). The third trail leads to the **Casa de Borman** – a ruined stone house where legend has it Nazi war criminal Martin Bormann hid out after escaping the Allies at the end of World War II (this despite overwhelming forensic evidence that Bormann committed suicide in 1945).

ARRIVAL AND INFORMATION   SAN IGNACIO

By bus Buses to San Ignacio all stop at the Terminal de Ómnibus on RN-12, opposite the main entrance into the village (Av Sarmiento); regular buses pass by to Posadas (1hr) and Puerto Iguazú (3hr).

By car Coming from Posadas on RN-12, take the first left turn at the Esso petrol station (Av Sargento Cabral) and four blocks along you'll see the sign to Parque Provincial Teyú

Cuaré (on the left). Another four blocks up Cabral is the road to Casa de Horacio Quiroga (also on the left).

Tourist information The tourist office (daily 7.30am–12.30pm & 1–6pm) is at the junction of RN-12 and the main entrance road into the village, opposite the bus station.

ACCOMMODATION AND EATING

Adventure Hostel San Ignacio Independencia 469 ☎ 03752 470955. Great location in the village, set around a garden with a pool and hammocks – very welcome after a day tramping round ruins. Spacious if ageing dorms, free wi-fi and breakfast included. Dorms $\underline{\$150}$; doubles $\underline{\$560}$

Carpa Azul Rivadavia 1295 ☎ 0376 447 0096. This is perhaps the most popular in a clutch of very similar large restaurants geared up for day-trippers around the entrance to the ruins, all of which serve snacks plus some more substantial dishes such as *parrilla*. It even boasts a swimming pool and shower facilities. Daily noon–3.30pm & 8.30pm–late.

Club de Río ☎ 03755 15 570843, ⓦ clubderio.com.ar. Several kilometres south of the village, signposted from the centre (on the same road as Parque Teyú Cuaré), with comfortable *cabañas* set around a huge swimming pool, in a quiet location on the river (with small sandy beach). Buffet breakfast and wi-fi included. $\underline{\$1400}$

San Ignacio San Martín 823 and Sarmiento ☎ 03752 470042, ⓦ hotelsanignacio.com.ar. A comfy, modern place with en-suite rooms, all with a/c and cable TV. There's also an adjoining restaurant (breakfast usually not included). Free wi-fi. $\underline{\$500}$

4

Iguazú Falls

Composed of over 250 separate cascades, and straddling the border between Argentina and Brazil, the **Iguazú Falls** are quite simply the world's most dramatic waterfalls. Set among the exotic-looking subtropical forests of **Parque Nacional Iguazú** in Argentina, and **Parque Nacional do Iguaçu** in Brazil, the Falls tumble for a couple of kilometres over a complex set of cliffs from the Río Iguazú Superior to the Río Iguazú Inferior below. At their heart is the dizzying **Garganta del Diablo**, a powerhouse display of natural forces in which 1800 cubic metres of water per second hurtle over a 3km semicircle of rock into the boiling river canyon 70m below.

The vast majority of the **Iguazú Falls** lie on the **Argentine side** of the border, within the **Parque Nacional Iguazú**. This side offers the most extensive experience of the *cataratas*, thanks to its well-planned system of trails and walkways taking you both below and above the waters – most notably to the Garganta del Diablo. The surrounding forest also offers excellent opportunities to view the region's wildlife. The main settlement on this side, **Puerto Iguazú**, lies approximately 18km northwest of the park entrance.

AROUND THE IGUAZÚ FALLS

ACCOMMODATION	
Cabañas Panambí	2
Camping Americano	4
Casa Yaguarete	1
Hostel Inn	3
Sheraton Iguazú Resort & Spa	5

Eldorado (75km), Posadas (280km) & Las Mercedes (580km)

Puerto Iguazú

Just under 300km northeast of Posadas, sitting high above the meeting of the Paraná and Iguazú rivers, at the most northern extremity of Misiones Province, **PUERTO IGUAZÚ** is a strange place. Originally a rather dull, backwater town, its popularity with Falls visitors has increasingly given it the feel of a lively resort in recent years, and, though it has little in the way of notable architecture, it has a certain simple charm that can grow on you. Its tropical vegetation and quiet streets seem more in keeping with the region than the high-rise concrete of the Brazilian city of Foz, and of the three border towns (the commercial settlement of Ciudad del Este in Paraguay, notoriously unsavoury and unsafe, is definitely best avoided), Puerto Iguazú is the only one to have a really secure and accessible riverfront area from which you can take in the surrounding panorama.

The town is bisected diagonally by **Avenida Victoria Aguirre**, which runs from Puerto Iguazú's modest **port** out towards RN-12 and the national park. From the centre the Avenida Tres Fronteras runs west for 1.5km to the **Hito Argentino de las Tres Fronteras**, a vantage point over the rivers with views over to Brazil and Paraguay that is marked by an obelisk painted in the colours of the Argentine flag. An alternative route is via Avenida Aguirre, which forks right just before the town's triangular grassy central square, **Plaza San Martín**. From here, Avenida Aguirre snakes down through a thickly wooded area of town to the port area; you can then follow the pleasant Costanera (Av Río Iguazú), popular with joggers and cyclists, left uphill towards the Hito.

ACCOMMODATION
Boutique Hotel de la Fonte	5
Garden Stone Hostel	2
Hotel Saint George	6
Iguazú Jungle Lodge	1
Jasy Hotel	3
Lilian	7
Porãmbá Hostel	4
Secret Garden B&B	8

EATING
Bocamora	1
María Preta	2
El Quincho del Tío Querido	3
Parilla Pizza Color	4
La Rueda 1975	5

DRINKING AND NIGHTLIFE
La Barranca	1
Icebar Iguazú	2

La Aripuca

RN-12 Km4.5 • Daily 9am–6pm • $70, children free • ☎ 03757 423488, ⓦ aripuca.com.ar

The bizarre attraction of **La Aripuca** lies on the outskirts of Puerto Iguazú, just over 4km along RN-12 towards the national park. An *aripuca* is an indigenous wooden trap used in the region to catch birds; La Aripuca is a giant replica of such a trap, standing over 10m high and constructed out of 29 species of trees native to Misiones Province (all obtained through unavoidable felling or from victims of thunderstorms) – it looks like a giant wooden temple. Above all, La Aripuca is a kind of eco-symbol: the friendly German- and English-speaking family who constructed the strange monument hope to change visitors' conscience about the environment through tours designed to explain the value and significance of these trees. Some very good crafts are on sale – mostly made of tropical wood – and you can snack, have a drink or try *mate*-flavoured ice cream.

ARRIVAL AND DEPARTURE
PUERTO IGUAZÚ

By plane Aeropuerto Internacional de las Cataratas del Iguazú lies 7km from the Falls and 20km from Puerto Iguazú on RN-12. There are regular flights to Buenos Aires with Aerolíneas Argentinas, Austral (who also fly to Salta), LAN and Andes. Taxis run to the Falls or into town according to fixed rates (around $250). Four Tourist Travel (☎ 03757 42068) runs a shuttle bus ($90), which meets all flights, and will drop off at your accommodation in town (not Brazil). Book the return trip 24hr before departure.
Destinations Buenos Aires (10 daily; 1hr 30min); Salta (1 daily; 1hr 20min).

By bus The Terminal de Ómnibus is at Córdoba and Misiones (☎ 03757 423006), and has a restaurant and a left-luggage service. There are frequent buses to/from the Argentine Falls (daily 7.20am–7.20pm, every 20–30min; return

7.50am–8pm; 30min; $50 one-way) – buy tickets at the terminal booth. Crucero del Norte buses run to/from the Brazilian Falls (hourly 8am–7pm; 1hr; $65 one-way) and to Foz do Iguaçu (Mon–Fri 7am–7pm, every 40min; Sat & Sun hourly; 45min; $35). Buses stop at Rua Mem de Sá (at Rua Taroba), the street just north of the Terminal de Transporte Urbano (the local bus station in the centre of Foz), where there are local buses to the Brazilian Falls (see p.264).
Destinations Buenos Aires (11 daily; 17hr 15min–19hr 20min); Córdoba (3 daily; 21hr–21hr 50min); Corrientes (7 daily; 9hr–9hr 30min); Posadas (hourly; 6hr); Rosario (7 daily; 17–19hr); San Ignacio (hourly; 5hr).

Car rental Europcar, Tareferos 111, ☎ 03757 421675 (also at airport); Hertz, Entre Ríos 66, ☎ 03757 425515 (also at airport).

4

INFORMATION

Tourist information Puerto Iguazú's tourist office is at Av Aguirre 337 (Mon–Fri 8am–1pm & 2–8pm, Sat & Sun 8am–noon & 4–8pm, sometimes open longer in high season; ☎03757 423951, ⓦiguazuturismo.gob.ar).

ACCOMMODATION

Puerto Iguazú's budget **accommodation** tends to be located in town, while the more upmarket places are set back among jungle vegetation on the road to the park and in the surrounding area. Note that camping inside the national parks is forbidden. The recommendations below (with the exception of camping) all include free wi-fi and breakfast.

IN TOWN

Boutique Hotel de la Fonte 1 de Mayo and Corrientes ☎03757 420625, ⓦboutiquehoteldelafonte.com; map p.261. This Italian-owned hotel offers six well-equipped a/c rooms (all with cable TV), one of which boasts an oversized jacuzzi, and an attractive garden with a pool. You can dine here too, with beautiful-looking and -tasting dishes incorporating local flavours. $1345

Garden Stone Hostel Córdoba 441 ☎03757 420425, ⓦgardenstonehostel.com; map p.261. Overall best hostel in town, a friendly, spotless place with four-bed dorms (with a/c) and doubles with or without private bathroom; there's a communal kitchen, TV room and pool, plus reception is open 24hr. Dorms $170; doubles $570

Hotel Saint George Córdoba 148 ☎03757 420633, ⓦhotelsaintgeorge.com; map p.261. A family-friendly hotel and one of the most comfortable in town, with some exceptionally light and attractive first-floor rooms with balconies overlooking the pool. Good restaurant downstairs, and good buffet breakfast. $1670

★**Iguazú Jungle Lodge** Hipólito Irigoyen and San Lorenzo ☎03757 420600, ⓦiguazujunglelodge.com; map p.261. Fabulous *cabañas* sleeping up to seven – plus a couple of doubles – in a landscaped plot overlooking the jungle on the edge of town. Extremely well equipped and tastefully appointed, they are really luxurious houses, with ample verandas, a huge kitchen and barbecue facilities. The decent breakfasts can be served either poolside or in the *cabañas*. $1565

Jasy Hotel San Lorenzo 154 ☎03757 424337, ⓦjasyhotel.com; map p.261. Fabulous accommodation in a series of ten rustic lodges set on a slope, all simply furnished but spacious and stylish (a/c and cable TV included). Free wi-fi in common areas only. The restaurant is also great (ⓦjasyrestobar.com). $875

Lilian Fray Luis Beltrán 183 ☎03757 420968, ⓔhotellilian@yahoo.com.ar; map p.261. Spotless and airy, if dated, rooms with good fans and modern bathrooms near the bus station. Free wi-fi in lobby only. $610

Porámbá Hostel El Uru 120 ☎03757 423041, ⓦporambahostel.com; map p.261. Excellent value (300m from the bus terminal), this friendly hostel offers comfy dorms with a/c, chilled-out garden with hammocks, small pool and decent shared kitchen. Dorms $180; doubles $600

★**Secret Garden B&B** Los Lapachos 623 ☎03757 423099, ⓦsecretgardeniguazu.com; map p.261. This marvellous B&B has just three small, perfectly maintained rooms set around a verdant little garden. Breakfasts are simple but excellent, and caipirinhas are offered in the evenings. John Fernandes, a photojournalist originally from India but long resident in Argentina, could not be a better host. $1730

OUT OF TOWN

Cabañas Panambí Violeta de los Alpes and Irupe ☎03757 497418, ⓦcabanaspanambi.com; map p.260. On the jungle-clad banks of the Río Paraná at the edge of town, these nine rustic cabins come with wooden balconies overlooking the river, simple but comfortable furnishings and free pick-up from the bus terminal. $885

Camping Americano RN-12 Km5 ☎03757 420190, ⓦcomplejoamericano.com.ar; map p.260. In a great leafy location off the main road towards the national park, the campsite has showers, a shop, telephones and large swimming pool. The associated *cabañas* and hotel next to the complex are not such a good deal. $150

Casa Yaguarete Posadas and El Dorado, Zona de Granjas ☎03757 450097, ⓦcasayaguarete.com; map p.260. Welcoming B&B just outside town, with cosy doubles and triples, all with hot showers and cable TV. The friendly owners can help arrange trips and tickets. $900

Hostel Inn RN-12 Km5 ☎03757 421823, ⓦhiiguazu .com; map p.260. A large, well-run HI-affiliated hostel with different-sized dorms, doubles and triples, in enormous grounds with a large swimming pool. HI members: dorms $95; doubles $420; non-HI members: dorms $105; doubles $465

Sheraton Iguazú Resort & Spa Parque Nacional Iguazú ☎03757 491800, ⓦstarwoodhotels .com; map p.260. Big, ugly modern hotel inside the national park. The crime of its construction is compounded by the fact that you only get a decent view of the Falls from a few of its rooms (for which you pay more), but it has to be admitted it is well located from the guests' viewpoint, with the Falls in walking distance and the possibility of exploring the jungle before most visitors arrive. $5000

EATING

Bocamora Costanera (Río Iguazú) 20 ☎ 03757 420550; map p.261. This grill and fancy restaurant is superbly located in a colonial-style house overlooking the river. On weekend nights it metamorphoses into a popular disco. Daily noon–midnight.

María Preta Brasil 39 ☎ 03757 420441; map p.261. A stylish bar-restaurant with outdoor seating and a comprehensive menu that includes *yacaré* (cayman) as well as more conventional pasta and *parrilla*; it also has live Brazilian music some evenings. The service can be quite slow. Daily noon–4pm & 9pm–late.

Parrilla Pizza Color Córdoba 135 ☎ 03757 420206, ⓦ parrillapizzacolor.com; map p.261. This local institution does excellent *pizza a la piedra* and good salads, plus decently priced *parrillas*. You can sit inside or out. Daily 11.30am–midnight.

El Quincho del Tío Querido Perón and Caraguatá ☎ 03757 420151, ⓦ eltioquerido.com.ar; map p.261. This spacious and airy restaurant always has huge skeins of sausages and *morcillas* (blood sausages) garlanded over the vast grill, a sign of the plentiful barbecued meat on offer, with nightly shows of tango, bolero or folk music. Mon 6.30–11.30pm, Tues–Sun 11.30am–3.30pm & 6.30–11.30pm.

★**La Rueda 1975** Córdoba 28 ☎ 03757 422531, ⓦ larueda1975.com.ar; map p.261. Undoubtedly the best *parrilla* in town, though the menu also features an enticing range of salads, fish dishes and succulent pasta, all served in especially congenial surroundings – all rustic wood and old photos. The wine list is impressive. Mains $190–230. Daily noon–3.30pm & 8.30pm–late.

DRINKING AND NIGHTLIFE

In Puerto Iguazú itself there's a handful of bars-cum-nightclubs on Avenida Brasil close to the junction with Avenida Aguirre, though many locals head over to Brazil for a big night out.

La Barranca Perito Moreno 269 ☎ 03757 423545; map p.261. Puerto Iguazú's only really fun bar (often packed with Brazilians), *La Barranca* offers, in addition to a plentiful supply of cold beer, powerful cocktails and sangría, plus occasional live music, mostly electronic and Brazilian pop-rock. Daily 8.30pm–late.

Icebar Iguazú RN-12 Km5 ☎ 03757 494047, ⓦ icebariguazu.com; map p.261. This is an obligatory stop for Brazilian and Argentine tourists, and if you haven't been to one before, the ice theme (frozen bar, ice sculptures, artificially controlled sub-zero temperatures), in-house thermal jackets and gloves, and themed vodka cocktails are a lot of fun. It's $200 to enter for 30min sessions (you can't stay longer), during which time it's an open bar. Daily 2pm–midnight.

DIRECTORY

Banks and exchange There are several banks with ATMs in Puerto Iguazú.
Consulates Brazil, Córdoba 264 ☎ 03757 421348

(Mon–Fri 8am–1pm).
Post office Near the plaza, at San Martín 384 (Mon–Fri 8am–1pm & 4–7pm).

Parque Nacional Iguazú

18km southeast of Puerto Iguazú, along RN-12 and RN-101 • $260 for foreigners (cash only); keep your ticket and have it stamped on the way out, which will entitle you to a fifty percent discount the following day • Daily 8am–6pm • ☎ 03757 491469, ⓦ iguazuargentina.com

As you get off the bus at the **Parque Nacional Iguazú**, you're greeted by the sound of rushing water from the Falls, the first of which lies just a few hundred metres away. There's a **visitors' centre** to the left of the bus stop, where you can pick up maps and information leaflets. There's also a small but interesting museum here with photographs and stuffed examples of the park's wildlife.

The Sendero Verde trail

From the visitors' centre, the so-called Sendero Verde ("Green Path") leads to the Estación Cataratas, from where two well-signposted trails, formed by a series of walkways and paths, take you past the Falls. The easiest approach is to tackle the **Circuito Superior** first, along a short trail (650m) through the forest above the first few waterfalls. For more drama, segue into the **Circuito Inferior** (1.6km), which winds down through the forest before bringing you within metres of some of the smaller but still spectacular waterfalls – notably **Saltos Ramírez** and **Bossetti** – which run along the western side of the river. Around the waterfalls, look out for the swallow-like *vencejo*, a remarkable small bird that, seemingly impossibly, makes its nest behind the gushing torrents. As you descend the path, gaps in the vegetation offer great views across the Falls: photo opportunities are numerous. Note that special walkways have made **wheelchair access** to all of the Circuito Superior and much of the Circuito Inferior possible, although there is little room to turn around in many sections.

Isla San Martín

Boats daily 9.30am–3.30pm • Free

Another signposted trail leads down to the jetty from where the boat rides depart, including a regular free boat service (suspended when the river is high) for **Isla San Martín**, a gorgeous, high, rocky island in the middle of the river. More trails circumnavigate the island, through thick vegetation and past emerald-green pools. There's a small sandy beach at the northern end of the island, though bathing is allowed only in summer.

The Sendero Macuco trail

Heading west from the visitors' centre, a well-marked path leads to the start of the **Sendero Macuco**, a 4km nature trail down to the lower banks of the Río Iguazú, past a waterfall, the **Salto Arrechea**, where there is a lovely secluded bathing spot. The majority of the trail is along level ground, through a dense wood, and is one of the best places to spot the area's fauna (see box opposite), especially early in the morning, before the helicopters on the Brazilian side get going.

Garganta del Diablo

To visit the **Garganta del Diablo** ("Devil's Throat"), you must take the Tren de la Selva ("Jungle Train"), which leaves regularly from Estación Cataratas for the Estación Garganta del Diablo, 3km southeast (fare included in park entrance fee). From here a 1.1km walkway with a small viewing platform takes you to within just a few metres of the staggering, sheer drop of water formed by the union of several immensely powerful waterfalls around a kind of horseshoe. As the water crashes over the edge, it plunges into a dazzling opaque whiteness in which it is impossible to distinguish mist from water. The *vencejos* often swirl around the waterfall in all directions, forming giant swarms that sometimes swoop up towards you and perform miraculous acrobatic twists and turns. If you're bringing your camera, make sure you've an watertight bag to stash it in, as the platform is invariably showered with a fine spray.

ARRIVAL AND TOURS

PARQUE NACIONAL IGUAZÚ

By bus Buses to the Parque Nacional leave from the Terminal de Ómnibus in Puerto Iguazú (daily 7.20am–7.20pm, every 20–30min; return 7.50am–8pm; 30min; $50 one-way), dropping you at the park entrance. Buy tickets at the terminal booth.

By taxi Taxis charge $250 one-way to get to the park from Puerto Iguazú (though you might be able to negotiate a lower rate).

Tours Guided tours (daily 8.45am–3.45pm, every 30min)

into the forest are organized at the offices of Iguazú Jungle (☎03757 421600, ⌨iguazujungle.com), located at the Circuito Inferior. A typical trip lasts one and a half hours, and involves being driven in the back of a truck along a rough 8km road through the forest, a walk down a narrow trail to the river, and a wild 6km boat ride down some rapids towards the Garganta del Diablo. Don't expect to see any wildlife (much of which is nocturnal), but guides may point out some of the flora. You can also just opt for a jet-boat ride.

The Brazilian side

To complete your trip to Iguazú, you should also try and visit the **Brazilian side**. You'll only need a few hours but it's worth crossing in order to take photos of the Falls – particularly in the morning – as it provides you with a superb panorama of the points you will have visited close up in Argentina, as well as its own close encounter with the Garganta del Diablo. The city of **Foz do Iguaçu** lies a good 20km northwest of the Brazilian Falls; much larger than Puerto Iguazú, Foz boasts little in the way of sights and the relative strength of the Brazilian real usually makes it expensive compared with Argentina – you can easily visit the Brazilian Falls on a day-trip in any case.

FLORA AND FAUNA AROUND THE FALLS

The Falls are not the only attraction in the parks. The surrounding subtropical **forest** – a dense, lush jungle – is packed with animals, birds and insects, and opportunities for spotting at least some of them are good. Even on the busy walkways and paths that skirt the edges of the Falls you've a good chance of seeing gorgeously hued, bright blue butterflies as big as your hand (just one of over 250 varieties that live around the Falls) and – especially on the Brazilian side – you will undoubtedly be pestered for food by greedy coatis (a raccoon relative). For a real close-up encounter with the parks' varied wildlife, though, head for the superb **Sendero Macuco** (see opposite).

Despite appearances, the jungle landscape around the Falls is not virgin forest. In fact, it is in a process of recuperation: advances in the navigation of the Upper Paraná – the section of the river that runs along the northern border of Corrientes and Misiones – in the early twentieth century allowed access to these previously impenetrable lands and economic exploitation of their valuable timber began. In the 1920s, the region was totally stripped of its best species and traversed by roads. Only since the creation of the park in 1943 has the forest been protected.

FLORA

Today, the forest is composed of several layers of **vegetation**. Towering above the forest floor is the rare and imposing *palo rosa*, which can grow to 40m and is identifiable by its pale, straight trunk that divides into twisting branches higher up, topped by bushy foliage. At a lower level, various species of palm flourish, notably the *pindó* palm and the palmito, much coveted for its edible core, which often grows in the shade of the *palo rosa*. Epiphytes – which use the taller trees for support but are not parasitic – also abound, as does the *guaypoy*, aptly known as the strangler fig since it eventually asphyxiates the trees around which it grows. You will also see lianas, which hang from the trees in incredibly regular plaits and have apt popular names such as *escalera de mono*, or "monkey's ladder". Closer still to the ground there is a stratum of shrubs, some of them with edible fruit, such as the pitanga. Ground cover is dominated by various fern species.

FAUNA

The best time to spot **wildlife** is either early morning or late afternoon, when there are fewer visitors and the jungle's numerous birds and mammals are at their most active: at times the screech of birds and monkeys can be almost cacophonic. At all times, you have the best chance of seeing wildlife by treading as silently as possible, and by scanning the surrounding trees for signs of movement. Your most likely reward will be groups of agile **capuchin monkeys**, with a distinctive black "cowl", like that of the monks they are named after. Larger, lumbering **black howler monkeys** make for a rarer sight, though their deep growl can be heard for some distance. Along the ground, look out for the tiny **corzuela deer**. Unfortunately, you've little chance of seeing the park's most dramatic wildlife, large cats such as the puma and the jaguar, or the tapir, a large-hoofed mammal with a short, flexible snout. **Toucans**, however, are commonly spotted; other birds that can be seen in the forest include the solitary **black cacique**, which makes its nest in the *pindó* palm, various species of woodpecker and the striking crested yacutinga. Of the forest's many **butterflies**, the most striking are those of the *Morphidae* family, whose large wings are a dazzling metallic blue.

Parque Nacional do Iguaçu

BR-469 Km22.5 (Av das Cataratas) • Daily 9am–5pm • R$56.30, includes buses inside the park (last bus departs Porto Canoas 6.30pm; pesos or dollars accepted) • ☎ 0055 45 3521 8383, ⓦ cataratasdoiguacu.com.br

The Brazilian Falls are protected within the **Parque Nacional do Iguaçu**. Buses terminate at the **visitors' centre** by the entrance, where you pay the entrance fee and transfer onto a shuttle bus. After passing drop-off points for boat and trail tours (see p.267), buses stop at the head of the waterfalls trail (bus stop #5, the "**Path of the Falls Stop**"), just opposite the *Hotel das Cataratas*. From here a walkway takes you high along the side of the river; it is punctuated by various viewing platforms from where you can take in most of the **Argentine Falls**, the river canyon and **Isla San Martín**. The 1.2km path culminates in a spectacular walkway offering fantastic views of the **Garganta del Diablo** and of the **Brazilian Santo Salto Maria**, beneath the viewing platform and surrounded by an almost continuous rainbow

4

created by myriad water droplets. You are likely to get soaked here – enterprising locals sell ponchos, for what they're worth; carry a plastic bag to protect your camera. At the end of the walkway you can take a lift to the top of a cliff for more good views. A little further along, the Porto Canoas complex has a shuttle bus stop, souvenir stores and restaurants, often plagued by stripe-tailed coatis (see box, p.265) that accost visitors, begging for food.

Parque das Aves

Av das Cataratas Km17.1 (100m north of the park entrance) • Daily 8.30am–5pm • R$30 • ☎ 0055 45 3529 8282, ⓦ parquedasaves.com.br

If you've not been lucky enough to see some of Iguazú's exotic birds at the Falls themselves, head for the **Parque das Aves**, where walk-through aviaries allow for close encounters with some of the most stunning (all birds have been rescued from traffickers and would not survive alone in the wild). The first of these is populated with various smaller species such as the noisy bare-throated bellbird, with a weird resonant call, the bright blue sugar bird and the blue-black grosbeak. For most people, though, the highlight is a sighting of the bold toucans – almost comically keen to have their photo taken. There is also a large walk-through butterfly cage – butterflies are bred throughout the year and released when mature.

CROSSING THE BRAZILIAN BORDER

You will need to enter Brazil via the Puente Internacional Tancredo Neves, the bridge that crosses the Río Iguazú between the two countries and where immigration formalities take place. Certain nationalities – US and Canadian, for example – need **visas** to enter Brazil (even for one day), which can be obtained for a fee at the consulate in Puerto Iguazú; check beforehand. When returning to Argentina, make sure you have enough days to continue your journey, as passport control often gives only thirty days here – though you can ask for the normal ninety. **You must stop** at both the Brazilian and Argentine immigration posts in both directions, even if your bus appears to be driving straight through (tell the driver you need to pass through Immigration). Wait times are rarely more than a few minutes, but if you don't get a Brazilian stamp going in, you will be fined up to US$200 when you try and leave. Taxi drivers will wait for you while you clear immigration, but buses may not; keep your ticket and take the next one coming through.

ARRIVAL AND INFORMATION   PARQUE NACIONAL DO IGUAÇU

Buses and taxis in Foz usually take currency from Argentina as well as Brazil, but don't count on it – they are not obliged to, so it depends on the individual driver. If you want to stay in Foz you'll need a supply of the Brazilian currency, the real – change can be obtained from various kiosks at Foz's bus terminal.

By plane Foz do Iguaçu Airport (☎ 0055 45 3521 4200) is 12km southeast of the city, just off the road to the Brazilian Falls. Inside the terminal you'll find an information booth and car rental desks. From here, bus #120 (R$3.20) runs to the Terminal de Transporte Urbano (TTU) in the centre of town on Av Juscelino Kubitschek (30min), and in the other direction, to the Brazilian Falls (40min). By taxi, the fixed fare into Foz is around R$50, and R$85–100 to Puerto Iguazú.

By bus Crucero del Norte runs direct buses between Puerto Iguazú's bus terminal and the Brazilian Falls, plus a service to Foz do Iguaçu (see p.264). From the Terminal de Transporte Urbano in Foz, bus #120 "Parque Nacional" runs

all the way to the Brazilian Falls via Parque de Aves and Foz airport (Mon–Sat 5.45am–12.40am, every 30min; Sun 5.30am–12.40am, every 45min; R$3.20). Foz do Iguaçu's long-distance bus terminal or *rodoviária* (☎ 0055 45 3522 3633) is located 4km north of the centre and is served by buses from throughout southern Brazil.

By Taxi Taxis in Puerto Iguazú should charge around $400–450 return for a trip to the Brazilian Falls, with stops at Immigration and the Falls.

Time difference Note that between Nov and Feb Brazil is one hour ahead of Argentina – this time difference could be vital for making sure you catch the last bus back into town.

TOURS

Iguaçu Falls has become a major adventure sports hotspot in Brazil, with a bewildering range of activities available. Martin Travel, at Travessa Goiás 200 in Foz (☎ 0055 45 3523 4959, ⓦ martintravel.com.br), is a reliable local Brazilian tour agency that specializes in ecotourism and puts together groups to go canoeing, rafting or mountain biking along forest trails.

Helicopter flights Helisul (☎ 0055 45 3529 7474, ⓦ helisul.com) operates helicopter rides from just outside

the park's entrance (Av das Cataratas Km16.5), across from the Parque das Aves, offering 10min flights over the Falls (daily 8.30am–5.30pm; R$308/person; minimum 3 people); sensational views, but controversial thanks to the noise pollution (which scares wildlife).

Boat tours Macuco Safari (daily 9am–5.30pm, every 15min; ☎ 0055 45 3529 6262, ⊚ macucosafari.com.br), at its own dedicated bus stop in the park, operates a jet-boat ride through white water right up to and into the Falls for R$198/person. Macuco also runs various guided boat tours along Paraná and Iguazú rivers (R$110), and can arrange guided hikes, rafting or fishing trips.

The Saltos del Moconá and around

The quiet village of **El Soberbio** lies in one of Misiones Province's most enchanting areas, best known as the access point for the **Saltos de Moconá**, an unusual but decidedly uncooperative set of waterfalls. One of Argentina's strangest but most spectacular sights, they spill down the middle of the Río Uruguay for around 3km, tumbling from a raised riverbed in Argentina into a 90m river canyon in Brazil.

The split-level waterfalls – the longest of their kind in the world – are formed by the meeting of the Uruguay and Pepirí-Guazú rivers just upstream of a dramatic gorge. As the waters encounter this geological quirk, they "split" once again, with one branch flowing downstream along the western side of the gorge and the other plunging down into it. This phenomenon is visible only under certain conditions: if water levels are low, all the water is diverted into the gorge, while if water levels are high the river evens itself out. At a critical point in between, however, the Saltos magically emerge, as water from the higher level cascades down into the gorge running alongside, creating a curtain of rushing water between 3m and 13m high. The incredible force of the water as it hurtles over the edge of the gorge before continuing downstream explains its Guaraní name – *moconá* means "he who swallows everything".

El Soberbio

About 322km south of Iguazú, the village of **EL SOBERBIO** is perched on the banks of the Río Uruguay. Its charm is derived not so much from its buildings, which are unassuming modern constructions, but from its gorgeous riverside setting, amid lush undulating sierras. There's also an intriguing **mix of cultures** – sunburnt, blond-haired Polish and German immigrants rub shoulders with Argentines of Spanish and Italian descent, all with a hefty dose of Brazilian culture thrown in. Locals have a refreshingly cavalier attitude to the idea of national boundaries, popping over to Brazil (Porto Soberbo) on the regular ferry for Saturday-night dances and listening to Brazilian country music on the radio; indeed, in many homes Portuguese is the main language. Note that there is no immigration post on the Brazilian side, so you can also go across just for the day or night, but you cannot continue on into Brazil from here.

ARRIVAL AND DEPARTURE   **EL SOBERBIO**

By bus El Soberbio's modest bus terminal is right in the village centre at the intersection of avenidas San Martín and Rivadavia. There are around 5–7 daily buses between Posadas and Soberbio (around 5hr 15min). You can also take a bus direct from Iguazú to Moconá (see p.269).

By colectivo Expreso Prox usually runs 2–3 colectivos daily between Soberbio and Moconá, starting at around 8am (1hr 15min).

ACCOMMODATION

If you can afford them, you're best off staying at one of the posadas and lodges deep in the nearby jungle (see box, p.268). Otherwise there are a few passable accommodation choices in and around the village itself. There's no ATM, so bring enough money to cover all your expenses.

Cabañas Saltos del Moconá Av San Martín 800 ☎ 03755 495179, ⊚ cabsaltosdelmocona.com.ar. Just outside the village on the way to the Falls, these rustic cabins are fairly plain but comfortable, with room for up to four people. Breakfast included. Per person **$250**

Hostal del Centro Rivadavia 313 ☎ 03755 495133. The least offensive of the poor accommodation in the village itself. Basic but adequate rooms (with fans or a/c), comfy beds, sketchy wi-fi and no breakfast included – it's very cheap, though. **$350**

4

The Parque Provincial Moconá and the waterfalls

Daily 9am–5pm • $30 • **Boat trips** daily 10am–4.30pm (15–30min) • $200 • ⓦ saltosdelmocona.tur.ar

The **Saltos del Moconá** themselves lie just over 80km northeast of El Soberbio in the **Parque Provincial Moconá**, accessed via the paved RN-2. They can be seen from both Argentina and Brazil (where they are known as Yucumã), the latter **only by taking a boat trip**. As with Iguazú, the better view is from Brazil, while the Argentine side wins out in the adventure stakes. Before setting out for the Saltos, you should **check the state of the river** with the police, who maintain a post nearby (☎03755 441001), and ask locals in El Soberbio about the condition of the road (which can be flooded and impassable) and for precise directions.

The first 40km of the road north takes you through tobacco plantations and communities of Polish and German immigrants clustered around numerous simple wooden Lutheran, Adventist and Evangelical churches. Despite the incredible lushness of the landscape, this is a region afflicted by considerable poverty, and local small farmers carry out much of their work using old-fashioned narrow wooden carts, pulled by oxen. If you are taking a **boat trip**, your guide will drive you down to the river and you will complete the journey by water – a fabulous experience in itself. Having surveyed the waterfalls from the spectacular Brazilian side, you will be transferred to land on the Argentine side, where you can look across the apparently "normal" river from the shore, swim in the shallows, admire the butterflies and, if possible, wade over to view the waterfalls from above.

Halfway to the Saltos the road strikes into the heart of an area of secondary forest, the last stretch of which is protected as the park, which was created in 1988. After another 40km or so, you arrive at the Centro de Interpretación for the Saltos, from where there are a number of short trails through the forest. A trail of just over 1km leads to the edge of the Río Uruguay, from where – compulsorily accompanied by a *guardaparque* or local guide, and conditions permitting – you can embark on an adventurous wade across 300m of knee-high water to reach the edge of the waterfalls, or take a boat trip.

POSADAS AND LODGES IN THE SELVA MISIONERA

To experience the awe-inspiring beauty of this area of remote, virgin jungle at its best, it is worth treating yourself to a couple of days being pampered at one of the lodges or posadas tucked away in the forest. Access is difficult, even in a 4WD, so you're advised to fork out the extra for a transfer to and from your accommodation; if you have a vehicle they will arrange for its safekeeping while you are away.

★**Don Enrique Lodge** 8km from Colonia La Flor, via RP-15 ☎011 4723 7020, ⓦdonenriquelodge .com.ar. Some 40km north of El Soberbio (1hr 20min) on the aptly named Río Paraíso, this place is run with dedication and affection by hospitable host Bachi and her family, offering fabulous service, delicious meals and, above all, peace and quiet. The individual wooden lodges, each with a balcony and sundeck, are furnished with impeccable taste. You can explore the jungle with a guide – on one side of the river up to a lookout, on the other to a waterfall to admire tree ferns and all manner of flora and fauna. Free wi-fi. Two-night minimum. $3000

La Misión Moconá RN-2 Km36, Puerto Paraíso ☎011 15 3415 0500, ⓦlodgelamision.com.ar. Located 45km north of El Soberbio on the banks of the Río Uruguay, *La Misión* is extremely convenient for visits

to the Falls; you can also use its mountain bikes or kayaks, or go fishing. The six *cabañas* are handsome cedar-and-stone constructions, the food is good, the welcome warm and the views of the river and jungle are fantastic. Free wi-fi. Two nights minimum and full board only – vital as there are no eating options within a large radius. $1510

Posada La Bonita 30km north of El Soberbio, off RP-15 ☎011 15 4490 8386, ⓦposadalabonita .com.ar. A fabulous construction smack in the middle of the jungle, this pioneering posada offers half-board deals (lunch is extra) Built from stone and timber, and furnished with rustic pieces made of dead wood, it sets the trend for the other lodges in the region. The three isolated units stand apart from the main house and have their own little verandas. No internet. $1940

ARRIVAL AND TOURS

By bus In addition to colectivos from El Soberbio (see p.267), Moconá is connected to Puerto Iguazú by a direct minibus service operated by Destino Moconá (departing Iguazú at 7am, returning at around 4pm; 4–5hr).

By car Now that RN-2 extension is complete, it should be straightforward to drive from El Soberbio in an ordinary car – check in Posadas about flooding before setting out.

Organized tours Tour companies in Posadas and

THE PARQUE PROVINCIAL MOCONÁ

Puerto Iguazú offer packages to Moconá involving at least an overnight stay, but these are expensive and only really worthwhile for a group. Better value is to make your own way to El Soberbio and then arrange a tour from there. A number of agencies in El Soberbio, such as Yabotí Jungle, at Av Corrientes 481 (☎03755 495266, ✉mocona4x4@yahoo.com.ar), offer 4WD and boat tours to the waterfalls.

The Gran Chaco

One of Argentina's forgotten corners, the **GRAN CHACO** is a land of seemingly unending alluvial plains and scrubby desert. It has little in the way of dramatic scenery, no impressive historical monuments and few services for the visitor, but if you have a special interest in **wildlife** you will find it rewarding, provided you avoid the blistering heat of summer. In the sizeable sectors not yet cleared for agriculture, it harbours an exceptional diversity of **flora and fauna** (see box, p.270), making it worth your while to break your journey for a day or two as you cross the region. Birdwatchers fare best: more than three hundred bird species have been recorded in the dry Chaco. Anglers come from all over the world in search of fish such as the *dorado*.

4

Wet Chaco scenery is mostly found near the river systems of the Río Paraguay and the Río Paraná, where the rainfall can be as high as 1200mm a year, causing heavy flooding at times. Narrow strips of jungle border the main rivers that cross the region from west to east: the Río Pilcomayo and the Río Bermejo, which, after a fairly energetic start in the Bolivian highlands, grow turgid with the heavy load of sediment they carry by the time they reach the Chaco plains. In some places they dissipate into swamps called *esteros* or *bañados*, or lagoons that can become saline in certain areas owing to high evaporation.

Rainfall diminishes the further west you travel from the Paraná and Paraguay rivers, and the habitat gradually alters into **dry Chaco** scenery, typified by dense **thornscrub** that is used to graze zebu-crossbreed cattle, but cleared in those areas where irrigation has made it possible to cultivate crops such as cotton. This zone was known to the conquistadors as **El Impenetrable**, less because of the thornscrub than for the lack of water, which only indigenous groups seemed to know how to overcome. Indeed, Formosa and Chaco provinces still have one of the most numerous and diverse indigenous populations in the country. These communities include the once-nomadic Toba or **Komlek** (*Qom-lik*) – part of the Guaycuru family of tribes, who mostly live on the banks of the Río Pilcomayo and in Formosa Province and make a living from manual labour and crafts such as basket-weaving and pottery – and the **Wichí** – part of the Matacoan language family – who still rely on hunter-gathering for their economic and cultural life but also sell beautifully woven *yica* bags made of a sisal-like fibre.

When to go

The Gran Chaco records some of the highest **temperatures** anywhere in the continent from December to February, often reaching 45°C or more. The best times to see wildlife are in the early morning or late afternoon and the best time of year to visit is from June to September: although night frosts are not unknown in June and July, daytime temperatures generally hover in the agreeable 20–25°C bracket. The **rainy season** generally lasts from October to May, but violent downpours are possible throughout the year.

WILDLIFE-VIEWING IN THE CHACO

The main reason for visiting the Chaco is to see its varied and fascinating **wildlife**. Despite the vast lists of elusive, endangered mammals given in the region's tourist literature, though, only the very luckiest or most patient observers will see a **jaguar**, maned wolf, giant armadillo or *mirikiná* (nocturnal monkey). The surest bet for seeing any animals is to hire the services of one of the region's few but excellent **tour operators** (see box, p.274).

PARQUE NACIONAL COPO

In the northeast corner of Santiago del Estero Province, the **Parque Nacional Copo** is the best remaining chunk of prime dry Chaco left in the country and the only area of protected land in the Argentine Chaco big enough to provide a sustainable habitat for some of the region's most threatened wildlife, including the elusive **Wagner's peccary**. Giant and honey anteaters also inhabit the park, as do the threatened crowned eagle, the greater rhea and the king vulture. Frequently parched, it's a huge expanse of approximately 1140 square kilometres, with 550 square kilometres of provincial reserve attached to the west.

PARQUE NACIONAL RÍO PILCOMAYO

The edges of the woodland patches of the **Parque Nacional Río Pilcomayo**, to the north of Formosa city, can be great for glimpsing the larger mammals, including giant anteaters, honey anteaters, peccaries, deer, three types of monkey and pumas. Capybara, the two species of cayman, and even tapir live in the wetter regions of the park. Jaguars are believed to be extinct here, but the maned wolf can, very occasionally, be found – indeed, this park offers one of your best chances of seeing one. Almost three hundred species of **birds** have been recorded here, including the **bare-faced curassow** and **thrush-like wren**, both highly endangered in Argentina.

COMPLEJO ECOLÓGICO MUNICIPAL (SÁENZ PEÑA)

The **Complejo Ecológico Municipal** (daily 8am–6pm; ☎03732 424284; $25, plus $25/vehicle), on RN-95 near **Presidente Roque Sáenz Peña**, however, is really the only place for guaranteed viewing of the endangered beasts of the Chaco, including the maned wolf, jaguar, puma, tapir, honey anteater, bare-faced curassow, giant anteater and giant armadillo. This zoo fulfils an important educational role in an area where ecological consciousness is sometimes acutely lacking. Poorly funded, it nonetheless does an excellent job at rescuing, releasing or housing wounded or impounded specimens that are the victims of road traffic accidents, fires, illegal hunting and unscrupulous animal trading.

Chaco Province

The **easternmost strip of Chaco Province**, along the Paraná and Paraguay rivers, is the heartland of the wet Chaco. Most of the original forests and swamps have fallen victim to agricultural developments, dedicated to the production of beef cattle and crops such as fruit, soya and sugar cane. The main highway through this region is **RN-11**, which connects Santa Fe with **Resistencia**, the starting point for trips along RN-16 to **Parque Nacional Chaco** and the interior of the province.

Resistencia

With about half a million inhabitants, **RESISTENCIA** is Chaco Province's sprawling administrative capital and the principal gateway to the Gran Chaco. Despite its commercial importance and lack of colonial architecture, the city is a pleasant enough place; it has a feeling of spaciousness about it and is known for the outstanding friendliness of its inhabitants. The city's self-styled nickname is "Ciudad de las Esculturas" ("City of Sculptures"), owing to the hundreds of outdoor **statues** scattered throughout town.

Fogón de los Arrieros

Brown 350 • Mon–Fri 8am–noon & 8–11pm, Sat 8am–1pm • $25 • ☎03722 426418, 🖵 fogondelosarrieros.com.ar

Aldo Boglietti, the man behind Resistencia's sculpture project, also founded a remarkable cultural centre called the **Fogón de los Arrieros** in 1943, the city's most famous attraction (its name means "The Drovers' Campfire"). You can visit during the day to look round the eclectic mix of paintings (including works by Fontana and Soldi) and sculptures left behind by visiting artists, but it's more fun in the evening, when you can have a drink or empanada at the cosy bar. Best of all, try to catch one of the **events** – concerts, poetry recitals and the like – staged once or twice a week in the main salon or, weather permitting, on the patio.

Museo del Hombre Chaqueño
Juan B. Justo 280 • April–Nov Mon–Fri 8am–noon & 3–8pm; Dec–March Mon–Fri 4–8.30pm • Free • ☎ 0362 445 3005

The **Museo del Hombre Chaqueño** has a clearly presented collection detailing provincial history, with information on the region's pre-Columbian cultures – before the arrival of the Spanish, the Gran Chaco was a melting pot of indigenous cultures from across the continent. The museum's highlights include models of figures from Guaraní mythology and beautiful nineteenth-century silver *mate* gourds.

Museo Regional de Antropología
Las Heras 727 • Mon–Fri 9am–noon & 4.30–7.30pm • Free

Resistencia's most extensive archeological and ethnographical collection is housed in the **Museo Regional de Antropología**; it displays objects recovered from the ruins of the failed sixteenth-century settlement of Concepción del Bermejo, the only serious attempt by the Spanish to colonize this area of hostile terrain and equally hostile inhabitants.

Fundación Chaco Artesanal
Pellegrini 272 • Mon–Fri 8am–1pm & 4–8pm, Sat & Sun 9am–noon & 5–8pm • ☎ 03722 459372

The best place in the Chaco to purchase crafts made by the area's indigenous groups is the **Fundación Chaco Artesanal**, a nonprofit outlet that sells items such as Wichí pottery, Komlek basketware and graceful *palo santo* crucifixes.

ARRIVAL AND INFORMATION
RESISTENCIA

By plane Resistencia Airport lies 5km southwest of the centre, off RN-11. Aerolíneas Argentinas and Austral operate one daily flight each to and from Buenos Aires Aeroparque (1hr 40min). Taxis (around $160) run into the city – there are no buses.

By bus The bus terminal (☎ 03722 461098) is at the junction of avenidas Malvinas and MacLean, 4km southwest of the main square, Plaza 25 de Mayo. A taxi from here to the centre costs around $150. You can get a *remís* to Corrientes ($7–8) from the south side of the plaza at Alberdi.

Destinations Buenos Aires (hourly; 12hr 20min–15hr 30min); Corrientes (hourly; 30min); Formosa (hourly; 2hr 30min); Posadas (hourly; 4hr 45min–5hr 25min); Puerto Iguazú (8 daily; 9–10hr); Rosario (hourly; 9–12hr); Santiago del Estero (4 daily; 8hr 30min–10hr 20min).

Tourist information There is a small tourist information kiosk on the Plaza 25 de Mayo (Mon–Fri 7.30am–12.30pm; ☎ 03722 458291).

ACCOMMODATION

★ **Amérian Hotel Casino Gala** J.D. Perón 330 ☎ 0362 445 2400, ⓦ hotelcasinogala.com.ar. Knocking spots off the competition and housed in a converted Neoclassical building, this hotel has comfortable and enormous rooms that are all effectively suites, a glorious swimming pool and an efficient spa offering massages and foot-rubs. Free wi-fi in public areas. $1400

Casa Mía Hotel Santa María de Oro 368 ☎ 0362 442 5026, ⓦ casamiahotel.com.ar. Excellent value, with simple but modern a/c rooms, free wi-fi and pleasant roof deck. Free parking. $635

Hotel Covadonga Güemes 200 ☎ 0362 444 4444, ⓦ hotelcovadonga.com.ar. A well-run hotel with rooms decorated in a simple but contemporary style, comfy beds, free wi-fi and breakfast included. Just one block from Plaza 25 de Mayo. $945

EATING

Kebon Don Bosco 120 and Güemes ☎ 0362 444 4111. Resistencia has a poor choice of restaurants, but this local favourite is definitely the best option: it has a tasteful ambience and serves well-cooked classics (roast chicken

"EL CHACO" AND THE CAMPO DEL CIELO METEORITES

An estimated five thousand years ago a meteor shattered on impact with the earth's upper atmosphere, sending huge chips of matter plummeting earthwards, where they fell on a 15km band of the Chaco. This cataclysmic spectacle and the subsequent fires that would have been triggered must have terrified the locals. When the Spanish arrived in South America, the Komlek called the area *Pigüen Nonraltá*, or "Field of the Heavens" – Campo del Cielo in Spanish. They venerated the "stones from the sky", whose surface, when polished, reflected the sun. Mysterious legends reached Spanish ears, arousing an insatiable curiosity for anything that smacked of precious metal, and even sparking illusions of the fabled City of the Caesars, a variant of the El Dorado myth. In 1576, Hernán Mexía de Miraval struggled out here, hoping to find gold, but, instead, he found iron. The biggest expedition of all came in 1783, when the Spanish geologist and scientist Miguel Rubín de Celis led an expedition of two hundred men to find out if the **Mesón de Fierro** – a 3.5m-long curiosity and the most famous of the **meteorites** – was in fact just the tip of a vast mountain of pure iron. When they dug below, they found only dusty earth. The latitude was recorded, but since there was no way of determining its coordinate of longitude, the Mesón de Fierro was subsequently lost – it's probable that the indigenous inhabitants reburied their "sunstone".

The largest of the meteorites you can see today, "**El Chaco**", has been reliably estimated to weigh 37,000kg, a strong contender for the second biggest in the world (the biggest, almost twice the size, is in Namibia). El Chaco and the Campo del Cielo (⊕ campodelcielo.com.ar) both lie in the southwestern corner of Chaco Province, 15km south of the town of Gancedo, in the Reserva Natural Pigüen N'onaxá.

4

$155) and tasty river fish (*surubí* $210). Tues–Sun 9.30am–2pm & 8pm–midnight; closed most of Jan. **Mirasoles Pastelería** Las Heras 730 ☎0362 448 8041. Bright, welcoming café and bakery, serving a range of tempting pastries, cakes, breakfasts and light meals (1.6km south of Plaza 25 de Mayo). Mon–Wed 7am–midnight, Thurs & Fri 7am–1am, Sat & Sun 8am–1am.

Peña Nativa Martín Fierro 9 de Julio and Hernández ☎0362 439 2085. If a full *parrilla* with all the trimmings is what you're after, or maybe just a filling empanada or two, this traditional place is the right choice – plus you sometimes get live music thrown in. Founded in 1945, and famous for its live TV shows (on Canal 9) recorded Thurs 12.30pm and Sun 2.30pm. Daily noon–3.30pm & 8.30pm–late.

Parque Nacional Chaco

Daily 6am–7pm • Free • ☎ 03725 499161, ⊕ parquesnacionales.gob.ar

Dedicated naturalists can spend a few days trying to track down the region's fauna in the **PARQUE NACIONAL CHACO** in the province's humid east. Within easy striking distance of Resistencia, the park conserves a mix of threatened wet and semi-dry Chaco habitat around the banks of the Río Negro. In quick succession, you can pass from riverine forest to open woodland, palm savannah and wetlands. Its 150 square kilometres are too restricted a space to provide a viable habitat for the largest Chaco predator, the jaguar, but plenty of mammals still inhabit the park, even if your chances of seeing them are slight. **Birdlife**, however, is plentiful and easy to spot.

The park has a camping area with toilets, fire pits and electricity, but there's no **food** to buy, and little in **Solari**, the nearest settlement, so bring supplies. A board by the park headquarters displays the trails, which are also marked on a pamphlet available from the *guardaparques*. A good introduction to the park is the well-shaded nature-trail loop that leads from a suspension bridge behind the park headquarters (1.5km). But the most popular walk is the one to the lookouts at the ox-bow lagoons of **Laguna Carpincho** and **Laguna Yacaré** (6km), with a deviation to see an enormous *quebracho* tree, El Abuelo, which is an estimated five hundred years old. A longer walk (9km) is to **Laguna Panza de Cabra**, a swamp choked with lilac-bloomed *camalote* waterlilies and offering excellent birdwatching opportunities.

ARRIVAL AND DEPARTURE

PARQUE NACIONAL CHACO

By bus/remís The turn-off to the park is 56km west of Resistencia along RN-16, from where the paved RP-9 heads 40km north to Capitán Solari; from Solari it's a further 6km on dirt roads to the park headquarters. There are five daily buses from Resistencia to Solari, from where you can pick up a *remís* to the park.

Formosa Province

Formosa Province is dominated by its eponymous capital city, at its eastern end and second in importance to Resistencia in the Argentine Chaco; it's really just a base for visiting the province's wildlife – but not in the height of summer. To the north is the internationally significant wetland site of **Parque Nacional Río Pilcomayo**, on the border with Paraguay. For those set on seeing deepest Argentina, the aptly named **El Impenetrable** poses a real challenge – the weather, bad roads and virtually nonexistent infrastructure being the main obstacles. The **Bañado La Estrella** is a remote wetland that rewards the most intrepid and determined with fine birdlife, but go on an organized tour to make it worthwhile.

Formosa city

The city of **FORMOSA**, the provincial capital, seems as though it has been pressed flat by the heat: few buildings rise above a single storey and many exhibit the grey mouldy stains of subtropical decay. Situated on a great loop in the Río Paraguay, it acts as a **port** for the entire province. Not a particularly attractive place, despite its name (an archaic form of *hermosa*, "beautiful"), it's given a pink facelift when the *lapacho* trees flower in September, the best time to see it. In Argentina it's perhaps best known for the "Operación Primicia" of 1975, the largest attack ever launched by the paramilitary group **Montoneros** (leading to 28 deaths and, indirectly, to the military coup the following year). Visiting a few years before, Graham Greene, in *Travels With My Aunt*, wrote that "there was a pervading smell of orange petals, but it was the only sweet thing about Formosa", for him "an ignoble little town".

The main commercial district is concentrated within a block or two either side of the **Avenida 25 de Mayo**, east of the central square, Plaza San Martín. A block inland from here, on the corner of 25 de Mayo and Belgrano, is the pink, hacienda-style **Museo Histórico** (Mon–Fri 8.30am–12.30pm & 5–8pm, Sat 9am–noon; free), housed in the former residence of General Ignacio Fotheringham, the English-born first governor of what was then Formosa Territory. It is an eclectic and poorly organized collection, and exhibits include a stuffed Swiss bear and Komlek artefacts, plus information on early exploration of the region.

ARRIVAL AND INFORMATION

FORMOSA

By plane Formosa Airport (aka El Pucú) lies 7.5km southwest of the city centre, on RN-11. Austral operates one daily flight to and from Buenos Aires Aeroparque (1hr 50min). Bus #25 runs to Plaza San Martín via Av Gutnisky, and taxis also meet flights.

By bus The bus terminal is at Av Gutnisky 2615 (Gutnisky becomes Av 25 de Mayo before it reaches the Plaza San Martín, nearly 2km from the terminal); several local buses run down to the plaza from here.

Destinations Buenos Aires (7 daily; 13hr 30min–17hr 15min); Corrientes (5 daily; 3hr–3hr 40min); Resistencia (15 daily; 2hr); Salta (1 daily; 16hr 15min); Santa Fe (5 daily; 9hr 45min–12hr 40min).

Tourist information There's a small tourist office on Plaza San Martín, at Uriburu 820 (Mon–Fri 8am–noon & 4–8pm; ☎ 03717 425192, ⊛ formosa.gob.ar/turismo), which can help with accommodation in the province, including a handful of estancias.

ACCOMMODATION AND EATING

Asterión Hotel Arturo Illia 4853 (RN-11, Km1170) ☎ 03717 452999, ⊛ asterionhotel.com.ar. The best place to stay in Formosa, this hotel's name comes from a Borges short story about the Minotaur, and you will find a small collection of Borges memorabilia on display in the lobby. Rooms are bright, spacious and appealingly decorated, with an ethnic touch, and all the facilities are impeccable, from the safe garage to the shady swimming pool. Free wi-fi. **$750**

TOURS IN THE GRAN CHACO

The logistics of **visiting the parks and reserves** in the Gran Chaco region, and Formosa Province in particular, are complicated to say the least. Argentina's hottest climate, poorest roads and most inaccessible terrain are likely to frustrate even the most adventurous of travellers. Signposts are erratic and wildlife lurks where you least expect it. You will certainly need a helping hand if you are to get the most out of the Chaco and you will be best off going on an **organized tour** with a reputable company. **Aventura Formosa**, Paraguay 520, Formosa (☎0370 443 3713, ✉fiznardo@hotmail.com), has extremely reliable tours run by an experienced local guide with a tremendous in-depth knowledge of the region, its geography, wildlife and culture. **El Jabiru** (☎03718 477001, ✉info@eljabiru.com.ar) runs birdwatching trips into the Bañado de la Estrella and other trips in Formosa, including to the Parque Nacional Río Pilcomayo; English spoken.

Casa Grande González Lelong 185 ☎03717 431612, ⓦcasagrandeapart.com.ar. An attractive little complex whose well-equipped rooms have kitchenettes. Its facilities include a pool and garden, massages and a gym, plus one of the best restaurants for many kilometres, *Mirita*, which specializes in delicious fish dishes and has a very decent wine list. Free wi-fi in public areas. $875

SHOPPING

Casa de la Artesanía San Martín 802 and 25 de Mayo. This nonprofit organization is the best outlet for the province's indigenous crafts, with a good selection of Wichí yica bags, Pilagá woollen carpets, tightly woven Komlek basketwork, plus *palo santo* carvings and *algarrobo* seed jewellery. Mon–Sat 8am–noon & 4–8pm.

Parque Nacional Río Pilcomayo

Administration office (for information), RN-86 at Av Pueyrredón, Laguna Blanca • Mon–Fri 7am–2pm • Free • ☎03718 470045, ⓦparquesnacionales.gob.ar

The 519-square-kilometre **PARQUE NACIONAL RÍO PILCOMAYO** was created in the 1950s to protect some of the best remaining subtropical wet Chaco habitat. Extensive areas are subject to spring and summer flooding, whereas in the winter months it is prone to droughts. In addition to swampy wetlands, it conserves some remnant gallery forest along the Río Pilcomayo, and large swathes of savannah studded with copses of mixed woodland.

The best times to **visit the park** are sunset and dawn, when it's cooler and you stand a better chance of seeing the wildlife. The park has **two entrances** – to the Estero Poí and the more compact Laguna Blanca sectors – both within striking distance of **Laguna Blanca**, a village some 175km northwest of Formosa.

Estero Poí sector

Guardaparques Mon–Fri 7am–2pm, Sat & Sun 7am–2pm or 5pm (subject to staff availability)

The turning for the **Estero Poí sector** lies 2km southeast of Laguna Blanca village on RN-86, from where 9km of dirt road leads to the *guardaparques'* house. An interpretation trail runs from a bush campsite through the adjacent scrub, and within easy walking distance is a pair of swamps, dominated by the attractive *pehuajó* reed with its banana-palm leaves, along with bulrushes, horsetails and mauve-flowered waterlilies. Further into the park lie swathes of savannah grassland and the gallery forest of the Río Pilcomayo – good for spotting wildlife. Note that after **heavy rain** this section is usually closed.

Laguna Blanca sector

Guardaparques Mon–Fri 8am–4pm, Sat & Sun 8am–6pm

Just outside Laguna Naineck, 14km southeast of Laguna Blanca village, a gravel road (5km) leads to the **Laguna Blanca sector**. Next to the *guardaparques'* office is a pleasant free **campsite**, shaded by *algarrobos* and palms, with drinking water and showers; bring all your own food supplies. From behind the toilet block, there's a 300m **nature trail** where you have a good chance of seeing howler monkeys, while an excellent boardwalk from the campsite takes you 500m through reedbed marshland to lookout points and a 10m **tower** on the shore of the shallow lagoon itself. If you swim here, wear shoes so the piranhas don't snack on your toes. There are excellent opportunities for **birdwatching**, especially at dawn.

ARRIVAL AND DEPARTURE
PARQUE NACIONAL RÍO PILCOMAYO

By bus and remís There are four daily Godoy company buses to/from Formosa to Laguna Blanca (departing Formosa 10am, 12.25pm, 2.15pm & 8pm; return from Laguna Blanca 5am, 1.40pm, 5.40pm & 7.10pm; 2hr 35min–3hr 30min), from where you can pick up a *remís* to the park. You'll have a lot more flexibility with your own transport, though.

El Impenetrable

The dead-straight RN-81 runs northwest of Formosa through an area so difficult to enter it has been dubbed **El Impenetrable**. Those with a specialist interest in wildlife – especially birdlife – may want to use the route to access the **Bañado La Estrella**, a fascinating wetland near Las Lomitas, 300km northwest from Formosa. Otherwise, avoid it: if you want to cross the Chaco region, take the much faster RN-16 from Resistencia.

Bañado La Estrella

About 45km north of the village of Las Lomitas, via the unpaved RP-28, lies the **Bañado La Estrella**, a huge swathe of swamp in the central northern part of Formosa Province fed by the waters of the Río Pilcomayo, a river that dissipates into numerous meandering channels. RP-28 crosses the Bañado by means of a long causeway (*pedraplén*), usually just beneath the water line, and runs some 70km to RN-86 at Posta Cambio A Zalazar. The scenery looks like a Dalí painting: tree skeletons (*champales*) swaddled in vines, as if the floodwaters had once completely submerged them and then receded, leaving them snagged with weeds; beneath their branches shines the mirror-smooth blue water, dotted with rafts of *camalote* water lilies. You might even get to see members of the **Pilagá community**, an indigenous people who number about five thousand, fishing for *sábalo* with spears; note that they are generally reluctant to be photographed, especially without permission.

ARRIVAL AND DEPARTURE
EL IMPENETRABLE

By bus Buses pass regularly along RN-81 in both directions (between Tartagal, Embarcación, Jujuy, Salta and Formosa) and can be flagged down at Las Lomitas, but access to RP-28 is difficult without your own transport.

By car Driving times on unpaved roads in this area of the world are dependent on rainfall. Many vehicles can't negotiate the mud, and the ones that do often take far longer than they would in good conditions (if in doubt, call the Vialidad Provincial in Formosa; ☎ 03717 426040).

The Northwest

THE QUEBRADA DE HUMAHUACA

5

The Northwest

Argentina's Northwest (El Noroeste Argentino – often referred to as NOA or simply "El Norte") is infinitely varied: ochre deserts where llamas roam, charcoal-grey lava flows, blindingly white salt flats, sooty-black volcanic cones and pristine limewashed colonial chapels set against striped mountainsides. The Northwest is also the birthplace of Argentina – a Spanish colony thrived here when Buenos Aires was still an unsteady trading post on the Atlantic coast and it remains a bastion of the nation's large (but oft-forgotten) indigenous population. Salta is indisputably the region's tourism capital, with some of the country's best hotels, finest architecture and tastiest food. From here, you can meander up the enchanting Quebrada del Toro on the Tren a las Nubes (Train to the Clouds), one of the world's highest railways, or head south, via the surreal canyon of the Quebrada de las Conchas, to visit some of the world's highest vineyards at Cafayate.

To the far northwest huddles boot-shaped **Jujuy Province**, one of the federation's poorest and most remote, shoved up into the corner of the country against Chile and Bolivia, where in the space of a few kilometres humid valleys and soothingly green jungles give way to the austere, parched altiplano (or *puna*), home to flocks of flamingoes, herds of guanacos and very few people. **San Salvador de Jujuy**, the slightly oddball provincial capital, is the gateway to the many-hued **Quebrada de Humahuaca**.

South of **Cafayate**, attractions include impressive pre-Inca ruins at **Quilmes**, a quirky museum dedicated to Pachamama, or Earth Mother, at **Amaicha**, and dramatic trekking around **Tafí del Valle**, while the nearby city of **San Miguel de Tucumán** has an addictively lively atmosphere and a smattering of historic sights. Equally enticing are the eternally snowy peaks that give their name to the Nevados del Aconquija, the natural border between Tucumán and Catamarca Province, where a plethora of picturesque villages, each more isolated than the last, reward patient visitors with rural hospitality, wondrous natural settings and some fabulous handmade crafts: **Belén** and **Londres** stand out. Try and make it all the way to **Antofagasta de la Sierra**, an amazingly out-of-the-way market town set among rock and lava formations and reached via some of the emptiest roads in the country.

Highlights

❶ Inca mummies Controversially displayed in high-tech fridges, three impeccably preserved Incan children, discovered on a lofty volcano, can be seen in the Northwest's best museum, MAAM. **See p.283**

❷ Tren a las Nubes The magical Train to the Clouds winds up a magnificent gorge, via countless tunnels, bridges and loops, hauling you higher and higher to an iconic viaduct in the altiplano. **See p.293**

❸ Tilcara You'll find charming hotels, an abundance of arts and crafts, a massive colonial church and even a pre-Incan fortress in this village, the best base for visiting the Quebrada de Humahuaca. **See p.302**

❹ Cuesta del Obispo Spiral up (or down) a mind-boggling mountain road, zigzagging between the sultry plains of the Valle de Lerma and the rarefied air of Cachi and the Valles Calchaquíes. **See p.312**

❺ Vineyards of Cafayate Try fruity cabernet sauvignons, earthy tannat and floral torrontés at the world's highest wineries. **See p.317**

❻ Antofagasta de la Sierra Far from anywhere, this high-altitude village huddles among out-of-this world volcanic landscapes. **See p.328**

HIGHLIGHTS ARE MARKED ON THE MAP ON P.280

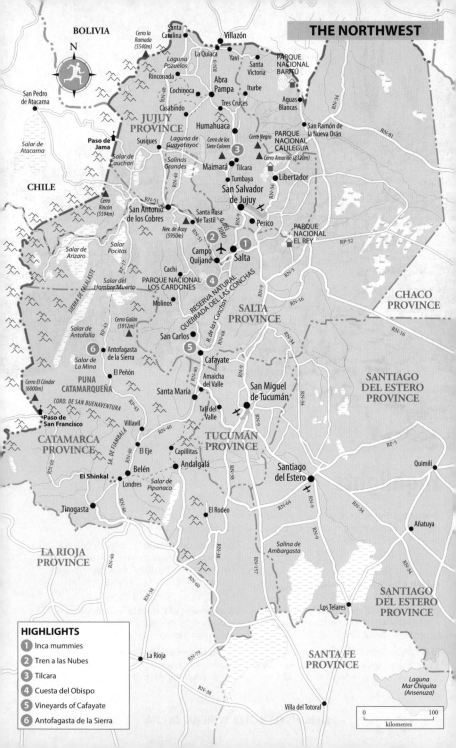

THE NORTHWEST

BOLIVIA

N

San Pedro
de Atacama

Salar de
Atacama

CHILE

Cerro la
Ramada
(5540m)

Santa
Catalina

Villazón

La Quiaca

Yavi

Santa
Victoria

Laguna
Pozuelos

Rinconada

Abra
Pampa

Tres Cruces

Iturbe

**PARQUE
NACIONAL
BARITÚ**

Aguas
Blancas

Cochinoca

Casabindo

**JUJUY
PROVINCE**

Humahuaca

San Ramón de
la Nueva Orán

RN-81

Paso de
Jama

Salar de
Cauchari

Susques

Laguna de
Guayatayoc

Salinas
Grandes

Cerro de los
Siete Colores

3

Cerro Negro

**PARQUE
NACIONAL
CALILEGUA**

Salar
de Atacama

Maimará

Tilcara

Cerro Amarillo (4320m)

Cerro
Rincón
(5594m)

San Antonio
de los Cobres

Santa Rosa
de Tastil

Nev. de Acay
(5950m)

Tumbaya

San Salvador
de Jujuy

Libertador

Perico

**PARQUE
NACIONAL
EL REY**

RP-52

Salar de
Arizaro

Salar
Pocitos

2

Campo
Quijano

1

Salta

Cachi

4

Molinos

**PARQUE NACIONAL
LOS CARDONES**

**RESERVA NATURAL
QUEBRADA DE LAS CONCHAS**

**SALTA
PROVINCE**

RN-16

**CHACO
PROVINCE**

Salar de
Antofalla

Cerro Galán
(5912m)

San Carlos

5

Cafayate

RN-16

6

Antofagasta
de la Sierra

El Peñón

Salar de
La Mina

Amaicha
del Valle

San Miguel
de Tucumán

**SANTIAGO
DEL ESTERO
PROVINCE**

Cerro El Cóndor
(6000m)

**PUNA
CATAMARQUEÑA**

Santa María

Tafí del
Valle

CORD. DE SAN BUENAVENTURA

Paso de
San Francisco

Villavil

**CATAMARCA
PROVINCE**

El Eje

Capillitas

**TUCUMÁN
PROVINCE**

RP-5

Santiago
del Estero

Quimilí

Belén

Andalgalá

El Shinkal

Londres

Salar de
Pipanaco

Santiago
del Estero

Tinogasta

El Rodeo

Añatuya

**LA RIOJA
PROVINCE**

Salina de
Ambargasta

**SANTIAGO
DEL ESTERO
PROVINCE**

La Rioja

Los Telares

**SANTA FE
PROVINCE**

Villa del Totoral

Laguna
Mar Chiquita
(Ansenuza)

HIGHLIGHTS

1 Inca mummies

2 Tren a las Nubes

3 Tilcara

4 Cuesta del Obispo

5 Vineyards of Cafayate

6 Antofagasta de la Sierra

0 ——— 100
kilometres

VISITING THE NORTHWEST

If you can, time your visit to the Northwest for the Argentine **spring** or **autumn**. Summers can be steamy in the valleys, making large cities like Tucumán unbearable, while heavy summer rains around Salta can wipe out roads and make exploring the area difficult. On the other hand, in July and August night-time **temperatures** at altitude are bitterly low, so your first purchase will probably be an alpaca-wool poncho. Salta and Jujuy are both well linked by public transport, as are the stops along the Quebrada de Humahuaca as far as Humahuaca town. Beyond this, transport is more sparse and you will have to plan in advance, or else rent a car or use tour agencies.

Salta and around

Historic capital of one of Argentina's biggest and most beautiful provinces, **SALTA** easily lives up to its well-publicized nickname of *Salta la Linda* (Salta the Fair), thanks to its festive atmosphere, handsome buildings and dramatic setting. Fifteen hundred kilometres northwest of Buenos Aires, at the eastern end of the fertile Valle de Lerma, and bounded by the Río Vaqueros to the north and Río Arenales to the south, the city is squeezed between steep, rippling mountains; at 1190m above sea level, it enjoys a relatively balmy climate. In recent years, Salta has become the Northwest's undisputed tourist capital, and its top-quality services include a slew of highly professional tour operators, some of the region's best-appointed hotels and liveliest youth hostels and a handful of fine restaurants. In addition to a cable car and a tourist railway, its sights include the ornate **Iglesia San Francisco**, and a raft of excellent **museums** dedicated to subjects as varied as pre-Columbian culture, anthropology, local history and modern art. A generous sprinkling of well-preserved **colonial architecture** has survived, giving the place a pleasant homogeneity and certain charm.

San Lorenzo, a self-contained suburb of Salta only fifteen minutes west, enjoys a slightly cooler mountain climate and is awash with lush vegetation, making it alluring for both visitors and locals who want to escape from the big city, especially in the summer – despite its tourist appeal, Salta is primarily a major commercial centre with more than 600,000 inhabitants.

Brief history

Notoriously violent Spanish *conquistador* Hernando de Lerma, the governor of Tucumán, founded the city of Salta in 1582. The site was chosen for its strategic mountainside location, and the streams flowing nearby were used as natural moats. In 1776, the already flourishing city was made capital of a huge administrative region that took in Santiago del Estero, Jujuy and even the southern reaches of modern Bolivia, becoming one of the major centres in the viceroyalty. During the War of Independence, local hero **Martín Miguel de Güemes** (1785–1821) based his anti-royalist forces in the town, creating the now traditional red-and-black-poncho uniform for his gaucho militia. Güemes served as governor of Salta province from 1815, but was killed during a royalist attack on the city in 1821. After Buenos Aires became the capital of the newly federalized country in 1880, Salta went into steady decline, missing out on the rest of Argentina's mass immigration of the late nineteenth century; the railway didn't arrive here until 1890. A belated urban explosion in the 1920s and 1930s has left its mark on the predominantly Neocolonial style of architecture in the city. Since the turn of the millennium, Salta has joined the ranks of Argentina's fastest-growing and most dynamic metropolises.

Plaza 9 de Julio

Salta's central square, **Plaza 9 de Julio**, is one of the country's most harmonious. Surrounded on all four sides by graceful, shady *recovas*, or arcades, under which several café terraces lend themselves to idle people-watching, it's a great place to

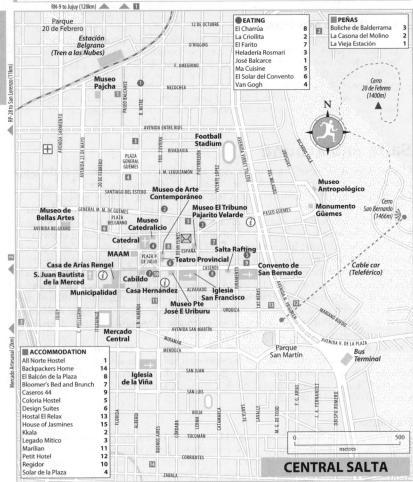

while away an hour or two. The well-manicured central part of the square is a collection of palms and jacarandas, fountains and benches, plus a quaint, late nineteenth-century bandstand and an equestrian statue of independence hero Juan Antonio de Arenales. Around it stand the city's Neoclassical **cathedral**, the **Teatro Provincial** (the beautifully renovated Cine Victoria of 1940), the snow-white **Cabildo** and two of the city's best **museums**.

Catedral Basílica de Salta

España 537 • Mon–Fri 6.30am–12.30pm & 4.30–8.30pm, Sun 7.30am–1pm & 5–9.30pm • Free • **Museo Catedralicio** Mon–Fri 9.30am–12.30pm & 4.30–6.30pm, Sat 9.30am–12.30pm (Jan & Feb afternoon hours 5–7pm) • $4

Towering over the northern side of the Plaza 9 de Julio like a giant wedding cake, the pink and white **Catedral Basílica de Salta** dates from 1882, the city's third centenary year. It's an impressive Italianate Neoclassical pile, with some well-executed interior frescoes painted in 1937 – the one of the Four Apostles around the cupola is particularly fine. Inside, and immediately to the left of the entrance, is the grandiose

5

Panteón de los Heroes del Norte, where local independence hero General Güemes is buried. The **Capilla del Señor del Milagro** and **Capilla de la Virgen del Milagro**, at the far end of the left and right aisles respectively, house the sacred images that are the centrepieces of major celebrations every September (see box below). With a separate entrance on Belgrano, the well-presented **Museo Catedralicio** contains two floors of religious art, including the usual vestments, chalices and quality silverware, though despite appearances, most of the exhibits date from the early twentieth century.

Museo de Arte Contemporáneo (MAC)

Zuviría 90 • Tues–Sat 9am–8pm, Sun 10am–2pm • Donation $2 • ☎ 0387 437 3036, ⓦ macsaltamuseo.org

Housed on the first floor of a handsomely renovated Neocolonial building, the outstanding **Museo de Arte Contemporáneo (MAC)** – all sleek white walls and dark parquet – puts on rotating exhibitions of mainly local artists, from up-and-coming wannabes straight out of art school to more established local names, who are often given shows of their own. Painting dominates, but sculpture, video and photography are also often on display.

Museo de Arqueología de Alta Montaña (MAAM)

Mitre 775 (Plaza 9 de Julio) • Tues–Sun 11am–7.30pm • $70 • ☎ 0387 437 0592, ⓦ maam.gob.ar

The **Museo de Arqueología de Alta Montaña (MAAM)** is the one museum in Salta that you should not miss. It was specially created to house the so-called **Llullaillaco Children**, one of the most important archeological finds ever made in Argentina and generally regarded as the best preserved **Inca mummies** ever found. In 1999, three naturally mummified Inca children were uncovered by an expedition of mountaineers and scientists on top of **Volcán Llullaillaco**, due west of Salta on the Chilean border and 6739m above sea level. They are a 6-year-old girl (*La niña del rayo*), visibly struck by lightning some time after her burial, her hair arranged in two small braids and with a metal plaque as an adornment (which attracted the lightning); a teenage girl

---

EARTHQUAKES AND THE FIESTA DEL MILAGRO

No earthquake as destructive as those that flattened the cities of Mendoza in 1861 and San Juan in 1944 has struck the Northwest region of Argentina within recent history, but this part of the country lies along the same fault line that was responsible for that seismic activity and is prone to occasional tremors, some of them violent. The **Nazca plate**, beneath the eastern Pacific, and the **South American plate**, comprising the whole continent, are constantly colliding – a continuation of the tectonic activity that formed the Andean cordillera. To make matters worse, the Nazca plate is subducting – nudging its way beneath the landmass – an action that accounts for the abundance of **volcanoes** along the range; some of them are extinct, others lie dormant, but none in the Northwest is very active. Nonetheless, frequent **earthquakes** of varying strength (but mostly mild for geological reasons) rock Northwest Argentina, accounting for the repeated displacement of many settlements and the absence of colonial architecture in some.

Salta still thanks its lucky stars for **El Milagro**, the legend according to which two sacred images have spared the city the kind of destruction caused by seismic disasters. An image of **Christ** and another of the **Virgin Mary** were found floating in a box off the coast of Peru in 1592, exactly a century after the Americas were discovered by Columbus, and somehow ended up in Salta. Precisely one century later, on September 13, 1692, a series of tremors began to shake the city, damaging some public buildings and houses. During that night, a priest named José Carrión dreamed that if the images of Christ and Mary were paraded through the streets for nine days the earthquakes would stop and Salta would be spared forever. Apparently it worked and, ever since, the **Fiesta del Milagro** has been a major event in the city's calendar. Festivities and religious ceremonies starting on September 6 reach a climax on September 15, when the now-famous images, which are kept in the cathedral, are paraded through the city's streets in a massive, solemn but colourful procession.

5

(*La doncella*) whose face was painted with a red pigment and who had small fragments of coca leaves above her upper lip; and a 7-year-old boy (*El niño*) wearing a white feather ornament tied around his head. Their incredibly well-preserved corpses – all three lived around 1490 AD – were at first kept in a university laboratory in the city while tests on their tissue and other remains were completed. They are now shown, one at a time, in a specially refrigerated case, and the effect is startling.

The jury is still out as to whether it is sacrilegious to display the bodies in a public museum: the decision to do so provoked a furore, including **demonstrations** by representatives of local indigenous groups, so bear in mind that this is a sensitive issue. The children were sacrificed to the Inca deities, possibly in a fertility ceremony or as an offering to the gods of the sun and moon. They were probably drugged unconscious with a concoction of coca leaves and maize beer or *chicha* (so their bodies were not rendered imperfect by wounds) and then buried, left to die of the lack of oxygen and the extreme cold (though the boy's death was far from peaceful, as he was tied up and vomit and blood were found on his clothing).

Over a hundred **artefacts**, part of the remarkably intact treasure-trove buried with the children at the end of the fifteenth century, are on display in the museum's other rooms, where the temperature and humidity are kept artificially low – bring something warm to wear. The exhibit is both scientific and didactic, including a video about the expedition, displays of textiles and the like (the English labels are also very good). Check out also the exhibit on **La Reina del Cerro** ("Queen of the Hill"), the deteriorated remnants of another Inca mummy discovered on Cerro Chuscha in 1920 and illegally trafficked in subsequent years.

Cabildo (Museo Histórico del Norte)

Caseros 549 (Plaza 9 de Julio) • Tues–Fri 9am–7pm, Sat 9am–1.30pm & 3–6.30pm, Sun 9am–1.30pm • $20 • ☎ 0387 421 5340, ⓦ museonor.gov.ar

On the southern side of Plaza 9 de Julio stands the white-facaded **Cabildo** (old town hall). The oldest parts date from 1717, but it took on its current appearance after a 1940s restoration. It now houses the highly eclectic **Museo Histórico del Norte**, whose collections are arranged chronologically on the ground floor, beginning with a decent selection of pre-Hispanic archeological finds that include pots, anthropomorphic jars, funeral urns and a replica of "El suplicante" a precious stone idol stolen from the museum in 2003. The Spanish colonial and early independence period are represented by a rather fusty collection of portraits, a replica of Güemes' sabre, antique weapons and wonderful horse-drawn carriages and hearses, parked in the cobbled back courtyard. Upstairs, galleries lead off a veranda with superb views across the plaza, with displays ranging from old coins and eighteenth-century paintings to wooden saints. Of the religious art up here, the moving *San Pedro de Alcántara*, by eighteenth-century Altoperuvian artist Melchor Pérez de Holguín, stands out. Note that there are no English labels.

Casa de Arías Rengel

La Florida 20 • Tues–Sun 9am–7pm • Free • ☎ 0387 421 4714

Featuring a brilliant white facade, with an elaborate arched doorway and handsome green door, the **Casa de Arias Rengel** was erected towards the end of the eighteenth century. The home of Sergeant-Major Félix Arias Rengel, who conquered the Argentine Chaco and had the house built, it has splendid patios, full of lush trees and plants, while the fine interior details include verandas, banisters and rafters of red *quebracho* timber. Inside there are temporary exhibitions of local arts (with selections of African art from the often travelling Colección Campomar), a permanent display of indigenous art and some contemporary sculptures by **Esdras Luis Gianella**, the Argentine artist who was based in Salta until his death in 2010.

Casa Hernández (Museo de la Ciudad)

La Florida 97, at Alvarado • Mon–Sat 9am–1pm & 4–8.30pm • Free • ☎ 0387 437 3352

Opposite Casa Rengel, the **Casa Hernández** is a typical Neocolonial corner house with a chamfered angle. Built around 1780, with a delightful patio at its heart, it now houses the **Museo de la Ciudad**, a rather motley collection of local donations of artefacts and documents related to the city's history, from antique cameras and eyeglasses to pianos and dresses.

Iglesia de la Viña

Alberdi 485, at San Juan • Mon–Fri 6.30am–12.30pm & 4.30–8.30pm, Sun 7.30am–1pm & 5–9.30pm

Just south of the centre, the brightly painted **Iglesia Nuestra Señora de la Candelaria de la Viña** (commonly known as the **Iglesia de la Viña**) is the opulent twin of San Francisco (see below). The Italianate church was completed in 1886 to house a sacred image of the Virgin Mary – Our Lady of Candelaria – thought to have been created in medieval Portugal. At 44m, the tower is one of the tallest in Argentina, added to the church in 1908.

Museo Presidente José E Uriburu

Caseros 417 • Tues–Fri 9am–7pm, Sat 9am–1.30pm • $20 • ☎ 0387 421 8174

A fine adobe mansion with one of the most charming patios in the city (enhanced with a lime tree, blossoms and a grape-laden arbor), the Casa Uriburu is now the **Museo Presidente José E Uriburu**, a museum of period furniture and decorative arts. Until 1947 it was owned by the influential Uriburu family, who produced two presidents of Argentina – José Evaristo Uriburu (1895–98) and nephew José Félix Uriburu (1930–32). Constructed around 1773, patriarch Don José de Uriburu acquired the house in 1810, though there is little here about the family, and the collection of antique tables, sofas, portraits, silverware and fans is overshadowed by the building itself. Limited English captions.

Iglesia San Francisco

Caseros and Córdoba • Mon–Sat 8am–1pm & 2–9pm, Sun 8am–1pm & 5–9pm • Free • ☎ 0387 431 0830,
ⓦ conventosanfranciscosalta.com

One of the most beautiful religious buildings in the country, the **Iglesia San Francisco** takes up a whole block at the corner of Caseros and Córdoba. Built between 1767 and 1872, it's an extravaganza of Italianate Neocolonial exuberance, with pure ivory-white columns contrasting with the vibrant ox-blood walls, while the profuse detailing of Latin inscriptions, symbols and Neoclassical patterns is picked out in braid-like golden yellow.

The church's most imposing feature is its slender 54m **campanile** (added in 1882), towering over the low-rise Neocolonial houses of downtown Salta and tapering off to a slender spire. The highly elaborate **facade** of the church itself, behind a suitably austere statue of St Francis in the middle of the courtyard, is lavishly decorated with balusters and scrolls, curlicues and pinnacles, Franciscan inscriptions and the order's shield, but the most original features are the organza-like **stucco curtains** that billow down from each of the three archways, nearly touching the elegant wrought-iron gates below. Inside, the decoration is a little more subdued, with a beautiful trompe l'oeil ceiling, Neoclassical altar and ornate side chapels. If you can, take a **guided tour** (Spanish only, but with English audio players; Mon–Sat 10.30am, 12.30pm, 2.30pm & 6pm), which will get you into the **cloisters** and fascinating **Museo del Convento**, where the surprising archeological section features a perfect terracotta Etruscan head dating from the fourth century BC.

5

Museo El Tribuno Pajarito Velarde

Pueyrredón 106, at España (two blocks east of Plaza 9 de Julio) • Mon–Fri 10.30am–2pm & 3.30–6pm • $20

The curious **Museo El Tribuno Pajarito Velarde** was the home of a colourful local personality, Guillermo Velarde Mors (born in Salta in 1895), who died in his magnificent wooden bed here in 1965. Nicknamed "Pajarito" ("little bird"), this controversial bohemian was born into a wealthy, influential family, then worked in turn as a lawyer, journalist and banker, but retired from his last job, at the Banco Provincial de Salta, at the age of 37 to create a kind of arts club. While promoting artists, writers and musicians, especially local folk singers and groups, at a time when they lacked social kudos, he also went out of his way to cause scandals – he particularly liked provoking the nuns who ran the girls' school opposite his house. Respected as a great patron of the arts, he was also marginalized by local society, owing to his outlandish lifestyle – he never married, had lots of affairs and his music sessions often degenerated into drunken orgies. Crammed full of his fascinating belongings – including his 1912 German piano and a hat donated by an admiring Carlos Gardel (two tangos were composed in Pajarito's honour) – this humble adobe house, built in the late 1700s, is a fitting tribute to both an original local character and the history of Salta's socio-cultural life in the twentieth century. The mischievous curator, Carol, delights in shocking visitors with some of Pajarito's prize trinkets, several of which are in dubious taste (a cup made from bull's testicles, for example) – her lively explanations are best in Spanish, but she does a good enough job in English.

Paseo Güemes

Tree-lined **Paseo Güemes** is the main thoroughfare of a leafy, well-to-do barrio crammed with big, Neocolonial houses, and climbs up towards a bombastic **monument** of General Güemes himself. Surrounded by a grove of eucalyptus, the bronze equestrian statue, dating from 1931, is decorated with bas-reliefs depicting the army that defended newly independent Argentina from several last-ditch invasions by the Spanish.

Museo Antropológico de Salta

Ejército del Norte and Ricardo Solá • Mon–Fri 8am–7pm, Sat 10am–6pm • $5 • ☎ 0387 422 2960, ⓦ antropologico.gov.ar

The centrepiece of Salta's illuminating **Museo Antropológico de Salta** is its extensive ceramics collection, especially the set of finds from Tastil (see p.294). Look out also for the petroglyph known as the **Bailarina de Tastil**, a delightful figure carved onto rock, removed from the *pucará*, or pre-Columbian fortress, to the safety of a glass case. A well-executed reconstruction of a pre-Columbian burial shows how the local climate preserved textiles and wood in perfect condition for centuries, and a row of decorative urns is another highlight of the museum.

Teleférico San Bernardo

Daily 10am–7pm (last car down 7.30pm) • $110 return ($55 one-way) • ⓦ telefericosanbernardo.com

A steep path featuring the fourteen Stations of the Cross (and around 1021 steps) zigzags up the overgrown flanks of **Cerro San Bernardo** (1471m) from behind the Museo Antropológico, but you might prefer to take the **Teleférico San Bernardo**, or cable car – walking down the shady, cement path is a lot easier. From the base station on Avenida Hipólito Yrigoyen (between Urquiza and San Martín, at the eastern end of Parque San Martín), the cable-car gondolas take you to the summit in under ten minutes, and from the small miradors at the top you can admire panoramic **views** of the city. You can usually buy drinks at the ticket office on the peak, but bring water if you intend to hike, just in case.

Museo de Bellas Artes

5

Av Belgrano 992, at Sarmiento • Tues–Sun 9am–7pm • Free • ☏ 0387 422 1745

Salta's **Museo de Bellas Artes** is housed in the elegant Casona Usandivaras, an Art Nouveau mansion built in the early twentieth century for a former mayor, just west of downtown. Its eleven beautifully restored rooms house a rich patrimony of local, national and international art, ranging from paintings from the Peruvian **Cusqueña School** to twentieth-century sculpture. Highlights are a Cuzco *St Matthew*; the eighteenth-century polychrome *Asunción de la Virgen* from the Jesuit missions; the large *City of Salta*, painted in 1854 by Giorgio Penutti; and some fine engravings by nineteenth-century artists Basaldúa, Spilimbergo and Quinquela Martín.

Calle Balcarce and around

Salta's modern nightlife area lies along two blocks of **Calle Balcarce** known as **Paseo Balcarce**, north of Avenida Entre Ríos. Arts and crafts are on sale in the evenings and at weekends, and this is also where you'll find the largest number of restaurants, bars, discos and folk-music venues.

Museo de Arte Étnico Americano Pajcha

20 de Febrero 831 • Mon–Sat 10am–1pm & 4–8pm • $20 • ☏ 0387 4229417, ⊕ museopajchasalta.com.ar

The quirky **Museo de Arte Étnico Americano Pajcha** is a real gem, a priceless collection of Andean folk art curated by Liliana Madrid de Zito Fontán, a local ethnologist. The artefacts are arranged thematically and geographically in seven galleries; indigenous Argentine art and handicrafts loom large, but there are many outstanding items from all over South America, along with some beautiful photographs. Painting, textiles, religious objects (Christian and pre-Columbian) and wooden articles represent all the main ethnic groups; the silver jewellery, crafted by the Mapuche of Chile, and Andean ceramics are undoubtedly the highlights. There is also a fine example of a *pajcha*, an Inca offering tray with several compartments, looking not unlike an ancient muffin-mould. If he's around, avail yourself of a guided tour by enthusiastic curator Diego Outes Coll.

San Lorenzo

Just 11km northwest of Salta along RP-28, **SAN LORENZO** is part dormitory town, part retreat for many Salteños, appreciated for its spotlessly clean *ceibo*-lined avenues and patrician villas. Plentiful walking and riding opportunities, a private nature

---

WALKS AND TOURS AROUND SAN LORENZO

It's a pleasant one- to two-hour walk up the **Quebrada de San Lorenzo** (at the western end of Av Juan Carlos Davalos), a rocky gorge down which a stream flows, sometimes forming falls and pools; the walk takes you through unspoilt woodland to the foot of the hulking mountains that form a natural barrier behind the village.

Another enticing stroll can be taken through the **Reserva del Huaico** (Mon–Fri 8am–noon & 2–6pm, Sat 8am–noon, by prior appointment only; guided walk in Spanish only, rates vary; ☏ 0387 497 1024, ⊕ reservadelhuaico.org.ar), a nature reserve set up to protect the native forest and its endemic flora and fauna (especially its birds); the exploration of its trails culminates at a viewpoint from where you can take in the whole valley to Salta city and beyond. The reserve is located at the western end of Mariano Moreno.

Turismo San Lorenzo at Juan Carlos Dávalos 960 (☏ 0387 492 1757, ⊕ turismo-sanlorenzo .com.ar) offers three-hour guided walks up the Quebrada de San Lorenzo as well as other local walking and horseback trips. It also runs excursions further afield, such as to the Quebrada de Humahuaca or Cafayate.

reserve and an excellent range of **accommodation** make it an ideal alternative to staying in downtown Salta.

ARRIVAL AND DEPARTURE   SALTA

BY PLANE

Salta's Martín Miguel de Güemes International Airport (☎0387 424 2904) is in El Aybal, about 10km southwest of the city centre, along RN-51. Minibuses meet most flights ($40) and will drop you off at your hotel, but you'll have to wait till they fill up. City buses #8A and #6 run between the airport and central Av San Martín every 30min or so, but you'll need to pay with coins ($3.75) as you cannot buy *tarjetas* (stored-value cards) at the airport; a *remise* will set you back about $120 (pay in advance at the *remises* counter in the terminal; normal taxis should use the meter but should be around the same, depending on location).

Destinations Buenos Aires (6 daily; 2hr); Córdoba (2–3 weekly; 1hr 20min); Mendoza (2–3 weekly; 1hr 43min); Puerto Iguazú (1 daily; 1hr 50min).

BY BUS

Salta's bus terminal is at Hipólito Yrigoyen 339 (☎0387 401

1143), just east of Parque San Martín, five blocks south and eight east of central Plaza 9 de Julio. There are usually three companies running buses to Chile (San Pedro de Atacama and beyond) via Jujuy and Purmamarca, all departing at 7am daily (arriving 4pm at San Pedro). Bus #7 ($3.75) runs every 15min from central Salta to the Camino de la Quebrada, in San Lorenzo just before the gorge, stopping along Av San Martín and Juan Carlos Dávalos.

Destinations Buenos Aires (hourly; 19hr 10min–21hr 45min); Cachi (2 daily; 4hr); Cafayate (6 daily; 3hr 30min); Córdoba (8 daily; 11hr 15min–14hr); Jujuy (hourly; 55min–2hr 20min); Resistencia (4 daily; 13hr); San Antonio de los Cobres (2 daily; 5hr); Tucumán (10 daily; 4hr–4hr 50min).

BY TRAIN

The Tren a las Nubes (see box, p.293) departs from the Estación Salta, Ameghino 690, at Balcarce; bus #5 ($3.75) links it with the bus terminal via Plaza 9 de Julio.

INFORMATION

Provincial tourist office Buenos Aires 93 (Mon–Fri 8am–9pm, Sat & Sun 9am–8pm; ☎0387 431 0950, ⓦturismosalta.gov.ar). Dispenses maps and accommodation information; some staff members speak English.

City tourist office Caseros 711 (Mon–Fri 8am–9pm, Sat & Sun 9am–9pm; ☎0387 437 3340, ⓦsaltalalinda.gov .ar). Attractively located in a converted Neoclassical building (Casa de Moldes), the city tourist office has a few leaflets and a good city map.

TOURS FROM SALTA

A number of outfits offering a wide variety of highly professional **tours**, **expeditions** and other **activities** in the Northwest region are based in and around Salta. The following is a selection of the best.

★**Clark Expediciones** Mariano Moreno 1950, San Lorenzo ☎0387 492 7280, ⓦclarkexpediciones .com. Supremely experienced and professional team that specializes in birdwatching trips in Northwest Argentina, to Calilegua and El Rey national parks, to the Laguna de los Pozuelos and further afield.

Marina Turismo Caseros 489 ☎0387 431 2097, ⓦmarina-semisa.com.ar. One of the most professional outfits in the region, Marina's friendly and dynamic team will bend over backwards to get you a vehicle (and driver-guide, should you need one), find a guided excursion, book your hotel, change your flight or even just give you useful tips about where to eat, sleep or drink. English spoken.

MoviTrack Buenos Aires 28 ☎0387 431 6749, ⓦmovitrack.com.ar. Offers the "Safari a los Nubes", a fun and adventurous way of discovering the Quebrada del Toro; there's an optional extension via the Quebrada

de Humahuaca, in a special vehicle giving all passengers panoramic views. It also does trips to Cachi and Cafayate.

Norte Trekking Gral Güemes 265 oficina 1 ☎0387 431 6616, ⓦnortetrekking.com. Federico Norte and his experienced team are a fount of knowledge on the local area and can take you on a safari into the *puna*, to the Valles Calchaquíes, to the Parque El Rey and elsewhere; they also run longer tours into Chile and Bolivia.

★**Salta Rafting** Caseros 177 ☎0387 421 3216, ⓦsaltarafting.com. Highly professional, youthful team of operators specializing in rafting in a bucolic setting on the Río Juramento, grade III rapids about a 2hr drive from the city. It also runs "canopy" (zipwire) rides over the canyon, and can organize horseriding and mountain-biking excursions.

Socompa Balcarce 998, 1st floor ☎0387 416 9130, ⓦsocompa.com. Excellent operator working out of Salta, but specializing in the Puna Catamarqueña.

ACCOMMODATION

Salta has a wide variety of **places to stay**, but if you have your own transport you'll also find a number of excellent accommodation options in nearby San Lorenzo (see below), only a 15min drive from the city centre, plus a good many **fincas** and **estancias** (see box, p.292) in the surrounding countryside. Holidays and weekends can get busy in Salta, and it's a good idea to book ahead at these times. All the options listed below offer **free wi-fi**, unless otherwise stated.

CENTRAL SALTA

★ **El Balcón de la Plaza** España 444 ☎ 0387 421 4792, ⓦ balcondelaplaza.com.ar. A fabulous boutique hotel in a colonial-style house built in 1896, with just ten rooms (blending original tiled floors and wood ceilings with stylish furnishings) and all the amenities (buffet breakfast included). $1245

Bloomer's Bed and Brunch Vicente López 129 ☎ 0387 422 7449, ⓦ bloomers-salta.com.ar. The five suites around a colonial patio – all with mod cons such as flat-screen TVs – ooze charm. Run by a British–Peruvian couple, this B&B serves brunch rather than breakfast, is welcoming, comfortable and brightly decorated. $865

Caseros 44 Caseros 44 ☎ 0387 421 6761, ⓦ caseros44 bandb.com.ar. Homely little B&B just like a private house. All the rooms have ceiling fans and en-suite bathrooms. Cash only. $600

Coloria Hostel Güemes 333 ☎ 0387 431 3058, ⓦ coloriahostel.com. One of Salta's better-value hostels, with an excellent central location, bright, contemporary dorms and private rooms (the more expensive ones en suite) and shared kitchen. Continental breakfast included. Dorms $85; doubles $290

Design Suites Pasaje Castro 215 ☎ 0387 439 5962, ⓦ designsuites.com. Housed in the carefully renovated Palacio Usandivaras, a 1913 mansion with a rather ugly modern adjunct. Inside it is all modern art and minimalism, with the best suites in the old palace, also home to a top-rate restaurant. $1230

★ **Legado Mítico** Mitre 647 ☎ 0387 422 8786, ⓦ legadomitico.com. Wonderfully inviting themed hotel in a well-located, converted 1930s townhouse – each of the huge, sumptuously decorated rooms is named after a figure of regional importance such as a writer, a gaucho or a member of an indigenous tribe. $2000

Marilian Buenos Aires 176 ☎ 0387 421 6700, ⓦ www .hotelmarilian.com.ar. Professionally run, attractively decorated central hotel with both heating and a/c, a decent *confitería* and room service. It has an *apart-hotel* branch at España 254 (usually cheaper). $600

Regidor Buenos Aires 8 ☎ 0387 431 1305. Cheap but charming place with character, a rustic *confitería* and very pleasant rooms (all with a/c). Rooms overlooking the square tend to be noisy. $475

★ **Solar de la Plaza** Leguizamón 669 ☎ 0387 431 5111, ⓦ solardelaplaza.com.ar. Definitely one of the classiest acts in the city, *Solar* is housed in a converted 1950s Neocolonial mansion with beautifully furnished, large rooms, rooftop pool, professional service and outstanding buffet breakfast featuring delicious local products. $1050

OUT OF THE CENTRE

All Norte Hostel Balcarce 1353 ☎ 0387 471 2960, ⓦ allnorte.com.ar. Some 2km north of Plaza 9 de Julio (but closer to the bars on Balcarce), this homely hostel is managed by friendly Fernando and his family, with spotless dorms, private rooms and showers. Simple breakfast included. Dorms $195; doubles $320

Backpackers Home Buenos Aires 930 ☎ 0387 423 5910, ⓦ backpackerssalta.com. The city's veteran hostel now has a pool, as well as a very friendly, international atmosphere and a strong tendency to have fiestas. There are simple doubles as well as cramped dorms. Internet access via ADSL cable, no wi-fi. Dorms $115; doubles $350

Hostal El Relax Pasaje Pedro Saravia 19 ☎ 0387 471 4691, ⓦ hostalelrelaxsalta.com. Justly popular hotel overlooking Parque San Martín (near the cable car), with simple but comfy rooms enhanced with bright local artwork (depicting local landscapes) and flat-screen cable TVs. Breakfast included and free parking nearby. $820

House of Jasmines RN-51 Km11, La Merced Chica, near Salta airport ☎ 0387 431 5454, ⓦ houseof jasmines.com. A colonial house tastefully transformed into a luxury lodge. It has just seven suites and a scattering of private dining areas. The food and wine are memorable, making it just the place for a romantic treat. $2700

★ **Kkala** Las Higueras 104 ☎ 0387 439 6590, ⓦ hotelkkala.com.ar. Fabulous boutique hotel in Tres Cerritos, a well-heeled barrio close to the centre but far from the hustle and bustle. The enticing rooms are beautifully furnished, while the views from the hotel, its pool/deck and tranquil public areas are stunning. $1550

Petit Hotel Hipólito Irigoyen 225 ☎ 0387 421 3012, ⓦ petithotelsalta.com.ar. Mid-range hotel, seven blocks from the centre, with clean rooms and good service. You can enjoy views of the Cerro San Bernardo from its café terrace and small swimming pool. $900

SAN LORENZO

Cabañas del Sol RP-28 Km11.5 ☎ 0387 492 1821, ⓦ saltacabanasdelsol.com. Wonderful complex of thirteen *cabañas*, some of them right down by the riverside, in a fabulous rural setting 4km from San Lorenzo; ideal for anyone who wants to have self-catering accommodation and good value for a group, with the

5

cabins sleeping up to seven. Breakfast included. $1045
★**Casa Hernández** José Hernández 406 ☎0387 492 2502, ⊚lacasahernandez.com.ar. This friendly B&B is superb value, with spacious, modern rooms (all with private toilets, with the cheapest rooms sharing showers), shared lounge with fireplace, small pool and delicious breakfasts. $440

El Castillo de San Lorenzo Juan Carlos Dávalos 1985 ☎0387 492 1052, ⊚hotelelcastillo.com.ar. This romantic property was built in the late nineteenth century as an Italian-style castle for businessman Luigi Bartoletti, and now offers bright, comfy rooms blending contemporary and period styles, all with balconies and stunning views. Buffet breakfast served in the former coach house. $980

Don Numas Posada Boutique & Spa Pompilio Guzmán 1470 ☎0387 492 1918, ⊚donnumas.com.ar. This home-from-home posada has spacious rooms with modern bathrooms, ultra-friendly service, two swimming pools, a fully equipped spa and a prime setting affording mountain views. The breakfast, complete with home-made cakes and pies, will keep you going all day, but other simple meals or *asados* are offered on request. $1095

★**Eaton Place** Av San Martín 2457 ☎0387 492 1347, ⊚eatonplacesalta.com.ar. As the name hints, this exquisite hotel – whose English-speaking owner has a collection of antiques – is inspired by London mansions, though what Belgravia townhouse boasts a palm-lined driveway? The plush rooms, classy service, dreamy swimming pool, toothsome food and marvellous grounds make this a plum choice. $950

Hostal El Cerrito Juan Carlos Dávalos 1683 ☎0387 492 2257, ⊚hostalelcerrito.com.ar. Simple but clean rooms with fan and bathroom, in a pleasant house surrounded by gardens and a small pool on the deck. $660

EATING

Salta has plenty of eating places to suit all pockets, ranging from simple **snack bars** where you can savour the city's famous **empanadas** to a growing number of classy **restaurants** where people dress smartly for dinner. The most traditional **cafés** huddle around Plaza 9 de Julio, while the city market (Mercado Central) at Florida and San Martín has a number of stalls selling snacks at super-cheap prices.

CENTRAL SALTA

El Charrúa Caseros 221 ☎0387 432 2222, ⊚parrilla elcharrua.com.ar. Best wood-fired *parrilla* in town, with most steaks priced around $200, but also a decent fish menu ($135–240). Daily 11am–4pm & 7.30pm–1am.

La Criollita Zuviría 306 ☎0387 431 7342. Local restaurant best known for its empanadas and Andean-themed dining room. Try the excellent spicy meat empanadas ($10), larger tamales ($30) and *humitas* ($45), plus the more substantial *locro* ($80), chicken soup ($65) and steaks ($120). Daily 10am–3pm & 7pm–midnight.

El Farito Caseros 509 ☎0387 421 5035. Tiny empanada joint on the main plaza, dishing out Salta's classic delicious piping-hot cheese and meat pasties, spiced with peppers, all day long. It's $95 for a dozen or just $8 for one; sit in the shady patio or take away. Tues–Sun 10am–late.

PEÑAS

Salta is famed for its lively **peñas**, informal folk-music clubs mainly found in the Northwest. Most open around 8pm to serve food – mainly local fare such as *locro* and empanadas. The musicians turn up and start jamming later, often at around 10pm but in some cases not till midnight. Many *peñas*, particularly the more touristy ones, charge extra for the music/show.

Boliche de Balderrama San Martín 1126, at Esteco ☎0387 421 1542, ⊚facebook.com/BalderramaSalta; map p.282. One of the most famous *peñas*; well known as a bohemian hangout – it was founded in 1954 by the late Juan Balderrama and his brothers, and immortalized by a *zamba* written by Manuel Castilla – nowadays it's a far more conventional place, attracting plenty of tourists. Shows can be good fun, but don't expect a truly authentic experience, despite its historic pedigree. Entry is usually $90 and the food is decent but quite pricey.

★**La Casona del Molino** Luís Burela 1, at Caseros ☎0387 434 2835; map p.282. Empanadas, *locro*, tamales, *humitas*, sangría and improvised live music after 11pm, all in a handsomely restored Neocolonial mansion. Cash only (but no cover). Usually open Tues–Sun 9pm–3.30am – get here early to secure a table.

La Vieja Estación Balcarce 875 ☎0387 421 7727, ⊚la-viejaestacion.com.ar; map p.282. Modern *peña* in one of the city's trendiest streets, dishing out food, draught beer and folk music shows. Shows cost around $100, but credit cards are accepted. Reservations recommended (taken from 7pm daily). Usually open daily from 9pm (till 3am Mon–Thurs, 5am Fri & Sat & 2am Sun). Shows usually start around 10.15pm (9.15pm Sun).

CLOCKWISE FROM TOP LEFT CHEESE, TAFÍ DEL VALLE (P.320); FESTIVAL CELEBRATING PACHAMAMA, SALTA PROVINCE; HORSES BY A STREAM NEAR TAFÍ DEL VALLE (P.320); MUSEO PACHAMAMA, AMAICHA (P.320) >

5

Heladería Rosmari Pueyrredón 202 ☎0387 431 3774, ⓦrosmariartesanal.com.ar. Best ice cream in the city (scoops from $22). Flavours range from *crema de coco* to Ferrero Rocher, tiramisu and *crema de portuguesa* (thick and creamy nougat custard). Daily 11am–11pm.

Ma Cuisine España 83 ☎0387 421 4378. Justly considered the best gourmet experience in town, this small, French-inspired restaurant serves perfectly grilled steaks but also vegetarian tagliatelle, grilled fish and a range of well-constructed pasta dishes. Reservations required (cash only). Mon–Sat 8pm–midnight.

★**El Solar del Convento** Caseros 444 ☎0387 421 5124. Elegant surroundings and classical music set the tone for this high-class but not so expensive restaurant, serving juicy steaks and with an excellent wine list (mains $125–140). The patio area in front is also good for coffee and pastries. Daily 11am–3pm & 8pm–1am.

Van Gogh España 502 (Plaza 9 de Julio) ☎0387 431 4659. The best coffee in town ($23), excellent cakes, quick meals, appetizing snacks and the location are the attractions here, plus live music late at weekends. The bar looks a bit tired now compared to some other spots nearby, but it does serve food all day. Daily 6am–3am.

OUT OF THE CENTRE

José Balcarce Necochea 594, at Mitre ☎0387 421 1628. José López presides over the "Andean Fusion" kitchen at this charming, Neocolonial corner restaurant and uses regional products such as quinoa and grain amaranth (another Andean cereal) to accompany llama; also try llama carpaccio or, for the less adventurous, the steak and roast potatoes. Cash only. Tues–Sun 5pm–1.30am.

SAN LORENZO

Campo Adentro Juan Carlos Dávalos 1401, at Gorriti ☎0387 492 1600. In a galleried building with a large terrace, the extensive menu of this *parrillada* includes empanadas, delicious *locro*, fresh trout (best simply grilled, rather than smothered in sauce) and pasta. Mon & Wed–Sun noon–3pm & 8pm–midnight.

Casa Pueblo Salta Juan Carlos Dávalos and Gorriti ☎0387 492 2688. Popular restaurant in a mock adobe palace serving a vast range of well-crafted dishes, from burgers and pizzas to Greek food. Mon–Thurs 11am–midnight, Fri & Sat 10am–1am, Sun 10am–11pm.

Confitería Don Sanca Juan Carlos Dávalos 1450 ☎0387 492 1580. A charming place serving tasty food, including a very good stab at tea. Enjoy with a slice of cake inside or on the grassy patio. Tues–Sun noon–9pm.

ENTERTAINMENT

Teatro Provincial Zuviría 70 (Plaza 9 de Julio) ☎0387 422 4515, ⓦteatroprovincial.gob.ar. Salta's world-class theatre began life in 1940 as the Cine Victoria. Now beautifully renovated with a plush interior, it's home to one of Argentina's best-regarded classical orchestras, the Sinfónica de Salta, which attracts leading musicians from around the globe. The theatre also hosts plays, dance and folklore concerts (the Ballet de la Provincia and Ballet Folklórico Martín Miguel de Güemes are also based here). Box office Mon–Fri 9am–1.30pm & 4.30–9pm.

ESTANCIAS AND FINCAS IN SALTA AND JUJUY PROVINCES

Salta and, to a lesser degree Jujuy, are provinces with a very long colonial history, which has left behind many **estancias** (traditional ranches), known locally as *fincas*, some of which now offer rooms to guests. Estancia stays are a wonderful way of combining rest – and sometimes even luxury – with a chance to get to know locals, tune in to nature and experience *criollo* customs and farming activities. Free wi-fi and breakfast are usually included. In all cases, reserve ahead.

El Bordo de las Lanzas Rivadavia 298, General Güemes ☎0387 5534 6942, ⓦestanciaelbordo .com. A historic tobacco farm located 80km northeast of Salta. The early seventeenth-century house maintains its colonial structures – the furniture and artefacts come from Jesuit missions in the Northwest, Peru and Bolivia – but with all modern conveniences. $1735

Finca Valentina RN-51 Km6, La Merced Chica ☎0387 15 415 3490, ⓦfinca-valentina.com.ar. Conveniently close to Salta's airport, this delightful, modern *finca* is run by an utterly stylish couple from Milan who combine flair (Valentina is an architect) with professional know-how (Fabrizio is an economist). Its handful of charming rooms are set among a green park near wonderful walking and riding country. There's memorably delicious food, too. $1240

Finca Santa Anita Piedras Moradas s/n, Coronel Moldes ☎0387 490 5050, ⓦsantaanita.com .ar. Located around 60km south of Salta by RN-68, on the west bank of the huge Embalse Cabra Corral reservoir. As well as swimming in the pool or taking organized horserides, you can watch tobacco being processed and visit the tobacco museum on the premises. $825

DIRECTORY

Banks and exchange Banco de la Nación, Mitre 151; Citibank, Balcarce 103, at España; there are plenty of ATMs around town. To change US$ at the best rates, look for the moneychangers outside Dinar Cambio, on España at the northwest corner of Plaza 9 de Julio.
Consulates Bolivia, Mariano Boedo 32 ☎0387 421 1040

(Mon–Fri 9am–2pm); Chile, Santiago del Estero 965 ☎0387 43 1857 (Mon–Fri 9am–1.30pm).
Laundry Laverap, Santiago del Estero 363.
Post office Deán Funes 160 (Mon–Fri 8.30am–7.30pm).
Visa extensions Dirección Nacional de Migraciones, Maipú 35 (Mon–Fri 7.30am–12.30pm; ☎0387 422 0438).

Quebrada del Toro

Whether you travel up the magnificent **Quebrada del Toro** by train – along one of the highest railways in the world (see box below) – in a tour operator's jeep, in a rented car or, as the pioneers did centuries ago, on horseback, the experience will be unforgettable, thanks to the gorge's constantly changing dramatic mountain scenery and multicoloured rocks. It is named after the **Río Toro**, normally a meandering trickle, but occasionally a raging torrent and as bullish as its name suggests, especially in the spring. The road and rail track swerve up from the tobacco fields of the Valle de Lerma, southwest of Salta, through dense thickets of **ceibo**, Argentina's national tree, ablaze in October and November with their fuchsia-red spring blossom, and end at the dreary but strategic mining settlement of **San Antonio de los Cobres**.

TOURS   QUEBRADA DEL TORO

Tour operators Many tour operators in Salta (see box, p.288) offer tours of the Quebrada del Toro by road, which shadows the train for part of the way, offering passengers the chance to photograph the handsome locomotive if it is running that day. MoviTrak can meet you at a station on the way back to guide you around the altiplano in a jeep; you miss out on the return train journey but get the best of both worlds – the train ride up in daylight plus a chance to explore the area more independently. It is also possible to combine excursions up the Quebrada del Toro with a return leg down the Quebrada de Humahuaca (see p.299), over two or three days (4WD only).

THE TRAIN TO THE CLOUDS

Travelling through the Quebrada del Toro gorge on the Tren a las Nubes, or **Train to the Clouds**, is an unashamedly touristic but jaw-dropping experience. Clambering slowly from the station in Salta (it never exceeds 35 km/hr) to the magnificent Meccano-like **La Polvorilla viaduct**, 4220m high in the altiplano, the comfortable train – with a leather-upholstered interior, shiny wooden fittings, spacious seats, a dining car, a post office and even altitude-sickness remedies – was originally built to service the borax mines in the salt flats of Pocitos and Arizaro, 300km beyond La Polvorilla. The viaduct lies 217km from Salta, and on the way the train crosses **29 bridges** and **twelve viaducts**, threads through **21 tunnels**, swoops round two gigantic **360° loops** and chugs up **two switchbacks**. La Polvorilla, seen on many posters and in all the tour operators' brochures, is 224m long, 64m high and weighs over 1600 tonnes; built in Italy, it was assembled here in 1930. There are brief stopovers near La Polvorilla (2.50pm), where the train doubles back, and in San Antonio de los Cobres (4pm), allowing you to visit the Mercado Artesanal, where locals will sell you llama-wool scarves and pose for photos (for a fee). Folk groups and solo artists interspersed with people selling arts, crafts, cheese, honey and souvenirs galore help while the time away on the way down, when it's dark for the most part (in winter).

The train leaves (and returns to) the Estación Salta (see p.288) once or twice a week (usually Fri & Sat) from late March to early December, with more frequent departures in July (Tues, Thurs & Sat) and August to November (Thurs & Sat); note that some days the train only runs **one-way** from Salta, meaning you must take the bus back from San Antonio. It's a long day either way – the train departs Salta at 7.05am and gets back around 9pm – the speedier bus back departs after the 4pm arrival in San Antonio (see p.295). **Tickets** cost $2600 for the round trip ($2300 for trips from late March to June 30) and should be reserved in advance at ⓦ trenalasnubes.com.ar or ☎0387 422 8021.

5

Campo Quijano to Ingeniero Maury

RN-51 begins its climb up the **Quebrada del Toro** a few kilometres northwest of **Campo Quijano**, a small town with plenty of places to buy food and drink some 30km southwest from Salta. The first 22km of the Quebrada road are unpaved – the gravel surface makes this usually passable for all vehicles, but check in advance if it's been raining (work is ongoing to surface this section but it is unlikely to be completed for several years). As the road follows the Río Toro up the valley (crossing the rail line several times), the tropical vegetation of the Yungas zone is swiftly replaced by cacti and arid, candy-coloured mountain slopes. The surfaced road resumes at the small hamlet of **Chorrillos**, where it's another 10.5km to the village (and police checkpoint) of **Ingeniero Maury** – a winding, dramatic section along the ever-narrowing Toro gorge. From Maury it's 27km to **Alfarcito**, along the most spectacular section of the route, with the explosion of colours, rock forms and vistas best appreciated in the afternoon (preferably coming down). Halfway along, the road breaks away from the rail line to follow the Quebrada Tastil.

Alfarcito

The first place worth visiting along RN-51 is the hamlet of **ALFARCITO**, a tiny Kolla (*Qolla*) community on the banks of the Tastil that's at the centre of an ambitious project to funnel tourist dollars to the indigenous population (⊕fundacionalfarcito.org .ar). The tiny chapel of **San Cayetano** is usually open during the day, its modern interior decked out with cosy benches topped with llama wool cushions. Nearby, the **Centro Artesanal** (Mon–Sat 9am–5pm; $5) provides background to the project and what they hope to achieve here in the coming years (Spanish labels only). There's also a crafts store, selling local products made of alpaca wool and *cardon* cacti, the flora and fauna most characteristic of the area.

EATING   **ALFARCITO**

Parador El Alfarcito ☎0387 578 4450. Next door to the chapel this small Kolla-run café is the only place to eat in the village, selling soft drinks, coffee and home-made snacks (empanadas $10, *humitas* $25). Mon–Sat 9am–5pm.

Santa Rosa de Tastil

The minute village of **SANTA ROSA DE TASTIL**, around 10km further up the narrowing Quebrada Tastil from Alfarcito, at 3100m above sea level, has only a handful of Kolla inhabitants but is the location of an intriguing **pre-Inca site**. In the village itself, just beyond the tiny **Capilla Santa Rosa de Lima**, the **Museo de Sitio Tastil** (Tues–Fri & Sun 9am–6pm, Sat 10am–7pm; free; ☎0387 4317657) is set beneath the gorge's cactus-clad rocks. It contains finds from the nearby excavations (Spanish labels only). There's a small craft shop opposite, with products handmade by the local community.

Sitio Arqueológico Tastil

Tues–Sun 9am–4pm • Free

Preserving the site of one of Argentina's largest pre-Inca towns, the **Sitio Arqueológico Tastil** is thought to have been inhabited by some two thousand people between 1000 and 1442 – it was traditionally thought to have been abandoned around 1430, but the Inca are now believed to have conquered the city and relocated its population. The entrance lies off RN-51 just beyond the village itself, on the left next to the cemetery. From here a trail leads up the hill to once-fortified heights commanding fabulous valley and mountain views. Low stone walls, snaking around the hillside and cacti, mark the ruins of various buildings, streets and plazas, and several stones are embellished with well-preserved petroglyphs.

San Antonio de los Cobres

RN-51 ends at **SAN ANTONIO DE LOS COBRES**, some 60km beyond Santa Rosa de Tastil at a dizzying 3775m above sea level. It's the small, windswept "capital" of an immense but mostly empty portion of the *puna*, rich in minerals, as its name ("of the coppers") suggests, but little else, except some breathtaking scenery. The Tren a las Nubes makes a short stop here on its way back down to the plains, with the only attraction the **Mercado Artesanal** (daily 9am–9pm), a market selling cheap local and Bolivian arts and crafts.

ARRIVAL AND INFORMATION   SAN ANTONIO DE LOS COBRES

By bus Ale Hermanos (☎0387 423 2226, ⓦalehnos.com /recorridoSaltaCobres.html) runs a twice-daily bus service between Salta and San Antonio (5hr), with the first departure 7.30am from Salta. At the time of writing there were no services onwards to San Pedro de Atacama (Chile) via the Paso de Jama. If you are taking the train (see p.293)

and want to take the bus back, get off in San Antonio at 4pm (on the return leg).
Tourist information The small visitor centre (daily 10am–6pm) in the Mercado Artesanal, on the edge of town, has information on a variety of ecotourism ventures being developed in the area (such as staying on a llama farm).

ACCOMMODATION AND EATING

Hostería de las Nubes Caseros 441 ☎0387 490 9059, ⓦhoteldelasnubes.com. Fairly basic, but the plumbing works, the meals are fine (breakfast included), and it's the

only really recommendable place in town. Free wi-fi in public areas. **$690**

San Salvador de Jujuy

The capital of Jujuy Province, **SAN SALVADOR DE JUJUY** lies 120km north of Salta and serves as the commercial centre for the entire region. It is the most Andean of all Argentina's cities: much of its population is descended from indigenous peoples (primarily Quechua, Aymara and Chiriguano), including recent Bolivian immigrants, and it's the powerbase of the **Asociacion Barrial Tupac Amaru**, the influential social organization and NGO founded by **Milagro Sala**, the "most powerful woman in the north of Argentina" (see p.298). A day or two will suffice to see the town's modest attractions, though its excellent spread of restaurants and a thriving cultural scene make it a good stopover or possible base to visit the rich hinterland that surrounds it.

Though the town is a typical blend of modern buildings interspersed with adobe homes and grander historic edifices, Jujuy's central streets and its Plaza Belgrano have a subtropical charm. Scratch the surface and you'll unearth some real treasures, among them one of the finest pieces of sacred art to be seen in Argentina, the **pulpit** in the **cathedral**.

Brief history

Jujuy was founded by the Spanish *conquistador* Francisco de Argañaraz y Murguía, after a couple of early false starts, in 1593. Earthquakes, the plague and conflict all conspired to hamper the city's growth during the seventeenth and eighteenth centuries and have deprived it of all its original buildings. General Belgrano ordered the **Jujuy Exodus** on August 23, 1812 – an event every Argentine schoolchild learns about – at the height of the Wars of Independence; the city's entire population was evacuated and Jujuy was razed to the ground to prevent its capture by the Spanish. Jujuy continued to bear the brunt of conflict, sacked by the royalists in 1814 and 1818. It then remained a forgotten backwater throughout the nineteenth century (made worse by a devastating **earthquake** in 1863), and the railway did not reach it until 1903. Since the 1930s, its outskirts have spilt across both rivers and begun to creep up the hillsides, and it now has a sizeable immigrant population, mostly from across the Bolivian border to the north. The province – and therefore the city, which lives off the province's agricultural production – have traditionally grown rich on sugar and tobacco, but earnings have declined in recent years and forced

5

farmers to diversify into other crops. NGO **Tupac Amaru** has a massive membership base here – protests against provincial governor **Gerardo Morales** (who was elected in October 2015) effectively shut down the main plaza in late 2015 through early 2016.

Plaza General Belgrano

Most of the Jujuy's main sights are near **Plaza General Belgrano**, at the eastern extremity of the compact centre. Planted with lime trees and palms, it's still the city's hub, partly occupied by craftsmen, mainly potters, displaying their wares. The elegant **Cabildo** runs along its northern side, now housing the city's main police station and a small museum of police history (Mon–Fri 8am–1pm & 2–9pm, Sat & Sun 9am–noon & 6–8pm; free; ☎0388 423 7715), which also offers a chance to see inside the ageing structure.

Casa de Gobierno

Plaza General Belgrano s/n • Mon–Fri 9am–noon & 4–8pm • Free

Plaza General Belgrano is dominated to the south by the **Casa de Gobierno** with its extremely Gallic-looking slate mansard roof, where the national flag donated to the city by General Belgrano, as a tribute to the Exodus, is proudly guarded in the **Salón de la Bandera**. Dotted around the building stand five large **statues** by renowned sculptress **Lola Mora** (see box, p.219). Representing Peace, Progress, Justice, Freedom and Labour, the set was originally designed for the Congreso Nacional in Buenos Aires, inaugurated in 1906, but the reactionary federal government vetoed the project and had the statues dumped in a store room. Luckily Jujuy's government at that time was less intransigent, and in 1915 it appointed Lola Mora as the city's director of parks and squares, in order to erect the statues in their present position.

Iglesia Catedral Basilica

Plaza General Belgrano s/n • Daily 8am–noon & 5–8pm • Free • **Museo Catedral** Tues–Fri 9.30am–12.30pm & 4–7pm, Sat 10am–1pm • $10

Jujuy's **Iglesia Catedral Basilica**, constructed in the 1760s, is topped by an early twentieth-century tower and extended by an even later Neoclassical atrium. The exterior is unremarkable, but the interior, a layer of painted Bakelite concealing the original timber structure, is impressive: a realistic mock-fresco of sky and clouds soars over the altar, while above the nave is a primitive depiction of the ceremony in which Belgrano awarded the Argentine flag to the people of Jujuy in 1812.

Two original doors and two confessionals, Baroque masterpieces from the eighteenth century, immediately catch the eye, thanks to their vivid red and sienna paint, picked out with gilt, but the undisputed highlight – and the main attraction of the whole city – is the magnificent *ñandubay* and cedar-wood **pulpit**. Decorated in the eighteenth century by indigenous artists from the Jesuit missions, it easily rivals those of **Cusco**, its apparent inspiration, with its harmonious compositions, elegant floral and vegetable motifs and the finesse of its carvings. Its various tableaux in gilded, carved wood, gleaming with an age-old patina, depict subjects such as Jacob's ladder and St Augustine, along with biblical genealogies from Adam to Abraham and David to Solomon. One curiosity is the error in the symbols of the four **Apostles**: Matthew and John are correctly represented by a human figure and an eagle respectively, but Mark, symbolized by a bull, and Luke, by a lion, are the wrong way round.

The **Museo Catedral** (enter via the shady patio) contains a couple of rooms filled with nicely presented religious art, including an eighteenth-century painting series of the life of Mary and a rare silver plate from 1695; labels are in Spanish only.

Iglesia San Francisco

Belgrano and Lavalle • Mon–Sat 9am–noon & 5–7.45pm • Free • **Museo del Arte Sacro** Mon–Fri 9am–1pm & 5–9pm • $10

Not of quite the same calibre as the cathedral's, but very striking nonetheless, is the Spanish Baroque **pulpit** in **Iglesia San Francisco**; also inspired by the pulpits of Cusco and almost certainly carved by craftsmen in eighteenth-century Bolivia, it drips with detail, with a profusion of little Franciscan monks peeking out from row upon row of tiny columns, all delicately gilded. Although the church and separate campanile are built to a traditional neo-Baroque style, the church was actually built in the 1930s. The church's **Museo de Arte Sacro** has a separate entrance at Belgrano 677, containing a small but precious collection of religious art saved from various Franciscan churches across the region, including an ornate eighteenth-century altar from Potosí, Bolivia.

Museo Histórico Provincial

Lavalle 265 • Daily 2–8pm • $10 • ☎ 0388 422 1355

Jujuy's premier museum, the **Museo Histórico Provincial** houses exhibits on the province's turbulent history with special focus on independence hero **General Juan Lavalle** – this is the colonial house where he died, mortally wounded after the Battle of Famaillá, in 1841. Other exhibits included the iconic kepi (caps) of the No. 12 squadron National Guards and a room dedicated to Dr Macedonio Graz, provincial governor and founder of the city's first newspaper in 1856.

Museo Temático de Maquetas Tupac Amaru

Alvear 1152 • Daily 8am–11pm • Free • ⓦ www.tupacamaru.org.ar

The enlightening **Museo Temático de Maquetas Tupac Amaru** at Tupac Amaru's

5

headquarters – the organization lead by Milagro Sala (see box, p.298) – presents local indigenous cultures and history as a series of charming dioramas, though you'll need to read Spanish to make the most of the explanations.

ARRIVAL AND DEPARTURE
SAN SALVADOR DE JUJUY

By plane Jujuy's Gobernador Horacio Guzmán airport (☎0388 491 1109) is over 30km southeast of the city, along RN-66 near Perico; the taxi fare is around $250. Minibuses to "Plaza Manuel Belgrano" are $100.
Destinations Buenos Aires (3 daily; 2hr 10min); Salta (1 daily; 20min).

By bus The bus terminal, at Av Dorrego 365 (☎0388 422 6299), just south of the centre, serves all local, regional and national destinations, and also runs a service to Chile. There's a left-luggage facility. Several city buses run between the terminal and the centre ($5.50); taxis are around $20–30.
Destinations Buenos Aires (hourly; 21–23hr); Córdoba (9 daily; 11hr 30min–16hr); Humahuaca (hourly; 2hr); La Quiaca (hourly; 2hr 45min–5hr); Purmamarca (hourly; 1hr 15min); Salta (hourly; 1hr 30min); Tilcara (hourly; 50min–1hr 30min); Tucumán (10 daily; 5–6hr).

INFORMATION

Tourist information For basic information, head for the Dirección Provincial de Turismo (Mon–Fri 7am–10pm, Sat & Sun 8am–1pm & 4–10pm; ☎0388 422 1325, ⓦturismo.jujuy.gov.ar), at the northeastern corner of central Plaza General Belgrano.

ACCOMMODATION

Jujuy has a wide variety of **places to stay**, though holidays and weekends can get busy – book ahead at these times. All the options listed below offer **free wi-fi** and breakfast.

★**Altos de la Viña** Pasquini López 50, La Viña ☎0388 426 2626, ⓦaltosdelaviña.com.ar. On the heights of La Viña, 4km northeast of the city centre, this refurbished hotel, with large, comfortable rooms and a shady garden, commands fabulous views of the valley and mountains. Shuttle service to and from downtown. $1090

El Arribo Belgrano 1263 ☎0388 422 2539, ⓦelarribo.com. A short walk from the centre, a remodelled nineteenth-century house, retaining original tiles and doors, has been turned into this pleasant and peaceful boutique hotel. Friendly service, a small garden and a (rather small) swimming pool are bonuses. $755

Augustus Belgrano 715 ☎0388 423 0203, ⓦhotel augustus.com.ar. Extremely friendly hotel, with modern,

clean rooms, spacious bathrooms and good breakfasts. The snack bar serves delicious sandwiches and *lomitos*. $900

★**D-Gira Hostel Jujuy** Juana Manuela Gorriti 427 ☎0388 15 408 0386, ⓦamvelas.wix.com/dgirahostel jujuy. This modern, cosy and comfy hostel beats all the competition in this price range, with friendly owners and free drinking water, shampoo and soap, and especially tasty breakfasts (fresh breads, fruits and so on). Dorms $100; doubles $330

Gregorio I Hotel Independencia 829 ☎0388 424 4545, ⓦgregoriohotel.com. Modern hotel with swish, contemporary-style rooms, cable TV, a/c, parquet floors and Andean artwork. Centrally located, but parking can be difficult. $765

Hostelina Hostel Alvear 529 ☎0388 424 8522, ⓦhostelina.com.ar. Spotless hostel offering simple,

---

TUPAC AMARU AND THE NORTH'S MOST POWERFUL WOMAN

The story of **Milagro Sala**, leader of the influential social organization and NGO Tupac Amaru, is a remarkable one. Born in Jujuy in 1964, Sala was abandoned as a baby in a cardboard box by her Kolla parents and adopted and raised by a "white" Argentine family. After a rough teenage life, Sala became active as a community organizer: her career took off when she started to coordinate food drives with her neighbours to feed the children of starving families. Founded in 2001, Tupac Amaru eventually channelled government funds (around $8 billion a month) into social projects such as low-income housing, parks and public swimming pools, and has done so at a record low cost; nevertheless, the new governor of Jujuy, Gerardo Morales – who has a long and fraught relationship with Sala – tried to pull funding in 2015, after claims of financial fraud. The subsequent protests, and legal and political battles, spilled on into 2016 – in January, Sala was arrested (the protests continued), resulting in calls from the United Nations and Amnesty International for her release. Visit the Tupac Amaru museum for more background (see p.297).

modern dorms with bunks and a family room that can fit four people. Basic breakfast included in the shared kitchen. Dorms $155; family room $620

Hostería Pascana El Tero Tero 456 ☎0388 426 0158, ⓦhosteriapascana.com.ar. Just across the river in the Los Perales neighbourhood, this tranquil guesthouse offers comfy, rustic-style cabins and suites with beamed ceilings and gas stoves, all with bathrooms and a/c. $645

Las Vertientes RN-9 Km17 ☎0388 498 0030. Excellent campsite in an area near the village of Yala, north of the city, that used to be a tobacco plantation. The complex has its own pool and restaurant. $60

EATING

Carena Belgrano 899, at Balcarce ☎0388 423 5109. Mellow, contemporary *confitería*, serving snacks and light meals (pastas $110–120, sandwiches from $35) and acting as a community centre – concerts, seminars and group meetings are held here. Free wi-fi. Mon–Thurs & Sun 7am–3am, Fri & Sat 24hr.

La Estancia Belgrano 630, ☎388 423 6213. Central *parrilla* serving excellent steaks ($105–125) and local trout ($150), accompanied by a large and tasty salad bar. Gets going late in the evenings. Mon–Fri noon–3.30pm & 9pm–12.30am, Sat & Sun noon–4pm & 9pm–1am.

★**Madre Tierra** Belgrano 619 ☎0388 422 9578. Delightful, airy vegetarian lunch-only spot with a $120 set menu ($50 for just one course) that will keep you going for hours. Even if you're not a vegetarian, you'll find the fresh salads, jugs of delicious fruit juices, soup and mains such as quinoa burgers and stuffed pumpkin a great change from the meat overdose, and you can stock up on all manner of goodies for a picnic from the onsite shop. Mon–Sat 7.30am–10pm.

★**Manos Jujeñas** Senador Pérez 379 ☎0388 424 3270. Absolutely fabulous Northwestern food, including memorable *locro* and delicious empanadas, accompanied by jugs of honest wine and, from time to time, by live folk music. Incredibly friendly service too. Mon 8pm–late, Tues–Sat noon–3pm & 8pm–late, Sun 8pm–late.

Pingüino Belgrano 718 ☎388 422 7247. This is Jujuy's finest *heladería*, scooping out delicious ice cream by the bucketful. You can enjoy every flavour imaginable from the outdoor seating on a pedestrianized stretch, and watch the town in full swing. Tubs $40–140, cones $10–35. Daily noon–8pm.

★**Viracocha** Independencia 994, at Lamadrid ☎0388 15 438 2605. Unusual dishes such as llama in dark beer sauce, or smoked llama ravioli, plus delicious classic Andean fare – lots of quinoa and native potatoes – make this one of Jujuy's top places to eat. Mains $68–115. Mon–Sat 11.30am–3pm & 8pm–midnight, Sun 11am–3pm.

Zorba Belgrano 802, at Necochea ☎0388 424 3048. Reasonably priced Greek food – feta salads, moussaka, *pastitsio* and stuffed vine leaves – along with Argentine favourites and delicious sandwiches in a bright, modern venue with a real buzz that would not look out of place in Kolonaki. Free wi-fi. Mon–Sat 8am–2am, Sun 6pm–1am.

DIRECTORY

Banks and exchange Masventas, Balcarce 223 (Mon–Fri 8am–1.30pm & 5–8pm). Several ATMs are dotted around, including HSBC on Belgrano, at Balcarce.

Consulate Bolivia (the most helpful in the Northwest), Av Senador Pérez and Independencia (Mon–Fri 9am–1.30pm).

Internet Free wi-fi available in Plaza Belgrano and at most cafés.

Laundry Laverap, Belgrano 1214.

Post office Belgrano 1136, between Necochea and Balcarce (Mon–Fri 8am–1pm & 5–8pm).

Quebrada de Humahuaca

North of San Salvador de Jujuy, the **Quebrada de Humahuaca** offers dazzling scenery all the way to the namesake town of **Humahuaca**, 125km from the provincial capital. While most day-trips along the gorge from Jujuy and Salta take you up and down by the same route, RN-9, you're actually treated to two spectacles: you'll have your attention fixed on the western side in the morning, and on the eastern flank in the afternoon, when the sun lights up each side respectively and picks out the amazing geological features: polychrome strata, buttes and mesas, pinnacles and eroded crags, more akin to the arid landscapes of northern Mexico or the southwestern US than the Pampas of central Argentina.

Highlights include the photogenic **Cerro de los Siete Colores**, overhanging the picturesque village of **Purmamarca**, and the small town of **Tilcara** boasting the best range of lodgings and restaurants in the whole area, plus an enigmatic pre-Inca fortress. Beyond Humahuaca, RN-9 crosses bleak but awe-inspiring altiplano landscapes all the way up to

5

La Quiaca on the Bolivian border, nearly 2000m higher yet only 150km further on. A side road off RN-9 climbs to the incredibly isolated and highly picturesque hamlet of **Iruya**, if you really want to get off the beaten track. From Purmamarca an alternative is the tantalizing side road (RN-52) across the *puna*, via enchanting **Susques**, to the Chilean border at the Paso de Jama, high in the Andes. The whole of RN-9 and some of the side roads are accessible by regular **buses** from Jujuy, many of them also serving Salta.

Tumbaya

Some 47km from Jujuy, where the Quebrada becomes an arid, narrow valley, gouged out by the Río Grande, lies **TUMBAYA**, a tiny, almost deserted Kolla village with dirt streets and low-slung adobe homes. On tiny Plaza Belgrano, the handsome colonial church, the **Iglesia Nuestra Señora de los Dolores**, houses some fine colonial art, including a painting of *Nuestra Señora La Aparecida*, another of *El Cristo de los Temblores*, and a *Jesús en el Huerto*. Originally constructed around 1796, it was partially rebuilt after two earthquakes in the nineteenth century and restored in the 1940s; its design is typical of the Quebrada de Humahuaca, a solid structure clearly influenced by the Mudéjar churches of Andalucía.

Purmamarca

The picturesque village of **PURMAMARCA**, 65km north of Jujuy, is now a major tourist destination thanks to the **Cerro de los Siete Colores**, a series of gorgeous multihued bluffs and hills that surround it. At its heart the village remains a small collection of adobe houses, mud walls and dirt streets, though the local Kolla community now shares it with boutique hotels, hostels, art and craft stores and restaurants.

Plaza 9 de Julio

Purmamarca's main square, **Plaza 9 de Julio**, is surrounded by stalls selling an array of indigenous textiles, ponchos and bags (daily 9am–1pm & 3–7pm), set up to compete with the growing number of boutique shops. The handsome church, the **Iglesia Santa Rosa de Lima** (Mon–Fri 9am–12.30pm & 4.30–6pm, Sat 9am–noon) was built around 1779 to the typically Mudéjar, single-towered design of the Quebrada, with a series of eighteenth-century Cuzco paintings lining the walls inside (Aug 30 is the main church fiesta). At the northeast corner of the plaza, the four graceful arches of the old nineteenth-century **Cabildo** embellish its otherwise simple white facade – it now serves as the Centro Cultural, with simple displays highlighting the region's history (daily 10am–noon & 5–7pm; free).

Cerro de los Siete Colores

Purmamarca's chief attraction, the **Cerro de los Siete Colores**, was formed over millions of years, the result of an unusually complex blend of rock types from ancient clay and limestone to more recent strata of sandstone and iron-rich claystone. As a result, the mountain's stripes range from pastel beiges and pinks to orangey ochres and dark purples, though you may not be able to make out all seven of the reputed shades. A loop road dubbed "Paseo de los Colorados" gently climbs around the back of the village for the best views of the polychrome mountainside (allow around 1hr on foot).

ARRIVAL AND INFORMATION	PURMAMARCA

Purmamarca lies 4km to the west of RN-9 on RN-52, the region's main trans-Andean route, heading northwest towards Susques and the Chilean border.

By bus Frequent buses to Tilcara, Humahuaca and Jujuy (1hr 30min) arrive/depart from a block east of the main square (Rivadavia and Libertad), and there's usually a 7am departure direct to La Quiaca. Note that many buses between Tilcara/Humahuaca and Jujuy only run on RN-9 and drop off at RN-52 junction, a 4km hike from Purmamarca – ask when you buy your ticket. *Hotel Manantial* (see opposite) sells tickets for the Geminis

(W geminis.cl) bus to Calama and San Pedro de Atacama, Chile (Mon, Thurs & Sat), and Salta (Tues, Fri & Sun).

Tourist information There is a helpful little tourist office (daily 8am–8pm) just off the main plaza on Florida.

Services The village has one Banco Macro ATM on the plaza, but bring plenty of cash, as it often runs out of money.

ACCOMMODATION

Casa de Adobe RN-52 Km4.5 ☎0388 490 8003, W casadeadobe.com.ar. A small set of hyper-luxurious *cabañas*, affording magnificent mountain views and with a terrific display of good taste. Gorgeous materials and textiles, plus plasma-screen TVs with international satellite channels. Free wi-fi and breakfast included. **$1065**

★ **Colores de Purmamarca** c/7 Colores (above Av San Martín 600) ☎0381 431 0700, W coloresdepurmamarca .com.ar. Stylish self-catering apartments with a wonderful Cerro de los Siete Colores mountain backdrop, fireplaces, kitchen, satellite TV and free bikes. Free wi-fi, plus breakfast delivered to your room. **$1075**

La Comarca RN-52 Km3.8 ☎0388 490 8001, W lacomarcahotel.com.ar. In a magical setting with unbeatable views of the coloured mountains, this stylish adobe-and-stone complex has huge rooms, a beautiful heated pool, a mini-spa and a top-rate gourmet restaurant (open to non-residents) with a cellar worth visiting in its own right. Free wi-fi and breakfast. **$1520**

Hostal El Cardón Belgrano s/n ☎0388 490 8672, W hostal-elcardon.com. Probably the best budget option, just off the plaza, with simple but spacious rooms, basic breakfast and reliable free wi-fi included. The spectacular view from the terrace, however, is the real bonus. **$550**

★ **Hostería del Amauta** Salta 3 ☎0387 15 524 7337, W hosteriadelamauta.com. Oozing with charm, this well-designed *hostería* has a selection of rooms impeccably decorated with soft linens, local timber and wrought-iron detailing. The buffet breakfasts (included) are delicious, healthy and copious. Free wi-fi. **$1130**

Huaira Huasi RN-52 Km5 ☎0388 490 8070, W huairahuasi.com.ar. Justly popular hotel, 2km from the centre of town (you'll need a car), with comfy, rustic *cabañas*, sensational views and simple breakfasts included (shared kitchen). Free wi-fi but no TV. **$960**

Manantial del Silencio RN-52 Km3.5 ☎0388 490 8080, W hotelmanantial.com.ar. This delightful, convent-like Neocolonial building in parkland a short distance out of the village houses small but comfortable rooms. The restaurant varies in quality, the swimming pool is unheated and the service leaves a lot to be desired, but as the pioneer boutique hotel in the area it has its merits. Free wi-fi and buffet breakfast included. **$1400**

La Posta de Purmamarca Santa Rosa s/n ☎0388 490 8029, W postadepurmamarca.com.ar. Simple modern beds in spacious, all-white rooms, plus a great central location. TV in common lounge only, with breakfast and free wi-fi included. **$1210**

EATING

★ **Comidas Gabriel** Belgrano, between Florida and Libertad ☎0388 496 5560. The premier culinary experience in Purmamarca is an evening with Chef Gabriel, who for around $250–300 conjures up daily menus based on the finest local ingredients and Andean recipes (served with water only); think llama ravioli, quinoa and avocado salad, chocolate cake with coca leaf and ice cream flavoured with local herbs. At the time of writing, Gabriel was operating out of *Sabores Jujeños* nightly (he takes it over for the evening), but check for his latest location. Daily 8.30pm–midnight.

Los Morteros by López Salta s/n ☎0388 490 8063. One of the region's best restaurants, a short stroll from the church, with gourmet cuisine using the valley's excellent natural produce – think goat's cheese empanadas and chicken fricassee with broad beans and quinoa – served in a classy dining room adorned with traditional textiles and other crafts. Noon–3pm & 8pm–late; closed Tues.

La Posta Plaza 9 de Julio (Rivadavia) ☎388 490 8040. Next to the Cabildo, *La Posta* serves simple Andean meals, snacks and drinks, and sells local crafts, in a rich red-ochre-walled building. Daily noon–3pm & 8pm–midnight.

Cuesta de Lipán and the road to Chile

Snaking west from Purmamarca, RN-52 quickly climbs up the remarkable zigzags and switchbacks of the **CUESTA DE LIPÁN**, one of the most dizzying roads in the region. The well-maintained and surfaced road runs on towards the Chilean border at Paso de Jama, crossing some of the country's most captivating landscapes – barren steppe alternating with crinkly mountains, often snow-peaked even in the summer. Some 30km west of Purmamarca, just after the Abra de Potrerillos pass, you reach the road's highest point, at nearly 4200m, and enter the *puna* (or altiplano): ahead you have open views to gleaming salt flats (see p.302) and to the north, beyond the valley of the Río Colorado, the shallow, mirror-like **Laguna de Guayatayoc** glistens in the sun.

5

Salinas Grandes

The aptly named **Salinas Grandes** are one of the country's biggest salt flats and certainly the most impressive, ringed by mountains on all sides and beneath almost perennial blue skies. From Purmamarca, RN-52 cuts right across them, affording sensational views on all sides. This huge rink of snow-white crystals, forming irregular octagons, each surrounded by crunchy ridges, crackling like frozen snow under foot, acts as a huge mirror. The salt, shimmering in the nearly perpetual blazing sunshine, often creates cruel water mirages, though there are in fact some isolated pools of brine where small groups of flamingoes and ducks gather. This is a likely place for spotting vicuñas and llamas, too, flocks of which often leap across the road to reach their scrawny, yellow pastureland, or *tola*, on either side of the road. At around 60km from Purmamarca there's a small viewing point and a cluster of local Kolla stalls selling the usual arts and crafts and basic refreshments. Just beyond here, you'll see the bone-white salt mounds of Mina Guayatayoc III, which still extracts salt here.

Where the road snakes between the **Cerro Negro** and the valley of the Río de las Burras, through the **Quebrada del Mal Paso**, it crosses the Tropic of Capricorn several times, before reaching Susques, some 130km from Purmamarca.

Susques and the Chilean border

The small and isolated mountain village of **SUSQUES**, occupied by Chile until 1899, lies at an altitude of 3620m, on a promontory between the Susques and Pastos Chicos rivers. It's worth a brief stop to peek inside the sumptuous church, the sixteenth-century **Iglesia de Nuestra Señora de Belén de Susques**, with its delicate thatched roof and rough adobe walls, like those of all the houses in the village, and the rare naive **frescoes** on the inside. From here it's around 130km to the border at **Paso de Jama** (4320m); Chilean and Argentine immigration now share the same building, 4.5km inside Argentina at the whistlestop hamlet of **Jama**, where there's also a petrol station. At around 4100m, a few travellers get altitude sickness here just waiting in the passport line, and medics are usually standing by with oxygen. From here it's another 160km to San Pedro de Atacama in Chile.

ARRIVAL AND DEPARTURE   SUSQUES

By bus Several bus companies, including Geminis (@geminis.cl), run daily buses between Salta (departing 7am) and cities in Chile, via Jujuy, Purmamarca and Susques.

ACCOMMODATION AND EATING

Pastos Chicos RN-52 Km140 (at RN-40 junction) @0388 423 5387, @pastoschicos.com.ar. Probably the best place to stay; it's 4km south of Susques, but conveniently next to a petrol station, with rooms that are comfortable and warm. The restaurant is cosy with tasty meals. Free wi-fi and breakfast included. $620

La Vicuñita San Martín 121 @03887 490207. Very basic but clean rooms with bathrooms, also serving simple food (empanadas and *humitas*) and located close to the village centre, opposite the church. $500

Tilcara

Some 23km north from Purmamarca lies **TILCARA**, another once sleepy indigenous community turned thriving tourist hub thanks to its charming adobe homes and great pre-Inca *pucará*, or fortress. At an altitude of just under 2500m and yet still dominated by the snaggletoothed mountains that surround it, this is one of the biggest settlements along the Quebrada and the only one on the east bank; it lies just off RN-9, where the Río Huasamayo runs into the Río Grande. The tiny centre of narrow, dusty streets lies around the main square, **Plaza C. Álvarez Prado**, a leafy space surrounded by craft stalls. Tilcara is always lively, but even more so during **Carnival**. Like the rest of the Quebrada, it also celebrates **El Enero Tilcareño**, a procession and feast held during the latter half of January, **Holy Week**, and **Pachamama**, or the Mother Earth festival, in

August. The festivities feature wild games, music, noisy processions and frenzied partying. If you dislike crowds and have not booked accommodation well ahead, though, then these times are best avoided.

Museo Arqueológico

Belgrano (Plaza C. Álvarez Prado) • Daily 9am–6pm • $60 (includes *pucará* and botanical garden), Mon free • ☎ 0388 495 5006

Housed in a beautiful colonial home, Tilcara's **Museo Arqueológico** contains a well-presented but rather dry collection of archeological finds organized by culture and region. The museum does at least provide a glimpse of the richness of pre-Hispanic cultures in the Andes, including artefacts not only from northwest Argentina but also from Chile, Bolivia and Peru, such as anthropomorphic Mochica vases, a bronze disc from Belén and assorted items of metal and pottery. You need to read Spanish to fully appreciate the collection, though there is one room – Sala VI – that offers an English introduction. There's also a small but poignant gallery dedicated to locals "disappeared" during the Dirty War (see p.541).

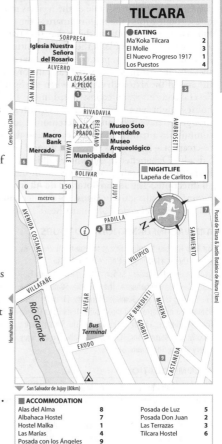

Museo Soto Avendaño

Belgrano (Plaza C. Álvarez Prado) • Mon & Thurs–Sun 9am–6pm • $10 • ☎ 0388 495 5354

Next door to the Museo Arqueológico (and often confused with it), the **Museo Soto Avendaño** displays 42 intriguing plaster sculptures by adopted son Ernesto Soto Avendaño (1886–1969). The collection includes *El Trabajo* and *España y América*, plus a maquette of Avendaño's controversial Humahuaca monument (see p.306). Temporary exhibitions of local artists take up the other galleries, as well as *ermitas* (religious images made of natural materials such as flowers and seeds), made for Semana Santa. The colonial building itself was once owned by independence leader Don Manuel Álvarez Prado (there's a small room dedicated to the gaucho hero).

Nuestra Señora del Rosario y San Francisco de Asis

Alberro 447 (Plaza Sargento Antonio Peloc) • Nominally Wed–Fri 9–11am & 5.30–7pm, but hours vary • Free

Tilcara's impressively large colonial church, **Nuestra Señora del Rosario y San Francisco de Asis**, stands one block back from the main square, on the smaller Plaza Sargento Antonio Peloc. Completed in 1797, it was rebuilt in 1865 with *cardón* cactus used in the doorway and interior furnishings.

Pucará de Tilcara and Jardín Botánico de Altura

Acceso al Pucará • Daily 9am–6pm (last entry 5.30pm) • $60 (includes Museo Arqueológico, *pucará* and botanical garden), Mon free

A kilometre or so southwest of the main plaza lies the **Pucará de Tilcara**, or

5

pre-Columbian fortress, one of the region's most complex, with row upon row of family houses built within the high ramparts – the rubble of foundations smothers the whole hill, dating primarily from the **Inca** period (late fifteenth century), though there has been a fortress here since at least the twelfth century. The original inhabitants were thought to have been the **Tilcaras**, part of the **Omaguaca** confederation that was later absorbed by the Inca empire – it may have served as a major Inca provincial capital, but was abandoned at the end of the sixteenth century when the Spanish assumed control of the valley.

Several sections were reconstructed in the 1950s, allowing a glimpse of what the stone houses might have looked like, along with a building known as La Iglesia or "church", thought to have been an Inca ceremonial edifice, possibly used for sacrifices. On the summit lies a truncated **pyramid**, though this is more fanciful monument than accurate re-creation – it honours the archeological pioneers of the site, Juan Ambrosetti and Salvador Debenedetti. The whole hill is spiked with a grove of cacti, and, with the backdrop of imposing mountains on all sides, it affords marvellous panoramic views in all directions. The **Jardín Botánico de Altura**, at the main entrance leading up to the *pucará*, is an attractively landscaped collection of local **flora**, mostly cacti, including the hairy *cabeza del viejo* ("old man's head") and equally hirsute "lamb's tail" varieties.

ARRIVAL, INFORMATION AND TOURS — TILCARA

By bus The bus terminal lies at the southern end of Av Alvear; there's a left-luggage office but little else.
Destinations El Aguilar (3.45pm daily, plus 7.45pm Fri–Sun; 3–4hr); Humahuaca (hourly; 30–50min); Iryua (3–4 daily; 3hr–3hr 30min); Mendoza (1 daily; 23hr 35min); Purmamarca (1–2 direct daily; 16min); La Quiaca (Bolivian border; 11 daily; 1hr 50min–3hr 50min); Salta (hourly; 3hr 45min–4hr 30min); San Salvador de Jujuy (every 30min; 1hr 15min–3hr).

Tourist information The Dirección de Turismo at Belgrano 360 (daily 8am–9pm; ☎ 388 495 5720, ⊛ tilcara .com.ar) offers basic information and maps.
Services Banco Macro has a branch and ATM on the main plaza.
Bike tours Mountain-bike tours around Tilcara and further afield can be arranged by Jujuy en Bici, Belgrano 763 ☎ 09388 504 5335, ⊛ jujuyenbici.com.ar.

ACCOMMODATION

Tilcara is not short of places to stay, including a couple of the region's best **youth hostels**, though prices tend to reflect the area's growing popularity. The options below include free wi-fi and breakfast unless otherwise stated.

Alas del Alma Padilla 437 ☎ 0388 495 5572, ⊛ alasdelalmatilcara.com.ar. Extremely comfortable, self-catering adobe-and-stone *cabañas* sleeping two or four, done out in an appealing traditional style with local textiles and ceramics. Conveniently located at the entrance to the village. **$645**
Albahaca Hostel Padilla, between Ambrosetti and Sarmiento ☎ 0388 15 585 5994, ⊛ albahacahostel .com.ar. One of the best-value hostels in town, with clean dorms and private rooms, decent shared kitchen and a breakfast of wholesome breads and home-made jams. Can arrange excursions plus Spanish and folk music classes. Dorms **$175**; doubles **$650**
★**Hostel Malka** San Martín s/n ☎ 0388 495 5197, ⊛ malkahostel.com.ar. An outstanding, well-maintained youth hostel with dorms and self-catering cabins, 400m up a steep hill; it commands sweeping views, is extremely comfortable and serves excellent breakfasts for an extra $95. The friendly owner runs treks and 4WD tours in the area. Dorms **$300**; cabins **$850**
Las Marías Sorpresa 573 ☎ 0388 495 5525,

⊛ lasmariastilcara.com.ar. Justly popular luxury hotel close to the centre, with rooms blending traditional stone and wood materials with a contemporary style and modern amenities, private balconies and panoramic views. **$1550**
Posada con los Ángeles Gorriti 156 ☎ 0388 495 5153, ⊛ posadaconlosangeles.com.ar. Built around an idyllic courtyard, with a quirky but attractive architectural-style decor, charming rooms, fine views and tip-top service. **$980**
★**Posada de Luz** Ambrosetti 661 ☎ 0388 495 5017, ⊛ posadadeluz.com.ar. Stellar views up the valley, inventive architecture and a friendly welcome are just some of the assets of this enticing posada, where each tastefully furnished and decorated room has its own cachet. Book well ahead as it fills up quickly. **$1050**
★**Posada Don Juan** Lavalle 1064 ☎ 0388 495 5422, ⊛ posadadonjuan.com.ar. Wonderful semi-detached units, each with a small terrace, spaced evenly around a tranquil park affording marvellous views of Tilcara and its surroundings. Simple, tasteful decor and professional staff. **$880**

Las Terrazas Sorpresa and San Martín ☎0388 495 5589, ⊕lasterrazastilcara.com.ar. Built into landscaped terraces near the edge of town, this gorgeous boutique hotel has large rooms decorated with local crafts, balconies and a small pool and sundeck, all of which command fantastic views of the rippling mountains. $1800

Tilcara Hostel Bolívar 166 ☎0388 495 5105. Set in

an historic house, this hostel has established a good reputation for friendliness (it's like a family home, complete with pet dogs) and comfort in its basic but adequate dorms. It has a pleasant common room, barbecue facilities (the village market is just next door) and the owners organize communal dinners. Dorms $110

EATING

★**Ma'Koka Tilcara** Belgrano and Bolívar ☎0388 509 5617. Cosy café, with wooden tables and an Andean theme, that also serves as a bookshop (Spanish titles only). Serves decent coffee ($22), cappuccino ($35), *El Molle alfajores* ($15) and $50 beers. Daily 8.30am–1pm & 3–9pm.

El Molle Belgrano 417 ☎0388 495 5614, ⊕alfajoreselmolle.com. Sample the tempting *alfajores* (cookies) at this local store, a family business founded in 2009. Numerous delicious varieties from *dulce de leche* and strawberry, to orange and nougat. Mon–Fri 9.30am–1.30pm & 4–8pm, Sat & Sun 9.30am–9pm.

★**El Nuevo Progreso** 1917 Lavalle 351 ☎0388 495

5237. This long-popular restaurant offers more unusual dishes such as lamb cooked in dark beer as well as plentiful salads – and occasional excellent folk music, on the smaller plaza opposite the church. Sharing plates from $250, steaks $175 and local trout $155. Daily 6–11.30pm.

Los Puestos Belgrano and Padilla ☎0388 495 5100. For a meal in exceptionally beautiful surroundings, with handsome photos on the walls, *Los Puestos* rules supreme: the varied menu features tender grilled llama, mouthwatering empanadas, juicy *humitas* and succulent pasta, all at reasonable prices. Daily 11.30am–3pm & 8.30pm–midnight.

NIGHTLIFE

Lapeña de Carlitos Lavalle 397 ☎011 4915 7746. It's a touch touristy but this is the best evening out in town, with enthusiastic folk bands, though the food can be hit or miss

($300-plus for a meal for two). Cover for most shows is $15 (starting daily around 9.30pm). Daily 10am–2am.

Tropic of Capricorn

Some 16km beyond Tilcara RN-9 crosses the **Tropic of Capricorn**, marked by a giant sundial monument built in the 1980s. It was meant to align with the noon shadow at the solstice, but was curiously installed at the wrong angle by mistake. A few craft stalls mark the otherwise windswept spot.

Uquía

Tiny **UQUÍA**, around 30km north of Tilcara, is worth a visit for its handsome colonial-era church, deceptively typical of churches in these parts, but with a real artistic treasure inside.

Iglesia de la Santa Cruz y de San Francisco de Paula

Plaza Coronel Juan Cáceres (just off RN-9) • Daily 10am–noon & 2–4pm • Free

Set against a vivid backdrop of brick-red mountains and surrounded by lush *quebrachos*, the **Iglesia de la Santa Cruz y de San Francisco de Paula** was completed in 1691, with its separate tower integrated in the churchyard wall. Though it features a simple design, with a plain, whitewashed facade (apart from the smart green door), the interior is a real surprise. The simple nave directs your gaze to the fine Baroque **retablo** (probably from Potosí, Bolivia). Nine beautiful and unusual **paintings**, also from the seventeenth century, line the walls; these are the celebrated "Ángeles Arcabuceros", warrior-like angels typical of the Cuzco School, featuring period Spanish dress and wielding arquebuses and other weapons of the time. Formerly they numbered ten, but one went missing while they were being exhibited in Buenos Aires, where the remaining nine were restored, excessively to some tastes – they may have lost their centuries-old patina, but remain just as intriguing.

5

Humahuaca

Some 44km north of Tilcara, the indigenous community of **HUMAHUACA** spills across the Río Grande from its languid centre on the west bank. Its delightful cobbled streets, lined with colonial-style or rustic adobe houses, lend themselves to gentle ambling – necessarily leisurely at this altitude, a touch below 3000m. Most organized tours arrive here for lunch and then double back to Jujuy or Salta, but you may like to stay over, and venture at least as far as the secluded village of **Iruya**; Humahuaca is also an excellent springboard for trips up into the desolate but hauntingly beautiful landscapes of the altiplano or **Puna Jujeña**.

Cabildo

Plaza Sargento Gómez • Statue appears daily noon & midnight

Most tours to and around Humahuaca aim to deliver you at the lush main square at midday on the dot, in time to see a kitsch **statue of San Francisco Solano** emerge from a niche in the equally kitsch tower of the whitewashed **Cabildo**, give a sign of blessing, and then disappear behind his door. A crowd gathers, invariably serenaded by groups of folk musicians; the saint repeats his trick at midnight to a smaller audience. The Cabildo itself is an incongruous Neocolonial, Moorish edifice completed in 1940.

Iglesia Catedral de Nuestra Señora de la Candelaria y de San Antonio

Plaza Sargento Gómez • Daily noon–1pm • Free

Opening each day after the noon statue show is over, and far more impressive, is the **Iglesia Catedral de Nuestra Señora de la Candelaria y de San Antonio**, the current incarnation built around 1723 on the western side of the plaza, and much restored since. Within its immaculate white walls is a 1680s *retablo*, and another on the north wall by Cosmo Duarte, dated 1790, depicting the Crucifixion. The remaining artworks include a set of exuberantly Mannerist paintings called the *Twelve Prophets*, signed by leading Cusqueño artist Marcos Sapaca and dated 1764.

Monumento a los Héroes de la Independencia

Jujuy and Córdoba

Looming over the church and the whole of Humahuaca is the controversial **Monumento a los Héroes de la Independencia**, a bombastic concoction of stone and bronze, built between 1933 and 1950 by Ernesto Soto Avendaño (see p.303). Triumphal steps lead up to it from the plaza, but the best thing about it is the view across the town and valley to the mountainside to the east. Built to honour the northern Argentine army, who fought fourteen battles in this region during the Wars of Independence, the 20m-high monument is topped by a bronze statue of an indigenous warrior in a ferocious pose – said to be either heroic messenger Pedro Socompa or Diego Viltipoco, an Omaguaca chief. Behind it, framed by two giant cacti, is an adobe tower decorated with a bronze plaque, all that remains of the Iglesia Santa Bárbara, whose ruins were destroyed to make way for the monument.

ARRIVAL AND DEPARTURE   HUMAHUACA

By bus Buses from Jujuy (8 daily; 2hr), Salta (5 daily; 4hr 30min), La Quiaca (8 daily; 2hr 30min) and Iruya (3 daily; 3hr–3hr 30min) arrive at the small bus terminal a couple of blocks southeast of the main plaza, at Belgrano and Entre Ríos.

ACCOMMODATION

Giramundo Hostel Salta 38 ☎0388 742 2056, ⓦgiramundohostel.com.ar. Friendly hostel decorated with colourful murals, with small, comfy dorms, clean, tiled bathrooms, shared kitchen and tranquil garden area. Free wi-fi and breakfast included. Cash only. Dorms **$235**; doubles **$590**

Hostal La Soñada Río Negro and San Martín ☎0388 742 1228, ⓦhostallasoniada.com. Cosy, rustic accommodation with bright rooms decorated with local arts and crafts. Free wi-fi and breakfast included. Cash only. **$645**

La Humahuacasa Buenos Aires 740 ☎0388 412 0868, ⓦhumahuacasa.com.ar. Popular hostel three blocks from the bus terminal, with clean dorms and a fun, communal atmosphere. Free wi-fi in common areas and breakfast included. Cash only. Dorms $\overline{\$160}$

★**El Sol** Barrio Medalla Milagrosa (off Salta) ☎0388 742 1466, ⓦelsolhosteldehumahuaca.com. Cute little posada that doubles up as an HI-affiliated youth hostel, with dorm bunks and neat doubles (some en suite and pricier). The house is built of adobe brick with a straw roof, and the atmosphere is young, with lots of guitar-centred evenings. Free wi-fi and breakfast included. HI members get a fifteen-percent discount. Cash only. Dorms $\overline{\$150}$; doubles $\overline{\$390}$

EATING

Casa del Tantanakuy Salta 370 ☎0388 742 1538. Serves regional dishes, wines and espresso coffee and holds literary, artistic and musical events. In its marvellous projection room it screens films by the likes of Orson Welles and Wong Kar Wai. Daily noon–3pm & 8pm–midnight.

Casa Vieja Buenos Aires and Salta ☎0388 742 1181. A rustic interior belies some very fine cooking, with the emphasis on Andean ingredients, and the stage is regularly graced by leading folklore singers and musicians. Daily set lunch menu for $75. Daily noon–3pm & 8pm–midnight.

Pachamanka Buenos Aires 457 ☎0388 742 1265. Peaceful, friendly place offering lots of takes on quinoa – cheese- and quinoa-stuffed ravioli, quinoa stew and so on – as well as some spicier Bolivian dishes and excellent empanadas ($10), tamales ($30) and *humitas* ($40). There are also Andean specials such as *locro*, llama steak and lamb stew (mains $90–130). Daily noon–late.

El Rosedal Buenos Aires 175 ☎0388 742 1318. Authentic, delicious fare based on llama and quinoa. Lunch menus from $80. Daily 8am–11pm.

Iruya

The indigenous Kolla community of **IRUYA** fits snugly into the side of the valley of the Río Iruya, in the far northern corner of Salta Province, around 75km northeast of Humahuaca. Reminiscent of certain Greek island villages, its fortified walls, steep cobbled streets, whitewashed houses and timeless atmosphere, accentuated by the rarefied air – at an altitude of 2780m – make it well worth a visit. The largely unpaved road here from Humahuaca is dramatic (and sometimes flooded Dec–April), crossing a couple of stony riverbeds before winding up a spellbinding valley, and then down again, via a twisting corniche road along which you wonder how two buses can pass each other. The point where you cross the border into Salta Province is the Abra del Cóndor pass, at a giddying and often gale-blown 3900m.

ARRIVAL AND DEPARTURE   IRUYA

By bus Transporte Iruya runs small buses (☎0388 742 1174) from Humahuaca to Iruya (3hr–3hr 30min) departing daily 8.20am, 10.30am and 4pm (no 4pm bus on Sat). Return buses depart Iruya 6am (Mon–Sat only), 1pm and 3.15pm. Panamericano (☎0388 425 4336) runs one daily service from San Salvador de Jujuy at 6am, passing Purmamarca at 7.30am, Tilcara at 8am and Humahuaca at 8.30am; it returns at 2pm. See ⓦiruyaonline.com.

CASABINDO AND THE FEAST OF THE ASSUMPTION

If you have your own transport, and are looking to get well off the beaten track, you may want to take a diversion to the unspoilt Kolla village of **Casabindo**, particularly if you can time your visit to coincide with the August 15 **Feast of the Assumption**, among the most fascinating and colourful of all the Northwest's festivals. Some 80km north of Humahuaca you pass through the crossroads village of **Abra Pampa**, a forlorn place of llama herdsmen living in adobe houses, from where the rough-surfaced RP-11 leads to Casabindo, 60km southwest. The tiny village is dwarfed by a huge church, the **Iglesia de la Asunción**, so large it's nicknamed La Catedral de la Puna ("the cathedral of the *puna*"). It houses a collection of Altoperuvian paintings of *ángeles militares*, or angels in armour, similar to those in Uquía (see p.305). Its several chapels are the theatre of major celebrations on the August 15 festival. Plume-hatted angels and a bull-headed demon lead a procession around the village, accompanied by drummers. The climax of the festival is a bloodless *corrida*, a colonial custom. The bull, representing the Devil, has a rosette hung with coins stuck on his horns and the Virgin's "defenders" have to try and remove it. Coca leaves and fermented maize are buried in another ceremony on the same day, as an offering to Pachamama, the Earth Mother.

5

IRUYA'S FIESTA DEL ROSARIO

On the first Sunday of October, Iruya's entrancing little **Iglesia de Nuestra Señora del Rosario y San Roque** – a typical Quebrada chapel built in 1690 to the familiar Mudéjar design – is the focal point for the exuberant **Fiesta del Rosario**, half Catholic, half pre-Columbian, culminating in a solemn procession of weirdly masked figures, some representing demons. Of all the Northwest's festivals, this is the most magical and mysterious.

ACCOMMODATION

Iruya San Martín 641 ☎0388 748 2002, ⊛hote liruya.com. Other than the hostel, the best place to stay is this comfortable, modern hotel, where rooms with a view cost a little extra ($1000) and there's a good restaurant. Free wi-fi in public areas and breakfast included. $820

Milmahuasi Hostel Salta s/n ☎0387 15 445 7994, ⊛milmahuasi.com. Warm blankets and hot showers are on offer at this friendly hostel with views over the Río Milmahuasi, comfy dorms and private doubles. Breakfast included and delicious vegetarian dinners available if requested. Free wi-fi. Dorms $160; doubles $720

The Puna Jujeña

Due north of Humahuaca and the turn-off to tiny Iruya, RN-9 begins its long, winding haul up into the remote **altiplano** of northern Jujuy, known as the **Puna Jujeña**; this is a raw wilderness of salt flats, **lagoons** speckled pink with flamingoes and tiny indigenous hamlets built of mud bricks around surprisingly big Quebrada-style chapels. Some 30km north of Humahuaca, RN-9 enters the **Cuesta de Azul Pampa**, a dramatic mountain pass peaking at 3730m and offering unobstructed views across to the jagged peaks to the east. Past the bottleneck of the Abra de Azul Pampa, where fords along the road sometimes freeze, causing extra hazards, the road winds along to the bleak little mining town of **Tres Cruces**, where there's a major *gendarmería* post – personal and vehicle papers are usually checked. Nearby, but out of sight, are some of the continent's biggest deposits of lead and zinc, along with silver mines, while overlooking the village is one of the strangest rock formations in the region, the so-called **Espinazo del Diablo**, or "Devil's Backbone", a series of intriguingly shaped stone burrows, clearly the result of violent tectonic activity millions of years ago, ridged like giant vertebrae. This road continues all the way to the Bolivian border at **La Quiaca**, 165km north of Humahuaca, unattractive in itself but close to **Yavi**, with its superb colonial church. La Quiaca livens up a little on the third and fourth Sundays of October, when the **Manca Fiesta**, also known as the Fiesta de la Olla, or cooking-pot festival, is staged; ceramists and other artisans show off their wares, while folk musicians put on concerts.

Yavi and around

Across the rolling Siete Hermanos mountain range, 17km east of La Quiaca, sits the charming Kolla community of **YAVI** (at 3516m), with sloping cobbled streets and weathered, adobe houses. There are also pre-Columbian petroglyphs and cave paintings in the nearby Cerros Los Ocho Hermanos (the **Petroglifos de Laguna Colorada**), although the 5km walk to get to them, through mesmerizing countryside, is just as rewarding as the sites themselves.

Casa del Marqués de Tojo

Marqués Campero (Plaza Mayor) • Mon–Fri 9am–noon & 2–5pm, Sat 9am–noon • $25

From a mirador at the top of main drag Avenida Senador Pérez, to the north of the village, you have a panoramic view, taking in the dilapidated but romantic eighteenth-century **Casa del Marqués de Tojo**, the erstwhile family home of the region's ruling

5

marqués, the only holder of that rank in colonial Argentina. The house is a museum of sorts, with a motley collection of artefacts and junk, such as the bedstead used by the last marqués, arranged in various rooms around an inviting patio shaded by a willow and an elm.

Iglesia de Nuestra Señora del Rosario y San Francisco

Marqués Campero (Plaza Mayor) • Opening hours erratic, but usually daily 2–9pm; ask for the lady who keeps the key • Free

Behind its harmonious white facade, the village's seventeenth-century church, **Iglesia de Nuestra Señora del Rosario y San Francisco**, is one of the region's best-preserved colonial interiors, lit a ghostly lemon-yellow by the unique wafer-thin onyx-paned windows. The ornate Baroque pulpit, three *retablos* decorated with coloured wooden statuettes of saints and a fine sixteenth-century Flemish oil painting that must have been brought here by early colonizers, seem like rare antiquities in the stark white nave.

ARRIVAL AND DEPARTURE   YAVI AND AROUND

By bus and taxi La Quiaca is the gateway to Yavi, with regular buses making the run to/from San Salvador de Jujuy (hourly; 2hr 45min–5hr) via Tilcara (1hr 50min–3hr 50min) and Humahuaca (2hr 30min). Once in La Quiaca, shared taxis (*taxis colectivos*) run to Yavi from the Mercado Municipal (Hipólito Yrigoyen and Rivadavia; $15–20; 20min) when full, usually in the early mornings; taxis will also make the trip ($200–250 return, with wait time). For Bolivia, take a taxi to the border bridge (Puente Internacional La Quiaca) and walk through immigration; the bus terminal in Villazón, on the Bolivian side, is 750m directly north along Av República Argentina.

ACCOMMODATION AND EATING

Apart from some grimly basic *hospedajes*, there are is one recommendable place to stay in Yavi itself, offering food as well as lodging – which is just as well, as there are only a couple of restaurants. Better options can be found in nearby La Quiaca.

YAVI

Hostería Pachama Senador Pérez and RN-5 ☎ 0388 749 0508. Comfy hotel, though the ultra-plain rooms come as a disappointment after the appealing decor of the main building. Staff can concoct a basic but tasty meal if required, served in an attractive dining room. Simple breakfast included. $485

LA QUIACA

Crystal Sarmiento 539 ☎ 03885 422255, ⊛ hotelcrystallaquiaca.com. Very basic rooms with wood furniture and bathrooms leading off a stark courtyard, with decent food served at low prices. Free wi-fi and breakfast included. $675

Munay Tierra de Colores Belgrano 61 ☎ 03885 423924, ⊛ munayhotel.com.ar. La Quiaca's best place to stay, this well-run *hostería* has pleasant rooms (with a/c and cable TV) in a modern building and a safe garage. Basic breakfast included but no internet/wi-fi. $630

The cloudforest national parks

A trio of the Northwest's cloudforests, or *yungas* – areas of dense jungle draped over high crags that thrust out of the flat, green plains of lowlands on either side of the Tropic of Capricorn – are protected by national park status. They are difficult to access, and a visit requires time and planning, but they reward with lush jungle scenery and, above all, an incredible range of fauna. The microclimates of all three *yungas* are characterized by clearly distinct dry and wet seasons, winter and summer, but relatively high year-round precipitation. The peaks are often shrouded in cloud and mist, keeping most of the varied plant life verdant even in the drier, cooler months.

The biggest of the three, the **Parque Nacional Calilegua**, is also the most accessible and best developed, within easy reach of San Salvador de Jujuy. **Parque Nacional El Rey**, in Salta Province, is much closer to the provincial capital, but its access roads are sometimes impassable after the heavy seasonal rains. **Parque Nacional Baritú**, away to

5

the north in a far-flung corner of Salta Province, is the hardest to get to, and therefore the most pristine. The lack of public transport, the need to cross into Bolivia in order to enter the park, zero on-the-spot facilities and the challenging terrain all but rule out individual travel, and no tour operators go there regularly, but if you're really determined Clark Expediciones or Norte Trekking in Salta (see box, p.288) should be able to help you arrange a visit.

The parks are best visited between May and October, as the summer months – December to March or April – can see sudden cloudbursts cut off access roads and make paths much too slippery for comfort. At all times bring **insect repellent** since mosquitoes and other nasty bugs are plentiful.

Parque Nacional Calilegua

Aguas Negras, Jujuy • Daily 8am–2pm • Free • ☎ 03886 422046, ⓦ parquesnacionales.gob.ar

Spread over 760 square kilometres, just south of the Tropic of Capricorn, the **PARQUE NACIONAL CALILEGUA** rises above rich fertile land that is home to some of the country's biggest sugar farms. It's the setting for amusing anecdotes in Gerald Durrell's book *The Whispering Land*; his tales of roads cut off by flooding rivers can still ring true but his quest for native animals to take back to his private zoo cannot be imitated – the park's rich flora and fauna (see p.554) are now strictly protected by law. The land once belonged to the Leach brothers, local sugar barons of British origin, whose family donated it to the state to turn it into a national park in the 1970s. This was a shrewd business move: sugar plantations need a lot of clean water and the only way to keep the reliable supplies which run through the park free of pollution, uncontrolled logging and the general destruction of the fragile ecosystem was through the state regulations that come with national park status.

The main access to the park is through **Libertador General San Martín**, an uninviting little town some 110km northeast from San Salvador de Jujuy via RN-34. It's dominated by the huge Ledesma industrial complex – the world's biggest sugar refinery – and usually referred to as Libertador or LGSM on signs. Just north of the town (across the Río San Lorenzo), the paved RP-83 branches off RN-34 and runs for 8km west to the **park entrance** at Aguas Negras (named after the river here), where there's a rangers' office and camping – once in the park, all roads are gravel. Just 3km beyond RP-83 turning, back on RN-34, the tiny village of **Calilegua** has a *hostería* and park information, but otherwise no facilities.

TREKKING IN THE PARQUE NACIONAL CALILEGUA

You will need to walk off the beaten track, well away from noisy trucks, if you want to have the slightest chance of spotting any of the wildlife in the Parque Nacional Calilegua. **Trekking** here takes time and it's a very good idea to spend a night or two in the park. Morning and late afternoon are the best times to see animals and birds by streams and rivers. Nine trails of varying length and difficulty have been hacked through the dense vegetation; ask the rangers for guidance.

The summits of the **Serranía de Calilegua**, marking the park's northwestern boundary, reach heights of over 3300m, beyond which lie grassland and rocky terrain. The trek to the summit of Cerro Amarillo (3320m) takes three days from the park entrance; the nearby shepherds' hamlet, **Alto Calilegua**, is certainly worth a visit. From the tiny settlement of San Francisco within the park it's even possible to link up with **Tilcara** (see p.302), a four-day trek; some of the organized trips arranged in Salta and Tilcara itself, including horserides, offer this amazing chance to witness the stark contrast between the verdant jungle and the desiccated uplands.

ARRIVAL, INFORMATION AND TOURS	PARQUE NACIONAL CALILEGUA

By car Cars can make it along the main road through the park, punctuated by numerous viewpoints, as far as the Mesada de la Colmenas, near a rangers' headquarters, but a 4WD will be required beyond here.

By bus Buses from Salta (2 daily; Balut departs 12.30am, arrives 3.15am; Flecha departs 11.45pm, arrives 2.20am) or Jujuy (hourly; 2hr) stop at Libertador's terminal on Av Antartida Argentina, 200m east of RN-34. Buses from Libertador to Valle Grande pass through the park, leaving the terminal at 8.30am (arriving 9.15am), and passing the park entrance in the other direction at 6.30–7.30pm (you can also hire taxis in Libertador).

Tourist information The park *intendencia* is in the village of Calilegua (San Lorenzo s/n ☎03886 422046, ✉calilegua@apn.gov.ar). It's definitely worth a visit before you head in for maps and extra information.

Tours Clark Expediciones (see box, p.288) regularly runs expert birdwatching safaris to the park.

ACCOMMODATION

Camping Aguas Negras Near to the park entrance. This free campsite 200m from the rangers' office offers only basic facilities (toilets, grills, tables and benches); take enough insect repellent, food and drinking water. Campers usually "shower" in the small waterfall on the San Lorenzo River.

Benitez Hostería 19 de Abril s/n, Calilegua ☎03886 433119. The best place to stay in Calilegua village, with spotless, modern rooms (with a/c and cable TV) and tasty, home-cooked meals. Free wi-fi and breakfast included. $805

Posada del Sol Av Los Ceibos 747, Libertador ☎03886 424900, ✇posadadelsoljujuy.com.ar. Plush modern posada offering top-notch service and excursion possibilities, with inviting rooms arranged around an attractive courtyard and swimming pool. $1236

Termas de Caimancito RP-1 (12km from Caimancito) ☎03886 15 650699, ✇termas decaimancito.com.ar. In a bucolic setting, this spa resort offers delicious meals and clean rooms, camping and the opportunity to splash around in various curative mineral pools. Located 30km northeast of Libertador along RP-1, which turns eastwards off RN-34 and passes the straggly village of Caimancito, this is an excellent place to relax, relatively near the park in an area rich in trails and scenery. $650

Parque Nacional El Rey

RP-20, Salta/Jujuy border • Daily 9am–dusk • Free • ☎0387 431 2683, ✇parquesnacionales.gob.ar

Straddling the borders of Salta and Jujuy provinces, **PARQUE NACIONAL EL REY** lies nearly 200km by road from the city of Salta. Covering 400 square kilometres of land once belonging to Finca El Rey, a farm established in the eighteenth century, the national park perches at an average of 900m above sea level and nestles in a natural horseshoe-shaped amphitheatre, hemmed in by the curving **Crestón del Gallo** ridge to the northwest, and the higher crest of the **Serranía del Piquete**, to the east, peaking at around 1700m. A fan-shaped network of crystal-clear brooks, all brimming with fish, drains into the Río Popayán. The **toucan** (*Ramphastos toco*) is the park's striking and easily recognizable mascot, but other birdlife abounds, totalling over 150 species – the park is also the best place in the region for spotting tapirs, peccaries and wild cats. A road of sorts follows the Río La Sala, while a path will take you on the two-hour climb from the rangers' station to **Pozo Verde**, a lakelet coloured green by lettuce-like *lentejas de água*, and a nearby pond where birds come to drink. The only **accommodation** option is to pitch your tent in the park campsite (free), which has water, grills, toilets, lights and electricity (but no food).

ARRIVAL AND TOURS	PARQUE NACIONAL EL REY

By car If you plan to come under your own steam, make sure you have a 4WD. The park's only access road is RP-20, branching left from RP-5, which in turn leads eastwards from RN-9/34, near the village of Lumbrera halfway between Metán and Güemes. *Guardaparques* at the entrance can advise you on how to get around in your vehicle.

Tours Public transport to the park is nonexistent and through traffic very slight, so an organized trip is the best option if you do not have your own vehicle. Norte Trekking (see box, p.288) can take you on an informative and enjoyable safari to the park; equally professional Clark Expediciones (see box, p.288) specializes in natural history and birdwatching trips here.

5

The Valles Calchaquíes

The **Valles Calchaquíes** are a series of beautiful highland valleys that enjoy more than three hundred days of sunshine a year, a dry climate and much cooler summers than the lowland plains around Salta. The fertile land, irrigated with canals and ditches that capture the plentiful snowmelt from the high mountains to the west, is mostly given over to **vineyards** – among the world's highest – that produce the characteristic **torrontés** grape. The valleys are named after the Río Calchaquí, which has its source in the Nevado de Acay (at over 5000m) near San Antonio de los Cobres, and joins the Río de las Conchas, near Salta's border with Tucumán.

Organized tours from Salta squeeze a visit into one day, stopping at the valleys' main settlement, the airy village of **Cafayate**, for lunch. However, by far the most rewarding way to see the Valles Calchaquíes is under your own steam, by climbing the amazing **Cuesta del Obispo**, through the **Parque Nacional Los Cardones**, a protected forest of gigantic *cardón* cacti, to the alluring village of **Cachi**; then follow the valley south through some mesmerizing scenery via **Molinos** and **San Carlos**, on to Cafayate, where plentiful accommodation facilitates a stopover. The alternative route to Cafayate from Salta runs through the spectacular **Quebrada de las Conchas**, snaking past some astonishing rock formations, optimally seen in the late afternoon or early evening light.

The Cuesta del Obispo

To get to the northern Calchaquí settlement of Cachi, 170km southwest of Salta, you travel along the partly sealed RP-33, a scenic road that squeezes through the dank Quebrada de Escoipe, before climbing the scintillating mountain pass known as the **Cuesta del Obispo**, 20km of hairpin bends, offering views of the rippling Sierra del Obispo. These bewitching mountains, blanketed in olive-green vegetation and heavily eroded by countless brooks, are at their best in the morning light; in summer, cloud and rain descend in the afternoon and evening storms can make the road impassable.

Valle Encantado

Just before you reach the top of the *cuesta*, a signposted track leads south down to the **Valle Encantado**, 4km away; this is a fertile little valley, set around a marshy lagoon, that becomes a riot of colour in September and October, when millions of wild flowers burst into bloom, but it's a rewarding detour all year round; its cool temperatures and delightfully pastoral scenery make it an ideal place for a break, especially if you're driving. Foxes, *vizcachas* and other small animals are often spotted here.

Back on the main road the **Abra Piedra del Molino**, a narrow mountain pass at 3457m, is marked by the mysterious "millstone" that gives the pass its name.

Parque Nacional Los Cardones

Daily 9.30am–6pm • Free • ☎ 03868 15 414365, ⓦ parquesnacionales.gob.ar

Some 20km west of the Abra Piedra del Molino, RP-33 cuts through the **Parque Nacional Los Cardones**, an official reserve set up to protect the forest of *cardón* cacti that covers the dusty valley and creeps up the arid mountainside, mingled with the parasol-like *churquis* and other spiny trees typical of desert regions. There are no facilities and you can wander as you like among the gigantic cacti, many of them more than 5m tall. *Cardones* grow painfully slowly, less than a couple of millimetres a year, and their wood has been excessively exploited for making furniture and crafts and for firewood; it's now protected, so don't remove any specimens.

FROM TOP CAFAYATE VINEYARD (P.317); LA POLVORILLA VIADUCT (P.293) >

5

Cachi

The charming village of **CACHI**, 2280m above sea level on the Río Calchaquí, is one of the region's most enticing destinations, overshadowed by the permanently snowcapped **Nevado del Cachi** (6380m), whose peak looms only 15km to the west. It's a pleasant place to wander, investigating the various local crafts, including ponchos and ceramics, or climbing to the **cemetery** for wonderful mountain views and a panorama of the pea-green valley, every arable patch of which is filled with vines, maize and capsicum plantations.

Plaza 9 de Julio

Cachi is centred on the delightful **Plaza 9 de Julio**, shaded by palms and orange trees. On the north side of the plaza stands the much-restored **Iglesia San José**, with its plain white facade, fine wooden floor and unusual cactus-wood altar, pews and confessionals. On the east side, in a Neocolonial house around an attractive whitewashed patio, is the **Museo Arqueológico Pío Pablo Díaz** (Tues–Sun 9am–6pm; free; ☎03868 491 1080), displaying a run-of-the-mill collection of locally excavated items (Spanish labels only).

Walks from Cachi

Scenic trails to **Cachi Adentro** and **La Aguada**, each 6km west of the village, lead from the end of Calle Benjamín Zorrilla (follow it west from the plaza), and take you through fertile farmland where, in late summer (March–May), the fields are carpeted with drying paprika peppers, a dazzling display of bright red that features in many postcards on sale in the region.

ARRIVAL AND INFORMATION   CACHI

By bus Cachi lies 160km from Salta, via mostly paved roads. Ale Hermanos (☎0387 4232226) runs 2–3 times daily from Salta to Cachi (first departure 7am; 4hr 15min), with buses arriving one block from the main plaza on Ruíz de los Llanos. There is no public transport between Cachi and Cafayate (see p.316), connected by primarily gravel roads, but the Hermanos bus continues on as far as Molinos (2hr) and Angastaco (4hr) on Wed and Fri departing at 11.30am (it also departs Cachi Mon 7.12am). From Angastaco you can take buses to Cafayate (2 daily at 5.35am and 5pm; 2hr 30min–3hr). Alternatively, taxis will drive from Cachi to Cafayate for $250–300 per person (minimum four people).

Tourist information There's a small tourist office on Plaza 9 de Julio, next to the municipalidad on Güemes (Mon–Fri 8am–9pm, Sat & Sun 9am–3pm & 5–9pm; ☎03868 491902).

Services Banco Macro has a branch and ATM on the plaza (at Ruíz de los Llanos and Güemes); the post office is on Güemes, one block south of the plaza.

ACCOMMODATION

Art Hostel Federico Suárez 504 ☎03868 491713, ⓦhostelcachi.com.ar. Best budget option (linked to the *Viracocha* restaurant), right in the centre of Cachi, with bright dorms and double rooms with private or shared bathrooms, free wi-fi and decent breakfast. Cash only. Dorms $175; doubles $420

El Cortijo Av del Automóvil Club Argentino s/n ☎03868 491034, ⓦelcortijohotel.com. In a colonial house at the bottom of the hill, this beautiful hotel features unusual native-style decor combined with sophisticated Neocolonial furnishings and very attentive service. Free wi-fi and breakfast included. $920

Hostería ACA Sol del Valle Av del Automóvil Club Argentino s/n ☎03868 491105, ⓦsoldelvalle.com.ar. Just outside the village with simple but elegant rooms and tiled floors in a Neocolonial mansion. It also has a swimming pool with a view and a passable restaurant (breakfast buffet included). Free wi-fi. $1120

La Merced del Alto Fuerte Alto s/n ☎03868 490030, ⓦlamerceddelalto.com. In a converted convent, this is Cachi's most luxurious accommodation; set in lush gardens with a pool and a spa, it enjoys outstanding views of the surrounding countryside, and has a very decent bar and restaurant serving top-notch breakfasts. Free wi-fi in public areas. $2340

EATING

Ashpamanta Bustamante s/n ☎0387 15 578 2244. Run by the local yoga instructor and her chef husband, this is currently the most popular restaurant in Cachi, for good reason – tasty, creative vegetarian dishes in a dimly lit,

tranquil dining room, everything from spicy curries to quinoa empanadas and home-made lemonade. Reservations recommended. Daily 12.30–3pm & 7.30–11pm.
Oliver Ruíz de los Llanos 160 (Plaza 9 de Julio) ☎ 03868

491052. For real espresso coffee, cold beer and all manner of snacks, this charming little café/wine bar, on the main square just along from the *Confitería del Sol*, is a good bet. Daily 8am–midnight.

From Cachi to Cafayate

The unpaved, gravel RN-40 from Cachi to Cafayate takes you along some stupendous corniche roads that wind alongside the Río Calchaquí itself, offering views on either side of sheer mountainsides and snowcapped peaks. It's only 180km from one town to the other, but allow plenty of time (at least 4hr) as the narrow track slows your progress and you'll want to stop to admire the views, take photographs and visit the picturesque valley settlements en route, oases of greenery in an otherwise stark landscape. Don't try it in wet weather (most cars can otherwise traverse the road, but vehicles with low clearance may have problems – ask a local before departing, and make sure you have a spare tyre).

Molinos

Some 60km south of Cachi, **MOLINOS** lies a couple of kilometres west of the main road, in a bend of the Río Molinos, and is worth the side-trip for a peek at its lovely adobe houses and the eighteenth-century **Iglesia de San Pedro Nolasco**. The village's artisan products are also regarded as among the finest in the region. Opposite the church, the refurbished Finca Isasmendi, the eighteenth-century residence of the last royalist governor of Salta, is now a rural inn, *Hacienda de Molinos* (☎ 03868 494094, ⓦ haciendademolinos.com.ar; $1400), with eighteen enchanting rooms, some with four-poster beds, set around a tranquil patio.

Quebrada de las Flechas

Around 50km or so south of Molinos, the already impressive scenery becomes even more spectacular as you enter the surreal **Quebrada de las Flechas**, where the red sandstone cliffs form a backdrop for the flinty arrowhead-like formations on either side of the road that give the gorge its name. For 10km, weird rocks like desert roses dot the landscape and, beyond the natural stone walls of **El Cañón**, over 20m high, the road squeezes through **El Ventisquero**, the "wind tunnel".

San Carlos

The oldest settlement in the valley, **SAN CARLOS** is 35km further on from the Quebrada de las Flechas, straddling RN-40. Established in 1551, the Spanish outpost was destroyed several times by the Calcahquies before Jesuit missionaries founded a permanent foothold in 1641. Most points of interest lie around central **Plaza 4 de Noviembre**, including the **Iglesia San Carlos Borromeo** (daily 8am–7pm), completed in 1854 and one of the biggest churches in the region. Stalls selling *locro* usually set up on the plaza for lunch, and there are several cheap restaurants here, as well as the **Mercado Artesanal** (daily 9am–1pm & 3–7pm). From here the road to Cafayate (22km) is paved, and you'll pass into wine country (see p.317).

Reserva Natural Quebrada de las Conchas

The main, paved route between Salta and Cafayate is RN-68, which traverses the **Reserva Natural Quebrada de las Conchas**, one of the region's most mesmerizing destinations. The road follows the gorge of the Río de las Conchas through a startling array of landscapes, which, apart from being a geologist's dream, provide a technicolour spread of giant cliffs and bluffs that look like ancient castles one way, and marble cake another. The gorge starts around 21km south of the town of **La Viña** (90km south from

5

Salta) where you should fill up – the next petrol station is at Cafayate (around 100km). The first major **viewpoint** is at around 32km from La Viña, a stunning panorama across the valley.

Posta de Las Cabras
RN-68 Km88 • Daily 8.30am–7pm • ☎ 0387 499 1093

Some 14km south of La Viña (and around halfway between Cafayate and Salta), a convenient stopoff is provided by the bucolic **Posta de Las Cabras**, where, in addition to the goat's cheese ($50) suggested by its name, you can sample all kinds of local cakes, coffee ($20–30), sandwiches ($70), or just observe the white goats ambling around the property.

La Garganta del Diablo
Some 55km from La Viña, just off the road, lies a giant semicircular fissure into the mountainside dubbed **La Garganta del Diablo** ("Devil's Throat"), where huge sinuous bands of red sedimentary rock have been pushed up in spectacular fashion like a geological fault line. It's one of the few sites in the region marked as sacred to the Diaguita, though day-trippers continually ignore the signs asking you not to clamber up to the top. Half a kilometre down the road is **El Anfiteatro**, a narrower but equally entrancing ravine.

Mirador Tres Cruces
Named after three crosses on the side of the road, 5km beyond La Garganta del Diablo, the **Mirador Tres Cruces** is notable for the stupendous views across the Quebrada and the towering walls of red stone that line the road here.

El Sapo and Casa de Los Loros
Around 7km south of Mirador Tres Cruces, the road passes a bulbous rock formation shaped like an animal-like figure and dubbed **El Sapo** (it really does look like a toad). Some 3km further on, the **Casa de Los Loros** are a series of holes pitted in giant pillars of mud along the roadside, where parrots (*loros*) come to nest in the spring.

El Obelisco and Los Castillos
Some 10km beyond Casa de Los Loros the road swings by a huge monolith dubbed **El Obelisco**. The reds, ochres and pinks of the sandstone make it all look staggeringly beautiful. The majestic Sierras de Carahuasi – the northernmost range of the Cumbres Calchaquíes – loom behind as a magnificent backdrop, while 2km further on, across the river, rock formations have been eroded and blasted by wind and rain to form buttresses, known as **Los Castillos**, or "the castles".

Cafayate
The self-appointed capital of the Valles Calchaquíes and the main settlement hereabouts, the town of **CAFAYATE** is the centre of the province's **wine industry** and the main tourist base for the valleys, thanks to its plentiful, high-quality accommodation, and convenient location at a crossroads between Salta, Cachi and Tucumán. It's a small but lively place, and apart from exploring the surroundings on foot, by bike or on horseback, you can shop for artisan goods and learn all about wine-making – trying out the final product – at an impressive wine museum and at numerous bodegas (see box opposite).

Plaza 2 de Febrero
The **Iglesia Catedral Nuestra Señora del Rosario**, a relatively recent creation completed in 1895, dominates the main, unusually large square, **Plaza 2 de Febrero**, but is

RUTA DEL VINO: CAFAYATE VINEYARDS

While Mendoza and, increasingly, San Juan are the names most associated with wines from Argentina, wine shops around the world are selling more and more bottles with the name **Cafayate** on their labels. These **vineyards**, which at around 1700m are some of the highest in the world, were originally developed by the Jesuits in the seventeenth century and by the 1800s were already producing commercial malbec and cabernet varieties. The local speciality, however, is a grape thought to have been brought across from La Rioja (Spain) in the late nineteenth century: the **torrontés**. The delicate, flowery white wine it produces, with a slight acidity, is the perfect accompaniment for the regional cuisine, but also goes well with fish and seafood. You can try it and see how the wine is made at one of the many bodegas in and around Cafayate. The following is just a sample (a list of all thirty bodegas is available from the wine museum or tourist office):

CENTRAL CAFAYATE

Nanni Silverio Chavarría 151 ☎03868 421527, ⓦbodegananni.com. Founded in 1897, this organic winery was the first here to make tannat, and its reserve is one of the best. Popular with bigger groups and has English-speakers; you can do tastings w(of four wines) without the tour ($30) but you usually have to wait. Daily 10am–1pm & 2.30–6.30pm; guided tours (Spanish) every 30min Mon–Sat 10.30am–6pm & Sun 11am–5.30pm; restaurant open daily 11.30am–3.30pm & 7–10.30pm.

El Porvenir Córdoba 32 ☎03868 422007, ⓦelporvenirdecafayate.com. The Romero Marcuzzi family winery produces especially good malbec and the excellent Laborum torrontés. Tour and tasting (three wines) for $50 (four wines $80). Best to reserve 24hr in advance. Mon & Sun 9am–1pm, Wed–Sat 9am–1pm & 3–6pm.

El Transito Belgrano 102 ☎03868 422385, ⓦbodegaeltransito.com. A more casual affair where you can walk in and try two basic wines for free (the torrontés is $55 a bottle and they have a blended red for $60). No tours. Daily 10am–1pm & 3.30–6pm.

Vasija Secreta RN-40, just north of town (just about walking distance) ☎03868 421850, ⓦvasijasecreta.com. Professional operation in a gorgeous Spanish-style hacienda dating from the 1850s. Has some English-speakers, with free tastings of two or three bottles. One of the few open all day Sunday. Daily 9am–7pm.

OUTSIDE CAFAYATE

El Esteco RN-40 and RN-68 (walkable from the centre) ☎03868 421139, ⓦelesteco.com. Founded in 1892 and boasting the grandest premises in the valley, with tastings and tours from $60. Mon–Fri 10am–1pm & 2.30–7.30pm, Sat & Sun 10am–1pm.

Finca Quara RN-40 Km4340 (just south of town) ☎03868 421709. The Llama brand, with beautiful premises and professional tastings (free) of one or two wines – the extra-dry torrontés is a must, and they do a decent malbec. Mon–Fri 10am–12.30pm & 2–5.30pm, Sat & Sun 10.30am–12.30pm.

Piattelli Vineyards RP-2 Km3 (off RN-40, north of town) ☎03868 154 18214, ⓦpiattellivineyards .com. Up-and-coming producer. Tours and tastings $75 (includes four reserve wines; Grand Reserva tastings $150). Daily tours in Spanish 10am, noon, 2pm & 4pm; English tours 11am & 3pm.

---

disappointingly nondescript inside; more interesting, perhaps, is the **Mercado Artesanal** (daily 8am–8pm) on the other side of the plaza, and the **Paseo de Artesanos** on the San Martín side, another craft market open similar times.

Museo de la Vid y el Vino

Güemes and Perdiguero • Tues–Sun 9am–7pm • $30 • ☎03868 422322, ⓦmuseodelavidyelvino.gov.ar

A stylish tribute to Cafayate wine-making, the **Museo de la Vid y el Vino** uses poetry and videos to bring to life the oenologist's craft and explain why the area is so good for the grapes (quality soil, 340 days of sunshine a year and the unusual 20°C average swing in temperature between night and day). Housed on the old Bodega Coll property (ancestor of today's Bodega Transito, above), highlights include a scale model of the town that moves through day and night, a re-creation of the fantastic starry skies the region enjoys, and a walkway over rushing "water". The second section provides some history and focuses on the wine-making process itself. Everything is labelled in English, though videos are in Spanish only and the final poem – *Soneto del Vino* by Borges, of

5

course – is left untranslated. A small shop and café, where you can taste *picadas* and most of the local wines, rounds things off.

Museo de Arqueología Calchaquí

Colón 191 (near Calchaquí) • Mon–Fri 10.30am–9pm, Sat 10.30am–6pm • Free (ring the bell to enter) • ☎ 03868 421054

The unusual **Museo de Arqueología Calchaquí**, one block southwest of the plaza, is a private museum literally set in a family home. It's the product of decades of collecting archeological remains from tombs – mostly ethnic **Diaguitas** and **Calchaquies** – by one Rodolfo Bravo, who opened this museum back in 1943. Today one large room just inside the main door is piled with **ceramics**, including some massive, painted urns – it's a startling, impressive collection taking in almost all the pre-Hispanic sub-cultures of the region around Cafayate.

ARRIVAL AND INFORMATION   CAFAYATE

By bus Buses to/from Salta (5–6 daily; 3hr 30min) and services to/from Tucumán (5 daily; 5–6hr) via Amaicha and Tafí del Valle should be using the new bus terminal at the northern edge of town (RN-40) by the end of 2016. There are currently no direct services to Cachi – two Flecha buses trundle daily as far as Angastaco (2–3hr) via San Carlos (30min), where there are three weekly buses to Cachi.

Tourist information The tourist office is rather inconveniently located on the edge of town on Plaza Michel Torino (daily 9am–9pm ☎ 03868 422442), next to a police station at the end of Buenos Aires, and dispenses information about where to stay, what to do and where to rent bikes or hire horses.

Post office Güemes and Cordoba (Mon–Fri 8.30am–1pm & 5–7pm).

ACCOMMODATION

You'll have little trouble finding a room except during the popular, but not very exciting, **folk festival**, the Serenata Cafayateña, held on the first weekend of Lent. All the options below include free wi-fi and breakfast unless stated otherwise.

★**Casa Árbol** Calchaquí 84 ☎ 03868 422238, ⓦ casaarbolhostel.com. This simple but beautifully maintained hostel is the best value in town, with dorms and private rooms all with tiled floors and shared bathrooms, plus a bar and lush garden to relax in. Book ahead. Dorms $155; doubles $410

Casa de la Bodega RN-68 Km18.5 ☎ 03868 421555, ⓦ lacasadelabodega.com.ar. Off the road to San Carlos (RN-68), but only 15min from Cafayate, this sumptuous wine-boutique hotel has only eight rooms, some of which are giant suites; the decor, comfort, service and, of course, the wine are all top-notch. $1275

Hostal Benjamin Catamarca 267 ☎ 03868 567408, ⓦ hostalbenjamin.com. Simple but clean budget hotel with fans, TVs, private bathrooms plus communal kitchen and lounge. Free wi-fi but breakfast is $40 extra. $765

★**Killa** Colón 47 ☎ 03868 422254, ⓦ killacafayate.com.ar. Only a block from the central plaza, this splendid hotel is charming, comfortable and incredibly classy – it successfully combines Neocolonial elegance with rustic cosiness; some of the upstairs rooms have dream-like views of the surrounding mountains. There is a fair-sized pool. $1385

Los Patios de Cafayate RN-40 and RN-68 ☎ 03868 421747, ⓦ patiosdecafayate.com. Handwoven carpets,

chandeliers, colonial tapestries, native textiles and local arts and crafts all give this beautiful hotel a feeling of luxury, enhanced by the swimming pool and the fabulous spa, housed in a modern annexe and offering wine and grape massages – it's part of the El Esteco vineyard (see box, p.317). $2545

Portal del Santo Silverio Chavarría 250 ☎ 03868 422500, ⓦ portaldelsanto.todowebsalta.com.ar. New hotel built in a Neocolonial style. The handsome rooms are well equipped, with mini-bars and cable TV, while breakfasts are delicious and generous, using home-made products. There's a swimming pool with jacuzzi. Paying cash gives a $200 discount. $1400

★**Rusty-K Hostal** Rivadavia 281 ☎ 03868 422031. Set in an old colonial house built by the owner's grandparents, two blocks northwest of the main plaza, this is the best hostel in Cafayate, with a fun atmosphere, comfortable dorm beds and some decent doubles too (with private bathrooms). Dorms $200; doubles $500

Los Toneles Camila Quintana de Niño 38 ☎ 03868 422301, ⓦ lostoneleshostal.com.ar. Friendly budget hotel half a block from the plaza with barrels of character – literally, with giant beer barrels serving as decoration, as tables in the small patios off each room and for a children's play area. A yard with benches that resembles an English pub garden completes the picture. $850

5

Villa Vicuña Belgrano 76 ☎03868 422145, ⓦvillavicuna.com.ar. Picturesque, slightly quirky hotel in a mustard-yellow Neocolonial house right next to the plaza. The rooms are delightful, as is the central patio where you can have breakfast or tea, weather permitting. **$1466**

EATING

Café de las Viñas Güemes 60 (Plaza 2 de Febrero). One of the better bars on the main plaza and an ideal place for people-watching, with a decent array of wines by the glass (though pricey at $95), beers, coffee and snacks (cheese and cold cuts) – tables outside or in the pleasantly decorated interior. Daily 11am–2am.

Carreta de Don Olegario Güemes 20 (Plaza 2 de Febrero) ☎03868 421004. Much frequented and well-priced *parrilla* on the east side of the plaza with regional fare (empanadas, *locro* and so on). It's one of the oldest restaurants in town, helmed by a big fan of Boca Juniors (you'll see the posters and memorabilia on the walls). Daily noon–3pm & 8–11pm.

★**La Casa de las Empanadas** Mitre 24 ☎03868 15 454111, ⓦcasadelaempanada.com.ar. Locally celebrated for its varied and delicious empanada menu (with fillings ranging from goat's cheese and beef to tuna and corn), but also knocks out tasty *humitas*, *locro* and tamales. Tues–Sun 11am–3.30pm & 8pm–12.30am.

Heladería Miranda Güemes 170 ☎03868 421106. Gourmet ice cream: as well as the usual *dulce de leche*, chocolate etc, this small ice-cream parlour serves wine sorbets, both cabernet and torrontés. Daily noon–10pm.

★**Terruño Gourmet** Güemes 28 (Plaza 2 de Febrero) ☎03868 422460. Justifiably regarded as the best restaurant in the centre, with plaza or indoor seating, this classy restaurant headed by Carlos Amante knocks out carefully crafted steaks ($200), local trout and goat's cheese empanadas ($16). The wine list is artfully curated, and the staff well versed (though not always in English). Mon–Sat 11am–3pm & 7pm–midnight.

Quilmes

Via a 5km dirt road heading in a westerly direction, off RN-40 (50km south of Cafayate) • Daily 9am–dusk • $30 • Buses to/from Cafayate running along RN-40 will drop you at the junction, leaving you to walk to the site

The major pre-Inca **archeological site** of **Quilmes** is one of the most dramatically sited in the country. Inhabited since the ninth century AD by the ancestors of the Calchaquí, the settlement of Quilmes had a population of over 3000 at its peak in the seventeenth century. These people resisted the Spanish for 130 years, capitulating only in 1667 when they were punished mercilessly – the remaining population was transported to Buenos Aires (eventually to today's Quilmes) where only four hundred survived.

In 1978 the stone walls of almost all the buildings here were reconstructed – though no buildings are complete, the effect is startling, with the settlement appearing to climb the mountain in a series of giant terraces. Follow the signs up to the northern viewpoint on the cliffside and the full scale of Quilmes becomes clear – the footprints of a multitude of dwellings and structures of all shapes and sizes spread across the plain and up the hillside, the whole site studded by giant *cardón* cacti. Though it's visibly stunning, there's no interpretation on site whatsoever – guides wait at the entrance (they work for tips) and are worth hiring (if you can speak Spanish); without them, one stone wall soon looks much like another.

The **museum** and **hotel** on site are closed for the foreseeable future – sadly, Quilmes is part of an all too common dispute between the local indigenous community, who consider this a sacred site, and its former private owner (artist Héctor Cruz). After a long legal battle, ownership of the whole site has been returned to the indigenous community, but the dispute rubbles on.

Amaicha del Valle

The indigenous Calchaquí community of **AMAICHA DEL VALLE**, 65km south of Cafayate over in Tucumán Province, is a peaceful little place that livens up once a year during the **Fiesta de la Pachamama** in carnival week, when dancers and musicians lay on shows while locals put on a kind of pre-Columbian Passion Play, acting the roles of

5

the different pagan deities, including Pachamama, or Mother Earth. The goddess is also the inspiration for one of the region's most impressive museums, the Museo Pachamama on RP-307 on the edge of town (near the YPL petrol station). The town centre lies another kilometre off the main road, set around sleepy **Plaza San Martín**, with a couple of simple places to eat and stay but little else.

Museo Pachamama

RP-307 Km118 · Daily 8.30am–1pm & 2–6.30pm · $40 · ☎ 03893 421004, ⓦ museopachamama.com · Buses between Tucumán and Cafayate will drop off at the museum entrance

The brainchild of local artist Héctor Cruz, the enlightening **Museo Pachamama** is actually several museums rolled into one, and it's worth a look to see the structure itself, built around fabulous cactus gardens and incorporating eye-catching stone mosaics, depicting llamas, pre-Hispanic symbols and geometric patterns. Each large room in turn displays an impressive array of local archeological finds, the well-executed reconstruction of a mine along with impressive samples of various precious and semiprecious ores and minerals extracted in the area, plus paintings, tapestries and ceramics from Cruz's own workshops, to modern designs inspired by pre-Columbian artistic traditions.

Tafí del Valle

Some 53km southeast from Amaicha, across the spectacular pass at Abra del Infiernillo (3042m), **TAFÍ DEL VALLE** is favoured by locals and tourists alike as a day-trip destination or longer retreat from the provincial capital of Tucumán (128km east), especially in the summer when the city swelters (the average temperature here is 12°C lower). Once over the pass, the dry, arid landscapes of the central mountains disappear and Tafí occupies a far greener valley in the western lee of the Sierra del Aconquija, sandwiched between the Rio del Chusquí and the Río Blanquita, both of which flow into the Río Tafí and then into the Dique La Angostura, a reservoir. Blue and sunny skies are virtually guaranteed year-round, though occasionally thick fog descends into the valley in the winter, making its alpine setting feel bleak and inhospitable. The village's main street is **Avenida Perón**, where most of the shops and restaurants are located, while the central semicircular plaza, **Plaza Ángel Miguel Estévez**, lies a block north.

The main attraction here is the opportunity to explore the beautiful mountain scenery and unspoilt riverbanks; the trekking hereabouts is very rewarding. Popular trails go up **Cerro El Matadero** (3050m; 5hr), **Cerro Pabellón** (3770m; 4hr), **Cerro Muñoz** (4437m; one day) and **Mala-Mala** (3500m; 8hr); go with a guide, as the weather is unpredictable.

As well as being at the heart of the province's arts and crafts industry, the town is also known for its delicious cow's and goat's cheese, and holds a lively **Fiesta Nacional del Queso**, with folk music and dancing and rock bands, in early February.

Museo Histórico "La Banda"

José Manuel Silva · Daily 8am–6pm · $15 · Guided tours included · ☎ 03867 421685

Just over 1km from the Plaza Ángel Miguel Estévez, across the Río Tafí, the **Museo Histórico "La Banda"** occupies a Jesuit complex, the Conjunto Jesuítico de La Banda ("La Banda" is the name usually given to locations across rivers from main settlements). Parts of the building date from around 1718–20 when the Jesuits began converting the local Diaguita here in earnest. The whole complex was reconstructed in 1940, with the first section now housing a small collection of pre-Hispanic archeological finds, mostly painted ceramic urns, from nearby Tafí culture digs. The second section is dedicated to the Jesuits and some of the illustrious residents who occupied the complex after the religious order was expelled in 1767; these include Governor José Manuel Silva (who bought it in 1816), and officials such as President Nicolás Avellaneda, who once stayed here in the 1870s. The structure itself is as interesting as the exhibits, its adobe walls, tiled floors and thatched roof evocative of early mission life. The informative guides generally speak Spanish only and there are no English labels. Other buildings in the complex are occupied by a high-quality arts and crafts market and café.

ARRIVAL AND INFORMATION   TAFÍ DE VALLE

By bus Aconquija (Ⓦtransporteaconquija.com.ar) buses from Tucumán (9–10 daily), Amaicha (7 daily) and Cafayate (5 daily) arrive at the terminal on Av Gobernador Critto, a short walk east of the main plaza and Av Perón.

Tourist information The large and informative tourist office lies on the southern edge of Plaza Ángel Miguel Estévez (daily 9am–6pm; ☏03867 421020, Ⓦtafidelvalle .com), with free local maps.

ACCOMMODATION

Accommodation in Tafí is plentiful, but rooms can get booked up at weekends in the summer, and during the cheese festival (early Feb). Other than the campsite, all the options below include free wi-fi and breakfast.

Camping Los Sauzales Los Palenques ☏03867 421084. This municipal campsite, attractively located at Los Palenques on the banks of Río El Churqu, at the edge of the village, has showers, grills and electricity – it also has very basic dorms ($120). $60 per pitch (plus $40 per person, and $30 per car)

Las Carreras RP-325 Km13 ☏03867 421473, Ⓦestancialascarreras.com. Around 2km from the centre via gravel road, in a colonial hacienda built by the Jesuits in 1718, this luxurious hotel is very much a family-oriented place. Guests have contact with farm animals, dogs and horses; there's a cheese dairy on the premises; and the rooms are large and beautifully decorated, with lots of locally produced textiles. $1735

Hostería ACA Sol del Valle San Martín and Gobernador Campero ☏03867 421027, Ⓦsoldelvalle .com.ar. This well-refurbished institution is reasonable value, with bright, clean and comfortable rooms. There is also a very good restaurant on the premises. $820

Hostería Castillo de Piedra De Los Jesuitas, Banda ☏0381 471 4087, Ⓦcastillodepiedra.com. This hotel (1.5km from the centre) is a quaint, stone, mock castle on the outside, but has designer rooms on the inside, with

exquisite furnishings, great views, a swimming pool, a sauna and, above all, a gourmet restaurant. $1530

★**Nómade Hostel** Los Castaños and María Lidia Chenaut ☏0381 307 5922, Ⓦnomadehostel.com.ar. The pick of the budget options and a short walk from the bus terminal, this welcoming hostel has basic but colourful en-suite rooms, rooms with shared bathrooms and clean dorms. HI members get a ten- to twenty-percent discount. Dorms $180; doubles $480

Nuestro Destino Bar & Hostel Túpac Amaru 140 ☏0381 563 1532, Ⓦnuestrodestinohostel.com. Another highly recommended budget option, a traditional adobe property with a range of private rooms (some with bathrooms) and comfy dorms, plus tranquil garden and spectacular views. Dorms $270; doubles $725; triples $1210

Posada Inti Watana Madre Teresa de Calcuta, El Churqui ☏03867 420178, Ⓦposadaintiwatana .blogspot.com. Around 2km from the centre, this cosy hotel run on sustainable principles by French-Argentine couple Fabienne and Juan has just four elegant rooms with tiled floors, bamboo thatched ceilings and wood beams, plus a gorgeous garden and sumptuous breakfasts. $725

EATING

El Portal de la Villa Perón 221 ☏03867 421065. Smart café and restaurant on the main drag with indoor and outdoor seating, set lunch menus of *locro*, *humitas* and mains such as steak for $80 (plus goat and llama steaks). Sells local Kkechuwa craft beer. Cash only. Daily 8am–1am.

Rancho de Félix Perón and Belgrano ☏03867 421022, Ⓦranchodefelix.com.ar. Contemporary *parrilla* in the heart of town, with solid but not always exceptional fare: huge steaks for two ($260) plus empanadas, *humitas* and *locro*. Daily 11.30am–3.30pm & 8.30pm–12.30am.

San Miguel de Tucumán

In the humid valley of the Río Salí, **SAN MIGUEL DE TUCUMÁN** (or simply **Tucumán**) is Argentina's fourth-largest city, 1190km northwest of Buenos Aires and nearly 300km south of Salta via RN-9. The capital of a tiny but heavily populated sugar-rich province, known popularly as the Garden of the Republic, Tucumán is by far the biggest metropolis in the Northwest, the region's undisputed **commercial**

SAN MIGUEL DE TUCUMÁN

RN-9 to Salta (300km) & Jujuy (330km)

Airport (9km)

Casino
Legislatura
Teatro San Martín
AVENIDA SARMIENTO
Train Station
Colegio Nacional
PLAZA URQUIZA
SANTA FE
P. GARCÍA
CATAMARCA
SALTA
JUNÍN
BORDABEHRE
MARCOS PAZ
MAIPÚ
MUÑECAS
25 DE MAYO
LAPRIDA
RIVADAVIA
MONTEAGUDO
BALCARCE
ESTADOS UNIDOS

ACCOMMODATION
A La Gurda Hostel ... 4
Hostel Backpackers ... 3
Hotel Boutique Don Abel ... 2
Posada Arcadia ... 1

CORRIENTES
HONDURAS
SANTIAGO DEL ESTERO
AVENIDA AVELLANEDA
HAITÍ
SAN JUAN
GUATEMALA

DRINKING AND NIGHTLIFE
El Alto de la Lechuza ... 3
Plaza de Almas ... 1
La San Juan Bar ... 2

Mercado del Norte
Correo Argentino
CÓRDOBA
CUBA
AVENIDA SOLDATI
Parque 9 de Julio

0 ... 250
metres

MENDOZA
ENTRE RÍOS
AVENIDA JACQUES
RÍO DE JANEIRO
S Santiago del Estero (155km)

Iglesia San Francisco
Casa de Gobierno
Casa Padilla
Museo Folclórico de la Provincia
SAN MARTÍN
PLAZA INDEPENDENCIA
Iglesia La Merced
FRANCIA
MORENO
AV. BENJAMÍN ARÁOZ

COLOMBRES
CATAMARCA
JUJUY
AYACUCHO
CHACABUCO
AVENIDA 24 DE SEPTIEMBRE
CONGRESO
Museo Provincial de Bellas Artes
Museo Histórico de la Provincia
LAS HERAS
CRISÓSTOMO ALVAREZ
AVENIDA SÁENZ PEÑA
CHARCAS
Bus Terminal

EATING
Cilantro ... 2
Sara Figueroa ... 3
Setimio Vinoteca & Wine Bar ... 1

Basílica Santo Domingo
BUENOS AIRES
9 DE JULIO
Catedral
Casa Histórica de la Independencia
SAN LORENZO
Former Belgrano Railway Station

capital and one of the liveliest urban centres in the country, with a thriving business centre and a youthful population. Tucumán also has a slightly boisterous image, perhaps partly since it's Argentina's rugby capital, but its confidence has been trimmed over the past two or three decades by municipal political and economic crises – and the city seems to have taken longer than the rest of the country to recover from the turmoil of 2001.

Despite its narrow, traffic-clogged streets and the slightly down-at-heel pedestrianized shopping area northwest of the centre, you could easily spend a full day visiting the city's sights, which include a couple of decent museums.

Brief history

Originally founded in 1565 by *conquistador* Diego de Villarroel and Spanish settlers from Santiago del Estero, Tucumán was moved to its current location in 1685. Its moment of glory came on July 9, 1816, when the city hosted a historic Congress of Unitarist politicians at which Argentina's independence from Spain was declared. British investment and climatic conditions favoured Tucumán's **sugar industry**, and most of the city's wealth, built up around the end of the nineteenth century, accrued from this "white gold". A slump in international sugar prices and shortsighted over-farming meant most sugar mills closed in the 1960s, devastating the local economy and ushering in a long period of instability – "**Tucumán is Burning**" was a landmark art exhibition held in Buenos Aires and Rosario in 1968 that sought to highlight the impoverished living conditions in the city. In the 1970s, **Montoneros** and **People's Revolutionary Army** (ERP) militants were active in the mountains near the city. Today things are far calmer, with Tucumán the world's biggest lemon-growing area, but also a major producer of mandarins, grapefruit and kumquats, its economy benefiting from the country's explosive growth since 2003. Not everything has changed, however; **Juan Manzur**'s victory (with 51.64 percent) in Tucumán's 2015 gubernatorial election was tarnished by allegations of ballot burning.

Plaza Independencia

Oozing tropical lushness, **Plaza Independencia** is Tucumán's focal point; a grove of native trees jostles with orange trees, while a large pool with a fountain, a statue to Liberty (by **Lola Mora**) and a monolith marking the spot where governor Marco Avellaneda's head was spiked, after his opponent Rosas had him executed in 1841, take up the remainder. In the southeast corner of the square is the mid-nineteenth-century Neoclassical cathedral, formally the **Catedral de la Encarnación de María**, its slender towers topped with blue-and-white-tiled domes. On the western side of the square is the elegant French-style **Casa de Gobierno** (Mon–Fri 8.30am–8.30pm; free), completed in 1910 and still home to the provincial government, as well as the tomb of **Juan Bautista Alberdi** (local architect of Argentina's Constitution of 1853), who was reinterred here in 1991.

Museo Folclórico de la Provincia

Av 24 de Septiembre 565 • Tues–Fri 9am–1pm & 4–8pm, Sat & Sun 4–8pm • Free • ☎ 0381 421 8250

Set in a beautiful eighteenth-century Neocolonial townhouse, the **Museo Folclórico de la Provincia** contains a quaintly eclectic collection that ranges from *mate* ware and textiles, including the typical local lace, known as "randas", to an exquisite set of traditional musical instruments, including little banjos or *charangos* made of mulita shell – a small species of armadillo – and *bombo* drums made of *cardón* cactus wood. There's also a room dedicated to local folk singer and Argentine legend **Mercedes Sosa** (1935–2009), aka "La Negra".

Museo Casa Histórica de la Independencia

Congreso 151 • Daily 10am–6pm (July 9am–7pm) • $30 • Tours (included in entry fee) daily 9am, 10am & 11am • **Sound-and-light show** Mon–Wed & Fri–Sun 8.30pm ($10; tickets from the tourist office at 6pm) • ☎ 0381 431 0826, ⓦ museocasahistorica.org.ar

The **Museo Casa Histórica de la Independencia**, with its gleaming white facade, is where Argentina officially declared its independence from Spain in 1816 and where its first Congress was held. Built in the 1760s, the house was originally a family home – all of it was demolished in 1904 save for the historic Salón de la Jura, the room where the Congress was held. This faithful replica of the house was completed around the *salón* in 1943. Between two grilled windows and mock-Baroque spiralling columns, the mighty *quebracho* doors lead into a series of large patios, draped with bougainvillea, jasmine and tropical creepers – in the third patio you can see bas-reliefs by Lola Mora (see box, p.219). The house contains a fine collection of colonial armour, furniture, paintings, silverware and porcelain, plus exhibits chronicling how the country gained its independence. There's a fun sound-and-light show dramatizing the site's history here every day but Thursday at 8.30pm.

ARRIVAL AND DEPARTURE

SAN MIGUEL DE TUCUMÁN

By plane Tucumán's international airport, Aeropuerto Benjamín Matienzo (☎ 0381 426 4906), serves Buenos Aires (8 daily; 1hr 45min) and is 13km east of the centre of town; a taxi will cost about $140 (there is no public transport).

By bus The bus terminal (☎ 0381 422 2221, ⓦ terminaltucuman.com) is at Brígido Terán 350, six blocks east and two south of Plaza Independencia. It contains a shopping centre ("Shopping del Jardín"), supermarket, restaurants, bars, post office, telephone centres, left-luggage and even a hairdresser – but no working ATMs: try the supermarket for cash withdrawals. Several city buses run between the centre and the bus terminal, and you'll

need a top-up card (Tarjeta Ciudadana; $15 or $25 stored value) for each trip, on sale at all kiosks.

Destinations Buenos Aires (10 daily; 14–17hr); Córdoba (10 daily; 7hr 45min–9hr 5min); Jujuy (10 daily; 4hr 50min–5hr 45min); Salta (10 daily; 4hr–4hr 50min); Tafí del Valle (6 daily; 3hr).

By train Trains (ⓦ www.sofse.gob.ar) run to and from Buenos Aires via Rosario from the station (☎ 0381 431 0725) at Catamarca and Corrientes; trains depart Retiro station Mon & Fri 8.47am, while trains return from Tucumán 4.16pm (Wed) and 9.01pm (Sat). The trip takes around 26–27hr.

5

INFORMATION

Tourist information The provincial office is at 24 de Septiembre 484 (Mon–Fri 7am–1pm & 5–9pm, Sat & Sun 9am–1pm & 5–9pm; ☎0381 430 3644, ⓦ tucumanturismo.gob.ar), on Plaza Independencia.

ACCOMMODATION

Downtown Tucumán has a wide selection of business **hotels**, but the quality in the mid-range is poor – you're better opting for one of the boutique hotels in the leafy suburb of Yerba Buena, 10km west of Plaza Independencia. In the centre, many mid-range hotels are conveniently clustered around the Plaza Independencia. At the budget end, you can choose from a number of decent *residenciales* and several excellent **youth hostels**. All options below include breakfast and free wi-fi.

★**A La Gurda Hostel** Maipú 490 ☎0381 497 6275, ⓦ lagurdahostel.com.ar. Exceptional hostel, with a/c rooms with spotless bathrooms (some en suite) and comfy mixed dorms with fans. You get kitchen use, shared TV room and pool table. Breakfast included. Dorms $130; doubles $340

Hostel Backpackers Laprida 456 ☎0381 430 2716, ⓦ backpackerstucuman.com. Decent HI-affiliated hostel with an outdoor bar and swimming pool, in a beautiful Neocolonial townhouse; there are colourful private rooms and dorms with shared kitchen. Dorms $120; doubles $320

Hotel Boutique Don Abel Aconquija 1400, at Güemes, Yerba Buena ☎0381 425 1230, ⓦ hotelboutiqueabel .com.ar. Handsome modern hotel, with an attractive garden; the four rooms are named after precious gems such as sapphire and ruby. $1072

Posada Arcadia Güemes 480, Yerba Buena ☎0381 425 22140, ⓦ posadaarcadia.com.ar. Excellent budget hotel in this sleepy suburb, with four rooms with Quechua names meaning "beauty", "wind", "pretty woman" and "blooming". There is a swimming pool in the relaxing garden and the owners can arrange for trips to pottery workshops nearby or horseriding in the surrounding hills. $580

EATING

Cilantro Monteagudo 541 ☎0381 430 6041. Fusion food and an excellent wine list at this highly regarded – and very fashionable – restaurant. Leave room for dessert and one of the delicious liqueurs on offer. Mon–Sat noon–3pm & 8pm–midnight, Sun noon–3pm.

★**Sara Figueroa** Opposite Museo Casa Histórica de la Independencia, Congreso 151. The now elderly Figueroa is a local legend, selling her delicious empanadas outside the museum for decades – usually beef or chicken, baked

and always served hot. Daily 8am–noon (or until she runs out).

Setimio Vinoteca & Wine Bar Santa Fé 512 ☎0381 431 2792, ⓦ setimio.com. As the name suggests, this pricey joint takes its wine seriously – either sample it by the glassful with a hearty *picada* or enjoy the braised lamb and other fine dishes with a bottle of top-quality malbec or syrah. Mon–Sat 10am–3pm & 7.30pm–1.30am.

DRINKING AND NIGHTLIFE

★**El Alto de la Lechuza** 24 de Septiembre 1199 ☎0381 421 8940. One of the oldest *peñas* in the country – improvised folk music in an ancient building where the empanadas are particularly succulent. Thurs–Sat 9.30pm–6am.

Plaza de Almas Maipú 791 ☎0381 430 6067. Popular place where locals flock to see the latest art exhibition, or just have a drink among friends. It also serves sandwiches,

pizzas and other simple dishes. Cash only. Mon–Sat 12.30–3pm & 8pm–2am.

★**La San Juan Bar** San Juan 1059 ☎0381 421 0261. The place to go for an evening of Latino musical fun, with DJs, live salsa dancers and sometimes bands. Tues & Sun 10pm–1.30am, Wed 10.15pm–3.30pm, Thurs–Sat 10.15pm–5am.

Catamarca Province

Studded with snowcapped mountains and volcanic peaks, **Catamarca Province** remained largely isolated from the rest of Argentina until 1888, when the railway first reached its capital, San Fernando del Valle de Catamarca. It's still one the poorest parts of the country, and tourism is far less developed here, with the most enticing attractions served via RN-40 from Salta and Cafayate. **Antofagasta de la Sierra** is especially intriguing, a remote Andean village surrounded by jaw-dropping volcanic landscapes.

Belén

Some 250km southwest of Cafayate, the indigenous community of **BELÉN** is best known as the **Cuna del Poncho** ("the birthplace of the poncho"). Its many excellent *teleras*, or textile workshops, turn out beautiful blankets and sweaters made of llama, vicuña and alpaca wool, mostly in natural colours, as well as high-quality ponchos. The wool is sometimes blended with walnut bark, to give the local cloth, known as *belichas* or *belenistos*, its typical rough texture. Squeezed between the Sierra de Belén and the river of the same name, the town offers the area's best accommodation and restaurants, and it's also a base for **adventure tourism**, including trekking and horseriding.

As for **festivals**, every January 6 a pilgrimage procession clambers to the **Monumento a Nuestra Señora de Belén**, a 15m statue of the Virgen de Belén, overlooking the town from its high vantage point to the west, the Cerro de la Virgen.

Iglesia Nuestra Señora de Belén

Plaza Olmos y Aguilera • Free

On the western flank of Belén's main square, **Plaza Olmos y Aguilera**, shaded by whitewashed orange trees and bushy palms and ringed by cafés and ice-cream parlours, stands the Greek Revival **Iglesia Nuestra Señora de Belén**. Designed and built by Italian immigrants between 1905 and 1907, its brickwork is bare, without plaster or decoration, lending it a rough-hewn but oddly elegant look. Belén was founded in 1681 by missionary priest Bartolomé de Olmos y Aguilera in honour of the Belén shrine in Spain – a venerated image of the Virgin Mary stands in front of the ornate church altar.

Museo Arqueológico Cóndor Huasi

San Martín 310 (Galería Misael) • Mon–Fri 9am–1pm & 5.30–8.30pm • $5

Housed on the first floor of a rather grim commercial arcade (Galería Misael), half a block from the main plaza, the **Museo Arqueológico Cóndor Huasi** contains one of the country's most important collections of **Diaguita** artefacts. The huge number of ceramics, and some bronze and silver items, trace the Diaguita culture through four archeological periods, from 300 BC to 1000 AD onwards, when the so-called Santa María culture produced large urns, vases and amphorae decorated with complex, mostly abstract geometric patterns, with depictions of snakes, rheas and toads. There are a few Inca artefacts, too, but everything is labelled in Spanish only.

ARRIVAL AND INFORMATION   BELÉN

By bus Buses to/from Antofagasta (2 weekly; 6–7hr), Catamarca city (6–7 daily; 5hr 30min) and Londres (hourly; 15–20min; some continue to Shinkal) arrive at the corner of Sarmiento and Rivadavia, near the museum.

Tourist information The small tourist office is at General Paz 180 (daily 7am–1pm & 2–10pm; ☎ 03835 461091).

ACCOMMODATION AND EATING

1900 Belgrano 390 ☎ 0381 461100. At the best restaurant here by far, smart waiters serve up lovingly prepared lunches and dinners in a room with cheery, brightly coloured decor – try the huge *bife de chorizo* with cheese and a potato tortilla plus the earthy house wine. It often gets filled up at midday with regulars. Daily noon–3pm & 8pm–midnight.

Hotel Belén Belgrano and Cubas ☎ 03835 461501, ⓦ hotelbelen.com.ar. The best place to stay in the area, this impressive hotel is part of a large complex that includes a convention centre and *Restaurante Mikhuy* – there are singles, doubles, triples and suites, but all are decorated in a sleek contemporary style, with dark wood furnishings and amusing ethnic bathrooms, with lots of stone and ceramic tiling, plus cable TV. Weak but free wi-fi and buffet breakfast included. $680

Jeremias Parrilla General Roca 92 ☎ 03835 461796. If *1900* is closed or full, you can fall back on this classic *parrilla*; it serves tasty empanadas and does a filling *locro* in addition to the usual slabs of beef. Daily noon–3pm & 8pm–2am.

5

Londres and around

Fifteen kilometres west of Belén and even more charming, with its partly crumbling adobe houses and pretty orchards, **LONDRES** lies 2km off RN-40 along a winding road that joins its upper and lower towns. Known as the Cuna de la Nuez, or "Walnut Heartland", the town celebrates the **Fiesta de la Nuez** with folklore and crafts displays during the first few days of February. Londres de Abajo, the lower town, is centred on Plaza José Eusebio Colombres, where you'll find the simple, whitewashed eighteenth-century **Iglesia de San Juan Bautista**, in front of which the walnut festival is held. The focal point for the rest of the year is Londres de Arriba's **Plaza Hipólito Yrigoyen**, overlooked by the quaint **Iglesia de la Inmaculada Concepción**, a once lovely church in a pitiful state of repair but noteworthy for a harmonious colonnade and its fine bells, said to be the country's oldest.

Londres' humble present-day aspect belies a long and prestigious history, including the fact that it's Argentina's second-oldest "city" (*ciudad*), founded in 1558, only five years after Santiago del Estero. **Diego de Almagro** and his expedition from Cusco began scouring the area in the 1530s and founded a settlement which was named in honour of the marriage between Philip, heir to the Spanish throne, and Mary Tudor: hence the tribute to the English capital in the village's name.

El Shinkal

6km west of Londres • Daily via guided tour only: 8am, 9.30am, 11.30am, 3.30pm, 5.30pm & 7pm (site closed noon–3pm) • $35

The remarkable **Inca** ruins of **El Shinkal** provide an insight into what pre-Hispanic settlements in the region must have looked like: the ruins date from the late Inca period (1471–1536), though the site was probably inhabited by the Diaguita for hundreds of years before that. Amazingly intact, though parts of it are over-restored in a zealous attempt to reconstruct the fortress, it was the site of a decisive battle in the **Great Calchaquí Uprising** (see box below). Splendid steps lead to the top of high

THE CALCHAQUÍ WARS

After the European invasions of this region in the late sixteenth and early seventeenth centuries, the indigenous tribes who lived along the **Valles Calchaquíes**, stretching from Salta Province in the north, down to central Catamarca Province, steadfastly refused to be evangelized by the Spanish invaders and generally to behave as their aggressors wanted; the region around Belén and Londres proved especially difficult to colonize. Even the Jesuits, usually so effective at bringing the "natives" under control, conceded defeat. The Spanish made do with a few *encomiendas*, and more often *pueblos*, reservations where the Indians were forced to live, leaving the colonizers to farm their "own" land in peace. After a number of skirmishes, things came to a head in 1630, when the so-called **Great Calchaquí Uprising** began. For two years, under the leadership of **Juan Chelemín**, the fierce *cacique* of Hualfín, natives waged a war of attrition against the invaders, sacking towns and burning crops, provoking ever more brutal reactions from the ambitious new governor of Tucumán, Francisco de Nieva y Castilla. Eventually Chelemín was caught, drawn and quartered, and various parts of his body were put on display in different villages to "teach the Calchaquíes a lesson", but it took until 1643 for all resistance to be stamped out, and only after a network of fortresses was built in Andalgalá, Londres and elsewhere.

War broke out once more in 1657, when the Spanish decided to arrest "El Inca Falso", also known as Pedro Chamijo, an impostor of European descent who claimed to be Hualpa Inca – or Inca emperor – under the nom de guerre of **Bohórquez**. Elected chief at an impressive ceremony attended by the new governor of Tucumán, Alonso Mercado y Villacorta, amid great pomp and circumstance, in Pomán, he soon led the Calchaquíes into battle, and Mercado y Villacorta, joined by his ruthless predecessor, Francisco de Nieva y Castilla, set about what today would be called ethnic cleansing. Bohórquez was captured, taken to Lima and eventually garrotted in 1667, and whole tribes fell victim to genocide: their only remains are the ruins of Batungasta, Hualfín and Shinkal, near Londres.

ceremonial mounds with great views of the oasis and Sierra de Zapata. The on-site **museum** and informative guides provide context (though you are unlikely to find an English-speaker). To find the ruins, just follow the well-signposted scenic road, next to the Iglesia de la Inmaculada Concepción.

The Puna Catamarqueña

The altiplano of northwestern Catamarca Province, known as the **Puna Catamarqueña** (*puna* is the Quichoa word for altiplano, a word of Spanish coinage), stretches to the Chilean border and is one of the remotest and most deserted, but most outstandingly beautiful parts of the country. Dotted with majestic ebony volcanoes and scarred by recent lava flows, with the Andean cordillera as a magnificent backdrop, the huge expanses of altiplano and their desiccated vegetation are grazed by hardy yet delicate-looking **vicuñas**, while **flamingoes** valiantly survive on frozen lakes.

The trip out here is really more rewarding than the main destination, **Antofagasta**, which is primarily a place to spend the night before forging on northwards, to San Antonio de los Cobres in Salta Province (see p.295), or doubling back down to Belén. As you travel, look out for *apachetas*, little cairns of stones piled up at the roadside as an offering to the Mother Goddess, Pachamama, and the only visible signs of any human presence.

Although a **bus** shuttles back and forth between Catamarca, Belén and Antofagasta twice a week, the surest way to get around is by 4WD, along RP-43, one of the loneliest roads in Argentina; it's quite possible not to pass another vehicle all day. RP-43 is now **completely paved**, but take all the necessary precautions including plenty of fuel, and don't forget warm clothing as the temperature can plummet several degrees below freezing at night in July. By far the best (and safest) way to explore this difficult region is with the Salta-based tour company Socompa (see p.288), which also runs the *hostería* in El Peñón, easily the best accommodation this side of Belén.

Hualfín

Some 50km north of Belén, RP-43 branches off from RN-40 at the small hamlet of **El Eje**, but if you need **accommodation** continue on for another 8km to **HUALFÍN**, where you can find rooms for rent. Most people use the village as their last **fuel stop** before the long haul to Antofagasta de la Sierra; provisions can also be bought here. Hualfín itself is famous for its paprika, often sprinkled on the delicious local goat's cheeses, and for a fine **colonial church**, dedicated to Nuestra Señora del Rosario and built in 1770; ask for the key at the municipalidad to see the pristine interior adorned with delicate frescoes.

Up to Antofagasta de la Sierra

The first stretch of RP-43 to Antofagasta de la Sierra (all of 207km from El Eje) takes you through some lightly farmed countryside, planted with vines and maize, with feathery acacias and tall poplars acting as windbreaks, and dotted with humble mud-brick farmhouses. Potentially treacherous fords at **Villavil** (28km from El Eje) and, more likely, at **El Bolsón**, 10km further on, are sometimes too deep to cross even in a 4WD, especially after spring thaws or summer rains; you'll either have to wait a couple of hours for the rivers to subside, or turn back. Just over 70km from El Eje, the road twists and climbs through the dramatic **Cuesta de Randolfo**, hemmed in by rocky pinnacles and reaching an altitude of 4800m before corkscrewing back down to the transitional plains.

Reserva Natural Laguna Blanca

Beyond the Cuesta de Randolfo, you're treated to immense open views towards the dramatic crags of the Sierra del Cajón, to the south, and the spiky rocks of the Sierra

5

Laguna Blanca, to the north. Impressive white **sand dunes**, gleaming like fresh snow against the dark mountainsides, make an interesting pretext for a halt. Down in the plain, the immense **salt lakes** stretch for many kilometres, and this is where you'll probably spy your first **vicuñas** – the shy, smaller cousins of the llama, with much silkier wool – protected by the **Reserva Natural Laguna Blanca**. All along this road, with photogenic ochre mountains as backdrops, whole flocks of vicuña graze off scrawny grasses. You could make a short detour to visit the shores of **Laguna Blanca** itself, a shallow, mirror-like lake fed by the Río Río and home to thousands of teals, ducks and **flamingoes**; it's clearly signposted along a track off to the north.

Portezuelo Pasto Ventura

After the Reserva Laguna Blanca, the road climbs steadily again up the often snow-streaked Sierra Laguna Blanca to reach the pass at **Portezuelo Pasto Ventura** (4000m), marked by a sign: this is the entrance to the altiplano, or *puna* proper. From here you have magnificent panoramas of the Andes, to the west, and of the great volcanoes of northwestern Catamarca, plus your first glimpse of wide-rimmed **Volcán Galan** (5912m), whose name means "bare mountain" in Quichoa.

El Peñón

Tiny **El Peñón**, 135km from Hualfín, is the first altiplano settlement you reach along RP-43: just a few gingerbread-coloured adobe houses, a good *hostería*, run by Socompa (see p.288), some proud poplar trees, and an apple orchard, surprising given the altitude. The village nestles in the **Carachipampa Valley**, which extends all the way to the Cordillera de San Buenaventura, to the southwest, and its striking summit **Cerro El Cóndor** (6000m), clearly visible from here in the searingly clear atmosphere.

Soon the chestnut-brown volcanic cones of **Los Negros de la Laguna** come into view, a sign that you're in the final approaches to Antofagasta. One of twin peaks, **La Alumbrera** deposited enormous lava flows when it last erupted, only a few hundred years ago. The huge piles of visibly fresh **black pumice** it tossed out, all pocked and twisted, reach heights of 10m or more. Just before Antofagasta, the road swings round **Laguna Colorada**, a small lake often frozen solid and shaded pink with a massive flock of altiplanic flamingoes which somehow survive up here.

Antofagasta de la Sierra

Perched 3440m above sea level, 260km north of Belén, **ANTOFAGASTA DE LA SIERRA** lies at the northern end of a vast, arid plain hemmed in by volcanoes to the east and south, and by the cordillera, which soars to peaks of over 6000m, a mere 100km over to the west. With a mainly indigenous population of just over a thousand, it exudes a feeling of utter remoteness, while still managing to exert a disarming fascination. It's a bleak yet restful place, an oasis of tamarinds and green alfalfa fields in the middle of the *meseta altiplánica* – a harsh steppe that looms above the surrounding altiplano. Two rivers, Punilla and Las Paitas, meet just to the south, near the strange volcanic plug called **El Torreón**, adopted as the town's symbol. Salt, borax and various minerals and metals have been mined in the area for centuries and Antofagasta has the hardy feel of a mining town, but most of its people are now subsistence farmers and herdsmen, scraping a living from maize, potatoes, onions and beans or rearing llamas and alpacas, whose wool is made into textiles.

The best views of the immediate surroundings can be enjoyed from the top of the Cerro Amarillo and Cerro de la Cruz, two unsightly mounds of earth that look like part of a huge building site and dominate the town's humble streets of small mud-brick houses. The **Cerro de la Cruz** is the destination of processions held to honour Antofagasta's patron saints, St Joseph and the Virgin of Loreto, from

DAY-EXCURSIONS FROM ANTOFAGASTA

Within easy excursion distance of Antofagasta are a number of archeological and historical sites, such as the ruins at **Pucará de la Alumbrera**, 8km south, and the **Pucará del Coyparcito**, 3km further away (both pre-Columbian fortresses). The **Petroglifos de La Peña** (mostly depicting llamas and human figures) are also worth a visit; you'll definitely need the services of a guide to find them, and for the necessary explanations to make a visit worthwhile, but they are all open to the public at all times and no entrance fee is charged. Ask at Antofagasta's museum for archeological information and guided visits. The abandoned onyx, mica and gold **mines** in the region such as the **Minas de Oro Incahuasi** are another intriguing target, while long treks on mule-back are the only way of seeing **Volcán Sufre** (5706m) on the Chilean border; 4WD trips to the **Antofagasta**, **Alumbrera** and **Galán** volcanoes are also popular. The mirage-like landscapes of the great **Salar del Hombre Muerto** salt flats, 75km to the north of Antofagasta are best explored using the services of a guide, as are the rainbow-coloured pumice fields of the **Campo de Piedra Pómez** (63km to the south, near El Peñón). The tiny community of **Antofalla** (some 50km to the northwest), at the foot of another volcano, is incredibly picturesque, close to some rarely visited ruins of a Jesuit mill.

December 8 to 10. Every March the town comes to life for the **Feria Artesanal y Ganadera de la Puna**, a colourful event attended by craftspeople and herdsmen from all over the province.

Museo del Hombre

RP-43 (Plaza 9 de Julio) • Mon–Fri 8am–1pm & 6–9pm • $5 • ☎ 03835 471001

The premier tourist attraction in town is the beautifully presented **Museo del Hombre**, created primarily to house two perfectly preserved, ancient mummies: an indigenous woman and a naturally mummified baby, found in the nearby Peñas Coloradas and believed to be nearly two thousand years old. Surrounded with jewels and other signs of wealth, the child may have belonged to a ruling dynasty. The museum's other exhibits, few in number but of extraordinary value, include an immaculately preserved pre-Hispanic basket, the pigment colouring and fine weave still intact.

Museo Mineralógico de la Puna

San Martín s/n • Mon–Fri 8am–6pm • $5

The privately run **Museo Mineralógico de la Puna** highlights the wondrous geology of the region, with all sorts of odd-shaped and coloured rocks and fossils presented by the enthusiastic, Hungarian-born owner, Zoltán Czekus (opening times vary according to his schedule).

ARRIVAL AND INFORMATION   ANTOFAGASTA DE LA SIERRA

By bus The twice-weekly bus (usually Wed & Fri) from Catamarca (departing 6.15am) and Belén (departing around 12.30pm) will drop you in the main street; it makes the return journey Mon & Fri at 10am.

Tourist information Antofagasta has no tourist office; for visiting the immediate and farther-flung surroundings ask at the municipalidad on Belgrano for the town's most experienced guides. Better still, contact Socampa (see p.288). There are no banks here – bring plenty of cash.

ACCOMMODATION AND EATING

Complejo Pucara ☎ 0381 15 089060, ⓦ complejo pucara.com.ar. Rustic but stylish accommodation in a tranquil compound just south of the centre (off RP-43), with fine views, friendly hosts (who can arrange trips) and compact but comfy rooms. Breakfast included. Cash only. **$640**

Hostería Incahuasi Belgrano ☎ 011 4945 8931. One block from the plaza, this is the best guesthouse in town, with simple, cosy rooms with tiled floors, helpful hosts (the Baldi family) who double as tour guides, excellent breakfasts (included) and delicious dinners if requested. Free wi-fi. **$640**

Mendoza
and El Cuyo

PLAZA DE ESPAÑA, MENDOZA

Mendoza and El Cuyo

Argentina's midwestern region, generally known as El Cuyo, is formed by the provinces of Mendoza, San Juan and La Rioja plus the neighbouring province of San Luís. This massive territory stretches all the way from the chocolate-brown pampas of La Payunia, on the northern borders of Patagonia, to the remote highland steppes of the Reserva Las Vicuñas, more than a thousand kilometres to the north. Extending across vast, thinly populated territories of bone-dry desert, they are dotted with vibrant oases of farmland and the region's famous vineyards. The sophisticated metropolis of Mendoza, one of Argentina's biggest cities, is the epicentre of the country's blossoming wine – and wine tourism – industry, with the two smaller provincial capitals, San Juan and La Rioja, still quiet backwaters by comparison.

The region's dynamics are overwhelmingly about its highly varied **landscapes** and **wildlife**. In the west loom the world's loftiest peaks outside the Himalayas, culminating in the defiant **Aconcagua**, whose summit is only a shade under 7000m. Ranging from these snowy Andean heights to totally flat pampas in the east, from green, fertile valleys to barren volcanoes – including the world's second-highest cone, extinct **Monte Pissis** – the scenery also includes two of the country's most photographed national parks: the sheer red-sandstone cliffs of **Talampaya** and the moonscapes of **Ischigualasto**. All this provides a backdrop for some of Argentina's best opportunities for **extreme sports** – from **skiing** in exclusive **Las Leñas** to white-water rafting, rock climbing, and even the ascent of Aconcagua or the **Mercedario** and **Tupungato** peaks.

European settlers have wrought changes to the environment, bringing the grape vine, the Lombardy poplar and all kinds of fruit trees with them, but the thousands of kilometres of irrigation channels that water the region existed long before Columbus "discovered" America. Pumas, vicuñas, ñandús and hundreds of colourful bird species inhabit the unspoilt wildernesses of the region, where some of the biggest-known dinosaurs prowled millions of years ago. Flowering **cacti** and the dazzling yellow *brea*, a broom-like shrub, add colour to the browns and greys of the desert in spring.

GETTING AROUND   MENDOZA AND EL CUYO

Tourism is well developed in Mendoza Province so it's possible to visit most places by **public transport** or on tours from Mendoza and other towns. In the two other provinces getting around is more difficult, though operators will take you to places like Talampaya from San Juan or La Rioja. To see the region at your own pace (and have much of it to yourself), consider renting a vehicle – preferably a **4WD**, since sometimes roads are, at best, only partly sealed. However, recently some of the main roads have received a significant facelift.

BODEGA SALENTEIN

Highlights

❶ Mendoza city Argentina's wine capital has a lot to offer, from top-class dining to vibrant nightlife. **See p.335**

❷ White-water rafting Expect exhilarating trips on the region's feisty rivers. **See p.344**

❸ Bodega Salentein Who said the Dutch can't make wine? This "Wine Cathedral" is one of the continent's most impressive wineries. **See p.347**

❹ Mountain climbing If Aconcagua – one of the world's tallest peaks – is too crowded, then take your tent and ropes to Mercedario or another of the Andes' great challenges. **See p.356 & p.375**

❺ La Payunia A secluded region of ancient volcanoes, dark and rust-red lava flows, and photogenic guanacos. **See p.368**

❻ Ischigualasto and Talampaya The pride and joy of San Juan and La Rioja provinces – the first an eerie moonscape and dinosaur graveyard, the second an awe-inspiring canyon with mighty red-sandstone walls. **See p.383 & p.386**

❼ Laguna Brava Head up into the strikingly coloured cordillera of La Rioja to see flamingoes on this wild, high-mountain lagoon. **See p.387**

HIGHLIGHTS ARE MARKED ON THE MAP ON P.334

MENDOZA AND EL CUYO

CATAMARCA PROVINCE

SANTIAGO DEL ESTERO PROVINCE

0   100
kilometres

Monte Pissis (6882m)
Cerro Bonete (6759m)

RESERVA PROVINCIAL LAS VICUÑAS

Laguna Brava

PARQUE NACIONAL SAN GUILLERMO

Aimogasta

Famatina

Chilecito

RN-40

Villa Unión

PARQUE NACIONAL TALAMPAYA

La Rioja

LA RIOJA PROVINCE

RESERVA PROVINCIAL SAN GUILLERMO

Angualasto   Rodeo   Huaco

Patquía

Chamical

RN-150

PARQUE PROVINCIAL ISCHIGUALASTO (VALLE DE LA LUNA)

Jáchal

Iglesia

RP-510

Valle Fértil

RN-150

SAN JUAN PROVINCE

RP-412

RN-141

CHILE

CÓRDOBA PROVINCE

RN-149

Calingasta

Talacasto

Chepes

RN-406

Barreal

San Juan

RN-141

Cerro Mercedario (6770m)

PARQUE NACIONAL EL LEONCITO

Difunta Correa

RN-20

RP-149

PARQUE PROVINCIAL ACONCAGUA

RN-40

Cerro Aconcagua (6959m)

RN-7

SAN LUIS PROVINCE

Río Mendoza

Cristo Redentor

RN-7

Mendoza

PARQUE PROVINCIAL VOLCÁN TUPUNGATO

RN-7

SANTIAGO DE CHILE

Cerro Tupungato (6570m)

Tupungato

Tunuyán

MENDOZA PROVINCE

Volcán Maipo (5323m)

RN-146

Laguna Diamante

RN-143

San Rafael

Río Diamante

RN-7

RN-40

General Alvear

RN-188

Río Atuel

Las Leñas

RESERVA PROVINCIAL LAGUNA DE LLANCANELO

Malargüe

RN-143

N

RESERVA PROVINCIAL LA PAYUNIA

LA PAMPA PROVINCE

RN-40

RN-151

Río Colorado

NEUQUÉN PROVINCE

HIGHLIGHTS

1 Mendoza city
2 White-water rafting
3 Bodega Salentein
4 Mountain climbing
5 La Payunia
6 Ischigualasto and Talampaya
7 Laguna Brava

EL CUYO – OUT WITH THE OLD AND IN WITH THE NEW

Mendoza, San Juan and La Rioja provinces – plus the less visited province of San Luís, to the east – make up the region known as **El Nuevo Cuyo**, or "New Cuyo", formed by a 1988 treaty. The much older term *Cuyo* and the adjective *Cuyano*, which originally did not include present-day La Rioja, are widely used in the names of travel companies, newspapers and other businesses. The etymological **origins** of the word *cuyo* are not entirely clear, but it probably comes from the native Huarpe word *xuyu*, meaning (sandy) riverbed. The original core area of the Intendencia del Cuyo, basically corresponding to modern Mendoza Province, has strong historical ties with **Chile** from where it was first colonized, and among other things the local accent still reflects this – with, for example, the "-ll" and "-y" being pronounced as the "y" in yellow, as in Chile, rather than the "j" sound you hear in Buenos Aires.

Mendoza Province

The southern half of El Nuevo Cuyo is taken up by **Mendoza Province**, the self-styled Tierra del Sol y del Buen Vino, the "land of sunshine and good wine". Within its borders are some of the country's most dramatic **mountain landscapes**, where you can try all sorts of adventure pursuits, from kayaking to hang-gliding. Its lively capital, **Mendoza**, supplies much-wanted creature comforts after treks, climbs into the Andes or a day of white-water rafting. While Mendoza Province shares many things with San Juan and La Rioja – bleak wildernesses backed by snow-peaked mountains, remarkably varied flora and fauna, an incredibly sunny climate prone to sudden temperature changes, and pockets of rich farmland mainly used to produce beefy red wines – it differs in the way it exploits them. Mendoza leads the way in **tourism** just as it does in the **wine industry**, combining professionalism with a taste for the avant-garde. The two industries come together for Mendoza's nationally famous **Fiesta de la Vendimia**, or Wine Harvest Festival, in early March, a slightly kitsch but exuberant bacchanal at which a carnival queen is elected from candidates representing every town in the province.

Mendoza Province can be divided into three sections, each with its own base. The north, around the capital, has the country's biggest concentration of vineyards and top-class wineries, clustered around **Maipú**, **Luján de Cuyo** and the up-and-coming **Valle de Uco**, while the scenic Alta Montaña route races up in a westerly direction towards the high Chilean border, passing the mighty **Cerro Aconcagua**, an increasingly popular climbing destination. Not far to the southwest are the much more challenging **Cerro Tupungato** (6570m) and the remote Laguna Diamante, a choppy altiplanic lagoon in the shadow of the perfectly shaped Volcán Maipo, which can only be visited from December to March. Central Mendoza is focused on the laidback town of **San Rafael**, where you can taste more wine, and from where several tour operators offer white-water rafting trips along the nearby **Cañón del Atuel**, or rivers like the Sosneado and Diamante. If you've always wanted to ski or snowboard in July, try the winter sports resort at **Las Leñas**, where you'll be sharing pistes with South America's jet-set. The third, least-visited section of the province wraps around the southern outpost of **Malargüe**, a final-frontier kind of place promoting itself as a centre for nature, scientific discovery and adventure. Within easy reach are the **Laguna de Llancanelo**, home to an enormous community of flamingoes (it can become dried out some years, though, so check with operators on its condition before visiting), the charcoal-grey and rust-red lava deserts of **La Payunia** and the karstic caves of **Caverna de las Brujas**.

Mendoza and around

MENDOZA is a mostly low-rise city, spread across the wide valley of the Río Mendoza, over 1000km west of Buenos Aires and less than 100km east of the Andean cordillera – whose perennially snowcapped peaks are clearly visible from downtown. Its airy microcentro is

6

less compact than that of most comparable cities, partly because the streets, squares and avenues were deliberately made wide when the city was rebuilt in the late nineteenth century (see p.338), following a major earthquake. Every street is lined with sycamore and plane trees – providing vital shade in the scorching summer, they are watered by over 500km of *acequias*, or irrigation ditches, which form a natural, outdoor air-cooling system. Watch out when you cross the city's streets, as the narrow gutters are up to 1m deep and often full of gushing water, especially in the spring when the upland snows melt.

The centre of the city is the vast **Plaza Independencia**, with its four orbital squares (plazas **Chile**, **San Martín**, **España** and **Italia**), each with its own distinctive character. The **Museo del Pasado Cuyano** offers an insight into late nineteenth-century life for the city's richer families, while the **Museo de Ciencias Naturales y Antropológicas "Juan Cornelio Moyano"** is filled with scientific and paleontological memorabilia. The latter sits in the handsome **Parque General San Martín**, which commands views of the city and its surroundings. The park is also the venue for the city's major annual event, the **Fiesta de la Vendimia**, held

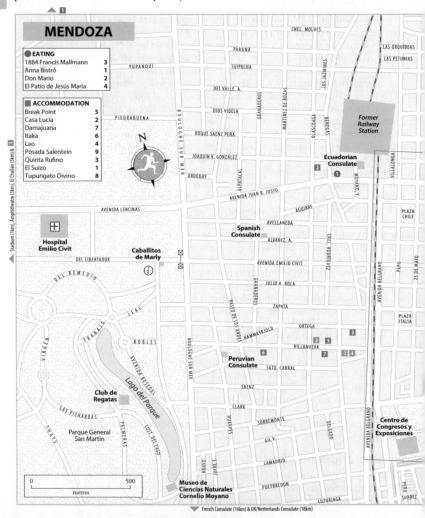

MENDOZA

EATING

1884 Francis Mallmann	3
Anna Bistró	1
Don Mario	2
El Patio de Jesús María	4

ACCOMMODATION

Break Point	5
Casa Lucia	2
Damajuana	7
Itaka	6
Lao	4
Posada Salentein	9
Quinta Rufino	3
El Suizo	1
Tupungato Divino	8

French Consulate (16km) & UK/Netherlands Consulate (18km)

every March. The ruins of colonial Mendoza's nucleus have been preserved as the **Área Fundacional**, where there's another small museum. The most impressive sight is the historic **Bodega Escorihuela**, a beautiful winery in a southern suburb.

Most people visit Mendoza principally to do a **wine-tasting tour** at the many **bodegas** in or near the city (see box, pp.346–347). Within easy reach to the south of the city are two small satellite towns, **Luján de Cuyo** and **Maipú**, where, in addition to the majority of the region's wineries, you'll find a couple more interesting museums, one displaying the paintings of Fernando Fader – a kind of Argentine Van Gogh – and the other focusing on the wine industry. The city also acts as a base for some of the world's most thrilling **mountain-climbing** opportunities.

6

Brief history

Before Mendoza was founded as a part of the **Spanish colony of Chile**, the indigenous Huarpe people, who lived off the land hunting and growing crops,

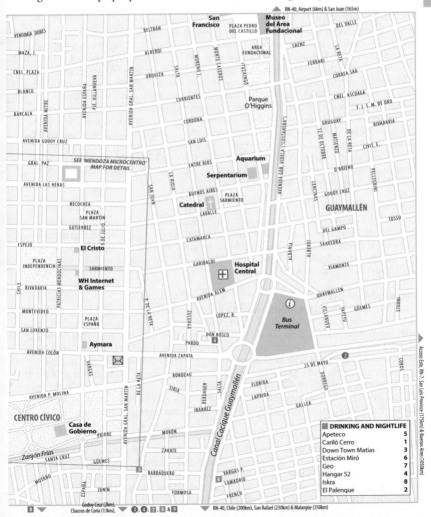

DRINKING AND NIGHTLIFE	
Apeteco	5
Cariló Cerro	1
Down Town Matias	3
Estación Miró	6
Geo	7
Hangar 52	4
Iskra	8
El Palenque	2

6

inhabited the area. However, in 1561 García Hurtado de Mendoza, captain-general of Chile, sent over an expedition led by Pedro del Castillo to establish a colony from which to "civilize" the Huarpe. Castillo named the town he founded after his boss, and soon-flourishing Mendoza continued to be ruled from across the Andes, though its isolation enabled it to live a life of its own. The extensive network of pre-Hispanic **irrigation canals** was exploited by the colonizers, who planted **vineyards** that soon became South America's most productive. By 1700, the city's merchants were selling wine to Santiago, Córdoba and Buenos Aires. After the Viceroyalty of the River Plate was created in 1777, Mendoza was incorporated into the huge **Córdoba Intendencia**. *Mendocinos* are still proud of the fact that San Martín's Army of the Andes was trained in their city before thrashing the Spanish royalist troops at the Battle of Maipú, Chile, in 1818. Once Argentina gained its independence, however, Mendoza began to suffer from its relative isolation, stagnating by the mid-nineteenth century.

The 1861 earthquake

Worse was to come, though: as night fell on March 20, 1861, three hundred years after the city's founding, an **earthquake** smashed every building in Mendoza to rubble, and some four thousand people, a third of the population, lost their lives. It's believed to have been one of the worst to have hit South America in recorded history, an estimated 7.8 on the Richter scale. Seismologists now believe that the epicentre lay right in the middle of the city, explaining why the damage was so terrible and yet restricted in radius. Pandemonium ensued, God-fearing *mendocinos* seeing the timing – the city's anniversary and Eastertide – as double proof of divine retribution. Remarkably, a new city was quickly built, overseen by the French urban planner **Ballofet**, who created wide streets, open squares and low buildings for the new-look Mendoza. The city's isolation ended soon afterwards, with the arrival of the railway in 1884. The earth continues to shake noticeably at frequent intervals, but all construction in modern Mendoza is designed to be earthquake resistant.

Mendoza today

Gran Mendoza (or "Greater Mendoza"), with a population of close to one million, includes the city centre – home to around 150,000 people – plus leafy suburbs such as Chacras de Coria and Las Heras, and industrial districts, such as Godoy Cruz. Wine, petrochemicals, a thriving university and, more recently, **tourism** have been the mainstays of the city's thriving economy.

Plaza Independencia

Four blocks in size, **Plaza Independencia** lies at the nerve centre of the city and at the crossroads of two of Mendoza's main streets, east–west Avenida Sarmiento and north–south Avenida Mitre. It's modern Mendoza's recreational and cultural focus, planted with shady acacias and magnolias, and bustles with life both during the day and on summer evenings. It is also the setting for festivals, concerts and outdoor cinema-screenings, and a crafts fair is held here at weekends. Right in the middle of the square are monumental fountains, backed by a mosaic mural depicting the story of Argentina's independence; just to their west stands a 17m-high steel structure, dating from 1942, on which a mass of coloured lights forms the national coat of arms at night.

Just north of the square, on the corner of Sarmiento, is the site of the illustrious 1920s **Plaza Hotel**, famous because the Peróns stayed here soon after first meeting in San Juan; it is now the Hyatt's five-star luxury establishment (see p.345). Next door is the Neoclassical facade of the **Teatro Independencia**, one of the city's more traditional playhouses, while over on the eastern side of the plaza is the grim **Legislatura Provincial**.

Plaza España

The small **Plaza España** lies a block east and a block south of Independencia's southeast corner. It's the most beautiful of all Mendoza's squares – its benches are decorated with brightly coloured Andalucian ceramic tiles, and the paths are lined with luxuriant trees and shrubs. Although Mendoza's population is of overwhelmingly Italian origin, the city's old, traditional families came from Spain, and they had the square built in the late 1940s. The mellow terracotta flagstones, picked out with smaller blue and white tiles, and the lily ponds and fountains set off

6

MENDOZA MICROCENTRO

0   200
metres

● **EATING**

Azafrán	4
Bröd	10
Chini	2
Ferruccio Soppelsa	3
La Florencia	5
Fuente y Fonda	9
La Marchigiana	1
Maria Antoineta	6
Sancho	7
Tasca la Plaza	8

■ **ACCOMMODATION**

Aconcagua	15
Alamo	2
Argentino	5
Balbi	1
B&B Plaza Italia	14
Campo Base	13
Cervantes	12
Crillón	9
Huentala	11
Internacional	8
International	16
NH Cordillera	3
Park Hyatt	7
Ritz	10
Square Independencia	4
Zamora	6

■ **DRINKING AND NIGHTLIFE**

Believe Irish Pub	3
Decimo	2
Uvas Lounge & Bar	1

6

> ## MENDOZA ADDRESSES
>
> Mendoza has the most complicated **street-name system** of any city in Argentina. Streets that run north–south keep the same name from end to end, but those that run west–east have up to four names within the city limits alone. From west to east, names change at Avenida Belgrano, Avenida San Martín and Avenida Gobernador R. Videla, the latter running along the Guaymallén canal, the city's eastern boundary. Beyond it lies the residential suburb of Guaymallén, itself divided into several districts, where you'll find the bus terminal, a cluster of budget accommodation, a number of restaurants and a couple of wineries. On all street signs is a useful number telling you how many blocks you are from the city's point zero, at San Martín and Sarmiento; 100 (O) means one block west, 500 (N) five blocks north. Paseo Sarmiento, a busy pedestrian precinct lined with loads of shops and cafés with terraces, joins Plaza Independencia, the city's centre-point, to Avenida San Martín.

the monument to the Spanish discovery of South America, standing at the southern end of the plaza. It comprises a *zócalo* or brightly tiled pedestal, decorated with scenes from *Don Quixote* and the Argentine gaucho epic *Martín Fierro*, along with Columbus's "discovery" and depictions of missionary work. At the centre of the plinth stand two female statues: one is a Spanish noblewoman clasping a book, the other a *mestiza* (part Spanish, part indigenous) woman, a *mendocina*, holding a bunch of grapes. Dancing and folk music take place here on October 12, the **Día de la Raza**, a celebration of *mestizo* culture.

Plaza Italia

One block south and then a block west of Independencia is **Plaza Italia**. On the south side of the square is a bronze statue of the mythical Roman wolf feeding Romulus and Remus, next to a marble pillar. The main monument in stone and bronze, to its west, represents La Patria – The Motherland – flanked by statues of an indigenous man and a Roman philosopher. A frieze running around the monument, showing scenes of building, ploughing and harvesting, is a tribute to the Italian immigrants whose labour helped build the country. In November, the park blazes with the bright red flowers of its *tipas*, and during the week leading up to the Fiesta de la Vendimia in March, the plaza hosts the **Festa in Piazza**, a big party at which stalls representing every Italian region serve their local culinary specialities. The climax is an extravagant fashion parade.

Museo del Pasado Cuyano
Montevideo 544 • Tues–Sat 9am–1pm • $30 • ☎ 0261 423 6031

Half a block east of Plaza Italia is the **Museo del Pasado Cuyano**, the city's history museum, housed in part of a late nineteenth-century mansion. The adobe house belonged to the family of a Francisco Civit, governor of Mendoza, and his son Emilio, who was a senator and was responsible for many of Mendoza's civic works, including the great park. It contains a large amount of San Martín memorabilia and eighteenth-century furniture, artworks and weapons, all rescued from the earthquake rubble. The most valuable exhibit, in the chapel, is a fifteenth-century polychrome **wooden altarpiece** with a liberal dose of rosy cherubim, that somehow turned up here from Sant Andreu de Socarrats in Catalonia.

Plaza San Martín

The square to the northeast of Plaza Independencia is the relatively nondescript **Plaza San Martín**; it's dominated by an early twentieth-century statue of General San Martín on a horse, looking towards the Andes, which he crossed with his army to defeat the Spanish.

Basílica de San Francisco

Daily 9am–noon & 6–8pm • Free

Near the plaza's northwest corner is the city's only church of note, the **Basílica de San Francisco**, one of the first buildings to go up after the 1861 quake. Its Belgian architect modelled it on Paris's Église de la Trinité, but part of the structure had to be demolished after another earthquake in 1927, leaving the church looking a bit truncated. It's venerated locally, as some members of San Martín's family are buried in simple tombs inside. A special chamber up the stairs next to the altar contains a revered image of Our Lady of Carmen, the patron saint of the Army of the Andes, along with San Martín's stylish rosewood staff, with a topaz hilt and a silver tip – it, too, has the status of a religious relic among the people of Mendoza.

6

The City district

The district surrounding the basilica is Mendoza's small "**City**", or financial district, whose opulent banks and insurance-company offices, most built in a "British" style, are among the city's most impressive buildings. The Banco de Galicia, the ex-Banco de Mendoza, and the Banco de la Nación – lying on the eastern side of Plaza San Martín, diagonally opposite the basilica – were all built in the 1920s and 1930s, the city's heyday.

Espacio Contemporáneo de Arte

9 de Julio and Gutiérrez • Mon–Sat 9am–9pm, Sun 4–9pm • Free • ☎ 0261 425 2543

The ex-Banco de Mendoza now houses the **Espacio Contemporáneo de Arte**, worth a look for its contemporary art exhibitions and the eight-sided lobby crowned with a huge stained-glass cupola.

Museo del Área Fundacional

Alberdi and Videla Castillo • Tues–Sat 8am–8pm, Sun 2–8pm • $30 • ☎ 0261 425 6927

The **Museo del Área Fundacional** is built on the Plaza Mayor, where the city was originally founded, 1km northeast of Plaza Independencia. The modern building houses an exhibition of domestic and artistic items retrieved from the rubble after the mammoth earthquake of 1861. It's built over part of the excavated colonial city foundations, which you can peer at through a glass floor. The exhibition relates the story of Mendoza's foundation and development before and after the great disaster. Nearby, across landscaped Plaza Pedro del Castillo, named for the city's founder, are the eerie ruins of the colonial city's Jesuit temple, popularly but erroneously known as the Ruinas de San Francisco.

Parque General San Martín

Av Sarmiento • Daily 24hr

Just over 1km due west of Plaza Independencia, on a slope that turns into a steep hill overlooking the city, **Parque General San Martín** is one of the most beautiful parks in the country, although you're advised not to visit after dark. As well as large areas of open land, used for impromptu football matches and picnics, its four square kilometres are home to the main football stadium, the amphitheatre where the finale of the Fiesta de la Vendimia is staged, a meteorological observatory, a monument to the Army of the Andes, a rowing lake, a tennis club, a hospital, the university campus, the riding club, an agricultural research centre, several restaurants, Mendoza's best jogging routes, a rose garden and an anthropological museum – in short, a city within the city.

The park was first created in 1897 by French botanist and landscape artist **Charles Thays** (see box, p.87). It contains over fifty thousand trees of 750 varieties, planted, among other reasons, to stop landslides from the Andean foothills. The aristocratic Avenida de los Plátanos and Avenida de las Palmeras, lined with tall plane trees and Canary Island palms, and the romantic Rose Garden, with its five hundred rose varieties and arbours of wisteria, are popular walks.

6

FIESTA DE LA VENDIMIA

Mendoza's main festival is the giant **Fiesta de la Vendimia**, or Wine Harvest Festival, which reaches its climax during the first weekend of March every year. Wine takes over the city and the tourist trade shifts into high gear. On the Sunday before the carnival proper (the last Sun in Feb), the *Bendición de los Frutos*, or Blessing of the Grapes, takes place, in a ceremony involving the bishop of Mendoza. During the week leading up to the grand finale, events range from folklore concerts in the *centro cívico* to Italian food and entertainment in the Plaza Italia. On Friday evening is the **Vía Blanca**, a parade of illuminated floats through the central streets, while on Saturday it's the *Carrusel*, when a carnival parade winds along the same route, each department in the province sending a float from which a previously elected beauty queen and her entourage of runners-up fling local produce, ranging from grapes and flowers to watermelons and packets of pasta, into the cheering crowds lining the road. On Saturday evening, the *Acto Central* is held in an amphitheatre in the Parque San Martín; it's a gala performance of song, dance and general kitsch-o-rama, hosted by local TV celebs, eventually leading up to a drawn-out vote to elect the queen of the festival. The same show is re-run on the same stage – minus the election, and therefore with less tedium – on Sunday evening. The spectacle costs millions of pesos and is a huge investment by the local wine-growers, but as it's attended by some 25,000 people it seems to be financially viable. The organizers boast that it's the biggest such festival in South America and one of the most lavish wine-related celebrations in the world. For more information contact the city's tourist office (see p.344).

The gates

The main entrance is through magnificent bronze and wrought-iron **gates**, topped with a condor, at the western end of Avenida Emilio Civit. They were not, as a popular legend would have it, ordered by Ottoman Sultan Hamid II then shipped here when he couldn't pay the bill; the crescent motif in their fine lace-like design, which led to the apocryphal anecdote, was simply a fashionable pattern at the time. The gates were actually ordered by city authorities in 1910 to celebrate the country's centenary, and were made by the McFarlane ironworks in Glasgow.

Caballitos de Marly and Fuente de los Continentes

A road open to traffic skirts the northern edge of the park after going round the **Caballitos de Marly**, an exact reproduction in Carrara marble of the monumental horses in the middle of Paris's Place de la Concorde. From here you can rent a bike, take a horse and cart or catch a bus to the park's furthest points (remember, it is huge). A short walk southwest of the entrance, near the northern shores of the rowing lake, the recently restored **Fuente de los Continentes** is a dramatic set of sculptures meant to represent the diversity of humankind, and a favoured backdrop for wedding photographs.

The zoo

Av Libertador s/n • Tues–Sun: Jan, Feb & Sept–Dec 9am–6pm; March–Aug 9am–5pm • $40; under-12s $20 • ☏ 0261 444 4411, ⓦ zoo.mendoza.gov.ar

A good 2km west of the park entrance you'll find the city's controversial (and generally mediocre) **zoo**. In 2014 concern about the welfare of Arturo the polar bear led to more than a million people signing a petition demanding his relocation. The zoo is set in landscaped grounds of eucalyptus, *aguaribay* and fir forest, built into the lower slopes of the Cerro de la Gloria.

Monumento al Ejército Libertador

A popular destination is the top of the Cerro de la Gloria, where there's an imposing 1914 monument to the Army of the Andes, the **Monumento al Ejército Libertador**. All cast in bronze, a buxom, winged *Liberty*, waving broken chains, leads General San Martín and his victorious troops across the cordillera. Around the granite plinth are bronze friezes depicting more picturesque scenes: the anti-royalist monk Luis Beltrán busy making weapons for the army, and the genteel ladies of Mendoza donating their jewellery for the good cause – these "Patricias Mendocinas", after whom a city street is named, were rumoured to have been particularly excited by the presence of so many soldiers billeted in the city; babies and infants sadly watch their valiant fathers head off to battle.

Museo de Ciencias Naturales y Antropológicas "Juan Cornelio Moyano"

Tues–Fri 9am–6pm, Sat & Sun 3–6pm • Free • ☎ 0261 428 7666, ⓦ facebook.com/Museo.Moyano.Mendoza

At the southern tip of the park's 1km-long, serpentine rowing lake, in its southeastern corner, is the **Museo de Ciencias Naturales y Antropológicas "Juan Cornelio Moyano"**, which was reopened in March 2015 after years of refurbishment. Built in the 1930s to imitate the shape of a ship's bridge by local architects who introduced German Rationalism to Argentina, the museum is a series of mostly private collections of taxidermy, ancient fossils, indigenous artefacts and mummies. The most interesting exhibits are a female mummy discovered – along with a brightly coloured shawl – at over 5000m in the Andes, shrunken heads from Ecuador and fossils of dinosaurs unearthed near Malargüe in southern Mendoza.

ARRIVAL AND DEPARTURE — MENDOZA AND AROUND

BY PLANE

Officially called Aeropuerto Internacional Ingeniero Francisco J. Gabrielli, but known popularly as "Plumerillo" after the suburb where it's located, Mendoza's modern and efficient airport (☎ 0261 520 6000) is only 7km north of the city centre, just off RN-40. Taxis and *remises* ($120) are in plentiful supply, and buses #62, #63, #64 and #67 take you to the centre ($8) and downtown; for information, ask at the Atención al Cliente office. Heading back to the airport, be sure to catch a bus that has an "Aeropuerto" sign in the windscreen.

Airlines Aerolíneas Argentina and Austral, Paseo Sarmiento 82 ☎ 0261 420 4101 or ☎ 0810 222 86527; LAN, Rivadavia 256 ☎ 0810 9999 526; American Airlines, Av España 943, 1st floor ☎ 0261 425 9078.

Destinations Buenos Aires (7–8 daily; 1hr 40min); Córdoba (1–2 daily; 1hr); Rosario (1–2 daily; 1hr 30min); Santiago (2–3 daily; 1hr).

BY BUS

Mendoza's very busy bus station (☎ 0261 431 5000 or ☎ 0261 431 3001) is slightly drab, but has plenty of facilities. There are buses to and from just about everywhere in the country, plus Santiago de Chile, Lima and Montevideo. It's due east of the microcentro, on the edge of the suburb of Guaymallén, at the corner of avenidas Gobernador Videla (usually referred to as the Costanera) and Acceso Este (RN-7); this is less than 1km from the city centre, but if the walk is too much, you can take the bus (any from group 2, leaving from Av Gobernador Videla; A21-A25, A27-A29 and B21-B27; $6) or a taxi (around $70).

Destinations Buenos Aires (16 daily; 13–14hr); Córdoba (16 daily; 9–10hr); La Rioja (12 daily; 8hr 30min); Las Leñas (June–Sept 1 daily; 5hr); Los Penitentes (3 daily; 4hr); Malargüe (5–7 daily; 5–6hr); Neuquén (10 daily; 12hr); Río Gallegos (3 daily; 40–44hr); Salta (4 daily; 18–19hr); San Juan (hourly; 2hr 20min); San Luís (hourly; 3hr 40min); San Rafael (hourly; 3hr 30min); Santiago de Chile (5–6 daily; 6–7hr); Uspallata (6 daily; 2hr 20min); Valparaíso, Chile (3 daily; 8hr 15min).

GETTING AROUND

By bus For finding your own way around, there are buses and trolley-buses – the latter mostly serving the inner suburbs plus the bus station. They have a complex numbering system, with a logic that escapes most people; study the map displayed at each stop. You pay a flat $6 fare for both, except for much longer distances such as the airport. You can only pay with the RedBus card, which you can buy and top up at *kioskos* around town. There is also a tourist bus with audio commentary in English, Portuguese or Spanish, which takes you around the city's main attractions (ⓦmendozacitytour.com; $159 for adults, $95 for under-13s; pass valid for 24hr).

By car For car rental, head to Alamo, Primitivo de la Reta 928 ☎ 0261 429 3111; Avis and Budget, Primitivo de la Reta 914 ☎ 0261 429 6403; Hertz, Espejo 391 ☎ 0261 423 0225; Localiza, Primitivo de la Reta 936 ☎ 0261 429 6800. There are also branches at the airport.

By taxi Brisas ☎ 0261 430 2225; Radiomóvil ☎ 0261 445 5855; Radiotaxi ☎ 0261 430 3300; Veloz del Este ☎ 0261 429 9999.

By bike You can rent bikes (daily 10am–7pm; $130 for 4hr, $150 for 6hr, $175 for 9hr) from Bike Cool Tours (Rivadavía 779 ☎ 0261 425 3461). Alternatively, if you bring your passport and a copy of your hotel booking, you can get an hour's free bike rental from various city bike rental spots (including Plaza Independencia, the bus terminal and Av Las Heras y Belgrano in town;

Parque Benegas in Godoy Cruz; Mon–Fri 8am–8pm & Sat 9am–3pm; ✉ enlabici@ciudaddemendoza.gov.ar, ⓦ ciudaddemendoza.gov.ar/en-la-bici).

INFORMATION AND TOURS

Tourist offices The main tourist office (daily 9am–9pm; ☎ 0261 413 2101, ⓦ turismo.mendoza.gov.ar) is at San Martín 1143; this is also the place to obtain Aconcagua climbing permits (see p.357). There's another city tourist office at Garibaldi and San Martín (daily 9am–9pm; ☎ 0261 420 1333), as well as one in the bus station

(7am–10pm; ☎ 0261 431 3001).

Walking tours The tourist office runs guided walks with themes such as history or religion – ask for the latest timetable. A number of tour operators (see box below) run half-day city tours.

ACCOMMODATION

Mendoza has plenty of places to stay, with more than enough beds for its needs, except during the Fiesta de la Vendimia in early March. It has several luxurious **hotels**, including branches of top-class international chains, as well as plenty of **youth hostels**, plus a fair number of **B&Bs**. In the middle range are countless nondescript but decent smaller hotels. At the higher end, particularly interesting options are **bodega hotels** or **posadas**, many of which are in the swish suburbs of Chacras de Coria and Maipú. The quiet, suburban location of these bodega hotels does mean that unless you have your own car you may be more or less limited to the delights the bodega has to offer. Always book bodega accommodation ahead, and let your hosts know if you don't have your own transport, as they will usually pick you up from Mendoza city or airport. If you haven't got anything booked, the best street to head for is Arístides Villanueva (usually referred to as Arístides), three blocks south and four blocks west of the Plaza Independencia – it's packed with both hostels and more upmarket options. You can also ask at the tourist office for its list of rooms to rent in private houses.

HOSTELS

Alamo Necochea 740 ☎ 0261 429 5565, ⓦ hostelalamo .com; map p.339. Sociable and clean hostel in a beautiful yellow villa on a quiet residential street. Dorms $150; doubles $400

Break Point Av Arístides Villanueva 241 ☎ 0261 423

9514, ⓦ breakpointhostel.com; map pp.336–337. At the heart of the city's *movida* zone, this lively hostel offers free internet, all kinds of tours, a large TV lounge and a small pool, plus added bonuses like an X-Box and table football. Dorms $160; doubles $360

Campo Base Mitre 946 ☎ 0261 429 0707,

MENDOZA TOUR OPERATORS

Popular tours include ones to wine bodegas, Alta Montaña and Villavicencio. Mountain-bike tours in the foothills and white-water rafting on the Río Mendoza are also possible. Many operators also offer longer trips to La Payunia, Cañón del Atuel, Talampaya and Ischigualasto, but Malargüe, San Rafael, San Agustín de Valle Fértil and Villa Unión are much closer bases for these.

Argentina Rafting Primitivo de la Reta 992 ☎ 0261 429 6325, ⓦ argentinarafting.com. This outfit is the regional expert at rafting, but also offers a wide range of adventure activities such as abseiling, parachute jumping and, for the less ambitious, horseriding.

Aymará Av España 735 ☎ 0261 424 4773, ⓦ aconcaguaaymara.com.ar. With years of experience leading expeditions up Aconcagua, Aymará also offers horse rides through upland terrain.

Backpackers Travel & Adventure Sarmiento 231 ☎ 0261 425 5511, ⓦ youthtravelargentina.com. Aimed at the younger, budget market, this tour agency offers trekking and excursions to Alta Montaña.

Cata Las Heras 601 ☎ 0261 425 1750, ⓦ cataturismo .com.ar. This agent offers a wide range of tourist

services, with the emphasis on group trips, offering everything from wine tours to rafting trips.

El Cristo Espejo 228 ☎ 0261 429 1911, ⓦ turismo -elcristo.com.ar. A highly professional team, El Cristo puts together excursions as far away as Malargüe, including interesting bodega tours.

Mendoza Viajes Sarmiento 129 ☎ 0261 438 0480, ⓦ mdzviajes.com.ar. This well-established agency offers reasonably priced wine tours throughout the province.

Sepean Primitivo de la Reta 1088 ☎ 0261 420 4162, ⓦ sepean.com. A general tour and travel agency, offering hotel packages in the region and across the border in Chile.

Trout and Wine Espejo 266 ☎ 0261 425 5613, ⓦ troutandwine.com. Run by a wine-loving Irishman, and specializing in upmarket wine tours.

6

W hostelcampobase.com.ar; p.339. The youth hostel is clean, friendly and laidback, with lots of barbecues, parties and general fun, though some of the dorms are cramped. Offers a wide range of activities including trekking, horseriding and paragliding. Dorms $160; doubles $500

Damajuana Arístides Villanueva 282 ☎0261 425 5858, W damajuanahostel.com.ar; map pp.336–337. Airy hostel in one of the city's main nightlife areas. One of its best features is the garden, which has a good-sized pool; the dorms are plain but clean. Organizes tours. Dorms $150; doubles $600

International España 343 ☎0261 424 0018, W hostelmendoza.net; map p.339. The best-established of all the hostels, with a bright patio, welcoming ambience, small dorms with private bathroom and an excellent kitchen; the staff can also fix you up with tours and sports activities in the whole region. Its *El Carajo* bar is a popular meeting place, and most evenings there's some sort of sociable activity on. Private rooms available. Dorms $180; doubles $550

Itaka Av Arístides Villanueva 480 ☎0261 423 9793, W itakahostel.com.ar; map pp.336–337. Fun and friendly place with pretty patio and leafy garden, above-average kitchen facilities and a small pool. In addition to excursions they lay on a daily wine tasting at 7pm. Dorms $150; doubles $450

★**Lao** Rioja 771 ☎0261 438 0454, W laohostel.com; map pp.336–337. Spotless and well-run English-owned hostel with incredibly helpful staff. Rooms and bathrooms are flawless and there's a small plunge pool and hammocks for lazy days. Dorms $200; doubles $400

Square Independencia Mitre 1237 ☎0261 423 1806, W squareindependencia.com.ar; map p.339. Nicely located in an attractive townhouse near the plaza of the same name, *Square Independencia* has a fully equipped kitchen, a patio, and pleasant dorms. Has free wine tasting every night (7–9pm), and the staff organize bodega tours and treks. Dorms $170; doubles $560

B&BS AND HOSPEDAJES

B&B Plaza Italia Montevideo 685 ☎0261 423 4219, W plazaitalia.net; map p.339. English-speaking B&B run by genuinely hospitable locals in an impeccably decorated family house with en-suite rooms and a/c, plus parking and a delicious breakfast. Also organizes wine tours. US$140

Casa Lucia Olascoaga 1561 344 ☎0261 515 9085, W casaluciamendoza.com; map pp.336–337. Small and very friendly B&B with three well-equipped rooms with tea-making facilities, fridge and wine glasses in a quiet, residential part of the city. Extra points for the cute garden. US$79

Quinta Rufino Rufino Ortega 142 ☎0261 420 4696, W quintarufino.com; map pp.336–337. A converted house in a quiet neighbourhood, with pleasant en-suite

rooms and friendly staff. The owners, who are outdoor specialists, can arrange adventure-sport outings. $620

Zamora Perú 1156 ☎0261 425 7537, @ hotelzamora @gmail.com; map p.339. A Neocolonial villa with clean rooms around a leafy patio; ask for the room with a roof terrace. Also rooms with four or five beds, and group discounts available. Popular with Aconcagua climbers. $500

HOTELS

Aconcagua San Lorenzo 545 ☎0261 520 0500, W hotelaconcagua.com; map p.339. Professionally run, modern hotel, with small but comfortable rooms with TV and mini-bar; it's worth paying extra for a room with a glorious mountain view. A swimming pool and sauna are welcome facilities in the summer and winter, respectively. $2070

Argentino Espejo 455 ☎0261 405 6300, W argentino -hotel.com; map p.339. Shiny place on the Plaza Independencia aimed squarely at the foreign tourist dollar, with ultra-stylish rooms, a small gym, a mini-swimming pool and highly attentive service; breakfast is served in an airy *confitería*. $1344

Balbi Av Las Heras 340 ☎0261 423 3500 or ☎0261 423 3610, W hotelbalbi.com.ar; map p.339. Hotel with old-fashioned decor, a lavish reception, huge breakfast area and large rooms. There is an attractive pool and terrace. $1200

Cervantes Amigorena 65 ☎0261 520 0400, W hotelcervantes.com.ar; map p.339. Traditional-style, comfortable three-star hotel, with plain decor and slightly old-fashioned bathrooms. In addition it has one of the best hotel restaurants in town, *Sancho* (see p.348). $1080

Crillón Perú 1065 ☎0261 429 8494, W hcrillon.com.ar; map p.339. An above-average three-star hotel, the *Crillón* has efficient service. Bathrooms are well kept, although showers are rather cramped. $1100

Huentala Primitivo de la Reta 1007 ☎0261 420 0766, W huentala.com; map p.339. Trendy, verging on glitzy, four-star boutique hotel with stylish lobby and plush rooms, plus a pool and a rather pretentious French restaurant, *Chimpay Bistró*. US$182

★**Internacional** Sarmiento 720 ☎0261 425 5606, W hinternacional.com.ar; map p.339. The best in its class in Mendoza, this hotel has understated, tasteful furnishings in spacious a/c rooms. A swimming pool and parking are two further assets. $1319

NH Cordillera España and Gutiérrez ☎0261 441 6464, W nh-hotels.com; map p.339. Jazzy hotel, one of the nicest of the Spanish chain in Argentina, with professional reception service, sleek rooms and standard bathrooms. Perks include a gym, sauna and swimming pool, plus a generous breakfast. US$142

6

BODEGAS IN AND AROUND MENDOZA

There are dozens of **wineries** in the **Mendoza area** that are open to visitors. The easiest way to visit bodegas is on a **tour** organized by an agency in Mendoza (see box, p.344). A typical half-day trip visits two or three bodegas, while a full day visits five or six and includes lunch; full-day trips are better value. Wine enthusiasts willing to splurge should contact Trout and Wine (see box, p.344), which does a range of small-group "premium" tours led by English-speaking guides; lunch is included.

Alternatively, you can rent a car and **drive** yourself; using **public transport** only works if you're planning on seeing a limited number of bodegas. Another option is to rent a **bike**, but always double-check the bike, take an emergency number in case of punctures, and ask which routes are the safest, as it's no rural idyll – some busy roads have bike lanes, but on others you are exposed to industrial traffic. In Maipú, try the friendly Mr Hugo Bikes, at Urquiza 2288 (☎0261 497 4067, ⓦmrhugobikes.com), or Maipú Bikes, at Urquiza and Gómez (☎0261 15 543 2941, ⓔmaipubikes@gmail.com).

If you're going under your own steam, make sure you call ahead to check times, to book a visit and to ask for an English-speaking guide, if necessary. The bodegas are concentrated in **Guaymallén**, in **Maipú** (see p.352) and in **Luján de Cuyo** (see p.350), plus the beautifully located wine region of **Valle de Uco** (made up of Tunuyán, Tupungato and San Carlos). Buses referred to below stop at the Mendoza bus terminal or along Avenida San Martín.

Most bodegas charge for tours (which include tastings), and you're pointedly steered to a sales area at the end (cash only; surcharge for the best tipples). Try and see different kinds of wineries, ranging from the old-fashioned, traditional bodegas to the highly mechanized, ultramodern producers; at the former you're more likely to receive personal attention and get a chance to taste finer wines. Best of all is staying the night at one of the several wineries offering accommodation – some of it highly luxurious (see p.344).

BODEGA TOURS

La Azul RP-89 s/n, Tupungato ☎02622 423 593, ⓦbodegalaazul.com. Very small bodega with a sweeping view of the Andes. Tours are quick and focus on tasting. The restaurant (five-course menu with wine $450) is well worth a visit if you have time, though it's only open for lunch (Tues–Sun 12.30–3.30pm). Booking essential. Tours Tues–Sun 10.30am, 11.30am, 4pm & 5pm; $150.

Domaine St Diego Franklin Villanueva 3821, Maipú ☎0261 15 539 5148, ⓔmlauritamza @hotmail.com; bus #20. Small, fairly intimate family-run winery. Visitors can try good-quality wines and olive oil after an hour in the vineyards and in the bodega (6 people max). Reserve (essential) at least 24hr ahead. Mon–Fri 9am–5pm, Sat 9.30am–1.30pm; $90.

Escorihuela Belgrano 1188 and Presidente Alvear, Godoy Cruz ☎0261 424 2282. Just 2km south of Mendoza's city centre, this historic bodega was founded in 1884. It is famous for its enormous barrel from France, housed in a cathedral-like cellar. The sumptuous buildings include huge vaulted storage rooms stacked with aromatic casks and a gourmet restaurant, *1884 Francis Mallmann* (see below). Tours Mon–Fri noon & 4pm; $100.

Giol ("La Colina de Oro") Ozamis 1040, Maipú ☎0261 497 4297; bus #160. A wonderfully old-fashioned place, with lots of antique barrels – including

Park Hyatt Chile 1124 ☎0261 441 1234, ⓦmendoza .park.hyatt.com; map p.339. The most central of Mendoza's luxury hotels, this modern block is located on the site of the *Plaza Hotel* where Perón and Eva once stayed; the Neoclassical facade is a replica of its predecessor. Apart from the much-vaunted casino, facilities include a luxurious spa specializing in wine treatments, a large outdoor pool, the stylish *Uvas* cocktail bar and *Bistro M*, one of the classiest restaurants in the city. Rooms are spacious, with luxurious en-suite bathrooms. **US$145**

Ritz Perú 1008 ☎0261 423 5115, ⓦritzhotelmendoza .com; map p.339. This place tries very hard to look British, and partly succeeds with its chintz furnishings and plush fitted carpets. Rooms have a/c. **$1100**

BODEGA ACCOMMODATION

Posada Salentein RP-89 s/n Km14, Tunuyán ☎02622 429 090, ⓦbodegasalentein.com; map pp.336–337. A posada belonging to the Salentein winery, which can also be visited on a tour (see box above). The price of a room includes a wine tasting in the fabulous bodega, plus free entrance to the art gallery. **US$520**

Tupungato Divino RP-89 and Calle Los Europeos, Tupungato ☎02622 15 448 948, ⓦtupungatodivino.com. ar; map pp.336–337. A beautifully located hotel, surrounded by young vines, and with fabulous Andean views. Its rooms blend rustic charm with eye-catching modernity, and the outstanding food served in the restaurant complements the fine wines made at the nearby bodegas. **US$150**

one of the biggest in South America – and the Museo Nacional del Vino y la Vendimia across the street. Mon–Sat 10am–6pm, Sun & public hols 10am–3pm; $60.

★**Carmelo Patti** San Martín 2614, Luján de Cuyo ☎0261 498 1379. Known as "El maestro del vino", local personality Carmelo has been working in the wine trade since 1971. His enthusiasm and knowledge make him one of the best wine guides in the area (Spanish only). Visits are informal. Mon–Sat 11am–1pm & 3–5pm; free.

Lagarde San Martín 1745, Luján de Cuyo ☎0261 498 0011, ⊛lagarde.com.ar. Lagarde is a major producer, one of the oldest bodegas in the province (founded 1897) and worth visiting for its beautifully quaint setting. There's also a gourmet restaurant on site with a courtyard. Tours Mon–Fri 11am, 12.30pm & 3pm, Sat 11am & 12.30pm; $170 to taste four wines.

Luigi Bosca San Martín 2044, Luján de Cuyo ☎0261 498 1974, ⊛luigibosca.com.ar. One of the best-known wine brands in Argentina, Luigi Bosca appears on many of the agency-run trips. The professional guides are keen to emphasize the winery's family credentials, but it all feels a bit too commercial. Tours Mon–Fri 9.30am, 11am, 12.30pm & 3pm, Sat 9.30am & 11am; $200.

Nieto Senetiner Guardia Vieja, Ruta Panamericana, Chacras de Coria ☎0261 496 9099, ⊛nietosenetiner.com.ar. Some of Argentina's finest wines are produced by this traditional winery. The 12.30pm tour can be followed by a delicious lunch (reserve in advance). It's also possible to explore the vineyard on horseback with advance booking. Tours (English and Spanish) Mon–Sat 10am, 11am, 12.30pm, 3pm & 4pm; $100.

Norton RP-15, Perdriel, Luján de Cuyo ☎0261 490 9760, ⊛norton.com.ar; bus #380. A prize-winning producer, making top-class if slightly old-fashioned wines, and well worth a visit. Also has a restaurant. Mon–Sat 9am–6pm; $150.

Pulenta Estate RP-89 s/n, Km6.5, Luján de Cuyo ☎0261 507 6426, ⊛pulentaestate.com. Modern winery with tours focusing mainly on tasting. Produces an excellent cabernet franc. Tours Mon–Fri 9.30am, 11am, 11.30am, 3pm & 3.30pm or 4pm, Sat 9.30am & 11am or 11.30am; $110.

★**Salentein** RP-89 s/n, Km14, Tunuyán ☎02622 429 500, ⊛bodegasalentein.com. One of the most beautiful wineries in the country. Visiting this magnificent state-of-the-art building – known as the "Cathedral to Wine" – and the private art collection makes for a memorable experience, and the wines are outstanding. Tours (English) daily 11am & 3pm; $150.

San Felipe ("La Rural") Montecaseros s/n, Coquimbito, Maipú ☎0261 497 2013, ⊛bodegalarural.com.ar; bus Línea 10 #171, #172 or #173. This magnificent traditional bodega stands among its own vineyards and has a small museum. An interesting contrast with some of the more urban wineries. Tours (English and Spanish; wine tasting not included) hourly Mon–Sat 9am–noon & 2–5pm; free.

Viña El Cerno Moreno 631, Coquimbito, Maipú ☎0261 481 1567, ⊛elcerno-wines.com.ar. Satisfying boutique, family-run winery, in a small country house with a tiny vineyard. The malbec and chardonnay are delicious and the tour highly personalized and enthusiastic. Tours (Spanish and English) Mon–Sat noon–6pm; $45 including glass of wine.

Weinert San Martín 5923, Chacras de Coria ☎0261 496 4382, ⊛bodegaweinert.com. One of Argentina's oldest and best wine producers, with an enormous antique barrel still in use, a fabulous cellar and mud-and-cane buildings – characteristic of the area's indigenous population – used to provide the perfect temperature for fermentation. Tasting tours are family-friendly, with grape juice on hand for the kids. Tours Mon–Sat 10am–12.30pm & 2.30–4.30pm; $90.

CAMPING

El Suizo Av Champagnat, El Challao, 6km northwest of the city centre ☎0261 444 1991, ⊛campingsuizo.com.ar; bus #114 and #115 run out to El Challao from Av Alem and San Martín; map pp.336–337. A campsite set among shady woods up in the cool heights above the city. It has a swimming pool, a small restaurant and even an open-air cinema. $100 charge per person. Per pitch $50

EATING

Mendoza is the prosperous capital of Argentina's western region, and the produce grown in the nearby oases is tiptop; as a result, the city's many, varied and often highly sophisticated **restaurants** are usually full, and serve some of the best food and drink in the country thanks to the nearby vineyards, fertile valley produce and relative proximity to the fishing ports of Chile.

★**1884 Francis Mallmann** Belgrano 1188, Godoy Cruz ☎0261 424 3336, ⊛1884restaurante.com.ar; map pp.336–337. This ultra-chic wine bar and award-winning restaurant with fashion-model staff, steep prices, swish decor and crystal wine glasses – rare in Argentina – is considered one of the country's finest. It is next to the Bodega Escorihuela, and serves its fine wines with a balanced menu that includes goat from Malargüe ($468),

6

rabbit ($429), spinach and mushroom ravioli ($364) and a gigantic ribeye ($507) cooked on the mesmerizing *parrilla* outside. Daily 8.30pm–midnight/1am.

Anna Bistró Av Juan B Justo 161 ☎0261 425 1818, ⓦannabistro.com; map pp.336–337. Popular and airy restaurant with a beautiful garden serving a fresh range of Argentine and international dishes. Good vegetarian options and set menus ($138). Daily 8am–1am.

Azafrán Sarmiento 765 ☎0261 429 4200, ⓦazafranresto.com; map p.339. A deli-cum-restaurant with an excellent cellar (you can walk in and choose a bottle), colourful decor and delicious food – like grilled octopus ($295) – plus home-brewed beer; portions are a bit on the miserly side, but the service is efficient and the quality is high. Daily noon–midnight.

Bröd Chile 894 ☎0261 425 2993, ⓦfacebook.com /Brodbakery; map p.339. Stylish bakery, although not very Swedish as the name might suggest. Try the delicious apple crumble ($35) and the refreshing lemonade with mint ($40). Serves brunch on Sundays. Mon–Sat 8am–9pm, Sun 9am–4pm.

Chini Av España and Las Heras ☎0261 425 5792; map p.339. One of the best ice-cream parlours in the city, with dozens of flavours. Daily 7am–1am.

Don Mario 25 de Mayo 1324, Guaymallén ☎0261 431 0810, ⓦdonmario.com.ar; map pp.336–337. An institutional *parrilla* in the neighbourhood of Guaymallén (east of the city centre), frequented by *mendocino* families in search of comforting decor and an old-fashioned *parrillada*. The meat comes in gargantuan portions at $200 a head. Daily 12.30–3.30pm & 8pm–12.15am.

Ferruccio Soppelsa Emilio Civit esq Belgrano, Espejo 299; map p.339. This *heladería*, run for years by the same Italian family, is guaranteed to give you enough calories to last you to the top of Aconcagua. Part of a local chain, with branches elsewhere in and around the city. Daily 10am–2am.

La Florencia Sarmiento 698 esq Perú; map p.339. A no-nonsense *parrilla* that's popular with tourists and locals

alike. Sit inside or street-side, and check out the extensive local wine list. Daily noon–4.30pm & 8pm–1am.

Fuente y Fonda Montevideo 675 ☎0261 429 8833, ⓦfuenteyfonda.com.ar; map p.339. A cosy restaurant serving Argentine food for sharing. All main courses are for two people and reasonably priced ($290–365). The menu changes daily, but can include dishes like *canelones* and *milanesas*. Daily noon–3pm & 8pm–midnight.

★ **La Marchigiana** Patricias Mendocinas 1550 ☎0261 423 0751, ⓦmarchigiana.com.ar; map p.339. This is *the* Italian-Argentine restaurant in the city, run by the same family for decades. You can eat fresh *caprese* salad ($71), followed by delicious cannellini ($136), and finish with one of the best tiramisus ($48) in the country. Mon–Thurs & Sun noon–3pm & 8pm–midnight, Fri noon–3pm & 8pm–12.30am, Sat noon–3pm & 8pm–1am.

Maria Antoineta Av Belgrano 1069 ☎0261 423 0751, ⓦmariaantonietaresto.com.ar; map p.339. French-inspired bistro (as the name suggests) with an affinity for kale, serving carefully prepared meat, fish and pasta dishes. Try their delicious home-made burger ($123). Mon–Fri 8am–midnight, Sat 9am–midnight, Sun 10am–5pm.

El Patio de Jesús María Arístides Villanueva and Boulogne Sur Mer; map pp.336–337. Well-known and respected classic *parrilla* with another branch out in El Challao on Cerro Bodeguita. Daily noon–3.30pm & 8pm–12.30am.

Sancho Amigorena 65; map p.339. Conventional meals such as *milanesas* and steaks, together with pasta and fish dishes, are on offer at this smart and old-school establishment in a hotel (see p.345), with an appealing patio seating area. Mon–Fri noon–11.45pm, Sat 8pm–12.30am.

Tasca la Plaza Montevideo 117; map p.339. Intimate little bistro, or *tasca*, conveniently located on the Plaza España and serving appropriately Hispanic food, including tapas, along with sangría and good wines. Charming service. Mon–Thurs 1–3pm & 7.30pm–midnight, Fri–Sun 7.30pm–midnight.

DRINKING AND NIGHTLIFE

Mendoza's **bars** are lively and it has a well-developed café-terrace culture, with Avenida Arístides Villanueva, to the west of the centre, a hotspot. **Clubs** are vibrant and mostly concentrated in outlying places such as El Challao, to the northwest, and Godoy Cruz and fashionable Chacras de Coria to the south (see p.350).

BARS

Believe Irish Pub Av Colón 241 ☎0261 666 1598, ⓦirishpub.com.ar; map p.339. This is where tourists and locals alike come to watch international sporting events. You can also just sit at the bar, have a gin and tonic and eat pizza. Mon, Sat & Sun 8.30pm–4.30am, Tues–Fri 12.30pm–4.30am.

Decimo Garibaldi 7 ☎0261 434 0135; map p.339.

Situated at the top of Edificio Gomez, this wine bar offers a spectacular view of the city from its roof terrace. Along with decent cocktails and wine it also has stand-up comedy shows some nights. Mon–Sat 8am–4pm & 6pm–3am.

Down Town Matias Av Arístides Villanueva 198 ☎0261 434 0071, ⓦdowntownmatias.com/mendoza; map pp.336–337. Spacious sports bar with two floors and

ARGENTINE WINE

Argentina is the world's fifth-largest wine producer (after Italy, France, Spain and the US), with three-quarters of the country's total production coming from **Mendoza** Province, focused on Maipú and Luján de Cuyo in the south of the city. **San Rafael**, **La Rioja** and **San Juan** are also major wine-growing centres.

Many wine experts would agree that Argentina's vintages are improving rapidly as a result of both a domestic market that's fast becoming more discerning and the lure of exports. **Table wines** still dominate, often sold at the budget end of the market in huge, refillable flagons called *damajuanas*, and sometimes marketed under usurped names such as *borgoña* (burgundy) and chablis. Younger Argentines often only drink wine on special occasions, plumping for lighter **New Wave** wines such as Chandón's **Nuevo Mundo**. Many upmarket restaurants offer extensive wine lists including older vintages, but bear in mind that the selection of servings by the glass is very limited. Be prepared to pay for the whole bottle if you want some wine with your meal (but you can always ask to bring the rest home if you don't finish it). Commonly found bodega names to look for include **Chandón**, **Graffigna**, **Navarro Correas**, **Salentein**, **Finca Flichmann** and **Weinert**.

Although the most attractive wineries to visit are the old-fashioned ones, with musty cellars crammed with oak barrels, some of the finest vintages are now produced by growers using the latest equipment, including storage tanks lined with epoxy resin and computerized temperature controls. They tend to concentrate on making varietal wines, the main grape varieties being riesling, chenin blanc and chardonnay for whites, and pinot noir, cabernet sauvignon and malbec for reds – the reds tend to be better than whites. **Malbec** is often regarded as the Argentine grape *par excellence*, giving rich fruity wines, with overtones of blackcurrant and prune that are the perfect partner for a juicy steak. The latest trend is for a balanced combination of two grapes: for example, mixing malbec for its fruitiness with cabernet for its body, which tones down the sometimes excessive oakiness that used to characterize Argentine wines. Growers have also been experimenting with varieties such as tempranillo, san gervase, gewürztraminer, syrah and merlot, and very convincing sparkling wines are being made locally by the *méthode champenoise*, including those produced by Chandón and Mumm, the French champagne-makers.

---

booths with flat-screen TVs. Mon 9am–2am, Tues–Sat 9am–3am, Sun 6pm–2am.

Hangar 52 Av Arístides Villanueva 168 ☎0261 666 1598, ⓦfacebook.com/Hangar52galponcervezero; map pp.336–337. A hip and extremely popular bar serving regional and national *cerveza artesanal* and a few mediocre cocktails. The crowd is young cool *mendocino* kids and the place often gets packed. Daily 6pm–3am.

El Palenque Av Arístides Villanueva 287, ☎0261 429 1814, ⓦfacebook.com/ElPalenquePulperiaCentro; map pp.336–337. A *pulpería*-style bar with bags of old-fashioned pampas atmosphere and a range of empanadas and wines; popular with the city's youth, although the service is a bit snooty. Daily noon–2.30am.

Uvas Lounge & Bar Chile 1124 ☎0261 441 1232, ⓦmendoza.park.hyatt.com; map p.339. Situated inside Mendoza's *Park Hyatt* (see p.345), this sophisticated hotel bar offers fine wine by the glass and tapas. Daily 11am–midnight.

NIGHTCLUBS

★**Apeteco** San Juan and Barraquero ☎0261 15 507 2457, ⓦapeteco.com; map pp.336–337. A city institution, this club has a great party ambience and is an essential stop on a midweek night out. Wed–Sat 10pm–5.30am.

Cariló Cerro Av Champagnat s/n, El Challao; map pp.336–337. The über-fashionable club during the summer season (Sept–March), spinning house and techno. Fri & Sat midnight–late.

Estación Miró Ejército de los Andes 656, Dorrego, Guaymallén ☎0261 511 9877, ⓦfacebook.com /ExtasisAlternative; map pp.336–337. The city's main LGBT nightclub throws a fun-loving, exhibitionist party every weekend. Cocktails, shows and even an alternative Fiesta de la Vendimia in March. Fri & Sat 11pm–late.

Geo San Martín Sur 576, Godoy Cruz ☎0261 15 550 6042, ⓦgeodiscoclub.com; map pp.336–337. Trendy club playing a mix of electronica, rock and reggaeton. Thurs–Sat midnight–late.

Iskra San Martín Sur 905, Godoy Cruz ☎0261 15 218 8781, ⓦiskradiscopub.com.ar; map pp.336–337. Varied mix of rock, reggaeton and dance music for a young crowd, most of whom are in their late teens and 20s. Thurs–Sat midnight–late.

6

DIRECTORY

Banks and exchange Supervielle, Av San Martín 1190; ICBC, Necochea 165; Cambio Santiago, Av San Martín 1199; Citibank, Sarmiento 20; Banco de la Nación, Necochea 101. ATMs everywhere.

Consulates ⓦ ccmdz.com.ar; Bolivia, M. Callejón Lemos 635 ☎ 0261 423 0413; Brazil, Rivadavía 628 ☎ 0261 423 0939; Chile, Belgrano 1080 ☎ 0261 425 5024; Ecuador, Francisco Moyano 1587 ☎ 0261 429 6416; France, Alzaga 3972 ☎ 0261 496 2417; Germany, Peatonal Sarmiento 165

☎ 0261 420 1077; Italy, Necochea 712 ☎ 0261 520 1400; Peru, Huarpes 629 ☎ 0261 429 9831; Spain, Agustín Alvarez 455 ☎ 0261 425 3947; UK/Netherlands, Roque Saenz Peña 3531 (Luján de Cuyo) ☎ 0261 498 9400.

Internet WH Internet & Games at España 1076 and Las Heras 61.

Laundry Lavasec Colón 470 ☎ 0261 423 8866.

Police Tourist police, San Martín 1143 ☎ 0261 413 2135.

Post office San Martín and Colón.

Luján de Cuyo

Nineteen kilometres south of Mendoza are two satellite towns, the first of which, sitting where the Guaymallén Canal meets the Río Mendoza, is Luján de Cuyo. Lying just west of the Ruta Panamericana, or RN-40, it's part residential, part industrial, with a huge brewery and some of the city's major **wineries**.

Iglesia de la Carrodilla

Carrodilla 11 • Mon 5–7.30pm, Tues–Fri 9am–noon & 5–7.30pm, Sat 9am–noon • Free

The northern district of Luján de Cuyo, known as Carrodilla, 7km south of downtown Mendoza, is an oasis of the colonial city that survived the 1861 earthquake. Here you'll find the **Iglesia de la Carrodilla**, usually included in the city's wine tours. Built in 1840, it's now a museum of seventeenth- and eighteenth-century religious art as well as the parish church. The naive frescoes depict scenes of grape harvesting, and the church's main relic is an oakwood statue of the Virgin and Child, star of the religious processions that precede Mendoza's Fiesta de la Vendimia. Artistically, the finest exhibit is the moving *Cristo de los Huarpes*, an exceptional piece of *mestizo* art carved out of *quebracho* wood in 1670 by local indigenous craftsmen.

Chacras de Coria

The western district of Luján de Cuyo is **Chacras de Coria**, a leafy suburb of European-style villas, golf courses, bodegas and several new, upmarket hotels. It's also full of outdoor *parrillas*, bars and nightclubs, frequented at weekends and in the summer by affluent *mendocinos*.

Museo Provincial de Bellas Artes Emiliano Guiñazú

San Martín 3651

On the town's eastern edge is the **Museo Provincial de Bellas Artes Emiliano Guiñazú**. The grandiose villa and luxurious garden are very appealing, but the main attraction is Fernando Fader's (see p.201) **Impressionistic murals**, which decorate the house's interior. His paintings also dominate the museum's collection. The museum was closed for renovation at the time of research; it's expected to reopen in 2017.

ARRIVAL AND INFORMATION   LUJÁN DE CUYO

By bus Bus #19 from downtown Mendoza or the bus terminal runs to Luján de Cuyo and stops along Av San Martín and Sáenz Peña.

Tourist office There's a small office at Sáenz Peña 1000 (daily 8am–5pm; ☎ 0261 498 1912).

ACCOMMODATION

★Cavas Wine Lodge Costa Flores s/n, Alto Agrelo ☎ 0261 410 6927, ⓦ cavaswinelodge.com.

Impeccably designed luxury lodge near Luján de Cuyo. Each of the fourteen individually designed rooms comes

FROM TOP EL HONGO (THE MUSHROOM) ROCK FORMATION, PARQUE PROVINCIAL ISCHIGUALASTO (P.384); RAFTING ON THE CAÑÓN DEL ATUEL (P.360); TWO GUANACOS IN LA PAYUNIA (P.368) >

with its own wooden deck, plunge pool and circular terrace with unobstructed views of the cordillera. The final Bacchanalian touch is a red-wine spa bath; this and other wine-based spa treatments, such as a torrontés wine wrap, can be booked by non-guests, too. Prices drop significantly in low season (early June to mid-Sept). **US$700**

Finca Adalgisa Pueyrredón 2222, Chacras de Coria ☎0261 496 0713, ⊚fincaadalgisa.com.ar. Small *finca* (ranch) now geared more towards tourism than wine production, though still with its own vineyard. The majority of the very attractive rooms are in an annexe with a jasmine-covered veranda running alongside; there's a swimming pool among the vines. **US$390**

Parador del Angel Jorge Newbery 5418, Chacras de Coria ☎0261 496 2201, ⊚paradordelangel.com.ar. A handsome and quiet adobe guesthouse with spacious and very tastefully decorated rooms. The owners are keen art collectors and share their exquisitely decorated home and peaceful garden with a great sense of hospitality. The breakfasts are memorable. Children (ie under-15s) not allowed. **US$94**

Posada Olivar Besares 978, Chacras de Coria ☎0261 496 0061, ⊚posadaolivar.com. Set in fine grounds, giving an insight into the typical *chacras* (smallholdings) that gave this leafy Mendoza suburb its name, this friendly posada run by an enthusiastic young English-speaking couple combines simplicity with comfort. There is a large pool in the garden. **US$120**

DRINKING AND NIGHTLIFE

Aloha Ruta Panamericana s/n, Chacras de Coria ☎0261 496 0557, ⊚facebook.com/Aloha.Oficial; map pp.336–337. Extremely fashionable club (best on Sat) playing Argentine rock music, frequented by a fairly young crowd. Fri 11pm–late, Sat midnight–late

La Guanaca Ruta Panamericana s/n, Chacras de Coria ☎0261 15 507 0070, ⊚pasionymatraca.com; map pp.336–337. A long-time favourite among Mendoza's club aficionados to dance the night away. Fri & Sat 10pm–5.30am.

Maipú

The self-styled "Cuna de la Viña", or birthplace of the grapevine, **MAIPÚ**, lying some 15km southeast of Mendoza via RN-7, is the city's other small satellite town. Founded in 1861 by the Mercedarian monks Fray Manuel Apolinario Vásquez and Don José Alberto de Ozamis as a new site for the earthquake-levelled Mendoza, it quickly became the centre of wine-making in the region, and is where many of the city's **wineries** are located today (see box, pp.346–347). The wine-growing district, to the north of the town's centre, is called Coquimbito, where vineyards alternate with dusky olive groves.

Museo del Vino

Bodega La Rural at Montecaseros • Mon–Sat 9am–noon & 2–5pm • Free • ☎0261 497 2013

The large Bodega La Rural at Montecaseros is where you'll find Mendoza's **Museo del Vino**, a summary explanation of the region's wine industry housed in a fabulous Art Nouveau villa, with elegant fittings and detailing, including some delicate stained glass – the venue far outstrips the contents, which won't teach you anything you won't find out in far more interesting bodegas.

ARRIVAL AND GETTING AROUND   MAIPÚ

By bus Buses #151, #172, #173, #174, #180, #181, #182 and #183 all go to Maipú, taking slightly different routes from downtown Mendoza.

By bike You can rent bikes for exploring the area at Urquiza 2288 (☎0261 497 4067).

ACCOMMODATION

Club Tapiz RP-60 Km2.5, Pedro Molina s/n ☎0261 496 3433, ⊚club-tapiz.com.ar. Affiliated with *Bodega Tapiz* in Maipú, *Club Tapiz* has seven tastefully appointed rooms in a renovated villa dating from 1890, as well as a spa, pool, gaucho-style *pulpería* and its own gourmet restaurant, *Tapiz*, surrounded by a vineyard. *Casa Zolo*

– a separate villa tucked away behind the vineyard (although closer to the main road), with its own pool – has an additional four rooms for those wanting more privacy. Price includes wine tasting at the hotel every night at 8pm and a free visit – including wine tasting – to Bodega Tapiz (no transfer). **US$206**

Alta Montaña

The Andean cordillera or **ALTA MONTAÑA** (High Mountains), which includes some of the world's tallest mountains, looms a short distance west of Mendoza, and its snow-tipped peaks are visible from the city centre almost all year round beyond the picturesque vineyards and fruit orchards. Even if you've come to the region for the wine, you'll want to head up into the hills before long: the scenery is fabulous, and skiing, trekking and highland walks are all possible, or you can simply enjoy the views on an organized excursion.

The so-called **Alta Montaña Route** – RN-7 – is also the international highway to Santiago de Chile, via the upmarket Chilean ski resort of Portillo, and one of the major border crossings between the two countries, blocked by snow only on rare occasions in July and August. If you're in a hurry to get to or from Santiago, try to travel by day, to see the stunning scenery in the area. Possible stop-offs along RN-7 to explore if you've more time include the pretty village of **Potrerillos** and **Vallecitos**, a tiny ski resort that caters for a younger crowd than exclusive Las Leñas (see p.364). As the road climbs further up into the mountains it passes another village, **Uspallata**, and then a variety of colourful rock formations – look for the pinnacle-like **Los Penitentes**. Closer to the border, **Puente del Inca** is a popular place to pause, both for its sulphurous thermal spring and its location – near the trailhead, base camp and muleteer post for those brave enough to contemplate the ascent of mighty **Aconcagua**, the continent's tallest peak, just to the north. The last settlement before you travel through a tunnel under the Andes and into Chile is **Las Cuevas**, from where an old mountain pass can be ascended – weather permitting – to see the **Cristo Redentor**, a huge statue of Christ erected as a sign of peace between the neighbouring countries, and for the fantastic mountain views.

Potrerillos

Sixty-four kilometres from Mendoza and some 50km along RN-7 from Luján de Cuyo is the village of **POTRERILLOS**, which styles itself as a centre for adventure tourism. Its picturesque valley is dotted with poplar trees that turn a vivid yellow in March and April, while the views up to the precordillera are fabulous: the colours form a blurred mosaic from this distance.

ARRIVAL AND TOURS   **POTRERILLOS**

By car To reach RN-7, the Alta Montaña road from Mendoza, first head south along RN-40, then turn westwards 15km south of the city, beyond Luján de Cuyo and Perdriel.

Tour operators A number of adventure-tour agencies operate from here, including Potrerillos Explorer, Manzana K Casa 4 (☎0261 609 5197, ⓦpotrerillosexplorer.com), and Argentina Rafting, Ruta Perilago s/n (☎0261 429 6325, ⓦargentinarafting.com), which runs exciting white-water rafting trips down the Río Mendoza in season.

Vallecitos

Eighty kilometres from Mendoza, and 25km west of Potrerillos via an unnumbered track, **VALLECITOS** is a relatively inexpensive resort nestling in the Valle del Plata, in the lee of the Cerro Blanco, at an altitude of around 3000m. Popular with young people, it functions as a small ski resort – with twelve pistes of varying levels of difficulty – in winter, and as a base for climbing and treks into the Cordón del Plata, as well as acclimatization for Aconcagua, in summer. The ski centre (☎02622 488810) is open daily from July to September, snow permitting.

Uspallata

Fifty-four kilometres north of Potrerillos by RN-7 and 105km northwest of Mendoza via RN-40 and RN-7, the village of **USPALLATA** has been an important crossroad between Mendoza, San Juan and Chile for centuries. It lies in the valley of the Río Uspallata, a fertile strip of potato, maize and pea fields, vineyards, pastures and patches

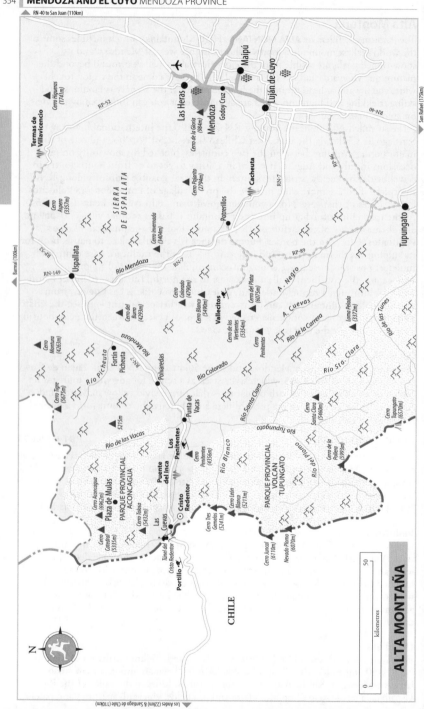

RN-40 to San Juan (110km)

Barreal (100km)

San Rafael (175km)

Cerro Higueras
(1741m)

Termas de
Villavicencio

Las Heras

Maipú

Godoy Cruz

Lujan de Cuyo

Mendoza

Cerro de la Gloria
(984m)

RP-52

RN-40

Cacheuta

Cerro Pajarito
(2794m)

RN-7

RP-96

Tupungato

Potrerillos

Cerro
Aspero
(3357m)

SIERRA
DE USPALLATA

Cerro Invernada
(3404m)

Uspallata

Río Mendoza

RN-7

RP-89

RN-149

Cerro
Colorado
(4790m)

Cerro del Burro
(4293m)

Cerro Blanco
(5490m)

Vallecitos

Cerro del Plata
(6075m)

A. Negro

A. Cuevas

Río de la Carrera

Loma Pelada
(3372m)

Río de los Tunes

Cerro
Montura
(4265m)

Cerro de los
Vertientes
(5354m)

Cerro
Penitentes

Río Sta. Clara

Cerro Tigre
(5675m)

Fortín Picheuta

Río Picheuta

Río Mendoza

Polvaredas

Río Colorado

Río Santa Clara

Río Tupungato

Cerro
Santa Clara
(5460m)

Cerro
Tupungato
(6570m)

5215m

Punta de Vacas

Río de las Vacas

Los Penitentes

Cerro
Penitentes
(4356m)

Río Blanco

PARQUE PROVINCIAL
VOLCÁN TUPUNGATO

Cerro de la
Pollera
(5993m)

Río del Plomo

Cerro Aconcagua
(6962m)

Plaza de Mulas

PARQUE PROVINCIAL
ACONCAGUA

Puente del Inca

Cristo Redentor

Cerro Tolosa
(5432m)

Cerro León Blanco
(5211m)

Cerro Tres
Gemelos
(5241m)

Cerro
Catedral
(5335m)

Las Cuevas

Túnel del
Cristo Redentor

Portillo

Cerro Juncal
(6110m)

Nevado Plomo
(6070m)

CHILE

N

Los Andes (22km) & Santiago de Chile (110km)

0   kilometres   50

ALTA MONTAÑA

of farmland where flocks of domesticated geese are kept. The village's cool climate, plentiful accommodation and stress-free ambience make it an ideal place for a few days' relaxation; otherwise there's really not much to do here.

The area east of the village called **Sierra de Uspallata**, which blocks Mendoza's view of Aconcagua, was described in the 1830s by Charles Darwin in the *Voyage of the Beagle*: "Red, purple, green and quite white sedimentary rocks, alternating with black lavas broken up and thrown into all kinds of disorder, by masses of porphyry, of every shade, from dark brown to the brightest lilac. It really resembled those pretty sections which geologists make of the inside of the earth."

Bóvedas de Uspallata

Daily 8.30am–8pm • Free • ☎ 02624 420045

The unusual **Bóvedas de Uspallata** are late eighteenth-century furnaces used for smelting iron mined in the nearby mountainside, a short way north of the village. Famously, the ovens were used by the patriotic monk Fray Luis Beltrán to make cannons and other arms for San Martín's army. Made of brick and adobe, with their egg-shaped white domes they look decidedly North African or Middle Eastern in style. Inside are exhibitions about the region's mining activity and the historical importance of the construction.

ARRIVAL AND INFORMATION   USPALLATA

By bus The centre of Uspallata is the junction of RN-7 and Las Heras, where buses arrive from Mendoza (7daily; 2hr 20min) and head towards Puenta del Inca and into Chile.

Tourist information A hut right by the junction serves as a rudimentary tourist office (daily 8am–10.30pm; ☎ 02624 420045).

ACCOMMODATION AND EATING

Café Tibet Near the junction of RN-7 and RN-149. Good coffee in a very imaginatively stylized Tibetan temple, done out in homage to the movie *Seven Years in Tibet*, some of which was shot near Uspallata. Daily 8am–11pm.

Hostal Los Cóndores Las Heras s/n, near the junction ☎ 02624 420002, ⓦ loscondoreshotel.com.ar. Has nice rooms (albeit with hard beds), enormous modern bathrooms and a *confitería*. The buffet breakfast is excellent, and they also offer horseriding and treks into the nearby mountains. **$950**

Hotel Valle Andino South of the village, just off RN-7 ☎ 02624 420095, ⓦ hotelvalleandino.com. A relatively luxurious hotel with spacious rooms, tennis courts and a

pleasant sitting room; it conveniently offers full board, with hearty rustic meals on offer. B&B **$1140**; half-board **$1420**; full board **$1700**

Hotel Viena Av Las Heras 240 ☎ 02624 420046, ⓦ hospedajeviena.com. This decent if modest hotel has simple, almost stark, rooms with private bathrooms, plus cable TV to while away the deadly quiet evenings. **$400**

Lo de Pato 1km south of the junction ☎ 02624 420610. The best place to eat hereabouts. It's a popular stopoff for coach trips and buses to and from Chile, which means it can get crowded at lunchtime, but the rustic, no-nonsense food is tasty. Daily 7am–midnight.

Up to Los Penitentes

From Uspallata, RN-7 swings round to the west and rejoins the Río Mendoza, whose valley it shares with the now-disused rail line, all the way to its source at Punta de Vacas. The road follows an ancient Inca trail; several mummified corpses have been found in the mountains to the south and are displayed in Mendoza at the Museo de Ciencias Naturales y Antropológicas (see p.343). The scenery is simply fantastic: you pass through narrow canyons, close by the Cerro del Burro (4293m) and the Cerro División (4603m) to the south, with the rugged ridges of the Cerros del Chacay culminating in the Cerro Tigre (5700m) to the north. Stripes of different-coloured rock – reds, greens and yellows caused by the presence of iron, copper and sulphur – decorate the steep walls of the cordillera peaks, while the vegetation is limited to tough highland grass and *jarilla*, a scruffy, gorse-like shrub gathered for firewood. The road climbs a gentle slope, slips through a series of tunnels, takes you through the abandoned hamlet of Polvaredas and past the police station at Punta de Vacas, at 2325m above sea level; the public customs post is further on at Los Horcones.

Los Penitentes ski resort

RN-7, Puente de Inca • ☎ 0261 429 953, ⓦ lospenitentes.com or ⓦ penitentesweb.com

Some 65km from Uspallata is the small ski resort of **Los Penitentes**, or more properly Villa Los Penitentes. The "penitents" in question are a series of strange pinnacles of rock, high up on the ridge atop Cerro Penitentes (4356m), towering over the small village of typical, brightly coloured ski-resort buildings to the south. The pointed rocks are thought to look like cowled monks, of the kind that traditionally parade during Holy Week in places such as Seville – hence the name. The resort's 28 pistes vary from nursery slopes to the black "Las Paredes", with most of the runs classified as difficult and the biggest total drop being 700m. The modern ski lifts also run in the summer, so you can enjoy the fabulous mountain and valley views from the top of Cerro San Antonio (3200m); the fissured peak looming over it all is the massive Cerro Leña (4992m).

ACCOMMODATION   LOS PENITENTES

Ayelén Hotel de Montaña RN-7 Km160 ☎ 0261 425 3443, ⓦ bit.ly/HotelAyelen. Functional hotel aimed specifically at winter sports enthusiasts, with games and TV rooms to keep skiers entertained in the evenings, plus a decent restaurant. **$1585**

Hostería Penitentes RN-7 Km160, ⓦ lospenitentes .com/en/hosteria-penitentes.html. This is the main alternative to the *Ayelén Hotel de Montaña*, and more amenable to one-night as opposed to full-week bookings in season. It is more about location than luxury, but is nonetheless comfortable, clean and efficient. **$1150**

Puente del Inca

Just 6km west of Los Penitentes is **Puente del Inca**, a traditional stop for anyone heading along the Alta Montaña route. Situated at just over 2700m above sea level, this natural **stone bridge** is an impressive sight, featuring on many a postcard. Formed by the Río de las Cuevas, it nestles in an arid valley, overlooked by majestic mountains; just beneath the bridge are the remains of a once sophisticated spa resort, built in the 1940s but swept away by a flood. The ruins, the bridge itself and the surrounding rocks are all stained a nicotine-yellow by the very high sulphur content of the warm waters that gurgle up nearby. Stalls sell souvenirs here, including all kinds of objects that have been left to petrify and yellow in the mineral springs: shoes, bottles, hats, books, ashtrays and statues of the Virgin Mary have all been treated to this embellishment, and are of dubious taste, but the displays make for an unusual photograph. Only 4km west of Puente del Inca is the dirt track that heads into the Parque Nacional Aconcagua.

ACCOMMODATION   PUENTE DEL INCA

Refugio El Nico RN-7 s/n Puente del Inca ☎ 0261 15 592 0736. A simple and small hostel just 50m from the ancient Inca bridge. Dorms **$245**; doubles **$475**

Vieja Estación 100m from RN-7. This mountaineers' refuge has basic bunk beds and shared bathrooms but is a perfectly fine place to rest your head. The views are breathtaking. **$250**

Aconcagua

At 6962m – or 6959m according to some maps – **Cerro Aconcagua** is the highest peak in both the western and southern hemispheres, or outside the Himalayas. Its glacier-garlanded summit dominates the Parque Provincial Aconcagua, even though it is encircled by several other mountains that exceed 5000m: cerros Almacenes, Catedral, Cuerno, Cúpula, Ameghino, Güssfeldt, Dedos, México, Mirador, Fitzgerald, La Mano, Santa María and Tolosa, some of which are easier to climb than others, and many of which obscure views of the great summit from most points around. The five glaciers that hang around its faces like icy veils are Horcones Superior, Horcones Inferior, Güssfeldt, Las Vacas and Los Polacos.

Although **climbing** Aconcagua is technically less demanding than climbing many lower-altitude peaks, it is still a challenge to be taken seriously. Fitness, patience and acclimatization are key, and, unless you're fairly experienced with high-altitude treks, you shouldn't even consider going up; despite what the agencies may tell you, both independent climbers and people climbing as part of organized treks often end up turning back.

MOUNTAIN-CLIMBING ESSENTIALS | ACONCAGUA

Equipment Given the huge amount of supplies needed to make the ascent, most people invest in a mule.

Hazards The two biggest obstacles are coping with the cold – temperatures can plummet to -40°C at night, even in the summer – and the altitude, and fickle weather is also a major threat. Expeditions always descend when they see milky-white clouds shaped like the lenses of eyeglasses, known as *el viento blanco*, which announce violent storms. On average, some two people a year die trying to climb Aconcagua. Frostbite and altitude sickness are the main health hazards, but proper precautions can usually prevent both.

Permits Unless you are arranging everything through a tour operator, the first place you need to go is the Dirección de Recursos Naturales Renovables (mid-March to mid-Nov: Mon–Fri 8am–6pm, Sat & Sun 8am–1pm; rest of the year

Mon–Fri 8am–1pm; ☎0261 425 8751, ⓦaconcagua .mendoza.gov.ar), located on the first floor of Mendoza's main tourist office at Av San Martín 1143. This is where you must apply for the compulsory permits to enter the Aconcagua reserve. For foreign trekkers these cost from US$200 for a single day's access to as high as US$944 for a twenty-day permit to climb to the summit in winter.

Seasons The main climbing season runs from mid-November to mid-March; January is the most popular month, and therefore most expensive, as it coincides with Argentine summer holidays and is when the weather is usually most settled. Allow three weeks for an expedition, since you should acclimatize at each level, and take it easy throughout the climb; many of the people who don't make it to the top fail because they try to rush.

Brief history

Aconcagua may be the highest Andean mountain, but for many mountain purists, it lacks the morphological beauty of Cerro Mercedario to the north or Volcán Tupungato to the south; it's also not as difficult a climb to the summit as some of the other Andean peaks. Nevertheless, ever since it was conquered by the Italian–Swiss mountaineer Matthias Zurbriggen in 1897 – after it had been identified by German climber Paul Güssfeldt in 1883 – Aconcagua has been one of the top destinations in the world for expeditions or solo climbs. In 1934, a Polish team of climbers made it to the top via the Los Polacos glacier now named after them; in 1953, the southwest ridge was the route successfully taken by a local group of mountaineers; and in 1954, a French team that had conquered Cerro Fitz Roy made the first ascent of Aconcagua up the south face, the most challenging of all – Plaza Francia, one of the main base camps, is named for them. In recent years, Aconcagua has become a major attraction for less experienced mountaineers, and of the seven thousand-odd people who try to reach the summit every year, about half make it.

Routes

Of the three **approaches** – south, west or east – the western route from the Plaza de Mulas (4230m) is the most accessible and most used, and is known as the Ruta Normal. Very experienced climbers take either the Glaciar de los Polacos route, with its base camp at Plaza Argentina, reached via a long track that starts near Punta de Vacas,

ACONCAGUA IN PRE-COLUMBIAN HISTORY

The origins of the name Aconcagua are not entirely clear, although it probably comes either from the Huarpe words *Akon-Kahuak* ("stone sentinel") or from the Mapuche *Akonhue* ("from the beyond"). That it was a holy site for these and/or other indigenous peoples is evidenced by the discovery in 1985 of an Inca mummy – now in the Museo del Área Fundacional, Mendoza (see p.341) – on the southwest face. Found at an altitude of 5300m, the presence of the mummy shows that ceremonies, including burials and perhaps sacrifices, took place at these incredible heights.

or the very demanding south face, whose Plaza Francia base camp is reached from Los Horcones, branching off from the Plaza de Mulas trail at a spot called Confluencia (3368m). For more details of the different routes, plus advice on what to take with you and how to acclimatize, consult the (dated, but still useful) Aconcagua website (ⓦaconcagua.com.ar). For more specialist information, especially for serious climbers who are considering one of the harder routes, the best publications are R.J. Secor's *Aconcagua, A Climbing Guide* (second ed. 1999) or Harry Kikstra's *Aconcagua – Summit of South America* (2005).

ARRIVAL AND TOURS · ACONCAGUA

By bus To get to either Los Horcones or Punta de Vacas, you can take the three daily buses (around 4hr) from the bus terminal in Mendoza.

By organized tour It's definitely preferable, whether trekking or climbing, to go with local guides on an organized trip, if only because of the treacherous weather. Several outfits in Mendoza specialize in tours, which cost around US$3975 per person plus around US$745 each for equipment rental and US$582–944 for permits (depending on season). Tour companies include Aconcagua Trek, at Av Colón 531 (☏0261 15 466 5825, ⓦaconcaguatrek.com); Inka Expediciones, at Juan B Justo 345 (☏0261 425 0871, ⓦinka.com.ar); Mallku Expediciones, at Perú 1499 (☏0261 420 4811, ⓦmallkuexpediciones.com.ar); South Face (Aconcagua Pared Sur), at Lamadrid 696 (☏0261 427 0825, ⓦaconcaguaparedsur.com); and Fernando Grajales (☏0261 428 3157, ⓦgrajales.net), where you can also hire mules if climbing independently.

ACCOMMODATION

Hostel Arco de la Cuevas This hostel with great mountain views, dorms and rooms with en-suite baths in an attractive Alpine-style stone building, arching over RN-7, is popular with Aconcagua climbers. It also has a restaurant. Dorms **$220**; doubles **$550**

Cristo Redentor

From January to March, but usually not for the rest of the year because of snowfalls or frost, you can drive up the several hairpin bends to the **Monumento al Cristo Redentor**, an 8m-high, six-tonne statue of Christ the Redeemer. It was put here in 1904 to celebrate the so-called May 1902 Pacts, signed between Argentina and Chile, under the auspices of British King Edward VII, to determine once and for all the Andean boundary between the two countries. Designed by Argentine sculptor Mateo Alonso, the statue was made from melted-down cannons and other weapons, in a reversal of Fray Luis Beltrán's project a hundred years before (see p.355). Nearby is a disused Chilean customs post – the Paso de la Cumbre, no longer used by international traffic. The views towards Cerro Tolosa (5432m), immediately to the north, along the cordillera and down into several valleys, are quite staggering; make sure you have something warm to wear, though, as the howling winds up here are bitterly cold. When the road is open, most Alta Montaña tours bring you up here as the grand finale to the excursion; would-be Aconcagua conquerors often train and acclimatize by clambering to the top on foot.

South of Mendoza

The cordillera south of Mendoza city contains two remote and little-visited but stunning provincial parks – the fabulous **Parque Provincial Tupungato**, 80km southwest from Mendoza and dominated by the soaring volcano of the same name, and the **Reserva Provincial Laguna Diamante**, with a turquoise altiplanic lake, the **Laguna Diamante**, at its heart. The latter is a further 140km southwest of Tupungato and only open during the summer; both are well worth the effort it takes to reach them.

Tupungato

There's little to see in the small market town of **TUPUNGATO**, 78km southwest of Mendoza – the town is reached from the provincial capital via RN-40 and RP-86.

This is, though, the best place to contract guides to take you to the top of the mighty Volcán Tupungato.

Parque Provincial Tupungato

Parque Provincial Tupungato, most accessible from Tupungato town, stretches along the Chilean border to the south of RN-7 at Puente del Inca. The virgin countryside within the park is utterly breathtaking, completely unspoilt and unremittingly stark, and this is where you find the much lesser-known peak of **Volcán Tupungato**. Now that Aconcagua has become almost a victim of its own success, anyone looking for a challenging mountain trek with fewer people crowding the trails and paths should head for the better-kept secret of this extinct volcano peaking at 6570m. You'll need plenty of time as the treks last between three and fifteen days, depending on how long you're given to acclimatize at each level – the longer the better. Calculate on US$3000 per person.

6

ARRIVAL AND INFORMATION   TUPUNGATO

By bus Buses run fairly regularly to and from Mendoza (hourly; 1hr 15min–2hr), stopping at Plaza General San Martín and along the main road.

Tourist information Ask at the *Hotel Turismo* (see below), which also acts as the town's tourist office (Mon–Fri 7am–7pm, Sat & Sun 8am–8pm), about trips to the volcano.

Tours Apart from the companies recommended for Aconcagua, which also arrange tours to Tupungato (see opposite), check out Rómulo Nieto at the *Hostería Don Rómulo* (see below).

ACCOMMODATION AND EATING

Hostería Don Rómulo Almirante Brown 1200 ☎ 02622 489020. Not only does owner Rómulo arrange reasonably priced tours in the area, including excellent highland horse treks, but you can stay at his small and cosy *hostería*, with decent rooms. There is an excellent *parrilla* attached. $600

Hotel Turismo Av Belgrano 1050 ☎ 02622 488007. This spacious hotel offers smart bedrooms, modern bathrooms and a full board option, thanks to its excellent restaurant

– where local goat is a speciality. $630

Patios de Correa La Costa s/n. The best of a bunch of campsites around the village – there's an excellent barbecue grill. $100

Pizzeria Ilo Belgrano and Sargento Cabral ☎ 02622 488323. This place is very popular with the locals and serves up an excellent margarita plus delicious home-made pasta; the wine list is surprisingly good for a pizzeria. Daily 11am–3pm, Wed–Sun 8.30pm–midnight.

Reserva Provincial Laguna Diamante

Some 220km southwest of Mendoza, **Laguna Diamante** is the destination of one of the least known but most unforgettable excursions in the area. The source of the Río Diamante, the lake is so called because the choppy surface of its crystalline waters suggests a rough diamond. One reason for its relative obscurity is that weather conditions make it possible to reach Laguna Diamante only from mid-December to the end of March. At Pareditas, 125km south of Mendoza by RN-40, take the reliable, unsurfaced RP-101, which forks off to the southwest. The drive is one marvellous panoramic view of the Andean precordillera, following Arroyo Yaucha through fields of gorse-like *jarilla* and gnarled *chañares*, looking out over the rounded summits of the frontal cordillera, before entering the Cañón del Gateado, through which the Arroyo Rosario flows past dangling willows. At another fork in the road, 20km on, take the right fork to the Refugio Militar General Alvarado, the entrance to the **Reserva Provincial Laguna Diamante**. Here, you'll catch your first sight of **Volcán Maipo** (5323m), the permanently snowcapped volcano that straddles the frontier, some 4000m above sea level. Nestling beneath the Cordón del Eje, a majestic range of dark ochre rock, and towered over by the snow-streaked Maipo opposite – a perfect cone worthy of a Japanese woodcut – this ultramarine lake is constantly buffeted into white horses by strong breezes and its waves noisily lap the springy, mossy banks. The silence is broken only by the howl of the wind.

ARRIVAL AND INFORMATION

By 4WD No public transport reaches this remote spot, so you'll need a 4WD.

By organized tour Try Nicolás García at Argentina Mountain, Coronel Rodriguez 1176, Mendoza (☏ 0261 425 0426), who offers day-trips from Mendoza ($1450/person) as well as longer horse treks and climbs up Maipo and Tupungato. You may also be able to pick up a tour from San

RESERVA PROVINCIAL LAGUNA DIAMANTE

Rafael, which is closer. Since the lagoon is in an area under military control, near a strategic point on the Chilean border, take your passport.

Tourist information Rangers at the *guardería*, which you pass on the final approach to the lagoon, can offer some information on the reserve and its wildlife, and appreciate the chance to share a *mate*.

San Rafael and around

The small city of **SAN RAFAEL** is the de facto capital of central Mendoza Province; around 230km south of Mendoza via RN-40 and RN-143, it's a kind of mini-Mendoza, complete with wide avenues, irrigation channels along the gutters and scrupulously clean public areas. The town was founded in 1805 on behalf of Rafael, Marqués de Sobremonte – hence the name – by militia leader Miguel Telles Meneses. Large numbers of Italian and Spanish immigrants flocked here at the end of the nineteenth century, but the so-called Colonia Francesa expanded further when the railway arrived in 1903. Favoured by French immigrants during the nineteenth century, San Rafael built its prosperity on vineyards, olives and fruit, grown in the province's second-biggest oasis.

In all, there are nearly eighty **bodegas** in San Rafael department, most of them tiny, family-run businesses, some of which welcome visitors. Tourism has been a big money-spinner over the past couple of decades, especially since adventure tourism has taken off. The **Cañón del Atuel**, a short way to the southwest, is a great place for gentle white-water rafting, or you can try the much more challenging, dramatic **Río Diamante**. If exploring the southern parts of the province, there's a wider choice of accommodation in San Rafael than in Malargüe, although the latter still makes a far more convenient base.

San Rafael has a flat, compact centre that lends itself to a gentle stroll, but otherwise there aren't any sights to speak of – the town is essentially a base for visiting the surrounding area. The main drag, with most of the shops and hotels, is a continuation of RN-143 from Mendoza. Within the town it's called **Avenida Hipólito Yrigoyen**, west of north–south axis **Avenida General San Martín** and **Avenida Bartolomé Mitre** to the east. Street names change either side of both axes.

Museo de Historia Natural

Daily 8am–7pm • $5 • ☏ 0260 442 2121 (ask to speak to someone at the museum and they will transfer you), ⓦ bit.ly/MuseoHistoriaNaturalSR • Take a taxi or a bus marked "Isla Diamante" from Av Ballofet

To fill an hour or so, head to Isla Diamante, a large island 6km south of the town centre, in the middle of the river of the same name, which is home to the **Museo de Historia Natural**. Among masses of bedraggled stuffed birds, moth-eaten foxes and lumps of rock, you'll find some fabulous pre-Columbian ceramics, the best of which are statues from Ecuador; there's also a small collection of crafts from Easter Island and

---

RAFTING IN SAN RAFAEL

Rafael is an excellent base for **rafting**, with the Cañón del Atuel being the most sedate option. More challenging experiences are available with rapids as tough as Grade IV–V in season (Dec–Feb), such as the Río Sosneado (booked through Bruni Aventura, Av Ballofet 98; ☏ 0260 442 3790, ⓦ bruniaventura.com.ar; min 4 people, $800/person). One- or multi-day adventures down the splendid and rarely visited canyon of the **Río Diamante** are also possible, or the Río Grande (Sport Star, RP-173 Km35, Valle Grande; ☏ 0260 15 458 1068, ⓦ sportstar.com.ar; prices from $1000/person, min 6 people).

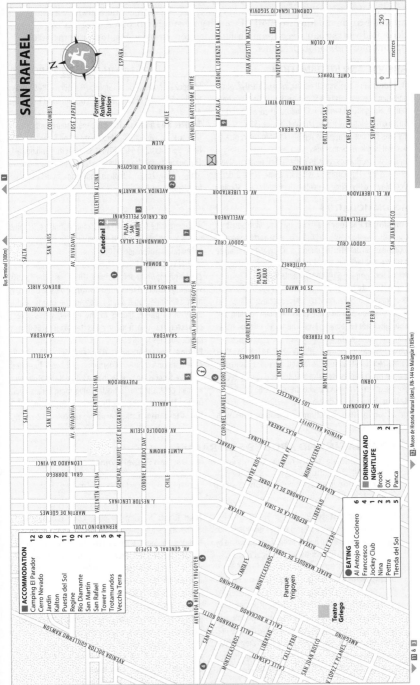

SAN RAFAEL

Former Railway Station

Catedral

■ ACCOMMODATION
Camping El Parador	12
Cerro Nevado	6
Jardin	8
Kalton	7
Puesta del Sol	11
Regine	10
Río Diamante	2
San Martín	1
San Rafael	3
Tower Inn	5
Trotamundos	9
Vecchia Terra	4

● EATING
Al Antojo del Cocinero	6
Franccesco	4
Jockey Club	1
Nina	2
Pettra	3
Tienda del Sol	5

■ DRINKING AND NIGHTLIFE
Brook	3
OX	2
Panca	1

Teatro Griego

Parque Yrigoyen

Bus Terminal (300m)

Champañera Bianchi (4km), Airport (5km) & RN-143 to Mendoza (230km)

Museo de Historia Natural (6km), RN-144 to Malargüe (185km)

some particularly fine ceramics from northwestern Argentina. You'll also see a mummified child dating from 40 AD and a gorgeous multicoloured leather bag decorated with striking, very modern-looking geometric designs, found in the Gruta del Indio in the Cañón del Atuel.

ARRIVAL AND INFORMATION
SAN RAFAEL AND AROUND

By plane San Rafael's small airport, with one daily flight to and from Buenos Aires (1hr 50min), is 5km west of the town centre, along RN-143 towards Mendoza. There are no buses, but taxi rides into town won't break the bank ($85).

By bus The bus terminal is ten blocks from the centre on General Paz, at Av Granadores.

Destinations Buenos Aires (4 daily; 13hr); General Alvear (9–11 daily; 1hr 45min); Las Leñas (June–Sept 2 daily; Oct–May 1 daily; 3hr); Malargüe (8–9 daily; 2hr 40min);

Mendoza (hourly; 3hr 15min); Neuquén (8–9 daily; 8–9hr); San Juan (2 daily; 5hr 40min); San Luís (1–2 daily; 4hr).

Tourist information The city's main tourist office is at the corner of avenidas Hipólito Yrigoyen and Balloffet (daily 8am–9pm; ☎ 0260 442 4217, ⬤ sanrafaelturismo.gov.ar). The bus terminal also has its own tourist information kiosk (daily 8am–2pm, although opening hours change frequently).

ACCOMMODATION

Camping El Parador Isla Río Diamante, 6km south of the centre ☎ 0260 443 6756. Set in an attractive wooded location on an island in the middle of the river, the campsite has excellent facilities and also offers apartments sleeping up to four. Camping $100; apartments $500

Cerro Nevado Hipólito Yrigoyen 376 ☎ 0260 442 8209, ⬤ cerronevadohotel.com.ar. This spotless place has rather stark rooms with white walls and plain bedding, but also a pleasant restaurant. Avoid the street-side rooms, as they can be noisy. $600

Jardín Hipólito Yrigoyen 283 ☎ 0260 443 4621. Very comfy rooms, all en suite, arranged around a lush patio shaded by an impressive palm tree. It's let down by details like the under-par breakfast and the minuscule TVs. $600

Kalton Hipólito Yrigoyen 120 ☎ 0260 443 0047, ⬤ kaltonhotel.com. Typical mid-range town hotel with

well-kept, albeit unremarkable, rooms. One of its plus points is the plentiful buffet breakfast, featuring home-baked cakes and breads. $1050

★ **Puesta del Sol** Deán Funes 998 ☎ 0260 454 0042, ⬤ complejopuestadelsol.com. One of the most stunning hostels in the country, with modern facilities, a huge swimming pool amid landscaped grounds, and a lively atmosphere, thanks to the owner, who's a real character. It's 4km from the bus terminal – $60 in a *remís*. Doubles $595

Regine Independencia 623 ☎ 0260 442 1470, ⬤ hotelregine.com.ar. Charming and well-furnished mid-sized rooms together with a beautiful lush garden and a small pool. The hotel's rustic dining room serves good food and the a/c works well. There is covered parking. $400

Río Diamante Pellegrini 330 ☎ 0260 442 2499,

BODEGAS IN AND AROUND SAN RAFAEL

Though Mendoza is undeniably Argentina's wine capital, **San Rafael's wineries** are among the finest in the country. Several open their doors to visitors, although tours are more informal than in Mendoza and often don't run at set times; don't be surprised if no one speaks English. Some of the best include:

Algodón Wine Estates RN-144 Km674 ☎ 0260 442 9020, ⬤ algodonwineestates.com. Beautiful but slightly commercial and luxury-loving bodega owned by an ex golf-player. Tours (English and Spanish) Tues–Sun 10am, 11am, noon, 3pm, 4pm and 5pm; $80.

Champañera Bianchi Hipólito Yrigoyen s/n ☎ 0260 444 9661, ⬤ casabianchi.com.ar. An interesting contrast with its old downtown bodega, this ultramodern, sparkling wine-production unit, housed in a postmodern steel and glass building, is 4km west of the town centre. Excellent sparkling wines made according to the *méthode champenoise*. Tours (English and Spanish; 30min) Mon–Sat 9.30am–noon & 2.30–5.30pm; $30.

Jean Rivier Hipólito Yrigoyen 2385 ☎ 0260 443 2675, ⬤ jeanrivier.com. Friendly, small winery, founded by Swiss wine-makers; their tiptop wines include an unusual cabernet sauvignon–fer blend. Delicious chardonnays, too. Mon–Fri 8–11am & 3–6pm, Sat 8–11am; free.

Suter Hipólito Yrigoyen 2850 ☎ 02627 421076, ⬤ bodegasuter.com.ar. Slightly mechanical guided visits, but you get to taste some decent sparkling wine. Traditional-style winery. Tours (every 30min) April–Nov Mon–Fri 9.30am–1pm & 2–5pm, Sat 9.30am–1pm & 2–4pm; Dec–March Mon–Fri 9.30am–1pm & 2–6pm, Sat 9.30am–1pm & 2–5pm; free.

ⓦriodiamantehotel.com. Very pleasant, good-value rooms with stainless-steel washbasins in gleaming bathrooms. They are very helpful at putting together excursions in the region. **$880**

San Martín Av San Martín 435 ☎0260 442 0400, ⓦsanmartinhotelspa.com. Well-equipped hotel with spa, gym, restaurant and both a heated indoor pool and a more refreshing one outdoors. Comfortable rooms, although slightly impersonal. **$1190**

San Rafael Coronel Day 30 ☎0260 443 0127, ⓦhotelsanrafael.com.ar. Relaxing mid-range hotel with a somewhat outdated interior. It has a bar, reception with log fire and cable TV in the rooms, some of which are triples and quadruples. **$1100**

Tower Inn Hipólito Yrigoyen 774 ☎0260 442 7190, ⓦtowersanrafael.com. This sandy-hued tower of stone and plate glass may be a bit of an eyesore, but the interior is airy, modern and well run, and a large swimming pool, spa, gym and patio bar make it San Rafael's only four-star hotel. **$1990**

Trotamundos Barcala 300 ☎0260 443 2795, ⓦtrotamundoshostel.com.ar. A rather cramped hostel, with not enough bathrooms, that's popular with young Argentines. Best enjoyed in low season when the hostel feels less crowded. Dorms **$160**; doubles **$400**

Vecchia Terra Castelli 23 ☎0260 442 4169, ⓦvecchiaterra.com.ar. A high-quality *apart-hotel* with apartments for up to six people. Luxuriously furnished throughout, with modern kitchens and great showers. Pool and gym across the street. Better value for money than the *Tower*. **$1550**

EATING

★ **Al Antojo del Cocinero** Av Ballofet 173 ☎0260 442 3264, ⓦbit.ly/AntojoCocinero. By far the town's best and most intimate restaurant, serving delicious *humitas* ($85) and hearty, contemporary dishes. Extra points for the beautiful garden at the back. Make sure to book ahead. Tues–Sun 8.30pm–midnight.

Franccesco Champagnat 31 ☎0260 443 7024. Minimalist restaurant serving inventive, though sometimes clumsily executed, dishes like grilled salmon ($195) or *degustación de pudding* ($60). Mon–Sat 9pm–midnight.

Jockey Club Belgrano 330 ☎0260 443 0237. Good old-fashioned service and hearty food at a reasonable price is served at this much-loved restaurant. Same owners as *Bon Vivant* (open for lunch and dinner) on Hipólito Yrigoyen, at Juan M. de Pueyrredón. Daily 9–11pm.

Nina San Martín and Olascoaga ☎0260 468 5173. Very smart cocktail bar doubling as a café and tearoom, so one of the best places to come for a shot of caffeine. Daily 7am–late.

Pettra Hipólito Yrigoyen 1750 ☎0260 443 9837. Very popular *parrilla* where you can eat big slabs of meat, washed down with good local wine at an affordable price. Mon–Wed 8.45pm–12.30am, Thurs–Sun 12.30–3pm & 8.45pm–12.30am.

Tienda del Sol Hipólito Yrigoyen 1663 ☎0260 442 5022, ⓦtiendadelsol.net. Trendy, postmodern resto-bar, serving seafood and pasta dishes (such as *panzeti* with salmon) alongside cocktails and other drinks, at slightly inflated prices. Daily noon–2.30pm & 8.30pm–12.30am.

DRINKING AND NIGHTLIFE

Brook Deán Funes and Sarmiento ☎0260 480 8038, ⓦfacebook.com/BrookSanRafael. Ultra-hip dance club, very popular with a young crowd, especially on Saturday nights. Fri & Sat midnight–late.

OX Olascuaga 10 ☎0260 15 458 7764. A good party choice, with themed nights including *noche de latina* and even *fiesta del turismo*. Wed–Sun 10.30pm–late.

Panca Day and Bombal ☎0260 423 0404, ⓦfacebook.com/PancaBar. Intimate bar serving excellent pisco sours and a good selection of wine, together with Peruvian dishes like ceviche ($90) and *lomo saltado* ($120). Daily 7pm–2am.

Cañón del Atuel

One of the area's main attractions is the **Cañón del Atuel**, a beautifully wild canyon linking two man-made lakes along the Río Atuel. Visits usually begin at the reservoir further from San Rafael, the **Embalse del Nihuil** (75km from the city along RN-144), and end up at the **Embalse Valle Grande**. On your way south along RN-144 you head over the 1300m Cuesta de los Terneros, which offers great views of the arid valley below. After about 50km, you turn left onto RP-180, which takes you to the reservoir.

The gorge

To get to the second reservoir from Embalse del Nihuil, and to make a full circuit back to San Rafael, you turn left off RP-180 at Villa Nihuil onto the windy **RP-173**.

6

> ## RELIVING *ALIVE*
>
> In 1972, a group of young **rugby players from Uruguay** caught the attention of the world after they survived a **plane crash** and over two months of brutal subzero temperatures in the Andes, at a place on the Argentine–Chilean border in the mountains west of the Cerro Sosneado and Río Atuel, now called the **Glaciar de las Lágrimas** (glacier of tears). The passengers survived by consuming snow and their colleagues' corpses and fashioning sleeping bags from the insulation in the plane's tail, before two of them finally made it west over the mountains and alerted the Chilean authorities, who had long since given them up for dead. Their incredible story was told in the 1993 movie *Alive* and the documentary *Alive: 20 Years Later*. It is now possible to **visit the site** of the crash, where parts of the plane are still scattered. Some may find the idea macabre, and getting there is obviously no walk in the park – count on at least three days of trekking and horseriding through the snow, although you'll also get to take a unique hot bath in the warm blue waters bubbling up out of the ground at the ruins of the old *Hotel Sosneado*. Tours are run by Risco Viajes in San Rafael (see below) or with guides from Malargüe, such as Karen Travel (see p.367).

The road heads northeast towards the city, squeezing through a narrow **gorge** whose cliffs and rocks are striped red, white and yellow, contrasting with the beige of the dust-dry mountainsides. Wind and water have eroded the rocks into weird and often rather suggestive shapes that stimulate the imagination: tour guides attach names like "the Nun" or "the Toad" to the strange formations. The road then passes a couple of dams, attached to power stations, before swinging round the **Embalse Valle Grande**. Sticking out of these blue-green waters are more strange rock formations, one of which does indeed look like the submarine its nickname suggests. From the high corniche roads that skirt the lakeside you are treated to some grand views of the waters, dotted with kayaks and other boats, and the mountains beyond. Near here is the start of the stretch of the Río Atuel used for **white-water rafting**; the scenery along the way is pleasantly pastoral along the more open parts and staggeringly beautiful in the narrower gorges.

ARRIVAL AND ACTIVITIES

By 4WD If you have your own vehicle you can get here under your own steam, but bear in mind that past the dam after Valle Grande RP-173 turns into a dirt road, so a 4WD is preferable.

By organized tour San Rafael is only 25km from the canyon by RP-173, but unless you have your own transport, you'll have to get here on an organized tour: try Risco Viajes, Av Hipólito Yrigoyen 284, San Rafael (☎ 0260 443 6439, ⓦ riscoviajes.com).

CAÑÓN DEL ATUEL

Hunuc Huar This wonderful crafts workshop (daily 9.30–1pm & 4–9pm), run by an indigenous family and specializing in fine ceramics, is set in an idyllic garden.

Raffeish Reliable and ecologically conscious operator offering white-water rafting trips (RP-173 Km35, Valle Grande; ☎ 0260 443 6996, ⓦ raffeish.com.ar). Trips last an hour, along an easy stretch for beginners, or a couple of hours or more, taking in a tougher Grade II section of the river. Take a change of clothes, as you'll get soaked.

ACCOMMODATION

Hotel Valle Grande RP-173 Km35 ☎ 0260 424 7598, ⓦ hotelvallegrande.com. This upmarket hotel offers all kinds of sports facilities and a fine swimming pool, but can get very crowded during the summer months; the hotel also has *cabañas* for rent that can sleep up to eight. Doubles **$1300**; *cabañas* **$1500**

Las Leñas and around

Two hundred kilometres southwest of San Rafael is one of Argentina's most upmarket ski resorts, **LAS LEÑAS** (accessed via RN-144, RN-40 and then RP-222). This is where the Porteño jet set comes to show off their winter fashions, get photographed for society magazines and have a good time. **Skiing** and **snowboarding** are only part of the fun – as in all exclusive winter resorts, the *après-ski* is just as important as the snow conditions.

SKIING IN LAS LEÑAS

Las Leñas is no Gstaad or St Moritz: it's a purpose-built **resort** built at an altitude of 2200m, with excellent **skiing** and **snowboarding** – when there is enough snow – and a breathtaking backdrop of craggy mountaintops, of which Cerro Las Leñas is the highest (4351m) and Cerro Torrecillas (3771m) the most daintily pinnacled. The whole area covers more than 33 square kilometres, with 29 pistes, ranging from several gentle nursery slopes to a couple of sheer black runs; cross-country and off-piste skiing are also possible.

Experienced skiers will want to head direct for **El Marte** lift, the only one which accesses the harder runs, but be aware that this is often closed due to the resort's characteristic high winds, which can be a source of some frustration. Contact the Ski School for information about off-piste excursions into the area's impressive **back country**. Nature is, of course, unpredictable, but **August to early September** is probably your best bet for serious powder, as well as for lower winds (and prices) and thinner crowds. Lessons are available in several languages, including English. The equipment-rental service (next to the *Hotel Acuario*) is pricey, as are the lifts – day-passes cost upwards of US$80, depending on the season – though many hotels offer discounts on these as part of packages. Your ski pass includes cover for getting you off the mountain in the event of an accident on piste, but only as far as the resort's medical centre. An early start to the day definitely pays off – the slopes are relatively empty, as many people are recovering from all-night partying.

More seriously, many ski champions from the northern hemisphere head down here during the June to October season, when there's not a lot of snow in the US or Europe; the Argentine, Brazilian and South American skiing championships are all held here in August, while other events include snow-polo matches, snow-rugby, snow-volleyball and fashion shows. Las Leñas is also trying to branch out into **summertime adventure travel**, such as mountain biking, rafting and horseriding, making the most of its splendid upland setting and pleasant daytime temperatures. Note that the resort is completely closed down, however, from March to June and from October to the end of December.

Pozo de las Ánimas

The road to Las Leñas heads due west from the Mendoza-to-Malargüe section of RN-40, 28km south of the crossroads settlement of El Sosneado. It climbs past the ramshackle spa resort of Los Molles, and the peculiar **Pozo de las Ánimas**, a set of two huge well-like depressions that make for a diverting photo stop (scheduled bus services don't stop here, and they can't be seen from the road). Caused by underground water erosion, each is several hundred metres in diameter, with a pool of turquoise water in the bottom. The sand-like cliffs surrounding each lake have been corrugated and castellated by the elements, like some medieval fortress, and the ridge dividing the two looks in danger of collapse at any minute.

ARRIVAL AND DEPARTURE

LAS LEÑAS AND AROUND

By plane The resort lies 50km from RN-40, a total of nearly 200km southwest of San Rafael. If you are booked at the resort, look to get a transfer from Malargüe airport (once-weekly charter flight from Buenos Aires, June to mid-Sept; US$750–780 return, depending on which hotel you're staying at), Mendoza or San Rafael.

By bus During the ski season you can take Iselín and CATA buses from Mendoza (1 daily; 7hr; $450), or the daily public bus or agency transfers from Malargüe – best to buy tickets from the terminal the night before and ask if they'll pick you up from your hotel. Otherwise, you'll need your own transport.

ACCOMMODATION

All accommodation in Las Leñas is under the same management and needs to be booked either online (W laslenas.com, E reservas@laslenas.com) or through the central office in Buenos Aires (Bartolomé Mitre 401 4th floor; T 011 4819 6060). Lodgings are usually booked as part of weekend or eight-day packages. All resort accommodation is within tramping distance of the slopes and, per person, costs upwards of US$3415/week (half board & ski passes included) in the peak weeks of July and August, though prices tend to drop by some fifty percent at either end of the season. Even though Las

6

Leñas is a playground for the rich and famous, it's possible to visit without breaking the bank; you could stay in a hostel, "dormy houses" (chalets grouped at the edge of the village that can sleep up to five and have simple kitchens and bedrooms), or overnight elsewhere nearby, such as in Los Molles (see p.365) or Malargüe (see below).

Hostel Leñas This newly built hostel is modern and aimed at a younger crowd, but expect it to be (and feel, especially in terms of bathrooms) packed in high season, as it is one of the few budget options in the ski resort. Dorms $410

Piscis Hotel Extravagant five-star hotel with gym, spa and casino. Prices per week. Half board US$3230

Virgo Hotel and Spa Pleasant hotel just next to the ski lifts, with some great amenities including a cinema and an outdoor swimming pool. Prices per week half board US$3415

EATING AND DRINKING

There are several expensive **restaurants** (hours vary by season) to choose from and a couple of on-site **discos**. There's also a supermarket, helpful if you want to save money by cooking your own meals.

Cuatro Estaciones ☎ 02627 471100 ext. 2722. Situated inside the *Hotel Piscis*, this upmarket (and expensive) restaurant serves international dishes and pizza. Make sure to reserve ahead. Open daily (winter only) for dinner.

Innsbruck ☎ 02627 471100 ext. 1206. Conveniently located at the base of the ski lifts, this no-frills restaurant dishes up standard Argentine food like *guizos* (stews) and

pasta at relatively reasonable prices. Open daily (winter only) for breakfast, lunch, dinner and for cocktails during the small hours.

UFO Point ☎ 02627 471100 ext. 1233. Food includes decent (but expensive) pizzas and sushi. After dinner, it turns into the local nightlife hotspot. Open daily (winter only) from lunch until late.

Malargüe and around

MALARGÜE is a laidback town 186km south of San Rafael by RN-144 and RN-40. The biggest settlement in the southernmost section of Mendoza Province, it's less of a destination in itself, and more – like San Rafael – a base for exploring the prime tourist sites in this region. It's more conveniently located for most of these than San Rafael, although it has a far more limited choice of accommodation.

The town is within day-trip distance of the black and red pampas of **La Payunia**, a nature reserve where flocks of guanacos and ñandús roam over lava flows. Far nearer – and doable as half-day outings – are some remarkable underground caves, the **Cueva de la Brujas**, and **Laguna Llancanelo**, a shining lagoon flecked pink with flamingoes and crammed with other aquatic birdlife. You could also consider staying here in order to go skiing at **Las Leñas**, 77km away (see p.364).

The core of the town lies on either side of RN-40, called Avenida San Martín within the town's boundaries, a wide, rather soulless avenue along which many of the hotels are located, as well as a couple of cafés, the bank and telephone centres. **Plaza General San Martín** is the focal point, with its benches shaded by pines and native trees, but it's nothing to get excited about. The town is extremely easy to find your way around, although it's fairly spread out. Its handful of attractions are clustered together at the northern reaches, beyond the built-up area.

Centro de Convenciones y Exposiciones Thesaurus

Av San Martín s/n • Mon–Sat 9am–9pm, Sun 4–9pm • Free • ☎ 0260 447 0027, ⓦ bit.ly/CentroConvencionesThesaurus

Malargüe's pride and joy is the fine little **Centro de Convenciones y Exposiciones Thesaurus**, subtly plunged underground in the middle of the centre's adjoining garden. Its postmodern design, incorporating some fine workmanship, is certainly impressive for a town of this size. The centre also houses an art gallery with small exhibition rooms linked by corridors, intended to echo a cave's labyrinth.

Observatorio Pierre Auger

Av San Martín Norte 304 • Mon–Fri 9am–12.30pm & 3.30–6pm, Sat 3.30–6pm • Free • ⓦ visitantes.auger.org.ar

The convention centre complements the **Observatorio Pierre Auger**, opposite, part of a fascinating twenty-year astrophysics project to measure the mysterious ultra-high-energy cosmic rays that bombard Earth. A grid of 1600 cream-coloured water tanks serving as particle detectors has been placed 1.5km apart across an area of the Pampas fifteen times the size of Buenos Aires – look out for them as you drive into town. It makes hunting for a needle in a haystack seem like child's play: only one such ray is likely to hit a square kilometre of the Earth's surface per century.

Museo Regional

Av San Martín s/n • Tues–Sun 9am–1pm & 4–8.30pm • Free

6

The town's **Museo Regional** consists of a four-room display in a neatly refurbished building, including objects as varied as ammonites, guanaco leather, clay pipes for religious ceremonies, jewellery and dinosaur remains. A new annexe to the museum houses Mi Viejo Almacén, a shop selling local artisan goods.

ARRIVAL AND DEPARTURE   MALARGÜE AND AROUND

By bus Buses from Mendoza and San Rafael stop at the bus terminal at Esquibel Aldao and Av General Roca, six blocks south and two west of central Plaza San Martín, but will also drop off and collect passengers at the plaza en route.
Destinations Las Leñas (June–Sept daily; 1hr 15min); Mendoza (3 daily; 6hr); San Rafael (10 daily; 2hr 45min).

INFORMATION AND TOURS

Tourist information Malargüe's excellent tourist office (daily 8am–9pm; ☎0260 447 1659, ⓦmalarguetegusta.com) is in a fine rustic building on RN-40 by the Parque de Ayer, four blocks north of the plaza. There's plenty of information on what to see and do, and on places to stay, tour operators and fishing in nearby rivers.
Tour operators Choique, Av San Martín and Rodríguez, 1st floor (☎0260 447 0391, ⓦchoique.net), knows the terrain inside out and offers excellent excursions to La Payunia and all the main sights of southern Mendoza; the long-established Karen Travel, Av San Martín 54 (☎0260 15 463 1594, ⓦkarentravel.com.ar), can get you to just about any site you might wish to see, in a group or on a

more personalized tour.
Ski equipment Equipment, including snowboards, can be rented from a number of outlets along Av San Martín, including Aires de Libertad (Av San Martín 129; ☎0260 447 1416) and Sport Center (Av San Martín 615; ☎0260 447 2088, ⓦsportcentermalargue.com.ar), which has a good range of skis. It makes sense to rent gear in Malargüe rather than at Las Leñas – it's cheaper and you'll avoid the queues – but try to avoid travelling with a second pair of footwear that you can't pop in a daypack as lockers at Las Leñas are expensive. Kitting yourself out fully will cost some US$70 or more a day, depending on the quality of skis. Rental shops are generally open until around 9pm.

ACCOMMODATION

The range of accommodation in Malargüe is expanding with every year, though higher-end options are still limited. Additionally, twice a year (in March and Nov), what decent options there are get packed out with physicists, who come for an international convention on the Pierre Auger experiment (see p.366).

Cisne Villegas and Civit ☎0260 447 1350. Clean, functional hotel in the centre of town, in an intriguing cuboid building. Rooms are well heated in winter. $800
Eco Hostel Malargüe Colonia Pehuenche I, Finca N. 65 (ask them for a taxi number for the transfer when booking) ☎0260 15 440 2439, ⓦhostelmalargue.com. Rustic HI hostel set on an organic farm 5km south of town. Horseriding excursions and laundry service offered. Dorms $160; doubles $500
Hostel La Caverna Cte Rodríguez 445 Este ☎0260 447 2569. This laidback hostel has a spacious common area and plenty of dorm beds. Dorms $200; doubles $650
Maggio Hotel Manuel Ruibal 592 ☎0260 447 2496, ⓦmaggiohotel.com. The most pristine mid-range option with large, well-furnished rooms in a contemporary style.

The whole hotel is done out in refreshing green tones and the bed linen is luxurious. $800
Nord Patagonia Fray Inalicán 52 ☎0260 447 2256. Pleasant, compact hostel right on the main square. Dorms $150; doubles $450
Río Grande Av San Martín 1500 ☎0260 447 1589, ⓦriograndemalargue.com.ar. Friendly owners, a choice between decent but very plain rooms and more commodious, tastefully decorated ones, and a restaurant serving delicious food, including local specialities such as trout and roast goat. $918
Rioma Fray Inalicán 68 ☎0260 447 1065, ⓦhotelriomacom.ar. Reasonable, if rather nondescript, hotel in the centre of town. There is an outdoor swimming pool and the owners lay on barbecues on request. $900

EATING

La Cima Av San Martín 886 (where RN-40 enters town from the north) ☎ 0260 429 0671. This *parrilla*, by far the best in Malargüe, serves up huge hunks of beef, lamb and goat – you can walk off the calories getting back into town. Mon–Sat noon–2.45pm & 9–11.45pm.

Cuyam-Co El Dique, 8km west of Malargüe ☎ 0260 15 466 1917. This is a commercial trout farm where you can catch your own fish, though you can also eat fish freshly caught by staff. It is then perfectly cooked and served with an excellent local rosé; try the delicious smoked trout or fresh trout pâté, too. It is worth booking ahead. Daily 12.30–2.30pm & 8pm–late.

Reserva Faunística Laguna de Llancanelo

Access to the reserve is via RP-186, which branches east off RN-40 some 20km south of Malargüe; it's then another 20km to the reserve entrance, near the shallow cavern known as the Cueva del Tigre

The **Reserva Faunística Laguna de Llancanelo** makes an easy half-day trip from Malargüe. It's an internationally recognized RAMSAR wetland, with large populations of waterfowl all year round, although you'll find the greatest concentrations in spring and summer, as many species come here to nest. On windless days, the shallow saline lagoon's mirror-still waters in the middle of a huge dried-up lake bed make for a fantastic sight. When the lake is not dried out you'd be very unlucky not to spot flocks of flamingo, at times so huge that whole areas of the lake's surface are turned uniformly pink. Other species of bird include black-necked swan, several kinds of duck, grebe and teal, gulls, terns and curlews. Parts of the reserve are out of bounds all year, and access to others is restricted to non-critical seasons. The park is patrolled by *guardaparques*, and it is best to go on an organized tour from Malargüe (see p.367), as you'll get more out of visiting the lagoon with someone who knows the terrain and the fauna. Preferably come very early in the morning or in the late afternoon and evening, when the light is fabulous and the wildfowl more easily spotted. Note, however, that in the last few years the water levels of the lake have dropped significantly, so check with operators on its latest condition.

Caverna de las Brujas

$165 • Karen Travel and Choique organize tours (around 6–8hr; $710/person including entry fee; no under-7s)

The **Caverna de las Brujas** is a marvellous cave that plunges deep into the earth, just 73km southwest of Malargüe, 8km off RN-40 along a marked track. The road climbs over the scenic **Cuesta del Chihuido**, which affords fantastic views of the Sierra de Palauco to the east, in a region of outstanding beauty enhanced by sparse but attractive vegetation. This area is covered by a thick layer of marine sedimentary rock, through which water has seeped, creating underground cave systems. The name Caverna de las Brujas literally means "witches' cave", and local legends say that it was used as a meeting place for sorcerers. Las Brujas is a karstic cave, filled with rock formations, including some impressive **stalactites and stalagmites**; typically they have been given imaginative names such as "the Virgin's Chamber", "the Pulpit" and "the Flowers". Water continues to seep inside, making the walls slippery, as if they were awash with soapsuds. Although the tourist circuit is only 260m long and never descends more than 6m below the surface, the experience is memorable.

The *caverna* lies within a provincial park, and a small *guardería* stands nearby; ask here for the key to the padlocked gates that protect the grotto. It's compulsory to enter with a guide. Wear good walking shoes and take a jumper – the difference in temperature between inside and out can be as much as 20°C – and a pocket torch, though miners' helmets are also supplied; a highlight inside the cave is experiencing the total darkness by turning out all lights and getting used to the spooky atmosphere.

La Payunia

The highlight of any trip to southernmost Mendoza Province, yet overlooked by most visitors because of its relative inaccessibility, **La Payunia**, protected by the Reserva Provincial

OPPOSITE PARQUE NACIONAL TALAMPAYA (P.386) >

La Payunia, is a fabulously wild area of staggering beauty, sometimes referred to as the Patagonia Mendocina. Dominated by Volcán Payún Matru (3690m), and its slightly lower inactive neighbour Volcán Payún Liso, it is utterly unspoilt apart from some remnants of old fluorite and manganese mines plus some petrol-drilling derricks, whose nodding-head pump-structures are locally nicknamed "guanacos". Occasionally, you will spot real guanacos, sometimes in large herds, standing out against the black volcanic backdrop of the so-called **Pampa Negra**. This huge expanse of lava in the middle of the reserve was caused by relatively recent volcanic eruptions, dating back hundreds or thousands of years rather than millions, as is the case with most such phenomena in the region. "Fresh" trails of lava debris can be seen at various points in the park, and enormous boulders of igneous rock are scattered over these dark plains, also ejected during the violent volcanic activity. The only vegetation is flaxen grass, whose golden colour is highlighted against the coal-coloured hillsides. Another section of the reserve is the aptly named **Pampa Roja**, where reddish oxides in the lava give the ground a henna-like tint. The threatening hulk of Volcán Pihuel looms at the western extremity of the reserve – its top was blown off by a particularly violent explosion that occurred when the mountain was beneath the sea. Note that there is no accommodation in the park. Your best option is to stay in Malargüe.

ARRIVAL AND DEPARTURE   LA PAYUNIA

By 4WD If you plan to drive there independently, you'll need a 4WD and a good map. You must also take a guide with you – ask in the travel agencies or tourist office in Malargüe.

By organized tour To visit the park, take one of the excellent day-trips run by Karen Travel in Malargüe (see p.367).

San Juan and La Rioja

San Juan and **La Rioja** provinces share some memorable countryside, with range after range of lofty mountains alternating with green valleys of olive groves, onion fields and vineyards, but they're the poorer cousins, in every sense, of Mendoza Province. The provinces' **bodegas**, for example, continue to take a back seat to those of Mendoza and San Rafael, even though their wine can be just as good and they export much of their grape harvest to Mendoza's wineries. **Tourism** has not fully got off the ground here, either, partly owing to poor transport services. To engineer tourist circuits you'll need your own transport, preferably a 4WD.

Outside the capital, La Rioja's population density is very low. It barely reaches one inhabitant per square kilometre, far lower than San Juan – around three people per square kilometre – which is itself only half as densely populated as Mendoza Province. Leaving the cities behind to scout around the outback, you'll experience a real sense of setting off into uncharted territory. Some unpaved roads peter out into tracks barely passable in the hardiest jeep, and the weather conditions can be inclement. However, this inhospitable nature does offer up fantastic opportunities for alternative tourism, such as 4WD trips or hiking.

Club-sandwiched between the precordillera and the two rows of cordillera – known as main and frontal ranges, a geological phenomenon unique to this section of the Andes – are successive chains of valleys. The higher ones over 1500m above sea level are known as the *valles altos*, of which the **Valle de Calingasta** is an outstanding example. Between them the two provinces have four natural parks. The highly inaccessible **Parque Nacional San Guillermo** in San Juan Province adjoins the **Reserva Provincial Las Vicuñas** across the boundary in La Rioja; respectively, they give you a sporting chance of spotting wild pumas, vicuñas and other Andean wildlife, amid unforgettable landscapes. Further east are the provinces' star attractions: **Parque Nacional Talampaya**, with vertiginous red cliffs that make you feel totally insignificant and – only 70km south – its contiguous, unidentical twin, **Parque Provincial Ischigualasto**, more commonly referred to as the Valle de la Luna, an important dinosaur graveyard in a highly photogenic site.

6

THE *ZONDA* EFFECT

San Juan, even more so than the rest of the Cuyo, is prone to the **zonda**, a legendary dry wind that blows down from the Andes and blasts everything in its path like a blowtorch. It's caused by a **thermal inversion** that arises when wet, cold air from the Pacific is thrust abruptly up over the cordillera and is suddenly forced to dump its moisture, mostly in the form of snow, onto the skyscraper peaks, before helter-skeltering down the other side into the deep chasm between the Cordillera Principal and the precordillera, which acts like a very high brick wall. Forced to brake, the *zonda* rubs against the land like tyre rubber against tarmac, and the resulting friction results in **blistering temperatures** and an atmosphere you can almost see. Mini-tornadoes can sometimes also occur, whipping sand and dust up in clearly visible spirals all along the region's desert-like plains. The Cuyo's answer to the *Föhn*, mistral or sirocco, ripping people's nerves to shreds, the *zonda* is one of the world's nastiest meteorological phenomena. Although it can blow at any time of year, the *zonda* is most frequent in the winter months, particularly August, when it can suddenly hike the temperature by ten to fifteen degrees in a matter of hours.

San Juan and around

Some 165km north of Mendoza, the city of **SAN JUAN** basks in the sun-drenched valley of the Río San Juan, which twists and turns between several steep mountain ranges. The city revels in its pet name, Residencia del Sol. In some of its barrios it has rained only a couple of times over the past decade, and the provincial average is less than 100mm a year. When it does rain, it's usually in the form of violent storms, as savage as the *zonda* wind that occasionally stings the city (see box above). All this sunshine – more than nine hours a day on average – quickly ripens the sweetest imaginable grapes, melons and plums, irrigated by the pre-Columbian canals that have helped the city to prosper over the years. But nature is also a foe: periodic tremors remind *sanjuaninos* that they live along one of the world's most slippery seismic faults; the Big One is dreaded as much here as in California.

One of South America's strongest earthquakes ever recorded flattened San Juan in 1944 and as a result the city has hardly any buildings more than 70 years old. It's modern and attractive, but San Juan is also quite conservative compared with its much bigger rival Mendoza. Around a third of a million people live in Greater San Juan, but in the compact microcentro everyone seems to know everyone else. Broad pavements, grand avenues and long boulevards shaded by rows of flaky-trunked plane trees lend the city a feeling of spaciousness and openness, making San Juan a comfortable starting point for touring some of the country's finest scenery. Destinations close to the city include an **archeological museum** in the southern suburbs and the mind-bogglingly grotesque pilgrim site of **Difunta Correa**, to the east.

The total area of San Juan city is extensive but easy to find your way around, as the grid is fairly regular and the streets don't change name. In all directions from the intersection of Calle Mendoza and Avenida San Martín, the city's point zero, the cardinal directions are added to the street name; for example, Avenida Córdoba oeste (west) or este (east), or Calle Tucumán norte (north) or sur (south).

Brief history

The city was founded by the Spanish aristocrat Juan Jufré as San Juan de la Frontera on June 13, 1562, during an expedition from Santiago de Chile, and since then it has had a persistently troubled history. In 1594, the settlement was washed away by floods, and in 1632 it was again destroyed, this time in attacks by the Huarpe people. The following year an uprising by the indigenous inhabitants was brutally put down; seventeen were hanged on the Plaza Mayor as an example. In the middle of the nineteenth century, San Juan found itself at the heart of the country's civil war when its progressive leader, Dr Antonino Aberastain, was assassinated by federalist troops.

In 1885 the arrival of the railways heralded a change to San Juan's backwater status, as Basque, Galician and Andalucian immigrants began arriving.

Like Mendoza, the city has had terrible luck with seismic shocks: several violent earthquakes struck the city in the 1940s, the strongest of all, reaching around 8.5 on the Richter scale, hitting San Juan on January 15, 1944. It flattened the city and killed more than ten thousand people; during a gala held in Buenos Aires to raise funds for the victims shortly afterwards, an as yet relatively unknown army officer, Juan Domingo Perón, met an equally obscure actress, Eva Duarte.

6

Plaza 25 de Mayo

Plaza 25 de Mayo is the city centre, surrounded by terraced cafés and shops. The controversial **cathedral**, too modern for many tastes, on the northwest edge of the plaza, has a 50m brick campanile, built in the 1960s, that takes its inspiration from the tower of St Mark's in Venice. You can climb or take the lift almost to the top of the **bell tower** (daily 9am–1pm & 5–9pm; $20) – which plays the national anthem on special occasions – for panoramic views.

Museo Casa de Sarmiento

Sarmiento 21 sur • Mon–Fri 9am–8.30pm, Sat & Sun 10.30am–4pm • $20 • Tours hourly in Spanish, twice daily in English; call ahead to confirm time • ⓦ casanatalsarmiento.cultura.gob.ar

Opposite the tourist office is the city's most famous historical site, the **Museo Casa de Sarmiento**. The house where Sarmiento, Argentine president and Renaissance man, was born on February 15, 1811, was only slightly damaged in the 1944 earthquake, thanks to its sturdy adobe walls and sandy foundations. It has since been restored several times, to attain its present gleaming state – for the Sarmiento centenary in 1911 it was declared a national historic monument, Argentina's first. It's a beautiful, simple whitewashed house built around a large patio, with a neat fig tree. The rooms contain an exhibition of Sarmiento relics and personal effects, plenty of portraits and signs of sycophancy, echoed by the gushing commentary of the guides who steer you round.

Museo Santiago Graffigna

Colón 1342 norte • Thurs– Sat 11am–4pm • Free • ☎ 0264 421 4227 • Bus #12A from Av Libertador San Martín, $5

The most notable bodega to visit is the **Bodega Graffigna**, now incorporating a wine museum – the **Museo Santiago Graffigna**. Located in a beautiful brick reconstruction of the pre-quake winery, it still produces red and white wines, among the best in the province. The displays use audiovisual techniques to give a guided tour (English included), and are a tribute to the Graffigna family, who went on producing wine despite major setbacks, not least the 1944 quake. The company is now owned by the French drinks company Pernod Ricard.

Museo Arqueológico Profesor Mariano Gambier

On RN-40 between Progreso and c/5 • Mon–Fri 8am–2pm • Free • ☎ 0264 424 1424 • Take bus number #50 from Laprida and Mendoza and ask the driver to drop you off at RN-40 and Boulevard Sarmiento. You can also take a taxi

Some 6km south of San Juan centre, the **Museo Arqueológico Profesor Mariano Gambier** in the Rawson neighbourhood is worth the trek. Don't be put off by its location in an industrial warehouse – inside, the highly academic presentation, by San Juan University, takes you through the prehistory and history of the provinces' cultures, from the so-called Cultura de la Fortuna (10,000–6000 BC), of which there are just a few tools as evidence, to the Ullum-Zonda civilization of the Huarpe people, whose land was invaded first by the Inca in the fifteenth century and then by colonizers from Chile in the sixteenth.

The museum's highlight, though, is a set of **mummified bodies** dating from the first century BC through to the fifteenth century AD, with the most impressive of all discovered in 1964 at over 4500m in the cordillera, in northern San Juan Province.

Kept in an antiquated fridge is **La Momia del Cerro el Toro**, probably the victim of an Inca sacrifice; the body is incredibly well preserved, down to her eyelashes and leather sandals. Other items worth a mention are a 2000-year-old carob-wood **mask**, some fine **basketwork** coloured with natural pigments and ancient ponchos with geometric patterns. All the exhibits are labelled in Spanish and English.

ARRIVAL AND INFORMATION

By plane Las Chacritas airport (officially called Domingo Faustino Sarmiento airport), small but functional, is 12km east of the city, just off RN-20 (☎0264 425 4133); there are plenty of taxis and *remises* to the centre ($110). There are frequent flights to Buenos Aires (3–4 daily; 1hr 40min).

By bus The city's user-friendly bus station, with regular services all over the province, region and country, is twelve blocks east of the central Plaza 25 de Mayo, at Estados Unidos 492 sur (☎0264 422 1604).

SAN JUAN AND AROUND

Destinations Barreal (2 daily; 5hr); Buenos Aires (10 daily; 16hr); Córdoba (5 daily; 8hr 30min–9hr 50min); Huaco (daily; 3hr); La Rioja (13 daily; 6hr); Mendoza (hourly; 2hr 20min); Rodeo (1–2 daily; 3hr); Salta (5 daily; 16hr); (San Agustín de) Valle Fértil (3 daily; 4hr); San José de Jáchal (5–6 daily; 2hr 15min); San Rafael (2 daily; 5hr 45min).

Tourist information The extremely helpful main provincial tourist office is at Sarmiento 24 sur (daily 8am–8pm; ☎0264 421 0004, ⊛turismo.sanjuan.gov.ar /sanjuanlaestrelladelosandes.com).

ACCOMMODATION

Albertina Mitre 31 este ☎0264 421 4222, ⊛hotelalbertina.com. Tastefully decorated, comfortable if rather cramped rooms in a refurbished hotel on the main square, with parking. Breakfasts are disappointing. **$605**

Alhambra General Acha 180 sur ☎0264 421 4780, ⊛alhambrahotel.com.ar. Medium-sized rooms, each with an en-suite bathroom, in this well-run but rather stuffy establishment with friendly staff. **$400**

Alkázar Laprida 84 este ☎0264 421 4965, ⊛alkazarhotel.com.ar. One of San Juan's few luxury hotels; although on the impersonal side, it does have extremely smart rooms, with modern bathrooms and sweeping views across the city, and a swimming pool in the grounds. The decor is quite dated, though. **$990**

América 9 de Julio 1052 este ☎0264 421 4514, ⊛hotel-america.com.ar. Agreeable, traditional, small hotel. Popular, so call ahead to reserve. All rooms have an en-suite bathroom. Guests are entitled to free use of a swimming pool, a 20min walk away. **$570**

Camping Municipal Rivadavia RP-12 ☎0264 433 2374. Located opposite the racetrack, with a swimming pool and very decent facilities, this site is popular with families from San Juan. **$120**

Camping El Pinar Within the grounds of the Parque Sarmiento, along RP-14 just before the Dique Nivelador ☎0264 433 2374. Set amid a refreshing wood of pines, cypresses and eucalyptus, this shady site has a bathing area, a canteen and well-kept facilities. Popular among young people and can get a bit too rowdy sometimes. **$110**

Gran Hotel Provincial José Ignacio de la Roza 132 este ☎0264 430 9999, ⊛granhotelprovincial.com. A conventional hotel with pool and old-fashioned polite service, right at the centre of San Juan, a few steps from the Plaza 25 de Mayo. Beige is the predominant colour. **$1000**

Jardín Petit 25 de Mayo 345 este ☎0264 421 1825 or ☎0264 421 1464, ⊛jardinpetithotel.com.ar. Small, functional rooms and a bright patio with a small pool overlooked by the breakfast room. Lots of bright colours in the public areas; the rooms are much duller. **$550**

Nuevo Suizo Salta 272 sur ☎0264 421 0067. Newly renovated hotel with modern design aspirations that looks better in photos than in reality. Good value, though. **$620**

El Refugio Ramón y Cajal 97 norte and San Luís ☎0264 421 3087, ⊛elrefugioaparthotel.com.ar. Attractive, professionally run *apart-hotel*, with car park, a refreshing little pool, and tastefully decorated duplex apartment-like rooms, with kitchenettes, bright bathrooms and breakfast served in the room or outside. **$700**

San Francisco Av España 284 sur ☎0264 422 3760. Very reliable place, with smart, simply decorated rooms, modern bathrooms and friendly service; the small bar is open 2pm–midnight. **$450**

Zonda Hostel Caseros 486 sur ☎0264 420 1009, ⊛zondahostel.com.ar. This relaxed and very helpful youth hostel has clean dorms, outdated bathrooms, and a small garden, with breakfast included. Dorms **$130**; doubles **$320**

EATING

San Juan has a wide range of **places to eat**, including one of the region's best vegetarian restaurants, as well as plenty of pizzerias, *parrillas* and *tenedor libre* joints. Most of the best places are in the western, residential part of the city, near the Parque de Mayo. **Café** life is all part of the *paseo* tradition, imported lock, stock and barrel from Spain, but later in the evening most *sanjuaninos* entertain themselves in their gardens, round a family *asado*.

Abuelo Yuyi Av José Ignacio de la Roza and Urquiza ☎0264 422 1011. The most popular pizzeria in town, offering delicious thick-crust pizzas with a variety of toppings. Daily 9pm–1/1.30am.

Baró Rivadavia 55 oeste ☎0264 420 3066, ⓦbarorestaurant.com.ar. Colourful and airy resto-bar with tasty Italian food. Also good for an Argentine *merienda* in the afternoon. Mon–Thurs 7.30am–2am, Fri 7.30am–3am, Sat 8am–3am, Sun 10am–8pm.

Bonafide Plaza 25 de Mayo, esq Mendoza y Rivadavia. A bustling meeting place for the city's movers and shakers near the cathedral. Part of an upmarket café chain famous for its chocolate and decent strong coffees. Mon–Sat 7am–9.30pm.

★**De Sánchez** Rivadavia 61 oeste ☎0264 420 3670, ⓦdesanchezrestoran.com.ar. San Juan's most fashionable restaurant, under the same ownership as and right next door to *Baró*. This chic belle époque-style restaurant serves imaginative contemporary cuisine and displays a connoisseur's selection of books, albums and CDs, many of which are for sale. Good-value lunchtime menus. Mon–Thurs 12.30–3.30pm & 9pm–12.30am, Fri 12.30–3.30pm & 9pm–1.30am, Sat 9pm–1.30am.

Freud Café Plaza 25 de Mayo ☎0264 427 2157. A popular establishment on the eastern side of the main square where the locals come for coffee, drinks, lots of gossip and football chat. Daily 24hr.

Remolacha Av José Ignacio de la Roza 199 oeste ☎0264 422 070. Traditional *parrilla* serving meat, pasta and *minutas*. Delightful garden and courteous old-school service, but has a tendency to overcook the meat. Daily noon–3pm & 8.30pm–1am.

Rigoletto Paula A. de Sarmiento 418 sur ☎0264 426 4331. This place offers a cosy atmosphere and friendly service, as well as delicious pizzas and pasta. Daily 9.30pm–late.

El Rinconcito Del Bono 321 sur ☎0264 426 5740. Offbeat place with psychedelic decor, Latino music and a range of Mexican tacos, Colombian *arepas* (corn pancakes) and Cuban rice dishes, plus tropical cocktails. Wed–Sun 9.30pm–late.

★**Soychú** Av José Ignacio de la Roza 223 oeste ☎0264 422 1939. Delightful vegetarian restaurant serving fabulous dishes, in a bright, airy space; office workers flock here to take food away, so come early. Mon–Sat noon–3pm & 8pm–midnight, Sun noon–3pm.

6

DRINKING AND NIGHTLIFE

San Juan's best **nightlife** is found in the outskirts of town, with just a couple of decent **bars** in the centre.

Flores Entre Ríos 145 sur ☎0264 408 4045, ⓦfacebook.com/FLoresMusicBar. One of few decent bars situated in the city centre with either live music or a DJ spinning tunes at night. Mixed *sanjuanino* crowd (although generally leaning towards a slightly younger clientele). Daily 9am–3pm & 7pm–4.30am.

★**Ilinca** Morón 1031 sur, Rivadavía, Marquesado ☎0264 416 2859, ⓦbit.ly/IlincaComplejoRural. Outdoor bar and restaurant 25 minutes from the city centre with a delightful atmosphere, live music every night and tasty pizzas. On site there are also shops selling artisan goods and organic food. Oct–April Thurs–Sun 9.30pm–3am.

DIFUNTA CORREA

As legend would have it, during the Civil War in the 1840s, a local man named Baudilio Correa was captured, taken to La Rioja and killed; his widow Deolinda decided to walk to La Rioja with their baby boy to recover Baudilio's corpse. Unable to find water, she dropped dead by the roadside, where a passer-by found her, the baby still suckling from her breast. Her grave soon became a holy place and lost travellers began to invoke her protection, claiming miraculous escapes from death on the road. The story of the widow Correa is believed to be indigenous in origin but has been mingled with Catholic hagiography in a country where the borderline between religion and superstition can often be very faint. The **Difunta Correa** – *difunta* meaning deceased – is now the unofficial saint of all travellers, but especially bus- and truck-drivers. Thousands of people visit the shrine every year, over 100,000 of them during Holy Week alone, many of them covering part of the journey on their knees; National Truck-Drivers' Day in early November also sees huge crowds arriving here. Some people visit the shrine itself – where a hideous statue of the Difunta, complete with suckling infant, lies among melted candles, prayers on pieces of paper and votive offerings including people's driving licences, the remains of tyres and photographs of mangled cars from which the occupants miraculously got out alive – while others just deposit a bottle of mineral water on the huge mountain of plastic built up over the years.

El Santuario de la Difunta Correa

65km east of San Juan by RN-141 • Regular buses to Vallecito stop here, but unless you're really curious, it's only worth the short stop you get on the bus route from San Juan to La Rioja, or if you're travelling under your own steam between San Juan and Ischigualasto

The most unusual site around San Juan lies some 65km east of the city: **El Santuario de la Difunta Correa** is both a repellent and an intriguing place and one of the most concrete examples of how indigenous legends and Roman Catholic fanaticism have melded together into one belief (see box, p.375). All around Argentina you'll come across mini-Difunta **shrines**, sometimes little more than a few bottles of mineral water heaped at the roadside – and easily mistaken for a particularly bad bout of pollution. But the original shrine is here. Past the suburbs, the landscape turns into desert-like plains, complete with sand dunes; to the north the reddish Sierra Pie de Palo ripples in the distance, relieving the monotony. Suddenly, in the middle of nowhere, amid its own grim complex of hotels, *confiterías* and souvenir shops and on top of a small hill, is Argentina's answer to Lourdes.

Valle de Calingasta

In the west of San Juan Province is the marvellous, fertile **Valle de Calingasta** – a bright green strip of land around 90km west of the city of San Juan as the crow flies, on the other side of the Sierra del Tontal range, but reached by a long road detour. Its major settlement of interest is **Barreal**, a pleasant, laidback little town set amid fields of alfalfa, onions and maize, with a stupendous backdrop of the sierra, snowcapped for most of the year. Barreal's environs are home to the **Complejo Astronómico El Leoncito**, one of the continent's most important space observatories, and the clay flats of the **Barreal del Leoncito**, used for wind-cart championships. To the east of town is a series of mountains, red, orange and deep pink in colour, known aptly as the **Cerros Colorados** (**Coloured Mountains**). To the southwest of Barreal, RP-400 leads to the tiny hamlet of Las Hornillas, the point of departure for adventurous treks and climbs to the summit of **Cerro Mercedario** (6770m), said by many mountaineers to be the most satisfying climb in the cordillera in this region. In the sedate town of **Calingasta** itself, north of Barreal, the main sight is a fine seventeenth-century **chapel**.

Since the closure of the old RP-12, the main paved route from San Juan to Valle de Calingasta is north via RN-40 to Talacasto, then along RP-436 for 23km, after which you branch left to Calingasta at the main RN-149 junction.

Barreal

The small oasis town of **BARREAL**, set alongside the Río Los Patos, 1650m above sea level, at the southern extreme of the Valle de Calingasta, is a fast up-and-coming, friendly place which makes a great base for adventure tourism in the surrounding area. The central square, **Plaza San Martín**, is the focal point, at the crossroads of Avenida Presidente Roca and General Las Heras. The town enjoys a pleasant climate, and the views to the west – of the cordillera peaks, including the majestic **Cerro Mercedario**, El Polaco, La Ramada and Los Siete Picos de Ansilta, seen across a beautiful plain shimmering with onion and maize fields – are superb. Barreal makes a good base if you want to conquer **Mercedario** – one of the Andes' most challenging yet climbable mountains. To the east you can climb up into the coloured mountains, or up to the high point of **Pircas**, which affords one of the most famous of all views of the cordillera, as well as panoramas across to San Juan city.

ARRIVAL AND DEPARTURE   **BARREAL**

By bus Buses to and from San Juan stop in Plaza San Martín (2–5 daily; 4hr 30min).

INFORMATION AND TOURS

Tourist information There's a helpful tourist office at Av Presidente Roca and Las Heras, just by Plaza San Martín (Daily 9am–12.30am). The offices for Parque Nacional El Leoncito (see opposite) are at Cordillera Ansilta s/n

(☎ 02648 441240, ⓦ elleoncito.gob.ar).

Fortuna Viajes For trips in the surrounding area try Fortuna Viajes (☎ 0264 15 404 0913, ⓦ fortunaviajes.com.ar), which

organizes treks and climbs, including that of Mercedario (US$4500/person for a 12-day expedition from Barreal, all-inclusive except food; minimum 2 people).

ACCOMMODATION

Barreal has a surprisingly wide choice of excellent accommodation. As this is spread out over a couple of kilometres – some of it on the northern and southern approaches into town – ask the bus driver to drop you as close to your lodging as possible.

6

Cabañas Doña Pipa Mariano Moreno s/n ☎ 02648 441004. Rents out *cabañas* for up to six people in pleasantly spacious grounds and has a simple hotel annexe. Doubles $\overline{\$400}$; *cabañas* $\overline{\$1100}$

Cabañas Kummel Presidente Roca s/n ☎ 02648 441206. A good option with friendly owners who are very knowledgeable about the area and can also help arrange trips. Sleeps up to six people. $\overline{\$650}$

Eco Posada El Mercedario Av Presidente Roca esq Los Enamorados ☎ 0264 15 509 0907, ⓦ elmercedario .com.ar. A lovingly restored adobe farmhouse, with high, cane ceilings and swept brick floors in the rooms, which are tastefully themed around famous Argentine women, renowned gauchos and others. There's a homely restaurant, horses graze in the garden and the owner runs 4WD tours. $\overline{\$720}$

Hostel Barreal Av San Martin s/n ☎ 02648 441144, ✉ hostelbarreal@hotmail.com. An excellent and restful hostel whose owner organizes rafting trips on the Río Los Patos. Rooms are spotless and there is a convivial atmosphere. Dorms $\overline{\$120}$; doubles $\overline{\$300}$

Hostel Don Lisandro Av San Martín s/n ☎ 0264 15 505 9122, ⓦ donlisandro.com.ar. A well-equipped and wonderfully sociable hostel. The neglected backyard

takes away from the atmosphere, though. Dorms $\overline{\$150}$; doubles $\overline{\$450}$

★ **Posada de Campo La Querencia** 4km south of the main plaza, on C/Florida ☎ 0264 541 6201, ⓦ laquerenciaposada.com. In a beautifully designed building, this posada offers charming, appealingly designed rooms with fabulous views of open country – it's worth paying a little extra for the west-facing ones, looking towards the cordillera. Breakfasts and other meals are irreproachable, as is the friendliness of the welcome. $\overline{\$1150}$

★ **Posada Don Ramón** 8km north of the village, on Av Presidente Roca s/n ☎ 0264 15 404 0913, ⓦ posadadonramon.com.ar. All of the huge rooms are designed to maximize the splendid panoramic views of the cordillera, including Aconcagua and Mercedario. Lie back in your bathroom jacuzzi – or the swimming pool – and enjoy. The place is luxuriously, if simply, furnished, and has a lovely bodega stocked with organic Sanjuanino wines. The proprietor also owns and guides for Fortuna Viajes (see above). $\overline{\$900}$

Posada San Eduardo Av San Martín s/n ☎ 02648 441046. Large, simple rooms set around an old, wisteria-lined colonial-style patio. Its restaurant serves well-cooked, if slightly unimaginative, food and there's a garden pool. $\overline{\$700}$

EATING AND DRINKING

El Alemán Belgrano s/n ☎ 02648 441193. The German-descended owners dish up servings of sauerkraut, smoked hams and goulash with well-prepared vegetables from the

garden and German-style beer, all in a bucolic setting – follow signs from the *Posada San Eduardo*. The owners also rent out *cabaña* accommodation. Daily 6.30–11pm.

Barreal del Leoncito

Immediately south of Barreal along the western side of RN-149 is a huge flat expanse of windswept, hardened clay, the remains of an ancient lake, known as the **Barreal del Leoncito**, the Pampa del Leoncito, or simply the Barreal Blanco. Measuring 14km by 5km, this natural arena, with a marvellous stretch of the cordillera as a background, is used for **wind-car** championships (*carrovelismo* in Spanish) – the little cars with yacht-like sails have reached speeds of over 130km an hour here; contact Sr Rogelio Toro in Barreal if you want to have a go (☎ 0264 671 7196, ✉ dontoro.barreal @gmail.com; main season Nov–Dec; $400 for 2hr with an instructor).

Parque Nacional El Leoncito

Park entrance daily 24hr • Information around 2km from RN-149, just after you turn left to Estación Astronómica Dr. Carlos U. Cesco; daily 8am–6pm • ☎ 02648 441240, ⓦ elleoncito.gob.ar

Some 15km or so further south along RN-149 is a turn-off eastwards up into the **Parque Nacional El Leoncito**, which is symbolized by the ñandú, or Andean rhea. Up on nearby hills are two space **observatories**, among the most important in the world because of the outstanding meteorological conditions hereabouts – averaging more than 320 clear nights a year. About 12km up this track is the park entrance: announce your presence to the *guardaparques*. Note that, frustratingly, there are no public buses south from Parque Nacional El Leoncito or Barreal along RN-149 to Uspallata in Mendoza Province (see p.353).

Complejo Astronómico El Leoncito

5km from the Park Information Office • Tours daily (English & Spanish) 10am–noon & 4–6pm; 30–40min; not permitted for people under 4 or over 70; no wheelchair access • $50 • ☎ 0264 421 3653, ⓦ www.casleo.gov.ar

Visible from far around thanks to its huge white dome, the **Complejo Astronómico El Leoncito**, at an altitude of over 2500m, affords fabulous views of the valley and the cordillera. Inaugurated in 1986, this space observatory was built to resist even earthquakes registering 10 or higher on the Richter scale, an absolute necessity in this area of violent seismic activity. The primary telescope weighs some 40 tonnes, and its main 2.15m-diameter mirror has to be replaced every two years. The guided tour, led by enthusiastic staff members, takes you through the whole process; take warm clothing as the inside is kept cold. Night visits, with food and lodging, are on offer (see below); arrive by 5pm.

Estación Astronómica Dr Carlos U. Cesco

Daily 10am–noon & 4–6pm; night visits 9.30–11pm • $50 • ⓦ www.oafa.fcefn.unsj-cuim.edu.ar

Off a turning 3km back down the track is the relatively modest-looking **Estación Astronómica Dr Carlos U. Cesco**, where the staff will be only too happy to show you the visitors' centre and explain the observatory's work. You can also make night visits (weather permitting), at which you can actually get to use telescopes; take a torch and warm clothing.

ACCOMMODATION	**PARQUE NACIONAL EL LEONCITO**

Complejo Astronómico El Leoncito ☎ 0264 15 459 8286, ⓔ elalemanbarreal@gmail.com. Located inside the observatory (see above) but booked through the *Apart Hotel Alémán*, these rooms make it easier to stay the night and gaze at the nocturnal sky; don't expect any great comfort and certainly not luxury, but everything works. Prices include breakfast and dinner. Book at least 24hr in advance. **$850**

Las Hornillas and Mercedario

The scenic RP-400 strikes out in a southwesterly direction from Barreal to **Las Hornillas**, over 50km away. This tiny hamlet is inhabited mostly by herdsmen and their families amid pastureland and gorse scrub and is effectively the base camp for the mighty **Mercedario**, which looms nearby. If you want to climb this difficult but not impossible mountain, regarded by many as the most noble of all Argentina's Andean peaks, contact Fortuna Viajes in Barreal (see p.377). The nearby rivers are excellent for fishing for trout; ask at the tourist office in Barreal.

Cerros Pintados

The mountainsides to the immediate east of Barreal, accessible by clear tracks, are a mosaic of pink, red, brown, ochre and purple rocks, and the so-called **Cerros Pintados**, or "Painted Mountains", live up to their name. Among the rocky crags, tiny cacti poke out from the cracks, and in the spring they sprout huge wax-like flowers, in translucent shades of white, pink and yellow, among golden splashes of broom-like *brea* shrubs. About 8km north of Barreal, another track heads eastwards from the main road, climbing for 40km past some idyllic countryside inhabited only by the odd goatherd or farming family, to the outlook atop the **Cima del Tontal**, at just over 4000m. To the east there are amazing views down into the San Juan Valley, with the Dique de Ullum glinting in the distance, or west and south to the cordillera, where the peak of Aconcagua and the majestic summit of the Mercedario are clearly visible.

Calingasta and around

The village of **CALINGASTA** is a peaceful place, 37km north of Barreal; its only attraction apart from its idyllic location is the seventeenth-century **Capilla de Nuestra Señora del Carmen**, a simple whitewashed adobe building, with an arched doorway and a long gallery punctuated by frail-looking slender pillars. The bells are among the oldest in the country, and the iron and wooden ladder leading onto the roof is a work of art, too.

From Calingasta it's 125km along RP-412 north to Iglesia, along a dry valley, through the occasional ford, with the Sierra del Tigre to the east and the Cordón de Olivares providing stupendous views to the west. No public transport runs on this stretch.

6

ACCOMMODATION   CALINGASTA

Hotel Nora Aldo Cantoni s/n ☎02648 421027. This simple, comfortable central hotel is by far the best in the region; extras include cable TV and parking. Breakfast not included. **$450**

Valle de Iglesia

The **Valle de Iglesia** is named after one of its main settlements, **Iglesia**, a sleepy village of adobe houses. It is a fertile valley separated from the Valle de Calingasta by the dramatic Cordón de Olivares range of mountains. You can get there from San Juan via RN-40, which forks off to the northwest at Talacasto, some 50km north of the city. From there a mountain road, RP-436, joins up with RN-149 heading north, taking you to Iglesia. More interesting than Iglesia itself is the small market town and windsurf hangout of **Rodeo** to the northeast, along RN-150. Further north still is the idyllic village of **Angualasto**, along the dirt track that leads to one of the country's most recent national parks, **San Guillermo**, the place in Argentina where you are most likely to spot pumas in the wild.

Rodeo and around

RN-150 arches round the pleasant, easy-going market town of **RODEO**. Windsurfing enthusiasts come from afar to take advantage of the superb, consistent winds on the **Dique Cuesta del Viento**, the local reservoir, during high season (Oct–April). Rodeo hosts one of the region's major folk festivals during the first weekend of February, the **Fiesta de la Manzana y la Semilla**, when you can try local specialities such as empanadas and *humitas* and watch dancing and musical groups in the Anfiteatro, just off Santo Domingo in the heart of the town.

North of Rodeo, you can head off towards Angualasto and the Parque Nacional San Guillermo (see p.380), while to the east RN-150 takes you to Jáchal (see p.380 it is an impressive, winding cliffside road that follows the stark valley of the Río Jáchal.

ARRIVAL AND INFORMATION   RODEO AND AROUND

By bus Buses to and from San Juan (3 weekly; 3hr) stop at the main plaza.

Tourist information The town's tourist office is at Plaza de la Fundación s/n (daily 8am–9pm; ☎0264 493 068).

ACCOMMODATION

50 Nudos El Puque s/n ☎011 15 3208 9864, ⓦ 50nudos.com. For relatively luxurious accommodation, aimed at the surfing crowd, this waterside posada offers comfortable rooms and a good restaurant and will get you kitted out to hit the reservoir's azure waters. **$500**

Finca El Martillo 2.5km from the plaza at the town's northernmost end ☎0264 459 0388, ⓦ fincaelmartillo .com. This marvellous farm, producing all kinds of herbs, fresh and preserved fruit and excellent jam and honey (sold at its shop and used in the on-site restaurant, which also specializes in trout and goat), rents out several delightful eight-bed *cabañas*. **$900**

Hostel Rancho Lamaral ☎0264 15 660 1197, ⓦ rancholamaral.com. An excellent place to base yourself if you're keen on joining the *windsurfistas* for real, this atmospherically breezy farmstead is set a short walk from the reservoir's northeastern shore; take a *remise* from town. The owner and staff exude a highly positive vibe, give lessons and will help sort you out with surfing rental gear. Dorms **$200**; doubles **$500**

Angualasto

From Rodeo, RP-407 heads north, cutting through a ridge of rock and sloping down into the valley of the Río Blanco. The little village of **ANGUALASTO**, which has preserved a delightful rural feel, seemingly detached from the modern world, is set among rows of poplars, orchards and small plots of maize, beans and vegetables. It is proud of its little **Museo Arqueológico Luis Benedetti** (Tues–Sun 8.30am–12.30pm & 2.30–6.30pm), whose tiny collection of mostly pre-Columbian finds includes a remarkable 400-year-old mummified corpse, found in a *tumbería* (burial mound), nearby.

El Chinguillo

The road northwards follows the Río Blanco valley, fording it once – often impossible after spring or summer rains or heavy thaws – to the incredibly remote hamlets of Malimán and **El Chinguillo**, the entrance to the Parque Nacional San Guillermo, in a beautiful valley surrounded by huge dunes of sand and mountains scarred red and yellow with mineral deposits. The Solar family's delightful farmhouse provides the only **accommodation** hereabouts (☎0264 443 5328 or ☎0264 671 1412), as well as delicious empanadas and roast lamb.

Parque Nacional San Guillermo

The **Reserva Provincial San Guillermo**, in the far northern reaches of San Juan Province, was the first region in the country to be declared a **UNESCO Biosphere Reserve**, in 1980. Part of the Provincial Reserve, on great heights to the west of the Río Blanco valley, later attained national park status, in 1998: the **Parque Nacional San Guillermo**. The Parque Nacional is home to a huge variety of wildlife. Guanacos and vicuñas abound, along with ñandús, eagles, condors, several different kinds of lizard, foxes and all kinds of waterfowl, including flamingoes, which match the seams of jagged pink rock that run along the mountainsides like a garish zip-fastener. Above all, this is a part of Argentina where if you stay for a number of days you stand an extremely good chance of spotting a puma – a very rare occurrence elsewhere in the country. For some reason the pumas living here are less shy of humans and often approach vehicles; treat these powerful and potentially dangerous creatures with caution. The highest peaks, at well over 5000m, are permanently snowcapped, and the high altitude of the park's roads – as high as 3700m – affects some visitors.

PARK ESSENTIALS	PARQUE NACIONAL SAN GUILLERMO
Planning a visit Visiting requires advance preparation – the park is isolated and the weather can be capricious. You'll need at least three days, and must register with the park office on the western outskirts of Rodeo on Calle La Colonia (Mon–Fri 8am–2pm; ☎02647 493 214, ✉ sanguillermo@apn.gov.ar). **Essentials** Make sure you travel with adequate clothing, fuel and supplies.	**Getting around** You will require a 4WD and a guide (roughly $1500/day), as negotiating the fords can be dangerous, plus you'll have to travel with at least one other vehicle in case of breakdown. Registered guides include Alberto Ramírez (☎0261 15 658 1527) and Ramón Ossa (☎0264 844 1004; book as far in advance as possible). Motorcycles and horses are not allowed.

ACCOMMODATION

Refugio Agua del Godo ☎02647 493214. Two-bedroom, basic bunkbed accommodation in the centre of the park. Bring suitably warm bedding and provisions. Contact the park office in Rodeo if you want to stay the night. Free

San José de Jáchal and around

The small town of **SAN JOSÉ DE JÁCHAL** (usually called simply Jáchal) lies in the fertile valley of the Río Jáchal, 155km due north of San Juan by RN-40. The town was founded in the seventeenth century on the site of a pre Columbian village. Destroyed in a severe earthquake in 1894, it was rebuilt using mud bricks in an Italianate style, with arched facades and galleried patios, focused on the Plaza San Martín.

Jáchal itself isn't much to write home about, but it makes for a convenient stopover. If you have a moment to spare, visit the astonishingly eclectic **Museo Arqueológico Prieto** (daily 9am–noon & 5–7pm), at 25 de Mayo 788 oeste, signposted along RN-150. It is a motley collection of all manner of odds and ends, but among the curios are some fine pre-Columbian artefacts, painstakingly collected and displayed by a local who handed it all over to the police. During the first fortnight in November, the town stages the **Fiesta de la Tradición**, a festival of folklore, feasts and music.

The flour mills

6

Sleepy Jáchal is most famous for a handful of nineteenth-century **flour mills** – now rightly recognized as historic monuments – scattered about attractive farmland immediately to its north. Their beige or whitewashed walls, wonderfully antiquated machinery and enthusiastic owners or managers make for a memorable visit; always offer guides a tip if shown around. **El Molino del Alto** (also called El Molino de García) is the best, as it is fully functioning, and – if he's around – the passion of Dionício Pérez, the manager, is a joy to behold (Spanish only).

The area in which the mills are located is worth a visit in its own right. North of Jáchal, RN-40 suddenly swerves to the east, and the road continuing straight ahead, RP-456, cuts through Jáchal's rural northern suburbs amid bucolic farmland, used to grow wheat, maize, alfalfa and fruit. With the stark mountain backdrop of the Sierra Negra to the east, Sierra de la Batea to the north and Cerro Alto (2095m) to the west, this dazzlingly green valley, dotted with adobe farmhouses, some of them with splendid sun-faded wooden doors, looks like parts of Morocco in the lee of the Atlas. Canals and little ditches water the fields, using snowmelt from the cordillera and precordillera, as rain is rare here.

ARRIVAL AND INFORMATION
SAN JOSÉ DE JÁCHAL AND AROUND

By bus Buses from San Juan stop at the terminal seven blocks southeast of the main plaza.

Tourist information There's a helpful tourist office on the plaza at San Juan 133 (daily 8am–10pm; ☎02647

420124); ask here for updates on which flour mills (see above) are open for visits. They'll also help sort out a *remís* for a tour of the mills (one recommended driver is Urriche Eduardo; ☎0264 15 415 2542).

ACCOMMODATION AND EATING

Hualta Picum Apart-Hotel Sarmiento 749 ☎02647 420774. The best place to stay in town has spacious, bright, well-furnished apartments for up to eight people. Thankfully, given the lack of good eating options in town, you can self-cater. **$600**

Tata Viejo San Martín, Echegaray and General Paz. The only real restaurant in Jáchal offers hearty, inexpensive food, although service is unexceptional – if not downright unfriendly – and the old papa of the name is nowhere to be seen. Daily 12.30–3pm & 8pm–midnight.

Huaco and around

The small village of **HUACO**, shaded by *algarrobos* and eucalyptus, is no more than a cluster of mud-brick houses. It's accessible from Jáchal by taking RP-456 north out of town, then turning right onto RP-49 – which hugs the Sierra Negra before skirting the Dique Los Cauquenes reservoir – and finally right again onto RP-40. Just before you get to the village itself you pass a splendid adobe **flour mill**, similar to those north of Jáchal. Built in the nineteenth century, it belonged to the Docherty family, descendants of an Irishman who fought in the British army that invaded Buenos Aires, was captured and decided to settle in Argentina; Buenaventura Luna (see p.382) was one of their descendants.

Cuesta de Huaco

RP-49 turns into RN-40 just before Huaco, and runs northeast for 145km from Jáchal to Villa Unión in La Rioja Province (see p.385). For part of its route (just before

Huaco), you squeeze along the **Cuesta de Huaco**, a narrow mountain road accurately described as a place "where the reddish dawn lingers on the even redder clay of the mountainside". Those words were sung by deep-voiced crooner **Buenaventura Luna**, real name Eusebio de Jesús Dojorti Roco; he was a highly popular star in the 1940s and 1950s, and is buried in Huaco.

The new **RN-150** is a slightly longer but faster way of reaching Villa Unión, but taking this road means missing out on the Cuesta de Huaco's magnificent views of the arid valleys to the north. It is, though, the safer option in poor weather; the Cuesta de Huaco runs through the Río Bermejo Valley, bone-dry for most of the time but suddenly flooding after storms. Beware of the many deep fords (*badenes*) along the road – if they are full of water, wait for the level to drop before attempting to cross. Even when dry, they can rip tyres if taken too fast.

ACCOMMODATION   **HUACO AND AROUND**

Hostería Huaco La Paz s/n ⓣ0264 518 0001, Ⓦhosteriahuaco.com.ar. This *hostería* sitting just back from the main through road is an airy adobe-style building offering pleasant a/c rooms and spacious *cabañas* (sleeping 5–15 people) with a garden featuring a pool and outdoor jacuzzi. Doubles $400; *cabañas* $600

Parque Provincial Ischigualasto and Parque Nacional Talampaya

San Juan and La Rioja provinces boast two of the most-photographed protected areas in the country, which together have been declared a UNESCO World Heritage Site, as the only place on the Earth's surface where you can see all stages of the Triassic geological era, which witnessed the emergence of the first dinosaurs. In San Juan is **Parque Provincial Ischigualasto**, better known as Valle de la Luna – Moon Valley – because of its out-of-this-world landscapes and apocryphal legends. The province has jealously resisted repeated attempts to turn it into a national park, and the authorities are doing a good job of providing easy access and looking after the fragile environment. While he was in office, President Menem, on the other hand, made sure that his native province of La Rioja got its first national park: **Parque Nacional Talampaya**, best known for its giant red-sandstone cliffs, which are guaranteed to impress even the most jaded traveller. It's also the country's best example of desert *monte* scrub – a vulnerable ecosystem with rare fauna and flora, and the only habitat endemic to Argentina.

While you can visit both parks in the same day from either **Villa Unión** in La Rioja (see p.385) or the more appealing town of **San Agustín de Valle Fértil** in northeastern San Juan Province, you can get more from the parks by splitting your visits; Talampaya especially merits a longer visit. In many ways it is wise to go to Talampaya in the morning, when the sun lights up the coloured rocks and illuminates the canyon, whereas Ischigualasto is far more impressive in the late afternoon and at sunset in particular. If possible, avoid the gruelling day-trips offered from San Juan, or even La Rioja.

San Agustín de Valle Fértil

Set among enticing landscapes some 250km northeast of San Juan by RN-141 and RP-510, the oasis town of **SAN AGUSTÍN DE VALLE FÉRTIL** is the best base for visiting Parque Provincial Ischigualasto, about 80km to the north, via Los Baldecitos. It's built around a mirror-like reservoir, the Dique San Agustín just up in the hills – cacti and gorse grow on its banks, and a small peninsula juts artistically into the waters. The town prospered in the nineteenth century thanks to the gold, iron and quartz mines and marble quarries in the mountains nearby, but it has now turned to tourism as its source of income, to supplement meagre farm earnings. The fertile valley that gives it its name – sometimes it's referred to simply as "Valle Fértil" – is a patchwork of maize fields, olive groves and pasture for goats and sheep. Unsurprisingly, the local cheese and roast kid are recommended.

ARRIVAL AND DEPARTURE

By bus Buses from San Juan (3 daily; 3hr 30min–4hr) and La Rioja (3 weekly; 4hr) arrive at the terminal, which is

SAN AGUSTÍN DE VALLE FÉRTIL

located at Santa Fe and Entre Ríos.

INFORMATION AND TOURS

Tourist information The tourist office (daily 7am–midnight; ☎02646 420104) on Plaza San Agustín is extremely helpful and can fix you up with guides and transport both to Ischigualasto and to other, less dramatic, sites in the nearby mountains, including pre-Hispanic petroglyphs.

Paula Tour Tour operator running trips to Ischigualasto

(Tucumán s/n; ☎0264 642 0096, ✉ali_tour@hotmail .com), which organizes a number of circuits in the park, including night-time ones around the full moon. You'll need to reserve an English-speaking guide in advance ($80 extra). It also offers tours of the town, the wider province, and Talampaya – the latter often in collaboration with the Runacay agency in Villa Unión (see p.385).

ACCOMMODATION

Altos del Valle Rivadavia 114 ☎02646 420194, ⓦaltosdelvallesj.com.ar. A cosy and intimate apartment hotel with impeccable en-suite rooms equipped with fridge and a/c. There's a peaceful garden with a small swimming pool in the corner. **$550**

Campo Base Valle de la Luna Tucumán and San Luis ☎0264 15 485 9236, ⓦhostelvalledelaluna.com.ar. This very good youth hostel can help organize reasonably priced tours in the area. Brand-new doubles across the road. Dorms **$110**; doubles **$350**

Doña Zoila Mendoza s/n, half a block from the main plaza ☎02646 420147. A decent but basic option, close to the main plaza. Rooms are simple. Dorms **$130**; doubles **$260**

Fatme Rivadavia s/n ☎02646 420014, ✉fatmehotel @yahoo.com.ar. Just three blocks from the central plaza, this is a clean and friendly place with very reasonably

priced rooms, but no meals apart from breakfast are served. Close to restaurants, though. **$400**

Hostería Valle Fértil Rivadavia s/n ☎02646 420015, ⓦhosteriavallefertil.com. A full seven blocks from the plaza, the *hostería* is situated on a high bluff, overlooking the Dique. A comfortable, three-star place, it has a decent restaurant (daily 8.30–11pm) specializing in goat casserole, and good, if cramped, rooms – the more expensive ones with reservoir views. It is a bit run-down though, and the bunker-like design has not aged well. **$532**

Rustico Cerro del Valle Santa Fe s/n ☎02646 420202, ⓦcerrodelvalle.com.ar. This aptly named *hostería*, conveniently located over the road from the bus terminal, has very tastefully decorated and rustic rooms with well-stocked mini-bars, a fine garden pool, hospitable owners and friendly dogs. **$850**

EATING AND DRINKING

A lo de Pepe Rivadavia and Sarmiento. One of the best restaurants in town (not that there are that many to compete with), *A lo de Pepe* is an intimate little place that serves a fine *parrilla*. Daily noon–5pm & 8pm–1am.

La Cocina del Zuma Tucumán 1576 ☎0264 15 562

2955. Just opposite the petrol station at the entrance of town, coming from San Juan along RP-510, lies this *parrilla* serving sizzling *bife de chorizos* ($210), big portions of salads ($60) and tasty *milanesas* ($85). Daily noon–3pm & 8pm–late.

Parque Provincial Ischigualasto

Park entrance daily Oct–March 8am–5pm; April–Sept 9am–4pm • $200 • ☎02646 491 100, ⓦischigualasto.gob.ar

Some 80km north of Valle Fértil, the **PARQUE PROVINCIAL ISCHIGUALASTO**, also known as the Valle de la Luna, or Moon Valley, is San Juan's most famous feature by far, covering nearly 150 square kilometres of desolate but astonishingly varied terrain.

For paleontologists, Ischigualasto's importance is primarily as a rich dinosaur burial ground: two of the world's very oldest species of dinosaur, the diminutive *Euraptor lunesis* and the *Herrerasaurus ischigualastensis*, both dating back some 230 million years, were found here, among many others. The park is also a joy for geologists, as most strata of the 45-million-year Triassic era are in plain view.

The park is in a desert valley between two ranges of high mountains, the Sierra Los Rastros to the west and Cerros Colorados to the east. As witnessed by the mollusc and coral fossils found in the cliffsides, for a long time the whole area was under water. Over the course of millions of years the terrain has been eroded by wind and water, and sections built of volcanic ash have taken on a ghostly greyish-white

6

hue. A set of red-sandstone mountains to the north acts as a perfect backdrop to the paler stone formations and clay blocks, all of which are impressively illuminated in the late evening.

At the entrance, an excellent **museum** exhibits some wonderful stories of forensic paleontology, unravelling some curious examples of dinosaur death (Spanish only).

The rock formations

The majority of visitors come to admire the spectacular lunar landscapes that give the park its popular nickname, and the much publicized and alarmingly fragile **rock formations** – some have already disappeared, the victims of erosion and the occasional flash floods that seem to strike with increasing frequency. **Cerro El Morado** (1700m), a barrow-like mountain that according to local lore is shaped like a man lying on his back, dominates the park to the east. A segmented row of rocks is known as El Gusano (the Worm); a huge set of vessel-like boulders is known as El Submarino; a sandy field dotted with cannonball-shaped stones is dubbed the Cancha de Bolas (the Ball-court). One famous formation, painfully fragile on its slender stalk, is El Hongo (the Mushroom), beautifully set off against the red sandstone cliffs behind.

Flora and fauna

Another of the park's attractions is its wealth of flora and fauna. The main plant varieties are the native *brea*, three varieties of the scrawny *jarilla*, both black and white species of *algarrobo*, the *chañar*, *retamo* and *molle* shrubs and four varieties of cactus. Animals that you are likely to spot here include European hares, Patagonian hares, the *vizcacha*, the grey fox, armadillos and small rodents, plus several species of bat, frog, toad, lizard and snake. Condors and ñandús are often seen, too, while guanacos may be spotted standing like sentinels atop the rocks, before scampering off.

Routes through the park

The main driving tour follows a set **circuit**, beginning in the more lunar landscapes to the south. Panoramic outlook points afford stunning views of weird oceans of hillocks. These are the typical moonscapes, but they look uncannily like the famous landscapes of Cappadocia, with their Gaudí-esque pinnacles and curvaceous mounds. The whole tour takes at least a couple of hours to be done at all comfortably. But be warned that sudden summer storms can cut off the tracks for a day or two, in which case you may not be able to see all of the park. Apart from the main vehicle circuit (which you can also arrange to do at night around full-moon time), there are a couple of other options: a **mountain bike** circuit or a **trek** to climb Cerro El Morado (contact an agency in Valle Fértil, such as Paula Tour; see p.383). RN-150 that skirts the park's southern boundary joins up Los Baldecitos with San José de Jáchal (see p.380), finally creating a much-needed tourist circuit, and providing an alternative route to Villa Unión.

ARRIVAL AND INFORMATION

PARQUE PROVINCIAL ISCHIGUALASTO

Arrival The park can be visited only in a vehicle – either your own or that of a tour operator. You'll be assigned a *guardaparque* – many of whom only speak Spanish – who will accompany your convoy. Convoys leave hourly, and at busy times (Jan–March) can sometimes involve more than thirty vehicles. If you're seeking more solitude, arrive when the park opens or later in the afternoon; big convoys can also generate a lot of dust and considerably reduce the time you get to spend at each stop. Visiting it by public transport is complicated and not advised.

When to visit The optimal time of day for visiting the

park is in the mid- to late afternoon, when the light is the most flattering. That way you also catch the mind-boggling sunsets that illuminate the park, turning the pinkish orange rock a glowing crimson, which contrasts with the ghostly greyish white of the moonscapes all around.

Tourist information The *guardería* (daily: Oct–March 8am–5pm last entrance; April–Sept 9am–4pm last entrance; you must leave by dusk; ☎02646 491 100; $200) lies at the entrance to the park, along a well-signposted lateral road off RP-510 at Los Baldecitos.

ACCOMMODATION AND EATING

There is no camping or accommodation and most people stay at either Villa Unión (see below) or, to be closer, Valle Fértil (see p.382). There's a restaurant at the entrance.

Villa Unión and around

The small town of **VILLA UNIÓN**, essentially strung out along the main RN-76 in the parched Valle de Vinchina, 120km northeast of Huaco, isn't much to write home about, but is fast developing as a convenient base for tours to Parque Nacional Talampaya 70km south, but also to the staggeringly desolate Reserva Provincial Las Vicuñas, wrapped around the beautiful Laguna Brava (see p.388), over 150km northwest. The town, formerly called Hornillos, received its name in the nineteenth century in recognition of the hospitality of its people towards peasants thrown off a nearby estancia by the ruthless *estancieros*.

Cuesta de Miranda

Agencies in Villa Unión (see below) do tours, or you can catch the local Ivanlor buses that travel once a day in each direction; from Chilecito, buses continue to La Rioja

A popular trip from Villa Unión is east along RN-40, over the 2025m mountain pass that crosses the Sierra de Famatina and down the fabulous **Cuesta de Miranda**, a sinuous, parapet-like mountain road, on towards Sañogasta and the old mining town of Chilecito. The Río Miranda snakes through a deep gorge, hemmed in by multicoloured cliffs and peaks, striped red, green, blue and yellow with oxidized minerals and strata of volcanic rock.

ARRIVAL AND DEPARTURE   VILLA UNIÓN

By bus At the entrance of town along RN-76 is the bus terminal, serving La Rioja, Chilecito and planned routes to Huaco. Coop Transporte Talampaya (☎03804 15 681114) runs transfers to the park, as well as a couple of circuits within it.

Destinations Chilecito (3 weekly; 4hr 30min); La Rioja (4 daily except Sun; 4hr); Patquía (4 daily except Sun; 3hr); Vinchina (4 daily except Sun; 1hr).

INFORMATION AND TOURS

Tourist information There's an obliging tourist office just before the bus terminal (daily 8am–10pm; ☎03825 470543). The park office for Talampaya (Mon–Fri 7am–2pm, or 6–10pm if the staff are required at the park during high season; ☎03825 470356, ⓦtalampaya.gob .ar) is at San Martín 150, half a block from the plaza.
Runacay First-rate travel agency, located on the main

plaza at Hipólito Irigoyen esq J.V. González (☎03825 470368, ⓦrunacay.com). It runs a variety of tours, prime among them its walking tours of Talampaya (including a night-time option around the full moon), but also other Talampaya options and adventure trips into the cordillera, such as to Laguna Brava. Tours are available in English, Spanish, French and German.

ACCOMMODATION

As with many provincial towns, the accommodation is spread out in the town and its approach roads, so get the bus driver to drop you off as close as possible to where you're staying. The less expensive options can be found in town, while the most luxurious accommodation is a couple of kilometres to the south on RN-76, near RN-40 junction.

Don Remo RN-76 s/n, Barrio San José ☎03825 477755, ⓦhoteldonremo.com.ar. This modern low-rise hotel, split into two buildings and divided by a well-kept garden, has nicely decorated rooms, a very decent restaurant and a swimming pool at the back with a view of the mountains. Service is friendly, and the rooms are very good value. **$600**
Hospedaje Doña Gringa Nicolás Dávila 103 ☎03825 470258. This tiny *hospedaje* has very clean rooms around a

delightful leafy patio. The laidback atmosphere is one of its assets. Breakfast costs extra. **$350**
Noryanepat Joaquín V. González 150 ☎03825 470133, ⓦhotelnoryanepat.com.ar. Basic but acceptable rooms with cramped bathrooms, where the toilets have a tendency to break away from their fittings. Cheap, and conveniently located one block east of the main plaza. **$350**
Pircas Negras RN-76 s/n ☎03825 470611, ⓦhotelpircasnegras.com. Modern hotel built to a

contemporary design with smart rooms, ample parking and a passable restaurant, though service can be sloppy. $\overline{\$1100}$ **Refugio del Condór** Nicolas Davila 121 ☎03804

675400. This hostel is a decent option if you're after a good-value budget choice in town. Dorms come with a/c and there's a very spacious back yard. Dorms $\overline{\$120}$; doubles $\overline{\$300}$

EATING

Laguna Brava Parrillada Plaza San Martín on Av San Martín ☎03825 410686. Don't let the simple look of this no-fuss *parrilla* put you off. Serves decent *milanesas* ($70) and regional delicacies such as *chivito* (goat; $110). Staff

are friendly, if overly laidback. Generous opening hours and one of the few places in town open for a late lunch. Daily 11am–4pm & 7pm–midnight/1am.

Parque Nacional Talampaya

The park's main entrance is a few kilometres down a well-signposted turning off RN-76 at the Puerta de Talampaya • Daily: May–Sept 8.30am–4.30pm; Oct–April 8am–5pm • $120 • ⑩ talampaya.gob.ar

The entrance to **Parque Nacional Talampaya** is 55km down RN-76 from Villa Unión, and then along a signposted road to the east. Coming from the south, it's 93km north of Ischigualasto and 190km from Valle Fértil. The park's main feature is a wide-bottomed canyon flanked by 180m-high, rust-coloured sandstone cliffs, so smooth and sheer that they look as if they were sliced through by a giant cheese wire. Another section of the canyon is made up of rock formations that seem to have been created as part of a surreal Gothic cathedral. Added attractions are the presence of several bird species, including condors and eagles, as well as rich flora and some pre-Columbian petroglyphs. The park's name comes from the cacán words *ktala* – the locally abundant *tala* bush – and *ampaya*, meaning dry riverbed. Avoid Easter if possible, when the park is at its busiest; the middle of the day in the height of summer, when it can be unbearably hot; and the day after a storm, when the park closes because of floods. The *zonda* wind (see box, p.372) can also cause the park to close. In midwinter, it can be bitterly cold. The best time of day by far to visit is soon after opening, when the dawn light deepens the red of the sandstone.

The cliffs and canyon

Talampaya's cliffs appear so frequently on national tourism promotion posters and in coffee-table books, you think you know what you're getting before you arrive. But no photograph really prepares you for the belittling feeling you have when standing at the foot of a massive rock wall, where the silence is shattered only by the wind. Even the classic shots of orange-red precipices looming over what looks like a toy jeep, included for scale, don't really convey the astonishment. The national park, covering 215 square kilometres, was created in 1997 to protect the canyon and all its treasures. Geologically it's part of the Sierra Los Colorados, whose rippling mass you can see in the distance to the east. The sandstone cliffs were formed at the beginning of the Triassic period, nearly 250 million years ago, and have gradually been eroded by torrential rain and various rivers that have exploited geological faults in the rock, the reason why the cliffs are so sheer.

The rock paintings and jardín botánico

Just south of the entrance to the canyon, huge sand dunes have been swept up by the strong winds that frequently howl across the Campo de Talampaya to the south. The higgledy-piggledy rocks at the foot of the cliffs host a gallery of white, red and black **rock paintings**, made by the Ciénaga and Aguada peoples who inhabited the area around a thousand years ago. The pictures include animals such as llamas, ñandús and pumas, a stepped pyramid, huntsmen and phallic symbols, and the nearby ink-well depressions in the rock are formed by decades of grinding and mixing pigments. There is a huge *tacu* (carob tree) here, thought to be more than one thousand years old. Inside the canyon proper, the so-called **jardín botánico**, or more accurately the *bosquecillo* – thicket – is a natural grove of twenty or so different native cacti, shrubs and trees.

They include *algarrobos*, *retamos*, *pencas*, *jarillas* and *chañares*, all labelled; occasionally grey foxes and small armadillos lurk in the undergrowth and brightly coloured songbirds flit past. Nearby, and clearly signposted, is the **Chimenea** (chimney), also known as the Cueva (cave) or the Canaleta (drainpipe), a rounded vertical groove stretching all the way up the cliffside; guides revel in demonstrating its extraordinary echo, which sends condors flapping.

The rock formations

Wonderfully shaped formations in the park have been given imaginative names – mostly with a religious slant, but many of them do fit. **El Pesebre** (the Crib) is a set of rocks supposed to resemble a Nativity scene, and appropriately nearby are **Los Reyes Magos**, the Three Kings, one of them on camel-back. A cluster of enormous needles and pinnacles is known as **La Catedral** – the intricate patterns chiselled and carved by thousands of years of erosion have been compared variously with Albi cathedral or the facade of Strasbourg cathedral, both built of a similar red sandstone. A set of massive rock formations is known as **El Tablero de Ajedrez**, or the Chessboard, complete with rooks, bishops and pawns, while a 53m-high monolith resembling a cowled human figure is El Cura, the Priest, or El Fraile, the Monk, depending on whom you ask. **El Pizarrón**, or the Blackboard, is 15m of flat rock-face of darker stone etched with more ñandús, pumas, guanacos and even a sea horse – suggesting that the peoples who lived here a thousand years ago had some kind of contact with the ocean.

ARRIVAL AND DEPARTURE   PARQUE NACIONAL TALAMPAYA

By bus There are regular buses from the terminal in Villa Unión (Mon–Fri & Sun 2 daily & Sat 1 daily; 45min–1hr).

TOURS

Private vehicles are not allowed into the park, so if you arrive here under your own steam you must choose between various guided tours. These should generally be arranged in advance, especially at busy times. Tours to Cañon de Talampaya depart from the service area – where you find a campsite, *confitería* and information office – at RN-76 Km148; tours to Cañon Arco Iris and Ciudad Perdida leave from RN-76 Km133.5, where you find toilets, a kiosk and another information office.

Cooperativa de Transporte Talampaya Local organization (☎03804 15 681114) offering transfers from Villa Unión, plus tours to the Ciudad Perdida and Cañón Arco Iris sectors of the park.

Rolling Travel Tour operator (☎03825 477713, ⓦ talampaya.com) offering trips around the two most commonly travelled vehicle circuits inside Talampaya. Tours leave roughly hourly, with the last one of the day setting off an hour or so before the park's closure. Both circuits visit the main points of interest – the shorter is 2hr 30min and

the longer 5hr 30min.

Runacay Travel agency (see p.385) offering a variety of excellent walking circuits, which enable you to avoid congested minibuses and explore the park at a much more sedate pace, as well as getting into some of its lesser-known recesses.

Mountain-bike tours Enquire at the entrance or contact the park guides' association (☎03825 470397, ⓔ sergiolei_guiatur @hotmail.com), but you need your own transport. Bring sun cream, headgear and water.

ACCOMMODATION AND EATING

Campsite RN-76 Km148. You can pitch a tent at the park's basic campsite (open 24hr) next to the parking area, but bear in mind that it's often windy (and dusty) and can get extremely cold at night. Camping – though possible – is not recommended during winter when night

temperatures can get down to -10°C. Free

Confitería RN-76 Km148. The park *confitería*, from where the tours to Cañón de Talampaya depart, serves simple, reasonably priced snacks, sandwiches and hot meals. Daily 8am–10pm.

Reserva Provincial Las Vicuñas and around

The **Reserva Provincial Las Vicuñas** is nearly 150km northwest of Villa Unión, via RN-76 and then a numberless track that twists and turns to the park's central feature, the wild and shallow **Laguna Brava**. The main attractions are fabulous altiplanic scenery

6

– most of the terrain is over 4000m – the magnificent, strikingly coloured mountainous backdrops and the abundant wildlife, mainly vicuñas, as the name suggests. Large herds of this smaller cousin of the llama graze on the reserve's *bofedales*, the typical spongy marshes watered by trickles of runoff that freeze nightly. The best times to visit are spring and autumn, since summer storms and winter blizzards cut off roads and generally impede travel.

Villa San José de Vinchina to the reserve

On the way to the reserve you pass through **Villa San José de Vinchina**, 65km north of Villa Unión, a nondescript village near which are six large, low, circular mounds. Made of a mosaic of pink, white and purple stones, these mysterious **Estrellas de Vinchina** form star-shapes and are thought to have had a ceremonial purpose for the pre-Columbian indigenous people of the area, perhaps serving as altars. Otherwise head on through the Quebrada de la Troya, a magnificent striped canyon, into the Valle Caguay, dominated by the majestic cone of Volcán Los Bonetes. From here the road is best negotiated in a 4WD – in any case it is wise to visit the reserve on an organized tour (around $850/person) from Villa Unión (see p.385). If you have your own vehicle you can only enter the park accompanied by an authorized guide (book ahead: Gaston Alguilar, ☎03825 15 400550). Getting to the park you'll need to pull off the main road into **Alto Jagüe** to show your passport at the checkpoint and pay the park entrance fee ($30/person plus $400/vehicle including a guide; don't forget to check back in when leaving the park so they know you're safe).

The track heads through to the southern banks of the Laguna Brava, a deep blue lake 17km by 10km, whose high potassium-chloride levels make its water undrinkable. When it's blowing a gale, huge waves can be whipped up; when there is no wind, the mirror-like waters reflect the mountainous backdrop. Behind stretches a panorama of 6000m peaks, including the enormous Pissis – the second-highest volcano in the world (6793m). Other lakes in the reserve are the smaller Laguna Verde – a green lake, as its name suggests – and the Laguna Mulas Muertas, often covered with pink flamingoes, Andean geese and other wildfowl. There's no public transport, no *guardería* and nowhere to stay: just you and the wilds.

La Rioja and around

LA RIOJA – or Todos los Santos de la Nueva Rioja, as it was baptized at the end of the sixteenth century – is an indolent place, built in a flat-bottomed valley 517km northeast of San Juan, watered by the Río Tajamar. It is not a sightseers' city, but you can find enough to occupy a full day if passing through; La Rioja's microcentro really is small and all the places of interest are not far from the two main squares, Plaza 25 de Mayo and – two blocks west and one south – Plaza 9 de Julio. Among the highlights are two of the country's best **museums** of indigenous art, one archeological and the other with a folkloric slant. It is best visited in the spring (Oct–Nov), when the jacaranda trees are in bloom, and the city is perfumed by the blossom of orange trees that have earned it the much-bandied sobriquet "Ciudad de los Naranjos". In spite of the plentiful shade of this luxuriant vegetation, the blistering summer heat is refracted off the brutally arid mountains looming to the west and turns the city, notoriously one of the country's hottest, virtually into a no-go zone. Whatever you do, avoid the midsummer, when temperatures can get up to 45°C.

Brief history

La Rioja came into being on May 20, 1591, when the governor of Tucumán, Juan Ramírez de Velasco, a native of La Rioja in Castile, founded the city in its strategic valley location. Today's main Plaza 25 de Mayo coincides exactly with the spot he chose. Ramírez de Velasco had set out on a major military expedition to populate the empty spaces of the Viceroyalty and subdue the native Diaguitas, who had farmed the fertile oasis for centuries. La Nueva Rioja, the only colonial settlement for many kilometres around, soon flourished, and Ramírez de Velasco felt justified in boasting in a letter that it was "one of the finest cities in the Indies".

From it, mainly Franciscan missionaries set about fulfilling Ramírez de Velasco's other aim of converting the indigenous peoples. Their convent and that of the Dominicans, the oldest in Argentina, both miraculously survived the earthquake that flattened most of the old colonial city in 1894. The whole city was rebuilt, largely in a Neocolonial style that was intended to restore its former glory, but long decades of neglect by the central government were to follow. La Rioja did not even benefit as much as it hoped it would when Carlos Menem, scion of a major La Rioja wine-producing family, was elected president in 1990. There are signs that La Rioja is beginning to diversify away from its agricultural base, although the city, with a current population of about 150,000, is still regarded by most Argentines as a rather arid backwater.

6

Catedral San Nicolás de Bari

Plaza 25 de Mayo • Daily 8am–12.30pm & 6–9pm • Free • ☎ 0380 442 6122

On the west side of Plaza 9 de Julio is the striking, white Casa de Gobierno, built in a Neocolonial style with a strong Andalucian influence, which contrasts with the **Catedral San Nicolás de Bari** on the south of the plaza. This Neoclassical hulk of a church – built at the beginning of the twentieth century in beige stone, with a huge Italianate cupola, neo-Gothic campaniles and Byzantine elements in the facade – is primarily the sanctuary for a locally revered relic: a seventeenth-century walnut-wood image of St Nicholas of Bari, carved in Peru (kept locked in a side room; to see it, ask in the cathedral for the key).

6

Iglesia San Francisco

25 de Mayo and Bazán y Bustos • Daily 9am–noon & 5–9pm (although not very strict) • Free

One block north of Plaza 25 de Mayo is the **Iglesia San Francisco**, an uninspiring Neoclassical building visited by St Francisco Solano, who played a key role in the sixteenth century converting the local indigenous population. The stark cell where he stayed, containing only a fine statue of the saint and a dead orange tree, said to have been planted by him, is treated as a holy place by *riojanos*.

Museo Arqueológico Inca Huasi

Juan B. Alberdi 650 • Tues–Sun 9am–1pm & 6–8pm • $15 • ☎ 0380 443 9268, ⓦ facebook.com/MuseoIncaHuasi

The **Museo Arqueológico Inca Huasi** was set up in the 1920s by a Franciscan monk who was interested in the Diaguita culture – rather ironic, considering that the Franciscan missionaries did all they could in the seventeenth century to annihilate it. One of the pieces of art on display is a quite hideous seventeenth-century painting of the conversion of the Diaguita people by St Francisco Solano, but the rest of the exhibition is a fabulous collection of **Diaguita ceramics** and other pre-Columbian art. The dragon-shaped vase near the entrance is around 1200 years old; another later piece, inside one of the dusty cases, is a pot with an armadillo climbing it, while fat-bellied vases painted with, among other things, phalluses and toads – symbols of fertility and rain – line the shelves. The current director is striving to give a more pre-Christian context to the collection while not offending the friars.

Museo Folklórico and around

Pelagio B. Luna 811 • Tues–Fri 9am–1pm & 5–9pm • $15 • ☎ 0380 442 8500

The wonderful **Museo Folklórico** contains a large display on local mythology; a set of beautiful terracotta statuettes representing the various figures brings to life the whole pantheon, such as Pachamama, or Mother Earth, and Zapam-Zucum, the goddess of children and the carob tree – she has incredibly elongated breasts the shape of carob-pods. Zupay is the equivalent of the Devil, while a series of characters called Huaira personify different types of wind. The museum also contains a reconstruction of a nineteenth-century Riojano house. Opposite, on the corner of Pelagio B. Luna and Catamarca, is one of the region's best **crafts markets** (Tues–Sat 9.30am–12.50pm); the *artesanía*, all of it local, is of high quality, especially the regional *mantas*, or blankets.

Iglesia Santo Domingo

Pelagio B. Luna and Lamadrid • Daily 7am–12.30pm & 6–8.30pm • Free • ☎ 0380 442 5318, ⓦ facebook.com/StoDomingoLR

One block east of Plaza 25 de Mayo, the **Iglesia Santo Domingo** is the only building of interest to have survived the 1894 earthquake; it's one of the oldest buildings in Argentina, dating from 1623. The extremely long, narrow, white nave is utterly stark, apart from a fine altar decorated with seventeenth-century statuary, as is the simple whitewashed facade – but the carob-wood doors, carved by Indian craftsmen in the late seventeenth century, are a fine example of **mestizo art**.

ARRIVAL AND DEPARTURE   LA RIOJA AND AROUND

By plane La Rioja's small airport, Vicente Almandos Almonacid, is 7km east of town along RP-5 (☎ 0380 446 2160), and the only transport from it into town is by *remís*. There are regular flights to and from Buenos Aires (Mon–Fri & Sun 1 daily; 1hr 40min).

By bus The new bus terminal is some 2.5km south of the central Plaza 25 de Mayo, at Av F.O. de la Colina s/n

(☎ 0380 442 5453; buses #2 or #8 to centre; $6), and serves the whole province plus other cities in the country.

Destinations Buenos Aires (4 daily; 14hr); Catamarca (13 daily; 2hr); Chilecito (8–9 daily; 3hr); Córdoba (10 daily; 6hr 30min); Salta (4 daily; 10hr); (San Agustín de) Valle Fértil (3 weekly; 4hr); San Juan (13 daily; 6–7hr); Villa Unión (3 daily; 4hr).

INFORMATION AND TOURS

Provincial tourist office Av Ortiz de Ocampo, at Av Felix de la Colina, just next to the bus terminal (daily 8am–9pm; ☎0380 442 6345, ⓦturismolarioja.gov.ar).

Corona del Inca For one- or two-day tours to Talampaya or Ischigualasto, contact this tour operator at Pelagio B.

Luna 914 (☎03822 422142, ⓦcoronadelinca.com.ar). Longer excursions, including to Villa Unión, are also offered.

Travel Git Another option for day-trips to Talampaya and Ischigualasto (25 de Mayo 74, Galería Sussex Loc 6A; ☎03804 431781).

ACCOMMODATION

You're unlikely to want to stay long in La Rioja, but it's not badly off for accommodation, covering the whole range with a few reliable options. Enquire about B&B-style *casas de familia*, the best bet at the budget end, at the tourist office.

Naindo San Nicolás de Bari and Joaquín Victor González ☎0380 447 0700, ⓦnaindoparkhotel.com. This sparkling five-star hotel, comprising a modern plate-glass block stuck on top of a handsome Neocolonial mansion, offers comfortable if characterless rooms and has its own restaurant, a decent pool and a well-stocked bar. $1742

Pensión 9 de Julio Copiapó 197 ☎0380 442 6955, ⓦpension9dejulio.com. Your best bet for basic, budget accommodation. The leafy patio gives some atmosphere and the rooms are cramped but acceptably clean. Street-side rooms are extremely noisy, especially at weekends. $350

Plaza Hotel San Nicolás de Bari and 9 de Julio ☎0382 242 5215, ⓦplazahotel-larioja.com. Everything is squeaky clean, almost clinically so, but the rooms are smart and the rooftop pool and terrace enjoy views of the cathedral and mountains beyond. Its well-located *confitería* is one of the places to be seen in La Rioja. $1025

Savoy San Nicolás de Bari and Av Roque A. Luna ☎0380 442 6894, ⓦhotelsavoylarioja.com.ar. This classic hotel is pulled down by its unimaginative neutral decor, but the staff are friendly and the rooms are quite spacious, with decent, functional bathrooms. $600

EATING

Café de la Plaza Rivadavia and Hipólito Yrigoyen ☎0382 246 5804. One of the most strategically located places to have a drink or snack – the service is a bit nonchalant, and the decor is resolutely late-1990s, all brushed metal and diffused lighting. Daily 7.30am–late.

Orígines Pelagio B Luna and Catamarcha ☎0380 15 462 0740. One of the city's finer places to dine, serving very reasonably priced national and international plates with a *riojano* touch, such as *carbonada* (meat and vegetable stew; $70), *humitas* ($95), Thai rice ($145) and

stuffed rabbit ($135). Service is slightly stiff. Daily 11.30am–3pm & 8pm–12.30am.

Ribera Av Perón and Pelagio B. Luna ☎03822 460424. This is a classic pizzeria with decades of tradition and a polished setting with attractive wooden tables. Big pizzas start at $95. Tues–Sun noon–3pm & 7pm–midnight.

La Vieja Casona Rivadavia 427 ☎0380 442 5996. La Rioja's best *parrilla*, serving outstanding meat (around $180/person) and delicious home-made pasta, with an excellent wine list from local bodegas. Daily noon–3pm & 8.30pm–midnight.

The Lake District

LAGO ESPEJO

The Lake District

Argentina's Lake District – the northwestern wedge of Argentine Patagonia – is a land of picture-perfect glacial lakes surrounded by luxuriant forests, jagged peaks and extinct volcanoes. Not so long ago it was a sparsely populated wilderness controlled by indigenous peoples; now, the undisputed modern capital, Bariloche, sees annual invasions of holiday-makers drawn to the alpine flavour of this "Argentine Switzerland", with its chalet architecture, breweries and chocolate shops. Yet the real attraction is the unspoilt beauty of the Parque Nacional Nahuel Huapi, the grandfather of all Argentina's national parks, packed with enough trekking and outdoor activities to last any enthusiast weeks.

7

To the north of **Bariloche**, alpine-style capital of Río Negro state, is the upmarket resort of **Villa La Angostura** and the stunning **Seven Lakes Route**. To the south is the more alternative resort of **El Bolsón**, with its excellent **beer**, and the splendid **Parque Nacional Los Alerces**, home to more fabulous lakes and ancient *alerce* trees. South from **Esquel**, a good base for seeing the park, lurks a trio of curiosities: **Butch Cassidy**'s cabin at **Cholila**, the Welsh settlement of **Trevelin** and the historic **La Trochita** steam train.

In the northern swathes of the Lake District the main hub is family-oriented **San Martín de los Andes**, with its admirable lakefront location. Both it and neighbouring **Junín de los Andes** – renowned nationwide for its angling opportunities – are perfect bases for exploring the rugged **Parque Nacional Lanín**. The park's focus is **Volcán Lanín**, a conical peak popular with mountaineers, while its **Pehuén region** is full of excellent treks and lakeside towns. **Neuquén**, the namesake capital of Argentina's only palindromically named province, is a pleasant enough city to relax in, but its indisputable draw has to be the nearby treasure-trove of giant dinosaur fossils. In recent years vines have been planted with considerable success in the desert-like areas nearby; **wineries** with dramatic names – like Bodega del Fin del Mundo ("winery at the end of the world") – have started making fabulous semillons and syrahs, which you can taste on the premises.

GETTING AROUND   THE LAKE DISTRICT

The Lake District is a popular Argentine tourist destination and served by generally excellent bus links during the high season (roughly Christmas to Easter and the July–Sept ski season); buses are less frequent out of season but most routes are still served, weather permitting. Consider renting a car if you want to visit some of the more off-the-beaten-path locations, such as Moquehue or the Chañar wineries.

HIKING CERRO CATEDRAL

Highlights

❶ **Bariloche** The region's principal town has some of the most handsome Lake District landscapes right on its doorstep. **See p.397**

❷ **Lake District beer** The Blest and El Bolsón breweries serve a variety of highly drinkable real ales from palest *rubia* to dark stout. **See p.401 & p.414**

❸ **Cerro Catedral** Whether you choose to hike it in summer or ski it in winter, this peak in Nahuel Huapi park affords fabulous views of craggy mountains and rich blue lakes. **See p.406**

❹ **Ruta de los Siete Lagos** The scenic Seven Lakes Route swings past at least a dozen meres whose waters range from deep ultramarine to delicate turquoise. **See p.410**

❺ **La Trochita** A much-loved steam train that featured in Paul Theroux's *The Old Patagonian Express* – follow his example and take a trip down the tracks. **See p.418**

❻ **Volcán Lanín** Climb the slopes of a woodcut-perfect volcano that reigns over its namesake national park – or just admire the views from a peaceful lakeside vantage point. **See p.430**

❼ **Giant dinosaurs** Gawp up at some of the biggest dinosaur remains ever found or check out a clutch of unique titanosaur eggs – all within reach of Neuquén city. **See p.438**

HIGHLIGHTS ARE MARKED ON THE MAP ON P.396

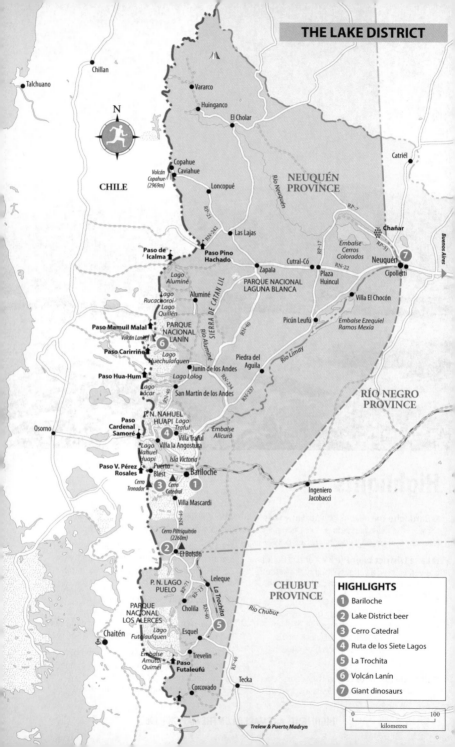

Bariloche

The holiday capital of the Argentine South, **BARILOCHE** (formally San Carlos de Bariloche) is one of those places that Argentines always tell you not to miss, the kind of hype that can easily lead to disappointment. Europeans familiar with the Alps – or North Americans or New Zealanders used to similar scenery – are unlikely to travel thousands of kilometres to see a simulacrum of Switzerland. The city is undeniably worth the trip, though – not because of the alpine style, but because it is the main base for visiting the stunningly pristine landscapes of the **Parque Nacional Nahuel Huapi** which surround it.

Bariloche rests up against the slopes of Cerro Otto, behind which rear the spire-tipped crests of the Cerro Catedral massif. Everything in Bariloche faces the mesmerizing Lago Nahuel Huapi, one of the scores of lakes that give the region its name, but something went massively wrong with the urban planning – the main road artery was built along the shore, severing the centre from the town's best feature. The **beach** is narrow but pleasant enough and the views are predictably spectacular, but the water is cold even in summer.

The town's lifeblood is tourism, with around a million visitors arriving annually. This is a place of secular pilgrimage for the nation's students, who flood here on their summer breaks, along with coachloads of young Israelis and Brazilians. None of these necessarily comes in search of the true mountain experience, but they often end up having one, pushed out of town by the inflated high-season prices of hotels. In winter, it's specifically the nearby **ski resort** of Cerro Catedral that draws the crowds. At peak times, the excesses of commercialization and crowds of tourists may spoil your visit. Nevertheless, the place does offer remarkably painless access to many beautiful and genuinely wild sections of the Andean cordillera, and out of season (March–June, excluding Easter, and Sept–Nov) the town is still big enough to retain some life of its own.

Brief history

Before the incursions of the Mapuche and Spanish, the area was the domain of the Tehuelche people, whose livelihood largely depended on hunting and trade (with their western, Mapuche, counterparts). The discovery of their mountain passes (the name Bariloche is derived from a Mapudungun word meaning "people from beyond the mountains") became an obsession of early Spanish explorers in Chile, many of whom were desperate to hunt down the wealth of the mythical City of the Caesars. Knowledge of the passes' whereabouts was a closely guarded secret until the 1670s. The history of the non-autochthonous presence in the region really began when the Jesuit **Nicolás Mascardi** was dispatched by the Viceroy to found a **mission** around that time. The area's indigenous groups put paid to Mascardi and his successors and, in 1717, the mission was abandoned. The local indigenous groups took one Jesuit introduction more to their hearts than Christianity: the apple (*manzana*). Used for cider, wild apples became so popular that the region's Mapuche communities became known as **Manzaneros**. In 1881 – in the aftermath of the brutal **Conquest of the Desert** (see p.535), which thousands of Patagonia's indigenous population captured or killed – Chile and Argentina signed a border treaty recognizing the Nahuel Huapi area as Argentine.

Modern Bariloche has its roots in the arrival of German settlers from southern Chile in the early twentieth century, but was tiny until the creation of the national park in 1934. In recent decades, the population has skyrocketed, and the town is now a major urban centre, though the homogeneity of its original alpine-style architecture has sadly been swamped by a messy conglomerate of high-rise apartments. In 2011, the eruption of **Volcán Puyehue** in Chile, just over 90km from Bariloche, carpeted the surrounding area in ash. There were severe disruptions to flights from airports as far away as Buenos Aires for months and the mess took time to clear up, with some people shutting up shop altogether and leaving town. By 2013, Puyehue was slumbering again and life had largely returned to normal – only for another Chilean volcano, **Cabulco**, to erupt in 2015. Although this one was not as severe as the 2011 eruption, Bariloche was still affected, with ash covering the city.

7

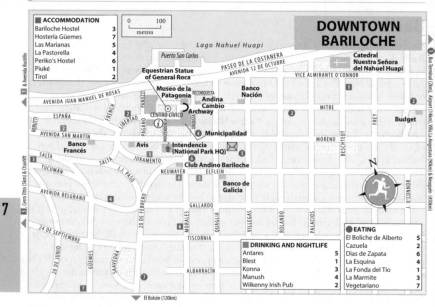

Centro cívico

Bariloche's focal point is the **centro cívico**, a set of buildings constructed out of timber and the local greenish-grey stone, resolutely facing the lake. Dating from 1939, it's a noble architectural statement by Ernesto de Estrada, who collaborated with Argentina's most famous architect, Alejandro Bustillo (after whom the main lakeside avenue is named), in the development of an alpine style that has come to represent the region. In the centre of the main plaza, around which these buildings are grouped, stands a graffiti-strewn equestrian **statue** of General Roca, whose horse looks suitably hangdog after the Conquest of the Desert. People bring Saint Bernards along, often with the famous cask around their necks, in readiness for photo opportunities at a small price. The pavement is adorned with painted white scarves, symbols of the Madres de Plaza de Mayo (see box, p.66), and the names of local *desaparecidos*.

Museo de la Patagonia

Centro Cívico s/n • Tues–Fri 10am–12.30pm & 2–7pm, Sat 10am–5pm • Free • ⓦ museodelapatagonia.nahuelhuapi.gov.ar

Of the plaza's attractions, the most interesting is the **Museo de la Patagonia**, which also rates as one of the very best museums on things Patagonian, from wildlife to modern history. Look out for the caricature of Perito Moreno as a wet nurse guiding the infant Theodore Roosevelt on his trip through the Lake District in 1913. Superb, too, are the engraved Tehuelche tablet stones that experts speculate may have been protective amulets, Aónik'enk painted horse-hides and playing cards made of guanaco skin, one of the Mapuches' famous lances and Roca's own uniform.

Catedral Nuestra Señora del Nahuel Huapi

Vice. Almirante O'Connor 500 • Mon–Fri 9am–8.30pm, Sun 9.30am–9pm • Free • ☎ 0294 443 4084, ⓦ iglesiacatedralbariloche.com

On the lake shore to the east of the Museo de la Patagonia is the Bustillo-designed **Catedral Nuestra Señora del Nahuel Huapi**, whose attractive stained-glass windows illustrate Patagonian themes such as the first Mass held by Magellan.

ARRIVAL AND DEPARTURE

BY PLANE

Bariloche's airport (☎0294 440 5016) is 14km east of town. There are always *remises* hanging around (approx $250 to town), or you can take local bus #72, which runs every 2hr (7am–10pm; $12).

Airlines Aerolíneas Argentinas, Mitre 185 ☎0810 2228 6527; LADE, John O'Connor 214 ☎0294 442 3562; LAN, Mitre 534 ☎0810 999 9526.

Destinations Buenos Aires (9–10 daily; 2hr); Córdoba (Mon–Sat 1 daily; makes a short stop in Rosario; 4hr); El Calafate (1 daily; 1hr 55min); Rosario (Mon–Sat 1 daily; 2hr 20min).

BY TRAIN

The train station (☎0294 442 3172, ⊛tren patagonico-sa.com.ar) is right next to the main bus terminal along Av 12 de Octubre (RN-237). The only service is a weekly overnight train, known as El Tren

BARILOCHE

Patagónico, to Viedma (Sun; 16hr; from $646).

BY BUS

The main bus terminal is next to the train station, 2km east of the city centre along Av 12 de Octubre (RN-237). The best local buses for the centre are #10 or #20 (every 15–20min; 10min; $8). You need to have a Sube or Santa Fé card, which you can buy in town; Kiosko PPI on Rolando 268 is the only outlet that sells both types of cards. Taxis to town from the terminal will cost around $80.

Destinations Buenos Aires (11 daily; 23hr); Córdoba (1 daily; 22hr); El Bolsón (15 daily; 2hr); Esquel (7–8 daily; 5hr); Junín de los Andes (2 daily; 3hr); Mendoza (1 daily; 17hr); Neuquén (15–17 daily; 6hr); Puerto Madryn (2 daily; 12–14hr); San Martín de los Andes (4 daily; 4hr); Trelew (2 daily; 11hr 30min–13hr); Villa La Angostura (9 daily; 1hr 15 min); Villa Traful (4 weekly; 1hr 45 min).

GETTING AROUND AND INFORMATION

By bus The city has a great bus system, especially in summer when buses to peninsula Llao Llao (#10 and #20), Villa Lago Gutierrez (#41) and Cerro Catedral (#55) run more frequently and make it straightforward to access hiking trails without a car. You must buy a bus card (Santa Fé or Sube) in advance from kiosks (Santa Fé cards at Mitre 91 and Moreno 480; Sube cards at Moreno 69 and Morales 501; both at Kiosko PPI on Rolando 268) and top it up before you travel ($8/journey). The exception is bus #55, which you pay for on board ($22).

By car Rental outlets include Avis, Av San Martín 162 (☎0294 443 1648), and Budget, Mitre 717 (☎0294 442 2482).

Tourist information Expect to queue in summer at the busy tourist office on the main plaza (centro cívico; daily 8am–9pm; ☎0294 442 9850, ⊛barilocheturismo.gob.ar). It keeps a list of available accommodation.

Intendencia The office for Parque Nacional Nahuel Huapi is by the centro cívico at Av San Martín 24 (Mon–Fri 8am–4pm, Sat 10am–4pm; ☎0294 442 3111, ⊛nahuelhuapi.gov.ar), which should be your first port of call if you are planning a visit to the park.

Club Andino Bariloche A block behind the *intendencia*, at 20 de Febrero 30 (daily 9am–9pm; ☎0294 442 2266, ⊛clubandino.org), this mountaineering institution can offer more detailed information on trekking routes.

ACCOMMODATION

Accommodation in Bariloche is plentiful but pricey (it can be as much as forty percent cheaper in low season), and you should reserve in advance throughout the year for the cheaper options, which fill rapidly – and in high season for all accommodation.

DOWNTOWN

Bariloche Hostel Salta 528 ☎0294 442 5460, ⊛barilochehostel.com.ar. Cosy hostel with wooden furniture, great lake views and spacious rooms. Dorms $350; doubles $850

Hostería Güemes Güemes 715 ☎0294 442 4785, ⊛hosteriaguemes.com.ar. Friendly and welcoming *hostería* on a quiet residential street a 10min walk from town. Rooms are a bit small and have slightly thin walls, but the beds are very comfortable. $1150

Las Marianas 24 de Septiembre ☎0294 443 9876, ⊛hosterialasmarianas.com.ar. Spotless and well-appointed hotel run by two ex-mountaineers. Rooms are clean and tastefully decorated and you can get scrambled eggs for breakfast. US$110

La Pastorella Av Belgrano 127 ☎0294 442 4656,

⊛lapastorelladelapatagonia.com. Tasteful French decor gives this place a homely feel. Rooms are tidy and spacious but lack the charm of the rest of the hotel. There's a small, tranquil garden and free parking. $500

★**Periko's Hostel** Morales 555 ☎0294 452 2326, ⊛perikos.com. Best of the youth-hostel-type accommodation, this excellent, well-built and well-run place is loaded with information about trips. Reserve well in advance. Dorms $200; doubles $600

Piuké Beschtedt 136 ☎0294 442 3044. An attractive chalet-style hotel with flowery gardens just a block from the cathedral. Rooms are simple but comfortable and breakfast is included. $600

Tirol Libertad 175 ☎0294 442 6152, ⊛hoteltirol.com .ar. In an ideal location a block from the centro cívico is this modern, tastefully decorated hotel. Rates include breakfast

ACTIVITIES AND TOURS AROUND BARILOCHE

The numerous excursions available from Bariloche can be roughly divided into two categories – land and water – with the city's **tour agencies** offering more or less identical packages and prices. Exploring the rivers and lakes via raft and boat is popular, as is fishing. Rafting can be arranged at **Aguas Blancas**, Morales 564 (☎0294 443 2799, ⓦaguasblancas.com.ar), and tours around the Circuito Chico and Grande at **Adventure Center**, Moreno 30 (☎0294 443 5040, ⓦadventurecenter.com.ar). For trips to Isla Victoria and Bosque de Arrayanes, contact **Turisur**, Mitre 219 (☎0294 442 6109, ⓦturisur.com.ar). If you prefer to take to the water in a kayak, try **Senzalimiti**, Julio Cortazar 5050 (☎0294 452 0597, ⓦslimiti.com). Inland, you can rent mountain bikes at **Patagonia Inhóspita** (☎0294 443 1164, ⓦpatagoniainhospita.com). Bikes for doing the Circuito Chico (see p.402) are best rented at **Bike Cordillera**, Av Bustillo Km18.6 (☎0294 452 4828, ⓦapurabici.com).

7

served in a dining room with huge windows and stunning lake views. $1150

AROUND THE LAKE

Avenida Bustillo runs for 25km along the lake shore to Puerto Pañuelo (served by buses #10 and #20) and is packed, at least for the first dozen kilometres, with bungalows and cabins. Some of these have sensational lake views, though most have been gentrified in the worst possible taste; below is a small selection of some of the best, along with one or two places to stay a little farther afield.

Aldebaran Av Bustillo Km20.4 ☎0294 444 8678, ⓦaldebaranpatagonia.com. Named after one of the brightest stars in the night sky, this hotel stands out for its stunning lakeside location, its spacious understated rooms and the original decor, which continues the astronomical theme. All rooms enjoy breathtaking views of the mountains and lake. US$290

Alun Nehuen Av Bustillo Km32 ☎0294 444 8005, ⓦalunnehuenbariloche.com.ar. This slightly old-fashioned lakeside hotel boasts spectacular views, and you can fish or take a boat trip from its dock. Big discounts offered in the low season. B&B $1200; full board $1700

Apart Hotel del Arroyo Av Bustillo Km4050 ☎0294 444 2082, ⓦdelarroyo.com.ar. Comfortable and functional cabins with well-equipped kitchens, in a convenient location. Situated over the arroyo (brook) that gives them their name, providing natural cooling in summers. Ask for promotions in low season if staying more than one night. $1000

Camping La Selva Negra Av Bustillo Km2.95 ☎0294 444 1013, ⓦcampingselvanegra.com.ar. A campsite within easy reach of the city, whose facilities include above-average bathrooms, a bar and café, wi-fi and the use of stoves. $180

★ **El Casco Art Hotel** Av Bustillo Km11.5 ☎0294 446 3131, ⓦhotelelcasco.com. Belonging to one of the country's leading art dealers, staying at this fabulous hotel, whose grounds are lapped by the lake's waters, is like staying in a private art gallery – indeed, the beautiful works, mostly by Argentine artists of the highest calibre, are for sale. Every detail refers back to this arty theme, without becoming heavy-handed; even the cocktails at the bar are inspired by specific painters and their palettes. US$309

Charming Luxury Lodge and Private Spa Hua Huan 7549, Av Bustillo Km7.5 ☎0294 446 2889, ⓦcharming-bariloche.com. The name says it all: it is charming and luxurious, and the bigger suites each have their own private spa, with jacuzzi, sauna, steam bath, aromatherapy and chromo-therapy. It's pricey, though. Doubles US$107; suites with spas US$468

★ **Estancia Peuma Hue** RN-40 Km2014, towards El Bolsón ☎0294 450 1030, ⓦpeuma-hue.com. Aptly named (it means "place of dreams" in Mapudungun), *Peuma Hue* is idyllically located at the head of the sapphire Lago Gutiérrez, and offers supreme comfort, exquisite and well-balanced food and the possibility of kayaking, horseriding, birdwatching, walking or just lapping up the beauty of the place (full board deals include horseriding, boat rides and sauna). The owner and staff are helpful and friendly. B&B US$250; full board US$450

Hostería Lonquimay Lonquimay 3672, Barrio Melipal ☎0294 444 3450, ⓦhosterialonquimay.com. Nicely appointed chalet-style hotel with an intimate feel not far from the Cerro Otto chairlift. $840

Llao Llao Hotel & Resort Av Bustillo Km25 ☎0294 444 8530, ⓦllaollao.com. One of Argentina's most famous hotels, designed and built by Alejandro Bustillo along the lines of an enormous Canadian cabin (see p.404). Excellent views and services, including indoor and outdoor pools, a golf course and even a "royal suite". The fine restaurant, *Los Césares*, serves superbly cooked grilled meat and pasta; reservations essential. US$245

EATING

Bariloche has a large and excellent selection of places to eat, most within walking distance of the centre. Calle Mitre is also lined with stores selling local specialities such as chocolate, smoked trout, ice cream and *alfajores*. Catering for large numbers of tourists, restaurants tend to have extended opening hours (but vary depending on the season). Some stay open between lunch and dinner in high season.

DOWNTOWN

El Boliche de Alberto Elflein 158 ☎0294 443 4564, ⓦelbolichedealberto.com. The best branch in the local chain, this is the juiciest and largest (but not the priciest) *parrilla* in town. Prepare to gorge yourself – and to wait for a table (reservations not accepted). Also runs a pasta restaurant under the same name at Elflein and Villegas, in case you fancy a change from meat. Daily noon–3pm & 8pm–midnight.

Cazuela Mitre and John O'Connor ☎0294 442 6518. Serving home-made pasta ($120), casseroles ($99) and the mandatory Argentine pizza ($130), this little corner restaurant is good value for money. Mon–Fri 8am–midnight, Sat & Sun 10am–midnight/1am.

Dias de Zapata Morales 362 ☎0294 442 3128. Mexican-run Mexican restaurant serving quesadillas, tacos and decent cocktails. Most portions are large, moderately priced and of high quality. The spicy sauce and the vegetarian fajitas ($195) deserve special mention. Daily 12.30pm–1am.

La Esquina Urquiza and Perito Moreno ☎0294 442 8900. Corner by name and corner café by nature, this popular local haunt is a good place to have a drink and while away the time with a newspaper or book. Mon–Sat 8am–1am, Sun 10am–1am.

La Fonda del Tío Mitre 1130 ☎0294 443 5011, ⓦbit.ly/LaFondaDelTio. A favourite among locals for their delicious, very generously sized *milanesas* – one is enough for three people. For other dishes, the menu changes daily. Mon–Sat noon–3.30pm & 8pm–midnight.

La Marmite Mitre 329 ☎0294 443 2198. Not a bargain by any means, the intimate, old-fashioned *Marmite* is nonetheless worth a visit for its regional and Swiss specialities, especially its fondues. Mon–Sat noon–midnight & Sun 8pm–midnight.

Vegetariano 20 de Febrero 730 ☎0294 442 1820. If you've had your fill of *parrillas* this excellent mid-range veggie restaurant will provide relief. Vegans beware, though – most dishes contain egg and dairy products, and there are also fish dishes. Mon–Fri noon–3pm & 8–11pm, Sat noon–3pm.

AROUND THE LAKE

★**Butterfly** Hua Huan 7831 and Av Bustillo Km7.9 ☎0294 15 453 4994, ⓦbutterflypatagonia.com.ar. High-end restaurant at Playa Bonita – a 15min taxi ride from the centre of Bariloche – serving a delicious seven-course menu ($720) with a Patagonian theme (wine pairings available; $270). Pricey, but well worth a visit just for the sautéed trout with black olives, prawns and beetroot and raspberry sauce. Bookings essential. Mon–Sat seatings 7.45pm & 9.30pm.

DRINKING AND NIGHTLIFE

With the constant influx of Argentine students mixing with an onslaught of thirsty backpackers, Bariloche has a lively *movida*. **Bars** are scattered around town, while the majority of the pub action is along Elflein and on Juramento. However, drinking can be expensive – plan on spending about a third more than elsewhere in Argentina in the trendiest bars.

Antares Elflein 47 ☎0294 443 1454. Bar/restaurant with a wide variety of Austrian-style homebrews on tap. Beer is included in some of the dishes on the menu – such as the venison stew with stout – and "minipints" are even served with desserts. Happy hour (half price) is every day, 6.30–8.30pm. Daily 6.30pm–late.

★**Blest** Av Bustillo Km11.6 ☎0294 446 1026. This out-of-town microbrewery has an excellent selection of very good home-made brews – its potent raspberry beer is worth sampling, as are all the ales. It also serves moderately priced meals, mostly with a Germanic flavour. Daily noon–midnight.

Konna Juramento 73 ☎0294 443 7883. Cute little microbrewery with an excellent seating area outdoors in summer, and live music on some nights. Pub grub is well prepared and filling – try the lamb burgers – and the beer is decent. Daily 7pm–late.

Manush Neumeyer 20 ☎0294 442 8905. English-style pub with gastro ambitions that fills up quickly. Homebrews, burgers and steak are on offer. Daily 5.30pm–3am.

Wilkenny Irish Pub San Martín 435 ☎0294 442 4444. Wannabe Irish bar that's the most famous party pub in Patagonia. Drinks are not cheap, although happy hour on selected drinks (daily 7–9pm) brings the price down a bit. Daily 7pm–late.

DIRECTORY

Banks and exchange Bank hours vary depending on the season (April–Nov Mon–Fri 9am–2pm; Dec–March Mon–Fri 8am–1pm). Banco Nación, Mitre 178; Banco Francés, San Martín 336; Banco de Galicia, Quaglia 307; Andina Cambio, Mitre 102.

Laundry Laverap, Quaglia 321.

Post office Moreno 175 (Mon–Fri 8am–1pm & 4–7pm).

Parque Nacional Nahuel Huapi

Neuquén–Río Negro border • Park border open daily 24hr • $120 entrance fee, which you can pay at various points within the park

The main goal of any trip to Bariloche is to see the natural wonders contained within the **PARQUE NACIONAL NAHUEL HUAPI**, the oldest of the Argentine national parks. Protecting a glorious chunk of the Andean cordillera and its neighbouring steppe, most of the park falls within the watershed of the immense **Lago Nahuel Huapi**, an impressive expanse of water that can seem benign one moment and a froth of seething whitecaps the next. Of glacial origin, it's 557 square kilometres in area but highly irregular in shape, with peninsulas, islands and attenuated, fjord-like tentacles that sweep down from the thickly forested border region. The lake's name is Mapudungun for Isle (*huapi*) of the Tiger (*nahuel*) and refers to the jaguars that once inhabited regions even this far south.

Heavy rainfall permits the growth of temperate rainforest and species such as the *alerce* (see box, p.420), here at the northernmost extent of its range in Argentina. Other species typical of the sub-Antarctic Patagonian forests also flourish: giant *coihues*, *lengas* and *ñire* among others. The dominant massif of the park is an extinct volcano, **Cerro Tronador**, whose three peaks straddle the Argentine–Chilean border in the south. Glaciers slide off its heights in all directions, though all are in a state of alarmingly rapid recession.

The strongest winds blow in **spring**, which is otherwise a good time to visit, as is the calmer **autumn**, when the deciduous trees wear their spectacular late-season colours.

Circuito Chico

The most popular, if not the most exciting, excursion from Bariloche is the short **Circuito Chico**, a 65km road course following Avenida Bustillo westwards. The first ten

---

THE ZONES OF PARQUE NACIONAL NAHUEL HUAPI

The park can roughly be split into three zones, all of which reward **trekkers** of any level of stamina and hardiness with a highly developed infrastructure of trails and refuges. A plethora of lakes, waterfalls, boat trips and chairlifts will entertain anyone not so keen on hiking.

THE CENTRAL ZONE

The most visited sites within the central zone, around **Lago Nahuel Huapi**, lie within easy reach of Bariloche. There are plenty of tours from the city (see box, p.400), though you may prefer to do it at your own pace using public transport or by car. In the middle of the national park and its eponymous lake lies Isla Victoria, an elongated, thickly forested island northwest of Bariloche. North of the island you find the peninsula of the Bosque de los Arrayanes (see p.410), which can also be reached from the exclusive upmarket resort of Villa La Angostura (see p.408). At the western end of Brazo Blest, the outpost of Puerto Blest is surrounded by some of the park's most impressive **forest**, where a scenic trail takes you to the Cascada Los Cántaros, a series of waterfalls in the forest.

THE SOUTHERN ZONE

It is in the south that you'll find most of the longer and more **mountainous treks**, either around Cerro Catedral or Pampa Linda; again, Bariloche can be used as a base. From Puerto Blest, a dirt road runs south for 3km to Puerto Alegre, at the northern end of tiny Lago Frías, with a launch crossing the lake daily to Puerto Frías. From here you can **cross to Chile** or hike south across the Paso de las Nubes, further into the southern zone.

THE NORTHERN ZONE

The zone to the north of Lago Nahuel Huapi, bordering the Parque Nacional Lanín, centres on **Lago Traful**. Its big attraction is the **Seven Lakes Route**, which runs from Villa La Angostura to San Martín de los Andes (see p.422). *Guardaparques* stationed at points along the route are helpful when it comes to recommending day-treks in their particular sectors. The *Guía Sendas & Bosques de Lanín y Nahuel Huapi* is a very useful guide (Spanish only) and comes with two reasonably reliable maps (1:200,000) of the region.

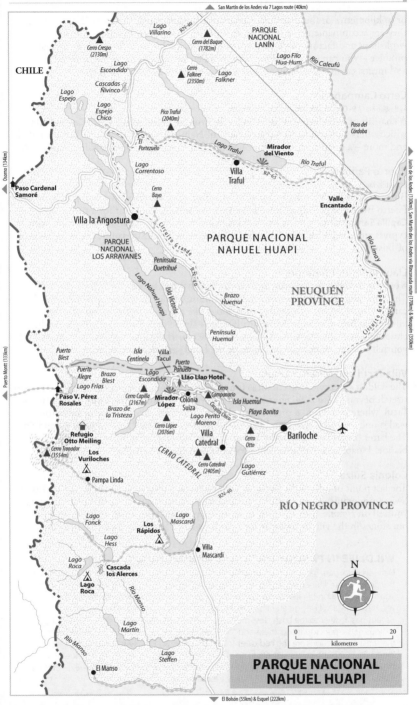

San Martín de los Andes via 7 Lagos route (40km)

CHILE

Lago Villarino
RN-40
Cerro del Buque (1782m)

PARQUE NACIONAL LANÍN

Cerro Crespo (2130m)
Lago Escondido
Lago Filo Hua-Hum
Río Caleufú

Cascadas Ñivinco
Cerro Falkner (2350m)
Lago Falkner

Lago Espejo
Lago Espejo Chico
Pico Traful (2040m)

Osorno (134km)

El Portezuelo
Lago Traful
Mirador del Viento
Río Traful

Paso del Córdoba

Lago Correntoso
Villa Traful
RP-65

Paso Cardenal Samoré

Cerro Bayo

Valle Encantado

Villa la Angostura

7

Circuito Grande

PARQUE NACIONAL LOS ARRAYANES

PARQUE NACIONAL NAHUEL HUAPI

Río Limay

Península Quetrihué
RN-40

Junín de los Andes (130km); San Martín de los Andes via Rinconada route (170km) & Neuquén (350km)

Lago Nahuel Huapi
Isla Victoria
Brazo Huemul

NEUQUÉN PROVINCE

Circuito Grande

Península Huemul

Puerto Blest
Isla Centinela
Villa Tacul
Puerto Pañuelo

Puerto Alegre
Brazo Blest
Lago Escondido
Llao Llao Hotel

Puerto Montt (133km)

Lago Frías
Paso V. Pérez Rosales

Cerro Capilla (2167m)
Mirador López
Colonia Suiza
Cerro Campanario
Isla Huemul

Brazo de la Tristeza
Cerro López (2076m)
Lago Perito Moreno
Circuito Chico
Playa Bonita

Refugio Otto Meiling
Cerro Tronador (3554m)
Los Vuriloches

Villa Catedral
Cerro Otto
Bariloche

CERRO CATEDRAL

Pampa Linda
Cerro Catedral (2405m)
Lago Gutiérrez

RN-40

RÍO NEGRO PROVINCE

Lago Fonck
Lago Mascardi

Lago Hess
Los Rápidos

Lago Roca
Cascada los Alerces
Villa Mascardi

Lago Roca
Río Manso

N

Lago Martín

0   20
kilometres

Río Manso
Lago Steffen

El Manso

PARQUE NACIONAL NAHUEL HUAPI

El Bolsón (55km) & Esquel (222km)

or so kilometres of the circuit are underwhelming: although the lake views are great, they are accompanied by a steady stream of twee boutiques, hotels, restaurants, workshops and factory outlets for cottage industries. It's great for buying regional produce – you can get everything from woollen sweaters to preserves, smoked trout and meats, ceramics, chocolates and wood-carvings – but not much else.

Cerro Campanario

Av Bustillo Km17.5 · Chairlift daily 9am–6.30pm · $150 return · ⓦ cerrocampanario.com.ar

A chairlift or stiff thirty-minute climb takes you up 200m to the **Cerro Campanario**, which offers panoramic 360-degree views of Nahuel Huapi, *Llao Llao*, Cerro Catedral and more – a good way to get your bearings and warm up before tackling longer treks.

Puerto Pañuelo

Av Bustillo Km25

Boats trips to Isla Victoria (see p.408), the Bosque de los Arrayanes (see p.410) and Puerto Blest (see p.408) all leave from **Puerto Pañuelo**. Look out for a tiny chapel, the **Capilla San Eduardo**, on the left-hand side just before you reach the port. Built with cypress and tiled with *alerce* shingles, it was designed by Estrada under the supervision of Bustillo.

Llao Llao Hotel & Resort

Av Bustillo Km25 · Booking essential for guided tours · Free · ☎ 0294 444 8530, ⓦ llaollao.com

The imposing **Llao Llao**, one of Argentina's most famous hotels (see p.400), and which can be visited as part of a **guided tour**, looks like a carbuncle set on top of a verdant knoll from below, though Alejandro Bustillo's alpine design strangely improves the closer you get. The sensational views alone are worth the hike up, and you can reward yourself with afternoon tea or dinner at the hotel's excellent restaurant.

Villa Tacul and Mirador López

The wildest scenery of the circuit is found along the road that runs through the forested stretch beyond *Llao Llao*. Four kilometres beyond the hotel a track heads north to **Villa Tacul**, where you'll find a pretty, sandy beach. There are also a couple of short forest walks, one around Cerro Llao Llao, the other between *Llao Llao* and **Lago Escondido**. The latter brings you to **Mirador López**, overlooking the deep blue waters of Lago Nahuel Huapi and with excellent views of **Cerro Capilla** (2167m).

Colonia Suiza

The last point of call on the circuit is **Colonia Suiza**, a pretty village originally settled by Swiss immigrants. There's nothing particular to see here, but it's a good place for gorging yourself on *curanto*, a sort of stew of mussels, meat and vegetables, prepared in a pit with hot stones in the village centre twice a week (Wed & Sun 11am; ☎0294 444 8605).

WILDLIFE IN PARQUE NACIONAL NAHUEL HUAPI

Nahuel Huapi park has abundant **birdlife**, with species such as the Magellanic woodpecker, the green-backed firecrown, the ground-dwelling Chucao tapaculo and the Austral parakeet. You'll hear mention of rare **fauna** such as the *huemul* (see box, p.421) and the *pudú*, though you have only a slightly greater chance of seeing them than you do of spying Nahuelito, Argentina's answer to the Loch Ness monster. Animals that make their home in the steppe regions of the park (guanaco, rheas and foxes) are more easily seen. Of the non-native species, the most conspicuous are the **red deer** (*ciervo colorado*) and the **wild boar** (*jabalí*), introduced by hunt-loving settlers. In an effort to curb their numbers, the authorities issue shooting permits, which continue to serve as a source of revenue for the park – expect to see roast boar and venison carpaccio on many a local menu.

TREKKING IN PARQUE NACIONAL NAHUEL HUAPI

To say **Parque Nacional Nahuel Huapi** is an ideal destination for **trekking** would be a sizeable understatement. Myriad spectacular trails lace the park, though its principal trekking region is in the southern zone (see box below), southeast of Cerro Tronador.

THE TREKS

In the **Cerro Catedral** area, a popular one-day hike takes you to **Refugio Frey**, reached by taking the chairlift from Villa Catedral to Refugio Lynch and then a rocky traverse (4hr); the terrain is wearing on the legs but the spectacular mountain vistas make it worthwhile. For more of a challenge, you could hike all the way from Villa Catedral rather than taking the chairlift and stay the night at Refugio Frey. To make it a circular trek, descend through magical forest and meadow back to the base of the lift (4hr).

In the **Pampa Linda** sector, the classic hike is to **Refugio Otto Meiling**, above even the summer snowline and with views of Cerro Tronador, where you can stay or camp. You can also hike up to the eastern slopes of Cerro Tronador and stay the night at *Refugio Agostino Rocca*, which has shower and cooking facilities. Much less frequented but also offering great views is the trek to **Refugio Tronador** (no services, light or running water), usually done as a two- or three-day hike, overnighting near the Chilean *carabineros*. You'll need a permit from both the Pampa Linda *guardaparque* and the nearby *gendarmaría*, since the trek takes you into Chile. The Club Andino Bariloche also runs its own trekking tour to Pampa Linda (summer 9am, runs on demand; $800, book in advance), which visits the Ventisquero glacier and then takes you on a guided 4hr 30min trek to Costano Overo.

As a rule, trails (*sendas*) to refuges are well marked. The high-mountain trails (*sendas de alta montaña*) are not always clearly marked, though, and the less-frequented paths (*picadas*) are not maintained on a regular basis, closing up with vegetation from time to time.

PRACTICALITIES

Before you set out, you should visit the Club Andino Bariloche (see p.399), which has extensive info and sells trekking **maps**. It is also obligatory to fill out a *registro de trekking* at the *guardaparque* station on entering the park and to check out again before leaving. The **trekking season** is basically between December and March, but you should always heed weather conditions and come prepared. **Snow** can fall unseasonally, as late as December and as early as March at higher altitudes, so it's inadvisable to hike certain trails outside the high season. Bear in mind the area is a long way west of Buenos Aires despite being in the same time zone, so the sun is overhead in summer at close to 3pm, rather than midday. Average temperatures are 18°C in summer and 2°C in winter.

An impressive network of well-run **refuges** ($185–300/person; reservations not possible) makes trekking appealing: you'll need to bring a sleeping bag, but can buy **meals** and basic supplies en route. In high season, refuges and trails in the more popular areas can get very busy, so carry a tent with you. There are authorized **campsites** that you need to pay for (no permit needed); the park has suffered a series of devastating **fires** in recent years, so restrictions have tightened up and free camping is only allowed in the vicinity of the mountain refuges. Campsites include: *Lago Roca*, near the Cascada Los Alerces; *Los Vuriloches* (☏0294 15 462 3125) at Pampa Linda; and *Los Rápidos* (☏0294 15 441 6120) at Lago Mascardi.

At Pampa Linda there are more luxurious **accommodation** options. Among the best are:

Hostería Pampa Linda Cerro Tronador ☏0294 449 0517 or ☏0294 449 0517, ⓦ hosteriapampalinda .com.ar. A well-cared-for *hostería* with friendly staff and comfortable rooms. Closed May & June. **$1920**

Hotel Tronador Cerro Tronador ☏0294 449 0556, ⓦ hoteltronador.com. Upmarket option with stunning lake views, at the northwestern end of Lago Mascardi. Closed mid-April to mid-Nov. Full board **$2728**

ARRIVAL AND GETTING AROUND   **CIRCUITO CHICO**

Organized tours from Bariloche (see box, p.400) do the circuit (4hr; $235), or you can go independently.

By bus Bus #20 from Bariloche goes to Cerro Campanario, Puerto Pañuelo and *Llao Llao*, and bus #10

heads to Colonia Suiza.
By car The best option for comfort, although costly

(around $1200/day). There are plenty of car rental options in Bariloche (see p.399).

By bike Take bus #20 towards *Llao Llao* and get off at Av Bustillo Km18.6, from where you can rent a bike (see p.400); this cuts out the initial traffic-heavy part of the route.

Circuito Grande

Renting a car is the best way to do the Circuito Grande, though full-day organized tours ($495) with Adventure Center (see box, p.400) are also available

The **Circuito Grande** is a 240km loop that leads east out of Bariloche on RN-237 past the incredible rock formations of the **Valle Encantado** ("Enchanted Valley"). Here you'll see pine forests lining the steep valley outcrops and stone fingers pointing skywards while the blue waters of the Río Limay flow below. The Río Traful joins the Río Limay at Confluencia, 70km from Bariloche. Here the RN-237 continues on towards Neuquén while RP-65 turns northwest towards Villa Traful. Past the lake, at El Portezuelo pass, the circuit joins the southern section of the Ruta de los Siete Lagos (see p.410) near Lagos Correntoso and Espejo, and then returns southwards to Bariloche via Villa La Angostura. Alternatively, you could turn right when you meet the Ruta de los Siete Lagos and head to San Martín de los Andes (see p.422).

Cerro Catedral

Cable car daily 9am–4.45pm • $120 return • Buses (marked "Catedral") run from Moreno 470 in Bariloche to Villa Catedral; alternatively, you could take a half-day organized trip to the village (4hr; $235) with Turisur (see box, p.400)

Some 20km south of Bariloche is **Cerro Catedral**, named for the Gothic steeples of rock that make up its craggy summit (2405m). In summer, the village of **Villa Catedral** is the starting point for a couple of fantastic treks up and around Cerro Catedral (see box, p.405), though you could just take a cable car and then a chairlift to reach Refugio Lynch near the summit (1870m). A short but steep climb takes you to the ridge, where the views are superb, and you just might catch a glimpse of condors.

Lago Mascardi and Cerro Tronador

Day-tours (around $615) are run by several travel agents, with some also offering the possibility of a boat trip on Lago Mascardi

In 2003, the path of the famous RN-40 (see box, p.491) was diverted to head through Nahuel Huapi rather than its original, less-scenic route further east, although some maps still show the old route numbers (RN-258 and 237). Leading south from Bariloche, it goes past handsome **Lago Gutiérrez** to the southernmost point on **Lago Mascardi**, where a dirt road strikes west around the lake shore and you must pay the park entrance fee. Further along, at Los Rápidos (where there's an organized campsite, the road forks. Both roads here become single-track, necessitating a timetable for travelling in each direction; check with the tourist office before setting out, as this changes seasonally. One fork takes you west along the southern Río Manso to Lago Hess and the Cascada de los Alerces – a 20m plunge of white water that is said to resemble a seated nineteenth-century lady with her dress spread out. The other fork takes you north towards **Pampa Linda**, with terrific views of the glaciers on **Cerro Tronador**. The "thundering" in its Spanish name refers to the echoing roar heard when vast chunks of ice break off the hanging glaciers and plunge down to the slopes below. The road goes on to the Ventisquero Negro lookout, a moraine-encrusted glacier and offshoot of Glaciar del Manso on the upper slopes of Cerro Tronador. Some tours include short walks to the 50m-high Saltillo de las Nalcas or Garganta del Diablo, while there are plenty of longer hiking options from Pampa Linda itself (see box, p.405).

SKIING IN THE LAKE DISTRICT

Along with Las Leñas (see p.364), Bariloche and the Lake District is Argentina's premier **ski destination**, packed in the winter with ski and snowboard fans from Argentina, Brazil and further afield. While it does get busy in peak season (July & Aug), the quality of the powder, infrastructure and après-ski is very good, with Bariloche acting as a hub for the surrounding area. The main ski resort is **Cerro Catedral** (w catedralaltapatagonia.com), served by Villa Catedral at its base, with plenty of accommodation, equipment rental, restaurants, comfortable lifts and easy access to the après-ski in Bariloche – not to mention outstanding views. There are more than 120km of runs in all, of varying grades of difficulty, some with descents of up to 4km in length. Other resorts in the area include the smaller, more upmarket **Cerro Bayo** (w cerrobayoweb.com) 10km east of Villa La Angostura (see opposite), and **La Hoya** (w skilahoya.com) some 13km northeast of Esquel (see p.415), a low-key family centre with moderately challenging pistes, nine lifts and good powder.

For five days in August, Bariloche celebrates the **Fiesta Nacional de la Nieve**, with ski races, parades and a torchlit evening descent on skis to open the season officially, although the season actually lasts from around mid-June to mid-October. If you want the probability of good snow conditions but prefer quieter slopes, go in September.

Isla Victoria

Trips run by Turisur twice daily • $680 (doesn't include $120 park entry fee, $150 Bariloche transfers or $37.25 port tax)

A very popular boat trip within the park heads to **Isla Victoria** from Puerto Pañuelo (see p.404), where there are rock paintings, beaches and a chairlift to Cerro Bella Vista with the requisite stunning views. The boat then continues north to the Bosque de los Arrayanes (see p.410).

Puerto Blest

Trips run by Turisur twice daily • $680 (doesn't include $120 park entry fee, $150 Bariloche transfers or $37.25 port tax)

Less crowded than the Isla Victoria boat and equally worthwhile, the boat-and-bus excursion to **Puerto Blest** in the western fringes of the Parque Nacional Huapi takes in lake vistas along the way and starts with a 75-minute boat trip from Puerto Pañuelo. A minibus continues the trip to the shores of Lago Frías, with its peppermint-coloured waters. During the early morning and late afternoon you can see condors gathering at their nearby roost. Returning to Puerto Blest, the boat crosses the channel to dock on the north shore, after which there is a forty-minute stroll to the stepped **Cascada Los Cántaros** waterfall.

Villa La Angostura

Spread along the northern lake shore of Nahuel Huapi, **VILLA LA ANGOSTURA** has grown enormously in the past decade, capitalizing on the Lake District's surging popularity. The settlement originally swelled owing to its proximity to the trout-fishing at Río Correntoso, one of the world's shortest rivers, but today caters mostly to upper-end tourists, with whole new areas of wooded hills giving way to luxury hotels, cabins and spas. The almost ubiquitous log-cabin architecture can feel a bit forced, rather like a mountain-village theme park, and the constant flow of traffic rather ruins the peace. However, it is smaller than Bariloche, has some top-notch accommodation (though few budget options), and provides the only land access to **Parque Nacional Los Arrayanes** (see p.410).

The town sprawls along the lakeside, with the centre known as **El Cruce**. Avenida Arrayanes transects the town; everything you are likely to need during your stay is concentrated in a 200m stretch between Boulevard Nahuel Huapi and Cerro Bayo. The park is reached by crossing the isthmus at **La Villa**, a 3km-long peninsula south of the centre – the old harbour.

Other than visiting the park or going on fishing trips, you can get good views from the summit of **Cerro Bayo**, 10km east from the centre of Villa Angostura, which you can hike up in summer. Another good local hike (or short drive) is to **Mirador Belvedere** and Cascada Inacayal, a delightful waterfall, both along the southeast shore of Lago Correntoso.

ARRIVAL AND DEPARTURE VILLA LA ANGOSTURA

By bus The cute wooden bus station is just off Av Arrayanes at Av Siete Lagos. Empresa 15 de Mayo (☎ 0294 449 5104 or ☎ 0294 449 4227) runs nine daily buses between La Villa and El Cruce. Quetrihue (Inacayal 13 1st floor, Villa La

Angostura ☎ 0294 449 4803) does transfers to Bariloche airport ($400/person).
Destinations Bariloche (10 daily; 1hr 30min); San Martín de los Andes (4 daily; 2hr 30min).

INFORMATION AND ACTIVITIES

Tourist information The helpful tourist office is at Av Arrayanes 9, next to the bus station (daily 8am–10pm; ☎ 0294 449 4124, ☜ villalaangostura.gov.ar), and can help you find accommodation if you haven't made reservations in advance.
Bike rental Aquiles, Av Arrayanes 96 and 150 (☎ 0294 449 4303).
Fishing trips Max Fishing, Río Litran 1433,

☎ 0294 15 431 1184.
Horseriding Cabalgatas Correntoso (Cacique Antriao; ☎ 0294 15 451 0559, ☜ facebook.com/cabalgata correntoso.com.ar) runs trips led by Tero Bogani, who adds just the right amount of gaucho to the rides.
Patagonia Sailing (☎ 0294 15 461 9781, ☜ patagoniasailing.com.ar). Runs small-group sailing trips, from 1hr to a full day, on Lago Nahuel Huapi.

7

ACCOMMODATION

The most affordable accommodation in Villa La Angostura tends to be in **El Cruce**, with more upmarket choices in the northern and southern suburbs – prices increase as the lake view improves.

La Angostura Barbagelata 157 ☎ 0294 449 4834, ☜ hostellaangostura.com.ar. One of the best and most central hostels, two blocks from the bus station, with modern and tastefully designed four- to six-bed dorms and double rooms – all en suite – and a pleasant communal area. Private apartments sleeping up to six people ($1350) also available. Dorms $300; doubles $850
Las Balsas Bahía Caballera de Benerice 2290 ☎ 0294 449 4308, ☜ lasbalsas.com. Part of the high-end Relais et Chateaux group, *Las Balsas* epitomizes Angostura, and is renowned for its sybaritic qualities: beautiful rooms, a relaxing spa and a perfect location, though the restaurant is disappointing. US$350
Camping Unquehué Av Siete Lagos 727 ☎ 0294 449 4103, ☜ campingunquehue.com.ar. The most convenient campsite, 500m west of the bus terminal. Priced per pitch, with a $130 surcharge per person. Apartments sleeping up to four also available. Camping $40; apartments $2000
Correntoso Av Siete Lagos 4505 ☎ 0294 15 461 9727, ☜ correntoso.com. The settlement's original fishing lodge, dating from 1917, was completely renovated before reopening in 2003 as this four-star hotel. Making the most of its spectacular setting overlooking the river for which it's named, the *Correntoso*'s historic charm, created by abundant natural light and highly tasteful decor, mixes well with its modern services, which include a herbal spa and gourmet restaurant. US$350

★**La Escondida** Av Arrayanes 7014 ☎ 0294 482 6110, ☜ laescondida.house. Exquisite *hostería* lounging in sumptuous grounds that slope down to the lakeside, where a heated pool, loungers, boats and even beds beckon. The rooms, named after typical Argentine game, are stylish in an understated fashion; each enjoys breathtaking views and is distinctly decorated and furnished. US$240
Hostería del Francés Lolog 2057 ☎ 0294 448 8055, ☜ lodelfrances.com.ar. A beautiful cabin with lake views and four double rooms with wooden bathrooms and balconies, 4km from the tourist office. An apartment sleeping up to three ($1500) is also available. $1150
Río Bonito Topa Topa 260 ☎ 0294 449 4110, ☜ riobonitopatagonia.com.ar. This spotlessly clean and pleasant *residencial* offers airy rooms, among the cheapest in town. $900
Traunco Las Frambuesas 52 ☎ 0294 449 5518, ☜ traunco.com.ar. Pleasant *hostería* in typical local style – wooden floors throughout, with tree trunks curling around the stairs and bar. The location is handy for the bus station and main street and the rooms are comfortable, if small. $1800
★**Verena's Haus** Los Taiques 268 ☎ 0294 449 4467, ☜ verenashaus.com.ar. White, wood-clad and homely establishment run with tender loving care. The breakfasts are excellent, with a selection of home-made breads, cakes and jams. $1190

EATING AND DRINKING

Most of Villa La Angostura's **restaurants** are located along a 200m stretch of El Cruce. Prices are high by Argentine standards – don't expect much change from $500 per head for a full meal with wine – and the gentrification can be a bit over the top, but the quality of food is generally good.

Los Amigos del Lado Sur Los Taiques 55 ☎0294 449 4829. The tables here have lovely garden views. Dishes include reasonably priced (by Angostura standards) wild boar and venison. Daily 8am–6pm.

Hub Arrayanes 21 ☎0294 449 5700. Trendy bar-restaurant with imaginative variations on a typically Patagonian theme, like trout ravioli, venison, and lamb stews. Live music some nights. Daily 8pm–late.

★ **La Luna Encantada** Belvedere 69 ☎0294 482 5999. Great home-brewed beer, cheese fondue ($360 for two people) and wood-fired pizzas (from $120) served in a well-appointed cabin. Popular with locals – a sure sign the prices are keen. Daily 1–3.30pm & 8.30pm–midnight.

Tinto Bistro Quetrihué ☎0294 449 4924. An almost royal place (The Netherlands' Queen Máxima's brother is the owner) serving up beautifully presented international dishes in a cute bistro setting. Try the ceviche ($195) and the wok-cooked vegetables ($235). Daily 8.30–11.30pm.

7

Parque Nacional de los Arrayanes

Daily 9am–2pm; stays open until 6pm for those arriving by boat • $120 • Hike or cycle from Villa La Angostura (12km each way), or take a boat from Bahía Mansa, Bahía Brava or Bariloche

The **Parque Nacional de los Arrayanes** is a park within a park, home to the **Bosque de los Arrayanes**, the world's best stand of myrtle woodland. The park is located on the narrow-necked Península Quetrihué, jutting out from Barrio La Villa in Villa La Angostura, with the Bosque situated at its far tip.

Quetrihué means "place of the *arrayanes*" in Mapudungun, and it is those trees that are the real draw here. The **arrayán** is a slow-growing tree characterized by flaky, cinnamon-coloured, paper-like bark and amazing spiralling trunks. It can reach heights of up to 15m and live for three hundred years (although some specimens here may be as much as 600 years old), and it only grows close to cool water. The canopy of the *arrayán* is made up of delicate glossy clusters of foliage, and in late summer it flowers in dainty white blossoms, with the edible blue-black berries maturing in autumn.

Boulevard Nahuel Huapi terminates in La Villa with the stretch that connects the two bays on either side of the peninsula's narrow neck: **Bahía Mansa** ("Peaceful Bay") on the eastern side and **Bahía Brava** ("Wild Bay") on the western side, both used as catamaran departure points. When seen from the lake, the Bosque doesn't look much different from the surrounding forest – it's when you're underneath the canopy that its magic envelops you. The much-told story that Walt Disney took his inspiration for the forest scenes in *Bambi* from this enchanted woodland is apocryphal (he actually took it from photographs of birch forests in Maine), but that doesn't much matter. The place certainly does have a fairytale feel, as you walk around the 600m **boardwalk** at your leisure while the contorted corkscrew trunks creak against each other in the breeze and the light plays on them like a French Impressionist's dream.

ARRIVAL AND DEPARTURE — PARQUE NACIONAL DE LOS ARRAYANES

By boat Futaleufú (☎0294 449 4405) runs three daily catamaran trips from Bahía Mansa ($450), and Patagonia Argentina (☎0294 449 4463) three daily trips from Bahía Brava ($450). Turisur (see p.400) runs two daily boat trips from Bariloche via Isla Victoria ($680).

By bike Bayo Aboyo offer bike rental both in Villa La Angostura (Av Siete Lagos 94; ☎0294 448 8383) and at Puerto Manzano (Av Arrayanes 6510).

Ruta de los Siete Lagos

The classic **Ruta de los Siete Lagos** ("Seven Lakes Route") connects **Villa La Angostura** with **San Martín de los Andes** (see p.422) in spectacular fashion, passing through forested valleys and giving access to many more than the eponymous seven lakes – lagos Nahuel Huapi, Espejo, Correntoso, Escondido, Villarino, Falkner and

Machónico. You'll also pass several fishing spots – buy permits before setting off (from tourist offices, YPF stations or campsites). The route is now all paved, and considered part of the classic RN-40; previously, it was RN-231 in the southern half and RN-234 in the northern half, and older maps still mark it as such.

Lago Nahuel Huapi to Lago Correntoso

Soon after leaving Angostura, RN-40 crosses Río Correntoso, famous for its fishing and, at barely 250m long, one of the planet's shortest rivers. The road then skirts the northernmost tip of **Lago Nahuel Huapi**, by far the largest lake on the route. As you turn north, you quickly see **Lago Espejo** ("Looking-glass Lake"), renowned as the warmest and smoothest (hence the name) lake hereabouts. Alongside the Seccional Espejo *guardaparque* post is a free campsite, by a beach that's good for swimming. Just before the *guardaparque*'s house is another site, with spacious pitches, a beach, and an easy forest trail opposite (30min), which heads through woods to an isolated spot on the western shore of magical **Lago Correntoso**. Beyond here you trace Lago Correntoso's northern shores and pass a lakeside campsite, run by one of the area's original indigenous families and offering *tortas fritas*, meals and provisions.

7

Cascadas Ñivinco

RN-40 swings sharply north from Lago Correntoso, before coming to RP-65 turn-off to Villa Traful (see p.412) via the Portezuelo pass. You then pass through a magnificent valley with sheer cliffs towering over 600m. It's worth stopping at the signposted track to a series of five waterfalls known collectively as **Cascadas Ñivinco**. Reaching them involves an easy 2km walk through *ñire* and *caña colihue* forest, but you'll get your feet (and possibly knees) wet when you ford the river.

Lago Escondido, Lago Villarino and Lago Falkner

Further north is pint-sized **Lago Escondido**, the most enchanting of all the lakes, hiding its emerald-green charms demurely in the forest. Before crossing the limpid waters of Río Pichi Traful, you pass through Seccional Villarino (open daily 24hr), where the *guardaparque* will give you information on recommended walks, such as the trek up Cerro Falkner.

Continuing north, you come to the eastern point of **Lago Villarino**, a popular place for fishing, with Cerro Crespo (2130m) as a picturesque backdrop and a free lakeside campsite. On the other side of the main road, **Lago Falkner** is a perennial favourite of fishermen, sitting at the foot of **Cerro Falkner** (2350m), and a campsite here (see p.412) provides accommodation. Just to the north of Lago Falkner you pass Cascada Vulliñanco, a 20m waterfall to the west of the road.

Lago Machónico to San Martín

Continuing on RN-40, you cross from Parque Nahuel Huapi into the neighbouring Parque Lanín (see p.430). You then skirt the eastern shore of **Lago Machónico** and, in the final meanders of the route, pass through handsome *ñire* and *coihue* woods. Make sure you stop at the Mirador de Pil Pil to take in the superb panorama of mighty Lago Lácar, whose waters lap San Martín de los Andes, the route's northern terminus.

ARRIVAL AND DEPARTURE

RUTA DE LOS SIETE LAGOS

By bus Several daily bus services travel the route between Villa La Angostura and San Martín; be sure you get a bus that follows the "7 lagos" route and not the alternative "Rinconada" route. La Araucana (☎02972 420285 or ☎02972 422131, ☻araucana.com.ar) runs minibuses three times a day ($200), but you need to change in Villa Traful. Albus (☎0294 449 4041, ☻albus.com.ar) also

operates buses along the same route four times a day in high season, less frequently out of season ($121).

By organized tour Many agencies in San Martín offer trips along the route, including Siete Lagos Turismo at Villegas 313 (☎02972 427877, ☻sietelagosturismo .com.ar). Bariloche-based tour operators (see p.400) also come here.

ACCOMMODATION

Camping Falkner On the shores of Lago Falkner. This large lakeside campsite has lots of facilities, including a restaurant and shop; it's popular with Argentine students and young families, who come to cool off in the lake, camp and party. $180

Lago Traful

A popular destination for trout and salmon fishermen, **Lago Traful** is a pure, intense blue, like a pool of liquid Roman glass. It's best accessed along RP-65, which follows its entire southern shore, with the most beautiful approach from the Ruta de los Siete Lagos, crossing the pass of El Portezuelo and heading through the **Valle de los Machis** (with its majestic *coihue* trees), beneath the heights of Pico Traful (2040m).

Midway along the lake on RP-65 is **Villa Traful**, a loose assemblage of houses spread out along several kilometres of the shoreline. Five kilometres east of the village on RP-65 is a particularly impressive lookout point: the **Mirador Pared del Viento** (or Mirador del Traful), a precipitous rockface with superb views over the azure waters 75m below.

Trekking options include hikes to various waterfalls, climbing **Cerro Negro** behind the village (1999m; 7–9hr) or making a trip to **Laguna Las Mellizas** on the northern side of the lake to see indigenous rock paintings. You'll need to hire a boat for the fifteen-minute crossing, preferably with a driver who can also guide you through the multiple tracks to the paintings (5hr return); the *Hostería Villa Traful* (see below) can often put you in contact with someone. There is a free wild campsite at Paloma Araucana, by the foot of the Mirador Pared del Viento.

ARRIVAL AND INFORMATION   LAGO TRAFUL

By bus Albus buses (☎0294 442 3552) run between Villa Traful and Bariloche (4 weekly; 2hr).
Park information Set back from the village's main jetty, a *guardaparque* post (daily 9am–8pm; ☎0294 447 9033) can provide you with information on local hikes – register before setting out.

Tourist information To the east of the village, near the YPF fuel station, is the tourist office (daily 9am–9pm; ☎0294 447 9099). As well as advising on accommodation, it sells fishing permits and has information on fishing guides.

ACCOMMODATION AND EATING

Hostería Villa Traful RP-65, Villa Traful ☎0294 447 9005, ⌨hosteriavillatraful.com. Homely, log-cabin-style hotel with a real fire and windows looking out onto expansive gardens. Also rents out cabins ($1800) for up to six people. $1250
Ñancú Lahuen RP-65, Villa Traful ☎0294 447 9017. Popular tearoom and restaurant, serving high-quality treats like chocolates and cakes, as well as meals like pasta

and trout. Daily noon–11pm.
La Vulcanche RP-61 s/n ☎0294 447 9028, ⌨vulcanche.com. A pleasant budget complex with dorms ($30 surcharge for bed sheets), camping and good-value self-catering cabins sleeping up to five. There's a restaurant on site and staff can help you organize fishing excursions. Camping $100; dorms $200; *cabanas* $800

El Bolsón

The 123km trip southwards along RN-40 from Bariloche to **EL BOLSÓN** offers yet more stunning mountain and lake views. Just inside Río Negro Province and set in the bowl of a wide, fertile valley, hemmed in by parallel ranges of mountains, El Bolsón is a thriving tourist centre with numerous trekking opportunities close at hand. It was Latin America's first town to declare itself nuclear free and an "ecological municipality". Owing to the claim that the jagged peak of the nearby **Cerro Piltriquitrón** (2260m) is one of the earth's "energy centres", El Bolsón became a popular hippy hangout in the 1960s, and while it's a bit more commercial these days, the laidback atmosphere persists. In summer it's particularly popular with young Argentine backpackers, since it's far easier on the wallet than nearby Bariloche.

OUTDOOR ACTIVITIES IN EL BOLSÓN

The Informes de Montaña, at Roca and Onelli (daily 8am–9pm; ☎0294 445 5810), can guide you through **trekking** possibilities in the area, most of which consist of considerable ascents. Among the most popular is the **Cerro Hielo Azul Circuit** (4–6hr), which brings you high enough to look out over views of glaciers. Further north you can make side treks to the less-visited areas of **Cerro Dedo Gordo** (4–5hr) and **Los Laguitos** (6–8hr). To the south, the hike to *Refugio Cerro Lindo* (5–7hr) takes in Lago Jovita, a lake with beautiful blue waters encased by sheer cliffs. Another interesting, relatively gentle hike, to **Cajón Azul** (4–5hr), starts from the same point as Dedo Gordo – 15km north of El Bolsón off RN-40 at Chacra Wharton, by the banks of Río Azul – and passes an excellent *refugio* that serves hot food. The Cajón (gorge) itself is an opening 1m wide and 40m deep; the Río Azul roars through the bottom. Local tour operators offer guided treks as well as horseriding, rafting and boating. Particularly good is Grado 42, at Av Belgrano 406 (☎0294 449 3124, ⊛grado42.com), which offers tours to the Bosque Tallado and other local sights.

Spiritual life in El Bolsón is cosmopolitan, and you'll find Buddhist temples as well as a variety of practitioners of alternative paths. Unsurprisingly, UFOs and spirits (*duendes*) are also said to stop off regularly, being guaranteed an especially sympathetic reception on the last Saturday of February, when the town's main party, the **Fiesta del Lúpulo** (Hops Festival), celebrates the harvest of an important local crop (and in particular the heady brew made from it) with music, food and an enjoyable, well-lubricated atmosphere.

The town is also worth visiting for its **crafts market** (Tues, Thurs, Sat & Sun 10am–dusk) on the Plaza Pagano, famous throughout the Lake District for the quality of its merchandise, including locally brewed beers.

Bosque Tallado

Taxi to Cerro Piltriquitrón ($800 return) plus a 40min uphill walk

East of town, on the wooded slopes of **Cerro Piltriquitrón**, is an unconventional and interesting site – the **Bosque Tallado** (Sculpted Forest) – 31 tree stumps carved by local craftsmen into a variety of fascinating and often grotesque figures.

ARRIVAL AND DEPARTURE   EL BOLSÓN

Arriving from the north, RN-40 is called Av Sarmiento; its southern end is called Av Belgrano. These two converge on the ACA fuel station in the centre of town on Av San Martín, the town's backbone. If you come in a car it's worth filling your tank here – fuel is cheaper in El Bolsón than in nearby localities.

By bus Buses from Bariloche and Esquel drop you off at their respective offices, most of which are on or just off Av Sarmiento. La Golondrina (Hube and Perito Moreno; ☎0294 449 2557) runs buses to Lago Puelo, Cholila and Wharton (for treks to Cajón de Azul) and stops at the south end of Plaza Pagano along Av San Martín.

Destinations Bariloche (13 daily; 2hr); Cholila (3 daily; 2hr 30min); Esquel (8 daily; 2hr 45min); Lago Puelo (hourly; 30min); Wharton (8 daily; 30min).
By taxi Taxis can be hard to find and should be booked in advance: try Remises Patagonia (☎0294 449 3907).
By organized tour Bariloche agencies such as Turisur (see p.400) run day-trips to El Bolsón ($615).

INFORMATION AND TOURS

Tourist office On the north side of the plaza, at the corner of San Martín and Roca, is the useful tourist information office (daily 8am–10pm; ☎0294 449 2604, ⊛turismoelbolson.gob.ar).

Fran's Remises Taxi company (☎0294 449 3041) offering return services and tours to local attractions like Cascada Escondida ($220) and Bosque Tallado ($800).

ACCOMMODATION

Albergue Gaia 7km north of the centre ☎0294 449 8331, ⊛alberguegaia.com.ar; take a Transporte Urbano bus to Km118. A stellar hostel, the airy, ecologically minded *Gaia* boasts laundry facilities, a swimming pool and very friendly staff. There's an extra charge for breakfast. Dorms __$250__; doubles __$690__

Cabañas Paraiso Subida a Piltriquitrón 2005 ☎0294 449 2766, ⓦcabaniasparaiso.com.ar. Ideally located for the Bosque Tallado, with well-equipped cabins for up to six people, and a heated indoor pool. The staff can organize rafting, trekking and horseriding excursions. $\underline{\$1700}$

La Posada de Hamelín Granollers 2179 ☎0294 449 2030, ⓦposadadehamelin.com.ar. A lovely brick building in town, with hops growing up the walls, adobe interiors and four tastefully furnished rooms. $\underline{\$720}$

El Pueblito Comarca Andina del Paralelo 42 ☎0294 449 3560, ⓦfacebook.com/ElPueblitoHostel. Located 4km north of the centre and reached by Transporte Urbano bus or a taxi, the well-run, HI-affiliated *El Pueblito* has a bar serving local beers, a restaurant and open fires, as well as great views of the surrounding area. Dorms $\underline{US\$20}$; doubles $\underline{US\$65}$

★**Valle Nuevo** 25 de May and Berutti ☎0294 449 2087. Small but clean and bright rooms with stunning mountain views. Well maintained, and with excellent customer care. $\underline{\$650}$

EATING AND DRINKING

El Bolsón is one of the few towns in Argentina where finding **vegetarian food** is not a problem. The valleys around are chock-a-block with *chacras* or smallholdings that produce organic vegetables, and fruits and berries for jams or desserts; the local honey and cheese are also good. In summer, the plaza heaves with open-air **bars**.

El Bolsón Brewery Km124 on the main road north ☎0294 449 2595, ⓦcervezaselbolson.com. The aficionado owner serves up a variety of beers, including fruity brews (if you like the similar ales from Belgium, you'll love these). Free guided tours of the brewery are sometimes given. Mon–Sat 9am–midnight, Sun 10am–10pm.

Humus de la Montaña Camino los Nagales ☎0294 449 2702. Famed for its organic yogurt, cheese and ice cream. Tours of the dairy are given three days a week (Tues, Thurs & Sat 4pm & 6pm; $25). Mon–Sat 9am–7pm.

★**Jauja** San Martín 2867 ☎0294 449 2448. Patagonian restaurant, ice-cream parlour and artisanal chocolate shop all in one; the ice cream, especially the red fruits flavour, is fantastic. The original home of what is now a small chain. Mon–Fri 8am–midnight, Sat & Sun 9am–midnight.

Cholila and around

Sitting amid prairie grasslands, 3km east of the junction of RP-71 and RP-15, the hamlet of **CHOLILA**, with its spectacular backdrop of savage peaks, seems to belong in the American West. So there's no better setting for one of Patagonia's most idiosyncratic sights – the **cabin** of Wild West outlaw **Butch Cassidy**. From Cholila, you can continue southwest through a glorious lush valley hemmed in by snowcapped mountains towards the northern gate of Parque Nacional Los Alerces (see p.418).

Butch Cassidy's cabin

Head 12km north of Cholila along RP-71 towards Leleque, and turn left at the police commissionaire's white house at El Blanco towards *La Casa de Piedra* teahouse. The cluster of three buildings is around 250m down the track

North of Cholila village is the area's main tourist attraction: the site of **Butch Cassidy's cabin**. This is where he lived after fleeing incognito to this isolated area at the start of the twentieth century with his partner, the **Sundance Kid**, who also lived here for a short while with his beautiful gangster moll, **Etta Place**. The buildings were already in a lamentable state of repair when Bruce Chatwin (*In Patagonia*) visited in the 1970s and were about to collapse when the local authorities finally set about restoration in 2007 – overdoing the job, to some tastes. Still, there is no visitors' centre, entrance fee, or much to do as such, other than take in the atmosphere, relish the remoteness, and conjure up the ghosts of the famous outlaws.

Museo Leleque

Down a track off RN-40, Km1440 • Mon, Tues & Thurs–Sun 11am–7pm (though hours change frequently) • $50 • ☎011 4326 5156, ⓦwww.benetton.com/patagonia

A couple of kilometres off RN-40 along a track that leads east from RP-15 turn-off to

BUTCH CASSIDY AND THE SUNDANCE KID

Butch Cassidy, Etta Place and the **Sundance Kid** were fugitives together in the Argentine frontier town of Cholila between the years 1901 and 1906, as attested to by both the **Pinkerton Agency** and provincial records of the time. Butch and Sundance had grown weary of years of relentless pursuit, and heard rumours that Argentina was the new land of opportunity, offering the type of wide-open ranching country they loved, and where they could live free from the ceaseless hounding of Pinkerton agents.

It appears that, at first, the *bandidos* tried to go straight – Sundance and Etta even living under their real names as Mr and Mrs Harry Longabaugh – and in this they succeeded, for a while at least. They were always slightly distant from the community and were evidently viewed as somewhat eccentric, yet decent, individuals. Certainly no one ever suspected they had a criminal past.

Various theories are mooted as to why the threesome sold their ranch in such a rush in 1907, but it seems as though the arrival of a Wild Bunch associate – the murderous **Harvey "Kid Curry" Logan**, following his escape from a Tennessee jail – had something to do with it. The robbery of a bank in Río Gallegos in early 1905 certainly had the hallmarks of a carefully planned Cassidy job, and a spate of robberies along the cordillera in the ensuing years has, with varying degrees of evidence, been attributed to the *bandidos norteamericanos*.

What happened to Cholila's outlaws next is a matter of conjecture. Etta returned to the US, putatively because she needed an operation for acute appendicitis, but equally possibly because she was pregnant, as a result of a dalliance with a young Anglo-Irish rancher. The violent deaths of Butch and Sundance were reported in Uruguay, and in several sites across Argentina and Bolivia. The least likely scenario is the one depicted by Paul Newman and Robert Redford in the famous 1969 Oscar-winning film. Bruce Chatwin in his classic *In Patagonia* proposes that the Sundance Kid was shot by frontier police in Río Pico, south of Esquel. Countless books have been written on the trio, including *In Search of Butch Cassidy*, by Larry Pointer, and *Digging Up Butch and Sundance*, by Anne Meadows.

Cholila, the Estancia Leleque lies within the Benetton estate, one of the largest private properties in the country, owned by the Italian fashion family. The only part of the estancia open to the public is the fabulous **Museo Leleque**, housed in a beautifully restored outbuilding. The handsome exhibits spread over four rooms trace the history of the indigenous peoples, local pioneers and the relations between them by means of a collection of memorabilia collected by the late Pablo Korscheneweski, born in Odessa in 1925, who founded the museum together with Carlo Benetton. The highlight, though, is the *boliche* – a typical rural inn combined with general store and canteen, where you can have a drink and something to eat while admiring a set of remarkably well-preserved old bric-a-brac. Save some money for the excellent museum catalogue.

ARRIVAL AND DEPARTURE

By bus Cholila's bus terminal is on the main square. **Destinations** El Bolsón (3 daily; 1hr 40min–2hr);

CHOLILA AND AROUND

Esquel (2 daily or 5 weekly depending on season; 2hr 30min–3hr 45min).

ACCOMMODATION

Hostería El Trebol 2.7km from the bus terminal along RP-15 ☎ 02945 498055. Comfortable, tranquil B&B, with simple rooms in lime-green cabins, and a bar area with homely hearth. There's also a restaurant serving dinner (from $180), with courses featuring vegetables grown in the hotel's garden. $800

Esquel and around

Heading south beyond Cholila you'll notice a distinct change in the scenery, as the lush pine forests are replaced by drier terrain that is home to the stunted *meseta*-style vegetation more typical of Patagonia proper. Some 90km south of the Cholila/Leleque turning off RN-40, **Esquel**, the main town in the area, is a starting point for visits to

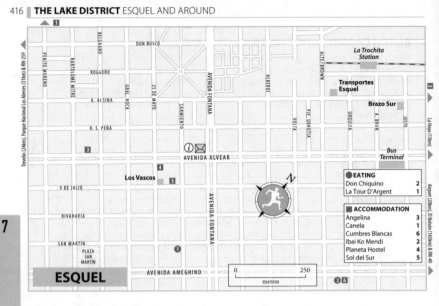

7

ESQUEL

Parque Nacional Los Alerces and a scattering of Welsh villages, of which **Trevelin** is the most appealing. This is also the stage through which the steam train **La Trochita** runs, one of the region's most enduring attractions.

Esquel

For a place so close to exuberant Andean forests, **ESQUEL** is surprising for the aridity of its setting. Enclosed in a bowl of dusty ochre mountains, it is a stark contrast to Bariloche and El Bolsón. The town itself is pretty drab and uninteresting – most people make the trip to access the nearby **Parque Nacional Los Alerces** (see p.418), with the trip on *La Trochita* (see box, p.418) as the next biggest attraction; it's also a popular place to stay for skiing in winter (see box, p.408). If you're looking to kill some time in town, it's worth popping into Los Vascos, the old-fashioned *almacen de ramos generales* (general store) at 9 de Julio 1000. Such stores were once common sights in the Argentine countryside, providing a one-stop shop for pioneers and estancia workers to get their supplies. The 90-year-old store, with its wooden shelves and stepladders, still sells everything from shampoo and talc to trousers and hats.

ARRIVAL AND DEPARTURE   ESQUEL

By air The town's airport (☎02945 451676), which has a daily flight to Buenos Aires (2hr), is 20km east of the centre. You can take a *remís* to town ($250).

By bus The stylish bus terminal (☎02945 451584) is on the main boulevard, at Av Alvear 1871, about 1km from the town centre.

Destinations Bariloche (8 daily; 4hr 30min); Cholila (2 daily or 5 weekly depending on season; 2hr 30min–3hr 45min); El Bolsón (8 daily; 2hr 30min); Trevelin (hourly; 30min).

By train *La Trochita* station (see box, p.418) is at Roggero and Brun, three blocks northwest of the bus terminal.

INFORMATION AND TOURS

Tourist information The excellent tourist office at Alvear and Sarmiento (high season Mon–Fri 8am–10pm, Sat 9am–10pm; low season Mon–Fri 8am–8pm, Sat 9am–8pm; ☎02945 451927 or ☎02945 453145, ⓦesquel.tur.ar) can help you find accommodation if you

haven't reserved.

Brazo Sur (AP Justo 982; ☎02945 15 466538) operates tours in the region, including trips to the Parque Los Alerces, horseriding and rafting.

ACCOMMODATION

There's a wide range of accommodation in town while *cabaña* complexes are found 2–3km from the centre. Outside summer (Dec–Feb) and the skiing season (July & Aug) you'll get large discounts.

Angelina Alvear 758 ☎02945 452763, ⓦbit.ly /HosteriaAngelina. This comfortable, family-run *hostería* is modern with stone-clad walls and a fountain. Ask for a room at the back, as the front can be a bit noisy. $750
★Canela Los Notros 1440 ☎02945 453890, ⓦcanelaesquel.com. Veronica and Jorge run a fabulous British-style B&B in a pleasant residential area a short way out of town. The tasteful rooms are extremely comfortable, the house is charming – as are the hosts – and the breakfast will keep you up and running all day. US$135
Cumbres Blancas Av Ameghino 1683 ☎02945 455100, ⓦcumbresblancas.com.ar. A classy motel feel pervades this upmarket establishment. Large airy rooms come with wi-fi and safe, and there's a sauna and "Scottish

shower" (lateral water jets). $2720
★Ibai Ko Mendi Rivadavia 2965 ☎02945 451503, ⓦibaikomendi.com.ar. Delightful rooms in the main *hostería* building, plus attractive wood and stone cabins sleeping up to seven, all set in a tranquil complex that includes a pool and spa. Doubles $1700; *cabañas* $1900
Planeta Hostel Av Alvear 1021 ☎02945 456846, ⓦplanetahostel.com. A clean, spacious and centrally located hostel with cosy duvets. Dorms $280; doubles $1000
Sol del Sur 9 de Julio 1086 ☎02945 452189, ⓦsoldelsurhotel.com.ar. A dependable mid-range choice, with standard, comfortable rooms and amenities (TV and fridge). Breakfast is included. $1250

EATING

Don Chiquino Av Ameghino 1641 ☎02945 450035. This reliable restaurant serves tasty Italian food in a cosy atmosphere, though it gets packed in high season. Daily noon–midnight.
La Tour d'Argent San Martín 1063 ☎02945 454612.

Cheap and filling menu featuring pastas (from $58) and chicken with mushrooms ($120), as well as a more adventurous, appetizing a la carte selection that includes trout with a variety of sauces ($155–188). Daily noon–2/2.30pm & 8–11.30pm.

Trevelin

The main Welsh settlement along the Andes (most of the Welsh towns in Patagonia are closer to the ocean), **TREVELIN** is a small, easy-going place that retains a pioneering feel, with several low brick buildings characteristic of the late nineteenth and early twentieth centuries. Lying 24km south of Esquel, it has beautiful views across the grassy valley to the peaks in the south of Parque Nacional Los Alerces. Welsh settlers from the Chubut Valley set off on a series of expeditions to this region, with the first group – led by Colonel Fontana of the Argentine army and John Evans – arriving in 1885. These settlers founded the village a few years later; the name comes from the Welsh *tre* (town) and *velin* (mill), in reference to the flour mill that was built by the settlers.

The town's heritage is evoked in the celebration of a minor **Eisteddfod** (two days in the second week of October), and two **casas de té**. The best in terms of atmosphere is *Nain Maggie* at Perito Moreno 179 (daily 3.30–8pm; ☎02945 480232; $220 for Welsh tea with cakes): the teahouse is named after owner Lucia Underwood's grandmother, who was born in Trelew, came to Trevelin in 1891 and died in the town ninety years later at the age of 103. For the best cakes head to *La Mutisia*, at Av San Martín 170 (daily 3.30–9pm; ☎02945 480165; $200 for Welsh tea with cakes).

Museo Cartref Taid

200m northeast of the plaza • Daily 3–7pm • $60

Clery Evans, granddaughter of the village's founder John Evans, relates the origins of the settlement in Spanish at the **Museo Cartref Taid** (Welsh for "grandfather's home"). In the garden is the **Tumba de Malacara**, part of the grave of her granddad's faithful horse, El Malacara – who leapt heroically down a steep scarp to save his master from the same grisly fate that befell his companions. They had been killed by enraged Mapuche warriors who, following an atrocity committed against their tribe during the Conquest of the Desert, were bent on reprisals against any Europeans. The house

LA TROCHITA: THE OLD PATAGONIAN EXPRESS

A trip on the **Old Patagonian Express** rates as one of South America's classic journeys. The steam train puffs, judders and lurches across the arid, rolling steppe of northern Chubut, like a drunk on the well-worn route home, running on a track with a gauge of a mere 75cm. Don't let Paul Theroux's disparaging book *The Old Patagonian Express* put you off: travelling aboard it has an authentic Casey Jones aura and is definitely not something that appeals only to train-spotters. Along the way you'll see guanacos, rheas, maras and, if you are lucky, condors, as you traverse the estate of Estancia Leleque, owned by Italian clothes magnate Benetton, one of Argentina's biggest landowners.

Referred to lovingly in Spanish as **La Trochita**, meaning the "little narrow gauge", or *El Trencito*, the route has had an erratic history. It was conceived as a branch line to link Esquel with the main line joining Bariloche to Carmen de Patagones on the Atlantic coast. Construction began in Ingeniero Jacobacci in Río Negro Province in 1922, but it took 23 years to complete the 402km to Esquel. Originally, it was used as a mixed passenger and freight service, carrying consignments of wool, livestock, lumber and fruit from the cordillera region. The locomotives had to contend with snowdrifts in winter, and five derailments occurred between 1945 and 1993, caused by high winds or stray cows on the track. Proving unprofitable, the line was eventually closed in 1993. The Province of Chubut took over the running of the 165km section between Esquel and El Maitén soon afterwards, and *La Trochita* has matured into a major tourist attraction.

For most people, a ride on *La Trochita* means the half-day trip north from Esquel to Nahuel Pan, 22km away ($580). The train departs every Saturday at 10am and puts on up to ten further journeys weekly depending on demand and the season – ask at the tourist office for the latest timetables or call ☎ 02945 451403. There is also an occasional service running the 165km to El Maitén and returning the following day. Renovations or strikes sometimes close the line completely, so check before you come to Esquel if the train ride is the main objective of your journey.

attracts a steady stream of Bruce Chatwin pilgrims, as the story features in his classic travelogue, *In Patagonia* (see p.564).

ARRIVAL, INFORMATION AND TOURS

By bus Buses from Esquel (1–2 hourly; 30min) drop you off near the town's main plaza. Getting back to Esquel, the bus picks you up along Av San Martín.

Tourist information RN-259 from Esquel arrives at the octagonal Plaza Coronel Fontana at the north end of town, where you'll find the tourist office (Jan–Feb Mon–Fri

TREVELIN

8am–10pm, Sat & Sun 9am–10pm; March–Dec daily 8am–8pm; ☎ 02945 480120, ⊛ trevelin.gob.ar).

Gales Al Sur (Av Patagonia 186; ☎ 02945 480427, ⊛ galesalsur.com.ar) runs excursions to Los Alerces national park, horseriding trips and other local interest tours.

ACCOMMODATION AND EATING

El Chacay Cacique Nahuel Pan s/n ☎ 02945 15 407376. This campsite has a rural feel and decent hill views, and facilities include showers and a shop. Near the south end of San Martín, turn left a block past *Oregón* restaurant. $130
Estefania Perito Moreno 215 ☎ 02945 480148. This *hostería* has frilly rooms and a small heated pool. $700

Oregón San Martín and John Thomas, about eight blocks south of the main plaza ☎ 02945 480408, ⊛ oregontrevelin.com.ar. Good *cabañas* in an orchard, each with a kitchen and sleeping up to four. There's also a decent, moderately priced *parrilla* restaurant (Mon & Wed–Sun noon–3pm & 8.30–11.30pm). $1000

Parque Nacional Los Alerces

Established in 1937, the huge **PARQUE NACIONAL LOS ALERCES** in Chubut Province protects some of the most biologically important habitats and scenic landscapes in the region. Its superb lakes are famous for both their rich colours and their fishing, while most have a backdrop of sumptuous forests that quilt the surrounding mountain slopes. In the northeast of the park these lakes form a network centred on **lagos**

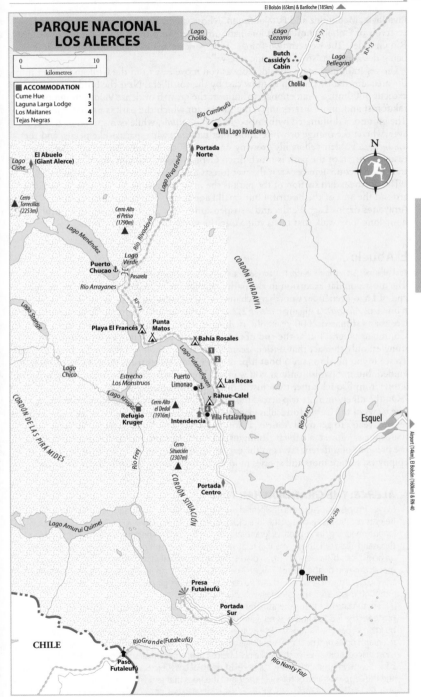

PARQUE NACIONAL LOS ALERCES

El Bolsón (65km) & Bariloche (185km)

0 ————————— 10
kilometres

ACCOMMODATION
Cume Hue	1
Laguna Larga Lodge	3
Los Maitanes	4
Tejas Negras	2

Lago Cholila

Lago Lezama

RP-71

Butch Cassidy's Cabin

Lago Pellegrini

RP-15

Cholila

Río Carrileufú

Villa Lago Rivadavia

Lago Rivadavia

Portada Norte

El Abuelo (Giant Alerce)

Lago Cisne

Cerro Torrecillas (2253m)

Cerro Alto el Petiso (1790m)

Río Rivadavia

N

7

Lago Menéndez

Lago Verde

CORDON RIVADAVIA

Puerto Chucao

Pasarela

Río Arrayanes

RP-71

Lago Stange

Playa El Francés

Punta Matos

Bahía Rosales

Lago Futalaufquen

Lago Chico

Estrecho Los Monstruos

Puerto Limonao

Las Rocas

Río Percy

Esquel

CORDON DE LAS PIRÁMIDES

Lago Kruger

Cerro Alto el Dedal (1916m)

Rahue-Calel

Refugio Kruger

Intendencia

Villa Futalaufquen

Río Frey

Cerro Situación (2307m)

CORDON SITUACIÓN

Lago Amutui Quimei

Portada Centro

RN-259

Airport (14km), El Bolsón (160km) & RN-40

Trevelin

Presa Futaleufú

Portada Sur

CHILE

Río Grande (Futaleufú)

Río Nanty Fall

Paso Futaleufú

Rivadavia, Menéndez and Futalaufquen, whose waters drain south to the dammed reservoir of **Embalse Amutui Quimei**, and from here into the Río Futaleufú (also called Río Grande). The western two-thirds of the park up against the Andes are off-limits, being designated a "strict scientific reserve".

The vegetation changes considerably as you move east from the Chilean frontier into the area affected by the rain shadow cast by the cordillera. Near the border, rainfall exceeds 3000mm a year, enough to support the growth of dense **Valdivian temperate rainforest** and, most interestingly, the species for which the park is named: the **alerce**. The ground is dominated by bamboo-like *caña colihue*, while two species of flower are everywhere: the orange or white-and-violet *mutisias*, with spatula-like petals, and the *amancay*, a golden-yellow lily growing on stems 50cm to 1m high. In contrast, the eastern margin of the park is much drier. Cypress woodland and *ñire* scrub mark the transitional zone here between the wet forests and the arid steppe near Esquel.

The **northeastern section** of the park is the most interesting for the visitor, especially around the area of the beautiful but small **Lago Verde**. The transcendental **Río Arrayanes** drains Lago Verde, and a suspension bridge gives access to a delightful hour-long loop walk that takes you along the riverbank to Puerto Chucao.

El Abuelo

Boat trips Daily (Sat only in low season) 11.15am • $680 • ☎ 02945 452119, ✉ info@ventalacustres.com.ar

The most popular excursion in the park is the lake trip ("Safari Lacustre") to the far end of Lago Menéndez's northern channel to see **El Abuelo** ("The Grandfather", also named *El Alerzal*), a gigantic *alerce* 2.2m in diameter, and 57m tall. This magnificent tree is an estimated 2600 years old, making it a sapling when Pythagoras and Confucius taught, but at the end of the nineteenth century it almost became roof shingles: only the fact that settlers deemed its wood rotten inside saved it from the saw. To see it you need to take a **boat trip**; the excursion leaves from Puerto Chucao and is guided, but in Spanish only. If you want an English translation, you'll need to organize a tour from Esquel rather than just turning up at the pier.

On the ninety-minute trip across the pristine blue waters of **Lago Menéndez** you get fine views of the Cerro Torrecillas glacier, which is receding fast and may last only another seventy years. To get to El Abuelo, a 3km trail takes you through dense Valdivian temperate rainforest, a habitat distinguished from the surrounding Patagonian forests by the presence of different layers to the canopy, in addition to the growth of lianas, epiphytes, surface roots and species more commonly found in Chile. Here a mass of

---

ALERCE: THE GRANDFATHER TREE

Similar in appearance to the Californian redwood, the **alerce**, or Patagonian cypress, can reach heights of 57m and is one of the four oldest species of tree in the world. To the Mapuche it is *lahuán*, meaning "long-lived" or "grandfather", and the oldest specimens are an estimated four thousand years old. They grow in a relatively narrow band of the central Patagonian cordillera, on acidic soils by lakes and only in places where the annual rainfall exceeds 3000mm, so are more common on the wetter Chilean side of the Andes than in Argentina. Growth is extremely slow (0.8–1.2mm a year), and it takes a decade for a tree's girth to gain 1cm in diameter – though the trunk may eventually reach 3m across.

From the late nineteenth century onwards, the *alerce* was almost totally logged out by pioneers: the reddish timber is not eaten by insects and does not rot, so was highly valued for building, especially for roof shingles. Other uses included musical instruments, barrels, furniture, telegraph poles and boats. In Argentina, the only trees to survive the forester's axe were the most inaccessible ones, or those like El Abuelo, a titanic millennial specimen whose wood was bad in parts. In Argentina, a few stands exist north of Los Alerces, in Parque Nacional Lago Puelo and the Lago Frías area of Nahuel Huapi, and the trees that remain are generally well protected.

THE ELUSIVE *HUEMUL*, ENDANGERED SOUTH-ANDEAN DEER

If you spend any time in the Argentine Lake District it won't be long before you hear talk of the almost legendary **huemul**. This little deer, which stands 1m at the shoulder, was declared a "National Monument" in 1996 in response to an alarming decline in population. A secretive denizen of high Patagonian forests, it once played an important role in the livelihood of indigenous groups who relied on it for food and often depicted it in cave paintings. The arrival of the Europeans and their firearms had disastrous consequences for the remarkably tame species, and there are even tales about them being killed with knives. With the increasing destruction of their forest habitat, their numbers declined rapidly and today only an estimated six hundred remain in Argentina. Your best chance of glimpsing one is in winter, when harsh weather may drive them down to lower altitudes and more open areas in search of food. One of the likeliest locations to spy a *huemul* is near Playa El Francés on the northeastern shore of Lago Futalaufquen – but even there you'll need luck on your side. They are also sometimes spotted further south, in Los Glaciares national park (see p.468) or Chile's Torres del Paine.

The *huemul* shows a series of adaptations to its tough environment, such as a thick, dense coat to protect against the cold, and short, strong legs to help it gain a foothold on rocky slopes. They are also remarkably good swimmers, and can cross lakes and rivers with ease.

vegetation is engaged in the eternal struggle of the jungle: height equals light. In addition to the *alerces*, look out for fuchsia bushes and *arrayanes* (see p.410). Despite its name, **Lago Cisne** is no longer home to any black-necked swans; they were wiped out by mink.

ARRIVAL AND INFORMATION

PARQUE NACIONAL LOS ALERCES

By boat Boat trips leave from Puerto Chucao to Puerto Sagrario (Sat only in low season) at 11.15am ($680); book in advance at Brazo Sur (see p.416).

Access points and entrance fees Entrance to the park is via three points of access: the most practical is the Portada Centro (or "central gate"; 33km from Esquel and 12km before the small village of Villa Futalaufquen), which gives access to the park headquarters and the useful information centre. The most scenic route is to take RP-71 to the Portada Norte, by the headwaters of Lago Rivadavia near Cholila (see p.414), although it is 55km from the central gate. The third entrance, Portada Sur (or Futaleufú), is in the southeast corner of the park, 14km southwest of Trevelin. There is a $120 entry fee.

Getting around Transportes Esquel on Av Alsina 1632 in Esquel (☎02945 453529, ⍵transportesesquel.com.ar) runs a useful daily bus service (summer only) along RP-71 between Esquel and Cholila, via Villa Futalaufquen. Out of season, you'll need your own transport.

Information Set on manicured lawns alongside the bus stop in Villa Futalaufquen is the *intendencia* (daily: high season 8am–9pm; low season 8am–4pm; ☎02945 471020) and visitors' centre (daily 8am–9pm), which supplies useful information on hikes, accommodation and fishing, and sells fishing permits.

Services Services in the village are limited and all food and provisions are far cheaper in Esquel; the sale of fuel within the park has been prohibited, so fill your tank in the nearby towns first.

When to visit Hordes of people descend on the park each year, most from late Nov until Easter, and it gets extremely busy in Jan and Feb – so visit off-peak, if possible. The park is accessible year-round, although RP-71 can, albeit rarely and temporarily, be cut off by snow, and most accommodation closes outside the fishing season (mid-Nov to Easter). The autumn months are perhaps best, as the deciduous trees put on a blaze of colour, but spring is also very beautiful, if subject to some fierce winds.

ACCOMMODATION

During the fishing season there's a wide choice of accommodation in the park, especially along Lago Futalaufquen's eastern shore, but most establishments close off-season. There are plenty of **campsites**, including a free one with fine swimming at Punta Matos, Km21. Those who don't want to camp have little choice but to splash out on private **hotels** and **lodges** or rent a **cabin** (the ones north of the park in Villa Lago Rivadavia are a good bet and often better value), though these tend to be geared towards families or groups of fishermen. All accommodation should be reserved in advance, especially in summer.

Cume Hue ☎02945 15 687916, ⍵cumehue .patagoniaexpress.com. This pretty house on the eastern shore of Lago Futalaufquen is popular with anglers and offers half-board packages with shared or en-suite bathrooms. The camping ground is spacious, but make sure to pitch along the sides of it if you want shade. Half board **$920**; camping **$80**

TREKKING IN LOS ALERCES

There are 130km of **public trails** in the Parque Nacional Los Alerces, which are generally well maintained and marked at intervals with red spots. You are required to **register** with the nearest *guardaparque* before setting off (remember to check back in afterwards). In times of drought, some trails are closed, while others can only be undertaken with a guide. Bring plenty of water, sun protection, and adequate clothing as the weather changes rapidly and unseasonal snowfalls occur in the higher regions. Insect repellent is worthwhile, especially after several consecutive hot days in December and January, as that's when the fierce horseflies (*tábanos*) come out.

THE TREKS

The super-easy pastoral 1200m **Pinturas Rupestres** circuit passes eroded indigenous geometric designs painted about three thousand years ago on a hulk of grey rock that's surrounded by *caña colihue* and *maitén* trees; the lookout from the top of the rock affords a fine view. A more challenging trip is to the *hostería* and campsite at the southern end of **Lago Kruger**. This can be reached in a fairly stiff day's trekking (12hr), returning next day either the same way or by boat (cost depends on number of passengers). However, it's better to make it into a three- or four-day excursion, breaking the outward-bound trek by putting up a tent by the beautiful beach at Playa Blanca – get permission at the visitors' centre. Fires are strictly prohibited and there are no facilities.

One of the most popular treks is the **El Dedal Circuit**. It involves some fairly tough climbs but you'll be rewarded with excellent panoramic views. The path starts as the "Sendero Cascada" (which runs up behind the visitors' centre) through thick *maitén* and *caña colihue*. It then enters impressive mature woodland and scrubland, from where you have a panoramic view of the scarified, rust-coloured **Las Monjitas** range opposite. The path continues along the ridge northwest towards the craggy El Dedal massif. Up here you'll see delicate celeste and grey-blue *perezia* flowers, and possibly even condors. Passing gorgeous **Lago Futalaufquen**, whose turquoise body is fringed, in places, by a frill of Caribbean-blue shallows, you'll dip down into an oxide-coloured glaciated cwm (valley). A tiring scramble takes you back up to the top of the ridge, which overlooks the *Hostería Futalaufquen* and Puerto Limonao. From the ridge, a poor path leads up to the summit of **Cerro Alto El Dedal** (1916m), about forty minutes away; don't attempt it in poor weather.

★**Laguna Larga Lodge** ☎02945 15 501936, ⓦlagunalargalodge.com.ar. Impeccably run by Andrés, an enthusiastic sports fisherman and lover of excellent wine and fine dining – hence the top-rate restaurant and enticing cellar – this secluded fishing lodge set on the shore of the attractive Laguna Larga is well worth the slightly difficult trip to get here (make sure you ask for clear directions when you book). US$215

Los Maitenes 400m from the *intendencia* ☎02945 471006. The closest campsite to Villa Futalaufquen is generally good, with great views of Lago Rivadavia. It can get packed, though. Closed from end of April to end of October. $150

Tejas Negras Lake Futalaufquen ☎02945 471012, ⓦtejasnegras.com. Attractive cabins for rent all year round, which sleep up to four people comfortably. $2000

San Martín de los Andes and around

Around 200km north of Bariloche lies the southern belle of Argentine towns and the northern terminus of the famous **Ruta de los Siete Lagos** (see p.410), **SAN MARTÍN DE LOS ANDES**. It is Neuquén Province's most-visited destination by far and gets very busy indeed in the high midsummer and midwinter seasons. Nestled between mountains on the eastern shores of jewel-like Lago Lácar, the relaxing resort of chalets and generally low-key architecture is an excellent base for exploring much of Parque Nacional Lanín (see p.430). There's a sandy, if often windy, beach on the lake's shores, and in spring, the introduced broom (*retama*) daubs the scenery on the approach roads a sunny yellow. The centre of town is relatively small and nearly everything you need is found along avenidas Roca and San Martín, or the parallel Villegas. Expansion has been rapid, but – with the exception of the hideous, now derelict *Hotel Sol de los Andes* that

SAN MARTÍN DE LOS ANDES

ACCOMMODATION	
Aparthotel Cascadas	9
Caupolicán	7
Gleb	3
Hueney Ruca	8
Laura	5
Lolen	6
Las Lucarnas	4
Puma	2
Refugio Melingo	1

EATING	
La Barra	5
Corazón Contento	2
La Costa del Pueblo	4
La Crêperie	1
Ku	3

overlooks town – by no means uncontrolled. Whereas the larger rival resort of Bariloche caters to the young party crowd, San Martín attracts a more sedate type of small-town tourism, aimed at families and professionals rather than students and backpackers. **El Trabún** (meaning the "Union of the Peoples") is the main annual **festival**, held in early December on the Plaza San Martín. Local and Chilean musicians hold concerts (predominantly folklore), and mighty bonfires are lit at the corners of the square to prepare delicious *asados* of lamb and goat.

Museo de los Primeros Pobladores

Centro Cívico • Tues–Sat 9am–1pm, Sun 7–9pm • Free

On the main square is the **Museo de los Primeros Pobladores**, a tiny museum that puts the area in a historical context with changing exhibitions. Good for a break from bar-hopping and sunning yourself on the small beach.

La Pastera Museo del Che

Sarmiento and Roca • Mon–Wed & Sun 10am–1pm & 5–9.30pm • $20 • ⓦ lapastera.org.ar

A historical curiosity, **La Pastera Museo del Che**, tucked away behind a whitewashed wall, is a simple building where Che Guevara spent a night or two at the end of January 1952 during his first trip across South America – later immortalized in *The Motorcycle Diaries*. Well restored, perhaps overly so, it now functions as a community and cultural centre with regular poetry recitals and music performances. The permanent exhibit is a tribute to Che, and includes a bale of hay on which the future freedom fighter apparently slept during his stay.

Mirador Bandurrias

Take the bridge across Arroyo Pocahullo on c/Juez del Valle, pass the water treatment plant and keep heading northwest through the woods (roughly 4km one way)

If you can muster the energy, it's worth dragging yourself away from the town's bars to take in its stupendous views. The compelling **Mirador Bandurrias** (named after the buff-necked ibis) is 4km along the northeast shore of Lago Lácar, with marvellous views of the lake along its length.

Mirador Arrayán

Taking the track from the lake shore, pass *Hotel Sol de los Andes* and take the right fork, following the signs for 1km

Mirador Arrayán, around 5km from town, is one of the resort's most scenic viewpoints. It overlooks Lago Lácar, with a lovely mountain backdrop. If you're driving, note that the last kilometre of the road is unsealed and only suitable for 4WD vehicles.

ARRIVAL AND DEPARTURE — SAN MARTÍN DE LOS ANDES

By air Chapelco Airport (T 02972 428388) lies 25km away in the direction of Junín de los Andes and serves both towns. La Araucana minibuses connect the airport with San Martín ($100), or you can take a *remís* ($290). If flying out of Chapelco, you could catch the hourly bus run by Castelli (T 0294 15 432 8659; $11), which goes in both directions between Junín and San Martín and will drop you off at the airport on request.

Destinations Buenos Aires (1–2 daily in high season, 5 weekly rest of year).

By bus The bus terminal is scenically located in the south-west of town, across the road from Lago Lácar and the pier.

Destinations Bariloche (7 daily; 4hr); Hua Hum (twice daily in Jan & Feb only; 1hr 10min); Junín de los Andes (hourly; 1hr); Villa La Angostura (7 daily; 2hr 30min).

By boat From the pier, Naviera Lácar Nonthue runs boat excursions to Hua Hum and back (daily at 12.30pm; $900; T 02972 427380), which stop off at Quila Quina and the Chachin waterfall. There are also ferries for Quila Quina daily, on the hour (first boat 10am, last boat 7pm; $300 return). Departures less frequent during autumn and winter (three daily 11am, 1pm and 4pm).

INFORMATION AND TOURS

Tourist office On the Plaza San Martín, the tourist information centre (daily 8am–9pm; T 02972 427347, W sanmartindelosandes.gov.ar) can lend a hand if you can't find a room in high season.

Intendencia The information centre for Parque Nacional Lanín (daily 8am–6pm; T 02972 420664) is on the plaza, opposite the tourist office – it should be your first stop if you are planning on trekking. It doesn't sell fishing permits any more, so head to the fishing shops in town for this.

Tour operators Deportes de Montaña at Coronel Pérez 830 (T 02972 412782,) offers guided trekking, kayaking, biking, rafting and diving excursions, as well as hikes up Volcán Lanín. Siete Lagos, Villegas 313 (T 02972 427877), and a handful of other local agencies do tours to Hua Hum, Quila Quina and other places of interest.

ACCOMMODATION

During the peak summer and skiing seasons you should **reserve rooms** as far in advance as possible. In case you haven't, the tourist office keeps a daily list of vacancies, though you may find these choices limited. Some hotels have three or four price brackets, with the ski season often more expensive than summer. Out of season, room prices can be as much as halved.

Aparthotel Cascadas Obeid 859 T 02972 420133, W apartcascadas.com.ar. Great-value, aesthetically pleasing *cabañas* – sleeping up to nine people – on a quiet street. Superb facilities for the price, including a heated pool and hydromassage. $1700

Caupolicán San Martín 969 ☎02972 427658, ⓦcaupolican.com.ar. Fancy three-star hotel in the centre of town with a range of facilities, including cable TV, a bar and a living room with log fire. $1900

Gleb Rivadavia 411 ☎02972 424485. Modern, safe and friendly hostel, with some double rooms available. Dorms $300; doubles $750

Hueney Ruca Obeid and Coronel Pérez ☎02972 421499, ⓦhosteriahueneyruca.com.ar. Spacious and airy *hostería* with attractive minimalist decor and modern bathrooms. Some rooms accommodate up to seven people and breakfast is included. There's a sauna and jacuzzi. $1200

Laura Mascardi 632 ☎02972 427271. Simple and pleasant with airy, wood-panelled rooms, this budget hotel is close to the town centre and among the cheaper places in town in summer. $800

Lolen 4km southwest of town, 1km off RN-40 at Km78 and down a very steep track to Playa Catritre. A lakeside campsite with superb views, run by the Curruhuinca Mapuche community. $180

Las Lucarnas Coronel Pérez 632 ☎02972 427085, ⓦhosterialaslucarnas.com. The best of the cheaper spots, *Las Lucarnas* boasts excellent, spacious rooms in a family-run, central but tranquil place. $800

Puma Fosbery 535 ☎02972 422443, ⓦpumahostel.com.ar. Small, well-scrubbed and modern hostel with dorms, a couple of double rooms and kitchen facilities. Dorms $300; doubles $900

Refugio Melingo Las Lengas 139 ☎02972 412221, ⓦrefugio-melingo.com. A 20min trek up the hill from town, but the zen-like view of the valley from this German-run *hostería* sure makes up for it. Home-made rolls for breakfast, and spotless rooms. US$85

EATING

La Barra Brown and Costanera ☎02972 425459. A superb wood-cabin restaurant on the lakeside. Patagonian specialities (not always that cheap) are the order of the day and the wine list is extensive. Artisanal pasta and stone-baked pizza will appeal to those who have had enough of trout and lamb. Daily noon–3.30pm & 8pm–midnight.

Corazón Contento San Martín 467 ☎02972 412750. Buzzing café and takeaway offering a delicious menu of sandwiches, burgers, *milanesas* and so on, though the veggie-stuffed quiches are the biggest hit with the locals. Jan–March & July–Oct daily 9am–midnight; April–June, Nov & Dec Mon–Sat 9am–midnight.

La Costa del Pueblo Costanera and Obeid ☎02972 429289. With good if slightly obscured lake views, *La Costa del Pueblo* is an excellent place to grab a snack while waiting for a bus. The food is abundant and cheap. Daily 12.30–3pm & 8pm–midnight.

★**La Crêperie** Roca and Sarmiento ☎02972 421226. This gem serves delicious savoury and sweet crêpes, as the name indicates (the Bahiano with salted bananas and stout is a must), as well as sandwiches. Daily noon–12.30am.

★**Ku** San Martín 1053 ☎02972 427039. This moderately priced restaurant offers a varied menu that includes *parrillas* and pastas as well as regional trout, venison and wild boar dishes in a rustic setting. Mon–Sat noon–3pm and 8pm–midnight.

Lago Lácar

Buses run twice daily (Jan & Feb only) along RP-48, north of the lake ($60), or you could rent a car. There are also boats from San Martín (see opposite)

Southwest of San Martín, **Lago Lácar** ("Lake of the Sunken City"), which lies entirely within the Parque Nacional Lanín (see p.430), is best explored by combining boat or road trips with the odd hike.

Cerro Colorado

Around 13km from San Martín is the trailhead for an excellent two-hour hike up **Cerro Colorado** (1774m). You'll go towards a broad V-shaped valley, then along the banks of a stream – a steep climb with views of the valley and lake below.

Quila Quina

Ferries leave San Martín's pier (see opposite) daily, every hour, year-round • $300 return • You can also reach the settlement by signposted dirt road off RN-40

The beautiful, sheltered bay at **QUILA QUINA**, on the southern shore of Lago Lácar, is an incongruous mix of agricultural smallholdings of the Curruhuinca Mapuche community and holiday homes. There's a beach and walks in the area, including a two-day trek to the western end of Lago Lácar at **Pucará**.

Hua Hum and around

The unsurfaced RP-48 runs for 46km along the northern shore of Lácar and the adjoining Lago Nonthue to **HUA HUM**, a small settlement at the western end of the lake, used as a base for walks and fishing. The beautiful trip there takes in lakeside views and white beaches. A few kilometres from Hua Hum is a 20m-high waterfall, **Chachín**; follow the signs to the car park, from which it's a thirty-minute walk through forest to reach the falls.

Paso Hua Hum

Customs open daily 8am–8pm

Around 10km from Hua Hum village the road continues on to the international border crossing, **Paso Hua Hum**. The crossing is one of the most enjoyable Andean routes through to Chile, leading towards the town of Villarrica, although there is no public transport behind Hua Hum so you will need your own vehicle. Following the Río Hua Hum northwest brings you to the slender, gorgeous Lago Pirehueico, which is crossed by **car ferry**. The timetable changes frequently; ask at the tourist office in San Martín (see p.424) or call the Panguipulli tourist office in Chile (☎0056 63 310436).

Termas de Queñi

To the southeast of Hua Hum, 12km by dirt track, is the *guardaparque*'s post at **Lago Queñi**. The area around this lake is one of the wettest places in Parque Nacional Lanín, and is covered with Valdivian temperate rainforest and dense thickets of *caña colihue*. The star attraction here is the enchanting **Termas de Queñi** – unadorned hot springs, set in lush forest near the southern tip of the lake. Late September to early May is generally the best time to visit the springs: register with the *guardaparque*, and you can **camp** just past the post, on the other side of Arroyo Queñi. You can walk to the springs on an easy route from the campsite (1hr 30min).

Junín de los Andes

Set in a dry, hilly area of the steppe at the foot of the Andes, **JUNÍN DE LOS ANDES** is aptly named – Junín means "grassland" in the Aymara language. This relaxed town to the northeast of San Martín is popular with fishermen, largely owing to the rivers in the region that teem with trout. RN-40 (rather confusingly called Blvd Rosas/Roca for the stretch through Junín) cuts across the western side of town, and nearly all you'll need lies to the east. Though not as attractive as its bigger neighbour, San Martín de los Andes (see p.422), Junín lacks the trappings of a tourist town and the high prices that generally accompany them. It is also better placed for making trips to the central sector of Parque Nacional Lanín (see p.430), especially if you plan to climb Volcán Lanín itself, or to explore the **Lago Huechulafquen** area. A good time to visit is mid-February, when the **Fiesta del Puestero** – with gaucho events, folklore music in the evenings, *artesanía* and *asados* – takes place. Pleasant **Plaza San Martín** is the hub of the town's activity.

Paseo Artesanal

The **Paseo Artesanal**, on the east side of the main square, is a cluster of boutiques selling a selection of crafts, among which Mapuche weavings figure heavily.

Santuario de la Beata Laura Vicuña

Ginés Ponte and Don Bosco • Daily 8am–9pm • Free

The imposing, alpine-style tower of the **Santuario de la Beata Laura Vicuña**, also called by its old name Iglesia Nuestra Señora de las Nieves, is splendid in its simplicity. Its airy,

sky-blue interior is suffused with light, and its clean-cut lines are tastefully complemented by the bold use of panels of high-quality Mapuche weavings, with strong geometric designs and natural colours. Laura Vicuña, born in Santiago de Chile in 1891, studied in Junín and died here, aged just 13, in 1904. She was beatified in 1988. As a rather macabre touch, one of her vertebrae resides in an urn at the entrance to the sanctuary.

Museo Mapuche

Ginés Ponte and Avenida Rosas • Mon–Fri 8am–2pm & 5–8pm • Free

The tiny **Museo Mapuche** displays Mapuche artefacts from the Neuquén region alongside some dinosaur bones, collected by priest Pascual Marchesotti during his travels around Patagonia and brought here in 1988.

Parque Vía Christi

At the end of Avenida Antártida Argentina (15 min walk west of Plaza San Martín)

At the base of Cerro Cruz, **Parque Vía Christi** vividly depicts – with its 22 sculptures and mosaics – the story of the Conquest of the Desert (see p.535), alongside Mapuche legends and the Stations of the Cross.

ARRIVAL AND DEPARTURE JUNÍN DE LOS ANDES

By air Chapelco airport serves both Junín and San Martín (see p.424).
By bus The bus terminal (☏ 02972 492038) is one block over from Blvd Roca, at Olavarría and F.S. Martín.
Destinations Aluminé (2 daily; 3hr 30min); Buenos Aires (4 daily; 20hr); San Martín de los Andes (hourly; 1hr).

INFORMATION AND TOURS

Tourist information Padre Milanesio and Coronel Suárez (daily 8am–9pm; ☏ 02972 491160). The information centre can help book accommodation and also sells fishing licences. A small kiosk also operates at the bus station.
Park information Padre Milanesio 570 (Mon–Fri 8am–3pm; ☏ 02972 492748).

Alquimia Helpful travel agency (O'Higgins 603; ☏ 02972 491355, ⓦ alquimiaturismo.com.ar) that organizes day-tours in the region, including one to lakes Huechulafquen and Paimún with a visit to a Mapuche community. It specializes in adventure tourism, such as climbing Lanín and rafting on the Río Aluminé, and rents out climbing equipment.

ACCOMMODATION

There are some good places on the main road but often the best bet is to head for the streets east of the plaza. It's worth reserving accommodation in advance in summer.

Cabañas Las Bandurrias Lanín s/n ☏ 02972 491295, ⓦ lasbandurriasjunin.blogspot.com. Two delightful cabins sleeping up to five set in extensive grounds in Jardines del Chimehuín, a quiet residential area of town. $1150
★**Chimehuín** Coronel Suárez and 25 de Mayo ☏ 02972 491151, ⓦ hosteriachimehuin.com.ar. A rare gem, this *hostería* combines excellent value with a cottage-like setting among well-tended gardens, and engenders great loyalty from its regular guests, especially fishing aficionados. A fine home-made breakfast is included in the price. Book well ahead in summer. $800
Complejo Caleufu Travel Lodge J. Roca 1323 ☏ 02972 492757, ⓦ caleufutravellodge.com.ar. Motel-style lodge on the main road, run by a fun-loving couple who lived in California for years – they have a true sense of hospitality and an equally great sense of humour. $800

Estancia Huechehue RN-40 Km4 ⓔ info@huechahue.com, ⓦ huechehue.com. 30km east of Junín, this working and largely self-sufficient estancia takes its guests fishing and on horserides to see condors and petroglyphs in the surrounding countryside; at cattle-rounding time you'll be taken along on horseback to help. Run by London-born Jane, the homestead offers large, comfortable rooms and plentiful food and there's a jacuzzi to soak in after a hard day's ranching. The price includes all meals, transfers and horseriding. US$400
La Isla ☏ 0294 15 428 8881. Campsite with shady pitches on an island in the Río Chimehuín that can be accessed from the eastern extreme of Ginés Ponte, a few blocks from the centre. $150
Marisa J.M. Rosas 360 ☏ 02972 491175. The best of the budget options and just around the corner from the bus terminal, this *residencial* is neat, amiable and not too noisy,

THE MAPUCHE

Calling themselves the people (*che*) of the earth (*Mapu*), the **Mapuche** were, before the arrival of the Spanish in the sixteenth century, a loose confederation of tribal groups who lived exclusively on the Chilean side of the cordillera. The aspiring conquistadors knew them as Araucanos, and so feared their reputation as indomitable and resourceful warriors that they abandoned attempts to subjugate them and opted instead for a policy of containment. Encroachments into Araucania sparked a series of Mapuche migrations eastwards into territory that is now Argentina, and they soon became the dominant force in the whole region, their cultural and linguistic influence spreading far beyond their territories.

By the eighteenth century, four major Mapuche tribes had established territories in Argentina: the **Picunche**, or "people of the north", who lived near the arid cordillera in the far north of Neuquén; the **Pehuenche**, or "people of the monkey puzzle trees", dominant in the central cordillera; the **Huilliche**, or "people of the south" of the southern cordillera region around Lago Nahuel Huapi; and the **Puelche**, or "people of the east", who inhabited the river valleys of the steppe. These groups spoke different dialects of **Mapudungun**, part of the Arawak group of languages. Lifestyles were based around nomadic hunter-gathering, rearing livestock and the cultivation of small plots around settlements of *rucas* (family homes that were thatched, usually with reeds). Communities were headed by a *lonco*, or cacique, but the "medicine-men", or *machis*, also played an influential role.

SPANISH INFLUENCE

The arrival of the Spanish influenced Mapuche culture most significantly with the introduction of **horses and cattle**. Horses enabled tribes to be vastly more mobile, and hunting techniques changed, with the Mapuche adopting their trademark lances in lieu of the bow and arrow. As importantly, the herds of wild horses and cattle that spread across the Argentine Pampas became a vital trading commodity.

Relations between the Mapuche and the Hispanic *criollos* in both Chile and Argentina varied: periods of warfare and indigenous raids on white settlements were interspersed with times of relatively peaceful coexistence. By the end of the eighteenth century, the relationship had matured into a surprisingly symbiotic one, with the two groups meeting at joint *parlamentos* where grievances would be aired and terms of trade regulated. Tensions increased after Argentina gained its independence from Spain, and the Mapuche resisted a military campaign organized against them by the dictator Rosas in the early 1830s, but they were finally crushed by Roca's Conquest of the Desert in 1879. Mapuche communities were split up and forcibly relocated onto reservations, often on marginal lands.

THE MAPUCHE TODAY

The Mapuche are one of the **principal indigenous peoples** in Argentina today, with a population of some forty thousand divided among communities dotted around the provinces of Buenos Aires, La Pampa, Chubut, Río Negro and, above all, Neuquén. Most families still earn their living from mixed animal farming, but increasingly, Mapuche communities are embarking on tourist-related ventures. These include opening campsites; establishing points of sale for home-made cheese or *artesanía* such as their fine woven goods, distinctive silver jewellery, ceramics and woodcarvings; offering guided excursions; or receiving small tour groups. Though Mapuche culture is not as visibly distinct or politically active in Argentina as it is in Chile, the Mapuche are one of Argentina's best-organized indigenous groups.

despite having some rooms facing the main road. $\overline{\$500}$
Tromen Lonquimay 195 ❶02972 491498. Nothing special, and slightly cramped, but a decent enough budget option. Dorms $\overline{\$150}$; doubles $\overline{\$450}$

EATING

Panadería La Ideal Lamadrid 259. Very popular bakery, where the *medialunas* always sell out quickly. Great pastries, bread and even scones. Perfect for sipping coffee and soaking up the local ambience. Mon–Fri 7am–1.30pm & 4.30–9.30pm, Sat & Sun 8am–1pm & 5–9.30pm.

★ **Ruca Hueney** Plaza San Martín ❶02972 491113. A local institution whose speciality is unforgettably delicious trout; it also offers some tasty Lebanese dishes and takeaway options. Daily noon–3pm & 8.30pm–12.30am.

Parque Nacional Lanín

Formed in 1937, **PARQUE NACIONAL LANÍN** (ⓦparquesnacionales.gob.ar) protects 420 square kilometres of Andean and sub-Andean habitat that ranges from barren, semiarid steppe in the east to patches of temperate Valdivian rainforest pressed up against the Chilean border. To the south, it adjoins its sister park, Parque Nacional Nahuel Huapi (see p.402), while it also shares a boundary with Parque Nacional Villarrica in Chile.

The park's *raison d'être* and geographical centrepiece – the cone of **Volcán Lanín** – rises to 3776m and dominates the entire landscape. Meaning "choked himself to death" in Mapudungun, it is now believed to be extinct. The park's other trump card is the **araucaria**, or monkey puzzle tree (see box, p.430), which grows as far south as Lago Curruhue Grande but is especially prevalent in the northern sector of the park, an area known as the **Pehuén region**. Parque Lanín also protects notable forests of *coihue* and, in the drier areas, cypress. Flowers such as the *arvejilla* purple sweet pea and the introduced lupin abound in spring, as does the flame-red *notro* bush. Fuchsia bushes grow in some of the wetter regions.

As for **fauna**, the park is home to a population of *huemules*, a shy and rare deer (see box, p.421). *Pudú*, the tiny native deer, and pumas are present but rarely seen: you're more likely to glimpse a coypu, a grey fox or two species introduced for hunting a century ago, the wild boar and the red deer, which roam the semiarid steppes and hills of the east of the park. Birdwatchers will want to keep an eye out for the active white-throated treerunner, a bizarre bird with an upturned bill adapted for removing beech nuts, while the acrobatic thorn-tailed rayadito is another regional speciality.

Lago Huechulafquen and around

Castelli (ⓣ02972 491557) operates two daily bus services from Junín de los Andes

RP-61 branches west off RN-40 (previously called RN-234) just north of Junín de los Andes, entering Parque Nacional Lanín and skirting the shores of **Lago Huechulafquen**. Just 4km from the junction is the **Centro de Ecología Aplicada de Neuquén** (Mon–Fri 8am–3pm), which undertakes studies of regional fauna and has a trout farm that raises fish for restocking the area's rivers.

THE ARAUCARIA, OR MONKEY PUZZLE TREE

The distinctive and beautiful **araucaria** (*Araucaria araucana*), more commonly known as the **monkey puzzle tree**, is one of the world's most enduring species of tree. It grows naturally only in the cordillera of Neuquén Province and at similar latitudes in Chile, where it favours impoverished volcanic soils at altitudes between 600m and 1800m. This prehistoric survivor has been around for more than one hundred million years.

Araucarias grow incredibly slowly, though they can live for over **a thousand years**. Young trees grow in a pyramid shape, but after about a hundred years they start to lose their lower branches and assume their trademark umbrella appearance – mature specimens can reach 45m in height. Their straight trunks are covered by panels of thick bark that provide resistance to fire. The female trees produce huge, head-size cones filled with up to two hundred fawn-coloured pine nuts called *piñones*, some 5cm long, and rich in proteins and carbohydrates.

Known to the Mapuche as the *pehuén*, the tree was worshipped as the daughter of the moon. Legend has it that there was a time when the Mapuche, though they adored the *pehuén*, never ate its *piñones*, believing them to be poisonous. This changed, however, during a terrible famine, when their god, Ngüenechén, saved them from starvation by sending a messenger to teach them both the best way of preparing these nutritious seeds (roasting them in embers or boiling), and of storing them (burying them in the earth or snow). *Piñones* became the staple diet of tribes in the area (principally the Pehuenche, named after their dependence on the tree), and have been revered by the Mapuche ever since.

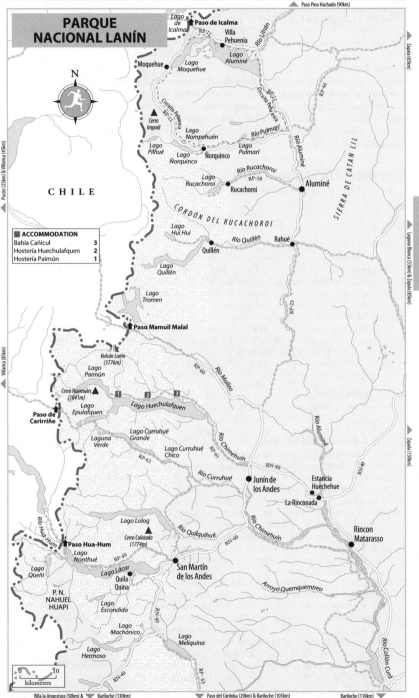

PARQUE NACIONAL LANÍN

N

CHILE

ACCOMMODATION
Bahía Cañicul	3
Hostería Huechulafquen	2
Hostería Paimún	1

Paso Pino Hachado (90km)

Zapala (65km)

Laguna Blanca (53km) & Zapala (85km)

Zapala (130km)

7

Pucón (25km) & Villarrica (45km)

Villarrica (85km)

Paso de Icalma
Lago de Icalma
RP-71
Villa Pehuenia
Río Litrán
Lago Aluminé
Moquehue
Lago Moquehue
RP-13
RP-46
Circuito Pehuenia RP-11
Cerro Impodi
Lago Nompehuén
Río Pulmarí
Lago Pulmarí
Río Aluminé
Lago Pilhué
Lago Ñorquinco
Ñorquinco
Río Rucachoroi
RP-18
Lago Rucachoroi
Rucachoroi
Aluminé
SIERRA DE CATAN LIL
CORDÓN DEL RUCACHOROI
Lago Huí Huí
Río Quillén
Rahué
Quillén
Lago Quillén
RP-23
Lago Tromen
Paso Mamuil Malal
Volcán Lanín (3776m)
Lago Paimún
RP-60
Río Malleo
Cerro Hüemules (1841m)
1 2 3
Lago Huechulafquen
Lago Epulafquen
Paso de Carirriñe
Laguna Verde
Lago Curruhué Grande
RP-62
Lago Curruhué Chico
Río Chimehuín
RP-61
Río Curruhué
Junín de los Andes
Río Aluminé
RN-40
Estancia Huechehue
La Rinconada
Río Hua-Hum
Paso Hua-Hum
Lago Lolog
Cerro Colorado (1774m)
Río Quilquihué
RN-40
Río Chimehuín
Rincon Matarasso
Lago Nonthué
RP-48
Lago Queñi
P. N. NAHUEL HUAPI
Lago Lácar
Quila Quina
San Martín de los Andes
Arroyo Quemquemtreu
Lago Escondido
RN-40
Lago Machónico
RN-40
Lago Meliquina
Río Collón Curá
Lago Hermoso
RP-63
RN-40

0   10
kilometres

The park's largest lake, Huechulafquen is an enormous finger of deep blue water extending into the steppe, its northern shores black with volcanic sand. The mouth of the Río Chimehuín, at the lake's eastern end, is a notable fly-fishing spot.

Puerto Canoa

At the western end of the lake is the settlement and jetty of **Puerto Canoa**, where you can look up at the fantastic, crevassed **south face** of Volcán Lanín. Puerto Canoa is the base for treks and boat trips in the area, including a fun **boat trip** with José Julian (☎02972 428029, ⊛catamaranjosejulian.com.ar) that plies a circuit that includes lakes Huechulafquen, Paimún and Epulafquen, where you'll see the solidified lava river of Volcán Achen Ñiyeu.

TREKKING IN PARQUE LANÍN

Before planning **treks** in the park you should check thoroughly with park officials in Junín or San Martín and fill out a *registro de trekking*, which must be presented at the *guardaparque* post before departure and on your return. Make sure your map is new – this is an area of active volcanoes, and trails and refuges change constantly.

THE TREKS

One of the most popular walks within striking distance of Junín is the four-hour hike to **Cerro del Chivo**, which starts opposite *Camping Bahía Cañicul*. It's a steep climb and you'll need to concentrate not to lose the trail above the tree line, but the views are spectacular. An excellent two-day option for losing the crowds is to cross the narrows linking the two lakes at La Unión near Puerto Canoa (there's normally a rowing-boat service) and head along the south shore of **Lago Paimún**. Initially, you strike inland skirting round the southern slopes of Cerro Huemules (1841m) before reaching the lake again midway along its length at **Don Aila**, where you can camp. From the *guardaparque* in Puerto Canoa there's another good, if somewhat arduous, day-hike to the **base of Volcán Lanín**. The last forty minutes are steep and there's no water source for the final hour. You can take a short detour to the waterfall at Cascada El Saltillo from *Camping Piedra Mala* at Km64, where there's space to pitch a tent.

CLIMBING LANÍN

Volcán Lanín is generally a good mountain to climb: easy to access, it also retains the balance between being possible for inexpert climbers to ascend while still representing a real physical challenge. Nonetheless, do not undertake it lightly – you should take a guide and be reasonably fit. The most straightforward route is from Lago Tromen; the heavily glaciated south face is a much fiercer option that's suitable only for experienced climbers.

The route **from Lago Tromen** takes two or three days in good weather – the two-day option involves a very tiring second day that includes the summit push and a complete descent. Group climbing through an agency is possible: try Alquimia in Junín (see p.428), or the park offices can email you a list of authorized guides. They also rent out all the essential mountaineering gear: good boots, waterproof clothing, helmet, ice axe, crampons, torch (or, better still, a headlamp) and cooker. UV sunglasses, high-factor sunblock, matches and an alarm clock are likewise essential. Optional items are gaiters (especially in late summer when you have to negotiate volcanic scree), black bin liners (for melting snow in sunny weather), candles, a two-way radio and an emergency whistle.

You'll need to register for the climb at the Lago Tromen **guardaparque's office** (daily 8am–6pm), and the *guardaparque* will check that you have all necessary equipment. If permission is granted you'll need to start the climb by 1pm. It will be necessary to acclimatize for a night in one of the three refuges on the mountain. The *guardaparque* will assign one to you, and try to accommodate your preference; get to Tromen early in high season, to ensure a place. The first refuge that you reach following the main trail is **Refugio RIM**. Its big advantage is that it has meltwater close by (Jan & Feb; if climbing outside high summer, you'll need to melt snow for water anyway). The smaller **CAJA**, further up the slope, is good if you plan to make the final ascent and total descent in one day, as it saves you half an hour's climb in the early morning. The **BIM** refuge, down from *RIM* via a second path, has pleasant tables and chairs, but is the lowest down the slope.

ARRIVAL AND INFORMATION

Access points The volcano and the central sector of the park around lakes Huechulafquen, Paimún and Tromen are best accessed from Junín de los Andes, while the park's southernmost reaches and the area around Lago Lácar (see p.425) are best visited from San Martín, or as part of the Siete Lagos circuit.

Entrance and fees The park has an open border, but note that there's a $120 entrance fee, and it's payable at the Lago Huechulafquen entrance only.

Maps and guides If you want to hike and can read Spanish, the *Guía Sendas & Bosques de Lanín y Nahuel Huapi* is very useful. Two reasonably reliable maps

PARQUE NACIONAL LANÍN

(1:200,000) accompany the guide.

When to go The whole park can be covered in snow from May to October, and it can snow in the higher mountain regions at almost any time of year. The best time to visit is in spring (especially Oct & Nov) or autumn (March to mid-May), when the deciduous trees adopt a spectacular palette, particularly in the Pehuenia area. Trekking is possible between late October and early May, although the season for some of the higher treks is shorter, usually from December to March. January and February see an influx of Argentine holiday-makers, but in general it is less crowded than Nahuel Huapi even in high season.

ACCOMMODATION

LAGO HUECHULAFQUEN
On the lake's north shore, between Km47 and Km60, there are plenty of places to camp, with no fewer than fifteen sites with varying facilities run by the Raquithué and Cañicul Mapuche communities.

Bahía Cañicul Halfway along Lago Huechulafquen at Km54. A campsite on top of the peninsula, with good, secluded pitches but basic toilets. $150

Hostería Huechulafquen Km56 ☎02972 427598, ⦿hosteriahuechulafquen.com. A snug fishing lodge

in full view of Volcán Lanín. Its restaurant is open to the public. $850

LAGO PAIMÚN
Hostería Paimún RP-61 Km58 ☎02972 491758, ⦿hosteriapaimun.com.ar. In a delightful spot on the shore of the lake, this peaceful inn offers half- and full board options, as well as guided fishing and boat trips. Closed April to end of October. Half board $1500; full board $1800

7

The Pehuén region

Northwards from Junín, **RP-23** runs mostly parallel to the turbulent waters of the Río Aluminé, carving through arid rocky gorges, before continuing on to Lago Aluminé and Villa Pehuenia. The **PEHUÉN REGION** is home to the **Circuito Pehuenia** and its trio of stunning lakes, and offers a plethora of outdoor experiences – you can choose between mountain biking, rafting and horseriding, or just hike along rewarding trails through beautiful woodland. To the east, parallel with the river valley, lies the **Sierra de Catan Lil**, a harsh and desiccated range that's older and higher than the nearby stretch of the Andes.

The area around **Villa Pehuenia** and **Moquehue**, northwest of slow-paced **Aluminé**, is one of the least developed yet most beautiful parts of the Argentine Lake District. This "forgotten corner" of Mapuche communities, wonderful mountain lakes, basalt cliffs and araucaria forests has largely escaped the commercial pressures found further south in the park system, although locals and recent settlers are fast waking up to its potential and tourists are arriving in ever-increasing numbers. However, infrastructure links are still fairly rudimentary, and having your own transport is a boon – otherwise, you'll need to take a taxi, as there is almost nothing in the way of public transport.

Aluminé

ALUMINÉ itself is a small but growing riverside town with a gentle pace of life. For a week in March or April it celebrates the **Fiesta del Pehuén** to coincide with the Mapuche harvest of *piñones*, with displays of horsemanship, music and *artesanía*. Its main claim to fame, though, is as a summer **rafting centre** (see p.434). A branch road heads west from the village to Lago Rucachoroi and (28km away) the *guardaparque* post.

ARRIVAL AND DEPARTURE | ALUMINÉ

By bus Aluminé's bus terminal is on Av 4 de Caballería. Albus (☎ 0299 445 2522, ⓦ albus.com.ar) runs services on a circuit from Neuquén to Zapala, on to Aluminé and Villa Pehuenia, and back to Zapala again.
Destinations Neuquén (2 daily; 5hr 30min); Villa Pehuenia (2 daily; 1hr 10min).

By taxi There is no public transport heading west of the village; you'll need to book a taxi (☎ 02942 496136) or ask at local travel agent Mali Viajes (☎ 02942 496310) about group transport – its office is just off the plaza.

INFORMATION AND ACTIVITIES

Tourist information From the bus terminal it's half a block to the Plaza San Martín, where you'll find the tourist office, Cristian Joubert 321 (daily 8am–10pm; ☎ 02942 496001, ⓦ alumine.gob.ar).

Aluminé Rafting This adventure operator, 2km south of town along RP-23, organizes rafting trips in the surrounding area (☎ 02942 15 695331, ⓦ interpatagonia .com/aluminerafting).

ACCOMMODATION AND EATING

Aluminé Cristian Joubert 336 ☎ 02942 496174, ⓦ hosterialumine.com.ar. A clean, straightforward hotel open year-round that is just off the main square; the place has its own restaurant, where breakfast is served ($40). $900
Hotel de la Aldea RP-23 and Capitán Crouzeilles ☎ 02942 496340, ⓦ hoteldelaldea.com.ar. A resort hotel a little out of place in the otherwise rustic village. Its

rooms are comfortable, if a little twee, and some have river views. The hotel rents out mountain bikes and arranges horseriding. $857
La Posta del Rey Cristian Joubert 336 ☎ 02942 496248. This hotel restaurant (see above) is a good place to try a sort of piñones pâté, while imaginative home-made pastas are the house speciality. Daily noon–3pm & 8pm–late.

Circuito Pehuenia

One of the most popular routes in the Pehuén region is the **Circuito Pehuenia**, linking Villa Pehuenia on the northern bank of Lago Aluminé with tiny Moquehue, at the lake's southwest. It passes along Lago Ñorquinco, which forms the northern boundary of Parque Nacional Lanín. Most people finish or start the circuit in Aluminé.

Trekking and other activities

The lack of convenient road routes acts as an encouragement to **trek**: there is great potential in the area around Moquehue and Ñorquinco, but local politics and unreliable weather mean you should carefully discuss your plans and route with local *guardaparques* or, even better, take a guide who knows the area. Remember that it is obligatory to register your departure with a *guardaparque* before setting out and clock in your arrival at the other end. If it's not safe, you will be refused permission to trek. The terrain is also ideal for **mountain biking**, and there's tremendous scope for other outdoor activities here as well, such as **horseriding** and **rafting** through the scenic gorge of the Río Aluminé.

Villa Pehuenia

Set among araucaria trees – and named after the Mapudungun word for these (*pehuén*) – on the shores of pristine Lago Aluminé, **VILLA PEHUENIA** is a splendid, fast-growing holiday village. *Cabañas* are the boom industry here, springing up in both the main part of the village and on the lumpy, tree-covered peninsula that juts into the lake's chilly waters. From the tourist office it is 700m to the commercial centre – a cluster of buildings selling food and other provisions. If you're walking around town, note that there are no street names and that the map provided by the tourist office lacks distinguishing features. To the north is **Volcán Batea Mahuida**, a mountain that has a minuscule Mapuche-run ski resort and a picturesque crater lake.

ARRIVAL AND INFORMATION | VILLA PEHUENIA

By bus A limited number of buses, operated by Destinos Patagonicos (☎ 02942 498067), run from the village centre.

Destinations Aluminé (2 daily; 1hr 30min); Neuquén (2 daily; 7hr).

Tourist information The well-informed tourist office (daily: summer 9am–9pm; winter 10am–6pm; ☎ 02942 498044, ⓦ villapehuenia.gov.ar) is at Km11 on the main road to Aluminé.

ACCOMMODATION AND EATING

The higher-end accommodation is on the peninsula, a picturesque 20min walk from the main village. Following the road west that runs by the side of the tourist office and then branches left at the lake brings you to a cluster of eating options.

Camping Lagrimitas RP-13 ☎ 02942 498003. Fantastic, tranquil pitches beneath araucarias by the lake shore. **$150**

Patagonia Bistró Golfo Azul ☎ 02942 547026. This beautifully located, good-value restaurant offers Patagonian dishes like wild boar and has views over the lake. Mon, Tues, Thurs & Fri 8pm–late, Sat & Sun 12.30–3pm & 8pm–late.

★ Posada La Escondida Down the road off RP-13 Km12 ☎ 02942 15 691166, ⓦ posadalaescondida.com.ar.

Luxurious accommodation on the west coast of the peninsula, where the suite-like rooms all have their own sun decks. Two-night minimum stay. **$3300**

La Serena By the east side of the lakefront, on the peninsula ☎ 02942 15 417942, ⓦ villa-pehuenia.com.ar/la_serena.html. A well-designed, rustic hotel. The rooms are on two levels, with enough space to sleep four, small kitchens and wonderful views. Passes to the hotel spa and breakfasts with home-made jams are included in the price. **$1290**

Moquehue and around

Villa Pehuenia is connected to the pioneer village of **MOQUEHUE** by an unsurfaced road (15km) that runs around the northwestern shores of **Lago Moquehue**, Lago Aluminé's sibling. The two lakes are joined at La Angostura by a 20m-wide, 500m-long channel of captivating turquoise waters.

A loose conglomeration of farmsteads set in a broad pastoral valley at the southwestern end of its lake, Moquehue is overlooked on both sides by splendid ranks of rugged, forested ranges and **Cerro Bella Durmiente**, so named because the summit supposedly looks like the profile of a sleeping beauty. As yet, there's none of the contrived feel that comes from an excess of holiday-makers, and most residents have deep roots here. There is also no electricity in the village, though some places have generators.

Hiking around Moquehue

Unguided **hiking** around Moquehue has created local political problems, with landowners complaining that hikers ignore private-property signs and are causing damage to the countryside. While the effects of hiking are probably exaggerated, the depth of feeling is not, and the tourist office strongly recommends all hikers be accompanied by an authorized guide. One of the best day-hikes takes you around the southeastern shores of **Lago Moquehue**, through land belonging to the **Puel Mapuche** community. The trail leads past several Puel farmsteads as well as diminutive, secluded lakes, including Cari Laufqué, and beautiful woodland of *ñire*, *radal*, *notro*, araucaria and *coihue*. This hike does require a guide, but there are also some excellent local walks that you can do independently: one short leg-stretch (35min one way) leads to an attractive waterfall in mystical mixed araucaria woodland; a slightly longer option is the hike up **Cerro Bandera** (2hr one way), with excellent views to Volcán Llaima.

ARRIVAL AND ACTIVITIES   MOQUEHUE

By car/taxi There is no public transport to Moquehue – you'll need to have your own car or organize a taxi from Villa Pehuenia.

Destinos Patagonicos (☎ 02942 498067, ⓦ facebook.com/destinos.patagonicos) organizes guided walks.

ACCOMMODATION

Bella Durmiente RP-13 ☎ 02942 660993, ⓦ bdurmientemoquehue.com.ar. A wonderfully authentic, wood-built guesthouse, with camping also available. There are wood fires and commanding vistas of the scenery in every room. Camping **$140**; doubles **$950**

Camping Trenel RP-11 ☎02942 15 664720, ⓦvillapehuenia.org/campingtrenel. Campsite located at the southeast corner of the lake on a slightly raised area with glorious views. Treks, zip-lining, climbing, kayaking and more can be organized from here; owner Fernando López is a well-known hiking guide in the area. **$150**

Central and northern Neuquén

Central and northern Neuquén Province is an area of desert-like *meseta* and steppe, home to Argentina's most important reserves of natural gas and petroleum. **Neuquén**, the eponymous provincial capital, is a good base for visiting the area's **dinosaur**-related attractions (see box, p.438), which include dinosaur footprints you can view *in situ*, bones from the largest dinosaur yet discovered, and the first fossilized dinosaur eggs ever found. Wine buffs will be more interested in the region's award-winning **wineries**, to the west of tiny Chañar.

Neuquén

The bustling provincial capital of **NEUQUÉN** sits at the confluence of the rivers Neuquén and Limay, whose waters unite to become the Río Negro. With a population of a quarter of a million or so, this plains metropolis functions as the commercial, industrial and financial centre of the surrounding fruit- and oil-producing region. It's a surprisingly attractive and friendly place to pass a day or two, with a couple of good museums and excellent restaurants. You'll find everything you need in the **microcentro**, which comprises the area north of RN-22, three blocks on either side of the central boulevard.

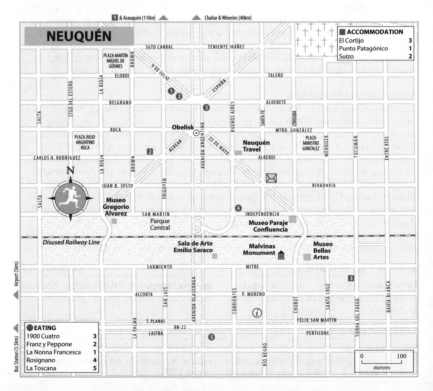

Parque Central

The centre of life in town is the vast **Parque Central**, bisected by an old railway line and home to four free museums, three of which are housed in abandoned railway buildings. From west to east these are: the **Museo Gregorio Álvarez** (Mon–Fri 8am–8pm, Sat & Sun 4–8pm), at San Martín and Brown, which contains several works by the local sculptor for whom the museum was named, as well as a small display on Patagonian history; the **Sala de Arte Emilio Saraco** (Mon–Fri 8am–8pm, Sat & Sun 4–9pm), an old cargo shed featuring temporary exhibitions by local artists; the **Museo Paraje Confluencia** (Mon–Fri 8am–8pm, Sat & Sun 6–11pm), which specializes in the city's history; and, the pick of the bunch, the **Museo Nacional de Bellas Artes Neuquén** (Tues–Sat 9.30am–8pm, Sun 4–8pm; free; ☎0299 443 6268, ⊛mnbaneuquen.gob.ar) at the southeast corner of the park. The only branch of the beautiful art museum (see p.84) outside of Buenos Aires, its displays include some fine South American art, plus examples from all the major European art movements. The most valuable painting is *La Última Copla*, by the great Valencian artist, Joaquín Sorolla.

Adjacent to the museum is an impressive **monument to the fallen** of the Malvinas/Falklands campaign of 1982 – the names of the dead are poignantly displayed on a glass wall that overlooks the serene fountain.

7

ARRIVAL AND DEPARTURE   NEUQUÉN

By air Neuquén's airport (☎0299 444 0980, ⊛anqn.com.ar) is 5km west of town off RN-22, with regular connections to Buenos Aires (2–4 daily; 1hr 30min). Indalo, under Autobuses Santa Fé, runs a bus to the city centre; it departs from the airport every 35min in front of the airport every 35min (pay on the bus; $7.50).

By bus Neuquén is a major transport nexus for the whole region. Its modern bus terminal, 3.5km west of the city centre on RN-22, is regarded as one of the best in the country; it's styled along airport lines (bags come through on a conveyor belt and passengers have to check in to platforms). Ko-Ko (☎0299 448 7606) runs a bus service to the centre every 15min; buy tickets from Kiosk 39 at the bus station before boarding. Alternatively, you can take a taxi into town ($70).

Destinations Bariloche (19 daily; 6hr); Buenos Aires (20 daily; 16hr 30min); Córdoba (2 weekly; 18hr 30min); Mendoza (3 daily; 10–11hr); San Juan (2 daily; 13–14hr); San Martín de los Andes (6 daily; 6hr 45min); Villa Pehuenia (2 daily; 7hr).

GETTING AROUND AND INFORMATION

By bus To use Neuquén's city buses, you must buy a *Sube* card in advance and top it up at the *kioskos* scattered throughout the city.

Tourist information There are tourist information booths at both the airport and the bus terminal, but the main tourist office (daily 8am–9pm; ☎0299 442 4089, ⊛neuquentur.gob.ar) is at Félix San Martín 182, two blocks east of Av Olascoaga. It is a mine of information on the whole province and runs an unusually informative and up-to-date website, although largely Spanish only.

ACCOMMODATION

Hotels in Neuquén are busy even during the week, so it's well worth booking in advance. Several unspectacular though centrally located mid-range places are clustered around avenidas Olascoaga and Argentina – a simple breakfast is generally included in the price.

El Cortijo Mitre 526 ☎0299 442 4324, ⊛bit.ly/El-Cortijo. Decent, newly built multistorey mid-range option. Heated rooms are clean and well maintained, if a little plain. $1250
Punto Patagónico Periodistas Neuquinos and Irigoyen ☎0299 447 9940, ⊛puntopatagonico.com. Homely and welcoming hostel with comfortable dorms and doubles and some good communal areas, including a spacious garden. Dorms $280; doubles $700
Suizo Carlos Rodríguez 167 ☎0299 442 2602, ⊛hotelsuizo.com.ar. Good-value option with bright rooms for up to four people, all with mini-bar and spacious bathroom. The reception area plays on the Swiss-chalet theme, but this is a classy and modern hotel. $1240

EATING

Neuquén's best places to eat and drink are scattered around Avenida Argentina between San Martín and Roca, where there are several pool bars and pizzerias in addition to more upmarket restaurants.

7

THE DINOSAUR SITES AROUND NEUQUÉN

Since 1988, the area around Neuquén has become a hotbed of dinosaur fever, with paleontologists uncovering **fossils** of both the largest herbivorous sauropod and the largest carnivorous dinosaur ever found. As you cross the Neuquén environs en route to the sites of discovery it is easy to imagine dinosaurs roaming the stunted plains and pterodactyls launching themselves into the air from the imposing cliff-faces. Getting to the sites by public transport is awkward – if you don't have your own car, your best bet is to go on a tour from Neuquén. These vary, but generally visit several sites of paleontological interest, with some tours also including winery stop-offs; try Arauquén (H. Yrigoyen 720; ☎0299 442 6476, ⓦarauquen.com) or Neuquén Travel (Alberdi 110; ☎0299 448 8570).

MUSEO ERNESTO BACHMANN

On the banks of the picturesque Embalse Ezequiel Ramos Mexía hydroelectric reservoir, 79km southwest of Neuquén along RN-237, the little oasis of **Villa El Chocón** is home to the **Museo Ernesto Bachmann** (daily 8am–8pm; $20; ☎0299 421 7858) where you can see a virtually complete, hundred-million-year-old skeleton of *Giganotosaurus carolinii*, discovered 18km away in 1993. This fearsome creature puts even *Tyrannosaurus rex* in the shade: it measured a colossal 13m long (its skull alone accounting for 1.8m), stood 4.7m tall and weighed an estimated eight tonnes.

PARQUE CRETÁCICO

Three kilometres further south along RN-237, a left turn-off leads another 2km down to the shores of Embalse Ezequiel Ramos Mexía. Here, at the northwest corner of the lake, is the **Parque Cretácico**, where you'll find some huge, astonishingly well-preserved **dinosaur footprints**. Not realizing what they were, fishermen once used them as barbecue pits. The footprints resemble those of a giant rhea, but were probably left by an iguanadon – a 10m-long herbivore – or some kind of bipedal carnivore. Other kidney-shaped prints are of four-footed sauropods, and smaller prints were probably left by 3m-long theropods.

1900 Cuatro First floor of the *Hotel Del Comahue*, Av Argentina 377 ☎0299 443 2040. Serves eclectic and imaginative foreign dishes and appetizing meals, though the overall ambience is somewhat formal and staid, and prices are predictably high. Daily noon–3pm & 8–11.30pm.

Franz y Peppone 9 de Julio and Belgrano ☎0299 448 2299. Another pizza, pasta and all things Italian restaurant, aimed squarely at those on a backpacker's budget. Mon–Sat noon–3pm & 8pm–late, Sun 8pm–late.

La Nonna Francesca 9 de Julio 56 ☎0299 430 0930. Atmospheric trattoria, on a similar theme to *Franz y Peppone*, though pricier. Large portions mean you won't go hungry. Mon–Sat noon–3pm & 8pm–midnight, Sun noon–4.30pm.

Rosignano Independencia and Buenos Aires ☎0299 443 6690. Hugely popular deli and takeaway joint (there's no room for eating in) packed with office workers at lunch time. Varied and inventive menu includes marinated squid, salads, vegetarian *milanesas* and grilled meats. Mon–Fri 11am–3pm & 8–11pm, Sat 11am–3pm.

La Toscana J.J Lastra 176 ☎0299 447 3322. One of the best restaurants in town, serving sizzling plates – like aubergine and courgette stuffed with ricotta ($278) – straight from the oven. Generous selection of tasty starters. Daily noon–3pm & 8pm–12.30am.

Chañar and the wineries

RP-7 follows the mighty Río Neuquén northwestwards from Neuquén across alluvial plains whose fertile lands feed the city with all manner of fruit and vegetables, while a series of reservoirs provides it with much-needed water. Artificial oases have been created in the desert-like terrain just west of tiny **SAN PATRICIO DEL CHAÑAR** (or **Chañar**), 41km from Neuquén, to support some of the country's newest and finest vineyards, producing highly palatable whites and reds, using grape varieties such as semillon and malbec.

A handful of outstanding wineries have sprung up in the region and some can be visited as part of the local **Ruta del Vino**, or wine route. Tours (with a small charge,

MUSEO CARMEN FUNES

Plaza Huincul, just over 110km west of Neuquén along RN-22, is where the region's petroleum reserves were discovered in 1918. Memorabilia from those pioneering days is displayed at the **Museo Carmen Funes** on the main street (Mon–Fri 9am–7pm, Sat & Sun 10.30am–8.30pm; $10; ☎0299 496 5486), though you'll find it impossible to concentrate on petroleum with the full-size reconstruction of *Argentinosaurus huinculensis* looming in the hangar next door. Walking between the legs of this beast – 40m long, 18m high and weighing 100 tonnes – is a bit like walking under a jumbo jet. The only fossils of this giant beast that have been found are the pelvis, tibia, sacrum and some vertebrae – the reconstruction of the rest is based on educated guesswork.

DINO PROJECT

Heading northwest from Neuquén 90km along RP-51 or RP-7 brings you to the shores of **Embalse Cerros Colorados**, the "**Dino Project**" at Lago Barreales (☎0299 449 0351, ⓦproyectodino.com.ar). Considered a "complete ecosystem of the Mesozoic era", the project, overseen by the University of Comahue, gives you the chance to help with the excavation. The most important finds are displayed at the on-site museum. The museum is closed at the moment, but still run on a voluntary basis; you can call the university in advance and ask if someone can show you around.

MUSEO ARGENTINO URQUIZA

Further afield, 250km northwest of Neuquén along RP-8, the isolated town of **Rincón de los Sauces** is home to the **Museo Argentino Urquiza** (Mon–Fri 9am–6pm, Sun 3–7pm; $3; ☎0299 15 631 9080), whose collection features the only known fossils of a titanosaurus, including an almost complete specimen. There is also a set of fossilized titanosaur eggs from nearby Auca Mahuida: the first set of **dinosaur eggs** ever to be found, they are approximately 14cm in diameter and have thin, porous shells through which the embryonic dinosaurs are thought to have breathed.

which is often reimbursed if you buy wine), tastings and fine dining are on offer; in all cases, reserve ahead. After leaving Chañar in the direction of Añelo, heading along RP-7, watch out on the right-hand side for the numbered lanes (*picadas*).

Bodega Familia Schroeder

Visits daily 10am–5pm, on the hour; 1hr • Tour and tasting $50 • ☎0299 489 9600, ⓦfamiliaschroeder.com

Picada no. 7 strikes off in the direction of **Bodega Familia Schroeder**. Tours (book ahead) with tastings include a visit to the "dinosaur cellar", where a dinosaur fossil was found during the winery's construction. The vineyard also has an acclaimed restaurant-bar, *Saurus* (Tues–Sun 10am–4pm; three-course lunch $500).

Bodega del Fin del Mundo

Visits Tues–Sun hourly 10am–4pm; 45min • Tour and tasting $30 • ☎0299 15 580 0414, ⓦbodegadelfindelmundo.com

Picada no. 12 leads to the dramatically named **Bodega del Fin del Mundo** ("Winery at the End of the World") – so-called because these wineries are in close competition with one or two in New Zealand for the title of the world's most southerly vineyard. These are the emblematic Patagonian wines, found throughout Argentina and further afield.

Bodega Malma

Visits Tues–Sun hourly 10am–4pm; 45min • Tour and tasting $30 • ☎0299 489 7500, ⓦbodeganqn.com.ar

Picada no. 15 is the approach to **Bodega Malma**, which has an excellent if pricey restaurant-bar (Tues–Sun 11am–4pm). "Malma", meaning "pride" in Mapudungun, is the name of the winery's flagship range of red and white varietals, such as pinot noir and sauvignon blanc.

Patagonia

GLACIAR PERITO MORENO

Patagonia

An immense land of arid steppe, seemingly stretching into infinity, Patagonia is famed for its adventures and adventurers, for marvellous myths and fabulous facts. Its geographical immensity is paralleled only by the size of its reputation – which itself has taken on legendary proportions, thanks partly to writers such as Bruce Chatwin, William Henry Hudson and Paul Theroux, as well as Charles Darwin. As a region of extremes, it has few equals in the world: from the biting winds that howl off the Southern Patagonian Icecap – the planet's largest area of permanent ice away from the poles – to the hearthside warmth of old-time Patagonian hospitality; from the lowest point on the South American continent, the Gran Bajo de San Julián, to the savagely beautiful peaks of the Fitz Roy massif; from the mesmerizingly sterile plains along the coastline to the astoundingly rich marine fauna that thrives just offshore.

One of southern Argentina's principal arteries, **RN-3** stretches from the capital all the way down to austral **Río Gallegos**. The highlight of this Atlantic fringe of Patagonia is the wildlife, especially at the **Península Valdés** reserve, famous for its **whale-watching**, but also at **Punta Tombo**, the continent's largest **penguin** colony. Further south, in Santa Cruz Province, colonies of sea birds perch on spectacular porphyry cliffs at **Puerto Deseado** and Commerson's dolphins frolic in the *ría*, or estuary, just outside the town. This coastal area helped define the Patagonian pioneering spirit: Welsh settlers landed on a beach just south of Península Valdés, at what is now **Puerto Madryn**, and gradually ventured into the **Lower Chubut Valley**. Their cultural legacy survives in settlements such as **Gaiman** and **Trelew**.

The second main road here is the famous **RN-40** (Ruta 40), which starts at Cabo Vírgenes, the most southerly point of mainland Argentina, and hugs the Andean backbone all the way up to the country's northerly tip. Some of the destinations in this western fringe are difficult to reach without your own transport (and not always that easy with it), but it is along or close by this route that you'll find Argentine Patagonia's hallmark features: impressive national parks brimming with wild beauty, great mountain lakes, the finest spit-roast lamb *asados* and some unique skies. The Cañón of Río Pinturas is home to one of Argentina's most famous archeological sites, the **Cueva de las Manos Pintadas**, with its striking, age-old rock art; to the west two beautiful, wind-whipped

CUEVA DE LAS MANOS PINTADAS

Highlights

❶ Whale-watching Enjoy close-up views of majestic southern right whales off the Península Valdés, one of the most important marine reserves on Earth. **See p.453**

❷ Welsh tearooms For a little taste of Wales, visit the town of Gaiman, which is famous for its wonderful tearooms. **See p.460**

❸ Magellanic penguins Watch tens of thousands of these charming birds waddling around their major nesting sites – the biggest is at Punta Tombo. **See p.461**

❹ Parque Nacional Los Glaciares The legendary Glaciar Perito Moreno dominates any visit to southern Patagonia, with world-class

trekking in the Fitz Roy sector a close second. **See pp.468–490**

❺ Lamb asados Succulent lamb cooked over an open fire defines Patagonia almost as much as the horizon-defying terrain and relentless gales. **See p.481**

❻ RN-40 Leave the crowds behind and head out onto the open road on the Patagonian stretch of Argentina's famous RN-40. **See p.490**

❼ Cueva de las Manos Pintadas Wonder at rock art executed hundreds or thousands of years ago, dramatically sited in the heart of a canyon. **See p.496**

HIGHLIGHTS ARE MARKED ON THE MAP ON P.444

lakes, **Posadas** and **Pueyrredón**, lie in a seldom-visited area in the lee of stately San Lorenzo peak. Further north is an outstanding geological curiosity, the **Bosque Petrificado Sarmiento**, a beguiling collection of ancient fossilized trees, while to the south stretches the wilderness of **Parque Nacional Perito Moreno**, one of the most inaccessible – and, consequently, untouched – of Argentina's national parks, with excellent hiking trails.

The region's climax is reached, however, with two of the country's star attractions: the trekking and climbing paradise of the **Fitz Roy** sector of **Parque Nacional Los Glaciares**, accessed from the laidback town of **El Chaltén**; and the patriotically blue-and-white hues of craggy **Glaciar Perito Moreno**, one of the world's natural wonders, within easy reach of the tourist hotspot of **El Calafate**.

Brief history

For over ten thousand years, before the arrival of European seafarers in the sixteenth century, Patagonia was exclusively the domain of nomadic **indigenous groups**. It was Ferdinand Magellan who coined the name "Patagonia" (see p.464) on landing at **Bahía San Julián**. The tales related by these early mariners awed and frightened their countrymen back home, mutating into myths of a godless, dangerous region.

European colonization

Two centuries of sporadic attempts to colonize the inhospitable coastlands only partially ameliorated Patagonia's unwholesome aura. In 1779, the Spanish established **Carmen de Patagones**, which managed to survive as a trading centre on the Patagonian frontier. In doing so, it fared considerably better than other early settlements: **Puerto de los Leones**, near Camarones (1535); **Nombre de Jesús**, by the Strait of Magellan (late 1580s); **Floridablanca**, near San Julián (1784); and **San José** on the Península Valdés (1779). All failed miserably, the last crushed by a Tehuelche attack in 1810 after braving it out for twenty years. Change was afoot, nevertheless. In 1848, Chile founded Punta Arenas on the Strait of Magellan, and in 1865, fired by their visionary faith, a group of **Welsh Nonconformists** arrived in the Lower Chubut Valley. Rescued from starvation in the early years by **Tehuelche** tribespeople and Argentine government subsidies, they managed to establish a stable agricultural colony by the mid-1870s.

Sheep farming and the oil industry

In the late nineteenth century, Patagonia changed forever with the introduction of **sheep**, originally brought across from the Islas Malvinas/Falkland Islands. The region's image shifted from one of hostility and hardship to that of an exciting frontier, where the "white gold" of wool opened the path to fabulous fortunes for pioneer investors. The transformation was complete within a generation: the plains were fenced in and roads were run from the coast to the cordillera. Native populations were booted out of their ancestral lands, while foxes and pumas were poisoned en masse to make way for gigantic estancias. By the early 1970s, there were over sixteen million sheep grazing the fragile pastures on over a thousand of these ranches. Later, the region's confidence and wealth blossomed further with the discovery of oil, spurring the growth of industry in towns such as **Comodoro Rivadavia**.

Plummeting international wool prices and desertification, though, eventually brought sheep farming to its knees, with the final blow being the eruption of Volcán Hudson in 1991, which buried immense areas of grazing land in choking ash. To make matters worse, the oil industry also went through a massive downturn.

Patagonia today

Today the picture is far more positive. Although there are hundreds of abandoned estancias in Santa Cruz alone, the Patagonian economy is once again on the up: in 2015 wool prices reached their highest for 35 years, and tourist numbers have steadily risen. However, serious challenges remain. In late 2015 work started on a controversial,

Chinese-funded US$5.7 billion **hydroelectric scheme** to create two massive dams and flood an area the size of Buenos Aires some 150km east of El Calafate. While the project promises to bring jobs and investment, there are serious and widespread concerns about the environmental and long-term political impact, not least on Parque Nacional los Glaciares (see p.468).

GETTING AROUND   **PATAGONIA**

Distances are huge, but most cities and towns are served by regular buses. However, to make the most of the more remote places, such as Península Valdés (see p.450) and along Ruta 40, you really need to rent a car. Note also that some bus services do not operate out of season (Easter–Sept), above all along and around Ruta 40, while others are severely curtailed.

RN-3 coastal route

A journey along the seemingly endless RN-3, with a few detours just off it, offers many opportunities – albeit at great distances from one another – to marvel at magnificent wildlife; nowhere is this easier or more rewarding than at the world-class **Península Valdés** reserve, best accessed from the seaside city of **Puerto Madryn**. In addition, you can explore Patagonia's fascinating Welsh legacy in the villages of the Lower Chubut Valley near **Trelew**, and the huge Magellanic penguin colony at **Punta Tombo**. The long trip can be broken up with stopovers in a trio of typical austral ports, **Puerto Deseado**, **Puerto San Julián** and **Puerto Santa Cruz**, each with its own wealth of marine wildlife and historical associations. A short way south of the last of these three, **Monte León** – the country's first national park to be created on the coast – is well worth a visit even if the marvellous estancia in its midst is beyond your budget. With your own transport, you could also fit in a side-trip to the curious petrified forests of the **Parque Nacional Bosques Petrificados de Jaramillo** (see p.463), or the **Bosque Petrificado Sarmiento** (see p.499), closer to RN-40 but accessible from the coast, too. The end of the road – and seemingly the end of the world – is reached at workaday **Río Gallegos**, a jumping-off point for travelling on to Tierra del Fuego or for starting a journey northwards along RN-40.

Puerto Madryn

Sprawling along the beautiful sweep of the Golfo Nuevo, Argentina's self-styled diving capital, **PUERTO MADRYN**, is the gateway to the ecological treasure-trove of Península Valdés; indeed, the superb **Ecocentro**, just east of town, makes a great introduction to the area's abundant marine life. Though Puerto Madryn was where the Welsh first landed in Patagonia in 1865, little development took place until the arrival of the railway from Trelew two decades later, when it began to act as the port for the communities in the Lower Chubut Valley. With the explosion of tourism, and the more recent increase in migration from northern Argentina, Puerto Madryn has undergone rapid growth, and the city's permanent population swells exponentially during the summer months.

Parque Histórico Punta Cuevas

Blvd Brown 3681, 4km south of the centre along the coast road • Daily 24hr • Free • Bus #2 from the bus station

The **Parque Histórico Punta Cuevas** marks the first Welsh settlement in Patagonia with the **Monumento al Indio Tehuelche**, a statue erected both to celebrate the centenary of the arrival of the Welsh and pay homage to the Tehuelche (see box, p.448), who provided invaluable help to the community. At sunset from here there is a glorious wide view of the arc of the Golfo Nuevo to the lights of the city. Close to the monument are the 3m-square **foundations** of the very first houses built by the pioneers, right above the high-water mark. At the time of research, a new museum telling the story of the Welsh arrival was under construction.

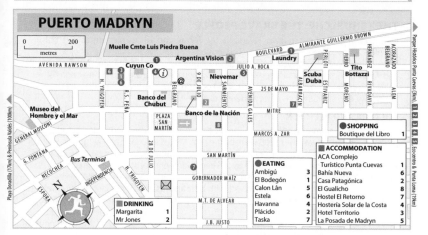

Ecocentro

Julio Verne 3784, just beyond Punta Cuevas • March–May 15 Wed–Sun 3–7pm; May 16–June 14 Sat & Sun 3–7pm; July 4–Sept Mon & Wed–Sun 3–7pm; Oct–Dec 20 Mon–Wed & Sun 3–8pm; Dec 21–Feb Mon & Wed–Sun 5–9pm • $125 • ☎ 0280 445 7470, ⓦ ecocentro .org.ar • Bus #2 from the bus station

Round the headland past the Monumento al Indio Tehuelche is Puerto Madryn's prime attraction, the excellent **Ecocentro**. An interactive museum set up to promote respect and understanding for marine ecosystems, it also houses a stunning life-size model of the orca Mel, who became something of a local celebrity after being captured on film in various wildlife documentaries. Be sure to go up the tower as well, to relax on one of the comfy sofas while enjoying panoramic views of the bay. There's also a lovely café.

Museo del Hombre y el Mar

D. Garcia and Menéndez • Mon–Fri 10am–4pm, Sat 3–7pm • $10, Tues free • ☎ 0280 445 1139

The rather staid **Museo del Hombre y el Mar** is not in the same league as Ecocentro, but the location – in the elegant, turreted Chalet Pujol, which dates back to 1915 – is grand. Among the exhibits are whale bones, a fearsome giant squid, relics from Welsh pioneering days, ancient arrowheads and Tehuelche textiles. There's also a mirador at the top with views across the city.

ARRIVAL AND DEPARTURE

PUERTO MADRYN

By plane The airport is 10km outside the city (around $100 by taxi), but only has a handful of flights; there is a far greater range from Trelew airport, 65km south (see p.458). Aerolíneas Argentinas has an office at Roca 427 (☎ 0810 2228 6527, ⓦ aerolineas .com.ar). LADE is at Roca 117 (☎ 0280 445 1256, ⓦ lade.com.ar).

By bus The bus terminal is at Ávila and Independencia, a short walk from the city centre. There's a café, lockers, and timetables on the wall.

Destinations Buenos Aires (12 daily; 18hr–21hr 35min); Puerto Pirámides (1–3 daily; 1hr 15min); Puerto San Julian (8 daily; 12hr 10min–13hr 10min); Río Gallegos (6 daily; 17–19hr); Trelew (every 30min–1hr; 1hr).

By car You can rent cars from Fiorasi, Roca 165 (☎ 0280 445 6300, ⓦ fiorasirentacar.com).

INFORMATION AND ACTIVITIES

Tourist information The tourist office at Roca 223 (daily 7am–9pm; ☎ 0280 445 3504, ⓦ madryn.gov.ar/turismo) has good maps, and a list of independent, multilingual guides. There's also a smaller, erratically manned office (☎ 0280 447 5971) in the bus station.

Tour operators Dozens of agencies run day-trips to the Península Valdés, all charging around $800 (excluding entrance fee and whale-watching trip): among the the best run are Argentina Vision, Roca 536 (☎ 0280 445 5888, ⓦ argentinavision.com); Cuyun Co, Roca 165 (☎ 0280 445

THE TEHUELCHE: THE BRAVE PEOPLE

Once spread throughout much of Patagonia, the **Tehuelche**, whose name, meaning "brave people", is derived from Mapudungun, the language of the Chilean Mapuche groups. Mapudungun actually consisted of three different groups – the Gününa'küna, Mecharnúek'enk and Aónik'enk – each of whom spoke a different language but shared common bonds of culture. Great intertribal parliaments were held occasionally, but any alliances would be temporary, and sporadic intertribal warfare broke out.

CULTURE AND RELIGION

The Tehuelche's **nomadic culture** – centred on the hunting of rhea and guanaco – had probably existed for well over 3000 years by the time Magellan landed on Patagonian soil, but contact with Europeans soon brought change. By 1580, Sarmiento de Gamboa had reported use of the horse by the Tehuelche, and by the early eighteenth century the animal had become integral to Tehuelche life. Intertribal contact and intermarriage became more common and hunting techniques evolved, with **boleadoras** and lances increasingly preferred to the bow and arrow. The boleadora consisted of two or three stones wrapped in guanaco hide and connected by long thongs made from rhea or guanaco sinew. Whirled around the head, these were thrown to ensnare animals at close quarters. Boleadoras are the main physical legacy of Tehuelche culture in today's Argentina.

Tehuelche **religious beliefs** recognized a benign supreme god (variously named Kooch, Maipé or Táarken-Kets), but he did not figure greatly in any outward devotions. In contrast, the malign spirit, **Gualicho**, was much-feared, the regular beneficiary of horse sacrifices and the object of shamanistic attentions. The main divine hero was **Elal**, the being who created man.

DECLINE AND FALL

The decline of **Tehuelche civilization** came fast: in 1870, there were estimated to be 1500 Tehuelche in Patagonia; a 1931 census in Santa Cruz Province (home to the greatest population of Tehuelche) recorded only 350. Wars with the huincas (white men) were catastrophic – above all, Julio Roca's Conquest of the Desert (see p.535) in 1879 – and were exacerbated by intertribal conflicts. Even peaceful contact with huinca civilization led to severe problems: disease wiped out whole tribal groups, while alcohol abuse led whites to replace one misconception (the "noble savage") with another (the "moral delinquent"), enabling them spuriously to justify attempts to settle ancestral Tehuelche lands as part of a greater plan to "civilize the indio".

Following the capitulation of the last rebel group to Roca in December 1884, the remaining Tehuelche were pushed into increasingly marginal lands. Guanaco populations plummeted and Tehuelche life became one of dependency. Many found the closest substitute to the old way of life was to join the estancias that had displaced them as peón shepherds. In this way, they were absorbed into the rural underclass. Whereas Mapuche customs and language have managed, tenuously, to survive, Tehuelche populations fell below that imprecise, critical number that is necessary for the survival of a cultural heritage. The last Gününa'küna speaker died in 1960. The Aónik'enk language can be spoken, at least partially, by fewer than a dozen people.

1845, ⓦcuyunco.com); Tito Bottazzi, Blvd Brown and Martín Fierro (☎0280 447 4110, ⓦtitobottazzi.com); and Nievemar, Roca 493 (☎0280 445 5544, ⓦnievemartours.com.ar).

Diving Diving trips that take in offshore wrecks and abundant marine life start at around $1200. The experienced Madryn Buceo, at Blvd Brown 1900 (☎0280 15 456 4422, ⓦmadrynbuceo.com), has English-speaking instructors and offers a wide range of dives (including with sea lions; around $1600) and courses. Scuba Duba, Blvd

Brown 893 (☎0280 445 2699, ⓦscubaduba.com.ar), is another good option.

Mountain biking Mountain bikes can be rented (around $150/day) from several places in town. There are a couple of good rides within easy reach: north to Playa Doradilla (17km from Madryn), where you can often see whales late in the afternoon between June and September, and to the sea-lion colony at Punta Loma (19km in the other direction).

ACCOMMODATION

Puerto Madryn has a wide range of accommodation, with good discounts available off season; high season (Oct–Dec), when prices are at their highest, is the best time for whale-watching. The better places tend to fill up quickly year-round, however, so advance bookings are recommended. Rates for all include breakfast, unless stated otherwise.

ACA Complejo Turístico Punta Cuevas Punta Cuevas ☎0280 445 2952, ⓦacamadryn.com.ar. This complex, 4km from the centre, has camping spots (tents provided), simple rooms and self-contained apartments suitable for groups. There are plenty of facilities, including a restaurant-bar. No breakfast. Camping $130; doubles $420; apartments $1500

Bahía Nueva Roca 67 ☎0280 445 1677, ⓦbahianueva .com.ar. A smart, red-brick hotel on the seafront, with comfortable rooms – try to get one of the few with an ocean view – and a nice lounge with an extensive library. The ample buffet breakfasts are also a cut above the rest. $1096

Casa Patagónica Roca 2210 ☎0280 445 1540, ⓦcasa -patagonica.com.ar. This cheerful, family-run B&B has a handful of rooms, one of which is en suite; they are simply decorated, but comfortable and good value. Guests have access to a microwave and a fridge, and there's a living room to relax in. $680

★**El Gualicho** Marcos Zar 480 ☎0280 445 4163, ⓦelgualicho.com.ar. Excellent HI-affiliated hostel with a lovely garden strung with hammocks, plus welcoming staff, a communal kitchen, private rooms (the cheapest ones have shared bathrooms) and mixed and female-only dorms. Tours, diving trips and bike rental are available. Dorms $200; doubles $700

Hostel El Retorno Mitre 798 ☎0280 445 6044, ⓦelretornohostel.com.ar. An attractive hostel whose whitewashed exterior is mirrored by the spick-and-span dorms and private rooms (some with shared bathrooms) and spotless communal areas. Kitchen and laundry facilities, barbecue, table tennis, bike rental and free bus station pick-ups are all provided too. Dorms $150; doubles $520

Hostería Solar de la Costa Brown 2057 ☎0280 445 8822, ⓦsolardelacosta.com. A popular beachfront guesthouse at the eastern end of town, Solar de la Costa has tastefully furnished en suites, many of which look out over the Golfo Nuevo. Staff are friendly, and there's a peaceful garden out back. $1015

Hotel Territorio Blvd Brown 3251 ☎0280 447 0050, ⓦhotelterritorio.com.ar. The top hotel in town has slick, contemporary en suites with plenty of space and sea views. There's a gym, spa, restaurant-bar, and decor that features artwork, historic photos, and even a whale skeleton (a combination that works far better than you might think). The only downside is the location, near Punta Cuevas, around 3.5km from the centre. US$210

La Posada de Madryn Abraham Matthews 2951 ☎0280 488 3467, ⓦla-posada.com.ar. One of the most stylish options in town, located close to a wooded area, La Posada de Madryn has compact, minimalist en suites that receive lots of natural light. There is also a comfortable communal lounge, plus a heated outdoor pool and a pleasant garden. $1020

EATING

Although Puerto Madryn is known for its seafood, and has several beachfront **restaurants** that serve nothing else – including the local speciality, *arroz con mariscos*, a variant of paella usually containing prawns, squid and clams – standards are mixed. Prices (see box, p.45) both here and in Patagonia as a whole are higher than in central and northern Argentina.

Ambigú Roca and R.S. Peña ☎0280 447 2541, ⓦambiguresto.com. The menu jumps from steaks, seafood and thinnish-crust pizzas to more exotic dishes, such as curries and stir-fries (mains $95–170). The walls are covered with old drinks posters and there are plenty of magazines to read. Daily noon–2.30pm & 7.30pm–midnight.

El Bodegón Brown 601 ☎0280 445 6326. This little joint has an unpretentious, local feel: the menu is chalked up on a board, with the fish- and seafood-based dishes particular highlights – for a bit of everything, try the *parrillada de mariscos*, or the $150 set lunch. Mon–Fri noon–3pm & 8pm–midnight.

Calon Lân Roca ☎0280 434 0957. If you don't have time to sample a traditional Welsh tea in Gaiman (see p.460) – and you really should – this first-floor café is a decent fallback. A mountain of cakes (including *torta galesa*) and sandwiches, accompanied by a pot of tea, will set you back $180. Tues–Sun 4–9pm.

Estela R.S. Peña 27 ☎0280 445 1573. This friendly, down-to-earth steakhouse serves top-notch *morcilla*, *chorizo* and *bifes de chorizo*, as well as a vast *parrillada*

($320 for two people). Steaks cost from $130, and there are some good weekday lunch deals. Daily noon–2pm & 8pm–midnight.

Havanna Roca and 28 de Julio ☎0280 447 3373, ⓦhavanna.com.ar. The Puerto Madryn branch of the venerable Argentine coffeehouse chain is a reliable spot for coffee ($27–44) at any time of the day – if you need a treat, the sugary *alfajores* are a good option. Daily 8/9am–10/11pm.

Plácido Roca 506 ☎0280 445 5991, ⓦplacido.com.ar. Elegant restaurant directly overlooking the Golfo Nuevo. It serves fine, though rather pricey, seafood, including hearty paellas and delicious prawn kebabs, as well as pasta dishes (mains $137–230). There's an excellent wine list, too. Daily noon–4pm & 8pm–1am.

★**Taska** 9 de Julio 461 ☎0280 15 499 4870. Unquestionably the best seafood restaurant in town, and good value for money (mains $110–170). Ask for the daily special, or sample a few Basque tapas (from $70), followed by a paella or *merluza* (hake) dish. The wine list is strong, as well. Daily 11.30am–3pm & 7.30pm–midnight.

8

DRINKING

Margarita Roca and R.S. Peña ☎0280 447 0885. Plenty of wood panelling gives this lively bar the feel of a pub. It's a great place for a pre- or post-dinner drink, though the food is also worth a look (sandwiches $55–135, pizzas $140–190). Live bands perform at the weekends. Mon–Sat 7.30pm–2/3am.

Mr Jones 9 de Julio 116 ☎0280 447 5368. This self-described "House of Beers" is a buzzing pub-restaurant, popular with locals and gringos alike. Most of the diners – who fill up the wooden benches and spill out onto the street-side tables – are here for a beer (from around $35) and a *picada* (cold meat and cheese platter). Mon–Sat 7pm–1/2am.

SHOPPING

Boutique del Libro 28 de Julio 20 ☎0280 445 7978, ⓦboutiquedellibro.com.ar. On the first floor of the mall is the best bookshop in town. There's a range of English-language non-fiction on Patagonia

and Tierra del Fuego – including Chatwin, Theroux and Musters – as well as some commercial fiction. Mon–Thurs 9.30am–9pm, Fri & Sat 9.30am–9.30pm, Sun 11am–9.30pm.

DIRECTORY

Banks There are plenty of ATMs, including at Banco de la Nación (9 de Julio 117) and Banco del Chubut (25 de Mayo 154).
Internet There are numerous internet cafés, including

TeleNetK on Belgrano and 25 de Mayo.
Laundry Lavandería Presto-lav on Brown and Gales (Mon–Sat 9am–12.30pm & 3.30–8.30pm; ☎0280 445 1526).

Península Valdés

The reserve entrance is halfway along the isthmus, 43km from Puerto Madryn • Daily 8am–8pm • $260 per person, plus $12 per car • ☎0280 445 0489, ⓦpeninsulavaldes.org.ar

PENÍNSULA VALDÉS, a sandy-beige, treeless hump of land connected to the mainland by a 35km isthmus, is one of the planet's most significant marine reserves, gaining World Heritage status in 1999. It was beautifully evoked by Gerald Durrell in *The Whispering Land*: "It was almost as if the peninsula and its narrow isthmus was a cul-de-sac into which all the wildlife of Chubut had drained and from which it could not escape." No description, however, prepares you for the astonishing richness of the marine environment that surrounds it – most notably the **southern right whales** that migrate here each year to frolic in the waters off the village of **Puerto Pirámides** – nor the immense animal colonies that live at the feet of the peninsula's steep, crumbly cliffs.

The first attempt to establish a permanent settlement here was made in 1779 by Juan de la Piedra, who constructed a fort on the shores of the Golfo San José. A small number of settlers tried to scrape a living by extracting salt, but the colony was abandoned in 1810 after attacks by the local Tehuelche; an extremely limited salt-extraction industry exists to this day in the saltpans at the bottom of Argentina's second-deepest depression, the **Salina Grande**, 42m below sea level, in the centre of the peninsula. However, it is nature tourism that's the pot of gold now, with **Punta Delgada**, **Punta Cantor** and **Punta Norte**, along with **Caleta Valdés**, providing some of the best opportunities on the continent for viewing marine mammals such as elephant seals and sea lions. How the recent discovery of oil and shale gas reserves in the vicinity of the reserve will affect this remains unclear at present.

Be warned not to collect your own shellfish in the area, because of the possibility of periodic **red-tide** outbreaks; all shellfish served in restaurants is safe to eat.

Isla de los Pájaros

Some 22km beyond the reserve entrance, you pass a signposted turn-off north that takes you 5km to the lookout point for the **Isla de los Pájaros** (Bird Island), a strictly controlled area where access is only permitted for the purposes of scientific research. From the shore, telescopes enable you to view sea birds in the nesting colonies 800m away. The most active months are between September and March, when you can spot egrets, herons, waders, ducks, cormorants, gulls and terns.

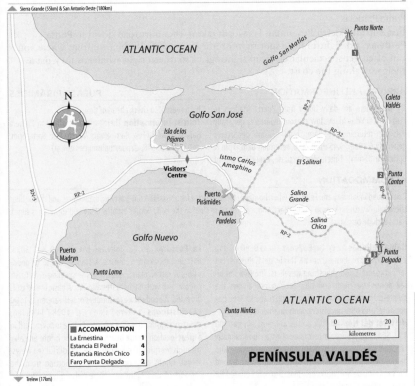

ATLANTIC OCEAN

Punta Norte

Golfo San Matías

Caleta
Valdés

Golfo San José

Isla de los
Pájaros

RP-3

RP-52

Istmo Carlos
Ameghino

El Salitral

Punta
Cantor

**Visitors'
Centre**

Puerto
Pirámides

Salina
Grande

RP-47

RN-3

RP-2

Punta
Pardelas

Salina
Chica

Punta
Delgada

Golfo Nuevo

RP-2

Puerto
Madryn

Punta Loma

ATLANTIC OCEAN

Punta Ninfas

0   20
kilometres

PENÍNSULA VALDÉS

8

■ ACCOMMODATION	
La Ernestina	1
Estancia El Pedral	4
Estancia Rincón Chico	3
Faro Punta Delgada	2

Trelew (17km)

Centro de Interpretaciones

Daily 8am–8pm • Free

Just past the turn-off to the Isla de los Pájaros is the **Centro de Interpretaciones**, which, although poor by comparison with Puerto Madryn's Ecocentro (see p.447), still has some interesting old photos and the skeleton of a young southern right whale that washed up at Caleta Valdés.

Puerto Pirámides and around

At the end of the asphalt road, 105km from Puerto Madryn, lies the tiny settlement of **Puerto Pirámides**, named after the pointed cliff at the mouth of the bay. This is *the* place for whale-watching: between June and mid-December the nearby waters are temporarily home to the most famous of all the peninsula's visitors, the **southern right whale**. Few experiences beat the thrill of watching these massive animals approaching your boat, breaching (leaping out of the water) or jutting their tails above the surface as they dive to feed. There are also good **diving** opportunities for humans (see box, p.453), with some trips attracting the attention of sea lions and whales, though it's officially illegal to dive with whales; locals refer euphemistically to "*excursiones especiales*". You can walk to the **sea-lion colony** (Jan is the best time) at Punta Pirámides, 5km round the headland to the northwest.

The village's orientation is straightforward: the main road you come in on, Avenida de las Ballenas, runs parallel to the beach, with two perpendicular streets descending to the water – the shorter, busier Primera Bajada and the much longer Segunda Bajada.

Punta Pardelas

Just outside Puerto Pirámides, it's worth taking the short road down to **Punta Pardelas**, a delightful little spot right on the shore of Golfo Nuevo, from where you can often get spectacular close-up sightings of southern right whales as they make their way along the coast.

ARRIVAL AND INFORMATION
PUERTO PIRÁMIDES

By bus There are daily buses from Puerto Madryn to Puerto Pirámides (daily: low season departures generally 9.45am, returning at 6pm; high season departures generally 6.30am, 9.45am & 4pm, returning 8am, 1pm & 6pm; 1hr 15min). Timetables fluctuate, especially out of high season, so check ahead of time.

Tourist information There's a tourist office on Primera Bajada (Jan & Feb 8am–8pm; March–Dec 8am–6pm; ☎ 0280 449 5048, ⓦ puertopiramides.gov.ar).

ACCOMMODATION

Book ahead in January and February when hordes of tourists arrive for a seaside-cum-partying experience, and throughout the whale-watching season (June–Dec). Some places close shop in the early winter months (May and sometimes June). Rates include breakfast.

Bahía Ballenas Av de las Ballenas s/n ☎ 0280 15 456 7104, ⓦ bahiaballenas.com.ar. This hostel is the best bet for backpackers and shoestring travellers. The two single-sex dorms are clean and tidy, though not always the quietest. The owners run the Tito Bottazzi agency (see box opposite) and offer guests discounts on their tours. $450

★ **Hotel del Nómade** Av de las Ballenas s/n ☎ 0280 449 5044, ⓦ ecohosteria.com.ar. This environmentally sensitive guesthouse is based in a handsome building and has lovely, minimalist en suites. Staff are ultra-friendly and the home-made breakfasts delicious. Discounts offered for stays of two nights or more. $1911

La Posta Av de las Ballenas s/n ☎ 0280 449 5036, ⓦ lapostapiramides.com.ar. A staggered line of good-value, if rather plain, apartments – sleeping two to six people – all with kitchenettes and TVs. A basic breakfast is provided. A good choice for families or self-caterers. $1600

Las Restingas Primera Bajada s/n ☎ 0280 449 5101, ⓦ lasrestingas.com. The smartest place in town, and in a great location on the beach. Most of the bright and airy (though overpriced) en suites have wonderful sea views, so you might even do some whale-spotting from the comfort of your bedroom. There's also a gym, spa and restaurant. $1680

VISITING PENÍNSULA VALDÉS

Many people see Península Valdés on a **day-trip** from Puerto Madryn (see p.446), following a fairly standard route that visits the lookout point for Isla de los Pájaros, Puerto Pirámides (where a whale-watching boat trip costs around $890), Punta Cantor and Caleta Valdés, and either Punta Norte or Punta Delgada. Be sure to find out exactly what sights you're visiting and how long you'll get in each place (most tours stay 1hr at each destination), whether the guide speaks English and the size of the group (some companies use large buses). Tours are long (10–12hr), so bring picnic provisions, though you can buy lunch in Puerto Pirámides.

If you want to visit the peninsula independently, the Mar y Valle **bus service** links Puerto Madryn with Puerto Pirámides (see p.451). However, it's difficult to get from Pirámides to the rest of Península Valdés without your own wheels.

Undoubtedly the best way to see the peninsula is to **rent a car** from Trelew or Puerto Madryn, allowing you to decide how long you want to spend wildlife-watching, and to time your arrival at Punta Norte or Caleta Valdés for high tide, when there's the best chance of seeing orcas; it also gives you the freedom to stay at an estancia, recommended for a better appreciation of what makes the peninsula so special (see opposite). Do not attempt to rush, however, especially if this is your first experience of driving on unsurfaced roads – serious crashes and fatalities happen with alarming regularity on the peninsula, especially after rain. When renting, check what happens if you break down or have a minor accident, as rescue bills can be hefty.

The whale-watching season runs from mid-June to mid-December, but the **best time to visit** the peninsula is from September to November, when elephant seals are also active, the penguin colonies have returned to breed and, if you're lucky, you stand a chance of seeing orcas cruising behind the spit at Caleta Valdés.

WHALE-WATCHING FROM PUERTO PIRÁMIDES, AND OTHER ACTIVITIES

In season (June to mid-Dec), you are almost guaranteed to come within a few metres of a southern right whale. If you're here towards the end of the season, there will be fewer specimens and you'll have to go farther out to sea to spot them, but you're also likely to see mothers with calves. Outside these dates, boat trips generally spot dolphins and sea lions. During the whale-spotting season, several companies offer daytime and sunset **whale-watching** trips (around $900) into the Golfo Nuevo: Hydrosport (☎0280 449 5065, ⓦhydrosport.com.ar), Tito Bottazzi (☎0280 449 5050, ⓦtitobottazzi.com) and Whales Argentina (☎0280 449 5015, ⓦwhalesargentina.com.ar) are all on Primera Bajada; Jorge Schmid (☎0280 449 5112, ⓦpuntaballena.com.ar) and Peke Sosa (☎0280 449 5010, ⓦpekesosaavistajes.com) are both on Segunda Bajada; while Southern Spirit (☎0280 449 5094, ⓦsouthernspirit.com.ar) is marked by a model whale on Las Ballenas at the top of Primera Bajada.

Services vary little, but check what type of boat you'll be using; the semi-rigid inflatable Zodiacs allow you to get closer to the animals, but bounce more in rough waters. Remember, though, that boat operators are meant to observe strict regulations about keeping a respectful distance from the cetaceans; the whales, especially the young, are highly inquisitive, however, and will often come up close or even plunge beneath the boat.

Another option is the whale-watching trips in a semi-submersible craft ($1780 in high season; prices come down a bit during the rest of the year) offered by Yellow Submarine (☎0280 449 5094, ⓦyellowsubmarinearg.com) on Av de las Ballenas.

DIVING AND KAYAKING

For **diving**, try Buceo Aventura (☎0280 15 460 7684, ✉buceoaventura@yahoo.com.ar) or Patagonia Scuba (☎0280 15 457 8779, ✉patagoniascuba@hotmail.com). Patagonian Brothers Expeditions on Avenida de las Ballenas (☎0280 15 434 0618, ⓦpatagoniaexplorers.com) runs excellent guided small-group **kayak** trips in both gulfs, from half-day paddles to nine-day expeditions. Huellas & Costas (☎0280 447 0143, ⓦhuellasycostas.com) also offers excellent kayaking trips lasting two to ten days.

8

EATING

★**La Estación** Opposite the petrol station ☎0280 449 5047. One of the best bars in the area, with a cosy ambience, laidback vibe and mix of old-time memorabilia and rock iconography. It also serves great home-made pastas and fresh fish and seafood (mains $90–200). Mon & Wed–Sun noon–midnight.

Hosteria The Paradise Av de las Ballenas and 2a Bajada ☎0280 449 5030, ⓦhosteriatheparadise.com .ar. One of the best restaurants in Puerto Pirámides, *Hosteria The Paradise* has excellent fish and seafood dishes ($100–240), and there's a varied wine list too. Daily noon–11pm.

Punta Delgada

From Punta Pardelas, it's 70km to **Punta Delgada**, at the southeasterly tip of the peninsula, past the pinky-white salt deposits of the **Salina Grande** and **Salina Chica** depressions. Punta Delgada itself is a headland topped by a lighthouse, part of the *Faro Punta Delgada* hotel (see p.454). The area affords excellent opportunities to view **sea lions** and, in high season, **elephant seals**. However, it is private property, and can only be visited on tours by Argentina Vision (see p.447), who own the hotel. Independent travellers need to buy lunch at the hotel's restaurant in order to access the beach on a short guided tour (free).

ACCOMMODATION   PUNTA DELGADA

★**Estancia Rincón Chico** Just southwest of Punta Delgada ☎0280 447 1733, ⓦrinconchico .com.ar. This estancia blends traditional Patagonian architecture with attractive modern rooms. The food served in the handsome dining room is delicious, while the lobby and living room are decorated with bric-a-brac like whale bones. The highlight is a guided visit (included in room rates) to the colonies of marine wildlife that gather on the estancia's private beach: up to 3500 sea lions and 10,000 elephant seals. You can also rent bikes to explore the steppe and admire the cliff-top ocean views. Closed Easter to mid-Aug. Rates include full board and excursions. Minimum two-night stay. US$376 per person

Faro Punta Delgada Punta Delgada ☎ 0280 447 1733, ⓦ rinconchico.com.ar. Perched on a cliff and buffeted by winds, this converted lighthouse is a very atmospheric place to stay. Rooms are comfortable, and there's a restaurant and pub. As well as tours of the nearby elephant-seal reserve (included in the rates, as is breakfast), staff can organize treks, bike rides and horseriding. Closed April–July. US$308

Punta Cantor and Caleta Valdés

North along the coast from Punta Delgada is a string of beaches bustling with marine mammals. **Punta Cantor**, midway up the peninsula, is a colony of seven thousand elephant seals at the foot of a high cliff. Walk down the cliff face of sedimentary deposits and fossilized oysters to the ridge just above the beach – don't try to climb down onto the beach, however, as it is strictly off limits. The best time to visit is from late September until early November, when the bull elephant seals fight for females – a display of bloodied blubbery bulk.

Two kilometres north is a viewpoint over the shifting curves of the shingle spits of **Caleta Valdés** – from September to November, orcas may be spotted entering the *caleta*, or bay behind the spit, at high tide – and there's a colony of Magellanic penguins 3km further on. This road is also one of the best for sighting *maras, choiques*, skunks and other terrestrial wildlife.

Punta Norte

Wild **Punta Norte**, the northernmost point of the peninsula, is famous for the **orca attacks** on baby sea lions that occur there during March and early April. In a spectacle rivalling anything in the natural world, the eight-tonne orcas beach themselves at up to 50km per hour and attempt to grab a pup; most efforts are unsuccessful, and an orca will sometimes settle for a snack of penguin. Attacks usually occur with the high tides – if you're so inclined, check with the Centro de Interpretaciones (see p.451) for times and plan your arrival to coincide with the hour either side of high tide to stand the best chance of witnessing one. These aside, the sight of ominous black dorsal fins of a pod of killer whales cruising just off the coast is thrilling enough. Serious photographers can buy an expensive permit to descend to the beach (contact the tourist office in Rawson; ☎ 0280 449 6887, ⓦ turismo.rawson.gov.ar), but the general viewing area can be as good a vantage point as any.

On the slope above the beach there's a small **visitors' centre and museum** (daily 8am–8pm; free). Inside, you can identify the distinguishing features of the different individual orcas.

ACCOMMODATION   **PUNTA NORTE**

La Ernestina Punta Norte ☎ 0280 466 1079, ⓦ laernestina.com. A charming but rather pricey estancia, *La Ernestina* has an excellent location right on the beach, making it a favourite haunt of wildlife photographers. Rates include full board, all drinks and excursions. US$300

Chubut Province: the Welsh heartland

If you're coming to Chubut Province looking for Argentina's answer to Snowdonia, think again. Not only is there not a mountain in sight, but also the **Welsh**, like the Tehuelche before them, have been absorbed almost seamlessly into Argentina's diverse cultural identity. Under the surface, though, vestiges of their pioneering culture remain and there's a real pride in the historical legacy – evident in the number of fine **Welsh chapels** dotted across the farmlands of the **Lower Chubut Valley** – and the current cultural connection that goes well beyond the touristy trappings.

Welsh is still spoken by some of the third- or fourth-generation residents in the main towns of **Trelew** and **Gaiman**, even if it isn't the language of common usage, and whereas it once seemed doomed to die out, the tongue now appears to be enjoying a

THE MARINE MAMMALS OF PENÍNSULA VALDÉS

Although diverse and significant populations of birds and terrestrial mammals exist on **Península Valdés**, it is the **marine mammals** here that are of particular interest.

SOUTHERN RIGHT WHALE

The **southern right whale** (*Ballena franca austral*) comes to the sheltered waters of the Golfo Nuevo and Golfo San José to breed. Weighing up to fifty tonnes and measuring up to 18m in length, these gentle leviathans are filter-feeders, deriving nutrients from plankton. Once favoured targets for the world's whalers – they were the "right" whales to harpoon, as they were slow, yielded copious quantities of oil and floated when killed – they have now been declared a "National Natural Monument", and are protected within Argentine territorial waters. This enabled the tourist industry to develop, reinforcing the economic value of keeping these creatures alive; their charming curiosity – a trait that once put them in danger – now makes them one of the most enjoyable cetaceans to view in the wild.

KILLER WHALES

The **killer whale**, or orca, is not in fact a whale at all, but the largest member of the dolphin family – it displays the high levels of intelligence we associate with such creatures, if not their cuteness. This is amply demonstrated in their unique hunting behaviour at Caleta Valdés and Punta Norte, where orcas storm the shingle banks, beaching themselves in order to snap up their preferred prey: baby sea lions and young elephant seals. Male killer whales have been known to measure over 9m, and weigh some eight tonnes, although the ones off Valdés do not reach these sizes. The dorsal fin on an adult male is the biggest in the animal kingdom, measuring 1.8m, and its size and shape are among of the factors used to identify individual orcas, along with the shape of the saddle patch and colour variations.

SEA LIONS

Sea lions (*Lobos marinos*) were once so numerous on the peninsula that 20,000 would be culled annually for their skins and blubber – a figure that roughly equals the entire population found here today. They are the most widely distributed of the Patagonian marine mammals and their anthropomorphic antics make them a delight to watch. It's easy to see the derivation of the name when you look at a 300kg adult male, ennobled by a fine yellowy-brown mane.

ELEPHANT SEALS

Península Valdés is the only continental breeding ground for the southern **elephant seal** (*Elefante marino*). Weighing some three tonnes and measuring 4–5m, bull elephant seals mean business. Though the average size of a harem for a dominant male ranges between ten and fifteen females, some super-stud tyrants get greedy. One macho male at Caleta Valdés infamously amassed 131 consorts. October is the best month to see these noisy clashes of the titans, but be prepared for some gore, as tusk wounds are inevitable. Adult females, much smaller than the males, are pregnant for 11 months of the year, giving birth from about mid-September. Pups weigh 40kg at birth, but then balloon to weigh 200kg after only three weeks. The elephant seal's most remarkable attribute, however, is as the world's champion deep-sea-diving mammal. Depths of over 1000m are not uncommon, and it is reckoned that some of these animals have reached depths of 1500m, staying submerged for a (literally) breathtaking two hours.

limited **renaissance**. In municipal schools today, young students have the option to study the language of their forebears: a team of **Welsh teachers** works in Chubut, and **cultural exchanges** with Mam Cymru are thriving – two or three pupils are sent annually from Chubut to Welsh universities and numerous delegations from different associations ply across the Atlantic. It's not all one way either: scholars have come from Wales to study the manuscripts left by pioneers and seek inspiration from what they pronounce to be the purity of the language that was preserved in Patagonia.

Trelew

The medium-sized town of **TRELEW** – its Welsh name means the "village of Lewis", in honour of founder Lewis Jones – rose to prominence after the completion, in 1889, of the rail link to Puerto Madryn, which allowed easy export of the burgeoning agricultural yields. Today it has a couple of excellent museums, while its good transport connections make it a convenient base from which to explore the surrounding Welsh settlements of the **Lower Chubut Valley** and, to the south, the famous penguin colony at **Punta Tombo**. The only downside is the shortage of appealing accommodation – nearby Gaiman has a far better selection.

Museo Regional Pueblo de Luis

9 de Julio and Fontana • Mon–Fri 8am–8pm, Sat & Sun 2–8pm • $10 • ☎ 0280 442 4062

The railway has since disappeared, but the old station is now home to the **Museo Regional Pueblo de Luis**, which does a good job of tracing the area's **Celtic** history and also explores the coexistence of the Welsh and the Tehuelche as well as the annual *eisteddfodau* (traditional Welsh literature, music and performance festivals).

Museo Paleontológico Egidio Feruglio (MEF)

Fontana and Lewis Jones • April–Aug Mon–Fri 9am–6pm, Sat & Sun 10am–7pm; Sept–March daily 9am–7pm • $95 • Tours (English) available; 1hr • Free • ☎ 0280 443 2100, ⓦ mef.org.ar

The excellent **Museo Paleontológico Egidio Feruglio (MEF)** houses one of South America's most important paleontological collections. It sets out to describe "300 million years of history" and contains beautifully preserved clutches of dinosaur eggs and skeletons from the region, including a 95-million-year-old argentinosaurus, one of the world's largest dinosaurs. Not to be missed.

Plaza Independencia

Trelew's urban centrepiece is its fine main square, the **Plaza Independencia**, with flourishing trees and an elegant gazebo, built by the Welsh to honour the centenary of Argentine independence; in September/October each year, the leafy plaza becomes the

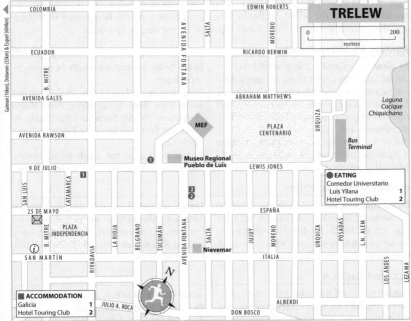

THE WELSH IN PATAGONIA

In July 1865, after two months at sea, 153 **Welsh** men, women and children who had fled Britain to escape cultural and religious oppression disembarked from their tea-clipper, the *Mimosa*, and took the first steps into what they believed was to be their Promised Land. Here they planned to emulate the Old Testament example of bringing forth gardens from the wilderness, but though the land around the Golfo Nuevo had the appearance of Israel, its parched harshness cannot have been of much comfort to those who had left the green valleys of Wales. Fired by Robert Fitz Roy's descriptions of the Lower Chubut Valley, they explored south and, two months later, relocated – a piecemeal process during which some groups had, in the words of one of the leading settlers, Abraham Matthews, to live off "what they could hunt, foxes and birds of prey, creatures not permitted under Mosaic Law, but acceptable in the circumstances".

The immigrants were mostly miners or small merchants from southeast Wales and had little farming experience. Doubts and insecurities spread, with some settlers petitioning the British to rescue them, but when all avenues of credit seemed closed, vital assistance came from the Argentine government by way of provisions and substantial monthly subsidies. And despite initial mistrust of the **Tehuelche**, the Welsh learned survival and hunting skills from their native neighbours, which proved invaluable when the settlers' sheep died and the first three harvests failed. By the early 1870s, 44 settlers had abandoned the attempt, and sixteen had died, but optimists pointed to the fact that ten new settlers had since arrived, and 21 Welsh-Argentines had been born into the community. They decided to stick it out.

With increasing awareness of irrigation techniques, the pioneers began to coax their first proper yields from the Lower Chubut Valley, and recruitment trips to Wales and the US brought a much-needed influx of new settlers in 1874, the year in which Gaiman (see opposite) was founded. Yet the best indicator of the settlement's progress was the international recognition received when samples of barley and wheat grown in Dolavon returned from major international expositions in Paris (1889) and the US (1892) with gold medals in their respective categories. The village's flour mill, built in the 1880s, still works today.

focus for the most important of the province's **eisteddfodau**, when two prestigious awards are made: the Sillón del Bardo (The Bard's Chair), for the best poetry in Welsh, and the Corona del Bardo (The Bard's Crown), for the best in Spanish.

ARRIVAL AND DEPARTURE

TRELEW

By plane Trelew's airport (W aeropuertotrelew.com) is 5km northeast of town; there's a Banco de Chubut ATM and a simple tourist-office counter that opens for flight arrivals. A taxi into town costs around $90. There's an Aerolíneas Argentinas office at 25 de Mayo 33 (T 0280 442 0170, W aerolineas.com.ar).
Destinations Buenos Aires (2–3 daily; 1hr 50min); El Calafate (3–9 daily; 1hr 50min); Mendoza (2–10 daily; 1hr 50min); Río Gallegos (3–7 daily; 50min); Ushuaia (1 daily; 2hr 15min).

By bus The busy bus terminal is opposite the main square, just off Urquiza.
Destinations Buenos Aires (11 daily; 19hr–21hr 40min); Gaiman (every 30min–1hr; 25–35min); Puerto Madryn (every 30min–1hr; 1hr); Puerto San Julián (8 daily; 9hr 55min–11hr 50min); Río Gallegos (8 daily; 15hr 40min–17hr 30min).

By taxi There's a taxi rank outside the bus terminal. Alternatively, call T 0280 442 0404 or T 0280 442 4445.

INFORMATION AND TOURS

Tourist information The helpful main tourist office is at San Martín and Mitre (Mon–Fri 8am–8pm, Sat & Sun 9am–9pm; T 0280 442 6819, W trelewpatagonia.gov.ar); the staff can provide you with a good leaflet on the various Welsh chapels of the Lower Chubut Valley.

Tours Several agencies run tours to the penguin colony at Punta Tombo, often combined with tours of Gaiman and Commerson's dolphin-watching in nearby Playa Unión, including Nievemar Tours, Italia 98 (T 0280 443 4114, W nievemartours.com.ar).

ACCOMMODATION

Galicia 9 de Julio 214 T 0280 443 3802, W hotelgalicia .com.ar. This well-run hotel, in a building that dates back to 1947, has a grand entrance and a lavish lobby, but the en-suite rooms, while perfectly comfortable, are a little on the small side. Breakfast included. $915
Hotel Touring Club Fontana 240 T 0280 443 3997.

Little Prince author Antoine de Saint-Exupéry and (reportedly) Butch Cassidy and the Sundance Kid have stayed at this faded Art Deco hotel, built in 1918. The compact rooms are pretty simple, but the atmosphere – especially in the high-ceilinged café-bar (see below) – is the real draw. Breakfast included. **$700**

EATING

Comedor Universitario Luis Yllana Just off 9 de Julio. If you're after an inexpensive breakfast, lunch or early dinner, join the students at this bustling university canteen, which serves simple, hearty dishes at prices that won't break the bank (around $70–100). Daily 10am–8pm.

★**Hotel Touring Club** Fontana 240 ☎ 0280 443 3997. Lively *confitería* and bar with faint touches of grandeur, offering standard snacks and meals like *milanesas* – as well as an array of *tragos* (from $40) from the extensive range of bottles lining the back of the bar. Daily 6.30am–midnight.

The Lower Chubut Valley

West of Trelew is the broad **LOWER CHUBUT VALLEY**, a fertile ribbon of land amid some barren steppe, thanks to the Río Chubut, which flows through here from the Andes. The river derives its name from the Tehuelche word "*chupat*", meaning clean or transparent. The Welsh began using the Chubut to irrigate the valley in 1867, and it was dammed a hundred years later to ensure a more predictable flow to the farm plots, while also generating electricity for industrial development around Trelew. A string of well-maintained **Welsh chapels** (*capillas galesas*) lines the Chubut, including – just south of Trelew – the Capilla Moriah; dating from 1880, it's the oldest in Argentina and many of the original settlers are buried in its cemetery. The small towns along the river's route are all charming and, though you're unlikely to hear Welsh spoken in the streets, the legacy of pioneering times is still evident.

8

Gaiman

The town of **GAIMAN**, 16km west of Trelew along RN-25, sits amid lush pastures and poplar trees that – in clement weather, at least – form a landscape more like a Monet watercolour than typical Patagonia. It's a pleasant place and the most eminently "Welsh" of the area's settlements. A visit to a Welsh tearoom (see box, p.460) is a must, and there are various monuments built by or dedicated to the settlers dotted around town: keep an eye out for the handsome brick **Capilla Bethel**, a chapel dating back to 1913, and the squat stone **Primera Casa** (First House). Mini-**eisteddfodau** are held in Gaiman in mid-September and the first week of May.

Museo Histórico Regional

Sarmiento and 28 de Julio • Tues–Sun 3–7pm • $10

Gaiman's old train station, dating back to 1889, now houses the **Museo Histórico Regional**, which focuses on the challenges of pioneer life and the development of the Welsh community in the region; among the exhibits are some particularly evocative old photos. After visiting the museum, railway buffs should walk over to the nearby tourist office, close to which is an abandoned 300m-long **railway tunnel**, which is open for exploration.

Primera Casa de Gaiman

Juan C. Evans 234 • Daily 11am–6pm • $15 • ☎ 0280 449 1571

Built in 1874 for David D. Roberts and his family, the **Primera Casa de Gaiman** (Gaiman's first house) provides an insight into the life – and hardships – of the town's early settlers. Once you've ducked into the low-roofed doorway you'll find a collection of old furniture, kitchen equipment and old photos.

ARRIVAL AND INFORMATION

GAIMAN

By bus Regular buses (every 30min–1hr; 25–35min) travel between the terminal in Trelew and Gaiman's main square.

Tourist information The helpful tourist office

(Mon–Sat 9am–8pm, Sun 11am–7pm; ☎ 0280 449 1571, ⓦ gaiman.gov.ar) is at Belgrano 574, a 5min walk from the central square.

GAIMAN'S WELSH TEAROOMS

The highlight of a visit to Gaiman is working your way through a mountain of cakes over afternoon tea at a **Welsh tearoom** (*casa de té*), some of which are owned and run by descendants of the original settlers. They all serve similar arrays of cake, toast, scones and home-made jams (around $180/person); the most traditional component is the *torta negra* (dark fruit cake), originally a wedding gift to be eaten on a couple's first anniversary. Among the best are:

Plas y Coed Michael D. Jones 123 ☎ 0280 449 1133. The walls of this charming *casa de té* are covered with a glorious array of Welsh-language posters, tea towels and photos. The cakes here are some of the best in town. Tues–Sun 2/3–7pm.

Ty Cymraeg Abraham Matthews 74 ☎ 0280 449 1010, ⓦ casagalesa.com.ar. At *Ty Cymraeg*, housed in a green-roofed building close to the river, a descendant of the pioneers serves tea in the original family home.

There are options available for children and coeliacs too. Tues–Sun 2–7.30pm.

Ty Nain Av Yrigoyen 283 ☎ 0280 449 1126. The ivy-clad *Ty Nain*, in a building dating back to 1890, is one of the most authentic of the teahouses. An abundant tea is served here by descendants of the first Welsh woman to be born in Gaiman. The dining area doubles up as a small museum, filled with fascinating knick-knacks. Daily 2/3–7pm.

ACCOMMODATION

Hostería Gwesty Tywi Chacra 202 ☎ 0280 449 1292. This cheerful guesthouse has a collection of comfortable en-suite rooms. There's a nice garden and (in the summer) guests can use the small swimming pool. It's a 10–15min walk from the main square on the other side of the river. Rates include breakfast. <u>$700</u>

Plas y Coed Av Yrigoyen 320 ☎ 0280 469 7069. The owners have done a good job of re-creating the homely atmosphere that pervades their original property – Gaiman's first teahouse – which lies just around the corner. The spacious living room is a good spot to recover from the massive, high-calorie breakfast (included in the rates). <u>$850</u>

Ty Gwyn 9 de Julio 147 ☎ 0280 449 1009, ⓦ tygwyn .com.ar. Located one block away from the main square and attached to a *casa de té* (see above), *Ty Gwyn* has clean and compact rooms with wooden floors and partial views of the Río Chubut. Breakfast included. <u>$800</u>

Yr Hen Ffordd Michael D. Jones 342 ☎ 02965 491394, ⓦ yrhenffordd.com.ar. *Yr Hen Ffordd* (*The Old Road*) is a good, clean budget option, although it could do with a bit of a face-lift. There are several twins and doubles with private bathrooms, as well as a family room sleeping six. Breakfast included. <u>$700</u>

EATING

Gwalia Lân Jones and Av Tello. If you're after lunch or dinner, rather than a Welsh tea, head to this restaurant, located diagonally opposite the main square, where there's

a typical Argentine mix of steaks, pasta and pizza on offer (mains from $120). Tues–Sat 12.30–3pm & 7.30pm–midnight, Sun 12.30–3pm.

Reserva El Pedral

73km southeast of Puerto Madryn • Day-trips $1200, including transfers and lunch • ☎ 0280 447 3043, ⓦ reservaelpedral.com

At Punta Ninfas, the privately owned **Reserva El Pedral**, surrounding the estancia of the same name, is home to a rapidly growing population of Magellanic penguins – there were over 1600 pairs at the end of 2015. As it's far less touristy than Punta Tombo, you have a less intrusive – and less rushed – encounter with these captivating birds. The reserve runs day-trips from Puerto Madryn, during which you're likely to spot guanacos and *choiques*, and maybe whales passing close to the beach, as well as the penguins. Alternatively, you can stay at the estancia (see below).

ACCOMMODATION   RESERVA EL PEDRAL

Estancia El Pedral Punta Ninfas ☎ 0280 447 3043, ⓦ reservaelpedral.com. Beautifully located, tranquil hotel, in a building dating back to 1923 and with a tragic backstory (which staff can tell you about), offering en suites, very comfortable and given character

by black-and-white photos of the estancia a century ago. The food is excellent, and you can go kayaking, mountain biking or hiking – or just laze by the pool. Rates include full board, a tour of the reserve and transfers. <u>US$500</u>

THE MAGELLANIC PENGUIN

The word "penguin", some maintain, derives from Welsh *pen gwyn* (white head), a name allegedly bestowed by a Welsh sailor passing these shores with Thomas Cavendish in the sixteenth century. In fact, **Magellanic penguins** don't have white heads and it's far more likely that the name comes from the archaic Spanish *pingüe*, or fat. The birds were a gift to the early mariners, being the nearest equivalent at that time to a TV dinner.

Though they're not exactly nimble on land, in water these birds can keep up a steady 8km an hour, or several times that over short bursts. An adult bird stands 50 to 60cm tall and weighs a plump 4–5.5kg. Birds begin arriving at their ancestral Patagonian nesting sites – which can be up to 1km from the sea – from late August, and by early October nesting is in full swing. Parents share the task of incubation, as they do the feeding once the eggs start to hatch, in early November. By early January, chicks that have not been preyed upon by sea birds, foxes or armadillos make their first sorties into the water. During the twenty-day February moult, the birds do not swim, as they lose their protective layer of waterproof insulation; at this time, penguin sites are awash with fuzzy down and sneezing birds. In March and April, they begin to vacate the nesting sites. Although little is known of their habits while at sea, scientists do know that the birds migrate north, reaching as far as the coast off Río de Janeíro, 3000km away.

Punta Tombo

107km south of Trelew • Sept to late March daily 8am–6pm • $120 • Unless you have your own car, the easiest way to visit is on a day-trip with a travel agency in Puerto Madryn or Trelew (around $800 plus entry fee)

Punta Tombo is by far the largest single colony of penguins on the continent, with a population of around half a million birds, though numbers are decreasing as overfishing affects food supplies; it is also one of the most commercialized. The noise from these black-and-white **Magellanic penguins** is immense; it's quite an experience to wander around this scrubland avian metropolis amid a cacophony of braying, surrounded on all sides by waddling, tottering birds. The penguins nest behind the stony beach in scrapes underneath the bushes, with a close eye on approaching strangers. Get too close and they'll indicate their displeasure by hissing or bobbing their heads from side to side – respect these warning signals, and remember that a penguin can inflict a good deal of pain with its sharp bill.

Late November to January is probably the best time to visit, as there are plenty of **young chicks**. The penguins are most active in the morning and early evening; tour agencies run morning trips from Trelew, allowing around one and a half hours with the birds. The nearby countryside is an excellent place to see **terrestrial wildlife**, such as guanacos, *choiques*, skunks, armadillos and *maras*.

Cabo Dos Bahías

260km south of Trelew • Daily 8am–8pm • $50

The remote coastal reserve of **Cabo Dos Bahías**, stuck out on a headland 30km from the tiny fishing village of **Camarones**, is home to 55,000 Magellanic penguins plus a colony of sea lions from August to April. Tame herds of guanacos are abundant in the park, which also has healthy populations of *choiques* and *maras*.

ARRIVAL AND DEPARTURE   CABO DOS BAHÍAS

By bus Unless you have your own wheels or are on an organized tour, you'll have to take a bus (3 weekly; 3hr) from Trelew to Camarones and then a taxi from there to the park (around $150).

ACCOMMODATION

Bahía Bustamante 88km south of Cabo dos Bahías ☎ 0297 480 1000, ⊕ bahiabustamante.com. Set in a beautiful, desolate coastal location, complete with its own petrified forest, this estancia once relied on the production of agar agar (used as a thickening agent in cooking) from the area's rich supplies of algae. Today the focus is on tourism: guests stay in seafront cottages and can partake in a range of activities – from sailing and kayaking, to horseriding and birdwatching. Rates include full board. **US$530**

Indalo Inn Roca and Sarmiento, Camarones ☎ 0297 496 3004, ⓦ indaloinn.com.ar. There's little accommodation choice in Camarones, so you'll probably end up in the no-frills, rather cramped en-suite rooms here. There's a restaurant, and staff also rent out more comfortable *cabañas*, located nearby on the *costanera*. A rather meagre breakfast is included in the rate for the rooms but not the cabins. Doubles $900; *cabañas* $1300

The coast of Santa Cruz Province

The stretch of RN-3 south of Cabo Dos Bahías encompasses some pretty dreary towns, not least the oil-hub of **Comodoro Rivadavia** – a dire place best avoided, despite its useful transport links, including an airport. While this section of eastern Patagonia must claim some of the most desolate scenery in Argentina, there are some natural gems threaded along it: the **Ría Deseado estuary** at **Puerto Deseado**, with its handsome porphyry cliffs and opportunities to view dolphins and penguins; the tremendous trunks of fossilized araucaria monkey puzzles in the **Parque Nacionales Bosques Petrificados de Jaramillo**; and **Puerto San Julián**, a historic town with access to one of the most conveniently situated penguin colonies in Patagonia. Farther south you could also break up the excruciatingly long distances of largely uneventful coastline by stopping at **Comandante Luis Piedra Buena**, known for its fishing, or **Parque Nacional Monte León**, Argentina's first coastal national park, in which a century-old estancia offers some of the area's finest lodgings.

Puerto Deseado and around

Avoiding grim Caleta Olivia, the first place worth visiting in Santa Cruz Province (albeit entailing a hefty detour) is easy-going **PUERTO DESEADO**, a straggly but engaging fishing and naval port on the flooded estuary, or *ría*, of the Río Deseado. Some spectacular coastal scenery and a couple of remarkable colonies of marine wildlife are within sight of town, most dramatically along the **estuary** itself. The town owes its name to the English privateer Thomas Cavendish, who baptized it **Port Desire**, in honour of his ship, when he stopped here in 1586.

Museo Regional Mario Brozoski
Colón and Belgrano • Mon–Fri 8am–5pm, Sat 4–8pm • Free

By the seafront, the **Museo Regional Mario Brozoski** displays items brought up from the *Swift*, a small English warship that sank off the coast of Puerto Deseado in 1770 and was discovered by divers in 1982. Among the exhibits are gallon-sized gin bottles.

Museo de la Estación del Ferrocarril
Arias s/n • Mon–Sat 4–7pm • Free, but donations welcome

Modern-day Puerto Deseado was largely shaped by the Ferrocarril Nacional Patagónico, a cross-country cargo route that ran northwest to Las Heras; the town's fine, porphyry-coloured, former train station operated as the route's terminus from 1911 until 1979. It now functions as the **Museo de la Estación del Ferrocarril** and houses a small collection of train memorabilia.

BOAT TRIPS FROM PUERTO DESEADO

Darwin Expediciones (based beside the Gipsy dock at España 2551, on the approach to town; ☎ 0297 15 624 7554, ⓦ darwin-expeditions.com) runs excellent **boat trips** around the Ría Deseado and, if the tide is high, up the **Cañadón Torcida**, a narrow and steep-sided channel of the estuary, dolphin-spotting on the way to **Isla de los Pájaros**, where passengers can disembark and observe the birdlife – dominated by Magellanic penguins – at close hand; to **Isla Pingüino**, one of the few places outside Antarctica where the punkish Rockhopper penguin can easily be spotted; and a trip up the estuary to the scenic **Miradores de Darwin**, retracing the scientist's 1833 journey and stopping to look at wildlife en route. The company also operates kayaking excursions and trips to the Parque Nacional Bosques Petrificados de Jaramillo (see opposite).

Ría Deseado

Stretching 45km inland from Puerto Deseado is the **RÍA DESEADO**, an astonishing sunken river valley, which, unlike most other estuaries on the continent, is flooded by the sea, like a shallow fjord. Opposite the town, its purple cliffs are smeared with guano from five species of **cormorant**, including the grey cormorant (*cormorán gris*), whose dull-coloured body sets off its yellow bill and scarlet legs. These birds are seen in few other places, and nowhere else will you get such a sterling opportunity to photograph them. The estuary also hosts several penguin colonies, small flocks of dazzling white snowy sheathbills (*Palomas antárticas*), a colony of sea lions and an estimated fifty playful and photogenic **Commerson's dolphins** (*toninas averas*); the undisputed stars here, these beautiful creatures torpedo through the water to rollick in bow waves just a metre or two from boats.

ARRIVAL AND INFORMATION

PUERTO DESEADO AND AROUND

By bus The bus terminal is inconveniently located at the far end of town. Caleta Olivia has more frequent buses to Río Gallegos than Puerto Deseado, as well as connections to Puerto Madryn and Trelew.

Destinations Caleta Olivia (2 daily; 2hr 50min–3hr); Río Gallegos (1–2 daily; 12hr).

Tourist information The main tourist office is at San Martín 1525 (Mon–Fri 7am–9pm, Sat–Sun 9am–9pm; opening hours shorten during the winter; ☎0297 487 0220, ⓦdeseado.gob.ar/turismo).

ACCOMMODATION

Residencial Los Olmos Gob. Gregores 849 ☎0297 487 0077. Shoestring travellers should head to this friendly little guesthouse, which has very clean – if rather drab and boxy – rooms with wall-mounted TVs, heaters and small private bathrooms. Rates include breakfast. **$450**

Tower Rock Pueyrredón 385 ☎0297 15 504 7504, ⓦtower-rock.com. These bright, modern studios and apartments – located a couple of blocks from the seafront, kitted out with kitchenettes and sleeping two to five people – feel pleasantly out of place in Puerto Deseado. There's a communal jacuzzi, but no breakfast. **$1350**

Parque Nacional Bosques Petrificados de Jaramillo

50km down a branch road leading west off RN-3, 80km south of the turn-off to Puerto Deseado • Daily: April–Sept 10am–5pm; Oct–March 9am–9pm • Free • Unless you have a rental car, you'll need to visit on an organized trip from Puerto Deseado or Puerto San Julián

The fossilized tree trunks at the **PARQUE NACIONAL BOSQUES PETRIFICADOS DE JARAMILLO** are strangely beautiful, especially at sunset, when their jasper-red expanses soak up the glow, as though they're heating up from within. The sheer magnitude of the trunks is astonishing, too, measuring some 35m long and up to 3m across. The primeval Jurassic forest grew here 150 million years ago – 60 million years before the Andean cordillera was forced up, forming the rain barrier that has such a dramatic effect on the scenery we know now. In Jurassic times, this area was still swept by moisture-laden winds from the Pacific, allowing the growth of araucaria trees. A cataclysmic blast from an unidentified volcano flattened these colossi and covered the fallen trunks with ash. The wood absorbed silicates in the ash and petrified, later to be revealed when erosion wore down the supervening strata.

Surrounding the trunks is a bizarre **moonscape** of arid basalt *meseta*, dominated by the 400m-tall **Cerro Madre e Hija** (Mother and Daughter Hill). A 2km trail, littered by shards of fossilized bark, leads from the park office past all the most impressive trunks, while the small **museum** has displays of some fascinating fossils, including araucaria pine cones.

Puerto San Julián and around

The small port of **PUERTO SAN JULIÁN**, just off RN-3 some 260km south of the turn-off to Puerto Deseado, is another convenient place to break the long journey down to Río Gallegos. The town lies 3km off RN-3, down a straight road that becomes Avenida San Martín, its main artery. This barren place, rich in historical associations, was once one of the few safe anchorages along the Patagonian coast. Today, there's little visible evidence of the port's history apart from a replica of Magellan's ship the *Victoria* moored along the *costanera*, but it's a good place to go on one of various **tours**, including a

THE BIRTHPLACE OF PATAGONIA

Puerto San Julián claims to be the birthplace of modern Patagonia (though, of course, it had an indigenous population for tens of thousands of years before the arrival of the Europeans). In 1520, during **Magellan**'s stay in the bay, the very first encounter occurred between the Europeans and the "giants" of this nameless land, when, it is believed, the explorer bestowed on them the name *"patagon"* (literally "big foot") in reference to their comparatively large build. As related by Antonio Pigafetta, the expedition's chronicler: "One day, without anyone expecting it, we saw a giant, who was on the shore of the sea, quite naked, and was dancing and leaping, and singing, and whilst singing he put sand and dust on his head… When he was before us he began to be astonished, and to be afraid, and he raised one finger on high, thinking that we came from heaven. He was so tall that the tallest of us only came up to his waist… The captain named this kind of people Patagon." On Palm Sunday, April 1, 1520, Magellan celebrated the first Mass on Argentine soil, near a site marked by a cross, down by the town's port.

recommended trip to view the **marine life** of the bay (see below). The penguins here live closer to human settlement than at any other site in the south.

Museo de los Pioneros (Rosa Novak de Hoffman)

Magallanes s/n • Officially Mon–Fri 8am–8pm, but it rarely sticks to these timings • Free

By far the most interesting exhibit at the small **Museo de los Pioneros (Rosa Novak de Hoffman)** is a paving slab that lay in the town square for many years until someone noticed that it had the distinct, prehistoric prints of a sauropod (a crocodile-like reptile) on it.

Bahía de San Julián

Pinocho Excursiones, Costanera and 9 de Julio, near the Victoria (☎ 02962 454600, ⌨ pinochoexcursiones.com.ar) run boat trips around the bay (around $600)

The best tour from Puerto San Julián is a trip around **Bahía de San Julián** in a zodiac launch to see the most conveniently situated **penguin colony** in Patagonia and all manner of flying sea birds. In addition, you stand a good chance of spotting **Commerson's dolphins**, a graceful, fun-loving species that regularly plays games with the boats. You'll also be taken to the protected island of **Banco Justicia** (Justice Bank) to see the cormorant colonies (home to four different species – rock, olivaceous, guanay and imperial), and other sea birds. Banco Justicia is thought to be where, in the sixteenth century, Magellan, and later **Francis Drake**, executed members of their crews who had mutinied, although others maintain it was at **Punta Horca** (Gallows Point), on the tongue of land that encloses the bay, opposite the town. You're not allowed to disembark at either, though you are allowed to get off at the misleadingly named **Banco Cormorán** where there is a colony of Magellanic penguins but no cormorants.

The best time for seeing dolphins and cormorants is December to Easter, especially early on, though the guide will generally give a scrupulously honest appraisal of your chances.

ARRIVAL AND INFORMATION

PUERTO SAN JULIÁN

By bus Most bus services arrive at or depart from the terminal at San Martín 1552 in the early hours.
Destinations Comandante Luis Piedra Buena (8 daily; 1hr 40min); Río Gallegos (10 daily; 4hr 20min–5hr); Trelew (8 daily; 10–12hr).

Tourist information There are a couple of offices – at the bus station and at San Martín and Rivadavia – but they're both erratically staffed (officially Mon–Fri 7am–9pm, Sat & Sun 9am–9pm; ☎ 02962 452353, ⌨ sanjulian.gov.ar).

ACCOMMODATION

Hostel Costanera 25 de Mayo 917 ☎ 02962 452300, ⌨ costanerahotel.com. This beige hotel has a seafront location overlooking the Bahía San Julián. The en suites are neat and tidy – those on the second floor have sea

views – and there's a bar-restaurant. Rates include breakfast. **$950**
Hotel Bahía San Martín 1075 ☎ 02962 454028, ⌨ hotelbahiasanjulian.com.ar. As good as it gets

accommodation-wise in Puerto San Julián – though that isn't exactly a ringing endorsement – *Hotel Bahía* has decent en suites, though the decor could do with refreshing. Breakfast included. $830

Comandante Luis Piedra Buena

Around 50km south of Puerto San Julián, the desolate monotony of the steppe is lifted briefly by the **Gran Bajo de San Julián**, whose Laguna del Carbón – 105m below sea level – is the lowest point in South America. It's another 70km from here to **COMANDANTE LUIS PIEDRA BUENA**, a sleepy town 1km off RN-3, with little to detain visitors unless you've come for the world-class **steelhead trout fishing** (licences available at the municipalidad, Avenida Gregorio Ibáñez 388, near the bus terminal).

The town is named after naval hero Piedra Buena, who was famed for his gentlemanly ways and determination to assert Argentine sovereignty in the south. In 1859, he made **Isla Pavón** (the island in the jade-coloured Río Santa Cruz) his home, building a diminutive house, from which he traded with the local Aónik'enk Tehuelche.

ARRIVAL AND DEPARTURE   COMANDANTE LUIS PIEDRA BUENA

By bus The bus terminal is at Gregorio Ibáñez Norte 130, near the town centre.

Destinations Puerto San Julián (8 daily; 1hr 40min); Río Gallegos (8 daily; 3–4hr).

ACCOMMODATION

Hostería El Alamo Lavalle 8 ☎02962 497249. Accommodation options are pretty limited in Comandante Luis Piedra Buena, but *El Alamo* is a reasonable place to spend the night. The rooms are simple and well kept, and there's a *confitería*. $700

Parque Nacional Monte León

33km south of Comandante Luis Piedra Buena • Nov–April daily 9am–7pm • Free • ☎02962 498184,

Beyond Comandante Luis Piedra Buena, the Patagonian plateau continues with unabating harshness for some 250km to Río Gallegos. An early detour, 33km out of Piedra Buena, leads to the **PARQUE NACIONAL MONTE LEÓN**, Argentina's first coastal national park. Created in October 2004, the magnificent 627-square-kilometre reserve encompasses sweeping cliffs, rocky islands and picturesque bays and, between September and April, the waters are awash with wildlife, including sea-lion and penguin colonies and three species of cormorant. The rugged cliffs that dominate the landscape are indented with vast caverns and rock windows – at low tide, you can walk out to **Isla Monte León**, a steep-sided islet filled with cormorants. Check first with the *guardafauna* office, 7km north of the park entrance on RN-3, for tide schedules. You have to register here before entering the park; they also have a list of guides.

ARRIVAL AND DEPARTURE   PARQUE NACIONAL MONTE LEÓN

Tours There's no public transport, so if you don't have your own car, you'll need to take a tour: try Nievemar in Trelew (see p.458) or Puerto Madryn (see p.446).

ACCOMMODATION

Monte León Lodge RN-3 Km2399 ☎011 15 6155 1220, ⓦmonteleon-patagonia.com. Unless you plan to camp (there's a free site in the park), the best place to stay in the park is at the glorious *hostería* in the former estancia homestead. It offers a taste of classy but simple, isolated country life in four large rooms with wooden floors and fireplaces, with two shared, old-fashioned bathrooms. Rates include half board, and advance reservations are necessary. Closed April–Oct. US$390

Río Gallegos

With its harsh climate and no-nonsense commercial feel, provincial capital **RÍO GALLEGOS** is not the kind of place where you'll want to stay for long, despite a few museums and some attractive early twentieth-century buildings. It is, however, an

RÍO GALLEGOS

important transport hub and many travellers pass through en route to or from El Calafate or Tierra del Fuego. The city's namesake river is also a top fly-fishing spot, with some of the world's biggest brown trout.

Avenida Kirchner (formally Av Roca) is the focus of city life; outdoor gear costs far less here than in the tourist hubs such as El Calafate, so stock up if you're off trekking. The attractive main square, **Plaza San Martín**, is marked by a fine equestrian **statue** of General San Martín and the quaint white-and-green Salesian **cathedral**, Nuestra Señora de Luján, a classic example of a pioneer church made from corrugated iron, and originally built in 1899 with a labour force composed of displaced Tehuelche.

Museo de Los Pioneros

Alberdi and Elcano • Daily 10am–5pm • Free • ☎ 02966 437763

The **Museo de Los Pioneros**, based in the city's oldest house and once owned by the city's first doctor, provides a great insight into life in the region at the beginning of the twentieth century, with curators playing ancient, crackly discs on a 1904 Victrola.

CROSSING THE CHILEAN BORDER TO TIERRA DEL FUEGO

It takes the best part of a day to travel overland from Río Gallegos to Río Grande (see p.523), the first major town in **Argentine Tierra del Fuego**, a tedious journey that crosses two borders and the **Strait of Magellan**; consider flying from El Calafate (see p.468) or Río Gallegos.

MONTE AYMOND BORDER CROSSING

At the Monte Aymond border crossing (April–Oct 9am–11pm; Nov–March 24hr), 67km south of Gallegos, formalities are fairly straightforward; don't try to bring fresh vegetables, fruit or meat products into Chile, though, as they'll be confiscated. On the Chilean side, the road improves and heads to Punta Arenas, Puerto Natales and, down a turning at Kimiri Aike, 48km from the border, Tierra del Fuego. This road, RN-257, takes you to Punta Delgada and the Primera Angostura (First Narrows) of the Strait of Magellan.

BY FERRY ACROSS THE STRAIT OF MAGELLAN

The ferry that crosses the Strait of Magellan (leaves daily every 45min; 8.30am–1am 20–30min; ⓦtabsa.cl) costs CH$1700 (US$2.40) per person, or CH$15,000 (US$21) for a car. As early mariners found, the currents here can be ferocious, but they're unlikely to be as disruptive to your plans as they were to sea-goers in the past – only in extreme weather does the ferry not leave. While crossing history's most famous straits, look out for Commerson's dolphins.

ON TO USHUAIA

Heading for Ushuaia, the road then traverses Chilean Tierra del Fuego to the border settlement of San Sebastián (April–Oct 9am–11pm; Nov–March 24hr), 80km from Río Grande. Check times carefully, as there may be a time difference between the Argentine and Chilean sides. Buses depart regularly from Río Gallegos for Punta Arenas (5–7hr), Río Grande (10hr) and Ushuaia (12hr); ferry crossings are included in the fare.

8

There are some evocative old photos – look out for the one of a group of British settlers nursing their pints outside the White Elephant pub (which sadly no longer exists).

Museo Regional Provincial Padre Jesús Molina

Ramón y Cajal 51 • Mon–Fri 9am–7pm, Sat & Sun 11am–7pm • Free • ☎ 02966 426427

The eclectic **Museo Regional Provincial Padre Jesús Molina** hosts temporary exhibitions of contemporary art, plus displays of Tehuelche artefacts, dinosaur remains and reconstructions of Pleistocene mammals. There's also a weaving workshop selling woollens.

ARRIVAL AND INFORMATION   RÍO GALLEGOS

By plane The airport is 7km west of town. There are no buses to the town centre – a taxi will cost around $160 – but there are services from the airport to El Calafate (2–3 daily; 3hr 30min–4hr 30min), some 300km away.

Destinations Buenos Aires (2–4 daily; 3hr 15min); Trelew (3–7 daily; 50min); Ushuaia (2 weekly; 1hr 15min).

By bus From the bus terminal, near the edge of town on RN-3, it's best to take a taxi 2km into the centre (around $80); alternatively, buses #1 or #12 will drop you on Av Kirchner.

Destinations El Calafate (4 daily; 3hr 45min–4hr); Puerto Madryn (6 daily; 17–19hr); Punta Arenas, Chile (1–2 daily; 5–7hr); Río Grande (via Chile; 1–2 daily; 10hr); Trelew (8

daily; 15hr 40min–17hr 30min); Ushuaia (via Chile; 2–3 daily; 13hr).

Tourist information Despite a distinct lack of attractions, Río Gallegos has numerous tourist offices. There are two in the centre: one at Beccar 126 (Mon–Fri 8am–8pm, Sat & Sun 8am–noon & 4–8pm; ☎02966 436920, ⓦturismo.riogallegos.gov.ar) and another in an old (formerly horse-drawn) wagon on the corner of Kirchner and San Martín (summer only: Mon–Fri 1–10pm, Sat & Sun 8am–10pm; ☎02966 422365). There's also a booth in the bus terminal (Mon–Fri 7am–8pm, Sat & Sun 7am–2pm & 4–8pm; ☎02966 442159).

ACCOMMODATION

All listings below include breakfast, which can come in handy given the town's limited eating options.

Apart Hotel Austral Kirchner 1505 ☎02966 435588, ⓦapartaustral.com. These spacious modern apartments

– each with bathroom, kitchenette and small dining area – are ideal for self-caterers or anyone planning to stay a

> ### RÍO GALLEGOS TO EL CALAFATE
>
> Much of the landscape between Gallegos and **El Calafate** is gale-blasted steppe, though there is the odd oasis, plus fabulous views of the austral Andes, including the baroque peaks of Torres del Paine on the Chilean side in clear weather. There are two main routes: the more scenic but far longer **RN-40**, which passes several crossing points into the far south of Chile as it curves round the southwesternmost reaches of Argentina; and the quicker, more direct **RP-5**, the "busiest" of the roads that cross the deep south of Santa Cruz Province. About halfway along RP-5 route is tiny **La Esperanza**, where you can refuel and eat.

few days, though the location can be a little noisy. $659
Hotel Colonial Urquiza and Rivadavia ☎02966 420020, ✉ines_frey@hotmail.com. The warmest welcome in town is provided here by owner María Clark, a descendant of one of the first British settlers in Río Gallegos. Rooms are spotless and very good value; all have TVs, and some are en suite. $400
Hotel Patagonia Fagnano 54 ☎02966 444969, ⓦhotel-patagonia.com. The smartest hotel in town,

aimed at business travellers rather than tourists. The en suites are comfortable, if expensive for what you get, and there's a gym, spa, bar and decent restaurant. $1392
Sehuén Rawson 160 ☎02966 425683, ⓦhotelsehuen .com. An efficient little hotel with a range of average but well-priced rooms; each has a TV, phone and boxy private bathroom, plus a bilingual copy of the New Testament, which may or may not prove useful. $590

EATING

Café Central Kirchner 923 ☎02966 424875. Next door to *Club Británico*, this cheerful café-restaurant is a good spot throughout the day, with various coffee-and-pastry deals (around $45), plus sandwiches, light meals, cakes and ice creams. Mon–Sat 8am–10/11pm.
Club Británico Kirchner 935 ☎02966 432668, ⓦbritishclub.com.ar. A port of call for Bruce Chatwin, this

atmospheric place dates back to 1911 and has more than a hint of a members' club about it. The club, which is decorated with photos of early pioneers, is still the favoured hangout for the area's small community of Anglo-Argentines. The attached restaurant is open to all and has a good range of meat and seafood dishes (mains $130–240), though don't expect many British flavours. Daily noon–3pm & 8pm–midnight.

Parque Nacional Los Glaciares

Declared a UNESCO World Heritage Site in 1981, the wild expanse of **Parque Nacional Los Glaciares** is a huge chunk of magical terrain shoved up against the Andes in the southwest corner of Santa Cruz Province. It encompasses a range of contrasting environments, from enormous glaciers that ooze down from the heights of the gigantic Hielo Continental Sur icecap to thick, sub-Antarctic woodland of deciduous *lenga* and *ñire*, and evergreen *guindo* and *canelo*; and from savage, rain-lashed, unclimbed crags to dry, billiard-table Patagonian *meseta* stretching as far as the eye can strain. Most people visit only the two sightseeing areas: the southern sector, around **Glaciar Perito Moreno**, one of the planet's most famous glaciers; and the **Fitz Roy** sector in the north for its superb trekking. Serving as bases for these two areas are, respectively, the towns of **El Calafate**, in the **south**, and **El Chaltén**, in the **north**, both lying on the fringes of the park and catering to burgeoning influxes of outdoor enthusiasts from across the world.

The park and its glaciers, however, have significant challenges ahead, thanks to a massive hydroelectric project (see p.556) on the Santa Cruz River.

El Calafate

The overriding reason to visit **EL CALAFATE** is to make it your base for seeing **Glaciar Perito Moreno** and the other world-class attractions in the southern sector of **Parque National Los Glaciares** (see p.475). Once a primitive staging post, the town is now one of Argentina's most-visited tourist destinations, with a rapidly expanding hotchpotch of neo-pioneer architecture, scores of hotels, restaurants and souvenir shops, and a huge casino. There has been significant investment here, not least because it is the fiefdom of

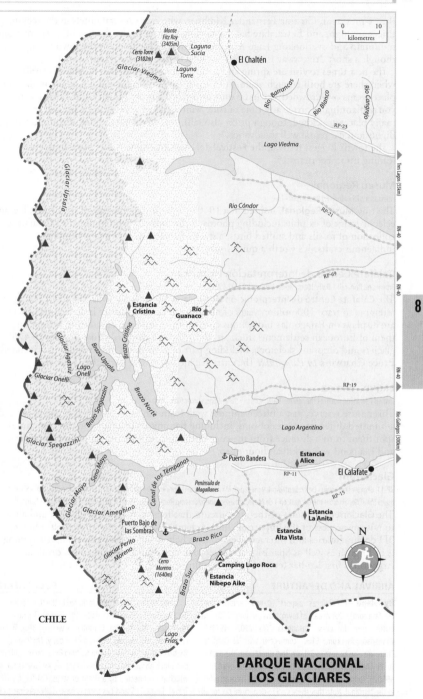

**PARQUE NACIONAL
LOS GLACIARES**

the ex-president, Cristina Fernández Kirchner, who owns several hotels in the region. Prices are high, and El Calafate has a sprawling feel, set in the shadow of its eponymous mountain and overlooking Lago Argentino. There's little to do in the town itself, though a short drive away is the excellent Glaciarium museum (see below).

The best **times to visit** are spring and autumn (Nov to mid-Dec & March–April), when there are both enough visitors to keep services running and not so many that the place seems overcrowded; it can be uncomfortably busy in January and February. If you're planning to arrive any time outside winter (when access can be limited and many places are closed, though prices also fall), it is advisable to book accommodation, flights and car rental well in advance.

The town's biggest festival, the **Festival del Lago Argentino**, takes place in the week leading up to February 15.

Museo Regional
Libertador 575 • Mon–Fri 8am–2pm • Free

The tiny **Museo Regional**, housed in a 1940s-era building, just east of the centre, has an eclectic range of exhibits including photos of the pioneers who founded El Calafate, a collection of fossils and stuffed birds, a stack of ancient typewriters, and some indigenous crafts. It's worth a quick look.

Calafate Centro de Interpretación Histórica
Brown and Bonarelli • Daily 10am–8pm • $100 • ☏ 02902 492799

The **Calafate Centro de Interpretación Histórica**, a 10min walk from the town centre, attempts to trace 100 million years of natural and human history in Patagonia. There are displays on Patagonia's indigenous communities (and the devastating impact on them of European settlement), rock art, the 1920–21 workers' strike (see box, p.476), glaciers and dinosaur skeletons, including part of a mylodon, the creature that inspired Bruce Chatwin's *In Patagonia*. The entry fee includes a free *mate* after your visit.

Laguna Nimez
Just off L.N. Alem, north of the centre • Daily: summer 9am–9pm; winter 9am–7pm • $100

This nature reserve, just a fifteen-minute walk from the town centre, is home to around a hundred different species of bird, including flamingoes (though you can sometimes spot them from a distance from the edge of the reserve without paying the entry fee), and is a good way to kill an hour or so.

Glaciarium
RP-11, 6km west of town • Daily: Sept–April 9am–8pm; May–Aug 11am–7pm • $200 • ☏ 02902 497912, ⓦ glaciarium.com • Shuttle buses (free) depart from the car park on 1 de Mayo, between Libertador and Roca, hourly 9am–7pm (reduced service May–Aug)

The **Glaciarium** is a state-of-the-art museum that focuses on ice and glaciers, and aims to raise awareness of the impact of climate change. It uses a range of models, photos, 3D documentaries and interactive exhibits to help bring the subject to life (everything is in English as well as Spanish), and after looking around you can sink a drink in Argentina's first ice-bar (entry $140, including a drink).

ARRIVAL AND DEPARTURE   EL CALAFATE

By plane El Calafate's airport (ⓦ www.aeropuertoel calafate.com) is 22km east of town; taxis (around $250) and buses run by Ves Patagonia (☏ 02902 497355, ⓦ vespatagonia.com; $120) connect it with El Calafate. There are also buses (1–3 daily; 3hr) direct from the airport to El Chaltén with the Las Lengas company (☏ 02962 493023, ⓦ transportelaslengas.com.ar), who have an office in the terminal. Note that there's a $76 departure tax for all

domestic flights (sometimes included in the ticket price). Destinations Bariloche (1 daily; 1hr 45min); Buenos Aires (4–7 daily; 3hr 20min); Córdoba (6 weekly; 3hr); Trelew (3–9 daily; 1hr 50min); Ushuaia (2–3 daily; 1hr 25min). **By bus** The bus terminal is on Av Julio Roca, on the hillside, one block above the main thoroughfare, Av Libertador, to which it's connected by a flight of steps. Cal Tur, Chaltén Travel, Taqsa, TPS and Las Lengas have daily services to El

RP-11 to Airport (20km), El Chaltén (210km) & Rio Gallegos (300km)

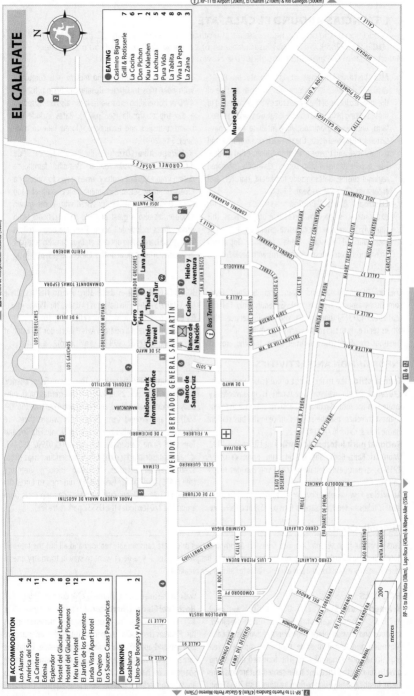

EL CALAFATE

N

● Centro de Interpretación Histórica (900m)

● EATING
Casimiro Biguá	7
Grill & Rotisserie	6
La Cocina	1
Don Pichon	2
Kau Kaleshen	5
La Lechuza	4
Pura Vida	8
La Tablita	9
Viva La Pepa	3
La Zaina	

Museo Regional

JOSE PANTIN

Lava Andina

Cerro
Frías
Thaler
Cal Tur

Chaltén
Travel

Hielo y
Aventura

Casino

Banco de
la Nación

Bus Terminal

National Park
Information Office

Banco de
Santa Cruz

AVENIDA LIBERTADOR GENERAL SAN MARTÍN

■ ACCOMMODATION
Los Alamos	4
América del Sur	2
La Cantera	11
Edenia	7
Esplendor	9
Hostel del Glaciar Libertador	8
Hostel del Glaciar Pioneros	10
I Keu Ken Hostel	12
El Jardín de los Presentes	1
Linda Vista Apart Hotel	5
El Ovejero	6
Los Sauces Casas Patagónicas	3

■ DRINKING
Casablanca	1
Libro-bar Borges y Alvarez	2

0   100   200
metres

RP-15 to Alta Vista (30km), Lago Roca (45km) & Nibepo Aike (55km)

RP-11 to Puerto Bandera (47km) & Glaciar Perito Moreno (75km)

8

ESTANCIAS AROUND EL CALAFATE

In addition to the options below, staff at the office of Estancias de Santa Cruz, Libertador 1215 (☎02902 492858, ⓦestanciasdesantacruz.com), can provide information on many other estancias in the area and throughout the province, and make reservations.

Alta Vista 35km west of El Calafate on RP-15 ☎02902 491247, ⓦhosteriaaltavista.com.ar. One of the more exclusive of the Santa Cruz estancias, catering to those seeking peace and quiet – it's also a working sheep farm, with 22,000 animals. Airy, intimate rooms have tasteful, restrained decor, the service is non-intrusive and professional, and there's a delightful, lupin-filled garden. The excellent restaurant serves classically prepared regional cuisine. Rates include full board, transfers and excursions. Closed May–Sept. **$5000**

Cristina Bahía Cristina ☎02902 491034, ⓦestanciacristina.com. Accessible only by boat, this superbly located, very expensive estancia is hidden at the end of remote Bahía Cristina. Top-notch accommodation – in spacious rooms with peak-framed views across the surrounding *meseta* – is combined with boat trips to Glacier Upsala and hiking, fishing, 4WD or horseriding excursions. It can also be visited on a day-trip to Upsala (see p.477). Rates include full board, transfers and excursions. Closed June to mid-Sept. **$14,200**

★**Nibepo Aike** 60km outside El Calafate ☎02966 422626, ⓦnibepoaike.com.ar. Beautiful farmhouse dating from early last century, when it was founded by a Croatian family, set in a stunning valley south of Lago Roca. Delicious meals are prepared with home-grown produce; it's also a great place to try traditional lamb *asado*. Rates include full board. There are also excellent hiking and horseriding options, and you can also take part in traditional ranching activities. Closed May–Sept. **$4500**

Chaltén, normally around 8am and 6.30pm (and sometimes around 1.30pm too). Generally only Cal Tur (☎02902 491368) operates a year-round service; the others tend only to run in the warmer months.
Destinations Bariloche (summer only; 1 daily; around 30hr); El Chaltén (2–6 daily; 3hr); Puerto Natales, Chile (2–3 daily; 5–6hr); Río Gallegos (4 daily; 3hr 45min–4hr).
By taxi Cóndor, 25 de Mayo 50 ☎02902 491655.
By car You can rent a car from Avis (Libertador 1078 and at the airport; ☎02902 492877, ⓦavis.com).

INFORMATION AND ACTIVITIES

Tourist office The main tourist office (daily 8am–8pm; ☎029024 91090, ⓦelcalafate.tur.ar) is inconveniently located on the rotunda, near the eastern entrance to town, so most travellers use the smaller office in the bus station (same hours; ☎02902 491476).
National park information office At Libertador 1302 (Mon–Fri 8am–6pm, Sat & Sun 9am–6pm; ☎02902 491545, ⓦparquesnacionales.gov.ar); you can get maps and buy fishing licences here.
Activities Few people allow for more time in El Calafate than it takes to see the glaciers (see p.475), but there are other worthwhile excursions. The Cerro Frías agency, Libertador 1144 (☎02902 492808, ⓦcerrofrias.com), runs daily trekking, horseriding, zip-lining and 4WD trips ($690–890) up and around Cerro Frías, from where there are stunning views, weather permitting, of Monte Fitz Roy and Torres del Paine. Calbagatas del Glaciar (☎02902 495447, ⓦcabalgatasdelglaciar.com) offers horseriding trips (from $240). Several agencies, including Hielo y Aventura (see p.475) and Cal Tur (see p.476), run trips to Torres del Paine in Chile: a (long, rather rushed) day-trip costs from around $1770 (excludes the US$32 park entry fee).

ACCOMMODATION

Outside of the high season (Jan, Feb & Easter) accommodation prices are considerably reduced and all but the top-end hotels become affordable; some places close during the height of winter. If you don't want to stay in town, try one of several nearby estancias (see box above). Rates for all include breakfast.

HOSTELS

★**América del Sur** Puerto Deseado 151 ☎02902 493525, ⓦamericahostel.com.ar. Well-designed, spacious and friendly place with wonderful views of Lago Argentino and knowledgeable staff who can help you organize a wide range of trips. The four-bed dorms and private rooms (the cheapest have shared bathrooms) are clean, bright and have under-floor heating. It's a 10–15min walk to the town centre. Dorms **$270**; doubles **$990**
Hostel del Glaciar Libertador Av Libertador 587 ☎02902 491792, ⓦglaciar.com. Under the same management as the *Pioneros* (see p.473), *Libertador* is based in an attractive building and appeals to a slightly older clientele. It has the same services as its sister hostel, though dorms are more spacious and have en-suite bathrooms. The private rooms are very comfortable, though feel a bit overpriced. The hostel

also runs its own travel service, including recommended alternative trips to Glaciar Perito Moreno, El Chaltén and Torres del Paine. Dorms US$22; doubles US$92

★ **Hostel del Glaciar Pioneros** Los Pioneros 255 ☏ 02902 491243, ⓦ glaciar.com. Opened in 1987, this is Calafate's original hostel and still the largest in town. Multilingual, friendly staff, laundry service, bright four- and six-bed dorms, excellent en-suite rooms (from singles to quads, shared and private bathrooms), communal kitchen, and accommodation-and-tours packages (including to Torres del Paine in Chile) all make *Pioneros* great value. Dorms US$17; doubles US$62

I Keu Ken Hostel F.M. Pontoriero 171 ☏ 02902 495482, ⓦ patagoniaikeuken.com.ar. This welcoming hostel (the name means "my ancestor" in Tehuelche) is justifiably popular, with a hilltop position that offers expansive views, economical four-bed dorms and *cabañas*, and a sociable living room and (small) bar. It's a 10min walk uphill from the bus terminal. Dorms $270; *cabañas* $805

HOTELS AND GUESTHOUSES

Los Alamos Gob. Moyano and Bustillo ☏ 02902 491144, ⓦ posadalosalamos.com. One of the most luxurious of the town's hotels, modestly posing as a *posada*, but with the feel of a village complex, surrounded by poplars. It has spacious, nicely furnished en suites, heated indoor pool, well-equipped spa, good restaurant and bar, tennis courts, and even an 18-hole pitch-and-putt golf course. US$270

★ **La Cantera** Calle 306 173 ☏ 02902 495998, ⓦ hotellacanteracalafate.com. A 10min walk south (uphill) of the bus terminal, *La Cantera* has a pioneer feel thanks to the cabin-like wooden walls, but inside the comforts are decidedly modern. The tasteful rooms feature huge beds, plush bathrooms and tremendous views of Lago Argentino or the mountains. There are also larger *cabañas*, plus a sizeable balcony scattered with comfy loungers, perfect for a sundowner. There's a free shuttle service to/from the town centre in the evening. US$181

★ **Edenia** Manzana 642, Punta Soberana ☏ 02902 497021, ⓦ edeniahoteles.com.ar. Impressive hotel with great bay views and whose out-of-the-way location is compensated by a regular minibus service to the centre and the fact that you are the last to be collected in the morning

on glacier tours. The en suites are bright and simply decorated, while the excellent restaurant-bar means you don't have to trek into town in the evening. There's a sauna, and massages are available. US$120

Esplendor Perón 1143 ☏ 02902 492485, ⓦ esplendorelcalafate.com. Sharp boutique hotel on the hill overlooking town. The rather forbidding exterior belies a sun-filled interior: a huge lobby – complete with antler chandeliers – a minimalist bar-restaurant, and rustically cool bedrooms awash with the colours of the Patagonian steppe. Corner suites have 270-degree views of El Calafate and Lago Argentino. A 10min walk into the town centre; free shuttle services also run every 30min. Closed June to mid-Aug. Doubles $1400; suites $1550

El Jardín de los Presentes Guido Bonarelli 72 ☏ 02902 491518. In a town with a real lack of decent mid-range options, *El Jardín de los Presentes* stands out for its clean, simple and reasonably priced en-suite rooms and self-contained apartments. It's a 15min walk from the town centre. Doubles $950; apartments $1150

Linda Vista Apart Hotel Agostini 71 ☏ 02902 493598, ⓦ lindavistahotel.com.ar. One of the best mid-range options, particularly for couples or groups who are planning to self-cater, *Linda Vista* has a collection of very clean, self-contained apartments (sleeping up to five) with bedrooms, bathrooms, kitchenettes and TVs. $1700

Los Sauces Casas Patagónicas Los Gauchos 1352/1370 ☏ 02966 495854, ⓦ casalossauces.com. One of El Calafate's top hotels, *Los Sauces* has impeccable en suites, all unique; a free bottle of champagne and a selection of fine chocolates are provided to help you to settle in. There's also a state-of-the-art spa and gym, as well as indoor and outdoor pools, a "club house" to relax in, a fine restaurant and bar, and expansive grounds. US$690

CAMPING

El Ovejero José Pantín 64 ☏ 02902 493422, ⓔ lamarca _parrilla@hotmail.com. This campsite, conveniently located 50m behind the petrol station at the entrance to El Calafate, has a pleasant riverside setting and is a good choice (during the warmer months of the year, at least). Very basic dorms and rooms are available, and there's a good-value *parrilla* on site. Camping $100; dorms $130; rooms $360

EATING

Most **restaurants** are clustered along or within a block of Avenida Libertador; with a few exceptions, prices are high by Argentine standards. Surprisingly, the choice of **bars** and late-night hangouts is limited – perhaps because everyone has to get up so early for the excursions. The opening times given here are for the high season; during the rest of the year, some places close and most of the rest operate reduced hours.

Casimiro Biguá Grill & Rotisserie Libertador 963 ☏ 02902 492590, ⓦ casimirobigua.com. Top-end joint serving cuts of prime beef and succulent Patagonian lamb in a slick but congenial atmosphere. It has one of the best

wine lists in town, and while the prices (steaks $197–298) are high, eating here is an experience, and there's often a better-value dish of the day for lunch (around $130). It closes during the winter but there is another branch (open

8

THE CALAFATE BUSH

Calafate, the indigenous name for what is known in English as the box-leaved barberry (*Berberis buxifolia*), is Patagonia's best-known plant. The bushes are protected by vindictive thorns, and the wood contains a substance known as *berberina*, which possesses medicinal properties and is used as a textile dye. From late October onwards, the bushes are covered with exquisite little bright yellow flowers. Depending on where they're growing, the berries mature between December and March. Once used by the indigenous populations for dye, they're nowadays often employed in delicious ice creams, appetizing home-made preserves or as a filling for *alfajores*. Remember the oft-quoted saying: "*El que come el calafate, volverá*" ("Eat calafate berries and you'll be back").

year-round) at Libertador 993. Daily 11.30am–1am.

La Cocina Libertador 1245 ☎02902 491758. Cosy diner with a tempting list of savoury crêpes ($135–155), as well as a selection of salads, pastas, risottos, fish and meat dishes. The place is a bit understaffed, so service isn't particularly quick. Mon & Wed–Sun noon–3.30pm & 6.30–11.30pm.

Don Pichon Puerto Deseado 242 ☎02902 492577. Top-notch *parrilla* on a hill a 10min walk northeast of the centre (call ahead for a free transfer) whose wraparound windows offer panoramic views of the city and the lake. Steaks are the big draw, but if you're feeling indulgent, go for the fondue. Mains $180–250. Tues–Sun 7pm–midnight.

★**Kau Kaleshen** Gob. Gregores 1256 ☎02902 491188. This charming restaurant and *casa de té* is the perfect place for a *merienda* – a copious high tea costs $100 for one person, $180 for two – or elegant dinner. The menu for the latter features osso bucco with quinoa risotto, lamb ribs in a red berry sauce, and fondue ($320 for two), plus toothsome desserts like roasted fruit kebabs with a calafate (see box above) and basil sorbet. Mon, Tues & Fri–Sun 4–11.30pm, Thurs 8–11.30pm.

La Lechuza Libertador and Primero de Mayo ☎02902 491610. This popular place serves up a huge range of pizzas ($96–224) from its wood-fired oven, plus pasta dishes, make-your-own salads and huge sandwiches. There are a couple of other branches dotted around town too. Daily noon–3.30pm & 7.30pm–midnight.

★**Pura Vida** Libertador 1876 ☎02902 493356. The owners provide traditional food with a modern touch in an

A-frame *cabaña* with a purple roof and green walls. The menu includes appetizing dishes such as shepherd's pie and "Granny's lentil stew"; there are numerous vegetarian options. Prices (for El Calafate at least) are reasonable too, with mains around $160–240. It's a 10min walk from the centre. Mon, Tues & Thurs–Sun 7.30–11.30pm.

La Tablita Cnel. Rosales 28 ☎02902 491065. Legendary *asado*, deservedly popular with locals and tour groups alike, who come here to gorge on delicious, serious-sized lamb or beef grills (the mixed *parrillas*, $440–485, could feed a small army). Sides are fairly expensive, but the massive mains (steaks $145–205) are generally big enough for two. Mon, Tues & Thurs–Sun noon–3.30pm & 7.30pm–midnight.

Viva La Pepa Emilio Amado 833 ☎02902 491880. Cheerful café with an extensive choice of savoury and sweet crêpes ($90–145) – from trout, dill and cream cheese to chocolate ice cream, cherries and *dulce de leche* – as well as soups, *tartines*, sandwiches, fresh juices and coffees. There's a whimsical air to the place: crudités are served in mini watering cans and children's paintings cover the walls. Mon–Wed & Fri–Sun noon–8pm.

La Zaina Gob. Gregores 1057 ☎02902 496789, ⊕facebook.com/LaZaina.AlmacendeVinos. Housed in an industrial-chic corrugated-iron cabin, this restaurant and wine bar is a great place for a drink: the *carta de vinos* is extensive (glasses from $39) and there are also interesting local tipples like a calafate berry liqueur. The food veers towards the hearty, with mains ($185–235) like braised lamb in a malbec sauce. Daily 5pm–midnight.

DRINKING

Casablanca Libertador 1202 ☎02902 491402. There's a local feel to this café-bar, which has classic film posters and signed rugby and hockey shirts on the walls, and though the food (pizzas, burgers, etc) is only okay it is reasonable value, and there's a good range of beers (from $40). Daily 11am–midnight.

Libro-bar Borges y Alvarez Libertador 1015 ☎02902

491464. This rapidly expanding café-bar – it now has two big terraces, a takeaway sandwich counter and a sizeable pub-style area on the first floor – has a range of Argentine and South American books (mainly in Spanish) crammed onto overstacked shelves that you can flick through while enjoying a craft beer (draught $85) or coffee. Plenty of snacks and light meals too. Daily 10am–2/3am.

DIRECTORY

Banks and exchange There are several ATMs including at the Banco de la Nación (Libertador 1133) and Banco de

Santa Cruz (Libertador 1285). Thaler (9 de Julio) exchanges all major international and South American currencies.

Internet There are several internet cafés, including Locutorio (Espora and San Martín). Prices are eye-watering – expect $25/15min, or more.

Laundry Lava Andina, Cmte. Espora 88 (Mon–Sat 9am–8pm; ☎02902 493980).
Post office Libertador 1133.

The southern sector of the park

The exalted glaciers in the **southern sector** of the Los Glaciares national park attract huge numbers of visitors from all over the world and it takes a bit of planning to find the magic and avoid the crowds. The main sites cluster around **Lago Argentino**, the largest solely Argentine lake, and the third biggest in South America, with a surface area of 1600 square kilometres.

The three hotspots in the southern sector of the park are: the easy-to-reach and not-to-be-missed **Glaciar Perito Moreno**, which slams into the western end of the **Península de Magallanes**; **Puerto Bandera**, from where boat trips depart to Glaciar Upsala and the other northern glaciers that are inaccessible by land; and, to the south down RP-15, the much-less-visited **Lago Roca** and the southern arm of Lago Argentino, the **Brazo Sur**.

Within the boundaries, be especially aware of the dangers of fire – an area of forest near Glaciar Spegazzini that burnt in the 1930s still hasn't recovered. **Mammals** in the park include the *gato montés* wildcat, pumas and the endangered *huemul*, although you are highly unlikely to see any of these owing to their scarcity and elusive nature. There is plenty of enjoyable **flora** on display, though, such as the ubiquitous *notro* (*Embothrium coccineum*, known in English as the Chilean firebush or firetree), with its flaming red blooms between November and March. Commonly seen **birds** include the majestic black and red Magellanic woodpecker (*Carpintero patagónico*).

8

TOURS OF GLACIAR PERITO MORENO

DAY-TOURS

Although it's easy to visit independently (see p.476), many people visit the Glaciar Perito Moreno on guided day-tours, which are offered by virtually all agencies in El Calafate and allow for around four hours at the ice face, the minimum required to fully appreciate the spectacle. The basic tour costs around $700, plus the park entrance fee of $260. Rather than having a fixed point of departure, companies tend to drive round town collecting passengers from hotels; to avoid having to get up much earlier than you need to, try to arrange that you're the last pick-up or go to the office yourself just before the bus leaves.
Tour agencies *Hostel del Glaciar Pioneros* (see p.473), Chaltén Travel (Libertador 1174; ☎02902 492212, ✆www.chaltentravel.com) and Rumbo Sur (Libertador 960; ☎02902 492155, ✆rumbosur.com.ar) run recommended tours.

BOAT TOURS

An excellent way of seeing the ice face from another angle is to take one of the boat trips that chug along near the towering heights of the ice wall. Safari Náutico heads to the southern face from Puerto Bajo de las Sombras (daily: Oct–May hourly, 10am–3pm; reduced service the rest of the year; 1hr; $250; ☎02902 492205, ✆hieloyaventura.com).

ICE-TREKKING

For an even closer look, you can walk on the glacier with Hielo y Aventura (Libertador 935; ☎02902 492205, ✆hieloyaventura.com), which organizes daily "Mini Trekking" trips (full day; 1hr 30min on the ice; $1200 including transfers but not the park entrance fee) and longer, more demanding "Big Ice" excursions (full day; 4hr on the ice; $2200 including transfers but not the park entrance fee), which include a boat trip across to the glacier. This is ice-trekking, not ice-*climbing* (try El Chaltén for that): you do not need to be in peak fitness. You'll be given crampons, but bring sunglasses, sun cream, gloves and a packed lunch, and wear warm, weatherproof clothes.

Glaciar Perito Moreno

The immense pack ice of the **GLACIAR PERITO MORENO** (also called Ventisquero Perito Moreno) is one of Argentina's greatest natural wonders. It's not the longest of Argentina's glaciers – nearby Glaciar Upsala is twice as long (60km) – and whereas the ice cliffs at its snout tower up to 60m high, the face of Glaciar Spegazzini can reach heights double that. However, such comparisons prove irrelevant when you stand on the **boardwalks** that face this monster. Perito Moreno has a star quality that none of the others rivals.

The glacier zooms down off the icecap in a great motorway-like sweep, a jagged mass of crevasses and towering, knife-edged séracs almost unsullied by the streaks of dirty moraine that discolour many of its counterparts. When it collides with the southern arm of Lago Argentino, the **Canal de los Témpanos** (Iceberg Channel), the show really begins: vast blocks of ice, some weighing hundreds of tonnes, detonate off the face of the glacier with the report of a small cannon and come crashing down into the waters below. These frozen depth-charges then surge back to the surface as icebergs, sending out a fairy ring of smaller lumps that form a protective reef around the berg, which is left to float in a mirror-smooth pool of its own.

That said, it's more likely you'll have to content yourself with the thuds, cracks, creaks and grinding crunches the glacier habitually makes, as well as the wonderful variety of **colours of the ice**: marbled in places with streaks of muddy grey and copper-sulphate blue, while at the bottom the pressurized, de-oxygenated ice has a deep blue, waxy sheen. The glacier tends to be more active in sunny weather and in the afternoon, but early morning can also be beautiful, as the sun strikes the ice cliffs.

With the wind coming off the ice, the temperature at the glacier can be a lot colder than in El Calafate, so take **extra clothes**. Do not stray from the boardwalks: people have been killed by ricocheting ice or wave surges.

Brief history

Perito Moreno, one of Patagonia's few growing glaciers, is famous for the way it periodically pushes right across the channel, forming a massive dyke of ice that cuts off the Brazo Rico and Brazo Sur from the main body of Lago Argentino. Isolated from their natural outlet, the water in the *brazos* (arms) would build up against the flank of the glacier, flooding the surrounding area, until eventually the pressure forced open a passage into the canal once again. Occurring over the course of several hours, such a **rupture** is, for those lucky enough to witness it, one of nature's most awesome spectacles.

The glacier first reached the peninsula in 1917, having advanced 750m in fifteen years, but the channel did not remain blocked for long and the phenomenon remained little known. This changed in 1939, when a vast area was flooded and planes tried (and failed) to break the glacier by bombing it. In 1950, water levels rose by 30m and the channel was closed for two years; in 1966, levels reached an astonishing 32m above normal. The glacier then settled into a fairly regular cycle, blocking the channel about every four years up to 1988; after that there was a sixteen-year gap until another rupture in 2004. Since then there have been major ruptures in 2006, 2008, 2012 and 2016.

ARRIVAL AND DEPARTURE   GLACIAR PERITO MORENO

By bus If you don't want to be restricted to a tour (see p.470), try the Cal Tur service from El Calafate's bus station (departing daily 8.15am & 1pm, returning 4pm & 7.30pm). If you get the morning departure you'll probably

---

ESTANCIA ANITA

About 30km from El Calafate, RP-15 passes historical Estancia Anita, the scene of one of Patagonia's most grisly episodes. In 1921, 121 men were executed here by an army battalion that had been sent to crush a workers' strike and the related social unrest; a monument by the roadside commemorates the victims. You can find out more about the event at the Calafate Centro de Interpretación Histórica (see p.470).

be among the first to arrive at the glacier – it's worth the effort to beat the crowds and glimpse the early morning sun shining on the west-facing snout.

By taxi You can hire a taxi from El Calafate to take you to the glacier (around $1700–2000, including a 4hr wait).

By car The other option is to rent a car from El Calafate (from $1100–14,000/day) and drive along the lesser-used RP-15 towards Lago Roca or along the paved RP-11. RP-15 is unsurfaced but by far the more picturesque. Turn right just after *Estancia Alta Vista* (see p.472), and then left after another 12km to the park's main entrance. The route along RP-11 heads straight down Av Libertador and along a paved road that lines the lake shore, then dropping down to the park's main entrance; the right turning here, down RP-8, leads to Puerto Bandera (see box, p.477), for boat trips to Upsala and other glaciers.

INFORMATION

Visitors pay the entry fee ($260) at the park's main entrance (daily: Jan & Feb 8am–9pm; March–Easter 8am–8pm; Easter–July 8am–4pm; Aug–Oct 8am–6pm; Nov 8am–7pm; Dec 8am–8pm), which lies at the edge of the peninsula; the trees nearby are a favourite evening roost of the austral parakeet (*cachaña*), the most southerly of the world's parrots. From here it's a 40min drive (around 30km) past picnic spots, a campsite, the *Los Notros* hotel (currently closed), and Puerto Bajo de la Sombras (see box, p.477) to a series of boardwalks in front of the glacier; there's also a café here, plus a gift shop and public toilets.

The Upsala, Spegazzini, Onelli and Agassiz glaciers

Glaciar Upsala is the undisputed heavyweight of the park, between 5km and 7km wide, with a 60m-high snout and a length of 60km. It's still South America's longest glacier, despite massive retrocession in recent decades, covering a total area three times larger than that of metropolitan Buenos Aires. Upsala played an important role in consolidating Argentine claims to its Antarctic territory – expedition teams used to acclimatize by living for months in a base on the glacier.

Navigating **Brazo Upsala** is a highlight in itself, though trips here are often cancelled due to the increasing number of **icebergs** that bob, grind and even turn occasional flips around you. For every one part of iceberg above the surface, it has six to seven parts

8

GLACIER CRUISES

FROM PUERTO BANDERA

Boat trips to see the Upsala, Spegazzini and Onelli glaciers are run from Puerto Bandera by Solo Patagonia (Libertador 867, El Calafate; ☎02902 491298, ⊛solopatagonia.com). When the weather's fine, the full-day excursion ($1350 plus park entrance fee) is an unforgettable experience; when it's rough, it can be memorable for the wrong reasons – if badly affected by motion sickness, take precautionary seasickness tablets. Dress in warm, waterproof and windproof clothing, and take your own food as prices on board are high.

Before booking, remember that your scope for refunds is limited: the weather has to be exceptionally foul for the trip to be cancelled entirely, and the company fulfils its legal obligations if only one of the main parts of the trip is completed; in windy weather especially, icebergs can block the channels, and Upsala is frequently inaccessible.

Mar Patag (9 de Julio 57, El Calafate; ☎02902 492118, ⊛crucerosmarpatag.com) runs excellent day-long cruises (from US$315), as well as the extended three-day "The Spirit of the Glaciers" tour (from US$1680/person); prices are high, but the service and the experience justify them. The trips give you close-quarter views of the Upsala and Spegazzini glaciers – as well as Perito Moreno – anchoring at Puerto las Vacas, off the Brazo Spegazzini, for the night.

TOURS OF BAHÍA CRISTINA

The one- and multi-day trips (from $1150, excluding transfers and the park entry fee) run by *Estancia Cristina* (see p.472) give you access to the central sector of the park and the windswept, desolate Bahía Cristina area. Boats visit Glaciar Upsala before heading up Bahía Cristina to the isolated estancia, a favoured point of entry for explorers of the icecap, including Padre de Agostini, and Eric Shipton, the famous mountaineer and explorer of the 1960s. Trekking, horseriding and 4WD excursions can be added on.

below, which gives an idea of the tremendous size of these blocks. Even in flat light, the icy blues shine as if lit by a neon strip-light – an eerie, incredible, cerulean glow.

Glaciar Spegazzini is many visitors' favourite glacier, with an imposing ice cascade to the right and the most dizzying snout of all the glaciers in the park (between 80 and 135m high). The **Onelli** and **Agassiz glaciers** are less impressive – but beautiful nonetheless – and are reached by an easy 800m walk to **Laguna Onelli**, a chilly lake dotted with small bergs. The walk itself is likely to appeal only to those who haven't had the opportunity to see Patagonian forest elsewhere, since the beauty of these woodlands is not enhanced by the presence of crowds of day-trippers.

Lago Roca

Overshadowed by the nearby glaciers, **Lago Roca**, a southern branch of Lago Argentino, tends to be frequented mainly by fishermen. Lying 52km from El Calafate, it offers good horseriding and trekking possibilities in stunning areas of open woodland and among the neighbouring hills of the Cordón de los Cristales. It also has rock art dating back three thousand years, which can be seen along a signposted trail to the left of the main road just before *Lago Roca* campsite (see below); from here, you can continue the four-hour hike to the summit of Cerro Cristales, with fine views of Torres del Paine to the south. There's no entry fee for this area of the park.

ARRIVAL AND DEPARTURE   LAGO ROCA

By bus/taxi Cal Tur and RP serve Lago Roca (summer only: 4 weekly; generally leaving El Calafate at 8.30am, returning 6.30pm; 1hr); a taxi from El Calafate costs $1700–2000, with waiting time. Alternatively, several travel agencies (see p.472) run day-trips taking in Lago Roca.

ACCOMMODATION

Camping Lago Roca Lago Roca ☏02902 499500, ⓦfacebook.com/CampingLagoRoca. This site has a mix of camping pitches and simple *cabañas*; the latter are heated and sleep two to four people. There's also a restaurant-bar, and you can rent fishing equipment and bikes. Camping/person **$150**; *cabañas* **$630**

El Chaltén

EL CHALTÉN, 90km west of RN-40 and 220km north of El Calafate, has undergone a convulsive expansion since it was established in 1985 in a (successful) attempt to claim the area from Chile. Today, it's a thriving tourist town showing regrettable signs of uncontrolled development. That said, the town's location is stunning, the atmosphere relaxed, and the population a friendly mix of Argentines, expats and travellers of all ages.

Rearing up on the opposite bank of the **Río de las Vueltas** is the curiously stepped, dark-grey cliff face of **Cerro Pirámide**, while you can glimpse the tips of the park's most daunting peaks, **Fitz Roy** and **Cerro Torre**, from the southern and eastern fringes of the village. In terms of specific sights, there is only the classically uncluttered alpine **chapel** on the western edge of the village. Built by Austrian craftsmen with Austrian materials,

---

LA LEONA: A HISTORIC WAYSIDE INN

En route from El Calafate to El Chaltén, by a modern bridge over the Río La Leona, stands one of RN-40's original inns, **Hotel La Leona** (daily 8.30am–9.30pm; ☏011 5032 3415, ⓦhoteldecampolaleona.com.ar). It's a wonderfully atmospheric place (despite heavy restoration), worth stopping at for a slice of home-made cake ($13–25); it also sells crafts, souvenirs and maps. You can try your hand here at the **juego de la argolla**, an old gaucho drinking game where you take turns to land a ring that's attached by a string to the ceiling over a hook mounted on the wall opposite: the first person to succeed wins a drink – try one of the **typical gaucho tipples**, such as sweet *caña ombú* or *caña quemada*. Buses travelling from El Calafate to El Chaltén generally stop briefly here.

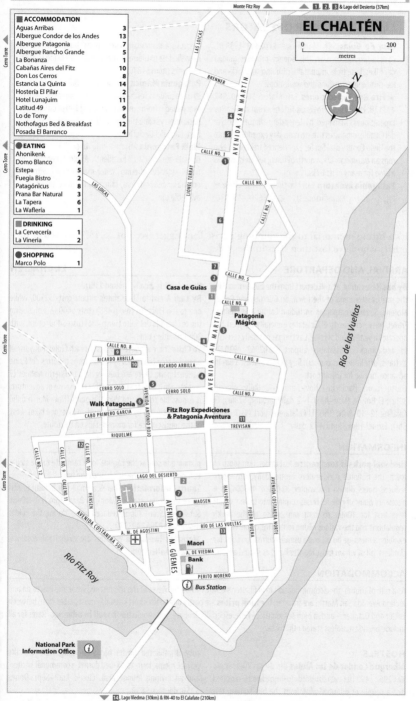

EL CHALTÉN

0 — 200
metres

ACCOMMODATION
Aguas Arribas	3
Albergue Condor de los Andes	13
Albergue Patagonia	7
Albergue Rancho Grande	5
La Bonanza	1
Cabañas Aires del Fitz	10
Don Los Cerros	8
Estancia La Quinta	14
Hostería El Pilar	2
Hotel Lunajuim	11
Latitud 49	9
Lo de Tomy	6
Nothofagus Bed & Breakfast	12
Posada El Barranco	4

EATING
Ahonikenk	7
Domo Blanco	4
Estepa	5
Fuegia Bistro	2
Patagónicus	8
Prana Bar Natural	3
La Tapera	6
La Waflería	1

DRINKING
La Cervecería	1
La Vineria	2

SHOPPING
Marco Polo	1

8

EL CHALTÉN TOUR OPERATORS

Casa de Guias San Martín s/n ☎02962 493118, ⓦcasadeguias.com.ar. This agency provides guided day hikes, long treks, mountain-climbing, and rock- and ice-climbing excursions and workshops.

★ **Fitz Roy Expediciones** San Martín 56 ☎02962 493178, ⓦwww.fitzroyexpediciones.com.ar. Fitz Roy Expediciones, managed by legendary climber Alberto del Castillo, organizes five- to nine-day expeditions onto the Hielo Continental Sur for experienced trekkers. It also runs an eco-lodge 17km north of town, which is used as a base for many of its treks.

Patagonia Aventura San Martín 56 (same office as Fitz Roy Expediciones) ☎02962 493110, ⓦpatagoniaaventura.com. Runs boat trips across Lago Viedma to Glaciar Viedma and ice-trekking trips on its flanks (from $1870).

Patagonia Mágica Fonrouge s/n ☎02962 493066, ⓦpatagoniamagica.com. This agency offers everything from mountaineering expeditions to backcountry skiing trips, as well as mountain-bike rides from Lago del Desierto.

Walk Patagonia Antonio Rojo 62 ☎02962 493275, ⓦwalk-trek.tur.ar. Excellent Anglo-Argentine-run travel agency offering tailor-made treks with an emphasis on local flora, fauna and history. Bike rental available too.

it's a fitting memorial to the climbing purist Toni Egger (see box, p.487), as well as to others who have lost their lives in the park.

ARRIVAL AND DEPARTURE
EL CHALTÉN

By bus Buses arrive at and depart from the bus terminal in the southeastern end of the town, on Güemes and Perito Moreno. Several companies, including Cal Tur and Chaltén Travel, have services to El Calafate; generally only Cal Tur operates a year-round service. Las Lengas has daily services to and from El Calafate's airport (☎02962 493023, ⓦtransportelaslengas.com.ar). Buy tickets at least a day in advance, or two for the airport.

Destinations Bariloche (Nov–April 1–2 daily; around 30hr); El Bolsón (Nov–April 1–2 daily; around $28hr); El Calafate (2–10 daily; 3hr); El Calafate airport (1–3 daily; 3hr); Esquel (Nov–April 1–2 daily; 22hr); Perito Moreno (Nov–April 1–2 daily; around 13hr).

By taxi A taxi to El Calafate's airport costs $2500, while one to Río Eléctrico (see p.488) costs $400. A sightseeing trip to Chorrillo del Salto (see p.486) costs $400 return, with 30min waiting time.

To Chile There are several ways to reach Chile: many travel agencies (see box, p.467) organize trips to Torres del Paine national park; there are bus services to Puerto Natales (3 weekly; 5hr); and, for those with a real sense of adventure, it is possible to cross to Villa O'Higgins (Nov–March only) via a two-day trip by bus, boat and on foot (or a bike) – ask at the tourist office for more details on the route.

INFORMATION

National park visitors' centre Just under 1km south of town, the national park visitors' centre (daily 9am–5pm; reduced hours during the winter; ☎02962 493004) is a necessary point of call. All buses coming into town stop off here first for 10min so staff can advise of the park's regulations and the various hiking routes. Inside are wildlife exhibits, a message board and a useful information book for climbers, all of whom must register here, as should anyone planning to stay at the Laguna Torre campsite to the south. Fishing licences can be purchased here too.

Tourist information There's a small but helpful tourist office in the bus station (Mon–Fri 8am–2pm & 3–10pm, Sat & Sun 9am–10pm; reduced hours during the colder months; ☎02962 493370).

Websites Two useful websites are ⓦchaltenhoy.com.ar and ⓦelchalten.com.

ACCOMMODATION

As a rule of thumb, the accommodation in El Chaltén's centre has better views of the mountains, while the places on and around Avenida San Martín are smarter. The **high prices** are partly due to the short season – most places close between Easter and October – and in high season (Dec–Feb), especially January, you should **book well in advance**. Rates for all include breakfast, unless stated otherwise.

HOSTELS

Albergue Condor de los Andes Río de las Vueltas s/n ☎02962 493101, ⓦcondordelosandes.com. Located just a couple of minutes' walk from the bus station, this cosy HI-affiliated hostel has welcoming staff, en-suite private rooms, four- to six-bed dorms, a communal kitchen, and an inviting lounge area. Closed April–Sept. Dorms $250; doubles $890

★**Albergue Patagonia** San Martín 493 ☎02962 493019, ⊛patagoniahostel.com.ar. This homely, HI-affiliated joint has decent dorms and private rooms, plus cooking facilities, laundry service, book exchange, bike rental and snug living room. The staff can make excursion and transport reservations and are a good source of information. Breakfast is included in the price for the private en-suite rooms, but not for dorm guests or those in private rooms with shared bathrooms. Closed April–Sept. Dorms US$25; doubles US$70

Albergue Rancho Grande San Martín 724 ☎02962 493005. There are better hostels in town, but as *Rancho Grande* is one of the few that stays open year-round, backpackers often end up here. There are acceptable dorms and private rooms, an inexpensive bar-restaurant and kitchen facilities. Breakfast costs extra. Dorms $210; doubles $800

HOTELS AND GUESTHOUSES

Cabañas Aires del Fitz Ricardo Arbilla 124 ☎02962 493134, ⊛airesdelfitz.com.ar. Friendly, family-run set of split-level wooden *cabañas* sleeping up to six people; each has a bedroom, bathroom, kitchenette, small dining area, and a TV and DVD player. Good value, especially for groups. No breakfast. $1200

Don Los Cerros San Martín 260 ☎02962 493182, ⊛hoteldonloscerrosdelchalten.com. In an elevated location right in the centre of town, this top-end option has spacious en suites with whirlpool baths perfect for soaking after a long trek and big windows to take advantage of the enviable views, as well as a spa (massages from $450), library and classy restaurant. $2800

Hotel Lunajuim Trevisán 45 ☎02962 493047, ⊛lunajuim.com. A well-run upper mid-range hotel, *Lunajuim* is an extremely pleasant place to rest your aching feet after a tiring hike: there are spacious en suites, a well-stocked library, bar-restaurant, and a roaring fire in the communal lounge. Closed May–Sept. US$165

Latitud 49 Arbilla 145 ☎02962 493347, ⊛latitud49 .com.ar. A justifiably popular *apart hotel* with cosy, well-equipped apartments; each one comes with a kitchen and living room, as well as bedroom(s). Staff are friendly, but breakfast costs extra. Closed June & July. $1600

Lo de Tomy San Martín 480 ☎02962 493254, ⊛lodetomy.com. With a striking pinky-purple and yellow exterior, *Lo de Tomy* is hard to miss. Look beyond the lurid colour scheme, though, and you'll find a very good-value place to stay, with pleasant cottages and larger apartments – both with kitchenettes, the latter sleep up to four people – and a restaurant specializing in lamb *asados*. Cottage $600; apartment $2500

★**Nothofagus Bed & Breakfast** Hensen and Riquelme ☎02962 493087, ⊛nothofagusbb.com.ar. As the name (the Spanish for the southern beech genus) suggests, wood features prominently in the interior of this welcoming B&B. The good-value, sun-washed double rooms come with or without bathroom, and there's a small library, book exchange and free afternoon tea. Closed Easter–Oct. $760

Posada El Barranco Lionel Terray and Calle 2 ☎02962 493006, ⊛posadaelbarranco.com. Charming Argentine–Kiwi-run B&B with attractive stone work on the outside and clean lines and smart furniture on the inside. The en-suite rooms are comfortable, and there are also two self-contained *cabañas* that each sleep up to four people; rates for the latter do not include breakfast. Closed May–Sept. Doubles US$129; *cabañas* US$129

OUT OF TOWN

Aguas Arribas Lago del Desierto, 37km from town ☎011 4152 5697, ⊛aguasarribalodge.com. In a tranquil lakeside location, just 5km from the Chilean border, *Aguas Arribas* is a wonderful spot for (wealthy) travellers who want to get away from it all. Great food, swish en suites, superlative views, and excellent hiking and fishing opportunities are all on offer. Rates include full board and activities. Closed May to mid-Oct. US$700

La Bonanza RP-23, 12km north of town ☎02962 493366, ⊛campingbonanzachalten.com. This charming campsite, useful if you have your own transport, is situated next to the Río de las Vueltas, where trees offer some shelter from the wind. There are hot showers and ample cooking facilities. If you're after more comfort, go for the futuristic-looking *domos* (permanently pitched geodesic tents) or rustic *cabañas*; both sleep up to five people. Camping $100; *domos* $350; *cabañas* $750

Estancia La Quinta 2km south of town off RP-23 ☎02962 493012, ⊛estancialaquinta.com.ar. A working cattle ranch in a lovely location whose thoroughly modern refurbishment belies its considerable history. The rooms are neat, if compact, and there's a peaceful lounge with views across the valley, plus a small museum, and a 100-year-old *casco* where home-cooked local dishes are served. Closed May–Sept. US$170

★**Hostería El Pilar** 15km north of town on RP-15 ☎02962 493002, ⊛hosteriaelpilar.com.ar. Delightful, old-fashioned corrugated metal *casco*, appealingly decorated in period style. Rooms are comfortable and peaceful, the homely living room has a wood-burning stove, and home-made treats are served in the tearoom, which has an enviable view of Fitz Roy. There is also a pleasant garden, and the owner is a knowledgeable guide. Closed April to mid-Oct. $1380

EATING

El Chaltén has several very good **restaurants** (although prices are relatively high), plus a few little **bars** (see p.482). Most hotels and restaurants make **lunch boxes** for day-treks. The opening times given below are for the high season, and should only be taken as a rough guide; many places close between Easter and October, and those that stay open have reduced hours.

Ahonikenk Güemes 23 ☎02962 493070. This no-nonsense little restaurant in the southern part of the town serves up a good range of pasta dishes, pizzas, stews and *milanesas* at reasonable prices (mains $130–220). Daily 11.30am–3.30pm & 7–10.30pm.

Domo Blanco San Martín 164 ☎02962 493036. Alongside the town's best ice cream (from $40) – flavours include *calafate* (see p.474), *maracujá* (passion fruit) and banana split – *Domo Blanco* also serves up an interesting range of panini, wraps and sandwiches. Daily 1/2pm–midnight.

Estepa Cerro Solo and Antonio Rojo ☎02962 493069, ⓦesteparestobar.com. Welcoming restaurant-bar in an adobe-style building lying in the shadow of Fitz Roy. The menu features a good selection of lamb dishes – try the stuffed lamb with pilaf rice and a mushroom sauce – as well as hearty calzones and pizzas from the wood-fired oven (mains $90–270). Tues–Sun noon–3.30pm & 7.30pm–midnight.

Fuegia Bistro San Martín s/n ☎02962 493019. Charming restaurant with a wide-ranging menu that calls in at India, Mexico, Italy, Spain, the Middle East, and even Scandinavia, as well as Patagonia (mains $130–240). The inventive fish dishes are particularly good. In the mornings a hearty buffet breakfast is on offer. Daily 7–10am & 7–11pm.

Patagónicus Güemes and Madsen ☎02962 493025. Local institution with a terrific range of pizzas ($70–220) – the best in town – served up at chunky wooden tables in a social, friendly atmosphere. They also produce their own beer (from $70), which is well worth a try. Mon & Wed–Sun 10.30am–11pm.

Prana Bar Natural Av San Martín 275 ☎02962 15 728074. Charming vegetarian teahouse-restaurant with an eclectic menu (mains $95–145) that features "power" smoothies, curries, stir fries, sweet and savoury crêpes, and a fine range of teas, coffees and desserts, including a mean tiramisu. They also do healthy lunch boxes for hikers. Daily 11am–11pm.

La Tapera Av Antonio Rojo s/n ☎02962 493195. Housed in an appealing log *cabaña*, *La Tapera* has friendly service and offers a menu featuring delicious and filling pastas, stews, salads and steaks (mains $140–265). The wine list is excellent and there are generally some tempting desserts too. Daily 12.30–3pm & 7.30–11.30pm.

La Waflería Av San Martín 640 ☎02962 493093. If you're in need of an energy boost before or after a trek, these waffles – 38 different types, savoury and sweet ($45–180) – hit the spot. Coffee and hot chocolate – some livened up with a shot of alcohol – are also on offer. Daily 11am–9am.

DRINKING

La Cervecería San Martín 564 ☎02962 493109. Top-notch microbrewery whose crisp, clean pilsners (draught $60) provide relief after a day on the trail. Genial staff, the occasional live-music session, and tasty snacks such as pizza, empanadas and the house speciality *locro* (a hearty stew; $140) add to the convivial atmosphere. Daily 11am–midnight.

★**La Vineria** Av Lago del Desierto 265 ☎02962 493301. With over 180 different wines (glasses from $40) from vineyards across Argentina, plus a good selection of craft beers and ales and a range of snacks and *picadas*, this cosy little joint is a fine place to begin or finish the night. Daily 4pm–2am.

SHOPPING

Marco Polo Güemes 23 ☎02962 493122, ⓦfacebook .com/MarcoPoloChalten. Excellent little bookshop with a strong range of English-language fiction, local trekking maps and guides, and non-fiction on Patagonia. There is a smaller range of German and French books, and plenty of Spanish-language texts. Mon–Sat 10.30am–1pm & 3.30–8.30pm, Sun 4–8.30pm.

DIRECTORY

Banks and exchange El Chaltén now has a bank (with an ATM), on the corner of Güemes and Viedma, and there's another ATM in the bus station; neither ATM is particularly reliable, however, so it's worth bringing some cash with you. Some hotels and restaurants will exchange US dollars.

Internet Internet cafés are thin on the ground, but virtually every hotel, hostel, restaurant and bar has (pretty slow) wi-fi.

Laundry There are several laundries in town; try Maori, Güemes and Viedma (daily 9am–7pm).

The northern sector of the park

The northern sector of Parque Nacional Los Glaciares, the **Fitz Roy sector**, is a trekking paradise. One of its main attractions is that those with limited time, or who are not in peak fitness, can still make worthwhile **day-hikes** using El Chaltén as a base.

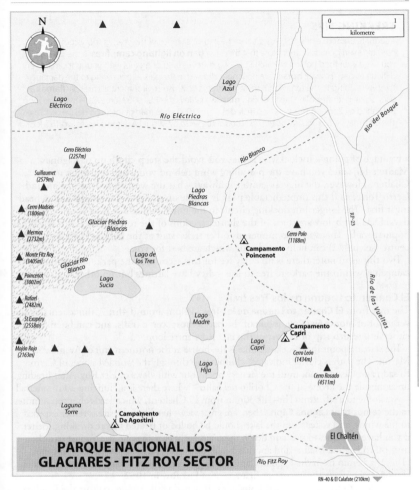

PARQUE NACIONAL LOS GLACIARES - FITZ ROY SECTOR

The sector also contains some of the most breathtakingly beautiful mountain peaks on Earth. Two concentric jaws of jagged teeth puncture the Patagonian sky with the 3405m incisor of **Monte Fitz Roy** at the centre of the massif. This sculpted peak was known to the Tehuelche as El Chaltén, "The Mountain that Smokes" or "The Volcano", owing to the almost perpetual presence of a scarf of cloud attached to its summit. It is not inconceivable, however, that the Tehuelche were using the term in a rather more metaphorical sense to allude to the fiery pink colour that the rock walls turn when struck by the first light of dawn.

Francisco Moreno saw fit to name the pagan summit after the evangelical captain of the *Beagle*, who, with Charles Darwin, had viewed the Andes from a distance, after having journeyed up the Río Santa Cruz by whaleboat to within 50km of Lago Argentino. Alongside Monte Fitz Roy rise **Cerro Poincenot** and **Aguja Saint-Exupéry**, while set behind them is the forbidding needle of **Cerro Torre**, a finger that stands in bold defiance of all the elements that the Hielo Continental Sur (see box, p.486) hurls against it.

For those who enjoy camping, the quintessential three-day **Fitz Roy/Cerro Torre loop** at the centre of the park makes a good option, and can be done in either direction. The

> ### TREKKING TIPS
>
> Adequate outdoor clothing is essential in the park at all times of the year, as snowstorms are possible even in midsummer. Note that there is a **ban on lighting campfires** in the park, so if you need your food hot, make careful use of gas stoves (and bring fuel with you, as it can be very difficult to get in town); **horses** are no longer allowed in the park either, owing to the damage they were doing to the terrain, but some operators now use environmentally friendly **llamas** as pack animals for treks. The best trekking **map** available is the 1:50,000 *Monte Fitz Roy & Cerro Torre* published by Zagier & Urruty, which includes a 1:100,000 scale map of the Lago del Desierto area. The informative *Trekking in Chaltén and Lago del Desierto* by Miguel A. Alonso is also worth a look.

advantage of going anticlockwise is that you avoid the steep climb up to Lagunas Madre e Hija and you have the prevailing wind behind you when returning to El Chaltén. However, the biggest gamble is always what the weather will be like around Cerro Torre, so if this unpredictable peak is visible on day one, you might like to head for it first. The longer interlocking circuit to the north will add at least another two days. Detailed below are some of the shorter sections of the route, as well as a few other popular trails. There are also numerous other treks; staff at the national park visitor centre (see p.472) can help you decide which are best for you.

Two things to note: there is no entry fee for this section of the park; and all the campsites within the park are free to use – they have latrines but no other facilities.

El Chaltén to Laguna de los Tres trail

The trek from **El Chaltén to Laguna de los Tres** (10km; around 4hr; 750m ascent), at the very foot of **Monte Fitz Roy**, is one of the park's most scenic trails, and can be hiked either as a return trip or as part of the Fitz Roy/Torre loop.

The starting point for this classic hike is the house at the northern end of Avenida San Martín. The path is clearly indicated, climbing up through the wooded slopes of Cerro Rosado and Cerro León, until the scenery opens out with views of Fitz Roy. After heading up alongside the ravine of the Chorillo del Salto – where there is a plunging 20m waterfall – you come to a left turn (1hr–1hr 30min from El Chaltén), which leads after ten minutes to the **campsite** at **Laguna Capri**. There are great views here, but the site is rather exposed to the winds, and water from the lake should be boiled or treated before drinking. Better, if you have the time, to push on down the main path, crossing one stream just past the turn-off to Laguna Madre, and another brook until you reach **Campamento Poincenot** (1hr–1hr 15min from the Laguna Capri turning), named after one of the team of French climbers who made the victorious first ascent of Fitz Roy in 1952.

According to the official story, Poincenot drowned while trying to cross the Río Fitz Roy before the assault on the mountain even took place, although another rumour hinted that this was no accident, but the work of a cuckolded estancia owner, enraged by his wife's infidelities with the Gallic mountaineer. The campsite covers a sprawling area on the eastern bank of the Río Blanco. Choose your spot well and you won't need to get out of your tent to see the rosy blaze of dawn on the cliffs of Fitz Roy.

To Laguna de los Tres

From *Campamento Poincenot*, follow the crisscrossing paths to the wooden bridge that spans the main current of the Río Blanco. A second, makeshift bridge takes you to the far bank, from where the path heads up through the woods, passing the **Río Blanco campsite** (intended for use by climbers), before pushing on past the tree line. The next section is tough going as the eroded path ascends a steep gradient, but mercifully it's not long before you come to the top of the ridge, cross a boggy meadow and then climb the final hurdle: a moraine ridge that hides a breathtaking panorama – perhaps the finest in the entire park – on the other side.

EMP R. P. Nº 5(EL CERRITO) 67
YAC RIO TURBIO 209
RIO GALLEGOS 274
40

THE HIELO CONTINENTAL SUR

Blanketing massive expanses of Parque Nacional Los Glaciares, the **Hielo Continental Sur** (Southern Patagonian Icecap) is the largest body of ice outside the poles, divided between Argentina and neighbouring Chile (which has around seventy percent of it). Climate change, however, is having a dramatic effect. In 1945 the icefield spanned an estimated surface area of 13,500 square kilometres; by 2010 fresh estimates suggested it had shrunk to 12,550 square kilometres. The Glaciarium museum (see p.470) near El Calafate has interesting – and concerning – displays on the icefield.

You now stand in the cirque of the rich, navy-blue **Laguna de los Tres** (1hr–1hr 15min from *Campamento Poincenot*), fed by a concertinaed glacier and ringed by a giant's crown of granite peaks, including Aguja Saint-Exupéry (named after Antoine de Saint-Exupéry, who drew on his experiences as a pioneer of Patagonian aviation when writing *Vol de Nuit*), Cerro Poincenot, Fitz Roy and a host of other spikes. Round the small rocky outcrop to the left for even more impressive views: this ridge separates the basins of Laguna de los Tres and Laguna Sucia, some 200m below the level of the first lake. The **Glaciar Río Blanco**, hanging above Laguna Sucia, periodically sheds scales of ice and snow, which, though they look tiny at this distance, reveal their true magnitude by the ear-splitting reports they make as they hit the surface of the lake. Retrace your steps and follow the path on the western (right-hand) bank of the Río Blanco (around 40min from the *Río Blanco* campsite).

Lagunas Madre e Hija trail

From *Campamento Poincenot*, there are two other trails: one crosses the Río Blanco and follows its western bank northward towards the Río Eléctrico and Piedra del Fraile (see p.488); the other path, from **Campamento Poincenot to Campamento De Agostini** (6km; 2–3hr; 100m descent), at the eastern end of Laguna Torre, leads past **Lagunas Madre e Hija** (Mother and Daughter Lagoons). To follow this trail, you'll need to double back towards Laguna Capri a little way, before finding the signposted route.

Walk due south of the campsite to the Chorrillo del Salto and follow the stream's eastern bank until you see a signpost directing hikers to the right. This route leads across a little bridge, and follow the boardwalk as it curves east to the turn-off to Laguna Madre, less than five minutes away. The route past the two lagoons makes for gentle walking and is easy to follow, pushing through knee-high bushes, and after a few hundred metres rising to and passing through the young forest to avoid the swampy ground for the most part.

Look out for upland geese (*cauquenes*), who like to graze by the lake shore. The path curls round to the right, squeezing between the far end of Laguna Hija and Laguna Nieta (Granddaughter Lagoon), and continues through mixed pasture and woodland before coming to the lip of the valley of Río Fitz Roy. Here, the path descends the steep slope and, if you look to your right, you may get your first glimpses of Cerro Torre through the *lenga* forest. Emerging from the trees, the slope levels out and you link up with the path from El Chaltén to *Campamento De Agostini* (see p.488), a forty-minute walk away.

El Chaltén to Laguna Torre trail

The most scenic route from **El Chaltén to Laguna Torre** (9km; around 3hr; 250m ascent), the silty lake in which – on perfect days – the imposing peak of **Cerro Torre** (3102m) is reflected, is reached by turning off Avenida San Martín by Viento Oeste and picking up the marked path at the base of the hill. This path climbs past the eerie skeleton of a large *lenga* tree (now a monument to the dangers of cigarettes), on to some rocks used by climbers for bouldering, and then weaves through hilly country for an hour, before arriving at a viewpoint where, weather permitting, you'll catch your first proper view of Cerro Torre.

THE CERRO TORRE CONTROVERSY

Even members of the French team that first ascended Fitz Roy in 1952 thought that summiting **Cerro Torre** was an impossible task. The altitude wasn't the problem – at 3102m, it wouldn't reach even halfway up some Andean peaks. Neither was the type of rock it was made out of – crystalline igneous diorite is perfect for climbing. Rather, it was the shape and the formidable weather: a terrifying spire dropping sheer for almost 2km into glacial ice, battered by winds of up to 200km/h and temperatures so extreme that ice more than 20cm thick can form on rock faces. Not only that, but the peculiar glaciers – "mushrooms" of ice – which build up on the mountain's summit often shear off, depositing huge blocks of ice onto climbers below.

MAESTRI, EGGER AND FERRARI

The Italian alpinist **Cesare Maestri** became the first to make a serious attempt on the summit. In 1959, he and Austrian climber **Toni Egger** worked their way up the northern edge. Caught in a storm, Egger was swept off the face and killed by an avalanche. Maestri somehow made it to the bottom, and announced that he had **conquered the summit** with Egger. The world, however, demanded proof, something Maestri could not furnish – the camera, he claimed, lay entombed with Egger.

Angered by the doubters, Maestri vowed to return. This he did, in 1970, and it was clear he meant business. Among his equipment was a 150kg compressor for drilling bolts into the rock. Torre couldn't resist in the face of such a determined onslaught, and Maestri's expedition reached the summit, making very sure that photos were snapped on top. A stake had been driven through Torre's Gothic heart.

Or had it? The climbing world was riven by dispute. Were Maestri's tactics in keeping with the aesthetic code of climbing or had the use of a machine invalidated his efforts? Did this represent a true ascent? On top of this, Maestri's photos revealed that although he had reached the top of the rock, he had not climbed the ice mushroom – the icing that topped the cake.

Enter **Casimiro Ferrari**, another Italian climber. Using guile where Maestri had favoured strong-arm tactics, Ferrari sneaked up on the beast from behind, from the Hielo Continental Sur. In the space of two days, Ferrari achieved his goal, and, elatedly, his team brought down photos of them atop the summit, ice mushroom and all.

Toni Egger's body was recovered in 1975, but no camera was found with him (he is now commemorated in the name of a jagged peak alongside Cerro Torre and a simple chapel in El Chaltén). But despite the controversy at the time, the bolts drilled by Maestri were used for many years, forming the most common route to the summit.

A BITTERSWEET IRONY

Nevertheless, this irony was a bittersweet triumph for Maestri, who feels he has been cursed. In the 1990s, he reputedly voiced his hatred for the mountain, claiming he wanted it razed to the ground. History has added its own weight to those who doubt Maestri's claims. The mountain has been scaled by routes of tremendous technical difficulty by modern climbers with modern equipment, culminating in the Slovenians Silvo Karo and Janez Jeglic's ascent of the south wall in 1988. However, it wasn't until 2005 that a team of climbers managed the route that Maestri claimed he and Egger took in 1959.

The controversy reignited in January 2012 when two climbers – American Hayden Kennedy and Canadian Jason Kruk – unilaterally decided to remove many of Maestri's bolts. On their return to El Chaltén, amid much local anger, they were briefly detained by the police, who confiscated the bolts. The reaction in the mountaineering community worldwide was mixed: while some praised their actions as returning the mountain to its natural state, many others accused them of destroying a piece of climbing history.

Along the Río Fitz Roy Valley

The path subsequently levels out along the Río Fitz Roy Valley, in whose ragged stands of southern beech you're likely to come across wrens and the thorn-tailed rayadito, a diminutive foraging bird. A signposted turn-off on the right leads to Lagunas Madre e Hija (see opposite), which you'll need to return to if hiking the central circuit in clockwise fashion. This path soon starts to climb a steep, wooded hillside, before levelling out, running along the right-hand (eastern) side of the shallow lakes and continuing on to *Campamento Poincenot* (1hr 30min–2hr 15min from turn-off).

Sticking on the trail towards Laguna Torre, the path climbs to another viewpoint, before dropping down onto the valley floor – covered here in puddles that, in good weather, mirror Cerro Torre. You'll see an area that burned in 2003, apparently due to a discarded cigarette. The last section crosses a hill in the middle of the valley and a small stream before coming to blustery *Campamento De Agostini*, the closest **campsite** to the mountain for trekkers. Occupying a beautiful wooded site on the banks of the Río Fitz Roy, it also acts as the base camp for climbers and can get very busy (especially in Jan), so plan accordingly. The only good views of Cerro Torre from the campsite are from a rocky outcrop at the back of the wood, where there's one extremely exposed pitch.

Otherwise, follow the path alongside the river, which brings you after about ten minutes to the moraine at the end of **Laguna Torre**. On top of the moraine, you can gaze at the granite needles of Cerro Torre, **Aguja Egger** (2900m) and **Cerro Standhardt** (2800m). Here, too, you'll find a **cable crossing** of the river: once used by climbers to go ice-trekking on **Glaciar Torre**. Although it looks easy enough to cross without a harness, people have drowned attempting to do just that – gusts of wind can be sudden and fierce.

To Mirador Maestri

You can get closer to the mountain by walking for forty minutes along the path that runs parallel to the northern shore of Laguna Torre to the **Mirador Maestri** lookout point, passing en route an expedition hut that contains moving commemorative dedications to climbers who never quite succeeded in their attempts on the various peaks (note that this is not a recognized camping spot). The mirador provides superb views of Cerro Torre and Cerro Grande, and the incredible peak-dotted ridge that runs between them.

Río Eléctrico, Piedra del Fraile and beyond

The area to the north of Fitz Roy, just outside the national park, makes for rewarding trekking and can be linked to the Fitz Roy/Torre circuit. Although much of this is private land, you are welcome as long as you observe the same regulations stipulated by the park, and camp only in designated sites.

The start of the trek

To get to the start of the trek from **RP-23 to Piedra del Fraile** (6km; 1hr 45min–2hr 15min; 80m ascent), take a Las Lengas (see p.494) **minibus** bound for Lago del Desierto (3 daily; 15min) and get off right next to the bridge over the **Río Eléctrico**, a tempestuous river; this saves having to struggle for five to six hours against the prevailing winds that sweep down the valley from the north. The path starts to the left of the bridge, although its first section is imperilled every time the river is in spate. Soon you peel away from the river and, following the fairly inconspicuous cairns, cross the flat gravel floor of the Río Blanco valley.

On the other side of the valley, the path joins the one heading south to Laguna Piedras Blancas and *Campamento Poincenot* (see p.484). Rather than turn south, aim right of the ridge ahead, into the valley of the Río Eléctrico, where you enter an enchanting, sub-Antarctic woodland, interspersed with grassy glades. Cross a brook and fifteen minutes further on you come to a gate in a ragged fence, followed shortly by another gate in another, equally dishevelled, fence. From the second gate, head right, towards the Río Eléctrico, and follow its bank. After approximately 35 minutes' gentle walk, you emerge from the woodland to be greeted with a terrific view of **Glaciar Marconi**; Piedra del Fraile is just five minutes further on.

Piedra del Fraile

At **Piedra del Fraile**, you'll find the *Piedra del Fraile* campsite (see opposite), set alongside the swift-flowing Río Eléctrico and sheltered by a vast erratic boulder – the *piedra* of the name. The *fraile* (friar or priest) was Padre De Agostini (1883–1960), a Salesian priest who was one of Patagonia's most avid early mountaineers and explorers, and who lends his name to the campsite at Laguna Torre (see p.488). He was the first person to survey the area, and chose this site for his camp.

ACCOMMODATION   PIEDRA DEL FRAILE

Camping Piedra del Fraile Piedra del Fraile ☎ 02962 493211, ✉ cabanasricanor@hotmail.com. This scenically located, privately run campsite, right next to the river, has places to pitch your tent, plus some basic dorm rooms and a small snack bar. Camping $̶1̶5̶0̶; dorms $̶2̶5̶0̶

To Glaciar Marconi

Two worthwhile treks lead from here, though you'll be charged $300 to continue your journey on through private land: the first, from **Piedra del Fraile to Glaciar Marconi** (10km return; 5hr–6hr 30min return; 35m ascent), takes you to the foot of the glacier, fording the Río Pollone and passing through the blasted scenery on the southern shore of Lago Eléctrico. There are fine views of the northern flank of Fitz Roy, especially from the Río Pollone Valley, but be warned that the trail is unmarked once you cross the river; keep tight to the shore of Lago Eléctrico as it curves right, then continue due north past *Campamento La Playita*, following the Río Eléctrico Superior upstream to Laguna Marconi and its glacier. Glaciar Marconi itself sweeps down off the **Hielo Continental Sur** (see box, p.486), and forms the most frequently used point of access for expeditions heading onto this frigid expanse, by way of the windy **Paso Marconi** (1500m).

To Paso del Cuadrado

The second hike, from **Piedra del Fraile to the Paso del Cuadrado** (6km return; 7–9hr; 1200m ascent), involves a much more difficult climb and should only be attempted by those with comprehensive mountaineering experience. From the camp, cross the small stream on the south side, walk through a wood and strike towards the gap between two streams, to the right of the wooded hillside. The path zigzags steeply up, though eventually levels out. After one and a half to two hours, you pass an oddly shaped boulder with a tiny pool just above it and then the path peters out further up, once it reaches the scree.

From here on you must make your own course, keeping the main stream to your right. When you reach the terminal moraine of the glacier, ford the river and work your way around the right-hand side of the col (2hr–2hr 30min from the boulder). Cross the exposed area of rock on your right and then make the tiring thirty-minute climb up the snow to the pass, which is not immediately obvious but lies in the middle of the ridge. Expect a ferocious blast of wind at the top of Paso del Cuadrado (approximately 1700m), but hold onto your headgear and look out at one of the most dramatic views you're likely to come across in Patagonia. Weather permitting, you'll be able to see Fitz Roy's north face, across to the steeple of Cerro Torre, and down, across deeply crevassed glaciers, to the peaks of Aguja and Cerro Pollone, named after Padre De Agostini's home village in the Italian Alps.

Piedra del Fraile to Campamento Poincenot trail

You can head back east from **Piedra del Fraile to Campamento Poincenot** (11km; 3hr–3hr 30min; 200m ascent) to join up with the Fitz Roy/Torre loop. The path follows the Vallé Río Blanco south but can be difficult to pick up due to a number of false trails created by meandering cattle. On leaving the woods and emerging into the valley plain of the Río Blanco, head back towards RP-23 until you reach a stream (about 20min). Turn right and follow its course until you see a faint path that heads south along the tree line. After about half an hour, you re-enter the national park and eventually pick up the line of under-ambitious cairns that mark the path: follow these until you come to the confluence of the Piedras Blancas stream and Río Blanco, an area strewn with chunks of granite.

8

THE ESTANCIAS OF SANTA CRUZ

In many people's minds, Argentina is composed of a vast patchwork of immense *latifundias* presided over by their *estanciero* owners. Although this image is no longer entirely true, landowning is still deeply embedded in the national consciousness, and an opportunity to stay at an **estancia** provides an excellent glimpse into this important facet of Argentine culture. Indeed, a stay on one of these farmsteads can be a holiday destination in itself. In the sheep-farming province of Santa Cruz a group of estancia owners runs the **Estancias de Santa Cruz** (ⓦestanciasdesantacruz.com), which can make reservations at their estancias and produces an excellent booklet detailing them all, available from the offices at Suipacha 1120, Buenos Aires (ⓟ011 4325 3098), and Libertador 1215, El Calafate (ⓟ02902 492 8580). The best of their estancias are listed in the relevant sections of this book.

It's worth making a short detour right (west) up this valley, scrambling across the boulders to see the **Glaciar Piedras Blancas** tumbling into its murky lake, backed by a partial view of Fitz Roy (20–30min one way). Otherwise, ford the Piedras Blancas stream a little way up from where it meets the Río Blanco and cross the moraine dump to regain the trail. From this point, it's less than an hour's walk along the deteriorated if fairly easy path to *Campamento Poincenot* (see p.484).

RN-40 and the Cordillera

The western boundary of Argentine Patagonia and the border with Chile are formed by the southern reaches of the Cordillera de los Andes, the world's longest mountain chain. These peaks are the feature that draws most visitors here, luring them along with a ring of beautiful lakes and a national park, albeit not as famous or as breathtaking as Los Glaciares. The nationally renowned RN-40 (often simply called "La Cuarenta" – "The Forty") zigzags up this mountainside swathe of inland Patagonia; indeed, it hugs the Andes all the way from the southern tip of the mainland to the Bolivian border in the far north. Most access roads for visiting the region run west from RN-40, to the wild trekking areas around lakes Posadas and Pueyrredón and into Parque Nacional Perito Moreno. The main exceptions are the major archeological site of the Cueva de las Manos Pintadas in the canyon of **Río de las Pinturas**, just east of RN-40; and the oasis town of **Sarmiento**, a very useful stopover for anyone travelling farther up to the Lake District.

The region's scenery is predominantly dry and flat, its occasional slopes densely cloaked in southern beech woods, with a narrow fringe of scrubland separating forest from steppe. in these areas that you stand your best chance of seeing the area's outstanding **fauna**: condors, and perhaps even a puma or *huemul*. As for **flora**, the brush looks dreary and anonymous for most of the year. Some bushes liven up considerably in the spring, however, not least the thorny calafate, which blooms with a profusion of yellow flowers, and the *lengua de fuego* with its gloriously bright orange flowers like clam shells. RN-40 also passes harsh *meseta*, rocky outcrops, patches of desert and the occasional river valley, usually accompanied by boggy pasture and lined in places with willow and poplar. Here you'll find the few people who live along the route, where old traditions and an unhurried pace still reign.

ARRIVAL AND GETTING AROUND
RN-40 AND THE CORDILLERA

By bus From November 15 to April 15, Chaltén Travel (ⓟ02962 493092, ⓦchaltentravel.com) operates buses (Nov & April 3–4 weekly; Dec–March 1 daily) between El Calafate and Bariloche via El Chaltén and Perito Moreno; some services also go via Los Antiguos. Also in the summer, Taqsa/Marga (ⓦtaqsa.com.ar) runs daily buses along the

same route; the whole journey takes around thirty hours. A couple of smaller operators sometimes run services on these routes too. Timetables are notoriously prone to change, so it's worth checking out the latest information before setting off.
By car To truly appreciate the mystique of the area, you can drive yourself. RN-40 is just about passable in a normal

THE LEGENDARY RUTA 40

Argentines fondly refer to RN-40, or Ruta 40, the country's longest road, as La Cuarenta (The Forty). Stretching from Cabo Vírgenes, the southernmost point of the Argentine mainland, to northernmost Ciénaga, on the Bolivian border, it's more than just a highway. Like Route 66 in the US, the road has its own ethos – inspiring songs, books and arguments – and is as central to a visit to Argentina as a football match or a *milonga*.

By far the best way to approach Ruta 40 is to rent a vehicle and drive yourself – it's worth investing in a **4WD**, even for the paved sections. Special care is required, though, especially further south where strong crosswinds and poorly maintained gravel (*ripio*) roads make it extremely easy to flip over.

A LONG AND WINDING ROAD

La Cuarenta runs a staggering 5224km – roughly the distance from Amsterdam to Kabul. Partly to make it more attractive for tourists, the road's route has been changed over the years. Ruta 40 now starts at the ocean at Cabo Vírgenes and winds north through eleven provinces, past twenty national parks and across 24 major rivers, before reaching the altiplano. There it breaks a record: the dizzying **Abra de Acay**, at 5061m, is the highest point on a national road anywhere in the world. Although sections are relatively busy, notably around Bariloche and between Mendoza and San Juan, most of La Cuarenta runs through Argentina's magnificent open spaces, seldom more than 100km from the majestic peaks of the Andes. Many visitors are drawn by the road's rugged mystique – a result of its inaccessibility and frequently poor condition – while others are put off for the same reason. The Argentine government has pledged to pave the entire road, but hasn't completed the task yet.

SOUTH TO NORTH: THE ROUTE

Between a navy lighthouse at **Cabo Vírgenes**, La Cuarenta's starting point, and Chos Malal, in Neuquén Province, the road zigzags across the Patagonian steppe, a barren, windswept expanse thickly blanketed with snow during the winter.

North of Neuquén Province, Ruta 40 enters **El Cuyo**, Argentina's western midlands. It meanders through La Payunia, in Mendoza Province (see p.468), a land of rosy lava and ebony gorges, deep karstic caves and flamingo-flecked lagoons, before passing near **Laguna Diamante** (see p.459), an all-but-inaccessible lagoon from where you can admire the silhouette of Volcán Maipo. Further north, in La Rioja Province, the road skirts sunny valleys and hugs the **Cuesta de Miranda** (see p.385), a serpentine corniche winding through polychrome mountains.

La Cuarenta's last – and highest – stretch cuts through the historic **northwest**. Rippling hills, herds of goats and crumbling adobe houses are typical sights here. For a top-notch poncho, stop off at **Belén**, in Catamarca (see p.325) – traditional methods of weaving have been maintained in this highland village since pre-Hispanic times. You'll also want to stop in **Cachi** (see p.314), for a photo of the surrounding snow-topped sierras and valleys. Just before Ruta 40 reaches Bolivia, it is spanned by the mighty **La Polvorilla viaduct** (see p.293), a fabulous feat of engineering.

8

car – if it doesn't rain, and if you don't mind having to drive at 30km/h along some sections for fear of crunching the undercarriage. Although the road is being steadily tarmacked, significant sections are still *ripio* (gravel), notably between Tres Lagos, Bajo Caracoles and Perito Moreno. They require careful negotiating but add greatly to the sense of adventure.

Websites ⓦ turismoruta40.com.ar is a useful website, with information on the route, itineraries, accommodation and services along RN-40.

Tres Lagos to Parque Nacional Perito Moreno

The taste of things to come, the paved RN-40 heading northeastwards from the El Chaltén turning is desolate and remote: the minuscule and rather depressing settlement of **TRES LAGOS**, 35km to the north, is little more than a road junction (unpaved tracks lead off RN-40, west towards the Andes and east into the heart of the steppe) but it

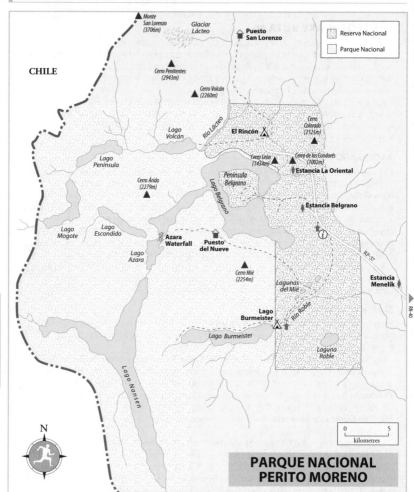

8

does have a few services for travellers, useful in emergencies: a free municipal **campsite**, shaded by cherry trees along a small stream; a couple of tyre-repair places (*gomerías*); and a supermarket.

The next 340km stretch of RN-40, between Tres Lagos and Bajo Caracoles, is the most rugged of all. High crosswinds can make driving hazardous, so always keep your speed under control and take breaks. There are virtually no fuel stations along this part of the route, and you should carry enough fuel for several hundred kilometres of motoring (invest in a jerry can or two) if you plan to make any side-trips. Journeys are now speedier thanks to the excellent tarmac section between the junction near Estancia La Verde – where you can make a detour to tiny **Gobernador Gregores** some 70km away for fuel and some basic accommodation – and **Las Horquetas**, the hamlet from which a road leads to the Parque Nacional Perito Moreno. *Estancia La Oriental* (see p.494) sells petrol and diesel; the supply is intended for guests only, but they will help out in an emergency.

ACCOMMODATION   **TRES LAGOS**

Huentru Niyeu Tres Lagos ☎02962 495 0060, ⓦturco_nazer@hotmail.com. If you need somewhere to stay, and don't fancy sleeping under canvas, try the simple

cabañas at *Huentru Niyeu*, located just beyond the municipal campsite in Tres Lagos. You can get home-cooked meals here, and have your laundry done. **$700**

Parque Nacional Perito Moreno

Extreme isolation means that, despite being one of Argentina's first national parks to be created, the **PARQUE NACIONAL PERITO MORENO** is also one of its least visited. Though replete with glorious mountains and beautiful lakes, this is not a "sightseeing" park like Nahuel Huapi or Los Glaciares. The bulk of its forested mountain scenery lies in its western two-thirds, which are reserved for **scientific study**, meaning that most of the area accessible to the public consists of arid steppe. Although visitor numbers are slowly increasing, the park still offers a solitude that few other places can match.

You can see much of the park by car in a day or two, but could equally spend much longer trekking through the starkly beautiful high pampas, past virulently colourful lakes and near the imperious snowcapped hulk of San Lorenzo – and still miss out on many of its hidden wonders. In the absence of humans, **wildlife** thrives here. Guanacos can be seen at close quarters, while the luckiest visitors may glimpse a puma (or at least its tracks) or an endangered *huemul*, of which about one hundred are thought to live in the park. Condors are plentiful, as is other **birdlife** including the Chilean flamingo, black-necked swan and the powerful black-chested buzzard eagle (*águila mora*). One of the park's most biologically interesting features is its **lakes**: the ones here have never been stocked with non-endemic species. Native fish are protected and no fishing is allowed.

The northern sector

From *Estancia La Oriental* (see p.494), a pass leads 10km on to the *guardaparque*'s house at **El Rincón**, once one of Argentina's most isolated estancias, where you can **camp**. Just before the buildings, a track branches west towards Chile. The first 3km can be covered by car, and from here it's a 5km walk to the desolate shores of **Lago Volcán**, a milky-green glacial lake. Although a pass (Paso de la Balsa) is marked on some maps, this is not a legal border crossing and you will be detained if caught.

From El Rincón, it's a stiff five- to six-hour walk to the **Puesto San Lorenzo** refuge, from where you can access the park's finest views of Monte San Lorenzo. Consult the *guardaparque* about conditions ahead before setting off. Take the winding track to the right of the house (traversable in a normal car for 5km; beyond this, you'll need a high-clearance 4WD, and even that will only get you a bit further), leaving the park's northern boundary. After one particularly tight hairpin down a small gravel scarp, you must ford two streams and pick up the track on the other side. Eventually, you reach a bluff with a steep moraine scarp, which is as far as you can get with a vehicle (9km from El Rincón).

From here, you have a fine view of the turbulent **Río Lácteo**, which you must keep on your left. The track drops down the bluff, passes a windbreak and then gives up entirely in the woods some 200m beyond. From here on, there's always a temptation to drop down onto the flat gravel bed of the Río Lácteo, but resist this and stay high, at least until you have passed the huge alluvial moraine fan that pushes the river far over to the eastern side of the valley. After this, the path drops and wends its way through the marshy grassland bordering the river valley. A little further on, the tin shack of Puesto San Lorenzo is easily visible.

With care, you can ford the Río Lácteo here. Beyond, a path leads west up the valley towards **Glaciar Lácteo** and the 2000m fortress wall of **San Lorenzo's southeast face** – if you are lucky enough, that is, to catch this notoriously temperamental mountain in one of its more benevolent moods.

8

The central sector

A kilometre or two north of the park administration building, at Estancia Belgrano, the track forks left towards **Lago Belgrano**, the most remarkable of the lakes accessible to visitors, with one of the most intensely gaudy turquoise colours anywhere in Patagonia. After 8km you reach the scrub-covered **Península Belgrano**; a leaflet is available from the park administration building for a self-guided two-hour circular trail through the *mata negra* bushes, detailing the behaviour of its graceful guanaco inhabitants. Look out for the mounds of guanaco dung at the animals' communal toilets, and the piles of bones pumas have left behind. Although it only takes three to four hours to walk to the other side, you can **camp** on the peninsula, allowing more time to take in the beauty – or worry about the predators.

A longer hike of two to three days can be made south of Lago Belgrano, accessed on a path that cuts through the Lagunas del Mié, but you must ask permission from park administration first to use the old shepherd's refuge, **Puesto del Nueve**, as a base. From here, you can visit the 10m waterfall that drains Lago Belgrano and explore the region around beautiful **Lago Azara**, where you stand a slim chance of finding footprints or traces of *huemules*, the endangered Andean deer that is the park's symbol.

Back on the main track, heading north from *Estancia Belgrano*, you reach the well-marked turn-off to *Estancia La Oriental*, which lies on the edge of a tranquil valley (see below). About 3km further north, on the other side of the valley, stands **Cerro de los Cóndores**, a cliff face stained by great white smears, indicating the presence of condors' nests. About thirty of the giant birds use the *condorera* regularly. To gain a similar perspective, you can climb nearby **Cerro León** (1434m; 4hr return), which affords excellent views of the heartland of the park.

ARRIVAL AND INFORMATION   PARQUE NACIONAL PERITO MORENO

Information The park is open daily 9am–9pm between October and April, but can be cut off by snow, sometimes for weeks on end; the weather changes moods like a spoilt child. Temperatures are bracing all year, and can drop to -25°C in winter, lower with wind chill. There is no entry fee. Note that lighting fires in the park is prohibited, and that it is strictly illegal to cross into Chile at Paso Cordoniz by Lago Nansen.

By bus/taxi Without your own transport, getting to the

park is difficult and expensive: guests at the *Estancia La Oriental* (see below) should be able to arrange a pick-up from RN-40 (around $1000 or so). A taxi from Gobernador Gregores, where there is a national park office at San Martín 882 (☎02962 491477, ✉peritomoreno @apn.gov.ar), costs around $1500–2000, though don't rely on finding one willing to go all that way.

By car The park is reached by a 90km *ripio* spur road, which joins RN-40 just west of Las Horquetas.

INFORMATION AND TOURS

Ruta-40 This travel agency, based in Bariloche (Juramento 190; ☎0294 452 3378, ⊛www.ruta-40.com), has a ten-day RN-40 tour that visits the park.

Tourist information On arrival you'll need to register at the park administration building (daily 8am–8pm), 5km

inside the park. You'll also be given a welcome talk and leaflets on the trails and wildlife (some in English); there are creative educational displays in the small museum. Apart from water, there are no facilities here.

ACCOMMODATION

There are a couple of free, basic **campsites** in great locations at Lago Burmeister and El Rincón; you must register first at the administration office.

Estancia La Oriental 7km north of the administration building (☎011 4152 6901 or ☎02962 15 407197, ⊛laorientalpatagonia.com.ar. *La Oriental* is a beautifully sited working estancia, looking out across the northern curl of Lago Belgrano. Standards of accommodation and service

are not always as high as they should be, but you're severely limited for choice in this area. You can camp, stay in a dorm or opt for a private room (rates for this last option include breakfast). Closed April–Oct. Dorms $325; doubles $2275; camping/pitch $390

Bajo Caracoles

From the Parque Nacional Perito Moreno turn-off, RN-40 swings north for around 110km across more desolate steppe – the Pampa del Asador to the west at least affords occasional glimpses of the cordillera as relief – to the tiny crossroads settlement of **BAJO CARACOLES**. This stretch of the road is currently being paved, leading to slight changes in the route. Nondescript Bajo Caracoles is only really useful for refuelling your vehicle (it's the first reliable petrol stop north of Gobernador Gregores or Tres Lagos) and grabbing a bite to eat.

Posadas

From Bajo Caracoles an unpaved road leads west to the larger village of **POSADAS**, which is home to around 300 people and has better facilities, especially in terms of accommodation, and a petrol station. It is a loosely grouped assemblage of modern houses, and is listed on some maps as **Hipólito Yrigoyen** (or even, confusingly, as Lago Posadas), but locals use the old name of Posadas.

The village can used as a base for visiting the turquoise **Lago Posadas**, and the stunning lapis lazuli **Lago Pueyrredón**, set among splendid landscapes and famed for their fishing. The lakes are separated by the narrowest of strips of land, the arrow-straight **La Península**, which looks for all the world like a man-made causeway. It was actually formed during a static phase of the last Ice Age, when an otherwise retreating glacier left an intermediate dump of moraine, now covered by sand dunes, which cut shallow Lago Posadas off from its grander neighbour. Most places of interest around the lakes are accessible only to those with their own vehicle.

Cerro de los Indios

Three kilometres south of Posadas, the low, rounded wedge of **Cerro de los Indios** lies beneath the higher scarp of the valley. Bruce Chatwin's description of this rock in *In Patagonia* is unerring: "…a lump of basalt, flecked red and green, smooth as patinated bronze and fracturing in linear slabs. The Indians had chosen the place with an unfaltering eye for the sacred."

Indigenous **rock-paintings**, some almost 10,000 years old, mark the foot of the cliff, about two-thirds of the way along the rock to the left. The well-known depiction of a "unicorn" – now thought to be a *huemul* – is rather faded; more impressive are the wonderful concentric circles of a hypnotic labyrinth design. The red blotches high up on the overhangs appear to have been the result of guanaco hunters firing up arrows tipped in pigment-stained fabric, perhaps in an ancient version of darts. However, the site's most remarkable feature is the polished shine on the rocks, which really do possess the patina and texture of antique bronze. There's also no fence screening off the engravings and paintings here, leaving the site's magical aura uncompromised.

8

ARRIVAL, DEPARTURE AND TOURS   POSADAS

By bus There are just a couple of weekly buses: one to Bajo Caracoles (every Tues; 2hr), the other to Perito Moreno (every Tues; 4hr). Note that timetables tend to fluctuate.

To Chile Five kilometres east of Posadas, the beautiful RP-41 runs north towards the Chilean border at Paso Roballos and Los Antiguos, though spring floods mean that it is usually only passable from mid-December to March.

Las Loicas (Las Lengas and Condor Andino; ☎02963 490272, ⓦlasloicas.com) offers a range of tours around Posadas and along RN-40, including trekking, horseriding, birdwatching, cycling, wild camping and abseiling.

ACCOMMODATION AND EATING

Río Tarde Casa Patagonica Las Lengas 450 ☎02963 490266, ⓦriotarde.com.ar. Run by the Richards family, who are a good source of local information, this charming little hotel is a great spot to break your journey, with comfy if compact en suites. Rates include breakfast, and lunch and dinner are available. <u>US$85</u>

Lago Posadas

Do not try to drive around the south shore of **Lago Posadas**, around 7km north of Posadas village, even though a road is marked on many maps: cars can easily get bogged down near the Río Furioso. Instead, take the route running around the north shore, which passes through a zone of blasted, bare humps, crisscrossed by lines of *duraznillo* bushes. Known as **El Quemado** (The Burnt One), it's one of the most ancient formations in Argentina, dating back 180 million years to the Jurassic Age, and there are spectacular contrasts between minerals such as green olivina sandstone and greyish-red porphyry iron oxides.

Lago Pueyrredón and the Río Oro

Ambitious engineers have somehow managed to squeeze a dirt road between the southern shore of pristinely beautiful **Lago Pueyrredón** and the hills that press up against it, without having to resort to tiresome infill projects. This precarious arrangement is compromised only by the occasional spring flood (September is the worst month). Just past the neat bridge over the **Río Oro**, a track wends its way up the mountainside and past the magnificent purple chasm of the **Garganta del Río Oro**.

Monte San Lorenzo

Further on, the road rises through the wild foothills of **Monte San Lorenzo** and towards the snow line. This is private land, and crossing the border here is illegal; climbers intending to ascend San Lorenzo from the Chilean side should cross over to Cochrane at one of the legitimate border posts further north and tackle the mountain from Padre De Agostini's base camp, owned by mountain guide Luís Soto de la Cruz. The best **maps** of the area (#4772-27 *Cerro Pico Agudo* and #4772-33 y 32 *Lago Belgrano*) are those from the Instituto Geográfico Militar in Buenos Aires (see p.52).

Cueva de las Manos Pintadas

The landscape between Bajo Caracoles and Perito Moreno best embodies most people's concept of Patagonia – sparsely populated and at times empty lands stretching to the horizon. Why most people venture to these parts at all is to see the magnificent **Cueva de las Manos Pintadas** (Cave of the Painted Hands), one of South America's finest examples of rock paintings and listed as a UNESCO World Heritage Site. It can be approached either by road along a sidetrack just north of Bajo Caracoles, or, better, by walking or riding up the canyon it overlooks, the impressive **Cañón de Río Pinturas**. From the canyon rim, it's a spectacular two-hour **walk** to the cave paintings. The path drops sharply to the flat valley bed, and continues to the right of the snaking river,

---

THE SIGNIFICANCE OF THE PAINTINGS

The earliest paintings were made by the Toldense culture and date as far back as 1100 BC, but archeologists have identified four later cultural phases, ending with depictions by early Tehuelche groups – notably geometric shapes and zigzags – from approximately 1300 AD. The significance of the paintings is much debated: whether they represented part of the rite of passage for adolescents into the adult world, and were thus part of ceremonies to strengthen familial or tribal bonds, or whether they were connected to religious ceremonies that preceded the hunt will probably never be known. Other tantalizing mysteries involve theories surrounding the large number of heavily pregnant guanacos depicted, and whether these herds were actually semi-domesticated. One thing is for certain: considering their exposed position, it is remarkable how vivid some of the colours still are – the colours were made from the berries of *calafate* bushes, earth and charcoal, with guanaco fat and urine applied to create the waterproof coating that has preserved them so well.

nestling up against rock walls and pinnacles that display the region's geological history in bands of black basalt, slabs of rust-coloured sandstone and a layer of sedimentary rocks that range in hue from chalky white to mottled ochre. Bring binoculars for viewing the finches and birds of prey that inhabit the canyon, plus food, water, a hat and sunscreen.

At the point where the course of the Río Pinturas is diverted by a vast rampart of red sandstone, you start to climb the valley side again to reach the road from Bajo Caracoles and the **entrance building** to the protected area around the paintings, where there's a modest display. Unfortunately, some parts of the site have been tarnished by tourists etching modern graffiti on the rock – hence the fence that now keeps visitors at a distance – and you can only access the cave accompanied by a *guardaparque* on a one-hour **guided walk**.

The *cueva* itself is less a cave than a series of overhangs: natural cutaways at the foot of a towering 90m cliff face overlooking the canyon below, a vantage point from which groups of Paleolithic hunter-gatherers would survey the valley floor for game. Despite the rather heavy-handed fence that now frames them, the collage of black, white, red and ochre **handprints**, mixed with gracefully flowing vignettes of guanaco hunts, still makes for an astonishing spectacle. Of the 829 handprints, most are male, and 798 are of left hands. They are all "negatives", being made by placing the hand on the rock face, and imprinting its outline by blowing pigments through a tube. Interspersed with these are human figures, as well as the outlines of puma paws and rhea prints, and creatures such as a scorpion.

ARRIVAL AND INFORMATION

By car To get to the paintings, take the turn-off just to the north of Bajo Caracoles, a rough 45km stretch of *ripio* leading to a car park, 600m from the entrance building.

By tour You can access the park on a tour from Perito Moreno (see p.498) or Posadas (see p.495).

CUEVA DE LAS MANOS PINTADAS

Information The park (ⓦ cuevadelasmanos.org) is open daily: May–Sept 9am–7pm; Oct–April 10am–6pm; the entry fee is $120. Guided walks are available May–Sept on demand, and Oct–April every hour.

ACCOMMODATION

Estancia La Cueva de las Manos 7km up a well-signed track off RN-40, 60km from Perito Moreno ☎02963 432207, ⓦ cuevadelasmanos.net. The *cueva* actually lies on land owned by the estancia, which has dorms, private rooms, and a *cabaña* sleeping up to six. There's a restaurant, and staff can organize horse rides, hikes and transport. The estancia also runs 4WD trips to the *cueva* as well as to nearby Charcamata, a similar rock-art site. Note that any visit to the paintings from the estancia side involves negotiating a steep and difficult climb down to the river valley and up again. Breakfast included. Closed May–Oct. Dorms <u>US$300</u>; doubles <u>US$100</u>; *cabaña* <u>US$160</u>

Perito Moreno and around

With around four thousand inhabitants, **PERITO MORENO** is the biggest town in this part of the world, which emphasizes just how thinly populated the region is. Lying 130km north of Bajo Caracoles, it's a typically featureless, spread-out Patagonian settlement whose main point of interest is as a base for excursions to places such as the **Cueva de las Manos Pintadas**, some 120km south. When there is enough water, black-necked swans and flamingos pass their time at the wildlife refuge in town, the **Laguna de los Cisnes** (free entry).

Some 70km south of town is Arroyo Feo ("Ugly Stream"), an area of great beauty and archeological interest, with a dramatic narrow canyon and 9000-year-old cave paintings.

ARRIVAL AND DEPARTURE

By bus Taqsa/Marga services (ⓦ taqsa.com.ar) use the bus terminal, just north of town on RP-43; from here, cross the road and walk down Av San Martín to reach the town centre in about 10min. Chaltén Travel buses (☎02962 493092, ⓦ chaltentravel.com) stop instead outside the

PERITO MORENO AND AROUND

Hotel Belgrano at the south end of San Martín.

Destinations Los Antiguos (Nov & April 3–4 weekly; Dec–March 1 daily; 1hr); Bariloche (summer 1–2 daily; 13hr); El Calafate (summer 1–2 daily; 16hr); El Chaltén (summer 1–2 daily; 13hr).

INFORMATION AND TOURS

Tourist information The tourist office is at San Martín and Gendarmería Nacional (daily 8am–8pm; ☎02963 432732).

Guanacóndor This English-speaking tour operator (Perito Moreno 1087; ☎02963 432303, ✉jarinauta@yahoo.com .ar) runs trips to the Cueva de las Manos Pintadas, the best of which includes a 3hr walk down into the spectacular canyon floor. It also offers a recommended tour to Arroyo Feo, and longer trips that take in RP-41, a scenic road that skirts striking Monte Zeballos.

Zoyen Turismo Tour operator on Perón 1008 (☎02963 432207, ⓦzoyenturismo.com.ar), a good alternative to Guanacóndor.

ACCOMMODATION AND EATING

Camping Municipal Mariano Moreno and Paseo Julio A. Roca ☎02963 432130. Travellers on a tight budget should head to the town's campsite, which lies off the shore of Laguna de los Cisnes in the southern part of Perito Moreno. As well as spots to pitch your tent, there are small, rustic *cabañas*, which are just about acceptable for a night. Camping/pitch $\underline{\$100}$; *cabañas* $\underline{\$600}$

Hotel Americano San Martín 1327 ☎02963 432074, ⓦhotelamericanoweb.com.ar. Small hotel with a collection of simply furnished rooms (with bright orange walls) and a decent restaurant – one of the better ones in town – serving Argentine standards like *milanesas*, steaks, and grilled chicken. $\underline{\$620}$

Los Antiguos

Set on the banks of deep blue Lago Buenos Aires (the second biggest in South America, after Lake Titicaca in Bolivia) and sheltering from the winds in the lee of the Andes, **LOS ANTIGUOS** is a good alternative to Perito Moreno, 60km to the east. Known as Argentina's "cherry capital", the town gets booked out in January for the Fiesta Nacional de la Cereza.

ARRIVAL AND DEPARTURE

LOS ANTIGUOS

By bus There's no bus terminal: local buses to Perito Moreno stop along the main street, Av 11 de Julio. Chaltén Travel buses to/from El Chaltén via Perito Moreno arrive at and depart from its office at Lago Buenos Aires 537 (☎0297 15 413 1836, ⓦchaltentravel.com). La Union (☎0297 491 078) runs buses across the frontier to Chile Chico.

Destinations Chile Chico (Mon–Fri 1 daily; 30min); El Chaltén (3–4 weekly; 14hr); Perito Moreno (3–4 daily; 40min).

INFORMATION AND TOURS

Tourist information The tourist office (☎02963 491261), at Av 11 de Julio 446, can recommend tour operators and local guides for Cueva de las Manos Pintadas.

Chelenco Tours Tour operator (Av 11 de Julio Este 584; ☎02963 491198, ⓦchelencotours.tur.ar) running a range of trips, including to the Cueva de las Manos Pintados.

ACCOMMODATION

Hostería Antigua Patagonia 2km east of town ☎02963 491038, ⓦantiguapatagonia.com.ar. The best place to stay in the area, this beautifully located hotel has smart rooms with views of the lake, plus a sauna, a small gym, and bikes for exploring the surrounding countryside. Breakfast included. $\underline{\$1400}$

Sarmiento

North of Perito Moreno, much of RN-40 is tarmacked. It heads northeast from Río Mayo to meet RN-26 at a junction 70km west of **SARMIENTO** (or Colonia Sarmiento), the first real town you reach if you travel up the whole RN-40 from El Calafate. Beyond RN-26 intersection, the (paved, but badly potholed) RN-40 heads northwest again, crossing some particularly bleak Patagonian pampa, towards **Tecka** and, eventually, Esquel (see p.415) in the Lake District.

A rough-and-ready but not unappealing pioneering settlement, Sarmiento can also be accessed along RN-26 from Comodoro Rivadavia, 150km to the east. Cutting through hilly steppe country covered in *duraznillo* bushes, this road provides ample evidence of the country's oilfields, with the nodding heads of hundreds of wells. In addition to agriculture, Sarmiento services a large military presence (this is border country), but tourism is relatively underdeveloped despite the vicinity of the petrified forest (see below). Over the second weekend in February, it hosts the **Festival Provincial de Doma y Folklore**, with equestrian events and folk concerts.

Museo Regional Desiderio Torres

20 de Junio • Daily 9am–7pm • $10

The excellent **Museo Regional Desiderio Torres**, in the old train station, is worth a visit for its sizeable collection of indigenous artefacts and well-explained displays of weavings by the Mapuche (see p.429) and Tehuelche (see p.448), plus dinosaur bones and other fossils. Part of the museum is given over to the town's pioneering immigrant communities.

Lago Colhué Huapi and Lago Musters

Sarmiento is irrigated by waters from the Río Senguer and the sizeable lakes it feeds, **Lago Colhué Huapi** (around 15km east of town) and **Lago Musters** (around 5km northwest of town), the latter named after a nineteenth-century English adventurer, Captain George Chaworth Musters, who put it on the map. Both lakes, shining royal blue on sunny days, are home to large numbers of birds, including flamingoes. The irrigation supports a strong farming community (keep an eye out for the early October cherry blossom or the December fruit harvest), originally founded by the Welsh, with an influx of Lithuanians and **Boers**, who fled here after the Boer War.

Bosque Petrificado Sarmiento

32km from Sarmiento; 2km from the town centre, a signposted gravel track off RN-26 leads to the site • Daily 10am–6pm • Free • Taxis from town will run you to the park and back for around $350 including 1hr 30min waiting time

The **BOSQUE PETRIFICADO SARMIENTO** is home to perfectly preserved 65-million-year-old tree trunks, randomly strewn across a near-lunar setting with a stunning purple-and-orange cliff backdrop. Formed by mineral-rich water permeating the wood over hundreds of thousands of years, effectively turning the trees into stone, the petrified forest has parallels with the Parque Nacional Bosques Petrificados de Jaramillo (see p.463), but its bands of "painted desert" soils are more striking and erosion processes are much more visible here. Traversing the 2km circuit is rather like walking around a sawmill, the ground covered by splinters of bark and rotten wood that chink underfoot – except that these woodchips are Mesozoic. The highlight is a famous and much photographed chunk of **hollow fossilized log** that looks like nature's take on a giant drainage pipe.

Take water, sunscreen and a hat; the sun can be very strong, as can the winds. There are toilets in the park, but no other services. The tourist office can put you in touch with guides.

ARRIVAL AND INFORMATION   SARMIENTO

By bus Sarmiento's main street, initially Av Regimiento de Infantería, later becoming Av San Martín, runs off RN-26 at a right angle. Buses pull into the terminal at the far end, at avenidas San Martín and 12 de Octubre.
Destinations Comodoro Rivadavia (1 daily; 2hr 30min); Esquel (1 daily; 6hr 45min).
Tourist information The tourist office at Regimiento

de infantería and Pietrobelli (Mon–Fri 8am–7pm, Sat & Sun 9am–5pm; ☎0297 489 2105, ⓦsarmientochubut .gob.ar) has a useful free map, sells trout-fishing permits (the season is Nov–April) and can provide details about visits to three local *chacras*, or market gardens (Labrador, San José and San Cayetano).

ACCOMMODATION

Camping del Búlgaro 5km northwest of town ☎0297 489 3114. Located on the shores of Lago Musters, set among a strand of poplars, *Camping del Búlgaro* is the most attractive of the town's campsites. There's a small shop selling provisions on site. $100
El Molle Hotel Boutique Gral. Roca 366 ☎0297 489

3636, ⓦelmollehotelboutique.com. Probably the smartest hotel in the town centre – though the "boutique" tag is something of an overstatement – with modern en suites featuring Ruta 40 novelties like minibars and flatscreen TVs, as well as a café-bar. Breakfast included. $920

Tierra del Fuego

SEALS IN THE BEAGLE CHANNEL

9

Tierra del Fuego

Across the Strait of Magellan from mainland Patagonia, Tierra del Fuego is a land of windswept bleakness, whose settlements seem to huddle with their backs against the elements: cold winters, cool summers, gales in the spring, frost in the autumn. Yet this remote and rugged archipelago, tucked away at the foot of South America, exercises a fascination over many travellers. Some look to follow in the footsteps of the region's famous explorers, such as Ferdinand Magellan, Charles Darwin or Bruce Chatwin. Others just want to see what it's like at the very end of the world. While it may be expensive, fast-developing and time-consuming to reach, Tierra del Fuego offers up an easily accessible national park, epic mountain scenery, diverse wildlife, a truly fascinating history, and an array of outdoor activities – from hiking and skiing to boat trips and dog-sledding. There's nowhere else quite like it.

The archipelago of Tierra del Fuego is dominated by the sum of its most developed part, **Isla Grande**, South America's biggest island. Its eastern section, roughly a third of the island, along with a few islets, belongs to Argentina – the rest is Chilean territory. The major destination for visitors is the Argentine city of **Ushuaia**, a year-round resort on the south coast. Beautifully located, backed by distinctive jagged mountains, it is *the* base for visiting the tremendous **Beagle Channel**, rich in marine wildlife, and the wild, forested peaks of the **Cordillera Darwin**. With the lakes, forests and tundra of **Parque Nacional Tierra del Fuego** just 12km to the west, and historic **Estancia Harberton** – home to descendants of Thomas Bridges, an Anglican missionary who settled here in 1871 – a short excursion from the city, you could easily spend a week or so in the area.

Lago Fagnano, and the village of **Tolhuin** at its eastern end, is the main focus of the island's central area, which is of considerably greater interest than the windswept plains and scrubby *coirón* grasslands in the north. The southeastern chunk of Isla Grande, **Península Mitre**, is one of Argentina's least accessible regions, a boggy wilderness with low scrub and next to no human habitation. To its east there lies the mysterious **Isla de los Estados**, known in English as Staten Island. It is an extremely difficult area to visit, even more so than **Antarctica**, which can be reached from Ushuaia (see box, p.515).

GETTING AROUND   **TIERRA DEL FUEGO**

Ushuaia is Tierra del Fuego's undisputed **transport hub**, with bus services to destinations throughout the region, a busy airport, and a dock served by numerous boats and ships. A car can be useful for reaching some of the more remote places.

Brief history

The earliest known human settlement in Tierra del Fuego was around 8000 BC, and a number of distinct – and sophisticated – societies (see p.524) lived here at the start of

PARQUE NACIONAL TIERRA DEL FUEGO

Highlights

❶ **Flying in to Ushuaia** The city's dramatic location – wedged between the tail end of the Andes and the Beagle Channel – makes this a landing to remember. **See p.510**

❷ **Fresh king crab** Plucked straight from the Beagle Channel, *centolla* appears on menus throughout Ushuaia, and is delicious in soups, baked in its shell or simply grilled. **See p.513**

❸ **Wildlife in the Beagle Channel** Spot albatrosses and sea lions, terns and whales as you brave the elements on a boat trip through this stunningly beautiful, mountain-fringed waterway. **See p.514**

❹ **Parque Nacional Tierra del Fuego** Parakeets and hummingbirds are some of the surprising inhabitants of this national park, which spans 630 square kilometres of mountains, lakes, forests and tundra. **See p.515**

❺ **Estancia Harberton** Get a unique insight into the life of some of the earliest European settlers – and their interactions with the local indigenous communities – at Estancia Harberton. **See p.519**

HIGHLIGHTS ARE MARKED ON THE MAP ON PP.504–505

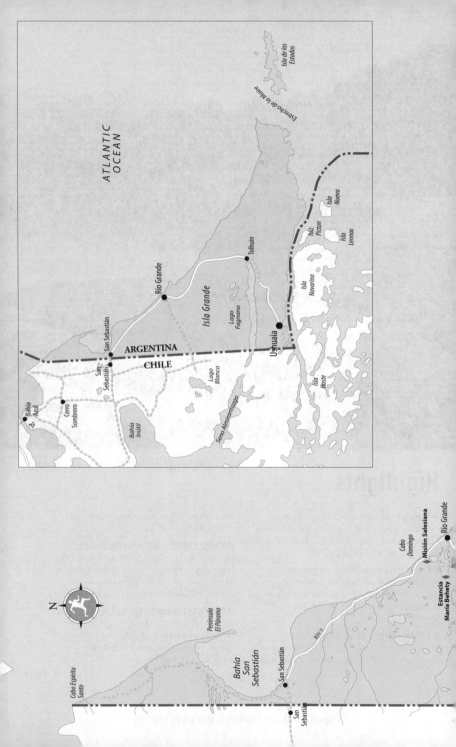

ATLANTIC
OCEAN

Isla de los Estados

Estrecho de la Maire

Río Grande

Tolhuin

Isla Grande

Lago Fagnano

Isla Nueva

Isla Picton

Isla Lennox

Ushuaia

ARGENTINA

CHILE

San Sebastián

San Sebastián

Lago Blanco

Isla Navarino

Isla Hoste

Bahía Azul

Cerro Sombrero

Lago Blanco

Bahía Inútil

Seno Almirantazgo

N

Cabo Espíritu Santo

Península El Páramo

Bahía San Sebastián

San Sebastián

San Sebastián

Cabo Domingo

Misión Salesiana

Río Grande

RN3

Estancia María Behety

TIERRA DEL FUEGO

ATLANTIC OCEAN

HIGHLIGHTS
1 Flying in to Ushuaia
2 Fresh king crab
3 Wildlife in the Beagle Channel
4 Parque Nacional Tierra del Fuego
5 Estancia Harberton

Estrecho de la Maire

Cabo San Diego
Bahía Thetis
Bahía Buen Suceso
Cabo Buen Suceso

Estancia Policarpo

Bahía Policarpo

Península Mitre

Puerto Español

Río Leticia

Cabo San Pablo

Estancia María Luisa
Río Irigoyen

Río Malenguena

Estancia Moat

Cabo San Pío

Isla Nueva

Río Ladrillero

Río San Pablo

Río Claro

Río Turbio

Río Moat

Isla Lennox

Isla Picton

RCA

Río Ewan Sur

Tolhuin

Río Cambaceres

ARGENTINA
CHILE

Isla Observatorio

Estancia Viamonte

Río Fuego

Estancia Rivadavia

RCH

Lago Chepelmuth

Río Ewan Norte

Estancia José Menéndez

RCF

Lago Yehuin

Río Indio

RCH

SIERRA LUCAS BRIDGES

Estancia Harberton

Isla Martillo

Isla Gable

Isla Navarino

RCB

RCE

TIERRA DEL FUEGO

Río Claro

Lago Fagnano

Lago Escondido

Paso Garibaldi

Río Lasifashaj

RC1

Puerto Almanza

Puerto Williams

RCD

SIERRA INJU-GOIYIN

Cerro Alvear (1425m)

Monte Olivia (1318m)

Beagle Channel

Radman

Glaciar Martial

Río Olivia

2 1

3

Ushuaia

PARQUE NACIONAL TIERRA DEL FUEGO

4

Lapataia

Lago Roca

Canal Murray

Isla Hoste

0   50 kilometres

9

WHEN TO VISIT

Most visitors arrive during the summer (Dec–Feb), when Ushuaia can get very busy. The best **time to visit** is between late March and the end of April, with the spectacular autumnal colours of the *Nothofagus* southern beech. Springtime (Oct to mid-Nov) is also beautiful, if rather windy. For **winter sports**, head for Ushuaia between June and August; the area is good for cross-country skiing, though the downhill facilities are best suited to beginners and intermediates. The **climate** is generally not as severe as you may expect, and temperatures rarely reach the extremes of mainland continental areas of Patagonia, though be prepared for blizzards and icy winds at any time of year.

the 1500s. In 1520, **Ferdinand Magellan**, in his attempt to be first to circumnavigate the globe, sailed through the strait. which was later named after him and saw clouds of smoke rising from numerous fires lit by the indigenous Selk'nam along the coast of Isla Grande. He called the land Tierra del Humo (Land of Smoke); it was the king of Spain who thought Tierra del Fuego (Land of Fire) would be more poetic. Early contact between indigenous groups and other **European explorers** was sporadic from then on, but this changed dramatically in the latter half of the nineteenth century, with tragic results. When Robert FitzRoy came here in the *Beagle* in the 1830s, an estimated three to four thousand Selk'nam and Mannekenk were living in Isla Grande, with some three thousand each of Yámana and Kawéskar in the entire southern archipelago. By the 1930s all four groups were virtually extinct, largely due to introduced diseases such as measles, and aggression from settlers.

Missionaries and sheep farmers

White settlement came to Tierra del Fuego in three phases. Anglican **missionaries** began to catechize the Yámana in the south, and Thomas Bridges established the first permanent mission on Ushuaia Bay in 1871. From the late 1880s, the Italian Roman Catholic Salesian Order began a similar process to the north of the Fuegian Andes. From the mid-1890s came a new colonizing impetus: the inauspicious-looking northern plains proved to be ideal **sheep-farming** territory, and vast *latifundias* (estates) sprang up. Croat, Scottish, Basque, Italian and Galician immigrants, along with Chileans, arrived to work on the estancias and build up their own landholdings.

Border disputes

The international border, as elsewhere along the Argentina–Chile boundary, has been a contentious issue over the years. Frontier disputes at the end of the nineteenth century required the arbitration of Great Britain, who in 1902 awarded Argentina the eastern section of Tierra del Fuego; land squabbles were still going on over eighty years later, the two countries almost coming to war in 1984 over three islands in the Beagle Channel. This time Pope John Paul II had to intervene, and gave the islands to Chile. A cordial peace has reigned since. In 1991, the Argentine sector gained full provincial status and is known as the **Provincia de Tierra del Fuego, Antártida e Islas del Atlántico Sur**. Its jurisdiction is seen to extend over all southern territories, including the Islas Malvinas/Falklands Islands (see box, p.544), which lie 550km off the coast, and the Argentine segment of Antarctica.

Tierra del Fuego today

Tierra del Fuego's **economy** depends on the production of petroleum and the natural gas, fisheries, forestry and technological industries, this last attracted by the area's status as a duty-free zone. Tourism, centred on Ushuaia, also plays a major role, and continues to expand. Luxury items are comparatively inexpensive (for Argentina), but basic items such as food cost much more than in other parts of the country.

Ushuaia and around 9

USHUAIA, the provincial capital and tourism hub for the whole of Tierra del Fuego, lies in the far south of Isla Grande. Dramatically situated between the mountains – among them **Cerro Martial** and **Monte Olivia** – and the sea, the city tumbles, rather chaotically, down the hillside to the encircling arm of land that protects its bay from the southwesterly winds and occasional thrashing storms of the icy **Beagle Channel**. Ushuaia is primarily a convenient base for exploring the rugged beauty of the lands that border the channel, a historically important sea passage, but be warned that it exploits tourism to the full – prices vary between high and astronomical.

Puerto Williams lies just across the channel, on the southern (Chilean) side of the strait, and there are other trips as well: to historic **Estancia Harberton** and its small penguin colony, and to nearby **Parque Nacional Tierra del Fuego**. In winter, there's decent skiing in the **Sierra Alvear** region north of town; in warmer seasons, it's also good for **trekking**.

Brief history

In 1869, Reverend Waite Stirling became Tierra del Fuego's first white settler when he founded his **Anglican mission** among the Yámana here; the city takes its name from the Yámana tongue, and means something akin to "bay that stretches towards the west". Stirling stayed for six months, before being recalled to the Islas Malvinas/Falklands Islands to be appointed Anglican bishop for South America. Thomas Bridges, his assistant, took over the mission in 1871, after which Ushuaia began to figure on mariners' charts as a place of refuge in the event of shipwreck. Bridges went on to found the first estancia in Tierra del Fuego (see p.523). A modest **monument** to the achievements of the early missionaries can be found where the first mission stood, on the south side of Ushuaia Bay.

The penal colony

In 1884, Commodore Augusto Lasserre raised the Argentine flag over Ushuaia for the first time, formally incorporating the area into the Argentine Republic. From 1896, in order to consolidate its sovereignty and open up the region to wider colonization, the Argentine state established a **penal colony** here. Forced convict labour was used for developing the settlement's infrastructure and for logging the local forests to build the town, but the prison had a reputation as the "Siberia of Argentina" and Perón closed it in 1947.

Ushuaia today

Nowadays, Ushuaia has a quite different reputation: the most populous, and popular, city in Tierra del Fuego, it depends largely on its thriving **tourist** industry, capitalizing on the beauty of its natural setting. You'll soon catch on that this is the world's most southerly resort, allowing you to amass claims to fame galore – golf on the world's most southerly course, a ride on the world's most southerly train, and so on. Ushuaia has plenty of sites worthy of a visit on their own merits, but unfortunately tourism has been allowed to develop with scant regard for the unique character of the town, and has changed it almost beyond recognition. At certain moments you can still get a sense of the otherworldliness that used to make Ushuaia special, but if you are coming expecting a Chatwin-esque frontier town, you will be disappointed.

Antigua Casa de Gobierno

Maipú 465 • Mon–Fri 10am–7pm, Sat & Sun 2–8pm • $130 (ticket also valid for Museo del Fin del Mundo) • Tours (Spanish) Mon–Fri 12.30pm & 5pm, Sat & Sun 5pm; 45min • Free • ☏ 02901 421863

The best place to start exploring Ushuaia is down by the pier, the **Muelle Turístico** (Tourist Dock), where an **obelisk** commemorates Augusto Lasserre's ceremony to assert Argentine sovereignty in this part of the world. Overlooking the sea from the other side

9

USHUAIA

Museo Marítimo &
Museo del Presidio

Banco de
la Nación

Museo del
Fin del Mundo

Museo
Yámana

Banco
Tierra del
Fuego

Main
Tourist
Office

Oficina
Antártica

Piratour

Trés Marías

Ushuaia Boating

MUELLE
TURÍSTICO

Antigua
Casa
Gobierno

Bus Sur

LADE

Canal &
Nature
Fun

Rumbo
Sur

Tolkar

Tagsa

Antarpply

Aerolíneas
Argentinas

Montiel

Buses
Pacheco

Lider

National
Park Office

PLAZA ISLAS
MALVINAS

ACCOMMODATION

Alto Andino	7
Antarctica Hostel	5
Arakur	3
B&B Galeazzi-Basily	1
B&B Nahuel	4
Los Cauquenes	11
Cruz del Sur	6
Cumbres del Martial	13
Hotel Austral	8
Martin Fierro B&B	9
Los Nires	12
Posada del Fin del Mundo	2
La Posta	15
Tierra de Leyendas	14
Yakush	10

● **EATING**

La Cabaña	8
Chez Manu	9
Kalma Restó	3
Kaupé	1
Ramos Generales	6
Tante Sara	2/5
Tierra de Leyendas	10
El Turco	7
El Viejo Marino	4

■ **DRINKING**

Bodegón Fueguino	4
Dublin	3
Küar	1/2

■ **SHOPPING**

Boutique del Libro	1
Renata Rafalak	2

0   200
metres

1 (2km)

2 (250m)

3 (3.5km)

1 (300m)

1 (500m), 6, 9, 11 & 12 ▶ Antigua Casa Beban (450m) ▶ Laundry (500m), 6, 9, 11 & 12 ▶ (600m), Chilean consulate (700m), Aero Club Ushuaia (1km), 13, 14, 15, 10 (1.5km) & Airport (4km)

Centro Hípico (3km) ▼

of the street is the late nineteenth-century **Antigua Casa de Gobierno**, originally the governor's house before being used by the local government and then the police. It has been restored to reflect its original use so you get an idea of how the wealthy would have lived in Ushuaia's early years.

Museo del Fin del Mundo

Maipú and Rivadavia • Mon–Fri 10am–7pm, Sat & Sun 2–8pm • $130 (ticket also valid for Antigua Casa de Gobierno) • Tours (Spanish) Mon–Fri 11am & 3.30pm, Sat & Sun 3.30pm; 45min • Free • ☎ 02901 421863

The worthwhile **Museo del Fin del Mundo**, a five-minute walk from the Antigua Casa de Gobierno, has exhibits on the region's history and wildlife, including the polychrome figurehead of the *Duchess of Albany*, an English ship wrecked on the eastern end of the island in 1883, and a rare example of a Selk'nam–Spanish dictionary.

Museo Marítimo y Presidio

Yaganes and Gob. Paz • Daily: April–Nov 10am–8pm, Dec–March 9am–8pm • $200 • Tours (Spanish) April–Nov 11.30am & 6.30pm, Dec–March 11.30am, 4.30pm & 6.30pm; 1–2hr • Free • ☎ 02901 437481, ⊛ museomaritimo.com

Ushuaia's former prison is now the must-visit **Museo Marítimo y Presidio**, and houses a motley collection of exhibits, including meticulous scale-models of famous **ships** from the island's history in the maritime section as you first enter. The prison building itself, though, is the main draw, an example of the panopticon style popularized by English philosopher Jeremy Bentham, its wings radiating out like spokes from a half-wheel, most of which have now been opened to the public.

The cells in wing four are complete with gory details of the notorious criminals who occupied them, and details of prison life, with informative panels in Spanish and English. The most celebrated prisoner was early twentieth-century anarchist Simón Radowitzsky, whose miserable stay and subsequent brief escape in 1918 are recounted by Bruce Chatwin in *In Patagonia*.

Upstairs, fairly dry displays tell something of Antarctica and the history of its exploration, as well as prisons around the world. Wing three has been given over to an art museum and a gift shop, while wing two contains an art gallery with regularly changing exhibitions.

Finally, wing one, which has not been restored and contains no exhibits at all, is perhaps the most interesting – the unheated and bare cells with peeling walls are quite spooky, and give something of an idea of what it must have been like to have been locked up or working here.

WINTER SPORTS AT THE END OF THE WORLD

If you want to **ski** or **snowboard**, you'll need to visit between late May and early September – June to August are the most reliable months. Most runs are for beginners and intermediates, but several companies, such as Gotama Expediciones (☎02901 15 605301, ⊛gotama -expediciones.com), offer more advanced back-country skiing. Equipment rental is reasonable and there are a couple of downhill (*esqui alpino*) pistes close to Ushuaia: the small Club Andino, 3km from town, and the more impressive one up by Glaciar Martial, 7km away.

Better runs are to be had, however, in the Sierra Alvear, the resorts of which are accessed from RN-3. These include the modern Cerro Castor centre (27km from Ushuaia; ☎02901 499301, ⊛cerrocastor.com), with 15km of pistes in runs up to 2km long, including a few black ones. The Sierra Alvear is also an excellent area for **cross-country** skiing (*esqui de fondo* or *esqui nórdico*). In addition, there are several winter-sports centres (*centros invernales*) along the **Valle Tierra Mayor** where you can try out snowmobiles, snowshoes, ice-skating and dog-sledding (*trineos de perros*), including Valle de Lobos and Nunatak (see p.519). Bear in mind that winter this far south entails short days and is bitterly cold.

9

Museo Yámana

Rivadavia 56 • Daily: summer 10am–8pm; winter noon–7pm; generally closed July & Aug • $110 • ☏ 02901 422874

The **Museo Yámana** is a charming little museum that charts the arrival of pre-Columbian and European settlers in the archipelago. Beautiful dioramas give an insight into indigenous habitats, culture and way of life, and they are aided by informative descriptions (in both Spanish and English). However, the displays go rather easy on the destructive role played by European colonists.

Antigua Casa Bebán

Maipú and Plüschow • Mon–Fri 10am–8pm • Free

Southwest of the centre, the **Antigua Casa Bebán** is a pavilion-style building with a steep roof and ornamental gabling prefabricated in Sweden in 1913. It hosts exhibitions of photos and artwork, as well as occasional films, and is the venue for the **Ushuaia Jazz Festival** (☸facebook.com/JazzAlFin) every November.

Glaciar Martial

7km above town at the end of Luis Martial • Chairlift daily: Nov–March 9.30am–4.45pm; June–Oct 10am–4.45pm • $70 • A taxi from the centre costs around $100

For first-rate Beagle Channel views, head up to the hanging (and fast receding) **Glaciar Martial**. A chairlift runs from beside the *Cumbres del Martial* hotel, which has a great tearoom (see p.513). During the winter, Glaciar Martial offers the closest decent skiing to Ushuaia (see box, p.509). There's also a zip line.

ARRIVAL AND DEPARTURE

USHUAIA AND AROUND

By plane The international airport, Malvinas Argentinas, is 4km southwest of town (☸aeropuertoushuaia.com). There's no public transport; a taxi to the centre costs around $100. There's a $28 departure tax on domestic flights and a US$20 one on international services; many flights include this in the ticket price. The Aerolíneas Argentinas office is at Maipú and 9 de Julio (☏02901 436338, ☸aerolineas.com.ar), and LADE is at Av San Martín 542 (☏02901 421123, ☸lade.com.ar).
Destinations Buenos Aires (3–8 daily; 3hr 30min); El Calafate (2–3 daily; 1hr 25min); Río Gallegos (2 weekly; 1hr 5min); and Trelew (6 weekly; 2hr 10min).

By bus There's no single bus terminal; buses depart from their respective company offices. Buses Pacheco (Av San Martín 1267; ☏02901 437073, ☸busespacheco.com) runs buses to Punta Arenas (Chile) via Río Grande and Tolhuin. Bus Sur (Av San Martín 409; ☏02901 430727, ☸bus-sur.cl) has services to Punta Arenas and Puerto Natales (Chile). Tecni Austral also has services to Punta Arenas and Río Gallegos; book through Tolkar (Roca 157; ☏02901 431408, ☸tolkarturismo.com.ar).

Lider (Gob. Paz 921; ☏02901 436421, ☸lidertdf.com.ar) has buses to Río Grande via Tolhuin. Montiel (Gob. Paz 605; ☏02901 421366) has services to Tolhuin and Río Grande. Taqsa (Godoy 41; ☏02901 435453, ☸taqsa.com.ar) has services to Río Gallegos. These timetables are for the Nov–March period; out of season, services are reduced drastically.
Destinations Puerto Natales (4 weekly; 15hr); Punta Arenas (1–3 daily; 12hr); Río Gallegos (2–3 daily; 13hr); Río Grande (every 30min–1hr 30min; 3hr 30min); Tolhuin (every 30min–1hr 30min; 1hr 30min).

By car Avis (☏02901 433323, ☸avis.com) and Hertz (☏02901 432429, ☸hertz.com) have offices at the airport. Most companies do not permit you to take your rental car out of Argentina. Roads are fairly reliable Oct to early May; outside this period, carry snow chains and drive with caution.

By boat Cruceros Australis (☏011 5199 6697, ☸australis.com) operates luxury, three- to four-night cruises (from US$1895/person in high season) between Ushuaia and Punta Arenas.

INFORMATION AND TOURS

Tourist information The tourist office is opposite the Muelle Turístico (☏02901 437666, ☸turismoushuaia.com; daily 9am–6pm). There's also a smaller branch at the airport (opens to meet incoming flights).
Trekking and climbing information Serious trekkers and climbers should contact the Club

Andino Ushuaia, at Leandro N. Alem 2873 (Mon–Fri; 10am–12.30pm & 3–8.30pm, ☏02901 442335, ☸clubandinoushuaia.com.ar), which can advise on longer treks outside the normally visited areas of the Parque Nacional Tierra del Fuego and put you in touch with qualified guides. Register here or at the

FROM TOP USHUAIA (P.507); PENGUINS ON ISLA MARTILLO (P.521) >

9

tourist office before embarking on any trek or climb. **Tours** Canal Fun & Nature, Roca 136 (☏ 02901 435777, ⓦ canalfun.com), and Rumbo Sur, Av San Martín 350

(☏ 02901 421139, ⓦ rumbosur.com.ar), offer a range of tours and day-trips, from kayaking and beaver-spotting to horseriding and dog-sledding.

ACCOMMODATION

Ushuaia has a wide range of **hotels**, **guesthouses** and **hostels**, many of which are clustered along the first four streets parallel to the bay. Nonetheless, most get booked up in the height of summer, and all are expensive. The most attractive options tend to be up the mountainside on the road to Glaciar Martial, west towards the national park, or on the northeastern outskirts; some of these have shuttle buses into the centre. Rates for all include breakfast. Note that the Argentine peso is notoriously prone to inflation, which has a knock-on effect on hotel rates (see p.45).

HOSTELS

Antarctica Hostel Antártida Argentina 270 ☏ 02901 435774, ⓦ antarcticahostel.com. One of Ushuaia's best hostels, with a sociable atmosphere, sunny lounge, communal kitchen, coin-operated washing machines, and lively bar. The simple upstairs six-bed dorms are a bit of a hike from the downstairs bathrooms, though. There are also a few (slightly overpriced) private rooms, with shared bathrooms. Dorms $300; doubles $1000

Cruz del Sur Gob. Deloqui 242 ☏ 02901 434099, ⓦ xdelsur.com.ar. A reliable if rather unexciting hostel with a well-equipped kitchen, relaxed lounge area and small library. The four-, six- and eight-bed dorms here are warm and clean, but rather compact. Dorms $250

La Posta Perón Sur 864 ☏ 02901 444650, ⓦ lapostahostel .com.ar. Although it's a 20min walk from the city centre, this hostel is an excellent choice; the four-, six- and eight-bed dorms are well maintained, and there are two kitchens, a laundry room and helpful staff. It also has private rooms with shared bathrooms, as well as self-contained apartments ($2300) sleeping up to six. Dorms $370; doubles $1115

Yakush Piedrabuena 118 ☏ 02901 435807, ⓦ hostel yakush.com. High-ceilinged hostel with a central location and a couple of good communal areas – an attic lounge room and a back yard with panoramic views. As well as the four- and six-bed dorms there are several private rooms. Dorms $350; doubles $900

B&BS AND HOTELS

Alto Andino Gob. Paz 868 ☏ 02901 430920, ⓦ altoandinohotel.com. A swish boutique hotel with a mix of contemporary suites (some with jacuzzis) and three-bed apartments (US$250) with kitchenettes; both have plasma-screen TVs. There's a bar with wraparound windows affording great views of the Beagle Channel and Glaciar Martial. Suites $3400

★**Arakur** Cerro Alarkén 1 ☏ 02901 442900, ⓦ arakur .com. Atop a 250m hill northeast of the centre, and backing onto a private nature reserve, *Arakur* is literally and figuratively the top hotel in town. The impeccably designed, spacious en suites have panoramic windows and high-tech features like automatic temperature adjustments and button-operated curtains. Facilities include a gym, games room, quality

restaurant and wonderful heated pool, with indoor and outdoor sections; the latter has superlative views. Free hourly shuttle buses run to and from the city centre (10min). $4150

B&B Galeazzi-Basily Gob. Valdez 323 ☏ 02901 423213, ⓦ avesdelsur.com.ar. Welcoming B&B with just two spick-and-span doubles sharing a spotless bathroom; guests have access to the kitchen and a lounge with a TV. The owners also rent out *cabañas* (each with private bathrooms and kitchenettes) sleeping up to four people. Doubles $1250; *cabañas* $2210

B&B Nahuel 25 de Mayo 440 ☏ 02901 423068. A bright green exterior makes this B&B easy to spot; inside are homely, rather frilly rooms (one of which has pink walls you'll either love or hate) with shared or private bathrooms. There's also a small lounge with a TV. $1450

Los Cauquenes De la Ermita 3462, 7km southwest of the city centre, towards the national park ☏ 02901 441300, ⓦ loscauquenes.com. A wood-framed luxury resort at the far edge of Ushuaia, right by the Beagle Channel. The classy channel-facing rooms (the cheaper options face the mountains) are so close that the sound of the waves lulls you to sleep. Entry to the spa, with its gorgeous indoor/outdoor pool and hot tub, is included in the rates. $4550

Cumbres del Martial Luis Martial 3560 ☏ 02901 424779, ⓦ cumbresdelmartial.com.ar. Situated by the glacier chairlift, this excellent hotel boasts a fabulous position, which affords amazing views of the city and the Beagle Channel. Choose between tasteful rooms and luxurious split-level *cabañas* – the latter have their own private jacuzzis, and are good for families. There's also a spa, a restaurant and a teahouse (see opposite). Doubles $5500; *cabañas* $7900

★**Hotel Austral** 9 de Julio 250 ☏ 02901 422223, ⓦ hotel-austral.com.ar. One of the better mid-range options in a town that is painfully short of them, *Hotel Austral* has a conveniently central location, very comfortable en-suite rooms with bright decor, queen-sized beds and TVs, and friendly service. Book well in advance. $1360

Martin Fierro B&B 9 de Julio 175 ☏ 02901 430525, ⓦ martinfierrobyb.com.ar. Centrally located, economically priced guesthouse, with a selection of comfy rooms – some with private bathrooms, and a few with kitchenettes – and a charming host, a font of local knowledge. A good choice all round. $1400

Los Ñires Av de los Ñires 3040 ☎02901 445173, ⓦlos nireshotel.com.ar. Located in the peaceful southwestern outskirts of town, this is a quality establishment. The en suites are cosy and have large windows that provide lots of light and views over the mountains or the channel. There's a decent restaurant and free shuttle buses into the centre, 5km away. __$3100__

Posada del Fin del Mundo Rivadavia and Gob. Valdez ☎02901 435062, ⓦposadafindelmundo.com.ar. Homely rooms (all with private bathrooms, flowery curtains, and TVs), good views, and a friendly welcome greet you at this guesthouse, a 10min walk uphill from the city centre. __$1500__

★ **Tierra de Leyendas** Tierra de Vientos 2448 ☎02901 443565, ⓦtierradeleyendas.com.ar. Located in a peaceful neighbourhood a 10min taxi ride from the city centre, and run by a charming couple, this wonderful boutique hotel is one of the best places to stay in Tierra del Fuego. All the en suites are immaculately designed, with huge windows to make the most of the stunning views. The food – at breakfast and in the restaurant (see below) – is outstanding, as is the service. __$3200__

EATING

The city centre has plenty of places to **eat** or grab a coffee, but many are tourist traps. You'll get better-quality food at lower prices – and, often as not, breathtaking views into the bargain – if you move around a bit. The quality of cuisine in Ushuaia is generally pretty high and there are several places where you can splash out on a memorable meal and sample the local gastronomic pride, *centolla* (see box below). **Prices** are high; those on a tight budget should consider self-catering.

La Cabaña Luis Martial 3560 ☎02901 424779, ⓦlacabania.com.ar. Part of the *Cumbres del Martial* hotel (see opposite), this flowery *casa de té* serves up an inviting array of cakes (including apricot tart and chocolate mousse cake; from $50), plus sandwiches, main meals such as lentil and sausage stew, and fondue. Daily 10am–11.30pm.

Chez Manu Luis Martial 2135 ☎02901 432253, ⓦchezmanu.com. Stunning panoramic views from huge windows and consistently good French cuisine that takes advantage of local produce – *centolla*, of course, plus other seafood, fish and melt-in-the-mouth lamb – ensure this continues to be one of Ushuaia's most sought-after dining spots. Tues–Sun noon–3pm & 8pm–midnight.

Kalma Restó Antártida Argentina 57 ☎02901 425786, ⓦkalmaresto.com.ar. Some of the most distinctive – and delicious – food in Ushuaia is served at this cool little joint. The inventive menu (mains $210–390) features dishes like a Tierra del Fuego-inspired paella, octopus ceviche, and a deconstructed chocolate tart. Mon–Fri noon–2pm & 7–11pm, Sat 7–11pm.

★ **Kaupé** Roca 470 ☎02901 422704, ⓦkaupe.com. ar. *Kaupé*'s service is friendly, the food delicious and the decor unpretentious, in what is just a family home with a fabulous view (the tables are packed in together). Seafood is the star; try the *centolla* in a mustard, cayenne and cream sauce. Reservations essential in high season. Mains $220–320. Mon–Sat noon–3pm & 8.30–11.30pm.

Ramos Generales Maipú 749 ☎02901 424317, ⓦramos generalesush.com.ar. Atmospheric bar-café-bakery decked out with an eclectic array of knick-knacks including model ships, old lamps, typewriters, sewing machines, musical instruments and toys. As well as good cakes, sandwiches and salads ($78–145), *picadas*, and main meals ($190–250), there's a strong wine and beer list. Daily 9am–midnight.

Tante Sara Av San Martín 175 ☎02901 433710, ⓦtantesara.com. Popular *confitería* and *panadería* which does a fine line in meal-sized sandwiches, wraps, burgers and salads ($145–206), as well as decent coffee and cakes, though prices are a bit steep. There's another branch on the same road (Av San Martín 701) which stays open until 1/2am. Mon–Thurs & Sun 8am–8.30pm, Fri & Sat 8am–9pm.

Tierra de Leyendas Tierra de Vientos 2448 ☎02901 443565, ⓦtierradeleyendas.com.ar. The intimate restaurant of this excellent hotel (see opposite) is well worth a visit for expertly prepared and presented dishes (mains $225–295), like lamb kebabs in a malbec reduction. Book a table in advance; you also have to let them know the day before if you want to sample one of the *centolla* dishes. Mon–Thurs & Sat 7.30–9pm.

El Turco Av San Martín 1410 ☎02901 424711. If you overlook the dubious cartoon of a Turkish man on the

THE KING OF THE CRUSTACEANS

A fixture on Tierra del Fuego menus, the **centolla** (king crab) has spindly legs that can measure over a metre from tip to tip, but the meat comes from the body, with an average individual yielding some 300g. The less savoury practice of catching them with traps baited with dolphin or penguin meat has been all but stamped out by the imposition of hefty fines by both Chilean and Argentine authorities, but despite controls on the size of crabs that can be caught, they are still subject to rampant overfishing. Tinned king crab is served off-season (late Oct to Dec), but is bland and not worth the prices charged; frozen *centolla* is only slightly better, so make sure it is fresh.

9

window, this low-key restaurant is good choice for a filling meal at reasonable (for Ushuaia) prices. The pizzas, *milanesas*, pastas and steaks (mains from $95) are nothing special, but won't break the bank. Mon–Sat noon–3pm & 8pm–midnight.

El Viejo Marino Maipú 227 ☎02901 15 418000. Owned by a fisherman who supplies many of the city's chefs, and with a tank of live *centollas* prominently displayed in the window, this is one of the more economical fish and seafood restaurants in town (mains $170–290). Try the crab empanadas, the seafood pasta, or the *merluza negra* (black hake). Daily 11am–2.50pm & 7–10.50pm.

DRINKING

Bodegón Fueguino Av San Martín 895 ☎02901 431972, ⓦtierradehumos.com/bodegon. An appealing restaurant-bar, whose sheepskin-covered benches get packed with travellers (and a few locals) enjoying a locally brewed beer, *picada*, or well-prepared meal; mains ($140–255) include peppered lamb and grilled salmon. Tues–Sun 12.30–3pm & 8pm–midnight.

Dublín 9 de Julio 168 ☎02901 430744. This green-walled, red-roofed pub is good for a beer (from $40), with a buzzing atmosphere and occasional live music. Apart from the Guinness posters, however, there isn't much in the way of Hibernian trappings. Daily 7pm–3/4am.

★**Küar** Perito Moreno 2232 ☎02901 437396, ⓦkuaronline.com. Set in an attractive stone-and-timber building right on the seafront, this youthful bar-restaurant has stupendous views and a blazing fire, as well as heaped *picadas* (from $280), snacks, main meals, and a wide range of beers (from $40) and wine (glasses from $40). It has another branch as well, less scenically located at Av San Martín 471. Mon–Fri 12.30–3pm & 6pm–late, Sat & Sun 6pm–late.

SHOPPING

Boutique del Libro Av San Martín 1120 ☎02901 424750, ⓦboutiquedellibro.com.ar. This outpost of the nationwide chain is the best bookshop in Ushuaia, with a selection of English-language books on Tierra del Fuego and Patagonia, plus a few novels. Mon–Sat 10am–1pm & 3.30–8.30pm.

Renata Rafalak Piedrabuenos 51 ☎02901 437254. This shop – there's no sign, so it's easy to miss – sells some of the finest crafts in the region; specialities include reproductions of Selk'nam and Yámana masks. Mon–Sat 10am–1pm & 3–5pm.

DIRECTORY

Banks and exchange Banco Tierra del Fuego, Av San Martín and Roca; Banco de la Nación, Av San Martín 190. There are also *casas de cambio* on San Martín.

Consulate Chile, Jainén 50 (Mon–Fri 9am–1pm; ☎02901 430909, ⓦchile.gob.cl/ushuaia/en).

Hospital Hospital Regional, Maipú and 12 de Octubre (☎02901 441000; emergencies ☎107).

Laundry Lavadero Qualis, Güiraldes 568 (Mon–Sat 9am–8pm; ☎02901 421996).

Police Deloqui 492 (☎02901 421773; emergencies ☎101).

Post office Av San Martín and Godoy.

Beagle Channel

No trip to Ushuaia is complete without a voyage on the legendary **Beagle Channel**, the majestic, mountain-fringed sea passage south of the city. Most **boat excursions** start and finish in Ushuaia, and you get the best views of town looking back at it from the strait. Standard trips visit Isla Bridges, Isla de los Pájaros and Isla de los Lobos, looping around Faro Les Eclaireurs, sometimes erroneously called the Lighthouse at the End of the World – that title belongs to the beacon at the tip of Isla de los Estados – on their way back. Look out for the black-browed albatross, the thick-set giant petrel, southern skuas and the South American tern, as well as **marine mammals** such as sea lions, Peale's dolphin, and the occasional minke whale.

ARRIVAL AND ACTIVITIES
BEAGLE CHANNEL

By boat Boats depart from the Muelle Turístico, where you'll find several huts housing travel agencies; trips tend to depart daily at 9.30/10am and 3pm, last 3–4hr, and cost $800–1000. There is also a $10/passenger dock tax. Try Tres Marías (☎02901 436416, ⓦtresmariasweb.com), the only company allowed to stop on the small Isla "H", a nature reserve home to Yámana shell middens (see p.524), or Patagonia Adventure Explorer (☎02901 15 465842, ⓦpatagoniaadvent.com.ar), who run the standard tour. These operators both use smaller boats so it's easier to see wildlife close up.

Diving Ushuaia Divers (Leandro N. Alem 4509; ☎02901 15 619782, ⓦushuaiadivers.com) run diving trips into the channel to look for king crabs and sea lions.

VISITING ANTARCTICA

Ushuaia lies 1000km north of **Antarctica**, but is still the world's closest port to the white continent. Most tourists pass through the city to make their journey across Drake's Passage, the wild stretch of ocean that separates it from South America; the two-day crossing is notoriously rough.

The grandeur of Antarctica's pack ice, rugged mountains and phenomenal bird and marine life will leave you breathless: whales, elephant and fur seals, albatrosses and numerous varieties of penguin are just some of the species. Kayaking, hiking, Zodiac boat trips, diving and snorkelling, cross-country skiing, snowshoeing and mountaineering are on offer.

Regular **cruise ships** depart from November to March and most cruises last 8–21 days. Some of the longer cruises also stop at the **South Atlantic islands** (Islas Malvinas/Falklands, South Georgia, the South Orkneys, Elephant Island and the South Shetlands) en route. Some ships are huge, carrying 500 passengers or more; travellers generally report a better experience on smaller vessels, plus the biggest ships are banned from landing passengers on Antarctica.

As an alternative to the cruises, several agencies, including Quark (see below), also offer packages in which you fly from Punta Arenas (Chile) to Antarctica, explore by Zodiac boat for several days, and then fly back.

BOOKING A CRUISE

Cruises are very expensive, but you can sometimes get last-minute discounts (bringing trips to around US$4000/person in some cases) in Ushuaia, especially on the newest ships. Ushuaia's **Oficina Antártica**, next to the tourist office (April–Oct Mon–Fri 9am–5pm; Nov–March Mon–Fri 8am–6pm, Sat & Sun 9am–6pm; ☎02901 430015, ☯tierradelfuego.org.ar/antartida /oficina_antartica), has details of current sailings and can advise on what each trip involves. Otherwise, try contacting the following agencies: Antarpply, at Gob. Paz 633 (☎02901 436747, ☯antarpply.com); Canal Fun & Nature (see p.512); Rumbo Sur (see p.512); or Puerto Williams-based Sim Expeditions (see p.520).

Whoever you book with, make sure they are a member of the International Association of Antarctica Tour Operators (IAATO; ☯iaato.org), which promotes safe and environmentally responsible travel.

RECOMMENDED CRUISE COMPANIES

Quark Expeditions UK ☎0808 120 2333, ☯quarkexpeditions.com. Offers a range of cruises, lasting 8–20 days; prices start at US$6000 per person. Some vessels take as few as twelve passengers, giving you a more private and intimate experience, though you have to pay more for this privilege. The company also offers flight-and-Zodiac packages (see above) from US$8995 per person.

National Geographic USA ☎1-888 966 8674 ☯nationalgeographicexpeditions.com. Very popular, well-established operator with 14- to 24-day cruises and leading photographers and naturalists on board; they have also been given special permission to visit Isla de los Estados (see opposite). The ships carry 102–148 guests and feature amenities such as spas, gyms and several dining options. Prices start at US$13,000 per person.

Parque Nacional Tierra del Fuego

PARQUE NACIONAL TIERRA DEL FUEGO, 12km west of Ushuaia, spans 630 square kilometres of jagged mountains, intricate lakes, southern beech forest, swampy peat bog, sub-Antarctic tundra and verdant coastline. The park stretches along the frontier with Chile, from the Beagle Channel to the **Sierra Inju-Goiyin** (also called the Sierra Beauvoir) north of Lago Fagnano, but only the southernmost quarter is open to the public, accessed via RN-3. Fortunately, this area contains much of the park's most beautiful – and wettest – scenery.

The accessible quarter of the park has three main sectors: Bahía Ensenada and Río Pipo in the east, close to the station for the Tren del Fin del Mundo (see p.518); Lago Roca further west; and the Lapataia area south of Lago Roca, which includes Laguna Verde and, at the end of RN-3, Bahía Lapataia. You can get a good overview of the park in a day, but walkers will want to stay for two or three days to fully appreciate the scenery and **wildlife**. The birdlife includes Magellanic woodpeckers (*Carpintero patagónico*), condors, steamer ducks, kelp geese – the park's symbol – and buff-necked

ibis, and there are also mammals such as the guanaco, the rare southern sea otter, the Patagonian grey fox and the Fuegian red fox.

Walking trails

The park is easy to walk around, with several relatively unchallenging though beautiful **trails** (*sendas*), many of which are completed in minutes; the best is arguably the scenic Senda Costera (Coastal Path) connecting Bahía Ensenada with Lago Roca and Bahía Lapataia. The spectacular climb up Cerro Guanaco from Lago Roca is comparatively tough, though hardened trekkers will find sterner physical challenges in the Sierra Valdivieso and the Sierra Alvear (see p.519). Obey the signs warning you to refrain from collecting shellfish – which are sometimes affected by poisonous red tides – and light fires only in permitted campsites, extinguishing them with water, not earth.

Río Pipo

North of the train terminus (see p.518) is the wooded valley of Cañadón del Toro, through which runs the **Río Pipo**. A gentle 4km walk along an unsurfaced road brings you to *Camping Río Pipo* (see p.518), and a couple of hundred metres on you come to a **waterfall**. Although a through-route north from here to Lago Fagnano is marked on some old maps, the area is off-limits and you will be fined if caught there. If you're heading south from Río Pipo back south to Bahía Ensenada, a more interesting alternative to walking between the two by road is to take the fairly demanding **Senda Pampa Alta** (5km; 1hr 30min), which is signposted off west on the way back to the train-station crossroads. This offers fine views over the Beagle Channel as it crosses RN-3 towards Bahía Lapataia 3km west of the crossroads, and then drops to the coast on a poor path through thick forest.

PARROTS AND HUMMINGBIRDS

The garrulous **austral parakeet** is the world's most southerly parrot, inhabiting these temperate forests year-round. The Selk'nam christened it *Kerrhprrh*, in onomatopoeic imitation of its call. Once upon a time, according to their beliefs, all Fuegian trees were coniferous, and it was *Kerrhprrh* who transformed some into deciduous forests, painting them autumnal reds with the feathers of its breast. The tiny **green-backed firecrown** is the planet's most southerly hummingbird, and has been recorded – albeit rarely – flickering about flowering shrubs in summer. Known to the Selk'nam by the graceful name of *Sinu K-Tam* (Daughter of the Wind), this diminutive creature was believed to be the offspring of *Ohchin*, the whale, and *Sinu*, the wind.

Bahía Ensenada

Two kilometres south of the crossroads, **Bahía Ensenada** is a small bay with little of intrinsic interest. It does, however, have the jetty for boats to Bahía Lapataia and Isla Redonda, and is the trailhead for one of the park's most pleasant walks, the **Senda Costera** (6.5km; 3hr). The route affords spectacular views from the Beagle Channel shoreline and takes you through dense coastal forests of evergreen beech, Winter's bark and *lenga*, some of their branches clad in *barba de viejo* (old man's beard) lichen. Look out, too, for the *pan de Indio* (Indian bread), a bulbous orange fungus. En route you'll pass grass-covered mounds that are the ancient campsite **middens** (see p.524) of the Yámana – these are protected archeological sites and should not be disturbed.

Lago Roca

Two kilometres after the Senda Costera rejoins RN-3, a turn-off to the right takes you across the lush meadows bordering the broad Río Lapataia to **Lago Roca**. Just past the campsite (see p.518) buildings there's a car park. From here, the gentle **Senda Hito XXIV** (8km return; 3hr) hugs the lake's northern shore and heads through majestic *lenga* forest to the Chilean border. This is a particularly good trail from which to spot the red-headed **Magellanic woodpecker**. Do not attempt to cross the border.

Cerro Guanaco

A spectacular, demanding trek is the climb up 970m-high **Cerro Guanaco** (8km return; 7hr), the mountain ridge on the north side of Lago Roca. There are superb **views** from the summit: the swollen finger of Lago Roca, flanked by the spiky ridge of Cerro Cóndor, with the jagged Cordillera Darwin beyond; to the east, Ushuaia and its airport; and to the north, a vertiginous cliff plunging down to the Cañadón del Toro. Even better, when you turn to the south you take in the tangle of islands and rivers of the Archipiélago Cormoranes, and Lapataia's sinuous curves. Beyond them are the Isla Redonda in the Beagle Channel and, separated by the Murray Channel, the Chilean islands, Hoste and Navarino. On a clear day, you can even make out the Islas Wollaston beyond the channel, the group of islands whose southernmost point is Cape Horn.

The weather on Cerro Guanaco can turn capricious with little warning at any time of year, so bring adequate clothing, even if you set out in glorious sunshine.

The Lapataia area

The absorbing Lapataia area is accessed by way of the final 4km stretch of RN-3, as it winds south from the Lago Roca junction, past **Laguna Verde**, and on to **Lapataia** itself, on the bay of the same name. This is one of the most intriguing sections to explore: in the space of a few hours, you can take a network of short trails past an incredible variety of scenery, including peat bogs, river islets, wooded knolls and sea coast.

9

Río Lapataia and the Archipiélago Cormoranes

Soon after the Lago Roca junction, you cross the **Río Lapataia** – over a bridge that's a favoured haunt of ringed kingfishers (*Martín pescador grande*) – onto the **Archipiélago Cormoranes** (Cormorant Archipelago). Signposted left off the road here is a short circuit trail, the **Paseo de la Isla** (600m), a delightful walk through tiny, enchanting islets.

Laguna Verde and beyond

Next you pass **Laguna Verde**, which is actually a sumptuous, sweeping bend of the Río Ovando, and makes a lovely setting for two campsites, *Camping Laguna Verde* and *Camping Los Cauquenes*. From Laguna Verde, it's only 2km to Lapataia, but there are several easy nature trails along the way, which you can stroll in half an hour allowing time to study the signs with ecological and botanical information (in Spanish). **Paseo Mirador** (1km) takes you to Bahía Lapataia via an impressive lookout over the bay; **Paseo del Turbal** (2km) takes you on a walkway across the peat bogs; and the **Senda Castorera** passes a beaver dam. You stand a good chance of spotting these rodents in the early morning or at dusk.

Bahía Lapataia and the end of the Pan-American Highway

RN-3 comes to its scenic end at Lapataia on **Bahía Lapataia**. For some this is not just the end of RN-3, but the end of the entire **Pan-American Highway** – around a mere 49,958km from Prudhoe Bay, Alaska. Deriving from the Yámana for "forested cove", Lapataia is a serenely beautiful bay studded with small islets. Near the car park is the **jetty** where boats arrive from Ushuaia.

ARRIVAL AND DEPARTURE

PARQUE NACIONAL TIERRA DEL FUEGO

By boat There are limited boat services running to the park from Ushuaia, usually going to Bahía Lapataia as part of a combined boat-and-bus tour – enquire at the Muelle Turístico.

By bus Buses (daily, hourly 9am–2pm to the park, returning 1pm, 3pm, 5pm & 7pm; 20–30min) shuttle throughout the day from the stand at Maipú and Fadul, to various points in the park; services are reduced, sometimes halted, during the colder months. There are also services to the Tren del Fin del Mundo station (daily 9am & 2pm, returning noon & 5pm; 20min).

By train The world's most southern railway, the Tren del Fin del Mundo (May–Aug 2–3 daily; Sept–April 3 daily;

40min each way; $530 round trip; ticket office at the Muelle Turístico; ☎02901 431600, ⊛trendelfindelmundo.com .ar), chugs its way through woodland meadows and alongside the Río Pipo to the park station, 2km from the main gate. Used to transport wood in the days of the penal colony, it's now little more than a tourist toy train. The main station is 8km west of Ushuaia on the road to the national park; take a bus (see above) or a taxi (about $400).

By taxi A taxi from Ushuaia costs around $550–700 one way, depending on where you want to be dropped off; a return trip with three hours' waiting time costs around $1300.

INFORMATION AND TOURS

Opening hours and entry fees The park is open daily 8am–8pm (shorter hours in winter). Entrance is $140; if you plan to visit again the next day, let the park staff know, and you won't have to pay twice. They can provide a simple

map of the park's trails, as well as info on its attractions.

Tours Virtually all travel agencies in Ushuaia (see p.510) offer park tours (around $800, plus entrance fee); most last 4hr and stop at all the major places of interest.

ACCOMMODATION

There are four main **camping** areas: the two nearest the entrance, *Río Pipo* and *Bahía Ensenada*, are free, but you're better off heading to Lago Roca and Laguna Verde, in the more exciting western section of the park. The best-equipped site is *Camping Lago Roca* (see below); there are also three free sites on Archipiélago Cormoranes – *Camping Las Bandurrias*, *Camping Laguna Verde* and *Camping Los Cauquenes* – which just edge it for beauty.

Camping Lago Roca Near Lago Roca ☎02901 433313, ⊛ confiterialagoroca@outlook.com. This site sits near picturesque Lago Roca and is the only one with facilities,

including a cafeteria. There's also a *refugio* with dorm beds and a couple of self-contained *cabañas*. Camping $150; dorms $130; cabañas $650

Central and northern Tierra del Fuego

The second-largest settlement in Tierra del Fuego, **Río Grande** is the only town of significance in Isla Grande's **central and northern sector**. The sterile-looking plains that surround it harbour fields of petroleum and natural gas. North of town RN-3 runs through monotonous scenery towards San Sebastián, where you cross the border into Chile or continue north on a dead-end route to the mouth of the Strait of Magellan at Cabo Espíritu Santo. On the way to Río Grande from Ushuaia, RN-3 passes a turn-off to **Estancia Harberton**, the region's most historic estancia and home to a penguin reserve.

The road then winds up to **Paso Garibaldi**, where you have majestic views over **Lago Escondido**, and passes through the woodland scenery of the central region. A string of *ripio* branch roads, the **rutas complementarias**, wiggles away from RN-3 in this area; those headed west take you to a couple of fine estancias, and those headed east into the **Península Mitre**, the windswept land that forms Isla Grande's desolate tip. One of the northern region's principal draws is its world-class **trout fishing**, especially for sea-running brown trout, which on occasion reach 14kg. The river, also named Río Grande, holds several fly-fishing world records for brown trout. The mouths of the Río Fuego and Río Ewan can also be spectacularly fruitful, as can sections of the Malengüeña, Irigoyen, Claro and Turbio rivers, and lakes Yehuin and Fagnano.

Ushuaia to Paso Garibaldi and the Sierra Alvear

The road from Ushuaia to **Paso Garibaldi** wends its way north and east through dramatic forested scenery, with great views of the valleys and savage mountain ranges that cross the southern part of the island. Many activity centres have sprung up along the route, primarily to cater to **winter-sports** enthusiasts, though they often also make excellent bases for adventurous **trekking** or horseriding. Above all, the serrated peaks of the **Sierra Valdivieso** and **Sierra Alvear ranges** make ideal bushwhacking territory. If rough-hiking independently, consult the Club Andino (see p.510) and arm yourself with a copy of Zagier & Urruty's *Ushuaia Trekking Map*, but do not underestimate the need for orienteering skills or the unpredictable weather: blizzards can hit at any time. Be prepared to get thoroughly soaked when crossing bogs and streams, but you'll be rewarded by the sight of **beaver dams** up to 2.5m high and probably their destructive constructors.

Heading northeast from Ushuaia, RN-3 curls up around the foot of **Monte Olivia** and heads into the **Valle de Tierra Mayor**, a popular area for winter sports and trekking.

Valle de Lobos and Nunatak

17km east of Ushuaia • Several travel agencies in Ushuaia run buses to Altos del Valle (☎ 02901 15 612319, ⓦ valledelobos.com) and Nunatak (☎ 02901 430329); check the latest timetable at the Muelle Turístico

Some 17km from Ushuaia is **Valle de Lobos**, a centre offering a range of activities, including dog-sledding. Nearby a trail leads to attractive **Laguna Esmeralda** (4.5km; 2hr), where you can camp (free), and a more challenging hike to **Glaciar Alvear** (another 3.5km; 2hr 30min). A kilometre or so beyond Valle de Lobos is the excellent Nunatak, a sports centre offering dog-sledding and snowmobile trips in the winter, and trekking and beaver-watching in the summer. Ask about the fascinating guided trek to **Lago Ojo del Albino** (10hr; guide, crampons and food included).

Estancia Harberton and around

Patagonia's most historic estancia, **Estancia Harberton** is an ordered assortment of whitewashed buildings on the shores of a sheltered bay. Though assuredly scenic, it's the historical resonance of the place that fleshes out a visit: this farmstead – or more particularly the family who settled here – played a role out of all proportion to its size in the region's history. Built by Reverend Thomas Bridges, the man who authored one

THE OTHER END OF THE WORLD: PUERTO WILLIAMS AND CAPE HORN

On the north shore of **Isla Navarino** on Chile's side of the border, 82km east and slightly south of Ushuaia along the Beagle Channel, is **Puerto Williams**. "Williams" is a thorn in Argentina's toe, since despite all the publicity and hype about Ushuaia being **the most southerly town in the world**, that privilege actually belongs to Puerto Williams. Founded as a military outpost and officially the capital of Chilean Antarctica, the town looks idyllic on a fine day, surrounded by the jagged peaks of Los Dientes. Though the settlement can be seen from RN-3, actually getting there from Argentina is a bureaucratic headache, meaning that companies that do the trip are expensive.

ARRIVAL AND ACCOMMODATION

Ushuaia Boating (Gob. Paz 233; ⓣ02901 436193 or ⓣ02901 15 609030, ⓔboatingushuaia @gmail.com) operates boats (Nov–April Mon–Sat, weather permitting) across the channel to Isla Navarino; passengers are then transported by bus to Puerto Williams. The whole journey takes around an hour and costs about US$130 one way. Fernandez Campbell (Juana Fadul 126; ⓣ02901 433232, ⓦfernandezcampbell.com) has direct boats (6 weekly Nov–April; 1hr 30min) to Puerto Williams for a similar price, as does Piratour (see opposite). Alternatively, cross the land border with Chile (see box, p.467) and travel across from Punta Arenas. Another option is Aero Club Ushuaia (Luis Pedro Fique 151; ⓣ02901 421717, ⓦaeroclubushuaia.com), which operates small planes that fly loops (from US$155/person for 30min, US$255/person for 1hr), without landing, over Puerto Williams and the surrounding area.

Among Puerto Williams' limited accommodation options, *Residencial Pusaki* at Piloto Pardo 222 (ⓣ061 621116, ⓔpattypusaki@yahoo.es) stands out for its welcoming family atmosphere, comfortable and economically priced dorms (CH$15,000/US$21) and private rooms (CH$35,000/US$50), and tasty home-cooked food.

ROUNDING THE CAPE

Many travellers like to go the whole hog and "round the Cape", erroneously translated into Spanish as *Cabo de Hornos* (literally "Ovens Cape"). Ask around in Puerto Williams – try SIM Expeditions (Ricardo Maragaño 168; ⓣ061 621150, ⓦsimexpeditions.com) – about **boat trips** to the most southerly point of the world's landmass, barring Antarctica. Weather permitting, you disembark on a shingle beach, and visit the tiny Chilean naval base, lighthouse and chapel; there's not much to do and it's quite desolate.

DAP (ⓣ061 616100, ⓦaeroviasdap.cl) has flights (3–6 weekly; 1hr 15min) between Puerto Williams and Punta Arenas; book tickets well in advance. These flights treat you to incredible views of Isla Navarino and the Darwin peaks, but, again, weather is a vital factor. The company also has flights over Antarctica.

of the two seminal Fuegian texts, the *Yámana–English Dictionary*, it was the inspiration for the other, Lucas Bridges' classic, *Uttermost Part of the Earth*. Apart from being a place where scientists and shipwrecked sailors were assured assistance, Harberton developed into a sanctuary for groups of Yámana and Mannekenk.

Today the estancia is owned by the fourth- and fifth-generation descendants of Thomas Bridges, and is open for **guided tours** that take in the copse on the hill – Tierra del Fuego's first nature reserve – where you learn about the island's plant life, and see reconstructions of Yámana dwellings, the family cemetery and the old shearing shed. Housed in a building at the entrance to the farmstead is an impressive marine-mammal museum, **Museo Acatushún** (ⓦacatushun.com), which displays skeletons of the main families of such animals found in the surrounding waters.

Harberton is **accessed** via the **RCj** branch road, whose turn-off is 40km northeast of Ushuaia on RN-3. Around 25km from the turn-off, you emerge from the forested route by a lagoon fringed by the skeletons of *Nothofagus* beeches, and can look right across the Beagle Channel to the Chilean town of Puerto Williams. A few hundred metres beyond here the road splits: take the left-hand fork heading eastwards across rolling open country and past a clump of **flag trees**, swept back in exaggerated quiffs by the unremitting wind. The estancia is a further 10km beyond the turn-off, 85km east of Ushuaia.

9

Isla Martillo

While at Harberton you can cross to the Reserva Yecapasela on **Isla Martillo**, the only island in the Beagle Channel that **penguins** call home – biologists think it's because the softness of the soil is perfect for their burrowing, and the sea currents in which they feed lead here, too. There are large colonies of two species – Magellanic, the same species but a different group from the larger colony in Punta Tombo (see p.461), and the orange-beaked sub-Antarctic gentoo. In recent years a few king penguins have also arrived. The sensitively run tours (see below) are a wonderful way to view the creatures.

The Lucas Bridges Trail

Opened in 1898 to drive herds of sheep from Harberton over the mountains to a new estancia, Viamonte, on the Atlantic coast, the **Lucas Bridges Trail** is a rewarding challenge for hardy travellers. Although you can attempt the trek on your own, it is not to be taken lightly – register first at Harberton, where you can obtain a basic map (there's more info on the Estancia Harberton website). Forest fires are a real danger: don't start a fire and be careful with cigarettes. Alternatively, take a guided tour (see below).

The RCj beyond Harberton

Beyond Harberton, the RCj runs for forty spectacular kilometres – accessible only with your own transport – to **Estancia Moat**, past the islands that guard the eastern mouth of the Beagle Channel: **Picton**, **Nueva** and **Lennox**. These uninhabited atolls have a controversial past, with both Chile and Argentina long claiming sovereignty over them. The track comes to an end at a naval outpost, beyond which Península Mitre (see p.523) stretches to Cabo San Diego, at the far tip of Tierra del Fuego.

ARRIVAL AND DEPARTURE
ESTANCIA HARBERTON AND AROUND

By bus From mid-Oct to March several travel agencies (mostly based at the Muelle Turístico) run buses from

Ushuaia to Harberton (1hr 30min–2hr).
By taxi A taxi from Ushuaia costs around $2000 one way.

INFORMATION AND TOURS

Estancia opening times and entry fee Estancia Harberton (ⓦ estanciaharberton.com) is open Oct to mid-April daily 10am–7pm. Entry is $180 (includes a 2hr guided walking tour of the homestead and the museum).
Estancia tours Travel agencies offer guided day-trips (around $1000) to Harberton, often combined with a tour of the Beagle Channel.

Isla Martillo tours The only operator permitted to land boats on Isla Martillo is Piratour (Muelle Turístico, Ushuaia; ☎ 02901 435557, ⓦ piratour.net); its half-day bus-and-boat trips depart from Ushuaia via Harberton but don't really visit the estancia.
Lucas Bridges Trail tours Luis Turi (☎ 02901 437753, ⓦ companiadeguias.com.ar) offers guided treks.

ACCOMMODATION AND EATING

★ **Estancia Harberton** 85km east of Ushuaia. Contact on Skype (estanciaharberton.turismo); ⓦ estancia harberton.com. Comfortable accommodation is provided in the old *Shepherd House*, which has recently remodelled en-suite rooms (each sleeping up to three people), a shared kitchenette and a large porch. More basic accommodation is on offer in the *Foreman's House Hostel*. Rates for the former

include full board, an Isla Martillo trip, an estancia tour and a museum visit (half-board packages also available); rates for the latter include breakfast, the estancia tour and museum visit. Camping (free) is permitted at three sites, though there are no facilities; register first at the estancia. There is a lovely teashop and restaurant. *Shepherd House* $8750; *Foreman's House Hostel* $755

Lago Fagnano

Cresting the **Paso Garibaldi** some 45km out of Ushuaia, RN-3 descends towards **Lago Escondido**, the first of the lowland lakes, accessible via a 4km branch road to the north, before heading alongside the southern shore of **LAGO FAGNANO**. This impressive lake, called Lago Kami by the Selk'nam, is flanked by hills, and straddles the Chilean border

9

at its western end. Most of its 105km are inaccessible to visitors, apart from anglers who can afford to rent a good launch.

ARRIVAL AND INFORMATION   LAGO FAGNANO

By bus Transportes Pasarela (25 de Mayo and Maipú in Ushuaia; ☎02901 433712) runs a daily bus (departs 10am, returns 2pm; sometimes extra services run in the high season; 1hr 15min) to Lago Fagnano.
Tours Several agencies offer day-trips (around $500) to Lago Fagnano and Lago Escondido.

ACCOMMODATION

Cabañas Khami Eastern end of Lago Fagnano ☎02964 15 566045, ☯www.cabaniaskhami.com.ar. Popular with anglers, this complex of cosy wooden *cabañas* is good value if you are in a big group. The *cabañas* sleep up to six, and there's a games room and a heated indoor pool. Minimum three-night stay over the weekend; two-night minimum stay during the week. **$1100**
Camping Hain Eastern end of Lake Fagnano ☎02964 15 603606. A well-run campsite, decorated with sculptures fashioned from old bottles and pitches, is protected from Tierra del Fuego's strong winds by wooden shelters. There's a communal kitchen and a snack bar. **$100**

Tolhuin

Near the eastern end of Lago Fagnano, the road splits: the left fork is the more scenic, old, unsurfaced RN-3 route, which cuts north across the lake along a splendid causeway; the right is RN-3 bypass, the more direct route to **TOLHUIN**, the region's oddest little town. Created in the 1970s, Tolhuin was designed to provide a focus for the heartland of Isla Grande – the name means "heart-shaped" in Selk'nam – but it has an artificial commune-like feel. It does, however, make a useful halfway point to break the journey – as most buses do – between Ushuaia and Río Grande.

ARRIVAL AND DEPARTURE   TOLHUIN

By bus There are regular buses from Ushuaia and Río Grande (both every 30min–1hr; 1hr 30min).

ACCOMMODATION AND EATING

Estancia Las Hijas 45km north of Tolhuin on RN-3 to Río Grande ☎02901 15 617022, ☯estanciaslashijas .com.ar. Dating back to the 1930s, this estancia is a great place to ride horses, help round up sheep, and learn about Selk'nam culture (see p.524). You can visit on a day-trip or stay the night (the accommodation is simple and basic). Rates for the latter include half board and activities. **$1400**
Panadería La Unión Jeujepen 450 ☎02901 492202, ☯www.panaderialaunion.com.ar. This bakery-restaurant is the hub of village life, and sells a range of delicious breads and other goodies, ideal if you are planning a picnic or just need a break from the road. Snacks from $20. Daily 24hr.

To Río Grande: RN-3 and the rutas complementarias

The main route between Tolhuin and Río Grande is the fast, paved RN-3, but if you have the time it's worth exploring one or more of the unsurfaced **rutas complementarias** (RC) that branch off it; they provide access to the heartland of Argentine Tierra del Fuego but are only really accessible to those with their own transport. Dotted around are some hospitable **estancias**, worth the journey for the authentic experience of seeing a working Fuegian farm or to gallop on horses across the steppe.

The RCh and RCf loop

The **RCh**, which branches off RN-3 22km north of Tolhuin, and the connecting **RCf**, which joins RN-3 some 10km south of the bridge over the Río Grande, form a 120km loop that passes through swathes of transitional Fuegian woodland and grassy pasture-meadows (*vegas*) populated by sheep. Along the RCh you'll see cone-shaped Mount Yakush and pyramid-like Mount Atukoyak to the south before the road joins the RCf by **Lago Yehuin**. This popular fishing locale is a good place for spotting **condors**, which nest on Cerro Shenolsh between the lake and its shallow neighbour, **Lago Chepelmut**.

The RCa

40km north of Tolhuin, the most beautiful of the central *rutas complementarias* – the **RCa** – branches east through golden pastureland towards the coast and the knobbly protrusion of **Cabo San Pablo**. A wonderful panorama stretches out from the south side of the cape, encompassing the wreck of the *Desdémona*, grounded during a storm in the early 1980s – at low tide, you can walk out to the ship – but the area is mainly of interest to fishermen. Beyond, the road continues for 17km through wetlands and "tree cemeteries" (collections of burnt tree stumps) and past the odd beaver dam to *Estancia Fueguina*, from where you'll need a high-clearance 4WD to progress any further.

Península Mitre

The public track eventually fizzles out at *Estancia María Luisa*, 18km further on, just beyond which run the famous fishing rivers, Irigoyen and Malengüeña. This is the beginning of the **Península Mitre**, the bleak toe of land that forms the southeastern extremity of Tierra del Fuego. This semi-wilderness – primarily swampy moorland and thickets fringed by rugged coastal scenery – was once the territory of the indigenous Mannekenk, whose presence is attested to by old shell middens. Before the 1850s, the only white men who came ashore were sailors and scientists, as well as shipwreck victims; the remains of wrecks line the shore, including the nineteenth-century *Duchess of Albany*, near **Bahía Policarpo**. The peninsula is effectively uninhabited, and the only way to explore is on guided **horseriding** excursions (see below).

TOURS AND ACCOMMODATION THE RCA

Centro Hípico Ushuaia Hipólito Yrigoyen 2260, Ushuaia ☎02901 15 568278, ⓦhorseridingtierra delfuego.com. This agency runs a range of horseriding trips across Tierra del Fuego, including one down the Costa de los Naufragios, from *Estancia María Luisa* to *Estancia Policarpo* and back.

Estancia Viamonte Just off RN-3, around 35km south of Río Grande ⓦestanciaviamonte.com. The historic *Estancia Viamonte*, founded by Lucas Bridges, is a wonderfully atmospheric place to spend a night. It was not accepting guests at the time of research, but may do so again in the future.

The RCb to Chile

The scenery north of *Estancia Viamonte* undergoes an abrupt transition, from scraggly clumps of Fuegian woodland to the forlorn, bald landscape of the steppe. South of Río Grande town, a few kilometres before you cross the river itself, you pass the turn-off for the **RCb**, worth detouring along for 1km to see the tiny village of **Estancia José Menéndez**.

The estancia was founded as *Estancia Primera Argentina* in 1896 by sheep magnate José Menéndez. The most notorious of its early managers was a hard-drinking Scotsman by the name of MacLennan, who earned himself the sobriquet of "Red Pig" for taking pleasure in gunning down the Selk'nam. Menéndez's second estancia, now known as **Estancia Maria Behety** (ⓦmaribety.com), is popular with anglers.

The RCb continues across the steppe for 70km to the Chilean frontier at **Radman**, where there's a little-used **border crossing**, known as Bella Vista (Nov–March 8am–9pm), which allows access to Lago Blanco, an excellent fishing destination, as well as providing an alternative route west to Porvenir in Chile.

Río Grande

RÍO GRANDE is a drab city that grew up on the river of the same name as a port for José Menéndez's sheep enterprises. The treacherous tides along this stretch of the coast can reach over 15m at the spring equinox, and low tide exposes a shelf of mud flats better for sea birds than boats. The city is a place to pass through quickly, unless you're a trout fisherman; the **Monumento a la Trucha**, a statue of a giant brown trout on RN-3, leaves you in little doubt as to what the town is famous for.

9

THE INDIGENOUS PEOPLES OF TIERRA DEL FUEGO

The lands at the end of the earth were home to several distinct societies before the arrival of the Europeans.

THE SELK'NAM

In 1580, Sarmiento de Gamboa became the first European to encounter the **Selk'nam**, one of the largest groups. He was impressed by these "Big People", with their powerful frames, guanaco robes and conical headgear. It wasn't long before their war-like, defiant nature became evident, though, and a bloody skirmish with a Dutch expedition in 1599 proved them to be superb fighters. Before the arrival of the Europeans, Selk'nam society revolved around the hunting of **guanaco**, which they relied on not just for meat – the skin was made into moccasins and capes, the bones were used for fashioning arrowheads and the sinews for bowstrings. Hunting was done on foot, and the Selk'nam used stealth and teamwork to encircle guanaco, bringing them down with bow and arrow, a weapon with which they were expert.

THE YÁMANA

The other sizeable group was the **Yámana** (Yaghan), a sea-going people living in the channels of the Fuegian archipelago. Their society was based on groups of extended families, who lived for long periods aboard their equivalent of a houseboat, a canoe fashioned of *lenga* bark. Out on the ocean, work was divided between the sexes: the men hunted seals from the prow while the women – the only ones who could swim – took to the icy waters, collecting shellfish with only a layer of seal grease to protect them. When not at sea, the Yámana stayed in dwellings made of *guindo* branches, building conical huts in winter (to shed snow), and more aerodynamic dome-shaped ones in the summer (when strong winds blow). Favoured campsites were used over millennia, and, at these sites, **middens** of discarded shells would accumulate in the shape of a ring, since doors were constantly being shifted to face away from the wind.

THE IMPACT OF THE EUROPEAN SETTLERS

The arrival of European settlers marked the beginning of the end for both the Selk'nam and the Yámana. To protect colonists' **sheep farms** in the late nineteenth century, hundreds of kilometres of wire fencing were erected, which the Selk'nam, unsurprisingly, resented, seeing it as an incursion into their ancestral lands; however, they soon acquired a taste for hunting the slow animals, which they referred to as "white guanaco". For the settlers, this was an unpardonable crime, representing a drain on their investment. The Selk'nam were painted as "barbarous savages" who constituted an obstacle to settlement and progress, and isolated incidents of attack and retaliation soon escalated into bloody conflict. Reliable sources point to bounty hunters being paid on receipt of grisly invoices, such as a pair of severed ears. The assault on Selk'nam culture, too, was abrupt and devastating, led by the "civilizing" techniques of the **Salesian missions**, who "rehoused" them in their buildings. By the late 1920s there were probably no indigenous Selk'nam living as their forefathers had done, and when pure-blooded Lola Kiepje and Esteban Yshton passed away, in 1966 and 1969 respectively, Selk'nam culture died with them.

THE MEASLES EPIDEMIC

Meanwhile, the arrival of settlers in 1884 triggered a **measles epidemic** that killed approximately half the estimated one thousand remaining Yámana. Damp, dirty clothing – European castoffs given by well-meaning missionaries – increased the risk of disease. Missionaries promoted a shift to sedentary agriculture, but the consequent change of diet, from one high in animal fats to one more reliant on vegetables, reduced the Yámana's resistance to the cold, further increasing the likelihood of disease. Outbreaks of scrofula, pneumonia and tuberculosis meant that by 1911 fewer than one hundred Yámana remained. Abuela Rosa, the last of the Yámana to live in the manner of her ancestors, died in 1982. Nevertheless, a few Yámana descendants still live near Puerto Williams on Isla Navarino.

ARRIVAL AND INFORMATION **RÍO GRANDE**

By bus The bus terminal is at Finocchio and Obligado, four blocks from the main avenue, San Martín. Several companies run services to/from Ushuaia (see p.510), and all have offices here. These timetables are for Nov–March; out of season, services are reduced drastically.

Destinations Punta Arenas (1–2 daily; 9hr); Río Gallegos

(1–2 daily; 10hr); Tolhuin (every 30min–1hr; 1hr 30min); Ushuaia (every 30min–1hr; 3hr 30min).

Tourist information The tourist office is on Plaza Almirante Brown (Mon–Fri 9am–8pm; ☎02964 430516,

ⓦriogrande.gob.ar).

Fishing For fishing licences and information, visit the Asociación Argentina de Pesca con Mosca at Montilla 1040 (☎02964 421268).

ACCOMMODATION AND EATING

Posada de los Sauces El Cano 839 ☎02964 432895, ⓦposadadelossauces.com. Located just across from the bus terminal, *Posada de los Sauces* has decent if rather plain

en-suite rooms, a restaurant serving up Argentine staples, and a lounge bar. $1100

Misión Salesiana Nuestra Señora de la Candelaria

Eleven kilometres north of central Río Grande on RN-3 is the **Misión Salesiana Nuestra Señora de la Candelaria**, a collection of whitewashed buildings grouped around a modest but elegant chapel. Río Grande's first mission, it was founded in 1893 by two of Patagonia's most influential Salesian fathers, Monseñor Fagnano and Padre Beauvoir, but their first township burnt down in 1896, and was relocated here. Originally built with the purpose of catechizing the island's Selk'nam, it in fact acted as part refuge and part prison, since local sheep magnates would round up the indigenous peoples on their land and pay the Salesians for their "conversion". In 1942, with virtually no Selk'nam remaining, the mission became an agricultural school, which it remains today.

Museo Monseñor Fagnano
Mon–Fri 8.30am–12.30pm, Sat & Sun 9am–12.30pm • $10 • ☎02964 430667 • Take Línea B "Misión" bus from Av San Martín (hourly; 25min)

The **Museo Monseñor Fagnano**, to the left of the chapel, has exhibits on local flora and fauna, and interesting homages to Don Bosco, founder of the Salesian movement, among which are some first-rate Fuegian indigenous items. Across the road is a **cemetery** with some vandalized tombs of Salesian fathers and unmarked crosses indicating Selk'nam graves, testaments to a culture that had been completely depersonalized.

North to San Sebastián and the Chilean border

North of the Misión Salesiano rears **Cabo Domingo**, and beyond that, the unforgiving plains of Patagonian shingle begin again, dotted by shallow saline lagoons that sometimes host flamingoes. RN-3 is paved as far as the **San Sebastián border post**, 82km north of Río Grande (see below), on the bay of the same name. Bahía San Sebastián itself is famous for its summer populations of migratory birds and is a vital part of the **Hemisphere Reserve for Shorebirds**. Oil companies operate here and access is restricted, but there are some birdwatching spots on the mud flats at Río Grande.

TO CHILE AND PATAGONIA

If you're planning on heading north into Patagonia via land, you'll need to cross first into Chilean Tierra del Fuego and then across the **Strait of Magellan** that separate Isla Grande from Patagonia. The main land **border crossing** is at **San Sebastián**, in the north of the island. The respective customs posts (April–Oct 7am–1am; Nov–March 24hr) are several hundred metres apart, 15km west of the Argentine village of the same name. Formalities are straightforward, if lengthy at times. There is also a smaller border post at Bella Vista (see p.523). You cannot take fresh fruit, meat or dairy products into Chile, and Argentine officers sometimes reciprocate. Once in Chile, you can either continue to Porvenir, where a long (2hr) and irregular crossing connects directly with Punta Arenas, or head to Bahía Azul, where there is a shorter (30min) and much more frequent crossing to Punta Delgada, although these ferries can't operate at low tide and involve a longer drive afterwards if you're planning to head further into Chilean Patagonia. Buses depart most days from Ushuaia (see p.510) or Río Grande (see p.524) to Punta Arenas and elsewhere in Patagonia.

Contexts

History

Argentina's past might best be summed up as "chequered". The modern nation is essentially a product of Spanish colonialism, initiated in the sixteenth century, and immigration from all corners of Europe and the Middle East during the late nineteenth and early twentieth centuries. Relatively little of its pre-Columbian civilizations has survived, other than archeological finds, though there is more indigenous influence on present-day Argentine culture than initially meets the eye, especially in the north. After independence in 1810, Argentina repeatedly took one step forward to progressive democracy and two steps back into corrupt lawlessness.

Twentieth-century Argentina produced its fair share of international icons – with Evita and Che Guevara leading the way, followed closely by Maradona (and, in the twenty-first century, Messi and Pope Francis) – but was often in the news for the wrong reasons. The country suffered under a series of brutal military dictatorships, including in the late 1970s, when a widespread campaign of state-sponsored terror became known as the "Dirty War". That regime eventually collapsed in 1983, after the Falklands/Malvinas fiasco. Argentina again hit the international headlines in a negative light when social unrest and economic recession lurched into chaos in late 2001. Two years later Néstor Kirchner became president, overseeing an economic recovery and a period of relative calm. Four years later, his wife, Cristina Fernández de Kirchner, became the country's first woman to be elected head of state – and was re-elected in 2011. However, amid economic stagnation and public dissatisfaction, the country moved to the right in the closely fought 2015 presidential election.

Pre-Columbian Argentina

The earliest records for human presence in what is now Argentina date back to around 10,000 BC. Over the millennia that preceded the arrival of Europeans, widely varying cultures developed. From around 4000 BC, distinct nomadic cultures like that of the **Yámana** (see box, p.524) emerged in the Tierra del Fuego archipelago. Other groups, such as the **Guaraní** of the subtropical northeast, evolved seminomadic lifestyles dependent on hunter-gathering and slash-and-burn agriculture.

The most complex cultures emerged, however, in the **Andean northwest**, where sedentary agricultural practices developed from about 500 BC. Irrigation permitted the intensive cultivation of crops like maize, quinoa, squash and potatoes, and this, combined with the domestication of animals such as the llama, facilitated the growth of rich material cultures. The most important early sedentary culture was the **Tafí**, whose people sculpted intriguing stone menhirs, which can be seen near Tafí del Valle, Tucumán Province. Later, this period saw the development of Catamarca's **Condorhuasi** culture, renowned for its distinctive, beautifully patterned ceramics. From about 600 AD, metallurgical technologies developed,

c.10,000 BC	**c.4000 BC**	**c.500 BC**
The earliest recorded human presence in the territory that is now Argentina.	Nomadic and seminomadic cultures appear in the extreme north and south.	The first sedentary peoples leave their mark in the northwest of present-day Argentina.

and bronze was used for items such as ceremonial axes and chest-plates, perhaps best by the **Aguada** civilization, also centred on Catamarca. The increasing organization of Andean groups after 850 AD is demonstrated by the appearance of fortified urban settlements. Three important **Diaguita** cultures emerge: Sanagasta, Belén and **Santa María**, whose overlapping zones of influence stretched from Salta to San Juan, and which are notable for their painted ceramics, anthropomorphic funeral urns and superb metalwork.

Tiahuanaco and Inca empires

Trade networks expanded vastly once the area came under the sway of pan-Andean empires: first Bolivia's great **Tiahuanaco** civilization, which probably influenced Condorhuasi culture; and, from 1480, that of the **Inca**, who incorporated the area into Kollasuyo, their southernmost administrative region. Incredibly well-preserved finds, including **three ritually sacrificed mummies** at the summit of 6739m Cerro Llullaillaco – the world's highest archeological discovery (see p.283) – have revealed the extent of this influence in terms of customs, religion and dress.

Tribal groups on the eve of the European arrival

According to estimates, in the early sixteenth century Argentina's **indigenous population** was around half a million, two-thirds of whom lived in the northwest. The central sierras of Córdoba and San Luís were inhabited by the **Comechingones** and Sanavirones. The Cuyo region was home to semi-sedentary Huarpe, while south and east of them lived various Tehuelche tribes (see p.448), often referred to generically by the Spanish as Pampas Indians or, further south, Patagones ("big feet") – giving rise to the name Patagonia. Tierra del Fuego was sparsely inhabited by Selk'nam, Mannekenk and the Yámana (see p.524). The Gran Chaco region was home to the nomadic Chiriguano, Lule-Vilela, **Wichí**, Abipone and Qom, while the northeastern areas were inhabited by Kaingang, Charrúa and Guaraní.

The first group to encounter the Spanish, however, were probably the nomadic **Querandí** of the Pampas. They lived in temporary shelters and hunted guanaco and rhea with *boleadores* (lassos with heavy balls attached). Though they put up determined resistance for several decades, their culture was eliminated during the subsequent colonial period – a fate shared by many others.

Early Spanish settlement

In 1516, Juan Díaz de Solís, a Portuguese mariner in the employ of the Spanish Crown, led a small crew to the shores of the River Plate in search of a trade route to the Far East. He was killed by the Querandí, or possibly the Charrúa, who inhabited what is now Uruguay. Another brief exploration of the region was made in 1520 by **Ferdinand Magellan**, who continued his epic voyage south to discover the famous straits that now bear his name, and the next significant expedition to this part of the world was made by an explorer of Italian descent, **Sebastian Cabot** (see box opposite).

The first foundation of Buenos Aires

In 1535, Pedro de Mendoza was authorized by the Spanish Crown to colonize the River Plate to pre-empt Portuguese conquest. In February 1536, he founded Buenos Aires,

600–850 AD	c. 1500 AD	1516
Andean groups begin to produce ceramics and other crafts, whose remains now grace the nation's many museums.	The northwest comes under the sway of the great Tiahuanaco and Inca empires and is incorporated into the latter.	Portuguese sailor Solís discovers the River Plate before being killed by the indigenous inhabitants.

CABOT – ARGENTINA'S UNWITTING BAPTIZER

Explorer **Sebastian Cabot** reached the River Plate in 1526 and built a small, short-lived fort near modern Rosario. He misleadingly christened the river the Río de la Plata ("River of Silver"), after finding bullion and believing there to be deposits nearby. Ironically, the metal had probably been brought here by a Portuguese adventurer, Aleixo García, who in 1524 had reached the eastern fringes of the Inca empire, but was killed with his Andean booty on his return journey.

Cabot's silver had its most lasting legacy in the word "Argentina" itself, which derives from the metal's Latin name, **argentum**. Its first recorded use was in a Venetian atlas of the New World produced in the middle of the sixteenth century. Martín del Barco Centenera, a member of a later expedition, published an epic poem in 1602 called *La Argentina*. The name also appeared in Ruy Díaz de Guzmán's 1612 book *Historia del descubrimiento, población y conquista del Río de la Plata* (History of the discovery, population and conquest of the River Plate), where he referred to the territory as Tierra Argentina, or "Land of Silver". However, "Argentina" was not adopted as the name of the Republic until the middle of the nineteenth century.

naming it Ciudad de la Santísima Trinidad y Puerto de Santa María de los Buenos Ayres, after the sailors' favourite saint, the provider of fair winds. However, his plans soon went awry, as it proved impossible to subjugate the Querandí. Mendoza was forced to send Pedro de Ayolas upstream to find a more suitable site for settlement, and in August 1537, Ayolas founded **Nuestra Señora de la Asunción del Paraguay** (Asunción). Mendoza died at sea on the way back to Spain, and authority for the colony devolved to Domingo de Irala, who ordered the evacuation of Buenos Aires in 1541. Spanish interest in colonizing this area of the world had decreased significantly after **Pizarro**'s conquest, in 1535, of Peru.

The creation of the Viceroyalty of Peru

In 1543, the new Viceroyalty of Peru, with its capital at Lima, was given authority over all of southern Spanish America. The northwest region of Argentina was first tentatively explored in the mid-1530s, but the impulse for colonizing the area came with the discovery, in 1545, of enormous **silver deposits** in **Potosí**, Alto Perú (modern-day Bolivia). This led to the establishment of the **Governorship of Tucumán**, covering a territory embracing most of today's northwest. Conquistadors crossed the Andes to press the locals into labour and find other overland routes to the Potosí mines. Francisco de Aguirre founded Santiago del Estero, Argentina's earliest continually inhabited town, in 1553, while other settlements were established at Mendoza (1561), San Juan (1562), Córdoba (1573), Salta (1582), La Rioja (1591) and San Salvador de Jujuy (1593).

Meanwhile, the Spanish in Asunción sent an expedition under the command of Juan de Garay down the River Paraná, founding Santa Fe in 1573 and **resettling Buenos Aires** in 1580, this time for good. Settlers benefited from one vital legacy of the Mendoza settlement – the feral **horses and cattle** that had multiplied in the area. Few then realized the significance these animals would have for Argentina's future.

Colonial developments

Buenos Aires and its environs were largely overlooked by the Spanish Crown until the late eighteenth century. Direct trade with Spain from the River Plate was prohibited

1526	**1536**	**1659**
Venetian navigator Cabot finds silver treasures on its shores, giving the River Plate its name.	The city of Buenos Aires is established by Pedro de Mendoza, but is not settled for four decades.	The Diaguita uprisings are quashed, presaging future moves to eradicate the region's indigenous peoples.

SLAVERY IN THE NEW COLONY

More important than the River Plate in the seventeenth and eighteenth centuries was the Governorship of Tucumán. The *encomienda* system of institutionalized slavery was more effective here and, to a lesser extent, in the Sierra de Córdoba, as the lands were more densely settled. Though some trade from this area was directed towards Buenos Aires, the local economy was run so as to provide the Potosí mine with mules, sugar, cotton textiles and wheat. Indigenous resistance to the colonizers erupted on occasion, as with the **Diaguita rebellion** of 1657, which was actually led by a Spanish rebel, Pedro Bohórquez. The rebellion was brutally crushed in 1659 and survivors were displaced from their ravaged communities and forcibly resettled as workers on haciendas. By the second half of the eighteenth century, demand for labour from both Potosí and the towns of Tucumán was so great that it led to the importation of **black slave labour**. It is estimated that by 1778 one in ten of Tucumán's regional population was a slave, while well over a quarter were of pure indigenous blood. Racial divisions were strongly demarcated, and the rights of whites to control land and political offices were reinforced by a dress code and a weapons ban for the non-white castes.

from 1554, and all imported and exported goods traded via Lima, which restricted growth of the port, but encouraged **contraband** imports. The potential of the Governorship of the River Plate was limited: there was no market in preindustrial Europe for agricultural produce, and the indigenous populations could not easily be yoked into the **encomienda** system of forced labour. It was the Society of Jesus – the Jesuits – who effectively pioneered Spanish colonization of this region (see box, p.193).

The economies of Buenos Aires, Santa Fe, Entre Ríos and Corrientes engendered strife with the indigenous peoples. Mounted raids by indigenous groups from the Gran Chaco, such as the Abipone, terrorized the northeastern provinces well into the eighteenth century, and Buenos Aires, dependent on its Wild West-style round-ups of wild cattle (*vaquerías*) for its **hide and tallow industries**, frequently came into conflict with groups of Tehuelche and, increasingly from the eighteenth century, Mapuche (Araucanians). These peoples relied on the same feral cattle and horses, driving vast herds of them to the northern Patagonian Andes for the purpose of trading with white settlers and other indigenous groups in present-day Chile. The mid-1800s also saw the emergence and apogee of **gauchos**, nomadic horsemen, often of *mestizo* origins, who roamed in small bands and lived off the wild herds of livestock.

The Viceroyalty of the River Plate

By the late eighteenth century, the British controlled the Caribbean and were blocking the Lima sea routes, so the establishment of another route to Potosí became vital. Owing to the obstacle that was Brazil, the River Plate seemed the logical choice, and the growing strategic value of Buenos Aires gained the recognition of the Spanish Crown, which, in 1776, made it the capital of the new **Viceroyalty of the River Plate**, whose jurisdiction included Alto Perú (modern Bolivia), Paraguay and the Governorship of Montevideo. Commercial restrictions were gradually loosened, and trade permitted with ports in Spain and Spanish America, but the Crown still clung to its monopoly on colonial commerce, prohibiting the sale of silver to foreign powers.

1776	1778	1797
The Spanish create the Viceroyalty of the River Plate, corresponding with much of northern Argentina.	José de San Martín, the country's future liberator, is born in Yapeyú, now Corrientes Province.	The Spanish Crown relaxes trade restrictions in the Viceroyalty, leading to a sharp rise in smuggling.

THE BRITISH INVASIONS

In **June 1806**, a force of 1600 men led by **General William Beresford** stormed into Buenos Aires hoping to assert British imperial control over the entire Viceroyalty. The Viceroy, the **Marqués de Sobremonte**, fled the city, and the remaining Spanish authorities grudgingly swore allegiance to the British Crown. Among the ordinary inhabitants, though, there was a sense of offended honour at the way such a tiny force had been allowed to overrun the city's defences.

The locals regrouped under a new commander-in-chief, the French-born **Santiago Liniers**, and ousted their invaders during the *reconquista* of August 12. Undaunted, the British captured Montevideo, from where they launched a second assault on a better-prepared Buenos Aires in July 1807. This battle led to the surrender of the British and came to be known as **La Defensa**, a name imbued with the bravura of Liniers' hastily assembled militia, whose cannon- and musket-fire peppered the enemy, while women poured boiling oil from the tops of the city's buildings onto the hapless British soldiers.

Tensions between **monopolist traders** and **free trade** advocates were becoming entrenched. The European wars of the late eighteenth century forced the Crown to loosen control and, in 1797, allowed its colonies to trade with neutral countries. To the dismay of monopolists, cheap European manufactures flowed freely into Buenos Aires courtesy of contraband merchants. Monopolists trading on the traditional Cádiz route suffered, and exports to Spain plummeted. It proved difficult to reinstate restrictions and attempts to do so caused anger among merchants, such as **Manuel Belgrano**, who argued for free trade with all nations, but not rebellion against the Crown. Although news of the French Revolution and the American Declaration of Independence circulated among Buenos Aires' elite, there was no significant revolutionary feeling against Spain. The **British**, however, caught wind of the commercial tensions in Buenos Aires, and, mistakenly interpreting them as revolutionary, **invaded** the city in 1806 (see box above).

Other changes in the economy of Buenos Aires became increasingly apparent during the Viceroyalty. Rich merchants (*comerciantes*) helped finance the growth of **estancias** (ranches) in the province, a shift away from the earlier practice of *vaquerías*. By the end of the eighteenth century, these estancias had become highly profitable enterprises.

The May revolution and independence

The victory over the British showed the people of Buenos Aires that they could manage their own affairs and not rely on the viceregal authorities. They had been united against a foreign invader and the feeling of pride carried over into defiance against the monarchy.

In 1808, **Napoleon Bonaparte**'s troops invaded the Iberian Peninsula. Napoleon forced the rival Spanish Bourbon kings – Carlos IV and his son, Ferdinand VII – to **abdicate**, and installed his own brother, Joseph Bonaparte, on the throne. This had massive repercussions in the Latin American colonies, ushering in two decades of upheaval. A new viceroy, **Viscount Balthasar de Cisneros** – appointed by a Spanish junta in Seville loyal to Ferdinand in 1809 – was unable to curb tensions between Spanish and *criollo* (creole) elites, and parallel tensions between various trading interests. The authority of Cisneros was fatally undermined when news came through of the fall of Seville to French troops.

1806–07	1810	1816
British troops attempt invasions of the Viceroyalty two years running, failing miserably both times.	Anti-colonial leaders form a government, known as the Primera Junta, on May 25.	In the city of San Miguel de Tucumán, independence from Spain is officially declared on July 9.

JOSÉ DE SAN MARTÍN

National hero **José de San Martín** is as ubiquitous as George Washington in the US, and has countless villages, barrios, streets, plazas, public buildings and even a mountain named after him, as well as innumerable statues in his honour. He's often simply referred to as **El Libertador** (The Liberator) and is treated with saint-like reverence. Yet he didn't even take part in the country's initial liberation from Spain, helped to free traditional rival Chile and spent the last 23 years of his life in self-imposed exile in France. This last fact is celebrated with streets and barrios named after **Boulogne-sur-Mer**, the town where he died on August 17, 1850. A slightly larger-than-original replica of his Parisian mansion, Grand Bourg, built on the edge of the leafy Palermo Chico neighbourhood in Buenos Aires, is now the Instituto Sanmartiniano, a library-cum-study-centre.

San Martín was born in 1778 in Yapeyú, Corrientes Province. He was sent to military school in Spain and later served in the royal army, taking part in the Spanish victories against Napoleon. He returned to his homeland soon afterwards, and assisted in training the rag-tag army that was trying to resist Spain's attempt to cling onto its South American empire. After replacing Manuel Belgrano as leader of the independence forces in 1813, he became increasingly active in politics, as a conservative, and attended the Tucumán Congress in 1816. He formed his own army, known as the **Ejército de los Andes**, basing himself in Mendoza. From there he crossed the Andes and obliterated royalist troops at Chacabuco, **freeing Chile** from the imperialist yoke – though his comrade-in-arms Bernardo O'Higgins got most of the credit – finally mopping up the remaining royalist resistance at Maipú in 1818, before moving on to Lima.

San Martín was not interested in political power, but was in favour of setting up a constitutional monarchy in the emerging South American states. In 1821, he signed the Punchanca agreement with the viceroy of Peru to put a member of the Spanish royal family on the throne, but when the royalists did not respond, he declared Peru's independence on July 12, 1821. Unable to hold the country together in the face of royalist resistance, he called upon **Simón Bolívar**, liberator of Venezuela, to come to his assistance. The only meeting between the two occurred in Guayaquil, Ecuador, in 1822. Bolívar's radical ideals clashed with San Martín's conservative mindset and San Martín opted to withdraw from Peru. Frustrated by a nascent Argentina that was a patchwork of disunited provinces led by brutish *caudillos*, San Martín took off to Europe and slipped into obscurity; all this changed after his death, and his remains were repatriated later that century. He now lies buried in Buenos Aires' Metropolitan Cathedral, where his tomb is a monument (see p.67). His death is commemorated with a national holiday.

The Primera Junta

On May 25, 1810, supporters of self-government gathered in front of the Cabildo in Buenos Aires, allegedly sporting sky-blue and white ribbons, the colours of the future **Argentine flag**. Inside, Cisneros was ousted and the **Primera Junta** sworn in. However, deposition of the viceroy and the establishment of self-government did not necessarily mean advocating republicanism. The new authority continued to proclaim loyalty to the deposed Ferdinand VII, although in reality this was a convenient fudge designed to win over conservatives.

The Primera Junta was headed by **Cornelio Saavedra**, who believed in sharing power with the provinces. Other members of the junta, including Belgrano and **Mariano Moreno**, were avowed free-trade enthusiasts, intent on bringing the rest of the territory under the central control of Buenos Aires. Moreno's views came to represent the position of the **Unitarists** (or **Azules** – "Blues") who favoured centralism, while

1826	1829	1833
After six years of political squabbling, Rivadavia becomes the first president of the United Provinces of South America, covering roughly the same area as the Viceroyalty.	Federalist *caudillo* (political-military strongman) Rosas, with his power base in Buenos Aires, triggers lengthy civil wars.	Rosas undertakes his Desert Campaign, with the aim of ridding the Pampas of non-European inhabitants.

Saavedra's contained the first seeds of the ideas of **Federalists** (the **Colorados** – "Reds"), promoting the autonomy of the provinces within the framework of a confederation. This dispute was to dominate nineteenth-century Argentine politics, causing bitter division and **civil war**. While the junta's internal disputes prevented unity in Buenos Aires, the May Revolution also failed to mark a clean break from the motherland. Royalists under Martín de Alzaga continued to press for the return of a viceroyalty.

As Unitarist and Federalist interests continued to battle for control of the capital, clashes between pro-royalist forces and pro-independence forces flared up across the old viceroyalty. After 1810, in the interior these struggles saw the emergence of Federalist **caudillos**, powerful local warlords. They recruited – or press-ganged – militias from among the slaves, indigenous peoples and gauchos of the countryside. Back in Buenos Aires, the royalist factions were effectively crushed by 1812, and a *criollo* front led by **José de San Martín** (see box opposite), the Sociedad Patriótica (Patriotic Society), sought full emancipation from foreign powers.

Declaration of Independence

Two congresses were convened to discuss the future of the former viceroyalty, but these were dominated by Unitarists and failed to produce a cohesive plan for the country. However, at the second, held on **July 9, 1816**, in the city of Tucumán, the independence of the **United Provinces of the River Plate** was formally declared, a title first adopted in Buenos Aires in 1813 and covering much of modern-day central and northern Argentina. The date, July 9, has since come to be recognized as Argentina's official **Independence Day**.

Later that year, San Martín led five thousand men across the Andes to attack the Spanish in Chile, one of the defining moments of Latin America's struggle against its colonial rulers. He was assisted in the north by another hero of Argentine independence, **Martín Miguel de Güemes**, an anti-royalist, Federalist *caudillo* whose gaucho army eventually liberated Salta. Though *caudillos* such as Güemes favoured independence, many resented the heavy taxes imposed to fund the struggle for autonomy, and tensions remained high.

Caudillismo and civil war

The 1820s began with infighting among *caudillo* groups but, in 1826, **Bernardino Rivadavia**, a Unitarist admirer of European ideals and bitter rival of San Martín, became the first outright president of what was then called the United Provinces of South America (covering roughly the same area as the United Provinces of the River Plate). He proposed a new constitution, which was rejected by the provinces, who objected to the call for dissolution of their militias and the concession of land to the national government. At the same time, conflict with Brazil over Uruguay led to a blockade of the River Plate and caused a financial crisis. These two issues brought Rivadavia's presidency to its knees by 1827. The bitter Unitarist/Federalist fighting that ensued only ceased when a *caudillo* from Buenos Aires, **General Rosas**, emerged victorious (see box, p.534). In 1829, he became governor of Buenos Aires, with power over the newly titled Confederation of the River Plate (also known as the Argentine Confederation), covering a similar area to the United Provinces of South America.

1850	1852	1853
On August 17, General San Martín, hero of the wars of independence, dies in exile in Boulogne-sur-Mer, France.	Rosas is defeated at the Battle of Caseros by Entre Ríos *caudillo* Urquiza and flees to England.	A new constitution effectively creates an Argentine Republic for the first time.

ROSAS – THE "CALIGULA OF THE RIVER PLATE"

General Juan Manuel de Rosas, one of the most controversial figures of Argentine history, was born into an influential cattle-ranching family, and was respected by his gauchos for his riding skills and bravery. He was an avowed Federalist, but his particular brand of Federalism focused more on opposing intellectual Unitarism, with its gravitation towards foreign, European influence, than on respecting provincial autonomy per se. After rising in the ranks in the Federalist army, he became governor of Buenos Aires in 1829, where he concentrated on centralizing his power.

He left office at the end of his term in 1832, but returned as dictator in 1835 as the country teetered on the brink of fresh civil war after the assassination of an ally of his, La Rioja *caudillo* **Juan "Facundo" Quiroga**. For seventeen years Rosas ruthlessly consolidated power using the army and his own brutal police force, the **Mazorca**, which used a network of spies and assassins to keep resistance in check. During this time, many opponents and intellectuals fled to Uruguay and Europe.

Rosas sought to improve his network of **patronage** through the expansion of territories available for farming in the Pampas. His 1833 **Desert Campaign** against the indigenous peoples was the precursor to Roca's genocidal Conquest of the Desert of the late 1870s (see opposite). The vast landholdings that Rosas dealt out to "conquerors" ensured he retained powerful allies.

However, Rosas alienated many of the interior provinces by not permitting free trade along the Paraná, increasing taxes on provincial trade, and allowing the import of cheap foreign produce into Buenos Aires. Rosas' bloody regime was brought to an end in 1852, at the Battle of Caseros. Defeat came at the hands of a one-time ally, the powerful *caudillo* governor of Entre Ríos, **Justo José de Urquiza**, who was backed by a coalition of interests who desired free trade on the Paraná, including the Brazilians, British and French. After defeat, Rosas left for England to become a farmer in Southampton, where he died in 1877.

The establishment of the Argentine Republic

The three decades following the defeat of Rosas in 1852 saw the foundations laid for the **modern Argentine state**. Economic expansion and the triumph of progressive Unitarism ensured the conditions for the boom that followed. Buenos Aires emerged from its struggles with the provinces and territorial conquest began in earnest. Urquiza attempted to establish a constitution sympathetic to Federalist interests, but Buenos Aires refused to renounce its privileged trading terms. Its rejection of the **1853 constitution** led to the de facto creation of two republics: one in Buenos Aires and the other, the Argentine Confederation, centred on Entre Ríos and headed by Urquiza.

The deadlock ended only in 1861, when the powerful governor of Buenos Aires, **Bartolomé Mitre**, defeated Urquiza militarily. The 1853 constitution was then ratified nationwide, with significant amendments to please Buenos Aires, and the basic structure of Argentine government was set. In 1862, Mitre was elected the first president of the new **Argentine Republic**. Trade restrictions were lifted throughout the country while colonization of the interior was promoted, one result of which was the small Welsh settlements in Patagonia (see box, p.458).

Mitre aimed for rapid **modernization**, focusing particularly on the capital. His achievements included the creation of a national army and postal system, and the expansion of the fledgling **railway network**. These initiatives were financed by investment from Britain, which contributed the capital to build railways, and by greater export earnings – the result, particularly, of the important expanding **wool trade**.

1854	1862	1865–70
The country's first railway links the capital to its agricultural hinterland.	Bartolomé Mitre becomes president. Later founds *La Nación* newspaper, in 1870.	The War of the Triple Alliance is fought, together with Brazil and Uruguay, against the despots of Paraguay, with huge loss of life.

Sarmiento and Europeanization

A significant event of Mitre's presidency was the start of the War of the Triple Alliance (see box below), the end of which overlapped with the presidency (1868–74) of **Domingo Sarmiento**, the man most identified with the drive to "Europeanize" Argentina in the nineteenth century. Sarmiento was an avid opponent of *caudillismo* and famous for pillorying the likes of Rosas. He believed they represented a "barbaric" era in Argentine history, and that their legacy impeded the country from adopting contemporary North American and European notions of progress and civilization. These theories of progress impacted heavily on the remaining indigenous populations of Argentina, as they inspired those who believed in "civilizing the Indian", and helped underpin the doctrine of the so-called "Generation of the Eighties" (the 1880s), which subscribed to imposing the nation-state by force – its leaders included Julio Roca (see below) and Nicolás Avellaneda. Sarmiento is also remembered for his highly ambitious **education policy** and for encouraging European immigration on a grand scale.

The Conquest of the Desert

With the near disappearance of wild herds of livestock and the movement of settlers into the Pampas, Mapuche and Tehuelche groups found it increasingly difficult to maintain their way of life. Indigenous raids – called **malones** – on estancias and white settlements increased, and debate raged in the 1870s as to how to solve the "Indian Problem". Two main positions crystallized. The one propounded by Minister of War **Alsina** consisted of containment, and aimed at a gradual integration of the indigenous tribes. The second, propounded by his successor, **General Julio Roca**, advocated uncompromising conquest and subjugation – Argentina could then concentrate on territorial expansion to the south, where it was believed the future of the nation lay.

Roca led an army south in 1879, and his brutal **Conquest of the Desert** was effectively over by the following year, leaving over 1300 indigenous people dead and the whole of Patagonia open to settlement. Roca subsequently swept to victory in the 1880 presidential election. He believed in a highly centralized government and consolidated his power base by using the vast new tracts of land as a system of patronage. With the southern frontier secure, he could, from the mid-1880s, back campaigns to defeat indigenous groups in the **Gran Chaco**, to stabilize the frontier with Paraguay.

THE WAR OF THE TRIPLE ALLIANCE

The **War of the Triple Alliance** (1865–70) had its origins in the expansionist ambitions of Paraguay's dictators and disputes over navigation rights on the Paraná and River Plate. In it, Argentina allied with Uruguay and Brazil to defeat Paraguay. Much of the fighting was left to the Brazilians, whose military ineptitude prolonged the conflict, during which most of the male population of Paraguay was decimated. By defeating its neighbour, Argentina secured control of the upper Paraná River and the territory (now Province) of Misiones.

1879	1880s	1891
General Julio Roca undertakes his short-lived but brutal Conquest of the Desert.	The first waves of full-scale European immigration arrive on Argentine shores.	The Unión Cívica Radical (Radical Civic Union), or Radical Party, is founded.

A LAND OF IMMIGRATION

While Argentina was expanding its trade and improving its infrastructure, European immigration began to rocket. Significant numbers of French people had already arrived in the 1850s and 60s, followed later by isolated groups of Italians, Swiss and Germans driven by poverty and an enterprising spirit. Many came in search of land but often settled for work as sharecroppers in estancias or as lowly shepherds, labourers and artisans. Between 1880 and World War I, another six million **immigrants** came to Argentina. Half of these were Italians (mostly from the north) and a quarter Spaniards, while other groups included French, Portuguese, Russians, Ottoman subjects (mostly Syrians and Lebanese), Irish, Scottish, English and Welsh.

In 1895, immigrants represented nearly a third of the population of Buenos Aires, which grew from 90,000 in 1869 to 670,000. This influx caused occasional resentment, particularly during periods of economic depression, which were usually sparked by events abroad. Growth depended largely on foreign investment, and the country was susceptible to slumps like the one in Britain in the 1870s, prompting debate about **protectionism** and tighter border controls. Immigrant participation in politics was not encouraged, and few took up Argentine citizenship on arrival, because citizens were obliged to perform military service. Generally, though, immigrants were welcomed as part of the drive towards economic expansion and colonization of the countryside.

Times of socioeconomic change

Agriculture and infrastructure continued to expand, benefiting from massive British investment. The first **railway** had been built in 1854, connecting Buenos Aires to the farms and estancias in its vicinity. In 1880, the railway network carried over three million passengers and over one million tonnes of cargo, and by 1890 nearly 10,000km of track had been built across the country. **Wool production** became such a strong sector of the economy in the second half of the nineteenth century that sheep outnumbered people thirty to one. The rise in the number of sheep farms – small, privately owned or rented family concerns – saw the growth of a strong middle class in the provinces. Also transforming the countryside was the boom in **export crops** such as wheat, oats and linseed. Another development of importance had been the invention of **refrigerator ships** in 1876, which enabled Argentina to start exporting meat to Britain and Europe. In Buenos Aires and other areas, the age of **latifundismo** had begun as huge tracts of land were bought up by speculators hoping to profit by their sale to railway companies. In the interim period they were rented out to sheep farmers and sharecroppers.

The age of Radicalism

At the turn of the nineteenth century, pressure for political change was increasing. Power still rested in the hands of the tiny landed and urban elite, leaving the rapidly expanding urban professional and working classes unrepresented; electoral fraud was rife. From 1891, a more progressive party, the **Radical Civic Union** (Unión Cívica Radical or UCR), agitated for reform but was excluded from power. A sea change came with the introduction of **universal male suffrage** and secret balloting in 1912 by reformist conservative president, Roque Sáenz Peña, giving into Radical pressure. Four years later, this allowed the victory of the first Radical president, **Hipólito Yrigoyen**, ushering in thirteen years of Radicalism, under him and **Marcelo T. de Alvear**.

1895	1912	1916
Nearly 250,000 immigrants are living in Buenos Aires, making up a third of the population.	Universal male suffrage is made law, ushering in several Radical governments.	Hipólito Yrigoyen is elected president, the first Radical to hold the post.

THE CENTENARY CELEBRATIONS

In 1910, the **centenary anniversary** was cause for great celebration. In its first hundred years Argentina had gone from being a fairly small colonial backwater to one of the world's richest countries, still in the throes of an unprecedented immigration and building boom, bursting with confidence, and destined for great things. Foreign nations gifted statues and other monuments, many of which are still standing in Buenos Aires, including the Torre Monumental (Britain; see p.87) and the Monumento de los Españoles (Spain; see p.100).

Turbulent labour relations

After World War I, economic growth picked up again, with the expansion of manufacturing industries, but its benefits were far from equally distributed. Confrontations between police and strikers in Buenos Aires led to numerous deaths in the **Semana Trágica** (Tragic Week) of 1919. This was followed by the 1920–21 **workers' strikes** in southern Patagonia. Most strikers were immigrant *peónes* (low-level estancia workers) from the impoverished Chilean island of Chiloe, but there were also a few labour activists, Bolsheviks and anarchists. A first strike in 1920 was sparked by the fact that *peónes* had been unable to cash in or exchange the tokens with which they were paid by sheep barons. The protest expanded to include a raft of other grievances concerning working rights and conditions, and anarchists and socialists got involved. Shaken, estancia owners promised to arrange payment, but when this was not forthcoming, a second strike was unleashed, this time releasing more in the way of pent-up anger and frustration. Incidents of **violent lawlessness** were used by opponents of the strike to panic the authorities, now better prepared, into **brutal repression**. The final tragedy came with the massacre in cold blood of 121 men by an army battalion at Estancia Anita. In response, the Radicals introduced social security and pro-labour reforms.

Before and after the crash

By 1925, Argentina was one of the world's richest nations and confidence was sky-high. Britain remained the country's major investor and market – as revealed in a confidential report by Sir Malcolm Robertson, ambassador to Argentina, in 1929: "Argentina must be regarded as an essential part of the British Empire. We cannot get on without her, nor she without us." This was a nation predicted to rival the United States in economic power. Within two or three decades, however, Argentina had fallen to the status of a developing world state. The loss of this golden dream of prosperity has haunted and perplexed the Argentine conscience ever since. The decline in status was not constant, but the **world depression** that followed the Wall Street Crash of 1929 marked one of the first serious blows. The effects of the crash and the collapse of export markets left the Radical regime reeling and precipitated a **military takeover** in 1930 – an inauspicious omen of events later in the century. The military restored power to the oligarchic elite, who ruled through a succession of coalition governments that gained a reputation for fraud and electoral corruption. By the late 1930s, the value of manufactured goods overtook agriculture for the first time. Immigration continued apace, with one important group being Jews fleeing persecution in Germany.

1920–21	1929	1939
Widespread workers' protests in Patagonia are violently repressed.	The Wall Street Crash devastates the Argentine economy.	The outbreak of World War II divides the country between supporters of the Allies and Fascist sympathizers.

The rise and fall of Perón

One of the major political developments of twentieth-century Argentina was the rise of **Juan Domingo Perón** (1895–1974), a charismatic military man of relatively modest origins who had risen through the ranks during the 1930s to the status of colonel. The outbreak of **World War II** severely affected Argentina's international trade. It stayed neutral for most of the war, as a split developed in the armed forces, with one faction favouring the Allies and a larger one, the Axis powers, admired mainly for their military prowess.

Perón's involvement with politics intensified after a **military coup** in 1943, in which the army replaced a weak conservative coalition led by Ramón Castillo, whose government had been elected amid allegations of fraud and had come to be seen as self-serving; moreover, it had been veering towards a declaration of support for the Allies. Perón was appointed Secretary for Labour and used this minor post as a platform to cultivate links with trade unions. His popularity alarmed his military superiors, who arrested him in 1945. However, Perón's second wife, Eva Duarte or **Evita** (see box, p.540), helped to organize mass demonstrations that secured his release, generating the momentum that swept him to the **presidency** in the 1946 elections. He subsequently founded the Justicialist party (more commonly referred to as the Peronist party). His first term in government signalled a programme of radical social and political change, but his philosophy of government, which came to be known as Peronism, defies easy definition (see box below).

Authoritarian rule

Controversy surrounds many aspects of Perón's regime. Dissident opinion had no place: these years were marked by a **suppression of the press**, increasingly heavy-handed control over higher education institutions and the use of violent intimidation. Though it is unclear to what extent he was personally involved, Perón's apparent willingness to provide a haven for Nazi refugees did little for his or Argentina's international

> **DEFINING PERONISM**
>
> Perón's brand of fierce **nationalism**, combined with an authoritarian cult of the leader, bore many of the hallmarks of fascism. Nevertheless, he assumed power by overwhelming democratic vote, and was seen by the poor as a saviour. Perón's scheme involved a type of "corporatism" that offered genuine improvements to the lives of the workers while making it easier to control them for the smooth running of the capitalist system. Perón saw strong **state intervention** as a way of melding the interests of labour and capital, and propounded the doctrine of **justicialismo**, or social justice, better known as **Peronism**. His administration passed a comprehensive programme of social welfare legislation that, among other things, granted workers a minimum wage, paid holidays and pension schemes, and established house-building programmes.
>
> Perón also supported nationalization and **industrialization** in an attempt to render Argentina less dependent on foreign capital. One of the most significant acts was, in 1947, to nationalize the country's railway system, compensating its British owners to the tune of £150 million. In so doing, he also capitalized on popular anti-British sentiment, which had been fostered over preceding generations during a period of disproportionate commercial influence wielded by the tiny class of British farming and industrial oligarchs. Nevertheless, some believe he paid over the odds for outdated stock.

1943	1946	1947
Juan Domingo Perón enters government for the first time and builds a popular base among trade unions.	Perón becomes president for the first time, with the support of second wife, Evita.	Women are granted the right to vote in elections on an equal footing with men.

reputation. Adolf Eichmann was one of the most notorious war criminals to settle here and, more recently, Erich Priebke was extradited from Bariloche to Italy to face trial for wartime atrocities. Some research suggests fewer Nazis actually fled to Argentina than previously thought, though many academics assert that various regimes, including Carlos Menem's (see p.545), had records relating to this period destroyed.

Perón's troubled second term

In 1949, Perón secured a constitutional amendment that allowed him to run for a **second term**. Though he won by a landslide in the 1951 elections, his position was severely weakened a year later by the death of Evita, a key political asset. It was becoming clear that his administration and the cult of personality that had swept him to power were losing impetus. He faced dissent within the army, resentful at what they saw as the subordination of their role. He had also incited the wrath of the powerful Catholic Church, whose privileges he had attacked. In addition, his successful wealth-redistribution policies had alienated influential sectors of society while raising the expectations of the less well-off – expectations he found increasingly difficult to fulfil. Agriculture had been allowed to stagnate in favour of industrial development, resulting in inflation and recession. Against a background of strikes and civil unrest, factions within the military rebelled in 1955, with the tacit support of a broad coalition of those interests that Perón had alienated. In the **Revolución Libertadora**, or Revolution of Liberation, Perón was ousted from power and went into **exile**.

Military governments and guerrilla activity: 1955–73

The initial backlash against Peronism was swift: General Aramburu banned it as a political movement, Peronist iconography and statues were stripped from public places and even mention of his name was forbidden. There followed eighteen years of alternate military and short-lived civilian regimes that lurched from one crisis to another. All the civilian administrations depended on the backing of the military, which was unsure of how to align itself with the Peronist legacy and the trade unions.

The Cold War in Argentina

Much of the 1960s was characterized by economic stagnation, strikes, wage freezes and a growing public disillusionment with the government, in an international climate dominated by the Cold War. Throughout this time, Perón hovered in the background, in exile in Spain, providing a focus for opposition to the anti-communist military. In 1966, a **military coup** led by General Juan Carlos Onganía saw the imposition of austerity measures to stabilize the economy, and repression to keep a tight rein on political dissent. This was not without consequences, and, in the city of radical politics, Córdoba, tension eventually exploded into violence in May 1969. In what became known as the **Cordobazo**, left-wing student protesters and trade unionists sparked off a spree of general rioting that lasted for two days, and left many people dead and the authorities profoundly shaken. Onganía's position became less and less tenable and, with unrest spreading throughout the country and an economic crisis that provoked currency devaluation, he was deposed by the army.

It was about this time that society saw the emergence of **guerrilla** organizations, which crystallized, over the course of the early 1970s, into two main groups: the

1949	1951	1952
Perón changes the constitution so that presidents can run for a second term.	Evita dramatically decides not to run for vice president but Perón wins his second term.	Evita dies of cancer of the uterus. At her funeral many mourners are trampled to death as they strain to catch a final glimpse of her.

EVITA

Eva Perón, in true rags-to-riches style, began life humbly. She was born **María Eva Duarte** in 1919, the fifth illegitimate child of Juana Ibarguren and Juan Duarte, a landowner in the rural interior of Buenos Aires. She was raised in poverty by her mother, Duarte having abandoned the family before Evita – as she was universally known – reached her first birthday. Aged 15, she headed to the capital to pursue her dream of becoming an actress, and managed to scrape a living from several minor radio and TV roles before working her way into higher-profile leading roles through the influence of well-connected lovers. Her life changed dramatically in 1944 when she met Juan Perón. She became his mistress and married him a year later, shortly before his election to the presidency.

PUBLIC LIFE

As first lady, Evita was in her element. She championed the rights of the working classes and underprivileged poor, naming them her **descamisados** ("shirtless ones"), and immersed herself in populist politics and social aid programmes. She would personally receive petitions from individual members of the public, distributing favours on a massive scale through her powerful and wealthy instrument of patronage, the Social Aid Foundation. She played the role of the devoted wife, and was, in many ways, a pioneering feminist: she has been credited with assuring that women were finally granted suffrage in 1947. She yearned to legitimize her political role through direct election, but resentment among the military forced her to pull out of running for the position of vice president to her husband in the election of 1951.

Another role she revelled in was that of **ambassador** for her country, and she captivated a star-struck press and public during a 1948 tour of post-war Europe, during which she was granted an audience with the pope. Hers was the international face of Argentina, dressed in Dior and Balenciaga, which assuredly compounded the jealousy of Europhile upper-class women at home. She was detested by the Argentine elite as a vulgar upstart who respected neither rank nor customary protocol. They painted her as a whore and as someone who was more interested in feeding her own personality cult than assisting the *descamisados*. Evita, in turn, seemed to revel in antagonizing the oligarchic establishment, whipping up popular resentment towards an "anti-Argentine" class.

LIFE AFTER DEATH

Stricken by **cancer of the uterus**, Evita died in 1952, aged 33. Her death was greeted with mass outpourings of grief never seen in Argentina before or since. Eight people were crushed to death in the crowds of mourners that gathered, and over two thousand needed treatment for injuries. In death, Evita led an even more rarefied existence than in life. After the 1955 coup, the military made decoy copies of her **embalmed corpse** and spirited the original away to Europe, all too aware of its power as an icon and focus for political dissent. There followed a truly bizarre series of burials, reburials and even allegations of necrophilia, before she was repatriated in 1974, during Perón's third administration and, later, afforded a decent burial in Recoleta Cemetery. To this day, Evita retains saint-like status among many traditionalist, working-class Peronists, some of whom maintain altars to her. Protests and furious graffiti greeted the casting of Madonna, fresh from a series of pornographic photo shoots, to portray her in the Alan Parker film *Evita*. For many, this was sacrilege – an insult to the memory of the most important woman of Argentine history.

People's Revolutionary Army (Ejército Revolucionario del Pueblo or **ERP**), a movement committed to radical international revolution in the style of Trotsky or Che Guevara; and the **Montoneros**, a more urban movement that espoused revolution on a more

1955	1966	1969
In the Revolución Libertadora, Perón is sent into exile by the military, who attempt to eradicate every trace of Peronism.	General Onganía heads one of the country's many military juntas, imposing strict censorship.	Inspired by similar uprisings in Europe, the Cordobazo riots mark the growing polarization of Argentine society.

distinctly national model, extrapolated from left-wing traits within Peronism: multinationals, landed oligarchs and the security forces were favoured targets.

The return of Perón and the collapse of democracy

By 1973, the army seemed to have recognized that its efforts to engineer some sort of national unity had failed. The economy continued to splutter, guerrilla violence was spreading and military repression was rising. Army leader General Lanusse decided to risk calling an election, and in an attempt to heal the long-standing national divide permitted the Peronist party – but not Perón – to stand. Perón, still exiled in Spain, nominated a proxy, **Héctor José Cámpora**, to stand in his place. Cámpora emerged victorious in the elections and forced a reluctant military to allow Perón himself to return to stand in new elections.

By this time, Perón had come to represent all things to all men. Left-wing Montoneros saw themselves as true Peronists – the natural upholders of the type of Peronism that championed the rights of the *descamisados* and freedom from imperialist domination. Likewise, some members of conservative landed groups saw him as a symbol of stability in the face of anarchy. Any illusion that Perón was going to be the balm for the nation's ills dissipated before his plane touched down in Buenos Aires. His welcoming party dissolved into a violent melee, with rival groups in the crowd of 500,000 shooting at each other. It's not known how many people died in the fracas; the total is thought to be in three figures. Cámpora quickly resigned and in May 1973 handed power to a stand-in, Raúl Lastiri, who called new elections in September. Perón was allowed to stand and as his running mate he chose his third wife, María Estela Martínez de Perón, a former dancer, commonly known by her stage name, **Isabelita**.

Perón's death and the doomed presidency of Isabelita

Perón was 78 and his health was failing; though he won the elections with ease, his third term lasted less than nine months, ending with his death in July 1974. Power devolved to Isabelita, who became the world's first female president. She managed to make a bitterly divided nation agree on at least one thing: her regime was a catastrophic failure. Rudderless, out of her depth and with no bedrock of support, Isabelita clung increasingly desperately to the advice of her Minister for Social Welfare, José López Rega, a shadowy figure who had been Péron's private secretary, became known as the "Wizard", and was even compared to Rasputin. Rega's notoriety stems from having founded the much-feared right-wing **death squads** (the "Triple A", or Alianza Argentina Anticomunista) that targeted intellectuals and guerrilla sympathizers. The only boom industry, it seemed, was corruption, and with hyperinflation and spiralling violence, the country was set to enter a particularly dark phase in its history.

Totalitarianism: the Dirty War

The inevitable **military coup** finally came on March 24, 1976 (now commemorated every year as a national holiday). Ousted President Isabelita Perón was imprisoned, returning to exile in Spain several years later. Under **General Jorge Videla**, a military junta initiated what it termed the Process of National Reorganization (usually known as the **Proceso**),

1973	**1974**
Perón returns from exile and is elected president, but old age and ill health make him weak.	After Perón's death on July 1, his widow "Isabelita" takes over and embarks on a disastrous two-year term in the Casa Rosada.

TORTURE AND DISAPPEARANCES

The most notorious terror tactic used by the dictators was to send hit squads to make people "disappear". Once seized, often by thugs driving unmarked cars, these **desaparecidos** simply ceased to exist – no one knew who had taken them or where they had gone. In fact, the *desaparecidos* were taken to secret detention camps – places like the infamous **Navy Mechanics School** (ESMA) In Buenos Aires, now a national memorial – where they were subjected to horrific torture, rape and, usually, execution. Many were taken up in planes and thrown, drugged and weighted with concrete, into the River Plate, the perverse idea being that they were not murdered directly by their executors. Most victims were between their late teens and 30s, but no one was exempt, even pregnant women; this triggered the foundation of human rights group the Madres and Abuelas de Plaza de Mayo (see p.66).

Jacobo Timerman, in *Prisoner Without a Name, Cell Without a Number*, an account of his experiences in a torture centre, gives an insight into the mind of one of his interrogators, who told him: "Only God gives and takes life. But God is busy elsewhere, and we're the ones who must undertake this task in Argentina."

which is more often referred to as the Guerra Sucia, or **Dirty War**. In the minds of the military, any attempt to combat opposition through the normal judicial process was sure to result in failure, so there was only one response to it: an iron fist. The constitution was suspended, and a campaign of systematic violence backed by the full apparatus of the state was unleashed. In the language of chauvinistic patriotism, they invoked the Doctrine of National Security to justify what they saw as part of the war against international Communism. These events were set against the background of **Cold War politics**, and the generals received covert CIA support. Apart from guerrillas and anyone suspected of harbouring guerrilla sympathies, those targeted included liberal intellectuals, journalists, psychologists, Jews, Marxists, trade unionists, atheists and anyone who, in the words of Videla, "spreads ideas that are contrary to Western and Christian civilization".

The World Cup and the Madres movement

The military junta had the opportunity to demonstrate its "success" by hosting the **1978 football World Cup**. Though the victory of the Argentine team in the final stoked national pride, few observers saw this as a reflection of the achievements of the military. Indeed, the event backfired in other ways. The tournament was a huge expense, draining public coffers, and provided a forum for human-rights advocates, including the courageous **Madres and Abuelas de Plaza de Mayo** (see box, p.66), to bring the issue of the *desaparecidos* to international attention. The Madres and Abuelas de Plaza de Mayo were one of the few groups to challenge the regime directly, organizing weekly demonstrations in Buenos Aires' central square. They continue to protest today.

Economic and military failure

A slight softening of the junta's extremist stance came when **General Roberto Viola** took control of the army in 1978 and then the presidency of the junta in 1981, but he was forced out later the same year by hardliners under **General Leopoldo Galtieri**. The military's grip on the country, by this time, was nonetheless increasingly shaky, with the economy in recession, skyrocketing interest rates and the first mass demonstrations against the regime

1976	1978
On March 24, the military overthrows Isabelita and ushers in six years of totalitarian dictatorship, the so-called "Dirty War".	Argentina hosts and wins the football World Cup.

since its imposition in 1976. Galtieri, with no other cards left to play, chose April 2, 1982 to play his trump: **an invasion of the Falkland Islands**, or Islas Malvinas. Nothing could have been more certain to bring a sense of purpose to the nation, and the population reacted with delight. This, however, soon turned to dismay when people realized that the British government, who had claimed sovereignty of the islands since the 1820s, was prepared to go to war. The Argentine forces were defeated by mid-June (see box, p.544).

The military had proved itself incapable of mastering politics and disastrous stewards of the economy, and now they had suffered ignominious failure doing what they were supposed to be specialists at: fighting. Perhaps the only positive thing to come out of this futile war was that it was the final spur for Argentines to throw off the shackles of the regime. While the junta prepared to hand over to civilian control, **General Reynaldo Bignone**, Galtieri's successor, issued a decree that pronounced an amnesty for all members of the armed forces for any alleged human-rights atrocities.

Alfonsín and the restoration of democracy

Democracy was restored with the elections of October 1983, won by the Radical **Raúl Alfonsín** – the first time in its four decades of existence that the Peronist party had been defeated at the polls. Alfonsín, a lawyer much respected for his record on human rights, inherited a precarious political panorama. He faced two great challenges: the first, to build some sort of national concord; and the second, to restore a shattered economy, with inflation at over 400 percent and foreign debt over US\$40 billion. In the midst of this, he solved a politically sensitive border dispute with Chile over three islands in the Beagle Channel – **Picton, Nueva and Lennox**. Papal arbitration had awarded the islands to Chile, but Alfonsín ensured, in 1984, that a public referendum approved this.

The issue of prosecuting those responsible for crimes against humanity during the dictatorship proved an intractable one. Alfonsín set up a **National Commission on Disappeared People** (CONADEP), chaired by the respected writer Ernesto Sabato, to investigate the alleged atrocities. Their report, *Nunca Más* (Never Again), documented nine thousand cases of torture and disappearance; human rights groups believe the actual figure for the number of deaths during the Dirty War is closer to thirty thousand. It recommended that those responsible be brought to **trial**. Those convicted in the first wave of trials included the reviled Videla, Viola, Galtieri, and Admiral Emilio Massera, one of the junta's most despised figures. All were sentenced to life imprisonment.

Alfonsín's concessions to the military

Military sensibilities were offended by the trials: defeat in the Falklands/Malvinas War had discredited them but they could still pose considerable danger to the fragile democracy and Alfonsín decided he couldn't risk full confrontation. In 1986, he caved in to military pressure and passed *Punto Final*, or End Point, legislation, which put a final date for the submission of writs for human rights crimes. However, in a window of two months, the courts were flooded with such writs, and, for the first time, the courts indicted officers still in active service.

Several short-lived uprisings forced Alfonsín to pull back from pursuing widespread prosecutions. In 1987, the **Law of Due Obedience** (*Obediencia Debida*) was passed, granting an amnesty to all but the leaders for atrocities committed during the

1982	1983
Argentine forces invade the Falklands/Malvinas islands in the South Atlantic but are defeated by a British task force.	Radical Raúl Alfonsín oversees the return to democracy but is forced to make humiliating concessions to the military.

A HISTORICAL DISPUTE: THE FALKLAND ISLANDS/ISLAS MALVINAS

The islands known to the British as the **Falklands** and to Argentines as **Las Malvinas** lie 12,500km from Britain and 550km off the coast of Argentina. Disputes have raged as to who discovered them, but the first verifiable sighting comes from a Dutch sailor in 1600. In 1690, Captain John Strong discovered the strait that divides the group's two major islands, and christened the archipelago the "Falkland Islands", after Viscount Falkland, then commissioner of the British Admiralty.

French sailors made numerous expeditions to the islands from 1698, naming them the **Iles Malouines**, from which derives the name "Malvinas". The first serious attempt at settlement came when a French expedition established a base at Port St Louis in 1764. A year later, claiming ignorance of St Louis, British sailors settled **Port Egmont** and claimed the islands for George III. The Spanish also believed they had legal title to the area, dating from the 1494 papal treaty that divided the Americas between Spain and Portugal. Reluctant to come to blows with an ally, the French negotiated a settlement, and, in 1767, Port St Louis was surrendered to Spain. In 1774, the British were persuaded to abandon their colony (though not, they would later maintain, their claims to sovereignty).

In 1820, the newly independent Argentine federation asserted what it saw as its right to inherit the Spanish title to the islands, but in the late 1820s Britain started reasserting its sovereignty claim. The Argentine federation, paralyzed by internal disputes, was powerless to prevent Britain from establishing a base. The colony developed significantly after the 1851 founding of the **Falkland Islands Company** and with the beginnings of serious commercial exploitation such as sheep farming and whaling. By 1871, eight hundred people were living in Port Stanley.

THE 1982 WAR

In April 1982 General Galtieri saw a chance to divert attention from his junta's failed policies with a campaign to "liberate" the islands. The British had been making preparations for scrapping its only naval presence in the South Atlantic, and Galtieri (wrongly) believed they would acquiesce in the face of an invasion. Following the arrival of a **British task force**, though, the conflict was short: poorly equipped Argentine teenagers on military service were

dictatorship. At a stroke, this reduced the number of people facing charges from 370 to fewer than fifty. This incensed the victims' relatives, who saw notorious Proceso torturers escape prosecution, including the "Blond Angel of Death", **Alfredo Astiz**, who attained international notoriety for the brutal murder of two French nuns and a young girl.

Economic collapse and the early handover

Alfonsín managed to secure some respite by restructuring the national debt and, in 1985, introducing a platform of stringent austerity measures, which were angrily received by many sectors of the population. The government deemed the **Plan Austral**, named after the new currency it introduced, to be essential, with inflation running at over a thousand percent annually. The country continued to be crippled by **hyperinflation**, however, even after a second raft of belt-tightening measures, or *australito*, in 1987. The inflationary crisis came to a head in 1989, when the World Bank suspended all loans: many shops remained closed, preferring to keep their stock rather than selling it for a currency whose value disappeared before their eyes. In supermarkets, shoppers listened to the tannoy to hear the latest prices, which would often change in the time it took to take an item from the shelf to the checkout. Elections took place in 1989, but, with severe **civil unrest**

1985	1987
The Official Story (*La historia oficial*), a film about the dictatorship, wins an Oscar.	Controversial amnesty laws are passed, resulting in the release of dozens of military officers found guilty of crimes against humanity.

expected to combat professional paratroopers. In the most controversial incident, widely considered a war crime, the *General Belgrano* was torpedoed outside the British-imposed naval exclusion zone, killing 323 Argentines – an event still viewed with considerable bitterness.

More than 900 people – the majority Argentines – died in the 74-day conflict, and negotiations on the sovereignty issue were set back decades. At the time of the invasion, the islands were essentially a forgotten British colony that had long suffered a dearth of development and were being gradually integrated into the Argentine economic sphere. This stopped abruptly with the war.

THE LEGACY OF THE WAR

The government of Margaret Thatcher – weak, divided and, according to many observers, on the verge of collapse prior to Galtieri's invasion – received a huge boost. In Argentina, by contrast, the war provoked the collapse of the military junta and the end of the Dirty War.

The issue of sovereignty remains highly emotive. It was only in 2009 that relatives of the Argentine war dead were allowed to visit the islands to dedicate a war memorial to their fallen. Britain insists the future of the islands depends on the desire of their inhabitants: in a 2013 referendum, 1513 out of 1517 residents voted to remain a British overseas territory.

There has been a series of flare-ups, particularly in the latter years of the CFK government, when British ships were prevented from docking in Ushuaia. Many suggest that stoking nationalism over the Falklands/Malvinas was an attempt to draw attention away from Argentina's deteriorating economy. The British, meanwhile, haven't helped. British companies starting to drill for oil offshore, Prince William's helicopter practice on the islands, and the decision to send a British warship to the South Atlantic around the war's thirtieth anniversary were all provocative moves.

Mauricio Macri came to power in 2015 and indicated that he would take a more constructive, less dogmatic approach to the future of the islands. Whether this happens – and is met by a similar response from Britain – remains to be seen.

Perhaps the most prescient analysis came from Jorge Luis Borges, who saw two countries increasingly unsure of their role in the world. "The Falklands thing," he said, "was a fight between two bald men over a comb".

breaking out, Alfonsín called a state of emergency and stood down early, handing control to his elected successor, **Carlos Saúl Menem**. Even so, it was the first time since 1928 that power had transferred democratically from one civilian government to another.

Menem's decade in power: 1989–99

The 1990s were dominated by **Carlos Menem** – the son of Syrian immigrants – and were characterized by radical reforms and controversy. Menem had been governor of La Rioja at the outbreak of military rule in 1976 and had spent most of the dictatorship in detention. His **Justicialist Party** (*Partido Justicialista* or PJ) was theoretically Peronist, but – once elected in 1989 – he embarked on a series of sweeping **neoliberal reforms**.

His first major achievement was to curb **inflation**. Backed by international finance organizations, Menem and his finance minister, **Domingo Cavallo**, introduced the *Plan de Convertibilidad* (Convertibility Plan), which pegged the restored peso, worth 10,000 australes, at parity with the US dollar, and guaranteed its value by limiting the Central Bank's power to print money. Inflation fell to eight percent by 1993 and remained in single figures throughout the 1990s.

1989	1992
Carlos Menem, a neoliberal Peronist, is elected president and takes office early after Alfonsín declares a state of emergency.	The Israeli embassy in Buenos Aires is attacked by jihadist suicide bombers, resulting in 29 deaths.

Menem also abandoned the Peronist principles of state ownership and state intervention, favouring the **privatization** of all the major utilities and industries: electricity, gas, telephones, Aerolíneas Argentinas and even the profitable YPF, the state-owned petroleum company, were sold off. Investment came primarily from European, mainly Spanish and French, corporations, and the sales allegedly benefited individuals (including politicians) rather than the state. All federal railway subsidies ended in 1993, coinciding with massive **public spending cuts**. In 1995, regional trade barriers fell, as a consequence of the full implementation of the **Mercosur** trading agreement, creating a **free-trade block** of Southern Cone countries – Brazil, Argentina, Uruguay and Paraguay, with other countries joining or developing close ties later on. Unemployment rocketed and acute financial hardship resulted in strikes and sporadic civil unrest.

Playboy president

One thing about Menem's brand of Peronism that stayed faithful to the original was his style of government. A cavalier **populist**, Menem never stopped trying to develop the "cult of the leader". He modelled his image, mutton-chop sideburns and all, on that of provincial *caudillos* such as Facundo Quiroga, the 1830s La Rioja warlord. Not known for his modesty, he preached austerity while developing a penchant for the life of a playboy.

The president increasingly became associated with trying to rule by **decree**. One of the most controversial aspects of this policy was the issuing of executive **amnesties** in 1989 to those guilty of atrocities during the 1970s. Although the amnesty included ex-guerrillas, public outrage centred on the release of former members of the junta, including all the leading generals. To Menem it was the pragmatic price to pay to secure the military's cooperation; to virtually all the rest of the country, it was a flagrant moral capitulation. His apparent failure to launch a serious investigation into two terrorist attacks against the **Jewish community** in 1992 and 1994 (see box, p.71) also showed him in a very poor light.

Menem's second term

In August 1994, Menem secured a **constitutional amendment** that allowed a sitting president to stand for a second term, though the mandate was reduced from six years to four. The voters, trusting his economic record, elected him to a second term the following year. **Human rights issues**, however, continued to surface. One of the most important developments was the start of a campaign to prosecute those guilty of having **kidnapped** babies of *desaparecidos* born in detention, in order to give them up for adoption to childless military couples. Recognition of this crime, not covered by Alfonsín's Punto Final legislation, resulted in the successful interrogation and detention of many leading members of the old junta, including Videla and Massera. In the mid-1990s, the armed forces acknowledged their role in the atrocities of the dictatorship, making a **public apology** – a symbolic act followed by similar repentance by the Catholic Church.

Austerity measures seemed to apply to anyone not in government, and foreign debt continued to balloon. When, in early 1999, Brazil's currency lost half its value, the government had to resist acute pressure to devalue the peso. Convertibility held, but Menem announced that Argentina should seriously consider the "**dollarization**" of the economy.

1994	1995
Argentina's worst-ever terrorist outrage, the bombing of the HQ of AMIA, a Jewish association, leaves 85 dead and hundreds wounded.	Menem is elected for a second term and makes the armed forces and Catholic Church apologize for their roles in the Dirty War.

As the end of his second term approached, Menem mooted the possibility of running for a third consecutive term of office, which alienated the populace from his Justicialist Party and contributed to the defeat of its eventual candidate, Eduardo Duhalde, in 1999. Duhalde was emphatically beaten by **Fernando de la Rúa**, the Córdoba-born mayor of Buenos Aires, who headed up the **Alianza** – a coalition of the Radicals (UCR), of which he was leader – and **FREPASO**, itself a coalition party of left-wingers and disaffected Peronists.

The de la Rúa government and the 2001 meltdown

Known for his stolid reliability rather than his charisma, de la Rúa was a complete contrast to his predecessor. On taking office he seemed to represent the **fiscal and moral probity** that Argentines felt their country – already showing signs of its worst-ever recession – needed. Once in charge, though, the Alianza coalition was hit by severe infighting, and public spending cuts forced by economic strictures led to major demonstrations.

By early 2001, de la Rúa had already appointed his third finance minister – bringing back Domingo Cavallo, Menem's henchman, who announced an unrealistic "zero deficit" drive to meet stiff IMF targets and protect convertibility. The country still wasn't pulling out of recession, with industrial production and exports dismally low owing to the phoney exchange rate, unemployment soaring and financial confidence on the wane. Then, in the national elections of October 2001, the Peronists gained control of both houses of congress. Private depositors began to pull their money out of banks, afraid the peso-dollar peg would be abolished. Under severe pressure to abandon convertibility and devalue the peso, Cavallo stood firm.

Corralito and chaos

In early December 2001, in a desperate bid to avoid devaluation and stop the cash drain from banks, Cavallo announced restrictions severely limiting access to private deposits, including salaries. This measure, known as the **corralito**, or "playpen", riled Argentines of all classes, though the wealthiest managed to get their money out in dollars and into accounts abroad. To cap it all, the IMF then announced the withdrawal of support owing to lack of confidence in the economy.

On December 13, a general strike was staged against the *corralito* by the Peronist-controlled unions and acts of looting were reported in the suburbs of Buenos Aires, a Peronist bastion. Despite de la Rúa's announcement of a state of emergency to deal with the crisis, on the evening of December 19 tens of thousands of protestors bashing pots and pans (the first of many noisy "**cacerolazos**", or saucepan protests) marched on the Plaza de Mayo. Although the police dispersed the huge crowd, more demonstrations took place the following day. De la Rúa found himself politically isolated, while brutal police efforts to clear the Plaza de Mayo and halt **demonstrations** in other cities ended in a bloodbath, with at least 25 people dead nationwide. De la Rúa left office ignominiously, fleeing the Casa Rosada by helicopter.

The Duhalde presidency: an interregnum

After a farcical series of short-lived presidential appointments, congress finally opted for **Eduardo Duhalde**, the Peronist presidential candidate defeated by de la Rúa in 1999,

1996   **1999**

Protests face Madonna when she shoots the film *Evita*, but she gets to appear on the balcony of the Casa Rosada.

Having failed to change the constitution, Menem cannot run for a third term and De la Rúa takes over.

who was sworn in on January 1, 2002. He heavily **devalued the peso** within days and then negotiated a new agreement with the IMF to avoid a humiliating default with international lending agencies. After *piqueteros* (see box opposite) clashed with police, leaving two people dead, in June 2002 he announced early **presidential elections** for 2003, pledging that he and his ministers would not stand for office.

After the worst of the crisis, Duhalde's finance minister, **Roberto Lavagna**, calmed financial markets, avoiding hyperinflation and stabilizing the US dollar exchange rate at just over three pesos, after a peak of nearly four. He also reached a short-term agreement with the IMF and, by early 2003, signs of economic recovery – in particular, increased exports – began to show. The downside to this was a **sharp rise in poverty** across the country, as the price of basic products and imports soared.

Menem's failed comeback

The Peronists failed to unite ahead of the 2003 elections, and warring factions fielded three separate contenders: former presidents Menem and Rodríguez Saá (the latter was head of state for a few days at the height of the 2001 crisis) and Duhalde's protégé, **Néstor Kirchner**, who enjoyed a narrow lead in opinion polls. In the event, **Menem** came first, with just under a quarter of the vote, with Kirchner going through to the second round, a couple of percentage points behind. But, as the run-off approached, opinion polls unanimously suggested that only three voters in ten would back Menem – who withdrew from the race to avoid a crushing defeat and, it was rumoured, spitefully prevent Kirchner from winning an overwhelming electoral mandate.

Néstor Kirchner and new-look Peronism

When Néstor Kirchner took power the political and economic situation he inherited was still grave and few were confident he had the skills or support to bring about recovery. However, against the odds, he grew to be a powerful force in Argentine politics. He and his family began to dominate the country to an extent that people talked of a "penguin" takeover; Kirchner, often known simply as "**K**" – easier on the tongue than his Swiss–German surname – was nicknamed "Pingüino", less for his bird-like appearance than for his Patagonian origins.

Kirchner soon emerged as one of a new generation of left-leaning **South American leaders**, including Chávez and Lula, set on forging regional independence and interdependence, strengthening Mercosur (a free trade association, made up of Argentina, Brazil, Paraguay, Uruguay and Venezuela), limiting the influence of multinationals, defying the IMF and largely thumbing his nose at Washington. Helped by Lavagna, he oversaw an astonishing economic revival, as the devalued peso provided a platform for Argentina's export sector to flourish; from 2003, the country registered one of the world's highest **GDP growth rates** (averaging over eight percent a year for several years). Favourable settlements were hammered out with the majority of Argentina's international creditors, and the government paid back billions of dollars in defaulted loans. Joblessness figures started to drop, dipping below ten percent by 2007. Argentina also had a string of record years for **international tourism**, matched by huge numbers of Argentine holiday-makers forced to discover their own country as travelling overseas was prohibitively expensive for many.

2001	2002
The government loses control of the economy and De la Rúa is airlifted from the Casa Rosada by helicopter.	Argentina's economy collapses and caretaker president Duhalde devalues the peso and restores order.

PIQUETEROS AND CARTONEROS – THE TOUGHER SIDE OF ARGENTINE LIFE

Piqueteros – "pickers" – came to prominence in the late 1990s and especially around the time of the 2001 crisis, staging often violent protests outside the houses of former junta members or banks and businesses, blockading roads and major access points to cities, in order to draw attention to social injustices such as job losses, poor working conditions or hospital closures. They've become a feature of Argentine life, with some pickets being organized on the spur of the moment in response to specific grievances, and other groups being linked to political movements – mainstream or otherwise.

Since the millennium, **cartoneros** – poor people who effectively act as semi-official refuse recyclers – have become a common sight on the streets of Buenos Aires. They rummage through rubbish bags, salvaging paper and cardboard to sell for scrap. The sight of whole families, including young children, sorting rubbish on the city pavements does not exactly make for a good image, and the poverty that fuels it is an ongoing challenge faced by the authorities.

"K" for Kirchnerism

As tax revenues swelled, Kirchner was able to reverse years of spending cuts in the education, welfare and public-service sectors, providing students with free computers, handing out child allowances and building better roads. While skilful macroeconomic management was a factor of the recovery, the government was helped along by record commodity and agriculture prices (especially **soya**), and Kirchner became the most popular resident of the Casa Rosada for many years.

He risked the wrath of some Peronists and the military, by repealing the **amnesty laws** that had made it impossible to prosecute anyone who had committed human rights atrocities. He closed the capital's **Escuela Mecánica de la Armada** (ESMA; the Navy Mechanics School, which had been a key torture centre during the Dirty War) and had it turned into a monument, excluding Peronist politicians with a dubious past from a memorial ceremony for the "disappeared".

Meanwhile, as poverty persisted (witness the *cartoneros* on the streets; see box above), the government faced an upsurge in violent **crime** in the capital and other large cities. Critics accused the government of massaging inflation figures through the state statistics office (**INDEC**), a situation that persisted for years, and a series of high-profile financial scandals hit the headlines in 2007. Rather than running for a second term that year, Kirchner stepped aside for his wife, **Cristina Fernández de Kirchner** (see box, p.550), to run as the candidate of their newly named Frente para la Victoria (Victory Front, or FPV). Beating rivals Elisa Carrió, a colourful ex-Radical, and Roberto Lavagna, the former economy minister, she swept to a resounding victory in the first round of the presidential election held in November 2007.

President Cristina Fernández de Kirchner

In many ways Cristina Fernández de Kirchner's electoral victory meant business as usual, with continued economic growth, booming exports and flourishing national and international tourism filling the government's coffers, aided by more efficient tax collection procedures. Cristina's first big hurdle loomed early in 2008, when she was

2003	2007
Despite an attempted comeback by Carlos Menem, left-wing Peronist Néstor Kirchner is elected president.	Kirchner's wife, Cristina Fernández, stands in the elections, and she becomes the country's first elected female president.

forced to back down in a major dispute with farmers over attempts to raise export taxes on agricultural produce; when her vice president, ex-Radical Julio Cobos, cast his vote against the government she cut off all relations with him for the next four years. Her administration successfully expropriated US$26 billion in private pension funds, in order to boost the state's own fund, to the consternation of foreign investors.

Although Latin America was not as hard hit by the global recession of 2009 as many countries, it was not left entirely unscathed – Argentina's economy grew by less than one percent in 2009, and has faltered ever since. Suddenly, Argentina was once again faced with the prospect of raising money on sceptical international financial markets to keep levels of public spending high – the same markets that had been burned by Argentina's massive debt default during the 2001 crisis.

Problems for Kirchnerism

Kirchnerism – as the new strand of Peronism began to be called, backed by a powerful youth movement known as La Cámpora – suffered defeat in the mid-term parliamentary elections of 2009, with its governing coalition losing its majority in both

LA PRESIDENTA

Cristina Fernández de Kirchner – commonly known simply as CFK or Cristina, and satirically as Kristina – is Argentina's most high-profile female politician since Evita. Born in 1953 in La Plata, she became involved in political activism while studying law there in the 1970s. She met Néstor Kirchner through anti-military politics and, after they married, moved to his native **Santa Cruz Province**, where they practised law and embarked on their political careers. After serving several terms as a representative of Santa Cruz Province in the national congress, Cristina was elected a senator for the province of Buenos Aires. In 2003, she became the country's first lady or, as she preferred it, "First Female Citizen". Glamorous and photogenic, she has a forthright manner and a sharp tongue – with a tendency to give long ad-libbed speeches laced with emotional outbursts and vitriolic rhetoric.

FROM FIRST LADY TO PRESIDENT

Both as the president's wife and as president in her own right, she has taken a firm and progressive stand on human rights (including justice for the victims of the dictatorship, same-sex marriage, transgender identity and gender equality) and the need for Latin America to assert itself on the world stage. Her popularity with the working classes (which secured her a landslide second electoral victory) and her high-profile **ambassadorial trips** abroad – together with a fashionable wardrobe – have led to inevitable comparisons with Evita. However, she told one newspaper early on, perhaps tongue-in-cheek, that she was both more intelligent and more beautiful.

She has also often been likened to **Hillary Clinton** – clever, tough and not afraid to make enemies. But Cristina dismissed that too, saying that Hillary only became a force in politics because she was married to Bill, whereas she is very much her own boss. Other observers, much to her horror, came to see her as an Argentine **Margaret Thatcher** – owing to her confrontational, anti-consensus approach and tendency to listen only to an ever-shrinking inner core of sympathetic advisers. Ironically, history might see her more as a reincarnation of Perón himself – a clever demagogue with authoritarian tendencies who made the most of the death of a consort but suffered from not knowing when, or to whom, to hand over power.

Although her presidency came to an end in 2015, it is unlikely that we've seen the end of Cristina in Argentine public life.

2009	2010
Argentine film *The Secret in Their Eyes* (*El secreto de sus ojos*) wins an Oscar.	Low-key bicentenary celebrations are held in May; Néstor Kirchner dies unexpectedly on October 27, aged 60.

houses of congress. Néstor Kirchner failed in his attempt to be elected as a member of the lower house of the national congress for Buenos Aires Province and stood down as Justicialist party leader. The presidential couple faced growing allegations of nepotism – Néstor's sister Alicia was made a minister – and repeated questions have been raised about how the Kirchners' personal declared assets rocketed since they came to power.

The 2010 bicentenary
One hundred years after its lavish belle époque centenary, Argentina hadn't exactly lived up to the heady promise of world domination and the bicentenary celebrations in 2010 were far more low-key. Even so, the government organized all manner of military processions and music-led festivities to entertain the crowds and launched a series of high-minded projects with logos and slogans galore (see box, p.63). The 2016 anniversary – two hundred years after the official declaration of independence – was an excuse for more pomp and circumstance.

Life after Néstor
When Néstor Kirchner stood aside in 2007, it was generally assumed he would run again for the presidency at the end of his wife's term in 2011, and would stand a good chance of winning. Those carefully laid plans were wrecked when Néstor's poor health took a turn for the worse and he died of a heart attack on October 27, 2010. His widow set about beatifying her late husband, donned mourning black and referred to Néstor mystically as "Él" – He. A mausoleum was built in their Patagonian home town of El Calafate, streets and public buildings were named after the former leader and a hagiographic biopic was released along with myriad books on his life and politics.

Despite favourable opinion polls, Cristina left it until the very last minute before announcing that she would run for a second term as president. In the build-up to the election her human rights record was challenged by members of the Qom indigenous community, who staged a hunger strike and blocked off one of Buenos Aires' main roads to call for the return of their ancestral land in Formosa (the group renewed their demonstration in the capital in 2015). However, undoubtedly benefiting from her widow status, a blip of good economic news and, above all, a divided opposition, she won the first-round ballot by a landslide. On December 10, 2011, she swore the oath of office, with former economy minister, Amado Boudou, as her vice president.

Cristina's second term
Cristina's second honeymoon period came to a sudden end in February 2012, when a commuter train failed to stop at the capital's busy Once station, killing 51 and injuring hundreds. The ensuing public outrage led the government to promise long-overdue modernization of the country's criminally neglected rail network.

The year continued to bring bad news, with a further string of corruption allegations in the increasingly hostile press, targeting the playboy vice president in particular. As longstanding energy and transport subsidies were lifted and unions demanded massive wage hikes, inflation continued unabated. The official rate of ten percent was widely contested (unofficial sources put it at 25 percent or higher), though financial consultants who did so were fined. Argentina's middle classes were annoyed by tight currency controls that restricted their ability to go on holiday, but a parallel market

2011	2012
Now widowed and clad in black, CFK wins a landslide re-election victory in November. Members of Qom indigenous group stage hunger strike in Buenos Aires over land rights issues.	A crowded commuter train crashes into the buffers at Once station on February 22, in one of the worst rail accidents in the country's history.

started selling US dollars for fifty percent more (the "blue" rate) than the state-imposed rate of just shy of five pesos to the dollar.

At the end of 2012, the government drove legislation through congress ostensibly designed to encourage plurality of the media, but opponents – above all the powerful *Clarín* media group – maintained that it was an attack on the free media intended to stifle legitimate dissent. A series of court appeals and counter-appeals further poisoned the already bitter relations between the president and her followers, on one side, and the media and judiciary on the other.

After Cristina

Although Cristina's popularity ratings were at an all-time low early in 2013, the opposition still seemed unable to unite behind a plausible leader. Political commentators warned that the only real opposition was coming from the media, the judiciary and alienated sectors of the trade union movement. Meanwhile, the president and her followers started to suggest they would favour changing the constitution to allow her to run for a third term.

However, the economy continued to flounder, with inflation surging to thirty percent, and Cristina was hit by a series of damaging controversies, notably the suspicious death of prosecutor Alberto Nisman, days before he was due to release a report condemning the government over the 1994 bombing of the AMIA Jewish centre. Nevertheless, the Peronists were still expected to triumph in the 2015 presidential election, with the president of the Justicialist party, Daniel Scioli, the candidate. However, in a shock result, the country moved to the right, with Buenos Aires mayor Mauricio Macri edging out Scioli by under three percent.

Macri, the scion of a wealthy family and ex-chairman of Boca Juniors, promised to tackle spiralling inflation, boost foreign investment, forge deals with foreign creditors, and reduce crime. Many fear that he will move to halt the human rights trials related to the brutal military dictatorship, and impose neoliberal austerity. With a divided country, an economy in the doldrums, and a Peronist party weakened but still dominant in congress, it remains to be seen how effective Macri will be.

ARGENTINA'S POPE

Argentina's recent history, including the dark years of the dictatorship, came under close scrutiny in 2013 when **Jorge Bergoglio**, an Argentine of Italian descent, became **Pope Francis I**. Bergoglio was known as a modest man who travelled by bus and lived in a simple apartment in Buenos Aires, although his past was tainted by allegations that he withdrew protection from two Jesuit priests who were jailed after carrying out social work in the city's slums during the Dirty War. His defenders deny the claims, saying there is no proof. In his first few years Pope Francis I has had a significant impact, speaking out on subjects like poverty and climate change, and taking a more progressive – though still far from liberal – approach to subjects such as homosexuality.

2013	2015
In March, the former cardinal archbishop of Buenos Aires, Jorge Mario Bergoglio, becomes Pope Francis I.	Prosecutor Alberto Nisman, who was investigating the 1994 AMIA bombing, is found dead on January 18. In November, centre-right candidate Mauricio Macri narrowly wins the presidential election.

Environment and wildlife

Argentina's natural wonders are some of its chief joys. Its remarkable diversity of habitats, ranging from subtropical jungles to subantarctic icesheets, is complemented by an unexpected juxtaposition of species: parrots foraging alongside glaciers; flamingoes surviving bitter subzero temperatures on the stark Andean altiplano. Though the divisions are too complicated to list fully here, we've covered Argentina's most distinctive habitats, along with the species of flora and fauna typical to each.

Pampas grassland

The vast alluvial plain that centres on Buenos Aires Province and radiates out into the surrounding provinces was once pampas grassland, famous for its clumps of brush-tailed *cortadera* grass. However, its deep, extremely fertile soil has seen it become the agricultural heart of modern Argentina, and this original habitat has almost entirely disappeared, transformed by cattle grazing and intensive arable farming.

Once, these plains were the home of **pampas deer** (*venado de las pampas*), but today only a few hundred individuals survive, mainly in Samborombón and Campos del Tuyú in Buenos Aires Province. The **coypu** (*coipo*) is a large rodent commonly found in the region's wetlands, especially in places like the Paraná Delta. The great *vizcacha* dens described in the nineteenth century by natural history writer W.H. Hudson (see p.565) have all but disappeared, but you may see an endemic bird named for the writer, Hudson's canastero, along with greater **rheas**, burrowing **parrots** (*loro barranquero*) and **ovenbirds** (*horneros*). Named after the domed, concrete-hard mud nests they build on posts, ovenbirds have always been held in great affection by gauchos and country folk.

Bordering the Pampas to the north and west is a semicircular fringe of **espinal woodland**, a type of open wooded "parkland". Common species of tree include **acacia** and the **ceibo**, Argentina's national tree, which in spring produces a profusion of scarlet blooms.

Mesopotamian grassland

The humid Mesopotamian grasslands extend across much of Corrientes and Entre Ríos provinces and into southernmost Misiones. Here you will find *yatay* palm savannah and some of Argentina's most important **wetlands**, notably the Esteros de Iberá.

The wetlands have a remarkable diversity of birdlife, including numerous species of duck, rail, ibis and heron. Some of the most distinctive species are the **wattled jacana** (*jacana*); the **southern screamer** (*chajá*), a hulking bird the size of a turkey; **roseate spoonbills** (*espátula rosada*); and **jabirus** (*yabirú*), the largest variety of stork, measuring almost 1.5m tall, with a bald head and shoe-horn bill. Up above fly **snail kites** (*caracoleros*), which use their bills to prise freshwater snails from their shells.

In the shallow swamps, among reed beds and long grasses, you will find the **marsh deer** (*ciervo de los pantanos*), South America's largest native deer, with multi-horned antlers. One of the most common wetland animals is the **capybara** (*carpincho*), the world's biggest rodent, weighing up to 50kg. **Reptiles** include the **black cayman** (*yacaré negro*), which grows up to 2.8m in length, and is the victim of illegal hunting.

WHERE TO SEE THE HABITATS

Subtropical Paraná forest

Subtropical Paraná forest (*selva paranaense*) is Argentina's most biologically diverse ecosystem, a dense mass of vegetation that conforms to most people's idea of a jungle. The most frequently visited area of Paraná forest is Parque Nacional Iguazú, but it is also found in patches across the rest of Misiones, and parts of Corrientes. It has over two hundred tree species, including the **palo rosa** (one of the highest canopy species, at up to 40m); the **strangler fig** (*higuerón bravo*); the **lapacho**, with its beautiful pink flowers; and the **Misiones cedar** (*cedro misionero*), a fine hardwood species that has suffered heavily from logging. Lower storeys of vegetation include the wild **yerba mate** tree, first cultivated by the Jesuits in the seventeenth century; the **palmito** palm, whose edible core is exploited as palm heart; and endangered prehistoric **tree ferns**. Festooning the forest are lianas, mosses, ferns and epiphytes, including several hundred varieties of **orchid**.

More than five hundred species of bird inhabit the Paraná forest, and you stand a good chance of seeing the **toco toucan** (*tucán grande*), with its bright orange bill.

This part of the country is also one of the few places you just might see the highly endangered **jaguar** (*yaguareté* or *tigre*). Weighing up to 160kg, this beast is the continent's most fearsome predator.

The dry chaco

The dry chaco refers to the parched plain of thorn scrub that covers most of central and western Chaco and Formosa provinces, northeastern Salta and much of Santiago del Estero. To early explorers and settlers, much of this area was known simply as the **Impenetrable** for its aridity. Everything, it seems, is defensive: the *vinal* shrub, for instance, is dreaded by riders for its brutal spikes, up to 20cm long. In places, there is a dense undergrowth of **chaguar** and **caraguatá**: robust, yucca-like plants that the Wichí process to make fibre for their *yica* bags.

Perhaps the hardest wood is that of the endangered, slow-growing **palo santo** (meaning "holy stick"). Its fragrant, green-tinged wood can be burnt as an insect repellent. The **palo borracho** (or *yuchán*) is the most distinctive tree of all, with a bulbous, porous trunk to store water; the tree protects itself, especially when young, with rhino-horned spikes.

The dry chaco is home to forty percent of Argentina's mammal species. An estimated two hundred **jaguars** hang on here. Less threatened are the **puma** and the **Geoffroy's cat** (*gato montés*). One of three species of native Argentine wild pig, the famous **Chacoan peccary** (*chancho quimilero*) was thought to be extinct until rediscovered in Paraguay in 1975, and later in a few isolated areas of the Argentine dry chaco. Another high-profile living fossil is the nocturnal **giant armadillo** (*tatú carreta*). Weighing as much as 60kg, a full-grown one is strong enough to carry a man.

The yungas

Yungas is the term applied to the subtropical band of the Argentine Northwest that lies between the chaco and the Andean precordillera, from the Bolivian border through Jujuy, Salta, Tucumán and into Catamarca. Abrupt changes of altitude give rise to radical changes in the flora here, creating wildly different ecosystems. The lowest altitudes are home to transitional woodland and lowland jungle (*selva pedemontana*), up to about 600m. Most of the trees and shrubs in these lower levels are deciduous and have showy blossoms: jacaranda, *palo blanco* and *amarillo*, *lapacho* and **ceibo**. Much of this forest has been hard hit by clearance.

Above 600m starts the most famous *yungas* habitat, the **montane cloud-forests** (*selva montaña* or *nuboselva*), best seen in the national parks of Calilegua, Baritú and El Rey. These forests form a gloomy canopy of tall evergreens, beneath which several varieties of cane and bamboo compete for sunlight. The tree trunks are covered in moss and lichen; lianas hang in a tangle; epiphytes and orchids flourish; and bromeliads, heliconias and succulents all add to the dank atmosphere.

More than three hundred varieties of **bird** inhabit the *yungas* forests. Species include the **toco toucan**; the rare **black-and-chestnut eagle** (*águila poma*); the **king vulture** (*jote real*), with a strikingly patterned head; and numerous varieties of **hummingbird**.

The streams are favourite haunts of crab-eating **raccoons** (called *mayuatos* here). Other mammals found close to the water include South America's largest native terrestrial mammal, the **Brazilian tapir** (*tapir*, *anta* or *mborevi*). The strange **tree-porcupine** (*coendú*) clambers around the canopy with the help of its tail, while the **three-toed sloth** (*perezoso*) depends on its sabre-like claws for locomotion. Felines are represented by **jaguars**, **margays**, **pumas** and **Geoffroy's cats**, but you will be lucky to see anything more than their tracks. This also applies to the most famous regional creature of all: the **taruca**, a stocky, native Andean deer.

The puna

The pre-*puna* and higher **puna** of the Andean Northwest encompass harsh, arid habitats. The most distinctive plant is the **cardón cactus** (also called *pasakán*), which indigenous folklore holds to be the reincarnated form of ancestors. On the higher slopes, you'll also find a type of rock-hard cushion-shaped prehistoric moss called **yacreta** that grows incredibly slowly – perhaps a millimetre a year – but lives for hundreds of years. It has been heavily exploited, partly for medicinal teas, but mainly because it is the only fuel found at these altitudes.

Of the fauna, birds are the most prolific; you can see all three varieties of **flamingo** – Andean, Chilean and James' – wading or flying together. Mammals spotted in the *puna* include **vizcachas**, looking like large rabbits with long, curly tails, and camelids (see box below).

LLAMAS, ALPACAS, GUANACOS AND VICUÑAS

The animals most associated with the Andes are the four species of South American **camelids**, especially the domesticated **llama**. Local people use llamas as beasts of burden, as well as for meat and wool. The other domesticated camelid is the slightly smaller **alpaca**, which produces finer wool, and the two other South American camelids are both wild. The short-haired antelope-like **guanaco** inhabits a wide area, from the northwest *puna* to the mountains and steppe of Tierra del Fuego; listen for their eerie, rasping call. The guanaco population is still relatively healthy, although it is hunted for its meat and skin. Its diminutive cousin, the **vicuña**, is the most graceful, shy and – despite its delicate appearance – hardy of the four camelids, capable of living at the most extreme altitudes. It's usually found between 3500m and 4600m, as far south as northern San Juan Province, although the biggest flocks are in Catamarca Province. Hunting brought them to the brink of extinction, but protection measures have helped ensure that their numbers have risen to a safe level. Attempts are being made to exploit their valuable fur (the second-finest natural fibre in the world after silk) on a sustainable commercial level.

Patagonian steppe

Typified by brush scrub and wiry *coirón* grassland, the Patagonian steppe (*estepa*) covers the greatest extent of any Argentine ecosystem. This vast expanse of semi-desert lies south of the Pampas and east of the Andean cordillera. Vegetation is stunted by gravelly soils, high winds and lack of water, except along rivers, where you find marshlands (*mallines*) and startlingly green willows (*sauces*). Just about the only trees, apart from the willows, are non-native Lombardy poplars, planted to shelter estancias.

Much of the scrubby brush is composed of monochrome *mata negra*, but in places you'll come across the resinous, perfumed *mata verde*, or the ash-grey *mata guanaco*, which blooms with dazzling orange flowers. You'll also see spiky **calafate** bushes, and *molle* – one of the largest bushes, covered with thorns and parasitic galls.

Your best chance of spotting some of the steppe's key species is in places such as Chubut's Península Valdés and Punta Tombo. **Guanacos** abound here. Look out too for the **mara** (Patagonian hare), the largest of Argentina's endemic mammals. This long-legged rodent, the size of a small dog, is becoming ever rarer. The **grey fox** (*zorro gris*) is regularly found around national park gates, waiting for scraps thrown by tourists. *Pichi* and *peludo* **armadillos** are often seen scampering across the plains.

Another characteristic bird of prey is the black-chested buzzard-eagle (*águila mora*), a powerful flier with broad wings and splendid plumage. The classic bird of the steppe, though, is the lesser or Darwin's rhea (*ñandú petiso* or *choique*). These long-legged, ashy-grey birds lay their eggs in communal clutches.

Patagonian forests

The eastern slopes of the Patagonian cordillera are cloaked in forests of **nothofagus southern beech**. Two species run from northern Neuquén to Tierra del Fuego: the **lenga** (upland beech) and the **ñire** (lowland or Antarctic beech). In autumn both species turn a variety of yellow and red hues. Associated with them are three intriguing plant species: false mistletoe (*farolito chino*), a semi-parasitic plant; verdigris-coloured **lichen beards** (*barba del indio* or *toalla del indio*); and **llao llao** tree fungus, also called *pan de indio* ("Indian's bread"). The *llao llao* produces brain-like knots on trunks and branches that are beloved of local artisans.

One of Argentina's most remarkable trees, the **araucaria monkey puzzle**, grows in central Neuquén on volcanic soils (see box, p.430). The most diverse range of plant and tree species in the region is found in the rare **Valdivian temperate rainforest** (*selva valdiviana*), found in patches of the central Patagonian Andes from Lanín to Los

---

ENVIRONMENTAL THREATS

Despite the protection afforded by a relatively well-managed national park system, the country's precious environmental heritage remains under threat. The most pressing issues are **habitat loss** and the protection of threatened forest, such as the Paraná forest in Misiones – a habitat that's been decimated over the border in Brazil and Paraguay. **Hydroelectric projects** in the northeast have destroyed valuable habitats along the Uruguay and Paraná rivers – and threaten to do the same in Patagonia (see p.556) – and **overfishing** has also severely depleted stocks. The phenomenal rise of **genetically modified soya** production in Argentina has also alarmed environmental campaigners, with particular concerns about the effects of monoculture on the country's biodiversity. Major oil and shale gas extraction projects pose further threats.

That said, **environmental** awareness is slowly gaining ground, especially among the younger generation. Greenpeace has thousands of members in Argentina; the national parks system is expanding with the help of international loans; and committed national and local pressure groups such as the Fundación Vida Silvestre in Buenos Aires (see p.40) are ensuring that ecological issues are not ignored.

Alerces, usually around low passes where rainfall is heaviest. Another tree species found only in the central Patagonian Lake District is the mighty **alerce**, or Patagonian cypress, which resembles a Californian redwood and is one of the world's oldest and grandest species.

Many of the birds that inhabit the steppe are also found in the cordillera. Typical woodland species include the world's most southerly parrot, the **Austral parakeet** (*cachaña* or *cotorra*) and two birds that allow you to get surprisingly close – the **Magellanic woodpecker** (*carpintero negro gigante*), and the **Austral pygmy owl** (*caburé*). Finally, if any bird has a claim to symbolizing South America, it's the **Andean condor**. With eyesight eight times better than a human's, and the longest wingspan of any bird of prey, it's the undisputed lord of the skies from Venezuela to Tierra del Fuego.

The principal predator of cordillera mammals is the **puma**, which has an extensive range in Argentina but is rarely seen. Perhaps the most endangered creature is the **huemul**, a thick-set native deer (see box, p.421). Almost as endangered is the **pudú**, the world's smallest deer, measuring 40cm at the shoulder. It has small, single-pointed horns, and is difficult to spot, as it inhabits the dense undergrowth of the central cordillera forests.

Introduced species include the European **red deer** (*ciervo colorado*) and **wild boar** (*jabalí*), both of which have reached plague proportions in some parts of the central Lake District. The **beaver** (*castor*), introduced to Tierra del Fuego in an attempt to start a fur-farming industry, has had devastating effects on the environment.

The Atlantic seaboard

Argentina has 4725km of **Atlantic coastline**, with several coastal areas integrated into a shorebird reserve network, designed to protect migrant waders across the Americas. Birds like the **Hudsonian godwit** (*becasa de mar*) and the **red knot** (*playero rojizo*) migrate from Alaska as far as Tierra del Fuego – over 17,000km. Other coastal species are **Magellanic penguins** (*pingüino magallánico*), whose major continental breeding colony is at Punta Tombo; **Chilean flamingos**; and the **South American tern** (*gaviotín sudamericano*).

Península Valdés is the main destination for marine fauna. Its twin bays, Golfo Nuevo and Golfo San José (Latin America's first marine park), are where as much as a quarter of the world's population of **southern right whales** (*ballena franca austral*) breed annually. The peninsula also hosts a forty-thousand-strong and growing colony of **southern elephant seals** (*elefante marino*). Other sightings might include **sea lions** (*lobos del mar*), found in colonies along the whole Atlantic coast, and possibly even a **killer whale** (*orca*). Further down the coast at Cabo Blanco, you can see the endangered **fur seal** (*lobo de dos pelos*); while Puerto Deseado and San Julián are fine places to catch the piebald **commerson's dolphins** (*toninas overas*). Sea trips on the Beagle Channel offer a slim chance of seeing **minke whale**, or perhaps even an endangered **marine otter** (*nutria marina* or *chungungo*).

Music

With the obvious exception of tango, Argentina's music has a low international profile. The country has a tradition that doesn't quite fit the popular concept of "Latin American" music: there is little of the exhilarating tropical rhythms of, say, Brazil, nor is there much of the panpipe sound associated with Andean countries. Within Latin America, however, Argentina is famed for its rock music, or rock nacional – a term which embraces an eclectic bunch of groups and musicians. Folk music, or folklore, is also popular throughout the country and provides a predominantly rural counterpoint to tango.

Tango

The great Argentine writer Jorge Luis Borges was a tango enthusiast and something of a historian of the music. "My informants all agree on one fact," he wrote. "The tango was born in the brothels." Borges' sources were a little presumptuous, perhaps, for no one can exactly pinpoint **tango**'s birthplace, but it certainly had roots in Buenos Aires. Early tango was a definitively urban music: a product of the melting pot of European immigrants, *criollos*, blacks and natives, drawn together when the city became the country's capital in 1880. Tango was thus forged from a range of musical influences that included Andalucían flamenco, southern Italian melodies, Cuban habanera, African *candombé* and percussion, European polkas and mazurkas, Spanish *contradanse* and, closer to home, the *milonga* – the song of the gaucho. In this early form, tango became associated with the bohemian life of bordello brawls and *compadritos* – knife-wielding, womanizing thugs. By 1914 there were over one hundred thousand more men than women in Buenos Aires (largely because significantly more men than women migrated to Argentina), and machismo and violence were part of the culture. Men would dance together in cafés and bars, practising new steps and keeping in shape while waiting for their women, often the *minas* (a slang term for a beautiful, sexy woman, though it can also be used pejoratively) of the bordellos. Their dances tended to have a showy yet predatory quality, often revolving around a possessive relationship between two men and one woman. In these surroundings, the *compadrito* danced the tango into existence.

The original **tango ensembles** were trios of violin, guitar and flute, but around the end of the nineteenth century the **bandoneón**, the tango accordion, arrived from Germany, and the classic tango orchestra was born. The box-shaped button accordion, now inextricably linked with Argentine tango, was invented around 1860 in Germany to play religious music in organless churches, and was reworked as the *bandoneón*.

In Argentina, an early pioneer of the instrument was **Eduardo Arolas**, remembered as the "Tiger of the Bandoneón". He recognized its immediate affinity with the tango – indeed, he claimed it was an instrument made to play tango, with a deep melancholy feeling that suited immigrants nostalgic for the homeland. It is not, however, an easy instrument to play, demanding a great deal of skill, with its seventy-odd buttons each producing one of two notes depending on whether the bellows are being compressed or expanded.

Vicente Greco (1888–1924) is credited as the first band leader to standardize the form of a tango group, with his **Orquesta Típica Criolla** of two violins, two *bandoneones* and a flute. There were some larger bands but the instrumentation remained virtually unchanged until the 1940s.

First tango in Paris

By the first decade of the twentieth century, the tango was an intrinsic part of the popular culture of Buenos Aires, played on the streets by organ grinders and danced in tenement courtyards. Its association with whorehouses and the low-down Porteño lifestyle, plus its saucy, sometimes obscene and fatalistic lyrics, didn't endear it to the aristocratic families of Buenos Aires, though, and they did their best to protect their children from the new dance, but it was a losing battle.

A number of upper-class playboys, such as poet and writer **Ricardo Güiraldes**, enjoyed mixing with the *compadritos* and emulating their lifestyle – from a debonair distance. It was Güiraldes who, on a European grand tour in 1910, is said to have been responsible for bringing the dance to Europe. The following year Güiraldes gave an impromptu performance in a Paris salon to a fashionable audience, for whom tango's risqué sexuality ("the vertical expression of horizontal desire", as one wag dubbed it) was highly attractive. Despite the local archbishop's admonition that Christians should not in good conscience tango, they did, and in large numbers. And, once it was embraced in French salons, its credibility at home greatly increased. Back in Argentina, from bordello to ballroom, everyone was soon dancing the tango.

And then came **Rudolph Valentino**, a charismatic Hollywood star whose image tango fitted to a T. A tango scene was gratuitously added to his film *The Four Horsemen of the Apocalypse* (1926): dressed in a gaucho's wide trousers, Valentino danced with a carnation between his lips (his own invention) and a whip in his hand. The scene was the hit of the film, and, travesty though the dance was, it meant the tango was now known all over the world. Tango classes and competitions were held in Paris, and tango teas in England, with young devotees togged up as Argentine gauchos. The greatest tango singer of all time, **Carlos Gardel**, became the darling of Parisian society, and later starred in Hollywood films, though he was forced to perform dressed as a gaucho. To this day, this image remains many people's primary perception of tango.

Tango's golden age

Back in Argentina, in the 1920s, tango moved out of the *cantinas* and bordellos and into cabarets and theatres, entering a classic era under band leaders like **Roberto Firpo**, **Julio de Caro** and **Francisco Canaro**. With their *orquestas típicas* they took the old line-up of Vicente Greco (two *bandoneones*, two violins and a flute) and substituted a double bass for the flute, thereby adding sonority and depth. It was during this period that some of the most famous of all tangos were written, including Uruguayan **Gerardo Hernán Matos Rodríguez**'s *La Comparsita* in 1917.

Early **tango-canciónes** (tango songs) used the language of the ghetto and celebrated the life of ruffians and pimps. **Angel Villoldo** and **Pascual Contursi** introduced the classic lyric of a male perspective, placing the blame for heartache firmly on the shoulders of a fickle woman. In its **dance**, tango consolidated a contradictory mix of earthy sensuality and middle-class kitsch. It depended on an almost violent friction, with the dancers passionate and sometimes seemingly out of control.

The second golden age

As an expression of the working classes, the progression of the tango has inevitably been linked with social and political developments in Argentina. The music declined a little in the 1930s as the army took power and suppressed what was seen as a potentially subversive force, but it enjoyed a second golden age with the rise of Perón and his emphasis on nationalism and popular culture. By the late 1940s Buenos Aires was a city of five or six million, and each barrio boasted ten or fifteen amateur tango orchestras, while the established orchestras played in the cabarets and nightclubs in the city centre. Sometime in this era, however, tango began to move away from the working class and into middle-class and intellectual milieus. It became a sort of collective reminiscence of a world that no longer existed – essentially nostalgia.

CARLOS GARDEL

Carlos Gardel (1887–1935) is a legend in Argentina. A huge influence in spreading the popularity of tango round the world, he came to be seen as a symbol of the fulfilment of the dreams of poor Porteño workers.

In Argentina, it was Gardel above all who transformed tango from an essentially low-down dance form to a song style popular among widely differing social classes. Everything about Gardel – his suavity, his arrogance and his natural machismo – spelt tango. The advent of radio, recording and film all helped his career, but nothing helped him more than his own voice – a voice that was born to sing tango and which became the model for all future singers of the genre.

His arrival on the scene coincided with the first period of tango's golden age and the development of *tango-canción* in the 1920s and 1930s. During his life, Gardel recorded some nine hundred songs and starred in numerous films, notably *The Tango on Broadway* in 1934. He was tragically killed in an air crash in Colombia at the height of his fame, and his legendary status was confirmed. His image is still everywhere in Buenos Aires, on plaques and huge murals, and in record-store windows, while admirers pay homage to his life-sized, bronze statue in Chacarita cemetery (see p.102).

After Gardel, the split between the **evolutionists**, who wanted to develop new forms of tango, and the **traditionalists**, who thought it was fine as it was, became more pronounced. Bands, as elsewhere in the world during this period, became larger, in the mode of small orchestras, and a mass following for tango was enjoyed through dance halls, radio and recordings until the end of the golden age around 1950.

In the 1950s, with the end of Peronism and the coming of rock'n'roll, tango slipped into the shadows once again.

Astor Piazzolla and tango nuevo

Astor Piazzolla dominates the recent history of tango, much as Carlos Gardel was the key figure of its classic era. From 1937, Piazzolla played second *bandoneón* in the orchestra of the master Aníbal Troilo, where he developed his feel for arrangements. (The first *bandoneón* takes the melody, and the second *bandoneón* the harmony.)

Troilo left Piazzolla his *bandoneón* when he died, and Piazzolla went on to ensure that tango would never be the same again. Piazzolla's idea was that tango could be a serious music to listen to, not just for dancing, and for many of the old guard this was a step too far. As he explained: "Musicians hated me. I was taking the old tango away from them. The old tango, the one they loved, was dying. And they hated me, they threatened my life hundreds of times. They waited for me outside my house, two or three of them, and gave me a good beating. They even put a gun at my head once." In the 1970s, Piazzolla was out of favour with Argentina's military regime and he and his family moved to Paris, returning to Argentina only after the fall of the junta. His influence, however, had spread, and his experiments – and international success – opened the way for other radical transformations.

Chief among these, in 1970s Buenos Aires, was the fusion of **tango-rockero** – tango rock. This replaced the flexible combination of *bandoneón*, bass and no drums, as favoured by Piazzolla, with a rock-style rhythm section, electric guitars and synthesizers. It was pioneered by **Litto Nebbia**, whose album, *Homage to Gardel and Le Pera*, is one of the most successful products of this fusion, retaining the melancholy of the traditional form in a rock format. Tango moved across to jazz, too, through groups such as the trio **Siglo XX**, while old-guard figures like **Roberto "Polaco" Goyeneche** and **Osvaldo Pugliese** kept traditional tango alive.

These days in Argentina, the tango scene is a pretty broad one, with rock and jazz elements along with the more traditional sound of acoustic groups. There is no shortage of good *tangueros* (tango musicians/singers) and they know each other well and jam together often. Big tango orchestras, however, are a thing of the past, and tango bands have returned to their roots, to an intimate era of trios, quartets and quintets – a sextet is serious business. Two of the best sextets, the **Sexteto Mayor** and **Sexteto Berlingieri**, joined together in the 1980s to play for the show *Tango Argentino*, and subsequent shows which revived an interest in tango across Europe and the US. The Sexteto Mayor, founded in 1973 by the virtuoso *bandoneonistas* **José Libertella** (1933–2004) and **Luis Stazo** (born 1930), is one of the best tango ensembles in Argentina today, though some of its founding members are no longer with us.

In a more modern idiom, singers like **Susana Rinaldi** and **Adriana Varela** are successfully renovating and re-creating tango, both at home and abroad. They are names to look out for along with *bandoneonistas* **Osvaldo Piro**, **Carlos Buono** and **Walter Ríos**; singer **José Ángel Trelles**; and **Grupo Volpe Tango Contemporáneo**, led by Antonio Volpe.

Lately tango is enjoying an upsurge of popularity in Argentina and other parts of the world, thanks in part to TV shows like *Strictly Come Dancing*, while the likes of the Buenos Aires-based Parakultural *milonga* and the band Bajofondo, which successfully melds tango with contemporary electronic music, are once again reinventing tango for a new generation. Incidentally, Gustavo Santaolalla, one of the founders of Bajofondo, won the Academy Award for Original Score in 2005 for *Brokeback Mountain* and again the following year for *Babel*.

Text courtesy of Jan Fairley

Rock nacional

Listened to passionately throughout the country, Argentina's home-grown rock music – known simply as **rock nacional** – began to emerge in the 1960s with groups such as **Almendra** (one of whose members, **Luis Alberto Spinetta**, went on to a solo career and until his death in 2012 was one of Argentina's most successful and original musicians) and **Los Gatos**, who in 1967 had a massive hit with the eloquent *La Balsa*. From a sociological point of view, though, the significance of *rock nacional* really began to emerge under the military dictatorship of 1976–83. At the very beginning of the dictatorship, there was an upsurge in rock concerts, during which musicians such as **Charly García**, frontman of the hugely popular **Serú Girán** and now a soloist, provided a subtle form of resistance with songs such as *No te dejes desanimar* (Don't be Discouraged), which helped provoke a collective sense of opposition among fans. It wasn't long, however, before the military rulers clamped down on what it saw as the subversive atmosphere generated at such concerts. The government issued recommendations that stadium owners should not let their premises be used for rock concerts, and by the end of the 1970s many bands had split up or gone into exile.

By 1980, cracks had begun to appear in the regime and a subtle freeing-up of the public sphere began. In December 1980, a concert by Serú Girán attracted sixty thousand fans to La Rural in Palermo, Buenos Aires: led by Charly García, the fans began to shout, in full view of the television cameras "*No se banca más*" (We Won't Put Up with it Any More).

By 1982 the rock movement was a loudly cynical voice, creating massively popular songs such as **Fito Páez**'s self-explanatory *Tiempos difíciles* (Difficult Times), Charly García's *Dinosaurios*, whose title is a clear reference to the military rulers, and *Maribel* by Argentina's finest rock lyricist, Spinetta, dedicated to the Madres de Plaza de Mayo.

Post-dictatorship rock

After the dictatorship ended, rock returned to a more apolitical role, typified by the light-hearted approach of 1984's most popular group, **Los Abuelos de la Nada**. One of the founding members of Los Abuelos, **Pappo**, went on to a solo career in heavy rock, appealing to a predominantly working-class section of society who felt that their lot had improved little with democracy; Pappo's music seemed to sum up their frustrations. One of the most popular groups of the 1980s was **Sumo**, fronted by charismatic **Luca Prodan**, an Italian raised in the UK who had come to Argentina in an attempt to shake off his heroin addiction. Sumo made sometimes surreal, noisy, reggae-influenced tracks, expressing distaste for the frivolous attitudes of Buenos Aires' upper-middle-class youth on tracks such as *Rubia tarada* (Stupid Blonde). Luca Prodan ultimately died of a heroin overdose in 1987, and is still idolized by Argentine rock fans.

Like Sumo, the strangely named and massively popular **Patricio Rey y Sus Redonditos de Ricota** (literally: Patricio Rey and His Little Balls of Ricotta) made noise with enigmatic tracks such as *Aquella vaca solitaria cubana* (That Solitary Cuban Cow), often touching on the dissatisfactions felt by many young Argentines in the aftermath of the dictatorship. Another success story of the 1980s and 1990s – albeit in a very different vein – was **Fito Páez**, whose 1992 album *El Amor después del amor*, with its sweet melodic tunes, one of them inspired by the film *Thelma and Louise*, sold millions throughout Latin America. One of Argentina's most original bands also emerged in the 1980s – **Los Fabulosos Cadillacs**, with their diverse and often frenetic fusion of rock, ska, dub, punk and rap. An irreverent and ironic sense of humour often underlies their politicized lyrics, all belted out by their charismatic, astringently-voiced lead singer, Vincentico, and backed up with a tight horn section and driving Latin percussion. Their classic album is *El León* (1992), on which you'll find their most famous anthem, *Matador*, a savage indictment of the military dictatorship.

Rock nacional's most enduring figures still include Charly García, whose wild exploits fill the pages of gossip magazines, include the internationally popular "sonic rock" band **Babasónicos**; experimental **Catupecu Machu**; punky **Attaque 77**; **Las Pelotas**, incorporating former Sumo members; melodic indie rockers **Estelares**; and the tropical rock sound of **Bersuit Vergarabat**.

Chamamé, cuarteto and folklore

Tango aside, Argentine music is mostly rooted in the rural dance traditions of the countryside, an amalgam of Spanish and immigrant Central European styles with indigenous music. Many of these dances – *rancheras, milongas, chacareras* and more – are shared with the neighbouring countries of Chile, Peru and Bolivia, while others like **chamamé** are uniquely Argentine. Argentina's indigenous roots are explored by singer-songwriter **Atahualpa Yupanqui**, who provided inspiration for the politicized *nueva canción* (new song) movement.

Chamamé

Chamamé is probably Argentina's most popular roots music. It has its origins in the rural culture of Corrientes – an Amerindian area that attracted nineteenth-century settlers from Poland, Austria-Hungary and Germany. These immigrants brought with them Middle European waltzes, mazurkas and polkas, which over time merged with music from the local Guaraní indigenous traditions, and African rhythms from the music of the region's slaves. Thus emerged *chamamé*, a music of poor rural *mestizos*, many of whom looked more Indian than European, and whose songs used both Spanish and the Indian Guaraní languages.

Chamamé's melodies have a touch of the melancholy attributed to the Guaraní, while its history charts the social, cultural and political relationships of *mestizo* migrants. Until the 1950s, it was largely confined to Corrientes, but during that decade many rural migrants moved to Buenos Aires, bringing their music and dances with them. *Chamamé* began to attract wider attention – in part, perhaps, because it was a rare folk dance in which people dance in cheek-to-cheek embrace.

The essential sound of *chamamé* comes from its key instrument – the large **piano accordion** (on occasion the *bandoneón*). It sweeps through tunes which marry contrasting rhythms, giving the music an immediate swing. Its African influences may have contributed to the music's accented weak beats so that bars blend and swing together. The distinctive percussive rhythms and haunting melodies are the music's unique, compelling features.

Argentina's reigning king of *chamamé* is **Raúl Barboza**, an artist who has also notched up a certain degree of success in Europe. Barboza's *conjunto* features a typical *chamamé* line-up of one or two accordions, a guitar and *guitarrón* (bass guitar). Perhaps one of the best-known *chamamé* artists internationally is **Chango Spasiuk**, an Argentine of Ukrainian heritage, who has been successful in producing a sort of *chamamé*-rock crossover, with a more modern feel that still preserves the music's essence.

Cuarteto

The Argentine dance style known as *cuarteto* first became popular in the 1940s. Named after the original **Cuarteto Leo** who played it, its line-up typically involves a solo singer, piano, accordion and violin, and its dance consists of a huge circle, moving counterclockwise, to a rhythm called *tunga-tunga*. In the 1980s it underwent a resurgence of interest in the working-class "tropical" dancehalls of Buenos Aires and Córdoba, where it was adopted alongside Colombian *guarachas*, Dominican merengue and Latin salsa. It slowly climbed up the social ladder to reach a middle-class market, notching up big sales. The most famous contemporary singer of *cuarteto* is **Carlos "La Mona" Jiménez**.

Folklore

In a movement aligned to *nueva canción*, dozens of folklore singers and groups emerged in the 1960s and 1970s, their music characterized by tight arrangements and four-part harmonies. The big *nueva canción* star was **Mercedes Sosa**, who passed away in 2009; other leading artists of these decades included the group **Los Chalchaleros**, guitarist **Eduardo Falú**, and **Ariel Ramírez**, notable for his *zambas* and Creole Mass. In more recent years groups have come through experimenting and re-evaluating the folk dance traditions, including the *zamba*, a national dance that involves the couple taking slow steps back and forth while waving handkerchiefs. Among this new wave were **Los Trovadores**, **Los Huanca Hua** and **Cuarteto Zupay**. The best place to see folklore music is at the annual **Cosquín national folklore festival** (see p.197), which has been a fixture since the 1960s.

Contemporary music

More current acts to keep an eye out for include singer-songwriter (and Hollywood actress) **Mia Maestro**, alt-rocker **Marilina Bertoldi** and indie outfit **Banda de Turistas**. Argentine-Uruguayan band **Bajofondo** and the Argentine-French-Swiss **Gotan Project** are also worth a listen; both fuse tango with electro, rock, hip-hop and jazz influences.

Books

Argentina's intellectual tradition is reflected in its many bookshops, especially the splendidly monumental ones in Buenos Aires. For non-Spanish-speakers, there are specialist sellers in the capital (see p.126), though if you're looking for specific books, such as the works listed below, your best bet is to get a copy before you depart.

TRAVEL

★ **Bruce Chatwin** *In Patagonia*. For many travellers, this is *the* Argentine travel book – in fact, the book that broke the mould for travel writing in general. Written in the 1970s, it's really a series of self-contained tales (most famously of the Argentine adventures of Butch Cassidy and the Sundance Kid) strung together by their connection with Patagonia. This idiosyncratic book has even inspired a "Chatwin trail", although his rather cold style and literary embellishments have their detractors too.

Bruce Chatwin and Paul Theroux *Patagonia Revisited*, published in the US as *Nowhere is a Place*. Two doyens of Western travel writing combine to explore the literary associations of Patagonia. Wafer-thin and thoroughly enjoyable, this book throws more light on the myths of this far-flung land than it does on the place itself.

Che Guevara *The Motorcycle Diaries*. Che's own account of his epic motorcycle tour around Latin America, beginning in Buenos Aires and heading south to Patagonia and then up through Chile. He undertook the tour aged just 23 and the resulting diary is an intriguing blend of travel anecdotes and an insight into the mind of a nascent revolutionary.

George Chaworth Musters *At Home with the Patagonians*. The amazing 1869 journey of Musters as he rode through Patagonia, becoming in the process the first outsider to be accepted into Tehuelche society. This book is our prime source for information on the Tehuelche, and gives a portrait of a culture about to be exterminated.

Paul Theroux *The Old Patagonian Express*. More tales about trains by the tireless cynic. In the four chapters on Argentina, which he passed through just before the 1978 World Cup, he waxes lyrical about cathedral-like Retiro station and has a surreal dialogue with Borges.

A.F. Tschiffely *Tschiffely's Ride*. An account of a truly adventurous horseback ride – described as the "longest and most arduous on record ever made by man and horse" – made by Tschiffely from Buenos Aires to Washington DC in the 1920s and providing an insight into rural Argentina at the time.

HISTORY, POLITICS AND SOCIETY

★ **Paul Blustein** *And the Money Kept Rolling In (and Out): Wall Street, the IMF, and the Bankrupting of Argentina*. The definitive account of the 2001 Argentine economic crisis. Authoritative, and a cracking read.

Lucas Bridges *The Uttermost Part of the Earth*. The genius of this classic text on pioneering life in Tierra del Fuego in the late nineteenth century lies less in its literary attributes than in the extraordinary tales of an adventurous young man's relationship with the area's indigenous groups, and the invaluable ethnographic knowledge he imparts about a people whose culture was set to disappear within his lifetime.

Jimmy Burns *The Hand of God*. A compelling read in which Anglo-Argentine journalist Burns charts the rise and fall of Diego Maradona, updated in 2010 as the bad-boy hero of football prepared to manage the national squad in the World Cup. Burns also wrote *The Land that Lost its Heroes*, a thoroughly researched account of the Falklands/Malvinas conflict, and *Francis: Pope of Good Promise*.

Steph Davies *Hiraeth: Stories from Welsh Patagonia*. A concise collection of stories about the Welsh experience in Patagonia, published in 2015 to coincide with the 150th anniversary of their arrival.

★ **Uki Goñi** *The Real Odessa*. A thoroughly researched investigation into the aid given by Perón (and the Vatican) to Nazi war criminals; hundreds infamously settled in Argentina. The government and Peronist party in particular have done little to address their previous sheltering of these men – Goñi finds evidence that incriminating documents were being burnt as late as 1996.

Marcela López Levy and Nick Caistor *Argentina: the Kirchners and the rise and fall of left populism*. Published by the Latin America Bureau, this is an up-to-date, expert analysis of the most influential – and controversial – political couple in Argentina since the Peróns.

John Lynch *San Martín: Argentinian soldier, American hero*. The first modern English-language biography of José de San Martín, arguably the greatest of all Latin American heroes, who led the continent's independence struggle against Spain in the nineteenth century. Lynch is a major Latin American scholar; his numerous books also include biographies of nineteenth-century dictator Rosas and of

THE DIRTY WAR IN BOOKS AND FILM

The tragedy of the bloody 1979–83 "Dirty War" has left deep scars on Argentine society that are yet to heal, and the experience and legacy of those years is a recurrent theme in books – fact and fiction – and films set in the country. As well as the works below, there's *Nunca Mas* (Never Again), the 1984 report (assembled by a truth commission – a model later used by other Latin American countries facing past demons), which was the first to reveal the horrors of what had taken place. It is available in English at ⓦdesaparecidos.org, with an excellent intro by novelist Ernesto Sabato.

BOOKS

Rita Arditti *Searching for Life*. Describes the ongoing search by their wider families for hundreds of children who were "disappeared", many given for adoption to military families after their parents were captured.

Nathan Englander *The Ministry of Special Cases*. A wry and tragic fictional story by a Jewish-American writer, which deals with the disappearance of a teenage son during the *proceso*.

Tomás Eloy Martínez *Purgatory*. Heart-wrenching semi-autobiographical tale of a woman and a country still haunted by the ghosts of the past.

Jacobo Timerman *Prisoner Without A Name, Cell Without A Number*. A powerful first-person account written by a prisoner who survived.

Horacio Verbitsky *Confessions of an Argentine Dirty Warrior*. Infamous account of the horrific practice of pushing drugged prisoners from airborne planes into the River Plate.

Andrew Graham-Yooll *A State of Fear*. Written by a former *Buenos Aires Herald* editor, this is a very readable account of a dark era by a journalist living through and reporting on it.

FILMS

Argentina's vibrant movie industry has received two foreign-language Oscars, both for movies that deal with this subject.

The Official Story (1985). A middle-class woman learns of events that have been hidden from her when she sets out to uncover her adopted daughter's real parents.

The Secret in Their Eyes (2009). Through the story of

a federal agent revisiting an old murder case, this asks the question pondered by many: isn't it time to move on now? The answer is no – not while there are still people who have to live with the painful events three decades on, and who still have unanswered questions.

San Martín's brother-in-arms Simón Bolívar.

★ **Gabriela Nouzeilles and Graciela Montaldo** (eds) *The Argentina Reader*. Compendium of essays and stories on Argentina's history and culture, including extracts from many of the books listed here. An excellent starting point for further reading, though a bit hefty for lugging around.

Domingo F. Sarmiento *Facundo, or Civilization and Barbarism*. Written as a fictional biography of real-life gaucho thug Facundo Quiroga, this is probably the most influential nineteenth-century Latin American book. The essay defines one of Argentina's major cultural peculiarities

– the battle between the provinces seeking to carve out their own power and a sophisticated metropolis more interested in what is going on abroad than in its vast hinterland.

Richard W. Slatta *Gauchos and the Vanishing Frontier*. Scholarly work that is the perfect cerebral accompaniment to the glossy coffee-table tomes sold on the subject. Slatta charts the rise, fall and rise again of the gaucho, his lifestyle, his maltreatment by the upper classes and the myths that grew around him.

NATURE AND WILDLIFE

Charles Darwin *The Voyage of the Beagle*. Very readable account of Darwin's famous voyage, which takes him through Patagonia and the Pampas. Filled with observations on the flora, fauna, landscape and people that Darwin encounters, all described in the scientist's methodical yet evocative style.

Gerald Durrell *The Whispering Land*. A light-hearted read detailing Durrell's observations while animal-collecting in Península Valdés, the Patagonian steppe and the *yungas*. Enduring good value, despite what now comes across as a

colonial tone: his capacity for making animals into characters is unsurpassed. See also *The Drunken Forest*, about his trip to the Chaco.

W.H. Hudson *Far Away and Long Ago*. A nostalgic and gently ambling portrait of childhood and rural tranquillity in the Argentine Pampas in Rosas' time, though some of the attitudes are rather dated.

Martín R. de la Peña and Maurice Rumboll *Birds of Southern South America and Antarctica*. A useful companion for even the non-specialist birdwatcher.

THE ARTS

Simon Collier (ed) *Tango! The Dance, the Song, the Story* (o/p). A glossy coffee-table book with a lively account of the history of tango and its key protagonists, well illustrated with colour and black-and-white photos.

★**Francis Mallman** *Seven Fires*. Beautifully illustrated recipe book, with a good dash of memoir, by a top Argentine chef, TV personality, and owner of one of the country's most applauded restaurants (see p.347). Includes

recipes for Argentine classics like empanadas and *dulce de leche* flan, as well as instructions on how to cook the perfect steak.

Alberto Manguel *With Borges*. Accomplished Argentine writer Manguel recounts the time he spent as a young man reading to Borges. Absolutely charming essay, with the kind of gentle humour, subtle poetry and sharp insights into Buenos Aires life that characterize the great man's own work.

SPORT

Andreas Campomar *¡Golazo!: A History of Latin American Football*. Argentina features prominently in this enjoyable journey through the continental obsession with football.

The section on the sport's introduction by British immigrants in the nineteenth century is particularly interesting.

FICTION

Roberto Arlt *The Seven Madmen*. Roberto Arlt captured the lot of the poor immigrant with his gripping, if idiosyncratic, novels about anarchists, prostitutes and other marginal characters in 1920s Buenos Aires. *The Seven Madmen* is the pick of his works – dark and at times surreal, it's filled with images of the frenetic and alienating pace of urban life.

★**Jorge Luis Borges** *Labyrinths*. Argentina's greatest writer, and one of the world's finest and most influential. His prose is highly original, witty and concise; rather than novels, he introduces his ideas through short stories and essays – ideal for dipping into – and *Labyrinths* is a good introduction to these, with selections from his major collections. It includes many of his best-known and most enigmatic tales, including *Library of Babel*, an analogy of the world as a never-ending library.

★**Julio Cortázar** *Hopscotch*. Cortázar is probably second only to Borges in the canon of Argentine writers, and *Hopscotch* is a major work, published in the 1960s. In this fantastically complex book, the author defies traditional narrative structure, inviting the reader to "hop" between chapters, which recount the lives of a group of friends in Paris and London.

Graham Greene *The Honorary Consul*. A masterful account of a farcical kidnapping attempt that goes tragically wrong. Set in the city of Corrientes and dedicated to Argentine literary doyenne Victoria Ocampo, with whom Greene spent time in San Isidro and Mar del Plata.

★**Ricardo Güiraldes** *Don Segundo Sombra*. A tender and nostalgic evocation of past life on the Pampas, chronicling the relationship between a young boy and his mentor, the novel's eponymous gaucho. Written in 1926, some decades after the end of the gaucho era, it helped to change the image of the Argentine cowboy from that of a violent undesirable to a strong, independent man with simple tastes, at the heart of Argentina's national identity.

José Hernández *Martín Fierro*. The classic gaucho epic, written in verse and traditionally learnt by heart by many Argentines. Written as a protest against the corrupt

authorities, it features a highly likeable gaucho outlaw on the run, who rails against the country's weak institutional structures and dictatorial rulers. Try to find the classic Walter Owen translation.

Manuel Mujica Láinez *Bomarzo*. Córdoba-born Láinez was one of the country's most influential twentieth-century writers. He is perhaps best known for his novel *Bomarzo*, set in a surreal town in Renaissance Italy, which was later turned into an opera libretto.

★**Tomás Eloy Martínez** *The Tango Singer*. Martínez was one of modern Argentina's most insightful journalists and novelists. The evocative descriptions of contemporary Buenos Aires in this tale of an American seeking an elusive tango singer make this an ideal literary companion to a visit. See also his books *Santa Evita* and *The Perón Novel*, about Argentina's famous couple, which masterfully mix historical fact and fiction.

Silvina Ocampo *Thus Were Their Faces*. Famously denied Argentina's top literary prize because her work was "far too cruel", Ocampo's writing pulls no punches – dark, fantastical, incisive. This is a bravura short story collection, though not for the faint-hearted.

Manuel Puig *Kiss of the Spiderwoman*. Arguably the finest book by one of Argentina's most original twentieth-century writers, distinguished by a style that mixes film dialogue and popular culture with more traditional narrative. Set during the 1970s dictatorship, this is an absorbing tale of two cellmates, worlds apart on the outside but drawn together by gay protagonist Molina's recounting of films to his companion, left-wing guerrilla Valentín.

Horacio Quiroga *The Decapitated Chicken and Other Stories*. Wonderful if sometimes disturbing gothic tales of love, madness and death. Includes the spine-chilling "Feather".

Colm Tóibín *The Story of the Night*. A moving tale of a young Anglo-Argentine trying to come to terms both with his sexuality and existential dilemmas in the wake of the Falklands/Malvinas War, and getting caught up in an undercover CIA plot to get Carlos Menem elected president.

Language

You'll find at least a decent smattering of Spanish very useful in Argentina. English-speakers are not uncommon, especially in big cities, but they are not ubiquitous and Argentines are appreciative of visitors who make the effort to communicate in Castellano, or Spanish. A good pocket dictionary is a vital accessory, but if you really want to refine your grasp of the language, a comprehensive grammar such as *A New Reference Grammar of Modern Spanish* by John Butt and Carmen Benjamin is a worthwhile investment.

Argentine Spanish is highly distinctive, especially the unmistakeable Porteño accent, characterized by a musical lilt and peppered with colloquialisms, betraying the strong Italian influence, as does the irresistible tendency to gesticulate. Beyond the River Plate region (in or close to the capital), certain regional variations take hold, though most rules of pronunciation, grammar and vocabulary apply for the whole country. Nowhere in Argentina will you hear the Iberian lisp in words like *cerveza* ("beer" – pronounced "sehr-bessa").

What really sets the local lingo apart, though, is the unique pronunciation of y/ll in words such as *yo* ("I/me") and *llave* ("key") as "zh" (the English equivalent is the "s" in "treasure"): "zho", "zhabe". A notable grammatical difference is the use of *vos* as the second-person pronoun ("you" singular), in place of *tú*, with correspondingly different verb endings – eg *vos sabés* = "you know", instead of *tú sabes*. *Ustedes* is always used as the second-person plural pronoun (the plural of "you"); *vosotros* and its derivatives are unheard of. The use of "*che*" (used when addressing someone; it loosely translates as "hey mate") in particular is so much identified with Argentina that other Latin Americans sometimes refer to Argentines as "*Los Che*". The word was most famously applied as a nickname of Ernesto Guevara.

Pronunciation

The Spanish pronunciation system is extremely phonetic – in other words, spelling follows rigid rules, unlike English, which seems to make them up as it goes along. Sounds in no two languages are exactly alike – be aware in particular that Spanish tends to be more fluid, less clearly enunciated and less staccato than English – but the following are examples of letters that are pronounced in a radically different way in (Argentine) Spanish and English. By the way, an (acute) accent written on a vowel denotes emphasis or stress – otherwise the tonic accent nearly always falls on the last syllable but one.

c is like "ss" before E and I, like "k" elsewhere.

g is like the h in "hill" before E and I, like "g" (as in "got") elsewhere.

h is silent, except after C when the two letters combine to make "ch" as in "Chile".

j is like the "ch" in "loch" but softer, closer to an aspirate H.

ll is like the "s" in "pleasure" (except in Corrientes and Misiones where it is pronounced "li" as in "pavilion"): *ella* sounds like "pleasure" (British pronunciation) without the "pl" but in the northeast sounds like "ell-ya".

ñ is pronounced "ni" as in "onion". Ñandú is pronounced "nyandOO".

r is trilled as in Italian or Scots; RR or R at the beginning of a word is doubly trilled (in parts of central and northwestern Argentina this sound is more like a "sh").

s is always soft as in "sign", never like a Z and not slushy as in much of Spain.

u after G and Q is silent. Miguel, the name, is "Mig-el", not "Mig-well".

v is basically pronounced like a B, though softened to a sound closer to English V in between two vowels: eg *Eva*.

y as a consonant (eg in *yacaré* – "alligator") is like the "s" in "pleasure", even in Corrientes and Misiones.

Y meaning "and" is an example of "y" as a vowel: it is pronounced like the "y" in "city".

z is a soft "ss" sound, never hard like an English Z: zorro (fox) sounds a little like the English word "sorrow".

ESSENTIALS

yes, no	sí, no
please, thank you	por favor, gracias
where, when	dónde, cuándo
what, how much	qué, cuánto
here, there	acá, allá
now, later	ahora, más tarde/luego
open, closed	abierto/a, cerrado/a
with, without	con, sin
good, bad	bueno/a, malo/a
big	grande
small	chico/a, pequeño/a (used less)
more, less	más, menos
a little, a lot	poco, mucho
very	muy
today, tomorrow	hoy, mañana
yesterday	ayer
nothing, never	nada, nunca
entrance, exit	entrada, salida
pull, push	tire, empuje
Australia	Australia
Canada	Canadá
England	Inglaterra
Great Britain	Gran Bretaña
Ireland	Irlanda
New Zealand	Nueva Zelanda
South Africa	Sudáfrica
United Kingdom	Reino Unido
United States	Estados Unidos
Scotland	Escocia
Wales	Gales

GREETINGS AND RESPONSES

hello, goodbye (adiós is used for goodbye, but is more formal)	hola, chau
good morning	buen día
good afternoon	buenas tardes
good night	buenas noches
see you later	hasta luego
how are you?	¿cómo está(s)? ¿cómo anda/andás?
(very) well, thanks	(muy) bien gracias
excuse me	(con) permiso
sorry	perdón, disculpe
cheers!	¡salud!

USEFUL PHRASES AND EXPRESSIONS

Note that when two verb forms are given. The first corresponds to the familiar *vos* form and the second to the formal *usted* form.

I (don't) understand	(No) entiendo
Do you speak English?	¿Hablás inglés?/¿habla inglés?
I (don't) speak Spanish	(No) hablo castellano
My name is…	Me llamo…
What's your name?	¿Cómo te llamás?/¿cómo se llama (usted)?
I'm British	Soy británico/a
…English	…inglés(a)
…American	…estadounidense/ norteamericano/a
…Australian	…australiano/a
…Canadian	…canadiense
…Irish	…irlandés(a)
…Scottish	…escocés(a)
…Welsh	…galés(a)
…a New Zealander	…neocelandés/a
…South African	…sudafricano(a)
What's the Spanish for this?	¿Cómo se dice en castellano?

I'm hungry	Tengo hambre
I'm thirsty	Tengo sed
I don't feel well	No me siento bien
What's up?	¿Qué pasa?
I don't know	No (lo) sé
What's the time?	¿Qué hora es?

HOTELS AND TRANSPORT

Is there a hotel/	¿Hay un hotel/banco cerca (de aquí)?
How do I get to…?	¿Cómo hago para llegar a…?
Turn left/right	Doblá/doble a la izquierda/derecha
On the left/right	A la izquierda/derecha
Go straight on	Seguí/siga derecho
One block/two blocks	Una cuadra, dos cuadras
Where is…?	¿Dónde está…?
the bus station	la terminal de omnibus

English	Spanish	Number	Spanish
the train station	la estación de ferrocarril	5	cinco
the toilet	el baño	6	seis
I want a (return)	Quiero un pasaje (de ida	7	siete
ticket to…	y vuelta) para…	8	ocho
Where does the bus for	¿De dónde sale el	9	nueve
…leave from?	micro para…?	10	diez
What time does it leave?	¿A qué hora sale?	11	once
How long does it take?	¿Cuánto tarda?	12	doce
far, near	lejos, cerca	13	trece
I want/would like…	quiero/quería…	14	catorce
Is there a discount	¿Hay descuento para	15	quince
for students?	estudiantes?	16	dieciséis
Is there hot water?	¿Hay agua caliente?	17	diecisiete
Do you have…?	¿Tiene…?	18	dieciocho
a single room	una habitación single	19	diecinueve
a double room	una habitación doble	20	veinte
with two beds	con dos camas	21	veintiuno
with a double bed	con cama matrimonial	30	treinta
with a private bathroom	con baño privado	40	cuarenta
with breakfast	con desayuno	50	cincuenta
It's for one person/	Es para una persona/	60	sesenta
one night/two weeks	una noche/dos semanas	70	setenta
How much is it?	¿Cuánto es/Cuánto sale?	80	ochenta
It's too expensive	Es demasiado caro	90	noventa
Do you have anything	¿Hay algo más barato?	100	cien/ciento
cheaper?		200	doscientos/as
Is there a discount	¿Hay descuento por	1000	mil
for cash?	pago en efectivo?	1,000,000	un millón
Is camping allowed here?	¿Se puede acampar aquí?	2008	dos mil ocho
		Monday	lunes
NUMBERS AND DAYS		Tuesday	martes
0	cero	Wednesday	miércoles
1	uno/una	Thursday	jueves
2	dos	Friday	viernes
3	tres	Saturday	sábado
4	cuatro	Sunday	domingo

AN ARGENTINE MENU READER

BASICS

Spanish	English	Spanish	English
aceite de maíz	corn oil	desayuno	breakfast
aceite de oliva	olive oil	guarnición	side dish
agregado	side order or garnish	harina	flour
ají	chilli	huevos	eggs
ajo	garlic	lata/latita	can or tin
almuerzo	lunch	manteca	butter
arroz	rice	mayonesa	mayonnaise
azúcar	sugar	menú del día	set meal
carta/menú	menu	mermelada/dulce	jam
cena	dinner	mostaza	mustard
comedor	diner or dining room	pan (francés)	bread (baguette or French stick)
copa	glass (for wine)		
cuchara	spoon	pimentón dulce	paprika
cuchillo	knife	pimienta	pepper
cuenta	bill	plato	plate or dish
		queso	cheese

sal	salt
sanduich	sandwich (usually made with very thinly sliced bread: *sanduich de miga*)
servilleta	napkin
taza	cup
tenedor	fork
vaso	glass (for water)
vegetariano/a	vegetarian
vinagre	vinegar

CULINARY TERMS

parrilla	barbecue
asado	roasted or barbecued; *un asado* is a barbecue
a la plancha	grilled
ahumado	smoked
al horno	baked/roasted
al natural	canned (of fruit)
al vapor	steamed
crudo	raw
frito	fried
picante	hot (spicy)
puré	puréed or mashed potatoes
relleno	stuffed

MEAT (*CARNE*) AND POULTRY (*AVES*)

bife	steak
bife de chorizo	prize steak cut
cabrito	goat (kid)
carne vacuna	beef
cerdo	pork
ciervo	venison
codorniz	quail
conejo	rabbit
cordero	lamb
chivito	kid or goat
chuleta	chop
churrasco	grilled beef
fiambres	cured meats – hams, salami, etc
jabalí	wild boar
jamón	ham
lechón/cochinillo	suckling pig
lomo	tenderloin/fillet steak
milanesa	breaded veal escalope
oca	goose
paletilla	shoulder of lamb
panceta	Italian-style bacon
pato	duck
pavo	turkey

pebete	sandwich in a bun or bread roll
pollo	chicken
ternera	grass-fed veal
tocino/beicon	bacon

OFFAL (*ACHURAS*)

bofes	lights (lungs)
chinchulines	small intestine
chorizo (blanco)	meaty sausage (not spiced like Spanish *chorizo* – *chorizo colorado*)
corazón	heart
criadillas	testicles
hígado	liver
lengua	tongue
mollejas	sweetbreads (thymus gland)
mondongo	cow's stomach
morcilla	blood sausage
orejas	ears
patas	feet or trotters
riñones	kidneys
sesos	brains
tripa gorda	tripe (large intestine)
ubre	udder

TYPICAL DISHES (*PLATOS*)

arroz con pollo	a kind of chicken risotto
bife a caballo	steak with a fried egg on top
bife a la criolla	steaks braised with onions, peppers and herbs
brochetas	kebabs
carbonada	a filling meat stew
cazuela de marisco	a seafood casserole
cerdo a la riojana	pork cooked with fruit
fainá	baked chickpea dough traditionally served with pizza
guiso	basic meat stew
locro	stew based on maize, beans and meat, often including tripe
matambre relleno	cold stuffed flank steak (normally filled with vegetables and hard-boiled eggs, and sliced; literally means "stuffed hunger killer")
matambrito	pork, often simmered in milk until soft

milanesa napolitana	breaded veal escalope topped with ham, tomato and melted cheese
milanesa de pollo	breaded chicken breast
mondongo	stew made of cow's stomach with potatoes and tomatoes
pastel de papa	shepherd's pie
provoletta	thick slice of provolone cheese grilled on a barbecue
puchero	a rustic stew, usually of chicken (*puchero de gallina*), made with potatoes and maize or whatever vegetable is to hand
vittel tonné	the Argentine starter *par excellence*: slices of cold roast beef in mayonnaise mixed with tuna

FISH (*PESCADO*)

abadejo	cod
atún	tuna
boga	large, flavoursome fish caught in the Río de la Plata
caballa	mackerel
corvina	sea bass
dorado	a large freshwater fish, with mushy flesh and loads of bones
lenguado	sole
lisa de río	oily river fish
manduví	river fish with delicate, pale flesh
manguruyú	oily river fish (best grilled)
merluza	hake
pacú	firm-fleshed river fish
pejerrey	popular inland-water fish
pirapitanga	salmon-like river fish
sábalo	oily-fleshed river fish
salmón	salmon
surubí	kind of catfish
trucha (arco iris)	(rainbow) trout
vieja	white, meaty-fleshed river fish

SEAFOOD (*MARISCOS*)

camarones	shrimps or prawns
cangrejo	crab
centolla	king crab
mejillones	mussels
ostras	oysters
vieira	scallop

VEGETABLES (*VERDURAS*)

aceitunas	olives
acelga	chard
albahaca	basil
alcauciles	artichokes
apio	celery
arvejas	peas
aspárragos	asparagus
berenjena	aubergine/eggplant
berro	watercress
cebolla	onion
champiñon	mushroom
chauchas	runner beans
choclo	maize or sweetcorn
chucrút	sauerkraut
coliflor	cauliflower
ensalada	salad
espinaca	spinach
garbanzo	chickpea
habas	broad beans
hinojo	fennel
hongos (silvestres)	(wild) mushrooms
lechuga	lettuce
lentejas	lentils
morrón	pepper
...dulce	sweet...
...rojo	red...
...verde	green...
palmito	palm heart
palta	avocado
papa	potato
papas fritas	chips/French fries
papines	small potatoes eaten whole
perejil	parsley
pimiento	green pepper
poroto	bean
puerro	leek
remolacha	beetroot
rúcula	rocket
tomate	tomato
tomillo	thyme
zanahoria	carrot
zapallito	gem squash – small green pumpkins that are a favourite throughout the country, usually baked and stuffed with rice and meat
zapallo	pumpkin

FRUIT AND NUTS (*FRUTA Y FRUTOS SECOS*)

almendra	almond
almíbar	syrup
ananá	pineapple
arándano	cranberry/blueberry
avellana	hazelnut
banana	banana
batata	sweet potato
castaña	chestnut
cayote	spaghetti squash
cereza	cherry
ciruela (seca)	plum (prune)
damasco	apricot
dátiles	dates
durazno	peach
frambuesa	raspberry
frutilla	strawberry
higo	fig
lima	lime
limón	lemon
maní	peanut
manzana	apple
melón	melon
membrillo	quince
mora	mulberry
mosqueta	rose hip
naranja	orange
nuez	walnut
pasa (de uva)	dried fruit (raisin)
pera	pear
pomelo (rosado)	(pink) grapefruit
quinoto	kumquat
sandía	watermelon
uva	grape(s)
zarza mora	blackberry

DESSERTS (*POSTRES*)

arroz con leche	rice pudding
budín de pan	bread pudding
crema	custard or cream
dulce	sweet in general; candied fruit or jam
dulce de leche	thick caramel made from milk and sugar, a national religion (see box, p.35)
ensalada de fruta	fruit salad
flan	crème caramel
helado	ice cream
medialuna	croissant-like pastry, more like the Italian "cornetto"
...dulce	sweet...
...salado	plain...

miel (de abeja)	honey
miel (de caña)	molasses
panqueque/crêpe	pancake
sambayón	zabaglione (custard made with egg yolks and wine, a popular ice-cream flavour)
torta	tart or cake
tortilla/tortita	breakfast pastry

DRINKS (*BEBIDAS*)

agua	water
agua mineral	mineral water
...con gas	sparkling...
...sin gas	still...
aguardiente	brandy-like spirit
botella	bottle
cacheteado	Coke and red wine spritzer (very popular in Córdoba)
café (con leche)	coffee (with milk)
cerveza	beer
champán	sparkling wine, usually Argentine, or champagne
chocolate caliente/ submarino	hot chocolate (often a slab of chocolate melted in hot milk, served in a tall glass)
chopp	draught beer
cortado	espresso coffee "cut" with a little steaming milk (similar to macchiato)
Fernet (branca)	Italian-style digestive drink, popularly mixed with Coke (the gaucho drink *par excellence*)
gaseosa	fizzy drink
jugo (de naranja)	(orange) juice
lata	can
leche	milk
licuados	juice-based drinks or milkshakes
liso	small draught beer (Litoral)
mate cocido	infusion made with *mate*, sometimes heretically with a bag
sidra	cider
soda	fizzy water
té	tea
vino	wine
...tinto	red...
...blanco	white...
...rosado	rosé...

Argentine idiom and slang

Anyone who has learnt Spanish elsewhere will need to become accustomed to the specific vocabulary in Argentina, as a familiarity with Argentine equivalents will certainly smooth things along. Many words for foodstuffs, especially fruit and vegetables, are not the same in Argentina as in other Spanish-speaking countries – you will find many of them in the Argentine menu reader (see p.569).

Though few terms used in Spain are actually taboo in Argentina, there is one major exception, which holds for much of Latin America. The verb **coger**, used in Spain for everything from "to pick up" or "fetch" to "to catch (a bus)", is never used in this way in Argentina, where it is the equivalent of "to fuck". In Argentina use *tomar* (to take) as in *tomar el colectivo* (to catch the bus) or *agarrar* (to take hold of or grab) as in *agarrá la llave* (take the key). Less likely to cause problems, but still one to watch, is **concha**, which in Spain is a perfectly innocent word meaning "seashell", but in Argentina is usually used to refer to the female genitals; the words *caracol* or *almeja* are always used instead for shells and Argentines never tire of finding the Spanish woman's name Conchita – short for Inmaculada Concepción – hilarious ("ita" at the end of a word means little).

Colloquial speech in Argentina, particularly in Buenos Aires, is extremely colourful, and it's good fun to learn a bit of the local lingo. There's a clear Italian influence in some words. Many colloquial expressions and words also derive from an Italian-flavoured form of slang known as *lunfardo*, originally the language of the Buenos Aires underworld (hence the myriad terms in *lunfardo* proper for police, pimps and prostitutes). There's also a playful form of speech, known as **vesre**, in which words are pronounced backwards (*vesre* is the word for *revés* – reverse, backwards); a few of these words, such as *feca* (coffee from *café*), have found their way into everyday speech. Though these expressions will sound odd coming from the mouth of a less-than-fluent foreigner, knowing a few of them will help you get the most out of what's being said around you. *Lunfardo* is also an important part of the repertoire of tango lyrics. Another feature to listen for is the widespread use of the prefix "re-", to mean "really" or "totally". *Re-lindo/a* means really good-looking; *re-malo/a* means really bad. *Recontra-* is even stronger: something that is *recontra-barato* means it is on sale at a rock-bottom price.

Words listed below that are marked with an asterisk (*) should be used with some caution as they are very familiar; those marked with a double asterisk (**) denote strong language and are best avoided until you are really familiar with local customs or know the person you are speaking to won't be offended.

afanar	to rob*	bombachas	knickers
almacén	grocery shop/store	bombilla	straw-like implement,
auto	car (*coche* is rarely used)		usually of metal, used for drinking *mate* from a gourd
bancar	to put up with*; *no me lo banco* ("I can't stand it")	bondi	bus
		bronca	rage*, as in *me da bronca* ("it makes me angry")
bárbaro/a	great!		
barra brava	(group of) hardcore football fans	cana	police officer (cop)*; prison*
birome	biro/ballpoint pen		
birra	beer*	cancha	football stadium
boliche	nightclub; also sometimes bar/store/shop in rural areas	canchero	smart (for clothes etc), sharp-witted, (over-)confident, cool
boludo/pelotudo	idiot (equivalent to prat, jerk etc)**	carpa	tent
		cartera	handbag/purse

cataratas	waterfalls, usually used to refer specifically to Iguazú Falls
caudillo	regional military or political leader, usually with authoritarian overtones
chabón	boy/lad*
chamuyo	conversation/chat*
chancho	ticket inspector*
chanta	braggart, unreliable person*
chata	pick-up truck*
chico/a	small (also boy or girl)
chorro	thief*
chupar	to drink (alcohol)*
colectivo	bus
combi	small minibus that runs urban bus routes
copado	cool, good*
despelote	mess*
estancia	farm, traditionally with huge areas of land
estar en pedo	to be drunk*
faso	cigarette*
feca	coffee*
fiaca	tiredness/laziness*, eg tengo fiaca ("I can't be bothered")
forro	condom/idiot**
gamba	leg*
gaucho	typical Argentine "cowboy" or rural estancia worker
gil	idiot*
guita/plata	money*
hincha pelotas	irritating person**
laburar	to work*
lapicera	pen
living	living room
luca	one thousand* (pesos)
mamado	drunk* (un mamado** means a blow-job)
mango	mango; peso*/monetary unit as in no tengo un mango ("I don't have a penny")
manyar	to eat*
mate	strictly the mate gourd or receptacle, but used generally to describe the national "tea" drink

medias	socks
micro	long-distance bus
milico	member of the military*
mina	woman/girl*
morfar	to eat*
negocio	shop (in general)
nene/a	child
onda	atmosphere/character, as in tiene buena onda ("there's a good atmosphere" or "she's good-natured")
palo	one million (pesos)*; un palo verde is a million US dollars (greenbacks)
pato	Argentine national sport; similar to handball on horseback
patota	gang*
pedo	fart**
pendejo	kid (mostly used derogatorily)**
petiso	small, also small person
pibe	kid
pinta	"it looks good"; la pinta means appearance, as in tiene pinta or tiene buena pinta
piola	cool, smart
pollera	skirt
pucho	cigarette*
quilombo	mess*
remera	T-shirt
subte	Buenos Aires' underground railway
suéter	sweater
tacho	taxi (tachero is taxi driver)
tapado	coat (usually woman's)
telo	short-stay hotel where couples go to have sex*
tereré	drink composed of yerba mate served with wild herbs (yuyos) and ice-cold water or lemonade/orange juice
trucho	fake, phoney
vereda	pavement
vidriera	shop window
vieja/o/os	mum/dad/parents*
zafar	to get away with*

A glossary of Argentine terms and acronyms

ACA (Automóvil Club Argentino) National motoring organization, which also runs decent hotels in many towns (pronounced A-ka).

Acampar To camp.

Aduana Customs post.

Aerosilla Chairlift.

Agreste Wild or rustic (often used to describe a campsite with very basic facilities).

Alerce Giant, slow-growing Patagonian cypress, similar to the Californian redwood.

Almacén Small grocery store, which in the past often functioned as a bar too.

Altiplano High Andean plateau.

Aónik'enk The southern group of Tehuelche, the last of whose descendants live in the province of Santa Cruz.

Araucaria Monkey puzzle tree.

Arepa Flat maize bread.

Arroba The @ sign on a computer keyboard.

Arroyo Stream or small river.

Autopista Motorway.

Bailanta Dance club, where the predominant sound is *cumbia* (see p.576).

Balneario Bathing resort; also a complex of sunshades and small tents on the beach, often with a bar and shower facilities, for which users pay a daily, weekly or monthly rate.

Baqueano Mountain or wilderness guide.

Barrio Neighbourhood.

Bofedal Spongy altiplano wetland.

Boleadoras/bolas Traditional hunting implement, composed of stone balls connected by thick cord, thrown to entangle legs or neck of prey. Traditionally used by gauchos, who copied it from Argentina's indigenous inhabitants.

Boletería Ticket office.

Boleto Travel ticket.

Bombachas de campo Baggy gaucho trousers for riding.

Bombilla Straw-like implement, usually of metal, used for drinking *mate* from a gourd.

Bonaerense Adjective relating to or person from Buenos Aires Province.

Bondi Colloquial term in Buenos Aires for a bus.

Botiquín Medicine kit.

C/ The abbreviation of calle (street); only rarely used.

Cabildo Colonial town hall; now replaced by municipalidad.

Cabina telefónica Phone booth.

Cacique Generic term for the head of a Latin American indigenous community or people, either elected or hereditary.

Cajero automático Cashpoint machine (ATM).

Calafate Type of thorny Patagonian bush, famous for its delicious purple berries.

Camioneta Pick-up truck.

Campesino Country-dweller; sometimes used to refer to someone with indigenous roots.

Campo de hielo Icecap or ice field.

Caña colihue Native Patagonian plant of the forest understorey; resembles bamboo.

Cancha Football stadium.

Cantina Traditional restaurant, usually Italian.

Característica Telephone code (eg 011 for Buenos Aires).

Carretera Route or highway.

Cartelera Agency for buying discounted tickets for cinemas, theatres and concerts.

Casa de té Tearoom.

Casco Main building of estancia; the homestead.

Cataratas Waterfalls, usually used to refer specifically to Iguazú Falls.

Caudillo Regional military or political leader, usually with authoritarian overtones.

Cebar (mate) To brew (*mate*).

Ceibo Tropical tree with a twisted trunk, whose bright-red or pink blossom is the national flower of Argentina, Uruguay and Paraguay.

Cerro Hill, mountain peak (often used in names).

Chaco húmedo Wet chaco habitat.

Chaco seco Dry chaco habitat.

Chacra Small farm.

Chamamé Folk music from the Litoral region, specifically Corrientes Province.

Chango Common term in the Northwest for a young boy; often used in the sense of "mate"/"buddy".

Chaqueño Someone from the Gran Chaco (or Province of Chaco).

Chata Slang term for pick-up truck.

China A gaucho girl or woman (often used as nickname).

Choique Common term, deriving from Mapudungun, for the smaller, southern Darwin's rhea of Patagonia.

Churro Strip of fried dough, somewhat similar to a doughnut, often filled with *dulce de leche*.

Colectivo Urban bus.

Combi Small minibus that runs urban bus routes.

Comparsa Carnival "school".

Confitería Café and tearoom, often with patisserie attached.

Conventillo Tenement building.

Cordillera Mountain range; usually used in Argentina to refer to the Andes.

Cortadera Pampas grass.

Costanera Riverside avenue.

Country Term for exclusive out-of-town residential compound or sports and social club.

Criollo/a Historically an Argentine-born person of

Spanish/European descent. Used today in two ways: as a general term for Argentine (as in *comida criolla*, traditional Argentine food) and used by indigenous people to refer to those of non-indigenous descent.

Cuadra The distance from one street corner to the next, usually 100 metres (see also *Manzana*).

Cuchilla Regional term for low hill in Entre Ríos.

Cuesta Slope or small hill.

Cumbia Popular Argentine "tropical" rhythm, inspired by Colombian *cumbia*.

Departamento Administrative district in a province; also an apartment.

Descamisados Term meaning "the shirtless ones", popularized by Juan and Evita Perón to refer to the working-class masses and dispossessed.

Despensa Shop (particularly in rural areas).

Día de campo Day spent at an estancia where traditional *asado* and empanadas are eaten and guests are usually given a display of gaucho skills.

Dique Dock; also dam.

E/ The abbreviation of entre (between), used in addresses.

Empalme Junction of two highways.

Encomienda Package, parcel; also historical term for form of trusteeship bestowed on Spaniards after Conquest, granting them rights over the indigenous population.

Entrada Ticket (for football match, theatre etc).

Estancia Argentine farm, traditionally with huge areas of land.

Estanciero An owner of an estancia.

Estepa Steppe.

Estero A shallow swampland, commonly found in El Litoral and Gran Chaco areas.

Facón Gaucho knife, usually carried in a sheath.

Federalists Nineteenth-century term for those in favour of autonomous power being given to the provinces; opponents of Unitarists (see p.578).

Feria artesanal/de artesanías Craft fair.

Ferretería Hardware shop (often useful for camping equipment).

Ferrocarril Railway.

Ficha Token.

Fogón Place for a barbecue or camp fire; bonfire.

Fonda Simple restaurant.

Galería Small shopping arcade.

Gaseosa Soft drink.

Gaucho The typical Argentine "cowboy", or rural estancia worker.

Gendarmería Police station.

Gomería Tyre repair centre.

Gomero Rubber tree.

Gringo/a Any white foreigner, though often specifically those from English-speaking countries;

historically, European immigrants to Argentina (as opposed to *criollos*), as in *pampa gringa*, the part of the Pampas settled by Europeans. Often used as a nickname.

Guanaco Wild camelid of the llama family.

Guaraní Indigenous people and language, found principally in Misiones, Corrientes and Paraguay.

Guardaequipaje Left-luggage office.

Guardafauna Wildlife ranger.

Guardaganado Cattle grid.

Guardaparque National park ranger.

Gününa'küna The northern group of the Tehuelche, now extinct.

Hacer dedo To hitchhike.

Humedal Any wetland swampy area.

IGM (Instituto Geográfico Militar) The national military's cartographic institution.

Impenetrable Term applied historically to the area of the dry *chaco* with the most inhospitable conditions for white settlement, due to lack of water; the name of a zone of northwestern Chaco Province.

Intendencia Head office of a national park.

Intendente Administrative chief of a national park.

Interno Telephone extension number.

Isleta de monte Clump of scrubby mixed woodland found in savannah or flat agricultural land, typically in the Gran Chaco and the northeast of the country.

IVA (Impuesto de Valor Agregado) Value-added tax or sales tax.

Jacarandá Tropical tree with trumpet-shaped mauvish blossom.

Jarilla Thorny, chest-high bush.

Junta Military government coalition.

Kiosko Newspaper stand or small store selling cigarettes, confectionery and snacks.

Kolla Andean indigenous group predominant in the northwestern provinces of Salta and Jujuy.

Lancha Smallish motor boat.

Lapacho Tropical tree typical of the Litoral region and distinguished by bright-pink blossom.

Leña Firewood.

Lenga Type of Nothofagus southern beech common in Patagonian forests.

El Litoral Littoral, shore – used to refer to the provinces of Entre Ríos, Corrientes, Misiones, Santa Fe and sometimes Eastern Chaco and Formosa.

Litoraleño Inhabitant of the Litoral (see p.212).

Locutorio Call centre, where phone calls are made from cabins and the caller is charged after the call has been made.

Lomo de burro Speed bump.

Lonco Head or *cacique* (see p.574) of a Mapuche community.

Madrejón A swampy ox-bow lake.

Mallín Swamp, particularly in upland moors.

Manzana City block; the square bounded by four *cuadras* (see opposite).

Mapuche One of Argentina's largest indigenous groups, whose ancestors originally came from Chilean Patagonia and whose biggest communities are found in the provinces of Chubut, Río Negro and especially Neuquén.

Mapudungun The language of the Mapuche.

Marcha Commercial dance music.

Mataco See Wichí.

Mate Strictly the *mate* gourd or receptacle, but used generally to describe the national "tea" drink.

Menú del día Standard set menu.

Menú ejecutivo Set menu. Tends to be more expensive than the *menú del día* (see above), though not always that executive.

Mesopotamia The three provinces of Entre Ríos, Corrientes and Misiones, by analogy with the ancient region lying between the rivers Tigris and Euphrates, in modern-day Iraq.

Micro Long-distance bus.

Microcentro The area of a city comprising the central square and neighbouring streets.

Milonga Style of folk-guitar music usually associated with the Pampas region; also a tango dance and a subgenre of tango, more uptempo than tango proper. Also a tango dancing event, often with tuition (see box, p.10).

Mirador Scenic lookout point or tower.

Monte Scrubby woodland, often used to describe any uncultivated woodland area. Also used to refer to the desertified ecosystem that lies in the rainshadow of the central Andes around the Cuyo region.

Mozarabic Spanish architectural style, originally dating from the ninth to thirteenth centuries and characterized by a fusion of Romanesque and Moorish styles.

Muelle Pier or jetty.

Municipalidad Municipality building or town hall.

Ñandú A common name, derived from Guaraní, for the greater rhea, but also used to refer to its smaller cousin, the Darwin's rhea.

Ñire Type of nothofagus southern beech tree common in Patagonian forests.

Ñoqui Argentine spelling of the Italian *gnocchi*, a small potato dumpling. Used to refer to phoney employees who appear on a company's payroll but don't actually work there, or idle civil servants; also slang for a punch (as in a fight).

Nothofagus Genus of Patagonian trees commonly called southern beech (includes lenga and ñire).

Ombú Large shade tree, originally from the Mesopotamia region and now associated with the Pampas, where it was introduced in the eighteenth century.

Paisano Meaning "countryman"; sometimes loosely used as equivalent to gaucho and often used by people of indigenous descent to refer to themselves, thus avoiding the sometimes pejorative *indio* (Indian).

Palmar Palm grove.

Palo borracho Tree associated especially with the dry-*chaco* habitat of northern Argentina; its name (literally "drunken stick") is derived from its swollen trunk in which water is stored.

Palometa Piranha/piraña.

Pampa(s) The broad flat grasslands of central Argentina.

Parquímetro Parking meter.

Parrillada The meat barbecued on a *parrilla* (barbecue).

Pasaje Narrow street.

Paseaperro Professional dog walker.

Pastizal Grassland, often used for grazing.

Pato The Argentine national sport; a kind of handball on horseback.

Payada Traditional improvised musical style, often performed as a kind of dialogue between two singers (*payadores*) who accompany themselves on guitars.

Peaje Road toll.

Peatonal Pedestrianized street.

Pehuén Mapuche term for monkey puzzle tree.

Peña Circle or group (usually of artists or musicians); a *peña folklórica* is a folk-music club.

Peón Farmhand.

Picada A roughly marked path; also a plate of small snacks eaten before a meal, particularly cheese, ham or smoked meats.

Planta baja Ground floor (first floor, US).

Playa Beach.

Playa (de estacionamiento) Parking area; garage.

Plazoleta/plazuela Small town square.

Porteño/a Someone from Buenos Aires city.

Prefectura Naval prefecture for controlling river and marine traffic.

Puesto Small outpost or hut for shepherds or *guardaparques*.

Pucará Pre-Columbian fortress.

Pulpería A type of traditional general-provisions store that doubles up as a bar and rural meeting point.

Puna High Andean plateau (see p.555; alternative term for altiplano).

Puntano/a Someone from San Luís.

Quebrada Ravine, gully.

Querandí Original indigenous inhabitants of the Pampas region.

Quinta Suburban or country house with a small plot of land, where fruit and vegetables are often cultivated.

Qom An indigenous group, living principally in the east of Formosa and Chaco provinces. The word means "people" in their language.

Rancho Simple countryside dwelling, typically constructed of adobe.

Rastra Gaucho belt, typically ornamented with silver.

RC (Ruta Complementaria) Subsidiary, unsealed road in Tierra del Fuego.

Recargo Surcharge on credit cards.

Recova Arcade around the exterior of a building or courtyard, typical of colonial-era buildings.

Reducción Jesuit mission settlement.

Refugio Trekking refuge or hut.

Remise/remís Taxi or chauffeur-driven rental car, booked through a central office.

Remise colectivo Shared cab that runs fixed inter-urban routes.

Represa Dam; also reservoir.

Río River.

Rioplatense Referring to people or things (including language) from the region around the River Plate (Río de la Plata) – Buenos Aires Province, Santa Fe Province and Uruguay, plus slightly further afield.

Ripio Gravel; usually used to describe an unsurfaced gravel road.

RN (Ruta Nacional) Major route, usually paved.

RP (Ruta Provincial) Provincial road, sometimes paved.

Ruta Route or road.

Salto Waterfall.

Sapucay Bloodcurdling shriek characteristic of *chamamé* (see p.562).

Selk'nam Nomadic, indigenous guanaco-hunters from Tierra del Fuego, whose last members died in the 1960s. Also called Ona, the Yámana name for them.

Sendero Path or trail.

S/N Used in addresses to indicate that there's no house number (*sin número*).

Soroche Altitude sickness.

Sortija Display of gaucho skill in which the galloping rider must spear a small ring hung from a thread.

Subte Buenos Aires' underground railway.

Tanguería Tango club.

Tasa de terminal Terminal tax.

Taxímetro Taxi meter.

Tehuelche Generic term for the different nomadic steppe tribes of Patagonia, whom early European explorers named "Patagones".

Teleférico Gondola or cable car.

Tenedor libre All-you-can-eat buffet restaurant.

Tereré Common drink in the subtropical north of the country and Paraguay, composed of *yerba mate* served with wild herbs (*yuyos*) and ice-cold water or lemonade.

Terminal de ómnibus Bus terminal.

Terrateniente Landowner.

Tipa Acacia-like tree often found in northern *yungas* (and along urban avenues).

Toba See Qom.

Truco Argentina's national card game, in which the ability to outbluff your opponents is of major importance.

Unitarists Nineteenth-century centralists, in favour of power being centralized in Buenos Aires; opponents of Federalists (see p.576).

Villa Short for *villa miseria*, a shantytown.

Wichí Seminomadic indigenous group, living predominantly in the dry central and western areas of Chaco and Formosa provinces, and in the far east of Salta. Sometimes referred to pejoratively as Mataco.

Yahganes See Yámana.

Yámana Nomadic indigenous canoe-going people who lived in the islands and channels south of Tierra del Fuego, and whose culture died out in Argentina in the early twentieth century.

Yerba (mate) The dried and cured leaves of the shrub used to brew *mate*.

YPF (Yacimientos Petroleros Fiscales) The principal Argentine petroleum company, controversially renationalized. It is often used to refer to the company's fuel stations, which act as landmarks in the less-populated areas of the country.

Zona franca Duty-free zone.

Small print and index

A ROUGH GUIDE TO ROUGH GUIDES

Published in 1982, the first Rough Guide – to Greece – was a student scheme that became a publishing phenomenon. Mark Ellingham, a recent graduate in English from Bristol University, had been travelling in Greece the previous summer and couldn't find the right guidebook. With a small group of friends he wrote his own guide, combining a contemporary, journalistic style with a thoroughly practical approach to travellers' needs.

The immediate success of the book spawned a series that rapidly covered dozens of destinations. And, in addition to impecunious backpackers, Rough Guides soon acquired a much broader readership that relished the guides' wit and inquisitiveness as much as their enthusiastic, critical approach and value-for-money ethos.

These days, Rough Guides include recommendations from budget to luxury and cover more than 120 destinations around the globe, from Amsterdam to Zanzibar, all regularly updated by our team of roaming writers.

Find travel information, read inspiring features and book your trip at **roughguides.com**.

Rough Guide credits

Editors: Rebecca Hallett, Ann-Marie Shaw
Layout: Anita Singh
Cartography: Rajesh Chhibber, Katie Bennett
Picture editor: Aude Vauconsant
Proofreader: Jan McCann
Managing editor: Mani Ramaswamy
Assistant editor: Payal Sharotri

Production: Jimmy Lao
Cover photo research: Roger Mapp
Editorial assistant: Freya Godfrey
Senior DTP coordinator: Dan May
Programme manager: Gareth Lowe
Publishing director: Georgina Dee

Publishing information

This sixth edition published October 2016 by
Rough Guides Ltd,
80 Strand, London WC2R 0RL
11, Community Centre, Panchsheel Park,
New Delhi 110017, India
Distributed by Penguin Random House
Penguin Books Ltd, 80 Strand, London WC2R 0RL
Penguin Group (USA), 345 Hudson Street, NY 10014, USA
Penguin Group (Australia), 250 Camberwell Road,
Camberwell, Victoria 3124, Australia
Penguin Group (NZ), 67 Apollo Drive, Mairangi Bay,
Auckland 1310, New Zealand
Penguin Group (South Africa), Block D, Rosebank Office
Park, 181 Jan Smuts Avenue, Parktown North, Gauteng,
South Africa 2193
Rough Guides is represented in Canada by DK Canada, 320
Front Street West, Suite 1400, Toronto, Ontario M5V 3B6
Printed in Singapore
© Rough Guides, 2016
Maps © Rough Guides

MIX
Paper from
responsible sources
FSC
www.fsc.org   FSC™ C018179

Help us update

We've gone to a lot of effort to ensure that the sixth
edition of **The Rough Guide to Argentina** is accurate
and up-to-date. However, things change – places get
"discovered", opening hours are notoriously fickle,
restaurants and rooms raise prices or lower standards. If
you feel we've got it wrong or left something out, we'd like
to know, and if you can remember the address, the price,
the hours, the phone number, so much the better.

Please send your comments with the subject line
"Rough Guide Argentina Update" to mail
@uk.roughguides.com. We'll credit all contributions and
send a copy of the next edition (or any other Rough Guide
if you prefer) for the very best emails.

Find travel information, read inspiring features and book
your trip at roughguides.com.

Readers' updates

Thanks to all the readers who have taken the time to write in with comments and suggestions (and apologies if we've
inadvertently omitted or misspelt anyone's name):

Lucia Álvarez de Toledo; Isobel Benand; Eleonora Bozzoni;
John Brzovic; Charlotte De Beule; Jamila Douhaibi; Peter
Forrest; Michael Hanna; Isabel; Melvin Jones; Jessica Kerrin;
Jeannette Korff; Tim Laslavic; Donna Murrell; M Pol-ewan;
Norman Skiba

ABOUT THE AUTHOR

Stephen Keeling first travelled across Argentina by bus in 1999. He worked as a financial journalist and editor for seven years before writing his first travel book in 2005, and has written many titles for Rough Guides. Stephen lives in New York.

Shafik Meghji is a travel writer, journalist and author based in south London. He first visited Argentina in 2004, and later lived in Buenos Aires. He has worked on over 25 Rough Guides, including guides to Bolivia, Chile, Costa Rica, Ecuador and Mexico, and his travel writing has been featured in four anthologies. Shafik writes regularly guides for publications including *The Guardian*, the *South China Morning Post* and *Time Out Buenos Aires*. A fellow of the Royal Geographical Society, member of the British Guild of Travel Writers, and trustee of the Latin America Bureau, he blogs at ⓦunmappedroutes.com and tweets @ShafikMeghji.

Sorrel Moseley-Williams is an award-winning journalist, based in Argentina since 2006. Also a sommelier, she navigates Latin America's southern cone to write about food, wine and travel, and edits her wine blog ⓦcomewinewith.me.

Madelaine Triebe developed her passion for Argentina in her early twenties while studying Spanish in Buenos Aires. It later led her to the hills of Córdoba to guide tourists on horseback, and on numerous travel adventures in Patagonia and Mendoza. When she's not dreaming of being a gaucho, she writes for various travel publications; you can find out about her latest adventures on ⓦmymaddytravel.com.

Acknowledgements

Stephen Keeling: Thanks to fellow author Shafik Meghji, to Rebecca Hallett and Ann-Marie Shaw in the UK for all their hard work and editing, and to Tiffany Wu for sharing the journey in northwest Argentina.

Shafik Meghji: Thanks to all the locals and travellers who helped out in big and small ways throughout my research. A special muchas gracias must go to: Mani Ramaswamy for the initial commission; Rebecca Hallett for her sterling editing work; my fellow authors Sorrel Moseley-Williams, Madelaine Triebe and Stephen Keeling; Juliana Estevez of Destino Argentina for her help with my travel arrangements; the Begg family at Estancia Los Potreros for their hospitality; everyone at Estancia Harberton for a wonderful night at the end of the world; María Paz Muriel

at Tierra de Leyendas; Jean, Nizar and Nina Meghji; and Sioned Jones, for her love and support.

Sorrel Moseley-Williams: With thanks to Mani for commissioning me, Becca for the editing learning curve, Argentina for keeping me on my toes and always being a land of opportunity, and Allan for understanding when I stretch my wings to clock up air, land and sea miles.

Madelaine Triebe: Muchísimas gracias a Mani Ramaswamy for the initial commission, to Rebecca Hallett for her invaluable guidance and sterling editing work and to my family and friends. A special thanks to Gustavo and Melanie in Patagonia, Linda in Cholila and Max in Buenos Aires for hosting me, as well as to Clery Evans in Trevelin for sharing some epic stories. Un abrazo fuerte a todos!

Photo credits

All photos © Rough Guides except the following:
(Key: t-top; c-centre; b-bottom; l-left; r-right)

Index

Maps are marked in grey

...bols

The symbols below are used on maps throughout the book

━ ■ ━ International boundary	Ⓜ Metro stop	Rocks	Marshland
━ ━ ━ State/province boundary	⚓ Ferry/boat station	Mountains	Bridge/pass
─ ─ ─ Chapter division boundary	⛽ Petrol station	Volcano	✡ Synagogue
Motorway	⊠ Gate	▲ Peak	Church (regional maps)
Pedestrianized road	♦ Place of interest	Spring/spa	Church (town maps)
Road	@ Internet	Cave	Mosque/muslim monument
─ ─ ─ ─ Path/walking route	ⓘ Tourist office	Viewpoint	Building
Railway	🕐 Telephone	Guadaparque/park ranger	Market
·─·─· Unpaved road	✉ Post office	Border crossing	Stadium
─── Ferry route	⊞ Hospital	Campsite	Christian cemetery
●─·─● Cable car	Golf course	Refuge	Park
✈ International airport	⊙ Statue	Ski area	Beach
✈ Domestic airport	🏛 Monument	Lighthouse	Swamp
★ Bus stop	∩ Arch	Vineyard	Glacier
P Parking	Waterfall	Ruin	Salt flat

Listings key

■ Accommodation	
● Eating	
■ Drinking/nightlife/tango	
● Shopping	